# A HISTORY OF
# AMERICAN MAGAZINES

## VOLUME IV: 1885–1905

# A History of
# AMERICAN MAGAZINES

## 1885–1905

BY

### FRANK LUTHER MOTT

THE BELKNAP PRESS OF

## HARVARD UNIVERSITY PRESS

Cambridge, Massachusetts

1957

LIBRARY OF CONGRESS CATALOG CARD NUMBER 39–2823

PRINTED IN THE UNITED STATES OF AMERICA

*To*

## ELMER ELLIS

**HISTORIAN, ADMINISTRATOR, FRIEND**

# PREFACE

THE arrangement of this volume follows the method used in those which have preceded it in this series. In the "running history," which furnishes the main part of the book, I have treated the leading events and characteristics of the period and (in successive chapters) the magazines of the various classes. But the more important magazines founded within the period I have treated in separate "sketches," which are not limited by the end-date of the period but are brought down to the present or to the magazine's own end-date. This is done to preserve the continuity of a magazine's story despite the arrangement in sections which the chronological treatment of the general work requires.

There is one exception to this rule. When a magazine is comparatively unimportant in its earlier life, its full treatment, or "sketch," is postponed to the volume devoted to the period in which it comes to its full power. Thus the history of the *Saturday Evening Post* was passed over in the first three volumes of this work and appears in the present one; and that of *Everybody's Magazine*, begun in 1899, is postponed to the next volume.

The scope of this history has been, from the first, very broad. It has seemed helpful to illustrate the main currents of the thought and feeling of the American people by some analysis of the contents of the magazines and by carefully chosen quotations from periodicals in order to give a proper idea of the integration of magazines with social movements. Also, the scope has been broadened by the most liberal possible interpretation of the term "magazine," which, so far as this work is concerned, means any serial that is not clearly a newspaper and is published oftener than semiannually.

It must not be thought, however, that there is any attempt here to mention all the magazines begun in the period 1885–1905. This is by no means a check list; that function is performed by Miss Gregory's admirable *Union List of Serials*. I have tried, in general, to limit my discussions to the more important periodicals in the various categories; but it is probable that my indexes of importance were not always reliable.

I am indebted to literally hundreds of people for help in the preparation of this volume. Some of the work on it was done as much as twenty-five years ago, before Volumes II and III were published. The libraries I have used chiefly are the Library of Congress, the libraries of the Universities of Missouri and Iowa, the New York Public Library, the Newberry and John Crerar Libraries in Chicago, and the St. Louis Public Library. But I have worked in many other libraries for shorter times, and still others have loaned me materials and answered questions for me. I am convinced that research librarians will have a special suburb of their own in the Heavenly City: I know they deserve it.

FRANK LUTHER MOTT

University of Missouri
December 1, 1956

# CONTENTS

## CHAPTER I

### THE END OF A CENTURY

## CHAPTER II

### THE COUNTING HOUSES

## CHAPTER III

### EDITORS AND CONTRIBUTORS

## CHAPTER IV

### THE GENERAL MONTHLY MAGAZINES

## CHAPTER V

### THE GENERAL WEEKLY MAGAZINES

## CHAPTER VI

### THE GENERAL QUARTERLIES

## CHAPTER VII

### LOCAL AND REGIONAL MAGAZINES

## CHAPTER VIII

### LITERARY TYPES AND JUDGMENTS

## CHAPTER IX

### THE GRAPHIC ARTS

## CHAPTER X

### POLITICS AND ECONOMICS

## CHAPTER XI

### SOCIAL ISSUES

## CHAPTER XII

### FOREIGN INTERESTS AND THE WAR WITH SPAIN

# CHAPTER XIII

### NEWSPAPERS AND ADVERTISING

# CHAPTER XIV

### MUSIC AND DRAMA

# CHAPTER XV

### EDUCATION

# CHAPTER XVI

### RELIGION AND PHILOSOPHY

## CHAPTER XVII

### GENERAL SCIENCE AND MEDICINE

## CHAPTER XVIII

### ENGINEERING, CONSTRUCTION, AND TRANSPORTATION

# CHAPTER XIX

### AGRICULTURE, HORTICULTURE, LIVESTOCK

# CHAPTER XX

### LAW, BANKING, AND INSURANCE

# CHAPTER XXI

### WOMEN'S ACTIVITIES

# CHAPTER XXII

### SPORTS AND RECREATION

## CHAPTER XXIII

### HUMOR AND HOBBIES

## SUPPLEMENT

### SKETCHES OF CERTAIN IMPORTANT MAGAZINES
### WHICH FLOURISHED 1885–1905

# CONTENTS

# ILLUSTRATIONS

# A HISTORY OF
# AMERICAN MAGAZINES

## 1885–1905

# CHAPTER I

## THE END OF A CENTURY

THE twenty years from 1885 to 1905 ended one century and began another. They seem to separate rather neatly into two periods — one centering on an extraordinary industrial and financial development, which met a temporary check in the panic of 1893, and the ensuing hard times; and the other having for its high lights the war with Spain and the discovery of gold in the Klondike, and ending in record-breaking prosperity and visions of world power. The entire double decade was characterized by the organization of industry and finance through consolidations; and that trend, so notable in the eighties, was accentuated amazingly at the very close of the century. But with all the mounting wealth and the growth of the industry and commerce that produced it, with all the triumphant self-confidence following the victory over Spain and the general prosperity of the first few years of the new century, there was a continuing counterpoint of dissent and protest and revolt, not only in discussion and debate but in industrial and political organization. The hard times of the mid-nineties dramatized the increasing gap between the proud battalion of new millionaires and Coxey's shambling army; but, as a matter of fact, there was no time in those twenty years when the cry of protest was not almost as loud as the shout of success.

This basic pattern of conflict became apparent to all — or almost all — observers of these years. Though a basic pattern, it was by no means the only figure in the intricate web woven by the activities of these two decades. American society was growing more and more complex, and economic and political problems were multiplying, as the century approached its end. What a variety of factors interacted to provide the colorful tapestry of those times! The catalogue includes the growth of large cities, the progress of the West and South, the immigration problem, new and often radical political movements, the growth of labor organizations, revolutionary inventions in transportation and industry, the new sociology, a shifting emphasis in religion, the emancipation of women, new movements in literature and art and the theater, and *fin de siècle* developments in education, in journalism, in publishing, in sports, and so on, and so on.

MAGAZINES AND NEWSPAPERS AS POPULAR INTERPRETERS

All these phenomena of the period became more readily apparent to contemporary observers because of the improvement in the media of communication. Newspapers flourished, books at low prices multiplied, the platform was active; but of all the agencies of popular information, none experienced a more spectacular enlargement and increase in effectiveness than the magazines.

This growth in the value of magazines as popular informers and interpreters, real though it was, must not be exaggerated. For many years before this, class periodicals had been intimately associated with practical problems in their own fields; the weekly journals of opinion had participated in the controversies of their times; and occasionally one or another of the great general magazines and reviews, like the *Century* under Gilder[1] and the *North American Review* after it was moved to New York,[2] had published incisive commentary on a lively issue. But as long as the general magazine was sold for thirty-five cents a copy, it was on the aristocratic level, for it had to be aimed, of course, at the moneyed and well-educated classes. In comparison with the newspaper, for example, it was leisurely in habit, literary in tone, retrospective rather than timely, and friendly to the interests of the upper classes. It retained a certain aloofness, as a serene observer of the passing scene.

But when the price of excellent, well-illustrated, general magazines was broken to fifteen and even ten cents, conditions changed radically. Editors locked up their ivory towers and came down into the market place.

This brought them into competition with the newspaper editors. Now, from the earliest times, it has been difficult to draw the line between newspapers and magazines; indeed, it has always been impossible to make the distinction wholly on the basis of content.[3] The confusion increased in the 1880's with the development of the Sunday editions of metropolitan newspapers, whose "supplements" contained literary miscellany that was sometimes comparable with magazine content. The 1890 census gave 400 as the number of Sunday papers, about two-thirds of them Sunday editions of dailies; in 1900 the figure was 639. In the summer of 1888, the editor of the *American Magazine* observed:

Much has been written in the past month in relation to the Magazine and Newspaper press, and efforts have been made to show that the Sunday and special

[1] See F. L. Mott, *A History of American Magazines* (Cambridge, Mass., 1938), v. 3, pp. 470–71.
[2] See Mott, *op. cit.*, v. 2, pp. 249–52.
[3] See Mott, *op. cit.*, v. 1, p. 8.

Saturday editions of the large dailies are, practically, weekly magazines, actively appealing to, and receiving the support of, magazine readers. . . . Many of the best writers contribute signed articles to the Sunday paper's columns.[4]

This invasion of the magazine field by the Sunday newspaper had little or no effect on the great "quality magazines," but those on a less esoteric level retaliated by a counterinvasion of the newspaper field. Joel Benton complained in the *Journalist* early in 1893, just before the major moves in the direction of cheap magazines began, that "each magazine and periodical now runs a neck-and-neck race to capture the first and freshest news, and thus beat its contemporaries. Priority in catching a current event is the overwhelming aim." The philosophical Benton thought this a great mistake, since the magazine tortoise could never overtake the newspaper hare.[5] The news-minded magazines referred to were, for the most part, comparative newcomers, such as the *Arena, Forum, Review of Reviews, Public Opinion, Literary Digest,* and so on. And now, having met the challenge of the newspaper in content, the magazine proceeded to set up a competition with it in price.

THE ADVENT OF THE GREAT TEN-CENT MAGAZINE

The low-priced magazine was by no means a new phenomenon in American publishing history, but the highly successful low-priced magazine was. In the cheap-publishing period of 1830–1850, there were weeklies selling as low as three cents, and monthlies at ten cents;[6] later there were other attempts at dollar-a-year monthlies, unsuccessful, mediocre to poor in quality, and mostly short-lived.[7] The only ten-cent magazine of the eighties that was fair in quality and moderately successful was *Drake's Magazine.*[8]

However, there was some retreat in the eighties from the higher price levels by magazines belonging to the "quality group." *Lippincott's*

---

[4] *American Magazine,* v. 8, p. 236, June 1888. Also see San Francisco *Argonaut* article quoted in *Printer's Ink,* v. 2, p. 51, Sept. 1, 1889; *Cosmopolitan Magazine,* v. 13, p. 635, Oct. 1892; *ibid.,* v. 14, p. 262, Jan. 1893; *Printer's Ink,* v. 1, p. 377, Nov. 1888; *ibid.,* p. 467, Dec. 1888.

[5] *Journalist,* v. 16, April 1, 1893, p. 6. Also see Benton's article in *Printer's Ink,* v. 11, Dec. 5, 1894, p. 11.

[6] Mott, *op. cit.,* v. 1, pp. 358–65. The most famous of the group was *Holden's Dollar Magazine* (1848–51); see *ibid.,* pp. 347–48.

[7] Such as *Church's Bizarre* (1852–55), for which see Mott, *op. cit.,* v. 2, p. 210, footnote; *Frank Leslie's Ten-Cent Monthly* (1863–66), which was published during its last year as *Frank Leslie's New Monthly, Devoted to Light and Entertaining Literature;* and *Ballou's Dollar Monthly* which dropped the word *Dollar* from its title and raised its price in 1866. For *Ballou's,* see Mott, *op. cit.,* v. 2, p. 31. Three mediocre dollar magazines were begun in New York in 1888: John B. Ketchum's *American Forget-Me-Not* (1888–92), William E. Hall's *International* (1888–1906), and Cornelia Redmond's *Continental Illustrated Magazine* (1888–94).

[8] See p. 44.

dropped illustration entirely, changed its editorial policy,[9] and reduced its price to twenty cents. About the same time, *Scribner's Magazine* was begun as a fully illustrated "quality magazine" in direct competition with the *Century* and *Harper's*, but at a single-copy price of twenty-five cents in comparison with their thirty-five. It took two or three years and the expenditure of a large sum to get *Scribner's* on a paying basis,[10] but its rivals felt the competitive pinch from the first.[11] Later in the year that saw the founding of *Scribner's*, the *Cosmopolitan Magazine*, which had been started as a thirty-five-cent, fully illustrated monthly, moved to New York and cut its price to twenty cents; it floundered about and almost perished before John Brisben Walker got it on the road to prosperity in 1890, raising its price to twenty-five cents in 1891.[12] In the latter year, Frank A. Munsey changed his *Weekly* to *Munsey's Magazine*, a fully illustrated monthly, at twenty-five cents.[13]

In England, the *Strand* was begun in January 1891 as an illustrated monthly selling for sixpence and with the "specific avowal" of its intention to beat *Harper's* on its own lines at half the price. But the American edition of the *Strand*, containing the same matter but dated a month ahead to allow for transportation time, was priced at twenty cents. It did not cut this to ten cents until competition forced the reduction in 1895.[14]

Probably the greatest encouragement for the publisher who was considering the chances of success for a magazine at ten or fifteen cents was the smash hit that had been made by the *Ladies' Home Journal* at a dime a copy. It had gained its first half-million circulation, indeed, at five cents a copy; then, with improvements in content and format that took it out of the cheap household-paper class, it had by 1893 built up a circulation of seven hundred thousand at ten cents a copy.[15] There were, of course, many five-cent weeklies largely supported by mail-order advertising, such as the *New York Ledger*, the *New York Weekly*, the *Yankee Blade*, the *Chicago Ledger*, and so on.

There were at this time economic and technological factors that also encouraged the entrepreneur with ideas about cheap general magazines. The hard times of the mid-nineties had already set in, and prices that were acceptable in a more inflationary period now seemed too high. And it has been demonstrated repeatedly that, although depressions

[9] See Mott, *op. cit.*, v. 2, p. 399.
[10] See p. 15.
[11] *Current Literature*, v. 1, p. 377, Nov. 1888.
[12] See Sketch 10.
[13] See Sketch 19.
[14] See F. W. Faxon, "The *Strand*: Its American and English Editions," in *Bulletin of Bibliography*, v. 1, p. 122, Jan. 1899.
[15] See Sketch 14.

kill off some older magazines, they do not greatly discourage new attempts, on the theory that new times, though hard, demand new measures and new magazines. Paper and printing costs were cheaper than ever before.[16] But the greatest promise held out for the success of a low-priced illustrated magazine for the general reader was that offered by the new, cheap technique of photoengraving known as the halftone. This process was developed in the eighties, largely through the successive inventions of Frederic E. Ives, experimenting in the laboratories of Cornell University, in 1878 and 1886.[17] By 1893 it was apparent that the halftone would soon displace the far more expensive fine-line engraving on wood. Even the *Century*, whose reputation depended in no small degree on its beautiful wood engraving by Timothy Cole and other artists of almost equal rank, was using some halftones by this time.[18] Small wonder, when the *Century* paid up to three hundred dollars for a page-size woodcut,[19] and it could buy a halftone for less than twenty dollars.

S. S. McClure founded his magazine in June 1893 as a copiously illustrated, well-edited monthly, containing fiction and articles on a literary level at least comparable with that of the established "quality group," and in an area of ideas more timely, lively, and journalistic. It sold for fifteen cents a copy, or a dollar and a half a year, and it boomed from the first.[20] The month after the first issue of *McClure's* appeared, the *Cosmopolitan* cut its price to twelve and a half cents a copy and a dollar and a half a year,[21] and two months later *Munsey's* went to ten cents a copy and a dollar a year. *Munsey's*, though it had more pages than *McClure's* or *Cosmopolitan*, was lighter in tone and more like the Sunday supplements. *Peterson's Magazine* went to ten cents at the end of 1893, and *Godey's* followed suit the next year; both were unprosperous general magazines that had once been great women's journals. In July 1895 both *McClure's* and *Cosmopolitan* followed *Munsey's* down to ten cents, where they were to remain until the general price increases of 1905–1909. The *Overland*, which had been reduced to twenty-five cents in 1891, adopted the ten-cent price five years later. Even *Harper's* came down to twenty-five cents in 1899.

From 1895 onward, there were many ten-cent magazines in the field.

[16] *Critic*, v. 24, p. 365, May 26, 1894.

[17] William T. Innes in *Inland Printer*, v. 79, p. 422, June 1927, discusses conflicting claims in the development of halftone engraving.

[18] Mott, *op. cit.*, v. 3, p. 472.

[19] *Journalist*, v. 12, Dec. 13, 1890, p. 3; *Quarterly Illustrator*, v. 1, p. 96, June 1893. Cf. Theodore L. Devinne "The Printing of 'The Century,'" *Century*, v. 41, pp. 87–99 (esp. p. 91), Nov. 1890; and Frank H. Scott's Quill Club speech on the making of the *Century* in *Critic*, v. 24, pp. 364–66, May 26, 1894.

[20] See Sketch 18.

[21] But it went up to 15¢ five months later, the price that it had held until 1895. See p. 596.

Frank Munsey wrote in 1899 that there were "a vast number of them," and added: "It is an off month that does not record the advent of several new ones."[22] And four years later Munsey estimated, probably with approximate correctness, that the ten-centers had 85 per cent of the circulation of American magazines; but he thought that of the "hundred or two" of such magazines, only four were big money-makers — his own *Munsey's* and *Argosy*, the *Cosmopolitan*, and *McClure's*.[23]

There was also a vogue in the nineties for five-cent magazines, and even for monthlies selling for one or two cents.[24] The great mail-order monthlies had annual subscription rates ranging from twenty-five to seventy-five cents a year, and after the turn of the century much of their distribution was free.

But it was in the weekly field that the nickel price was to become important, when the Curtis Publishing Company, having taken over the virtually defunct *Saturday Evening Post* in 1897, made a resounding success of it as a five-cent weekly magazine.

### THE NATURE OF THE TEN-CENT MAGAZINE

What was the appeal of these ten-cent magazines, which caused a revolution in the field of periodical publishing? What did they have, besides the attraction of price, to make them so popular? What were they like? We must not generalize too easily, for there were many differences among these newcomers; but they had some characteristics in common.

H. L. Mencken once declared that "what McClure, a shrewd literary bagman, did was to apply the sensational methods of the cheap newspaper to a new and cheap magazine." Tracing the pedigree of the new type of publication, he added that its "real father was the unknown originator of the Sunday supplement."[25] If this were said of *Munsey's*, one might agree readily enough; but if we accept such a pedigree for *McClure's*, we shall have to add the observation that the son was far superior to the father. Sensationalism cannot be said to have characterized generally these ten-cent magazines of the nineties.[26] What did characterize them were copious and well-printed illustration, liveliness and freshness in presentation of nonfiction articles, variety in subject matter, a serious treatment of contemporary problems, a keen interest in new inventions and progress in general, and attention to major world

---

[22] *Munsey's Magazine*, v. 20, p. 661, Jan. 1899.
[23] *Munsey's Magazine*, v. 30, pp. 151–52, Oct. 1903.
[24] See pp. 47–51.
[25] H. L. Mencken, *Prejudices: First Series* (New York, 1929), p. 175.
[26] Muckraking, with its sensationalism, came later.

events. These magazines had also, we must not forget, the attraction of success; there was a popular appeal in the numbers fat with advertising.

William Archer, the Scottish critic and playwright, once wrote competently, in an English review, of the "American Cheap Magazines." After speaking of their "extraordinarily vital and stimulating quality," he added: "There is nothing quite like them in the literature of the world — no periodicals which combine such width of popular appeal with such seriousness of aim and thoroughness of workmanship."[27]

### THE EFFECTS OF THE TEN-CENT MAGAZINE

The older magazines did not welcome the ten-cent monthlies with open arms. The managers of the top "quality magazines" could not believe that the newcomers could attract enough advertising to make up for their low price to readers.[28] The *Nation,* in its superior way, poked fun at them.[29] The *Independent* may be allowed to speak for all the critics:

> The revolution in the art of engraving, not to say its destruction, is threatening a change in the conduct of monthly magazines. . . . With July the *Cosmopolitan* and *McClure's* will reduce their price to ten cents. . . . What will be the effect on the higher-priced illustrated magazines, like *Harper's,* the *Century,* and *Scribner's,* it may not be easy to foresee; but it seems probable that they will not find it wise to reduce their price to a like figure. . . . The reason is that they will wish to maintain that higher, purer literary standard which succeeds in securing the best but not the most numerous readers. . . . They cannot change their constituency beyond the comparatively cultivated class which appreciates them. They cannot, half a dozen of them, secure half a million purchasers apiece, for there are not so many families of their sort in the country. The fit audience in an educated country like ours is not few, but it is not yet unlimited; nevertheless, it is the only audience worth addressing, for it contains the thinking people. The rest may or may not be sturdy citizens, may count in the militia and the population and the lower schools; but they are not the ones who delight to seek the instruction they need most.[30]

Replying to this argument, S. S. McClure wrote: "We confess that we are befogged. Either the venerable editor of the *Independent* [H. C. Bowen] is poking fun at his esteemed contemporaries — the high-priced monthlies — or he ignores the comparative quality of *McClure's Magazine.*" Then McClure names a long list of his own contributors, who, he contends, have about as high and pure a literary standard as any conceivable list of contemporary writers: among them are Stevenson, Kipling, Howells, Gladstone, Conan Doyle, Edward Everett Hale, and

---

[27] *Fortnightly Review,* v. 93, pp. 921-32, May 1910.
[28] Scott, *op. cit.,* p. 365.
[29] *Nation,* v. 61, p. 342, Nov. 14, 1895.
[30] *Independent,* v. 47, p. 867, June 27, 1895 (p. 11).

so on. And as to the possible audience for high-class literature, McClure points out that he has been supplying such material to a million families through his literary syndicate for ten years past.[31]

But soon circulation figures were making an even more convincing reply. The advent of the ten-cent monthlies created a vast new audience for the American general magazine in the nineties. In 1885 there were only four general monthly magazines with circulations of a hundred thousand or more, and their aggregate circulation was six hundred thousand. They were all priced at thirty-five or twenty-five cents per copy. In 1905 there were twenty such magazines, all but four of them selling for ten or fifteen cents, and their aggregate circulation was over five and a half million. The cheaper price had recruited millions of new readers.

But if Bowen had lived to see this magazine revolution, he would probably have persisted in his contention that there had been a decline in the high and pure tone of magazine literature. For the millions of new readers recruited by the cheaper price reacted on the magazines and, as has been pointed out, brought them down to the level of practical affairs. Their fiction and poetry were doubtless about as high and pure as ever; but in the nineties magazines were made or unmade not by fiction but by what editors called "solid matter" — history and biography, economic and political articles.[32]

The competition with the newspapers grew more and more pronounced. The invasion of the news field by the ten-cent magazines was met directly by the Sunday newspapers, which exploited their feature content as superior to the matter printed in the rival medium. "Magazines Made Obsolete!" shouted an advertisement of New York *Sunday World*, and "Better Illustrated Than Any Magazine!"[33] The *Saturday Evening Post* thought that the only difference between the magazine and the newspaper was in format: "A good magazine is a good newspaper in a dress suit," it declared.[34] A striking illustration of the integration of newspaper and magazine is afforded by the literary and pictorial supplements of scores of great daily papers over the country which were begun in the last few years of the decade and sold separately, such as the *Saturday Review* of the *New York Times*.

This merger of newspaper and magazine fields was not without its effect on the old "quality monthlies." It was a shock to many when the *Atlantic Monthly*, in 1898, turned to political controversy, social reforms, and the exposure of corruption in government. Under Walter

---

[31] *McClure's Magazine*, v. 5, p. 287, Aug. 1895.
[32] Scott, *op. cit.*, p. 365.
[33] *New York World*, April 25, 1896.
[34] *Saturday Evening Post*, prospectus, v. 170, May 28, 1898, p. 8.

Hines Page and Bliss Perry, America's premier literary monthly, which originally had been planned as a political force but had long since resigned such controversy to the newspapers and the weekly journals of opinion, reëntered the arena of timely public affairs.[35] The *Century* was edited by Richard Watson Gilder, a trained newspaperman, and the *Journalist* said of it, "It deals with matters of contemporaneous human interest; it leads thought, but never gets out of sight. The journalistic side of the *Century* has kept it in touch with the people."[36] This "journalistic side" of the *Century* was emphasized in the latter nineties. An acute observer wrote in 1899 that "now it often seems as if it were the aim of the magazines to be edited like newspapers." He reported that a count of articles in the *Century*, *Scribner's*, and *Harper's* showed a 10 per cent increase in "journalistic articles" in the preceding twenty-five years.[37] This gain was due chiefly to the *Century* and *Scribner's*; certainly *Harper's* made a point of eschewing articles closely related to the news. Editor Alden, after tracing the history of his magazine to show that its present policy was consistent with its past, wrote in 1902: "Now, in its appeal to its third generation of readers, it has still further limited its scope by the exclusion of the acutely journalistic article that used to be classed as 'timely.'" And this being the year of the eruption of Mount Pelée and the coronation of a new English king, Alden added: "By way of illustration, *Harper's* is the only magazine which during recent months has contained nothing about volcanoes or about Edward VII."[38] But *Harper's* was, by admission, an exception. A writer in the *Dial* in 1900 pointed out that the subjects demanding attention in magazines at that time were

those of political administration, of good government, of municipal socialism, of economics as they relate to social and individual prosperity and comfort. Notwithstanding the gains of the literary periodicals, the marked growth has been in the literature of practical subjects. . . . Periodical literature is taking a livelier and more intelligent interest in the larger affairs of life.[39]

That puts the matter very well. A few years later, an interviewer for the *Saturday Review* found that the editors of the leading monthlies were unanimous in the opinion that the use of articles dealing with current events and situations was still increasing.[40]

[35] Mott, *op. cit.*, v. 2, p. 512.
[36] *Journalist*, v. 12, Dec. 13, 1890, p. 3.
[37] *Atlantic Monthly*, v. 86, p. 124, July 1900. This study by A. R. Kimball really ended with 1897, and was reported in the *Journal of Social Science*, v. 37, pp. 26–43, 1899. The quotation is from the excellent article in the *Journal*, p. 36.
[38] *Harper's Magazine*, v. 105, pp. 646–47, Sept. 1902. See also *ibid.*, v. 106, p. 817, April 1903, etc.
[39] Henry Loomis Wilson in the *Dial*, v. 28, p. 352, May 1, 1900.
[40] *New York Times Saturday Review*, v. 17, p. 9, Jan. 2, 1904.

Leaders in this movement, of course, were the monthlies and weeklies dealing primarily with current events and comment, such as the *Review of Reviews*, the *Literary Digest, Public Opinion*, and *Current Literature*. Almost as closely related to the news were such monthly reviews as the *Forum*, the *Arena*, and the *North American Review*. The weekly journals of opinion were closer to the newspapers than were other classes of periodicals; indeed the *Nation* was a weekly edition of the *New York Evening Post* throughout the period now under consideration. Henry Loomis Nelson observed in 1900 that *Harper's Wekly*, of which he had recently been editor, and *Collier's, Leslie's*, the *Outlook*, the *Independent*, and other weekly miscellanies were stimulated to improvement by the Sunday supplements. They could not compete in timeliness, he pointed out, and so "they must excel in quality — especially quality of illustration."[41]

### THE ERA OF "MORE OF EVERYTHING"

With all this emphasis on news, the problems of the times, and "the larger affairs of life," the magazines came to represent as never before the complex currents of thought and feeling in the closing years of the century. And every interest had its own journal or journals — all the ideologies and movements, all the arts, all the schools of philosophy and education, all the sciences, all the trades and industries, all the professions and callings, all organizations of importance, all hobbies and recreations. Especially in the fields of the trade magazine and the scientific journal, the offerings multiplied. "There is scarcely a province in the entire realm of science and scholarship which is now without an official organ in America," wrote President Schurman in introducing his *Philosophical Review* in January 1892.

It was an era of multiplicity, if not of plenty. There were more money and leisure than ever before, and more slums in the cities and misery on the farms. There was more ambition, even among a traditionally ambitious people, than ever before, leading to its climax in a "success" cult at the end of the century. There were more sports, more popular songs, more humor than ever before. There was a deeper social consciousness and there was a greater enthusiasm for adult education than America had known before. In short, the nineties were an era of more of everything in America.

Out of it all, two conflicting ideologies emerged at the end of our period — one an exaltation of the American accomplishment, with an

---

[41] *Dial*, v. 28, p. 351, May 1, 1900. For any of the magazines mentioned in this paragraph, see further treatment in this volume by consulting the index.

emphasis on the doctrine of manifest destiny; and the other a deep concern over the increasing chasm between wealth and poverty, culminating in a literature of exposure to be known as "muckraking." The expression of the leading magazines on these matters will be noted in later sections of this study.

### NUMBERS OF PERIODICALS

The rapidity with which magazines are started in this country is equalled only by the suddenness of their disappearance. Periodicals of all sorts and kinds and devoted to the interests of everything under the heavens . . . come and go. . . . By far the greater number either fail or ruin their proprietors.[42]

That is what the editor of the *Journalist* thought in 1889. Nevertheless, the total of American periodicals seems to have increased by more than a thousand between 1885 and 1890; and though the rate appears then to have slowed somewhat, the *Nation* reported in shocked tones in the mid-nineties that magazines were being born "in numbers to make Malthus stare and gasp."[43] Another observer exclaimed a few years later: "Magazines, magazines, magazines! The news-stands are already groaning under the heavy load, and there are still more coming."[44]

There were about 3,300 periodicals[45] in publication in the United States during 1885.[46] By 1890 the number had increased by about one-third, to a little over 4,400; but in the ensuing lustrum that rate of increase was virtually cut in half, and there were about 5,100 periodicals by 1895. In the next five years the increase was again almost halved; there was an actual loss in monthlies in 1895–1896. By 1900 there were somewhat over 5,500 periodicals. There was a slight rise in the rate of increase during 1900–1905, with about 6,000 periodicals in the course of publication in the latter year.[47]

It seems likely that there were some 7,500 periodicals founded in this twenty-year period, and that in those years about half that number were discontinued or merged with others in similar fields.[48] This would

[42] *Journalist*, v. 8, Jan. 12, 1889, p. 8.

[43] *Nation*, v. 61, p. 342, Nov. 14, 1895.

[44] *National Magazine*, v. 7, p. 191, Nov. 1897.

[45] The term is here defined as non-newspaper serials published oftener than semiannually. For definitions of periodical, magazine, and related terms, see Mott, *op. cit.*, v. 1, pp. 5–6.

[46] Mott, *op. cit.*, v. 3, p. 5.

[47] These figures are based on the tables in *N. W. Ayer & Son's American Newspaper Annual* for the various years. One-seventh of the weeklies are counted as periodicals. See computations for other periods in earlier volumes of this work.

[48] These estimates are based on various counts, but especially on counts of the "births" listed in the *Bulletin of Bibliography*. It is known that the *Bulletin* record is incomplete, and in the present computation the figures derived from this source are arbitrarily increased 20 per cent.

mean that nearly 11,000 different periodicals were published in the course of the period.

*Current Literature*, which battened upon the best in the magazines, declared in 1889:

> The American magazines are perfect. In matter, in the range of subjects, in the illustration, in presswork, and in the general appearance of the periodicals, a reader simply cannot think of anything better.[49]

Such unmeasured praise borders, of course, upon the absurd; but most observers, both at home and abroad, thought very well of American magazines in this period. The Chicago *Graphic*, a good journal of opinion, said:

> The development of the magazine in the last quarter of a century in the United States has been marvelous, and is paralleled by no literary movement in any country or in any time. Every field of human thought has been entered and as the field has broadened new magazines have arisen to occupy the territory, and the magazine has become not only a school of literature but of science, art and politics as well.[50]

The English novelist and critic, Walter Besant, writing in the July 1894 number of the London *Author*, discussed the "great success" of the American magazines, which were more popular even in London than their English rivals. But the American *Critic* complained that Besant ascribed this ascendancy to the illustration, and "fails to mention the most important thing concerning them — their quality."[51] However, the *Dial*, always more austere in its criticism, held a position similar to Besant's, saying of American magazines: "In point of illustration they have no superiors anywhere, but much of their text appears to exist only for the sake of the pictures."[52] This was just before the advent of the cheaper halftone "cuts" in the magazines, which emphasizes the fact that even in the early nineties the quantity of illustration in the *Century*, *Harper's*, *Scribner's*, and the great weeklies was strongly objected to in some quarters. In 1890 A. H. Noll, in the *Writer*, dubbed this abundance of pictures "Grangerism," after the Reverend James Granger, inventor of the fad of "extra-illustration" of published books.[53] Julian Hawthorne advocated the complete elimination of pictures from magazines, in order to give literature its proper opportunity, as early as

[49] *Current Literature*, v. 2, pp. 1–2, Jan. 1889.
[50] *Graphic*, v. 6, p. 107, Feb. 6, 1892.
[51] *Critic*, v. 25, p. 97, Aug. 11, 1894.
[52] [Francis F. Browne] in *Dial*, v. 13, p. 204, Oct. 1, 1892.
[53] *Writer*, v. 4, pp. 219–22, Oct. 1890.

1888.[54] *Lippincott's Magazine*, which had been forced to abandon illustration in 1885 because it could not afford to keep up with the leaders in that department, wrote plaintively ten years later of "The Tyranny of the Pictorial."[55] We shall have more to say in a subsequent chapter of the part which illustration played in American magazines in this period; for the present, let us pursue the *Dial's* appraisal somewhat further.

Francis F. Browne, editor of that journal, looking askance at the "great circulations" of the leading magazines in the early nineties, which amounted sometimes to as much as two hundred thousand, believed that such mass readership forced a magazine's editorial content "into mediocrity; they are bound to be conservative" because they cannot afford to offend.[56] This doctrine was widely held by the more highbrow critics. Near the end of our period, Byron R. Newton, well-known journalist and public relations man, writing in the *Era Magazine*, argued that the camera and newspaper journalism had usurped the place of sound magazine work, and declared, "No country in the world is so prolific in mediocre magazines as our own United States."[57] Thus the nearness to current events, the direct appeal to the interests of the general public, and the distinctively journalistic quality, which were so much admired by some critics, were anathema to others.

One thing which worried Browne and which, as it has become more and more striking, has continued to afford anxiety to many critics, was the brevity of articles. "The *Forum*," said Browne, "is not without a certain dignity, but its articles are too brief to allow serious discussion." And the *Atlantic Monthly*, sacrarium of the literary-minded, was subjected to the same kind of criticism.[58] But Walter Hines Page, who had been editor of both of the magazines that thus came under Browne's reprobation, spoke approvingly of this very trend when he addressed the American Library Association in 1902.

> Effective style is changing [he said]. The somewhat leisurely style of a generation or two ago pleased the small circle of readers within its reach . . . a company who had leisure and liked to read that kind of writing. . . . The man who would write convincingly and entertainingly of things of our day and our time must write with more directness, with more clearness, with greater nervous force. . . . A magazine deserves to die that is not interesting.[59]

Yes, the time of the ninety-page review article[60] was long past. The

[54] *Belford's Magazine*, v. 1, p. 32, June 1888.
[55] *Lippincott's*, v. 55, p. 861, June 1895.
[56] Browne, *op. cit.*
[57] *Era Magazine*, v. 12, pp. 485–86, Nov. 1903.
[58] Browne, *op. cit.*
[59] *World's Work*, v. 4, Oct. 1902, pp. 2562–63.
[60] See Mott, *op. cit.*, v. 2, p. 238.

article that ran to twelve or fifteen pages, even with copious illustration, was now the exception; three- and four-page articles were common. Symposiums, in which authorities presented varying points of view on a leading issue, were very frequent in the magazines of the nineties; but even the authority must hold himself to a few pages, or a few paragraphs.

But if a critic found much that was good in the journalistic point of view, if he felt that the people could willingly forego the expansive dissertations characteristic of the magazines of a past generation, and if he believed that lavish illustration added not only attractiveness but fuller understanding, he was likely to take a position like that of *Literary Life*:

> Our magazines are outrivalled by none in respect to both text and illustration. With *Harper's*, *Scribner's* and *Century* easily taking the lead, we may boast of a weekly and monthly output that reaches the high-water mark of journalistic enterprise.[61]

One of the most comprehensive surveys of American periodicals printed during our period was done by the young librarian-editor Emma Helen Blair for the *Andover Review* in 1892. It concluded with the statement that periodical literature is "exercising an almost incalculable influence upon the moral and intellectual development of individuals, upon home life, and upon public opinion. Its great increase and improvement may be regarded as one of the most important signs of the times."[62]

[61] *Literary Life* (no vol.), n.s., March 1903, p. 20.
[62] *Andover Review*, v. 18, p. 154, Aug. 1892.

# CHAPTER II

## THE COUNTING HOUSE

THE wave of magazine prosperity that came with the growth of national advertising and increases of circulation from about 1885 to 1892 caused thousands of adventurers to invest their money in new periodicals. Millions were lost in such ventures in the early nineties, often a hundred thousand dollars or more at a throw. To mention but one illustration, R. T. Bush lost a quarter of a million on the *American Magazine*.[1] It was a good try, and might have been a success if its owner had been willing to risk further capital. *Cosmopolitan* spent more than that before it met with any success,[2] and *Munsey's* probably lost almost that much before it turned the corner.[3] Curtis had to borrow three hundred thousand dollars to supplement his own resources before he was able to make the *Ladies' Home Journal* a sucess.[4] *Scribner's Magazine* spent half a million to establish itself soundly as a quality magazine in the late eighties.[5]

E. W. Bok, who knew whereof he spoke, wrote in the *Epoch* in 1891: "I should think a man would weigh carefully the chances before putting any money into new magazine schemes. It is not so much a survival of the fittest as the survival of the largest capital."[6] There were thousands of periodical failures in the panic of 1893 and in the ensuing years; and when the publishing business picked up again, it was to the tune of increased costs. Something has already been said as to the expensiveness of engraving, and something will be said later about increased fees to writers. By 1898, Frank H. Scott was justified in stating that "Every number of a modern magazine costs more than ten thousand dollars for contributors and pictures before it goes to press."[7]

### CIRCULATIONS

The editor was dying, but when the doctor placed his ear to the patient's heart and muttered sadly, "Poor fellow — circulation almost gone!" he raised himself up and gasped, " 'Tis false! We have the largest circulation in the country!" Then

---

[1] See pp. 44–45.
[2] See Sketch 10.
[3] See Sketch 19.
[4] See Sketch 14.
[5] See Sketch 28.
[6] *Epoch*, v. 10, p. 296, Dec. 11, 1891.
[7] *New York Tribune*, Holiday Supplement, 1898, Part 2, p. 6. Scott referred, of course, to the general illustrated monthly.

he sank back on his pillow and died, consistent to the end — lying about his circulation.[8]

It was an agricultural monthly that printed the above fable in 1885, but it was applicable to any class of publication at any time before the Audit Bureau of Circulations was founded in 1914. Both N. W. Ayer & Son and George P. Rowell & Company, publishers of the two leading directories of periodicals, tried to induce honesty in circulation claims by encouraging itemized and sworn statements by publishers. Rowell finally resorted to the method of never quoting exact circulations unless satisfactory itemized data and records were received, but assigning code letters indicating circulation categories. This kept Rowell continually in hot water with publishers who claimed they were mistreated. But even by 1905, the proportion of publishers who made affidavits to the accuracy of their circulation figures was very small. However, the insistence of advertisers on confidential itemized statements and the skepticism of agencies made it awkward, if not impossible, for an important periodical to maintain fraudulent circulation claims over any considerable period.

Henry Ward Beecher, speaking to the New York Editorial Association in 1873, expressed the belief that competition and varieties of interests were such that the time would never come "when a journal will exist with half a million regular subscribers."[9] No journal did reach that figure until 1891, when the *Ladies' Home Journal*, stimulated by a big advertising campaign, went to about six hundred thousand. The *Youth's Companion*, of Boston, with its great premium list for amateur solicitors, passed the half-million mark two or three years later; and the *Delineator* was claiming that figure by 1895. The first periodical to pass the million mark was the famous fifty-cent mail-order journal *Comfort*, of Augusta, Maine, which made the grade in 1895. *Munsey's* was the first general illustrated magazine to reach half a million circulation — a point it attained in 1897. Five or six periodicals sold at very low subscription prices and supported by mail-order advertising reached half a million circulation in the late nineties; and by the end of our period in 1905, there were ten such publications which claimed (usually by sworn statement) half a million, and two (*Comfort* and the St. Louis *Woman's Magazine*) with over a million. The *Ladies' Home Journal* reached a million in 1903, and the *Saturday Evening Post* passed a half-million in that same year. The *Delineator* was claiming a million and a half by 1906. Two Methodist Sunday School lesson serials, sold to the schools in lots, had over half a million distribution each in 1905.[10]

[8] *Western Plowman*, v. 6, April 1885, p. 64.
[9] Charles F. Wingate, ed., *Views and Interviews on Journalism* (New York, 1875), p. 233.
[10] For further information on any of the periodicals mentioned in this paragraph, see index.

Such were the circulation leaders in the years 1885–1905. In Frank Munsey's famous Sphinx Club address in 1898, he asserted, "There never was anything deader in this world than the old idea of big profits and small volume. Small profits and big volume have driven this antiquated theory to the wall."[11] The growth of the large-volume theory is illustrated by the increase in the number of periodicals circulating a hundred thousand copies in successive five-year periods: in 1885 there were 21; in 1890, 39; in 1895, 68; in 1900, 85; in 1905, 159. The circulation leaders at these five-year dates, in order of size, were: 1885, *Youth's Companion, Fireside Companion, Century*; 1890, *Ladies' Home Journal, Comfort, Youth's Companion, Delineator*; 1895, *Comfort, Ladies' Home Journal, Hearthstone, Youth's Companion*; 1900, *Comfort, Ladies' Home Journal, Hearthstone, Munsey's Magazine*; 1905, *Delineator, Comfort, Ladies' Home Journal, McCall's Magazine, Saturday Evening Post, Munsey's Magazine.*

### PREMIUMS AND REWARDS

Techniques of circulation building were many and various. The Curtis Publishing Company made its great successes largely by advertising in newspapers. Many of the standard monthly magazines, including *Scribner's, McClure's, Cosmopolitan,* and *Review of Reviews,* furnished free subscriptions to editors of weekly and small daily papers throughout the country in exchange for the printing of one or more "reading notices" per month. Such short pieces usually included extracts from interesting articles which had appeared in the magazines.

The old method, and the one used with great success by such circulation leaders as the *Youth's Companion,* most of the women's magazines, and all of the mail-order journals, was that of the premium list. Premiums ranging from cheap books to sewing machines, jewelry, and clothing were offered for "clubs" of new subscribers. Portfolios of large photographs of the Chicago Columbian Exposition were popular, as well as the color pictures known as "chromos." Sometimes prizes were given for the largest "clubs," as when the *Farm Journal,* of Philadelphia, offered as a first prize, payment of the winner's taxes for one year (not to exceed a hundred dollars); a second prize of fifty dollars in gold; for the third man, payment of the interest on his mortgage (not over forty dollars); fourth, a milk cow; and fifth, a silk dress, Brussels carpet, or sewing machine.[12] Premium offers were advertised off and on throughout the year, but in the fall a big illustrated premium list of many pages

[11] *Munsey's Magazine,* v. 20, p. 47, Dec. 1898.
[12] *Farm Journal,* v. 15, pp. 230–31, Dec. 1891.

was issued. The "club" device made the solicitor virtually a local subscription agent for the periodical.

The premium system, however, showed signs of wearing out by 1905. The cheap and sentimental chromolithographs had become a subject of satire, though the popular expression, "You deserve a chromo for that!" was commonly not sarcastic but a commendation. The announcements in some periodicals that they did *not* offer premiums signalized the beginning of the end. *Brann's Iconoclast* ran a banner line on its front page saying: "No chromos, World's Fair Photos, or A. H. Belo sewing machines go with the *Iconoclast*. We are running a magazine, not a plunder store." [13]

The *Cosmopolitan* was a pioneer in offering college scholarships as rewards to subscription solicitors. Such miscellanies as the *Chicago Ledger* and *Saturday Blade*, the *Yankee Blade*, and the *Pennsylvania Grit* employed the carrier boys who delivered their weekly issues to solicit new readers; and this technique, with its premiums of money, bicycles, scholarships, and so on, was used with great success by the *Saturday Evening Post* in the early years of the twentieth century.

### NEWSSTAND SALES

The American News Company had held a monopoly on the national distribution of periodicals since it had become established in the sixties.[14] In 1872 the A.N.C.'s subsidiary, the Railroad News Company, bought an interest in the Union News Company, which was the leading newsstand owner; [15] thus the chief retail and the only wholesale business in periodical distribution came into the same hands. Early in our period the A.N.C. was said to be doing a business of seventeen million dollars annually.[16] The only important challenge to its sometimes dictatorial methods was that of Frank Munsey, who, when he made the historic reduction of the price of his monthly to ten cents, was told that the company would not handle *Munsey's Magazine* at a price low enough to make the venture possible. Munsey offered three and a half cents, to cover both agency and dealer shares, which was more than A.N.C. got from the ten-cent weeklies; but he was refused. He then defied the monopoly, with its thirty-two regional branches, which had "hitherto controlled the entire periodical business of the country," and got enough orders by direct-mail advertising and newspaper announce-

[13] The statement appeared through much of 1896. A. H. Belo was a famous Dallas and Galveston newspaper publisher.

[14] F. L. Mott, *History of American Magazines* (Cambridge, Mass., 1938), v. 2, p. 13.

[15] Roy Quinlan, "The Story of Magazine Distribution," in *Magazine Week*, v. 1, p. 4, Oct. 19, 1953.

[16] *Current Literature*, v. 1, pp. 283–85, Oct. 1888.

ments to start his new policy successfully.[17] Munsey finally formed the Red Star Agency for all his publications, and handled his own distribution for many years. When other magazines reduced their price to ten cents, they received only five cents of it, two cents going to the agency and three to the newsdealer. Likewise, twenty-five cent magazines got only about half that price from the agency, ten cents going to the dealer. There was some trend toward irregular shipments of bundles to independent dealers in the late nineties,[18] but Munsey was the only publisher in our period to declare his independence from the American News Company.

Newsdealers and their newsstands, originally devoted to the sale of newspapers, reached out more and more toward an emphasis on magazines during the years at the turn of the century. Before the middle nineties a very large proportion of magazine circulation was by annual subscription. A competent observer remarked in 1894 that "many weekly and monthly journals which have enormous circulations have insignificant newsstand sales."[19] A reporter for *Printer's Ink*, having visited the stands at the stations on the Elevated Railroad in New York, wrote that only a dozen or so of each of the leading monthly magazines were sold at each stand, though the weeklies *Puck* and *Truth* did much better.[20] Throughout most of the eighties, newsstands were generally found only in hotels, railroad stations, and ferry houses. "Butchers" on the trains did a good business in magazines. But by the end of the nineties, there were said to be three or four thousand newsdealers throughout the country, most of whom handled some periodicals.[21]

Many periodicals provided posters for display by the newsdealers; of these, the most artistic were those of the larger magazines. Said the *Critic* in 1894:

It is quite the thing nowadays to make collections of the monthly advertising posters of *Harper's*, the *Century*, and *Scribner's* magazines. *Harper's* are mostly done by one man — young Edward Penfield. . . . *Scribner's* has several people doing its posters. Dana Gibson has done some, and the Morans — Leon and Percy — have done a great many. . . . The *Century's* are pretty and artistic, but . . . they are lithographs rather than color prints. . . . *McClure's Magazine* does not issue a monthly poster, but it has a very good one that answers for all seasons by that clever young draughtsman, Harry McCarter.[22]

[17] *Munsey's Magazine*, v. 12, p. 111, Oct. 1894; also Frank A. Munsey, *The Founding of the Munsey Publishing House* (New York, 1907), pp. 42–47.

[18] Quinlan, *op. cit.*, v. 1, p. 4, Oct. 5, 1953.

[19] *Printer's Ink*, v. 11, p. 748, Oct. 31, 1894.

[20] G. A. Sykes, "Periodicals on the Elevated Railroads," in *Printer's Ink*, v. 7, p. 830, Dec. 21, 1892; John Z. Rogers, "As Seen at the News Stands," *ibid.*, in three parts beginning pp. 703–94, Nov. 30, 1892.

[21] *Printer's Ink*, v. 24, p. 62, Dec. 14, 1898.

[22] *Critic*, v. 24, p. 111, Feb. 17, 1894. For data on these posters, see F. Weitenkampf, *American Graphic Art* (New York, 1924), pp. 275–78.

Later, the *Chap-Book's* posters, by Will Bradley and others, were among the best.

Since the bulk of magazines was ordinarily circulated by mail, postal rates were very important. After the enactment of the Post Office Act of 1874, the rate for monthly and quarterly periodicals had been three cents per pound or fraction thereof, and two cents a pound for weeklies. But 1885 became an epochal year in magazine publishing when Congress passed a law reducing these rates to one cent a pound for all second-class mailings.[23] This cheap postage had much to do with the boom in magazine publishing during the eight years preceding the panic of 1893.

The rural free delivery system, begun experimentally in 1897, was rapidly increased during the first few years of the new century. It was of immense help to agricultural periodicals, to household and women's magazines, and to the cheap mail-order publications.

Club and agency rates for subscriptions sent by mail were usually a little above the amount received from newsstand sales. Thus, in 1885, the thirty-five-cent magazines got from $3.10 (*Harper's Magazine*) to $3.50 (*Century*), and a twenty-five-cent magazine like *Frank Leslie's Popular* received $2.10.

Census reports in these years did not separate newspaper advertising from that which appeared in magazines, but the increases of the grand total in all publications is instructive. It increased 80 per cent in the eighties; in the nineties, slowed down by hard times, it gained about one-third; and in the five years 1900–1905 it increased more than half. In the last-named year the total of $145,517,591 was more than double the 1890 figure. Though probably only about a fourth of this went to the magazines, it was far more than they had enjoyed a decade earlier, and it seemed stupendous then. It marked the beginning of an era in which advertising was not only to exert a great influence on American living, but was also to work an important change in the publishing economics of all periodicals.

The magazines were beginning to get their share of the advertiser's dollar by the beginning of the nineties. They were fattest with ad-

[23] United States Statutes at Large, 48 Cong., 2 Sess., ch. 242, March 3, 1885 (effective July 1, 1885).

vertising pages in December, because of Christmas announcements, and it may be noted that *Harper's Magazine* for December 1891 carried 177 pages of "ads," and the *Century* 150 pages. The rate for each was $250 a page. *Scribner's*, with a $150 page rate, had 136 pages; and the *Atlantic*, charging about $100, had 101 pages. The *Ladies' Home Journal* filled 13 of its quarto pages with advertising at a little over $2,000 a page. *Lippincott's* had 87 pages, the *North American Review* and *Popular Science Monthly* each 79, *Cosmopolitan* 75, *Forum* 55, and *Current Literature* 48. Some of the weeklies (especially *Youth's Companion*) and all of the mail-order journals were heavy with advertising.

When John Adams Thayer became advertising manager for the *Ladies' Home Journal* in 1892, its annual advertising revenue was about a quarter of a million dollars; when he left it to go to the *Delineator* some six years later, it was double that. In the fall of 1902 the *Delineator* boasted "more advertising than was ever inserted in any magazine published for women at any time, anywhere," [24] but it did not reach the million-a-year mark until ten years later.

By 1905 *McClure's* was printing an average of 165 pages of advertising a month (411,697 lines in the year) at $400 a page. *Munsey's*, with a much larger circulation, got $500 a page, but it had long been behind *McClure's* in the amount of advertising carried. *Review of Reviews*, with a rate of $225, was prosperous and fat, carrying an average of 150 pages of advertisements, sometimes as many as 200. *Harper's* had 134, and *Scribner's* 130. But *Collier's*, in that year of 1905, was the nation's advertising leader, at least in space, with an average of over 13 quarto pages a week (429,434 lines for the year). The *Saturday Evening Post* was rapidly overhauling it, with only about 8 per cent less linage.[25] The *Woman's Home Companion* estimated in 1904 that magazine advertising totaled about $30,000,000 a year.[26]

What happened to the advertising business in the latter eighties and the nineties may be explained in terms of the marketing process. In general, the sales stream for many years had flowed from manufacturer to jobber to retailer to consumer. Advertising, which was aimed (except in trade papers) to reach the consumer, was pretty much limited to the last part of this stream, and was performed by the retailer to produce the final objective of the whole process — purchase by the consumer. And since the retailer's market was a local one, the news-

[24] Quoted from the Butterick house organ by Frank Presbrey, *The History and Development of Advertising* (New York, 1929), p. 476.
[25] *Collier's* advertisement in *Ayer's Newspaper Annual*, 1907, p. 1269.
[26] *Woman's Home Companion*, v. 30, p. 8, Sept. 1904.

papers, with their close-to-home circulations, were used for advertising, rather than the nationally or regionally distributed magazines. This is the reason that few magazines carried any large amount of advertising before about 1885.

The marketing-advertising pattern described above is subject to some important exceptions, however. It had been demonstrated at a very early date that consumer advertising by the manufacturer could, in some cases, create such a demand that retailers would require large quantities of the advertised article from the jobbers; and jobbers, passing the demand back, would turn the manufacturer's advertising dollar into many profit dollars. This was so well recognized in the fields of proprietary medicines and cosmetics that new remedies, soaps, and so on commonly had to be backed by advertising to get themselves established in any large way. An important addition to manufacturers' advertising in the sixties and seventies was the sewing machine, and there was some piano and organ, as well as typewriter, advertising in the latter seventies. Book publishers were among the earliest advertisers, and periodicals themselves took a considerable amount of space, usually on an exchange basis.

Another exception to the formula stated above must be made in behalf of certain classes of weekly periodicals. Indeed all weeklies, being more closely related to the newspapers than the monthlies, were regarded as better advertising media. But farm papers were logical for the use of manufacturers of farm implements, seeds, and so on; and the cheap household monthlies were so completely adapted and committed to the announcements of producers who wished to bypass both jobber and retailer and sell to the consumer directly, that they came to be called "mail-order papers."

### GROWTH OF NATIONAL ADVERTISING

Then in the eighties, a phenomenal industrial development, along with the appearance of certain new inventions and some increase in magazine circulations, led to a gradual enlargement of consumer advertising on the part of manufacturers. Typewriters, which had begun tentatively in other decades, now became prominent, with the "ads" of the Caligraph and the Remington, and soon the Smith-Premier, Hammond, the eight-dollar American, and a half-dozen other makes. Waterman's Ideal Fountain Pen was a pioneer advertiser, as were Estabrook and Spencerian Steel Pens. "The W. L. Douglas $3 Shoe for Gentlemen" helped show the way in the eighties for the new national advertising by manufacturers. Douglas shares with Mrs.

Pinkham the distinction of pioneering the "portrait ad." Mrs. Pinkham's motherly but refined features doubtless reassured hesitating purchasers of her Vegetable Compound for Female Complaints, but to understand why the balding, mustached face of shoeman Douglas should sell so many three-dollar shoes, one must realize the sense of personal guarantee which a portrait gave to a product. Both Douglas and Mrs. Pinkham used their pictures not only in their advertising but on their packages: Mrs. Pinkham's lineaments were on her bottles, and those of Douglas were stamped into the sole of every shoe he made. In 1890 a San Francisco reader cut the Douglas picture from an advertisement, pasted it on an envelope containing his order, and stamped and mailed it without further address. The order was received promptly, and duly filled. Let us remember, too, that portraits of famous personages were much less common and far more prized in the eighties (and even in the nineties) than in later years.[27]

Royal Baking Powder, which was soon to take the upper left quarter-pages of the back covers of many magazines, with its cut of the package can and its motto "Absolutely Pure," was one of the early food and cooking products to advertise nationally. Dr. Price's Cream Baking Powder was a competitor. Another product in the food division was Baker's Breakfast Cocoa, with its picture of "La Belle Chocolatière," a small line drawing from a Dresden Gallery painting showing an old-fashioned maid carrying a cup of what was presumably cocoa (though in some advertisements it was Vanilla Chocolate) on a tray. "W. Baker & Co., Dorchester, Mass." was a very old firm, established in the year the Imperial Stamp Act was imposed upon the American colonies. Epp's Cocoa and Wilbur's Cocoa-Theta were competitors of the eighties, while Van Houten's Cocoa and Huyler's Cocoa and Chocolates came later. Durkee's Salad Dressing, "Unequalled for Excellence," began advertising widely about 1885, as did Armour's Extract of Beef, said to produce "That Feeling of Contentment." The first important soup advertising was that of Huckins, of Boston. The Great Atlantic and Pacific Tea Company, progenitor of all A&P stores, used its trade-mark of a grandmother (a rather grim beldame) pouring tea, also to advertise coffee and baking powder.

Apparel, as well as food, got a good start in national advertising in the eighties. In that decade, the promotion of Warner's Celebrated Coraline Corsets varied from full-page presentations, including pictures of graceful and tightly laced ladies, to smaller "ads" in which the woodcut showed an empty corset, which thus appeared less an article of apparel than an instrument of torture in a modern Inqui-

[27] See p. 152.

sition. The R & G Corsets were a close second; and there were the more "sensible" Ferris Waists, as well as Dr. Scott's Electric Corsets with their supposed curative values. For the men, there were the "made-to-order" Plymouth Rock $3 Pants and the competing Bay State Pants, the latter always heading its "ads" with the line "If You Wear Pants." Also there were Cluett Shirts and Collars, Armstrong Suspenders, and Regal and other brands of shoes.

In the eighties and early nineties the magazines contained the announcements of such pianos as Chickering, Ivers & Pond, Sohmer, Vose, Knabe, Everett, Emerson, Decker, Weber, and Fischer. The Estey Organ was widely advertised, especially in religious periodicals. As long as Knabe could buy half an inch across the bottom or the side of the back cover-page of a magazine, that was what it preferred; and Vose also used that style. In 1894 Steinway began the one-to-four-page reader type of ad; it was very attractive and was later used by Aeolian and other competitors. Several makes of music boxes were widely advertised. Other household luxuries promoted in the magazines of the eighties were Rogers Silverware and John Rogers statuary groups. Bathtubs were pictured and described in the latter eighties by the J. L. Mott Iron Works and others. Garland Stoves and Bay State Ranges, as well as Hartshorn Rollers for window shades, were early advertisers.

It was in the late eighties that the modern "safety" bicycle began its course of extraordinary popularity, largely aided by advertising. The Pope Manufacturing Company, of New Haven and Boston, had been using the magazines to promote its high-wheeled product; now Pope's ad-writer, Nathaniel C. Fowler, turned his bucolic pencil to the delineation of romantic country scenes traversed by riders of the new Columbia model. Pope's Columbia was paced by the Overman Wheel Company's Victor, but competition came thick and fast in the nineties. The March 1896 number of the *Cosmopolitan*, for example, contained the advertisements of 38 bicycle manufacturers. In that year the Monarch Cycle Manufacturing Company, of Chicago, spent $125,000 in advertising and sold 50,000 bicycles, which retailed at $80 to $100 each.[28]

ADVERTISERS OF THE 1890's

In the nineties came the tremendous upsurge in advertising that grew from the modest beginnings of the preceding decade. Only a few

[28] See pp. 377–80 for a review of the bicycle "craze."

of the leaders can be mentioned here.[29] The Eastman Kodak Company began the use of the words "You press the button; we do the rest" in 1889; in the latter nineties it had to abandon its famous slogan because the amateur had learned to do his own developing, and also because the appearance of a spate of competitors — Premo, Hawkeye, Bull's Eye, Quad, the three-dollar Kombi, and so on — had suggested a new slogan: "If it isn't an Eastman, it isn't a Kodak." By the end of the century Eastman was spending a record-breaking $750,000 a year in advertising.

The earliest breakfast foods to use advertising widely were Quaker Oats and H-O (Hornby Oats), both of which came into the magazines in the early nineties, the former with the figure of the well-nourished Quaker holding a package of the food in one hand and a scroll marked "Pure" in the other, and the latter with its Oliver Twist trade-mark showing the boy begging for more porridge. At the turn of the century the producers of H-O brought out Force, with its "Sunny Jim" trade-mark. C. W. Post, an invalid at a Battle Creek, Michigan, sanitarium, invented Postum Cereal and Grape Nuts ("There's a Reason") and poured large sums of money into their establishment shortly after 1900. Pettijohn's and Wheatena began somewhat earlier, and a smiling chef was calling attention to Cream of Wheat by 1896.

The National Biscuit Company offered a cracker with a name that addressed the consumer directly — Uneeda Biscuit. The H. J. Heinz Company advertised its pickles to the magic number of forty-seven varieties. Van Camp's Boston Baked Pork and Beans came from Indianapolis. The seed companies bought space not only in the farm and home periodicals but in the general magazines: early leaders in these announcements were W. Atlee Burpee, Philadelphia; Peter Henderson, New, York; and James Vick, Rochester. A host of others came on later, including D. M. Ferry & Company, Detroit; Vaughn's Seed Store, Chicago; and Starrs & Harrison, Painesville, Ohio.

Phonograph advertising on a national scale began in 1899 with the announcements of the Columbia Graphophone, followed three years later by the first Victrola advertising. "His Master's Voice" became one of the most famous of American trade-marks in the early years of the new century.

Soaps had long been standard advertising in America when Pears' Soap, an English product, began its first campaign in the United States in 1883. Though Pears' advertising was sometimes straight text, it usually employed large, attention-compelling pictures, with the slo-

---

[29] Presbrey, *The History and Development of Advertising*, chs. 38–53. This work is richer and more reliable for this period than for any other.

gan: "Good morning, have you used Pears' Soap?" Procter & Gamble's
Ivory Soap ("99 44/100 per cent. pure" and "It floats") was an advertising leader in the eighties and nineties. The three slogans just quoted,
with that of the Eastman Kodak and the De Long Hook and Eye
("See That Hump?") were the most famous of all of the early advertising catch lines. One that came in the latter nineties was "Have you a
little Fairy in your home?" — the slogan of Fairy Soap, always accompanied by charming illustrations of little girls. Cuticura's Soap
sometimes (though not always) pictured a man desperately scratching
his leg. Dr. Woodbury's Facial Soap showed the doctor's face and
head without a neck in its early advertising. Packer's Tar Soap, a
pioneer advertiser, was a leader in good illustration, with Louis
Rhead's poster art and E. W. Kemble's drawings of colored people.
Finally, well-posed human-interest photographs prevailed, and a picture of a little girl shampooing her brother's hair became famous.
Wool Soap's picture of two little girls became even better known:
"My mama used Wool Soap," says the child in the proper chemise;
"I wish mine had," says the one whose shirt has shrunk embarrassingly.

The three great cleaners represented heavily in the advertising of
the nineties were Sapolio, Pearline, and Gold Dust. For the first-named,
Artemas Ward supplied a long series of "ads," featuring proverbs, and
later James K. Fraser provided his "jingles." Pyle's Pearline, an old-
timer, was one of the first to use color art in its campaigns. The Gold
Dust Twins, devised by Kemble, made their product a top leader in
the nineties and later.

There were safety razor advertisers in the eighties and early nineties
— such as Diamond and Dr. Scott's Electric — but it was King C.
Gillette, using his portrait trade-mark, who started large campaigns in
that field about the end of our period. Williams and Colgate were
leading advertisers of shaving soaps in the nineties.

Chief dentifrices of the period were Sozodont, with its brilliantly smiling young lady, and the "deliciously flavored" Rubifoam. Others were
Dr. Lyon's Tooth Powder and Zonweiss Tooth Cream. Mennen's
toilet powders competed with Pozoni's Complexion Powder in the
pages of many magazines.

Mellin's Food was one of the great advertisers of the times. An
immigrant from England, it was a consistent space-buyer in the
eighties, using the picture of a healthy-looking child and the legend,
"This child was raised on Mellin's Food." Later its slogan was the line
from Shakespeare's *Henry VI*, "We are advertised by our loving
friends," and it led in large-space color advertising of fine quality.

A copy of the most elegant bicycle catalogue ever issued, descriptive of our new styles for 1892, will be sent to any address on receipt of three two-cent stamps.

## POPE MFG. CO.
### 221 COLUMBUS AVENUE,
### BOSTON, MASS.

( my mama used Wool Soap )    ( I wish mine had )

*WOOLENS* will not shrink if

# WOOL SOAP
### Is used in the laundry

## MAGAZINE "ADS" FAMILIAR TO READERS OF THE 1890's

See page 24 for the bicycle advertising, page 26 for mention of the Wool Soap "ads,"
and page 23 for Mrs. Pinkham and W. L. Douglas.

TYPES OF ILLUSTRATION IN THE ADVERTISING OF THE 1890's

See page 27 for Scott's Emulsion, and page 29 for Pears' Soap.

Such similar products as Lactated Food and Imperial Granum, early offerings in our period, fell by the way.

Leading advertised medicines were Castoria, St. Jacob's Oil, and Scott's Emulsion. Charles H. Fletcher bought small space in many media for Castoria ("Children Cry for It") in the seventies and eighties, building up a large business; but in the last few years of the century he plunged — and profitably — with full pages. Charles A. Vogeler's St. Jacob's Oil also began advertising in small space units in the seventies, to become in the succeeding decade one of the country's largest advertisers. H. D. Umbstaetter wrote its copy, brief and set without display lines or illustration, for a number of years.[30] Another liniment, Pond's Extract, had its advertisement in most of the magazines of the eighties; Omega Oil and Sloan's Liniment joined the procession a little later. Scott & Bowne's cod-liver oil known as Scott's Emulsion, with its trade-mark of the fisherman carrying a giant codfish over his back, came to be one of the best-known of medicines in the eighties and nineties. John E. Powers, one of the greatest advertisement writers of the period, did the Scott's Emulsion "ads" of the latter eighties, at a salary reported as a hundred dollars a day.[31] Syrup of Figs, with attractive illustration; Hostetter's Stomach Bitters, with its trade-mark of St. George and the Dragon; Dr. Pierce's Favorite Prescription; and that "powerful nerve tonic," Buffalo Lithia Water, were all prominent among the proprietary medicines of the times. Beecham's Pills were an old standby from England, and Ayer's Sarsaparilla and Cherry Pectoral were recommended tonics.

Liquors were not much advertised in the magazines, because the national circulation of such announcements encountered strong prohibition sentiment in many localities, and even laws against advertising liquors in certain states. But wines and ales were advertised in some magazines; and Pabst Malt Extract (the "Spring Medicine") and Anheuser-Busch's Malt Nutrine (the "Food Drink") had their virtues spread abroad pretty freely.

The railroads and the insurance companies learned to advertise largely in the nineties. By 1895 *McClure's*, for example, commonly carried six or eight pages of railroad advertising in each number. Leader among advertisers of life insurance was the Prudential, with the Rock of Gibraltar as its symbol. Book advertising, important in periodicals from their beginning, occupied much of the front "ad section" of most nationally circulated magazines. The International

---

[30] See Sketch 5 for further material on Umbstaetter.
[31] Presbrey, *The History and Development of Advertising*, p. 392.

Correspondence Schools became a large advertiser by the end of the century, as did the Swoboda Physical Culture System, with its pictures of manly muscularity. To make an end (when there really was no end), the Ingersoll watch at one dollar was shown in many magazines.

### PIONEER AUTOMOTIVE ADVERTISING

Though automobiles were advertised in the trade magazines in the latter nineties, it was not until the turn of the century that the first tentative consumer advertising of the new vehicles began to appear.

A pioneer "automobile number" of an American periodical was *Collier's* for January 17, 1903. This issue printed some articles about the new automotive vehicles, including Thomas A. Edison's startling prediction that eventually 40 per cent of the New York suburbanites would have their own cars, and a contribution to the debate as to the relative values of steam, electricity, and gasoline as the source of power. The following cars were advertised, usually in rather small space: Oldsmobile, Detroit, $650, which a commentator in the magazine calls merely "a gasoline motor under the bed of a buggy"; Winton, Cleveland, $2,500, 2 cylinders and 20 horsepower; General, Cleveland, 8 horsepower, "the only reasonably priced two-cylinder machine on the market"; Columbia, Hartford, 4 cylinders and 20 horsepower, "five speeds up to fifteen miles per hour"; National, Indianapolis, electric; White Steam Car, White Sewing Machine Company, Cleveland, $2,000, 10 horsepower, "with the distance of a gasoline and the ease of operation of an electric"; Hoffman, Cleveland, $800 to $950, 1 cylinder, 7 horsepower; Toledo, named after the city in which it was manufactured, $3,000, 18 horsepower; Waverly Electric, offered by the manufacturers of the Toledo, who also had a steam-driven car; Rambler, Kenosha, Wis., $750, 1 cylinder; Studebaker Electric, South Bend, Ind.; Stevens-Duryea, J. Stevens Arms and Tool Company, Chicopee Falls, Mass., $1,200, 2 cylinders, 7 horsepower; Haynes-Apperson, Kokomo, Ind., $1,200 to $1,800.

### IMPROVEMENTS IN ADVERTISING

Space units bought by national advertisers in the magazines during the eighties and nineties were small compared with those used later. Though full-page advertisements are found occasionally in magazines published in the first half of the nineteenth century, such space did not become common until the last few years of that century. Pears'

Soap's full pages became common in the standard magazines in the latter eighties. But the average size before the latter nineties was less than a quarter-page; while there were many half-pages, there were even more which measured only an inch or two. In September 1891 the *Ladies' Home Journal* filled eight of its large quarto pages with 243 advertisements, only two of which amounted to a quarter-page in size.[32] Twice in 1891, however, an advertiser took over its entire back cover; and when J. A. Thayer became advertising manager, full pages began to appear within the magazine: one for Hire's Root Beer in July 1892, and in December one for Pearline and another for Scott's Emulsion. Larger space gradually became the rule in the nineties. A leading advertising agent wrote in the trade journal *Printer's Ink* in 1900 that nothing less than a half-page would attract attention any more.[33] By 1903 the *Saturday Evening Post's* two-page "center spreads" were making a sensation in the advertising world — as that of the Victor Talking Machine, featuring the "His Master's Voice" picture, in the issue for April 25, 1903.

A growing artistry in American advertising was repeatedly noted by *Printer's Ink* in the early nineties. Increased space gave opportunity for a more skillful handling of white space in typographical design. The popular poster art was utilized by several advertisers; Packer's Tar Soap, Pabst Malt Extract, and the Monarch, Victor, and other bicycle-makers used striking poster effects for a time. Occasional two-color presentations were used on the back covers of such magazines as *Ladies' Home Journal* and *Youth's Companion* in the early eighties; and *Puck* and *Truth*, which used chromolithography lavishly, on a few occasions gave that kind of treatment to cover advertisements. But by far the most striking irruption of color into magazine advertising came in the *Youth's Companion's* World's Fair number for May 4, 1893. In that issue Mellin's Food took the back cover to reproduce in full color by the lithographic process Perrault's Paris salon picture, "The Awakening of Cupid." For that advertisement Doliber & Goodal, of Boston, the American agents of Mellin's Food, paid fourteen thousand dollars, long a record price for a single insertion.[34] The use of paintings for the illustration of advertisements was an English technique, and the first to use it to any considerable extent in the United States were Pears' Soap, Mellin's Food, and Pearline. The pencils of comic artists — notably E. W. Kemble — were often employed by American advertisers in the nineties.

[32] This computation does not include the half-page occupied by the *Journal's* own announcement. It does include cover-pages.
[33] J. W. Barber in *Printer's Ink*, v. 30, Jan. 17, 1900, p. 8.
[34] Presbrey, *The History and Development of Advertising*, p. 386.

JINGLE, JINGLE

The sudden outburst of rhymed advertising, or "jingles," in 1900–1905 was an interesting phenomenon. Copy writers had occasionally given way to the wiles of the muse throughout the nineteenth century, but perhaps there was more doggerel in the advertising of the nineties than previously. Charles M. Snyder's rhymes for the De Long Hook and Eye advertising caught the public attention, to wit:

> He rose, she took the seat and said:
> "I thank you," and the man fell dead.
> But ere he turned a lifeless lump,
> He murmured: "See that hump?"

But the leaders in the explosion of rhyme at the turn of the century were Sapolio, the breakfast food Force, and the Lackawanna Railroad. James Kenneth Fraser devised the advertisements of Sapolio's "Spotless Town," charmingly illustrated with quaint houses and quainter characters. We introduce the mayor:

> I am the Mayor of Spotless Town,
> The brightest man for miles around.
> The shining light of wisdom can
> Reflect from such a polished man,
> And so I say to high and low:
> The brightest use Sapolio.

Jim Dumps, *alias* Sunny Jim, was the character used to advertise Force, and to make one of the most spectacular advertising successes of the times. He was the invention of Minnie Maud Hanff, who wrote the verses, and Dorothy Ficken, who drew the pictures, and he soon became familiar to every reader of periodicals, a stage character, and an epithet and nickname.

> Jim Dumps was a most unfriendly man,
> Who lived his life on the hermit plan.
> In his gloomy way he'd gone through life,
> And made the most of woe and strife,
> Till Force one day was served to him.
> Since then they've called him Sunny Jim.

When the Lackawanna, a freight line between New York and Buffalo, put on passenger trains, it advertised cleanliness of travel in its cars, because the track was ballasted entirely with rock and its locomotives burned anthracite instead of bituminous coal. Wendell P. Colton, advertising manager, invented the epithet, "The Road of Anthracite," and the character of Phoebe Snow, dainty girl in white:

> Says Phoebe Snow,
> About to go
> Upon a trip to Buffalo:
> My gown stays white
> From morn to night
> Upon the Road of Anthracite.

Such were the leaders, but there were many others.[35]

### ADVERTISING ABUSES

The tremendous growth of advertising at the century's end served to emphasize some of the abuses that had grown up in the industry. Most of the cheap publications known as "mail-order papers" (because their advertisers sold their products, their agencies, and their "secrets" directly to readers by mail) had few or no limitations of honesty, taste, or even decency. In many media the announcements of manhood restorers, bust developers, contraceptives, patent medicines composed largely of opiates and alcohol, and consumption and cancer cures were multiplied. Many very respectable periodicals advertised No-to-bac with the revolting slogan "Don't Tobacco Chew and Spit Your Life Away!" Fraudulent stock-selling schemes flourished by the aid of advertising.

Some periodicals began protecting their readers against fraudulent advertising as early as 1880,[36] and gradually reliance on the *caveat emptor* rule was abandoned by the better class of periodicals. By the end of the century obvious frauds and fakes were barred from most reputable magazines. Leadership in the reform of advertising was assumed by magazine publishers and their advertising managers, who realized that unreliable and disreputable announcements imperiled the entire business. The *Ladies' Home Journal* began its crusade against fake remedies in 1904, to be joined the next year by *Collier's*; the result was the National Food and Drug Act of 1906.[37]

Probably no crusading will ever dislodge the testimonial, with its direct personal appeal; of course, some of them are honest — even when paid for. A certain world-famous clergyman was probably an actual user of Pears' Soap when he wrote:

[35] See *Printer's Ink*, Fiftieth Anniversary Number, v. 184, July 28, 1938, Part II, p. 174; Presbrey, *op. cit.*, pp. 374–81, 384–85.
[36] Mott, *op. cit.*, v. 3, pp. 12–13.
[37] See Sketches 14 and 9.

If cleanliness is next to Godliness, soap must be considered as a means of Grace, and a clergyman who recommends moral things should be willing to recommend soap. I am told that my commendation of Pears' Soap has opened for it a large sale in the United States. I am willing to stand by every word in favor of it that I ever uttered. A man must be fastidious indeed who is not satisfied with it.

Henry Ward Beecher.[38]

There was widespread complaint about the use of the female figure in the advertisements of the nineties. The Illinois Federation of Women's Clubs declared in 1899 that such illustration "lowers the standard of womanhood, detracts from womanly dignity, and corrupts the youth of the land." [39] All this referred chiefly to advertisements of corsets and underwear, but also to some art reproductions. Oneita Elastic Ribbed Union Suits were advertised with a figure posed much like a statue. Another firm used the "jingle":

> Though love be cold, do not despair —
> There's Ypsilanti Underwear.

The *Ladies' Home Journal*, which announced in 1898 its determination to abandon the discussion of women's underwear in its articles and departments because the subject was "offensive to refined and sensitive women," [40] allowed its advertisers to continue, however, to exploit the female form divine. It must be remembered that complete coverage, except in the ballroom, was Item Number One in decorum for the female of the nineties.

A very different subject of complaint was the "tailing" of fiction into the advertising pages in order to give a higher readership value to those pages. E. W. Bok claimed that he invented that device on the *Ladies' Home Journal* in 1896.[41] Within a few years nearly all the quarto-size periodicals were following the fashion thus set, and even the standard-size magazines often had special departments set down in the midst of their advertising sections. Wrote the editor of *Current Literature* in 1903: "It is certain that the art of advertising has become one of the most important in the conduct of business, but it is not reasonable that the art should be foisted upon the face of the literature of which magazines are the exponents." [42] Reasonable or not, the technique was to continue and to become more elaborate and extensive.

---

[38] In a Pears' advertisement doubtless widely published, but noted in *American Magazine*, v. 8, Oct. 1888, advertising section, p. 44.

[39] *Printer's Ink*, Fiftieth Anniversary Number, *op. cit.*, p. 132.

[40] *Ladies' Home Journal*, v. 15, Feb. 1898, p. 28.

[41] E. W. Bok, *The Americanization of Edward Bok* (New York, 1923), p. 234.

[42] *Current Literature*, v. 34, p. 9, Jan. 1903.

### THREAT OF TRUST COMBINATIONS

The trust mergers that came to a climax in the last year or two of the century constituted a great threat to the expanding advertising industry. Such combinations were frank attempts to eliminate competition, and competition is certainly the life of the advertising trade. The formation of the "baking-powder trust," which included nearly all of the leading advertisers in that field, occurred in 1899 and was followed by an immediate decline in their advertising. Similar trusts in the tobacco, chewing gum, biscuit, and other fields drove the advertising men to something like despair.

But in the opening years of the new century the balance sheets in these industries began to reveal the fact that lack of competition within a field did not result in total loss of business. It was realized that there was such a thing as competition between desires on a broader basis, so that candy and chewing gum actually competed with smoking tobacco and cigarettes. It was also discovered that a new organization outside a trust could build up a formidable opposition by using money and brains on a new product; such was the challenge of the Frank H. Fleer Company and their Chiclets to the chewing gum trust in the years 1898–1905. As a result of such object lessons and experiences, advertising made a quick recovery, and was ready for its major development.

### TRADE-MARKS

But probably the one factor that contributed most to bring magazine advertising to a high peak in 1905 was the increasing use of trade-marked goods. The development of standard brands by national advertising offered a fantastic opportunity to the producer who had a good product, the facilities for mass production, and the sense to employ good advertising men.

Many of the outstanding trade-marks, characteristic pictures, and slogans have been mentioned already in this chapter. The boy in the slicker advertising Uneeda Biscuits, Hire's Root Beer's curly-headed boy, Cottolene's "Pigs in Clover," "Jones, He Pays the Freight" on his scales, Cascarets that "Work While You Sleep," Dr. Williams' "Pink Pills for Pale People" will do for examples here.

In a 1905 issue, *Printer's Ink* displayed a summary of the advertising situation at the close of the period presently under survey, 1885–1905, from which the following sentences may be quoted:

Suddenly the manufacturing world has developed an intense, anxious interest in both advertising and the consumer. It is glad to talk plans of advertising and discuss trade-marks with solicitors, where a year ago the latter would have got no hearing. Several influences have created this interest. The work of the agencies for one, and the newspaper advertising of Cyrus Curtis, for another.[43] The trade press in every manufacturing field is giving attention to advertising, too. But the prime factor in this new attitude is the success of certain trade-marked goods. The trade-mark has offered a method of disposing of a product so broad, and individual trade-marks have in many instances become so valuable, that all manufacturers are interested, big and little.

They now realize that this is a golden age in trade-marks. . . .[44]

[43] This refers to the advertising of the *Saturday Evening Post* in the newspapers, but Curtis had made almost as spectacular a showing when he had put on big campaigns in the papers for his *Ladies' Home Journal*. See Sketches 27 and 14.

[44] *Printer's Ink*, v. 54, May 31, 1905, pp. 36–37.

## CHAPTER III

## EDITORS AND CONTRIBUTORS

SOME of the greatest editors in the history of American magazines were at work in the 1890's. The *Century's* Gilder and *Harper's* Alden were veterans of many years' service. Page made a distinguished record first on the *Forum*, then on the *Atlantic Monthly*, and finally on *World's Work*. Bok, of the *Ladies' Home Journal*, and Lorimer, of the *Saturday Evening Post*, were outstanding in ability and success. McClure was an editorial genius, and Munsey was (at the least) an acute and successful magazine publisher. Walker, of the *Cosmopolitan*, was a strong character and a great editor. Burlingame, of *Scribner's*, Shaw, of the *Review of Reviews*, and Flower, of the *Arena*, were distinguished editors of great magazines. One could lengthen the list without impairing its quality very much.

Editorial salaries of that time sound low to modern ears. Bok thought that the $10,000 a year which he, in common with Gilder and Alden, received in 1890 was liberal; and so it was in comparison with the $4,000 which the *Atlantic* paid Aldrich at that time.[1] One may quote, for comparison's sake, some figures which Bok cited in an article published in the *Cosmopolitan* in 1894, to the effect that young men of thirty or under in business in New York city rarely received salaries exceeding $2,000 a year.[2]

### CONTRIBUTORS' COMPLAINTS

Though the editor did not always love his contributors, nor was he invariably beloved of them, the relations of professional and semi-professional writers with the editorial office had to be reasonably pleasant if the magazine was to prosper. Editor Bird, of *Lippincott's*, wrote a little article in 1895 pointing out that there were inevitable cross-purposes, if not a natural enmity, between editors and contributors.[3] One thinks, on the other hand, of the close friendships that often existed between certain editors and contributors over many years — Gilder's with John Burroughs and others, Flower's with Hamlin Garland, McClure's with Miss Tarbell, Alden's with William Dean

[1] *Author*, v. 2, p. 7, Jan. 1890.
[2] *Cosmopolitan*, v. 16, p. 332, Jan. 1894.
[3] *Lippincott's*, v. 56, p. 859, Dec. 1895.

Howells, and that of Bob Davis and other Munsey editors with Will Porter.

But writers nearly always think themselves underpaid. An exception is found in the extraordinary action of Andrew Lang, the English poet and critic, who once wrote to the newly launched *America*:

Gentlemen:

I have received your cheque for £13, which I venture to think is too large, and I will therefore send you another piece of verse (when I write a piece) or of prose, for which I will ask you to be kind enough to send no payment.

Yours truly,

A. Lang.[4]

Many others complained bitterly, of course, not only about low rates but about having their work refused when other contributions that they were convinced were inferior found favor with the editors. Aldrich once received a letter from an irate would-be contributor who threatened the editor with a "public horsewhipping" because he declined to apologize for keeping an article on "Shakespeare's Viola" for seven weeks and then returning it (the author believed) unread.[5] More reasonably, a writer in the *Atlantic's* "Contributor's Club" in 1900 complained of current restrictions as to topic, method, and length.[6] This was much like Howell's complaint against the usurpation of magazine pages by "science, politics, economics, and the timely topics which I will call contemporanics."[7]

The editor must always be the victim of a pincers movement, receiving pressures from both contributors and readers. This is especially true of writing that comes under suspicion of being indecent or indelicate. A correspondent of the *Illustrated American*, for example, complained that this weekly had printed something "which might cause thoughts to arise in a young lady's mind."[8] Presumably, he meant impure thoughts, but was reluctant to write the word "impure." Alden once declared that "the magazine goes to an audience to which it is committed by a pledge, in part explicit, but for the most part a matter of implicit understanding" to print nothing improper. And improprieties he described by an eloquent but not very explicit sentence:

There are doubtless authors who revel in brutalities, who enjoy an infernal habitation not for its purgatorial fires but for its sulphurous airs, and who complain because they may not make their descents before a polite audience; but

---

[4] *America*, v. 6, p. 758, Sept. 24, 1891.
[5] Ferris Greenslet, *The Life of Thomas Bailey Aldrich* (Boston, 1908), pp. 149–50.
[6] *Atlantic Monthly*, v. 68, pp. 425–26, Sept. 1900.
[7] William Dean Howells, *Life and Letters* (New York, 1902), p. 11.
[8] *Illustrated American*, v. 4, p. 386, Nov. 15, 1890.

these things do not come within the scope of the demand of any species of human culture.[9]

The *Century* was criticized rather more often than *Harper's* for false delicacy in this period; James L. Ford's series of satires on the former, published in *Truth* in 1894, was at once amusing and biting. But many periodicals were more prudish than the *Century*.[10] Bok once deleted "a goodly portion" of a story by Mark Twain. In his autobiography he wrote, with singular lack of perception:

> Twain evidently saw that Bok was right, for he wrote: "Of course, I want every single line and word of it left out," and then he added: "Do me the favor to call the next time you are in Hartford. I want to say things which — well, I want to argue with you." Bok never knew what those "things" were, for at the next meeting they were not referred to.[11]

Kipling's similar assent to deleting the drinking of liquor in "William the Conqueror" and the doubtless apocryphal suggestion of the author to substitute Mellin's Food are well known. Bok apparently thought Brander Matthews invented the yarn, and he sought and received Kipling's confirmation that it was not strict fact: "No, I said nothing about Mellin's Food. I wish I had."[12] Julian Hawthorne once had a quarrel with *Collier's* because he found, upon reading his story of a seduced maiden in that weekly's columns, that the editor had spared his readers' feelings by revealing that the girl had been secretly married; thus the little stranger was legitimized for the columns of *Collier's*.[13] Walker "edited" Tolstoi's novel *Resurrection* in the course of its serial publication through the *Cosmopolitan*, and finally suspended it entirely. Walker is also said to have increased the demand for Richard Le Gallienne's version of the *Rubaiyat* in book form by bowdlerizing it (with asterisks) when he printed it in the magazine.[14]

### THE MAGAZINIST

The profession of magazinist was fully developed by the nineties. Magazine staffs were largely filled by recruiting from newspapers and from the ranks of promising contributors, but more and more maga-

[9] Henry Mills Alden, *Magazine Writing and the New Literature* (New York, 1908), p. 68. See Alden's statements regarding deletions in Hardy's "Jude the Obscure," in *Harper's*, v. 102, p. 809, April 1901; and Mary Ellen Chase, *Thomas Hardy from Serial to Novel* (Minneapolis, 1927), pp. 115–77.

[10] Note Arthur L. Scott, "The *Century Magazine* Edits *Huckleberry Finn*," in *American Literature*, v. 27, pp. 356–62, Nov. 1955.

[11] Edward Bok, *The Americanization of Edward Bok* (New York, 1920), pp. 382–83. Other examples are here given of agreement to editorial revision on the part of famous authors and public men.

[12] *Ibid.*, pp. 219–20.

[13] *Journalist*, v. 9, March 16, 1889, p. 18; *Critic*, v. 14, pp. 120–21, March 9, 1889.

[14] Charles Hanson Towne, *Adventures in Editing* (New York, 1926), pp. 39–40.

zines came to place in their top positions men who had been schooled in editorial work in other magazine organizations. Thus a group of workers on the staffs of periodicals developed. At the same time, an even larger number of writers came to devote a major share of their time to the preparation of magazine material, with ultimate printing in book form often in mind, but with magazine publication the direct first object. They usually began as free lancers, and sometimes remained in that independent position; but many of them formed some connection, as departmental editors or regular contributors, with one or more periodicals.

Once a writer had appeared in two or three of the leading magazines, he was likely to go on, hit the stride of the successful contibutor, become adept in furnishing the editors with what they wanted, and make himself a good income and a certain amount of fame. Brander Matthews once boasted that there had been times when he had "had five contributions in a single number of a magazine; and I have contributed in a single month to five different magazines."[15] With the passing of the anonymous periodical article, a writer who furnished more than one piece to a given issue had to use pen names — which was what Theodore Dreiser did in *Success*.[16] Such busy writers based much of their work on editorial suggestions. This was the case even with the poets, and Charles Hanson Towne tells how Theodosia Garrison supplied verse immediately on demand for the Butterick magazines.[17] Many others must have turned it out quite as freely.

Julian Hawthorne, one of the active magazinists of the period, estimated in 1888 that five thousand Americans earned their living by the pen.[18] This apparently did not include newspapermen, but it did take in the writers and editors of the weekly story papers, the contributors to syndicates for Sunday papers, and the hack writers of serials and departments for the cheap mail-order periodicals. It was twelve years later that W. J. Lampton estimated in the *New York Times* that there were twenty thousand persons in the United States then writing for publication — most of them "either not successful or only apparently so."[19] "The mere itch for authorship," said the *Chautauquan*, "— the *cacoëthes scribendi* — has become a pestiferous epidemic against which there appears to be no adequate and practicable guarantee."[20]

But editors and publishers seemed never to have too many writers

[15] *Unpartizan Review*, v. 14, p. 97, July 1920.
[16] Dreiser correspondence, University of Pennsylvania Library.
[17] Towne, *Adventures in Editing*, p. 161.
[18] *Belford's Magazine*, v. 1, p. 29, June 1888.
[19] Quoted in *Writer*, v. 13, p. 99, July 1900.
[20] *Chautauquan*, v. 16, p. 350, Jan. 1892.

besieging them, for, as the *Writer* pointed out in the mid-nineties, prize offers were nothing less than rife: "The prize offer for manuscripts is one of the prominent features of literary life today." [21] Such contests were believed, doubtless, to be good advertising; but there was always the great hope springing in the breast of the editor that he might discover new talent of the first order. Walter Hines Page, in his A.L.A. address, said:

> The reason you have rubbish in the magazines is because the editors cannot get anything better. . . . I should, as poor an editor as I am, undertake to make a better magazine than you have ever seen if I could find writers who could write well enough about contemporaneous things.[22]

On the other hand, the writers looked upon the mounting stockpiles of manuscripts with alarm, and some of them did what they could to discourage beginners. Junius Henri Browne, writing in the *Forum* in 1886, said: "There is not a magazine in the country but has enough accepted articles for the next two years without any additions." [23] Two years later Hawthorne made about the same calculation regarding the overstock then.[24] The *Ladies' Home Journal*, said the *Writer*, received 15,205 manuscripts in 1890, of which it accepted 497; and only about 200 of those accepted had come from free lancers.[25]

### PAYMENT OF AUTHORS

There was a great diversity in the rates of payment by magazines for literary material. In the course of the twenty years included in the present treatment, the rate to the unknown writer increased very little: in the best magazines it appears to have ranged from half a cent to a little over one cent a word throughout the period. In the late eighties the standard rate of the "quality magazines" (except for the *Atlantic*, which paid less) was ten dollars a page, or three-quarters of a cent a word. *Cosmopolitan, Drake's, Frank Leslie's Popular Monthly*, and the *American Magazine* paid about half of that; and *Belford's* and *Outing* about a quarter of a cent a word. Among the weeklies, *Harper's Weekly* and the *New York Ledger* paid a cent a word; and *Truth, Frank Leslie's Illustrated Newspaper, Once a Week, Munsey's Weekly*, and *Town Topics* about half of that, or five dollars a column.[26]

[21] *Writer*, v. 8, p. 45, April 1895.
[22] *World's Work*, v. 4, Oct. 1902, p. 2562.
[23] *Forum*, v. 1, p. 479, Aug. 1886.
[24] *Belford's Magazine*, v. 1, p. 29, Jan. 1888.
[25] *Writer*, v. 5, p. 108, May 1891.
[26] For the data about the late eighties, see *Journalist*, v. 8, Oct. 6, 1888, p. 7; *ibid.*, v. 9, July 13, 1889, p. 5. For the beginning of the new century, we may accept the generalization in Howells, *Life and Letters*, p. 11: "five or six dollars a thousand words for the work of the unknown writer."

It might be expected that the prosperity which came to the ten-cent magazines would be passed on to the contributors in the form of increased rates. This doubtless happened to some big-name writers, but the unknowns and the hack writers continued to receive about a cent a word from the first-line magazines and less from the cheap papers.[27] *Smart Set*, for example, almost never paid over a cent a word: it got O. Henry stories at that rate. It paid twenty-five cents a line for verse, on the theory that "poets are born, not paid." [28] Jack London, who once received five dollars in cash and five free subscriptions for a story from the *National Magazine*,[29] wrote an amusing scene for his novel *Martin Eden*, in which his hero visits the office of the "Transcontinental," seizes the business manager by the throat, and shouts, "Dig up, you venerable discourager of rising young talent! Dig up, or I'll shake it out of you, even if it's all in nickels!" He gets four dollars and a quarter from the business manager, and sixty cents and a ferry ticket from the trembling editor.[30] Even established writers were often badly paid. Kate Field pointed out in her *Washington* in 1893 that "It is quite possible for a man to achieve a national reputation for literary work by faithfully devoting his whole time to it, and still earn less than a thousand dollars a year." Kate, who was something of a shrew on occasion, added: "To be moderately hungry once in a while is certainly more stimulating to the imagination than to dine out four times a week." [31] How now, good Kate, sweet Kate, "that feed'st me with the very name of meat"!

In the eighties the sums mentioned above as "standard rates" were paid rather generally even to the magazine's more valued writers. The two most celebrated high-water marks in payments to contributors in that decade were made by the *Century* — the $50,000 paid Nicolay and Hay for their life of Lincoln and the $15,000 paid George Kennan for his articles on Siberia; [32] but both of these payments were on the basis of a cent a word, each series running for over two years. Undoubtedly the *Century* sometimes paid a little more than that to favorite authors, as when it gave John Burroughs $450 for three articles in 1886, which Burroughs said, in a letter to a friend, was "too much." [33] But a cent a word was standard, and two cents was unusual even to the most valued contributors.

[27] *Cosmopolitan* wrote Theodore Dreiser, Feb. 26, 1898, that their rate was a cent a word (Dreiser Collection, University of Pennsylvania Library).
[28] Towne, *Adventures in Editing*, pp. 65, 76.
[29] Charmian London, *The Book of Jack London* (New York, 1921), v. 1, p. 307.
[30] Jack London, *Martin Eden* (New York, 1909), p. 296.
[31] *Kate Field's Washington*, v. 8, p. 216, Oct. 4, 1893.
[32] William W. Ellsworth, *A Golden Age of Authors* (Boston, 1919), pp. 260–67.
[33] Clara Barrus, *The Life and Letters of John Burroughs* (Boston, 1925), v. 1, p. 282.

But when the ten-cent magazine revolutionized periodical publication, and when large circulations and heavy advertising patronage brought prosperity to leading magazines, much larger sums began to be paid to star contributors. *McClure's* bought the American serial rights to Kipling's rather short "Captains Courageous" for $12,000 in 1896,[34] and two years later paid $25,000 for the longer "Kim."[35] *Harper's* was said to have paid Mrs. Humphrey Ward $15,000 for the American serial rights of each of her novels which it ran.[36] The *Ladies' Home Journal* contracted with William E. Gladstone in the mid-nineties for his recollections at $15,000, but the statesman's death prevented the fulfillment of the contract.[37] Gladstone is said to have refused to furnish the *Cosmopolitan* a short article at a dollar a word.[38] That offer, if made, was freakish; Howells was doubtless right in pointing out that fifteen cents a word was virtually the upper limit for even the most famous literary contributors at the turn of the century.[39]

### MAGAZINE TO BOOK

In the same essay in which he made this statement, Howells asserted that

in belles-lettres at least, most of the best literature now sees the light in the magazines, and most of the second-best appears first in book form. . . . Many factitious and fallacious literary reputations have been made through books, but very few have been made through the magazines, which are not only the best means of living, but of outliving, with the author; they are both bread and fame to him. . . . They are ephemeral in form, but in substance they are not ephemeral, and what is best of them awaits its resurrection in the book, which, as the first form, is so often a lasting death.[40]

This was a striking declaration, but it set forth a state of facts that had long been recognized in the publishing trade. As early as 1885, Dana Estes, of the Boston book house of Estes, Lauriat & Company, testified before the Senate Committee on Patents, which had the matter of international copyright under study, in the following terms:

It is impossible to make the books of most American authors pay unless they are first published and acquire recognition through the columns of the magazines. If it were not for that one saving opportunity of the great American magazines, which are now the leading ones of the world and have an international reputation

[34] *Bookman,* v. 4, p. 95, Oct. 1896.
[35] S. S. McClure, *My Autobiography* (New York, 1914), p. 229.
[36] Walter Hines Page, *A Publisher's Confession* (New York, 1905), p. 22.
[37] Bok, *The Americanization of Edward Bok*, pp. 198–99.
[38] *Bookman,* v. 3, p. 98, April 1896.
[39] Howells, *Life and Letters*, p. 11.
[40] Howells, pp. 9–10.

and circulation, American authorship would be at a still lower ebb than at present.[41]

It may be doubted whether the international copyright agreement, when it became effective in 1891, had any decisive effect on American authorship as a trade or business. But at any rate, the investigation pursued at the time of its adoption served to emphasize the importance of the magazine as an aid to literary effort in this country.

[41] Senate Report 1188, 49 Cong., 1 Sess., v. 7, p. 55, 1885–86.

# CHAPTER IV

## THE GENERAL MONTHLY MAGAZINES

AT THE beginning of the twenty-year period 1885–1905, the leaders in the field of national illustrated monthlies devoted to the publication of literary miscellany were two New York magazines, *Harper's* and the *Century*; and at the end of the period, though more or less battered by competition of many kinds, these two, with the addition of *Scribner's*, were still leaders in what they liked to call the "quality magazine" class.

Though it did not drop the word *"New"* from its full title of *Harper's New Monthly Magazine* [1] until it was half a century old in 1900, the chief of the Harper group of periodicals was the oldest of general monthlies even in 1885. Henry Mills Alden had then been its editor for sixteen years, and he was to round out the longest term of service for the editor of any major American general magazine — a full fifty years. William Dean Howells was important in *Harper's* in these years, as the writer of the influential "Editor's Study" for some ten years, and as a contributor of serial fiction. The magazine's greatest hit, and the greatest fiction success of the decade in any magazine, was du Maurier's "Trilby," of 1894.[2] Perhaps the most brilliant decade in the long history of *Harper's Magazine* was that of the 1890's.

The *Century Magazine* [3] was edited throughout our period by Richard Watson Gilder, poet, reformer, and able editor. The great *Century* series of Civil War memoirs continued through most of the eighties and was followed by Nicolay and Hay's long life of Lincoln. The magazine was very strong in serial biography and in short fiction. It was beautifully illustrated and well printed. Timothy Cole's fine woodcuts continued to appear long after halftones had made the graver almost obsolete.

*Scribner's Magazine* [4] was founded in 1887 to compete in the "quality group," but at twenty-five cents a copy as against the prevailing thirty-five cents. The versatile E. L. Burlingame was its editor for more than a quarter of a century. *Scribner's* placed its emphasis on the fine arts, urbane criticism, and travel, with excellent illustration. Perhaps its outstanding contributors during its first twenty years

---

[1] See Sketch 16 in F. L. Mott, *A History of American Magazines* (Cambridge, 1938), v. 2.
[2] See p. 133.
[3] See Sketch 21 in Mott, *op. cit.*, v. 3.
[4] See Sketch 28 in this volume.

were Robert Louis Stevenson, James M. Barrie, and Theodore Roosevelt.

The *Atlantic Monthly*, of Boston,[5] occupied, in the words of the *Dial*, "a place by itself." And that old-school critic went on to say that the *Atlantic* stood "more distinctly for culture than any other American magazine."[6] Whether because of this distinction or in spite of it, the Boston monthly's circulation dropped to the remarkably low figure of about seven thousand before Walter Hines Page took over the editorship in 1898. Page and Bliss Perry, his successor, broke the literary calm of the *Atlantic* by introducing political and social controversy, and thus gave the old magazine a new lease on life.

## DOWN A NOTCH OR TWO OR THREE

*Lippincott's Magazine*,[7] of Philadelphia, was without illustration after 1885, and in the late eighties it adopted the plan, to be followed throughout the remainder of its long life, of printing a novel in each issue. They were usually good novels; but this policy, reducing as it did the space available for other matter, tended to take *Lippincott's* out of the class of the the the general literary monthly.

*Frank Leslie's Popular Monthly*,[8] a good magazine of the second class, declined when Mrs. Leslie leased it to Frederic L. Colver and went abroad for a holiday. Returning in 1898, she demonstrated again her uncanny managerial ability by taking the magazine over, reducing the price from twenty-five to ten cents, brightening the contents, and building circulation and advertising in less than six months to a point that placed it among the more prosperous periodicals.[9] It was not until 1906 that the name of the monthly was changed to *American Magazine*.

*Drake's Magazine*[10] was a ten-cent monthly begun in November 1882 and distinguished by an excellent department of humor entitled "Quacks." It was published for more than a decade, had good variety, some sharp editorial comment, and a limited amount of illustration. *Leisure Hours* (1885–1902), by Charles A. Dixon of Philadelphia, was another early ten-center. The *Brooklyn Magazine* (1884–1889)[11] was

[5] See Sketch 30 in Mott, *op. cit.*, v. 2.
[6] *Dial*, v. 13, p. 204, Oct. 1, 1892.
[7] See Sketch 4 in Mott, *op. cit.*, v. 3.
[8] See Sketch 28 in Mott, *op. cit.*, v. 3.
[9] *Journalist*, v. 23, p. 193, Sept. 24, 1898; Madeleine B. Stern, *Purple Passage: The Life of Mrs. Frank Leslie* (Norman, Okla., 1953), pp. 170–72.
[10] Published in New York by John N. Drake, in ten annual volumes and five numbers of v. 11. It published 48 to 64 pages per issue, with cheap paper toward the end in March 1893.
[11] Bok and Colver began this magazine as the organ of a club of young men connected with Plymouth Church. At first it was very much a local periodical. It had no money to pay contributors, but Bok was a skilful beggar and short pieces by Generals Grant, Sherman, and Sheridan, William Dean Howells, Harriet Prescott Spofford, Lucy Larcom, Cardinal Gibbons,

founded by two boys later famous in the magazine world, largely as the vehicle for publication of Henry Ward Beecher's sermons. The boys were Edward Bok and Frederic L. Colver, but Standard Oil's R. T. Bush moved their monthly to New York and attempted unsuccessfully to make a national magazine of it under the not unfamiliar title of *American Magazine*. A Brooklyn magazine of longer life was conducted by the poet Will Carleton under the name *Every Where*.[12] It had no little variety, with home departments and so on, as well as the contributions of Margaret E. Sangster, Kate Upson Clark, and other writers for family journals; but its characteristic contents were the poems and homely philosophy of Carleton, and it died soon after he did. *Belford's Monthly* [13] was a Chicago magazine devoted largely to Democratic party measures, such as free trade. It printed much fiction, however, together with poetry, book reviews, science items, and notes on the theater. During its first three years, 1888–1891, it printed a novel in each number. These were rather poor stuff; but in *Belford's* latter years, such contributors as Richard Henry Stoddard, Junius Henri Browne, Kate Field, Edgar Saltus, Edgar Fawcett, Julian Hawthorne, Julia Magruder, and Hamlin Garland improved the standard. But Belford, Clarke & Company, the book publishers who issued the magazine, gave it up during the panic of 1893. That was the year in which *Worthington's Illustrated Monthly Magazine* [14] was founded

Canon Farrar, and others, appeared. Even President Hayes wrote a two-page article, favoring Federal aid to education, for the magazine. A feature was the publication of the weekly sermons of the two most famous preachers of the times — Beecher and Talmadge. In April 1886 the magazine took over the *Plymouth Pulpit*, which had been published, with interruptions, since 1868 (see Mott, *op. cit.*, v. 3, p. 426). Circulation of the *Brooklyn Magazine* increased to 8,000 by 1886, when it was bought by Rufus T. Bush in order to give his son, who was just finishing college, a chance in the publishing business. Illustration was added, the name was changed to *American Magazine* in May 1887, and about $250,000 was spent to make the handsome new magazine, under W. C. Wyckoff's editorship, a success. It had some first-class contributors. Though it reached a circulation of 50,000 for a time, it was a bankrupt when it issued its last number in February 1889.

[12] Published Sept. 1894 through Feb. 1913, ending with v. 31, no. 2. "Will Carleton's Magazine" was displayed on the cover. It began as a small-folio of 16 pages, became a quarto of 32 pages in 1901, and a royal octavo of 64 pages in 1905. It sold for 50¢ a year at first, but was raised to $1.00 (10¢ on the stands) in 1908. The title was printed as *Everywhere* beginning Sept. 1907.

[13] Published June 1888 to July 1893. Donn Piatt was editor throughout most of the magazine's history, though he was out for about two years after a disagreement with the political bosses of the magazine in June 1889 (see *Writer*, v. 3, p. 190, Aug. 1889). During that time Alvah Milton Kerr was editor. The publishing firm changed name several times after various reorganizations, but Robert J. Belford was the controlling figure as publisher throughout. He once had to sue the Democratic National Committee for the cost of copies that it had bought for distribution in a campaign.

[14] Published Jan. 1893 through June 1894, by Alfred D. Worthington. It was a good magazine, publishing Mary A. Livermore's recollections, departments by Charlotte Perkins Stetson and Lilian Whiting, and a variety of contributions by Junius Henri Browne, Albert Bigelow Paine, Olive Thorne Miller, Kate Sanborn, S. G. W. Benjamin, Richard Burton, Helen Campbell, and Clinton Scollard. The single-copy price was 25¢, and there were 92 to 112 royal octavo pages.

at Hartford, Connecticut, with high hopes, only to perish after eighteen months of struggle.

It was in 1900 that Colonel William D. Mann, publisher of *Town Topics*, founded a monthly which he called *Smart Set* [15] and which he probably intended to have somewhat the same snob appeal that his weekly society paper had. Arthur Grissom, young poet and journalist, was installed as editor; and under his guidance and that of another poet who was associate editor, Charles Hanson Towne, the new monthly quickly drew together a group of contributors who gave it a reputation for good and clever writing, which it enjoyed long after Grissom's untimely death. The *Smart Set* was a twenty-five cent magazine begun after the ten-centers had obtained the upper hand. Another one that kept the old price was the *Reader*,[16] which began in November 1902 as a critical journal but soon became a general magazine. Purchased in 1904 by the Bobbs-Merrill Company, Indianapolis book publishers, it ranked for a few years among the leading magazines of the country. It was merged in *Putnam's* in 1908.

THE TEN-CENT MAGAZINE REVOLUTION

Enough has been said in Chapter I to place the three leading ten-cent magazines with relation to the history of periodical publication in the nineties, and each of them will have a special chapter in the supplement of this volume.[17] Of the three, *McClure's* was the best all-round magazine; *Cosmopolitan*, though perhaps as stimulating and vital, lacked something on the literary side; and *Munsey's*, with its excellent variety, made much of its appeal on a somewhat lower intellectual level than the others — and garnered the largest circulation.

A ten-cent magazine that began in New York in 1895 but did not achieve a position of much importance until after 1903 was Blakely Hall's *Metropolitan Magazine*.[18] For its first two or three years its chief attraction was pictures of "the nude in art," "artists' models," "the living picture craze," and so on. By 1898 it was becoming more respectable, with Theodore Dreiser and Alfred Henry Lewis as contributors, and articles on notable persons and institutions. It was in

[15] A separate sketch of the *Smart Set* will appear in the next volume of this series.

[16] In its first phase, the *Reader* was strong in verse and in wit. Bliss Carman, Henry Tyrrell, Herbert Croly, Sewell Ford, Carolyn Wells, Charles G. D. Roberts, and others were contributors. In the second phase, fiction was prominent, with many midwestern writers, such as Meredith Nicholson, Harold MacGrath, Brand Whitlock, Herbert Quick, Octave Thanet, and Emerson Hough. In its last year or two, it gave much attention to public affairs: notable was a series of debates between Bryan and Beveridge on "The Problems of the People."

[17] See for *McClure's*, Sketch 18; *Cosmopolitan*, Sketch 10; *Munsey's*, Sketch 19.

[18] A separate sketch of the *Metropolitan* will appear in the next volume of this series.

that year that Roland Burke Hennessey, an assistant editor of the *Metropolitan*, left it to found the *Broadway Magazine*,[19] a ten-center that also followed the somewhat risqué pattern of near nudity just described. After a short period of ownership by Courtland H. Young, during 1904–1905, the *Broadway* was purchased by Benjamin B. Hampton; and as *Hampton's Magazine* it became a brilliant and aggressive monthly. Doubtless the worst of the "naughty picture mags" was *Vanity Fair*, which was associated with Hennessey's *Saturday Standard*.[20]

*Everybody's Magazine* was founded in 1896 by the New York branch of Wanamaker's store.[21] It sold for ten cents a copy, and its contents for the first year or two were derived, by purchase, from the London *Royal Magazine*. Much American material had already been introduced before the sale of the magazine in May 1903 to Erman J. Ridgway and his two associates — John A. Thayer, one of the most aggressive advertising men of the times, and George W. Wilder, president of the Butterick Publishing Company and financial magnate. *Everybody's* now took its place among the leading ten-cent general illustrated magazines in contents, circulation, and advertising. But its greatest prosperity was derived from the serial "Frenzied Finance" and its sequels, contributed by Thomas W. Lawson from July 1904 through 1907.

There were also such ten-cent miscellanies as J. Reber's *Kansas City Illustrated World*,[22] a quarto whose columns were filled, in the main, with cheap syndicated matter printed from the stereotypes known as "boiler-plate"; and an *American Magazine*[23] produced in octavo from Hearst Sunday newspapers, badly selected, badly made up, badly printed. Both these periodicals lasted for a comparatively long time, apparently because it cost little to produce them.

### MONTHLIES AT FIVE CENTS OR LESS

Five-cent magazines were a part of the low-price movement of the nineties, but no monthly made any conspicuous success at that price.

[19] A sketch of *Broadway* and *Hampton's* will appear in the next volume of this series.

[20] In 1895, the *Standard*, a weekly which began in 1889 as *Weekly Sports*, changing title three years later to *Sports, Music and Drama*, and which in the mid-nineties flourished on the *Police Gazette* type of illustration, began a *Standard Quarterly*, which became *Vanity Fair* the next year. Blakely Hall, New York, was its publisher in the new phase, and illustration was much better in quality, with color lithographs by Charles Howard Johnson and Archie Gunn. Less successful, however, than Hall's *Standard*, *Vanity Fair* was received into the bosom of its progenitor after Jan. 1902. After various changes of ownership and title, it was succeeded by the distinguished *Vanity Fair* of 1913–36.

[21] A separate sketch of *Everybody's Magazine* will appear in the next volume of this series.

[22] Apparently published 1889–1927.

[23] Apparently published 1891–1907.

"The numerous five-cent magazines — the *Black Cat* and its latest rival the *Owl*, the *Nickell Magazine, Sothoron's*, etc. — being but half the price of the ten-cent magazines, are usually twice as bad," said the *Bauble*, itself a five-cent monthly and twice as bad as most of its contemporaries, in 1896.[24]

The *Monitor*,[25] of Cincinnati, was an odd, didactic magazine by the Loth brothers, which began in 1892 at five cents but was raised the next year to ten. In Boston the *Whole Family* was founded in October 1892 by the Russell Publishing Company; its name was changed in January 1894 to the *Nickell Magazine*.[26] It was well printed and fully illustrated, with an emphasis on the theater and "nude art." Most of its authors were unknown to the general reader. It was moved to New York in March 1901, to Buffalo in October 1904, and to limbo after November 1905. In its last two or three years it was an all-fiction magazine, specializing in "snappy stories." *Sothoron's Magazine*, of Philadelphia, was a creditable general literary miscellany of sixty-four pages octavo, published for thirteen months beginning May 1896. The *People's Monthly*,[27] of the same city, had an even shorter life. The *Half Hour*,[28] issued by George Munro's Sons, well-known producers of cheap books and periodicals, was chiefly fiction, though it published some music, a few pictures of actresses, and so on. *Concordia Magazine*, a sixteen-page octavo from York, Pennsylvania, was devoted to "mutual helpfulness and inspiration for manly men and womanly women": it also had something for boyish boys and girlish girls. It sold for five cents during its first series, but after a suspension it became a quarterly at fifteen cents.[29]

But the most important of the five-cent magazines — not for itself, indeed, but for what grew out of it — was the *Yellow Kid*,[30] a semi-

---

[24] *Bauble*, v. 2, p. 82, Aug. 1896. See Sketch 5 for the *Black Cat*. The *Owl* is noticed in the section on fiction magazines, p. 117. For *Bauble*, see p. 390, footnote.

[25] It was continued through June 1909. Paul V. Loth was editor at first, and Moritz Loth wrote curious didactic, family novels for the magazine. Later it was largely given over to the reprinting of "gems" from the classics, with some current events and opinion. It was a 32-page octavo.

[26] There was a good deal about the war with Spain, a bicycle department beginning in 1896, translations of Maupassant, stories by Max Pemberton, Robert Barr, and others. I. J. Potter and W. L. Kendall bought it Aug. 1899; A. S. Zabriskie, New York, March 1901; Universal Encyclopedia Co., Buffalo, Dec. 1904.

[27] A quarto of 24 pages, illustrated. Joseph P. Reed was editor and Frank Lee Benedict associate editor. Opie Read and Madison Cawein were among the contributors. It began March 1900, and was merged with the *Ledger Monthly* after Nov. 1900.

[28] Published Oct. 1897 through March 1900. The short stories were by unknowns or by English writers whose work was in the public domain. Mary E. Bryan was editor and wrote much for the magazine.

[29] C. Arthur Lutz was editor and publisher. It was a cheap magazine in many ways; perhaps even its idealism was cheap, and certainly its boiler plate was. Monthly, Dec. 1902–Nov. 1903; quarterly, Jan.–March 1919 through April–June 1922.

[30] Joe Kerr was editor. There were 48 large-octavo pages. It began with a $1,000 contest

monthly periodical begun March 20, 1897, by Howard, Ainslee & Company, of New York. It was chiefly humorous and satirical; but it included some of the "nude art" in the current style, notes on the theater, and short stories, with some illustration by the better artists. In August 1897 the name was changed to *Yellow Book* [31] and monthly publication was adopted; and in February 1898 new serial numbering was begun with another new title — *Ainslee's Magazine.*[32] The price was increased to ten cents in October of that year. There were now eighty pages. Editor Richard Duffy brought many of the most popular writers in America and England into the pages of *Ainslee's* within the next few months, with good illustration; but the circulation seemed to stick at about a hundred thousand, and the magazine was sold to Street & Smith at the end of 1898. It soon came to look much like *McClure's,* and at the turn of the century it belonged to the top group of ten-cent general illustrated monthlies. Articles mildly critical of business and industry, by John Gilmer Speed and Peter MacArthur, were never quite enough to make *Ainslee's* a real muckraker. Always strongest in short fiction, it published some of O. Henry's earliest stories and many by Stephen Crane, Jack London, W. W. Jacobs, and so on. In the fall of 1902, an all-story policy was adopted, the number of pages doubled, and the price increased to fifteen cents. As "A Magazine of Clever Fiction," it continued until 1926.

Nor should we entirely forget certain magazines that began business with a single-copy price of less than five cents. Most important

---

for short-story writers. M. Quad, Morley Roberts, and Will S. Gidley were among the contributors; and Harrison Fisher and Penrhyn Stanlaws among the artists.

[31] As a monthly, it pursued much the same policy. Ellis Parker Butler, Richard Duffy, and Hall Caine were contributors.

[32] Street & Smith sold the magazine to Ainslee Magazine Company, controlled by Ormond G. and George G. Smith, Oct. 1902. The latter had been *de facto* editor, or manager, over Richard Duffy, with Gilman Hall as assistant editor and Theodore Dreiser as a kind of consulting editor; Hall became editor in 1904 and Archibald Sessions in 1911. In the period of 1898–1902, when *Ainslee's* was a general magazine, there were covers by such artists as Harrison Fisher, Henry Hutt, and Will Grefé; and contributions by Anthony Hope, Rudyard Kipling, Conan Doyle, Ian Maclaren, F. Hopkinson Smith, F. Marion Crawford, Robert W. Chambers, Gen. A. W. Greely, Capt. Charles King, Lincoln Steffens, Eugene Wood, Theodore Dreiser, Bret Harte, Richard Hovey, and Albert Payson Terhune. It absorbed Dreiser's *Bohemian* in 1898. Priding itself on its national scope, it called itself "An American Magazine for the American People." After the change of policy in 1902, there were still some essays, verse, and theatrical notes by Harry Thurston Peck, H. C. Chatfield-Taylor, John Kendrick Bangs, Carolyn Wells, Paul Lawrence Dunbar, Frank Dempster Sherman, and Ella Wheeler Wilcox. Dorothy Parker edited the stage department 1920–22. Complete novels and short stories were contributed by Edgar Saltus, Elizabeth Duer, Joseph C. Lincoln, William J. Locke, May Sinclair, and Mrs. Wilson Woodrow. As "The Magazine That Entertains," *Ainslee's* gained about 250,000 circulation, and carried 20 to 30 pages of advertising per number at $250 a page. In 1914 paper prices forced it to the use of wood-pulp stock; soon there were few quality writers left. In 1925 it was filled chiefly with famous stories reprinted — "stories that charm and always will." Street & Smith merged *Ainslee's* with the *Far West Magazine* at the end of 1926. They revived the name *Ainslee's,* however, for a sex-story magazine Dec. 1934, changed it to *Ainslee's Smart Love Stories* April 1935, and then dropped it Oct. 1936.

of these was the *Penny Magazine*, founded in New York by Thomas C. Quinn, publisher, and Charles Frederick Stansbury, editor, as a fiction magazine. It carried stories by Edward Everett Hale, Hamlin Garland, Amélie Rives, Julia Magruder, and so on. Senator Chauncey M. Depew was the financial "angel," advancing, it was said, fifty thousand dollars for the project.[33] Though the little magazine (it had sixty-four small pages) began at a penny a number, or ten cents a year, in March 1896 (seven months later) it doubled that price. It kept its original name, however, until November 1900, when it became the *Unique Monthly*.[34] By then it was a general miscellany of information, fiction, and amusement, with some illustration, and had reached a circulation of a hundred thousand.[35] It was never successful, however, and was in a receivership during 1898–1899. It changed hands in 1900, and almost immediately got into trouble with the Post Office Department over the mailing of free copies.[36] The fact is, it became a mail-order paper in 1901; it ended in 1905.

*Browning's Magazine* [37] was a rather attractive monthly, well printed and illustrated, that began in January 1900 at three cents a copy. Carolyn Wells was an assistant editor, writing serials and conducting a puzzle department for it. It was published by Browning, King & Company, owners of a chain of clothing stores in fourteen cities — "The best fin-de-siècle clothing at moderate cost." By calling at a Browning store, patrons might obtain the magazine for three cents less than others paid — i.e., gratis. *Browning's* lasted for nine years. Shorter-lived was *Wisdom Monthly*, edited and published in Boston by John Foster Benyon for twenty-two months beginning March 1902. It was well illustrated, published short stories by Charles E. Van Loan, Cy Warman, and others somewhat less known, together with some verse and articles. *Wisdom Monthly* began at two cents a number, increasing the price to five cents in August 1903. The editor, with wisdom gained from nearly two years of the folly of publishing too cheap a magazine, called his final number *Wisdom and Folly*.

Many of the mail-order journals [38] were priced at twenty-five to fifty cents a year, and five cents a copy was a common rate among those

---

[33] *Printer's Ink*, v. 34, Feb. 13, 1901, pp. 19–25.

[34] W. L. Breadnell was editor and publisher 1900–03, and James J. Johnson, publisher of *Modern Stories*, owned it thereafter. It was made a 36-page quarto in 1900, and a small-folio on cheap paper the next year.

[35] *Journalist*, v. 21, p. 149, Aug. 28, 1897. See also Rowell and Ayer directories for 1898.

[36] *Printer's Ink*, v. 34, Feb. 13, 1901, pp. 19–25.

[37] The editor was C. M. Fairbanks. A photography department, with prizes, was a feature. The magazine began as a quarto, but was reduced to square-octavo in 1901. At the beginning, the title was *Browning, King & Company's Illustrated Monthly*, and its entire distribution was free. The name was shortened and the three-cent price adopted in July 1902.

[38] See Chap. XXI.

little magazines known as *bibelots,* or modern chapbooks, which flourished toward the end of the century.[39]

THE MONTHLY REVIEW

Editor F. F. Browne lamented in his *Dial* in 1892 that America had no first-class reviews:

> When we take a general survey of the American monthlies, the most noticeable fact is the absence of any review for a moment comparable with any of the three great English monthlies [*Nineteenth Century, Fortnightly,* and *Contemporary*]. We have never had anything fully equal to them, although a standard not greatly inferior was maintained by the *North American* in the days when that periodical stood for culture and scorned to be sensational at the cost of dignity. . . . The *Forum* is not without a certain dignity, but its articles are too brief.[40]

Here is the recurrent complaint against the shorter articles of the times.[41] By the "sensationalism" of the *North American,* Browne perhaps meant such things as the essays on contemporary life and manners by Grant Allen, Ouida, Sarah Grand, Gail Hamilton, and other facile and clever writers, though he doubtless felt that all exploitation of current events and the contemporary scene was beneath the dignity of a review. The *North American*[42] under Lloyd Bryce, from 1889 to 1896, was lively and successful; and its discussions of the great problems of the day were often important, such as the Gladstone-Blaine debate on free trade in January 1890. The symposiums and joint debates that had been so popular during A. T. Rice's editorship continued through the nineties. George B. M. Harvey gained control of the review in 1899, and introduced an even greater variety into the content; Mark Twain's astringent essays, and even a serial by Henry James, gave distinction to the *North American* at the turn of the century.

The *Forum,*[43] founded in 1886 by a man trained on the *North American* staff, L. S. Metcalfe, followed somewhat the same lines, and made even more prominent the joint debate in print. Walter Hines Page was editor for a few years, but toward the end of the nineties, the *Forum* declined; and in 1902 it became a quarterly, written largely by members of its own staff. The *Arena,*[44] founded in 1889 by B. O. Flower, was one of the most interesting reviews of the nineties, largely because Flower was a man of strong humanitarian feelings and bold,

---

[39] See Chap. XXIII. There were also several all-fiction magazines at this price; see p. 117.
[40] *Dial,* v. 13, p. 204, Oct. 1, 1892.
[41] See pp. 13–14.
[42] For the *North American Review,* see Mott, *op. cit.,* v. 2, Sketch 1.
[43] See Sketch 12 in this volume.
[44] See Sketch 2 in this volume.

reformatory impulses. He was editor during all the twenty years of the magazine's life except three at the close of the nineties. Uneven in quality, the *Arena* was always liberal and well meaning; and it was probably an effective propagandist for freedom of thought in some circles.

The *Review of Reviews*,[45] of New York, was the American offspring of W. T. Stead's London *Review of Reviews*. Albert Shaw began it in New York in 1891, and was its editor to its end in 1937. It differed from the reviews mentioned above by its emphasis on current events and its use of digests of articles which had appeared in other periodicals. It also printed articles of its own, and these increased toward the end of the nineties.

*Our Day: A Record and Review of Current Reform* [46] was a monthly edited by the famous Boston preacher, Joseph Cook. In its first number, issued for January 1888, Cook promised: "It will be conducted and owned by a syndicate of specialists in the discussion of leading reformatory movements, and will be independent of partisan or denominational control." And so it was. "There is hardly an American magazine," wrote the English W. T. Stead in 1890, "which touches at so many points the moral and social questions which command attention today." [47] There were many distinguished contributors, but *Our Day* suffered from lack of editorial attention; and in 1892 it was moved to Chicago, to be issued by the Temperance Publishing Association there. In 1895 it was wedded to the *Altruistic Review*,[48] H. A. Cuppy's magazine; but the marriage was unsuccessful, and divorce followed after one year. Resumed in 1896 as a bimonthly by Frederick L. Chapman, it kept the same broad reformatory base with which it had begun, and for a few years it was well illustrated and attractive. It came to give increasing space to current events, and in 1908 was combined with *World's Events*,[49] which had begun as a cheap paper designed to furnish information about current happenings and situa-

[45] See Sketch 25 in this volume.

[46] Title changed in 1895 to *Our Day: The Altruistic Review*; but former title resumed in 1896. Octavo, about 80 pages; several pages of advertising. Price began at $2.00; raised to $2.50 in 1890. Contents included Cook's "Monday Lectures," with their "Preludes" on current events, which had been widely circulated as a separate publication. Associate editors included Frances E. Willard, national president of the W.C.T.U.: Edmund J. James, University of Pennsylvania (labor reform); Anthony Comstock, secretary New York Society for the Suppression of Vice; and G. F. Pentecost, evangelist. Among contributors were Carroll D. Wright, Richard T. Ely, Neal Dow, Charles F. Thwing, George F. Magoun, George P. Fisher, Bishop W. C. Doane, J. E. Rankin, and Lucy Larcom. There was much against Mormonism, saloons, Sunday desecration, and so on, as well as material on religion and reform abroad, book reviews, and verse.

[47] *Review of Reviews* (London), v. 1, p. 61, Jan. 1890.

[48] See p. 284.

[49] Founded Oct. 1900 at Dansville, N. Y., by F. A. Owen, at 30¢ a year, or five years for $1.00. "The original idea" was to provide a cheap paper "for the use of teachers . . . and for

tions to high-school students, and was now much improved as a ten-cent monthly. It claimed a hundred thousand circulation in May 1907, and flourished for a few years; but in 1912 it made another change in title, and as the *Household Guest* became a family paper at twenty-five cents a year, devoted mainly to current events and mail-order advertising. It perished the next year.

A predecessor and later a rival of *World's Events* in serving the schools was *Our Times*,[50] a current events monthly selling for twenty-five cents a year in clubs.

More important was *World's Work*,[51] established toward the end of 1900 in time to greet the new century, by Walter Hines Page. A well-illustrated, lively magazine, it immediately took a position among the leaders. It bore a considerable resemblance to the *Review of Reviews*; on the whole, it was more vigorous and attractive, though a little smaller.

*Current Topics*[52] was a short-lived Chicago review of little importance. The *Rostrum*[53] was a dignified review, which began in Chicago as [S. R.] *Winchell's Quarterly* and ended as *Home Education*.

class use," with the hope of a "demand from the larger field — the general public" (v. 5, p. 185, March 1905). The publisher was a dealer in cheap but good books in series and sets, and he also issued the *Normal Instructor*. The full title, in the beginning, was *The World's Events: A Monthly Journal of Current News and Choice Selected Reading*; and besides its treatment of the news it contained a current biography department, with portraits, pieces on science and invention, reprints of famous poems, occasional special articles on timely subjects, and a few short stories. By the end of 1903 the quality of paper was better, illustration (including maps) increased; a year later the price was raised to $1.00 a year and the number of pages increased from 40 to 48. In Aug. 1905 the journal was sold to a new publishing company headed by D. C. Kreidler; and Simeon D. Fess became editor in chief. The subscription rate went back to 50¢ a year, and the title became *World's Events Magazine*. A. K. McClure's reminiscences were published in 1906, and other contributors were Robertus Love, E. E. Slosson, James Melvin Lee, and Edgar L. Vincent. It was an improved journal when it was moved to Dayton, Ohio, in Aug. 1907 and raised to $1.00 a year. After Chapman bought it and merged it with *Our Day*, it was attractive, well printed, fairly well illustrated, various, and still designed for schools. Frequent contributors were Bruce Barton, Edwin L. Sabin, and Sherwood Eddy.

[50] Begun in 1890 by the United Educational Company, later C. W. Barnes & Company, *Our Times* was merged in 1895 with the *Week's Current*, which had been published by E. O. Vaile in Oak Park, Ill., since 1883. But a semimonthly edition (later weekly) of *Our Times* was begun in 1896 by E. L. Kellogg & Company in New York. This was at first a small-folio of 8 pages, but in 1898 it became a large octavo of 16 pages, at 50¢ a year. It was merged with the *Pathfinder* in Dec. 1907, but resumed separate publication Sept. 9, 1909; again, and finally, it was merged with the *Pathfinder* in March 1911.

[51] See Sketch 34 in this volume.

[52] Conducted by David Wever as "part of an advertising device for selling pianos." But Paul Shorey contributed an article on Taine, and some other University of Chicago professors lent a hand. Begun in 1893, its name was changed to *Chicago Magazine* before it ended in 1895. It had a Texas edition in 1893. See Herbert E. Fleming, "The Literary Interests of Chicago," in *American Journal of Sociology*, v. 11, pp. 820–21, May 1906, issued separately under the title "Magazines of a Market-Metropolis" (dissertation, Chicago, 1906).

[53] It began in 1898, and became "A Monthly Magazine Devoted to Science, Literature, Politics, and Current Events" in 1901–02. It was a small-quarto of 68 pages at $1.50 a year until Aug. 1902, when the rate was lowered to $1.00, and it changed title to *Home Education* (1903–07). Israel Smith Clare, the historian, and Thomas Whitson were joint editors and publishers at first, but Clare dropped out Oct. 1902.

*Twentieth Century Review* was issued at Detroit by William E. Bolles; it gave much attention to current events and was in some respects a "success magazine." [54]

There were also monthly reviews issued for certain religious denominations, others published under the sponsorship of colleges and universities, and still others limited to special fields, such as literature, the drama, and science. Some will be described in the sections devoted to such categories in the following pages. And some American reviews were not monthlies, but quarterlies — the frequency which had once seemed best suited to the more dignified periodical literature — and will therefore be treated in Chapter VI.

THE INFORMATION MONTHLIES

Closely related to the reviews, and perhaps not properly divisible from them, were the magazines of information. Among these were several that were the organs of the organized adult education projects so important in this period.[55] The *Chautauquan* [56] was the foremost of these; it was made a well-rounded, comprehensive magazine in October 1889, with a distinguished list of contributors and a wide and liberal outlook. The *Bay View Magazine*,[57] of Flint, Michigan, was the organ of the Bay View Reading Circle, founded in 1893 by John M. Hall. The circle had seven thousand members by the end of its first year. The magazine carried well-illustrated reading courses, often centered upon foreign lands and civilizations, but containing other material as well.

Chicago was a leading center for home study periodicals. *Self Culture* [58] was "A Magazine Devoted to the Interests of the Home University League" in the mid-nineties. It was issued in Chicago by the Werner Company, American publishers of the ninth edition of the

[54] It began as a 5¢ weekly Nov. 9, 1901, became a monthly Jan. 1900, and ended as a mail-order journal in 1909.

[55] See Chap. XV.

[56] See Sketch 34 in Mott, *op. cit.*, v. 3.

[57] The magazine cost $1.00 a year; $3.00 bought the magazine and three textbooks. August and September were omitted each year. The publication house was moved to Detroit in 1904, where it eventually became little more than a bulletin of the B.V.R.C. It appeared to be a war casualty in 1917, but was renewed in Jan. 1918 as *Bay View Reflector*. By 1919 it had taken back its old name; and, with George G. Bechtel as editor and W. D. McClintock as business manager, it revived reading courses. It then specialized in contemporary history, with three history professors as contributing editors. It ended with the number for Jan. 1922 (v. 27, no. 4).

[58] Edward C. Towne was editor, 1895–96; G. Mercer Adam, 1896–1900; William W. Hudson, 1900–02. It was a small-quarto of 32 pages, and sold for $2.00 a year, or 20¢ a number. It was moved to Akron, Ohio, in 1896, and to Cleveland in 1901. It published 14 semiannual volumes, April 1895 through Feb. 1902. The title was changed to *Modern Culture* in Sept. 1900, when Hudson took over as editor. There was also a *Self Culture* in St. Louis 1893–97, edited by F. M. Ray.

*Encyclopaedia Britannica,* and its reading program was based largely, though not wholly, upon articles reprinted from that work. More material on timely problems was gradually introduced, and the Home University League idea was dropped in 1898. The magazine continued until 1902. *Progress* [59] was scarcely a periodical, though its "home study" lessons were issued in monthly parts. It was the organ of the University Association, of Chicago, which was an outgrowth of an educational auxiliary of the World's Fair. Bishop Samuel Fallows was head of the teacher-writers who produced the publication. Related to both *Self Culture* and *Progress* was *Current Encyclopaedia,* a digest of *Britannica,* edited by William E. Ernst, who had been an official of the Werner Company. Out of this heavy reprint, Ernst developed the *World To-Day,* [60] pride of Chicago magazine journalism for several years. It later became *Hearst's Magazine.* The *People's Magazine and Home University,* [61] a ten-cent monthly that specialized in serial reprints of standard works in science and the humanities, and included some matter on current events, made a good appearance. *Cram's Magazine* [62] was "A Monthly Journal of History, Geography and Topics of the Day," published by George F. Cram and edited by Israel Smith Clare and Eugene Murray-Aaron. It was an attractive magazine, for which the publisher and editors wrote much. These five were the main Chicago periodicals for home study in the present period, though there were several others. [63]

In Buffalo a monthly called *Queries* [64] published long quizzes in various fields of knowledge and offered prizes for correct answers. It also printed biographical sketches, book reviews, and so on. The *Progress of the World,* [65] New York, was a good "Monthly Summary of the Leading Facts in Current History and Achievement"; but it lasted only through the year beginning with October 1895. General Franz

---

[59] W. E. Ernst was secretary and treasurer of the association, and Fallows was chancellor. *Progress* was published 1895–1902. See Fleming, "Magazines of a Market-Metropolis," p. 77.

[60] See pp. 499–500.

[61] A quarto of 48 pages, published Oct. 1901–Nov. 1907. It enlarged its page size in 1906 and was then a handsome and well-printed magazine.

[62] A 96-page quarto at $3.00 a year, Nov. 1899–Sept. 1901. There were reprints from recent books, book reviews, a serial history of the world in large type for children by Lou V. Chapin, and a little fiction and verse.

[63] For example, *National Magazine,* a 32-page octavo published by National University at $1.00 a year; *University,* which began as a monthly at Ann Arbor in 1882, was made a biweekly when it absorbed the *Weekly Magazine, Educational News,* and *Fortnightly Index* in 1884, and was merged in *Unity* after its number for Feb. 27, 1886; *Correspondence University Journal,* 1884–86; *Home Library Magazine,* 1887; *Information,* 1904.

[64] This was a small-quarto of 32 pages at $1.00 a year. Charles Welles Moulton was editor for its first five years, 1885–89, and there was a succession of publishers. It was discontinued in 1892.

[65] Small-quarto, 60 pages, at $1.00 a year. James B. Best was publisher, and probably editor.

Sigel's *New York Monthly* [66] was a cheap nonfiction journal that gave much attention to the history of the Civil War.

Finally, the monthly eclectics were represented by the bright and beautiful *Current Literature* [67] and the decaying old *Eclectic Magazine*,[68] now edited by E. R. Pelton. The latter was sold in 1898 to the weekly *Living Age*, which issued it as a "monthly edition" for a few years. In 1905 the two parted company, but the *Eclectic* survived only two years thereafter. *Best in Print from Book and Journal* was issued during 1896–1898 at Albany, New York.

[66] A quarto of 24 pages at $2.00 a year. About half the magazine was in the German language. Some syndicated matter was printed from stereotyped plates.

[67] See Sketch 11.

[68] See Sketch 32 in Mott, *op. cit.*, v. 1.

# CHAPTER V

## THE GENERAL WEEKLY MAGAZINES

IT WAS an opinion widely held in the 1890's that the general weekly periodical had been caught between the upper and the nether millstones of the Sunday newspaper and the ten-cent magazine.[1] The high-class illustrated weekly was losing ground, the old story papers were dying, and the miscellanies published on Saturday or Sunday for week-end reading were in the doldrums. Weekly newspapers in small towns were doing as well as usual, and farm papers, religious organs, and the bulletin type of weekly in special fields were all prosperous enough; but the only type of great weekly miscellany of general circulation that was really flourishing was the cheap family journal of news and entertainment sold by newsboy carriers.

### THE GENERAL ILLUSTRATED MISCELLANIES

*Harper's Weekly* [2] was, nevertheless, an excellent paper throughout the nineties — the best of its class. It was handsome and freighted with rich materials. It lost something in editorial influence with the death of Editor George William Curtis in 1892, and perhaps more with the financial failure of the Harper house in 1899, but George B. M. Harvey was a forceful editor when he took over in 1901.

A real competitor of *Harper's Weekly*, even though on a lower level, was *Leslie's Weekly*,[3] which was called *Frank Leslie's Illustrated Newspaper* until 1894. The most extraordinary woman of her times in the magazine business, Mrs. Frank Leslie, had borrowed fifty thousand dollars from another widow, Mrs. Thomas K. Smith, to get the paper on its feet after her late husband's bankruptcy; but she had made enough to pay the debt by a single coup, and thereafter it was very profitable. Mrs. Leslie sold the paper in 1889, and for some years cavorted about Europe and America, lecturing and displaying her diamonds and wit. In 1891 she married Willie Wilde, brother of Oscar, with Marshall P. Wilder, the humorist, as best man (*Town Topics*

---

[1] *Journalist*, v. 6, Jan. 7, 1888, p. 4; *Fourth Estate*, quoted in *Printer's Ink*, v. 29, Dec. 13, 1899, p. 12; Frank Munsey's statement, *Munsey's Magazine*, v. 19, p. 221, May 1898; Edward Bok, *The Man from Maine* (New York, 1923), pp. 158–59.

[2] See Sketch 28 in F. L. Mott, *A History of American Magazines* (Cambridge, 1938), v. 2.

[3] See Sketch 26 in Mott, *op. cit.*, v. 1. See also *Literary Life*, v. 5. p. 5, Feb. 1886; *Kate Field's Washington*, v. 3, p. 185, March 25, 1891; Madeleine B. Stern, *Purple Passage: The Life of Mrs. Frank Leslie* (Norman, Okla., 1953), pp. 100–04.

could not miss the opportunity to say that the bride was Wildest) ;[4] but soon she discovered that neither Willie nor the stock she had received in payment for the *Weekly* were worth anything. So she divorced the former, marked off a loss of a hundred thousand dollars on the latter, and proceeded to recoup through other ventures.[5]

Another important weekly of the nineties was the *Illustrated American*,[6] founded in New York in 1890 by Lorillard Spencer. It called itself "A Weekly News Magazine"; but it contained much general miscellany, political comment, and even fiction, in addition to its current events. It was very well illustrated by many of the best artists, and it sold for twenty-five cents a number, or ten dollars a year. At the end of its first year, the *Writer* said that "nearly a quarter of a million dollars has been spent already on the enterprise, . . . [but] the subscription price is necessarily so high as to be beyond the reach of many."[7] After a few months, the size was reduced from small-folio (*London Graphic*) size to the quarto (*Harper's Weekly*) page; in 1892 the price was brought down to ten cents. The *Illustrated American* then gained a circulation of some forty thousand. It was a high-class periodical, but it must have lost a fortune for Spencer before he sold it in 1897. Sold again the next year, it deteriorated rapidly, to perish in 1900.

*Collier's*[8] began under the name of *Once a Week* in 1888, as a copiously illustrated miscellany at seven cents. It had reached a quarter of a million circulation in 1892, when it became more a news magazine, with emphasis on the new photo-journalism, though not neglecting fiction and other miscellany. Under that policy it continued

---

[4] *Town Topics*, v. 26, Oct. 8, 1891, p. 4. This paper printed a scurrilous piece entitled "From Puddle to Palace" about Mrs. Leslie in v. 15, March 27, 1886, pp. 13–14.

[5] See *Journalist*, v. 23, p. 193, Sept. 24, 1898; Stern, *Purple Passage*, p. 170.

[6] It published four volumes a year 1890–92, and two volumes yearly thereafter. A. B. de Guerville purchased it from Spencer, but sold it to Patterson and Hennessey in 1898. The Illustrated Biographical Company was publisher in 1900. Maurice M. Minton was editor 1890–94; C. F. Nirdlinger, 1894–96; Francis Bellamy, 1897–98; Roland Burke Hennessey, 1898–1900. The *Illustrated American* had many departments — for books, art, music, drama, science, education, religion, women's fashions, and others. News and pictures from abroad were a feature. A serial novel by Edgar Fawcett in 1890, illustrated by Thomas Nast, brought in William M. Tweed and his compeers as characters. The *American* was independent in politics; but it opposed high tariffs, Tammany, Mormonism, and prohibition. Its fight on the New Haven Railroad resulted in its sale being banned on Vanderbilt lines. Colored lithographs were used as supplements for the first five months. A few large woodcuts of old masters by W. Kurtz were also used in early volumes; but most illustration was by halftone. There were many pictures of the World's Fair, and later of the war with Spain. For the latter, Walter Russell and C. D. Graves were leading artists. Valerian Gribayédoff and H. Albrecht were foreign contributors. Under Hennessey there were, of course, many artist's models and bathing beauties; and in the periodical's final stage it was mainly a repository of portraits.

[7] *Writer*, v. 5, p. 8, Jan. 1891.

[8] See Sketch 9 in this volume.

O. HENRY'S BURLESQUE ON THE COUNTRY-TOWN WEEKLY

A page from his comic paper, the *Rolling Stone*. See page 668.

THE "YELLOW KID" USED IN POSTER ADVERTISING

The dress of this creature is printed in yellow. For the "Yellow Kid" craze, see pages 196–197.

to outdistance competitors. The name was changed to *Collier's Weekly* in 1895; and Robert J. Collier, son of the founder, became editor three years later. Coverage of the Spanish-American War was brilliant. Under Norman Hapgood's editorial direction, which began in 1902, the paper's influence on national affairs doubtless exceeded for a time that of any other single publication. Illustration continued copious, and both fiction and articles excellent.

By 1905 *Collier's* had nearly a million circulation, but the *Saturday Evening Post* [9] had passed that figure some three years before. Of course, the *Post* sold for a nickel and *Collier's* for a dime. The Curtis Publishing Company had taken over the *Post* in 1897, when it belonged to the moribund class of fiction-and-miscellany papers published for week-end reading referred to at the beginning of this chapter. The *Post* was indeed drawing its last breath when Curtis afforded first aid and resuscitated it. Ordinarily it is harder to revive a dying magazine than to start a new one, but Curtis performed the most remarkable job of resuscitation in the history of American magazines. With the aid of a great editor, George Horace Lorimer, and largely on the basis of appeal to young men, the *Post* soon made an immense success, which it was later to extend to proportions scarcely dreamed of in those experimental years at the turn of the century.

Though the *Independent* [10] was rather sparsely illustrated until about 1902, it may be included in the present category. It printed some fiction, much comment on public affairs, and departments devoted to the fine arts, literature, music, education, science, and so on; and it was more hospitable to good poetry than any other of its class. Henry C. Bowen, long-time editor of the *Independent*, died in 1896, two years before the paper celebrated its semicentennial.

Another weekly, which had been founded as a religious and denominational journal but which later turned to the broader fields of public affairs and general miscellany, was the *Outlook*.[11] Founded as the *Christian Union* in 1870, it did not adopt the new name and the new editorial policy until 1893. Four years later, it made one issue in the month a fully illustrated number about double the size of the others, and put more miscellany, including fiction, into it. Under Lyman Abbott's editorship, the *Outlook* in these years was strong in serial biography and autobiography, in literary criticism, and in comment on national affairs.

[9] See Sketch 27 in this volume.
[10] See Sketch 14 in Mott, *op. cit.*, v. 2.
[11] See Sketch 16 in Mott, *op. cit.*, v. 3.

### THE WEEKLY REVIEWS

Of course, the *Independent* and the *Outlook*, and indeed *Harper's Weekly*, might be classed as review periodicals, or journals of opinion; but all printed some fiction, and all emphasized the general miscellany in their content. In fact, the pure review was sparsely represented among American weeklies in the years 1885–1905.

The *Nation* [12] was perhaps such a paper, but it was in this period an adjunct of the *New York Evening Post*. It held many of the writers who had made it a great force in the seventies, and maintained a circulation of about ten thousand. It emphasized politics and current literature, with Edwin Lawrence Godkin in charge of the former and Editor Wendell Phillips Garrison looking after the latter.

In Boston, the old *Commonwealth*, which had been founded by Moncure D. Conway in 1862, was continued by Edward Everett Hale and F. E. Goodrich until 1896; but it had little claim to a national circulation. In Philadelphia, Wharton Barker's *American* [13] was continued, after a suspension, from 1894 through 1900. Independent in politics, giving much attention to books and art, both of these weeklies were of high grade and low circulation. Another notable Philadelphia weekly was Herbert Welsh's reformatory *City and State* (1895–1904), a high-minded journal of opinion.

The *Epoch* was begun by DeWitt Seligman in New York on February 11, 1887, as a general weekly similar to the *Nation* in format, and selling for ten cents. Its first number was a brilliant one, including contributions by such men as Elihu Root, Carl Schurz, Julian Hawthorne, Richard Henry Stoddard, H. H. Boyesen, and Robert Grant. At first H. T. Finck had a music department, George Edgar Montgomery wrote on the theater, George Parsons Lathrop surveyed the books, and John Foord did politics. Later Alan Dale covered both music and the theater, and Edward Bok's literary gossip supplanted Lathrop's reviews. The *Epoch* was Democratic in the national campaign of 1888. It could not keep the pace it had first set and was absorbed by *Munsey's Weekly* after the issue for March 11, 1892.

In Chicago, Slason Thompson founded a political and literary journal, the weekly *America*,[14] on April 5, 1888, and conducted it through

---

[12] See Sketch 4 in Mott, *op. cit.*, v. 3. Also note Daniel C. Haskell, comp., *The Nation, Vols. 1–105, New York, 1865–1917. Indexes of Titles and Contributors*, 2 vols., published by the New York Public Library.

[13] See Mott, *op. cit.*, v. 3, pp. 41–42.

[14] *America* was a small-quarto of 32 pages selling for 10¢ (or $3.00 a year) throughout most of its life, though in its first year it was a larger quarto at $3.50 a year. Its file is in six volumes, the first of which is annual and the other five semiannual. Subtitle: "A Journal for Americans, Devoted to Honest Politics and Good Literature." For its history, see its

September 24, 1891. Hobart Chatfield-Taylor is said to have advanced between fifty and a hundred thousand dollars to get it off to a good start, and he was joint editor and publisher for the first six months of the journal. Other editors were Reginald de Koven, who conducted a department of musical criticism; M. L. Scudder, financial editor; Harry B. Smith and Charles P. Bryan, assistant editors; and Maurice Thompson, literary critic in the latter half of the paper's life. During the period when Taylor was pouring his money into it, *America* published many famous authors, such as James Russell Lowell, Oliver Wendell Holmes, Charles Dudley Warner, Theodore Roosevelt, A. C. Swinburne, Andrew Lang, Bret Harte, Frank R. Stockton, James Whitcomb Riley, Eugene Field, and Hamlin Garland. This was a brilliant list, but after the first year the journal was largely staff-written. Its chief political mission was opposition to the liberal immigration laws, which was associated with an anti-Catholic bias and with a plan for certain limitations on the suffrage. Throughout most of the journal's life, each number opened with a full-page cartoon and carried a two-page, center-spread picture, usually political. Thomas Nast was *America's* chief cartoonist; but "Chips," T. E. Powers, and other artists contributed.

Another Chicago political periodical, but a fortnightly and cheaper, was *Up to Date*,[15] a free silver advocate, published during 1895–1898 by John Dilg at five cents a copy. Four of its twenty-four pages were occupied by chromolithographic cartoons by Champe and others. It was an attractive and often amusing journal.

*Kate Field's Washington*[16] (1890–1895) was subtitled "A National Independent Weekly Review"; and though it sometimes seemed rather local, its interests were essentially national, and in its last year it was published in both Washington and Chicago. Kate Field was a well-known lecturer, daughter of a St. Louis journalist, and a chatty, witty, prejudiced, and sometimes peevish commentator on public affairs and Washington doings. She was assisted by "two bright Vassar girls" — Caroline Gray Lingle, managing editor, and Ella S. Leonard, business manager — both of whom wrote for the weekly, along with Charlotte Perkins Stetson, Cornelia Atwood Pratt, and other well-known woman publicists. Miss Field was always forthright and definite. She was for

---

last number, v. 6, pp. 758–60, Sept. 24, 1891; also Herbert E. Fleming, "The Literary Interests of Chicago," *American Journal of Sociology*, v. 11, pp. 524–28, April 1906.

[15] John Mahon and Alvah Milton Kerr were successive editors, the latter leaving to become editor of *Belford's*, a political monthly.

[16] Kate Field's paper was a 16-page quarto at 5¢ a number, published in 10 regular semi-annual volumes (beginning Jan. 1, 1890) and 16 numbers of an eleventh. See Lilian Whiting, *Kate Field* (Boston, 1899), chap. 8, for much about this paper. Miss Whiting says that Francis Leupp was managing editor at the start.

women's rights, justice to the Indians, free trade in art objects, the preservation of the Yosemite as a national park, and better manners in Congress; and she was against prohibition, excessive tariffs, and Grover Cleveland. The paper usually contained a short short story, offered much about the Columbian Exposition, did the theaters and books pretty well, and printed many notes about American life the country over, based on Miss Field's lecture travels.

When the New York *Globe* was begun, on March 31, 1888, it was owned by the North American Exchange Company and emphasized its "Wall Street Letter" and information on stocks and bonds. But when, on June 1, 1889, it came under the management of the well-known journalist George F. Parker, it became known and respected for its conservative Democratic opinions, its "Globe Interviews" with public men, and so on. At that time its name was changed to *Saturday Globe* and its sixteen small-folio pages were enlarged to twenty. But it declined in a year or two, and ended July 18, 1891. It was a five-cent paper throughout.

*Waterman's Journal*, a Boston weekly devoted to current events and books, was sold by A. A. Waterman to J. Morrison-Fuller, who continued it under the title *To-Day*; [17] but the life span of both was less than three years. More important was *The Public*, edited and published by the social reformer and labor leader Louis F. Post in Chicago beginning in 1898. This was a good weekly review, resembling the *Nation* in appearance, financed by Daniel Kiefer and Joseph Fels. "A National Journal of Fundamental Democracy, and a Weekly Narrative of History in the Making," ran its subtitle. It gave some three pages to a concise summary of current events, and devoted the remainder of its sixteen pages to articles and editorials with strong social and labor leanings. It declined somewhat after Post resigned to become Assistant Secretary of Labor in 1913; it moved to New York at the beginning of 1917, and ended the next year.[18]

NEWS AND INFORMATION WEEKLIES

Most important of the news weeklies of the period was the *Path-*

---

[17] *Waterman's Journal* was issued May 16, 1889 through Feb. 6, 1890, and *To-Day*, March 27, 1890 through Jan. 7, 1892. The paper advocated fewer laws and less political humbug and more individual liberty.

[18] Alice Thatcher Post was managing editor of *The Public*, Angeline L. Graves associate editor, and Stanley Bowmar business manager. On the resignation of Post, Samuel Danziger became managing editor, and Miss Graves and Stoughton Cooley associate editors. When it moved to New York Danziger and Cooley were editors at first, and then George P. West and Mrs. Joseph Fels, widow of the paper's chief "angel." Post was primarily a labor journalist. He had been editor of the New York *Leader* before it was taken over by the socialists, and later associate editor of the United Labor Party's *Standard* under Henry George.

*finder*,[19] founded in Washington, D.C., by George Dean Mitchell on January 6, 1894. It began at three cents a copy and a dollar a year; though it soon advanced the single-copy price to five cents, it kept to the one-dollar rate for annual subscriptions for more than half a century. *Pathfinder* was originally called "A National Newspaper for Young Americans," and was designed for use in teaching current events in schools; but within a few years its aim was broadened somewhat, so that while it was still sold in package lots to schools, it was essentially a family magazine. It printed some fiction in the nineties, though not enough to change the emphasis on information. Its editors were highly skilled in condensation; and although there were a few pieces in an issue that ran to two columns of the little paper, there were a great many short items, all neatly departmentalized, and all amazingly interesting. The *Pathfinder* was filled with curious bits of science, invention, biography, geography, what-not. It gained slowly but steadily in circulation, reaching an average of twenty-eight thousand by 1901; in the final years of our period it declined somewhat.[20]

A similar paper was *Current Events*,[21] founded on May 20, 1902, by

[19] See Semicentennial Number, Jan. 10, 1944, p. 28; also Ellsworth Chunn, "History of News Magazines" (doctoral dissertation, University of Missouri, 1950), pp. 319–48. There was no volumning, but issues were numbered serially. Edwin S. Potter was associated with Mitchell in founding the *Pathfinder*, and remained as president of the company until 1900, when he was succeeded by David S. Barry. Potter had been a newspaperman, while Mitchell was a lawyer and had been secretary to his father, United States Senator John Inscho Mitchell, of Pennsylvania. At first a small-folio of eight pages and four 14-inch columns to the page, it was later smaller with more pages, printed on newsprint stock. Advertising, after the first few years, was not above criticism; and in the early decades of the new century there was too much space given to patent medicines, announcements of "free" gifts, courses in hypnotism, and so on. But the magazine now had a cover, it displayed its stories better, it presented opinion polls of its own, and it was in many ways a bright paper. In 1936 Mitchell, who was approaching 70 and impoverished by the Great Depression, sold the paper to Sevellon Brown, publisher of the *Providence Journal and Bulletin* and a son-in-law of Barry. Two years later Brown sold it to James M. Bray, former publisher of the *United States News*, who kept it less than a year before disposing of it to Emil Hurja, former executive director of the Democratic National Committee. Hurja made John Robey editor, and, abandoning competition for urban circulation, made the *Pathfinder* a news magazine for rural readers. In 1943 Hurja sold it to the *Farm Journal*, of Philadelphia, which moved it to that city, gave it good paper stock at last, fuller illustration, better typography, and enterprising editing. In June 1946, with Wheeler McMillen as editor, the *Pathfinder* was made a fortnightly. Circulation went up to 1,000,000 in 1947, and the price was raised to $2.00. It reached 1,250,000 in 1952, and the price was raised to $2.50. It was made a monthly the next year and the title was changed to *Pathfinder . . . the Town Journal*, and circulation and advertising continued to grow. The *Farm Journal* and *Town Journal* in the summer of 1954 had 5,500,000 circulation, concentrated in 2,623 counties where half the population live in the country or in towns under 10,000.
[20] See Rowell's Directory for 1908.
[21] Subtitle: "A Condensed Newspaper, Weekly, for Use in Public and Private Schools." It moved to New York, Chicago, and Columbus, and was published in the twenties in editions issued from all three cities. In 1910 it claimed "a larger circulation than any other school paper in the world," but it did not document the claim. After the death of the founder in 1921, *Current Events* was edited and published by his son, Preston Davis. It went up to 60¢ a year in the twenties, and to 75¢ in the early thirties, but came back again to 40¢. During most of its life it was a four-page paper. It ended May 28, 1948. Another *Current*

the newspaperman Charles Palmer Davis in Springfield, Massachusetts. It was destined for a long life, most of it at forty cents a year, and for many changes in ownership and homes. It was really a school paper, and so was the *Great Round World* [22] when it was begun in New York, by William Beverley Harrison, on November 12, 1896; but the latter periodical, after it had passed through bankruptcy proceedings in 1899, became an excellent news magazine for adults in the early years of the new century. It changed title to *The Week's Progress* in 1903, and to *Search-Light* the next year; and it was merged into the *Independent* in May 1906. Another current events periodical was *Our Times*, a monthly which had a weekly edition for several years.[23] Still another was *World's Chronicle* (1900–1919), of Chicago, which began as *Little Chronicle*.

The *Literary Digest* [24] and *Public Opinion* [25] were not, in basic intention, current-events periodicals, but rather weekly eclectics that surveyed editorial opinion and condensed and arranged it for the information of readers. They gave increasing attention, however, to statements of the news and public issues, and they ranked among the most important weeklies of the period. Another eclectic was the old *Littell's Living Age*.[26] On the death of Robert Littell, son of the founder, in 1896, the periodical became more simply the *Living Age*, and broadened its scope somewhat.

*Knowledge* was a short-lived New York periodical of 1890 designed as a weekly supplement to the encyclopedias. *Information*, another brief five-cent weekly, published by J. M. Stoddart in New York in 1896, was subtitled "A Cyclopedia of Current Events."

*American Notes and Queries*, of Philadelphia, was founded by William S. Walsh in May 1888 and edited by him for a year, for another year by W. H. Garrison, and then to its end in April 1892 by Samuel R. Harris. This repository of curious information, chiefly literary and historical, was a weekly of twelve square octavo pages. It had a sequel in the *Searcher* (1895–1896), also issued from Philadelphia.

---

*Events*, with strong sociological bent, was published monthly in Cleveland, 1893–97, by C. Elton Blanchard, and was merged in the *Great Round World*.

[22] This was at first a square duodecimo of 24 pages, with all the news in one breezy article. In Feb. 1899 it was bought at sheriff's sale by Edward J. Wessel, whose recently founded *Universe* was merged with it. The Gates Publishing Company bought it in 1901, the Wilson Company in 1903, and Robert Gillis Handy the next year. For several months in 1900–01, the price was 10¢ a number, but throughout most of its career the *Great Round World* was a 5¢ weekly. Genie H. Rosenfeld was editor in its first phase, and Henry Bannister Merwin later.

[23] See p. 53.

[24] See Sketch 16 in this volume.

[25] See Sketch 23 in this volume.

[26] See Sketch 88 in Mott, *op. cit.*, v. 1.

## MISCELLANEOUS MISCELLANIES

The *New York Ledger*,[27] for years "the weekly printed pabulum for scores of thousands of homes,"[28] lost its director in 1887, with the retirement of Robert Bonner; but the three sons of the founder carried this famous story paper on. Its circulation, however, declined to about a hundred thousand by 1890 and half of that in 1895.[29] In 1898 it was made a family mail-order monthly at fifty cents a year — an indignity it survived five years. The *New York Weekly*[30] was conducted from the latter eighties by two sons of Francis S. Smith, of Street & Smith — Ormond G. and George C. — continuing throughout the present period as a kind of flagship of the Street & Smith fleet. It was not then or ever a distinguished periodical, but it had been the first Street & Smith success and it continued through the nineties to claim two hundred thousand circulation.

In Chicago, the *Current*[31] came upon misfortunes in 1885 when its editor and manager left it between days; and though it published some very interesting matter by good authors in 1886, including the Hinton-Piatt debate over Richard Realf, it declined, and in 1888 it gave up the ghost.

An unusual magazine, no less than brilliant in its prime and surely deserving greater success than it ever achieved, was the *Criterion*, the voice of new ideas in twentieth-century letters and art. It was begun in St. Louis in 1889 as a pleasant and attractive journal of society and amusements called *St. Louis Life*.[32] It so continued until 1896, when it was acquired by Mrs. Grace L. Davidson, a widow of limited means, who changed the name to *Criterion*. Then, as occasionally happened with such local journals, this one struck a vein that made it a distinguished magazine and attracted national attention. A French-born literary adventurer named Henri Dumay came to St. Louis, offered some clever contributions to Mrs. Davidson's paper, and was shortly invited to join its editorial staff. He transformed it into a scintillating literary journal, and assured Mrs. Davidson that if she could interest some "angel" in moving the paper to New York, he would enlist a brilliant lot of contributors, and they would together make literary

[27] See Sketch 12 in Mott, *op. cit.*, v. 2.
[28] Editorial in *Cosmopolitan*, v. 27, p. 567, Sept. 1899.
[29] Rowell's directories are more reliable and conservative than Ayer's for these figures. John Elderkin, who had been connected editorially with the publication for 25 years, gave place in Nov. 1902 to George R. Knapp. This was just a year after the Bonners had sold out to a stock company (*New York Tribune*, Nov. 16, 1902, p. 3, col. 3).
[30] See Mott, *op. cit.*, v. 2, p. 38.
[31] See Mott, *op. cit.*, v. 3, p. 54.
[32] See p. 100.

and journalistic history. Mrs. Davidson, herself a mild and reserved lady of uncertain age, did succeed in interesting "a dear schoolmate of her girlhood," the sister and heiress of "a greatly successful newspaper man of St. Louis," who, if a later editor is to be believed, put a thousand dollars a week into the journal for at least two years.[33] It moved to New York in 1897. George Henry Payne and Rupert Hughes became associate editors; and all the most brilliant young writers of the "mauve decade" were enlisted as contributors. Thirty years later, H. L. Mencken wrote: "How, as a youngster, I used to lie in wait for the *Criterion* every week, and devour Pollard, Huneker, Meltzer, and Vance Thompson!"[34] Other writers for the journal were James L. Ford, Gelett Burgess, Charles J. Nirdlinger, A. C. Wheeler ("Nym Crinkle"), James Metcalf, James Gilmore Speed, Charles Battell Loomis, and Charles de Kay. Such were the critics, satirists, and essayists of the weekly; but it was especially strong in verse, with Carman, Hovey, Guiterman, Masson, Scollard, Lampton, and so on, as contributors. A twenty-four-page quarto at ten cents a copy, handsomely printed, its illustrations in this phase were by Hy Mayer, C. D. Fornaro, Rob Wagner, Thomas Nast, Howard Cort, and others.

But the magazine had trouble with its distributors, the American News Company; it was over the heads of many readers; when Editor Dumay "rhapsodized the little sanitary stops of a French dancer's dog,"[35] Mrs. Davidson was shocked and remonstrated; libraries thought it too improper for their tables; and it never succeeded in selling more than ten thousand copies, going down rather than up in the last years of the decade. Early in 1898 Mrs. Davidson abruptly discharged Dumay (who later made a journalistic success in Paris), and Hughes ran the paper for a few weeks before Joseph I. C. Clarke, Irish journalist and poet, was installed as editor. He carried on the *Criterion* pattern very well, with more restraint than Dumay had shown, but with excellent "untechnical criticism" of literature, drama, art, and music;[36] and with good fiction, timely articles, and much verse. Eventually the inevitable occurred: the St. Louis "angel" got tired of paying. In 1900 Clarke was succeeded by Emery Pottle, and the *Criterion* was made a ten-cent monthly. Though it declined in zest and brilliance, it was still a good magazine when it perished in 1905.

Julian Ralph's *Chatter* was a New York weekly on yellow paper in 1890. It started out brilliantly with Conan Doyle, Thomas Hardy, Jerome K. Jerome, John Kendrick Bangs, and Eugene Field as contribu-

---

[33] Joseph I. C. Clarke, *My Life and Memories* (New York, 1925), pp. 262–63. See the whole of Chap. XXIX for the *Criterion*.

[34] H. L. Mencken, *Prejudices*, First Series (New York, 1919), p. 129.

[35] Thomas Beer, *The Mauve Decade* (New York, 1926), pp. 154–55.

[36] Zona Gale in *Critic*, v. 44, pp. 325–26, April 1904.

tors; but it ran into financial trouble with its distributors and ended after six months.

*Broadway Weekly* [37] began as a society and satirical journal by Frank Parker, very handsome and well illustrated, but it soon deteriorated into a sensational paper with a series on the "vice trust," love affairs of actors, and so on. Politically it was for Tammany and against Theodore Roosevelt. Roland Burke Hennessey, who had a hand in most of the "spicy" periodicals of the times, was editor in its last year. There were entirely too many such papers in the nineties. Hennessey's *Saturday Standard* [38] enjoyed a certain popularity because of its pictures of ladies in tights or décolleté, scenes from Sam T. Jack's burlesques, and slangy gossip of sports and the theater. It was merged in 1904 with *Vanity Fair*, "A Magazine for the Home" — what a home! And there was the *Sunday Flash,* an indecent paper published in New York in 1887–88 "by a clever but unscrupulous Bostonian named Snelling." [39] A later "flash weekly" in New York was the *Tenderloin,* of 1899, which bore as subtitle the more or less respectable designation, "A Weekly Society Journal," but which did not last long after the Mazet Investigating Committee got after it.

THE CHEAP "FAMILY" PAPERS

There was also a notable class of cheaply printed, low-priced miscellanies designed for week-end reading in the family. These carried much mail-order advertising, but they differed from the general run of mail-order publications in their method of distribution: the papers referred to were sold by newsboys the country over. It was from the circulation methods of these papers that the *Saturday Evening Post* at the end of our period derived its technique of distribution by "boy merchants." [40] These family journals usually furnished news in somewhat sensational form, cheap fiction, and departments for home and family.

Several of these papers were "Blades," probably named after the old *Yankee Blade,*[41] of Boston. Sam Walter Foss, the popular poet, was editor of the *Yankee Blade* during its last seven years, 1887–1894. Greatest of the group in the nineties was W. D. Boyce's *Saturday Blade,* founded in Chicago in 1887. By 1890 Boyce had recruited, through prizes and liberal payment, over six thousand newsboys, especially throughout the Midwest, to sell his paper on Saturday after-

[37] Issued Feb. 18, 1903, through Nov. 2, 1904, thus ending with the national political campaign. It probably had Tammany backing.
[38] See footnote, p. 47.
[39] *Journalist*, v. 6, p. 2, Jan. 7, 1888.
[40] See Sketch 27.
[41] See Mott, *op. cit.*, v. 2, p. 36.

noons. The boys kept two cents out of the nickel paid for each copy, and the papers were returnable.[42]

The *Saturday Blade* was an eight-page folio combining news with fiction and departmented miscellany. It had about a quarter-million circulation through most of the nineties, chiefly in the small cities and villages. Boyce handled the circulation and advertising of the *Saturday Blade*, the *Chicago Ledger*,[43] a story paper; and the *Chicago World*,[44] a sporting weekly, in one group in the early nineties. The last-named was suspended in 1893, but the other two were continued until 1924 as "Boyce's Big Weeklies," with a combined circulation of half a million or so. Another famous weekly with the magic name was the *Toledo Weekly Blade*. This had begun as the weekly edition of a great Ohio daily in 1847, and had between one and two hundred thousand circulation in the nineties. It continued until 1923.

There were three papers of this type in upstate New York. The *Utica Saturday Globe*, founded in 1881 by two brothers, William T. and Thomas F. Baker, was built up to a circulation of two hundred thousand by 1890 through its copiously illustrated features. Amusement, sensation, the farm, and the family were its metier. It declined to a hundred thousand in the nineties, but lasted until 1924. Another New York paper, the *Elmira Telegram*, was founded in 1879 and claimed in 1885 "the largest weekly circulation of any provincial paper in America," namely, well over a hundred thousand. Later it reached a hundred and seventy thousand, at a dollar and a half a year, and in the twenties it became the Sunday edition of the daily *Star-Gazette*. And the Troy *Northern Budget*, oldest of all, having been founded in 1797, was published in the nineties by C. L. MacArthur and Son.[45]

The most successful, as well as the most excellent, of the periodicals of this general type was *Grit*,[46] of Williamsport, Pennsylvania. Begun as a week-end newspaper on December 10, 1882, it was about to perish

[42] *Printer's Ink*, v. 4, pp. 22–23, Jan. 7, 1891.

[43] See Mott, *op. cit.*, v. 2, pp. 53–54.

[44] This paper was begun in 1891 by A. B. Adsit. Boyce did not own it but handled it in conjunction with the *Blade* and *Ledger*. It was not the same *Chicago Saturday World* that W. Henry Welch edited; that was a society and family journal founded in 1870 and published in conjunction with Welch's monthly *World Magazine*, which had been founded a year later and sold for 50¢ a year. They ended with the World's Fair.

[45] It was merged in 1926 with the *Observer*, and is now issued as the *Observer-Budget*, a Sunday paper. See Clarence S. Brigham, *History and Bibliography of American Newspapers, 1690–1820* (Worcester, Mass., 1947), v. 1, pp. 599, 745–46, for its early history.

[46] It was first titled *Williamsport Grit*; but in 1887 its spreading circulation called for the name *Pennsylvania Grit*, and twenty years later its national distribution called for the simplest form — *Grit*. However, *Grit* still has city, state, and national editions. Circulation in the middle fifties was about 750,000. Dietrick Lamade died in 1938, leaving his sons George R. and Howard J. in charge. The price was raised from 5¢ to 7¢ in 1944, when the periodical adopted a tabloid form; five years later it went to 10¢. See *PNPA Bulletin*, Sept. 1949, p. 74; *Printer's Ink*, v. 66, March 31, 1909, p. 35; *Editor & Publisher*, Dec. 4, 1943, p. 54.

after its first year or two, when Dietrick Lamade and partners bought it, made it a bright, newsy, entertaining family paper, and brought it to fifty thousand circulation by 1890. It went on to four or five times that by the end of our period, and later to much greater heights, all distributed by an army of some thirty thousand boys in towns of less than twenty-five hundred population.

A somewhat different type of periodical was the *National Tribune*, of Washington. It was founded in 1877 as a paper for Civil War veterans and their families. It was mainly distributed by mail, at a dollar a year, and it emphasized G.A.R. news; otherwise it was similar to the large class of family news weeklies. It gained a quarter of a million circulation by 1891, but later declined somewhat.[47]

But what about the once prosperous Saturday and Sunday papers of news and miscellany in all the great cities? In New York, what about the old sensational *Dispatch*,[48] that more respectable friend of the sports fan, the *Sunday Mercury*,[49] the *Sunday Times and Messenger* (1843–1892), the *Sunday Courier* (1846–1901), and the *Sunday Democrat* (1870–1924)? Not one of these papers was really prosperous in the nineties; all were living on borrowed time or funds, or outright subsidies. They were already crowded into a corner by the Sunday editions of daily papers. The *Sunday Mercury* gained a few years' respite by starting a daily, of which it was the Sunday edition during 1893–1896. The New York pattern was repeated, *mutatis mutandis*, in Philadelphia,[50] Boston,[51] Washington, [52] and other large cities.

### MAGAZINE SUPPLEMENTS OF NEWSPAPERS

On the other hand, the great newspapers, feeling the competition which the ten-cent periodicals offered to their Sunday editions, fre-

[47] John McElroy was editor from 1884 until his death in 1929. In 1926 the *National Tribune* absorbed the Washington continuation of World War I's *Stars and Stripes*, and it is still published as *National Tribune — Stars and Stripes*.

[48] See Mott, *op. cit.*, v. 2, p. 37. It gained additional life in the early nineties by featuring special departments for the G.A.R., the Masons, the fire and police services, and so on.

[49] See Mott, *ibid.*

[50] In Philadelphia, besides the story papers, there were the *Sunday Dispatch*, founded in 1848 and now in its second century; the *Sunday Mercury* (1851–91); *Taggart's Sunday Times* (1863–1901), by John H. Taggart; *Sunday Transcript* (1858–1932) and many others of shorter life.

[51] Famous Boston weekly of this class was the *Saturday Evening Gazette* (1814–1906), notable for its sound character and literary tone, conducted 1880–94 by Col. Henry G. Parker; and 1895–1901 by Dr. Philip Woolf.

[52] There were many political-literary weeklies in Washington. Among them were the *Sunday Gazette* (1868–91); the *Sunday Herald and National Intelligencer* (1866–96), successor of the old Gales and Seaton paper and latterly a free-silver organ; the *National View* (1879–95), a Greenback paper edited by Lee Crandall; A. P. Beatty's *Courant* (1885–1905); the *National Republican* (1882–92) and the *National Democrat* (1889–95); Louis Schade's *Sentinel* (1873–1910); and the once famous *Forney's Sunday Chronicle* (1861–1911), conducted in the nineties by J. Q. Thompson. See also p. 88.

quently set up "magazines" in quarto or small-folio size, which featured content of somewhat more literary quality than was to be found in the familiar "Sunday supplements," but were included in the regular Saturday or Sunday issues.

Examples of this device in New York were the *Tribune Illustrated Supplement* (1897–1904), which had been preceded by *Twinkles* (1896–1897); the *Times Supplement* (later *Magazine*), begun in 1896; the *Saturday Evening Mail* (1897–1913), of the *Mail and Express*; the *Commercial Advertiser Pictorial Review*, which began as an illustrated supplement on Saturdays in 1898; the *Sunday Magazine of Intelligence and Entertainment* (1897–1900), which succeeded *Iroquois: A Modern Magazine* as a supplement of the *Press*. Many other newspapers followed this example, such as the *Lewiston* (Maine) *Journal*, the *Omaha Bee*, the *Chicago Daily News*, and the *Chicago Chronicle*. These Sunday supplements were sometimes sold separately, as were the *Pictorial Review* and *Sunday Magazine* named above.

These independent magazine supplements were fated to succumb rather generally to the syndicates in the early decades of the new century. It was in 1902 that Joseph P. Knapp, then manager of the American Lithograph Company and later the leading figure in the Crowell-Collier Company, arranged for thirteen leading Sunday newspapers in as many cities to carry a magazine supplement identical but for the name plates.[53] In New York, for example, this inserted section supplanted the *Tribune Illustrated Supplement*. By the end of our period, the Associated Sunday Magazines were claiming a combined circulation of over a million in eight cities.

Meanwhile the great weekly editions of prominent dailies were obsolescent. The *New York Weekly Tribune*, once the chief sounding board of Horace Greeley, had the greatest vitality of all the weekly editions of New York newspapers; but by the century's end it was reorganized into the *Tribune Farmer* and a triweekly newspaper, and the latter was soon dropped. The *Boston Transcript's* weekly edition ran for seventy years, from 1852 to 1921. The *Echo*, weekly edition of the Scripps papers, which had been issued for fourteen years, was abandoned in 1892. A few southern papers, such as the *Chattanooga News*, the *Memphis Commercial Appeal*, the *Atlanta Constitution*, and the Louisville *Courier-Journal*, maintained weeklies of fair circulation in the nineties and for several years afterward.

[53] John Arberry Haney, "A History of Nationally Syndicated Magazine Supplements" (doctoral dissertation, University of Missouri, 1953), pp. 169–71.

# CHAPTER VI

## THE GENERAL QUARTERLIES

THE heyday of the quarterly review was past long before the years with which we are now dealing. The single survivor of the group of great reviews of the past was the *North American*, which had been a monthly since 1879. A generation which moved more and more swiftly on the wheels of trains and even of automobiles could not abide the "slowcoach quarterlies." Though a few religious denominations still maintained quarterlies, most of them were now served only by monthlies, fortnightlies, and weeklies. About 2 1/2 per cent of the total periodicals in the period 1885–1905 were quarterlies, and they were chiefly devoted to special fields of learning in the sciences and the humanities.

A few quarterlies published in the hope of reaching fairly wide audiences must be discussed, however, in this short chapter. Additional quarterlies in special fields will be mentioned later; many scholarly journals have been published four times a year.

### INDEPENDENT JOURNALS

Though most quarterlies were sponsored by colleges, universities, or associations, there were several which were independent ventures; and a few were designed for popular rather than scholarly reading. The Boston publishers D. Lothrop and Company, who specialized in juveniles, published during the early nineties a periodical called *Best Things*, which was subtitled "A Quarterly Illustrated Journal of Literature and Timely Topics for Family Reading." It was a quarto illustrated by handsome woodcuts; it had some good contributors, and it sold for ten cents a copy or thirty cents a year.[1] Most important of all the compendiums of current events was the one which began in 1891 as the *Quarterly Register of Current History*, but which was known for the ten years beginning in 1893 as the *Cyclopedic Review of Current History*. The versatile Alfred Sidney Johnson was its founder, as well as its editor during most of its life of some twelve years.[2]

[1] *Best Things* was published Dec. 1890–March 1893. Its first number was small-folio in size, with 24 pages; by its fourth number it was a small-quarto of 32 pages. Among contributors were Charles G. D. Roberts, Mary E. Wilkins, J. T. Trowbridge, Edith M. Thomas, and Margaret Sidney, all of whom were represented in the first number.

[2] Quarterly, 1891–99; monthly, 1900–03. It was published in 12 vols., Feb. 1891–Feb. 1903, after which it was merged with *Current Literature*. At first it was sponsored by the

Shortly after Elbert Hubbard had begun his *Philistine*, he published, less successfully, three numbers of a *Roycroft Quarterly* in 1896. This attractively printed periodical is notable chiefly for the fact that Number One is a Stephen Crane issue and contains seven poems and a sketch by that author. The *Bohemian* (1899–1907), issued by a literary club in Fort Worth, Texas, and edited by Mrs. Henrie Clay Ligon Gorman, was well printed but undistinguished in content. The *Hesperian*, of St. Louis, was a modest critical quarterly that was largely written, as well as edited and published, by Alexander N. De Menil, poet, lawyer, and public servant. This was a little pamphlet of only forty or fifty pages, selling for fifteen cents, but De Menil was a good writer and sound critic.[3]

De Menil was an admirer, and occasionally a sharp critic, of William Henry Thorne's *Globe Quarterly Review*, of which he wrote:

> Virtually, the *Globe* is Mr. Thorne, and Mr. Thorne is the *Globe*. Eliminate from its pages the Thorne flavor, and the *Globe* would present the melancholy spectacle of the average trite, commonplace, and conventional eastern review of the present day. We cannot agree with Mr. Thorne in many of his judgments, but we cheerfully bear testimony to his originality, his vigor, and his thorough honesty.[4]

Thorne wrote about a third of his *Globe* — a ninety-page quarterly — discussing philosophy, politics, literature, and theology with equal facility and assurance. He was sometimes lively and acrimonious in his attacks on persons he disapproved, as in this sentence about women reformers: "The screaming blatherskite speechifyings and platformings of the Miss Anthonys, the Miss Willards, and the Lady Somersets of our times are the grotesque somersaults of female clowns."[5] Thorne hated Theodore Roosevelt and opposed the war with Spain. He was converted to Catholicism in 1892, but often attacked Archibishops Ireland and Ryan. He was troubled by illness, and issues were sometimes postponed because the editor was in hospital. By 1905 Thorne had run out of both health and money; but the *Globe*, which now ended, had been in the better tradition of the old personal review.[6]

---

*Detroit Evening News*, but it moved to Buffalo (where Garretson, Cox & Co. published it) in 1893, and to Boston (where it was successively issued by the New England Publishing Co. and Current History Co.) in 1897. Johnson left it at the end of 1901, and Clarence A. Bickford, William W. Hudson, and Nathan Haskell Dole became editors.

[3] July 1894–Sept. 1917, 92 numbers. De Menil had been editor of the *St. Louis Illustrated Magazine* (see p. 101) 1883–90.

[4] *Hesperian*, v. 1, pp. 159–60, April 1895.

[5] *Globe*, v. 4, p. 663, June 1894.

[6] Throughout most of its file this quarterly was called simply *The Globe*. It was begun in Philadelphia, was published through most of the nineties in New York, and returned to Philadelphia for its last volume. It sold for $2.00 a year. It published 14 annual volumes, Dec. 1889–Midwinter 1905.

There was more variety and brilliance in the short-lived *Conservative Review*, edited and published in Washington at the turn of the century by Walter Neale, who had set up a general publishing house in that city. This journal seems to have been started to oppose Republican "imperialism," and there were three antiexpansionist articles in the first number — one by Champ Clark. It also had strong southern interest; it printed several pieces on the Civil War, the autobiography of Richard Malcolm Johnston, and articles by John S. Bassett, James A. Harrison, and Philip Alexander Bruce. Politically, the *Conservative Review* aligned itself with the Sound-Money Democrats, religiously with the Catholics. Essays on literary figures were frequent. William Lyne Wilson, then president of Washington and Lee University, was editor at first, but he died in 1900 and Neale took over.[7]

Another turn-of-the-century review was the *International Quarterly*, founded and edited at Burlington, Vermont, as *International Monthly*, but later made a quarterly and moved to New York. It had excellent variety and balance, and a distinguished list of contributors; but it survived only six years. This review lived up to its name by its treatment of foreign relations and by printing such foreign scholars as Salvatore Cortesi, Edouard Rod, Bertrand Russell, Max Nordau, and Cesare Lombroso.[8]

### UNIVERSITY QUARTERLIES

Of the dozen or more university quarterlies published in this period, three stand out as having importance for the wider audience — the *Yale Review* and the *Sewanee Review*, both begun in 1892, and the *South Atlantic Quarterly*, founded in 1902. These are all treated in separate sketches.[9] The *Yale Review* began as a journal of history and politics, but later greatly broadened its scope. The *Sewanee Review* was founded by William Peterfield Trent as a journal with a broad purview and literary trend at the University of the South, Sewanee, Tennessee. The *South Atlantic* began at Trinity College (Duke University since 1924) under the editorship of John Spencer Bassett.

[7] An octavo of 200 pages, the *Conservative* sold for 50¢ a number, or $2.00 a year. It published ten numbers in five volumes, Feb. 1899–Sept. 1901. Among the better-known contributors were Frank B. Sanborn, David Starr Jordan, Fabian Franklin, Hamlin Garland, and Louise Imogen Guiney.

[8] Published Jan. 1900–Jan. 1906, in 12 vols., omitting July–Aug. 1902. It became a quarterly with its Sept.–Dec. 1902 number. The Macmillan Company acted as publisher in 1900, and Fox, Duffield & Co. in 1904–06. It moved to New York in 1904. Among contributors were N. S. Shaler, Norman Hapgood, W. J. Stillman, Harry T. Finck, C. H. Toy, W. P. Trent, Brander Matthews, Russell Sturgis, Josiah Royce, George Santayana, and C. W. Eliot.

[9] For the *Sewanee Review*, see Sketch 34 in this volume. The *South Atlantic Quarterly* and the *Yale Review* will be treated in separate sketches in the next volume of this series.

The *Columbia University Quarterly* (1898–1919) continued the old *Columbia University Bulletin* (1890–1898) and was more parochial than the three mentioned above, containing convocation addresses, historical and biographical matter pertaining to Columbia, news, and so on. Calvin Thomas, Brander Matthews, and Charles Sears Baldwin were in the succession of managing editors. The *Princeton College Bulletin* (1889–1904), edited by the president and faculty, was intended to "deal editorially and through signed articles with educational questions," [10] but it soon broadened its content. In 1896 it changed its name to *Princeton University Bulletin* and was devoted chiefly to addresses at the university, abstracts of Ph.D. theses, news, and announcements. *Union University Quarterly* (1904–1908) was a good but short-lived repository of faculty addresses and papers. Somewhat the same may be said of the *Vanderbilt University Quarterly* (1901–1915), though it had a longer life.

The *University of Texas Record* and the *University Record* at Chicago were both begun in 1896; the former lasted fifteen years and the latter twelve. Both were parochial in nature.[11] The *Kansas University Quarterly* (1892–1901) was "devoted to the publication of research by members of the University of Kansas." Its contents were largely scientific.[12] *Park Review* (1899–1907), a small quarterly of some fifty pages, was edited by professors at Park College at Parkville, Missouri.[13] Originally designed for faculty papers, it later found both contributors and readers outside the college community. It was especially strong in history, literature, and religion. The *University of California Chronicle* (1898–1933) was at first devoted largely to announcements and news, but it later published many university addresses, papers read before the Berkeley Club, some verse, and so on, in considerable variety. Joseph Le Conte, William James, William Henry Hudson, John Dewey, William Rainey Harper, Benjamin Ide Wheeler, Whitelaw Reid, and many other famous scholars and publicists are represented in its pages. Though it began as a bimonthly, it became a quarterly in 1902.

ALUMNI QUARTERLIES

The most distinguished of alumni quarterlies in the United States has been the *Harvard Graduates' Magazine* (1892–1934). This was

---

[10] *Princeton College Bulletin*, v. 1, p. 1, Jan. 1889.

[11] The *University Record* at the University of Chicago began as a weekly, and changed to monthly publication in 1902, and quarterly in 1906.

[12] It carried a Series B on philology and history, however, in 1897–99.

[13] Thomas Gregory Burt was the leading editor. E. Benjamin Andrews, Henry MacCracken, and Charles E. Jefferson were among the outside contributors.

largely because William Roscoe Thayer, its editor during its first twenty-three years, set a high standard.[14] In his very first number he had such Harvard "greats" as Charles W. Eliot, Theodore Roosevelt, A. P. Peabody, and Wendell Phillips Garrison. One of the most controversial articles in the *Magazine's* history appeared in the number for December 1905, in which Yale was attacked as having made no single "important contribution" to educational progress in the preceding third of a century.

The *Michigan Alumnus* (1894–current) was at first a quarterly review of wide interest,[15] and other alumni organs doubtless were quarterlies at times. Many universites have published series of "studies" in special fields, and some of these have had more or less regular quarterly issues.

[14] Thayer was editor through June 1915; William Richards Castle, Jr., Sept. 1915–June 1917; M. A. De Wolfe Howe, Sept. 1917–June 1918; Arthur Stanwood Pier, Sept. 1918–June 1930; Bernard De Voto, Sept. 1930–June 1932; Theodore Morrison, Sept. 1932–June 1934.

[15] It soon became a monthly, and in 1921 a weekly. Wilfred B. Shaw was editor for many years.

# CHAPTER VII

## LOCAL AND REGIONAL MAGAZINES

"MAGAZINES have greatly widened their horizons in recent years," remarked a skilled observer in the *Dial* in 1892, "and the West and the South of the present are less in need of publications" of their own than formerly.[1] It was true that the East had become acquainted with the rest of America. Some of the reasons for this shift of attention will be pointed out in this chapter; but in general it may be said that it was due to the movement of population, the growing economic importance of the West and South, the strident political voices from those regions, and the impressive showing of western and southern literature and education.

The broadened geographical interests of the national magazines, virtually all of them issued from eastern cities, did not prevent the publication of a large number of periodicals of many kinds throughout the land — north, south, east, and west. Some of these aspired to national circulation and influence — especially certain ventures in Chicago — but such breadth of distribution always seemed to be reserved for periodicals published in New York, Philadelphia, or Boston. The facts are that facilities for editing and publishing tended to center more and more in New York, and that it was coming to be recognized generally that New York was the national capital for the publishing of both books and magazines. Wrote the editor of the *Writer* in 1899: "No one section of this country can or will support a magazine of general literature, and the country as a whole will not support such a magazine if it is published as the representative of any single section."[2]

But local magazines for local audiences had been published since the beginning of periodicals in America, and in the nineties they were issued in greater numbers than ever before. The chief type of local periodical was that which served professional and occupational groups, such as the medical, legal, and insurance reporters. The farm papers were mainly state-wide in distribution, and many of the religious and educational journals were regional. Most large cities, the country over, produced one or more cheap monthlies for women and the home, of the type known as "mail-order journals." And there were also

[1] *Dial*, v. 13, p. 204, Oct. 1, 1892.
[2] *Writer*, v. 12, p. 102, July 1899.

comics, bicycling magazines, journals of secret orders, and so on, scattered through all parts of the country.

But attention must be given here to certain local and regional magazines of general appeal, uneven in merit but often interesting and significant. Some were little more than "booster" pamphlets, and most of them were too much given to "mug" articles. A "mug" story was a complimentary "write-up" of a local man decorated with his picture (or "mug"); a "mug" issue was filled with such stories, paid for in cash or merchandise. It is said that when Jack Sullivan, business manager of *Reedy's Mirror*, of St. Louis, came to die, he received the sacrament of extreme unction from the priest and then sank back on the pillow, murmuring: "Thanks, Father. I'll mug you in our next issue." [3] Nevertheless, many of these magazines had real importance, and there was one type — the urban weekly — which became one of the most interesting phenomena of the period.

### THE URBAN WEEKLY

The urban weekly, as it developed in the nineties, was primarily a journal of society, amusement, politics, and literary miscellany. It might, however, stress any one of those departments, according to the preferences of the editors or publishers. It might also omit any one, or any two or three of them, though a certain amount of news and chit-chat of local society was really the trade-mark of the genre.

The urban journal of society news and miscellany was not new. There had been many of them, and even some famous ones, in earlier periods — such as the New York *Home Journal*, the *Boston Budget*, and the lively San Francisco trio — the *News-Letter*, *Argonaut*, and *Wasp*. But the thing that made this class of papers so important in the nineties was the growing tendency to do precisely what the San Francisco *Wasp* had done — to break away from the conventional and rather dull pattern, and develop some phase or type of content which would make it, for a short time at least, a brilliant weekly journal. This flowering was nearly always the result of the discovery of unusual talent, in some field, of some local editor or contributor. Thus Ambrose Bierce and Frank Pixley had stirred up criticism and literature in San Francisco. Thus William Marion Reedy emphasized poetry and the critical essay in his St. Louis *Mirror*; thus Vance Thompson exploited smart criticism in his *M'lle New York*; thus Thomas J. Creamer played up politics in his New York *Citizen*; thus George Creel fought the Pendergast machine in his Kansas City *Independent*. These urban

---

[3] Obituary of Sullivan in *Mirror*, v. 15, n.s., June 1946, p. 5.

weeklies had a kind of adaptability that enabled them to change general policy as opportunities presented themselves or the need arose. Some eventually became mainly household or club journals for women and the home, and some went off on the path of the humor weekly. They were a various lot.

But many of them adhered, for long periods, to the chronicle of social happenings, with news of the local theaters and musical events and something of local sports, and were never more than society newspapers. Of these, some gained circulation by adding sophisticated short fiction and "spicy" sketches of the stage. Such papers were likely to emphasize the scandals in society; and even to invent such things, and to indulge in free comments on social leaders which some believed to be connected with blackmailing practices. In New York, this situation was worse than in any other city. The *Bookman*, welcoming Nugent Robertson's *Vanity*, said that the new weekly was attempting to prove "that a bright, up-to-date society organ can be successful without the aid of scurrilous innuendo and teacup scandal," but it added: "We do not envy Mr. Robertson his attempted Herculean task to cleanse the Augean stable of the society press." [4]

As we survey the more or less local periodicals in the various regions and cities, we shall find these urban weeklies in all the large cities.

### NEW ENGLAND

It was in 1887 that the *Critic* referred to "that perennial theme — Boston as a literary center." [5] The New England metropolis gave up its literary preëminence with much reluctance and argument. The *Brooklyn Magazine* printed in 1885 a symposium entitled "Is Boston Losing Its Literary Prestige?" in which Frederick H. Hedge called the roll of famous Boston men of letters in the eighties — Lowell, Holmes, Whittier, Aldrich, Howells, Hale, Parkman, Higginson, Fiske, Norton. But George Parsons Lathrop asserted dogmatically: "The loss of prestige is evident in the fact that we no longer accept the literature which comes from Boston as setting the standard." [6]

Certainly in magazine literature, Boston had long ago lost its leadership. It had been forced to give up the *North American Review* to New York, though it had kept the *Atlantic Monthly*, which it supported most inadequately in the nineties. Other Boston magazines were some-

---

[4] *Bookman*, v. 1, p. 82, March 1895.

[5] *Critic*, v. 11, p. 1331, Dec. 24, 1887.

[6] *Brooklyn Magazine*, v. 3, pp. 91–97, Dec. 1885. See also *American Magazine*, n.s., v. 3, pp. 51–65, May 1888. *Once A Week* published a series on American literary centers in 1895.

what down in the scale. The *Arena*, a leading liberal review, was published in Boston during the first half of its life, and then moved to New York. The *Living Age* kept on its even but inconspicuous course. The *Literary World* was a fortnightly of merit and small circulation. The *Youth's Companion*, the country's leading juvenile, was Boston's only national periodical of large circulation — except for a few cheap mail-order papers.[7]

An important regional magazine issued from Boston was Edwin Doak Mead's *New England Magazine* (1884–1917). Mead, who took over the magazine in 1889 after it had made a false start,[8] had spent nine years in the Fields publishing house during the time it issued the *Atlantic Monthly*; he was himself an industrious author and editor, a social and political reformer, and a member of the Free Religious Association. Edward Everett Hale promised to edit the revived magazine when Mead took it over, but he continued with it only about a

---

[7] The magazines mentioned in this paragraph, except the *Arena* (*q.v.* Sketch 2), are treated more or less fully in earlier volumes of this work. So are certain minor periodicals that were begun before 1885, as *Ballou's Magazine*, a 15¢ miscellany in the eighties, ending 1893; and three that continued throughout the present period — *Waverley Magazine*, beloved of amateur scribblers; John W. Nichols' *True Flag*, a famous miscellany which was taken over by G. H. Howard shortly before its end in 1908 and made a cheap mail-order paper; and the *Yankee Blade*, well-known cheap newspaper and miscellany (*q.v.* p. 67). Frederick Gleason's *Home Circle* (1871–90) was an illustrated eight-page folio, which sold for $2.00 a year or 5¢ a copy.

[8] It began as *Bay State Monthly*, edited and published by John N. McClintock for two years, specializing in biographies illustrated by portraits engraved on steel, in historical articles, and in descriptions of New England churches and colleges. Some of the numbers of *Bay State Monthly* were reprinted by J. A. Cline & Co., Boston, under the title *Massachusetts Magazine*, of which McClintock was listed as editor, and the file of which ran as follows. Vol. 1, no. 1, appeared in Aug. 1885 (original); there were no further numbers in v. 1. Vol. 2 has six numbers as follows: (1) reprint *Bay State*, Oct. 1884; (2) reprint *Bay State*, Nov. 1884; (3) reprint *Mass. Mag.*, Aug. 1885; (4) Nov. 1885; (5) April 1886; (6) June 1886. Vol. 3, no. 1, appeared in June 1887. The last four numbers were original. The *Bay State Monthly* seems never to have been a success. It was suspended four months in 1886, but Arthur P. Dodge came to McClintock's rescue. In Mead's regime, there was a business reorganization in the panic year of 1893, and Warren F. Kellogg, young journalist and author, became chief owner. In 1901 Kellogg and Mead sold it to James A. Garland, a young Harvardian who was almost as much interested in authors and authorship as he was in horses and horsemanship. Under Garland there was more effort to gain popularity with fiction, and William McLeod Raine, Eleanor H. Porter, and Willa Sibert Cather were contributors; while colonial and patriotic societies had departments. In 1907 the magazine was offered for sale at auction and purchased by Bertrand L. Chapman and associates, who owned it in its last decade. Editors were Winthrop Packard (1905–08), Rhey T. Snodgrass (1908), Charles Everett Beane (1908–09), Frederick M. Burrows (1909–17). In 1907–08 there were some famous contributors, as George Santayana, G. Stanley Hall, Frederick Orin Bartlett; and full-page New England landscapes in halftone were a feature. Thereafter quality declined. The complete file runs as follows: v. 1, Jan.–June 1884; 2, Oct. 1884, Jan.–March 1885; 3, April, May, Aug.–Nov. 1885; 4, Jan.–June 1886; 5, Nov. 1886–April/May 1887; 6, June/July 1887, Feb.–March, Aug.–Oct. 1888; 7–53, new series 1–47 semiannual vols., Sept. 1889–Aug. 1912 (Nov. 1887–Aug. 1889 omitted); n.s. 48, Sept. 1912–Jan. 1913; n.s. 49, March–July 1913; n.s. 50, Aug. 1913–Feb. 1914 (Aug./Sept. double number); n.s. 51, March–Aug. 1914; n.s. 52, Sept. 1914–April 1915 (Jan.–Feb. omitted); n.s. 53, May–Oct. 1915; n.s. 54, Nov. 1915–April 1916; n.s. 55, May–Sept. 1916 (July, Aug., Oct. omitted); 56, Nov. 1916–Feb./March 1917.

year, after which Mead himself was editor throughout the decade of the nineties. Though it maintained a New England tone and emphasis,, the magazine printed much about the South, the West, and Canada.. Social, economic, and literary matters were discussed, and a mildly reformatory spirit shown. Though not so fully illustrated, the *New England* in the nineties was not unlike the *Century* and *Scribner's*. Frank B. Sanborn, Walter Blackburn Harte, James K. Hosmer, George Willis Cooke, Rose Terry Cooke, Charlotte Perkins Stetson, Lucy Larcom, and Sam Walter Foss may be named as representative contributors.

A local monthly with the name *Bostonian: An Illustrated Magazine of Local Interest* was begun in October 1894 by Arthur Wellington Brayley. It was a well-printed quarto, with many illustrations. It set out to exploit the interest of Bostonians in the history of their city and state, and sometimes advertised itself as "An Illustrated Historical Monthly Magazine"; but it also gave attention to the theater, to women's clubs, and to book reviews. It reprinted serially the first American novel, *The Power of Sympathy*, William Hill Brown's curious contribution to the eighteenth-century literature of seduction, which it credited in the first two installments to Sarah Wentworth Morton — a common error. In 1896 Brayley changed the policy of his periodical, made a bid for national coverage and circulation, and called it the *National Magazine*. The next year he sold out to the W. W. Potter Company; and Arthur Winslow Tarbell, a recent Harvard graduate, became editor, while Joseph Mitchell Chapple and his three brothers, young midwestern newspaper men, came into the organization. In 1899 Joe Chapple became both editor and publisher; and though Potter kept an interest for several years, Chapple was the *National Magazine* from 1899 until its end in 1933.

Joe Chapple was a remarkable personality — a Chautauqua lecturer, a humorist, a famous after-dinner speaker, a natural "mixer" and promoter, a busy writer of inspirational books and articles. For the first few years after the big change of 1897, the magazine was mostly about Washington, the war, and people, with one short story, several poems, and some wit and humor in each issue. It was a handsome quarto, with good illustration, selling at ten cents. There were contributors like Vance Thompson, Eben E. Rexford, W. J. Lampton, Francis Lynde, Hezekiah Butterworth, and Ellis Parker Butler. After Chapple took complete charge, there was a persistent effort to be national in scope as well as name. The editor's "Affairs at Washington," the lead section, was one of the best of chatty letters from the national capital to appear anywhere; and there were articles about cities in the West,

Midwest, and South. The *National Magazine* specialized in small-city circulation throughout the country, but never reached more than about three hundred thousand. It maintained its character as a handsome illustrated monthly pervaded by the witty, conversational personality of Joe Chapple, with a national outlook and an emphasis on Washington affairs, as long as it lived.[9]

Boston was well supplied with periodicals of the urban weekly type. The veteran *Boston Budget*[10] was going strong through the nineties — a sixteen-page, small-folio Sunday paper selling at five cents and filled with society news, reports of local drama and music, fashions, household hints, and literary miscellany. Lilian Whiting's column of sweetness and light was a feature. The *Budget* absorbed the *Boston Beacon: A Weekly Magazine of Social Progress*, and the *Boston Home Journal*, two old literary and society papers,[11] in 1905, and the old *Saturday Evening Gazette*[12] the next year. Caroline T. Pilsbury's *Boston Ideas* began September 18, 1892, as the usual type of urban weekly, but with only eight pages and selling for three cents. In 1898 it broadened its coverage to the society and amusement news of other leading cities, and used the subtitle "The Nation's Weekly." It then carried correspondence from New York, Washington, San Francisco, and other cities; but it never achieved more than a few thousand circulation. It later became a spiritualist organ and led a strange, itinerant existence.[13]

The *Happy Thought* was a brief semimonthly designed chiefly for clubwomen, which occasionally carried excellent literary and dramatic

[9] The cover title *Joe Mitchell Chapple's National Magazine* was used 1899–1933. Vols. 1–46, Oct. 1894–Sept. 1917, regular semiannual vols. except 32 (April–Oct. 1910), 33 (Nov. 1910–April 1911), 34 (May–Sept. 1911). Vols. 47–61, Oct. 1917–May/June 1933, irregular volumes, mainly annual, with occasional combined numbers. A new series began Dec. 1917, when there was a change in size to larger-quarto; but this was later disregarded. The *Bostonian* began at the price of 15¢ a number, with a cloth-bound edition selling for 25¢. It sold for 10¢ 1896–1907, and then varied between 15¢ and 25¢, usually with changes in size, until its end. It never emphasized fiction, though it sometimes published both short stories and serials. It gave much attention to the development of radio, and in the spring of 1922 it started an organization of "hams" called the National Radio Circle. Chapple was mildly Republican in politics.

[10] See F. L. Mott, *A History of American Magazines* (Cambridge, 1938), v. 3, p. 42.

[11] Cyrus A. Page was editor of the *Beacon* from the paper's founding in 1884 until 1898, when he was succeeded by Huntington Smith. Under Smith, it claimed a circulation of 10,000. For the *Home Journal*, see Mott, *op. cit.*, v. 3, p. 101; Samuel T. Cobb was editor in the early nineties, and William W. Waugh and Atherton Brownell later.

[12] See footnote 51, p. 69.

[13] In 1915 *Boston Ideas* began printing Sunday morning "addresses" by John McCullough, "the distinguished actor who passed through the change called death Nov. 8, 1885," with the assistance of Frank A. Wiggin, of Unity Church (Spiritualist) in Boston. The journal was also interested in theosophy, telepathy, and so on. But in the twenties it became a kind of city "booster" paper, being published irregularly in various cities. The editor apparently traveled about the country, and published an issue in each city in which she sojourned — Miami, St. Petersburg, and Pensacola in Florida; Florence, Alabama; St. Louis, and San Diego. It ended in 1929.

notes.[14] G. L. Richards' *Brown Book of Boston* [15] (1900–1905) was a ten-cent home monthly promoted by prize competitions; it had some good contributors. *Suburban* was begun as a Cambridge monthly in January 1903 by George Marsh. In two or three months it was moved to Boston and made a weekly with local news of various suburbs as its chief feature, and some home and garden material. It later became the widely circulated monthly magazine *Suburban Life*.[16]

The *Granite Monthly* [17] was a New Hampshire magazine devoted to history, biography, and the promotion of state resources, published at Concord. The *Vermonter* [18] was a state monthly founded in August 1895 by Charles Spooner Forbes, in St. Albans, at a dollar a year. It moved to White River Junction at the turn of the century and was there conducted by Charles R. Cummings. It sometimes published literary material outside its scope as a promotional and historical journal. The *Pine Tree Magazine*, of Portland, Maine, began in February 1904 as *Our Home Companion*, but was changed two years later to a good monthly recorder of Maine's history and resources under the new name, edited by Charles Dunn, Jr., and illustrated by excellent pictures from photographs made by F. H. Thompson. It contained some fiction and verse and was an attractive magazine, but it perished in August 1907. The *Connecticut Quarterly* began in 1895 at Hartford under the editorship of W. Farrand Felch, who was followed the next year by George C. Atwell. It carried some fine illustration, and specialized in genealogical notes and news of the historical societies. In 1899, under the editorship of H. Phelps Arms, it became a monthly, changing its name to *Connecticut Magazine*, and attempted to compete in the general magazine field. In its last few years, under Francis Trevelyan Miller, it moved to New Haven and indulged in unusual typography and rich illustration; but it gave up the struggle in 1908.

### NEW YORK

"That New York . . . is now the center of literary activity can

---

[14] It was published Dec. 1, 1894, through March 20, 1897. Beginning as a large-quarto of 8 pages at 75¢ a year, it changed in 1896 to a regular quarto of 16 pages at $1.00.

[15] This was a large-quarto of 20 pages with brown cover. George Bernard was Richards' partner at first. Edwin C. Drew was the first editor, but he was succeeded after a few months by Arthur Winslow Tarbell. There were the regular departments for the home magazine. The *Brown Book* was merged in *Modern Women*.

[16] A trial issue without title was published in Dec. 1902. In Dec. 1904 it became "A Monthly Magazine of Country Life," with the title *Suburban Country Life*, changed Feb. 1905 to *Suburban Life*.

[17] See Mott, *op. cit.*, v. 3, p. 36.

[18] A quarto in the nineties, it became a royal octavo in 1901. It was moved to Montpelier in 1945 and there was conducted by Merle MacAlister.

hardly be gainsaid," wrote Brander Matthews in Philadelphia's *Lippincott's Magazine* in 1886. He continued:

> More than half the solidly established publishing houses are permanently fixed in New York. Nearly all the weekly papers of any weight, and all the foremost monthly magazines, with two or three exceptions only, are issued from New York. . . . There are now more literary men living in and around New York than in or near any other city in America.[19]

Bostonians often spoke of Harvard as a literary asset, and of the superior libraries and museums of their city; [20] but Matthews writes of "the ripening and expansion of Columbia College . . . the increase of libraries . . . the founding of the Authors' Club" in New York. George Parsons Lathrop remarks in *Harper's*, at about the same time, that "New York remains, as it always was, fickle and indifferent, a conglomerate of incongruous masses, caring nothing for the honor of developing a worthy literature." [21] But Richard Watson Gilder sees that very agglomeration of population as an attraction for authors: "The metropolis, as such, will always allure writers, and be a stimulus to them." [22] The *Journalist*, noting that William Dean Howells "has given up his Boston residence and moved to New York," is impatient with the whole debate. "Why not give the city in which three-fourths of the magazines are published credit for being the literary center?" it asks.[23]

New York was certainly the magazine center of the nation, with *Harper's, Century, Scribner's, Forum, North American Review*, and *Cosmopolitan* in the eighties; and then, coming along in the nineties to add to the New York list, *Review of Reviews, McClure's, Munsey's*, and *World's Work*. These were only the leaders among the general monthlies; the great metropolis was just as strong in the general weekly field, and even stronger with its class periodicals — industrial, financial, religious, and professional.

Oldest of the urban weeklies of the metropolis was the *Home Journal*,[24] with its literary tradition, which celebrated its semicentennial with its number for February 26, 1896.

A brilliant weekly of the New York of the nineties was *Truth*, a journal that suffered many changes but was at its best a lively, enterprising, and beautiful periodical. It began in 1881, with Maurice D.

---

[19] *Lippincott's Magazine*, v. 37, p. 106, Jan. 1886. See also *Belford's Magazine*, v. 7, p. 90, June 1891; here the Botta, Stedman, and Fawcett literary salons are discussed.
[20] See T. W. Higginson's assertion in *Brooklyn Magazine*, v. 3, p. 94, Dec. 1885.
[21] *Harper's Magazine*, v. 73, p. 832, Nov. 1886.
[22] *Brooklyn Magazine*, v. 3, p. 96, Dec. 1885.
[23] *Journalist*, Sept. 19, 1891, p. 6.
[24] See Mott, *op. cit.*, v. 2, Sketch 11.

Flynn as manager, but it was suspended at the end of 1884. "Truth at present cannot be found without going to the bottom of a well," remarked Editor Creamer in his *Citizen* on January 3, 1885. It was virtually a new paper which began with the new year of 1886 under the management of Davison Dalziel. A ten-cent quarto of twenty-four pages, *Truth* was subtitled "A Journal of Society, the Clubs, Sports, Drama, and the Fine Arts," and resembled *Town Topics*, its chief competitor, in appearance. At its beginning it experimented with suburban editions,[25] but these were soon abandoned. In fact, the paper grew shabbier, its size was reduced by one-third, and at last *Truth* seemed to be, if not at the bottom of a well, at least crushed to earth. But in 1891 there was another reorganization, and enough money was advanced to make the periodical a rival of *Puck* in brilliance. Like that great weekly, it came into the field of social satire — though it still maintained its chronicle of high society. It enlisted some well-known authors — especially those with reputations for sophisticated writing, like Edgar Saltus, Edgar Fawcett, William Le Queux, Ella Wheeler Wilcox — and some personages in the public eye, like Lord Tennyson and Senators Chauncey M. Depew and John J. Ingalls. There were some full-page portraits, with a few in color lithography. The first colored cover came with the issue for December 12, 1891; but in a few years not only the front and back covers but also the center spread were brilliant with chromolithography. Jay Hambidge, Archie Gunn, W. Granville Smith, and Thure de Thulstrup were leading artists.

Blakely Hall, who was to be associated throughout the nineties with various periodicals which exploited "spicy" content, became editor. Actresses and bathing girls were standard in *Truth* in the early nineties. The number for August 3, 1892, was refused by the American News Company, monopolistic distributor of magazines and whilom censor, because of a double-page pictorial spread that showed an interesting comparison of classical and modern naughtiness — a satyr spying on nymphs disporting themselves in the water, and a nattily dressed young man taking a kodak snapshot of bathing girls. By the mid-nineties *Truth's* circulation was doing better, at fifty thousand or more. Under a succession of editors and with various changes in ownership,[26] it carried on with color illustration, news and comment, and,

---

[25] Called the *Sunday Bugle* in Brooklyn, the *Sunday Transcript* in Jersey City, and the *Sunday Citizen* in Westchester.

[26] Blakely Hall was out by 1895, to be followed by Tom Hall as editor, 1896–98; E. H. Sylvester, 1898–1901; R. Bennett, 1901–02; Fannie Humphreys Gaffney, 1902–03; Charles Edward Barns, 1903; George William Hanna, 1904–05. The American Lithograph Company got a controlling interest in 1895, according to James L. Ford (*Forty-Odd Years in the Literary Shop*, New York, 1921, p. 300). George M. S. Horton, a newspaperman, was president in that year. Doubtless Mrs. Gaffney and Hanna owned it in its last years.

in 1897, a new sports department and both long and short fiction. At the end of that year the price per copy was dropped to five cents.

*Truth* gave its readers color pictures of battles during the war with Spain, including folding inserts of Manila Bay and other important fights, said to have been drawn by its artists from telegraphic reports. Then at the beginning of 1899, it was made a monthly [27] at twenty-five cents, with a big quarto page and folded chromolithographs for framing, full-page color portraits of actresses, and so on. It now was turning toward the woman's magazine field, with much of fashions, clubs, household helps, and the like. In this phase it was decidedly literary and artistic, with a serial by Henry James, a good book department, and articles on painters illustrated in color. In 1902 it was reduced to ten cents a copy, and had the subtitle "The Woman's Forum"; it was still bright with color, and its contents were varied. But it did not prosper, and after a suspension it had only one more short episode — this one as a five-cent monthly largely given over to reprints from English sources.

But the best-known urban weekly in America was New York's *Town Topics*, whose career, with certain unsavory incidents, is recounted in a separate chapter (Sketch 36) in this volume. The best of the New York gossip-sheets emphasizing politics was the brief *Citizen* (1884–1885), which was conducted by Thomas J. Creamer, leader of the Young Democracy in the state. As a state senator, he had opposed Tweed; he was a Cleveland man, and he thought Tilden "a political impostor, with a record as dirty as any man can have outside prison walls." [28] The pages of the *Citizen* were full of lively and intelligent gossip about politics, the theater, journalism, literature, and personalities. George F. Parker's *Saturday Globe* (1888–1891) was also a distinguished journal of opinion, though short-lived. Another brief attempt was the *New York Saturday Review* (1889–1891), devoted to "science, art, literature, society, politics, music, and drama," and edited by Elita Proctor Otis, a well-known society woman and excellent amateur actress. *Vanity* (1895–1896) was published by Eugene and Thomas Kelly, sons of a wealthy banker, with Nugent Robinson as editor. It was a clean and respectable society journal, with notes about amusements and the arts, and some satirical pieces. [29] Begun in the same year was *Form* (1895–1899), a monthly society magazine edited and published by Dempsey and Carroll. It purported to be "The

[27] In the fall of 1897 it had begun the custom of making one issue each month a "magazine" number, with 64 pages of a smaller size.
[28] *Citizen*, v. 1, p. 55, Jan. 10, 1885.
[29] See Ford, *Forty-Odd Years in the Literary Shop*, p. 305; *Bookman*, v. 1, p. 82, March, 1895.

Glass of Fashion and the Mould of Form," and was a handsomely illustrated quarto at a dollar a year; but the glass was not highly polished, and the magazine was deficient in wit and cleverness.

The *New-Yorker*, on the other hand, was smart and attractive. It began March 6, 1901, under the editorship of Harry Wilson Walker, a newspaperman with wide acquaintance in the Midwest, New York, and London, and a fresh and lively style. "It is a rare thing," wrote the editor of the *Journalist*, "that a man can write so varied a budget of gossip every week and make it all bright, spicy, and interesting, but the *New-Yorker* seems to get better each week."[30] This was a five-cent weekly, but it seems never to have exceeded twenty thousand circulation. R. W. Criswell became editor and publisher in 1904, and the paper perished two years later. The *Man of the World* was an 1899 weekly of club news, society, sports, finance, theaters, music, and literature, published by an English journalist trying his luck in New York. The journalist was Adolphus Rosenberg, and his luck was not very good. Perhaps his paper was distinguished chiefly by some sensational attacks on insurance companies. How many, many society weeklies there were in New York in the nineties! Mrs. Roger A. Pryor, a society leader, wrote in the *Cosmopolitan* in 1891 that a score or more were being published at the time: "their existence is by permission, because they are too insignificant to be worth crushing."[31] The above statistic probably includes suburban papers. In the mid-nineties William J. and Harvey M. Bloomer published *Harlem Life* and seven other society papers in suburbs of New York, all of the same size and style.

Different from all the others, and different from all other American magazines except perhaps the *Chap-Book* of Chicago, was *M'lle New York*,[32] a fortnightly begun August 1895 by Vance Thompson. It was small-quarto in size, distinguished by the drawings of T. E. Powers and Thomas Fleming, and well printed. Its imitative French posturing, its championship of Negro art, and its doctrine of "autolotry" in the arts were characteristic. Most important of its contents were the critical essays of James Gibbons Huneker on esthetics, music, American prejudices, and contemporary ideas in general. Huneker was an associate editor during most of the little magazine's brief life: it published only eleven numbers in its first series, ending with its first number for January 1896, and then a new series of four numbers, November 1898–January 1899.

[30] *Journalist*, v. 29, 452, April 27, 1901; and p. 513, June 22, 1901.
[31] *Cosmopolitan*, v. 11, p. 575, Sept. 1891.
[32] See F. C. Hanighan, "Vance Thompson and *M'lle New York*," *Bookman*, v. 75, p. 472, Sept. 1932.

*Brooklyn Life* [33] began March 8, 1890, as an imitation of the great New York weekly of that name; but it eventually became less literary and satirical and more an urban weekly of society, the theater, sports, art, and music. Frederick Mitchell Munroe and John Angus McKay were the original conductors, and the former remained with the journal for twenty years. It lasted until 1931.

In Syracuse, New York, Percy McCarthy Emory's *Remarques* [34] (1895–1899), which aspired to be "The Home Journal of Central New York," was in the main a local city periodical, well printed and illustrated.

### PHILADELPHIA AND PITTSBURGH

A spokesman for "Literary Life in Philadelphia" in the *American Magazine* for July 1887 names as the most illustrious writers of that metropolis at that time Walt Whitman, who was actually living at Camden; George H. Boker, dramatist and poet; Charles Godfrey Leland, humorist and essayist; John Bach McMaster, the historian; S. Weir Mitchell, poet and novelist; and the Davises — L. Clark and Rebecca H. and their son Richard Harding. It was not a very impressive showing. Of general magazines, *Lippincott's* was the only one of high grade that Philadelphia could boast in the eighties, and it was on the decline. Of course there were also *Godey's*, *Peterson's*, and *Arthur's*, Philadelphia's trio of once famous women's magazines; but all of them were to move to New York in the nineties, hoping for prosperity in the business of the larger city but not finding it. There were also the weekly miscellanies *Saturday Night* and *Saturday Evening Post* and the juvenile *Golden Days*, all making large claims and unwilling to face their evident failure. It was the Curtis Publishing Company that made Philadelphia important in the magazine world during the present period, with the smashing success of the *Ladies' Home Journal* and later the revival of the *Saturday Evening Post*. Besides, Philadelphia was a notable publishing center for class and professional journals, especially Sunday School periodicals.

Doubtless J. M. Munyon hoped to produce something more than a local magazine when he began *Munyon's Illustrated World* in 1884 as a handsome quarto. Three years later the title was changed to *Mun-*

[33] In 1902 Sherman Adams came in as associate editor and Frederick H. Timpson as business manager; McKay had dropped out. Adams did not remain long, but Munroe and Timpson ran the paper 1904–10. Munroe was replaced by G. Herbert Henshaw in 1910, and he and Timpson conducted it until its end.

[34] *Remarques* was a semimonthly selling at 5¢ a copy or $1.00 a year. In addition to society news and notes on the theater, sports, etc., this journal carried style and fashion articles, humor, and some news and comment. In 1898 the page was enlarged by new managers, Frederic R. and Mark A. Luescher, respectively business and editorial directors.

*yon's Magazine,* and it became a family monthly with a circulation of a hundred thousand at a dollar and a half a year in the early nineties; but it ended in 1894. The *Fortieth Street Station Leisure Hours* (1885–1902) was a ten-cent monthly published by Charles A. Dixon for West Philadelphia.[35] Beginning with eight quarto pages of short miscellany for commuters, it eventually published thirty-two pages of the home magazine type, with fiction and household departments. *Society* (1888–1897) was founded as a ten-cent monthly by Conrad Engel, Jr. as publisher and John Irving Dillon as editor, but was sold in 1892 to A. M. Miller, who made it a weekly; with various changes it survived five years longer. Another society monthly, with a strong infusion of Republican politics, was E. R. Clark's *Chin* (1890–1892), a five-cent monthly. More ambitious, but about as short-lived, was Frank A. Bisbee's ten-cent *To-Day* (1894–1897).

Two urban weeklies of long standing in Philadelphia were the *Sunday Mercury* (1851–1897) and the *Saturday Review* (1867–1899). The *Busy Bee* was founded by C. Joseph Dacey in 1890. It emphasized humor in its earliest phase, but it soon came to feature local events and literary miscellany; it became simply *Bee* in 1897, and lasted until 1919. Of weekly story papers, Philadelphia always had more than its share.

Pittsburgh had two urban weeklies of some importance in this period, as well as its quota of mail-order journals. The *Bulletin* had begun in 1876 as a week-end paper dealing with society news and the arts and amusements. Under John W. Black as publisher and G. F. Muller as editor, it was a good twenty-four-page quarto in the nineties.[36] The *Index* was begun September 1, 1895, as a quarto of sixteen pages and cover, at a dollar a year. It chronicled society, literature, and current events, and was well edited by Robert Galloway Paull. Its price was increased to a dollar and a half in 1900, and its scope was enlarged in various directions. In the next twenty years it had many editors,[37] dabbled much in politics, and carried on until it was merged with the *Bulletin* in 1931.

A year before its demise the *Index* absorbed the short-lived but handsome and interesting *Library*, a five-cent weekly published for seven months beginning in March 1900 by Charles S. Clarke, the file of which is now chiefly important as the repository of some stories by

[35] Dixon died in Feb. 1902, and *Leisure Hours* was sold to H. Logan Golsan. Under the title *Leisure Hours and the Inner Set* it was published through Oct. 1902.
[36] Black died in 1899, and his executors continued as publishers. Called *Bulletin-Index* after 1931, it lasted until 1948.
[37] *Index* editors after 1900 included William Templeton Mossman, Townsend DeWolf, Frank E. Gannett, P. W. Shephard, John R. Wright, Thomas C. McCune, H. D. Hart, George R. Pearson, and Catherine M. Patterson.

Willa Sibert Cather. Miss Cather's chief magazine connection during her life in Pittsburgh, however, was that with the *Home Monthly*. This was a rather well printed five-cent periodical in quarto size, which had begun as *Ladies' Journal* in 1894 and had been taken over and improved by T. E. Orr two years later. Miss Cather was a staff member, and wrote both fiction and prose for the magazine through 1896–1898. There was much of Pittsburgh in the *Home Monthly*, but it was moved out of the city to nearby Burgettstown six months before its end in the fall of 1900.

### WASHINGTON AND BALTIMORE

The Federal capital has never aspired to be the literary capital of the United States. In the nineties it was the publication point for the organs of a number of national associations and movements, for a few mail-order journals, and for many weeklies of varying types.

Washington was notable for its weeklies. In 1885 more than a score of them, chiefly devoted to news and comment, with some literary miscellany, were in course of publication. A paper of long standing even then was the *Sunday Capital* (1871–1890), in which society and literature competed with politics. The *Republic* [38] (1877–1899) was a "Sunday Journal of Literature and Events," with Republican leanings. Many others were published from Washington in the late eighties that had more politics and less literature than the two just mentioned. The *Washington Hatchet* (1883–1906) began with an emphasis on politics (Republican) and later turned to sports and the theater.

The chief Washington society journal at the turn of the century was the *Washington Mirror*, which began December 4, 1899, as a five-cent weekly in small-quarto form "Devoted to Amusements, Society, Sports, Fun, and Capitol News." It gave special attention to the theaters, printed an occasional short story and some verse, and used a colored cartoon on the cover. The front department, signed "The Gossip," carried many strong political editorials: it was anti-Negro, liked to poke fun at Minister Wu, and was generally free and independent in its criticism. James H. Frazier was editor and Martin Kastle chief owner. The management tried to meet deficits by raising the price to ten cents in 1905, but later in the year sold out to the New York *Club-Fellow*.[39]

[38] T. Edward Clark was editor and Rufus H. Darby publisher during most of the nineties; but in the last two years the Reverend J. B. North (with John W. Echols as publisher) made an A.P.A. organ of it.

[39] The *Club-Fellow and Washington Mirror: The National Journal of Society* was a gossipy 10¢ quarto published in New York 1905–30. The *Club-Fellow* had been founded in New York in 1900 by Percival L. Harden. He died in 1930, having sold the paper the year before. It was a monthly in 1930, but was merged with the *Tatler and American Sketch* in October of that year.

*Washington Life* began October 10, 1903; two years later it followed the usual pattern of Washington periodicals and solicited national circulation, adopting the title *American Spectator.* After September 22, 1906, it was merged with *Ridgway's,* of New York.

Several periodicals were published from time to time in Washington with the purpose of summarizing the work of governmental departments, such as the *United States Gazette* (1873–1897), a monthly in folio form conducted by J. H. Soule; and the *Reporter* (1881–1891), a monthly by A. A. Thomas.

Baltimore had a number of professional and learned journals, as well as several weeklies devoted to society, amusements, and the arts. Of the urban weeklies, the *Telegram* [40] (1862–1915), published by James Young in the nineties, was the oldest. Its chief rivals for many years were the *Baltimorean* (1872–1898), by Crutchfield & Haas, and T. J. Wentworth's *Every Saturday* [41] (1877–1910). These were eight-page folios in the eighties, and two-dollar quartos in the nineties. E. S. Judge's *Free Press* (1893–1900) and William H. Richardson's *Argus* (1887–1905) were of the same type, but sold for a dollar a year. But the best of the lot was *Baltimore Life* (1890–1901), a sprightly illustrated periodical of society, sports, and the stage, edited by George S. Steuart. Outcault, Gibson, and other well-known artists drew pictures for it. Like its namesake in New York, it featured polite humor and satire. Its emphasis on sports made it the organ of the Century Cycling Club, and brought it a baseball column by George V. Hobart, then known chiefly for his sparkling sports writing in the newspapers. Hobart became editor in 1898, and the next year he changed the title from *Life* to *Time.* It probably was too good (and expensive) for the urban weekly class, which commonly had to get along with less than ten thousand circulation.

Two local Baltimore monthlies should be mentioned — the *No Name Magazine* (1889–1892), edited by Eugene Lemoine Didier, which was notable chiefly for emphasis on Poe material; and the *Baltimore Herald* (1873–1911), Tom Wash. Smith's prolonged family paper, which, in its latter years, sold for twelve cents a year.

### THE NEW SOUTH

How sweetly the old moon shines upon our magnolias! Sometimes, poor Harlequin that I am, I almost think it is Fairyland. Sometimes I would kiss the earth,

---

[40] Edited by William I. Cook in the early nineties, and then by Miss Irene Cook and Mrs. James Young. It began as the *Sunday Telegram,* 1862–77, and ended as the *Democratic Telegram,* 1907–14.

[41] Title was changed to *Every Saturday Review* in 1895, and to *Saturday Review* in 1900. It was reduced to $1.00 a year in 1900.

it is so sweet. It is my home. I love it; I love its stinks, its blemishes. . . . These things are as the mole upon my mother's breast.[42]

Thus, in the spirit of pure patriotism, rhapsodized J. M. Leveque, editor of a little New Orleans magazine called the *Harlequin.* Throughout the South, from Maryland to Texas, there was more of this sentimental devotion to region than in any other part of the United States.

But the movement for a new southern economy, the doctrine for which was crystallized in Henry W. Grady's famous address entitled "The New South," delivered in New York December 22, 1889, gained great impetus in the early nineties. Shortly before Grady's oration was delivered, *Belford's Magazine,* of Chicago, commented on the country-wide interest in the matter: "The New South! The phrase is enormously popular. It is a prime favorite with newspapers, magazines, and politicians." [43] It was a leading topic, also, in the industrial press. The *Manufacturer's Record* devoted much attention to it, especially in 1890, and several southern industrial periodicals were published.[44]

In literature — or at least in the field of fiction — the South came into its own in the latter eighties and the nineties. "It has been reserved for a score or more of recent writers . . . to firmly establish a worthy and characteristic Southern literature," observed a contributor to *Harper's* in 1887. He named George W. Cable, Grace King, Richard Malcolm Johnston, Joel Chandler Harris, Thomas Nelson Page, Amélie Rives, Julia Magruder, and others.[45] More were to come later, until there was virtually a "craze" for southern dialect stories. Wrote a critic in the *New England Magazine* in 1894: "The presses teem today with books from Southern pens, and the great magazines announce every few months some newly discovered Southern writer." [46]

But the South was still inhospitable to its own magazines. William M. Baskervill, writing on "Southern Literature" in *PMLA,* in 1892, quoted a conversation overheard on the streets of Nashville. " 'Who is that man?' — 'Oh, he is nobody but the editor of a magazine.' " [47] A writer in an early number of *Fetter's Southern Magazine* remarked that "For years the reproach has been cast into the face of the South that she cannot have a standard literary periodical," and then he begged for support of *Fetter's,* whose managers were "expending a

---

[42] *Harlequin,* v. 1, p. 4, June 28, 1899.
[43] *Belford's Magazine,* v. 3, p. 365, Aug. 1889.
[44] See Chap. X. New York had a periodical called *The South,* 1871–89, and another of the same name 1903–09, both exploiting southern resources.
[45] Charles W. Coleman, Jr., in *Harper's Magazine,* v. 74, pp. 837–55, May 1887. See also Albion W. Tourgée's article in the *Forum,* v. 6, pp. 404–13, Dec. 1888.
[46] S. A. Link in *New England Magazine,* n.s., v. 10, p. 14, March 1894. See also *Critic,* v. 10, pp. 322–24, June 25, 1887.
[47] *Publications of the Modern Language Association,* v. 7, no. 2, p. 90, 1892.

fortune in an effort to give the South a creditable publication." But two years later *Fetter's* renounced its allegiance to the South, declaring that "the literature of any country is a national literature." [48]

There were, however, several attempts at regional magazines in the South, and many literary weeklies, chiefly local. Henry Clayton Hopkins edited the literary monthly *Dixie* in Baltimore 1899–1900. It was notable for a good art department, with fine portfolios of reproductions of paintings. Edward A. Uffington Valentine was book editor. It absorbed the *Southern Magazine,* which was published during the last seven months of 1899 at the village of Manassas, Virginia. For an even shorter period (May–July 1895), the honored name of *Southern Literary Messenger* was revived in Washington by Mrs. A. Truehart Buck. In Richmond, Daniel Murphy's *Every Saturday Journal* (1879–1905) was a good family weekly, and the monthly *Woman,* "edited by Mrs. General 'Stonewall' Jackson," lasted for a little over two years, 1894–1897.

In Atlanta John H. Seals's *Sunny South* had been a popular home weekly since 1875. In 1903 it became a weekly edition of the *Constitution,* but it was discontinued four years later. *Dixie* (1885–1908) was begun by Charles H. Wells as a monthly devoted to the exploitation of Southern industrial resources, but contained some miscellany; it was *Dixie Wood-Worker* in its last years. Good in illustration and typography, it was a promoter and historian of the Cotton States Exposition in Atlanta in 1895. The Atlanta *Illustrator* was a beautifully produced monthly of fiction, verse, history, essays, and so on, finely illustrated — and too ambitious to last more than a few months in 1896.

The *Florida Magazine* was a ten-cent miscellany of mediocre quality, issued at Jacksonville. In the midst of a forty-thousand dollar guessing contest on the outcome of certain elections, it merged with an Atlanta magazine, and they died in each other's arms.[49] The *Tatler of Society in Florida* (1892–1908) was Anna M. Marcotte's weekly of society, amusements, and miscellany; it was an octavo of twenty-four pages and sold at the low price of a dollar a year.

New Orleans was the center for much trade publishing. *The South Illustrated* (1886–1889) was a monthly largely about agricultural and industrial opportunities, and there were various specialized periodicals.

---

[48] *Fetter's Southern Magazine,* v. 3, p. 542, Dec. 1893; *Mid-Continent Magazine,* v. 1, p. 92, May 1895.
[49] The merger was with the *Alkahest* in Oct. 1903, and that *bibelot* ended a month or two later. The contest may have killed both. The *Florida Magazine* began as *Sunny Lands* at St. Augustine, Jan. 1900; but only one number was issued there, and it changed name when it was issued at Jacksonville, beginning Nov. 1900. F. A. Mann was the original projector, but G. D. Ackerly was sole publisher from Dec. 1900.

More literary were two ten-cent monthlies conducted by women —
*Current Topics for Leisure Hours* (1890–1895), by Mrs. P. W. Mount
(Ruth Ramay) ; and *Men and Matters* (1894–1904), by Marie Evans.
The latter was reduced to cheap reprint in its final years. Among the
weeklies were two hard-hitting satirical and political periodicals which
offered some literary miscellany and were illustrated by cartoons on
political and social matters. They were the *Mascot* (1882–1895) and
the shorter-lived *Lantern* (1886–1889). The *Advance* (1889–1903) was
a cheap Sunday paper for the family. *Harlequin* (1899–1909) was J.
M. Leveque's five-cent journal of politics, the theater, literary criticism, and so on. It was a distinguished periodical because its editor
was a brilliant writer on occasion, and very bold and outspoken. *Harlequin* was Democratic and hated McKinley, but he fought local graft
in government. The *Elite* (1899–1902) was a much milder journal of
society, music, and the drama. Political, professional, and religious
periodicals flourished in New Orleans in great variety.[50]

*Fetter's Southern Magazine* [51] was founded in Louisville, Kentucky,
by the poet George Griffith Fetter in August 1892. Partner in publishing the magazine was Charles Ernest Shober, a short-story writer ; but
he retired after less than a year in favor of Sam Stone Bush, who put
enough money into the venture to make it an attractive magazine for a
year or two. General Basil W. Duke, who had been editor of the *Southern Bivouac* at Louisville, was the new editor, and Opie Read, James
Lane Allen, F. Hopkinson Smith, Frank L. Stanton, Maurice Thompson, John Fox, Jr., and Grace Macgowan Cooke were leading contributors. "We shall aim to represent the new and catholic South," the
editor promised. But the magazine went into bankruptcy December
1894, and was sold to F. C. Nunemacher, who renamed it the *Mid-Continent Magazine* in May 1895. It now promised to be less sectional and
less "bitter and unkind," but it ended with the number for August
1895. Louisville was a periodical publishing center of some importance
and many class magazines were issued from its presses. *Cockrill's
Magazine* (1901–1907) was a ten-cent publication devoted to religion
and literature; its editor and publisher was H. B. Cockrill. *North and
South* was begun in 1903 to exploit the resources of the region served
by the Louisville and Nashville Railroad; it was called *Southland*
after 1929. In nearby Lexington, Mrs. Eugenia Dunlap Potts edited the

[50] See Max L. Griffin, "Bibliography of New Orleans Magazines," *Louisiana Historical
Quarterly*, v. 18, pp. 491–548, July 1935.
[51] Fetter's name was dropped and the title became the *Southern Magazine*, Aug. 1893. It
was suspended Nov.–Dec. 1894, April 1895. V. 1, Aug. 1892–Jan. 1893; 2, Feb.–July 1893;
3, Aug. 1893–Jan. 1894; 4, Feb.–July 1894; 5, Aug. 1894–March 1895; 6, May–Aug. 1895.
Merged with *Scribner's Magazine*.

*Illustrated Kentuckian* (1892–1894), a literary monthly of sixteen pages selling for a dollar a year.

During the period now under review, 1885–1905, Texans founded at least a score of literary, historical, household, and general magazines.[52] Dallas was the most prolific of the state's publishing centers. There the literary miscellany called the *Round Table* (1889–1893) had its all-too-brief life.[53] Olive B. Lee's *The Period* (1893–1906) was called *Lee's Texas Magazine* after its first half-dozen years, and *Lee's Magazine* after it moved to Boston in 1901. It was largely eclectic, clipping from southern newspapers and periodicals somewhat in the *Literary Digest* fashion.[54] The *Texas Monthly Magazine* (1896–1898) was published for a year in Austin by Robert E. McCleary, and during the remainder of its short life by William D. Scarff in Dallas. It was written by Texans, including the locally famous poet, John P. Sjolander. *Dixieland* (1904–1906) was a Dallas monthly "dedicated to those who died for Dixie." It was edited by Mrs. May Guillot Potter and called itself "The Illustrated Home Magazine of the South."

Two rough-riding Texan reform journals of the time were *Brann's Iconoclast*,[55] of Waco, and *Reed's Isonomy*,[56] of San Antonio. A society miscellany of long life was R. C. Johnson's *Opera Glass* (1879–1916) of Galveston.

### THE MIDDLE WEST

James Baldwin, writing in *Scribner's Magazine* in the late eighties about the east-central states, asserted: "In respect not only of position, but of wealth, of natural fertility, of political influence, of intellectual strength, of literary promise, it [the area of the old Northwest Territory] may well be regarded as the Centre of the Republic." [57] The growth of midwestern cities had done much to shift that center westward, but it was realized in the nineties that politics had also moved westward. Wrote Sherwin Cody in *Self Culture*:

> In the elections of 1892 we suddenly discovered that the West had the balance of power in politics. . . . The War with Spain has been the power that finally awakened the West. That war was largely promoted and managed by the West.

---

[52] See Imogene Bentley, "Texas Literary and Educational Magazines" (doctoral dissertation, George Peabody College for Teachers, 1941).

[53] Mrs. Sydney Smith was editor 1889–92; Charles D. O. Malloy, 1892–93. It began at $1.00 a year, but doubled its price after its first year.

[54] It succeeded the Texas edition of *Current Topics* (see p. 53), filling out unexpired subscriptions. About half its pages were filled with excerpts from editorials of newspapers (chiefly southern), and the other half with fiction, verse, and criticism. It sold for 10¢ a copy, and averaged less than 20 pages an issue.

[55] See Sketch 7 in this volume.

[56] Subtitled "A Journal of Justice"; issued from 1883 to 1905(?).

[57] *Scribner's Magazine*, v. 3, pp. 408ff, 589ff, May, June 1888. Quotation is from p. 600.

. . . The people of the East are against expansion, but the feeling in the West is precisely the reverse.[58]

Moreover, such other factors as the increased political importance of the Midwest's farmers, the spectacular appeal of the Columbian Exposition at Chicago, and the developments in manufactures, trade, and transportation in "the Great Valley" did much to bring the region between the Ohio River and the Rocky Mountains to the country's attention.

In Ohio, Cleveland and Cincinnati were the leading magazine centers, though Springfield was notable as the home of the Crowell Publishing Company, which issued the nationally distributed *Woman's Home Companion* and *Farm and Fireside*, which had larger circulations than any other periodicals published in the state. The *Chautauquan* had moved out to Ohio, first to Cleveland and then to Springfield.[59] Big mail-order journals were published in Cleveland and Cincinnati; and both these cities, with Dayton, were centers for religious publishing. Notable society journals were Cleveland's weekly *Town Topics* (1887–1916), edited successively by Felix Rosenberg and Norman C. McCloud, and emphasizing both society news and literary content; and *Mrs. Devereux's Tips* (1893–1909), of Cincinnati, which was a society-and-humor paper by Mrs. C. A. R. Devereux. The *New Bohemian* (1895–1896), by Walter S. Hurt, was a ten-cent monthly of good appearance, but local and amateur. The *Roller Monthly*, of Canton, began in 1885 as a weekly newspaper for workingmen called the *Roller*, and changed to monthly publication in 1898. It was a cheap miscellany published by T. B. C. Vosges, and ended in 1917 after many variations in price, format, and editorship.

In the summer of 1901 the *Book-Lover* quoted an editorial from the *Boston Globe* to the effect that the city which was once so jealous of its claims as a literary center was willing to pass that honor westward to Indianapolis.[60] Indiana was indeed making a serious bid for such a position. It was the home of the author of the immensely popular *Ben-Hur* and of the new best seller, *When Knighthood Was in Flower*. James Whitcomb Riley, "the Hoosier Poet," was writing the most popular verse being offered to readers. *The Gentleman from Indiana* had made Tarkington's initial hit. And there were many other active literary Hoosiers.

The *Indianian* (1897–1900) was an illustrated monthly magazine

[58] *Self Culture*, v. 8, p. 585, Jan. 1899.
[59] See Sketch 33 in this volume for the *Companion*. For *Farm and Fireside*, see Mott, *op. cit.*, v. 3, p. 156; for the *Chautauquan*, see *ibid.*, Sketch 34.
[60] *Book-Lover*, v. 2, p. 366, Summer 1901.

of history and literary miscellany published in Indianapolis — a thin small-quarto at a dollar a year, raised to a dollar and a half shortly before its early death. E. E. Stafford's *Illustrated Indiana Weekly* (1895–1902), which began as *Indiana Woman* and ended as *Mid-Continent*, printed political comment as well as matter on fashions, the theater, and sports. It opposed the Tom Taggart machine with vigor. A state magazine was established for Michigan by John F. Hogan in 1903 in Detroit. It was called the *Gateway*; and though it was promotional in type at first, it eventually became largely a journal of opinion.[61] *Yenowine's Illustrated News* (1885–1897) was a week-end paper of some note in Milwaukee. It was devoted to society, humor, and miscellany; and its editor and publisher was George H. Yenowine.

An interesting Minneapolis journal of the urban weekly class was the *Courant* (1899–1902), edited by P. J. Smalley, which became so much interested in women's club work that it was virtually the federation organ for that region. In 1900 it moved to St. Paul and called itself a "Journal for the Women of the Northwest," but it soon folded. An earlier society weekly in St. Paul was the *Eye* (1889–1890). Issued from St. Paul was the great promotional magazine of the Northwest, which exploited the beauties and resources and opportunities of the region all the way to the coast. It was called *The Northwest: An Illustrated Journal of Literature, Agriculture, and Western Progress* (1883–1903), and was edited and published by E. V. Smalley.[62] It was an attractive and interesting periodical of its class. The *Literary Northwest* (1892–1893) was a handsome, varied, dignified literary monthly published by the D. D. Merrill Company, a book house, and edited by Mrs. Mary Harriman Severance and H. T. Carpenter. The *South Dakotan* (1898–1904) was a monthly begun at Mitchell and moved to Sioux Falls in 1901; Doane Robinson was editor.

Iowa's literary magazine in the nineties was the *Midland Monthly*, edited and published in Des Moines by Johnson Brigham, a newspaperman with strong literary inclinations. The first number of the *Midland*, for January 1894, contained contributions of Hamlin Garland and Octave Thanet, Iowans most prominent in current literary production. Emerson Hough, Edwin L. Sabin, Ellis Parker Butler, Frank W. Calkins, and S. H. M. Byers were later *Midland* contributors. There were occasional articles, well illustrated, about travel

[61] Joseph Greusel was editor for the first six months or more. Hogan broadened it, eventually using the subtitle, "A Magazine Devoted to Literature, Economics, Social Service." It was strongly antilabor, anti-English, anti-Bolshevik, and so on, and too much inclined to hysteria in capitals.

[62] It was a 10¢ magazine of 32 large-quarto pages until May 1903, when Victor H. Smalley became editor and reduced the size of the pages. In its last 10 years it was titled *Northwest Magazine*.

abroad, while the war with Spain and the Yukon gold rush supplied material for many pages; but the *Midland Monthly* was definitely a state magazine, and its circulation never exceeded thirteen thousand.[63] It had a fine mood and quality, derived chiefly from its editor, who was a sound but gentle critic and whose reviews and editorials were of the magazine's essence. When Brigham was appointed state librarian in 1898, he had to give up the *Midland*; and he turned it over to his printers, who sold it the following January to John L. Settle and H. M. Whitener, of Fredericktown, Missouri. They moved it at once to St. Louis, where it survived only through June 1899.

The *Omahan* (1900–1903) was a ten-cent monthly of promotion and belles-lettres conducted by C. C. Tennant Clary. The leading Omaha weekly of society, politics, and amusements was the *Examiner* (1900–1924), edited by Alfred Sorenson. The *Omaha Bee*, a daily paper which had issued a weekly edition since 1873, took over in June 1900 a paper called *Omaha Illustrated*, which had been published for one year, and called it the *Illustrated Bee* through 1904.

The only important Kansas venture of the period in the field of general priodicals was *Agora: A Kansas Magazine* (1891–1896), which was begun in Salina by C. B. Kirtland, was moved to Topeka at the end of its first year and edited by T. E. Dewey, and in 1895 was taken to Lawrence by Dewey and made a monthly. It contained some of William Allen White's early political writing, a series on Coronado's march by Eugene F. Ware, and many symposiums on political questions. After it moved to Lawrence, there were several articles on Kansas history. The *Mid-Continental Review* (1890–1891), by John Hay, of Junction City, Kansas, was amateurish, though it had much variety.

Kansas City had three or four urban weeklies,[64] most important of which was the *Independent* [65] (1899–current), founded by George Creel and Arthur Grissom. These young men, Missourians at the be-

---

[63] It took over the small list of the *Literary Northwest* (*supra*) when it began. In 1896 it absorbed *Tainter's Magazine*, which had been published briefly in Galena, Ill., and Lancaster, Wis.; and also the *New Bohemian* (*supra*), of Cincinnati. Just before Johnson retired from the management of the *Midland*, he took over a monthly called *Illustrated Iowa*, which J. E. Clarey had founded in Des Moines in 1890 as the *Saturday Review*, and which he had made an illustrated monthly with the altered title in 1897. For the *Midland Monthly*, see Luella M. Wright's articles about it in *Iowa Journal of History and Politics*, v. 45, pp. 2–61, Jan. 1947; and *Palimpsest*, v. 33, pp. 225–56, Aug. 1952.

[64] Including *Progress* (1888–94), which became *Progress and Western Farm Journal* in 1893; and *Life* (1894–1908).

[65] See George Creel, *Rebel at Large* (New York, 1947), pp. 42–76. For three months in 1908 Creel called his periodical the *Newsbook*. This was part of a grandiose scheme fathered by Charles Ferguson for a National Fellowship of the University Militant, one of the activities of which was to publish weeklies in the chief cities of the country. Creel's brief *Newsbook* was the only periodical actually issued in connection with the Fellowship plan.

ginning of notable careers, had sought their fortunes in New York and one day met and agreed they both wanted to go back to Kansas City and start a periodical. Grissom made a runaway match with the daughter of a Kansas City banker and thus was able to finance the *Independent*, which he invited Creel to help him conduct. But the banker was already trying to rid himself of an unwelcome son-in-law; and soon Creel was left with the paper, while Grissom recovered forty thousand dollars from the banker for alienation of his wife's affections and returned to New York to help start the *Smart Set*. The *Independent* was an example of the better society-politics-amusement weeklies. It was notable during a year or two for its humor, verse, and book reviews; among contributors were Ella Wheeler Wilcox, R. K. Munkittrick, Charles Battell Loomis, Albert Bigelow Paine, and Winifred Black. But the most striking thing about the Creel editorship was a continuing attack on the Pendergast political machine and its outrageous election activities. Other enterprises beckoned Creel, however, and in January 1909 he gave the paper to Clara Kellogg and Katherine Baxter, who owned a printing business. It has since continued, mainly as a society and club organ.

The *Lotus* (1895–1897) began as a bimonthly edited jointly by undergraduates of Kansas colleges and issued in a Roycroft-type format. In May 1896 it left the collegians, became a monthly, and greatly improved its contents; [66] but it never had much chance of success.

### CHICAGO AS A MAGAZINE CENTER

The tremendous growth of Chicago as a manufacturing, wholesaling, and transportation center was one of the great American phenomena in the years around 1890. Its population had doubled in the eighties, bringing it to second place in the nation, and twice the size of any rival except first-place New York and third-place Philadelphia. "The country tributary to Chicago is increasing more rapidly in wealth and population than any other part of the nation," noted, in 1892, the *New England Magazine*,[67] whose native Boston had dropped to tenth place among the cities. The railroads fought for terminal facilities in the great midwestern capital, thus contesting for the chance to make Chicago richer. The *Economist*, of New York, complained in 1888: "Chicago has never contributed a dollar for the construction of rail-

---

[66] Collegiate editor was F. Hilliard Johnson. Clarence T. Southwick edited three numbers in the summer of 1896, and then the widely known magazinist Walter Blackburn Harte edited it for a year. Frank A. Gailey then edited it from Aug. 1897 to the end in Nov. 1897.

[67] Franklin H. Head in *New England Magazine*, n.s., v. 6, p. 567, July 1892.

roads, but of late years the roads themselves have been contributing immense sums to that city for rights of entrance." [68] And then in 1893 the eyes of the world were turned upon Chicago. The Columbian Exposition, one of the greatest of world's fairs, brought millions of visitors to the city; total admissions were 27,539,521.

The exposition was a great stimulus to art and literature in Chicago itself, but there were other cultural forces active in this aggressive city. A shrewd critic wrote many years later, "The strongest influence of the whole American movement [of the nineties] was started when young Herbert Stone came back to Chicago from Harvard with his head full of all that was going on in England." [69] What Stone and his partner Ingalls Kimball did was to start the *Chap-Book* and a general publishing business. When the *Chap-Book* ended, after a brief but brilliant life,[70] it was, very naturally, merged with the *Dial*, that more conservative but well-established journal of literary criticism edited by Francis F. Browne.[71] Other Chicago monthlies and weeklies have been mentioned in preceding chapters, such as the *World To-Day*,[72] but a few which were more definitely local may be given brief attention here.

The World's Fair received space in nearly every magazine in the country, but there were some Chicago periodicals which were largely devoted to the exploitation of the great show. *Halligan's Illustrated World's Fair* (1890–1893) was a small-folio of thirty-two pages issued monthly at two dollars and a half a year. It was copiously illustrated by halftone pictures of the fair, and it is said to have cost its publisher, Jewell Halligan, ten thousand dollars a year in losses during its three-year life.[73] John McGovern was editor, and he brought in a number of good contributors. The *World's Columbian Exposition Illustrated* (1891–1896) was another monthly devoted largely to pictures. It was published by James B. Campbell, a printer, and had virtually no literary content until, in 1894, it became *Campbell's Illustrated Monthly*. Later it had a longer existence as a mail-order paper under the title *Campbell's Illustrated Journal*.[74] A third Chicago periodical which capitalized on the fair, and the best of the lot, was the *Graphic* (1890–1894), published by G. P. Engelhard. A small-folio, printed on good

---

[68] *Economist*, v. 8, Oct. 20, 1888, p. 3.

[69] Seward Collins in *Bookman*, v. 70, p. 530, Jan. 1930.

[70] See Sketch 11 in this volume.

[71] See Sketch 33 in Mott, *op. cit.*, v. 3, pp. 539–43.

[72] See Chap. IV; also Sketch 10.

[73] Herbert E. Fleming, "The Literary Interests of Chicago," *American Journal of Sociology*, v. 11, p. 789, May 1906.

[74] It tried weekly publication 1895–96 under the title *Campbell's Illustrated Weekly*, and ended in 1907.

paper, it resembled *Harper's Weekly*. News and comment, editorials with Republican bias, fiction, and departments of art, music and drama, and books made up its contents.[75] It issued a "World's Fair Series" during 1892–1894, also distributed as a quarterly *Exposition Graphic*. *Life*, too, had a World's Fair edition, called *Chicago Figaro* (1890–1893), with much local society news, along with reprint from the parent periodical. Also there was a *World's Fair Puck* for six months in 1893.

The outstanding urban weekly of Chicago for many years was the *Saturday Evening Herald* (1874–1908). The chief founder, John M. Dandy, was the publicity manager of the World's Fair. He was succeeded by Edward Freiberger as editor of the *Herald* in 1898. An ill-judged venture was *Carter's Monthly* (1886–1899), which was a weekly miscellany in Wichita, Kansas, until its publisher, John Carter, moved it to Chicago, making it first a fiction magazine with Opie Read as editor, and then a kind of "booster" journal. *Gaskell's Literary Review* (1886–1890) was a curious monthly by C. A. Gaskell. It printed some good matter and was sponsored by the Gaskell Literary Club, but it was conducted chiefly as a means for selling books, music, and so on, by mail.

### ST. LOUIS

The *Critic* (1876–1900), conducted in St. Louis until 1898 by William Freudeneau, was a political and literary weekly. *St. Louis Life* (1889–1897) looked like a somewhat inferior New York *Life*; in addition to humor, it contained society news and comment on city affairs.[76] The *Censor* (1896–1943) was founded by George C. Dyer and long conducted by him. It was an urban weekly of politics, society, art and music, and literature. Dyer called the *Censor* "A Journal of Protest," and he was very outspoken. "That is a fine bunch that represents St. Louis in the present Legislature!" he exclaimed derisively in 1903, and added, "With a few exceptions, they are all there for the graft." [77] But he was anti-Folk and anti-T. R.

[75] It was edited for a time by J. A. Spencer Dickerson. Among contributors were Mary Hartwell Catherwood, Vance Thompson, and Florence Wilkinson; and among its artists, Will Bradley, Henry Reuterdahl, and T. Dart Walker. The *Graphic* grew out of a suburban Hyde Park paper published by Engelhard. It could not survive the financial troubles of 1893.

[76] Mrs. S. V. Moore was editor and publisher 1889–91; W. D. Alexander was publisher and Ballard Turner editor in 1892. Mrs. Grace L. Davidson bought it in 1896, changed the name to *Criterion*, and the next year moved it to New York, where it made a great reputation. See pp. 65–66.

[77] *Censor*, v. 9, p. 5, March 12, 1903.

The *Milwaukee Magazine,* which had been published in that city during the period 1870–1876 by Charles Whittaker and Thomas J. Gilmore, was transferred to St. Louis by the latter, after a suspension of a year or two, and resumed as the *St. Louis Illustrated Magazine* in 1878. Dr. Alexander N. De Menil was enlisted as editor in 1883, and under him this became the best St. Louis monthly of the period. It contained a variety of general literature, with household and fashion notes, and some emphasis on the popular interest in the occult. Its name was changed to *Midland Magazine* in 1894; it perished in 1897, just before the Des Moines *Midland Monthly* was moved to St. Louis, presumably to supplant it.

The most important of the several St. Louis weeklies was the *Mirror,* later called *Reedy's Mirror* after its famous editor and publisher.[78] Both in literature and politics, William Marion Reedy was a force of undeniable influence. The *Valley Magazine* (1902–1907) was a less successful Reedy venture. It was intended to be a popular monthly, and was priced at five cents a copy. Vance Thompson, Percival Pollard, Arthur Stringer, H. de Vere Stacpoole, John L. Didier, and others joined the editor in writing for the new magazine. But it did not make a success, and about the end of 1903 the L. F. Smith Publishing Company took it over and made it a weekly, with Claude H. Wetmore and Robertus Love as editors; it was a monthly at the end.[79] It featured the Louisiana Purchase Exposition. Liberal in politics, it favored Folk the reformer, though Reedy was generally against him. *Wetmore's Weekly* (1904–1905) was largely political.

Editor Francis G. Thornton announced the *Commonwealth* (1901–1904) as "a magazine of the so-called heavy class." It sold at ten cents a copy and tried to be a monthly, though it missed some numbers. Contributors were mostly local, and the scope was general. Frank G. Terrell's *Optimist* (1901–1903) was a dollar monthly. *Events* was a semimonthly, published by Mrs. Frances Armstrong Woods in 1903, mainly to exploit the exposition.

The *Journal of Speculative Philosophy,*[80] a quarterly which ended in 1893, was one of the most distinguished periodicals of a city which was the home of many professional, technical, and class journals.

---

[78] See Sketch 24 in this volume. For all early St. Louis periodicals, see Dorothy G. Holland, *An Annotated Checklist of Magazines Published in St. Louis Before 1900* (St. Louis, 1951).

[79] It had been an octavo of 60 pages until May 1903, when it was changed to a quarto of 24 pages and cover. It was a 10¢ monthly of 32 pages Nov. 1903, but it switched to weekly publication Dec. 15, 1903, and back to monthly in Dec. 1904. W. L. Harn was its last editor.

[80] See Sketch 8 in Mott, *op. cit.,* v. 3.

THE GREAT WEST

In the period 1885–1905, no less than seven western states were admitted to the Union. The frontier was driven back until there was no longer any significant amount of free land for homesteading. The old cattle-and-mining economy had given way pretty largely to diversified crops and stock, fruit-raising, and truck gardening. This meant that irrigation and the preservation of natural resources became major issues.

"The opening of Oklahoma was one of the most important events that has occurred in the development of the West. It marks an epoch," said a writer in the *Cosmopolitan* [81] who had taken a part in that remarkable land rush of April 22, 1889. Kate Field was more lyrical:

> Startling and beautiful is this idea of the sudden production of a complete cosmos — this birth, Minerva-like, of a commonwealth which knows no infancy. . . . This is an interesting miracle, and it is a little depressing to reflect that we shall probably not see it performed again.[82]

Despite their wonder at western progress, eastern periodicals were inclined to emphasize the aridity of both western lands and western culture. The *Harvard Monthly* insisted that there was much that Harvard could offer westerners — "a true refinement . . . which, amidst the haste of western progress, they could never find." [83] And a writer in the *New England Magazine* declared in 1890, with the lack of foresight not uncommon among would-be prophets, that "the farmer cannot now go further west with advantage. . . . The fight for a free life and a true home must be fought out where he is." [84] And irrigation, which had flourished from 1887 to 1892, and which seemed the answer to the *New England's* pessimism, was "materially checked, and in many cases disastrously so" by the hard times of 1893–1896, as *Irrigation Age* mournfully recorded.[85] However, by 1897, an observer could write in the *Arena* that "once again the people are talking of going west" and making the arid lands fruitful.[86] Another *Arena* writer some years before had looked forward to irrigation as the chief factor in making the West habitable for a hundred million persons.[87]

[81] Hamilton S. Wicks, "The Opening of Oklahoma," in *Cosmopolitan*, v. 7, p. 460, Sept. 1889.

[82] *Kate Field's Washington*, v. 8, p. 184, Sept. 20, 1893.

[83] *Harvard Monthly*, v. 17, p. 83, Nov. 1893.

[84] Edward B. Williams in the *New England Magazine*, n. s., v. 3, pp. 14–15, Sept. 1890.

[85] *Irrigation Age*, v. 10, p. 55, Aug. 1896.

[86] Judge J. S. Emer, "Our Arid Lands," in *Arena*, v. 17, p. 389, Feb. 1897.

[87] Richard J. Hinton in *Arena*, v. 8, p. 618, Oct. 1893.

Settlers who took up land in Dakota and Wyoming had no easy way of life. The Chicago *Graphic* told their story:

A few of the "boomers" will succeed. The majority will have to endure sufferings and hardships before their claims pass into the hands of mortgage sharks. The building up of a new country requires great sacrifices. . . . The American "boomer," though often thoughtless and irrational, is entitled to credit. . . . In the centuries to come he may be pointed out as the pathfinder.[88]

### COLORADO AND UTAH

Colorado entered the Union in 1893. It received much attention about that time because of the collapse of its silver-mining industry caused by the monetary policy adopted by Congress, and later because of the state's shift to gold-mining.

Its most interesting magazine during this period was the *Great Divide* (1889–1896), a sixteen-page small-folio at a dollar a year. This monthly contained much material about western fauna and flora, minerals and resources, the Indians and the early settlers, and so on, illustrated by woodcuts; and there was some fiction and poetry. It was published by H. H. Tammen, later famous as one of the publishers of the *Denver Post*, but at this time proprietor of a curio shop; and it was edited by Stanley Wood. Tammen used his cabinet of mineral specimens as the chief premium with which he built up the *Great Divide's* subscription list, and he described his elk heads, gem collections, and such in his fairly well filled general advertising columns. Some of the articles about the cliff dwellers and some halftones from William Henry Jackson's photographs (perhaps the first pictures by that artist to be published) gave the *Great Divide* real importance. But it reached less than fifty thousand circulation, and in the fall of 1895 it sought greater fame and prosperity in Chicago. There it adopted a handsome chromolithographic cover with cartoons by Frank Beard commenting on social and political matters, a page of humor, and some art studies; but it also kept its western interests. After a year of this, it had to abandon its expensive covers, and it suspended publication with the number for July 1896.[89]

Denver's leading weekly in the nineties was *George's Weekly* (1884–1908), founded by Herbert George and devoted to society, the stage, politics, automobiles, and state promotion. It was subtitled "A

---

[88] *Graphic*, v. 6, p. 319, April 30, 1892.

[89] See *Great Divide*, v. 11, p. 66, March 1894, for an account of the founding of the magazine. Gene Fowler, *Timber Line: A Story of Bonfils and Tammen* (New York, 1933) is wrong (p. 61) in calling this magazine a "pamphlet" and a "catalog" of Tammen's curios. The name was later used as that of a weekly edition of the *Post*, 1902–27.

Thought-Provoker," and was a lively journal at a dollar a year.[90] The *Commonwealth* (1889–1891) was a short-lived monthly which moved to Chicago for its last six months. P. A. Leonard's *Western World* (1902–1910) was a dollar monthly of mediocre quality and small circulation. In Colorado Springs, the *Garden of the Gods Magazine* (1902–1906) was begun as the organ of the local Chautauqua assembly, with John T. Burns as editor and John Vance Cheney and Captain Jack Crawford as leading contributors. In 1903 its title was changed to *Frontier Monthly*, and in the next year to *The Frontier*.[91]

Mormonism was a favorite subject in the magazines. The sensational nature of the polygamy theme and the advance of Utah toward statehood made a combination which few magazines resisted. The Mormon church maintained several periodicals, mentioned in the section on religious journals.

*Truth* (1901–1908) was an urban weekly at Salt Lake City conducted by John W. Hughes. It dealt in politics with much independence, but it was generally Democratic and anti-Mormon. Hughes died early in 1908.[92] *Goodwin's Weekly* (1902–1929) was similar in scope. It was edited by C. C. Goodwin, was Republican in its sympathies, and opposed the participation of the Mormon church in politics.[93] The *Western Galaxy: Tullidge's Monthly* was published by Edward W. Tullidge for only four months beginning with March 1888, and dealt with state resources and pioneer life.

### "OUR GREAT PACIFIC COMMONWEALTH"

William E. Smythe, founder and editor of the *Irrigation Age*, wrote an article with the above title for the *Century Magazine* in 1896, in which he told of the transition of the Golden State from speculation in mines and fruit lands, and the exploitation of wheatland monopoly, to farming and fruit-raising for the common people.[94] This was the most significant fact about California in the nineties.

The *Overland Monthly*, of San Francisco, now in a second series,

[90] In 1906 William H. Griffith became editor, and the next year he changed its title to *Coloradoan*. Griffith was out by the fall of 1907 and the subtitle was "Sam Wood's Paper." "Polly Pry" O'Brien wrote scandal for it in this phase. In April 1908, Lea. Mitchell White and Mortimer I. Stevens bought it and changed title to *Denver News Letter and Colorado Advertiser*; again it was a typical urban weekly, with special emphasis on motoring and the promotion of Colorado's mining interests. But it ended in the fall of 1908.

[91] This was a 10¢ magazine. Sept., Nov., Dec. 1903, and Jan.–March 1904 were omitted. In Dec. 1905 it was enlarged to quarto; Robert L. Hubbard became editor, and George Bent's "Forty Years With the Cheyennes" and other interesting Indian material were published.

[92] Hughes was succeeded by his widow, and in May 1908 by other managers, who changed the name in the periodical's last months to *Western Weekly*.

[93] The name was changed to *Citizen* in 1919 by new managers. Editorship and ownership changed often in later years.

[94] *Century*, v. 53, pp. 300–07, Dec. 1896.

was still the most important magazine of the Pacific Coast. Though definitely a regional periodical, it printed some good writers from the East. When Frederick Marriott bought it in 1900, he made it more a "booster" magazine for California; as such it was handsomer and more prosperous but lower in literary quality.[95]

Charles Frederick Holder began his *Californian Illustrated Magazine* at San Francisco as a good-looking twenty-five-cent monthly in October 1891, and then skipped two months before continuing. The magazine had some good illustration, mainly from halftones. All the good western writers, and some from the East, were contributors of fiction, verse, criticism of literature and art, and articles on science, politics, foreign affairs, and sports. Charles F. Lummis, David Starr Jordan, John Bonner, Joaquin Miller, Edwin Markham, Gertrude Atherton, and Ina Coolbrith were prominent in the *Californian's* pages. Dan De Quille's recollections of Mark Twain and Artemus Ward were interesting. California scenery was staple. Professor Holder became director of the Santa Catalina Zoological Station in 1894, and sold his magazine to Edward J. Livernash, who soon discontinued it.[96]

*Sunset* was begun in San Francisco in May 1898 by the Passenger Department of the Southern Pacific Company, to exploit "the wonders of California." It was well illustrated, sold for ten cents, and, though chiefly promotional, offered some short fiction and verse. It began with only some thirty pages in each number, but in 1903 it was increased to a hundred pages and its contents much improved. There were departments of the theater, books and writers, amateur photography. Charles Warren Stoddard's series on old missions was printed in 1906. By that time it was subtitled "The Magazine of the Pacific" and covered the coastal states of the Northwest as well as California. Short stories by Jack London were published, and serials by Owen Wister, Stewart Edward White, Mary Austin, and others. Charles Sedgwick Aiken was editor during the first decade of the twentieth century. *Sunset* was the only general western magazine to continue prosperously past the middle of the twentieth century.[97]

San Francisco was notable for its urban weeklies. The *Golden Era*, with its memories of Mark Twain and Bret Harte, was moved to San

---

[95] See Sketch 12 in Mott, *op. cit.*, v. 3.

[96] Vol. 1, Oct. 1891, Jan.–May 1892; 2, June–Nov. 1892; 3, Dec. 1892–May 1893; 4, June–Nov. 1893; 5, Dec. 1893–April 1894. Only the last two numbers were published by Livernash.

[97] Vols. 1–20, semiannual beginning May and Nov. (May 1898–April 1908); 21, May–Dec. 1908; 22–current, semiannual beginning Jan. and July (Jan. 1909–current). E. H. Woodman was the first editor; Aiken served 1901–10; Chas. K. Field, who had been associate editor, was editor 1911–26; Joseph Henry Jackson, 1927–29; Lou Richardson, 1930–37; W. I. Nichols, 1937–39; W. L. Doty, 1939–53. L. W. Lane became publisher in 1930, later the Lane Publishing Company. Colored illustration was introduced in 1910, along with a "Development Section" at the end of the book, with departments of western people

Diego by Editor Harr Wagner in 1887, to end there six years later.[98] The *Argonaut,* now without Ambrose Bierce's "Prattle," lost also its editor, Frank M. Pixley, by death in 1895, and was continued under less distinguished management.[99] The *News-Letter* celebrated its fiftieth anniversary in 1906; during the period 1885–1905 it was a journal of criticism of the arts and comment on politics. The younger Frederick Marriott was its manager; associated with him were such brilliant writers and critics as Kirk Ward, Ashton Stevens, Gellett Burgess, Jack London, Wallace Irwin, and others. In politics, the *News-Letter* was anti-Schmitz and anti-Hearst. The *Wasp* was the illustrated weekly of the trio, and sold for five dollars a year while the others were priced at four. These three and the *Wave,* a fourth urban weekly, had about the same circulation — fourteen to eighteen thousand. The *Wasp* in these years did less stinging and more reporting of society, the theater, art, politics, and finance.

The *Wave* (1887–1901) was a San Francisco society paper with literary leanings, conducted throughout the nineties by John O'Hara Cosgrave, the Australian-born journalist who was later editor of *Everybody's Magazine* in New York. It was a fully illustrated small-folio of sixteen pages, priced at ten cents. It published some important things — such as Frank Norris's "Moran of the Lady Letty" in 1898 — and for a time Gellett Burgess wrote interesting gossip for it from New York.[100] *Town Talk* (1892–1921) was an urban weekly of strongly political trend during its early years. It was conducted by S. B. Carleton in those years and was reformatory in state politics and gold-standard in national alignment. Theodore Firmin Bonnet bought a half-interest in it in 1900 and became editor and later sole proprietor. He emphasized society gossip and literature: such California writers as Frank Norris, Jack London, George Sterling, and Yone Noguchi were occasional contributors. Bonnet died in August 1920, and his widow continued the paper thereafter for only six months. Shorter-lived week-

---

and events. There was much of the Panama-Pacific Exposition in 1915, and of Villa and the Mexican troubles. David Starr Jordan, an old and faithful contributor, wrote on public questions during the first World War. About 1916 the magazine deteriorated into promotion at the expense of literature; and though there was much of interest about the Old West, the new Hollywood, Hawaii, and western events, architecture, gardens, and personalities, *Sunset's* quality had declined. The May 1918 issue was on the presses at the time of the earthquake and fire, and the *Sunset* building was destroyed; the next issue contained Aiken's story of the disaster, with pictures. In 1928, Field, long the magazine's chief owner, sold out to L. W. Lane, who made it into a "service" magazine for the West, dedicated to the task of illustrating how West Coast men and women can live happily in modern homes and surroundings. In this new phase, *Sunset* attained over 500,000 circulation by the mid-century. See *Magazine Week,* v. 1, Oct. 19, 1953, p. 7. Proctor Mellquist became editor in 1954.
[98] For the *Golden Era,* see Mott, *op. cit.,* v. 2, p. 117.
[99] For *News-Letter, Argonaut,* and *Wasp,* see Mott, *op. cit.,* v. 3, pp. 56–57.
[100] Suspended in the summer of 1900, it was resurrected briefly by Fred Healy in 1901.

lies were the *American Standard* (1888–1891) and the even briefer paper by a famous Hearst man called *Arthur McEwen's Letter*, which ran to thirty-nine numbers in 1894–1895.

An early Los Angeles magazine was the *Pacific Monthly* (1889–1891), edited by Charlotte Perkins Stetson. But the chief Los Angeles monthly was *Out West*, which was begun in June 1894 under the name *Land of Sunshine: An Illustrated Monthly of Southern California.* Charles F. Lummis was editor during the magazine's first decade, and wrote much for it, including an outspoken editorial department and a serial history of California. Among the contributors were David Starr Jordan, Joaquin Miller, Ina Coolbrith, C. H. Shinn, Edwin Markham, Grace Ellery Channing, and Charlotte Perkins Stetson. Benavides' "Narrative," articles on Indian and Mexican art, stories of the old Wild West, and Los Angeles promotional pieces distinguished the magazine, the name of which was changed to *Out West* in 1902. It was eventually merged with the *Overland*.[101]

Los Angeles had several weeklies in the period, including Horace Bell's *Porcupine* (1882–1898); George Rice's *Western Graphic* (1893–1918), merged with the *Capital* in 1901–1903 but later resumed as the *Graphic*; and the *Capital* (1895–1903), managed by H. W. Patton and a succession of other editors. The *Pacific Outlook* was begun in Los Angeles in 1895 by A. M. Dunn as a five-cent weekly of political opinion, the theater, music, and society. Later it was to become a notable leader of the Progressives in California.[102]

## THE NORTHWEST

The *Pacific Monthly* (1898–1911) was begun in Portland with Alexander Sweek as president of the publishing company, William Bittle Wells as manager and editor, and Lischen M. Miller assistant. It was a bright, well-printed magazine, with little illustration but good variety. It was strong in the history of the Northwest, in politics, and in literary notices.[103] Portland weeklies were H. D. Chapman's *Lantern* (1893–

[101] Lummis and Charles Amadon Moody were editors 1906–09; Charles Lawrence Edholm, 1909–10; George Wharton James, 1910–14; George Vail Steep, 1915; Lannie Hayes Martin and Cruze Carriell, 1915–17. F. A. Pattee was chief publisher to 1903.

[102] It absorbed the *California Weekly* (1908–10), of San Francisco, at the beginning of 1911, and with it obtained A. J. Pillsbury, its manager, as an editorial writer. The name was changed to *California Outlook: A Progressive Weekly*, and the paper became the organ of the political revolution in the state led by Hiram Johnson. C. D. Willard was one of the owners and a leading writer, and William Allen White and Chester H. Rowell were contributing editors. Meyer Lissueris was editor in 1915. It ended in 1918, its mission accomplished.

[103] In 1907 Lute Pease became editor and Charles H. Jones general manager. Pease did a notable series on conspiracies against the conservation laws. Illustration improved. Charles Erskine Scott Wood was a prominent contributor, and editor during the last year or more

1908) and the *Pacific Empire* (1895–1898). Abigail Scott Duniway was first editor of the latter paper, and wrote serial fiction and suffrage editorials for it; in the latter half of its life Lischen M. Miller and C. C. Coggswell were editors. It was merged in the *Pacific Monthly*.

Three Seattle monthlies dedicated to promoting the Northwest while furnishing some literary fare to their readers were Lee Fairchild's *Pacific Magazine* (1889–1891), Honor L. Wilhelm's *Coast* (1901–1911), and Edgar L. Hampton's *Westerner* (1904–1915). Will Carson was editor and publisher of a weekly of society and literature called *Soundings* (1890–1894). But Seattle's chief urban weekly was the *Argus*, which was well printed, active in politics on the Republican side, and full of interesting miscellany. Begun February 17, 1894, it eventually came under the control of H. A. Chadwick, who had bought an interest when it was only six weeks old.[104] Leonard Forbes's *State* (1898–1902) was a monthly of literature and promotion at Tacoma.

J. M. White began the *Rocky Mountain Magazine*, dealing with regional history, literature, and mining, in September 1900 at Helena, Montana, moving it a year later to Butte, where eight monthly numbers were published.[105] The *Nevada Magazine* (1899–1900) was published at Winnemucan by C. D. Van Duzer.

### THE YUKON

Alaska's earliest magazine-like periodical was Sheldon Jackson's *North Star* (1887–1898), first issued from the press of Alaska's only newspaper, the Sitka weekly *Alaskan*. Jackson was a great organizer; he set up the first Alaskan mail service by canoe, established a school for Eskimos, and so on. His *North Star* was a missionary paper designed chiefly for circulation in the states — a monthly of eight quarto-size pages.[106]

Some years before this, Jackson, as a special agent of the government at Washington, had reported on the agricultural possibilities of the Yukon Valley. As early as 1890, a writer in the *Arena* had called attention to unexploited gold fields in Alaska.[107] But when the world really

---

of the magazine's life. Ira E. Bennett was Washington correspondent, and William Winter wrote of the New York stage. Charles F. Holder, Arthur Chapman, and Randall R. Howard wrote much for the magazine. It was merged in *Sunset*.

[104] It began as a 5¢ paper, but it later sold for 10¢. Also it adopted the "Independent" label in politics. H. A. Chadwick died in 1934, and was succeeded by his son H. D., who still conducts it.

[105] It was followed by a very different *Rocky Mountain Magazine* in Denver, 1903–06; this was more a general family journal.

[106] Dr. B. K. Wilbur was its editor in its last two years. It was merged with the *Northern Light* (1893–1903), a similar periodical at Fort Wrangel.

[107] John H. Keatley, in *Arena*, v. 1, pp. 730–41, May 1890.

discovered Alaska, it was in a golden blaze of glory. When "the richest gold strike the world has ever known" was made in the Klondike in August 1896, communication had just been cut off by the seasonal closing in of the ice, and it was not until four months later that news got out; then began the sensational stampede to the gold fields.[108] A writer in the *Review of Reviews*, basing his estimate on what had happened in 1897, said that "at least a hundred thousand prospectors will advance on Dawson City and its vicinity in the first six or seven months of 1898."[109] For the next few years, the magazines were full of the Klondike gold rush and life in the Far North. In September 1897, *McClure's*, *Cosmopolitan*, and *Forum* all offered practical advice for prospectors in the Klondike. But the fullest and best of the early articles on the subject appeared in *Frank Leslie's Popular Monthly* for February 1898.[110] It was accompanied by a folded-in map, a table of distances, a list of supplies and equipment necessary to the prospector, and many pictures. The *National Geographic Magazine* eclipsed this in April, with a number devoted to Alaska and the Klondike, including big colored maps and an article by Hamlin Garland.[111] *Popular Science Monthly* had a fine illustrated two-part article by Angelo Heilprin in 1899.[112] Nearly all magazines had something about the Klondike rush.

With these activities in Alaska came many newspapers, including a few dailies; but there was no time for magazines until in later years. Eight numbers of an *Alaskan Magazine* were issued in Tacoma, Washington, in 1900; thirteen numbers of the weekly *Young Klondike* in New York in 1898, and four issues of *Alaska and Northwest Quarterly* in Seattle in 1899.

### PARADISE OF THE PACIFIC

Frank L. Hoogs's Hawaiian promotional monthly entitled *Paradise of the Pacific* began its long life in 1888 at Honolulu as a sixteen-page illustrated quarto. William M. Langton took it over about the turn of the century, and it was later to grow into a beautiful and prosperous magazine.

At the time of annexation in 1898, Hawaii had several monthlies, chiefly religious and agricultural.

[108] *Cyclopedic Review of Current History*, v. 7, pp. 554–68, July-Sept. 1897. Quotations are from pp. 554 and 555. In this article and those in the next four or five numbers of this review is an excellent factual summary of the gold rush.

[109] S. S. Bush in *Review of Reviews*, v. 17, p. 289, March 1898.

[110] *Popular Monthly*, v. 45, pp. 123–43, Feb. 1898. The *Bay View Magazine* calls this article by Henry Clay Colver, "The Gold Regions of the Klondike," "the most practical and best illustrated article on the Klondike" (v. 5, p. 210, March 1898). It was accompanied by one on "Alaska, the Land of the Klondike," by R. H. Herron.

[111] *National Geographic Magazine*, v. 9, p. 113ff, April 1898.

[112] *Appleton's Popular Science Monthly*, v. 55, pp. 1, 163, May, June, 1899.

# CHAPTER VIII

## LITERARY TYPES AND JUDGMENTS

A S THE decade of the 1880's ended, the *Critic* presented to its readers an unusually sound and comprehensive review of the literary history of those years. It was noted that:

In France, England, and the United States, the most obvious recent changes are the result of what may be called the democratization of literature. Never before has reading been so general; never have so many people been able to write so variously and so well. . . . Literature and journalism have joined hands as never before. . . . The scientific spirit of the age has popularized the love of accurate description, of "human documents."[1]

The trend toward a merger of journalism and literature has already been noted in this volume.[2] In 1892 Hamilton Wright Mabie, writing in the *Forum*, had similar ideas: "If there are not, as of old," he said, "a few writers of very high rank, there is an increasing number of thoroughly equipped men and women whose work, in its range and sincerity, indicates a general advance in skill and taste."[3]

The *Critic* article pointed out how "fertile in encyclopedias, dictionaries, and useful compendiums of every kind" the decade had been;[4] and other observers rather overemphasized the "scientific spirit" in realistic fiction. But surely one of the most striking aspects of the literature of the late eighties and early nineties was its preoccupation with social and economic problems, as well as with religion, psychology, and so on. Two of the most popular novels of the times were Mrs. Ward's *Robert Elsmere* and Bellamy's *Looking Backward*. The theme of the former was the hero's abandonment of the theology of the churches for practical social work — much the same theme as that of an even more popular but poorer novel by an American clergyman, published in 1897: Sheldon's *In His Steps*. *Looking Backward* was a fantasy of strong socialistic trend. "The growth of socialistic literature of the higher order," said *Current Literature* in 1891, "is something phenomenal"; and it named Bellamy's fable, William Morris's *News From Nowhere*, Albion W. Tourgée's *Murvale Eastman, Christian Socialist*, the translations of Marx's *Das Kapital*, and so on.[5] A best seller of the times was Henry

---

[1] George Pellew in tenth anniversary number of *Critic*, v. 18, p. 29, Jan. 17, 1891.
[2] See Chap. I.
[3] *Forum*, v. 10, p. 799, Feb. 1892.
[4] Pellew in *Critic*, v. 18, p. 29, Jan. 17, 1891.
[5] *Current Literature*, v. 6, p. 319, Feb. 1891.

George's *Progress and Poverty*; and in the mid-nineties George M. Harvey's *Coin's Financial School*, the free-silver manual, was immensely popular.

Also there was Helen Hunt Jackson's moving plea for the Indian called *Ramona* — "unquestionably the best novel yet produced by an American woman," wrote Tourgée in the *North American Review*.[6] And Marie Corelli's *A Romance of Two Worlds*, a curious mélange of many "isms," was a great best seller of the early nineties.[7]

### TRENDS IN FICTION

It was a period notable for the popularity of fiction. A writer in *Belford's Magazine* in 1888 observed: "The great stream that swells day by day in the form of prose fiction is simply appalling. . . . Every female born under the stars and stripes comes into the world prepared to write a novel."[8] True enough, but there was no need for animadversion respecting the ladies. In the *Critic's* review of American literature during the eighties mentioned above, most of the novelists listed are men. Ten years later the flood had not abated. "The preponderance of fiction in the literature of the closing decades of this century," predicted the *Arena*, "is the most salient feature in the literary history of our times which will strike the future historian."[9]

Ah, the thousands of novels of this period which are now completely erased from the memory of man — and woman, too! Written with high hopes of fame and royalties, hand-set into type by printer-slaves, distributed by shining-eyed publishers, given the paragraph-review treatment in magazines and newspapers, read and immediately forgotten by a few, and then dropped like so many blocks of lead into the deep sea of oblivion! Even such a selective review as the *Bookman* printed hundreds of pages about novels which have never even been heard of by modern students of the history of fiction.

The great literary debate of the times was the one about realism in fiction. Said a writer in the *Forum*:

For a long time a wordy war has raged in the magazines and the newspapers between so-called realists and romanticists. In *Harper's Monthly* Mr. Howells has been asserting the importance of novels that keep close to the facts of life; and the critics and criticasters have daily attacked his teaching and practice as

---

[6] *North American Review*, v. 143, p. 246, Sept. 1886.

[7] For the best sellers mentioned in this paragraph, see F. L. Mott, *Golden Multitudes: The Story of Best Sellers in the United States* (New York, 1947).

[8] *Belford's Magazine*, v. 2, p. 102, Dec. 1888. See also Pellew in *Critic*, v. 18, p. 29, Jan. 17, 1891.

[9] *Arena*, v. 19, p. 670, May 1898.

materialistic and debasing. . . . The ground is strewn with dead and dying reputations. . . .

— such as those of Saintsbury, Lang, Symonds, and Robert Louis Stevenson.[10] Howells was indeed captain of the forces contending for realism; from his chair in the *"Editor's Study"* of *Harper's*, he directed the campaign. Hamlin Garland, writing on "veritism" in the *Arena*, was an able lieutenant. As early as 1886, the *Dial* was claiming that Tolstoi's *War and Peace* had decided the issue and won the war: "It seems that for the present literary generation the victory is won, and the war virtually over," wrote Editor Browne.[11] But the *Dial* was a highbrow, and besides, it was premature in its claims. The lowbrow *Munsey's Magazine* admitted no such defeat, and by 1894 it could print this statement: "These are the days when the romantic in literature — the strong, the shining, the imaginative, the ennobling — flourishes, and holds the ear of the world, while 'realism' and 'veritism' are the languishing cults of the select few."[12] That the war for the realists had been, indeed, far from won is shown by the chorus of criticism that greeted Tolstoi's *Resurrection* and Norris's *McTeague* at the turn of the century.

And the liveliness of romanticism at the very end of the nineties is illustrated in the lists of "Books in Demand" — the first best-seller compilations — in the *Bookman*. Swashbuckling historical romance suited well the martial spirit of '98, and in that year the *Dial* confessed that "the romantic revival is at full tide," and added, "We have learned the limitations of literary photography."[13] Even the *Atlantic Monthly* made much use of historical romance in serial form at the turn of the century. But by 1903 the *Booklover's Magazine* suggested that the country had had enough of such literature for a while: "We humbly raise the question if the production of American historical novels has not reached the point where it would be wise for the authors to give the public a rest."[14] It was a timely word; and from Winston Churchill's *The Crossing*, of 1904, to the 1920's there were no more big successes in the field of historical romance.[15]

A minor war, compared with that waged over the new realism, was the conflict of opinion concerning the use of dialect in fiction. The book

[10] George Pellew, "The New Battle of the Books," in *Forum*, v. 5, p. 564, July 1888. See also *Life's* complaint about the tiresomeness of the controversy, v. 10, p. 1888, Oct. 6, 1887.

[11] *Dial*, v. 7, p. 81, Aug. 1886.

[12] *Munsey's Magazine*, v. 12, p. 330, Dec. 1894. See also N. H. Banks's review of *McTeague* in the *Bookman*, v. 9, p. 356, June 1899, a strong arraignment of realism.

[13] *Dial*, v. 25, p. 389, Dec. 1, 1898. Cf. Francis E. Lester in *Critic*, v. 28, p. 35, Jan. 18, 1896.

[14] *Booklover's Magazine*, v. 1, p. 28, Jan. 1903. T. T. Munger is the writer.

[15] See editorial by Alexander N. De Menil in the *Hesperian*, v. 4, p. 559, Oct. 1905, noting the disappearance of historical novels and giving reasons therefor.

reviewer George Merriam Hyde wrote a good article on the subject for the *Bookman* in 1897, in which he compared the reader to a "central office," where, "over converging wires, the discordant messages of the dialect hunters die in the large and charitable air of no Volapük." Hyde cites more than a dozen different "dialects" that had become more or less familiar in popular fiction, and then he looks toward the future:

> Of course, the chatter of these types is nothing now to what it will be when they all intermarry and produce other types. If Johnny or Chimmy should be spared to wed an Hungarian lady, or Ole should become enamoured of Miss Li Sing, or one of Mr. Cahan's Poles should seek the hand of a Bowery "loidy," can anyone foresee the consequences? [16]

### THE SHORT STORY

One of the three chief changes in the content of American magazines in the quarter-century 1872–1897 as shown in the Kimball study[17] is in the increase of short fiction. By 1882, the *Ladies' Home Companion* was observing editorially: "That magazine is liked best which has the best short stories";[18] while two years later the *Literary World* noted: "There has been a spurt this year in short stories, the demand for which is always greater than the supply."[19] About the same time *Life*, which had printed some fine examples of this type of literature, made similar note of "the unusual demand for short stories." This, it explained, was not limited to the magazines, but included newspapers and book publishers.[20]

As early as 1890, there was complaint by the enlightened writer of the "Point of View" department in *Scribner's Magazine* about the emphasis on "the short-story form (note well the hyphen)" and "the whole disproportion of the cackle to the be-cackled eggs."[21] This was because Brander Matthews, in his famous article entitled "The Philosophy of the Short-Story," in *Lippincott's Magazine* in 1885, had insisted on the hyphen to distinguish what he conceived to be the art form of the genre from a story that was merely short.[22] There was also much criticism of "dialect," which found its native habitat in the short story, and of abuse of "local color." James Lane Allen, who may be regarded as a liberal user of that element himself, wrote an article for the *Critic* in which he

---

[16] *Bookman*, v. 6, p. 56, Sept. 1897.
[17] See Arthur Reed Kimball in *Atlantic Monthly*, v. 86, p. 124, July 1900. Tables are in the annual *Journal of the American Science Association*, 1899.
[18] *Ladies' Home Companion.* v. 29, Nov. 1882, p. 1.
[19] *Literary World*, v. 15, p. 465, Dec. 27, 1884.
[20] *Life*, v. 5, p. 18, Jan. 8, 1885.
[21] *Scribner's Magazine*, v. 8, p. 129, July 1890.
[22] See F. L. Mott, *A History of American Magazines* (Cambridge, 1938), v. 3, pp. 225–26.

protested that "Fiction is not the proper literary form in which to furnish the reader miscellaneous information of flora, climate, and other
scenic features"; though more actual color, he said, would improve
most short stories.[23]

These abuses, and at length even the shackles of a prescribed art
form, tended to fall away from the short story at the end of the century.
Alden wrote in his "Editor's Study" in *Harper's* in 1901:

> The latest development of the short story is not only away from the old con-
> ventional pattern, but into an infinite variety of effects . . . the character sketch
> . . . a single dramatic situation, a succession of humorous incidents . . . a quick
> comedy . . . an equally quick tragedy . . . a brief glimpse of special life . . .
> a spiritual revelation . . . a picturesque view of some old time.[24]

Another development of the nineties in this field was the "storiette,"
later called the "short short story." *Munsey's Magazine* had a department devoted to them in 1896; *Everybody's* specialized in them; *Collier's* later became famous for its selection of them, and many other
magazines found them popular with their readers.

### ALL-FICTION MAGAZINES

Munsey's *Golden Argosy*[25] became an all-fiction monthly in 1896.
Within the next ten years it built up half a million circulation and became the first really successful magazine of its class. An earlier all-
fiction monthly — and an excellent one — was *Short Stories*;[26] but it
was almost altogether a reprint periodical until the end of the period
now under study. F. M. Somers, editor and publisher of *Current Literature*, founded it in 1890. The stories were very well selected from foreign sources, the classics, Sunday newspapers, and so on. "Twenty-five
stories for twenty-five cents!" it advertised. It was still published in the
1950's. The Current Literature Publishing Company also took over in
1895 a fiction reprint magazine called *Romance*,[27] which had been pub-

---

[23] *Critic*, v. 8, p. 13, Jan. 9, 1886. Cf. Maurice Thompson in *America*, v. 3, p. 471, Jan.
9, 1890.

[24] *Harper's Magazine*, v. 104, p. 170, Dec. 1901; also cf. v. 103, p. 1012, Nov. 1901.

[25] See Sketch 3 in this volume.

[26] Originally it had a striking format as a tall twelvemo on antique-finish paper, but it
changed to octavo in 1892. It printed stories by such writers as Kipling, Quiller-Couch,
Turgenev, Maupassant, Zola, Halévy, Harte, Anna Katherine Green, and Opie Read. In 1892
it began reprinting some of the older classics. There were always a few originals, for which
prize contests were held after the *Black Cat* set that fashion. The magazine was sold to a
new organization in 1904; and Doubleday, Page & Company took over its management in
1910, making it a "pulp" of the better class. It was a semimonthly 1921–49, and then
resumed monthly publication. Harry E. Maule was editor 1911–36, and D. McIlwraith
thereafter. Such outstanding "pulp" writers as H. Bedford-Jones, W. C. Tuttle, H. H. Knibbs,
James Francis Dwyer, Charles Tenney Jackson, William McLead Raine, Achmed Abdullah,
and H. C. Witwer have been contributors of novelettes, serials, and short stories.

[27] It began Feb. 1891 at 25¢, was reduced to 10¢ Aug. 1894, raised to 15¢ March 1895,
brought down to 5¢ in 1896, and back up to 10¢ before it ended July 1897.

lished by W. H. Benton in New York, and continued it with the same policy. Two years later they sold it to Gilson Willets, who soon merged it in the *Parisian*. D. Lothrop, of Boston, issued the *Story-Teller*, a good all-fiction monthly, 1890–1893. An excellent all-fiction monthly of the latter nineties was the *Pocket Magazine*,[28] a ten-cent magazine of some hundred and sixty small-size pages. Frederick A. Stokes Company published it, and Irving Bacheller was its editor. It published one novelette, five short stories, and a poem or two in each number; and most of the contributors were well-known magazinists, some of them in the top rank.

The *10 Story Book*[29] was founded in Chicago in June 1901 by Dwight Allyn, a newspaperman who had started a syndicate to furnish stories to daily newspapers. It was a small-octavo of sixty-four pages monthly, illustrated by line-cuts, and selling at ten cents; and it made a hit when it was first introduced by red-coated salesmen on the Chicago streets. Its emphasis at first was on the clever and "clean" original story; with its thousand-dollar prize contests, it was not unlike the famous *Black Cat* for its first few years. It carried no serials, but it did print a series "world masterpieces" chosen by Sherwin Cody. It was not long, however, until naughty tales — usually short and inferior — became the chief offering of *10 Story*, bringing it a circulation of sixty thousand by 1905. It lasted until 1916.

*Wayside Monthly*[30] was like that lady with a record whose career was rather checkered. Born *Detroit Monthly*, it was for six months a local periodical devoted to society, amusements, and "topics of the town." But in September 1901, after it had been published for six months, it became a five-cent all-fiction magazine under the title of *Wayside Tales*, with stories by Eben E. Rexford, William Heyliger, William Wallace Cook, and so on. Like the others of its class, it used the prize contest to bring in new writers and buyers. The price was raised to ten cents in 1902, and the publishers tried to sell stock in the magazine to readers at a dollar a share; but publication was suspended May 1903. Three months later the Sampson-Hodges Company, a news-

---

[28] It was reduced to the 5¢ price Feb. 1898, and Abbot Frederic succeeded Bacheller in August of that year; soon thereafter it was a bimonthly at 10¢.

[29] James S. Evans was associated with Allyn in the early years. Henry L. Blaisdell was editor for some years. See Herbert E. Fleming, "The Literary Interests of Chicago," *American Journal of Sociology*, v. 11, pp. 89–90, 101–03, June 1906.

[30] Lewis D. Sampson, former teacher and newspaperman, was president of the Sampson-Hodges syndicate. Gertrude N. Murdock was editor under that management. Schloss was the son of a wealthy retired merchant. Mrs. Marguerite Warren Springer was joint editor and manager with him. Such writers as Robert Barr, Jeffery Farnol, Stanley Waterloo, Frank H. Spearman, Josiah Flynt, Opie Read, and Edwin L. Sabin wrote for the *Wayside* in 1904. In August of that year the Altgeld-Cleveland papers, edited by Mrs. Altgeld, were printed. See Fleming in *American Journal of Sociology*, v. 11, pp. 105–06, June 1906.

paper feature syndicate, revived *Wayside* and took it to Chicago with the issue for October 1903. Many good writers now contributed to the magazine, and some nonfiction articles were inserted; but the publishers were forced into bankruptcy at the end of 1904. Murray S. Schloss then purchased the *Wayside* at receiver's sale, and built it up until failing health caused him to suspend it finally in 1906.

In May 1903, a firm of Chicago retail merchants went into the magazine business, under the leadership of Louis Eckstein, and founded the *Red Book*.[31] They discovered a brilliant young newspaperman and adventurer named Trumbull White and made him editor, published some fine short stories (no serials) and a section of "photographic art" devoted to popular actresses, and at the end of two years saw the magazine on a paying basis with a circulation of some three hundred thousand. In November of the year in which the long and successful career of *Red Book* began, Street and Smith, New York publishers of magazines and paper-backed books, started the *Popular Magazine*,[32] a small-quarto of ninety-six pages, designed "for boys and 'Old Boys,'" and selling for ten cents. It did not last long as a juvenile, however; in 1904 it became a fiction magazine of the *Argosy* type, stressing action, adventure, and the outdoors. Each number contained an installment of a serial, a complete novelette, and several short stories. The circulation was about a quarter-million in 1905. In that year George Agnew McLean became editor of *Popular*, to serve it for more than twenty years.

The leading amateur story magazine of the times was the *Black Cat*,[33] whose success with contests for fiction writers led many other periodicals to adopt such schemes for the double purpose of promotional advertising and the cheap purchase of stories.

Courtland H. Young began a magazine in New Orleans in January 1897 called the *American Clubman*, and changed the name in November to *Young's Magazine*.[34] This periodical belonged to the widespread class

[31] A separate sketch of the *Red Book* will appear in the next volume of this series.

[32] It became a semimonthly Oct. 1909, and a weekly Sept. 24, 1927, returning to semimonthly publication July 7, 1928. In Feb. 1931, it became a monthly again, at 25¢. Title changed to *Popular Stories* Sept. 24, 1927; to *Popular* Jan. 7, 1928; and back to *Popular Magazine* Oct. 20, 1928. It had good contributors in its short life as a juvenile, such as Ralph H. Barbour, Edward S. Ellis, Capt. Charles King, Upton B. Sinclair, Jr. (who later dropped the B. and the Jr.). Later some of the best "pulp" writers contributed, such as B. M. Bower, H. H. Knibbs, Morgan Robertson, H. B. Marriott Watson, Ralph D. Paine, H. C. Witwer, Frederick R. Bechdolt, Peter B. Kyne, Henry C. Rowland, and Rex Beach. *Popular Magazine* ended with the issue for Oct. 1931.

[33] See Sketch 5 in this volume.

[34] It was a 10¢ magazine until Feb. 1907, when it increased to 15¢; Nov. 1918 it went to 20¢. It adopted wood-pulp paper in 1917. Its advertising by this time was handled in the Newsstand Group, composed of several of Young's magazines with similar appeal; it carried only a half dozen pages of advertisements, offering French Love Drops, books on flagellation, Figure Studies, articles of "feminine hygiene," and so on. After Young's death in 1931, Cashel Pomeroy was editor. After Sept. 1933 it was merged in *Breezy Stories*, another of the group.

of local social and amusement periodicals, including some current events, some politics, and a few essays and short stories. But Young moved it to New York in 1903, and there it became more famous, specializing in "snappy stories."

The *New York News Library* was a serial that published four novels in each issue for ten cents. Pirated from English publications, these stories were by such authors as Rider Haggard, George M. Fenn, and Florence Marryat. It was printed on cheap paper in a small-folio format.

There were a number of all-story magazines selling at a nickel a copy. *Gray Goose* was a magazine for amateur contributors somewhat after the style of the *Black Cat* but not so good; it was published in Cincinnati by James Knapp Reeve during 1894–1906, and then sold to the Outing Company, which raised its price in 1908 to ten cents, and discontinued it the next year. The *Owl* (1896–1899), like the *Gray Goose* and *Black Cat,* throve on contests for short-story writers; it was a good-looking Boston magazine and claimed over a hundred thousand circulation at one time. The *White Elephant* (1896–1897) was issued by Frank Tousey, of New York. The *Rough Rider,* published for fourteen months from October 1900 by W. H. Crabtree, of Butte, Montana, was a quarto of sixteen pages, which printed Cutcliffe Hyne and some other notables.

Munsey's *Quaker*[35] began as a thirty-two-page small-folio at two cents a copy, then changed to a two-hundred-page pocket-size magazine at five cents, and finally came to the normal octavo size at ten cents. And there were a number of other short-lived all-fiction magazines in the period.[36]

### "DIME NOVEL" SERIALS

During the period 1885–1905, the dime novel tradition was carried on in two forms. First there was the weekly story paper, such as Beadle's *Banner Weekly* (1882–1897), Elverson's *Saturday Night* (1865–1902) and *Golden Days* (1880–1907), George Munro's *Fireside Companion* (1866–1907), and Norman L. Munro's *New York Family Story Paper*

[35] Title was changed to *Junior Munsey* April 1900. Matthew White, Jr., was probably the editor. At its end, when it was merged in *Munsey's,* it claimed 150,000 circulation. As *Junior Munsey* it was not all fiction, but had stage, literature, and current events departments, travel articles, and so on. Myrtle Reed, Edwin Lefèvre, James L. Ford, Juliet Wilbor Tompkins, E. W. Mayo, Mary Austin, and Albert Bigelow Paine were contributors.

[36] The *Outpost* (1903), Kansas City, began at 7¢ a copy and ended five months later at 5¢; Victor Murdock contributed serial fiction to it. More important was *Two Tales* (1892–93), Boston, a weekly of 24 to 32 pages at 10¢ a number, well printed and carrying some of the best authors then writing. The *Bohemian* (1900–09), Boston, was bought by James Knapp Reeves in 1904 and made a prize-story magazine. Later the Outing Publishing Company took it over and made it a good general magazine. The *Author's Magazine* (1901–03) was issued from Detroit; its contributors were all shareholders. There were also the *Idol* (1901), San Francisco; *Pearl Magazine* (1901), Boston; Mary Lambert's *Raven* (1899–1905), Oakland, Calif.; *White Owl* (1901–02), Philadelphia; and *Blackboard* (1902), St. Paul.

(1873–1921) and *Golden Hours* (1888–1911).[37] Some of these, it will be noted, continued past the end of the century, but they tended to merge with the cheap mail-order journals.[38]

The other class was composed of the many weekly "libraries," each number of which contained a novelette. Most of these were of quarto size with slashing action pictures on the front title pages, though a few were small-folios or octavos. In 1896 Street & Smith began the use of garish covers with the picture in three colors; soon all publishers were following this pattern, because probably nine-tenths of these periodicals were sold from the newsstands and the gaudy covers made a brave show there. A strict enforcement of postal regulations in 1901 denied the second-class mailing privilege to these "libraries," but it was soon discovered that all it was necessary to do to avoid the increase of mailing costs from one to eight cents a pound was to drop the word "library" from the title. And so this class of serial publication continued for many years of the twentieth century to stimulate the imagination of youth, often read behind the shelter of a geography at school or in a haymow hideaway.

Oldest and most durable of this type were *Beadle's Dime Library* and *Beadle's Half-Dime Library*, which began in 1878 and 1877 respectively; both ended in 1905. The same firm published *Waverley Library* (1879–1886), *Beadle's Boys' Library* (1881–1899), and *Beadle's Pocket Library* (1882–1893). In the eighties, and even more in the nineties, the Beadles had strong competition, chiefly from Frank Tousey, George and Norman L. Munro, and Street & Smith. We kidnap and torture a quip from a good commentator on this phase of our periodical literature as we point out that the Beadles had a hard time when, with

> Munros to the left of them,
> Tousey to right of them,
> Street & Smith behind them,
> Onward they blood-and-thundered.[39]

The Beadle firm dropped out of the race in 1897; the old wheel horses were dead, and the "libraries" were declining toward their graves.[40] *Bookseller and Newsman*, giving out the news that the Beadle plates were to be sold, remarked that this all belonged to a past age. Of similar tenor was an article in the *Writer* headed "The Degeneration of the

[37] All these are discussed in Mott, *op. cit.*, v. 3, pp. 42, 43, 178, except the two last-named, which became important in the mid-nineties, reaching large circulations. The *Family Paper* claimed over 250,000 in 1896, and was perhaps more a mail-order journal than a "dime novel" paper. It was priced at $3.00 a year.

[38] For mail-order journals, see pp. 364–68.

[39] See Bob Brown, "Swell Days for Literary Guys," *American Mercury*, v. 27, p. 484.

[40] For the Beadles, as well as some notes on related publishers, see Albert Johannsen, *The House of Beadle and Adams and Its Dime and Nickel Novels*, 2 vols. (Norman, Okla., 1950); and Frank P. O'Brien, *The Beadle Collection of Dime Novels* (New York, 1922).

Dime Novel"[41] — a title that would have bewildered critics of the preceding generation, who thought that the dime novel was degeneracy itself. But these prophets of doom were wrong, for both Tousey and Street and Smith were already launching a new fleet of these series of novelettes for men and boys.

A few of the "libraries" of Beadle's competitors may be mentioned here. The most famous of those issued by George Munro was *Old Sleuth* (1882–1905); and by Norman L. Munro, *Old Cap Collier* (1883–1890). Tousey seems to have begun with the *Wide Awake Library* (1878–1891) and to have continued with many others that ran through part or all of the nineties, and a few that lasted much longer. *Young Sleuth*, which began in 1892, stole a title from the older Munro series; but by that time there were "sleuths" behind every tree. *Secret Service* was a Tousey title beginning in 1899 that took over the achievements of the hero of one of his earlier series, *Old King Brady*. *Pluck and Luck* and *Work and Win* began in 1898. The *Frank Reade Library* began in 1892, the *James Boys Weekly* in 1900, and the *Wild West Weekly* in 1902. And there were many other Tousey series.[42]

Street and Smith were in the cheap fiction business long before Frank Tousey, having published the *New York Weekly* since ante-bellum days.[43] They also had a long list of the dime novel type of weekly, which they sold for a nickel instead of a dime, and which carried some thirty-two pages of thrilling narrative. Top of their list, by title and fact, was *Tip-Top Weekly*, begun in 1896, which gave to literature the priceless character of Frank Merriwell. To American youth at the threshold of the twentieth century, Burt L. Standish's creation had somewhat the same relation to experience and aspiration that the "parfait gentil knight" had to Chaucer's audience. A poetaster in *Tip-Top* (Chaucer's inferior, it must be admitted) once celebrated Frank in song:

> Who makes our youth, with resolution strong,
> Push toward the top, unmindful of the throng?
> Who stands with flashing eyes to greet
> Our struggling heroes, as they meet?
>     Oh, Merriwell!
>
> When all this earthly work is done —
> Life's victory, death's ransom, all are won —
> Who shall be crowned a noble king?
> Why, he of whom we sweetly sing,
>     Our Merriwell![44]

[41] Robert Peabody Bellows, in *Writer*, v. 12, pp. 97–99, July 1899. For *Bookseller and Newsman* item, see v. 14, Feb. 1898, p. 12.

[42] For Tousey, see Mott, *op. cit.*, v. 3, p. 179. Other titles: *Bob Brooks Library*, *Young Wild West*, *Happy Days*, *Blue and Gray*, *Liberty Boys of '76*, *Comic Library*.

[43] Mott, *op. cit.*, v. 2, p. 38.

[44] *Tip-Top Weekly*, no. 468, April 1, 1905, p. 31.

Quite as popular, however, with old and young was the *Nick Carter Library*, begun in 1891, and followed by the *Nick Carter Weekly* five years later, to publish throughout its long career literally thousands of novelettes about the exploits of its detective-hero. *Diamond Dick* (1896) was cut out of the same bolt of cloth. *Log Cabin* and *Nugget*, both started in 1889, were westerns; but they did not achieve the long life of one which began later — *Buffalo Bill Stories* (1901). *Rough Rider Weekly* began in 1903; it carried Ned Taylor's stories about "Ted Strong, the King of the Wild West" and a cowgirl named "Stella."

There were other publishers,[45] and many other series. Publication of this cheap literature continued until after outlets were filled with pocket-books.

"THE TWILIGHT OF POETRY"

An editorial in the *Saturday Evening Post* entitled "In the Twilight of Poetry" asserted in 1898 that "The taste for poetry is becoming a lost accomplishment."[46] This was, of course, an overstatement, but the lack of poetical production of importance was pointed out by many critics. The point was too much labored, thought an editor of *Scribner's Magazine*;[47] but the *Writer* believed that "The quality of magazine verse has grown so poor, and its substance so thin, that critics have ceased to regard it — other than as dainty tailpieces and convenient mechanical interludes."[48] Bliss Perry told the *Writer* that the *Atlantic Monthly* "would give relatively little space to verse," since it hoped to keep up the magazine's tradition in that field.[49] *Current Literature* and the *Literary Digest* made a feature of reprinting the best fugitive verse of the time.

It is probable that the leading magazine poet of our entire period, if we take the number of contributions as our criterion, was Clinton Scollard, a professor of English at Hamilton College, who was well-nigh omnipresent in the magazines. Bliss Carman, Theodosia Garrison, and Ella Wheeler Wilcox were runners-up. The publishers of Mrs. Wilcox's *Poems of Passion*, a rather innocuous *succès du scandale* of the eighties, claimed that "not another book of poems published in this country has had so large a sale."[50]

In January 1889 two reviews devoted to the publication of poetry and

---

[45] For example, the Sibley Publishing Company, with their *Golden Library* (1885), *Cricket Library* (1888), and *Gem Library* (1891).

[46] Editorial signed by M. S. McKinney in *Post*, v. 171, p. 426, Dec. 31, 1898.

[47] *Scribner's Magazine*, v. 11, p. 130, Jan. 1892.

[48] *Writer*, v. 2, p. 144, May 1888.

[49] *Writer*, v. 17, p. 200, Nov. 1904; see also p. 11, Jan. 1905.

[50] Advertisement on cover of *Belford's Magazine*, Nov. 1888.

its criticism were founded, the *Magazine of Poetry* and *Poet-Lore*. The former was begun in Buffalo, New York, by the editor and publisher Charles Wells Moulton, as a quarterly illustrated with portraits of the poets. Each number carried several pages of selections from each of a score or more of poets, with introductory notes, bibliographies, and so on, a department of verse for children, and some pages of single poems. It published both old and new poets, but the emphasis was on the contemporary. Unfortunately, Ione L. Jones neighbors with W. B. Yeats, and George W. W. Houghton with Walt Whitman. It changed to monthly publication in 1893; Moulton lost control of it in 1895, and it was merged with *Poet-Lore* the next year.

*Poet-Lore* was founded in Philadelphia by Charlotte Porter and Helen A. Clarke as a monthly "devoted to Shakespeare and Browning and comparative literature." It served the Browning and Shakespeare clubs by providing reading lists and programs and good critical articles by W. J. Rolfe, H. H. Furness, Oscar L. Triggs, L. A. Sherman, William G. Kingsland, and other scholars in those fields. It also offered serially translations of plays by such Europeans as Hauptmann and Sudermann, Maeterlinck, Björnson, and D'Annunzio. In 1892 Richard G. Badger, of Boston, took over the publication of the magazine, which increased in variety, with verse by the new American writers, more dramatic translations, and much criticism and literary notes of uneven quality. *Poet-Lore* was one of the early partisans of Ibsen, and printed many of the Russian playwrights. It became a quarterly in 1896, when it absorbed the *Magazine of Poetry*; and it was a handsome exponent of contemporary drama and poetry long past the end of the present period.[51]

### LITERARY CRITICISM AND BOOK REVIEWING

"The criticism of criticism is one of the marked literary characteristics of the last ten or fifteen years," wrote John Burroughs in the *North American Review* in 1899.[52] Certainly the perennial disparagement of book reviewing was in evidence in the nineties. "In all the wilderness of reviewing, how seldom do we encounter a real review!" exclaimed Arthur Waugh in the *Critic*. "How many books a year are treated to sound criticism from a man who really knows more about the subject

---

[51] In 1916 Badger published an index of the first 25 volumes, calling attention to the fact that it had published 86 dramas in those years. Later it printed the work of Benavente, Vazquez, Von Kotzebue, and many others. Badger dropped it after 1930, and it published only eight numbers 1931–37. Ruth Hill became one of the editors in 1921, and soon *de facto* editor. John Heard was editor 1933–48, and the quarterly was suspended during the next year; then Edmund R. Brown became editor. It was issued regularly 1950–51; then it expired with numbers for Spring 1952 and Spring 1953.

[52] *North American Review*, v. 168, p. 42, Jan. 1899.

than the writer he is estimating? There is very little such criticism now-adays. . . ." [53] And an *Atlantic* contributor thought that reviews were "written more like advertisements than otherwise." [54] Norman Hapgood joined the chorus in the *Bookman*: "In no country is the current comment on books more lacking in thought and workmanship. . . . In comment on the drama the same low level is unbroken." [55] And yet there was more writing in the magazines about books, literary figures, the drama, and publishing than ever before. Monthlies and weeklies alike carried notes and gossip about such matters, and full-length articles on writers of the past and present and on critical questions were common. The leading controversy in the field was the one over the sins and virtues of the new realism, which had come to us mainly from France and Russia — a wordy quarrel that is discussed earlier in this chapter  Another was the debate between the defenders of the purposeful novel or poem and the art-for-art's-sake advocates. The *Arena* was the most vocal of those who attacked the "arty" school; [56] but there were many to disagree. Said a *Bookman* writer in 1895: "The theory which is known as 'art for art's sake' has long been preached to deaf ears, but the ears are opening." And he added a declaration of conviction that such a doctrine would "inspire and persuade writers of the future." [57]

Many critics were concerned with a growing "immorality" in popular literature. The motherly Amelia E. Barr, a popular novelist herself, wrote in 1894 in the *North American*: "The one thing to be regretted in many of the lighter novels of the day is their kind of heroine. She is not a nice girl. . . . She is frank, too frank." [58] More shrill was *Belford's*, which often inveighed against popular sins: "This country is flooded with a nasty literature that is not only crude, but as low in tone as it is atrocious in taste." [59] Some writers ascribed the prevalent immorality in fiction and drama to French influence, as did Joshua W. Caldwell, writing in the *New England Magazine* on "Our Unclean Fiction." This literary lawyer traced the bad influence "directly to Paris," to Balzac and Zola, to "Sardou and his high priestess of indecency, Sara Bernhardt." [60] Arlo Bates, writing in *Scribner's Magazine*, asserted that "No Frenchman is able to feel himself fully sincere in fiction unless he is indelicate." [61] Others blamed the Russians, Ibsen, or Swinburne. "We

[53] *Critic*, v. 28, p. 413, June 6, 1896.
[54] *Atlantic Monthly*, v. 84, p. 314, Sept. 1899.
[55] *Bookman*, v. 6, p. 45, Sept. 1897.
[56] See p. 408.
[57] H. B. Watson in *Bookman*, v. 2, p. 186, Nov. 1895.
[58] *North American Review*, v. 159, p. 592, Nov. 1894.
[59] *Belford's Magazine*, v. 1, p. 263, July 1888.
[60] *New England Magazine*, v. 3, n.s., pp. 436–39, Dec. 1890.
[61] *Scribner's Magazine*, v. 2, p. 244, Aug. 1887.

are becoming sick of sin," declared William A. Page in his *Bauble* —
"the beautiful, the leprous, the Swinburney sin. It is the fashion nowadays, but the tide is already ebbing."[62]

*Current Literature* lists some of the shockers of 1888. It names Edgar
Saltus and the English Edward Heron-Allen, but it thinks the outstanding thing is

the development of the novel of physical passion as written by young women.
. . . a flood of animal lust . . . . Mrs. Amélie Rives-Chanler broke the ice with
*The Quick or the Dead*, which had been slightly cracked before by Miss Curry,
with her *Bohemian Tragedy*; and Miss Laura Daintrey smashed it into small
pieces in *Eros*.[63]

In its very first number *Current Literature* had remarked on "the
literary sensation of the last two months," the production of "the auda-
cious Virginia girl who wrote *The Quick or the Dead*, as *Puck* wittily
puts it, 'with a low-necked pen.' "[64] Wittily but misleadingly, for there
was no naughty exposure in Miss Rives's passionate, melodramatic
novelette, which had been published originally in *Lippincott's Magazine*
for April 1888. Ella Wheeler Wilcox, who had suffered under the cen-
sorious lash five years earlier for her *Poems of Passion*, came to the
defense of her sister-author with wild laudation in *Current Literature*:

Never before in the history of the civilized world has any author been so
grossly misconstrued, so unfairly criticized, so shamelessly abused without cause
as Amélie Rives, that marvellously endowed girl with the soul of Sappho and the
brain of Shakespeare.[65]

But Edgar Saltus was as severely and widely criticized as Miss Rives.
He should have his name changed to "Edgar Assaulted," said *Belford's*,[66] which was inclined to defend him, doubtless because its own
publishing firm had brought out his first novels in the late eighties. *Life*
called him "that particularly nasty young writer."[67] But by 1896, *Echo*
could refer to Saltus heroes as "the dark mustachio'd darlings of the
dear damsels that thought Saltus novels 'so deliciously wicked.'" Then
it added: "Alas, the years have gone, and Mr. Saltus is no longer the
idol; his novels no more seem impossibly daring; the dear damsels have
taken to novel-writing themselves."[68]

Tolstoi's *Kreutzer Sonata* and *Resurrection* were much criticized by
the moralists, and, on another level, Max Nordau's *Degeneration*.

[62] *Bauble*, v. 1, pp. 7–8, July 1895.
[63] *Current Literature*, v. 1, p. 463, Dec. 1888.
[64] *Ibid.*, p. 3, July 1888.
[65] A "syndicated letter" quoted in *Current Literature*, v. 2, p. 94, Feb. 1889.
[66] *Belford's Magazine*, v. 1, p. 265, July 1888.
[67] *Life*, v. 13, p. 370, June 27, 1889.
[68] *Echo* (no vol.), May 1, 1896, p. 5.

George Saintsbury, reviewing the latter work in the *Bookman*, calls its author "degenerate," while Editor Peck condemns it because "it brings to many persons a knowledge of certain things whose very existence was quite unsuspected before," in quotations from Zola's *Nana* and Ibsen's *Ghosts*, for example.[69] Nordau himself replies to his critics in the *North American Review*, calling them vulgar and ignorant. In the same number, Edmund Gosse, secure in his own elegant intelligence, takes somewhat the same view when he ascribes literary decadence to "the vast and Tartar hordes of readers that now devastate the plains of literature."[70] Literature, he implied, is for the cultivated. But Albert Ross, author of a novel of a roué in the Tweed regime entitled *Thou Shalt Not*, found encouragement in the "broadening" of public taste. "It is but a little while ago," he wrote in the *Arena*, "that women of refinement were afraid to admit that they had read certain books which they now discuss with the greatest freedom."[71]

Even in the early nineties there was reaction against the censors. When New York teachers charged poor dead Longfellow with eroticism in "The Launching of the Ship," some thought the idea silly.[72] "These fault-finding opinions are getting to be about as ridiculous and tiresome as the trashy material complained of," complained *Current Literature*. Theodore Dreiser pointed out the hard lot of the author: "Immoral! Immoral! Under this cloak hide the vices of wealth as well as the vast unspoken blackness of poverty and ignorance; and between them must walk the little novelist."[73]

### LITERARY PERIODICALS

The most important journals of this period devoted to criticism of current literature were the *Literary World*, of Boston, edited in these years by Edward Abbott and N. P. Gilman, and rather dull until enlivened in the year or two before its merger with the *Critic* by a new editor, Bliss Carman; the dogmatic but usually sound Chicago *Dial*, still edited by Francis F. Browne; the New York *Critic*, cultivated, varied, and gossipy under the able editorship of Jeanette L. Gilder; Harry Thurston Peck's *Bookman*, most brilliant of the monthlies; and *Current Literature*, which contained much criticism, along with its rich treasury of reprint material.[74]

[69] *Bookman*, v. 1, p. 180, April 1895; v. 1, p. 371, July 1895.
[70] *North American Review*, v. 161, pp. 80, 118, July 1895.
[71] *Arena*, v. 3, p. 444, March 1891.
[72] *Arena*, v. 5, p. 333, Nov. 1890.
[73] *Booklovers Magazine*, v. 1, p. 129, Feb. 1903.
[74] These magazines are treated in separate sketches in the present volume or the one preceding it in this work.

The *Literary Review* (1897–1901), of Boston, was founded by Edwin Ruthven Lamson as a little five-cent monthly, but as in some sort a competitor of the more pretentious *Chap-Book*, which said of its rival in February 1897:

> People who have been waiting for something that would lift them above the sordid reality of everyday existence — something sweet and pure and true — are advised by the *Review* that they need wait no longer: Mr. Lamson has arrived and has begun to lift.

Percival Pollard contributed a Chicago letter; and Vance Thompson, Richard Le Gallienne, Edwin Arlington Robinson, William Blackburn Harte, and Elbert Hubbard were contributors. But the lifting was not easy. Richard G. Badger became publisher in September 1897, and Karl Stephen Hermann was the new editor in 1900; but the end came the next year.

*Literary Life*[75] was begun in Cleveland, flourished as a general magazine in Chicago for two or three years, and was then suspended during 1887–1898. Revived as a New York Saturday paper of four pages, it became a monthly at fifty cents a year in December 1899. The Abbey Press took it over the next year and made it a handsome royal octavo. Designed for booksellers, libraries, and buyers, it was a rather severe critic. Anna Randall-Diehl merged her *Shakespeare Magazine* with it and became its editor in its final years, 1902–1903.

Even more markedly a victim of changing phases designed to catch the winds of popular favor was the *Literary Era* (1892–1905), which began in Philadelphia as the monthly organ of Porter & Coates, publishers of reprints and mail-order book dealers. For several years it consisted of some twenty-four pages of reviews taken from other periodicals and announcements of the new books. James Walter Smith's London letter appears to have been the only original contribution in the nineties; but in 1901 there were original articles by William S. Walsh and others, and illustrations from new books reproduced on "slick" paper, Joseph Stoddard, Jr., becoming editor. In the fall of that year came the big change in the fortunes of the *Era,* as it was now called: it blossomed out as an illustrated general magazine, with articles about foreign travel, wild animals, the stage, newspapers, and so on. Will M. Clemens' series of "Unsolved Murder Mysteries" was a feaure during 1904–1905. Among contributors were Theodore Dreiser, James Oliver Curwood, Josiah Flynt, Beatrice Harraden, and Joaquin Miller. It was quick to pick up the muckraking challenge of these years. John W. Ryckman was publisher, and he wrote some stories on city politics

[75] See Mott, *op. cit.*, v. 3, p. 234.

obviously modeled on those in *McClure's*. But the *Era* did not have *McClure's* resources, and it failed in the midst of its exposures, in October 1905.[76]

In 1899 Nathan Haskell Dole edited a rather charming little five-cent monthly in Boston called *Book Culture*. The *New York Times* began its *Saturday Review of Books*, earliest of the great modern book review weeklies, October 10, 1896, as a Saturday supplement.[77] But Saturday readers, handling the paper on their way to work, often dropped the insert on the floors of cars or the platforms of the subway; and in 1911 the supplement was made a part of the Sunday paper. Francis W. Halsey was the first editor (1896–1902), and he was succeeded by Edward Dithmar (1902–1907). Good advertising patronage soon forced the publishers to double the size of the original eight-page tabloid, and later to enlarge it further.

*East and West*, though it lasted only a year from November 1899, had a refreshing soundness, and made a good appearance as a small-quarto of thirty-two pages. It was edited by two young men just out of Columbia University, William Aspenwall Bradley and George Sidney Hillman; and it had the concrete encouragement, through contributions, of Professors Odell, Trent, Spingarn, Woodberry, and Erskine, and of other outstanding writers and scholars as well.

In San Francisco two short-lived literary periodicals were attempted at the beginning of the new century: *Literary West* (1902–1904), edited first by Herbert Bashford and then by John G. Jury, and specializing in poetry and economics; and *Impressions* (1900–1905), edited by Paul Elder, devoted largely to book reviews and critical articles. The latter was a handsome magazine, with a good list of contributors, mostly Californians; it turned from monthly to quarterly publication in 1902. In Birmingham, Alabama, the *Bookworm* (1900–1901) was a dollar monthly devoted largely to book reviews and "matters of interest to the South."

BOOKSELLERS' JOURNALS

Also there were many small periodicals issued by publishers and booksellers, some of them much more than house organs. Scribner's *Book Buyer*, and Leypoldt's (now Bowker's) *Literary News*, had been furnishing reliable information about book publication before the

---

[76] Lauriston Ward's exposures of loan sharks (June 1904) and naturalization frauds (Nov. 1904) were notable. Antilabor, the *Era* printed an article on "Lawless Unionism" by D. M. Parry, president of the National Association of Manufacturers (Aug. 1904) and had just begun a series on the labor question by C. W. Post when it quit, merging with the *New England Magazine*. It began exposures of life insurance companies' abuses before Lawson, whom it accused of stealing its thunder. Ryckman suggested a third party in January 1905.

[77] Elmer Davis, *History of the New York Times, 1851–1921* (New York, 1921), pp. 213–17.

eighties began; and they continued through the present period. Wana-maker's *Book News Monthly*, also an older periodical, furnished out-lines for readers' clubs in the nineties, as well as its regular reviews and announcements. *Book Notes for the Week*, of Providence, Rhode Island, continued its interesting career as a local critic.[78]

Dollar monthlies begun in the latter eighties by New York dealers were William Evarts Benjamin's *Book Lover* (1888–1890), edited by Ingersoll Lockwood; and Brentano Brothers' *Book Chat* (1886–1893), edited successively by William George Jordan and Adrian Schade van Westrum. The latter quoted much from new books, as well as literary comment from periodicals; it was especially interested in the novel and in the current magazine. George D. Smith's lively and outspoken *Literary Collector* (1900–1905) had some fine contributions.[79]

*Book Notes* (1898–1902) was a Chicago monthly published at fifty cents a year by the book section of a big department store.[80] *Book Reviews* (1893–1901) was a Macmillan trade journal, and always gave the chief position to Macmillan books, but it reprinted reviews of books issued by other publishers; and it carried some original articles and many news notes.

A few publications were maintained by the book and periodical trade. *Bookmart* continued until 1890, edited by R. Halkett Lord; and the American News Company's *American Bookseller* was issued until 1893,[81] when it was superseded by the *Bookseller, Newsdealer, and Stationer* (1894–1923), a semimonthly at a dollar a year. John J. Daly's *Newsman* (1884–1901) became *Bookseller and Newsman* in 1896. All these were New York periodicals.

The *Book and News Dealer* (1890–1906) began in San Francisco and was later moved to New York; it was a very newsy journal. The Chicago *Bookseller* (1896–1910), published by R. P. Hayes and edited by C. A. Huling, was called *Bookseller and Latest Literature* in its last five years.

### LEARNED JOURNALS OF LITERATURE AND LANGUAGE

On a far higher level of general significance is a group of learned quarterlies dealing with literature and language. The *American Journal of Philology* continued under the humane and able direction of Basil L.

---

[78] See Mott, *op. cit.*, v. 3, pp. 234–36.

[79] See Charles F. Heartman's brochure, *George D. Smith* (Hattiesburg, Miss., 1945), pp. 8–9.

[80] It was called "New Series" from the first, to distinguish it from the Providence *Book Notes*, but changed its name in 1900 to *Book World*. Madison C. Peters was editor until 1901, when he was succeeded by Mrs. Lester Wallack, writing under the name of Florence Gerald (*Journalist*, v. 29, p. 450, April 27, 1901). Siegel Cooper Company was the publisher.

[81] See Mott, *op. cit.*, v. 3, pp. 235–36 for both.

Gildersleeve at Johns Hopkins. *PMLA* (to use the cryptic title that is generally given to the *Publications of the Modern Language Association of America*) grew from the modest beginnings of 1884 to a quarterly of much distinction in its body of contributors and of much variety in its content. The "direct influence" of *PMLA* articles, says one scholar, "has not been monumental"; but he hastens to add that "there is no measuring their indirect influence on the culture of this country. . . . Not a student in our schools, colleges and universities could escape, even if he wished, the influence of the MLA." [82] *Modern Language Notes* was founded at Johns Hopkins by Aaron Marshall Elliott and others as a repository for shorter pieces, reviews, and so on. *Dialect Notes* began at New Haven in 1889 as the organ of the American Dialect Society; [83] it consisted mainly of word-lists. The *Journal of Germanic Philology* was founded by Gustav E. Karsten at the University of Indiana in 1897. In 1903 it was moved to Evanston and its title changed to *Journal of English and Germanic Philology*, Albert S. Cook becoming joint editor. Julius Goebel moved it in 1909 to the University of Illinois, where it has since flourished as a repository of the best scholarship of its field. *Modern Philology* began at the University of Chicago in 1903, and is still published there. The *Journal of Comparative Literature* was a short-lived quarterly published by McClure, Phillips & Company in New York and edited by the Columbia scholars, George E. Woodberry, J. B. Fletcher, and Joel E. Spingarn.

The *Journal of American Folk-Lore* began in 1888, with the Houghton Mifflin Company, Boston, as publishers for the American Folk-Lore Society, which had been organized mainly to publish this quarterly. Francis James Childs was first president of the society, but William Wells Newell was founding editor of the journal. It gathered ballads, tales, superstitions, dialects, of English, Negro, and Indian origin, as well as materials from Canada, the Eskimos, Mexico, the West Indies, and so on. The journal was moved to New York in 1910, Franz Boas being editor at that time, and later to Philadelphia. The Chicago Folk-Lore Society published the *Folk-Lorist* during 1892–1893.

### LEADING AMERICAN WRITERS

Four major American poets died in the early nineties, and the magazines were full of articles about their work. These were Whitman, Lowell, Whittier, and Holmes.

[82] Allen W. Porterfield, "Praise for Professors" in *Sewanee Review*, v. 43, p. 278, July–Sept. 1935. This is a good summary history of *PMLA*. For both *AJP* and *PMLA*, see Mott, *op. cit.*, v. 3, p. 236.

[83] It was issued irregularly through 1935; later it was continued as *Publications of the American Dialect Society*.

Whitman was most discussed. His "Goodbye, My Fancy" had attracted much attention in 1891, and the comment called forth by his death the next year revealed a critical uncertainty expressed by the *Californian Magazine*: "Whitman is dead, and leaves the world undecided as to whether he was a genius or merely a crude laborer in literature."[84] Charles D. Lanier wrote in the *Chautauquan* that it was probable "fifty years hence *Leaves of Grass* will be but a literary curio," and added that Whitman's "utterances may be prophetic, but they are not poetry."[85] But the *Arena* was indignant at such criticism. "It is a shame," wrote the editor, "that the country Whitman loved so well should withhold her praise."[86] So the debate continued throughout our period. Disciple Horace L. Traubel edited and published his monthly *Conservator* in Philadelphia during 1890–1919, eventually devoting it mainly to Whitmaniana — a unique tribute to a poet. In 1897 Traubel's journal admitted as "doubtless true" the *Dial's* opinion that the world was as yet unable to decide whether Whitman was a major or a minor poet, though the *Conservator* had, of course, never shared that uncertainty.[87]

There was no controversy over the greatness of Lowell. In the *Critic's* number celebrating Lowell's seventieth birthday there were scores of tributes. Thomas Nelson Page said he had "enriched the literature of English-speaking people, upheld the honor of the American people abroad, and illustrated that of American citizenship at home."[88] And in the introduction to a symposium of sketches about him in the *Review of Reviews*, just before his death, Lowell was named as "the most eminent American who has lived in the last decade of the century."[89]

Whittier was called "the most national of American writers" by the *Literary News*. On his death, the *News* said:

Sorrow is felt throughout the length and breadth of the land. No other poet has so read the hearts of his own people, interpreted their emotions, and powerfully affected their convictions. Perhaps the most remarkable thing about Whittier was the extent and variety of his influence . . .

with respect to national movements, revelations of the beauty of nature, and directions given to patriotic and religious feelings.[90]

Dr. Holmes's 1886 tour of England, which the *Brooklyn Magazine*

[84] *Californian Illustrated Magazine*, v. 1, p. 669, May 1892.
[85] *Chautauquan*, v. 15, p. 313, June 1892.
[86] *Arena*, v. 5, p. 236, Jan. 1892.
[87] *Conservator*, v. 8, p. 2, March 1897. For fuller discussion of this journal, see pp. 379–80.
[88] *Critic*, v. 14, p. 87, Feb. 23, 1889.
[89] *Review of Reviews*, v. 4, p. 287, Oct. 1891.
[90] *Literary News*, v. 13, n.s., p. 299, Oct. 1892.

called a "triumphal march,"[91] received much attention from American papers and magazines. A writer in *Once a Week* seemed to express the general opinion after his death when she guessed that the ultimate place of Oliver Wendell Holmes "in English literature" would be "well up among the immortals."[92]

A new poet made a dramatic success in 1899 when his "The Man with the Hoe" was printed in magazines and newspapers throughout the land. Said the *Literary Review*: "By a single poem, Edwin Markham leaped to a height of fame that no poet of our time, save Kipling, has attained."[93]

We return to controversy in surveying the contemporary reputation of Mark Twain. The *Literary World*, noting that the Public Library of Concord, Massachusetts, had excluded *Huckleberry Finn* from its shelves, said: "We are glad to see that the recommendation to this sort of literature by its publication in the *Century* has received a check."[94] *Life* called *Huckleberry Finn* "coarse and dreary fun."[95] About the same time the *Critic* reprinted an editorial from the *Springfield Republican* saying that *Tom Sawyer* and *Huckleberry Finn* are "no better in tone than the dime novels that flood the blood-and-thunder reading population"; but it prints in a parallel column the London *Saturday Review's* praise of Mark Twain as "a humorist who is yearly ripening and mellowing."[96] Acceptance of Mark Twain increased during most of the nineties, reaching its peak shortly before the end of that decade.[97] It was in the fall of 1898 that the editor of the *Critic* asked the question, "Who are the four most famous of living authors?" and answered it by naming Mark Twain, Tolstoi, Zola, and Ruskin.[98]

However, most literary Americans of the time would have ranked Howells at the top of writing men this side of the Atlantic. The editor of the *Bookman* in 1896 asserted that Howells was "universally admitted to hold the primacy among living American men of letters."[99] Henry James was still exasperating the general run of critics. William Marion Reedy wrote in his *Mirror*, in reviewing *The Wings of the Dove*: "Like everything else that he has produced, it is one mass of

[91] *Brooklyn Magazine*, v. 4, p. 216, Aug. 1886.
[92] Lily E. F. Berry, in *Once A Week*, v. 14, p. 5, Oct. 20, 1894.
[93] *Literary Review*, v. 3, p. 172, Nov. 1899.
[94] *Literary World*, v. 16, p. 106, March 21, 1885.
[95] *Life*, v. 5, p. 146, March 12, 1885; also see *ibid.*, p. 119, Feb. 26, 1885.
[96] *Critic*, v. 6, p. 155, March 28, 1885.
[97] See unpublished thesis of Maude Humphrey Palmer, "History of the Literary Reputation of Mark Twain in America" (State University of Iowa, 1925), esp. pp. 43–64.
[98] *Critic*, v. 33, p. 224, Oct. 1898.
[99] *Bookman*, v. 2, p. 525, Feb. 1896. Note similar statement by Albert Haw, *Review of Reviews*, v. 5, p. 607, June 1892. But there were dissidents: see *Mahogany Tree*, v. 1, p. 89, Feb. 6, 1892; *ibid.*, pp. 147–48, March 5, 1892.

bewildering abstractions, of verbal legerdemain, of fleshless and blood-less characters."[100]

But not James, nor Howells, nor even Mark Twain led the procession of novelists in mass popularity. E. P. Roe died in 1889, when his books were selling in greater numbers than those of any other novelist in America. Archibald Clavering Gunter was another phenomenal best seller: "From San Francisco to Paris and from Paris back to New York, I saw nothing but *Mr. Barnes of New York*," wrote one reporter in *Current Literature*, and added: "Foreigners persist in regarding it as 'the great American novel.'"[101]

An essayist who was ranked very high in the nineties was Thomas Wentworth Higginson; he had a runaway vote in the essayist class of *Literary Life's* famous voting contest for membership in a proposed American Academy of Immortals.[102]

### ENGLISH WRITERS IN AMERICA

The passing of the great Victorian writers resulted in hundreds of pages of criticism — mostly eulogistic — in American magazines. Arnold died in 1888, Browning in 1889, Tennyson in 1892, Christina Rossetti in 1894, Morris in 1896, Ruskin in 1900, and Spencer in 1903. Tennyson was the giant among them all, thought the *Literary News*, which said, somewhat magisterially:

> It has been conceded by those having authority, as well as by the scribes, that in the whole of English literature the names of Shakespeare, Milton and Shelley can alone stand with his, and the literature of the world can add but few such immortal names.[103]

But as far as popularity was concerned, Shakespeare was challenged, thought some, by Robert Browning. "Will the study of Browning cast out the study of Shakespeare?" asked *New Shakespeareana*.[104] But it was a rhetorical question, and an absurd one, for that journal, which found it strange that the number of Browning clubs multiplied in the nineties while that of the Shakespeare clubs remained static. Arlo Bates thought the explanation lay in the fact that a Browning poem was regarded as "a sort of prize rebus" by these clubs, and it was fun to solve

---

[100] *Reedy's Mirror*, v. 2, p. 4, Feb. 1903. Note a similar complaint in the Cleveland *Index*, v. 1, Oct. 1, 1898, p. 6. But, said *Dixie* (v. 1, p. 56, Jan. 1899), "one must concede that he is literature."

[101] *Current Literature*, v. 1, p. 9, July 1888.

[102] *Literary Life*, v. 1, n.s., Jan. 1, 1900, p. 6.

[103] *Literary News*, v. 13, n.s., p. 341, Nov. 1892.

[104] *New Shakespeareana*, v. 6, p. 92, Feb. 1899; also *ibid.*, v. 7, p. 233, Oct. 1890. For this magazine, see Mott, *op. cit.*, v. 3, p. 237. When it was revived in 1899 it corrected its spelling to *Shakespeareana*.

them.[105] But a similar problem-interest had developed in Shakespeare study as the Baconian theory had excited increasing interest. The *North American Review* gave much space to the Shakespeare-Bacon controversy, including a two-part article by Ignatius Donnelly on Baconian cryptography June–July 1887. "*Life* is ready to prove," declared that irrepressible journal, "that the real author of Ignatius Donnelly is Mark Twain." [106] The *Arena* carried a series on the matter in 1892–1893; and then, the articles having been submitted to a jury of twenty-five famous men, they returned a verdict of twenty for Shakespeare's authorship of Shakespeare.[107] *Shakespeariana* gave much space to what it called "the Baconian Comedy of Errors," and the English *Baconiana* was reprinted in Chicago in 1892. Anna Randall Diehl's *Fortnightly Shakespeare* (1895–1898) became, after its first year, the monthly *American Shakespeare Magazine*. After six years' suspension, *Shakespeariana*, the New York Shakespeare Society's journal, was renewed as *New Shakespeareana*, with Appleton Morgan still editor.

After Tennyson's death there was much discussion about the succession to the poet-laureateship. Morris and Swinburne were understood to have refused it. Rudyard Kipling, Sir Edwin Arnold, and William Watson had their partisans, along with the successful candidate, Alfred Austin.

There were three "literary crazes" in the nineties that came to America from England, but had their origins in other countries — the Kipling craze, weighted with life and lore from India; the *Trilby* craze, founded on adventures of English art students in the Latin Quartier of Paris; and the Omar craze, based on the Fitzgerald translation of the quatrains of a Persian poet.

"Kipling arose, meteoric, like a god out of India," wrote Edmund Gosse in the *North American Review*.[108] In 1897, S. S. McClure told a *New York Tribune* interviewer that Kipling was "the first magazine writer alive — with no Number Two." [109] In 1898, William Marion Reedy referred to Kipling in the *Mirror* as "the greatest living Englishman." [110] But that was not enough, and in 1899 William Dean Howells wrote in the *North American* that Kipling was "at this moment the most famous man in the world . . . all must own this, whatever any may think of his work." [111] Perhaps this judgment, as well as the one that

[105] *Bookmart*, v. 4, p. 20, June 1886, which quotes the *Providence Journal*.
[106] *Life*, v. 8, p. 7, July 1, 1886.
[107] *Arena*, v. 8, p. 746, Nov. 1893.
[108] *North American Review*, v. 165, p. 144, Aug. 1897.
[109] *New York Tribune*, Oct. 10, 1897, supp., p. 7, col. 1. See *Book News*, v. 17, p. 425, April 1899 for similar statement.
[110] *Reedy's Mirror*, v. 8, June 9, 1898, p. 3.
[111] *North American Review*, v. 168, p. 582, May 1899.

follows, was affected by America's anxiety over the famous writer's illness in New York at the height of his popularity. Of this the *Journalist* said:

We have passed through ten days of anxiety and suspense during which we were threatened with the greatest calamity which could fall upon English literature. It seemed more than likely that our greatest living writer — many of us believe the greatest writer the English language has ever known — was to be taken from us at the very beginning of his career — a writer who has won the love and personal regard of his readers as no other writer in any language has done.[112]

Of course, there were Kipling critics. Theodore Roosevelt once called *American Notes* "silly and unintelligent" in the *Cosmopolitan Magazine*.[113] But the reaction was to come later; at the turn of the century Kipling was a Colossus bestriding this narrow world of letters. *Kipling Note Book*, issued also under the title *Kiplingiana*, was a small monthly published for the first nine months of 1899 in New York by Milburg F. Mansfield and A. Wessels.

Of all the fiction serials of the 1890's the greatest success was made by George du Maurier's "Trilby," which appeared in *Harper's Monthly* with the author's own memorable illustrations.[114] As a book, it was an immediate best seller; heated arguments were waged about its morality, clergymen preached about it, songs were written about it, and parodies flourished. Virginia Harned and Wilton Lackaye starred in a successful stage version, and touring companies were soon organized. A new three-dollar shoe was appropriately named after the heroine, and "trilbies" became slang for "feet." A new town in Florida was named Trilby, with streets called for characters in the novel. A patent medicine company published a rhymed synopsis of the story ending:

> Had she spurned Svengali's offer
> When her headache made her sick,
> And just taken Bromo-Seltzer,
> 'Twould have cured her just as quick.

All these curiosities of a popular fad were duly chronicled in a special department of the *Critic* called "Trilbyana," and later published separately under that title.[115]

Edward Fitzgerald's translation of Omar Khayyám's verses was rapidly gaining disciples in the late eighties, with very cheap and

[112] *Journalist*, v. 24, p. 182, March 4, 1899.

[113] *Cosmopolitan Magazine*, v. 14, p. 229, Dec. 1892. See also *Literary Life*, v. 1, n.s., Oct. 14, 1899, p. 4; Cleveland *Index*, v. 1, July 1, 1899, p. 10, quoting several attacks, including one in the June *Arena* by Adachi Kinnosuke.

[114] See Mott, *op. cit.*, v. 2, p. 400.

[115] For data on the popularity of Kipling, *Trilby*, and Omar, see F. L. Mott's *Golden Multitudes* (New York, 1947).

very expensive editions appearing at short intervals. In 1899, Edward Heron-Allen was quoted to the effect that American reprints were appearing "almost daily." Fred Lewis Pattee wrote in the *Booklovers' Magazine* that Omar had "displaced Browning as the literary fad of the hour," and added: "To be able to quote patly from old Omar is supposed to be proof that one has entered a certain esoteric circle wherein are to be found only the elect." [116] Parodies of the *Rubáiyát* were not difficult: one of the most amusing was written and illustrated for *Collier's* in 1904 by Oliver Herford — "The Rubáiyát of a Persian Kitten."

There was much enthusiasm also for the work of Robert Louis Stevenson. The Scribner house published Stevenson in the United States; and *Scribner's* was the chief Stevenson magazine, printing serials and essays by him and articles about him.[117] R. L. S. developed a very loyal personal following, and his disciples could not praise him too highly: wrote one of them in the *North American*, "He will hold a place in the goodly fellowship of the immortals, with Balzac and Defoe and Cervantes and the rest." [118] Thomas Hardy had his partisans, too; and we find a writer in *Munsey's* declaring him the greatest English novelist of the nineties.[119] Ian Maclaren and other members of the "Kailyard School" were popular, and Maclaren had a very successful lecture tour in this country. His lavish Scottish dialect was criticized by many, and *Life* announced a project to translate him into English.[120] A. Conan Doyle, popular on a somewhat different level, had a less successful American tour. Charles Garvice, writer of high-society melodrama for the cheap papers, was rarely mentioned by the critics, most of whom probably knew nothing about him, for his work appeared mainly in the cheap mail-order papers; but *Half-Hour* pointed out in 1897 that he had "won such popularity as is enjoyed by only a few contemporary writers," and it added: "It is a question whether any English author has received as much money from America as Charles Garvice." [121]

### EUROPEAN WRITERS

Said the conservative spokesman for *Scribner's Magazine* in its "Point of View" department in 1891:

One of the most amusing features of the current activity in American fiction is

---

[116] *Booklovers' Magazine*, v. 2, pp. 200–01, Aug. 1903.
[117] See Sketch 28.
[118] *North American Review*, v. 171, p. 358, Sept. 1900.
[119] Anna Leach in *Munsey's Magazine*, v. 10, p. 602, March 1894. Cf. Chicago *Graphic*, v. 10, p. 238, March 24, 1894.
[120] *Bookman*, v. 5, p. 365, July 1897; *Life*, v. 28, p. 544, Dec. 31, 1896.
[121] *Half-Hour*, v. 1, Dec. 1897, p. 4.

surely the attempt to Frenchify it. That such an attempt is being made must, I think, be plain to everyone who follows the literary movement. . . . Reviewers are constantly holding up French models to our writers of stories, and much of the talk in our half-critical, half-gossipy papers is about current French literature; probably more people, literary and other, have recently received a new and stimulating sensation from Maupassant's stories than a short time ago had heard of his name.[122]

But not all critics held up French writers as models; indeed, there was much outright condemnation. "French novels," said *Literary Life*, "with a few notable exceptions, are decadent to the last and most forbidding degree. They almost always portray moral nastiness and end in catastrophe — rise in a cesspool and empty into a sewer." [123]

Émile Zola was more discussed than any other French writer of the day. Condemnation of his work on moral grounds seems to have been almost universal until the latter eighties; it has been suggested that Henry James's article on Turgenev in the *Atlantic*, in which an incidental reference is made to the values of Zola's contribution to the new realism, may have been a turning point.[124] At any rate, there was thereafter more than a little attempt to interpret him fairly. "There is no arguing away such a writer as Zola," contended Edgar Fawcett in 1889.[125] Some of his works of the nineties seemed heavy and revolting to many, but his dramatic defense of Dreyfus raised him greatly in American estimation. William Marion Reedy, in his *Valley Magazine*, called Zola "a coarser Balzac . . . deficient in inspiration"; but he was impelled to add: "He stood up before the world as a champion of Dreyfus. . . . Honor, then to Zola!" [126]

Chief interest in contemporary Spanish writers centered on the work of Palacio Valdés, the naturalistic novelist repeatedly praised in *Harper's* by Howells.[127]

"The interest in Russian literature, especially fiction, has amounted to a positive feature of the year," noted the *Literary World* in its summary of 1886.[128] The Russian authors it mentioned were Turgenev, Tolstoi, Dostoevski, and Gogol. Of these, it was Tolstoi who continued throughout the nineties to keep American attention and excite the highest admiration. "The greatest living novelist, and one of the con-

---

[122] *Scribner's Magazine*, v. 10, p. 394, Sept. 1891.

[123] *Literary Life* (no vol.), Aug. 1901, p. 20.

[124] Herbert Edwards, "Zola and the American Critics," in *American Literature*, v. 4, p. 114, June 1932.

[125] *Belford's Magazine*, v. 3, p. 722, Oct. 1899. Note also E. A. Vizetelly's claim that Zola was making more money than any other writer in the world (*Book Reviews*, v. 4, p. 39, June 1896); and the *Journalist's* disapproval (v. 18, Nov. 19, 1889, p. 8).

[126] *Valley Magazine*, v. 1, p. 117, Oct. 1902.

[127] See also William Henry Bishop, "A Day in Literary Madrid," in *Scribner's Magazine*, v. 7, pp. 187–201, Feb. 1890.

[128] *Literary World*, v. 17, p. 480, Dec. 25, 1886.

spicuous figures of the age," was the evaluation of an *Arena* critic.[129]

German literature was, comparatively at least, neglected in America.[130] It received conspicuous attention in the *Cosmopolitan* in the mid-nineties, a critical series in the *Bookman* in 1900, and so on. But Emil Blum was right when he wrote in the *Arena*:

> While, on the one hand, they [the American people] are cognizant of the changes that have occurred in English and also in French literature . . . they are, on the other hand, hardly aware that a similar process has revolutionized German literature.[131]

The German writers of whom Americans heard most were two dramatists, Hauptmann and Sudermann, who, with Ibsen, will be noticed in Chapter XIV.

### HISTORY AND BIOGRAPHY

The centennial of the establishment of the United States of America in 1789 brought out many special historical editions of periodicals, and there was even more interest in the quadricentennial of the Columbian discovery of America.[132] Echoes of the Civil War were still heard in the magazines of the latter eighties — a kind of postscript to the *Century's* famous series of generals' recollections. Also there was a "wave of 'patriotic hereditary' enthusiasm" through the nineties, which resulted in many genealogical studies.[133] The death of Francis Parkman in 1893 brought forth a number of tributes to that great historian. But it was thought by many that historical writing had changed greatly under the influence of "the scientific method," Winsor, Henry Adams, and the Johns Hopkins scholars being cited. "History seems to be becoming more and more a department of rigid science and less associated with literature," wrote one critic.[134]

Biography was very strong both in the magazines and in book publication. "The last half of the present century has developed an extraordinary mania for heroes and hero worship," wrote the author-adventurer Chaillé-Long in the *North American Review* in 1887.[135] And George Pellew said in the *Critic* a few years later that "it is in

---

[129] *Arena*, v. 15, p. 279, Jan. 1896. Ernest Howard Crosby, the critic quoted, later wrote a book on Tolstoi. Cf. statement in *Munsey's* that "no other Russian writer has ever enjoyed so wide a popularity in this country" (v. 19, p. 281, May 1898); and the *Unitarian's* gratitude to Howells for his defense of Tolstoi (v. 3, p. 247, June 1888).

[130] See J. P. von Grueningen, "Goethe in American Periodicals, 1860–1900," *PMLA*, v. 50, pp. 1155ff, Dec. 1935.

[131] *Arena*, v. 8, p. 212, July 1893.

[132] There was a short-lived *Discovery of America* magazine published at St. Paul in 1892; in it both Columbus and Ericsson had their innings.

[133] *Genealogical Advertiser*, v. 4, p. 98, Dec. 1901.

[134] George Pellew in *Critic*, v. 18, p. 30, Jan. 17, 1891.

[135] *North American Review*, v. 144, p. 507, June 1887.

biography and autobiography that the best work, excepting fiction, has been done of late years." [136] Series of biographies were popular with the book publishers. In the magazines the personal, or confessional, type of autobiographical article was common, especially in series. Thus the *Forum* in 1886 had articles by famous men on their educations, and about the same time the *North American Review* published a series on the religious experiences of men of note ("Why I Am a Methodist," for example), while *Lippincott's* was printing a series on how literary men got their start, and the *Ladies' Home Journal* was devising all kinds of personal questions for well-known people. The longest biographical serial of the period was Nicolay and Hay's "Abraham Lincoln: A History," which ran through more than two years of the *Century*, during 1887–1890. And what Flower called in the *Arena* "the Napoleonic craze" [137] was perhaps the most noticeable of all the biographical phenomena of the nineties.

Periodicals in this field were virtually all supported in whole or in part by historical or genealogical associations. Such organizations often published irregularly, whenever they had material on hand to send to the printer. No attempt will be made here to list such associations, or their "Collections," "Registers," "Records," "Publications," and "Proceedings," nor will the ventures of short life be named unless they have peculiar importance. But in the latter half of the nineteenth century, a number of the great historical societies began to publish the papers read at their meetings in quarterly numbers, which may be regarded as periodicals, and which continued for many years.[138] The periodicals in the field fall into four classes: (1) those of national scope, (2) organs of state or regional historical societies, (3) genealogical collections and magazines, and (4) archeological journals.

Ten historical and genealogical journals that had been founded before 1885 were published throughout the whole of the present period; the oldest of them was the perennial *New England Genealogical and Historical Register*.[139]

[136] Pellew, as above.

[137] *Arena*, v. 15, p. 347, Jan. 1896. Also see p. 230 of this volume.

[138] See unpublished dissertation by Maxwell Otis White, "History of American Historical Periodicals" (State University of Iowa, 1946). The American Antiquarian Society seems to have been the first to regularize the publication of its *Proceedings*, which began in 1812, with regular semiannual issues in 1849.

[139] Others were *Firelands Pioneer, Now and Then, New York Genealogical and Biographical Record, Pennsylvania Magazine of History* and *American Catholic Historical Researches*, named in the order of their founding. For these, see Mott, *op. cit.*, v. 3, pp. 159–62, where there are also notes on the *New Amsterdam Gazette* (1883–95) and the *Maine Historical and Genealogical Recorder* (1884–98).

The *Records of the American Catholic Historical Society of Philadelphia* is a quarterly founded in 1884. It absorbed the same organization's *American Catholic Historical Researches* in 1912. The *United States Catholic Historical Magazine* was conducted from 1887 to 1892 by the United States Catholic Historical Society, of New York, and was then succeeded by the *Historical Studies and Records* of that society. Historical and biographical studies, documents, notes and queries, and proceedings of their respective associations characterized these journals.

The *American Historical Review* was founded in October 1895 by a guarantee fund to run for three years; after that time it was taken over by the American Historical Association and the subscription price included in the membership fee. Editors were elected by the association. The managing editor for many years was John Franklin Jameson, who was a professor of history at Brown when first chosen.[140] Some of America's ablest historians served on the board of editors for a few terms — among them, Albert Bushnell Hart, John Bach McMaster, James Harvey Robinson, and Frederick Jackson Turner. Contributors have likewise included from time to time the great historians, and the range of topics has been wide. Departments are provided for documents, reviews, and notes of progress and news in the field. The book reviews furnish an important part of the journal, being authoritative and scholarly. On the whole, this review, well produced by the Macmillan Company in New York, has been, though sometimes dullish, in the top rank of learned journals.

Joseph W. Porter's *Bangor Historical Magazine* (1885–1894) broadened its scope and became *Maine Historical Magazine* in its last two years. The *Dedham Historical Register* (1890–1903), Julius H. Tuttle, editor, was produced quarterly by the Historical Society of Dedham, Massachusetts. The *Essex Antiquarian* (1897–1909), Sidney Perley, editor, was strong on graveyard inscriptions and on illustration. The *Jerseyman* (1891–1905) was published at Flemington, New Jersey. The *Pennsylvania-German* (1900–1914), founded at Lebanon by P. C. Croll, was a pleasant and valuable journal with a character of its own. Its folklore and dialect verse were especially interesting.[141] The *His-*

---

[140] Except for Andrew C. McLaughlin's service 1901–05, Jameson was managing editor 1895–1928; Dana C. Munro followed 1928–29, Henry E. Bourne, 1929–36, Robert Livingston Schuyler, 1936–43; Guy Stanton Ford, 1943–53; Boyd C. Shafer, 1953–current.

[141] An illustrated monthly at $1.00 a year, it was "devoted to the history, biography, genealogy, poetry, folk-lore, and general interests of the Pennsylvania-Germans and their descendants." It had several changes of ownership and place of publication after 1906, and for the last three years was called *Penn Germania*. It was suspended April 1913–Aug. 1914, but the war finally killed it.

*torical Record of Wyoming Valley* (1886–1908) was published at Wilkes-Barre under the editorship of F. C. Johnson.

Out in the Midwest, a second series of the *Annals of Iowa*, published at Iowa City, was succeeded in 1885–1902 by the *Iowa Historical Record*, of the State Historical Society; and that was followed in 1903 by the *Iowa Journal of History and Politics*, a repository of scholarly studies and notes in the field, now called *Iowa Journal of History*. Meantime, the State Historical Department at Des Moines began a third series of the *Annals* in 1893.[142] A journal of much the same character is the *Oregon Historical Quarterly*, founded in Salem by the Oregon Historical Society, later moved to other cities and finally back to Portland. The *Magazine of Western History* (1884–1895) was a good journal while it was published at Cleveland, but it later deteriorated.[143]

The *Publications of the Southern Historical Association* (1897–1907), of Atlanta, was at first a quarterly and later a bimonthly; it was broad in scope, published many documents, and had some distinguished editors and contributors. The *William and Mary College Quarterly Historical Magazine* (1892–current) was long edited by President Lyon G. Tyler. The *Lost Cause* (1889–1904) was begun as a monthly at seventy-five cents a year in Louisville, to "record the history of the Southern side during the Civil War." Ben La Bree was the founder, but the periodical was soon taken over by the United Daughters of the Confederacy. The *Virginia Magazine of History and Biography* (1893–current) is published by the Virginia Historical Society at Richmond. Its file contains much documentary material and is much used by genealogists. Philip Alexander Bruce was its first editor. The *South Carolina Historical and Genealogical Magazine* (1900–current) is published at Charleston by the state's historical society. The *Quarterly of the Texas State Historical Association* (1897–current), Austin, changed its title to *Southwestern Historical Quarterly* in 1921. The *American Historical Magazine* (1896–1904), of Nashville, Tennessee, was the quarterly organ of the Tennessee Historical Society.

The *Gotham Monthly Magazine* (1890) became *Adams' Magazine of General Literature and Authorized Exponent of the Daughters of the Revolution* (1891–1892), and that became in turn the *Magazine of the Daughters of the Revolution* (1893–1896), New York. Likewise,

---

[142] The first series of the *Annals* was published in Burlington by the State Historical Society of Iowa 1863–74; the second series was published in Iowa City by Samuel Storrs Howe, 1882–84.

[143] See Mott, *op. cit.*, v. 3, p. 262.

the *American Monthly Magazine*, begun in 1892 by the Daughters of the American Revolution, changed title repeatedly; but it was, on the whole, more literary than its sister magazine.[144] The *Mayflower Descendant* (1899–1940) was issued quarterly by the Massachusetts Society of Mayflower Descendants, George Ernest Bowman, editor. The *Genealogical Quarterly Magazine* (1890–1917), of Salem, Massachusetts, had several titles.[145] Other genealogical-record magazines were shorter-lived, and many were devoted to individual families.[146]

The *American Journal of Archaeology* was begun in 1885 by the Archaeological Institute of America, A. L. Frothingham, of Princeton, being its first editor. It has been a quarterly except for an experiment in bimonthly publication during 1897–1899. The institute was and is concerned chiefly with classical archeology; and this *Journal* has, for the most part, comprised reports to the members and technical matter. *Biblia* (1888–1905), of Meriden, Connecticut, was mainly a reporter of the discoveries in "biblical archeology" made under the Egypt and Palestine Exploration Fund. The *Journal of American Ethnology and Archaeology* (1891–1908) was edited through most of its life by J. Walter Fewkes, who was later Chief of the Bureau of American Ethnology; it was less a periodical than a series of monographic reports on the Hemenway Southwestern Archeological Expedition. *Records of the Past* (1902–1914) was a good-looking magazine founded by Henry Mason Baum as the organ of an exploration society in Washington, D. C.; George Frederick Wright was associated with it editorially for several years. There were a number of state and regional archeological journals.[147]

[144] The novelist Natalie Sumner Lincoln was editor 1917–35. The magazine ended in 1946.

[145] See Library of Congress Catalog for changes, index, and so on. It was *Putnam's Historical Magazine* 1892–99, published by Eben Putnam.

[146] Among the more important were *American Ancestry* (1887–99), Albany; *Magazine of New England History* (1891–93), Newport; *American Historical Register and Monthly Journal of the Patriotic-Hereditary Societies of the U.S.A.* (1894–97), published first in Philadelphia and later in Boston, well printed and illustrated, and edited in its latter years by James Grant Wilson; *"Old Northwest" Genealogical Quarterly* (1898–1912), Columbus, Ohio; *New Hampshire Genealogical Record* (1903–10), Dover; *Genealogical Exchange* (1904–11), Buffalo.

[147] The *Ohio State Archaeological and Historical Quarterly*, begun in 1887, is the organ of the society of that name. It published contributions from many well-known scholars, such as A. B. Hart, G. F. Wright, and W. H. Venable, on archeology, biography, early land companies, pioneer life, the Indians, political history, and so on. The *Wisconsin Archaeologist* (1901–current), Milwaukee, is also a local Archaeological Society organ. The *Quarterly Journal of the Berkshire Archaeological Society* (1889–95) was succeeded by *Berks, Bucks and Oxon Archaeological Journal* (1895–1930), later *Berkshire Archaeological Journal*. For lists of historical journals, see White, "History of American Historical Periodicals," and Augustus H. Shearer, "American Historical Periodicals," in *Annual Report of American Historical Association*, 1916.

Though the cheap libraries of the latter seventies and the eighties came to grief in the hard times of 1893 and thus ended what had been the country's longest period of low-price publishing,[148] a new era of cheap books came in at the turn of the century, with the offerings of Street & Smith, F. M. Lupton, Henry Altemus, A. L. Burt, and so on. Their books are advertised in the mail-order magazines. Lupton listed in a "Bargain Sale" of books in the *Boston Home Magazine* of May 1900, such popular numbers as *Dr. Jekyll and Mr. Hyde* for one cent, *A Study in Scarlet* and *Treasure Island* for three cents apiece, *Vanity Fair* for five cents, and Dickens' *Works* in twelve volumes for forty-eight cents.[149] Though cheaply printed and paper bound, these were not abridgements.

This type of publication had a profound effect on the establishment of best sellers as such. The term "best seller" was not used in application to books in the period now under consideration, but several magazines showed an active interest in large sales in the publishing field — *Current Literature*, the *Critic*, and the *Bookman* especially. The last-named published, from the time of its first appearance in 1895, lists of books "in the order of demand" at the bookstores, in imitation of the practice of the London *Bookman*. The *Bookman's* monthly and yearly lists excited much interest.[150] They did not include mail-order sales.

Best sellers are mentioned on many pages of this volume, but it may be useful to insert here a brief list of titles that were at the top in sales through the years 1885–1905. They include some published before 1885, such as *Ben-Hur, Tom Sawyer, Treasure Island*, and the *Rubái-yát*. Among the books from England that were top best sellers in the United States were Haggard's *She* and *King Solomon's Mines*, Corelli's *Thelma* and *A Romance of Two Worlds*, Mrs. Ward's *Robert Elsmere*, Conan Doyle's *Adventures of Sherlock Holmes*, Kipling's early tales, du Maurier's *Trilby*, Anthony Hope's *Prisoner of Zenda*, and Ian Maclaren's *Beside the Bonnie Brier Bush*. The outstanding best seller from European literature was *Quo Vadis*. Two best sellers of the eighties by American authors were written about children — but what different types! They were Mrs. Burnett's *Little Lord Fauntleroy* and Mark Twain's *Huckleberry Finn*. Among top best sellers by American authors were Gunter's *Mr. Barnes of New York*, Westcott's *David Harum*, Winston Churchill's historical novels, Ford's *Janice Meredith*,

---

[148] See F. L. Mott, *Golden Multitudes* (New York, 1947), ch. 23, for an account of that period.
[149] *Home Monthly*, v. 23, p. 23, May 1900.
[150] See Sketch 8 in this volume.

Wister's *The Virginian*, London's *The Call of the Wild*, and Sheldon's *In His Steps*.[151]

### WRITERS' MAGAZINES

A number of periodicals intended to aid the beginning writer appeared during the eighties and nineties. Most important of these was the *Writer* (1887–current), of Boston, which was founded and long conducted by William H. Hills. Hills was a busy man, editor of a local weekly at Somerville, conductor of a literary syndicate, director of the Writer's School of Journalism and Literary Training (which he operated by correspondence), and sole editor and publisher (after he bought out a partner) of the *Writer*. In his new monthly Hills printed "experience talks" by well-known writers, much news and notes about successful authors, all kinds of advice to beginners in literature, including some by Eugene Didier on the proper qualities for an author's wife (November 1888), and lists of the prize contests current in the nineties. In 1889 Hills started the *Author* as a kind of eclectic supplement of the *Writer*; it continued for three years. Margaret Gordon relieved Hills as editor of the *Writer* from 1902 to 1925.

The *Bulletin of the Society of American Authors* began at Dobbs Ferry, New York, December 1899, and changed its name to *American Author* two years later. Mrs. M. P. Ferris, editor, wrote most of it, and it ended with a number for November 1903–March 1904. Like the *Writer*, it was illustrated with portraits of successful authors. *Editor* (1895–1942) was a monthly "journal of information for literary workers."

### DEVELOPMENT OF LIBRARIES

In the period 1885–1905 occurred a phenomenal expansion of the free public-library system, which was due to a combination of municipal expenditures with many generous gifts from the wealthy. Andrew Carnegie, who distributed a large part of his philanthropy to smaller cities, was the dramatic figure in this movement.

In 1885, according to the *Library Journal*, there were only about three thousand libraries in the United States having as many as a thousand volumes on their shelves,[152] and few of these were free public libraries. By 1903, Helen E. Haines, managing editor of *Library Journal*, could write of the expanding system of such libraries as follows, in *World's Work*:

It is working toward the development of a national institution as distinctive

---

[151] See Mott's *Golden Multitudes* for fuller lists.
[152] *Library Journal*, Jan.–Feb. 1887, contains a list of these libraries.

and influential as our public school system. Ten years have seen the beginning and progress of this development. . . . The last five years count for most of all in their remarkable record of endowments and gifts — so largely the result of Mr. Carnegie's "investments" in library futures. . . . Each year an increasing number of cities and towns accept the maintenance of a public library as a proper municipal charge.[153]

The *Library Journal*,[154] of which R. R. Bowker was publisher after 1884 and editor after 1893, continued to be the leading journal in the field. *Public Libraries* (1896–1931) was a Chicago monthly edited by Mary Eileen Ahern chiefly for the smaller libraries and the associations of librarians. It later broadened its field somewhat, and was called *Libraries* after 1925. *Library Notes* was a little journal by Melville Dewey (or Melvil Dui), published very irregularly during 1886–1898 in Boston, and devoted mainly to time-saving methods and mechanical devices for librarians. *Medical Libraries* (1898–1902) was the organ of the Medical Library Association.[155] The *Bulletin of Bibliography* (1897–current) was begun by the Boston Book Company, which later became the F. W. Faxon Company. The first two quarterly numbers were edited by Thorvald Solberg, after which Frederick Winthrop Faxon conducted the journal until his death.[156] It has published many valuable special bibliographies, and has given much attention to periodicals.

[153] *World's Work*, v. 5, p. 3086, Feb. 1903.
[154] See Sketch 29 in Mott, *History of American Magazines*, v. 3.
[155] This was followed briefly by a *Bulletin*, and then by the *Medical Library and Historical Journal* (1903–07), which was in turn succeeded by the *Aesculapian* (1908–09), described as "A Quarterly Journal of Medical History, Literature and Art."
[156] After Faxon's death in 1936, Mary E. Bates was editor for eight years, and Anne Sutherland has occupied that position since 1945. This periodical began publishing a Magazine Subject-Index in 1907; and two years later a "Dramatic Index," which was continued until 1953.

# CHAPTER IX

## THE GRAPHIC ARTS

OUR great national and international fairs and expositions have always been effective stimulators of popular interest in art. A writer in the *Park Review* in 1901, looking back at the preceding quarter-century with pride in America's artistic progress, gave to the Centennial Exposition of 1876, at Philadelphia, which "stimulated native talent by its large collection of foreign paintings," credit for inaugurating that period of growth.[1] The Columbian Exposition of 1893, at Chicago, was recognized from the first as epochal in American art. "The fair at Chicago," wrote Charles de Kay in the *Cosmopolitan* shortly after the gates opened, "is one of those events which are rightly regarded as fixing dates in the history of the fine arts . . . a turning point in the fine arts for the nation."[2] And the *Nation* said that the Buffalo exposition displayed "the most complete and representative exhibition of American art ever got together."[3]

Long before the World's Fair, there had been a revolt against the National Academy of Design and its conservatism by the Society of American Artists. Declared *Life*: "A national academy it is not. No such institution is national when run by a handful of men ten or twenty years behind their brother artists."[4] This was said in a notice of the exhibition of 1885; six years later a critic in *Scribner's* was declaring "the present time an epoch of impressionism, so almost universal is the impressionistic attitude at present, and so novel is it as well. . . . A few years ago neither the name nor the thing was known at all."[5] This was progress in American art, which steadily developed new personalities and new techniques.

Art criticism is a field from which the dogmatist should be barred; yet an essay in the *New England Magazine* in the mid-nineties, called "Later American Masters," is worth quoting, opinionated though it is. "We possess," say the coauthors, "five American masters." They are named as "Winslow Homer, the recluse; George Innes, the seer; John La Farge, the colorist; James Whistler, the symphonic; and, lastly, A. P. Ryder." They place Sargent, Volk, Vedder, and Eastman Johnson with others in a second class; while Eakins, Blashfield, Chase, and

---

[1] Paul P. Boyd in *Park Review*, v. 1, p. 86, Jan. 1901.
[2] *Cosmopolitan*, v. 16, p. 265, July 1893.
[3] *Nation*, v. 73, p. 127, Aug. 15, 1911.
[4] *Life*, v. 5, p. 230, April 23, 1885.
[5] *Scribner's Magazine*, v. 9, p. 657, May 1891.

Kenyon Cox were not even in the second class.[6] Both Chase and Sargent were highly praised as portraitists in the nineties, and toward the close of the decade the former enjoyed a high reputation in other genres. According to Perriton Maxwell, writing in the *Saturday Evening Post* in 1899, Chase was "a master-painter who does superbly all that he tries to do, and some things better than any man living." [7]

Our present period ends a few years before the revolution of the "moderns" began, but the influence of French painters, salons, and schools was important through study abroad on the part of our artists. "Our adolescent art," wrote a *Scribner's* editor in 1891, "is forming itself on Gallic lines." [8] Thereby American representationism was being undermined by the impressionism of Manet, Degas, Renoir, Monet, and the rest. But the movement for realism in literature also affected painting. At any rate, we find *Brush and Pencil* declaring in 1897: "Art must step out of the picture gallery . . . and go into the streets." [9]

Though "art" was generally thought of as painting in oils or water colors, growing appreciation of sculpture, architecture, and even home decoration was widening the concept. "Good sculpture is becoming *la mode* in this western land," wrote Lorado Taft in the *Chautauquan* in 1896; and added, "The change wrought in the last twenty-five years is something wonderful." [10] Though William P. P. Longfellow complained in *Scribner's* that "the current of public interest" had drifted away from architecture as an art, a new and inspiring American type of high building for the large city — the "sky-scraper" — was developed in the early nineties. "Through it the thoughts of our architects are being turned to new principles of design," said another *Scribner's* writer. "Through it our cities are being transformed. . . . It is changing our business methods and our daily life." [11] But home decoration was not in step with the revolutions in the other arts. "Decorative Jim-Jams" was the title of an article in *Woman's Column* in 1890:

Throughout the length and breadth of the land, female America is busy decorating the interior of her domicile with a sort of artistic erysipelas. . . . Fans and feathers, plaques and palettes, ribbon-bowed tambourines with their sheepskin heads containing tableaux of Faust and Marguerite, who closely resemble the historical figures of Jack and Jill, or the allegory of "Mary Had a Little Lamb,"

[6] William Howe Downes and Frank Torrey Robinson in *New England Magazine*, v. 14, pp. 133–34, April 1896.
[7] *Saturday Evening Post*, v. 172, p. 347, Nov. 4, 1899; cf. Ernest Knauff in *Theatre*, v. 5, p. 165, Feb. 23, 1889.
[8] *Scribner's Magazine*, v. 9, p. 261, Feb. 1891.
[9] *Brush and Pencil*, v. 1, p. 14, Sept. 1897.
[10] *Chautauquan*, v. 22, p. 387, Jan. 1896.
[11] *Scribner's Magazine*, v. 9, p. 127, Jan. 1891; *ibid.*, v. 15, pp. 297–318, March 1894.

the lamb distinguishable from Mary only by its possession of four legs . . . spinning wheels in their holiday dress of paint and furbelows, churns converted into umbrella stands, decorated with flowers that resemble the contents of a chiropodist's showcase. . . .[12]

On the whole, in spite of the challenge of world's fairs, and in spite of certain aggressive movements which showed that fine arts were very much alive in America, there was a serious lack of popular appreciation of, and interest in, such matters. *Municipal Affairs* pointed out in 1898 that there was not a single municipal art gallery in the United States, though steps in that direction were presently being taken.[13] *Truth in Boston* declared in 1896 that "the real reason why artists starve in Boston is the fact that Boston has no genuine love for art"; [14] and the same could be said for nearly all American cities. The *Artist* pointed out about the same time that the great newspapers, which gave their readers news and comment on books, the theater, and music, gave very little space to painting, sculpture, and architecture; and it explained: "It is simply because the public is not supposed to be very greatly interested in them." [15]

### FINE ARTS IN THE MAGAZINES

The magazines did somewhat better by the fine arts than the newspapers, though even they did not make art a major subject. *Scribner's* was more intelligently devoted to the various art movements than were any other of the general magazines. The *Century* continued Timothy Cole's famous procession of engravings of old masters, and its series on cathedrals by Joseph Pennell was notable. Many other magazines reproduced art subjects, but usually with an eye to attractive illustration rather than with the intention of presenting significant art criticism.

The only art periodicals that maintained a circulation of as much as ten thousand throughout our period were the *Art Amateur* and the *Art Interchange*, of New York, both of which had been begun in the seventies.[16] The London *Studio* began the publication of an American edition in 1897 under the name of *International Studio*. It carried an American section in addition to the complete London magazine.[17] The

---

[12] *Woman's Column*, v. 1, Jan. 11, 1890, p. 1.
[13] *Municipal Affairs*, v. 2, p. 1, March 1898.
[14] *Truth in Boston*, v. 1, Feb. 29, 1896, pp. 2–3.
[15] *Artist*, v. 23, p. xvii, Oct. 1898; cf. similar conclusions in *Belford's Magazine*, v. 6, p. 121, Dec. 1890.
[16] See F. L. Mott, *History of American Magazines* (Cambridge, 1938), v. 3, p. 185.
[17] Peyton Brothers took over the publication of the American edition, making it independ-

London *Artist* also had an American edition, including an eight-page supplement called "The American Survey," edited by Charles H. Caffin. A quarto, with beautiful halftones, it lasted only from September 1898 through January 1902. Two New York art journals devoted, at least during this period, to the sales and collecting field, must be named here. The *Collector* (1889–1899) was a monthly conducted by Alfred Trumble; it was continued as *Collector and Art Critic* (1899–1907). *Hyde's Weekly Art News* began in 1902 as a weekly giving news of exhibitions and sales; James Clarence Hyde sold it two years later to James B. Townsend, who changed its title to *American Art News*.[18]

In Boston the famous lithographing firm headed by Louis Prang published the quarterly *Modern Art* (1893–1897); and Eugene Ashton Perry, who conducted a big business in halftone prints of famous art masterpieces at low prices "for home and school," published the monthly *Perry Magazine* (1898–1906) to promote his mail-order sales. Another Boston monthly was *Masters in Art* (1900–1909), a series of monographs on famous artists, each illustrated by some twenty full-page reproductions of the work of the artist treated.

Out in Chicago, *Brush and Pencil* (1897–1907) was closely related, at its inception, to the Chicago Art Institute. Charles Francis Browne was its editor during its first three years, and he was followed by Frederick W. Morton. Lorado Taft, John H. Vanderpoel, and James William Pattison were chief contributors at first. As it proceeded, the journal broadened its scope to international interests and increased its illustration, using some color plates.[19] The *Fine Arts Journal* (1899–1919), later to be likewise connected with the institute, began obscurely as a trade publication.[20]

*Art Education* (1894–1901) was conducted by James Clell Witter, of New York, for the cause of art teaching in the schools. Another New York magazine was the *China Decorator* (1887–1901), edited by Mrs. O. L. Baumuller. *Keramic Studio* began in Syracuse, New York;

ent, in 1921. William B. McCormick was president and editor 1921–28; H. J. Whigham conducted it 1928–31, after which it was merged in the *Connoisseur*. Vols. 1–32 of London *Studio* correspond to 10–41 of *International Studio*. It was well printed and edited, with sketches of artists, reviews of exhibitions, and attention to crafts.

[18] It became *Art News* in 1923. Townsend gave the journal variety and richness of content, with fine illustration. It acquired some millionaire backers (Marshall Field III, Thomas J. Watson) in 1941 and changed from a $7.00 weekly to a semimonthly at $4.50; later it became a monthly devoted to art and antiques.

[19] See Herbert E. Fleming, "Magazines of Chicago," *American Journal of Sociology*, v. 11, pp. 794–96, May 1906. Later it was planned to issue *Brush and Pencil* in Chicago simultaneously with *Salon of Dilettanti* in New York; but the former ended with April 1907 and the latter was issued only Jan.–June 1907 and Jan.–April 1908.

[20] Pattison, a teacher at the institute, was editor for some years. It was a fine, well-printed magazine in its latter years, broad in scope, but much devoted to the West and to the Chicago Plan of civic improvement.

it adopted the title *Design* in 1924, and has been published latterly in Columbus, Ohio. The *Craftsman* (1901–1916) was begun at Eastwood, New York, by Gustave Stickley, a disciple of Morris and Ruskin and a manufacturer of furniture. It abandoned its Morris format in 1904, broadened its scope to include much about houses and gardens, and even printed some fiction and poetry. Another magazine which followed Morris and Ruskin was the *Artsman* (1903–1907), organ of the Rose Valley art and craft center near Philadelphia, of which Horace Traubel was one of the editors. And there were many other periodicals devoted to varied phases of art.[21]

### THE GROWTH OF PHOTOGRAPHY

The development of the rapid dry plate in the eighties was an invitation to the amateur photographer. The coming of the handy Kodak, relieving the amateur from the trouble of developing his own negatives, was an even greater incentive. Both of these developments were due largely to the genius of George Eastman. The *American Amateur Photographer* declared in 1902 that to Eastman

more than to any other, or perhaps than to all the others together, and especially to the happy thought that evolved the catch sentence, "You press the button, we do the rest," is to be attributed the omnipresence of the camera today.[22]

The 1889 convention of the Photographers' Society of America at Boston attracted much attention because it celebrated at once the fiftieth anniversary of Daguerre's first success and the twentieth birthday of the society.[23] Photography at the Columbian Exposition, however, was "grossly mismanaged," according to the *Photo Beacon*.[24] The progress of illustration by photoengraving and the interest of amateurs were both tremendous stimulants to photography in the nineties. The camera was important in the coverage of the war with Spain by magazines and newspapers.[25] By the end of our period the use of cameras had become a great popular diversion. Wrote "The Cynic" in *Town Topics*:

---

[21] Ernest Knaufft's *Art Student* (1892–1907) was a modest, well-printed journal designed to teach drawing at home. *Arts for America* (1892–1900) was edited by Mrs. T. Vernette Morse in Chicago. *Sketch Book* (1902–07) was another Chicago monthly "devoted to the fine arts." *Art Review of Pictures and Frames* (1900–13) was a trade journal published first in St. Louis and then in New York. *American Art in Bronze and Iron* (1902–19) was a New York journal.

[22] *American Amateur Photographer*, v. 14, p. 99, March 1902.

[23] See *Photo Beacon* for 1889, "the Jubilee Year of Photography." J. F. Ryder, of Cleveland, was the society's first president, and its first convention-exhibition was held at Boston.

[24] *Photo Beacon*, v. 6, p. 2, Jan. 1894.

[25] See, for example, Sketch 9.

Click! Click! Click!
Look at the crowds and the cameras!
Everybody posing, smirking, attitudinizing!
Trying to look their best while being photographed,
Trying to look intellectual, unconscious, beautiful!
Good Lord, what are we coming to?
Is the world going to be one vast Rogues' Gallery? [26]

### JOURNALS DEVOTED TO PHOTOGRAPHY

The number of periodicals devoted to photography in the years 1885 to 1905 ran well into the hundreds, including those designed for the amateur and those for the professional, the short-lived and unsuccessful and the bigger and more prosperous ones. But all had comparatively small circulations, and subsisted chiefly on the advertising of the supply houses. Several that had begun in the seventies lasted well into the nineties or beyond [27] with not much over a thousand circulation.

The *Photographic Herald and Sportsman* (1889–1907), later the *Photo-American,* began at Stamford, Connecticut, but eventually moved to New York. It had good contributors and was well illustrated. The *American Amateur Photographer* was begun at Brunswick, Maine, by W. H. Burbank, in 1889. There were a few photogravures, woodcuts, and such, in its early numbers, plus correspondence with camera clubs and articles of a technical nature. It was purchased by the Outing Company of New York, in 1892. Alfred Stieglitz was one of the editors during 1893–1896, and Frederick C. Beach was an editor throughout the journal's history. The first color photograph (by Stieglitz) was reproduced in January 1894. There was much about exhibitions, salons, and competitions. Some attention was given to photography abroad, and there was some English correspondence. The most popular department was one in which the editors criticized prints sent in by readers. This journal ended in 1907.[28] *Photo-Beacon* (1889–1907) was a Chicago monthly which was almost wholly technical. John Nicol and F. Dundas Todd were successive editors.

*Camera* (1897–current) was mainly a professional journal, long published in Philadelphia, but later in Baltimore. *Photo-Era* (1898–1932), of Boston, was a profusely illustrated journal that served for

[26] *Town Topics,* v. 54, Aug. 10, 1905, p. 13.
[27] See Mott, *op. cit.,* v. 3, p. 186.
[28] It absorbed at the beginning of that year the *Camera and Dark Room* (1899–1906), which had been begun as the organ of the New York Society of Amateur Photographers in Brooklyn, and was later moved to New York. Walter G. Pierson was the chief conductor of this well-illustrated journal. The *American Amateur Photographer* ended with the issue of June 1907, but was continued by a merger called the *American Photographer.*

many years as official organ of the Federation of Photographic Societies and other organizations. The technical and art sides of the profession were well represented, but it was also designed for amateurs. It began its own contests in 1903. *Photo Miniature* (1899–1936) was a monthly twelvemo published in both New York and London; it devoted each issue to one subject within its field, and thus became a series of monographs, with a department of notes. *Camera Work* (1903–1917) was a distinguished quarterly conducted by Stieglitz in New York. Others doubtless deserve more discussion than they can receive here.[29]

LEADING MAGAZINE ILLUSTRATORS

"It is confessed," declared a writer in the *New York Tribune* in 1885, "that no literary magazines in the world equal ours in the matter of illustration."[30] And as events developed, the American general magazine went on increasing its pictorial content in richness and variety. "Nowadays it is often the text which is illustrative, rather than the pictures," said the Kimball survey at the end of the century.[31] The editor of *Bauble,* one of the chapbooks, voiced a common critical opinion of the latter nineties when he referred to the "picture-phobia" of the magazines: "Modern publishers," he said, "seem to think that the eye measures the depth of the popular mind." He thought that in *Munsey's,* for example, "the writers are only space-fillers."[32]

But all critical protests were vain: the people liked copious illustration. There is no doubt that a considerable proportion of these pictures were artistically mediocre or worse, represented careless and unintelligent editing, and were poorly engraved and printed. On the other hand, many of them were attractive and finely printed, and performed their illustrative function well.

The nineties saw a far larger number of good artists at work illustrating the better monthlies and weeklies than had ever before been known. It would be useless to catalogue them here, since they are named in connection with many magazines on other pages of this

[29] An early New York journal for amateurs was *Sun and Shade* (1888–91). *Camera Notes and Proceedings of the Camera Club of New York* (1897–1903) was preceded by a small *Journal of the Camera Club* and was published mainly under the direction of Alfred Stieglitz. Other New York journals were *Photo Critic* (1901–06) and *Down-Town Topics* (1902–13); the latter was called *Photographic Topics* during its last five years. *Professional and Amateur Photography* (1896–1911) was a Buffalo magazine. *Paine's Photographic Magazine* (1899–1901) had an unusually large circulation for one of its kind, but it did not last. *Western Camera Notes* (1899–1907) was issued from Minneapolis, and *Camera Craft* (1900–42) from San Francisco.

[30] *New York Tribune,* Dec. 21, 1885, p. 6, cols. 1–2.

[31] Arthur Reed Kimball in *Journal of Social Science,* v. 37, p. 37, 1899.

[32] *Bauble,* v. 2, p. 83, Aug. 1896.

work; but mention of a few of them will serve to indicate the quality of the better illustrators. John La Farge was both a talented writer and a thoughtful illustrator; and the same may be said of Joseph Pennell, whose sketches of European life and art were accompanied by his charming pen-and-ink pictures. Another artist-writer was Howard Pyle, whose richly romantic illustration was a feature of the magazines at the turn of the century. Rufus F. Zogbaum, Thure de Thulstrup, and William Henry Shelton were good artists in many fields, but are perhaps remembered chiefly for their pictures of the war with Spain. Charles Dana Gibson made his fame with illustration of society life: the "Gibson girl" was the ideal of the times; and scarcely less admired was his clean, square-jawed, broad-shouldered young man.[33] Howard Chandler Christy, Henry Hutt, Harrison Fisher, and James Montgomery Flagg soon followed in the procession of the artists who furnished pretty girls for the fiction and the covers of the magazines. Frederic Remington is best remembered for his magnificent westerns. William T. Smedley began as a genre painter, later working in a variety of fields. E. H. Blashfield, who emphasized historical research; the charming and picturesque Robert Blum; Edwin A. Abbey, sympathetic and appealing in his simplicity; and John W. Alexander and Wyatt Eaton, both strong in portrait work, were all notable magazine illustrators of the nineties. Will H. Low and Kenyon Cox became famous for their decorative and poetic performances. Arthur B. Frost amused a whole generation of readers by his humorous delineations of rural characters, and he shared with Edward W. Kemble the highest rank in illustrations of Negro life.

### PHASES OF MAGAZINE ILLUSTRATION

Poster art became a cult in the nineties. Wrote a critic in *Bradley His Book*:

The poster . . . giving its services all through the range of our complex interests and needs (for soaps as well as for books) has assumed a distinct place in art which all the horror of the conservative, the burlesque of the comic paper, and even the blind worship of collectors cannot destroy.[34]

Another fad — on a different level, to be sure, but not without its importance — was the extraordinary popularity of Palmer Cox's Brownies." These tiny characters, representing the "dude," the policeman, the Irishman, and so on, appeared and reappeared in Cox's draw-

[33] For Gibson, see pp. 363–64. For the Gibson man, note comment in *Munsey's Magazine*, v. 15, p. 501, July 1896.
[34] Van de Dater in *Bradley His Book*, v. 2, Nov. 1896, p. 21.

ings — always a lot of them in one picture, at the ball game, celebrating the Fourth, or just going though funny antics. Originally designed for children, these creatures became familiar to everyone after they were introduced in *St. Nicholas* in 1887; they got into other magazines, into the advertising pages, into books and newspapers. "Few books for children have been so successful as the Brownie books," said the *Bostonian* in 1895, announcing that a hundred thousand of them had been sold.[35]

In these latter days, when everyone has his picture in the paper now and then, it is hard to understand the passion for portraits that was general in the nineties. But it was possible then, for the first time, for middle-class readers to collect portraits of the great; and thousands of them did. The movement was tied up with the study of history and current events that belonged to the widespread adult education movements of the times. *McClure's Magazine* was able to base its first great success on its publication of pictures of Napoleon, and an even greater success on its Lincoln portraits. Several magazines —notably *Demorest's* — printed series of portraits of famous men and women on pages which were blank on the other side so that they could be removed without injuring the magazine, and sold scrapbooks in which their readers could paste them.

### THE NUDE IN MAGAZINE ART

*Munsey's* seems to have shown the other magazines that reproductions of the nude in art could be reproduced in popular magazines with impunity and favorable newsstand reaction. Its success in this kind was followed by that of the *Broadway* and the *Metropolitan*, though none did as well (perhaps because none edited so judiciously) as *Munsey's* with this type of content. *Peterson's*, which was grasping at straws just before it went under in 1895, "out-Heroded Herod in presenting nude pictures, and few Christian people will merit its demise," said the *Angelus*.[36]

Portraits of actresses in tights or décolleté were very common in the magazines as a regular offering. Bathing girls and "living pictures" were also common. *Truth*, which, like *Life*, presented some rather charming bathing beauties, did far better with the clumsy bathing dress of the period than did the cheaper magazines that used photographs actually made at the beach. *Truth* confessed that the bathing girl had to be idealized for its pages, because "in the water she is a

[35] *Bostonian*, v. 1, p. 456, Jan. 1895.
[36] *Angelus*, v. 8 (n.s. 1), p. 56, Nov. 1895.

fright. . . . If she wore anything that clung too closely she would be tabooed by her sisterhood in any seaside resort in America." [37]

"Living pictures," which began as posed reproductions of famous masterpieces, became immensely popular in the theaters,[38] where, said a writer on "The New Paganism" in the *Angelus,* they "were encored again and again," and then reappeared in shop windows and magazines.[39] Photographers exploited the fad. *Saroni's Living Pictures* (1894–1895) was a New York monthly carrying ten or twelve full pages of the pictures in each number. *Great Pictures* (1897–1902), of Chicago, went directly to the masterpieces themselves and exploited the nude in art by reproductions for its pages.

It was photography that revolutionized magazine illustration in the nineties. This was a double revolution. First, photography furnished the copy for the picture in many cases without any need of a drawing or painting. Second, not only was the artist thus eliminated, but so was the engraver, for the print could be re-photographed on a sensitized plate through a fine screen, and acid baths would remove or reduce the printing points of the whites in order to make a plate by "automatic" process. By this double revolution, a great flood of timely and apposite pictures was made available by the photographers, and then plates were prepared for printing at a fraction of the former cost.[40]

Printing in the quality magazines by what was at first called "the Ives process," after its inventor, Frederick E. Ives, and later "the halftone plate," began when the *Century* used it to reproduce some brush drawings made to illustrate John Vance Cheney's ballads in 1884. Soon *Harper's* was experimenting with the new process.[41] Though such beginnings were tentative, halftones were established in the magazines by the beginning of the nineties. Those which reproduced Burne-Jones' "The Six Days of Creation" for the December 1891 number of the *Magazine of Art* were highly praised.[42] When the *Quarterly Illustrator* issued its first number at the beginning of 1893, its editor referred to the halftone reproduction of drawings as "an invaluable factor in national progress" in illustration. At that time, the *Century's* illustra-

---

[37] *Truth,* v. 12, July 1, 1893, p. 7.
[38] See Chapter XIV.
[39] *Angelus,* v. 8 (n.s. 1), p. 16, Oct. 1895.
[40] See p. 5.
[41] See *New York Tribune,* Dec. 21, 1885, p. 6, cols. 1–2. Reference is to pictures in *Century Magazine,* v. 29, pp. 393–95, Jan. 1885.
[42] *New York Tribune,* Nov. 25, 1891, p. 9, col. 1.

tion was about one-third halftone, that of *Harper's* about one-half, *Scribner's* two-thirds, and the *Cosmopolitan* almost 100 per cent.[43] An editorial statement in the *Century* in January 1895 referred to "an entirely new development — a halftone plate originally, worked over by the engraver" to bring up "the highest lights and deepest darks." [44] Improvements in the process eventually sharpened the contrasts, however, and made such handwork unnecessary.

Richard Watson Gilder, who had edited the *Century* through the great period of fine-line engraving on wood, said wishfully in the *Outlook* in 1899: "I think there is to be a great reaction soon in public taste — that people will tire of photographic reproduction, and those magazines will find most favor which lead in original art." [45] The *Century* clung longest to wood engraving, but the art was doomed. Soon after the turn of the century, a writer in *Brush and Pencil* mourned: "Steel engraving, the glory of a former generation, is today an art of the past, and wood-engraving has but few representatives." [46]

### THE QUARTERLY ILLUSTRATOR

Harry C. Jones began the *Quarterly Illustrator* in New York in 1893 to review the illustration of the country's periodicals in each number. It was itself copiously illustrated by pictures from other magazines; and its quarterly reviews by different art critics — Perriton Maxwell, F. Hopkinson Smith, Henry Martyn, Charles de Kay, and others — as well as its biographical sketches of artists and little histories of the magazines, were excellent. A "Photographic Appendix" was added in 1894. In January 1894 a change was made to monthly publication: the *Monthly Illustrator* had more variety — a serial story by George Parsons Lathrop, a condensation of *Les Misérables* in order to use the famous illustrations, and so on. Among contributors were John Gilmer Speed, Royal Cortissoz, Julian Hawthorne, and Richard Harding Davis.

In October 1895 *Home and Country* (1885–1895), which had had a checkered career as a family magazine, was absorbed, its title added to that of the *Monthly Illustrator*, and its older numbering adopted. But the magazine now lost its special position as a critic of the arts; its departments of personalities, the stage, and poetry gave it variety but not distinction. It perished with the number for May 1897.

[43] *Quarterly Illustrator*, v. 1, pp. 1, 21, March 1893.
[44] *Century Magazine*, v. 49, p. 479, Jan. 1895.
[45] *Outlook*, v. 61, p. 320, Feb. 4, 1899.
[46] William C. Whittam in *Brush and Pencil*, v. 7, p. 92, Nov. 1901.

"OUR POPULAR BUT OVER-ADVERTISED AUTHORS"

*Life* asks (May 27, 1897), "Do they (we) need a rest?" Left to right: William Dean Howells, George W. Cable, John Kendrick Bangs, James Whitcomb Riley, Mark Twain, Mary E. Wilkins, Richard Harding Davis, F. Marion Crawford, Frances Hodgson Burnett, Joel Chandler Harris. See pages 128–131, as well as index under each name.

"MUST WE TAKE THE LAW IN OUR OWN HANDS?" ASKS *LIFE*

A dramatic comment on the feeling against early automobiles on the highways from *Life*, November 28, 1901. See page 329.

# CHAPTER X

## POLITICS AND ECONOMICS

A N EDITOR of the *Forum*, casting his eye over a listing of magazine contents in the fall of 1898, observed that it showed "a deepening of the popular interest in political economy and politics." He was convinced, not by this alone, but by his general observation, that "there can be no doubt that the great movements of the present age are economic and political."[1] He should have added the category of social problems. Certainly American magazines for the entire period of twenty years from 1885 to 1905 show a paramount interest in political, economic, and social questions. No longer did travel articles, history, and criticism of literature and the arts lead in the nonfiction content of the magazines. The progressive narrowing of the gap between the magazine and the newspaper[2] made political issues standard material in both, and of course many economic and social questions became involved in political action. The distinctively social issues will be treated in a separate chapter, but we shall here consider industry, business, and currency reform, along with political activity.

### GROVER CLEVELAND

As 1885 began, Chester A. Arthur was getting ready to move out of the White House. He would have liked another four-year lease on it; but his party had chosen the more colorful Blaine as its candidate in 1884, and Blaine had lost, and now the White House was to have a Democratic tenant for the first time in nearly a quarter of a century. Though Arthur, unexpectedly called upon to assume the executive duties, had not made a bad President, he had lacked the personal magnetism which seems to be necessary to success in that position. The Washington correspondent of that sparkling journal, the New York *Citizen*, wrote of him the week before his retirement:

As is generally known, he stands six feet in his undarned widower stockings, and is of florid and rather hectic complexion. . . . His manners are extremely courteous, especially to women, with whom he delights to converse on the small scandals and bohea gossip of New York and the Capital. There is now something stately and mournful in his isolation, for he seems not to have one warm, familiar friend.[3]

---

[1] *Forum*, v. 26, pp. 212, 216, Oct. 1898.
[2] See Chap. I.
[3] *Citizen*, v. 1, p. 170, Feb. 28, 1885.

So the widower's regime gave place to a bachelor's. The bitterness of the hatred that had been generated against Cleveland in the 1884 campaign was long-lasting, and even four years later Senator John J. Ingalls wrote in the *North American Review*:

> The alleged election of Grover Cleveland to the Presidency in 1884 was the most astounding phenomenon in American politics, and it is doubtful whether its parallel can be found in the history of any nation. Obscure men, ignorant men, degraded men, have been elevated to power; but it has never before occurred that a man possessing every acknowledged disqualification has been selected because of them.[4]

But more judicious observers found President Cleveland's industry, his accessibility, his sturdy honesty, his careful appointments, and his firm decisions reassuring.[5] In the campaign of 1888 the President was "his own platform," said *Harper's Weekly*, a warm supporter; [6] and such seemed to be the general opinion. But he was not a winning platform, though it was also generally agreed that it was his stand against high protective tariffs which defeated him that year. However, prophesied *Life* with perfect foresight, "he will lead his party to victory upon the same issue in 1892." [7]

Cleveland's second term was filled with events that called forth voluminous magazine commentary. This was partly because such matters as the Venezuelan dispute, the settlement of the Pullman strike, and the repeal of the Sherman Silver Act were of great public interest, but also because the magazines were following current affairs more and more closely. After his retirement, Cleveland wrote many articles for the periodicals, all of them rather dull and stuffy.

GROWTH OF THE TRUSTS

Railway and industrial combinations had been common ever since the Civil War; but the merger through the trust company technique did not attract great public attention before the late eighties. The development in manufacturing and industry that characterized those years, the growth of monopolies through trust organizations, and the multiplication of millioniares were phenomena much exploited in the magazines.

---

[4] *North American Review*, v. 146, p. 651, June 1888. An earlier article (*ibid.*, v. 143, pp. 616–27, Dec. 1886), by its editor, A. T. Rice, writing under a pen name, was almost as severe.

[5] See *Harper's Weekly* editorials and the "Topics of the Times" in the *Century* 1885–88; as well as *Arena*, v. 3, pp. 150–55, Dec. 1890; and *Citizen*, v. 1, p. 225, March 28, 1885, and v. 1, p. 266, April 11, 1885.

[6] *Harper's Weekly*, v. 32, p. 506, July 14, 1888. Cf. *North American Review*, v. 146, p. 211, Feb. 1888.

[7] *Life*, v. 12, p. 270, Nov. 15, 1888.

"A thorough examination of the nature, history, and methods of trusts is the most timely of all topics," wrote George F. Parker in his *Saturday Globe*,[8] in 1889, and many of his fellow-editors seemed to agree. "The word *trust* as now used," explained the editor of the *Arena*, "means an organization of capital for the production and distribution of any one product." [9] The development of the early mergers, such as the sugar combine, Standard Oil, and the tobacco trust, may be traced in the successive quarterly numbers of *Current History*, beginning in 1890. A writer in the *Chautauquan* asserted that "the objection to trusts is not based upon what they have done so much as upon what it is feared they may do." [10] Morrison I. Swift, writing in the *Andover Review* in 1888, advocated the acceptance and the regulation of combinations.[11] Andrew Carnegie protested against the fear of mergers: under the title "The Bugaboo of Trusts," he wrote in the *North American*, "There is not the slightest danger that serious injury can result to sound principles of business" from trusts, combinations, or the use of trade differentials.[12] But the *Franklin Review* saw a danger in "the abuse of the power of colossal fortunes controlled by a few individuals," and advocated "a statute limiting private fortunes." [13] *Belford's Magazine* agreed, but somewhat more militantly, as was its wont, "that these combinations are a menace to the liberties and material prosperity of the people." [14] That was the *Arena's* position, year after year. The *Journalist* added another thought: it suggested that the magazines themselves should get together. "A magazine trust is what we need to hold up rates and prevent cutting," it said.[15]

THE HARD TIMES

Trusts and combinations, especially in their phases of speculative investment and exploitation of agriculture and labor, were widely blamed for the financial crash of 1893, though the causes were many and various. Distress was evident enough in the West and the South and in the large cities in the early nineties. The *Arena* reported 2,650 foreclosures of farm mortgages in Kansas alone in the last six months of 1890, and over 33,000 evictions for nonpayment of rent in New

---

[8] *Saturday Globe*, v. 3, p. 238, July 13, 1889.
[9] *Arena*, v. 2, p. 627, Oct. 1890.
[10] *Chautauquan*, v. 10, p. 572, Feb. 1890.
[11] *Andover Review*, v. 10, pp. 109–26, Aug. 1888.
[12] *North American Review*, v. 148, pp. 141–50, Feb. 1889. The title of the article is very similar to Henry Wood's "The Bugbear of Trusts," *Forum*, v 5, pp. 584–96, July 1888.
[13] *Franklin Review*, v. 1, pp. 47–48, Feb. 1886.
[14] *Belford's Magazine*, v. 3, p. 66, June 1889.
[15] *Journalist*, v. 8, Feb. 9, 1889, p. 8.

York City in the same period.[16] Yet at the beginning of 1893, on the brink of disaster, the *Commercial and Financial Chronicle*, while admitting that the preceding year had not been "conspicuously prosperous," boasted that it had set a new record in its volume of business transactions.[17] When the break occurred, through successive failures of corporations in the summer, it came not as a panic, as had the similar catastrophe twenty years before, but as a slow and stupefying collapse. James H. Eckels, comptroller of the currency, wrote in the *North American* in August:

> There has been nothing approaching a panic . . . no unusual excitement, despite the general distrust of the stability of our moneyed institutions evidenced in every portion of the country; the daily failure of banks, national, state, and private; of great commercial enterprises, trust companies, corporations, and manufacturing establishments.[18]

Unexpected by nearly everyone, the situation seemed inexplicable. "The world today is confronted by a strange phenomenon," said the *Arena*. "The freest and richest country in the world is experiencing a business depression, one of the severest in its history. . . . Nobody seems to know the cause." [19] Nobody but Andrew Carnegie, of course, who always came up promptly with the answers, such as they were: in the *North American* he blamed the Silver Purchase Act of 1890 for the current hard times.[20]

A picturesque phase of the hard times was the march of Coxey's Army on Washington in 1894. Although the demonstration of the "army" in the nation's capital, and the "marches" of the dozen or more other "armies" that got their cue from Coxey's, semed generally ineffective, nevertheless the magazines took the whole movement rather more seriously than the newspapers. The daily papers, as may be seen in the *Literary Digest* and *Public Opinion*, were inclined to stress the comic side of the ragtag battalions. As one of them remarked: "The movement has assumed the burlesque stage and is destined to go down in history as one of the biggest humbugs of the age." [21] Two discussions of the episode in the magazines may stand here for all: the liberal W. T. Stead pointed out in the *American Review of Reviews* that Coxey's Army had the sympathy of the "masses," who recognized it as a gesture of economic desperation; [22] and the conservative *North American Re-*

[16] *Arena*, v. 3, p. 375, Feb. 1891.
[17] *Commercial and Financial Chronicle*, v. 56, pp. 5, 11, Jan. 7, 1893.
[18] *North American Review*, v. 157, p. 129, Aug. 1893.
[19] *Arena*, v. 9, p. 493, March 1894.
[20] *North American Review*, v. 157, pp. 354–70, Sept. 1893.
[21] *Pittsburgh Dispatch*, quoted in *Public Opinion*, v. 17, p. 43, April 12, 1894.
[22] *American Review of Reviews*, v. 10, p. 52, July 1894.

*view*, alarmed and defensive, printed a symposium on "The Menace of Coxeyism." [23] An interesting contribution was a paragraph by a Washington correspondent of the *Journal of the American Medical Association*, describing the camp of the "army" — about a thousand, and more expected, without shelter, fatigued and ill-fed, with open sewers, and so on.[24] A lighter note is furnished by the *Happy Home*, a cheap monthly of South Bend, Indiana, which offered words and music for the song "Coxey's March to Washington." The chorus ran:

> Led by Brown and Coxey,
> Both so shrewd and foxy,
> They strode on,
> They rode on,
> To make a grand appeal!

There was a special significance in the last lines:

> Stories of their tricks and capers
> Fill the space in daily papers
> On Coxey's famous March to Washington! [25]

Hard times always bring out a deal of philosophizing about thrift, and so it was in the nineties. "Living beyond one's resources is a hazardous experiment, to which fact alone may be attributed the present alarming state of affairs in many households," observed the *Bohemian* in the fall of 1893, and on this note it expired.[26] The individualistic *Farm Journal* declared, "Hard times are good for a nation; they teach economy and thrift; they mean easier times in the future." And again, "Economy, patience, and true American pluck will gradually bring back prosperity." [27] Will Carleton, poet and homely philosopher, in his magazine *Every Where*, pointed out that "as soon as times get good, people go to work making them bad again" by extravagance, recklessness, pride, and vice; and "as soon as they get bad, the movement begins to make them good once more" through economy, prudence, and invention.[28]

Though the rate of increase of magazines in the United States declined greatly in the five years of hard times that followed 1890,[29] many successful ones were started; and since the deceleration continued in more prosperous times, it is doubtful if it was caused by the financial stringency. Indeed, none of our depressions seems to have had

[23] *North American Review*, v. 158, pp. 687–705, Dec. 1894.
[24] *Journal of the American Medical Association*, v. 23, p. 212, Aug. 4, 1894.
[25] *Happy Home*, v. 1, pp. 6–7, May 1894.
[26] *Bohemian*, v. 1, p. 124, Sept. 1893.
[27] *Farm Journal*, v. 19, pp. 21, 56, Feb., March 1895.
[28] *Every Where*, v. 1, p. 8, Sept. 1894.
[29] See Chap. I.

much influence on the numbers of our periodicals, though they have greatly affected profits and conditions of publication. Will Carleton's belief that "invention" is stimulated in hard times is supported by the fact that the immensely successful general illustrated magazines selling at ten cents a copy began in the hard times of the nineties.

### FREE SILVER

As the rigors of the depression receded, it was thought by some that such vagaries as Coxeyism, government ownership, and free silver would fade away and disappear in the new dawn of prosperity. Wrote one of the editors in the Christmas number of *Scribner's Magazine* for 1895:

> We are beginning to feel richer. Already our circumstances are much easier than they were; mills that were closed are running again, wages that were cut down in the hard times have moved up to their former levels, the bugbear of free silver has been chased out of sight. . . . Christmas is not so hard to meet this year.[30]

Perhaps Free Silver's unwelcome form was hiding behind Santa Claus; but if so, it was only for the Christmas season. Kate Field had predicted, in the last issue of her *Washington*, a year and a half before the event, that the silver issue would split the party in power, and that the Republicans would win the 1896 campaign.[31]

Bimetallism had been before the people ever since the passage of the Currency Act of 1873, denounced ever afterward as "the crime of '73," which demonetized silver. But it had been an issue upon which the "haves" and "have-nots" had divided rather than one between the two great political parties. The depression of the seventies forced the enactment of the Bland-Allison silver purchase bill in 1878. And then agrarian and labor distress in 1890 forced the passage of the Sherman Silver Purchase Act, which doubled the amount of silver required to be purchased for coinage. But this satisfied neither side: the silver men thought it did not go far enough, and the capitalists were for the single gold standard. "Possibly no issue before the people of late has been of greater importance than that of the free coinage of silver," recorded *Current History* in 1891.[32] "Thick as leaves in Vallombrosa fall essays on silver, finance, and coinage upon a bewildred public," said the *Social Economist* in introducing a symposium on those topics in its number for March 1892.[33] The free-silver discussion took place on

[30] "Point of View" department in *Scribner's Magazine*, v. 18, p. 787, Dec. 1895.
[31] *Kate Field's Washington*, v. 11, p. 248, April 20, 1895.
[32] *Quarterly Register of Current History*, v. 1, p. 131, May 1891.
[33] *Social Economist*, v. 1, p. 328, March 1892.

all levels — in Populist papers, in general magazines, in the reviews, in the learned journals. The financial stringency of 1893 stimulated the discussion. "The silver problem is being discussed as never before," said the Chicago *Graphic* in July of that year.

In August President Cleveland summoned a special session of Congress to repeal the Silver Purchase Act, an accomplishment that took nearly three months because of filibustering against it. "We can scarcely find words strong enough to express our satification at a result for which we have been working since 1878," exulted the editor of the *Commercial and Financial Chronicle*,[34] who thought silver purchases had "acted so as to paralyze commerce and had finally brought disaster." But the repeal defined the alignment for the struggle to come. In May 1894, Senator Richard P. Bland wrote in the *North American Review* that "the people's money, under the operation of the gold standard, is now wholly at the mercy of the few who, by their great wealth, are able to own and control the scanty gold supply." [35]

When the national Democratic convention met in Chicago in July 1896, the free-silver men were in control two to one, and William J. Bryan, who had delivered his famous "cross of gold" oration in the heat of the debate over the silver plank, defeated Bland on the fifth ballot for the presidential nomination. Josiah Quincy lamented in the *North American* that the convention had been swept off its feet.[36] The nomination of William McKinley by the Republicans the month before had been less dramatic, though the "bolt" of the free-silver minority led by Senator H. M. Teller had lent some excitement. More important than this break in Republican solidarity, however, was the secession of the "Sound Money Democrats," as was to be proved in what Albert Shaw, in his *Review of Reviews*, called "the most remarkable presidential campaign since our Civil War," [37] and Senator Thomas C. Platt said in the *North American* was "a political battle having no parallel in our history." [38]

The *Commercial and Financial Chronicle* declared that the Chicago convention had "favored radicalism and lawlessness of the worst sort," and said that its platform "means an utter disregard of property rights. It means anarchists' operations legalized. It means the promoting of riots like that in Chicago in 1894." [39] Against such talk there was sharp protest. "It is not creditable to any of us to dub half the American

---

[34] *Commercial and Financial Chronicle*, v. 57, p. 740, Nov. 4, 1893.
[35] *North American Review*, v. 158, pp. 654–52, May 1894.
[36] *Ibid.*, v. 163, p. 183, Aug. 1896.
[37] *American Review of Reviews*, v. 14, p. 515, Nov. 1896.
[38] *North American Review*, v. 163, p. 513, Nov. 1896.
[39] *Commercial and Financial Chronicle*, v. 63, pp. 48, 50, July 11, 1896.

people 'anarchists' and 'pirates,' " complained the liberal editor of the *New England Magazine*.[40] The sarcastic paragrapher of *Life* thought that everyone short of money had to "squirm on the cross," and that it made no difference whether the cross was made of gold or silver.[41] Among the most effective arguments for free silver were those given in the form of blackboard "lessons" in a little paper-covered book by one William Hope Harvey, later called "Coin" Harvey. With pictures, narrative, and clear exposition, *Coin's Financial School* was a hit. "As a precipitant and reagent, nothing else was half so effective as the entry of Mr. Harvey with his little yellow-covered book," wrote Shaw in the *Review of Reviews*.[42] Bryan himself was, of course, an able campaigner, and there was a phenomenal quantity of public speaking. Reviewing the campaign in the *North American Review* just after its close, Bryan wrote:

> Men who had never spoken in public before became public speakers; mothers, wives, and daughters debated the relative merits of the single and double standards; business partnerships were dissolved on account of political differences; bosom friends became estranged; families were divided — in fact, we witnessed such activity of mind and stirring of heart as this nation has not witnessed before for thirty years. . . . And what was the result? Temporary defeat, but permanent gain for the cause of bimetallism.[43]

The free-silver issue was not dead when Bryan ran again for the presidency in 1900, though it was overshadowed by imperialism and the tariff, and affected by the newly mined gold coming in from the Klondike. But when he founded his own weekly journal of opinion, the *Commoner*, Bryan found comparatively little space for bimetallism.

The *Commoner* was begun January 1, 1901, at Lincoln, Nebraska. At first it was an eight-page quarto; but, attaining some 30,000 circulation immediately, it was doubled in size in its second year. It sold for a dollar a year, and by 1905 had nearly 150,000 distribution. It was strongly antitrust, antitariff, anti-imperialism, and antiwar. It included Bryan's "Bible Talks," news, and home departments.[44]

Charles H. Bliss started a propaganda serial for the free-silver cause at Auburn, Indiana, in 1894 called *Bliss' Quarterly*; it was later pub-

---

[40] *New England Magazine*, v. 15, pp. 252–53, Oct. 1896.
[41] *Life*, v. 28, p. 170, Sept. 3, 1896.
[42] *American Review of Reviews*, v. 14, p. 131, Aug. 1896.
[43] *North American Review*, v. 163, p. 703, Dec. 1896.
[44] Charles W. Bryan, brother of the editor, was publisher and later associate editor. Other causes of the *Commoner* were the popular election of United States Senators, woman suffrage, prohibition, and the income tax. When William J. Bryan entered the Cabinet, the periodical became a monthly (Aug. 1913), and when Charles W. Bryan became governor of Nebraska it was discontinued (April 1923). Its founder, said the *Bulletin of Bibliography* (v. 2, p. 3, May–Aug. 1923) was "evidently too busy fighting the Darwinian theory to edit a political weekly." Its subscription list was taken over by *Capper's Farmer* and the *Household Magazine*.

lished at Pensacola, Florida, as *Bliss' Magazine*, ending in 1905 as a promoter of the Florida land boom. Lee Crandall's *National View* (1879–1895) was a reform weekly published at Washington; it was at first allied with the Greenback party and the temperance cause, but was devoted to free silver in its last few years. It was superseded by Senator William M. Stewart's *Silver Knight* (1895–1901), which was merged in 1896 with the *National Watchman* (1892–1896).[45] There were other free-silver periodicals in the nineties, and a few special gold-standard journals.[46]

THE ISSUE OF IMPERIALISM

The war with Spain produced an issue which, if it did not overshadow free silver, at least equaled it. Writing in the *Independent* before his nomination for the presidency on the Democratic and Populist tickets, Bryan declared that the issues were imperialism, trusts, and the money question [47]; and in the Democratic platform imperialism was declared to be the "paramount issue" of the campaign.

The administration in power preferred the term "expansion" to "imperialism." War was no sooner declared against Spain than Senator John T. Morgan was advocating in the *North American Review* that the United States should take over and hold Cuba, Porto Rico, the Philippines, the Caroline Islands, and Hawaii.[48] One of the editors of *Munsey's Magazine*, writing on "The Prizes of Victory" before victory was assured, said: "The acquisition of the Spanish West Indies would be a momentous and magnificent step toward what scores of our

[45] Titles of the *Silver Knight* after the union with the *Watchman* were: *Silver Knight-Watchman*, 1896–98; *National Watchman*, 1898–1901. It had much variety for farmers and for the home circle.

[46] The *National Bimetallist* was first published in Chicago 1895–96; it was superseded by the Washington paper of the same name published 1897–98 by George E. Bowen and edited by H. F. Bartine. A. L. Graves's *Broad-Axe* (1891–96) was a free-silver paper in St. Paul, Minn. The *American Bimetallist* (1895–96) was edited at Huntington, Indiana, by Fred T. Liftin. The *Non-Conformist* (1896–98) was a free-silver paper at Omaha, Nebraska. The *Bryan Democrat* (1898–1900), New York, was a campaign paper, as was the *Jeffersonian* (1899), Brooklyn. *Sound Currency* (1891–1905) was published by the Reform Club, of New York; at first a semimonthly, then a monthly, and finally a quarterly, it contained a special article in each number by men like Horace White, Henry Loomis Nelson, and L. Carroll Root. *Sound Money* (1897–1900), Chicago, was published monthly by the National Sound Money League.

[47] *Independent*, v. 52, p. 291, Feb. 1, 1900. The Republicans, however, preferred the free-silver issue, and Editor Page wrote in *World's Work* (v. 1, p. 16, Nov. 1900): "The renomination of Mr. Bryan thrust the old silver controversy into foremost place." The *Yale Review*, opposing both free silver and imperialism, called for a third party (v. 9, pp. 123–201, Feb. 1901).

[48] *North American Review*, v. 166, p. 648, June 1898. But Faithful Contributor Carnegie opposed territorial expansion in the same review (v. 167, pp. 239ff, Aug. 1898), and there was much discussion pro and con in the *North American* for the next several years. Bryan's contributions seemed to give this journal some Democratic slant in 1900.

ablest statesmen, from Thomas Jefferson downward, have foreshadowed as the manifest destiny of the United States of America." [49] About the same time, an editorial in the *Saturday Evening Post* explained the spirit of expansionism: "This war has come along. It will give us a lift out of the rut. It makes the world, for us, a larger world; and it shows a need of preparation on our part for living in a larger world." [50] Indeed, the expansion idea "seemed to run over the country like the flame of a furious prairie fire," [51] as the *New England Magazine* said. Judge H. H. Powers, writing on "The War and Manifest Destiny" in the *Annals of the American Academy of Political and Social Science* in the fall of 1898, described the phenomenon in more detail:

> The past few months have witnessed one of the most remarkable developments of public opinion ever observed in this or any other country. A year ago we wanted no colonies, no alliances, no European neighbors, no army, and not much navy. . . . Today every one of these principles is challenged, if not definitely rejected. Proposals to enter into alliance with Great Britain, to annex Porto Rico and the Philippines, and to assume responsibilities for Cuba which may lead to annexation are seriously discussed, and entertained with surprising favor. Plans for enlarging our navy far beyond anything previously contemplated . . . are considered favorably and greeted with general acclaim.[52]

It was on January 9, 1900, that Albert J. Beveridge delivered his famous manifest destiny speech in the United States Senate: that utterance and the contributions that the handsome young orator made to the *Saturday Evening Post* made him a hero in the eyes of thousands of young men throughout the country.

But Beveridge's declaration that the United States was "a trustee under God of the civilization of the world" was interpreted by the *Workers' Call* as "pure exploitation," and the "lying rot about 'the white man's burden' " as an effort to ennoble "a purely business proposition." [53] William Marion Reedy referred in his *Mirror* to President McKinley's "colonial policy" as "Imperialism gone mad." [54] John Clark Ridpath, new editor of the *Arena*, exclaimed in 1898: "Imperialism is openly advocated in high places as though it were not rank treason. The Republic may be seen swaying and rocking under the stress like a shaken tower struck by the assults of a powerful enemy." [55] The *Conservative Review*, published in Washington for two and a half

---

[49] *Munsey's Magazine*, v. 19, p. 553, July 1898.
[50] In the *Post* also, Carnegie protested (Jan. 21, 1899), but Henry Watterson defended expansion (Jan. 28, 1899).
[51] *New England Magazine*, v. 19, p. 85, Sept. 1898.
[52] *Annals*, v. 12, p. 1, Sept. 1898.
[53] *Workers' Call*, v. 1, p. 1, March 11, 1899.
[54] *Mirror*, v. 10, p. 1, Feb. 22, 1900.
[55] *Arena*, v. 20, p. 363, Sept. 1898. But five months later another ownership brought the *Arena* in line with the expansionists.

years at the turn of the century, was devoted largely to the attack on imperialism. Champ Clark was a frequent contributor. "In the great Judgment Day," exhorted Clark, "the blood of all our soldiers who die there [in the Philippines] will be upon the heads of the men who are rushing our country into this monstrous folly. Far better for us were an earthquake to swallow the Philippines!"[56] But perhaps the most powerful arraignment of the American colonial policy was Mark Twain's "To the Person Sitting in Darkness," which appeared in the *North American Review* early in 1901.[57] Also there were a few short-lived periodicals opposing imperialism.[58]

But Editor Walter H. Page was probably right when he declared in his *World's Work*: "The truth seems to be that the mass of men simply do not believe that our liberties are in danger because of our occupation of Porto Rico and the Philippines."[59]

### THE PROTECTIVE TARIFF AND THE TRUSTS

No politico-economic question occupied more space in the magazines and reviews of 1885–1895 than the tariff in its many phases. One of the most spectacular magazine discussions of the issue was the debate in the *North American Review* of January 1890 between William E. Gladstone and James G. Blaine, which was continued through several succeeding numbers by other well-known economists and statesmen. Though Cleveland was elected in 1892 largely because of his opposition to surplus-producing high tariffs, he was unable to force a satisfactory tariff reform bill through Congress, and when the schedules were revised under a Republican administration in 1897, they went up rather than down.

That high tariffs stimulated trust organization, as *Harper's Weekly* argued in 1889,[60] was a general belief. In those times, *Public Opinion* headed one of its running résumés of editorial expression throughout the country "Trusts and Tariff,"[61] for it could not separate the two streams of commentary. But the great wave of prosperity that swept over the nation in the last three or four years of the century, together with the war and its issues, tended to allay public concern about both tariffs and trusts. That prosperity and the schedules of the Dingley Tariff brought a remarkable boom in new trust organizations. An

[56] *Conservative Review*, v. 1, p. 100, Feb. 1899.
[57] *North American Review*, v. 172, pp. 161–76, Feb. 1901.
[58] The *Anti-Imperialist* (1899–1900), Brookline, Mass.; *Anti-Imperialist Broadside* (1898–1900), Washington, D. C.; and others.
[59] *World's Work*, v. 1, p. 17, Nov. 1900.
[60] *Harper's Weekly*, v. 33, p. 678, Aug. 24, 1889.
[61] *Public Opinion*, v. 7, pp. 385, 405, Aug. 17, 24, 1889.

economist writing in the *Chautauquan* noted an increase of more than 50 per cent in the capital stock and bonded debt of trust organizations in the first two months of 1899, and remarked: "The tremendous rush for forming new combinations this year is of a nature to arouse consideration, even if it has not, as one alarmist puts it, created as much excitement as the blowing up of the *Maine*." [62]

Many writers declared that trusts, like high tariffs, tended to raise wages and lower prices. Thus William Coleman, of New York, defended the "general principle of centralization" in the *Journal of Political Economy*; [63] and the piano manufacturer, Alfred Dolge, asserted: "The trust will still further reduce the length of the day's work and increase the rate of pay. Moreover, it means the end of adulteration and of inferior manufacture because it removes the terrible stress of competition." [64] Dolge was writing in the *Saturday Evening Post* in 1898; two years later the *Post* printed Speaker Thomas B. Reed's exasperated "If monopoly is a crime, then you must give up your continued demand for lower and lower prices." [65] But at that time the *Post* editorially was suspicious of the trusts. Lorimer was all for the widest opportunity for young men, and he thought "aggrandized wealth" placed limitations on that opportunity. "Time alone will show," he wrote in 1902,

whether a good trust is productive of good to the people. . . . But there is no doubt about the sentiment of the American people: they not only distrust, but they fear vast accumulations of money in the hands of a few.[66]

Longest-lived of all periodicals devoted to the tariff question were the *American Economist*, published by the American Protective Tariff League, of New York, from 1887 to 1930,[67] and the *Protectionist*, published by the Home Market Club, of Boston, from 1889 to 1941.[68] On the other side, *Tariff Reform* (1888–1894) was issued by the Tariff Committee of the Reform Club, New York; and *Tariff-Trust Letters* (1894–1903) came from the American Free-Trade League, with headquarters at Boston.[69] *People's Cause* (1889), edited by R. R. Bowker in New York, advocated other reforms as well as lower tariffs. *National*

[62] *Chautauquan*, v. 29, p. 347, July 1899.
[63] *Journal of Political Economy*, v. 8, p. 19, Dec. 1899.
[64] *Saturday Evening Post*, v. 170, March 26, 1898, p. 8.
[65] *Ibid.*, v. 172, p. 706, Feb. 10, 1900.
[66] *Ibid.*, v. 174, Jan. 4, 1902, p. 12.
[67] Called *Tariff League Bulletin* 1887–88, *American Economist and Tariff League Bulletin* 1889–91, *American Economist* 1891–1926, and *Tariff Review* 1926–30. At first it was a monthly quarto of 8 pages, later a 16-page weekly, and finally a monthly again.
[68] Called *Home Market Bulletin* 1889–99. This was a well-printed monthly of octavo size.
[69] Called *Tariff-Trust Articles* 1901–03. Merged with *Free-Trader Bulletin* (1902–05), which was followed by *Free-Trade Broadside* (1905–19).

*Reciprocity* (1902–1903) was published in Chicago by the National Reciprocity League.

### SUCCESS AND A NEW CENTURY

The country's abounding prosperity, the victories at war, a new sense of world leadership, and high hopes for the future based on what seemed unlimited American resources, all combined to produce an uprecedented national exaltation in the years 1900–1901. The United States — and especially its youth and its rulers in government and industry — faced the twentieth century with unbounded confidence.

There was, of course, no little talk about whether the new century began January 1, 1900, or January 1, 1901. *Current Literature* called it "an almost endless discussion." The *Scientific American* carried an article in December 1899 that should have made the matter clear to anyone, but the "9" in "1900" misled many. Said San Francisco's *Town Talk* on January 6, 1900:

> Those deluded people who believe we are now in the Twentieth Century have the satisfaction of knowing that even though they are wrong, their judgment is in harmony with that of Leo XIII and Emperor William. . . . Many wise men are, like them, believers in the Year Zero.[70]

All through the nineties there had been much talk about *fin de siècle,* a term used by Paul Bourget and others, but popularized in France by Ernest Blum's play, *Paris Fin-de-Siècle.* As early as 1891 a writer in the *Atlantic Monthly's* "Contributor's Club" was complaining:

> Everywhere we are treated to dissertations on fin-de-siècle literature, fin-de-siècle statesmanship, fin-de-siècle morality. . . . People seem to take for granted that a moribund century implies, not to say excuses, disenchantment, languor, literary, artistic, and political weariness.[71]

Not so in America in 1900, where and when it was the fashion to talk about how rich and wonderful we were. Two outstanding magazine articles may be noted. Ray Stannard Baker, writing on "The New Prosperity" in *McClure's,* said:

> The years 1898 and 1899 were in many respects the most remarkable in the history of the nation. . . . In less than three years — that is, between 1897 and 1900 — so great were the trade balances in our favor that over a billion dollars of American indebtedness was wiped from the ledgers of Europe. . . . The bank clearings were billions of dollars greater than ever before in the history of the nation in 1899. . . . Wages for labor increased rapidly in every part of the country.

Then Baker detailed the figures of record-breaking production of gold

[70] *Town Talk,* v. 8, Jan. 6, 1900, p. 3.
[71] *Atlantic Monthly,* v. 67, pp. 859–60, June 1891.

and other metals, and "the largest wheat crop in the history of America" in 1898. And "perhaps the most notable thing about the recent upward trend is the way in which it has swept the entire country." [72]

The other article is the remarkable salutatory editorial by Walter Hines Page in *World's Work*, from which a few sentences may be taken:

> The United States is become the richest of all countries. . . . We have developed the skilled workman whose earnings are larger and whose product is cheaper than any of his competitors, because he is a better master of himself and of the machinery that he uses. Our commercial supremacy is inevitable. . . . All wise plans for the future must rest on the changes wrought by modern machinery, the organization of industry, and the freedom of the individual; for the perfection of method and of mechanism has done more than to spread well-being among the masses and to enrich and dignify labor: it has changed social ideals and intellectual points of view. It is in fact changing the character of men.[73]

It was great to be young and an American. Our young men, wrote Edward Bok in the *Cosmopolitan*, live "in a country where every success is possible, where a man can make of himself just what he may choose. . . . All success is possible." But, adds Bok, who had turned momentarily from advising young women to spare a word for young men, they must be honest, alert, willing to learn, teetotallers all, and respectable.[74] "Success" was a word that was sprinkled through all the magazine tables of contents during these years. In 1900, for example, we had Theodore Roosevelt on "Character and Success" in the *Outlook* for March 31, the artist John Holme on "Successful Personalities" in the *Cosmopolitan* for November, the single-taxer and poet Joseph Dana Miller on "False Ideals of Success" in the *Arena* for December, and many others. Miller thought money and power were not the right ideals, but for most of his readers "success" and "wealth" were virtually synonymous. Thomas W. Lawson, never distinguished as a scrupulous financier, wrote "A Formula for Money Making" for the *Twentieth Century Review* of 1901.[75] William Marion Reedy wrote in his *Valley Magazine* a year later that "Money-madness has taken the world of today as the world was never taken before," and he gives examples.[76]

The two leading professional preachers of success in the nineties were the Reverend William M. Thayer and Orison Swett Marden.

[72] *McClure's Magazine*, v. 15, pp. 86–94, May 1900.

[73] *World's Work*, v. 1, p. 3, Nov. 1900. Cf. *North American Review*, v. 161, p. 617, May 1895; *Saturday Evening Post*, v. 72, p. 1230, June 30, 1900 (editorial by Robert Ellis Thompson); *Bradstreet's*, Dec. 30, 1899, business summary for 1899.

[74] *Cosmopolitan*, v. 16, pp. 338–39, Jan. 1894.

[75] *Twentieth Century Review*, v. 1, Sept. 21, 1901, p. 1.

[76] *Valley Magazine*, v. 1, p. 59, Sept. 1902.

Thayer was not a magazinist but an anthologist: he collected anecdotes about successful men under such book titles as *Men Who Win* and *Pluck and Purpose*, and he edited a grade-school reader called *The Ethics of Success*. Marden was even more prolific in his production of little sermonizing books about success, which themselves achieved the thing they talked about. Marden's magazine *Success* had a harder time, however. After a year as a big ten-cent monthly of forty quarto pages, it tried selling as a five-cent weekly for another year; but it was not until new financing at the turn of the century that it began to reach the goal set by its title.[77] Other magazines of this type were less successful. There were Eugene L. Didier's Baltimore monthly called *Success: An Illustrated Magazine for the People*; William Cauldwell's biographical *Successful American* (1900–1907), New York; *Eternal Progress* (1901–1911), Cincinnati and Chicago, which eventually progressed into *Opportunity*; and *Successward* (1902–1903), of New York.[78]

In this connection the optimism of the publishers and editors of the great ten-cent magazines of the period should be noted. Sam McClure, Frank Munsey, and John Brisben Walker were ambitious young men with big ideas. A later critic, H. L. Mencken, points out that they all failed;[79] and so they did, in one way or another. But they were all immensely successful in this expansive, buoyant, self-vaunting generation, whose prototype was the youth who bore, 'mid snow and ice, a banner with this strange device — Success!

### THEODORE ROOSEVELT

Perhaps it is not straining the figure too much to think of that youth as Theodore Roosevelt, whom the headline writers knew as "T. R." and affectionate followers called "Teddy." He had attracted wide attention before he was thirty; in 1889 *Current Literature* introduced him as "a gentleman a little over thirty who has distinguished himself as a lawyer, politician, author, and player of polo."[80] A few years later, when he was Police Commissioner of New York, the *Chautauquan* spoke of him as "one of the most conspicuous young men in the country,"[81] and *Life* reported that "Every morning Mr. Roosevelt steps into the ring, and stays there all day. He does not go around looking for opponents, but to all who offer contention he is hospitality

---

[77] *Success* (1897–1911) will be treated in a separate sketch in the next volume of this work.
[78] An interesting work on this general subject is Irvin G. Wyllie, *The Self-Made Man in America* (New Brunswick, 1954).
[79] H. L. Mencken, *Prejudices*, First Series, (New York, 1929), pp. 175–76.
[80] *Current Literature*, v. 3, p. 11, July 1889.
[81] *Chautauquan*, v. 22, p. 588, Feb. 1896.

itself." [82] There was truth and error and Hubbardry in the following word caricature from the *Philistine* of 1899:

He's only a boy — don't take him too seriously — Teddy of Oyster Bay. Just a kid is our own Teddy, with his thirst for adventure & itch for turning things upside down, his ruf riding, big game killing and broncho busting! Only an over-grown fighting kid, with dirty face, buttons off all his clothes thru much "rastling," and a casual suggestion of shirt-tail that he neglected to tuck in. . . .
  Teddy is as high now as he will ever get. To promote him further would be to invite him to swing his chapararros astride the neck of Freedom & ride a hell-to-split race thru our fondest hopes of the Ideal Republic.[83]

As high as he would ever get, eh? Exactly two years and two weeks after this was printed, T. R. was President of the United States. He was well hated by many, and we may note in passing the remark of the clerical gentleman who edited the *Globe* review in 1904: "The accident of Hell made him President of the United States." [84] But he was the best single representative of the second half of the period under consideration in this volume. His ebullience, his youthful activity, his fighting idealism suited those times. In 1900, when he was a candidate for the vice-presidency, *World's Work* said truly that he was "by all odds the most interesting personality in our public life . . . the best public hero that has come in this generation." [85]

PARTY MAGAZINES

The only important monthly of the period that can be said to have been largely devoted to Democratic party doctrine was *Belford's*, a Chicago magazine published in 1888–1893, which is discussed in an earlier chapter because its contents were, after all, literary and mis-cellaneous.[86] The *Tammany Times* (1893–1914) was a ten-cent weekly, sixteen pages quarto, edited for many years by Fred Feigl. It carried society, theatrical, and sports news, with a woman's department, and thus might be classified with our "urban weeklies"; but its main pur-pose was to answer such critics of Tammany as *Harper's Weekly* and Godkin's *Evening Post*. George F. Parker's *Saturday Globe* has al-ready been mentioned; [87] and George W. Blake's anti-Hearst *De-*

[82] *Life*, v. 28, p. 474, Dec. 10, 1896.
  [83] *Philistine*, v. 9, pp. 125–26, Sept. 1899. A few months later, Hubbard, having received a visit from Roosevelt in the Roycroft Shop, was so pleased that he wrote a poem about the event.
  [84] W. H. Thorne in the *Globe*, v. 14, p. 212, Sept. 1904.
  [85] *World's Work*, v. 1, p. 21, Nov. 1900. Cf. Roosevelt Number of *Saturday Evening Post*, v. 177, March 4, 1905.
  [86] See Chap. IV.
  [87] See p. 85 for *Globe*; see also p. 69, footnote.

*mocracy* (1903–1910) was a good paper, organ of the party in New York City.[88]

The Republican monthly was *Gunton's Magazine* (1891–1904), which was called *Social Economics* during its first five years. It was subsidized by the Standard Oil Company and was frankly the spokesman of trusts, a high protective tariff, and what the Democrats called "special privilege." [89] Most of its contributors were obscure writers, though Senator George F. Hoar, President J. G. Schurman, Carroll D. Wright, and Horace White wrote for it in its early years. A news chronicle, book reviews, and some miscellany made it less a series of propaganda tracts and more a magazine.[90] A *Republican Magazine* published six attractive monthly numbers in New York in 1892 under the editorship of F. G. B. Curtis; it was a campaign periodical, and ended with the November issue. The *Basis* (1895–1896) was a Buffalo weekly (later a monthly) edited by Albion W. Tourgée; it had a considerable literary content.

## ANARCHISM

Much was written in these years about equality of opportunity,[91] but spokesmen of the poor in the slums and the failures on the farms disagreed — sometimes violently. In the face of the nation's proud wealth and militant optimism, elements of discontent were active not only in the hard times but in the succeeding years of better wages and bigger crops. The growth of sociology as a science and of social service as a systematic procedure will be noticed in the following chapter, but here we must discuss communistic anarchism and those phases of socialism which were distinctively political.

In 1885 the *Age of Steel* warned its readers of the menace of the revolutionary anarchists who had recently arrived from Europe:

The last few years have opened our eyes to the fact that from the off-scourings of Europe we have acquired some very bad citizens — men who are not in sympathy with our institutions but are enemies of society in general, who would overthrow law and order and apply the torch to property and the sword to slaughter.[92]

[88] Horatio P. Witherstine was editor for the first four years; he was followed by Joseph S. Mulroney. It was a good 5¢ paper. The fashion, household, farm, and garden departments that it carried at first were later crowded out by politics.

[89] *McClure's*, v. 26, p. 451, Feb. 1906; *Arena*, v. 41, p. 447, July 1909; *Twentieth Century Magazine*, v. 2, p. 126. The first-named says that Standard Oil subsidized *Gunton's* "to the tune of fifteen to twenty-five thousand dollars a year."

[90] George Gunton was president of the "College of Social Economics," Union Square, New York, and later manager of a speakers' institute on the order of Chautauqua. Associate editors were S. H. Nichols, 1891–92, Hayes Robbins, 1902–03; Stanhope Sams, 1903–04.

[91] See *World's Work* (J. G. Schurman), v. 1, p. 173, Dec. 1900; *ibid.* (W. H. Page), v. 3, p. 1473, Jan. 1902; *Forum* (Carroll D. Wright), v. 19, p. 309, May 1895.

[92] *Age of Steel*, v. 37, May 14, 1885, p. 2. Cf. Richard T. Ely's article in *North American Review*, v. 142, pp. 516–25, June 1886.

It was on May 4 of the next year that the Haymarket bombing occurred. The *Current*, of Chicago, declared that the act "disgraced liberty," and begged the strikers to go back to work and the authorities to close the saloons while "the populace is in a state of alarm and is not fitted to settle the questions that are up for solution." [93] When the anarchists were hanged, *Lucifer*, the Kansas paper of individualistic anarchy (or personal freedom) published a bitter article entitled, "Why Expect Justice from the State?" [94] and the *Workman's Advocate*, organ of the Socialistic Labor party, headed its article on the execution: "Foulest Murder — Brave Men Die Bravely for Labor's Cause — Not Ended." [95]

The matter was indeed "not ended." Though four of the anarchists were hanged, three lived to receive their pardons in 1893 from Governor John P. Altgeld. Only three months before the pardon the *Century Magazine* had published a long account of the trial by the presiding judge, Joseph E. Gary, which concluded:

> For nearly seven years the clamor, uncontradicted, has gone round the world that the anarchists were heroes and martyrs, victims of prejudice and fear. . . . Right-minded, thoughtful people . . . who may have had misgivings as to the fate of the anarchists, will, I trust, read what I have written, and dismiss those misgivings. . . .[96]

The pardon was a great shock to all conservatives. The *Journal of the Knights of Labor* declared that it "has roused the capitalistic press to something like fury." [97] The *Graphic*, of Chicago, thought it doubtful "if any other official act in the history of any American state has met with so general condemnation from every class of citizens," and it added: "Time has justified the Chicago verdict. Will it do the same for Governor Altgeld's intercession?" [98] Dr. Shaw, in the *Review of Reviews* thought not; in fact, Shaw was convinced that the pardon was "sure to make Altgeld's very name odious." [99] Sleep gently, Eagle forgotten.

The leading journal of communistic anarchy in English was the *Alarm*; *A Socialistic Weekly*, of Chicago, which was edited from the spring of 1884 for a little over two years by Albert R. Parsons. "Workingmen of America," advised Parsons, "learn the manufacture and use of dynamite — a weapon of the weak against the strong, the poor

[93] *Current*, v. 5, p. 305, May 8, 1886.
[94] *Lucifer*, v. 1, Sept. 18, 1886, p. 4.
[95] *Workmen's Advocate* (no vol.), Nov. 19, 1887, p. 1.
[96] *Century Magazine*, v. 45, p. 837, April 1893.
[97] *Journal of the Knights of Labor*, v. 15, July 6, 1893, p 4.
[98] *Graphic*, v. 9, p. 38, July 15, 1893.
[99] *American Review of Reviews*, v. 8, p. 135, Aug. 1893.

against the rich. Then use it unstintedly, unsparingly."[100] And a few months later, "Assassination, properly applied, is wise, just, humane, and brave."[101] When Parsons was arrested for the Haymarket bombing, the *Alarm's* press was seized. Dyer D. Lum revived it the week before Parsons was hanged,[102] and ran it for fifteen months.[103] Six numbers of a monthly *Rebel*, said to be "devoted to the exposition of anarchist-communism," were published in Boston, beginning in September 1895.

Some labor papers, especially those affiliated with the Socialistic Labor party, and all the individualistic anarchism periodicals had strong sympathies with their most spectacular cousin, communistic anarchism.[104]

### THE RISE OF SOCIALISM

"A few years ago the word 'socialism' was rarely heard in this country," wrote the editor of the New York *Citizen* in 1885, adding: "Now it is very common. A spectre of the old world, it is no longer confined to the land of its birth. But it is well to bear in mind that there are socialists and socialists, and also that socialism is not anarchy."[105] The next year Professor Richard T. Ely, who was shocking students at Johns Hopkins by his attacks on laissez-faire economics, contributed a comprehensive and informative article to the *North American Review* on anarchism and socialism in the United States.[106] He thought it doubtful if the enrolled members of the Socialistic Labor party numbered as many as ten thousand, but he believed there might be a million "who accept their economic philosophy." President Francis A. Walker, of the Massachusetts Institute of Technology, wrote articles on socialism for both *Scribner's* and the *Forum* in 1887 expressing his alarm at the world-wide growth of the movement. Walker regarded all economic theory not comprehended within the laissez-faire doctrine as socialism, including both the protective tariff and "that piece of wretched demagogism known as the Eight-Hour Law, passed by Congress without any intention that it should be enforced."[107] The fourth number of the *Political Science Quarterly* (December 1886) carried an article on "Scientific Socialism," which concluded that

[100] *Alarm*, v. 1, Nov. 8, 1884, p. 2.
[101] *Alarm*, v. 2, April 18, 1885, p. 2.
[102] Parsons contributed to Lum's first numbers from his Prison Cell 29. The story of the hanging appears on p. 1 of the issue for Nov. 19, 1897.
[103] It was later revived and published as a monthly in New York, Oct. 1915–Aug. 1916.
[104] An example of the individualistic anarchists is *Lucifer* (see p. 277).
[105] *Citizen*, v. 1, p. 130, Feb. 14, 1885.
[106] *North American Review*, v. 142, pp. 516–25, June 1886.
[107] *Scribner's Magazine*, v. 1, p. 114, Jan. 1887; *Forum*, v. 3, p. 230, April 1887.

socialism "has little to offer which views of a more moderate character cannot supply."

Throughout the nineties the general magazines and reviews published many articles about the various types of socialism. The *Arena* was especially hospitable to such discussions; indeed, one of its later editors, Paul Tyner, was president of the socialistic group called Union Reform League. Ely wrote much about socialism for the magazines, especially the *Outlook*. The appearance of his book *Socialism and Social Reform* in 1894 brought out some sharp criticism; for example, Arthur T. Hadley, Yale professor of political economy, protested in the *Forum* against "the attempt to 'popularize' economics by giving too much weight to the conclusions of unrestrained public sentiment." [108] In the seven years or so immediately following the Spanish-American War, which constituted, if not a truce, at least a quieter episode in the long conflict between labor and capital, even conservative magazines occasionally published sympathetic expositions of socialism. Notable were the 1901 series of articles in the *Chautauquan* and Upton Sinclair's presentation of the subject in *World's Work* in April 1906. We must, however, quote the reply of the *Saturday Evening Post* to what it considered the broad socialistic doctrine of the leveling of individuals. "One day in the dim and forgotten past," said a *Post* editorial, "a star fell from heaven and ambition was born." [109] Yet even the *Post* printed a sympathetic piece on socialism by Joseph Medill Patterson, when that journalist was having his fling with the new ideas in 1906.

Named as official organ of the Socialistic (later Socialist) Labor party in 1886 was the New Haven *Workmen's Advocate*, which had been founded as a labor weekly the year before. J. F. Busche, the first editor, was dismissed in 1890 because of his Lassallean emphasis on political action, to be followed by a Socialist schooled in French journalism, Lucien Sanial. The new editor worked with a new party leader, Daniel De Leon. The paper's name was changed to *People* in 1891 and it was moved to New York, to be published as an outsize folio of eight pages, filled with labor news, Marxian propaganda, and cheap miscellany. Later that year Sanial's eyes failed, and De Leon took over. In all the bitter quarrels of Socialist factions and leaders, De Leon remained for many years the outstanding editor in this field. He used the *People* to lead his party into active political work, to promote labor union infiltration, and always to spread Marxist doctrine. When the great schism in the Socialist Labor party occurred in 1899, the

[108] *Forum*, v. 18, p. 191, Oct. 1894.
[109] *Saturday Evening Post*, v. 170, June 18, 1898, p. 8.

anti–De Leon minority, which was soon to unite with the Social Democrats, kept the *People*, changing its name to *Worker* [110] in 1901, when the Socialist party was formed and the Social Democrats disappeared as a group. But when the anti–De Leonists "stole" the *People*, the Socialist Labor party set up another publication for their leader, called the *Weekly People*, which De Leon continued to edit until his death in 1914.[111]

Two midwestern attempts were made to supplant the *People* — one by the *St. Louis Labor* in 1893 and the other by the Chicago *Worker's Call* in 1899,[112] but neither succeeded. In San Francisco the *New Charter* was a Socialist Labor party organ conducted by the aggressive M. W. Wilkins. First published in San José in 1895, it was moved to San Francisco two years later and its name changed to *Class Struggle*. In 1900 it was called *Advance*, but it ceased with the union of 1901.[113]

Meanwhile, socialistic periodicals representing groups outside the Socialist Labor party were published in some profusion. Some were newspapers with strong propagandic slant, and many were in the German language. The leading journal of the Social Democracy was the *Social Democrat*, which in 1894 succeeded the *Railway Times* as Eugene V. Debs's organ. It became the *Social Democratic Herald* after the party split of 1898, which resulted in the formation of the Social Democratic party.[114]

In 1900–1901 a determined effort was made to bring together in one party the various socialistic groups — a difficult task in view of the emphasis among them all upon individualism. The *Yale Review* pointed out that all factions "clamor for unity"; but, it added, "we venture to guess that no real union will be brought about." [115] A bad guess, for the Socialist party, which emerged from a series of con-

[110] N. I. Stone was the first editor after the schism, but he was soon replaced by Algernon Lee, a Minneapolis newspaperman. The *Worker* changed its name to *Socialist* in 1908, but perished at the end of that year.

[111] It continued as the Socialist Labor party organ, advocating social revolution in a position between the violent revolutionaries and the political-action partisans. There was a *Daily People* 1900–14. See Arnold Peterson, *Daniel De Leon* (New York, 1931), a prejudiced but informative pamphlet; also Anniversary Edition of *Weekly People*, v. 30, May 3, 1930.

[112] The former, under Albert Sanderson, founded the Socialist Newspaper Union to publish local editions in 35 cities; but De Leon was too strong and *Labor's* Marxism too weak. The St. Louis Section of the S.L.P. was dissolved in 1897; it was later purged and reinstated, and *Labor* continued to 1930. *Worker's Call* also fought De Leon, M. L. Klauber, editor; it then joined in the Socialist party union, A. M. Simons becoming editor in 1901. The name became *Chicago Socialist* in 1902, and it was absorbed into the *Chicago Daily Socialist* in 1907.

[113] G. B. Benham was editor and publisher 1899–1900, and C. H. King in 1900. King sold the paper to the San Francisco Section of the S.L.P. Originally the paper was the successor of two labor journals, the Santa Cruz *New Charter* and the *San José Tribune*.

[114] W. P. Borland, a Kropotkin anarchist, was editor 1897–98; and A. S. Edwards, former editor of the *Coming Nation*, became editor with the change in name under the new organization. In 1900 the paper became an organ of the Socialist party.

[115] *Yale Review*, v. 9, p. 372, Feb. 1901.

ferences and conventions, represented a workable union of the strongest elements of the Marxist persuasion. The new party at once established many regional journals, most of them short-lived.[116] More important was the *International Socialist Review* (1900–1918), a Chicago
monthly edited by the scholarly and radical A. M. Simons. A ten-cent
magazine of sixty-four octavo pages, the *Review* carried articles by
nearly all the Socialist leaders of the time. It absorbed the monthly
*Comrade* (1901–1905), of New York.

Besides the periodicals that have been mentioned as exponents of
political socialism, there were many labor, reform, Christian socialist,
nationalist, and free-lance anarchistic journals, some of them treated
in other chapters of this volume,[117] which supported socialistic measures in political campaigns but were not consistently political.

### POPULIST CRUSADE

The People's party advocated socialistic reforms, while keeping
clear of Marxism. As *Current History* pointed out in the year of the
new party's organization, Populism had its nucleus in the Farmers'
Alliances, north and south.[118] The alliance movement brought out an
extraordinary number of small papers the country over. The *National
Economist* claimed in 1892 that there were nearly nine hundred such
papers at that time; [119] they were newspapers and small agricultural
sheets, but the main purpose of each was to serve its regional farmers'
alliance, whatever the precise name of that organization was. The
*National Economist* (1889–1892) itself was the official organ of the
Southern Farmers' Alliance and was edited in Washington by its leader, Dr. C. W. Macune. Another prominent periodical of that organization, edited by Colonel L. L. Polk, for several years its president, was
the *Progressive Farmer* (1886–1893), of Raleigh, North Carolina. The
*Western Rural* (1880–1890), of Chicago, edited by the founder of the
Northern Farmers' Alliance, Milton George, was chief spokesman for
that organization. The *Farmers' Alliance* (1889–1892), of Lincoln,
Nebraska, was edited by Jay Burrows, for some years president of the
Northern Alliance. Leading Grange organ of the period was the *Ameri-*

[116] For example, *Missouri Socialist* (1901–02), merged in *St. Louis Labor*; *Iowa Socialist*
(1902–04), Dubuque; *California Socialist* (1902–03), San Francisco; *Los Angeles Socialist*
(1902–09), which changed title to *Common Sense* in 1904; *Vanguard* (1902–08), Milwaukee.

[117] An excellent reference for socialistic groups and their journals is Howard H. Quint, *The
Forging of American Socialism* (Columbia, S.C., 1953). See also Donald Drew Egbert and
Stow Persons, eds., *Socialism and American Life* (Princeton, 1952), v. 2; and Edward Silvin,
comp., *Index to Periodical Literature on Socialism* (Santa Barbara, Cal., 1909), a pamphlet.

[118] *Current History*, v. 1, p. 280, Aug. 1891.

[119] *National Economist*, v. 7, p. 328, Aug. 6, 1892.

*can Grange Bulletin and Scientific Farmer* (1874–1907), conducted by Frederick Wolcott in Cincinnati.

The *Arena* carried more articles about the Alliance-Populist movement than did any other general magazine. General Weaver, Senator Peffer, and Congressman Davis, leaders in the cause, were contributors. In the *Forum* Peffer wrote on "The Farmers' Defensive Movement" in December 1889, claiming a million members for the alliances. About a year later Washington Gladden wrote in the same magazine about "The Embattled Farmers," and a little later Frank Basil Tracy described the first general political effort of the alliances: "The excitement and enthusiasm were contagious, and the Alliance men deserted their former parties by thousands . . . in that wonderful picknicking, speech-making Alliance summer of 1890." Two years later, the People's party was in the field, with Weaver as candidate for President; but times were a little better on the farms, and another *Forum* writer declared: "All the farmers want is more money. They are fast getting it, and the faster they get it the more reluctant they are to ride forty miles in a lumber-wagon to hear Mrs. Lease and General Weaver make speeches." [120]

In 1896, when Bryan fell heir to Populism, many conservative commentators classified him as a socialist. *Harper's Weekly* editorialized on "Mr. Bryan's Sectional and Class War," and after the election declared: "We have had our first general encounter with socialism." [121] Albion W. Tourgée wrote in the *North American* about "The Western Crusade Against the Trusts," [122] but there was more to Populism than that. The *Agora*, Kansas monthly review, printed in 1895 an article which stated some of the party's aims with eloquence:

It will not stop at the remonetization of silver, nor at the system of bonding the nation and the nation's children to the millionaires. It will demand the restitution of Nature's gifts — the land and all which the term implies — to the equal use of all. It will take from private corporations all public utilities and operate them for the benefit of all. It will emancipate woman from economic dependence and political nonentity. It will make it possible for men who are willing to work to live, accumulate wealth, and become prosperous. All this it will accomplish by the irresistible force of education, agitation, and peaceable revolution.[123]

Ballot reforms, primary elections, the initiative and referendum, recall of officials, income taxes, labor unionism and the eight-hour day, and

---

[120] *Forum*, v. 8, pp. 464–73, Dec. 1889; v. 10, pp. 315–22, Nov. 1890; (F. B. Tracy), v. 16, p. 243, Oct. 1893; (C. S. Gleed), v. 16, p. 257, Oct. 1893.

[121] *Harper's Weekly*, v. 40, p. 994, Oct. 10, 1896; v. 40, p. 1114, Nov. 14, 1896.

[122] *North American Review*, v. 157, p. 40, July 1893.

[123] *Agora*, v. 4, p. 252, April 1895. The author was C. B. Hoffman, who was a member of the Board of Regents of the Kansas State Agricultural College.

currency reform were among other objectives of the loosely organized movement known as Populism.[124]

Leading journals of the People's party were the *Representative* (1893–1901), St. Paul, conducted by that picturesque Populist, Ignatius Donnelly; the *People's Party Paper* (1891–1894), Atlanta, conducted by the equally picturesque Thomas E. Watson, leader of the southern Populists; the *American* (1895–1900), Philadelphia, edited by Wharton Barker, Populist candidate for the presidency in 1900; and *Jerry Simpson's Bayonet* (1899–1900), Wichita, Kansas.[125]

An early antimonopoly monthly was *True Commonwealth* (1890–1891), of Washington, which "demanded" government ownership of railroads and utilities. The *Public Ownership Review* (1897–1900), of Los Angeles, was also a monthly,[126] *Public Ownership* (1899–1901) was an Erie, Pennsylvania, weekly. There were several short-lived cooperative association journals at the close of the century.

The *Proportional Representation Review* began as a quarterly published in Chicago by the American Proportional Representation League in 1893. C. G. Hoag, secretary of the league, was editor, and John R. Commons, W. D. McCrackan, and other scholars contributed articles. In 1901 it was merged with the *Direct Legislation Record*, which had been published by the National Direct Legislation League at Newark, New Jersey, since 1894. Beginning in 1904, the merged periodical became a part of the quarterly *Equity* (1898–1919), of Philadelphia, a journal of the A. P. R. League. The *Referendum News* (1905–1906), of Washington, was also merged with *Equity*. *Referendum* (1899–1917) was a weekly edited and published in Faribault, Minnesota, by E. B. Ford.

The *Twentieth Century* (1888–1898) began as a weekly leaflet containing the Sunday sermon of Hugh O. Pentecost, the clergyman-lawyer who was at the time pastor of the liberal Unity Congregation, of New York. It soon became "A Weekly Radical Magazine" with contributions by Edward Bellamy, John W. Chadwick, and so on. In 1892 its publishers sold it, Pentecost was supplanted as editor, and the magazine devoted itself to direct legislation, proportional representation, and cooperative trade associations.

An anti-Populist journal was the *Conservative*, J. Sterling Morton's

---

[124] See list in John D. Hicks, *The Populist Revolt* (Minneapolis, 1931), pp. 456–57, for other alliance, Populist, and radical weeklies.

[125] In May 1900, Simpson turned the paper over to his associate editor, F. A. Peltret, and its title was merely *The Bayonet* for its remaining four months. The price was lowered to 50¢ a year, or half of that in clubs, but there was not enough response to avert failure.

[126] The title of its first five numbers was *Social Review*, and of the last five, *United Socialism, Anti-Imperialism*.

weekly, published in 1898–1902 at Nebraska City, Nebraska. Its sub-title described it as "A Journal Devoted to the Discussion of Political, Economic, and Sociological Questions," but it was given over mainly to Morton's replies to the arguments of the Populists. It derived force and influence from Morton's remarkable personality and from his authority as a spokesman for agriculture.

### THE SINGLE-TAX ARGUMENT

When the *Free-Soiler* [127] was discontinued, M. Battle's New York monthly paper called *Spread the Light* (1885–1889) carried forward the single-tax cause; its name was happily changed to *Tax Reformer* in 1887. In 1885 also began the *Leader*, New York daily and weekly, which supported George when he ran for mayor in the following year under the banner of the United Labor party. Louis F. Post, active young lawyer-journalist, was editor; but when the Socialistic Labor party took the journal over in January 1887, he was supplanted by the exiled Russian nobleman, Serge Schevitsch.

The *Leader* did not outlast the year, and Post became associate editor of the new single-tax weekly set up by George himself in January 1887, called the *Standard*. It was an eight-page folio, priced at two dollars and a half a year, at first; but it later became a quarto of sixteen to twenty-four pages at three dollars. George devoted much space in the early issues of the *Standard* to his quarrel with Archbishop Corrigan, who was attempting to discipline Father McGlynn for his socialistic views. Hamlin Garland contributed fiction, verse, and articles to the *Standard*. There was much of the single-tax crusade, of course, as well as tenement reform, antimonopoly, free trade, and so on. The journal became the official organ of the National Consumers' League, the Anti-Poverty Society, the Single-Tax League, and the United Labor party. In 1891 William T. Croasland became editor and sub-titled the paper "A Weekly Review of Free Trade," but he died in August of that year, and Post was editor during the *Standard's* remaining year.

The *Single-Tax Courier* was begun in St. Louis in 1891 by W. E. Brokaw, a sixteen-page quarto issued weekly at a dollar and a half a year. In 1896 George F. Hampton bought it and published it for three years in Minneapolis as the *National Single-Taxer* before moving it to New York. It was supplanted in 1901 by the *Single Tax Review*, a bimonthly conducted by the poet-politician Joseph Dana Miller from 1901 to his death in 1939; the title was *Land and Freedom* from

[127] See F. L. Mott, *History of American Magazines* (Cambridge, 1938), v. 3, p. 294.

1924 to its end in 1943. The *New Earth* (1889–1900) was a New York monthly published at fifty cents a year by the New Churchmen's Single Tax League.

## JOURNALS OF POLITICAL SCIENCE

Said the *Century Magazine* in January 1886: "The New Political Economy signalized by the American Economic Association organized at Saratoga last September depends on scientific investigation, not speculation." Such was in fact the aim. The *Publications* of the Association, first edited by Richard T. Ely, secretary, contained many papers and addresses of value. And within the next few years other scholarly journals were begun in the field.[128]

The *Political Science Quarterly* began in March 1886 under the editorship of the political science faculty of Columbia University. Its managing editor during most of its first quarter-century was Munroe Smith.[129] Though most of its articles were contributed by its editors, it also published papers by Woodrow Wilson, Arthur T. Hadley, Albert Shaw, Horace White, and others. Among the Columbia men, perhaps Edwin R. A. Seligman was most prolific in the early history of the *Quarterly*, though John Bassett Moore, Franklin H. Giddings, James Harvey Robinson, Samuel McCune Lindsay, and Charles A. Beard were prominent. The contents of the journal had a wide scope in politics, economics, sociology, and history. Its nonpartisan character was well maintained. The book review department was important, and a "Record of Political Events" ran semiannually from 1888 to 1916, and then for nine years more in an annual supplement.

The American Academy of Political and Social Science at Philadelphia, under the leadership of Edmund J. James, began its *Annals*, published in quarterly numbers in 1890. The file of this journal is a monumental contribution to its subject.[130]

When J. Laurence Laughlin came to the University of Chicago to head its Department of Political Economy in 1892, he founded at once a quarterly journal with the title *Journal of Political Economy*, "to be devoted largely to a study of practical problems of economics, finance, and statistics."[131] In the early numbers there was much about

---

[128] Quotation is from *Century Magazine*, v. 31, pp. 475–76, Jan. 1886. *Publications* were bimonthly 1887–99, quarterly 1900–11. Called *American Economic Association Quarterly*, 1908–10. Succeeded by *American Economic Review*.

[129] Smith was managing editor 1886–93, 1838, 1904–13. Other managing editors: William Archibald Dunning, 1894–97, 1899–1903; Thomas Reed Powell, 1914–16; Henry Raymond Mussey, 1917–18; Robert Livingston Schuyler, 1919–20; Parker Thomas Moon, 1921–36; John A. Krout, 1937–52; Dumas Malone, 1953–current. Ginn & Company were publishers 1886–1916; thereafter the Academy of Political Science of New York.

[130] See pp. 192–93.

[131] *Journal of Political Economy*, v. 1, p. 19, Dec. 1892. It became a monthly (missing

the silver question, currency, tariffs, taxes, banking, trusts, insurance, railways, trade unionism, and farm problems. The *Journal's* general attitude was conservative — against free silver, against the attacks on trusts, critical of labor unions. Later it inclined more to economic theory, and to the relations of politics and economics with sociology, psychology, history, and so on.

The *Michigan Political Science Association Publications* (1893–1905) consisted of papers read at the meetings of the association, many of which were valuable; but its issues were very irregular. Henry C. Adams was editor.

The *American Journal of Politics* was founded in 1892 as a substantial monthly of some hundred and twenty pages by Andrew J. Palm, of New York. Though nonpartisan, it was liberal in its attitude, printing an article by Eugene V. Debs in its first issue, and betraying a free-silver trend in 1893–1894. Leading topics were free trade, women's rights, strikes, immigration, penology, and corruption in municipal politics. Many governors and congressmen were contributors, along with such well-known reformers and publicists as Frances E. Willard, Anna Shaw, George E. Vincent, Edward Everett Hale, and John P. Altgeld. In 1894 the *Journal* became the organ of the American Institute of Civics, and its president, Henry Randall Waite, became an associate editor. In 1895 the title was changed to *American Magazine of Civics*; two years later it was merged in the *Arena*.

An earlier organ of the American Institute of Civics was the Boston monthly *Citizen* (1886–1888), dedicated to "good government through good citizenship." The first article in the first number was one by Woodrow Wilson condemning the system of "senatorial courtesy," and J. Laurence Laughlin and Herbert B. Adams were notable contributors. *Public Policy* (1899–1905) was a Chicago weekly by Allen Ripley Foote; it was called *The Other Side* during its first year.

SCHOLARLY REVIEWS OF ECONOMICS

The *Publications of the American Economics Association* formed a bimonthly serial from 1886 to 1910. The *Bulletin of the A.E.A.* for 1911 is sometimes called a Fourth Series of the *Publications*, but it is really a separate periodical issued from 1908 to 1911. The file constitutes less a review than a series of monographs, supplemented by the proceedings of the association. It was founded by Richard T. Ely,

---

August and September) 1906–21, and a bimonthly in 1922. After Laughlin's retirement, James Alfred Field was managing editor 1916–19; and John Maurice Clark, 1920–21. The "Department" took over the editorship 1922–28; Jacob Winer and Frank H. Knight, 1929–45; William H. Nicholls, 1946–48; Earl J. Hamilton, 1948–54; Albert Rees, 1954–current.

secretary of the A.E.A.; but an editorial committee was set up in 1891.[132] The association also published a supplementary bimonthly, edited by F. W. Taussig during 1896–1899 and called *Economic Studies*.

The *Quarterly Journal of Economics* (1886–current) was "published for Harvard University," first by George H. Ellis, Boston, and since 1910 by the university press; but its contributors were by no means limited to Harvard scholars. Charles Franklin Dunbar was editor for the *Quarterly's* first decade, and then Taussig was chief editor for forty years. The leading economists of the country have been contributors, and the perennial economic and political controversies have found place in *Quarterly* pages — labor, tariff, trusts, currency, immigration, railways, agriculture — as well as the economic theory of the schools.[133]

The development of financial organization was marked by such journals as the *National Corporation Reporter* (1890–current), of Chicago, and *Trust Companies* (1904–current), of New York.

### INDUSTRIAL AND MANUFACTURING JOURNALS

It is difficult to draw the line between the journals serving manufacturers and processors and those intended for retail merchants, especially since some are expressly intended for both classes. However, we can gain a better idea of the class-periodical picture if we attempt the distinction.

Probably the *Journalist* had both groups in mind when it printed the following paragraph on September 13, 1890:

> The multiplication of trade and class papers during the past ten years has been something enormous. Almost every line of industrial endeavor has one or more organs which represent, or misrepresent, its interests. They are for the most part handsome publications, rich in heavy paper, fine press work and tasteful typography, well edited. . . . They are pretty generally successful.

They were generally folio or quarto in size, and looked much like newspapers. They were successful not only because they performed real services for their subscribers, but because they were excellent specialized advertising media. Though subscription rates were low,

---

[132] The following were chairmen of the board: Franklin Henry Giddings, 1891–94; Horace Henry Powers, 1894; Frank William Taussig, 1895–1900; Sidney Sherwood, 1901; Jacob H. Hollander, 1902–10. Series as follows: Old Series, vols. 1–11 (March 1886–Nov. 1896); New Series, only two numbers (Dec. 1897 and March 1899); Third Series, vols. 1–11 (Feb. 1900–Nov. 1910). Third Series, v. 10 (1909) was called *American Economic Association Quarterly*.
[133] See C. J. Bullock, "The Quarterly Journal of Economics, 1886–1911," in *Harvard Graduates' Magazine*, v. 20, p. 281 *et seq.*, Dec. 1911.

circulations rarely exceeded ten thousand; but that was usually enough to bring large advertising patronage.

The official bulletin of the National Association of Manufacturers was *American Trade*, begun in New York in 1898. It became the bimonthly *American Industries* in 1902, and a monthly seven years later, ending in 1931. It gave most of its space to the fight against the "closed shop" and other labor union proposals. The *Exponent* (1904–1911), of St. Louis, was conducted by James W. Van Cleave, president of the Bucks Stove and Range Company, and later of the N.A.M. It had varied contents, but was mainly devoted to a feud with Samuel Gompers. The *Manufacturer* (1888–1908) was a Philadelphia weekly (later fortnightly) issued by the Manufacturers' Club of Philadelphia. It was long edited by the historian and journalist, Ellis Paxon Oberholtzer. The longest-lived of general industrial journals is the Baltimore *Manufacturers' Record*, begun in 1882 and for many years a prosperous weekly under B. H. Edmons. It has served southern manufacturers especially, as did the semimonthly *Dixie Manufacturer* (1896–1940), of Birmingham, Alabama.

The *Iron Age*, of New York, was conducted throughout the period by David Williams, son of the founder, and was the leading journal of the iron industry.[134] *Ice and Refrigeration*, of Chicago, founded by H. S. Rice in 1891, was a leader in its group.[135] The implement and vehicle fields were affected by the movement to automotive power only after the turn of the century; for example, the *American Blacksmith* (1901–1924), of Buffalo, ultimately merged with the *American Garage and Auto Dealer*.[136]

[134] For *Iron Age* and the other journals begun in former periods mentioned in this footnote, see Mott, *op. cit.*, v. 2, p. 92, and v. 3, p. 128. *American Manufacturer and Iron World*, Pittsburgh, was edited by John D. Phillips during most of the nineties; it is the present *Steel and Iron*. *Iron and Machinery World*, Chicago, was formed in 1902 by the union of the St. Louis *Age of Steel* and the Chicago *Iron and Steel*; four years later it was merged in the *Iron Trade Review*. The *Review* had already absorbed the Pittsburgh *Industrial World and Iron Worker*; in 1930 it changed title to *Steel*. The *American Metal Market* began as a New York weekly in 1882, going to daily publication in 1902. *Foundry* was begun in Detroit in 1892 by John A. Penton as a monthly and moved to Cleveland in 1901. The *Journal of the American Foundry-men's Association*, containing its Transactions, was published in Detroit monthly from July 1896 through 1901, irregularly in 1902, and quarterly 1903–04. The *Metallographist* (1898–1906) was founded as a Boston month'y by Albert Sauveur; it became the *Iron and Steel Magazine* in 1904. The *Metal World* (1891–1902), Pittsburgh, was called during its first two or three years *Tin and Terne and the Metal World*; it was merged with *Metal Market* when that periodical became a daily. *Metal Industry* (New York) was really a continuation of the *Aluminum World* (1894–1902), which took in the *Brass Founder* (1902–03) and the new *Electroplaters' Review*; in 1940 it became *Metal Finishing*. The *Open Shop* (1902–08), Cincinnati, and the *Open Shop Review* (1904–32), Detroit, Chicago, were organs of the National Metal Trades Association.

[135] Note also that *Refrigerating World* (1899–1934), New York, which began as *Cold Storage*, absorbed the Philadelphia *Ice Trade Journal* (1877–1904), adding its name and adopting its numbering, changed its title to *Refrigerating World* in 1907, and ended in 1934.

[136] Important also were *Implement and Vehicle News* (1900–10), Cincinnati, merged into

Oil and gas journals were many and various.[137] Perhaps the most important were the *American Gas-Light Journal,* [138] published throughout the period by A. M. Callender in New York, first as a semimonthly and then as a weekly; and the *Gas Age,*[139] issued in the nineties as a New York semimonthly under E. C. Brown's editorship and with the title *Progressive Age — Gas, Electricity, Water.*

Glass, pottery, wood, and package manufacturers supported a number of periodicals. The veteran was the *Crockery and Glass Journal,* New York weekly published in the nineties by George Whittemore.[140] The monthly *India Rubber World* was founded in New York in 1889 to meet the "extent and growing importance of the caoutchouc industry in the United States" by Arthur Clemens Pearson, who was associated with it as editor and publisher until his retirement in 1928. The *India Rubber Review,* of Akron, Ohio, became the Chicago *Tire Review* in 1934 and continues in the auxiliary automotive trade. Paper products, brushes, soap, and so on had their publications.[141]

---

*Implement Age,* later *Implement and Tractor; Implement and Vehicle Record,* begun in San Francisco in 1904, now called *Implement Review; Sewing Machine Times* (1882–1924), New York; *Sewing Machine Advance* (1897–1918), Chicago.

[137] *Petroleum Gazette* began at Titusville, Pa., in 1897 and later moved to Pittsburgh; it continued after 1918 as *Along the Way. Light, Heat and Power* (1885–94) was a Philadelphia weekly. The *Acetylene Journal,* Chicago, has been published since 1899, with some changes of title; and the *Compressed Air Magazine* was issued in New York and Easton, Pa., since 1896, also with slight title changes. *Light* began in Buffalo in 1901 and became *Light, Heat and Power* three years later; since 1910 it has kept the title *Gas Industry,* with slight changes. A periodical which obtained a striking leadership in later years was founded by Holland S. Reavis as *Oil Investor's Journal* in Beaumont, Texas, in 1902; its title was changed in 1910 to *Oil and Gas Journal,* and it was moved to Tulsa, Okla. (See Sara S. Bangert, "The Oil and Gas Journal," master's thesis, University of Missouri, 1956).

[138] See Mott, *op. cit.,* v. 3, p. 92.

[139] *Ibid.,* p. 31.

[140] See Mott, *op. cit.,* v. 3, p. 127. The *National Glass Budget,* a Pittsburgh weekly begun in 1884, was sold by John Ehmann in the mid-nineties to Frank M. Gessner. The *Journal* and *Budget* are still published. The *Glass and Pottery World* (1893–1909), Chicago, was merged into what is now the *Pottery and Glass Salesman.* The *American Potter's Journal* (1888–1905) was a weekly at Trenton, N. J. The *Ceramic Monthly* (1895–1900) was a small Chicago publication. *Wood Craft* (1904–15), Cleveland, was published for its first year and a half as *Patternmaker. Dixie* (1885–1906), Atlanta, was devoted chiefly to sawmilling and woodworking, but in its earlier years to broader industrial interests of the South; it was called *Dixie Wood-Worker* in its last year or two. A group of journals served the packaging trade, as *Box-Maker* (1892–1917), Worcester, Mass.; *Shears: A Journal for the Paper Box Trade* (1892–current), Lafayette, Ind., and later Chicago; and *Barrel and Box,* founded in Louisville, Ky., in 1895, and later moved to Chicago, becoming *Barrel and Box and Packages* on absorbing *Packages* (1898–1929), of Milwaukee. The *National Cooper's Journal,* a monthly begun at Buffalo in 1885, was moved to New York in 1901 by its owner, John A. McCann.

[141] Such as *Paper and Paper Products* (1884–current), which began as the *United States Paper Maker,* and the *Pulp and Paper Magazine* (1893–current). *Brooms, Brushes and Mops* (1898–1948) was a Milwaukee journal; it underwent some changes of title. The *American Soap Journal* (1890–1907) was a monthly founded in Chicago by Henry Gathman; it later added such subtitles as *Perfume Gazette* and *Manufacturing Chemist,* and in its latter years moved to Milwaukee. *Starchroom Laundry Journal* is the organ of the Laundrymen's National Association, founded in 1893 at Cincinnati and now published in New York. *Playthings* was founded by Henry C. Nathan in New York in 1903.

Leading journals in the shoe and leather industry [142] were Boston's weekly *Boot and Shoe Recorder* and monthly *Leather Manufacturer*. The *Recorder* was the largest trade and industrial paper in the country in the early nineties, sometimes issuing fat numbers of two hundred pages. *American Shoemaking* was founded in the same city by E. D. Deming in 1901, eventually absorbed the *Superintendent and Foreman of the Shoe Manufacturing Trade* (1896–1919), and continues prosperously. But perhaps the greatest journal in the field was a Boston paper transplanted to New York — the *Shoe and Leather Reporter*, which the *Tribune* of that city declared had "no superior in the world, either as regards the scope and value of the information supplied, or the commanding position and success attained in class journalism." Many other periodicals crowded this active field.[143]

Boston was the great textile center. There the *Textile World* was founded in 1888 by Henry G. Lord and Curtis Gould the younger as a ten-page monthly; it grew in time to a weekly of over a hundred and fifty pages.[144] The great flour-mill magazines were in the Midwest, and the three leaders had been started in the seventies — the *American Miller*, Chicago; the *Northwestern Miller*, Minneapolis; the *Southwestern Miller*, Kansas City.[145] There were many other food processing and packing journals,[146] and several serving export divisions of industries.[147]

---

[142] See Mott, *op. cit.*, v. 3, p. 127, for the *Recorder* (which is now published in New York) and for the *Reporter* and other journals in this field which were begun before 1885 and lasted through most or all of the next two decades. The quotation in this paragraph about the *Reporter* is from the *New York Tribune*, Jan. 30, 1897, Sec. II, p. 9, col. 3.

[143] The *Weekly Bulletin of Leather and Shoe News* began in 1896 and is now published at Manchester, N. H. The *Northwestern Shoe and Leather Journal* (1896–1905), St. Paul, was the organ of the Northwestern Shoe and Leather Association; and the *New England Shoe and Leather Industry* (1899–1917), Boston, was the organ of the New England Shoe and Leather Association and was long called the association's *Gazette*. The *American Review of Shoes and Leather* (1903–39) was a Philadelphia monthly founded and conducted by Samuel Deemer.

[144] It became a weekly in 1915, moved to New York, and was sold in 1928 to McGraw-Hill Publishing Company. It had three or four slight changes of title. In 1896 it absorbed the oldest journal in the field, the monthly *Textile Manufacturers' Review*, founded in New York in 1868; and later it took in the *Textile Record of America* (1880–1903), a Philadelphia monthly, and the *Textile Manufacturers' Journal* (1894–1915), a New York monthly. In Boston appeared *Textile Advance News* (1888–1920), *American Wool and Cotton Reporter* (1887–current), *Fibre and Fabric* (1885–current), and *Textile American* (1904–current). In New York: *American Knit Goods Review* (1898–1901), *Lace Maker* (1903–12), *Textile Colorist* (1879–1948, formerly Philadelphia), *Dyestuffs* (1898–current). In the South, the *Southern and Western Textile Excelsior* was published at Charlotte, N. C., 1893–1907, and was then issued as *Textile Manufacturer* until 1921; *Cotton* was published in Atlanta 1899–1928, *Cotton Gin* in Dallas since 1889, and *Cotton Trade Journal* in Memphis since 1901.

[145] See Mott, *op. cit.*, v. 3, p. 128 for this trio. *Miller's Review* (1882–1934), of Philadelphia and later New York absorbed *Dixie Miller* (1892–1924), of Atlanta (formerly of Nashville) and was finally merged with *American Miller*. *Operative Miller* (1896–1921) was a Chicago monthly; *Milling and Grain News* (1902–23) was an Omaha weekly.

[146] The *Baker's Helper* began as a house organ of Chapman & Smith, manufacturers of materials in Chicago, in 1887, when most baking was done in homes; H. R. Clissold bought it

There was no great over-all merchants' magazine in this period, but there were dozens of fairly prosperous city, state, and regional commercial reviews, trade journals, and merchants' magazines, from the *Board of Trade Journal* (1888–1922), of Portland, Maine, to the *Oregon Merchants' Magazine*, (1904–1944). Two early journals of this character ended in 1908, after the current financial alarm — the *Merchants' Review*, of New York, and the *Boston Journal of Commerce*.[148]

Several magazines were published for traveling salesmen, most important of which was the *Commercial Travelers' Home Magazine* (1893–1902), which began in Syracuse, New York, as the organ of an association for building a home for indigent traveling salesmen. At first its contents were mainly eclectic, but well chosen, under the editorship of William Mill Butler; but in its last three or four years, when it was published in New York under the title *Home Magazine* and edited by Arthur T. Vance, it was a good ten-cent magazine for the general reader. Among the contributors then were Albert Payson Terhune, Alfred Henry Lewis, Cutcliffe Hyne, Joaquin Miller, Edgar Fawcett, and William J. Lampton; and there were good departments of books, the stage, women's interests, and so on. But it did not have the resources to carry on in the general field, and was finally merged with *Book-Lover*. *Sample Case* (1891–current) is the organ of the

after a few years and made it the first bakers' journal in the industry. The *National Baker* (1896–1922) was a Philadelphia monthly. The *National Provisioner* was founded in New York in 1889, became the organ of the American Meat Institute, and was moved to Chicago. The Kansas City *Packer* was begun in 1893 and later established editions in New York, Chicago, Cincinnati, and Los Angeles. The Chicago *Canner* began in 1895. The *Provisioner, Packer,* and *Canner* are still published (1956). *American Creamery* (1888–97) was begun in Chicago, and later moved to New York, to be merged finally in the New York *Produce Review* (1895–1939). The latter journal soon became the *American Produce Review,* and in 1939 it was divided into three independent New York weeklies — *Butter and Cheese Review, Milk Review,* and *Egg and Poultry Review.* The Waterloo, Iowa, *Cramery Journal* has been issued since 1890; and *Western Creamery,* of San Francisco, was published 1895–1902. *Cheese Reporter,* of Sheboygan Falls, Wis., was begun in 1876 as part of a newspaper, and is still issued by the local newspaper publisher. *American Cheesemaker* (1886–1917) was a Grand Rapids, Mich., monthly. *Macaroni and Noodle Manufacturers' Journal* (1903–19) was a Cleveland monthly; *Rice Industry* (1900–11) was a Houston, Texas, monthly. *Oysterman* (1902–16) was a weekly published at Hampton, Va., and called *Oysterman and Fisherman* in its last six years; and *Pacific Fisherman* (1903–current) is a Seattle paper. *American Brewers' Review* (1887–1918), Chicago, and *Letters on Brewing* (1901–16), Milwaukee, were both monthlies.

[147] For example: *Trade and Export Journal* (1875–1920), St. Louis; the N.A.M.'s *Export* (1901–24), New York; *Exporters' and Importers' Journal* (1892–1932), Boston, Chicago, and finally New York; *World Trade* (1898–1926), Chicago; and *Export Implement Age* (1899–1907), Philadelphia, an auxiliary of *Implement Age. International Trade Developer* (1900–31) was a Chicago journal. The *Weekly Export Bulletin* (1900–31) was issued by the Philadelphia Commercial Museum. The *American Globe: Pacific Trade Review* (1903–34) was published in Los Angeles.

[148] Mott, *op. cit.*, v. 3, p. 147.

*PUCK* PRESENTS "THE EVOLUTION OF THE ANARCHIST"

The first picture of this double-page spread shows the immigrant as he is when he arrives, the second "As We Find Him Six Months Later." From *Puck*, May 11, 1887. See pages 171–173.

VOL. XII.—No. 8.   PUBLISHED BY JAMES McCALL & CO., NEW YORK.   { Published eight times a year, viz.: March, April, May, June, Sep., Oct., Nov. and Dec.

## Hints as to the Value of the French System.

As in music, *discord* offends the educated ear and has a demoralizing effect on the symphonious aspirations of the uncultured, so in dress, a *badly fitting garment* is very offensive to the artistic eye, and detrimental to the growth of the æsthetic sentiment in those whose artistic taste have not been educated and developed. It is like a weed in the garden of Fashion, marring the beauty of its surroundings and encouraging the growth of more. How requisite it is, therefore, to encourage an art, the requirement of which makes it easy to avoid the defects and imperfections which result from the clumsy though probably labored efforts of the unskilled. When that art can be acquired at so small a cost in money (seven dollars being the price of the French System), and when so little time is required for its thorough study, it does seem inexcusable for any lady to be without it. No dressmaker should be excused for making a badly fitting garment, for with a knowledge of the rules laid down in the French System and their careful application no misfit can be made, and no lady should be excused for wearing a dress that does not fit properly, for a perusal of the French System will not only convince her that the imperfections need not be, but it will enable her to criticise her dressmaker's work with intelligence.

The distinctive characteristics which have gained for the French System so great a celebrity, the entire confidence of the most eminent dressmakers, and an unprecedented amount of public patronage, may be thus concisely enumerated.

I. The elegant fitting dresses which are produced by the French System surpass everything hitherto known in the art of cutting and fitting.

II. Nothing can approach the efficiency, the accuracy, and perfect adaptation of the French System to fit any form.

III. A correct measure or impression will always produce a perfect fit, no matter how difficult the form or how fastidious the customer.

IV. The simplicity of the French System is so remarkable that a few minutes will suffice to instruct a dressmaker in its use.

V. The immeasurable superiority of the French System has obtained for it the general approval and unqualified confidence of the most eminent dressmakers, and in nearly every instance beginners, starting business, have attributed their entire success to its use.

VI. It is the only system known to have found favor with dressmakers in England, or to be patronized by the mantua-makers of Paris.

VII. In numberless instances, where other systems have failed, and where business has been reduced to the lowest ebb, the French System has been the means of restoring immediate confidence, and its introduction has marked the beginning of a large and prosperous business.

**2470.—CHILD'S COAT.**

This pretty Coat is here depicted as made of plush and satin. The waist is cut off as far as the side back seams, and four large side pleats form the front and sides of skirt, while the back is cut all in one, finishing in two box pleats. The fronts are turned back with revers of the plush, showing a full front of satin, pleated a few inches below the collar and then allowed to fall in fullness over the belt, which extends across the front of waist only. For back and front view see inside pages.

**2466.**

**Ladies' Wrap.**

Velvet Brocaded Ottoman Silk, with the flowers enriched with jet beads and a handsome garniture of fur and passementerie ornaments are

combined in this elegant garment. The fronts are cut without a dart, and the sleeves are in box form, the back is finished with two box pleats falling loosely over the fur, the lining should be satin, either quilted or plain. Other illustrations of this garment will be found on the inside

**2461.**

**Ladies' Coat.**

This coat is made of seal brown plush, finished with handsome ornaments to correspond, and lined with quilted satin. It is exactly modelled after the sealskin coats of the same shape, has exactly the same number of seams and darts, making it equal in every respect to a sealskin coat. It is illustrated in two views in other pages of this publication, with full directions for making, quantity of material, etc.

(2470   2466   2461)

FORERUNNER OF *McCALL'S MAGAZINE*

*The Queen* measured about 12 by 18 inches. This is the front page of the issue for December 1885. See pages 580–582.

Order of United Commercial Travelers of America. *Commercial Travelers' Magazine* (1894–1927) edited by Charles Clark Munn, was the journal of the Commercial Travelers' Club, with headquarters at Springfield, Massachusetts. The *T.P.A. Magazine* (1897–1945?) was issued from St. Louis for the Travelers' Protective Association of America.[149]

The "big four" among grocers' journals in the nineties were the *American Grocer*, New York; the *New England Grocer*, Boston; the *Grocers' Criterion*, Chicago; and the *Grocer and General Merchant*, St. Louis.[150]

The *Journalist* named in 1889 the three journals which, in its estimation maintained the highest standards in the men's furnishings trade — *Clothier and Furnisher* (1880–1926), *Haberdasher* (1886–1931), and *Men's Outfitter* (1878–1906), all of New York. Three years later the same periodical took occasion to name as the two "most successful magazines devoted to men's fashions and technical tailoring in the world" — the *Sartorial Art Journal* (1874–1929) and *American Tailor and Cutter* (1880–1916), both published by John J. Mitchell, of New York. Their editor, J. O. Madison, was described as "the most graceful, forceful, and original writer connected with the trade press." [151]

The *Dry Goods Economist*, which was the new name for one of the

---

[149] An interesting and doubtless helpful journal was *Sheldon's Business Philosopher* (1904–23), conducted by Arthur Frederick Sheldon, of the Sheldon School of Business Science. It absorbed W. C. Holman's *Salesmanship* (1903–08), of Meadville, Pennsylvania. Window dressing had its chief exponent in the *Merchants' Record and Show Window* (1897–1938), of Chicago, which absorbed four others in that field, including *Harmon's Journal* (1893–99), of Chicago.

[150] See Mott, *op. cit.*, v. 3, pp. 134–35, not only for these but for other grocery and produce journals begun 1865–85 and continued in the present period. Leading grocery journals begun in the late eighties were the *Grocery World* (1887–1914), of Philadelphia, and the *Interstate Grocer* (1889–1938), of St. Louis. The *Modern Grocer* (1898–1928) was a Chicago weekly. L. J. Callanan's *Monthly* (1897–1908), of New York, was an advocate of "pure and full-weight groceries." The *Tea and Coffee Trade Journal* (1901–current) and the *Spice Mill* (1878–current) are both New York periodicals, the latter now called *Coffee and Tea Industries*. The Philadelphia *Confectioner's Journal* (1873–current) was the leader in its field. *Grocers' Review* (1891–1927) Philadelphia, organ of the Retail Grocers' Association; *Trade Register* (1892–1917), Seattle, Wash.; *Retail Grocers' Advocate* (1896–current), San Francisco; *Grocers' Magazine* (1900–38), Boston; and *Wholesale Grocery Review* (1900–30), New York, were among the more important in the grocery field. The *Butcher's Advocate* (1879–current), New York, was still the leading journal in its field; it absorbed the *American Meat Trade and Retail Butchers' Journal* (1898–1920), New York. Important confectionery journals begun in this period were *International Confectioner* (1892–current), New York; *Candy and Ice Cream Retailer* (1899–1927), Chicago; and *Confectioners' Review* (1902–45), Cincinnati.

[151] *Journalist*, June 13, 1889, May 7, 1892, May 14, 1892. The *Sartorial Art Journal* was absorbed by the *American Gentleman*, which added the *Journal's* name to its own and took over its numbering. Several of the journals mentioned in this paragraph are described as to origins and lineage in Mott, *op. cit.*, v. 3, p. 134. The *Cloak and Suit Review* (1882–1900) was named by the *New York Tribune* (March 7, 1897, sec. II, p. 2, col. 1) as the "authority" in its field. The *Chicago Apparel Gazette*, begun in 1896, has been continued since 1924 in New York as *Men's Wear*. *Clothiers' and Haberdashers' Weekly* (1892–1901) and *American Furrier* (1904–36) were New York publications.

oldest of the business journals, continued throughout the period as a New York weekly. While that city was most prolific in organs of the garment trades, Chicago and St. Louis were not far behind.[152] The *Druggist's Circular*, which was conducted throughout the whole of our period by William O. Alliston in New York, was the veteran in its field.[153] The leading publication in the jewelry trade was the *Jewelers' Circular* (1869–current), New York, which has absorbed most of its competitors.[154] It has been a weekly and a daily, and is now a monthly. The *Furniture World* (1895–1930) was another New Yorker that was a leader in its field.[155]

Plentiful also, though often short-lived, were the periodicals serving the agricultural machinery trade; [156] the harness, leather goods, and

---

[152] Three publications of some importance founded near the turn of the century were *Milliner* (1898–1928), Chicago; *Dry Goods* (1899–1922), New York; and *Illustrated Milliner* (1900–34), New York. *Drygoodsman and Southwestern Merchant* (1898–1930), St. Louis, merged in the *Dry Goods Economist* after many variations of title. *American Modiste* (1903–14) was a Chicago quarterly; *Garment Buyer and Manufacturer* (1899–1908) and *Dry Goods Guide* (1898–1921) were New York monthlies. See Mott, *op. cit.*, v. 3, p. 134 for several drygoods and millinery journals begun in the seventies and continued in this period.

[153] Mott, *op. cit.*, v. 3, pp. 133–34. This entry includes other druggists' journals begun in the seventies and early eighties and continued in the nineties. Four of the most important begun in this period were the Philadelphia *Drug, Oil and Paint Reporter* (1885–current), after 1939 the *Paint Industry Magazine*; *Pharmaceutical Era* (1887–1931), founded by D. O. Haynes in Detroit, but later moved to New York; *Retail Druggist* (1893–1931), Detroit; and *Practical Druggist* (1896–1935), New York. There were also some lively journals dealing with drugstore sundries. For current and leading stationery and paper journals, see Mott, *op. cit.*, v. 3, pp. 128, 135. *American Paper Trade and Wood Pulp News* (1890–1900), New York, was merged into *Guyer's Stationer*. *Soap Gazette and Perfumer* (1899–1940) and *Soda Fountain Magazine* (1902–46) were New York monthlies.

[154] These included *Jewelers' Weekly* (1885–1900) and the *Jewelers' Review* (1887–1902), both of New York; and much later the famous old *Keystone* (1883–1934), of Philadelphia. The *American Jeweler* (1882–1929) continued as a prominent journal. The *Kansas City Jeweler and Optician* (1901–current) is now *Mid-Continent Jeweler*. *China, Glass and Lamps* (1890–current), Pittsburgh, and *Pottery, Glass and Brass Salesman* (1899–1942), New York, made some changes in their inclusive titles in later years.

[155] The *World* eventually absorbed the old *Furniture Buyer and Decorator* (see Mott, *op. cit.*, v. 3, p. 136). *Furniture Journal* (1888–1931), Rockford, Ill.; *Painting and Decorating* (1885–98), Philadelphia; *Decorative Furnisher* (1901–42), New York; and *Furniture Index* (1900–current), Jamestown, N.Y., should also be mentioned. The *World* also absorbed the *St. Louis Furniture News* (1889–1931) and the *Grand Rapids Furniture Record* (1892–1940).

[156] Many midwestern cities were homes of journals serving dealers in agricultural machinery. Chief of such publications were *Farm Implement News* (1882–current), Chicago; *Farm Machinery* (1886–current), St. Louis, now *Farm Equipment Retailing*; *Threshermen's Review* (1892–1928), St. Joseph, Michigan. *Gas Power* (1903–27) was another St. Joseph periodical. Later the two came under the same ownership and the *Review* was published as *Power Farming* and *Gas Power* as *Power Farming Dealer*. The former was eventually moved to Detroit. Other implement journals of some importance were *Implement and Hardware Age*, begun in Kansas City in 1886 and now called *Implement and Tractor*; *Farm Implements*, begun in Minneapolis in 1887 and now the *Northwest Farm Equipment Journal*; *Implement and Tractor Age* (1892–1922), begun in Springfield, Ohio, and later moved to Philadelphia; and *Implement Journal* (1896–current), which eventually became *Southwest Hardware and Implement Journal*, of Dallas, Texas. Chief hardware journals were *Hardware Trade* (1890–current), Minneapolis and St. Paul; *Hardware* (1890–1909), New York; *Hardware Dealers' Magazine* (1893–1929), New York; and *Hardware Retailer* (1901–current), Indianapolis.

shoe business; [157] and the grain, feed and coal retailers.[158] There were journals also for the dealers in sporting goods,[159] in tobacco,[160] and in liquors.[161] The daily hotel reporters had their fling in the eighties, but later hotel journals were mostly weeklies or monthlies.[162]

Finally, *Casket* and *Sunnyside*, not yet combined, were leaders in a field which they brightened as they could.[163] *Embalmers' Monthly* (1891–current) was published in Chicago and absorbed *American Undertaker* (1890–1904). *Monumental News* (1889–current) was originally published in Chicago by Rufus James Haight, and later moved to Buffalo.

[157] The harness trade was tied in with the carriage business, which will be treated in a later chapter. The *Harness World* (1888–1922), of Cincinnati, was combined in 1922 with *Harness and Spokesman*, which had begun in 1884 as *Spokesman of the Carriage and Associate Trades*, to form the present *Spokesman and Harness World*. *Trunks and Leather Goods Record*, begun in Philadelphia in 1898, is now *Luggage and Leather Goods*; and *Hide and Leather*, begun in Chicago in 1890, is now *Leather and Shoes*. Two shoe journals designed wholly for dealers were *Shoe Trade Journal* (1893–1910), Chicago, and *Shoe Retailer* (1898–1929), begun in New York but soon transferred to Boston.

[158] Chief grain and feed journals begun in the nineties were *Hay Trade Journal* (1892–1929), Canajoharie, New York; *Grain Dealers' Journal*, begun in Chicago in 1898 and now *Grain and Feed Journals Consolidated*; and *Flour and Feed* (1900–current), Milwaukee. There were also the *National Hay and Grain Reporter* (1900–14), of Chicago; and *Feeding-stuffs* (1901–22), New York, which had various titles, absorbed *Flour Trade News* (1902–07), and was followed by *Feed Stuffs* (1922–26). See also Mott, *op. cit.*, v. 3, p. 135. Oldest of the journals in the coal business was *Coal Trade Journal* (1869–1937), of New York; in longevity *Black Diamond*, of Chicago, founded in 1885, has now surpassed its record. Others were *Coal and Coke* (1894–1911), Baltimore; *Coal Trade Bulletin* (1898–1926), Pittsburgh; *Retail Coalman* (1900–current), Chicago; and *Coal Dealer* (1904–current), Minneapolis.

[159] *Sporting Goods Gazette* (1888–1926) was a Syracuse, New York, monthly; and *Sporting Goods Dealer* (1899–current), a St. Louis monthly.

[160] *Printer's Ink* (v. 11, Dec. 12, 1894, pp. 34–35) named the leading tobacco journals of "general circulation, as distinguished from the growers' papers," as *Tobacco* (1886–current), New York, specializing in the retail trade; *Tobacco Leaf* (1865–current), New York, a real veteran, edited through much of this period by the cigarmaker-songwriter Edward Burke; the *United States Tobacco Journal* (1874–current), New York, once edited by Oscar Hammerstein, later a famous impresario; and the *Tobacco World* (1881–current), Philadelphia. Two years after this listing *Cigar and Tobacco* (1896–current), Minneapolis, St. Paul, joined this long-lived group.

[161] Three or four wine and beer journals begun in the seventies were prominent later (see Mott, *op. cit.*, v. 3, p. 135). In the eighties began *Midas' Criterion of the Wholesale Whiskey and Wine Market* (1885–1917), Chicago; the *Wine and Spirit Bulletin* (1886–1918), Louisville, Ky.; and the *Wine and Spirit Gazette* (1887–1905), New York. The *American Wine Press* (1897–1918) was a New York monthly founded by L. J. Vance.

[162] Among them were the *Chef and Steward* (1891–1920), Chicago; the *Hotel Monthly* (1893–current), Chicago; *Caterer and Hotel Proprietor's Gazette* (1893–current), New York; and *Hotel Bulletin* (1900–current), originally issued from Chicago but now from New York. The *National Barber and Druggists' Gazette* (1890–1909) was E. T. Tyndall's Philadelphia monthly specializing in cosmetics. The *Barbers' Journal* (1902–current) was a New York monthly.

[163] Mott, *op. cit.*, v. 3, pp. 132–33.

# CHAPTER XI

## SOCIAL ISSUES

THE *Arena*, though it was probably never in any of its phases a really good magazine, was more bold and persistent in its presentation of current social issues than any other general review of the nineties. Its editor in 1890 printed the following paragraph about what he considered the Great Awakening of his times:

The unprecedented sale of Henry George's works on social problems; the formation of "single tax" societies throughout the land; the almost simultaneous appearance of numerous journals devoted to the exposition of multitudinous means and measures calculated to relieve the condition of the masses and abridge the almost supreme power of the money kings; the marvelous sale of Mr. Bellamy's *Looking Backward*, which, according to the publishers, some weeks ago was averaging a thousand copies a week; the rapid growth of numerous Socialistic and Nationalistic societies throughout the length and breadth of the land — these are signs which reveal most eloquently that the moral nature of man is being awakened.[1]

The first number of the *Annals of the American Academy of Political and Social Science*, beginning a long series of invaluable publication in its field, pointed out the functional position of magazines and newspapers in this development of the thought of the people: "The increase in public interest is amply evidenced by the attention given to such problems by our daily and weekly papers and by our leading monthlies and reviews."[2] Of course, as Henry Mills Alden, editor of *Harper's Monthly*, once stated magisterially, "the law of the magazine makes it the journal which records the social movements throughout the world."[3]

Several movements joined in forcing the serious consideration of social issues upon the American people at this time. At the risk of overclassifying a stream of thought and publication which does not lend itself well to bounds and limits, five categories are here set up to describe the social studies of the latter eighties and the nineties. First, there was the growth of charities, with the trend toward carefully organized social work. Second, there was the whole lot of non-Marxian, nonpolitical socialistic groups, unorganized except for such a temporary and incomplete bond as was furnished by the Union Reform League. Of these groups, the Christian Socialists were perhaps more

[1] *Arena*, v. 1, p. 242, Jan. 1890.
[2] *Annals*, v. 1, p. 133, July 1890.
[3] *Current Literature*, v. 1, p. 105, Aug. 1888.

effective, in their way, than any other; surely they received much publicity. The Fabian Socialists, with their long-term educational objectives, the Bellamy Nationalists, more aggressive in their educational methods and clubs, and some free-lance individualists belonged to this second movement. The third was that of the Marxian Socialists, of whom the public was kept well aware. It is useless to distinguish them here from the radicals who followed the Lassallean doctrine of direct political action. Their participation in politics (Socialist Labor, Democratic Labor, and Socialist parties) and certain relationships with the anarchists and with militant labor unions kept this general movement in the papers and magazines. Fourth came the Populists, members of the non-Marxian People's party, whose aims were properly termed socialistic (with a small *s*) and whose methods were political. And finally in this listing, the order of which bears no relation to the importance of the movements, we have the growth of sociology as a science, based on investigation, measurements, and analysis.

Of these five movements, the journals of the third and fourth, with their political connections, have been discussed in the preceding chapter, and the Christian Socialist publications will be considered with the journals of religion and philosophy (Chapter XVI). However, some phenomena of the times closely related to important groups of magazines remain for discussion here, including one of the chief causes of the movements mentioned above — the growth of the great cities.

But first let us note a few general periodicals in the field.

## SOCIOLOGY AND SOCIAL WORK

The related disciplines of sociology and social work (or social service) were both born in the nineties, and sociology had no learned journal until the *American Journal of Sociology* was founded in 1895 at the University of Chicago. Albion Woodbury Small, chairman of the faculties of sociology, anthropology, and home economics at Chicago, headed this pioneer journal's first board of editors — a distinguished one, made up chiefly of men at the beginning of brilliant careers, such as Charles R. Henderson, William I. Thomas, George E. Vincent, Charles Zueblin, Lester F. Ward, Edward A. Ross, and W. G. Sumner. The aims of the magazine, as expressed in its first number, were to exchange views among the world's scholars, to "translate sociology into the language of ordinary life," to support "every wise endeavor" for the social welfare, and to restrain "premature sociological opinion." The last aim is explained by the fact that the purposes of the new "science" were at that time often vague and its methods irresponsible and immature. In its early numbers the *Journal* presented Shailer Mathews' "Christian Sociology" serially, but social reform occupied less and less space as sociology tended to separate itself from social service in the universities. Social psychology, human ecology, and other sciences maintained or increased their space. Social surveys began to appear after the turn of the century, many of them studies of the Chicago scene by doctoral candidates; but the *Journal* did not lack for distinguished by-lines, such as those of Jane Addams, Franklin H. Giddings, Paul Monroe, Thorstein Veblen, and Edward T. Devine. Dean Small remained editor until his death in 1926.[4]

The old and respected *Journal of Social Science*,[5] which published the proceedings of the American Association for the Promotion of Social Science, was much concerned in the nineties with economic and political topics. The *Publications of the American Statistical Association* began in 1888 in Boston; somewhat irregular at first, it was later a quarterly and substituted *"Journal"* for *"Publications"* in its title.

The *Annals of the American Academy of Political and Social Science* (1890–current) was founded by a group of Philadelphians in connection with an academy designed to hold forums and annual meetings, but the journal soon surpassed the forums in importance. Head of the editorial group was Edmund Janes James, professor of political and social science at the University of Pennsylvania. Among the others were Henry C. Lea, book publisher and historian; Simon N. Patten, professor of political economy at Pennsylvania; Franklin H. Giddings,

---

[4] In 1905 the *Journal* was improved physically, and it was adopted as the organ of the newly formed American Sociological Society, which lent the magazine its national officers as "advisory editors" — an arrangement that persisted until the society established its own *American Sociological Review* in 1926. Even then the relation between the society and the *Journal* remained close. After its first decade, there was more emphasis on specialized research and statistical studies, and on what Dean Small called "applied sociology" — for example, in 1913–14 Roscoe Pound wrote on social legislation, Charles E. Merriam on social politics, G. Stanley Hall on social psychology, and Shailer Mathews on social origins of theological doctrine. Robert E. Park's "The City" in the March 1915 number was significant in the development of American sociology. Dean Small, who exercised commanding leadership in the field through his editorship of, and contributions to, the *Journal* for nearly a third of a century, was succeeded by Ellsworth Faris for a ten-year period. Distinctive were symposiums on social trends edited by William Fielding Ogburn, a new emphasis on population studies, and reliance on statistics, charts, and "precision devices." In the later thirties there was more attention to larger concepts. Studies in races and minorities, and on methodology and operational techniques, increased in the forties. Ernest W. Burgess was editor from 1936 to 1940, and he was followed by Herbert Blumer. International interests, always prominent in the *Journal*, were conspicuous in the forties and fifties. Louis Wirth wrote in 1947: "The contents of the *American Journal of Sociology* . . . reflect fairly accurately the proliferation of the science, its changing major interests, methods of operation, significant findings, and its new place in the academic world" ("American Sociology, 1915–1947," in *Index to Vols. I–LII*, p. 273). This is putting it mildly and carefully: few learned journals have served their own fields of scholarship more faithfully or with more nicely balanced stimulation and restraint. (See Ethel Shanas, "The *American Journal of Sociology* Through Fifty Years," in the *Journal*, v. 50, pp. 522–33, May 1945.)

[5] See F. L. Mott, *A History of American Magazines* (Cambridge, 1938), v. 3, p. 313.

young Bryn Mawr professor. James Harvey Robinson, who came to Pennsylvania as a lecturer in history in 1891, became an associate editor in that year. Foreign studies, constitutional law, railway rates, and money and credits were prominent topics in the early years. From the beginning, each annual volume included one or more supplementary issues, such as one in September 1893 devoted the subject of inland waterways. Roland Post Falkner became editor in 1895. The *Annals* increased in size, making two volumes of three numbers each per year. During and immediately following the war with Spain, there were many articles about Cuba and about the economic and social effects of war. Contributors were often famous authorities: the supplement for May 1899 on "The Foreign Policy of the United States" included articles by Minister Wu Ting-fang, former Senator Carl Schurz, and Harvard President A. Lawrence Lowell. Emory Richard Johnson, who had joined the staff as an associate editor while still an instructor in economics at Haverford, but who was now professor of transporation and commerce at Pennslylvania, became editor of the *Annals* in 1902, and survey "problems" numbers in various fields became common.[6]

The leading magazine of social work was *Charities*, organ at its beginning in 1897 of the Charity Organization Society of the City of New York. *Charities* was later to become the well-known magazine *Survey. Lend a Hand*, Edward Everett Hale's Boston magazine, was merged in *Charities Review*, another and earlier organ of the New York society, which was itself merged in *Charities* in 1901.[7]

Several states and cities published proceedings and reports of their boards of charities and corrections, such as the *Indiana Bulletin of Charities and Correction* (1890–1935), the *New Jersey Review of*

[6] In 1912 the semiannual volumes were abandoned, and each bimonthly issue was given a volume number and published in either paper covers or in boards as the subscribers wished. The latter provision was mainly for libraries, which found the *Annals* increasingly valuable. The nonmember subscription price ($6.00) had long been abandoned, and $5.00 was the rate for both individuals and libraries. Emphasis on separate units made the *Annals* less a magazine and more a series of symposiums, but it retained its important review department. There were many special numbers dealing with social, political, and economic phases of both world wars. Clyde Lyndon King was editor during 1915–30. When Thorstein Sellin succeeded him, he made a further step in the authoritativeness of the *Annals* by dispensing with the editorial council and asking specialists on various topics to arrange symposium numbers dealing with those topics, invite contributors, and edit the articles. Students will always be grateful to scholars in the social sciences at the University of Pennsylvania, who have borne the responsibilities of the editorship of the *Annals*. King wrote, without exaggeration, in the *Index* of 1916: "It is not too much to say that among the contributors are all the leading economists, sociologists, political scientists, and social workers of the country. . . . Business men, labor leaders, and public officials have presented their own points of view. Thus we have at various times numbered among our contributors presidents, senators, members of the House of Representatives, governors, mayors, leaders in national and international affairs, labor leaders, educators, eminent jurists, and publicists."

[7] For the journals mentioned in this paragraph, see history of *Survey*, Sketch 30 in this volume.

*Charities and Corrections* (1902–1918), and *Co-Operation* (1901–1908), organ of Chicago's Bureau of Charities.[8] Other bulletins and reviews were issued by church or private benevolent organizations, such as *St. Vincent de Paul Quarterly* (1895–1916), which was to be succeeded by the current *Catholic Charities Review*; and *Sea Breeze* (1888–current), published by the Boston Seamen's Friend Society.[9] The American Institute of Social Service, of New York, published *Social Service* (1899–1906) and *Social Progress* (1901–1918).

Among journals for the deaf were the veteran *American Annals of the Deaf*, a bimonthly published in Washington since 1847; the *Deaf Mutes' Journal*, now called *New York Journal of the Deaf*; and *Mentor: A Magazine for Teachers and Friends of the Deaf* (1898–1935), of Malone, New York. A number of cities had deaf-mutes' journals, usually the organs of clubs. There were also some journals dealing with the education of the blind, mostly short-lived. The *Training School Bulletin* has been published since 1904 by the New Jersey Training School for Feeble-Minded Children. The *Open Window* has been published faithfully since 1885 by the Shut-In Society of New York.

### THE PROBLEMS OF THE GREAT CITY

"The rapid growth of cities is one of the most striking facts of the century," declared a writer in the first number of the *Publications of the American Statistical Association*.[10] John Coleman Adams, writing in the *New England Magazine* in 1891, observed:

> The problems of city life thrust themselves persistently upon public attention. They dominate the social field. They try the patience and ingenuity of political thinkers. They tax to the uttermost the resources of the church. They are therefore presented from almost every imaginable point of view, and discussed in relation to almost every phase of national life and development.[11]

The editor of the *Chautauquan* was most concerned with the dangers the city offered to American youth; he believed that "the rush into thriving centers of trade, commerce, social activities, and the whirl of dissipations is the most marked and most alarming feature of American life." [12] But probably the most impassioned indictment of the city's

---

[8] Note also *Proceedings of Illinois Conference of Charities* (1896–current), called during 1910–15 *Institution Quarterly*, and later *Welfare Bulletin*; and *Bulletin of Iowa Institutions* (1899–1937).

[9] Another sailors' aid society was the Boston Port and Seamen's Aid Society, which published the *Mariners' Advocate* (1899–1919).

[10] *Publications of American Statistical Association*, v. 1, p. 49, June–Sept. 1888. Cf. *Arena*, v. 17, p. 1039, June 1897.

[11] *New England Magazine*, v. 4, n. s., p. 570, July 1891.

[12] *Chautauquan*, v. 22, p. 477, Jan. 1896.

vice was that delivered in *Everybody's Magazine* by the Rev. Percy Stickney Grant, of New York, in 1901:

Cities have been called ulcers. They swell and fester on the surface of human population, which is healthy only by its sparser distribution. They are full of filth, poverty, and vice. They breed criminals. They graduate thieves, murderers, and panderers as naturally as universities graduate scholars.

This is not the worst. Cities not only produce vice and crime; they also consume virtue. More horrible than a disease, they appear like diabolical personalities which subsist upon the strength, health, virtue, and noble aspiration produced in the country. A city is a Moloch; the fagots of its fires are human bodies and souls.[13]

That housing was one of the chief urban problems was admitted on every side. Thomas Byrnes, chief inspector of the New York police, wrote in the *North American Review* that "the lodging houses of New York have a powerful tendency to produce, foster, and increase crime." [14] Among the general magazines, the *Century* was preëminent in its editorial advocacy of reform in city government; and Editor Gilder in 1896 headed a civic movement promoted by Jacob Riis for improved housing in New York.[15] *Scribner's* also turned its attention occasionally upon the "flophouses" and the tenements of city slums, as did most magazines. The *Arena* published in 1894 some bibliographies of current literature on tenements, parks, and municipal reform; and in them are noted articles in nearly all the prominent general magazines as well as studies appearing in the specialized journals. That all this activity produced some results is indicated in an article by Edward T. Devine in the *Annals* in 1897, telling of the municipal lodging houses, the city supervision of the cheap places, and the campaign against mendicancy — all New York reforms.[16]

Settlement houses were looked upon as furnishing valuable basic aid to social and moral reform in slum districts. *Charities* and *Commons* discussed all such institutions; and Jane Addams, of Hull House, Chicago, was a frequent contributor to the magazines. The *Hull House Bulletin* was issued from 1896 to 1906, and several other settlement houses had similar modest periodicals.[17]

[13] *Everybody's Magazine*, v. 5, p. 555, Nov. 1901.
[14] *North American Review*, v. 149, p. 355, Sept. 1889.
[15] See *Review of Reviews*, v. 14, p. 693, Dec. 1896.
[16] *Annals of the American Academy of Political and Social Science*, v. 10, pp. 1–16, Sept. 1897.
[17] The Northwestern University Settlement had its *Neighbor* (1897–1925); the Nazarene home in Philadelphia had its *Neighborhood House* (1902–14); the New York Colored Mission had its *Milestones* (1893–1915); and the Henry Street Settlement in New York had its *Settlement Journal* (1904–15). There were also the *New York City Mission Monthly* (1887–current) and the *Mission Bulletin* (1886–1909), of Washington, as well as such church society journals as *Home Mission Echo* (1885–1909), Baptist, of Boston; *Home*

A curious outgrowth of the popular interest in city slums was the rise of a school of fiction devoted to portraying the street gamin and tenement life in general. In its number for March 1895, the *Bookman* reviewed three books from this movement — Edward W. Townsend's *Chimmie Fadden and Other Stories*, Henry W. Nevinson's *Slum Stories of London*, and (also from London) Arthur Morrison's *Tales of Mean Streets*. The next year *Munsey's Magazine* was talking about "the gamin fad," which was being encouraged by the Chimmie Fadden stories in slang, George Ade's *Artie: A Story of the Streets and the Town*, and Stephen Crane's much more serious *Maggie*. It also found "society girls" making much of the "street arabs," and painters and photographers exploiting their picturesqueness: they seemed to *Munsey's* critic unnaturally clean in the paintings of John George Brown.[18] Both the *Bookman* and *Munsey's* had articles about the slums in fiction in 1899, the former treating its more serious phase and discussing Gerhard Hauptmann's *Hannele*, Edwin Pugh's *Tony Drum*, and W. Pett Ridge's *Mordemly*, as well as some American books.[19] Israel Zangwill's *Children of the Ghetto* was widely discussed; perhaps the ghetto was not "slums," but Alvan Francis Sanborn's settings were, in his *A Daughter of the Tenement* and *The Lodging House and Other Stories*.

The enormous popularity of "The Yellow Kid," which began as the pioneer colored comic called "Hogan's Alley," in the sensational Sunday newspapers,[20] extended to the theater and popular songs and finally gave the name "yellow journalism" to all sensational papers. It was a part of this popular interest in slum life. Joe Kerr's short-lived *Yellow Kid* of 1897 was a fortnightly comic that later had further developments,[21] and is mentioned here chiefly because of the quotation it carried from Max Nordau. Nordau's *Degeneracy* was one of the literary sensations of the nineties; essentially a defense of degeneracy, the book seems related to the view of the miseries of the slums as entertainment. At any rate, it is at least interesting that this more or less philosophical statement from the German doctor-philosopher should appear on the title page of the ephemeral comic, *Yellow Kid*:

The Yellow Kid is the exact and ultimate expression of degeneracy in the *Type of Gamin*. Notice the bald head (on a boy), the two teeth, the abnormal head and abnormal feet, the formless shirt of yellow — color of decay — covering a multi-

*Mission Monthly* (1886–1925), Presbyterian, of New York; *American Home Missionary* (1895–1918), of Cincinnati; and *Home Missionary* (1900–19), of Philadelphia.

[18] *Munsey's Magazine*, v. 16, p. 379, Dec. 1896. See also pp. 373–74 in the same number.
[19] *Bookman*, v. 9, pp. 165–68, April 1899. Article by Grace Isabel Coldron.
[20] See F. L. Mott, *American Journalism* (New York, rev. 1950), pp. 325–26, 586.
[21] See pp. 48–49.

tude of other abnormalities. Every street gamin possesses the same characteristics in a less exaggerated degree, and that is why the Yellow Kid cannot exist [persist?] while degeneracy exists and degenerates.[22]

While the tenement houses of the poor were a subject for alarm among the social-minded, the apartment houses for the middle classes were a new marvel for admiration. An article on "The Cliff-Dwellers of New York" in the *Cosmopolitan* in 1893 tells the whole story. "To-day," we are told, "New York contains about seven hundred apartment houses, nearly all equipped with electricity and steam appliances." Though this type of living quarters has "attained almost perfection" only in New York, other cities, such as Boston, Philadelphia, and Chicago, are "just beginning to imitate the magnificent work done by New York architects in this direction." [23] Skyscraper office buildings were also beginning to cut the horizon, but the *Journal of the American Medical Association* warned early in 1897: "Tall buildings are in experiment, and it is too early to say with assurance whether the predictions of those who condemn them may be fully justified." [24]

Related to the social, economic, and even literary aspects of the city were the problems of municipal government. "It is a familiar remark in America that we have succeeded in doing nearly everything else better than governing our municipalities," wrote E. P. Oberholtzer in the *Annals* in 1893.[25] The *Saturday Globe*, speaking of the foulness of New York's streets in 1888, declared: "The death rate in this city is at least one-fourth larger than it would be under efficient municipal management." [26] "How long can this state of affairs continue without a revolution?" asked another New York weekly,[27] discussing the city's politics; and Editor Albert Shaw, who was a specialist on municipal affairs, wrote in 1892: "Everybody declares that the government of the City of New York is a stench and a sink of pollution, a hissing and a byword, a world-wide synonym for all that is iniquitous and abominable." [28] But the *Review of Reviews* was soon able to record the election of William L. Strong as a reform mayor,[29] and the spread of revolt against corruption in the cities over the country:

The organized reaction of good citizenship against municipal misrule, and the various positive movements for improved physical, social, and moral conditions in our American towns and cities, have together constituted the most significant

[22] *Yellow Kid*, title page of no. 1, March 2, 1897, and of the next six numbers.
[23] Everett N. Blanke in *Cosmopolitan*, v. 15, pp. 355, 362, July 1893.
[24] *Journal of the American Medical Association*, v. 28, pp. 321–22, Feb. 13, 1897.
[25] *Annals of the American Academy of Political and Social Science*, v. 3, p. 736, May 1893.
[26] *Saturday Globe*, v. 1, p. 116, May 26, 1888.
[27] *Citizen*, v. 1, p. 52, Jan. 10, 1885.
[28] *Review of Reviews*, v. 5, p. 286, April 1892.
[29] See Julian Ralph's article on Parkhurst, *ibid.*, v. 12, pp. 159ff, Aug. 1895.

and hopeful feature of our national life during the past season [winter of 1894–1895]. Municipal reform agitation has taken powerful hold of almost every considerable community in the entire land.[30]

Shaw's journal watched these reforms closely. The weekly *Christendom* maintained, a little later, a department of news of such reforms. But city political machines rarely perish; they accept defeat as affording a period of recuperation. Thus new crusades are called for. The opening guns in the great muckraking attack on corruption were fired at urban misrule in the *McClure* series on "The Shame of the Cities," by Lincoln Steffens, in 1903. The muckraking campaign will be discussed later in this chapter.

*Municipal Affairs* (1897–1903), a New York quarterly, began its career by observing that "the 'Civic Renaissance,' as the recent widespread revival of interest in municipal affairs has been aptly termed" was educational in nature. Therefore journals devoted to the subject were appropriate. *Municipal Affairs* itself was an able and well-produced review. Leading contributors were Professor Robert C. Brooks, Edwin Lawrence Godkin, and R. R. Bowker. Bowker contributed a comprehensive study of ownership of utilities in December 1897.[31] Brooks contributed bibliographies and digests of magazine articles. Each number contained a "debate" on some problem of city management.

*City Government* (1896–current), of New York, became *Municipal Journal* in 1900, and later *Public Works*; a monthly periodical during most of its life, it was a weekly from 1908 to 1922. Several engineering journals gave special attention to the needs of the cities.[32] *Midland Municipalities* was begun in Marshalltown, Iowa, in 1900 by Mayor Frank G. Pierce, as the official organ of the League of Iowa Municipalities; it later became the organ also of the Minnesota and Nebraska leagues, and then of the League of American Municipalities, changing its name to *American Municipalities* in 1912. It was always, however, more or less a midwestern journal. There were other regional publications of like character.[33]

[30] *Ibid.*, v. 11, p. 415, April 1895.
[31] E. McClung Fleming, *R. R. Bowker: Militant Liberal* (Norman, Okla., 1952), pp. 288–90.
[32] See Chap. XVIII.
[33] A monthly *Bulletin* of the League of American Municipalities, with a central office at Des Moines, Iowa, began in 1898, becoming *City Hall* in 1908; it was merged with *Midland Municipalities* in 1911. *Municipality* (1900–current) is the organ of the League of Wisconsin Municipalities at Madison. *California Municipalities* began at San Francisco in 1899, became *Pacific Municipalities and Counties* in 1903, and perished in 1932. For the *Arena Quarterly: A Magazine of Civic Progress*, see p. 414. *Detective* is the "official journal of the police authorities and sheriffs of the United States," begun in 1885 at Chicago.

### CRIME AND VICE

Crime, a perennial newspaper subject, was discussed in the magazines mainly as a social problem. The increase of crime during the depression of the early nineties was occasionally a theme. "An epidemic of train robbery seems to be spreading over the whole country," wrote Wade Hampton in the *North American Review* in 1894; and William A. Pinkerton a few months earlier in the same magazine wrote on "Highwaymen of the Railroad" — the James, Younger, and Dalton gangs. He ascribed "the recent epidemic of train robbing" to the hard times and the reading of "yellow covered novels." [34] Anthony Comstock's articles on the Louisiana lottery in *Our Day* called it a "national scourge" and may have had something to do with its banning shortly after their appearance.[35] S. S. McClure was much alarmed at the end of our period over "The Increase of Lawlessness in the United States," pointing out the rise of murders from about twenty-five per million population per year in the early eighties to considerably over a hundred per million in the late nineties.[36]

Crime as a subject for magazine fiction increased somewhat at the turn of the century under the stimulation of the immense popularity of "Sherlock Holmes."

The *Police Chronicle of Greater New York* (1897–1920) was to become *Civil Service Chronicle* in 1911. The title of the *National Police Gazette*, famous sensational weekly, which had become a guide to the prize ring and burlesque show for customers in barbershops, was now rather a misnomer, though the paper still featured the big crime stories as they came along.[37] The *Star of Hope* (1899–1921) was published at Ossining, New York, and was written and edited by prisoners who signed only their numbers. "He's in again — we hope for life," wrote the editor in welcoming Warden Thomas Mott Osborn back in August 1916.[38] The magazines printed much on prison reform; a bibliography in the *Arena* for August 1894 cites articles in a score of journals of various types.

The *Philanthropist* (1886–1914) was a little periodical published by the Society for the Prevention of State Regulation of Vice, "for social purity" and against the licensing of houses of prostitution; it became *Vigilance* in 1910. *Light* (1898–1936) was published at LaCrosse, Wisconsin, by B. S. Steadwell, who declared in the first number that

[34] *North American Review*, v. 159, p. 665, Dec. 1894; v. 157, p. 537, Nov. 1893.
[35] *Our Day*, v. 4, p. 436, Nov. 1889; v. 5, pp. 472–77, June 1890.
[36] *McClure's Magazine*, v. 24, p. 168, Nov. 1904.
[37] See Sketch 9 in Mott, *A History of American Magazines*, v. 2.
[38] This monthly was called *Star Bulletin*, 1918–20, and *Sing Sing Bulletin*, 1920–21.

a young girl was ruined every eight minutes in this country, and who cited cases and printed much about white slavery and sex hygiene. The Florence Crittenton Missions published small periodicals in various cities and the *Florence Crittenton Magazine* (1899–1917), later called *Girls*, as the national organ at Washington. The subject of prostitution was boldly discussed in many of the reviews, and especially the *Arena*. *Christian Life* (1887–1916), of Morton Park, Illinois, was latterly called *Purity Journal*.

The observation may be appropriately made here that there was much discussion of divorce in the magazines in the first half of our period. In 1890 Felix Adler, head of the new Society for Ethical Culture in New York, declared that "the divorce movement has gained headway to an alarming and unprecedented extent"; he thought that education, and not changes in laws, was the answer.[39] Three months later Elizabeth Cady Stanton was arguing in the *Arena* that divorce should be made respectable and "recognized by society as a duty as well as a right." [40] In the following number of the same magazine, the editor pointed out that "magazines, periodicals, and even daily newspapers have of late been discussing" uniform national regulation of divorce.[41] Perhaps none of the reviews was more concerned with this problem than the *North American*, which printed repeated symposiums and comments on it in 1889–1890.

The problem of homeless children was also mentioned often. David Dudley Field made the statement in the *Forum* in 1886 that twelve thousand homeless children under twelve years of age were living in the streets of New York.[42] Several home-finding societies published official bulletins, such as *Orphan's Cry* (1900–1911), San Francisco, and *Our Homes and Our Homeless* (1900–1905), Chicago.

### REFORMS: BELLAMY NATIONALISM

The knowledge of the degradation of the poor in the slums and of overworked farmers raising mortgaged crops on mortgaged land, plus the news of increasing numbers of trusts and combinations of great wealth, all coming upon the country at a time of economic depression, induced in the early nineties attitudes unusually favorable to reform theories and movements.

Most of the magazines in the late eighties and early nineties com-

[39] *Ethical Record*, v. 3, p. 202, Jan. 1890.
[40] *Arena*, v. 1, p. 566, April 1890.
[41] *Arena*, v. 1, p. 682, May 1890. Cf. similar statement in *Chautauquan*, v. 10, p. 589, Feb. 1890.
[42] *Forum*, v. 1, p. 113, March 1886.

mented on the growing number of millionaires in the country: they "seem to spring up between showers in New York," said a writer in the *Cosmopolitan*.[43] *Harper's Weekly* ran a series on "Men Who Control Millions" in August 1889. William Dean Howells, who had been influenced by the Boston Nationalist Club, decided that the United States had become a plutocracy.[44] W. T. Stead wrote in the *Review of Reviews* that, with over four thousand millionaires in the United States, "the greatest task which lies before Christian civilization today is a mission to millionaires" to show them their duty to make benefactions.[45] On the other hand, the theory of "tainted wealth" acquired some vogue, so that an institution was conceived to have infected itself with the sins of its benefactor when it accepted his ill-gotten gains for benevolent or educational purposes. The writer of a letter to the new *American Journal of Sociology*, edited by the University of Chicago faculty, said: "I can look for no lasting good from a work that is conducted by an educational institution founded by the arch-robber of America."[46] Edwin Lawrence Godkin pointed out in *Scribner's* that American fortunes, "now said to be greater than any of those in Europe," had "introduced among us the greatest of European curses — class hatred."[47] Benjamin O. Flower put it more picturesquely in his combined review in the *Arena* of Ward McAllister's *Society As I Have Seen It* and William Booth's *In Darkest England*, which showed "idlers who eat, drink, dance, and are consumed in a butterfly existence" in contrast with "the gaunt, hungry, hollow-eyed millions to whom life is an awful curse."[48]

Among the many types of reform movements which sprang up in our period under the influence of such ideas was the plan of utopian socialism known as Nationalism, based largely on Edward Bellamy's novel *Looking Backward*. The name of the movement came from the belief of its founder, as illustrated in the story and later expounded in magazine articles, that "the entire capital and labor of the nations should be nationalized and administered by their people through their chosen agents, for the equal benefit of all."[49] The chief difference from

[43] *Cosmopolitan*, v. 5, p. 385, Sept. 1888.
[44] *North American Review*, v. 158, p. 185, Feb. 1894.
[45] *Review of Reviews*, v. 7, pp. 7, 48–60, Feb. 1893.
[46] *American Journal of Sociology*, v. 1, p. 210, Sept. 1895.
[47] *Scribner's Magazine*, v. 20, pp. 497, 500, Oct. 1896.
[48] *Arena*, v. 3, p. 341, Feb. 1891. Cf. *Forum*, v. 10, pp. 546–57, Jan. 1891; *Californian Magazine*, v. 2, pp. 272–77, Nov. 1892.
[49] Bellamy in *North American Review*, v. 154, p. 742. For other Bellamy expositions of Nationalism in the general reviews, see *ibid.*, v. 150, pp. 351ff, March 1890, which was a reply to an article in the *Atlantic Monthly* (v. 65, pp. 260ff, Feb. 1890) by Francis A. Walker, who attacked socialism; and "The Programme of the Nationalists," *Forum*, v. 17, pp. 86–91, March 1894, which is followed by a reply by W. G. Sumner entitled "The Absurd Attempt to Make the World Over."

Marxism was in the Bellamy rejection of the class-struggle principle. That the times were ripe for revolt, in ideas if not in action, was apparent to many. The scholar, clergyman, and journalist N. P. Gilman, writing in the *Quarterly Journal of Economics* the year after *Looking Backward* was published, said that its "wide circulation is due to the fact that the earnest feeling with which it is written coincides with a very deep and widespread discontent with existing social conditions." [50] The book sold about a half a million copies, a large proportion in paper covers, during this period — an amazing distribution for those times.[51]

Some observers insisted on thinking of Nationalism as essentially a literary movement, and *Current Literature* referred to it in August 1889 as "Boston's latest literary fad." [52] Indeed, many of the early members of the first Nationalist Club were Boston men of letters, like William Dean Howells, Edward Everett Hale, and Thomas Wentworth Higginson; and Bellamy's original intention had been definitely literary. "In undertaking to write *Looking Backward*," he once noted in the *Nationalist*, "I had at the outset no idea of attempting a serious contribution to the movement for social reform. The idea was a mere literary fantasy." [53] But, as the *St. Louis Life* observed in 1890, "Mr. Bellamy has suddenly found himself the apostle of a new social creed" [54] — a creed which, as Congressman William McAdoo pointed out in *Belford's* about the same time, "is likely to bring mighty causes and forces into play." [55]

Nationalism was an educational rather than a direct-action movement. Wrote Rabbi Solomon Schindler, a Nationalist leader, in the *Arena*:

> A great many things will have to be unlearned, and a great many lessons will have to be patiently drilled into the minds of people before they will be ripe to take matters into their own hands and go even to the extent of nationalizing railroads, telegraph, etc.[56]

It was therefore logical to publish Nationalist periodicals. The first official organ was the *Nationalist* (1889–1891), a Boston monthly

[50] *Quarterly Journal of Economics*, v. 4, pp. 50–76, Oct. 1889.

[51] See F. L. Mott, *Golden Multitudes* (New York, 1947), p. 169. Cf. *Journal of the Knights of Labor*, Feb. 6, 1890. Also note Laurence Grönlund's claim in the *Arena* (v. 1, p. 153) in Jan. 1890 that 200,000,000 copies of the book had then been sold. Bellamy had probably derived some of his socialistic ideas from Grönlund's *The Co-Operative Commonwealth* (see Howard H. Quint, *The Forging of American Socialism*, Columbia, S. C., 1953, p. 78).

[52] *Current Literature*, v. 3, p. 93, Aug. 1889.

[53] *Nationalist*, v. 1, p. 1, May 1889.

[54] *St. Louis Life*, v. 2, Aug. 23, 1890, p. 5.

[55] *Belford's Magazine*, v. 4, p. 53, March 1890.

[56] *Arena*, v. 13, pp. 27–28, June 1895. See also Schindler's "What Is Nationalism," in *New England Magazine*, v. 7, n. s., pp. 53–61, Sept. 1892.

edited by Henry Willard Austin. Occasional contributors were Bellamy, Higginson, Hale, E. H. Sanborn, W. D. P. Bliss, Sylvester Baxter,
Helen Campbell, and John Orvis. There were "Club Notes," letters
to the editor, and general news of the movement. When this magazine
got into less satisfactory hands late in 1890, Bellamy began a new
periodical of his own called the *New Nation* (1891–1894). It was a
sixteen-page quarto written largely by the ailing Bellamy, and all in
a spirit of remarkable kindliness. Henry R. Lagate was Bellamy's
editorial assistant. The paper was eventually given up because it lost
money.[57] But in the heyday of the movement there were a hundred and
sixty-five Nationalist Clubs scattered throughout the country,[58] and
many papers were published that were devoted wholly or in part to
the cause. At one time as many as five such papers were being issued in
California,[59] where Nationalism flourished most luxuriantly after it
spread from its native Boston.

Meantime much was published in the magazines and reviews about
this reform movement, though by 1894 its more aggressive elements
had been drawn off into Populism. When Bellamy died in 1898, many
high-flown statements were made about him and his work. For example, the Christian Socialist W. D. P. Bliss thought it "doubtful if
any man, in his own lifetime, ever exerted so great an influence upon
the social beliefs of his fellow beings as did Edward Bellamy." [60] It was
generally recognized that the Bellamy type of Fabian Socialism had
done more to make the American middle class think seriously about
social principles than any other force in the latter part of the nineteenth century.

### REFORMS: FABIAN AND FREE-LANCE SOCIALISM

English Fabian Socialism, with its long-term objectives, never did
achieve a country-wide organization in America, despite the efforts of
W. D. P. Bliss to that end; but there were Fabian Societies in Boston,
New York, Philadelphia, and other cities in the mid-nineties. The fact
that Bliss was a Christian Socialist emphasizes the close relationship
between that group and the Fabians. Bliss founded the *American*

---

[57] *New Nation*, v. 4, p. 49, Feb. 3, 1894.
[58] *New England Quarterly*, v. 11, p. 754, Dec. 1938.
[59] *California Nationalist*, v. 1, May 24, 1890. The leading Nationalist papers in California were the *Pacific Union*, begun in 1889 at Los Angeles, to become the *Pacific Union
Alliance* in 1891 and to end soon thereafter; and the *California Nationalist* (1890–93) in
San Francisco. A *Bellamy Review* (1900–01) was published briefly at Kearney, Neb.; it
began as *Socialist Review*.
[60] *American Fabian*, v. 4, p. 1, June 1898. See also *Social Democratic Herald*, July 9,
1898; *People*, May 29, 1898; *Social Democrat*, June 2, 1898; *Appeal to Reason*, June 4,
1898. Cf. Arthur E. Morgan, *Edward Bellamy* (New York, 1944).

*Fabian* (1895–1900) as a Boston monthly, but he turned it over to the New York Fabian Society after the first year, and a succession of editors directed the remainder of its short life.[61] Leading contributors were Bellamy, Bliss, Henry Demarest Lloyd, Helen Campbell, Frank Parsons, and Charlotte Perkins Stetson.

Oldest of the American journals that may be loosely designated as Fabian was Daniel O'Loughlin's *Twentieth Century* (1888–1898), a New York weekly, which followed the People's party into the free-silver camp in 1896. Charles P. Somerby's *Commonwealth* (1893–1902) was also a New York weekly; at first it was largely devoted to reprinting Fabian documents from England, but later most of its space was given to news of socialism at home and abroad. The *Public*, [62] of Chicago, was edited by Louis F. Post, single-taxer, labor advocate, and free-lance socialist. *New Occasions* (1893–1897) was another Chicago independent socialistic publication — a dollar monthly conducted by Charles H. Keer. It was followed by *New Time* (1897–1898), edited by Frederick Upham Adams, who was joined in the latter numbers by Benjamin O. Flower, temporarily separated from the *Arena*.[63] The Reverend John E. Scott had a short-lived Fabian weekly in San Francisco called *Socialist* (1895–1897), which became *Social Economist* shortly before its end.

Most famous of all the free-lance socialistic periodicals was *Appeal to Reason*, J. A. Wayland's paper at Girard, Kansas.[64] Wayland, the "One-Hoss Editor," began his work as propagandist of socialism on the *Coming Crisis* at Pueblo, Colorado, in 1892. This was a Knights of Labor and Populist paper established three years earlier under the name *Colorado Workman*, and conducted by E. S. Moore and the famous Kansas lecturer for the People's party, Mrs. Mary Elizabeth Lease. Having helped elect a Populist governor in Colorado, Wayland resigned his unpaid editorial job; and in 1893 he founded the *Coming Nation* in Greensburg, Indiana, as a four-page weekly paper, folio in size, at fifty cents a year, designed for national circulation. He built

[61] Prestonia Mann, William J. Ghent, and John Preston. The periodical was a quarto of 12 to 16 pages during most of its life, and sold for only 50¢ a year.

[62] See p. 62.

[63] See Sketch 2. *New Time* was succeeded by *Coming Age*, which turned to spiritism (see p. 413, footnote).

[64] The authority on Wayland and the *Appeal* is Howard H. Quint, whose article in the *Mississippi Valley Historical Review*, "Julius Augustus Wayland, Pioneer Socialist Propagandist" (v. 35, pp. 585–606, March 1949), was elaborated somewhat as ch. 6 in his *The Forging of American Socialism*, cited above. See also George Milburn's "The *Appeal to Reason*," in *American Mercury*, v. 23, pp. 359–71, July 1931; Wayland's autobiography, *Leaves of Life* (Girard, Kan., 1912); George D. Brewer, *The Fighting Editor; or, Warren and The Appeal* (Girard, rev. 1910); A. M. Simons, "J. A. Wayland, Propagandist," *Metropolitan Magazine*, v. 32, pp. 25ff, Sept. 1910; and George A. England, "The Story of *The Appeal*," *Appeal to Reason*, Sept. 6, 1916.

up a circulation of sixty thousand, much of it through blocks of gift subscriptions. The editor's ability to write pungent paragraphs and his uncompromising hatred of the "ghoulish plutocrats" won his new paper many friends who wished to aid his propaganda effort. After a year in Indiana, Wayland moved his paper to a Tennessee community which he had planned, and which he set up chiefly through the earnings of his paper; [65] but the communistic experiment — or rather Wayland's connection with it — lasted only about a year, and in August 1895 he abandoned both the Ruskin Co-Operative Association and the *Coming Nation* to his quarrelsome fellow-communitarians.[66]

The village of Girard, Kansas, was then chosen for Wayland's next venture, and there he founded the *Appeal to Reason* with the number for August 31, 1895. A big four-page sheet on cheap paper, garish with scareheads, the *Appeal* sold for fifty cents a year, reduced occasionally to twenty-five cents; and by 1904 it had a circulation of a quarter of a million. In spite of this large distribution, it barely avoided deficits,[67] since it offered twenty-five copies a week to any address for a dollar and a half a year, or a hundred copies of any number for fifty cents. Wayland did not know his Marx and did not want to; he printed some Marx, but much more Bellamy, Grönlund, and Lloyd. He was also a strong Debs supporter, and printed many contributions from that socialist leader. He believed in political action for the socialist cause, and put the *Appeal* successively behind the People's party, the Socialist Labor party, the Social Democratic party, and the Socialist party. The paper's basic causes were government ownership of all means of production and distribution, and direct rather than representative legislation. Most of each weekly number was written by the editor. Many of the editorials were illustrated by small cartoons by Ryan Walker. There were several "columns" of paragraphic wit and propaganda, such as "Musings of a Mossback," "Yeast," and "Thoughts for Your Uncle Sam." When Fred D. Warren became managing editor shortly after the turn of the century, there were more red ink in the headlines, more sex sensations, and more attacks on public men.

*Wayland's Monthly* (1899–1915), a little five-cent periodical designed for reprinting important socialistic statements, was not much

---

[65] Wayland also had a modest personal fortune that he had accumulated in real-estate dealings before he turned to socialism.

[66] The *Coming Nation* was continued at Ruskin, Tenn. A. S. Edwards followed Wayland as editor, to serve for three years. After a period of suspension, the paper was revived at Girard in 1902–03. It was again revived in a new series in 1910–13, under the editorship of A. M. Simons. The Chicago *Progressive Woman* (1907–14), which had begun as *Socialist Woman*, was published at Girard under the old *Coming Nation* title for its last two years.

[67] *Wayland's Monthly*, Oct. 1904, p. 12. Wayland used no voluming for his serials.

more than a series of pamphlets. The number for October 1903, for example, contains the *Communist Manifesto* by Marx and Engels.

Wayland committed suicide in 1912; but the *Appeal* continued for several years, and still longer under some changes of title.[68] The position and influence of Wayland have been exaggerated by some of his admirers: to call him "a reincarnate Tom Paine" is to give him too much credit as a thinker.[69] He was a slashing writer — not highfalutin, like Brann, but quite as extreme, and a specialist in the cracker-barrel-philosophy approach.

Another independent socialist — though he was long allied with the Socialist Democrats and later with the Socialist party — was H. Gaylord Wilshire, of Los Angeles. He was the son of a wealthy father, but had become a nationalist, and from there had gone into various phases of radicalism, especially government ownership. He was aggressive and handsome, wore a Vandyke beard and loud waistcoats, and had a flair for making headlines.[70] He began the *Challenge,* a weekly, in Los Angeles in 1900, but made it a monthly under the title *Wilshire's Magazine* the next year, moving it then to New York. When he got into trouble with the Post Office Department, ostensibly over free mailings under a second-class permit, he moved the magazine to Toronto for a few years; but it was back in New York in 1904 and continued to 1915 as a sixteen-page monthly at ten cents a year. Wilshire, commonly referred to as "the millionaire socialist," seems to have possessed a certain arrogance that alienated many, both socialists and capitalists. Elbert Hubbard wrote of his troubles with the Post Office:

> And now Mr. Madden, Third Assistant Postmaster General, has very properly denied Willie's "Poo-Bah" the privileges of Second Class Matter, claiming that the contents are certainly Third Class at the least. Wilshire's magazine is entirely devoted to advertising Wilshire's van dyke whiskers, his check pants and tan

---

[68] In 1919 E. Haldeman-Julius, publisher of "Little Blue Books," took it over; but Louis Kopelin continued a *New Appeal* for two years. The *Haldeman-Julius Weekly* ran for ten years, 1919–29, and then became the *American Freeman* 1929–51. It was a monthly in its latter years. Fred D. Warren, who had been Wayland's assistant since 1901, and *de facto* editor from 1904 on, succeeded Wayland after the latter's death; but he was followed in 1916 by Kopelin. Haldeman-Julius was editor after he purchased the paper. Conviction of Warren for inciting to violence and crime in 1910 was the aftermath of the *Appeal's* crusade against the judiciary as a protest against the illegal extradition of the labor leaders Moyer and Haywood for trial in Idaho — the so-called "kidnapping" of those men. Warren printed and circulated offers of rewards for the kidnapping of ex-Governor Taylor of Kentucky, whose extradition from Indiana had been refused when he was accused of the assassination of Governor Goebel, "to show to the world that it was perfectly legal to kidnap workmen but utterly illegal to kidnap a retainer of capitalism" (W. J. Ghent, "The *Appeal* and Its Influence," *Survey*, v. 26, p. 26, April 1, 1911). President Taft pardoned Warren before he began to serve his sentence.

[69] Quint, *The Forging of American Socialism*, p. 175.

[70] See Ralph Hitchcock, *Fabulous Boulevard* (New York, 1949), pp. 85–112.

shoes — no other possible reason for its existence being disclosed anywhere in its pages.[71]

Nevertheless, Wilshire's periodicals were, at their best, lively and well produced, with some good occasional contributors.

### REFORMS: MUCKRAKING

The exposure of political corruption in city, state, and national government by magazines, which assumed the proportions of a "movement," came to a climax about 1905–1906, and was tagged "muckraking" by President Theodore Roosevelt. Of course, exposures had appeared now and again for many years. Something has been said already in this chapter about magazine criticism of city government, especially as directed at Tammany's control of New York; and certain of that city's weekly papers of opinion, society, and so on, were quoted in that connection. The urban weeklies [72] throughout America often raised their voices against misrule in the metropolitan centers. The services of this class of periodicals in such criticism, so often honorable to themselves and to journalism, have generally been forgotten. Only one quotation will be given here. Out in Kansas City, George Creel described the primary election of 1900 with a vivid pen:

Policemen were crowded thick at every polling place, and urged on by the Police Commissioners and favorite saloon keepers, bullied those whom they could, and battered those whom they could not. Many were drunk, and all were fully armed; that the day passed without bloodshed was a wonder. It was the last stand of the Police Machine, and like a pack of wolves brought to bay, they fought fiercely and ignobly. Police Commissioner Gregory and Saloon Keeper Pendergast, riding behind a pair of blooded bays, drove from place to place, whipping recalcitrants into line, mouthing threats and maledictions at every turn.[73]

The reviews and the general magazines also printed an increasing number of articles of exposure throughout the nineties. The *Arena*, *Forum*, and *North American Review* were especially active in this field. The summary already given in this and the preceding chapter has indicated the number and variety of peridocials engaged in criticism of the *status quo* in government and economics. Even the staid *Atlantic Monthly*, the humorous but conservative *Life*, and the usually complaisant *Saturday Evening Post* made their contributions to the growing critical trend by the turn of the century — the *Atlantic* in Mark Sullivan's "The Ills of Pennsylvania" in October 1901, and *Life* in the same year in its widely reprinted squib:

[71] *Philistine*, v. 14, pp. 18–21, Dec. 1901.
[72] See pp. 77–78 for discussion of this type of publication.
[73] *Independent*, v. 3, Aug. 25, 1905, p. 8.

*Query*: Who made the world, Charles?
*Charles*: God made the world in 4004 B.C.; but in 1901 it was reorganized by
James J. Hill, J. Pierpont Morgan, and John D. Rockefeller.[74]

The *Post*, which was primarily interested during these years at the
beginning of the new century in success — success in all its facets, but
mainly business success — printed some articles which, though not
severely critical, were actually of the exposure type. One example was
David Ghaham Phillips' "The Making of a Billionaire" in the number
for October 14, 1902, a factual and not unfair study of John D. Rockefeller's career.

Miss Tarbell's "History of the Standard Oil Company" began in
*McClure's* the next month; Lincoln Steffens' "Shame of the Cities"
series was started by the same magazine the following March; and
then came the great flood of "the literature of exposure." The details
are recounted in the separate histories of *McClure's, Collier's, Cosmopolitan, Arena, Everybody's*, and so on, in this work.[75]

In general, there were two types of muckraking in this period: that
which was based on painstaking investigation at great expense, for
which *McClure's* was distinguished; and the more impressionistic
kind, full of sound and fury, which was exemplified in the Lawson
series in *Everybody's*. Some magazines, of course, partook of both
varieties. It would be pleasant to think that all this crusading against
corruption in government, in industry, in finance, and even in religion
and education, was motivated by altruism; but it seems clear that
S. S. McClure, in the inspired experimentation that was a characteristic
of the man, discovered a formula of exposés which was found so immediately popular that it was followed at once by the editors of the
competing popular magazines. This does not mean that there was not
much sincerity on the part of writers of this "literature of exposure,"
or that the whole movement did not perform a great service to the
people. It means only that the materials and the skills to get a quick
popular response are commonly necessary to any significant performance by the magazines.

The rush of lesser muckrakers to reap the benefits of the taste
for exposure which had been created in 1903 and 1904 soon cheapened
the movement. *Collier's*, in a signed editorial by Hapgood in 1905,
disapproved the current "epidemic of exposure" and pointed out that

[74] *Life*, v. 37, p. 66, Jan. 24, 1901.
[75] The separate sketch of *Everybody's* has been postponed to the next volume of this
work, since nearly all of its career fell within the years to be covered by that volume; but
the other magazines here listed are treated separately in the supplement to the present volume.

"true investigators of the Steffens and Tarbell type find their authority diminish" in the turgid flood of abuse and calumny.[76] In the *American Magazine,* "Mr. Dooley" wrote a little later:

Time was whin th' magazines was very ca'ming to th' mind. Th' idea ye got fr'm these publications was that life was wan glad, sweet song. Ye don't need to lock th' dure at night. Hang yer watch on the knob. Why do the polismen carry clubs? Answer, to knock th' roses off th' trolley poles. But now, whin I pick up me fav'rit magazine, what do I find? Iv'rything has gone wrong. Th' wurrld is little bether than a convict's camp. Here ye arre! Last edition! Just out! Full account iv th' crimes iv th' Incalculated! Did ye read Larsen last month? Graft ev'rywhere. "Graft in th' Insurance Comp'nies"; "Graft in Congress"; "Graft in Lithrachoor," by Hinnery James; "Graft in Its Relations to th' Higher Life," by Dock Eliot.[77]

In 1906 President Roosevelt gave to the movement as a name the "smear word" *muckraking,* provoked thereto by a *Cosmopolitan* series entitled "The Treason of the Senate." Criticism of the cult for exposure grew, and at length the drawing power of such articles declined. The muckraking period ended, not so much because of pressures exerted by big business, but chiefly because readers tired of shrill-voiced criticism.[78]

REFORMS IN VARIETY

Yes, the twenty years from 1885 to 1905 formed a great period for reform movements of all kinds. "This is an age of reforms!" exclaimed young Dr. Woods Hutchinson, who was just beginning a long career as a journalist in the medical field. "The spirit of the Star-Eyed Goddess," he continued, "is everywhere active, and the lists are thronged with her eager champions, bearing every imaginable device." [79] There were not only the socialists of all types, ranging from anarchism to Fabianism; the currency reformers, with their slogan of "sixteen to one"; the single-taxers, who did more than any other group in the country to stimulate the study of economics; [80] and tariff reformers in government, social reformers in the churches, "veritists" in literature, and expressionists in art — but there were also the old persistent movements for temperance, women's rights, civil service reform, and so on.

---

[76] *Collier's,* v. 34, March 25, 1905, p. 23.
[77] *American Magazine,* v. 68, p. 539, Oct. 1909.
[78] C. C. Regier, *The Era of the Muckrakers* (Chapel Hill, 1932) is a useful book. Muckraking continued as a magazine technique until about 1912, when *Hampton's* gave up the ghost and *Cosmopolitan* quit the muckrake for the ladle of romantic sex fiction.
[79] *North American Review,* v. 145, p. 187, Aug. 1887.
[80] See J. Laurence Laughlin in *Journal of Political Science,* v. 1, p. 13, Dec. 1892.

The organization of the Prohibition party in 1884 and the several experiments with prohibitory laws caused a renewal of this old debate in the latter eighties. Leonard W. Bacon wrote in the *Forum* in 1886 that the "clamor for prohibition is so widely renewed as to force a thorough, persistent, relentless discussion of its claims."[81] The *North American Review* had a symposium on prohibitory legislation in August 1888. Anthony Comstock said in *Belford's Magazine* that liquor and licentiousness were twins.[82] The activities of the Prohibition party and the Women's Christian Temperance Union, and the interest in experiments with prohibitory laws in Canada and the dispensary system in the South, attracted no little attention in the magazines as the century came to an end;[83] and shortly thereafter the spectacular exploits of Mrs. Carrie Nation, of Kansas, drew much comment in both magazines and newspapers. The magazines took Carrie and her hatchet more seriously than did the daily papers, and one of the best articles written about the famous antisaloon crusader was one by William Allen White in the *Saturday Evening Post*. "Is it altogether impossible," asked her fellow Kansan, "that this frantic, brawling, hysterical woman in the Kansas jail, brave, indomitable, consecrated to her God, may be a prophetess whose signs and wonders shall be read and known of men by the light of another day?"[84]

There was a host of temperance periodicals, many of them journals of state units of the W.C.T.U. The important ones had continued from earlier periods,[85] but *Life and Health* (current), of Washington, began in 1885. Two Templar journals were the *International Good Templar* (1888–1916), which began in London, Ontario, and was soon moved to Milwaukee, and later Independence, Wisconsin; and the *Royal Templar* (1890–1905), of Buffalo. Among antiprohibition weeklies, the old *Champion*,[86] once called *Mixed Drinks*, continued at Chicago; *Truth* (1882–1912) at Detroit; and *Both Sides* (1895–1917) at Minneapolis.

Tobacco was commonly coupled with liquor in the crusades of the temperance journals. However, *Kate Field's Washington* attacked the prohibitionists in a stinging article entitled "Prohibition in All Ages a Ghastly Farce," while it commended Secretary Hoke Smith, of the Interior Department, for forbidding cirgarette smoking in his offices.

---

[81] *Forum*, v. 2, pp. 232–42, Nov. 1886.
[82] *Belford's Magazine*, v. 5, p. 64, June 1890.
[83] Canadian prohibition may be followed in the *Encylopedic Review of Current History*, and there is a good article on the dispensaries in the Carolinas in the *Outlook*, v. 66, pp. 193–94, Sept. 22, 1900.
[84] *Saturday Evening Post*, v. 173, April 6, 1901, p. 2.
[85] Mott, *A History of American Magazines*, v. 3, p. 310.
[86] *Ibid.*, p. 311.

"Is it not questionable," asked Kate, "whether a man who cannot curb his appetite for cigarettes is fit to be trusted?" [87] A terrific indictment appeared in the *Journal of the American Medical Association* under the heading, "Some Minor Immoralities of the Tobacco Habit"; though it was published in the number for April 1, 1899, it was by no means an April Fool joke.

Civil service reform, though it gained great victories in the act of 1883 and in President Cleveland's actions in extending the number of places protected by the law, was still a subject of discussion in the reviews and the journals devoted to government and political science. The file of *Good Government* is one long chronicle of the fight for the merit system. Its editors realized the truth that the professional politicians always fight for the spoils system, and that it is hard to keep the public interested in the crusade against that essentially venal procedure. They believed that most voters were opposed to the evils of the system, though "no one in his senses will claim that the masses of the people are ideal Civil Service reformers." [88] Among the general magazines, *Harper's Weekly*, the *Independent*, and the *Century Magazine* were seasoned fighters for the reform of the civil service.

The socialistic reform of taxes on incomes had few champions among writers for the general reviews. There was some talk about such drastic measures in the hard times of 1893. Wrote the editor of the Chicago *Graphic*:

It is rumored that President Cleveland, in his message to Congress, will advocate a tax on incomes. We can hardly bring ourselves to believe that the President will do anything of the kind. For of all methods of raising national revenues, none has ever proved more unpopular than that of taxing incomes. [89]

Though Cleveland did not advocate the measure, others did, and it was tacked on the high tariff bill passed in 1894 as a concession to the Populists, only to be declared unconstitutional the next year by a Supreme Court which apparently agreed that it was communistic in tendency.

But by the turn of the century reforms and reformers were nearly all doing badly, and not until the outburst of muckraking and the panic of 1907 did they experience an upturn. Hard times for the people are prosperous times for the reformers; but public prosperity means hard times for reforms, as the *American Fabian* pointed out in its swan song. [90] Of course, the perennials managed to survive, such as

[87] *Kate Field's Washington*, v. 1, p. 249–51, April 16, 1890; v. 8, p. 353, Dec. 6, 1893.
[88] *Good Government*, v. 13, p. 49, Nov. 15, 1893.
[89] *Graphic*, v. 8, p. 408, June 24, 1893.
[90] *American Fabian*, v. 5, Jan. 1900, p. 3.

some of those just mentioned. Women's rights and dress reform will be discussed in a later chapter.[91]

One reform movement which subsided somewhat at the turn of the century, to be resumed later with greater vigor, was that which concerned spelling. The Spelling Reform Association had begun in 1876, and had gained distinguished support in the universities. When the *Bulletin of the Spelling Reform Association* published its last issue in September 1886, it looked back on ten years of the reform with some satisfaction. It pointed out that two great New York weeklies, the *Independent* and the *Home Journal*, and a leading juvenile, *Little Folks*, of Chicago, were using the "amended spelling" of the S.R.A., and that C. W. Larison's *Journal of American Orthoepy* was printed in a special alfabet, as indeed were a number of fonographic journals issued mainly for students of shorthand. The *Bulletin* was continued by *Spelling* (1887–1894), of Boston; *Our Language* (1891–1894) was a New Yorker at fifty cents a year; and there were several shorter-lived periodicals devoted to the cause. The *Chautauquan* took some interest in the movement, printing an article by the most devoted advocate of the reform, Francis A. March, of LaFayette College, in its number for June 1887, and three years later an editorial which pointed out that discussion of spelling reform "is being carried on more clamorously than ever before."[92] About the same time the *Proof Sheet*, a printers' journal, declared that "Like it or dislike it as one may, indications point to the fact that the time is near at hand when there will be a considerable change in the methods of spelling English words." In the same issue James Medill, whose *Chicago Tribune* was later to go further than any other major newspaper in the use of "simplified spelling," wrote with much wisdom: "Invincible conservatism will defeat any revolutionary changes in the existing orthography. It would be much easier to establish a monarchy in the United States than a phonetic system."[93] An industrious clerk in the United States Pension Office contributed to the *American Anthropologist* in 1893 the interesting statistic that Civil War veterans applying for pensions had misspelled the word "diarrhoea" in 1,690 different ways.[94]

RACIAL PROBLEMS

"It is evident," wrote the scientist N. S. Shaler in 1890, "that the greatest questions of national conduct which our race has ever had to

[91] See pp. 355–56, 358–59.
[92] *Chautauquan*, v. 11, p. 188, April 1890.
[93] *Proof Sheet*, v. 2, pp. 9–12, Oct. 1895.
[94] *American Anthropologist*, v. 6, pp. 203–04, April 1893. This number contains a symposium of 13 articles by the leading spelling reformers.

consider" arise from the presence of Negroes in the United States.[95] Magazine commentary on this pervasive set of problems in the present period centered on the issues of Negro suffrage, education, and lynching.

There was a tendency throughout the North to leave the suffrage question in the southern states to decision by the whites in power, with no attempt to enforce the Fifteenth Amendment. The *Andover Review's* editor spoke for this point of view in 1890 when he wrote that there was "a growing appreciation" in the North of "the inherent difficulties of the situation." However, said the *Review*, "we do not admit that the Fifteenth Amendment was a mistake."[96] And so devices were found in the various states of the South by which the Negroes were disfranchised, as W. C. Hamm explained in the *North American* in 1898.[97]

Many magazines (perhaps the *Arena* most of all)[98] were concerned with the mob execution of Negroes. The education and industrial betterment of the colored race were given much attention both north and south. The *Atlantic Monthly* printed several articles on this topic during the nineties, including a notable one by Booker T. Washington.[99] Walter Hines Page, who was doubtless responsible for the publication of most of the *Atlantic's* articles on southern matters in the later nineties, found room for a number of such discussions in *World's Work* just after the turn of the century.[100] But it was a southern review which stirred up the Negro question most effectively in these latter years. The first number of the *South Atlantic Quarterly*, issued in January 1902, contained a strong article against lynching by John C. Kilgo, president of Trinity College, the institution that sponsored the journal. The seventh number carried an even stronger article, by the *Quarterly's* editor, John Spencer Bassett, attacking the attitudes toward Negro problems held by Southerners generally. "There is today," he said, "more hatred of whites for blacks and of blacks for whites than ever before." That was bad enough, but he added his opinion that Booker T. Washington was "the greatest man, save General Lee, born in the South in a hundred years."[101] Bassett nearly lost his job for his boldness, but Trinity College (now Duke University) kept him, to continue his acute commentary in various fields. And finally, we may note the tremendous eruption of denunciation when President Roosevelt invited Washington to dinner at the White House

---

[95] *Arena*, v. 3, p. 23, Dec. 1890.
[96] *Andover Review*, v. 13, pp. 305, 306, March 1890.
[97] *North American Review*, v. 168, pp. 285–96, Feb. 1899.
[98] See, e.g., *Arena*, v. 7, p. 630, April 1893.
[99] *Atlantic Monthly*, v. 78, pp. 322–28, Sept. 1896.
[100] See Sketch 34.
[101] *South Atlantic Quarterly*, v. 2, pp. 299, 304, Oct. 1903.

on October 18, 1901; this comment may be followed in the *Literary Digest, Public Opinion*, and other periodicals. Washington's "Up From Slavery" was a serial in the *Outlook* in 1900–1901.

Newspapers issued by and for Negroes numbered in the hundreds in the 1890's but the number of magazines of any considerable circulation and a life of more than a year or two is very small.[102] Most important was the *Colored American Magazine*, founded in Boston in 1900 by Walter W. Wallace. "American citizens of color have long realized," said Wallace in the first number, "that there exists no monthly magazine distinctively devoted to their interests and to the development of Afro-American art and literature."[103] Washington, T. Thomas Fortune, William Stanley Braithwaite, and Pauline E. Hopkins were leading contributors. The magazine carried short stories and serials, verse, articles chiefly on racial matters, and some illustration. It reached a circulation of fifteen thousand, but went bankrupt in 1903. It managed to continue, however, after missing an issue or two in the spring of that year. The next year, faced by a similar fate, it was rescued by John C. Freund, the music publisher, and moved to New York, where it continued until 1909.[104] An Afro-American Press Association held annual meetings in the early nineties.[105]

Chief events during this period in the long, sad history of our government's dealings with the Indians were the passage of the Dawes Act in 1887, by which tribal lands were parceled out to individual holders; and the Battle of Wounded Knee, which represented the last stand of Sitting Bull and the irreconcilable Dakota Sioux. Magazines gave some attention to these matters; one of the most important articles on the subject in the nineties was Henry L. Dawes's "Have We Failed With the Indians?" in the *Atlantic* in 1899.[106] He did not think we had. A number of national and regional societies devoted to religious and industrial education for the Indians issued magazines, chiefly of

[102] Three besides the *Colored American* may be mentioned: *Southland* (1890–91), of Salisbury, and later Winston, N. C.; *Howard's Negro American Monthly* (1890–1901), of Harrisburg, Pa., later called *Howard's American Magazine*; and *Voice of the Negro* (1904–07), of Atlanta, Ga., moved to Chicago and called *Voice* for its last five months. See Charles S. Johnson, "The Rise of the Negro Magazine," *Journal of Negro History*, v. 13, pp. 7–21, Jan. 1928.

[103] *Colored American Magazine*, v. 1, p. 60, May 1900. Harper S. Fortune, Walter Alexander Johnson, and Fesse W. Watkins were members of the first staff. The first reorganization was under William H. Dupree as president and William O. West as manager. Editors were William H. Wallace, 1900–02; Pauline E. Hopkins, 1903–04; Fred R. Moore, 1904–08; George W. Harris, 1909.

[104] Miss Hopkins and Jesse W. Watkins, treasurer, were connected with the magazine from its beginning to 1904. "We shall support the policies of Booker T. Washington, irrespective of critics, because we believe in them," it said in v. 8, p. 343, June 1905.

[105] See *Our Day*, v. 7, p. 379, May 1891.

[106] *Atlantic Monthly*, v. 84, pp. 280–83, Aug. 1899.

the bulletin type.[107] Chief of these was the *Red Man*, of the Carlisle Indian Industrial School, which began in 1880 under an Indian name, changed to *Morning Star* from 1882 to 1887, and ended in 1900, to be superseded by the *Carlisle Arrow* (1904–1918). The *Indian's Friend* (1888–1941) was the organ of one of the most prominent of the Indian aid societies, the Women's National Indian Association. Founded in Philadelphia, it was moved about in its early years, but was published from New York after 1906.

Racial emigrant groups have generally had their American journals in their own languages. Some that were published in English are discussed in the following chapter, while others are considered in connection with religious periodicals.

THE LABOR MOVEMENT

Aside from free silver and the war with Spain, the two national problems that received the greatest attention in the magazines of this period were, first, the consolidation of capital in the form of trusts and monopolies; and, second, the organization of labor, carried on mainly in order to attack capital in strikes. At the beginning of the period the editor of the *Current* observed that "the editor who writes with a free pen may lay his mind to Gladstone, to silver, to the admission of new states, but his thoughts ever return to the crisis in the affairs of Capital and Labor. This is the question of the hour." [108] A few years later Editor Pentecost, of the *Twentieth Century*, wrote in the *Arena*:

> How to insure the worker the fruits of his labor is the social problem of today. . . . One can hardly listen to a speech or a sermon, or direct his eyes to a page of current literature, without having this social question thrust upon him.[109]

The terms in which Pentecost describes the situation would imply that the chief public concern was in getting proper wages for labor, but what he probably meant was that the labor question in general commanded the universal interest that he had observed. As a matter of fact, the sympathies not only of the upper classes but of the great middle class seem to have been on the side of capital in the big strikes waged before the end of the century; and if the prevailing attitude of

---

[107] *Indian Helper* (1885–1900), of Carlisle, was merged with the *Red Man*. *Indian Bulletin* (1888–1901), of Hartford, was organ of the Connecticut Indian Association. *Indian Leader* has been issued by the Haskell Institute, Lawrence, Kas., since March 1897. The *Chilocco Beacon* began in 1900 and was later continued as *Indian School Journal* by the United States Indian Service in Oklahoma. *Cherokee Gospel Tidings* (1898–1902), of Siloam Springs, Ark., and other points, published part of its contents in the Cherokee alphabet. *Indian Sentinel* (1902–current) is issued from Washington by the Bureau of Catholic Indian Missions.

[108] *Current*, v. 5, p. 241, April 17, 1886.

[109] *Arena*, v. 2, p. 373, Aug. 1890.

the daily, weekly, monthly, and quarterly press is a criterion, labor reform on issues of basic policy was generally disapproved in those years. Of course, there were, as has been seen in this chapter, many reformatory magazines, reviews, and weekly papers. The general magazines of a reform cast were led by the *Arena*, while the *Forum*, *North American Review*, and others tried to present both sides in symposiums. It is true that Editor Walker, of the *Cosmopolitan*, was sometimes illuminated by a reformatory zeal, especially before his magazine became greatly prosperous; and that *McClure's*, the *Century*, the *Review of Reviews*, and the *Chautauquan* had a social sense and a perception of what was going on, and printed articles sympathetic to labor's struggle.[110] But three considerations were especially influential in alienating the middle class from the labor movement before the latter nineties: (1) labor groups were considerably affected by foreign agitators who advocated an un-American method of settlement by violence; (2) strikes not only involved such violence, but victimized the public, which was largely the middle class itself; and (3) wars between labor and capital went contrary to the old American tradition of getting ahead, which called not for violence but for industry and perseverance until the humble laborer was himself a tycoon.

Thus Henry Clews, famous banker, wrote in the *North American* in 1886: "The laboring man in this bounteous and hospitable country has no ground for complaint." [111] And the editor of *Fetter's Southern Magazine* declared, with a comparably complete assurance: "It is safe to say that popular sentiment now emphatically discountenances all strikes." [112] Some of the basic ideas involved were brought strongly to the attention of the public, oddly enough, by a poem published in a newspaper and then widely reprinted and discussed — Edwin Markham's "The Man With the Hoe." This "notably fine poem," observed the *Saturday Evening Post*, "has made a strong impression upon the public mind." But someone, argued the *Post*, has to do the labor of the world, and it continued:

It may be that those who engender discontent in the hearts of laboring men are worse than the heartless taskmasters who wring the sweat-pennies from the honest muscle. At all events, education . . . Love, brotherhood, charity, fellowship, humane liberality we can all cultivate; but we can never obliterate The Man

---

[110] The magazines named in this paragraph are treated in separate chapters in this or a former volume of the present work.

[111] *North American Review*, v. 142, p. 601, June 1886.

[112] *Southern Magazine*, v. 3, p. 428, Nov. 1893.

[113] *Saturday Evening Post*, v. 172, p. 58, July 22, 1899. This editorial was signed by Maurice Thompson. See also an article by him in the issue for July 8, 1899, in which he urges that education should not take men away from labor (p. 27).

With the Hoe until the necessity for the labor-product, of which he is the representative sign, shall cease to exist.[113]

The church joined with virtual unanimity in derogation of strikes and "radicalism." Editor Arthur Edwards, of the *Northwestern Christian Advocate,* a great Methodist weekly, contributed a sour note, however, to the general anthem of the nineties, as did the Christian Socialists. It was the famous Brooklyn preacher T. DeWitt Talmage who, in a series of "Labor Sermons," expressed the common opinion when he testified against some of the strike techniques in an eloquent passage:

> The torch put to the factories that have discharged hands for good or bad reasons; obstructions on the rail-tracks in front of midnight express trains, because the offenders do not like the president of the company; strikes on shipboard the hour they were going to sail, or in printing offices the hour the paper was to go to press, or in the mines the day the coal was to be delivered, or on the house scaffoldings so the builder fails in keeping his contract — all these are only a hard blow on the head of American labor, and cripple its arms, lame its feet, and pierce its heart.[114]

But Talmage was very severe, in the pulpit, on employers who did not have kind hearts. The *Andover Review,* a great religious monthly, thought the balance of popular sympathy between labor and capital was very delicate: it inclined to the former, but "at the suggestion of unfairness or violence it passes instantly to the other side." And most unfair, thought the *Review,* were the closed shop and the boycott: "when an organization . . . assumes the authority to prevent any individual from working or buying as he pleases, it invades the domain of personal right."[115] There was much against the closed shop in the magazines of the nineties. Picketing was another invasion of personal right; and a *Life* cartoon showed labor leaders riding clouds around Heaven's gate, shouting, "We got da place picketed. Dey're usin' a non-union kind of harp in dere!"[116]

The era under consideration saw three great strike periods. The first was that of 1885–1886, distinguished by the southwestern railway contests and the A.F. of L. strikes for shorter hours in Chicago, the latter climaxed by the Haymarket riot. Bishop J. L. Spalding, writing in the *Forum* in July 1886, said: "The report of the Chicago bomb, through the cannon-mouth of the press, has filled multitudes with

[114] *Brooklyn Magazine,* v. 4, separately paged "Tabernacle Pulpit" supplement, May 23, 1886, p. 54.
[115] *Andover Review,* v. 5, p. 532, May 1886.
[116] *Life,* v. 43, p. 269, March 17, 1904.

dread lest the foundations of our social fabric should be on the point of giving way"; [117] and Andrew Carnegie in the same review the next month, pointing out the obvious fact that the Chicago strikes had constituted "the most serious labor revolt that ever occurred in this country," added that "our magazines, reviews, and newspapers have been filled with plans involving radical changes. The pulpit has been equally prolific." [118]

The second period was that of 1892–1894, including the great Homestead strike of steel-mill workers, scarcely less sensational than the Chicago general strike and involving more loss of life. It was in comment upon the war of the steel-mill workers and the hired Pinkerton men that John Brisben Walker wrote with restrained passion in his *Cosmopolitan Magazine* that American "distribution of wealth has become frightful in its inequalities," adding: "The fact is, we have two separate worlds in this country, and the man who lives in what is known as the world of society has no conception of what the world of labor is thinking." [119]

Shocking as the Homestead war was, the Pullman strike attracted more comment in the magazines, probably because the Federal government was drawn into it. In 1892 Eugene V. Debs was boasting in the *American Journal of Politics* that "three million men and women are now marching under the banners of organized labor," and that by such confederation justice for labor would be obtained.[120] Two years later Kate Field in her weekly *Washington* wrote, in regard to the Pullman dispute: "Drunk with power . . . Dictator Debs ordered the strike." [121] At any rate, he led it, with the *Railway Times* as the organ of his American Railway Union.[122] Carroll D. Wright, United States Commissioner of Labor, writing in the *Publications of the American Economic Association*, called the railway strikes in Chicago in 1894 "an epochal event in the labor movement and the industrial development of the country." [123] H. P. Robinson, editor of the *Railway Age*, called them "the greatest and most extensive labor struggle that has ever taken place among the wage-earners of America, and possibly of the world," and thought that they were the result of a conspiracy to gain control of the government.[124] But one of the *Arena* editors thought that the burning of the freight cars was a modern Boston Tea

[117] *Forum*, v. 1, p. 409, July 1886.
[118] *Forum*, v. 1, p. 539, Aug. 1886.
[119] *Cosmopolitan*, v. 13, p. 574, Sept. 1892.
[120] *American Journal of Politics*, v. 1, p. 69, July 1892.
[121] *Kate Field's Washington*, v. 10, p. 17, July 11, 1894.
[122] See p. 175.
[123] *Pubs. Am. Econ. Asso.*, v. 9, n.s., p. 33, Oct.–Dec. 1894.
[124] *North American Review*, v. 159, p. 195, Aug. 1894.

Party; [125] and after the interposition of the Federal powers, there was a shrill chorus of denunciation of President Cleveland, Attorney-General Olney, and Special Counsel Edwin Walker, of Chicago, led by the demands of the *Journal of the Knights of Labor* for the impeachment of Olney.[126]

The great coal strike of 1894 was analyzed and justified in the *Charities Review*.[127] Two hundred thousand miners were engaged — a greater number of laborers than had ever before joined in any strike. In the language of Samuel Gompers in his *American Federationist*, "this vast army of toilers are engaged in the most momentous battle which has ever been waged between the forces of labor on one hand and capitalists on the other." [128] In short, every big strike seemed greater than the last.

The third period of major labor unrest was during the coal strikes of 1901–1902. In the latter year, with the great contest in the Pennsylvania anthracite fields so stubbornly contested, and with such arrogance on the part of George F. Baer, president of the Reading Railway System and a chief operator (especially striking when President Roosevelt intervened), there were strong inclinations of public thought toward government operation, compulsory arbitration, and such socialistic measures. Even *Current History*, usually a mere recorder, was stirred up about arbitration. "Can it be," it asked, "that any private interest would have suffered a hundredth part as much from the enforcement of compulsory arbitration at the inauguration of the present strike as the innocent public suffers daily from its prolongation?" [129] But no such laws as those urged by *Current History* were enacted, though this strike was finally settled on the basis of arbitration. That a change had taken place in public sympathy, which was now more generally on the labor side, and that the blame for strikes was more likely to be ascribed to management, seems to be fairly clear in these years after the turn of the century.

Though strikes dramatized labor problems, it would be wrong indeed to think that the magazines did not discuss such questions independently of the battles in which issues were joined and fought. The eight-hour day was the subject of much discussion: "The whole civilized world is interested in the eight-hour movement," declared *Dawn* in 1890, when it was a revolutionary principle.[130] Child labor

---

[125] Walter Blackburn Harte in *Arena*, v. 10, p. 494, Sept. 1894.

[126] *Journal of Knights of Labor*, v. 15, Sept. 13, 1894, p. 1.

[127] *Charities Review*, v. 4, p. 41, Nov. 1894.

[128] *American Federationist*, v. 1, p. 74, June 1894.

[129] *Current History*, v. 12, p. 654, Oct. 1902. See also *ibid.*, p. 496, Aug. 1894; pp. 779–82, Dec. 1902.

[130] *Dawn*, v. 2, p. 36, May 1890.

was often discussed. "Swarms of diminutive figures stand at the whirring machines ten hours a day for a trifle that would scarcely maintain a well-fed dog," wrote an observer in the *Publications of the American Economic Association*.[131] Organizational problems, political and ideological infiltration, the effects of immigration, compulsory arbitration of disputes, cooperative management, and government ownership were among the ideas widely discussed.

Hundreds of labor periodicals were begun in the period 1885–1905, most of them perishing within those twenty years. This had been the story of labor publications for fifty years, except that not so many were attempted before the nineties. *John Swinton's Paper*, a distinguished periodical which was to die the next year, said in 1886 that some forty labor papers had failed in New York alone in the preceding forty years, and added, "We do not know of more than ten labor papers in the United States that have enough income to pay expenses." [132] Even when subsidized, union funds and management were unlikely to be consistent throughout a long term of years. Most of the labor journals were quarto or folio in size, and were little more than bulletins of union news and comment by union leaders for a given city or district.

Aside from the journals of socialism and political action, treated in the preceding chapter, the leading publications in the general labor field were the *Journal of the Knights of Labor* [133] and the American Federation of Labor's *American Federationist*. The A.F. of L. had its *Report* of proceedings from its organization in 1881, issued irregularly,[134] but the *Federationist* was created at the Chicago convention of 1894 as a monthly to be widely distributed among unionists. A quarto of twenty pages, it was edited by the successive presidents of the organization. Begun in New York, and moved to Indianapolis the next year, it found its home in Washington in 1898. It was the spokesman for the federation on all issues. Other A.F. of L. journals were the current *American Labor World*, begun in 1899 on the basis of the old New York *Union Printer* (1882–1899); and the Kansas City *Labor Herald* (1904–1940). There were many obscure and now forgotten

---

[131] *Pubs. Am. Econ. Asso.*, v. 5, p. 216, March 1890. *Arena* has a bibliography listing articles in a number of magazines, in v. 10, p. 143, June 1894.

[132] Quoted in *Journalist*, July 24, 1886, p. 181. For *John Swinton's Paper*, see Mott, *op. cit.*, v. 3, p. 299.

[133] See Mott, *op. cit.*, v. 3, p. 300.

[134] Also rearranged under the title *Proceedings*. In his autobiography, Gompers speaks of the *Trade Union Advocate* beginning in 1887 as the A.F. of L.'s first official organ; but the present author has found no trace of this paper. (See Samuel Gompers, *Seventy Years of Life and Labor*, New York, 1925, v. 1, p. 273.)

labor journals that never were included in the directories.[135] Unions in the various industries and trades nearly always maintained official journals, though some were merely records of proceedings and news.[136]

An amazing number and variety of journals serving American secret societies were published during the present period. *Printer's Ink* counted thirty Masonic periodicals in course of publication in 1890, and almost as many for the Odd Fellows and for the Knights of Pythias.[137] More than eighty new Masonic journals were begun between 1885 and 1905, and almost half of them lasted for ten years or more.[138] Among the other well-established fraternal organizations,

[135] The *Union Labor Advocate* is one of the longer-lived general labor journals; begun in Chicago, it has long been published at Elizabeth, N.J., as a dollar monthly. J. G. Schonfarber, former editor of the *Journal of the Knights of Labor*, began a paper in Baltimore in 1888 called the *Critic*; later it was edited by others, and favored the single tax, ballot reform, and so forth, until its end in 1893. *Hammer and Pen* (1899–1909), of New York, was the organ of the Church Association for the Advancement of Labor; it was a small periodical supposed to be issued quarterly, but actually irregular. Harriette A. Keyser was editor and publisher, and also organizer and secretary of the association. *Unionist* began in Green Bay, Wis., in 1899; it was published in Los Angeles as *Fellowship* in 1906, and was merged three years later with *Twentieth Century*.

[136] See *Employees' Magazines in the United States*, 86-page list issued in 1925 by the National Industrial Conference Board, Inc., New York; and *Employees' Magazines*, a 24-page list issued in 1931 by the Policyholders' Service Bureau, Metropolitan Life Insurance Company, New York. Among union periodicals begun in 1885–1905, the following were some of the leaders: *Amalgamated Journal* (1900–39), of Pittsburgh, which served the Amalgamated Association of Iron, Steel and Tin Workers; *United Mine Workers' Journal* (1891–current), of Washington, which began at Rochester, New York; *Brotherhood of Maintenance of Way Employees Journal* (1890–current), of Detroit, long published as *Advance Advocate*, the railway trackmen's monthly; *Railway Telegrapher* (1885–current), of St. Louis and other cities; *Commercial Telegraphers' Journal* (1903–current), of Chicago; *Garment Worker* (1902–current), a New York weekly, which virtually succeeded the monthly *Garment Worker* (1893–1903) and represents the United Garment Workers of America; *Typographical Journal* (1889–current), of Indianapolis, which serves the International Typographical Union of North America; *Paper Makers' Journal* (1901–current), which began at Watertown, New York, as *Paper and Pulp Makers' Journal*, and is now published at Albany, the organ of the International Brotherhood of Paper Makers; and *International Musician* (1901–current), which began in St. Louis and is now published in Newark, New Jersey, at 30¢ a year, as the official monthly of the American Federation of Musicians. Some representatives of national unions not listed above which were begun in the period 1885–1905 and still continue at midtwentieth century are *Lather* (1900), *Painter and Decorator* (1887), *International Engineer* (1901), *Boilermakers' Journal* (1888), *Bridgeman's Magazine* (1901), *Plumber, Gas and Steamfitters' Journal* (1898), *American Pressman* (1890), *Machinists' Monthly Journal* (1889), *Railway Carmen's Journal* (1895), *Motorman and Conductor* (1895), *Journal of the Switchmen's Union* (1898), *Railway Clerk* (1900), *Potters' Herald* (1901), *International Book-Binder* (1900), *Bricklayer, Mason and Plasterer* (1898). The *Barber's Journal* (1892–1904), of Cleveland, has been continued as *Journeyman Barber, Hairdresser and Cosmetologist* in Indianapolis since 1905. The *Mixer and Server* (1890), of Cincinnati, has been called *Catering Industry Employee* since 1929.

[137] *Printer's Ink*, v. 2, p. 775, May 14, 1890.

[138] See Josiah H. Drummond, *Masonic Historical and Bibliographical Memoranda* (Brooksville, Ky., 1922); cards of Iowa Masonic Library, Cedar Rapids, Iowa. Perhaps the most

older periodicals generally retained preëminence.[139] The insurance business utilized the predilection of the people for regalia, secret forms, and so on, as the basis for social functions, by organizing policyholders into "lodges." The *Modern Woodman* (1883–current) was the official journal of the Modern Woodmen of America. The *Modern Maccabee* (1887–1914) began as the *Michigan Maccabee* at Port Huron, Michigan; and the *Ladies' Review* (1895–current), called *W.B.A. Review* since 1932, was issued by the same publishers in behalf of the Ladies of the Maccabees of the World. There were many other orders and many organs representing them.[140]

---

important of those begun in 1885–1905 was the *New Age Magazine* (1904–current), the Scottish Rite journal, published in Washington by the Supreme Council of the Thirty-Third Degree. Two from California were the *Trestle Board* (1887–1924), of San Francisco, and *Southwestern Freemason* (1896–1927). The *Square and Compass* (1892–current) was a Denver contribution. The *Eastern Star* (1888–current), of Indianapolis, was for the women's auxiliary. The older *Masonic Review* and *Voice of Masonry* were merged in 1900 as *Masonic Voice-Review* (Chicago); and the old *Keystone* was merged in 1905 with the *American Tyler* (Detroit), which had been started in 1888, as *Tyler-Keystone*.

[139] For fraternal journals founded in earlier periods, see Mott, *op. cit.*, v. 2, p. 215; v. 3, p. 134.

[140] For example, *Elks-Antler* (1895–1927), Benevolent and Protective Order of Elks; *Chariot* (1895–current), Tribe of Ben-Hur; *Mystic Worker* (1896–1913), Mystic Workers of the World; *Yeoman Shield* (1897–1932), Brotherhood of American Yeomen.

# CHAPTER XII

## FOREIGN INTERESTS AND THE WAR WITH SPAIN

AN OUTSTANDING phenomenon of magazine tables of contents in the 1890's was a change in the outlook on foreign countries. The old travel article, emphasizing the curious and picturesque elements of foreign life in the mood of the carefree observer, tended to give place to more statistical and less literary discussions of the economics and politics of other countries.[1] Those old leisurely, stylized, well-illustrated articles that had been staple in American magazines for nearly a hundred years did not drop out all at once, but they gradually disappeared. Perhaps the very fact that so many more Americans went on trips to Europe in the 1890's — a hundred thousand a year, according to the *International*[2] — made reading about other people's trips commonplace rather than romantic. Less visited spots, like Japan and South America, fared better in the magazine travel essays than the older Cook's Tour places.

But on the subjects of foreign trade, international relations, and political crises abroad, there was a constantly increasing number of articles in the leading magazines;[3] and when the American victory over Spain in 1899 brought the United States recognition as a world power, such monthlies as the *Forum, North American Review*, and *Review of Reviews*, and such weeklies as the *Nation* and *Harper's Weekly* gave more and more space to our foreign interests. It was not unusual for the monthly reviews just named to devote half their space to material bearing on foreign affairs at any time in the nineties. The *Chautauquan, Bay View Magazine,* and *Current History* and other news periodicals performed constant and effective service in their interpretation of foreign cultures to American readers; the first-named had a French year during 1896–1897, followed by German and English years. During the war with Spain and afterward, such weeklies as *Collier's, Leslie's*, the *Outlook,* and the *Independent*, gave much attention to foreign matters; *World's Work*, later than these in beginning, kept a view consonant with its title. *Literary Digest* and

---

[1] Obsolescence of the old-fashioned travel article is indicated by the measurements of Arthur Reed Kimball (see *Atlantic Monthly,* v. 86, p. 124, July 1900; also Kimball's tables in *Journal of the American Social Science Association,* 1899).

[2] *International,* v. 3, p. 176, Aug. 1897.

[3] James C. Bowman, "Trends of American World Consciousness, 1890–1900, as Shown by Nine American Magazines" (unpublished thesis, University of Missouri, 1952) is helpful throughout this chapter.

*Public Opinion*, leading compendiums of press comment, carried much international news and discussion.

An all-too-brief monthly of travel, exploration, and science was *Around the World* (1893–1895), a well-illustrated fifteen-cent magazine edited by the naturalist Angelo Heilprin. There was some difficulty in publishing it in New York while the editor, who wrote no small part of it, lived in Philadelphia.

The Chicago *International* (1896–1901) was much more than a travel magazine, since it published translations from foreign periodicals, reviews of books, and so on. A. T. H. Brower started it as a ten-cent magazine filled with such material, but it was soon increased in price to twenty-five cents, and much travel matter was added — even the register of first-class passengers on ships leaving American ports, elementary courses in foreign languages, and gossip about Americans abroad. It had some good contributors, such as Ernest Seton Thompson, William Eleroy Curtis, and Edwin L. Sabin. It reduced its price again in 1898 and tried a theater department and more original miscellany, but it was never very successful.

The *Four-Track News* was founded July 1901 by George H. Daniels in New York as a ten-cent illustrated magazine of "travel and education." It had such contributors as Cy Warman, Nixon Waterman, Minot J. Savage, Kirk Munroe, and M. Imlay Taylor. In 1906 it became *Travel Magazine* and is current as *Travel. The 400* (1893–1906) was an irregular urban journal published in Chicago, which gave some attention to society and the theater but was chiefly devoted to travel. A handsome paper, edited by H. E. Persinger and published by E. C. Sullivan at the turn of the century, it was merged in the *Saturday Evening Herald*. The *Globe Trotter* (1902–1913), a curious little Milwaukee monthly, was the organ of the Cosmopolitan Correspondence Club.

There were several geographical journals in the period 1885–1905. The *National Geographic Magazine* did not attain its traditionally high level until after Gilbert Grosvenor became editor in 1903.[4] The *Journal of Geography* is the result of a union of the *Journal of School Geography* (1897–1901) and the *Bulletin of the American Bureau of Geography* (1900–1901). It has been published in various cities, is low in price and well illustrated, and appears monthly except for the summer vacation; it is the organ of the National Council of Geography Teachers.

4 See Sketch 20.

[William M.] *Goldthwaite's Geographical Magazine* (1891–1895) was a New York monthly. Several local geographical societies published bulletins.[5]

Journals devoted to world commerce and published for exporters were not uncommon, but they were usually no more than bulletins. (See note 147, Chapter X.)

The *International Monthly* was founded in January 1900 by Professor Frederick A. Richardson at Burlington, Vermont, and conducted by him throughout its career of five and half years. It was designed for the interchange of ideas among the world's thinkers, and comprised twelve departments — history, philosophy, psychology, sociology, religion, fine arts, industrial art, physics, biology, medicine and hygiene, and geology and geography. A large and impressive "advisory board" was divided among these departments; it included such men as Josiah Royce, N. S. Shaler, John Bassett Moore, Charles Seignobos, Alois Brandl, Karl Lamprecht, Ernest von Halle, Salvatore Cortesi, Baron Kentaro Kaneko, Richard Garnett, and Sir Archibald Geike. The articles were scholarly, without being too technical for the average reader. Art and literature were prominent fields; and John La Farge, H. T. Finck, W. P. Trent, George Brandes, Paul Elmer More, and Brander Matthews were contributors. The journal became *International Quarterly* in December 1902, and the price was raised from three to five dollars; despite the excellence of much of its contents, it failed to make a permanent place for itself.

### INTEREST IN ENGLAND

Americans were more interested in the English than in any other people because they had more and closer dealings with them, in a greater variety of fields. The popularity of books by Englishmen in the United States, for example, has been noted in Chapter VIII. Commerce with England and its dependencies was discussed in many aspects: as casual illustrations we may mention Brooks Adams's "England's Decadence in the West Indies," in the *Forum* for June 1899, and Worthington C. Ford's "Commercial Superiority of the United States," *North American Review*, January 1898. English traits and customs were of continuing interest; for example, Julian Ralph, whose travel articles were found in many of the magazines of the nineties, and who preserved more than most the mood of the older, gossipy essays in this field, wrote on "Eating and Drinking in London" for *Harper's*

---

[5] Most important was the *Bulletin of the Geographical Club* (later *Society*) *of Philadelphia* (1893–1938), irregular before 1904 and quarterly thereafter.

*Weekly* (November 8, 1890). Articles on significant developments in English society and government appeared in American periodicals with remarkable frequency, though not all were as stimulating as "Conservation of the British Democracy," in the *North American* for February 1897, by the English historian W. E. H. Lecky.

The United States enjoyed visits from many distinguished Englishmen in the nineties; nearly all of them lectured while in this country, and wrote articles or books about the Americans when they returned to their own island, which, very naturally, most of them greatly preferred to the sprawling country they had briefly visited. Few were as ill-mannered about it, however, as some earlier visitors. Dean F. W. Farrar, Professor Henry Drummond, the poet Edwin Arnold, the Greek historians R. C. Jebb and John P. Mahaffy, and the novelists Walter Besant, Conan Doyle, Hall Caine, Rider Haggard, James Barrie, Ian Maclaren, and Anthony Hope Hawkins were lecturer-visitors in the nineties. Kipling made his home in the United States for a few years, and found his wife in this country. Henry M. Stanley, who had for years been thought of as an American, occupied a high position in American popular esteem. When he was in Africa on the Emin Pasha expedition, and had not been heard from for months, the *North American Review* (December 1888) published a symposium with the title "Is Stanley Dead?" A writer in the *Cosmopolitan* in 1891 declared that the "most remarkable men of today" were two explorers, one in the physical and the other in the geographical world — Edison and Stanley.[6] English actors were prominent on the American stage — Booth, Irving, Tree, Ellen Terry, and so on.

"Do We Hate England?" was the title of an article in the *Forum* in March 1891; and the author, Bishop A. Cleveland Coxe, showed that some of us did. But it must be recognized that Americans had almost as much regard for Queen Victoria as did Englishmen. Wrote the editor of *Current History* in 1897: "When the record of the nineteenth century shall have been finished, it will be said that its last decade witnessed two of the most significant celebrations in history, the World's Columbian Exposition, and the Diamond Jubilee of her Majesty Queen Victoria."[7] In articles and pictures the American public was told all about that great spectacle of empire. Andrew Carnegie wrote in the *North American*: "Certainly the world has never seen such a procession" as that of the jubilee, "nor is it likely to see anything like this again."[8] True indeed.

[6] *Cosmopolitan*, v. 11, p. 150, June 1891.
[7] *Cyclopedic Review of Current History*, v. 7, p. 314, April–June 1897.
[8] *North American Review*, v. 165, p. 497, Oct. 1897.

The three historical episodes that caused the chief stock-taking of American attitudes toward England were the dispute about the Behring Sea fisheries, the threat of war over the Venezuelan boundary question, and the Boer War. Nearly all leading magazines and reviews printed articles on the Venezuelan issue, and some of them carried symposiums. By no means all were on the side of President Cleveland and Congress: examples that might be cited include Lord Bryce's article, with its peaceful tone, in the *North American* in February 1896, and Theodore S. Woolsey's bold espousal of the chief British argument in the same month, in an article entitled "The President's Monroe Doctrine," in the *Forum*. The Boer War of 1899–1901 divided American sympathies, and the press reports ranged from those which featured Boer "atrocities" to William J. Bryan's *Commoner*, which headed an editorial in its very first number, "The Boers — God Bless Them." One of the most significant discussions of foreign affairs to appear in American reviews in these years was Theodore Mommsen's article on the European fiscal implications of the South African War, which suggested the possibilities of intervention by European nations. Professor Mommsen boldly asserted the decline of British world policy. "We begin to doubt," he wrote, "if Britain, even Greater Britain, may in the long run be able to cope with the great nations."[9]

The Irish question was also widely discussed in American periodicals. Here was a matter very close to the hearts of the Irish immigrants who formed considerable segments of the American population, especially in eastern cities. Many Catholic periodicals gave special attention to the Irish cause.[10] The Ancient Order of Hibernians issued the weekly *Hibernian* (1899–1918) at Boston, and the monthly *National Hibernian* (1901–1918) at Camden, New Jersey, and Columbus, Ohio. The *Celtic Magazine* (1879–1899) was a New York illustrated monthly designed for Irish-American readers.

An interesting ten-cent illustrated monthly "for Scottish homes in America" was the *Caledonian* (1901–1923), New York, founded by the Reverend David Macdougall and edited by him until his death in 1920. It carried correspondence from Scottish organizations in the homeland and America, and specialized in sketches of American notables of Scottish lineage (for example, President McKinley). The Order of the Scottish Clans published the *Fiery Cross* (1894–current).

*St. George's Journal* (1876–1928), Philadelphia, was long published

[9] *Ibid.*, v. 170, p. 241, Feb. 1900.
[10] See former volumes of this work for the *Irish-American*, the Boston *Pilot*, and *Dona-hoe's Magazine*. *Irish Echo* (1886–94) was a small and irregular periodical devoted to Irish culture. *Gaelic American* (1902–37), published by John Devoy in New York for many years, was devoted to Irish interests chiefly.

as a monthly for Americans of British origin. The monthly *Anglo-American Magazine* (1899–1902) was published at twenty-five cents in New York and a shilling in London. It was a literary magazine of no great distinction. Out in San Francisco, the *British Californian* (1897–1932) claimed to "represent" fifty thousand (the number was later almost doubled) British-born residents of that state. The magazine offered in 1904 "a new and correct history of the American Revolution" entitled "The Cleavage of an Empire," but it was chiefly devoted to reports of current British affairs.

The magazines most effective in promulgating British ideas and attitudes, however, were the great English publications regularly reprinted on this side of the water. The Leonard Scott Publication Company, which had for many years issued English journals for American consumption, moved its office in 1889 from Philadelphia to New York. It was then reprinting, line for line and page for page, *Nineteenth Century*, *Contemporary Review*, *Westminster Review*, *Edinburgh Review*, *Scottish Review*, *Quarterly Review*, *Blackwood's Magazine*, and *Fortnightly Review*. Though they had long paid English publishers for advance sheets, the Leonard Scott enterprises suffered from the international copyright; and the multiplication of American reviews, as well as the declining taste for the stodgier style of review, spelled the doom of such large-scale ventures in America. The *Review of Reviews* began in New York as an auxiliary of Stead's monthly of the same name in London, but it soon achieved independence.[11]

More popular English periodicals did better in the United States. The *Illustrated London News*, published in the early nineties in New York by Ingram Brothers, was later taken over by the International News Company, which also issued the ten-cent *English Illustrated Magazine* and other Londoners.[12] The American edition of *Cassell's Family Magazine* began in 1884. It was not very attractive at first; but in the nineties it carried authors like Jerome K. Jerome, Barry Pain, Bret Harte, and Gertrude Atherton. It continued past the end of our period.[13] The *Strand* (American edition, 1891–1916) was wholly English in content.[14] *Pearson's Magazine* began an American edition in 1899; it varied from its English edition from the start and later became an entirely separate

---

[11] See Sketch 25.

[12] The name of the *English Illustrated* was changed in 1900 to *New Illustrated Magazine*, but it perished in that year. The International News Company issued *The Sketch, Young Ladies' Journal*, and *Family Library Monthly*.

[13] Until 1907, in its American edition, of which v. 1 (1885) was new series, v. 2, of the English edition.

[14] See p. 4.

publication.[15] A few English religious and literary periodicals also were reproduced in America.[16]

Further, in the eighties many Americans subscribed directly to certain English magazines — a fashion that was soon to decline. But in 1885, W. H. Moore, the leading independent American dealer in subscriptions, catalogued nearly three hundred British periodicals for his customers.

Meantime American magazines gained an important foothold in England. As early as 1886, when it was still a matter of reprinting from advance sheets, a writer in the *Cosmopolitan* observed that "more copies of *Harper's* and the *Century* are sold in Great Britain than of any British monthly of equal price." [17] *Scribner's* prosperous English edition should have been mentioned. Some years later, when the shift had been made to interchange of home-printed magazines, Brander Matthews wrote an illuminating note on the situation:

> The reputation of American authors has been spread abroad in England largely by the agency of the great American illustrated magazines, which have now an enormous circulation on the other side of the Atlantic. A few British magazines and reviews continue to be imported into the United States, but they are very few indeed; and certainly the total number imported is less than the number exported of any one of the American illustrated monthlies.[18]

In the latter nineties cheaper illustrated American monthlies invaded London at sixpence and made a great hit. In those years class magazines published in America sometimes had their English editions, as the juvenile *St. Nicholas*, the *Ladies' Home Journal*, the comic *Texas Siftings*, and many more.

Advocacy of international copyrights grew strong and emphatic in the latter eighties. The *Critic* reported a series of "Authors' Readings" in Chickering Hall in the winter of 1887–1888 in behalf of the cause. Virtually all leading American men of letters joined in this demonstration. The *Century* carried a series of open letters on the subject February 1886, and there were other notable pronouncements.

The long-sought reform went into effect, on July 1, 1891, and seemed to have no immediate revolutionary impact on American book or maga-

---

[15] *Pearson's* will be treated in a separate sketch in the next volume of this work.

[16] *Quiver* was "an illustrated magazine for Sunday and general reading." Its American edition began in Dec. 1894, as v. 20 was beginning in London. The Cassell Company was publisher. A "companion journal" to the *British Weekly Pulpit* was published in New York 1888–90. An American edition of the Duke of Newcastle's *English Church Review* was issued in Philadelphia for a brief term beginning in April 1901. *Literature* was reprinted in New York during 1897–99; it was composed largely of original matter in its final year.

[17] *Cosmopolitan Magazine*, v. 2, p. 41, Sept, 1886.

[18] *Ibid.*, v. 13, p. 350, July 1892.

zine publishing, especially in the early nineties. In the best-seller field, those years were dominated by Kipling, Stevenson, du Maurier, Anthony Hope, and Ian Maclaren; toward the turn of the century, American writers took over. The *Eclectic Magazine*, which depended largely on English reprint, had its troubles in the latter nineties, but *Littell's* went on bravely.

EUROPE'S PROBLEMS AND CULTURES

Such French visitors to America as Paul Bourget, Ferdinand Brunetière, Paul Blouet, and René Doumic helped to increase American interest in things French during the nineties. Few historical cults have ever attained the scope and zeal of that for Napoleon in our period. The furor of publication about him spread from France to America. An early series about him was the one by John C. Ropes in *Scribner's*. By 1894 the *Century* could say:

> The interest in Napoleon has had a revival that is phenomenal in its extent and intensity, as evinced in a flood of publication, the preparation of works of art dealing with the period, and the demand for autographs, portraits, and relics of Napoleon. Even the theater has taken up the theme.[19]

In November of the same year, a serial life of Napoleon by William M. Sloane began in the *Century*, and another by Ida M. Tarbell started in *McClure's*. But the French serial that American readers found most enthralling in the latter nineties was the news and discussion of the *cause célèbre* of that generation — the Dreyfus trial. "The hero of the hour is Alfred Dreyfus," wrote the correspondent whom the *Cosmopolitan* sent to Paris to cover the trial.[20] It was France that was on trial, declared James B. Eustis, former ambassador to that country, in the *Conservative Review*: "France has been arraigned at the bar of public opinion of the civilized world."[21] This was the general American attitude; there was wide agreement with the verdict of *Current History* that the conviction of Dreyfus was a sign of "national decadence." That review prophesied truly that "cruelty and cowardice combined have inscribed upon French history a page of scandal over which posterity will long pore in amazement and perplexity."[22]

Allan Forman pointed out in his *Journalist* in 1889 a fact that was long true: certain French periodicals surpassed in engraving, presswork, and color anything that was being done in either America or Eng-

[19] *Century Magazine*, v. 47, p. 949, April 1894.
[20] *Cosmopolitan Magazine*, v. 24, p. 481, March 1898.
[21] *Conservative Review*, v. 2, p. 14, Aug. 1899.
[22] *Cyclopedic Review of Current History*, v. 10, pp. 509, 527, 3rd quar., 1899.

land.[23] The language bar, however, prevented the sale of many of these interesting and sometimes exquisite magazines in the United States. The leading exponent of Gallic life and letters in the United States at the turn of the century was the *Parisian* (1896–1901), a New York monthly edited by M. L. Dexter. It was made up mainly of translations from French periodicals.[24]

Foreign-language periodicals are outside the scope of the present study; there were a score of them, chiefly local, in French at the end of the century, and about a hundred in German. The leading German personalities in the standard American magazines were Kaiser Wilhelm II and Prince Bismarck; on the death of the latter in 1898 there were many articles about him. Socialism and anti-semitism in Germany were leading topics; German trade relations with the Untied States were much discussed; and German political dealings with this country and with England, Austria, and Russia were subject matter for many American magazine and review articles. German educational ideas were often explored, as in John Tilden Prince's "American and German Schools" in the *Atlantic Monthly* for September 1890; and German military tactics were a constant source of interest, as illustrated in Poultney Bigelow's "Pictures from the German Manoeuvres" in *Harper's Weekly*, November 8, 1890. A "popular journal of German history and ideals in the United States" was *Pennsylvania-German* (1900–1914), published at Lebanon, Pennsylvania. It was a fifteen-cent monthly, handsome and well printed.

One of the best of American magazines representing a European culture in the new world was *Scandinavia* (1883–1886), published in Chicago by N. C. Fredericksen, a Danish-American. It published some translations, many news notes about politics and literature, and in 1885 some letters by the editor "From Home."

Said the *Journalist* in 1888:

There have been very few series printed or projected by any magazine which have attracted as much attention, excited as widespread an interest, and held promise of as permanent a literary and historical value as the series of papers already begun in the *Century Magazine* upon Siberia and the exile system, by George Kennan.[25]

This great travel series, which has been called "the *Uncle Tom's Cabin* of the Siberian exile," caused the *Century* to be banned by the Russian

---

[23] *Journalist*, v. 10, Nov. 2, 1889, p. 11.

[24] It changed title in 1900 to *Parisian Illustrated Review*. It ended in June 1901, and was succeeded a few months later by the short-lived *Cosmopolite. France: A Monthly Magazine for the Study of the French Language and Literature* (1900–02) was published by the New England College of Languages in Boston.

[25] *Journalist*, v. 7, May 19, 1888, p. 8.

government.[26] It marked the beginning of a sharper American interest in Russian life and affairs than had been known before. The year after its publication, the *Cosmopolitan* noted "the present mania in this country for things Russian" — nihilism, czarism, famine, Russian literature and music.[27] And a few years later the *Arena* spoke of the continuing spread of the Russian cult:

> The growing interest taken in Russian affairs and the appreciation recently evinced for Russian literature is very marked in the United States. Almost every magazine and newspaper contains articles treating of some phase of Russian government, life, customs, or habits of thought. Translations of great Russian works are appearing at short intervals, while lecturers have found it immensely profitable to treat of the real or supposed social and political conditions of this great empire. Russian teas, suppers, dinners, and dances are becoming popular.[28]

In 1899 the *Atlantic* published Kropotkin's "Autobiography of a Revolutionist." But the greatest Russian personality in American magazines in this period was Tolstoi. His *Confession* appeared in 1884, marking his conversion, and many interpretations of his teachings were offered in the United States. Though he did not visit America, many writers from this country made the pilgrimage to Yasnaya Polyana to talk with him.

The Russo-Japanese War of 1904–1905 received remarkable news coverage in such American weeklies as *Collier's*, *Leslie's*, and *Harper's Weekly*, and was discussed and described in most magazines. The anti-czarist movement that culminated in the uprising of 1905 had some organs in the Untied States, notably a New York edition of *Free Russia*, issued from 1890 to 1894 with much the same material as the London paper.

The "Eastern Crisis" of 1897, followed by the war between Greece and Turkey, was widely discussed in the American reviews, especially in articles of the type of Professor Woolsey's "The Powers and the Graeco-Turkish War" in the *Forum* of July 1897.

#### ASIAN PEOPLES AND CULTURES

The Sino-Japanese War of 1894–1895 brought the attention of America almost violently to the Far East. Wrote Secretary of the Navy H. A. Herbert in the *North American Review*: "Japan has leaped, almost at one bound, to a place among the great nations of the earth. Her recent exploits in the war with China have focussed all eyes upon her."[29] At

[26] See F. L. Mott, *History of American Magazines* (Cambridge, 1938), v. 3, p. 473.
[27] *Cosmopolitan Magazine*, v. 6, p. 557, April 1889.
[28] *Arena*, v. 3, p. 658, May 1891.
[29] *North American Review*, v. 160, p. 685, June 1895.

the same time, the weakness of China in defense presented her as a kind of grab bag of the nations. Julian Ralph wrote in *Harper's Weekly* (January 15, 1898) of "The Dissection of China." In the next two years, American reviews and magazines were full of the Hay "open-door policy," by which the United States hoped to save China's territorial integrity. The Boxer Rebellion of 1900 and the growing enmity between Russia and Japan, as well as immigration and trade problems, kept the reviews and magazines well aware of Oriental problems as the new century began. A Chinese personality interesting to the American people was that of Minister Wu Ting-fang.

In 1900 the *National Geographic Magazine* began a long and richly illustrated series of articles about China and Japan. John Barrett's two-part article, "China: Her History and Development," and several pieces about China by Commander Harrie Webster and James Mascarene Hubbard appeared in 1900–1901. Stimulated by the interest in the Russo-Japanese War, the *National Geographic* published no less than eleven articles about Japan in the years 1904 and 1905.

*Artistic Japan* was a well-illustrated journal published from 1888 to 1890 in London and New York. The *Asiatic Journal of Commerce* (1902–1911) was a San Francisco monthly. The *Journal of the American Asiatic Association* began in 1898, to become *Asia* many years later;[30] and there were other serials of a scholarly nature about the Orient. *Armenia* (1904–1929), of Boston and later New York, was at one time called *Oriental World*.

THE WAR WITH SPAIN

"We meet on every hand a marked revival of the cry for peace," observed the *Arena* in 1894, and furnished a bibliography on the subject, which listed a score of magazines of the period.[31] It seemed to many in the early nineties that war was likely to be abolished in that generation. *Current History* pointed out in 1895 that the United States had arbitrated its disputes with foreign nations no less than thirty times in the preceding half-century.[32] An International Arbitration Congress was held in Washington in the spring of 1896, and the May 7 issue of the *Independent* carried a symposium of opinions as to the desirability of a world court. With some, of course, arbitration was merely a means to isolationism, as when Senator Chauncey M. Depew wrote in *Congress*: "The political mission of the United States is purely internal."[33]

[30] Issued under that title in 1917–42. The Oriental Club of Philadelphia issued its *Studies* in 1888–94, and Vanderbilt University its *Oriental Series* in 1899–1918.
[31] *Arena*, v. 11, p. 118, Dec. 1894.
[32] *Cyclopedic Review of Current History*, v. 5, p. 860, 4th quar., 1895.
[33] *Congress*, v. 1, p. 54, April 1888.

But the peaceable men did not have it all their own way by any means. In fact, the scientist N. S. Shaler saw in the mid-nineties "a strange tide which is setting our nation toward warfare." He wrote in the *North American* early in 1896:

We appear to be driven by a blind impulse into modes of thought and action concerning our neighbors that will, if unchecked, bring us to contests of arms. A trifling fracas with Chile, an insurrection in Cuba, a matter of fishing in Newfoundland, of sealing in Alaska, or the confused questions of a wilderness boundary in [Venezuela] South America, each and all serve to set the dogs of war baying up and down the land.[34]

Before this, there was warlike talk about the Cuban outrages, and it grew fast. "The time is ripe for the interference of the Untied States in the affairs of Cuba," declared the martial John Brisben Walker in his *Cosmopolitan* in 1895;[35] and the next year *Harper's Weekly* reported that the Cuban troubles were "the most engrossing question of national hysteria,"[36] while the *Bookman,* viewing magazines, newspapers, and books all together, thought that "the growing interest in whatever relates to battle make the explosion seem inevitable."[37] In a serial begun in October 1897, *Cosmopolitan* offered a "looking backward" narrative entitled "Our Late War with Spain"; as prophecy it was a poor performance, showing, as it did, a coalition of European powers attacking the United States from Canada.[38] One of the strongest of the scores of articles appearing in American magazines on the Cuban question was one by Hannis Taylor, former minister to Spain, in the *North American Review* late in 1897. "Spain herself has demonstrated," he wrote, "that she is powerless either to conciliate Cuba or conquer it."[39]

On the night of February 15, 1898, occurred the explosion that had been heard by the prophetic ear of the *Bookman*; to be precise, there were two of them, and the naval board of inquiry later reported that they came from "under the bottom" of the battleship *Maine* in Havana Harbor, destroying the ship and killing most of the crew. On April 11, President McKinley asked for a declaration of war against Spain; and part of his message to Congress on that occasion was a paraphrase of Hannis Taylor's article in the *North American*.[40] "Everybody turned out to see the volunteers parade the streets," we read in the *Anglo-*

---

[34] *North American Review*, v. 162, p. 328, March 1896.
[35] *Cosmopolitan Magazine*, v. 19, p. 470, Aug. 1895.
[36] *Harper's Weekly*, v. 40, p. 1115, Nov. 14, 1896.
[37] *Bookman*, v. 3, p. 153, April 1896.
[38] Later, on March 23, 1898, just before the declaration of war, *Truth* came out with a chromolithograph of New York ablaze under bombardment, and an article by General Miles on our coastal defenses.
[39] *North American Review*, v. 165, p. 610, Nov. 1897.
[40] *Ibid.*, v. 166, p. 687, June 1898.

*American Magazine*, "and hear their voices proclaim, to the tune of Sousa's march and the tread of countless feet:

> "The Maine, the Maine,
> Remember the Maine!
> Hurrah for Cuba,
> And down with Spain!" [41]

On the whole, it was a popular war. It produced a galaxy of heroes — President McKinley, "Teddy" Roosevelt, Richmond P. Hobson, Admiral Dewey, and so on. An editorial in the *Saturday Evening Post* declaimed eloquently after the loss of the *Maine*:

> In the presence of our great national calamity and in the fierce light of the Maine's terrible explosion, the dignity, the courage, and the serene self-possession of our Chief Magistrate stands forth in bold relief. . . . We believe that the honor and welfare of the Nation are safe in his hands. [42]

But there were dissenting voices. The new socialistic *Public*, referring in the early autumn of 1898 to "the ghastly mismanagement of the war," asserted roundly: "President McKinley is no king, whose delinquencies are to be loaded off upon the shoulders of his ministers." [43] And the robustly individual W. H. Thorne, with an unusual access of fury, wrote in his *Globe* review about "those brainless, selfish, purchasable, ignorant, unprincipled, dastardly wildcats known as patriotic members of Congress, who forced the Spanish-American War resolutions upon a willing President and a gullible people, when we had no case or cause of war with Spain." [44]

All but the most staid of American reviews and magazines devoted large proportions of their space to the war during 1898 and 1899. A Philadelphia monthly described the "coverage":

> Certainly it is no fault of the editors if the public is not thoroughly conversant with every possible phase of the present war. The lightest "Illustrated" and the gravest review alike offer timely articles which range from "Lovers' Day at a State Camp" to profound studies of questions of weightiest import. *McClure's*, indeed, is wholly given over to belligerency from cover to cover. [45]

*Munsey's* and *Cosmopolitan* had been dedicated to the war long before it began. The camera reporters did excellent work both for the ten-cent monthlies, which always kept closer to current events than the "quality magazines," and for the great weeklies. *Collier's* made its position se-

---

[41] *Anglo-American Magazine*, v. 1, p. 25, Feb. 1899.
[42] *Saturday Evening Post*, v. 170, March 12, 1898, p. 8.
[43] *Public*, v. 1, Sept. 24, 1898, p. 1.
[44] *Globe*, v. 8, p. 463, Dec. 1898.
[45] *Citizen*, v. 4, p. 122, July 1898.

cure as a great national weekly by what was probably the best "picture coverage" given any war by a magazine up to that time.[46]

But soon "Dewey was the morning down in Manila Bay." "Dewey is the greatest of fleet commanders, the grandest of all the heroes of the sea," declared one current-events magazine; [47] and one hero eulogized another when T. R. wrote in *McClure's*, "Admiral Dewey performed one of the great feats of all time."[48]

America was surprised by her new responsibilities, however. "Very few people," wrote Albert Shaw in his *Review of Reviews*, ". . . had for a moment supposed that armed intervention for the pacification of Cuba would begin with a campaign for the conquest of the Philippine Islands, which lie in the Pacific Ocean between Hong Kong and New Guinea."[49] But Shaw was an expansionist, as was Walter Hines Page, editor of *World's Work*, who pointed out aptly a few years later just what had really happened to America:

> We do not mean by "expansion" a thing that happened when we acquired the old Spanish colonies and then stopped, for geographical enlargement is one of the least important phases of it. In commercial, political, and intellectual ways it is going on more rapidly every year. We are honorably winning foreign markets . . . extending our political influence . . . and our intellectual horizon. It has an increasing influence on our national character.[50]

A flood of magazine articles about the Philippines appeared in the winter of 1898–1899. Two may be cited as typical — Charles Denby's "Shall We Keep the Philippines?" in the *Forum* for November 1898, and Max L. Tornow's "Economic Condition of the Philippines" in the *National Geographic* for February 1899. The Philippine Information Society, of Boston, published *Facts About the Filipines* (1901–1902), later called *Philippine Review*; and Americans in Manila soon began journals of education and religion there for the Filipinos.[51] *Cuba: Political Weekly* (1897–1898) was a prewar propaganda sheet, and the *Cuba Review* (1903–1931) was a trade monthly; both were New York periodicals.

LATIN AMERICA

Besides the extensive interest shown in the Spanish West Indies, there were other matters that drew American eyes southward — the

[46] See p. 455.
[47] *Up to Date*, v. 7, June 4, 1898, p. 1.
[48] *McClure's Magazine*, v. 13, p. 490, Oct. 1899.
[49] *Review of Reviews*, v. 17, p. 643, June 1898.
[50] *World's Work*, v. 3, p. 1367, Nov. 1901.
[51] Such as *Philippine Christian Advocate* (1902–11), which was succeeded by *Philippine Observer* (1911–34); *Philippine Teacher* (1904–45), which changed title to *Philippine Education* in 1906 and to *Philippine Magazine* in 1928.

Trans-Isthmian Canal project, trade with South America, and the efforts toward Pan-American unity. There were such expansionists as Henry Cabot Lodge, who criticized "Our Blundering Foreign Policy" in the *Forum* because, in 1895, we had a weak navy, had not acquired a Nicaraguan canal, had not annexed Cuba, had not taken steps to take over the Spanish West Indies, and had not dominated Pacific commerce.[52] The need for an Isthmian canal was sharply emphasized by the necessity that the battleship *Oregon* faced when it was in the Atlantic and was urgently needed in the Pacific. "The cruise of the *Oregon* . . . around Cape Horn . . . awakened the nation to a full realization of the importance" of the canal in time of war as well as in peace, said a writer in the *North American*.[53] All the reviews debated the various questions connected with the building of such a waterway until the decisive action of 1903; later the construction operation itself engaged the fascinated attention of many readers.

The *Monthly Bulletin of the Bureau of the American Republics* began in 1893 as a trade periodical, later to become an attractive magazine.[54] The *Pan-American Magazine* (1900–1931), published at various times in half a dozen or more different cities in North and South America, printed illustrated articles and much news and comment.[55] *Modern Mexico* (1895–1909) was started in St. Louis, moved to Mexico City, and was last published in New York.

MISSIONARY PERIODICALS

Increased attention to foreign affairs in the 1890's stimulated interest in Christian missions abroad.[56] In both secular magazines and church periodicals, there was much about foreign missions, and scores of periodicals devoted to this field and designed chiefly to win financial support for such projects were published. Among the leading missionary periodicals begun in earlier periods and still issued in the nineties were the *Baptist Missionary Magazine* and the American Board's *Missionary Herald*, the veterans,[57] the Congregational *American Missionary*, the Methodist *Woman's Missionary Friend*, and the interdenominational *Missionary Review of the World*.[58]

[52] *Forum*, v. 19, pp. 8–17, March 1895.
[53] *North American Review*, v. 167, p. 698, Dec. 1898.
[54] It adopted illustration in 1908 and became a travel magazine in part. In 1910 it became *Bulletin of the Pan-American Union*.
[55] The *Bulletin of Bibliography* (v. 13, p. 65, Sept.–Dec. 1927) called the *Pan-American Magazine* "the greatest traveler among magazines." Though surpassed in itinerancy by others, it was published, within three years, in New York, San Antonio, Lima, Panama City, and New Orleans.
[56] See Ortha May Lane, *Missions in Magazines* (Iowa City, 1935), p. 21.
[57] See Mott, *op. cit.*, v. 1, p. 134.
[58] See Mott, *op. cit.*, v. 2, p. 71; v. 3, pp. 70, 72.

Two specialized periodicals in the field were the *Double Cross and Medical Missionary Record* (1886–1900), of New York, and the *Medical Missionary* (1886–1914), of Battle Creek, Michigan. *Liberia* (1892–1909), published by the historic American Colonization Society, superseded the old *African Repository*. *Voice of Missions* (1892–current) was the organ of the African Methodist Episcopal Church's missionary activity. Nearly all sects, indeed, had their missionary bulletins or magazines.[59]

### THE IMMIGRATION PROBLEM

"Immigration has been of immense gain to the United States," wrote Hugh McCulloch in *Scribner's* in 1888, but "if the effect should prove to be deleterious to the character of the population, the gain would have been dearly acquired."[60] And the *Andover Review* about the same time doubted whether "America can long continue to be a receptacle for the overflow of Europe."[61] The weekly *America* put it more strongly when it referred to "the pollution of our national life-blood by the stream of ignorance, misery and vice pouring into it from the lowest strata of European life."[62] H. H. Boyesen, himself an immigrant from Norway, was more specific in the *Forum*:

> These immigrants are no longer, as formerly, absorbed into the native population, . . . but a large portion of them become a disturbing element, an unexpended surplus in the labor market which unsettles all economic relations.[63]

Other reviews were alarmed because leadership in anarchy, communism, and socialism in this country was so often in the hands of comparatively new immigrants.

The new *Journal of Political Economy* looked into the statistics of the increase of immigration in the eighties over that of the preceding decade, to find that while new arrivals from England, Ireland, and

[59] Representative ones in the nineties were the Presbyterian *Woman's Work* (1886–1924); the Methodist *World-Wide Missions* (1888–1912); the Southern Methodist *Review of Missions* (1879–1903), which had begun as *Missionary Reporter*; the Methodist Protestant *Woman's Missionary Record* (1885–1940); the Congregational *Pilgrim Missionary* (1888–1909), of Boston; *Missionary Intelligencer* (1887–1918), by and for the Foreign Christian Missionary Society; *John Three Sixteen* (1891–current), Hepzibah Faith Missionary Association; *Christian Missionary* (1894–1928), of the Christian church; the German Evangelical *Missionary Messenger* (1886–1917); *Mission Field* (1887–1922), of the Reformed Church in America; the Reformed Presbyterian *Herald of Mission News* (1887–1928), which changed title to *Olive Trees* in 1897; the United Brethren *Missionary Monthly* (1897–current); *Prophetic and Mission Record* (1896–1920), of the American Advent Mission Society; *Friends' Missionary Advocate* (1885–current); and *Missionary* (1896–current), of the Catholic Missionary Union.
[60] *Scribner's Magazine*, v. 4, p. 432, Oct. 1888.
[61] *Andover Review*, v. 9, p. 303, March 1888.
[62] *America*, v. 1, March 28, 1889, p. 3.
[63] *Forum*, v. 3, pp. 533–34, July 1887.

France had increased 41 per cent, which was plenty, immigration from the more submerged Italian, Polish, Russian, and Hungarian classes had increased 435 per cent.[64] Others thought that the "yellow peril" was the greatest: Thomas Magee wrote in the *Forum* in October 1890 about "China's Menace to the World." But the *North American*, which discussed the Oriental problem frequently, carried an article by Yan Phon Lee in April 1889 titled "The Chinese Must Stay," and the very last number of the *Californian Magazine* (April 1894) had a good article by John Bonner protesting against the Chinese Exclusion Act. And so the debate on the various phases of immigration, with its sometimes acute effect on foreign relations, continued.

By 1897 Joseph H. Senner, United States Commissioner of Immigration, wrote in the *Annals of the American Academy of Political and Social Science* that "heavy" immigration was no longer possible under new restrictive measures.[65] But he was wrong, for despite further regulation the numbers of immigrants admitted mounted again in the closing years of the century, and in 1905 reached a million in one year for the first time.

[64] *Journal of Political Economy*, v. 1, p. 433, June 1893. Also see Francis A. Walker in *Forum*, v. 11, pp. 634–44, Aug. 1891, for a study of the census figures on immigration.
[65] *Annals*, v. 10, pp. 1–19, July 1897.

## CHAPTER XIII

## NEWSPAPERS AND THE ADVERTISING BUSINESS

SINCE magazines and newspapers were closer together in the 1890's than ever before in the history of either, their relationship had many interesting phases. Perhaps the most important of these were the invasion of the magazine field by the Sunday newspaper and the criticism of the newspaper (especially as to its sensationalism) by the magazines.

"It is difficult to see how the better Sunday newspaper can very much more nearly approximate to weekly magazines," declared John A. Cockerill, managing editor of the *New York World*, in 1892.[1] The *World* was, at that time, the country's foremost newspaper, with the most ambitious of Sunday editions. The statement was made in the *Cosmopolitan*, whose editor observed some months later that magazines did a better job of selection than Sunday papers.[2] In general this was true; but on certain levels there was so much similarity between Sunday paper and magazine miscellany that discussion of the phenomenon and what might come of it was common.[3]

The magazines published a vast deal of material about newspapers in this period, most of it sharply critical. "No other profession is so wept over," observed a writer in the *Bookman*.[4] The *Arena*, which paid much attention to newspaper problems in the latter nineties, recorded that

> One of the signs of the times is a loud and rapidly swelling cry of protest . . . against the sensational journal. The protest has reached such a volume that it must be met, and it is met by a majority of the editors and managers with the statement that "sensationalism is what the people want."[5]

Boston's *Happy Thought* had some unhappy thoughts about the competition in sensationalism between the *Journal* and *World* in New York in 1896. It congratulated its readers that "Boston has fortunately escaped with but slight contamination," but it feared that it was "only a question of time when some foreign newspaper capitalist will descend

---

[1] *Cosmopolitan Magazine*, v. 13, p. 645, Oct. 1892.

[2] *Ibid.*, v. 14, p. 262, Jan. 1893.

[3] See Chap. I for fuller discussion of this matter.

[4] F. M. Colby in the *Bookman*, v. 15, p. 534, Aug. 1902. See also *Dial*, v. 22, p. 229, April 16, 1897 (typical of much in this journal); *Conservative Review*, v. 5, p. 228, Sept. 1901; *Scribner's Magazine*, v. 6, pp. 760–68, Dec. 1889; Major J. W. Powell's comment on "monstrous lies" in his address on becoming president of the Washington Anthropological Society (*American Anthropologist*, v. 1, p. 321, Oct. 1888).

[5] *Arena*, v. 18, p. 681, Nov. 1897; see also J. C. Ridpath in *ibid.*, v. 20, p. 141, July 1898.

upon us."[6] It was eight years. *Life* itemized the faults of the journalism of the times with conscious naïveté:

> Almost everyone seems to agree that newspapers are dreadfully demoralizing and objectionable. . . . The newspapers print too much gossip; they invade privacy; they get up panics by croaking and circulating bad news; their pictures are bad as art and worthless as illustration; they are so big that it takes all day to read them, but small enough to print the meanest items; they don't tell the truth, and again, they do tell the truth, but tell it with too little discrimination.[7]

Many magazines (and indeed many newspapers) condemned the vulgar enterprise of those reporters who, assigned to cover the marriage of President Cleveland, were refused entrance to the White House but pitched their tents on the front lawn of the couple's honeymoon cottage at Deer Park, Maryland.[8] The *Journalist*, chief spokesman for the press, called this "a disgusting exhibition of impertinence."[9] The *Critic* was much concerned with immoralities in the press. "Day by day the offense grows ranker," it declared.[10] Said the *Philistine*:

> At the publishers' convention recently held at San Francisco the delegates were treated to a steamboat ride down the Bay, where a picnic was held. Police were on hand to see that the delegates did not all rush down a steep place into the sea and perish in the waters.[11]

Many articles about the press were more restrained, however, and better advised. The *Era Magazine* often discussed the newspapers intelligently. Edward Bruce Channing, telling "The Story of Hearst" in the *Era*, found him "the most interesting individual in the United States," and "perhaps the most influential editor in the world today."[12] An anonymous "Reformed Yellow Journalist," writing in the *Saturday Evening Post* in 1904, declared with much truth that "yellow journalism was at its height a few years ago and has now subsided to near-sanity, except in a few conspicuous spots." He added: "Yellow journalism never represented anything but the extremes of the real journalism of the country."[13] But the *Post* had commented intelligently on one of the phases of the "yellow journalism" of the latter nineties when it had declared editorially: "The Spanish-American War is a newspaper-made war."[14] Arthur Brisbane wrote an extremely valuable contribution to

[6] *Happy Thought*, v. 3, March 19, 1896, p. 4.
[7] *Life*, v. 22, p. 116, Aug. 24, 1893.
[8] See *Public Opinion*, v. 1, p. 174, June 12, 1886.
[9] *Journalist*, v. 3, June 5, 1886, p. 8.
[10] *Critic*, v. 10, p. 49, Jan. 29, 1887.
[11] *Philistine*, cover of issue for Sept. 1895.
[12] *Era Magazine*, v. 13, p, 99, Feb. 1904.
[13] *Saturday Evening Post*, v. 178, April 14, 1904, p. 1.
[14] *Ibid.*, v. 170, June 4, 1898, p. 8.

the *Cosmopolitan* for September 1898 called "The Modern Newspaper in War Time," telling about the remarkable activities of the *New York Journal* in covering that war, which included publishing as many as forty editions a day, totaling over a million copies.[15]

It was the Sunday paper at which the bitterest criticism was directed throughout the period now under consideration. As early as May 1888 the famous preacher Joseph Cook called for a boycott against Sunday journalism:

> Let reputable people refuse to receive into their houses Sunday journals, and cause it to be known that advertisements in these papers do not reach the better class of home, and a financial chill may be thrown into the lawless, mercenary heart of an irresponsible Sunday press. . . . The loafer's journal is peculiarly loaferish, and the Satanic press peculiarly Satanic, on Sunday.[16]

Then, with the coming of "yellow journalism," the torrent of criticism of the Sunday supplements increased. "Some of these days," said *Brann's Iconoclast*, "the American people will be blessed with a renaissance of common sense, and then such papers as the *Sunday World* will frizzle up like Jonah's gourd and make place for legitimate journalism."[17]

Women, according to one *Arena* writer, "have entered and occupied the field of journalism, and they are there to stay"; but another contributor to that review, writing under the title "Women in Gutter Journalism," declared that "in the world of modern wildcat journalism, the woman reporter lasts about four years."[18] The *Journalist* gave no small attention to women workers in the field, issuing a special women's number as early as January 26, 1889.

Mechanical developments of importance to journalists were the telephone and the typewriter. Both were accepted by newspaper offices throughout the nineties much more slowly than might have been expected. The *Journalist* reported in 1891:

> With the rapid improvements in typewriters and their approach toward reasonableness in price, their use is becoming more common among newspaper workers and writers generally. It is quite possible that the time is not far off when the reporter will hand in his copy neatly executed on the typewriter. . . . It saves the eyes, avoids pen-cramp, and does away with the back-ache which comes from bending over a desk.[19]

[15] *Cosmopolitan Magazine*, v. 25, p. 541, Sept. 1898. Cf. *Bookman*, v. 7, p. 323, June 1898.

[16] *Our Day*, v. 1, pp. 44–45, May 1888; also *ibid.*, v. 3, p. 121, Feb. 1889; *Current Literature*, v. 2, p. 460, June 1889; James Parton, "Newspapers Gone to Seed," *Forum*, v. 1, pp. 15–24, March 1886.

[17] *Brann's Iconoclast*, v. 5, p. 117, Aug. 1895.

[18] *Arena*, v. 17, p. 127, Dec. 1896; *ibid.*, v. 17, p. 568, March 1897.

[19] *Journalist*, v. 12, Jan. 3, 1891, p. 8.

In the same year, an article in *Electricity* pointed out the typewriter's contribution to the telegrapher's work. "The use of the typewriter in telegraph work," it was said, "has doubled the value of every live newspaper in the country by enabling it to print twice as much news and better, because later, news."[20]

<h2 style="text-align:center">JOURNALISTS' JOURNALS</h2>

The *Publishers' Auxiliary* and *American Press* were useful and newsy weeklies issued by ready-print and boiler-plate houses during our period. The *National Printer-Journalist* was the organ of the National Editorial Association, an organization dominated by the small-city dailies and the weeklies.[21]

The *Journalist* was founded in 1884 by Allan Forman and conducted by him as a New York weekly throughout most of its stormy career. Several other men were associated with Forman, in one capacity or another;[22] but he was the *Journalist*, for good or ill. His paper was a newsy, well-illustrated quarto of sixteen pages, very free with praises of its friends and criticism of its enemies. Libel suits and personal assaults marked its early years. There were those who thought it inclined to blackmailing, and it was noticeable that it was unkind to those who would not advertise with it. In the competition among the composing machines in the nineties, for example, Forman was markedly unfriendly to the Mergenthaler interests when they did not advertise; and so it was with the typewriters, the wire agencies, and so on.[23] The paper was suspended for two years from 1895 to 1897, while Forman recuperated from illness abroad; when he resumed the *Journalist*, it had three weekly competitors in New York, all striving for national circulation. But these were prosperous times, and it survived for ten years more.[24] The file of the *Journalist* is an invaluable record of the newspaper events and personalities of the latter eighties and the nineties. Its unusual holiday editions were remarkable for variety and interest.

[20] *Electricity*, v. 1, p. 264, Dec. 9, 1891.

[21] For the periodicals mentioned in this paragraph, see F. L. Mott, *A History of American Magazines* (Cambridge, 1938), v. 3, p. 273-74.

[22] Forman's original associates were Charles A. Byrne and Leander Richardson, well-known theatrical journalists. After the first year, Byrne and Richardson sold to Charles J. Smith, one of the founders of the *New York Star*, who became associate editor, and to William G. McLaughlin, later conductor of the *Metropolis*, who became business manager of the *Journalist*. Late in 1886 Forman bought out the others. H. Clay Lukens then became associate editor until he was succeeded by C. C. Starkweather in April 1888 (see v. 28, pp. 369-71, Feb. 10, 1901).

[23] See strong implication, if not accusation, of blackmailing in *Printer's Ink*, v. 11, p. 584, Oct. 10, 1894.

[24] Forman took a partner, Arthur E. Harrell, in 1906, and made the paper a monthly; but early the next year it was merged in *Editor & Publisher*.

*Newspaperdom* (1892–1925) was founded in New York as a modest monthly by Charles S. Patterson, with the design of appealing mainly to publishers of weeklies and small-city dailies. It was a helpful and sensible quarto. Patterson sold it in 1901 to John Clyde Oswald, and it later had a succession of proprietors and forms, until it disappeared into the capacious maw of *Editor & Publisher.*[25]

*Fourth Estate* was founded in 1894 by Ernest F. Birmingham in New York as "a weekly newspaper for the makers of newspapers and investors in advertising." It specialized in conciseness, brief mention, short "write-ups" of papers, with half-column wide portraits. Though never very prosperous, it made many friends. Its annual list of advertising agencies was valuable. In 1927 it was absorbed by *Editor & Publisher.*[26] Frank H. Lancaster, who had been Birmingham's editor from 1894 to 1895, started his own weekly, the *Newspaper Maker*, in 1895; it lasted six years.

*Editor & Publisher* was founded in 1901 by Colonel J. B. Shale, New York representative of the Scripps-McRae wire agency known as the Publishers' Press Association. Frank L. Blanchard was associate editor. From the first it was newsy and attractive. Later it absorbed its rivals and became the national spokesman for the country's daily newspapers.[27]

The American Newspaper Publishers' Association began issuing a *Bulletin* for its members in 1895. State editorial associations sometimes printed their proceedings, and a few tried to issue regular publications. The *Massachusetts Editor* began in 1897, became *New England Editor* the next year, and perished in 1900.

### ADVERTISING AND ITS PROBLEMS

In a retrospective editorial published near the end of the present period, the *Woman's Home Companion* pointed out that "what might be called the 'New Advertising'" dated from the beginning of the nineties, "when magazines first became national in their scope." [28] The growth of magazine circulations had much to do with it, but the nationwide increase of industry even more.[29] After all, the newspaper publishers got by far the largest part of the advertiser's dollar.

[25] It was a weekly at times, but a semimonthly through most of its career. H. Craig Dare bought it in 1912, and after his death in 1923, it was continued by Mrs. Dare. James Wright Brown, of *Editor & Publisher*, bought it in 1925 and issued it for a short time as *Advertising*.

[26] H. M. Newman bought it in 1926, broadened its scope, but sold out the next year. He is said to have lost $60,000 on it.

[27] A separate sketch of *Editor & Publisher* will appear in the next volume of this work.

[28] *Woman's Home Companion*, v. 30, Sept. 1940, pp. 8–9.

[29] See pp. 20–24.

The amazing growth of advertising brought out various problems. Wrote one critic: "This is a veritable age of puffery, devoted to the exploiting of the unworthy, and forcing the ignorant, the money-grabber, and the incompetent into the great white light of publicity." [30] The playwright Dion Boucicault argued in the *North American* in 1887 that advertising had corrupted the newspaper, and the newspaper had corrupted the drama.[31] Another writer in the same journal complained bitterly a few years later because advertising had distended the newspaper, and the proper eight-page size had now been swelled to sixteen, and sometimes even to twenty.[32]

But quack medicines were still, very properly, the chief object of the attacks of the reformers of advertising. It was not until the very end of the present period that the crusade of the *Ladies' Home Journal* and *Collier's* brought about the enactment of the Pure Food and Drug Act of 1906. Throughout the nineties, complaints were often made that many of the smaller medical journals were supported by the advertisements of disreputable nostrums. Dr. E. R. Squibb, of the famous pharmaceutical house of that name, wrote in the *Journal of the American Medical Association*: "The medical journals are themselves largely responsible for the existence of patent medicines. If those journals would cease to distribute their advertisements, the sales would fall off seventy-five per cent." [33] But even the *JAMA* advertised proprietary medicines. A more glaring inconsistency is found in the file of *Brann's Iconoclast*, which rails thus against the nostrums:

Take up almost any paper published in this country, and you will find staring you in the face display advertisements for the cure of criminal complaints, charlatans promising to restore the worn-out roué's power for evil, abortion recipes, gambling devices, love philtres, quack dream-books filled with suggestive pictures — especially designed for the young — and finally to crown the crime, a "personal column" wherein the lawless libertine sets his snares for foolish schoolgirls — the whole making a symposium of reeking rottenness that might cause the gorge of the very Prince of Hell to rise.[34]

But in the same number with this diatribe, we find the "ad" of Veno's Electric Fluid, "the only medicine that will make cripples walk," and Veno's Curative Syrup, "warranted to cure malarial fever, nervousness, dyspepsia, liver, kidney, blood and stomach disorders, sleeplessness, and bad appetite."

The "quality" literary magazines were careful about their advertis-

[30] James L. Ford, "The Golden Age of Puffery," *Bachelor of Arts*, v. 1, p. 502, Sept. 1895.
[31] *North American Review*, v. 145, p. 37, July 1887.
[32] Julian Proctor in *ibid.*, v. 149, p. 123, July 1889.
[33] *JAMA*, v. 29, p. 586, Sept. 18, 1897.
[34] *Brann's Iconoclast*, v. 6, p. 74, April 1896; ad on p. 83.

ing. Nearly all of the better class of magazines were made more conscious of their responsibilities as censors of their own pages by the
*Collier's* crusade referred to above, and patent medicines were banned
by many of them in 1903 and thereafter.

ADVERTISING JOURNALS

The leading periodical devoted to the multiple phases of advertising
was *Printers' Ink*, founded in 1888 by the famous advertising agent,
George Presbury Rowell.[35] It had a small page, but it was packed
with the wit and wisdom, the news and personalities of the advertising
business. Someone named it "The Little Schoolmaster of Advertising,"
and the name was picked up as a kind of slogan. Its early years were
enlivened by a long fight with the Postmaster General over its alleged
abuse of the second-class mailing privilege. *Printers' Ink* was furnished
to all newspapers that did business with the Rowell agency, and much
of its circulation was made up of "block subscriptions" formed when
a medium would put all of its chief advertising patrons down to receive
the little magazine with the hot tips for advertisers. Rowell would
sometimes take payment for this in newspaper space, which he would
fill with the advertising of his clients. Agencies also bought blocks for
their clients: E. C. Allen, of Augusta, bought four thousand subscriptions in 1890. Postmaster General Wanamaker did not consider all
this legitimate circulation. After much bitter recrimination, compro-
mises were made, *Printers' Ink* was readmitted at second-class rates,
and it went on gaining business and reputation. The little magazine
became a "schoolmaster" by printing many single articles and serial
dissertations on phases of advertising; and as research in the field
developed, these came to be more valuable. It became the recognized
spokesman for advertising. It helped to develop an ethical consciousness in the profession, and was a leader in advertising reforms. Its
own advertising was almost as interesting as its text, and it carried a
large volume of copy from the country's leading media. It had begun
with eight to sixteen of its small pages, but by the end of the present
period, it occasionally issued nearly a hundred pages in one of its
weekly numbers.[36]

---

[35] The name of the first editor, Charles Love Benjamin, appeared as publisher of the first
few numbers; but the whole undertaking was Rowell's. See Rowell, *Forty Years an Advertising Agent* (New York, 1906), pp. 355–65, for the story of the beginnings and of the
fight with Wanamaker. For the latter, see also *Printers' Ink*, v. 7, pp. 205–23, Aug. 24, 1892.
The editors have been Benjamin, 1888–89; John Irving Romer, 1891–93, 1908–33; Oscar
Herzberg, 1894–1901; Charles J. Zingg, 1901–06; Charles B. Larrabee, 1933–current.

[36] Later it printed an occasional number with 200 pages. Under Romer, it kept up with
the stupendous growth of advertising. For a summary of its leading accomplishments in its

Rowell claimed that by 1905 there had been two hundred *"Printers' Ink* babies,"* as he called the imitators of his journal.[37] Many of these were short-lived, and most of them had circulations under ten thousand. *Profitable Advertising* was begun in 1891 by C. F. David, Boston. Kate E. Griswold conducted it from 1897 to 1909, when it was combined with *Selling Magazine* (1906–1909), of New York, and became *Advertising and Selling*. It later absorbed *Advertising News* (1893–1918). H. C. Brown's *Art in Advertising* (1890–1909), of New York, was a specialist, and a quarto in size. *Fame* (1892–1938), of New York, organ of the agency of the well-known Artemas Ward, was similar to *Printers' Ink*, though a monthly and devoted in the nineties largely to card advertising in the subway.

*Advertising World* (1896–1930), of Columbus, Ohio, and *Ad Sense* (1896–1906), of Chicago, were founded in the same year and were among the leaders in this overcrowded field at the turn of the century. Chief journal of outdoor advertisers was the *Billboard* (1894–current), of Cincinnati. *Agricultural Advertising* (1894–1918) was begun in Chicago and ended in New York. Among the periodicals in this field that emphasized wit and humor was Herbert Booth King's *The King's Jester* (1891–1892).[38]

### PRINTING AND ALLIED TRADES

The *Inland Printer*, of Chicago, was the outstanding journal in the printing field.[39] *Printers' Ink* said with enthusiasm in 1899 that the *Inland* was "head and shoulders above any and every similar publication now appearing or that ever has appeared." [40] Exceptionally well produced itself, it was an authority on good typography, presswork, and printing stock. When John Clyde Oswald purchased the *American Printer* in 1899, he made it a rival of the *Inland* in excellent production; it had been founded by Howard Lockwood in 1885. In 1903 Henry Lewis Johnson began *Printing Art* at the Harvard University Press as a highly illustrated monthly at five dollars a year. It was a beautiful periodical, including reproductions in full color, etchings,

---

first half-century, see its great semicentennial number, v. 184, July 28, 1938, sec. 2, pp. 448–50.

[37] Rowell, *Forty Years an Advertising Agent*, p. 359.

[38] Other advertising journals of importance: *American Advertiser Reporter* (1885–93), of New York; *Mail Order Journal* (1897–1925), of New York, called *Advertising Age* 1916–21, and later *National Advertising*; *Pacific Advertising* (1897–1907), of Los Angeles; *White's Sayings* (1899–1909), by C. V. White, of Seattle; *Rhode Island Advertiser* (1899–1907), of Providence; *Common-Sense* (1901–10), of Chicago; *Judicious Advertising* (1902–25), of Chicago.

[39] See Mott, *op. cit.*, v. 3, p. 132.

[40] *Printers' Ink*, v. 21, p. 55, July 10, 1899.

wood engravings, and so on. Richard Garnett, Theodore L. DeVinne, Will Bradley, and Alfred W. Pollard were among the contributors.[41]

There were many other periodicals for printers, some of which enjoyed comparatively long lives. A number of labor journals were published as organs of unions in the printing field, as were several specialized periodicals, such as *Linotype Bulletin* (1902–current), the Mergenthaler house organ.[42]

[4.] It later became less ambitious under a succession of editors, turned more to advertising, changed title to *Printed Salesmanship* in 1925–36, moved to Chicago, perished in 1944.

[42] *Paper and Press* (1885–1906), of Philadelphia, became *International Press* in 1896. *American Art Printer* (1887–93) was a handsome New York monthly edited by William J. Kelly. St. Louis produced two journals in this field at the end of the century: *Progressive Printer* (1898–1911) and *Practical Printer* (1899–1911). Three in the engraving trade were *Engraver and Printer* (1891–96), of Boston; *Illustrator and Process Review* (1896–1905), of Buffalo; and *Engraver and Electrotyper* (1897–1916).

# CHAPTER XIV

## MUSIC AND DRAMA

THE latter eighties saw a great triumph for Wagnerian opera in the United States. The critics still discussed the matter pro and con, but opera lovers had decided. Walter Damrosch, writing on "German Opera and Every-Day Life" in the *North American* in 1889, said: "Five years ago the German opera at the Metropolitan Opera-House in New York was founded by Dr. Leopold Damrosch, and these five years have witnessed one of the most remarkable phenomena in the art-history of America" — namely, the enthusiastic acceptance of Wagner by American opera-goers.[1] Another writer in the same review had observed a little earlier that "Italian opera — rest its soul — is dead, very dead" in this country.[2] But a few years later the fickle public was changing its idols; and *Music* remarked in 1893 that "a principal feature of the season in purely musical circles is a strong revulsion against Wagnerism."[3] French, Italian, and even American opera won much favor in the later nineties; Wagner came back; and it was a cosmopolitan offering that Foster Coates wrote about in the *Chautauquan* when he said in 1897 that "For the past few years the opera has become the fashionable fad in New York . . . the most fashionable amusement we have."[4]

To the great symphony orchestras of New York and Boston were added in the nineties those of Chicago, Cincinnati, and Pittsburgh. Critics were high in their praises of Theodore Thomas, who left New York for Chicago in 1891, thus gaining for the new Chicago Symphony "one of the most distinguished orchestral leaders in the world," said *Music*.[5] And the *Illustrated American* declared: "To no man, living or dead, are American lovers of good orchestral music under as great obligations as to Theodore Thomas."[6]

Many singers, violinists, and pianists from abroad made American tours, but perhaps the greatest sensation of all was made by Ignace Jan Paderewski, the Polish pianist. "Paderewski marks a new epoch

---

[1] *North American Review*, v. 149, p. 699, Dec. 1889, Cf. *Critic*, v. 9, p. 236, Nov. 13, 1886; *Current History*, v. 1, p. 72, Feb. 1891.
[2] Edgar J. Levey in *North American Review*, v. 144, p. 650, June 1887.
[3] *Music*, v. 4, p. 242, July 1893. Cf. Henry T. Finck, "German Opera in New York," *Scribner's Magazine*, v. 5, p. 8, March 1888.
[4] *Chautauquan*, v. 24, p. 707, March 1897.
[5] *Music*, v. 1, p. 81, Nov. 1891.
[6] *Illustrated American*, v. 19, p. 253, Feb. 22, 1896.

in the development of piano playing," asserted *Music*;[7] and William Mason and James G. Huneker, collaborating on an article for the *Century*, agreed that he was "unquestionably an inspired and phenomenal pianist."[8]

### POPULAR SONGS

In the nineties occurred the greatest development in popular songs America had ever known. They came from several sources: there were "coon songs" from the minstrel shows, sentimental ballads from the musical comedies, and ragtime pieces from the vaudeville stage. Reginald de Koven, writing on "Music Halls and Popular Songs" in the *Cosmopolitan* in 1897, named as the most popular: "Daisy Bell," better known to a later generation by its refrain line "On a bicycle built for two"; "Little Annie Rooney," which shared honors with two other New York songs, "The Sidewalks of New York" and "The Bowery"; the ragtime song, "Ta-ra-ra Boom-der-ay!"; the minstrel song, "I Want Yer, Ma Honey"; and the sentimental ballad, "Sweet Rosy O'Grady."[9] Harry Thurston Peck, who loved to discourse learnedly in the *Bookman* on popular foibles, talked in 1896 about the origins and migrations of such popular tunes as "Linger Longer, Lou," "Down Went McGinty," and the chief sentimental songs of that year — "Two Little Girls in Blue," "Only One Girl in the World for Me," and "Her Golden Hair Was Hanging Down Her Back."[10] Then came the war with Spain, bringing "There'll Be a Hot Time in the Old Town Tonight," as well as Paul Dresser's "The Blue and the Gray."[11]

At the very end of our period, the phonograph was contributing something to the quick popularity of songs; but throughout the nineties it was mainly a curiosity and a concert instrument. For example, in the Boston *Opera Glass* for January 1895, a Professor A. I. Newhall advertised that he would give "phonograph concerts adapted to lodges, churches, societies, clubs, lyceums, lecture courses, receptions, and theaters."

### MUSICAL JOURNALS

There were two main audiences for the musical journals — the "music trade" and the teachers and students. The latter included

[7] *Music*, v. 1, p. 587, April 1892.
[8] *Century Magazine*, v. 43, p. 721, March 1892.
[9] *Cosmopolitan Magazine*, v. 23, p. 536, Sept. 1897.
[10] *Bookman*, v. 3, p. 106, April 1896.
[11] Many songs of the nineties are discussed by E. C. May, in "Words and Music," *Evening Post*, v. 197, Oct. 18, 1924, pp. 11ff.

THE GIBSON MAN AND THE GIBSON GIRL, AND A DISCORDANT ELEMENT

A *Life* (March 18, 1897) double-spread by Charles Dana Gibson. See pages 563–564.

## THE GLORIFICATION OF THE "AMERICAN GIRL"

In this case, the Gibson girl.
From a double spread in *Life*, June 30, 1892 — a Fourth of July tribute.

church choirs. In addition to periodicals provided for these groups, there were many literary miscellanies that published sheet music in order to introduce it; for it must be remembered that in the years before the phonograph, radio, and television, publishers of songs had to find slower roads to popularity. Also, many urban weeklies gave special attention to music. There was some distinguished music criticism in certain periodicals of the various classes named, but in general this was subordinated to more practical uses. *Printers' Ink* called attention in 1894 to the fact that over fifty musical journals were being published currently,[12] a situation that held true throughout the nineties.

The *Musical Courier* (1880–current), of New York, was the leader in the trade and an important critical journal. A generous rival said in 1892 that the *Courier* was "the largest weekly periodical in the world devoted to music, also the most comprehensive, and by far the most profitable. . . . Its annual earnings amount to as much as fifty thousand dollars."[13] Its chief critic was James G. Huneker until 1902, when he was succeeded by William J. Henderson. Among music teachers' magazines, *Etude*, of Philadelphia, was the leader. Other musical magazines begun before 1885 that were among the top ten in circulation as the century ended were *Kunkel's Musical Review* (1879–1909), of St. Louis; *Werner's Voice Magazine* (1879–1902), New York; and *Echo* (1883–1901), Lafayette, Indiana.[14]

Perhaps the greatest name in musical journalism in these years was that of John C. Freund. Born in London and educated at Oxford, he came to New York as one of the editors of *Bonfort's Wine and Spirit Circular* in the early seventies, but soon began founding and editing musical journals.[15] In 1893 Freund supplanted his *Music and Drama* with the more definitely trade-aimed *Freund's Musical Weekly*, which became *Musical Age* in 1896 and lasted until 1914. In 1898 he established *Musical America*, a high-class weekly of criticism and news of music in the United States. A later editor, writing of Freund some years after his death, said that he

made *Musical America* utterly unfettered in its editorial policies and distinct in character and purpose from the traditional trade journals of the music field. He drove blackmail and the bludgeoning of artists out of musical journalism in America. He, more than any other single influence, definitely turned the tide of music study for Americans back from Europe to their own land. His pen was a

[12] *Printers' Ink*, v. 11, p. 22, Aug. 15, 1894.
[13] *Music*, v. 2, p. 240, July 1892.
[14] For *Werner's*, see F. L. Mott, *A History of American Magazines* (Cambridge, 1938), v. 3, p. 170; for the others mentioned in this paragraph, see *ibid.*, pp. 196–98.
[15] *Musical America*, v. 23, p. 210, Oct. 8, 1898.

tireless force for the recognition of the American composer, the American artist, the American teacher.[16]

Freund feuded with Otto Floersheim, of the *Musical Courier*, over some of the matters named in the paragraph just quoted. It was in 1902 that Victor Herbert recovered fifteen thousand dollars in a libel suit against the *Courier*, which had called him a plagiarist. Such was the musical journalism of the period.

When Theodore Dreiser was at loose ends in New York in the mid-nineties, it occurred to him that he could do something for himself and his composer-brother (who wrote his songs under the name of Paul Dresser) by publishing one of those hybrid musical and literary miscellany magazines which had some vogue at the time. He went to his brother's publishers, Howley, Haviland & Company, with the idea and, upon receiving substantial encouragement, he founded *Ev'ry Month* in October 1895. It was not a very good magazine, leaving much to be desired, from its oddly contracted title throughout its thirty-two to forty-eight quarto pages of poorly made-up content. It contained short stories (including one each from the pens of Stephen Crane and Bret Harte), some verse, a variety of articles (largely dealing with current events and art subjects), some book reviews, and departments of fashions and household hints (increasingly emphasized), besides two features that deserve our special attention. These were Paul Dresser's songs in sheet-music form and Theodore Dreiser's editorials. There were commonly four songs in a number, comprising a fourth to a third of the total pages, and including such Dresser classics as "On the Banks of the Wabash, Far Away," "Just Tell Her That You Saw Me," and "I Believe It, For My Mother Told Me So." The editorial department, headed "The Prophet," contained some notably Dreiserian comment on contemporary life, as for example:

> Like a sinful Magdalen, the city decks herself gayly, fascinating all by her garments of scarlet and silk, awing by her jewels and perfumes, when in truth there lies hid beneath these a torn and miserable heart, and a soiled and unhappy conscience that will not be still but is forever moaning and crying "for shame."[17]

Late in 1897 Dreiser was forced out of the editorship of the magazine he had planned, but in which he had no financial interest. It absorbed the *J. W. Pepper Piano Music Magazine* (1900–1902), of Philadelphia, but was itself merged into what then remained of the old

---

[16] *Ibid.*, v. 46, Aug. 20, 1927, p. 8. Freund died in 1924; a few years later there was a reorganization under Milton Weil, who had been Freund's business manager. *Musical America* changed from weekly to semimonthly to monthly.

[17] *Ev'ry Month*, v. 3, Oct. 1896, p. 6.

*New York Ledger* early in 1903. But the *Ledger* did not survive the year. Dreiser was never proud of his connection with this curious magazine.[18]

Boston was the home of several musical periodicals of some note. The *New England Conservatory Quarterly* (1894–1904) was soon made chiefly an alumni magazine for the institution it represented. The *Musician* was begun in Philadelphia by the Hatch Music Company in 1896 to popularize its compositions for students of the piano; in 1903 the Oliver Ditson Company, Boston, purchased it and merged with it their older *Musical Record*, attaining a circulation of forty thousand before the end of our period — the largest of all music journals except *Etude* and *Pepper's*.[19] *Masters in Music* (1903–1905) devoted each monthly number to the work of a single famous composer, offering thirty pages of music and sixteen of text. Daniel Gregory Mason was editor and Bates & Guild publishers.

Chicago was also a music-publishing center. Perhaps its most distinguished musical magazine was William S. B. Mathews' monthly *Music* (1891–1902). This was a high type of miscellany, offering articles on music and musicians, past and present, aids for teachers, and reviews of new music and of books in the field. In addition, it printed some fiction and verse, offered a "Trade Department," told much of music at the World's Fair and of Thomas's controversies, and so on. In later issues there was much about public-school music. This journal was finally merged in *Philharmonic* (1901–1903), Charles E. Nixon's bimonthly, which forthwith changed its title to *Muse,* and perished soon thereafter. The *Musical Review* (1891–1894) was Clayton F. Summy's monthly, which did a comprehensive service of reviewing "music and works pertaining to music." In later numbers it printed much eclectic matter from other journals, a serial manual for music teachers, and some sheet music.

One of the magazines that was more a literary miscellany than a music journal was *Conkey's Home Journal* (1897–1903), published by the W. B. Conkey Company, Chicago. It was one of those highly departmentalized monthlies, published at fifty cents a year with the assistance of premiums and mail-order advertising. It had some good contributors, especially in its early years; and about a third of its pages were given to musical compositions.[20] The *Will Rossiter*

---

[18] See John F. Huth, Jr., "Theodore Dreiser: 'The Prophet,'" *American Literature,* v. 9, pp. 208–17, May 1937.

[19] The *Musician* was sold to New York publishers in 1919 and was still published there in the 1950's. It came to publish much less music and more teaching helps and miscellany.

[20] It was called *American Home Journal* during its first year. Though a mail-order journal, it used good printing and paper to the end.

*Monthly* (1900–1901) contained Rossiter music in each issue, with stage gossip and pictures, as well as some fiction that surely was borrowed. In the Chicago trade field the older *Musical Times* found a strong competitor about the turn of the century in the *Musical Leader,* which had begun in 1895 as *Musical Leader and Concert-Goer* — one of a number of papers in various cities entitled "Concert-Goer."

## CHURCH AND SCHOOL MUSIC

There were a score of choir journals containing anthems for church use, usually monthly or semimonthly, priced at something less than a dollar a year and sold chiefly in block subscriptions to church choirs. Chief of these for a number of years was the *Choir Leader* (1894–1935), conducted by E. S. Lorenz, of Dayton, Ohio. Official publication of the American Guild of Organists was the *New Music Review* (1901–1935), New York.

"Devoted to the interests of bands and orchestras" was Carl Fischer's *Metronome* (1885–current), of New York. It began as a small monthly at fifty cents a year, but improved greatly as the years went on, and raised its price. *Harmony* (1894–1901), of New York, was a handsome monthly designed for town bands and school orchestras. *Dominant* (1893–1925) was another New York monthly published for orchestra teachers and players. *Pepper's Musical Times and Band Journal* (1877–1912) was mainly a trade journal.

Two leading violin journals were the *Violin World* (1892–1928), New York, and the *Violinist* (1900–1937), Chicago. *Gatcomb's Musical Gazette* (1887–1899), Boston, was "devoted to the interests of the banjo, mandolin, and guitar," as was *Cadenza* (1894–1924), which was begun in Kansas City and later moved to Boston.

The *Two-Step* (1894–1935), Chicago, was a magazine of dance music and dancing.[21] There were many other musical journals of some importance.[22]

---

[21] It was called *Terpsichorean* during 1920–28, and *Dancing Master* during 1928–35.

[22] The following may be listed: *Acme Haversack of Patriotism and Song* (1887–96), of Syracuse, N.Y., originally designed for the G.A.R.; *American Music Journal* (1900–07), of Cleveland; *Choir* (1899–1922), of Cincinnati; *Choir Journal* (1899–1908), of Boston; *Choir Herald* (1893–current), of Chicago and Dayton; *Church Choir* (1897–1920), of Chicago; *Concert-Goer* (1897–1903), of New York; *Home Music Journal* (1891–99), of Logansport, Ind.; *Messenger* (1889–1905), of Boston, organ of Music Teachers' National Association; *Music Trades* (1890–current), of New York; *Musical Echo* (1894–1909), of Savannah, Ga.; *Musical Enterprise* (1888–1931), of Camden and Milwaukee; *Musical Messenger* (1904–24), of Chicago and Cincinnati; *Pacific Musical Review* (1901–33), of San Francisco, which began as *Bohémienne; School Music* (1900–36), of Quincy, Ill., and Keokuk, Iowa; *Trifet's Monthly Galaxy of Music* (1887–94), of Boston; *Vocalist* (1888–97), of New York; *Western Musician* (1901–07), of Dixon, Ill.

There can be no doubt as to the marvelous growth of public interest in theatrical matters during the last few years. The space devoted to the subject in all
classes of periodical publications, from the dailies to the ponderous quarterlies,
proves this very conclusively.[23]

This opinion, expressed in 1888 by the *Stage*, is borne out by the
magazine files of the latter eighties; and the absorbing interest in the
theater then asserted continued to the end of the century and longer.
There is commentary on the drama, the stage, and shows of all kinds
almost everywhere; and an important element in the formula for a successful cheap magazine always was a department of pictures of
actresses, accompanied by a page or two of stage gossip.

All this was not distinctively literary. "Is the divorce of literature
and the stage complete?" asked Charles Dudley Warner in the *Critic*
at the beginning of the nineties, and he added:

How long is it since a play has been written and accepted and played which has
in it any so-called literary quality, or is an addition to literature? . . . The stage
can be amusing, but can it show life as it is without the aid of idealizing literary
art?[24]

And at the end of the nineties Mark Twain, apologizing for preaching
"because the rest of the clergy seem to be on vacation," urged that
at least something serious be devised to mix with comedy and "shows"
in the theaters.[25] The decline of great drama is blamed by Norman
Hapgood, a leading critic of the theater throughout his career as
writer and editor, on "what is commonly called the Theatrical Trust."
This was a syndicate formed in the mid-nineties for the control of the
country's theaters by six men — Samuel F. Nirdlinger (Nixon) and
J. Frederick Zimmerman, of Philadelphia, and Al Hayman, Charles
Frohman, Marc Klaw, and Abraham L. Erlanger, of New York.[26] The
fight against the theater monopoly was led by the *New York Dramatic
Mirror*, whose editor, Harrison Grey Fiske, found himself defendant
in a suit for criminal libel that was backed by the trust magnates. The
action was dismissed, however, and the *Mirror* continued its attacks,
issuing a weekly supplement devoted to its crusade for some months
in 1898.[27]

[23] *Stage*, v. 1, Sept. 29, 1888, p. 2. Cf. Charles Wyndham in *North American Review*, v.
149, p. 607, Nov. 1889.
[24] *Critic*, v. 15, p. 286, Dec. 7, 1889. Cf. *Illustrated American*, v. 3, p. 85, Aug. 2, 1890;
*North American Review*, v. 144, p. 169, Feb. 1887; *ibid.*, v. 145, p. 36, July 1887; and
Dion Boucicault in *Arena*, v. 2, p. 641, Nov. 1890.
[25] *Forum*, v. 26, p. 151, Oct. 1898.
[26] *International Monthly*, v. 1, p. 99, Jan. 1900.
[27] *New York Dramatic Mirror*, v. 39 *passim*, esp. March–April 1898.

Encouraging to advocates of a more literary drama, however, was the success of James A. Herne's *Marjorie Fleming* and *Shore Acres*, lauded by Howells in *Harper's* and by Garland and Flower in the *Arena*.[28] The *Tammany Times*, a reporter of the theater that was impressed more by box-office than literary values, pointed out in 1894 that *Shore Acres* was "filling every seat at Daly's Theater nightly," and declared, "Mr. Herne is one of America's greatest actors." [29] Bronson Howard's *Shenandoah* was a great triumph, "artistically and dramatically," said *Theatre*; [30] and most critics agreed. In *Literary Life's* contest for membership in its "Academy of Immortals," Howard was far ahead in the drama class.[31]

Among dramatists from abroad, Ibsen was most popular and most discussed. "His ideas and works are an issue," declared Hamlin Garland in the *Arena*.[32] Modjeska and Duse did much in the roles of the early controversial Ibsen plays to make the great Norwegian dramatist famous in this country, where his work "became associated in the popular mind with the sort of progressive culture which had previously found its only adequate expression in Emerson readings and Browning clubs." [33] "In Boston everyone is positively Ibsen-mad this winter," said Miss Cracklethorpe in J. L. Ford's story "The Ibsen Fad" in the *Illustrated American* in the 1890 season.[34] Other importations were Sudermann's *Magda*, Hauptmann's *The Sunken Bell*, and Maeterlinck's *Monna Vanna*; and in 1899 the *Critic* spoke of "the Rostand epidemic which has laid hold so vigorously of the American public." [35]

There were many revivals of classical plays, too — especially of Shakespearean tragedy. On May 22, 1888, at the Metropolitan Opera House, occurred an all-star presentation of *Hamlet*, in honor of Lester Wallack. Booth played Hamlet; Barrett, the Ghost; John Gilbert, Polonius; Frank Mayo, the King; Mme. Modjeska, Ophelia; Gertrude Kellogg, the Queen; Rose Coghlan, the player Queen; and Joseph Jefferson, the First Gravedigger. "There was a terrible jam," said *Theatre*.[36] The frequent visits of Henry Irving, Ellen Terry, Johnston

---

[28] *Harper's Magazine*, v. 81, pp. 152–57, June 1890; *ibid.*, v. 83, pp. 478–79, Aug. 1891; *Arena*, v. 4, p. 247, July 1891; *ibid.*, v. 4, p. 543, Oct. 1891; *ibid.*, v. 8, p. 306, Aug. 1893; Herbert Edwards, "Howells and Herne," in *American Literature*, v. 22, pp. 432–34, Jan. 1951.
[29] *Tammany Times*, v. 3, May 19, 1894, p. 11.
[30] *Theatre*, v. 4, p. 465, Dec. 1, 1888; *ibid.*, v. 5, p. 464, Sept. 21, 1889.
[31] *Literary Life*, v. 1, n.s., Jan. 1, 1900, p. 6.
[32] *Arena*, v. 2, p. 72, June 1890.
[33] *Munsey's Magazine*, v. 19, p. 273, May 1898. Cf. Wilbur L. Cross in *Arena*, v. 3, p. 81, Dec. 1890.
[34] *Illustrated American*, v. 1, p. 19, Feb. 22, 1890. Cf. *Illustrated Day's Doings* on "the Ibsen Influenza," v. 10, Jan. 18, 1890, p. 7.
[35] *Critic*, v. 34, p. 94, Jan. 1899.
[36] *Theatre*, v. 4, p. 305, June 16, 1888.

Forbes-Robertson, Eleanora Duse, and Sara Bernhardt were memorable; and they all appeared chiefly in the classics. "It is something, good reader," said the *Illustrated American*, "to live in the time of Henry Irving and Ellen Terry." [37]

Thus there was much of real worth in the theater of the nineties, in spite of the trash that was the object of running criticism. The *Dramatic Mirror* printed in 1896 a series of answers to the question, "What is the present condition of the actor's art?" Wilton Lackaye said, "Better than ever." Henry Talbot said, "At the lowest possible ebb." William Gillette said, "Good, bad, and indifferent — as it always has been and always will be." [38] But dramatic criticism would not have been normal without many voices constantly crying that the stage was bankrupt.

Immorality in the current drama was the object of attack not so much of professional critics of the theater as of the *censores morum* in general. It is interesting to note that two famous women, writing in American reviews within a year or two of each other on the threshold of the nineties, took opposite views of the situation. Mary Anderson spoke in the *North American* of "the rapidly growing respect and esteem of the world for the art and artists of the stage"; [39] but Elizabeth Stuart Phelps wrote in the *Forum* that "our stage today exhibits moral monstrosity to the edge of abomination." [40] The *Dramatic Mirror*, which fought the professional moralists all through the nineties, had to confess in 1904 that "A bigoted prejudice against the theatre and all concerned with it still survives in small communities" and occasionally bursts out in the cities. [41]

Chief of the successful plays of the nineties to come under the fire of the censors was Pinero's *The Second Mrs. Tanqueray*, [42] but the biggest flare-up of feeling against increasing "immoralities" of the stage came when Olga Nethersole presented Clyde Fitch's adaptation of Daudet's *Sapho* in February 1900. "It has been denounced from pulpits, condemned by women's clubs, branded as fatally demoralizing to young men and young women," reported *Current History*, adding: "But Miss Nethersole keeps it on the stage, and protests that she does so distinctly in the interest of moral purity; she considers herself to

---

[37] *Illustrated American*, v. 19, p. 5, Jan. 4, 1896. See also Arthur Hobson Quinn, *A History of the American Drama from the Civil War to the Present Day* (New York, rev. 1936); Glenn Hughes, *A History of the American Theatre, 1700–1950* (New York, 1951) — both *passim*.

[38] *New York Dramatic Mirror*, v. 35, April 18, 1896, p. 23.

[39] *North American Review*, v. 148, p. 16, Jan. 1889.

[40] *Forum*, v. 9, p. 672, Aug. 1890.

[41] *New York Dramatic Mirror*, v. 51, Jan. 2, 1904, p. 12.

[42] The English Clement Scott inveighs against it in *North American Review*, v. 157, p. 476, Oct. 1893.

be engaged in a 'holy work.' " [43] She sued the Reverend Dr. Easton, of Philadelphia for slander when he called her "a lewd actress" in his pulpit; however, she had to suspend her play when the police arrested her for presenting an "indecent" show, though she continued her "holy work" with *The Second Mrs. Tanqueray*. It seems that what the police objected to mainly was the scene in which the hero carried the heroine up stairs that were shown on the stage to a bedroom that was not shown on the stage. "Tammany!" exclaimed William Marion Reedy, who had come on from St. Louis for his periodic view of Broadway shows, and had confessed that *Sapho*, though good, was not a play for young girls — "Tammany! Gathering its strength, financial and otherwise, from blackmail, from the lowest dives of the metropolis, Tammany as a censor of morals! Ye gods!" [44] When the case came to trial, the court made short work of it, and everyone concerned was declared not guilty; the play immediately went back on the stage of Wallack's Theatre, and a new version opened at the Theatre Comique.[45]

BURLESQUE, VARIETY, SPECTACLES

"Burlesque" in 1885 still meant travesties on the classics and satires on accepted ideas. Wrote the busy theater reporter for the *Citizen*, of New York, in that year:

> It is sheer nonsense to say that burlesque is decaying; it will always live in some form. There are fashions in burlesque as in dresses; and burlesque, like Egypt or the New York Central, has its ups and downs. . . . The great difficulty with burlesque is the scarcity of good subjects. When you have been through the Arabian Nights and exhausted the nursery legends, your vein of ore is worked out. . . . Some of the best artists have appeared in burlesque — Joe Jefferson in *Ivanhoe* here with Mrs. John Wood, Harry Beckett with the British Blondes. . . . Miss Farren is the most popular artist in London, as Lillian Russell is here.[46]

But legs, tights, and lingerie seemed to edge out art in the latter eighties; and though the "refined burlesque" of the London Gaiety Company might be praised at the expense of the "scant dresses" of local coryphees,[47] the exploitation of the female figure steadily increased. The development doubtless represented a consolidation of the "Black Crook" type of light opera with the traditional burlesque, which had always been pretty free in its manners.[48] "Traddles," the

[43] *Current History*, v. 10, p. 119, March 1900. For the trial, see *ibid.*, p. 307, May 1900.
[44] *Reedy's Mirror*, v. 9, Nov, 16, 1899, p. 4; *ibid.*, v. 10, March 1, 1900, p. 3.
[45] *Will Rossiter's Monthly*, June 1900, no pp.
[46] *Citizen*, v. 1, p. 313, May 2, 1885.
[47] *America*, v. 2, p. 28, April 4, 1889.
[48] See Bernard Sobel, *Burleycue* (New York, 1931), *passim.*

correspondent of the Boston *Opera Glass*, was an enthusiastic reporter of this new burlesque. He tells of how managers "engage a large number of really beautiful girls who abound in concave curves," and dress them in lingerie and incandescent lights.[49] He waxes lyrical about "tights under lace and tights under tulle":

> There is a language of tights like the language of flowers. When Marie Rostelle leads the march of the Gay Hussars, she wears white, and when Lillian Washburne sings that ghastly ballad "In the Baggage Car Ahead," she does it in black tights with a heliotrope garter, and there is always a responsive tear in the gallery.[50]

A note in *Munsey's* extensive theater department declared: "This is the period and ours is the country of the Stage Beauty, who triumphs over critics and wins the golden favor of the public, even though her histrionic abilities are of the slenderest." [51] The two Lillies were types of high popularity — Lillian Russell and Lillie Langtry — both famed for beauty rather than ability. "Living Pictures" became the rage in the mid-nineties. *Town Topics* reported in 1894: "Koster & Bial's is doing a tremendous business. Every seat is being taken, and the standing room so fully occupied that one has to crane his neck to get even a peep at the living pictures." [52]

Though *Theatre* thought the minstrel show had deteriorated in the eighties, "a bang and an uproar" having supplanted the "tuneful song which breathed of sugar-cane and cotton," [53] the burnt-cork performances continued to flourish through the nineties. The Theatre Comique's distinctive "Mulligan Plays," a series with typed characters developed by Harrigan and Hart, made an immense success in New York in the eighties.[54] The number of traveling troupes multiplied in the nineties, but the increase was chiefly among those offering cheap attractions.[55] It was also the period in which the great vaudeville circuits began; and at the very end of the century came the great spectacles, beginning with *Ben-Hur.* "The most remarkable dramatic production in many respects known to theatrical history is *Ben-Hur*," declared the *Overland Magazine*. "More than 25,000 people had seen the play by the time of its hundredth performance in February

---

[49] *Opera Glass*, v. 4, p. 24, Feb. 1897.

[50] *Ibid.*, p. 44, March 1897.

[51] *Munsey's Magazine*, v. 14, p. 294, Jan. 1893.

[52] *Town Topics*, v. 3, May 14, 1894, p. 11.

[53] *Theatre*, v. 1, p. 274, May 24, 1886.

[54] There is an excellent account of these shows on the occasion of their opening at a new theater after the Comique was burned, in *Town Topics*, Jan. 10, 1885, p. 7. Also see E. J. Kohn, Jr., "Partners," part IV, *New Yorker*, April 9, 1955, pp. 41ff.

[55] *Remarques* (v. 5, June 1, 1898, p. 16) points out, on the basis of an examination of "Dates Ahead" in the *Dramatic Mirror*, that there were 88 cheap touring companies of the "ten-twent'-thirt'" kind, compared with 62 troupes with "first class attractions."

1900." [56] The great chariot race on the stage was the climax of the play. It was so realistic that it is said some people attended night after night, with the idea that at some performance Messala might edge out Ben-Hur in the contest. In 1903 Charles Frohman wrote in the *Broadway Weekly*, "The Public now demands large productions exclusively." [57] In the summer of 1900 *Quo Vadis* was being presented in two New York theaters at the same time, and both were doing a good business.[58]

Though flickering short films were commonly shown on the programs of vaudeville houses by the end of the period presently under consideration, moving pictures were looked upon as an incidental novelty. Advertisements of them were found abundantly in the *New York Clipper*, but there were no serious reviews of them.

### PERIODICALS OF THE THEATER

The *New York Dramatic Mirror* continued throughout the present period; its leadership in the field was challenged for a time by the *Dramatic Times*, which was merged in the *New York Dramatic News* in 1896.[59] For professionals, however, Frank Queen's *New York Clipper* was, in the *Journalist's* figure, "the distinctive monarch of the theatrical seas" at the end of the century.[60] It still gave some attention to sports, especially baseball, and it was remarkable for its advertising of actors seeking jobs, managers seeking actors, song-writers seeking professional singers, carnival and circus "calls," and so on. F. T. Low's *New York Amusement Gazette* (1885–1893) was also chiefly for professionals.

*Theatre* (1886–1893) was an ambitious New York weekly edited by Deshler Welch and carrying full-page portraits of actors and cartoons by Denslow. A handsome illustrated monthly with the same name began in 1900, with Arthur Hornblow as editor and prominent critics and actors as contributors — quite the most ambitious attempt

[56] *Overland*, v. 36, ser. 2, p. 39, July 1900. Cf. Acton Davies in *Impressionist*, v. 1, Jan. 1900, p. 13; *Saturday Sprite*, v. 1, April 27, 1901, p. 8.

[57] *Broadway Weekly*, v. 1, Feb. 18, 1903, p. 9. Frohman credits Joseph Brooks's "imported melodramatic spectacle, *The World*" as being the first of the series, and also says Brooks persuaded Wallace to allow Klaw and Erlanger to produce his novel on the stage. Frohman was planning a production to be called *Ulysses*.

[58] *Will Rossiter's Monthly*, May 1900, no pp.

[59] These papers, and the *Clipper*, are discussed in Mott, *op. cit.*, v. 3, pp. 198–99. Leander Richardson dropped out of the management of the *Dramatic News* in 1893, "tired of debts" (*Journalist*, Sept. 9, 1893), and was followed by A. P. Dunlop, who had been publishing *Dunlop's Stage News* (1891–93). Richardson later ran *Leander Richardson's Illustrated Dramatic Weekly* (1894–96). There was a Chicago edition of the *Dramatic News* in the early nineties.

[60] *Journalist*, Jan. 26, 1901. Cf. *Printers' Ink*, v. 31, May 9, 1900, p. 12.

in American theatrical history to present adequate representation of the stage in a periodical.[61] The *Stage* (1888–1890) was a Philadelphia weekly edited by Morton McMichael III, with young Richard Harding Davis as associate editor. This pleasantly written journal was followed by one of the same name edited by Albert Ellery Berg in New York in 1891–1894, and that by another *Stage* (1904–1906) by Roland Burke Hennessey, devoted largely to theater gossip and pictures. The *Impressionist* (1899–1900) was a short-lived New York monthly, with good contributors, devoted to the theater and literature. *Billboard* was founded by W. H. Donaldson in Cincinnati in 1894 as an "amusement weekly" specializing in billposting, circuses, fairs, carnivals, and vaudeville. It was a professional journal, and carried correspondence about "business" in various cities, timetables of routes, directories of professional people, and so on.

In Boston, the *Opera Glass* (1894–1898) was a lively little monthly at fifty cents a year, and the *Dramatic Review* (1895–1901) was an unprosperous monthly. Chicago's *Dramatic Magazine* (1897–1903) was a monthly, but issued quarterly cumulative editions. The Chicago *Dramatic Journal* (1880–1897) was a weekly that had once included the word *Sporting* in its title. The *San Francisco Dramatic Review* (1899–1906) absorbed *Music and Drama* (1882–1901), of that city. The urban weeklies of society and politics the country over almost always gave much attention to the local theaters,[62] while newspapers in the leading cities (and especially New York) employed notable, and often distinguished, critics to report critically the plays and concerts.[63]

---

[61] Two initial quarterly numbers were entitled *Our Players' Gallery*; and the name was changed to *Theatre Magazine* in 1927, when Perriton Maxwell became editor. Stewart Beach was editor in the last two years of the magazine, 1929–31. The colored gravure covers were long a feature. See *Critic*, v. 44, pp. 328–30, April 1907.

[62] See pp. 77–78.

[63] For example, in New York in 1886 the *Tribune* had William Winter for drama and H. E. Krehbiel for music; the *World*, L. U. Reavis, drama; the *Times*, E. A. Dithmar, drama, and William J. Henderson, music; the *Star*, Harrison Grey Fiske, drama; the *Evening Post*, J. Ranken Towse, drama, and H. T. Finck, music; the *Mail and Express*, Maybury Fleming, drama, and Gustav Kobbe, music (*Theatre*, v. 1, p. 197, May 3, 1886).

# CHAPTER XV

## EDUCATION

THE magazines frequently commented at length on educational problems and on various phases of the work of schools and colleges during the twenty-year period that began in 1885. Especially interested were the "quality" magazines and the reviews, to which leading educators contributed many suggestive and critical articles in this field.

In 1890 Charles W. Eliot, of Harvard, declared in the *Arena* that "no state in the American Union possesses anything which can be properly called a system of secondary education." [1] George T. Ladd, of Yale, writing in *Scribner's* about the same time, found the whole American educational system "inchoate and unformed"; he advocated a "reconstruction of secondary education," and expressed the conviction that "no form of institution which we can call the American University" had yet been developed, and, further, that there should be no effort to develop more than half a dozen universities in this country "in the next generation." [2] But the country was entering upon a period of great advances in all departments of education. High schools developed tremendously in the nineties in cities large and small, and even in the villages. Universities varying more or less in "form of institution" developed remarkably in that decade, especially in the Middle West and the West. David Starr Jordan was able to write at the close of the century:

> The Universities of America have grown enormously in wealth and power within the last twenty-five years. The next twenty-five years will tell the same story. They have the confidence of the people. . . . In the University at last the history of democracy must be written. [3]

The founding and early growth of the University of Chicago was a remarkable phenomenon. "There has been no instance . . . in the history of education," wrote H. H. Boyesen in the *Cosmopolitan*, "of such a full-grown Minerva-birth." [4]

Problem areas were certain southern states and the rural districts throughout the nation. Controversial questions included those dealing with changing curricula, the preparation of teachers, and political

---

[1] *Arena*, v. 2, p. 24, June 1890.
[2] *Scribner's Magazine*, v. 2, pp. 346–60, Sept. 1887.
[3] *Conservative Review*, v. 2, p. 261, Nov. 1899.
[4] *Cosmopolitan Magazine*, v. 14, p. 665, April 1893.

control of the schools. Mobile teaching personnel, especially in country schools, was a great threat to efficiency: John T. Prince pointed out in the *Atlantic Monthly* in 1890 that 65 per cent of the positions in certain midwestern states changed occupants annually.[5] Another subject often discussed in newspapers and magazines was that sometimes called by contemptuous epithets like "educational frills" and "pedagogic fads." Manual training had been introduced in the late seventies, and *Science* spoke of the debate over those elements of the curriculum as being prominent in 1888.[6] In the late eighties and early nineties, what Editor Flower, of the *Arena*, called "the new education" included "music, drawing, color work, modelling, folding and pasting, and physical culture"; and the *Arena* defended the teaching of such arts against critics.[7]

### UNIVERSITY EXTENSION

The *American Review of Reviews* for July 1891 contained a remarkable article by Herbert B. Adams, of Johns Hopkins University, detailing the development of adult education in the United States and England. Though the various movements in this field were described, the article was entitled "University Extension and Its Leaders," and this activity of certain universities (especially Chicago, Wisconsin, Pennsylvania, and Hopkins) was represented as one of the liveliest directed at the education of adults. "University Extension has been called the Salvation Army of education," said Adams. Eighteen months later, Adams told readers of the *Review of Reviews* of "far more important developments" along this line.[8]

An American Society for Extension of University Teaching was organized in Philadelphia, where from 1891 through 1894 Edmund J. James was president, and periodicals called *University Extension* and the *Bulletin* were published. These were superseded by the *Citizen* (1895–1898), edited by a committee which tried to give it somewhat the same kind of position in Philadelphia that the *Critic* had in New York and the *Dial* in Chicago. It had some comment on local affairs, but also much on national and foreign matters, many book reviews, articles on sociology, psychology, old authors, and so on, as well as news of the university extension movement, public libraries, and adult education in general. It was a ten-cent monthly, and liberal in politics. John Nolen, W. P. Trent, Henry A. Beers, Albert A. Bird, and C. H. Hinton were among the leading contributors. The *University Extension*

---

[5] *Atlantic Monthly*, v. 66, p. 415, Sept. 1890.
[6] *Science*, v. 11, p. 1, Jan. 6, 1888.
[7] *Arena*, v. 8, p. 512, Sept. 1893.
[8] *Review of Reviews*, v. 3, pp. 593–609, July 1891; v. 6, pp. 701–12, Jan. 1893.

*Bulletin* was begun at Chicago in May 1892, but its name was immediately changed to *University Extension Magazine*. This was superseded in 1893 by the *University Extension World*, an attractive monthly edited by Francis W. Shepherdson, which became a quarterly in 1894 and ended the next year.

Conservatives in the educational field criticized university extension as undignified, superficial, and tending to overload faculty members who already had enough to do with regularly enrolled students, but the better magazines were by nature allied with the new movement.[9]

THE C.L. & S.C.

Editor Albert Shaw declared in the *Review of Reviews* in 1891 that the Chautauqua Literary and Scientific Circle was "the greatest popular educational movement of modern times." [10] H. H. Boyesen called it "the nearest realization of democracy . . . in the United States," and "in the noblest and broadest sense the work of civilization."[11] Many more encomiums from the magazines might be quoted.[12] Elbert Hubbard in his *Philistine* had to belabor the movement, of course: "They offer culture at so much a pound, and sell tons of it."[13] But Professor Adams, of Hopkins, was certain of the actual values of Chautauqua: "No one who has ever seen the practical and local working of Chautauqua reading circles will ever doubt the beneficial influence of the C.L.S.C."[14] It spread from coast to coast, and by the end of the century some fifty thousand men and women had been graduated from the four-year course, and over a quarter of a million had been enrolled for shorter periods.[15]

The monthly *Chautauquan* was the organization's periodical, and a subscription to it was included with the membership fee. It set forth the programs, and also supplied articles relating to the courses. But in 1889 it burgeoned into a full-fledged general magazine of high quality, adding much timely material to its former offering. Theodore L. Flood conducted it with ability through the nineties.[16] Some of the local Chautauqua associations had bulletins of their own. The *Chautauqua Quarterly*, of Cleveland, continued from 1901 to 1936. The

[9] See George Herbert Palmer's "Doubts About University Extension," *Atlantic Monthly*, v. 69, pp. 367–73, March 1892, and a defense in *Christian Union*, v. 47, p. 961, May 20, 1893.
[10] *Review of Reviews*, v. 4, p. 87, Aug. 1891.
[11] *Cosmopolitan Magazine*, v. 19, pp. 147, 158, May 1895.
[12] Notably "The Most American Thing in America," by John Habberton, in the *Illustrated American*, accompanied by an editorial, v. 20, p. 3, June 27, 1896; and Edwina Spencer's "The Chautauqua Movement," in *Munsey's Magazine*, v. 31, pp. 523ff, July 1904.
[13] *Philistine*, v. 1, p. 23, June 1895.
[14] *Review of Reviews*, v. 3, p. 601, July 1891.
[15] *Chautauquan*, v. 31, p. 429, Aug. 1900.
[16] See F. L. Mott, *A History of American Magazines* (Cambridge, 1938), v. 3, pp. 544–47.

*Catholic Reading Circle Review* (1891–1906) was published in New York; later titles were *Mosher's Magazine* and *Champlain Educator*. A Jewish Chautauqua was begun at Atlantic City in 1896, and the *Menorah Monthly*[17] became its organ.

The C.L. & S.C. had imitators, of course. Prominent among them was the Bay View Reading Circle, with headquarters at Flint, Michigan, and its *Bay View Magazine*.[18] The Northampton (Massachusetts) Home-Culture Clubs published a short-lived monthly called *Symposium* (1896), edited by the well-known southern writer George W. Cable. Many magazines and reviews fell into step with the adult education movement by offering monthly outlines for reading clubs.

LYCEUM LECTURES

Hundreds of communities throughout the land set up Chautauqua "assemblies" for two weeks or more each summer, in which series of lectures were given by invited speakers, and discussions were held — all modeled on the parent "assembly" at Chautauqua Lake, New York. In the winters, the old lecture lyceums[19] continued, but with diminishing popularity. The bureaus had commercialized the lyceum courses, and concerts and other entertainments had crowded out more serious offerings, until by 1892 only about half the numbers were lectures,[20] and even these had to be enlivened by humor, recitations, or songs. By the middle nineties, what with this decline and the hard times, the leading lecture impresario, James B. Pond, declared in the *Cosmopolitan* that "There is seldom a lecture course nowadays that can get support."[21] An observer writing in the *New England Magazine* about the same time said:

> We have now not over a dozen lecture courses in those states which at one time carried on from three to four hundred courses. The lyceum, what is left of it, is no longer the New England conscience bound on a voyage to convert the world to political or social righteousness. Efforts are invariably made to book anyone who has made a sensation in either politics or criminal life.[22]

But when the era of expansion and prosperity, with its success gospel, burst upon the country in the closing years of the century, lectures again became popular, and the winter lyceum courses, under new bureau leadership, flourished once more. Writing on "The Rage for Lectures" in the *Saturday Evening Post* in 1900, William Matthews

[17] See p. 300.
[18] See p. 54.
[19] See Mott, *op. cit.*, v. 3, pp. 171–73.
[20] *Chautauquan*, v. 14, p. 694, March 1892.
[21] *Cosmopolitan Magazine*, v. 20, p. 595, April 1896.
[22] *New England Magazine*, v. 15, n.s., p. 212, Oct. 1896.

said: "Instead of diminishing, through the satiety of the hearers, the number of courses of lectures in our large towns is steadily increasing, and the throngs of listeners are swelling with each successive season." [23] And this was soon the case with the smaller towns, which furnished ticket buyers who were even more faithful throughout the years, if smaller in number.

*Talent* (1890–1907) was founded in New York as a quarterly organ for the lecture bureaus and committees by S. M. Spedon. In 1903 Paul M. Pearson took it to Philadelphia, made it a monthly, and greatly improved it. The *Lyceumite* (1902–1933) was begun as a handsome monthly in Chicago by Edwin L. Barker, absorbed *Talent* in 1907, and continued to flourish as the leading lyceum magazine for several years.[24]

### EXPOSITIONS AND FAIRS

Though the great expositions of the times were founded to a considerable extent on entertainment and on industrial promotion, it was generally understood that their chief aim was education in a broad sense. "The Fair is a great school, a university," said William Dean Howells, writing of the Columbian Exposition at Chicago in *Harper's*.[25] All the great fairs of the period, beginning with the one in Chicago in 1893, were given extensive treatment in the magazines — the Trans-Mississippi Exposition at Omaha in 1898, the World's Fair in Paris in 1900, the Pan-American Exposition at Buffalo in 1901, the Louisiana Purchase Exposition in St. Louis in 1904, and the Lewis and Clark Exposition in Portland in 1905.

But the great Chicago show eclipsed them all. The magazines began giving much space to the coming World's Fair while it was still in the planning stage. The quarrel over its site was bitter: New York, Chicago, St. Louis, and Washington "struggled fiercely" over it, according to *Current History*.[26] *Belford's Magazine* printed a symposium on the question.[27] Other magazines printed wholesale advice about the fair. P. T. Barnum wrote in the *North American Review*: "Make it bigger and better than any that have preceded it. Make it the Greatest Show on Earth — greater than my own Great Moral Show — if you can." He suggested among other things exhibiting the mummy of the daughter of Rameses II, who found Moses in the bulrushes. "Think of

[23] *Saturday Evening Post*, v. 172, p. 1206, June 23, 1900.
[24] Ralph Parlette was editor of the *Lyceumite and Talent* in the prosperous years before World War I. In May 1913 it adopted *Talent's* volume numbering, but changed title to *Lyceum Magazine*. In 1929 it became *Platform World*.
[25] *Harper's Magazine*, v. 87, p. 801, Oct. 1893.
[26] *Current History*, v. 1, p. 42, Feb. 1891.
[27] *Belford's Magazine*, v. 4, p. 1, Dec. 1889; v. 4, p. 754, April 1890.

the stupendousness of the incongruity!"[28] The year before the fair opened, many magazines were already giving large space to it. *Current Literature* had a regular department for it during 1892.

Many periodicals gave over at least one number to the fair during 1893, usually with copious illustration. The management of the exposition, alive to the value of so much free publicity, cooperated liberally with writers and publishers. The educational, artistic, and industrial value of the great show made a tremendous impression on all observers. One of the most interesting magazine features among those which attempted to sum up the exposition was the *Dial's* symposium of "literary tributes." From these we may quote H. H. Boyesen's dictum, "The Fair is the completest and most magnificent résumé of the world's work and thought that ever has been gathered in one place"; and Charles Dudley Warner's statement: "The sight of it has changed the world, has changed the aspect and the estimate of life for tens of thousands of home-keeping people. It has introduced into practical lives the element of beauty."[29]

There were criticisms, of course. Director General George R. Davis replied in the *North American Reviw* to "the recent and very general agitation" over Chicago rates and charges for visitors.[30] Some moralists were shocked by the dances in "Little Egypt" on the midway; *Town Topics* gleefully represented Anthony Comstock as viewing the *danse du ventre* and the "wine-jelly wobble" with disapproval.[31] There was also a great "to-do" over the question of opening the fair on Sundays.[32]

### EDUCATIONAL JOURNALS

The number and range of education periodicals in the period 1885–1905 was very great. There were probably at least a thousand of them, including both general and specialized journals, organs of associations, state and regional journals, bulletins and reviews of colleges and universities, student and alumni magazines, and others. Some had been founded in the mid-nineteenth century and lasted throughout the present period; others perished after only a few months of publication. Probably not a fifth of them lived to be five years old.[33] The great majority of them had very small circulations. In 1900 less than a

[28] *North American Review*, v. 150, p. 401, March 1890.
[29] *Dial*, v. 15, pp. 176–77, Oct. 1, 1893.
[30] *North American Review*, v. 156, p. 385, April 1893.
[31] *Tales from Town Topics*, v. 31, p. 141, March 1899.
[32] See Elizabeth Cady Stanton, "Sunday at the World's Fair," *North American Review*, v. 154, pp. 254–56, Feb. 1892; J. W. Chadwick, "Why the Fair Must Be Open on Sundays," *Forum*, v. 14, pp. 54–60, Dec. 1892.
[33] Sheldon Emmor Davis, *Educational Periodicals During the Nineteenth Century* (Bureau of Education Bulletin, 1919, no. 28), p. 89.

hundred circulated over a thousand copies each, and only eleven over twenty thousand.[34] Advertisements of school supplies kept many of them going, and sponsoring institutions supported others.

But the general educational journals, as distinguished from teachers' trade papers, were comparatively few. The former dealt with the broader problems in the field, with practices and theories in Europe, with the history of education, and with applications of psychology, sociology, and ethics. The latter were concerned chiefly with the methods and devices of teaching, outlines and helps, news of the field, and even verse and light literature. The two types of content were not strictly confined to the two classes, but tended to identify them.

Two Boston journals founded in the preceding period continued as important leaders throughout the nineties — *Education*, under the editorship of F. H. Kasson and F. H. Palmer during the nineties; and the *Journal of Education*, New England's most widely circulated weekly teachers' magazine, edited for nearly half a century by A. E. Winship. In nearby Worcester was published the *Pedagogical Seminary*, long edited by G. Stanley Hall as "an international record of educational institutions, literature and progress." [35] This was a distinguished journal, devoting itself largely to child psychology.

Perhaps the leading scholarly journal in the field of general education was the *Educational Review* (1891–1928), edited through its first thirty years by Nicholas Murray Butler, of Columbia University. It gave special attention to European education and to what it called "the philosophy of education." The leading educators in America were contributors, and many thinkers outside the professional field wrote for it.[36]

A distinguished series in the field of secondary education was begun by *Academy* (1886–1892), founded at Syracuse by the Associated Academic Principals of the State of New York, but moved to Boston in 1890. It was a handsome and valuable magazine, of which George A. Bacon was editor. It was followed by *School and College* (1892), published by Ginn and Company of Boston and edited by Ray Greene Juling. This was superseded in turn by the *School Review* (1893–current), which was begun in Hamilton, New York, by Jacob Gould

[34] These statistics are based on Rowell's newspaper directory, which is more conservative than Ayer's.

[35] It was published irregularly through the nineties, and was thereafter a quarterly. Following Hall's death in 1924, Clark Murchison became editor and the Clark University Press publisher, and the words *and Journal of Genetic Psychology* were added to the title. It was still published in the fifties.

[36] Published by Henry Holt & Co. in 1891–99; monthly except Aug.–Sept. Frank Pierrepont Graves was editor in 1920–23, and William McAndrew in 1924–28. It was merged in *School and Society*.

Schurman, who had just become president of Cornell University, and Charles Herbert Thurber, who was about to leave Cornell for Colgate. But in 1896 it was moved to the University of Chicago and for many years edited by the faculty of the School of Education there. John Dewey was editor-in-chief in 1902. The *School Review* was the leading journal in its field of secondary education in America, and had many distinguished contributors.

There were many other journals designed for general circulation in the educational field, but for one reason or another not in the first rank.[37]

TEACHERS' TRADE PAPERS

The largest circulation of any educational periodical of the period belonged to the *Normal Instructor* (1891–current), F. A. Owen's fifty-cent monthly "teachers' trade paper," to use its own designation. It absorbed the *Teachers' World* (1887–1903), published by Mrs. Elizabeth P. Bemis in New York.[38] It had at that time passed the hundred thousand circulation mark and was a prosperous quarto of forty-eight pages. In Boston, *Popular Educator* was founded in 1885 by Edward James Norris, Sr., and continued by his son as a dollar monthly much like the *Normal Instructor*. There Norris began also *Primary Education* in 1893 as a separate monthly, with Eva D. Kellogg as editor. Both were successful, having a combined circulation of over a hundred thousand by the end of the century.[39] A third group of teachers' periodicals was the one published in New York by E. L. Kellogg. It was the oldest of such groups, the *School Journal* and *Teachers' Institute* having survived from the seventies.[40] Kellogg's *Primary School* (1890–1905) was merged into *Teachers' Institute* in 1905, when it became *Teachers' Magazine*. Through the nineties the three Kellogg teachers' magazines held some ninety thousand combined circulation, the high-

[37] The *Journal of Pedagogy* (1887–1907) was an upper level review when it was published and edited by the Ohio University faculty at Athens; later, as it moved successively to Binghamton, N.Y., Syracuse, N.Y., and Ypsilanti, Mich., and changed from monthly to quarterly publication, it declined somewhat. Albert Leonard was one of its founders and later its editor and manager, and its peregrinations followed his changes in educational positions. The monthly *School World* (1899–1918), of London and New York, was eventually merged in the *Journal of Education*. Mary H. Simpson's *New Education* (1888–1909), of New York, was published for its first four and a half years as *Teacher*. A. P. Chapin's *Educational Gazette* (1885–1910) was issued first from Rochester and then from Syracuse. A. N. Raub's *Educational News* (1885–1900) was published successively in Harrisburg, Philadelphia, and Newark.

[38] It separated from the *Teachers' World* in 1906 but consolidated again the next year. Owen, with Mrs. Bemis as editor, published three periodicals during 1906–07 — the *Instructor*, the *World*, and *Primary Plans*. The last, founded in 1903, was absorbed in 1914. Owen also published *World's Events* (1901–08) for high-school readers (see pp. 52–53).

[39] They were consolidated as *Primary Education and Popular Educator* in 1926, title changing two years later to *Grade Teacher*. It is still current in the 1950's, with publication office at Darien, Conn.

[40] See Mott, *op. cit.*, v. 3, p. 168.

school newspaper *Our Times* [41] an additional thirty thousand, and *Educational Foundations* (1889–1936) some twenty thousand.

Three other educational journals complete the list of those whose circulations exceeded twenty thousand. H. S. Fuller's *School* (1889–1933) was a New York paper publishing eight quarto pages weekly. W. Hazleton Smith's *Educator* (1889–1905) was a modest Buffalo monthly at fifty cents a year. The *American Journal of Education* [42] published at St. Louis nine editions for eleven states, chiefly in the South and Midwest, during the nineties; in 1902 it was moved to Milwaukee by new owners and the multiple-edition policy discontinued.

### COUNTY, STATE, AND REGIONAL JOURNALS

Oldest of all educational periodicals in the present period were two state journals founded in 1852 — the *Ohio Educational Monthly* and the *Pennsylvania School Journal*. Almost as old were the *Indiana School Journal* and the *Wisconsin Journal of Education*. Many other states had their own journals before 1885,[43] and in the latter eighties and the nineties most of the states not already so provided acquired journals published by state departments of education or teachers' associations, or by private publishers who invited the coöperation of such official organizations.[44] Not a few teachers' magazines were the recipients of state subsidies, and others benefited by less direct aid. City, county, and state superintendents, for example, brought pressures to bear upon teachers to subscribe for chosen journals.[45]

There were many consolidations, some of which invited interstate or regional audiences. Of these, the more important ones have already been mentioned. Most of the educational periodicals with regional names, however, were state journals with regional ambitions.[46]

[41] See p. 53.

[42] See Mott, *op. cit.*, v. 3, p. 168.

[43] See Mott, *op. cit.*, vols. 2 and 3 for those founded within the periods thus defined.

[44] Some of the longer-lived ones may be listed here: *Connecticut School Journal* (1896–1903), Meriden; *Virginia School Journal* (1892–1905), Richmond; *Georgia Teacher* (1886–95), Atlanta; *Florida School Journal* (1894–1922), Cocoa, etc.; *Florida School Exponent* (1894–1914), Miami, etc.; *Alabama School Journal* (1889–current), Birmingham, issued until 1921 as *Educational Exchange*; *Mississippi School Journal* (1896–1911), Jackson; *Progressive Teacher and Southwestern School Journal* (1895–current), Morristown, etc., Tenn.; *Louisiana School Review* (1895–1911), New Orleans; *Texas School Magazine* (1898–1914), Dallas; *Oklahoma School Herald* (1892–1922), Norman, etc.; *Educator-Journal* (1900–24), Indianapolis; *Teachers' Journal* (1901–20), Marion, Ind.; *Midland Schools* (1885–current), Des Moines, first issued as *Iowa School Journal*; *Nebraska Teacher* (1898–1922), Lincoln; *State Normal Monthly* (1889–1901), Emporia, Kan.; *Common School* (1889–99), Grafton, N. D.; *South Dakota Educator* (1888–1925), Mitchell, S. D.; *Associate Teacher* (1899–1918), Pierre, S. D.; *Colorado School Journal* (1885–current), Denver; *New Mexico Journal of Education* (1903–20), Santa Fe; *Oregon Teachers' Monthly* (1897–1928), Salem. See also Davis, *Educational Periodicals*, ch. 3 and Bibliography B.

[45] *Ibid.*, pp. 24–36.

[46] *Southern Educational Journal* (1891–1907), Atlanta, Ga.; *Southern School Journal*

A remarkable development in the field of the teachers' paper was that of the county school journal, usually associated with a local newspaper and the office of the county superintendent of schools. It was designed for parents as well as teachers, was usually published monthly at fifty cents a year, and was filled with news of the schools, teachers' helps, quotations from educational classics, and so on. Such papers had not been unknown in former years, but they reached their greatest popularity about 1890; during the entire period now under consideration over two hundred and thirty such papers were begun.[47] Most of them lasted only a few years, or less, though there were those, like the *Christian County School News* (1887–1934), of Taylorville, Illinois, that broadened their fields, found good audiences, and persisted for many years.[48] So common did this type of paper become in the Midwest that the Educational Newspaper Union, of Chicago, provided ready-print pages for them, and the *Iowa Teacher* (1885–1910), of Charles City, furnished at one time no less than sixty-five ready-print editions for towns in Iowa and neighboring states.

There were also city teachers' papers, such as the Philadelphia *Teacher* (1896–1921), later *Current Education*; the *Chicago Teacher* (1899–1910); and the *Cook County School News* (1904–1915), Winnetka, Illinois.

### SPECIALIZED JOURNALS

The only magazine of the times devoted largely to "university interests" was John Seymour Wood's *Bachelor of Arts* (1895–1898), a chapbookish kind of periodical that carried some news of the larger universities, comment thereon by Edward S. Martin, sports articles by Walter Camp, and contributions by such writers as H. H. Boyesen, E. C. Stedman, Theodore Roosevelt, Norman Hapgood, Joel Benton, and Jesse Lynch Williams. It was an attractive periodical, but it printed little of importance on higher education.

The chief journals devoted to secondary education have already been mentioned in preceding categories. Many normal schools and teachers' colleges had their own journals, which were commonly de-

---

(1889–1927), Louisville, Lexington, Ky.; *Southern Teacher* (1887–94), Chattanooga, Tenn.; *Southern School Journal* (1890–96), followed by *Arkansas School Journal* (1896–1913), Little Rock; *Interstate School Review* (1891–1900), Danville, Ill.; *Western Teacher* (1892–1920), Milwaukee; *Western School Journal* (1885–1916), Topeka, Kan.; *Western Journal of Education* (1895–1949), San Francisco; *Northwestern Journal of Education* (1890–99), Lincoln, Neb.; *Northwest Journal of Education* (1889–1921), Seattle, Wash.

[47] Davis, *Educational Periodicals*, pp. 42–44.

[48] It later became *School News and Practical Education*; C. W. Parker was editor for about 30 years. The *Educational Independent* (1893–1902), published in the office of the local newspaper at Edinboro, Pa., reached a circulation of 30,000; but it was edited by the faculty of a state normal school.

voted mainly to elementary and secondary education.[49] Outstanding was the *Teachers' College Record* (1900–current), of Columbia University, edited through its first twenty-seven years by James E. Russell. The *Child Study Monthly* (1895–1902), Chicago; the University of Chicago's *Elementary School Journal* (1900–current); and *Pilgrim Teacher* (1885–1917), Boston, dealt with elementary education.

*Primary Education* and the *American Primary Teacher*, both of Boston, were the leaders in their field.[50] *Kindergarten Magazine* (1888–1933) was begun in Chicago by Alice B. and Cora L. Stockham to promote kindergarten methods; after it changed owners in 1892, there was less of this insistence and more on primary education in general. The *Kindergarten Review* (1891–1915) of Springfield, Massachusetts, began as a little monthly at fifty cents a year called *Kindergarten News*, but it was improved and the name changed in 1896.

The *Catholic School Journal* (1901–current) has long been a prosperous periodical; it is issued from Milwaukee. The *Improvement Era* (1897–current) is a Mormon publication at Salt Lake City.

Special branches of the curriculum often had their own journals, usually mentioned in this volume in connection with the arts and sciences concerned.[51]

### COLLEGE MAGAZINES

Most college magazines have been the result of the literary ambitions of small groups of students willing to give time and effort to their production; after these enthusiasts disappear from the college scene, others carry on for a few years, and the magazine is finally abandoned amid mourning over the state of literature on the campus. Some years later another group of enthusiasts starts another cycle, and so it goes. But a few magazines designed to publish students' literary work have long survived, perhaps because of firm traditions and consistent faculty en-

[49] Two of the longer-lived were *State Normal Monthly* (1889–1901), Emporia, Kan.; and *Normal Seminar* (1904–24), Cheney, Wash. See Davis, *Educational Periodicals*, pp. 60–61.

[50] For the former, see p. 269, above; for the latter, Mott, *op. cit.*, v. 3, p. 167.

[51] But a few may be noted here. *Correct English* (1899–1951), Chicago, was designed for the classroom, teacher's desk, and public. The *English Leaflet* (1901–current), Boston, was issued by the New England Association of Teachers of English. *School Science* (1901–current), which added *and Mathematics* to its title in 1905, has been published in or near Chicago under the sponsorship of the Central Association of Teachers of Science and Mathematics. The *Manual Training Magazine* (1899–1939) began in Chicago, but ended in Peoria as *Industrial Arts Magazine*. *School Arts Book* (1901–current) varied between Boston and Worcester, and, like many such magazines, was published only during the school year. The *American Physical Education Review* (1896–1929) was published first at Boston and then at Springfield by the American Physical Education Society; and *Physical Training* (1901–current) was published at New York by the Physical Directors' Society of the Y.M.C.A. Three journals that specialized in school management may be mentioned: *School Economy* (1887–98), Chicago; *American School Board Journal* (1891–current), Milwaukee; *County Superintendents' Monthly* (1899–1908), Fremont, Neb.

couragement.[52] Of those begun in the present period, few are worthy of note. The *Harvard Monthly* (1885–1918) numbered among its editors such men as William Vaughn Moody and Robert M. Lovett, and had many contributors who were to become famous. The *Inlander* (1891–1899) was the handsome and often excellent magazine of the students of Michigan University.

When S. S. McClure, then a student at Knox College, was president of the Western College Press Association, he compiled *A History of College Journalism* (Chicago, 1882), which listed two hundred and twelve college and university periodicals, and gave summary histories of journalism in twenty-three institutions, mostly in the Middle West.

### JUVENILE PERIODICALS

At almost any time within the period 1885–1905, a count in the directories shows some seventy-five English-language juveniles in course of publication in the United States. Of these two-thirds were religious in nature, about half of this class being intended for distribution to Sunday School teachers and scholars.

The great juvenile of the period was the *Youth's Companion*, which maintained a circulation of half a million. Its owner and chief editor for a third of a century, Daniel Sharp Ford, died in 1899, leaving an estate valued at two and a half million dollars.[53] The great monthly *St. Nicholas*[54] was still edited by Mary Mapes Dodge and published by the Century Company, but its circulation declined sharply about the turn of the century.[55] D. Lothrop & Company, of Boston, continued several of their juveniles into the nineties.[56] One of the chief adventurers in the field of the juvenile in that decade was Frank A. Munsey, whose *Golden Argosy*[57] was founded as a boys' paper, and whose *Junior Munsey* (1897–1902), begun as *Quaker*, was merged into the *Argosy*. It was in 1899 that the *American Boy*,[58] which was to be the leader in its field in the first half of the twentieth century, was founded in Detroit.

On another level was a galaxy of lesser lights, among which were some old-timers like *Golden Days*,[59] of Philadelphia, whose name had been imitated in Norman L. Munro's *Golden Hours* (1888–1911), of New

---

[52] See Mott, *op. cit.*, v. 1, pp. 488–89.
[53] See Mott, *op. cit.*, v. 2, Sketch 2. For death of Ford, see *Printer's Ink*, v. 30, Jan. 10, 1900, pp. 23–24.
[54] See Mott, *op. cit.*, v. 3, Sketch 25.
[55] *Printer's Ink*, v. 30, March 28, 1900, p. 22, estimated its circulation at 5,000, though Ayer at the same time recorded it at 65,000.
[56] See Mott, *op. cit.*, v. 3, p. 1777.
[57] See Sketch 3 in this volume.
[58] To be treated more fully in a separate sketch in the next volume of this work.
[59] See Mott, *op. cit.*, v. 3, p. 178.

York, which had begun as a paper for young ladies, but was soon appealing to youth in general; [60] and in Frank Tousey's *Golden Weekly* (1889–1891) and *Happy Days* (1894–1910), both of New York. These were all five-cent weeklies, with sixteen four-column pages in small-folio, providing much fiction and miscellany. A big picture on the front page, action stories, and low price attracted many purchasers. Street & Smith's *Good News* (1890–1897) was similar in type, but had better authors. W. B. Lawson, author of the Diamond Dick series, and Edward Stratemeyer, of the Tom Swift series, served stints as editor. Oliver Optic wrote its first serial; and Harry Castlemon, Edward S. Ellis, and Horatio Alger were early contributors. A cheaper paper, of the mail-order monthly type, was *Sunshine for Youth*, issued at Augusta, Maine, from 1886 to 1908 by E. C. Allen & Company. It sold at fifty cents a year during most of its life, and at fifteen cents a year at the end. A paper of a similar kind was the *Star Monthly* (1894–1908), of Oak Park, Illinois, which ended in bankruptcy.

Sunday School papers were distributed in blocks, each school taking as many as it had scholars in the age group served and passing them out free each Sunday. The Methodist *Classmate*, the Presbyterian *Forward*, and the Baptist *Young People* continued their excellent content in good format.[61] And there were many others, both continuants and beginners, in this period. Sunday School study serials, most of them issued quarterly for the help of teachers, counted circulations of a hundred thousand; those edited by the Rev. F. N. Peloubet and published in Boston since 1879 at five cents a number for classes on different age levels were the most popular interdenominational periodicals of this kind. The Methodists had a battery of such journals, published in New York; and the one for intermediate classes claimed well over half a million circulation. Other denominations had similar publications. Of the interdenominational *Sunday School Times* a writer in the *Review of Reviews* in 1895 said it occupied "a position of authority never approached by any similar publication." H. Clay Trumbull was its editor, and it numbered the English Gladstone and Farrar among its contributors.[62]

David C. Cook, who had been publishing for Sunday Schools since 1875 — papers for the scholars, helps for the teachers, and books for the Sunday School libraries — began his most successful paper in 1887. This was the *Young People's Weekly*, interdenominational, which attained a circulation of a quarter of a million. For younger scholars there were

[60] W. C. Dunn was editor for its first ten years. In 1904 it became a monthly family magazine of the mail-order type, at 25¢ a year.

[61] See Mott, *op. cit.*, v. 3, p. 180.

[62] *Ibid.*, p. 67, for the group; *Review of Reviews*, v. 12, p. 426, Oct. 1895, for the *Sunday School Times*.

the *Boys' World* (1902–1914) and *Girls' Companion* (1902–1949).[63]
The Society of Christian Endeavor was represented by more than a
dozen periodicals at one time in the latter nineties. The first official
organ was the *Golden Rule* (1886–current), Boston, called *Christian
Endeavor World* since 1897. The *Baptist Union* (1890–1904), Philadelphia and Chicago, represented a combination of Baptist young people's
societies. The Methodist society for youth known as the Epworth League
issued several periodicals, among them *Our Youth* (1885–1890) and
*Epworth Herald* (1890–1940); and for the Methodist Episcopal Church
South the *Epworth Era* (1894–1931). The Latter-day Saints in Salt
Lake City were active publishers; two of their juveniles begun in this
period were *Children's Friend* (1902–current) and *Character Builder*
(1900–1932).

There were a number of Catholic juveniles. The most important one
begun in the nineties was the monthly *Rosary* (1891–current), founded
by the Dominican Fathers in New York; it had excellent variety, good
illustration, and some good contributors, who did not "write down" to
their young readers. The *Catholic School Journal* (1901–current) is a
Milwaukee monthly mainly for elementary schools.

Some papers designed for supplementary reading in the schools had
some importance. A few of these have been mentioned above. In St.
Louis, the city's school board bought some fifty thousand copies of a
local semimonthly called *School and Home* (1884–1900) for several
years. Several weekly newspapers for children had wide circulation,
mainly in the schools. The *School Weekly* (1898–1908), of Oak Park,
Illinois, was absorbed into *World's Chronicle*. Grace Sorensen's *Children of the United States* (1900–1907), of Omaha, was a unique monthly
written "for and by school children." There were several nature study
magazines for children, the most important of which was the *Junior
Naturalist Monthly* (1899–1907), published under the auspices of Cornell University. Other periodicals were correlated more or less closely
with the schools.[64]

Certain institutional periodicals have some interest. *Junior Republic*
(1898–1916), called *Citizen* in its latter years, was the organ of the
George Junior Republic at Freeville, New York. *American Youth*
(1889–1898) was a mission weekly in Chicago. *Association Boys* was
sponsored by the Young Men's Christian Association. Leading humane
society publications were the same as in the preceding period.[65]

[63] In his *Who's Who* sketch, Cook claimed to issue a list "growing to 43 separate titles,
combined circulation exceeding 4,500,000."

[64] For example, *Young Idea* (1887–1914), published mainly in Boston by Charlotte and
Mary I. Allen; and the excellent *Holiday Magazine* (1903–13), New York, called *Children's
Magazine* after 1905.

[65] See Mott, *op. cit.*, v. 3, p. 312.

# CHAPTER XVI

## RELIGION AND PHILOSOPHY

PROTESTANT church membership increased in the twenty years from 1885 to 1905 approximately three-fourths, which represents considerably more than the proportional increase of total population.[1] It seems to have been generally agreed that church attendance, however, had declined greatly long before the close of the century. A writer in *Belford's Magazine* in 1889, pointing out that there was only one Protestant church for every four thousand people in New York, claimed that not one-tenth of the Protestant population were church attendants.[2] Others called attention to the great lag in church building,[3] though the *Church Economist* seemed to think that the quarter of a billion dollars which it estimated was spent annually for the support of Protestant churches in the late nineties was liberal.[4]

The first article in the first number of that lively review the *Arena* was about the religious changes of the time, by Minot J. Savage. "The fact that we are in the midst of a great theological change is unquestioned," he declared. This was on the threshhold of the nineties. The writer gave four causes of this phenomenon, which Benjamin O. Flower, editor of the magazine, termed a "revolution." These were historical and literary criticism of the Bible, the new conception of the universe that the physical sciences had given to thinking men, new knowledge brought forward by geology and anthropology about man's origins, and the contemporary "growth of the moral nature" of man.[5]

One of the signs of change was the prevalence of heresy in the churches. Doubtless the growing belief in evolution had been an entering wedge; that doctrine was now common in many religious periodicals. It was fully accepted, for example, in such widely circulated religious leaders as the *Independent* and the *Christian Union* (later the *Outlook*). Even the old *Bibliotheca Sacra* was now arguing that the Bible story of creation was only allegorical.[6] But in the late eighties and early nineties certain heresy trials attracted wide attention. Two of them became especially famous — that of the Andover professors, and that of Charles

---

[1] Daniel Dorchester, "The Evangelical Churches at the Close of the Nineteenth Century," *Christian Advocate*, v. 76, pp. 52–53, Jan. 10, 1901.

[2] *Belford's Magazine*, v. 2, p. 549, March 1889. Cf. *Arena*, v. 2, p. 604, Oct. 1890.

[3] For example, T. B. Wakeman, "Our Unchurched Millions," *Arena*, v. 2, pp. 604–13, Oct. 1890.

[4] *Church Economist*, v. 1, p. 3, April 22, 1897.

[5] *Arena*, v. 1, pp. 1–14, Dec. 1889; v. 8, p. 647, Oct. 1893.

[6] *Bibliotheca Sacra*, v. 51, p. 159, April 1894.

A. Briggs, of Union Theological Seminary. Out of the former controversy grew the *Andover Review*.[7] The latter produced hundreds of columns of newspaper copy and numberless pages of magazine comment. "For several weeks," observed the *Chautauquan* in the summer of 1891, when the Briggs case was at its height of interest, "the press of the country has been proving that religion is still the most interesting subject — by the amount of attention and by the prominence it has given theological matters."[8]

AGNOSTICISM

Robert G. Ingersoll was the spokesman and symbol of agnosticism in the nineties. He wrote for many magazines on many subjects, but for his freethinking articles the *North American Review* was his chief forum. His famous two-part apologia, "Why Am I an Agnostic?" appeared there in 1889–1890.[9] After his death a paper called the *Ingersoll Memorial Beacon* (1904–1913) was conducted in Chicago to continue the expression of his views. It eventually absorbed Singleton Waters Davis' *Humanitarian Review* (1903–1911), of Los Angeles.

Similarly, the *Free Thought Magazine* (1882–1903) was combined with the *Torch of Reason* (1896–1903) to form the *Liberal Review* (1904–1906), Chicago. Of these the *Torch* was the most distinguished. It was begun in Silverton, Oregon, but moved to Kansas City in 1902 to be edited by Thaddeus B. Wakeman, president of Liberal University. Wakeman, a prolific writer for the periodicals, was the first to suggest and adopt the Era of Man chronology as a substitute for Anno Domini, dating it from 1600 for various interesting reasons, including the martyrdom of Bruno on that date. Thus the *Torch* under Wakeman was dated E. M. 302–303.

The reform paper *Lucifer* also used E. M. dating. *Lucifer* was devoted to free sex, free thought, and individual anarchism. In 1897 it was moved from Kansas to Chicago, where it was often held up by postal authorities. Its editor, Moses Harmon, was convicted of obscene publication in 1906.

The *Blue Grass Blade* was a freethinking weekly consisting of four pages in newspaper form, conducted by Charles C. Moore, chiefly at

[7] See Sketch 1 in this volume.

[8] *Chautauquan*, v. 13, p. 524, July 1891. See also *Nation*, v. 56, pp. 412, 414–15, June 8, 1893. The Briggs case was not the only heresy trial in these years by any means. See Philip Schaff, "Other Heresy Trials and the Briggs Case," *Forum*, v. 12, pp. 621–33, Jan. 1892. "Heresy is in the air," said the *Arena*, v. 4, p. 385, Sept. 1891.

[9] *North American Review*, v. 149, pp. 741–49, Dec. 1889; v. 150, pp. 330–38, March 1890. See also F. L. Mott, *A History of American Magazines* (Cambridge, 1938), v. 2, pp. 252–53.

Lexington, Kentucky. It had two short trial runs there in 1884–1885; then it was published in 1890 in Cincinnati, but moved back to Lexington the next year. It crusaded for prohibition of the liquor traffic, for woman suffrage and free love; it was against all churches and against organized government and religion as then existing. Moore entitled the account of his visit to the Holy Land "Dog Fennel." He was arrested, fined, and whipped, without much effect on the conduct of his paper. In 1898 he was tried in a Federal court in Cincinnati for publishing obscenity, refused counsel and defended himself unskillfully, and was convicted and sent to prison. He wrote for the *Blade* while incarcerated; and after President McKinley pardoned him in five months, he continued his paper for a year or two.[10]

Rowell's *Directory* listed six to twelve "freethinking" periodicals each year through the nineties. The lists changed rapidly. The old Boston *Investigator* was edited by L. K. Washburn in the nineties.[11]

### THE ETHICAL CULTURE MOVEMENT

An article in one of the ethical culture journals pointed out that this movement was "begun in New York in 1876, when Felix Adler, the son of a Jewish rabbi of that city, founded the Society for Ethical Culture." The first branch societies were founded in Chicago (1883), Philadelphia (1885), St. Louis (1886), and London (1887).[12]

In 1890, a Russian scholar wrote of the movement abroad:

> This new interest in Ethics seems to have awakened almost simultaneously throughout the entire civilized world. . . . A marked difference, however, is already to be noted in the kind of interest which the subject calls forth. While in the older countries of Europe it is treated in a calm, objective spirit, in Russia and the United States the problems of Ethics are discussed with deep feeling and made the subject of heated controversy.[13]

In the United States, at least, this was because the ethical culture societies, with their rejection of creeds and supernaturalism, were regarded as a sharp challenge to orthodox religion. William Marion Reedy, concise and dogmatic as was his wont, declared: "They think they have found in ethics a substitute for faith, but they are mistaken. Their cult is worthless save insofar as they have a certain unacknowledged faith in something beyond themselves."[14] But the movement grew in scope and influence in the present period.

---

[10] There was much irregularity in issue. See T. D. Clark, "Editor of Blue Grass Blade," *Lexington Leader*, June 30, 1938, p. 46.

[11] See F. L. Mott, *op. cit.*, v. 3, p. 301.

[12] *Conservator*, v. 2, p. 82, Jan. 1892.

[13] W. Kawelin in *Ethical Record*, v. 3, p. 228, Jan. 1890.

[14] *Reedy's Mirror*, v. 8, Dec. 8, 1898, p. 3.

The pioneer journal of the Union of Ethical Societies was the *Ethical Record* (1888–1890), a quarterly published for the union by S. Burns Weston, lecturer of the Philadelphia society. It printed contributions by Adler, president of the union; Stanton Coit, writing from London; William M. Salter, lecturer of the Chicago society; Josiah Royce, of Harvard, and others. There was also some news of the movement. The *Record* was followed by the *International Journal of Ethics*, which was founded in Philadelphia in October 1890, on a broader base. The new *Journal* was intended to serve not only the ethical culture societies but also the social settlements and the expansion of the sociological sciences.[15] The editorial board carried out the international purpose of the review; it included Franz Jodl, of Prague, Alfred Fouillée, of Paris, G. von Gizycki, of Berlin, Coit, Royce, and others. Weston was the first managing editor and publisher.[16] Weston also published at Philadelphia *Ethical Addresses* (1894–1914), which absorbed the New York society's *Ethical Record* (1899–1904). *Cause* (1895–1899) was still another journal of the active Philadelphia society.

Another Philadelphia publication which gave much attention to the ethical culture movement in the early nineties was that remarkable monthly journal called the *Conservator*, founded by Horace Traubel in 1890 and edited and published by him (with assistance from his family and friends) until his death in 1919. Though it denied being an "organ" of the local society or the union,[17] the *Conservator* gave much news of the movement during its first three or four years. In 1894, however, Traubel asserted that the societies were becoming as dogmatic as the churches they had deserted. His own views on sex, communism, and so on, had become too radical for the societies, which rather generally repudiated the *Conservator* by this time.[18] Thereafter, though Traubel's journal kept its allegiance to the international ethical movement, it abandoned the American societies.[19] This created a crisis for the journal, but its friends rallied to its support, and it turned to another cult — the promotion of Walt Whitman and his poems and essays. The editor's own editorial notes often had pungency and wisdom, but there was too much utterance from the tripod — too great an affectation of the prophetic. Of course, Traubel's self-emphasis was consistent with his Whit-

[15] See brief historical sketch, *International Journal of Ethics*, v. 34, pp. 1–5, Oct. 1923.

[16] James H. Tufts took Weston's place in 1914, and in 1923 the journal was taken over by the University of Chicago Press and edited thereafter chiefly by professors of that institution.

[17] *Conservator*, v. 1, p. 1, March 1890.

[18] *Conservator*, v. 4, *passim*, but especially pp. 182–84, Feb. 1894.

[19] Sara Alice Pollock, "The Conservator, the Exponent of Whitman" (unpublished master's thesis, University of Chicago, 1919), pp. 6–7. See also David Karsner, *Horace Traubel* (New York, 1919).

manism; in fact, the *Conservator* was consistent throughout not only in its emphasis on individuality but in its radicalism, its internationalism, and its literary tone. Among its common topics were Whitman, sex, feminism, pacifism, imperialism, socialism, communism, labor unionism, and vivisection. Though there were many famous contributors to the review, Traubel not infrequently wrote a whole number himself. Some of his editorials and poems were later collected into volumes, entitled respectively *Collects* (1915) and *Optimos* (1910). The *Conservator* has some importance for Whitman students; but it contains, alas, a little too much Traubel for most tastes.

### CHRISTIAN SOCIALISM

The increasing interest of the churches in social problems was inspired and supported by a remarkable series of literary performances. Two of these were published in 1888 — *Looking Backward* and *Robert Elsmere*. The former, with its sequel of the Nationalist movement, has already been discussed; [20] it had a tremendous and lasting effect on middle-class men of good will, most of them church members. The latter was a novel by an Englishwoman, Mrs. Humphry Ward, which told why and how a young rector rejected contemporary theology and church forms and turned instead to social work for the underprivileged. In a symposium which the *North American Review* published about the book, Julia Ward Howe noted: "Sermons have been preached about it in various places. Religionists of varying opinions have spoken for and against it. I know of no book since *Uncle Tom's Cabin* whose appearance has excited so much comment." [21] William E. Gladstone's grandfatherly review of the novel, with its learned attitude and kindly admonition to the bold young authoress, had much to do with the precipitation of *Robert Elsmere* into a maelstrom of controversy. Gladstone said, "It certainly offers us a substitute for revealed religion," [22] but, like nine-tenths of the book's critics, he showed a remarkable disinterest in Mrs. Ward's positive philosophy. As a later writer observed:

> The unorthodox portions of *Robert Elsmere* created a vast amount of animadversion at the time, and people overlooked one of the chief teachings of the book: that Christians could work together for the uplifting of the struggling toilers, irrespective of religious creeds. [23]

But the great controversy helped get the book read, and its positive

20 See Chap. XI.
21 *North American Review*, v. 148, p. 110, Jan. 1889.
22 It appeared first in the *Nineteenth Century* for May 1888; in America it was reprinted in *Our Day*, v. 2, pp. 311–32, Oct. 1888.
23 Louise A. Nash in *Womankind*, quoted in *Hesperian*, v. 1, p. 473, April 1897.

teachings had their effect. One of the oddities of the discussion about *Elsmere* on all levels was that the venerable James McCosh, president of Princeton University, wrote an article about it for that sensational story paper, the *New York Ledger*, in which he said that its theological arguments "could be pulled down, as a castle of cards, by a Junior in theology." But no, let us refrain, he continued, for "the new religion is presented to us by a gifted lady with all sorts of fine arts and attractions, which it would be most ungallant to attack." So he did not attack, though he did make it plain that he held it against her that she was a niece of Matthew Arnold, whom McCosh had disliked ever since he came to Princeton to give a lecture late and all muddy from the road, having missed, first, the train in New York, and, second, the station hack at Princeton Junction.[24]

A third novel attacking orthodoxy to appear in 1888 was Margaret Deland's *John Ward, Preacher*. More important, Tolstoi was becoming known in America in the nineties. Hall Caine's best seller, *The Christian*, was also an attack on the churches. William T. Stead published his *If Christ Came to Chicago* in 1895, and Edward Everett Hale's *If Jesus Came to Boston* was issued the next year. Then came Charles M. Sheldon's immensely popular *In His Steps*, which brought the social gospel home to the reader by challenging him to do as he believed Jesus would do. One is inclined to agree with *Reedy's Mirror* that "As a story, it is somewhat of a bore"; [25] but it enjoyed a wonderful vogue, selling over two million copies in the United States and more than that abroad.[26]

Christian Socialism in the nineties was of two kinds — a general, Fabian type of sympathy with the poor, which involved support of the city missions, setting up institutional churches, "home missionary" work in general, and a more or less active siding with labor unionism; and, on the other hand, an aggressive attitude, which included organizational activity, certain political work for the recognized objectives of socialism, and sometimes alliance with Marxist groups. The mission movement has already been discussed, and the "home missionary" periodicals will find a place later in this chapter.[27] The general, unorganized Christian Socialist idea is well set forth in a remarkable article in the *Andover Review* by a young English professor at Wellesley. Socialism, Miss Vida M. Scudder thought, would render possible, for the first time in centuries, literal obedience to the commands of the Master;

[24] *New York Ledger*, Dec. 29, 1888. The *Ledger* began in the next issue a serial entitled "Robert Elsmere's Successor," by Dr. Joseph Parker, City Temple, London.
[25] *Reedy's Mirror*, v. 9, April 20, 1899, p. 1.
[26] See F. L. Mott, *Golden Multitudes* (New York, 1947), ch. 28.
[27] See p. 195 for city missions, p. 305 for home missionary periodicals.

it would enable men to "take no thought for the morrow," for it would remove from them the necessity of constant thought for what they shall eat, what they shall drink, wherewithal they shall be clothed.[28]

Some church leaders did not stop with such speculations, but embroiled themselves in reform fights, strikes, and political debate. Washington Gladden, minister of a Congregational church at Columbus, Ohio, and R. Heber Newton, rector of All Souls Episcopal Church, New York, were defenders of labor unions and active in church reform through the eighties and nineties.[29] Famous for his reform utterances, and especially for his war against the Tammany organization, was Charles H. Parkhurst, whom *Once a Week* properly called "a good, consistent, stick-to-it, thoroughbred social reformer."[30] There was a tremendous amount of genteel sympathy with socialism in the nineties, much of it based on primitive Christian ideology. But the other type of Christian Socialism was institutional, organizing groups to join in some of the bitterest conflicts of the decade.

One of the chief leaders of this second type was W. D. P. Bliss, who began his career as a Congregational minister, went over to the Protestant Episcopal church because he thought it offered more sympathy to his liberal ideas, and finally cut loose from the churches altogether to devote himself to radical organization. In 1889 Bliss and several other members of the Boston Nationalist Club organized the pioneer Society of Christian Socialists, immediately founding as its organ *Dawn* (1889–1896). This dynamic little periodical, which subtitled itself variously "A Magazine of Christian Socialism and Social Progress," "A Journal of Revolution Toward Practical Christianity," and so on, began as a fortnightly, became a weekly, and then was a monthly first at a dollar a year and then at fifty cents. The entire Boston group financed it at first, but in 1891 Bliss took over control in order to make it more belligerent. *Dawn* labored to show the identity of socialism and true Christianity, the need for church reform in both theology and social attitude, and the theory of labor unionization. In connection with the great strikes of the period, it was always with the unions. It deprecated violence, and advocated the ballot as the only weapon of labor:

Workingmen are learning fast that American justice and American laws exist mainly to keep workingmen down and protect property, while capitalists can disobey the laws *ad infinitum*. It is well. Workingmen must learn that they can

---

[28] "Social and Spiritual Progress, A Speculation," *Andover Review*, v. 16, p. 61, Jan. 1891. Cf. Chas. W. Shields and H. C. Potter, "The Social Problem of Church Unity," *Century Magazine*, v. 40, pp. 687–97, Sept. 1890.

[29] See Charles H. Hopkins, *The Rise of the Social Gospel in American Protestantism, 1865–1915*, v. 14 of "Yale Studies in Religious Education" (New Haven, 1940), pp. 65–78.

[30] *Once a Week*, v. 12, Jan. 13, 1894, p. 7.

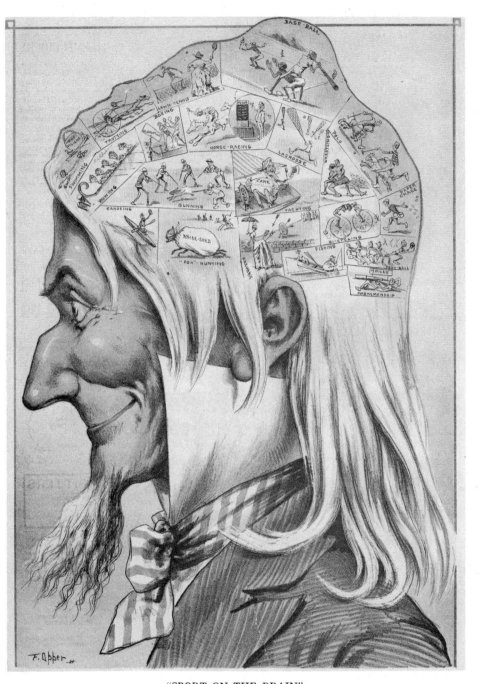

## "SPORT ON THE BRAIN"

*Puck* presented this "American Phrenological Chart" in its issue for June 1, 1887, to illustrate the craze for sports of all kinds that had struck the country. See pages 369–380.

BEACH COSTUMES — AND POOR OLD DAD

Given a pretty girl and a good artist, and even those heavy old bathing suits looked attractive. Gibson in *Life*, August 26, 1897. See pages 152–153.

gain nothing by appeal either to violence or legal proceedings. Their only way is to strike through the ballot and overcome the capitalistic ownership of the country.[31]

After the election of 1896, Bliss continued to urge political action on Fabian groups.

Even more prominent than Bliss in the organizational efforts of the Christian Socialists was George D. Herron, professor of Applied Christianity at Iowa (Grinnell) College. Shortly after he had been installed in that chair, Herron, President Thomas A. Gates, and others took over the new *Northwestern Congregationalist,* of Minneapolis, and rechristened it *The Kingdom: A Weekly Exponent of Applied Christianity* (1894–1899). Herbert W. Gleason was editor of this paper, which reflected the great variety of opinion characteristic of Christian Socialism. Herron encouraged the founding of the Christian Commonwealth Colony, a communitarian group which published in Chicago a periodical called *Social Gospel.*[32] After his support of Eugene V. Debs carried Herron into political socialism, he founded the *Social Crusader* (1898–1901), published by a religious group calling itself the Social Crusade, a more sympathetic medium.[33] Meantime, the *Kingdom* was killed by a libel suit against Gates for an attack on the textbook monopoly, in which he was successfully defended by Clarence Darrow. Herron's marital tangles, which culminated in 1901, ended his career as a prophet of Christian Socialism, and he retired to Fiesole, Italy, where his new wife had a luxurious villa.[34]

The *New Ideal Magazine* (1888–1890), which began life as *Progressive Pulpit,* was a monthly conducted by James H. West, of Boston. It had many famous contributors, and represented a liberal religious attitude, with strong social consciousness. The *Christian Socialist* (1903–1922), called in its latter years *Real Democracy,* was edited by Edward Ellis Carr and associates, of Chicago.

### NEW THOUGHT

New Thought was a cult that flourished in the 1890's and subsequently. Founded on the transcendental doctrine of the immanence of the divine in each individual, it undertook to realize the divine qualities through such means as the exercise of optimism, mental control of health, and existence on high spiritual planes. It had certain sympathies

[31] *Dawn,* v. 7, Feb. 1895, p. 2.
[32] Published at Commonwealth, Ga., until April 1900, when the community dissolved, and at South Jamesport, N.Y., from then through June 1901.
[33] This was followed by *Socialist Spirit* (1901–03).
[34] See Hopkins, *Rise of the Social Gospel,* pp. 185–200, for the Herron story.

with theosophy, Christian Science, and a somewhat primitive psychiatry.[35]

Since tight definition is contrary to the nature of New Thought, it is easy to make highly inclusive lists of periodicals more or less dedicated to the cult. Many enthusiasts (some of them clergymen) tried their hands at little magazines which sought to inculcate the highly inspirational teachings of New Thought, but most such experiments were cut short by lack of cash response. Sydney Flower began the *Hypnotic Magazine* in Chicago; it became *Suggestive Therapeutics* in 1898. Three years later it was merged with the *Journal of Magnetism*, which Flower continued (1902–1910) as *New Thought*. John Emery McLean's *Mind* (1897–1906) was published chiefly in New York, as an exponent of "science, philosophy, religion, psychology, metaphysics." One of the leading New Thought magazines was the *Nautilus* (1898–current), conducted by Elizabeth Towne, which expounded "the joy philosophy" and preached "self-help through self-knowledge."[36] *Suggestion: The New Psychology Magazine* (1898–1914) was published in Detroit by Herbert A. Parkyn; it moved to Chicago in 1906, changing title to *Stellar Ray*. Its arresting slogan was "Do you ever think?"

Hazlitt Alva Cuppy, a young man of thirty just returned from study in German universities, arrived in Chicago in the summer of the hard times year of 1893 with a hundred and sixty-four dollars in his pocket, and next month published the first issue of the *Altruistic Review*, which he called "an attempt to organize the good impulses of the world."[37] It was strong in philosophical articles, character sketches, and reviews of periodicals and books. In 1895 it was merged with *Our Day*,[38] but the partnership was dissolved the next year and a new one was formed under the title *Pulpit Herald and Altruistic Review*, to be changed to *Twentieth Century Monthly* shortly before the end in 1897.[39]

Four short-lived magazines of New Thought tendencies were merged in the *Arena* in the late nineties.[40] At least a score of such periodicals, often interesting and attractive, but usually unable to match their

[35] See Albert Whitney Griswold, "New Thought," *American Journal of Sociology*, v. 40, pp. 309–18, Nov. 1934.
[36] Mrs. Towne was Elizabeth Lois Struble when she founded the magazine in Portland, Ore. In 1899 she moved it to Sioux Falls, S.D.; next year she married William E. Towne and they moved the *Nautilus* to Holyoke, Mass., where it has since been published.
[37] *Altruistic Review*, v. 1, p. 1, July 1893; also preliminary pages of July 1894 number.
[38] See p. 52.
[39] The *Review* was for a time published in Springfield, Ohio, and edited in Chicago. Cuppy became director of the University of Chicago Press in 1896. For bibliographical problems in these combinations, see *Bulletin of Bibliography*, v. 1, p. 153, July 1899. The *Twentieth Century Monthly* was, among other things, the organ of a coöperative buying club for clergymen.
[40] See Sketch 2.

optimism with success, were being published in the year the century ended.[41]

"The faith cure and the mind cure are at the present time attracting a great deal of popular attention," observed *Science* in 1887, and added: "Mistaken prognosis accounts for many cases" of such cures.[42] Christian Science had made a spectacular beginning by 1890, with only two hundred churches scattered throughout the country. It was violently attacked in many quarters. Mark Twain, after a preliminary blast against Mary Baker Eddy, the founder, in the *Cosmopolitan* in October 1899, followed with a series of articles in the *North American Review* in 1902–1903. There were defenses, of course, but in general the magazines of the nineties inclined to agree with a dogmatic Congregational clergyman writing in the *Chautauquan* that Christian Science was "a disgrace to the intelligence of the age."[43]

Amid all the controversy in the magazines, the membership of the Christian Science church quadrupled in the nineties.[44] Its gains were made in some part through active publication.[45] Its chief review was the monthly *Christian Science Journal*, founded in 1883 by Mrs. Eddy, as the "Official Organ of the First Church of Christ, Scientist," in Boston. Beginning as a modest pamphlet, it was enlarged to twenty-four pages octavo in 1885, and again increased in size (and price) in 1888. Through the nineties it carried forty or fifty pages, filled with doctrinal articles, essays, poetry, and news of organizations and of cases of healing. There was much by and about Mrs. Eddy. The *Christian Science Sentinel* (1898–current), conducted for the first few months under the title *Christian Science Weekly*, also grew in size from its initial four pages to sixteen; it was a doctrinal and literary weekly newspaper. Many of the churches in the larger cities had their own weekly papers during this period.

Out in Kansas City, Charles Fillmore and his wife Myrtle brought out in April 1889 the first issue of a monthly called *Modern Thought*,

[41] Following are a few New Thought magazines not mentioned above: *Annular World* (1895–99), Los Angeles, etc.; *Exodus* (1896–1904), Chicago, etc.; *Free Man* (1897–1901), Bangor, Maine; *Good News* (1901–04), Columbus, Kan.; *Ideal American* (1897–1907), Yonkers, N.Y., etc.; *Independent Thinker* (1900–02), New York; *New Man* (1895–1901), Beloit, Wis., etc.; *Now* (1900–28), Santa Fe, N.M.; *Optimist* (1903–08), Philadelphia; *Radiant Centre* (1900–03), Washington, D.C.; *Universal Truth* (1888–98), Chicago; *Washington Newsletter* (1897–1921), Washington, D.C.; *Wise-Man* (1903–11), New York; *Weltmer's Magazine* (1901–38), Nevada, Mo.

[42] *Science*, v. 9, p. 504, May 27, 1887.

[43] *Chautauquan*, v. 10, p. 721, March 1890.

[44] *Christian Science Journal*, v. 12, pp. 90–93, May 1894; v. 12, pp. 451–54, Dec. 1894.

[45] See *Christian Science Monitor*, Nov. 24, 1933, part 5, for a review of this publication activity.

which seemed initially to belong to the New Thought group. But Mrs. Fillmore had experienced a faith cure, and both Fillmores were committed to that doctrine. They had come under the influence of Emma Curtis Hopkins, editor of the *Christian Metaphysician* (1887–1897), and a former member of the *Christian Science Journal* staff. After its first year the Fillmores changed the title of their magazine to *Christian Science Thought*, but upon objection from Mrs. Eddy they deleted the term which she had adopted as the name of her church, and called it *Thought* until it was merged with *Unity* in 1895. *Unity* was established by the Fillmores' Society of Silent Unity, a prayer group which centered in Kansas City but eventually attained national scope, in 1891. Its creed is that prayerful concentration will overcome sickness, financial need, and all the bars to perfect happiness. It is an attractive magazine, and is said to enjoy a very large circulation, partly distributed by friends for propaganda purposes. *Wee Wisdom*, another Fillmore periodical, was begun in 1893 as a Sunday School leaflet, but it is now much more than a juvenile.[46]

This may be the place for a note about Alexander Dowie, whose claims as a healer were the basis for an organization of bearded zealots at Zion City, near Chicago. "People began to tell him he was a prophet," said the little magazine called *Chum*, "so he wondered whether he was, then guessed yes, and pinned his faith to his guess. It was a good guess, particularly from a business standpoint."[47] *Leaves of Healing* (1894– current) and *Zion Banner* (1901–1906) were issued from Zion Ctiy.

### THEOSOPHICAL PERIODICALS

Theosophy was founded on the Vedic and Brahman scriptures of India, though Helena Petrovna Blavatsky, its founder, brought into it also certain elements of occultism from Egypt and other quarters of the world. In an article in the *North American Review* in 1890, it was claimed there were then thirty-eight "chartered branches" in the United States. This was the year before the death of the talented, adventurous, widely traveled, obese founder; six years later the president of the American society claimed, also in the *North American*, that the number of chapters in this country had tripled.[48] Readers of the nineties were an inquiring generation, though often it was only an amused curiosity that looked into such phenomena as theosophy. Thus, *Life* asked in 1893 :

---

[46] Five other magazines are published by the Unity Society. Since 1940, Lee's Summit, near Kansas City, has been the publication center. Fillmore died in 1948, and was succeeded by his son Lowell as president of Unity. See James Dillett Freeman, *The Story of Unity* (Lee's Summit, Mo., 1954).

[47] *Chum*, v. 1, p. 14, May 1904.

[48] *North American Review*, v. 151, p. 173, Aug. 1890.

What is this about theosophy? Does it really bite? Has any otherwise reliable person looked into it? Are its germs discernible under the microscope? . . . *Life* has never had it and wants to know. Is it a member of Tammany Hall? [49]

The *Path* (1886–1903) was founded in New York by William Q. Judge, one of Madame Blavatsky's associates in the establishment of the cult. Judge quarreled with the lady in a break symbolic of basic differences between East and West; he died in 1896, and the periodical was carried on by others, first as *Theosophy* and later as *Universal Brotherhood Path*, being moved to the theosophical headquarters at Point Loma, California. *New Century* (1897–1911) was also begun in New York, but moved to Point Loma after a few years; Katherine Tingley, "reorganizer" of theosophy, was its founder. It absorbed the *Path* in 1903, becoming *New Century Path*.[50] The *Metaphysical Magazine* (1895–1913), of New York, tried to keep free of cults, but printed many pieces on theosophy by C. H. A. Bjerrgaard, librarian of the Astor Library. It changed title frequently.[51] Harold W. Percival's *Word* (1904–1917), New York, and M. E. Cramer's *Harmony* (1888–1906), San Francisco, should also be mentioned.

Buddhism was represented in America by the *Buddhist Ray* (1888–1894), Santa Cruz, California; and *Light of Dharma* (1901–1907), San Francisco. Chief interpreter of Islam was the *Moslem World*, founded in New York in 1893 by Mohammed Alex Russell Webb.

### THE Y.M.C.A. AND THE SALVATION ARMY

The leading periodical of the Young Men's Christian Association was one that was published successively in three cities under five names, but longest under that of *Association Men*.[52] Local associations often had their own papers, especially in the early nineties. In 1892 Rowell's *Directory* listed an even fifty such periodicals, most of them monthlies. *Association Notes* (1886–1937), of the New York club, called *Men of New York* after 1919, was perhaps the most prominent of these.

The nineties were a great decade in Salvation Army history. That

---

[49] *Life*, v. 21, p. 394, June 22, 1893.

[50] It became *Century Path* in 1906 and ended in 1911. It was continued by the *Theosophical Path* (1911–35), which was merged into *Theosophical Forum* (1889–current), begun in New York, moved to Point Loma.

[51] Variant titles: *Intelligence*, 1897–98; *New Cycle*, 1900; *Ideal Review*, 1900; *Man*, 1911–13. The magazine's first editors were Leander Edmund Whipple, J. Elizabeth Hotchkiss, and J. Emery McLean. Elliott Coues was a contributor. It contained some excellent matter, but too much about astrology, symbolism, and so on.

[52] It began as *Watchman* in Chicago in 1874, was later moved to Cleveland and then to New York. It was called *Young Men's Era*, 1890–96; *Men*, 1896–99; *Association Men*, 1899–1930; *Young Men*, 1930–33. It was merged during 1899–1923 with *The Y.M.C.A.'s*, New York.

organization was lauded and assisted by religious leaders who were trying to instill a greater social consciousness in Protestant church members. Wrote Charles A. Briggs in the *North American Review*: "The Salvation Army is one of the most remarkable religious organizations of modern times." Its chief periodical was the *War Cry*, the New York edition of which was begun in 1882. By the end of our period it was published all over the world in thirty different languages and in various editions in this country.[53] Sold on the streets by uniformed members of the army, it disseminated the gospel of helpfulness to urban derelicts. Several other Salvation Army papers were published in the United States in the period.[54]

### THE DENOMINATIONAL PAPERS

In the latter eighties the religious press completed the change-over begun in the seventies [55] by which emphasis on news, both secular and religious, gave place to emphasis on religious reading for the family, with an important supplement of denominational news. This transformation from newspaper to class periodical was illustrated by the change in form; for example those three sterling New York religious journals, the *Evangelist, Examiner*, and *Observer*, were still adhering to the blanket-folio page size of the older newspapers (about 36 by 52 inches); in the latter eighties they all dropped to small-folio (about 18 by 24); and in the early nineties they all adopted a quarto size (about 10 by 14), which had nothing of the newspaper about it. Long before 1885 many religious periodicals, as the *Independent*, the *Christian Union*, and the *Christian Advocate* (to keep to the New York press) had adopted quarto format.

The fact is that the growth and improvement of the daily newspapers had driven the religious press from the field of secular news, except for résumés and commentary, and forced it inexorably into the category of class periodicals. Said the *New York Tribune* in 1890:

> Religious papers have found a formidable competitor in the secular press, which now treats religious questions and news with an ability and a fulness that no religious paper can hope to excel. This has compelled the religious papers . . . to develop new features of their own, in which the secular press cannot compete with them.[56]

[53] *North American Review*, v. 159 p. 697, Dec. 1894.
[54] Such as the *Conqueror* (1892–97) and *Harbor Lights* (1898–1900), both of New York. The army was active in England, and several of its London publications were circulated in America.
[55] See Mott, *op. cit.*, v. 3, p. 66.
[56] *New York Tribune*, April 27, 1890, p. 19.

That this change marked a decline in both the prosperity and the prestige of the religious press there can be no doubt. The editor of *Zion's Herald* declared in 1904 that "the decline of religious journalism in this country in recent years has been marked by the suspension and consolidation of religious papers." Pointing out specific losses suffered by some of the survivors, he sighed: "The old-time religious paper is gone."[57] Suspensions and consolidations were destined to go on much more rapidly in succeeding years, but observers were well aware of the trend in the early nineties.[58]

George Perry Morris, an editor of the *Congregationalist*, contributed a comprehensive article on "Religious Journalism and Journalists" to the *Review of Reviews* in 1895, in which he noted newspaper remarks to the effect that "the influence of the religious press is waning." To this, Morris replied that the influence of the poor papers was waning, and deserved to wane; but that the better papers were making great improvements: they had better editing, better typography, better printing, with illustration and covers — and that the prestige of such papers was being maintained.[59]

This observation points to a fact that few, if any, contemporary critics seem to have realized: namely, there were so many different kinds of religious publications that generalizations about them were almost impossible. More than a dozen classes could easily be set up, including (1) magazines of comment and literature with church backgrounds, such as the *Independent* and *Outlook*; (2) journals of liberal variety, but still denominational, such as the *Churchman* and *Christian Register*; (3) well-edited denominational spokesmen, such as the *Congregationalist* and *Christian Advocate*; (4) the hundreds of regional Protestant denominational journals, which attempted with indifferent success to combine, as the *Andover Review* put it, prophetic utterance with news and gossip;[60] (5) the many interdenominational journals, of which the *Christian Herald* was foremost; (6) organs of religious action groups, such as the Salvation Army's *War Cry*; (7) the great array of missionary society journals, including those devoted to "home missions"; (8) the quarterly and monthly theological reviews of the denominations; (9) the undenominational scholarly reviews in biblical and religious fields; (10) the great Catholic press, which divided into some of the above categories; (11) the press representing the Jewish faith, some of

[57] *Writer*, v. 17, p. 22, Feb. 1904.
[58] *Current Literature*, v. 1, p. 3, July 1888; *Review of Reviews*, v. 12, pp. 428–29, Oct. 1895.
[59] *Review of Reviews*, v. 12, pp, 416–17, Oct. 1895. Cf. *New York Tribune*, Jan. 15, 1899, p. 8, col. 4.
[60] *Andover Review*, v. 13, p. 556, May 1890.

it in German; (12) the foreign-language religious press, which also was divided into some of the foregoing categories; (13) the large and various group of peripheral journals, which have been discussed already in this chapter. When a clerical writer in the *Arena* complained that a man might as well "look in hades for an ice crop" as to look in the religious press for help on social and economic questions,[61] he was doubtless referring to the class numbered (4) above, but certainly he was disregarding (1), (2), (6), (7), (13), and perhaps others.

Further, the heterogeneous nature of the religious press makes it hard to define, and therefore hard to furnish with statistics. The lists in the directories indicate, however, that about a thousand journals dealing largely with religious matters were in course of publication at any time during the early 1890's.[62] Consolidations reduced the total somewhat in the latter part of the decade. Papers with small circulations often had good advertising patronage. Said the advertising authority, *Printers' Ink*:

Of all the class publications, those devoted to religion are regarded with the most favor by general advertisers and used more largely than any others. . . . It is said they are more thoroughly read, and each copy has a larger number of readers than most secular papers. . . . As a class, they demand a higher rate for advertising space.[63]

Subscription prices were low, ranging, for the weeklies, from a dollar to two and a half a year. Less than 10 per cent had circulations of over ten thousand.

In the following review of the denominational journals 1885–1905, the leaders surviving from earlier periods will be mentioned;[64] and data will be given about the most important of those begun in the period under treatment.

### METHODIST AND BAPTIST PERIODICALS

The Methodist Episcopal Church led in the number of its periodicals; but during the decade many of its papers were suspended or consolidated, reducing its total from about a hundred and fifty to half of that.[65] Its leading weekly was the New York *Christian Advocate*, still edited by that sterling controversialist and well-informed commentator, James

---

[61] Rev. Robert E. Bisbee in *Arena*. v. 20, p. 212, Aug. 1898.

[62] Rowell listed about that number early in the decade, but fewer in the late nineties. Ayer, which omits all periodicals not carrying advertising, and which places peripheral journals in other classes, has 700–800 throughout the decade.

[63] *Printer's Ink*, v. 6, p. 55, Jan. 13, 1892.

[64] The full indexes in the preceding volumes of this work make it unnecessary to furnish cross references to journals already discussed.

[65] Compare the Rowell figures in *Printer's Ink*, v. 6, p. 55, Jan. 13, 1892, with Rowell's *Directory* lists for the latter nineties.

Monroe Buckley. Its circulation, though only fifty thousand (and decreasing toward the end of the century), was national in scope. Of the fifteen regional *Christian Advocates*, perhaps the social-minded *Northwestern*, edited by Arthur Edwards, is the only one that requires mention — though several were prosperous.[66]

The bimonthly *Methodist Review* had become, under William Valentine Kelly's editorship, a more literary than theological journal. In St. Louis, the Reverend Naphtali Luccock, then pastor of the Union Methodist Episcopal Church and later a bishop, edited (with J. W. Lee) a short-lived but attractive monthly called the *American Illustrated Methodist Magazine* (1899–1905). The *Christian Student* (1900–1940) was a quarterly published by the Methodist Educational Fund on behalf of the colleges of the church.

The Methodist Episcopal Church South also published several periodicals. Its leading weekly continued to be the Nashville *Christian Advocate*, edited during the nineties by E. E. Hoss. The *Florida Christian Advocate* (1886–1941) was founded at Sanford by James P. De Pass, and was later moved to other towns. In 1892 the *Methodist Advocate* (1871–1930) absorbed its brash new Chattanooga rival, the *Methodist Journal*, and became the *Methodist Advocate-Journal* for the next thirty years.

Second only to the Methodists in the number of periodicals published, and perhaps even surpassing them as the new century opened, were the Baptists. This fecundity may have been due not only to an increase of communicants but also to sectarian differences that encouraged the issue of a full complement of publications for each sect. The Ayer *Directory* listed over a hundred Baptist publications in 1900. Three-fourths of the states had one or more; Mississippi had eight.

The leading Baptist weekly was the New York *Examiner*, which in 1895 absorbed the *Christian Inquirer*, itself the result of a merger of the *Baptist Weekly* (1872–1888) and the *Gospel Age* (1886–1888). Important regional journals were the Boston *Watchman* and *Morning Star*, the Chicago *Standard*, and the Portland *Pacific Baptist*, all of them long and well established. In Philadelphia the *Baptist Commonwealth* (1882–1917) was the leading paper after the *National Baptist* was merged in the New York *Examiner* in 1894. In the Southeast, the old *Christian Index*, of Atlanta, continued to have the largest circulation and the

---

[66] New ones were *Kansas Christian Advocate* (1888–96), Topeka, which merged with *Methodist Herald* (1887–1903), Minneapolis, to fill out the latter's file as *Midland Christian Advocate*; *Rocky Mountain Christian Advocate* (1887–1900), Denver; and *Omaha Christian Advocate* (1889–1900). In the nineties *Zion's Herald*, of Boston, was edited by Charles Parkhurst; it was one of more than a dozen "unofficial" Methodist papers. For data about Methodist periodicals in the nineties, see *Chautauquan*, v. 20, pp. 313–20, Dec. 1894.

greatest prestige. In the Southwest, the Dallas *Baptist Standard* (1888–current) was the chief Baptist weekly; it had begun as *Baptist News* at Honey Grove, Texas, with Lewis Holland as editor, then had moved to Dallas as *Western Baptist*, and in 1892 to Waco, where it assumed its present name. J. B. Cranfill was its editor through the stormy era of Texas Baptist history climaxed by the assassination of W. C. Brann.[67] In the Ohio Valley were the Cincinnati *Journal and Messenger*, the St. Louis *Central Baptist*, and the Louisville *Western Recorder*. The last-named was a widely circulated family journal published by the Baptist Book Concern. Most of the Baptist periodicals founded in the present period were state or local papers.[68]

After the death of the *Baptist Quarterly Review* in 1890, the denomination had no theological journal until the *Review and Expositor* began its long career in 1904 under the care of the faculty of the Southern Baptist Theological Seminary, of Louisville.

### THE CONGREGATIONAL AND PRESBYTERIAN PRESS

Congregational weeklies had a tendency to become more literary than religious, more journals of opinion than church papers. Thus those great and often brilliant periodicals, the *Independent* and the *Christian Union*, became nonsectarian by the end of the century — and indeed some unkind critics called them nonreligious.[69] That was untrue, however; even after the *Christian Union* changed title to the more secular word *Outlook* in 1893, it was rather more preoccupied with religious points of view than were such journals as the Methodistic *Harper's Weekly*. The *Independent* and *Outlook* did not forget their Congregational upbringing.

The Boston *Congregationalist*, under the editorship of Albert E. Dunning in the nineties, was also distinguished for literary content, Lucy Larcom, Gail Hamilton, Rose Terry Cooke, and Elizabeth Stuart Phelps being constant contributors. In the West, the Chicago *Advance* continued its prosperous career, publishing much family material, including

---

[67] See Sketch 9.

[68] The more important ones were *Baptist Banner* (1889–1934), Huntington, Parkersburg, W. Va.; *Baptist Advance* (1902–current), Little Rock, which became *Arkansas Baptist* in 1932; *Baptist and Reflector* (1899–current), Nashville, Tenn., a merger of the *American Baptist Reflector* (1876–88), Chattanooga, and *Tennessee Baptist* (1844–89); *Baptist Chronicle* (1886–1948), Shreveport and other Louisiana towns; *Baptist Observer* (1902–current), Indianapolis; *Baptist World* (1897–1919), Louisville, called *Baptist Argus* 1897–1908; *Florida Baptist Witness* (1884–1904), various Florida towns; *New Jersey Baptist Bulletin* (1891–current), Newark, etc.; *Word and Way* (1896–1949), Kansas City. Two long-lived Negro papers were *Christian Banner* (1888–1919), Philadelphia; and *National Baptist Union Review* (1899–current), Nashville, Tenn. See Gaines S. Dobbins, "Southern Baptist Journalism" (Southern Baptist Seminary Thesis, 1914).

[69] See Mott, *op. cit.*, v. 2, p. 373.

serials by E. P. Roe, Charles M. Sheldon ("In His Steps"), and J. S. C. Abbott. There were more than a dozen Congregational papers in course of publication in 1895.[70]

The Congregationalists were strong in reviews. *Bibliotheca Sacra* was being published at Oberlin under George Frederick Wright's editorship; the career of the distinguished *Andover Review* falls within the present period;[71] and the grand old *New Englander* ended in 1892, to give place to a more brilliant *Yale Review*.[72] The *Yale Divinity Quarterly* (1904–1914) was a student-edited bulletin, printing alumni news, a few articles by distinguished leaders of the denomination, and so on.

The two great New York Presbyterian weeklies were the *Observer* and the *Evangelist*. After the death of Samuel Irenaeus Prime in 1885, his son-in-law Charles Augustus Stoddard succeeded to the control of the *Observer*. The new editor's "Augustus" letters became as famous a weekly feature of the paper as the "Irenaeus" column had been for so many years. Through the nineties the *Observer* did not call itself Presbyterian, but "evangelical" or "undenominational." The *Evangelist* continued until 1899 under the distinguished editorship of Henry Martyn Field, whose travel letters and defense of the "New School" Presbyterianism were notable. In 1894, the management was reorganized and the format improved, with the help of Cyrus H. McCormick and Philip Armour, of Chicago.[73] In 1899 Field withdrew in favor of Louise Seymour Houghton; and three years later the paper was merged in the undenominational *Christian Work*, which was to absorb the *Observer* also ten years later.

Presbyterians McCormick and Armour were also strong supporters of the Chicago *Interior*, which was a handsome and clever paper of some thirty thousand circulation, edited by William C. Gray until his death in 1901. The Philadelphia *Presbyterian*, the Cincinnati *Herald and Presbyter*, and the Louisville *Christian Observer* were leading Presbyterian papers; and there were forty or more others published within our period.[74]

[70] Addiston P. Foster, "Journalism in the Congregational and Presbyterian Churches," *Chautauquan*, v. 20, pp. 585ff, Feb. 1895.

[71] See Sketch 1 in this volume.

[72] To be treated in a separate Sketch in the next volume of this work.

[73] *Printer's Ink*, v. 11, pp. 155–56, Aug. 1, 1894.

[74] See Foster in *Chautauquan*, v. 20, pp. 585ff, Feb. 1895. Regional papers begun within the period were *North and West* (1884–1902), Minneapolis, which began as *Northern Presbyterian* and ended as *Western Presbyterian*; and *Michigan Presbyterian* (1894–1914), Detroit, which moved about to New York and Chicago in its last few years, changing title to *Presbyterian Examiner*. A monthly bulletin called *Assembly Herald* was begun in Rochester, N.Y., in 1893, later moving to Philadelphia. In 1899 it was merged with *Church at Home and Abroad* to form what was titled variously *Assembly Herald* and *Presbyterian Herald*. This became *New Era Magazine* 1919–21, and *Presbyterian Magazine* 1921–33. At a yearly price of 25¢ in the later nineties, it had a circulation of considerably more than 100,000.

Chief United Presbyterian papers were two in Pittsburgh — *United Presbyterian*, independent, and *Christian Union Herald*, published by the church. The *Midland* (1884–1903) was the chief western organ. The Cumberland Presbyterians were served by the St. Louis *Observer* and the Nashville *Cumberland Presbyterian*.

The decline of theological reviews is illustrated by the deaths of all the old Presbyterian quarterlies early in the present period. The *Southern Presbyterian Review* perished in 1885, the *Princeton Review* in 1888, the *Presbyterian Review* in 1889, and the *Cumberland Presbyterian Quarterly* in 1892. The only theological quarterly of the church in the nineties was a sequel of the *Presbyterian Review* in New York called the *Presbyterian and Reformed Review* (1890–1902), which was soon moved to Philadelphia. It was succeeded by the *Princeton Theological Review* (1903–1929), which published contributions on theology, the history of religion, and philosophy, by church leaders.

THE EPISCOPAL, UNITARIAN, AND LUTHERAN PRESS

The *Churchman*, said the *New York Tribune* in 1890, was the only successful Episcopal paper;[75] it was under the editorship of George S. Mallory. But the *Living Church*, of Chicago, somewhat outside the *Tribune's* diocese, was also doing very well, considering what success in the religious field meant; C. W. Leffingwell was its editor and publisher through the nineties. Several local Episcopal monthlies were begun in our period.[76] The *Protestant Episcopal Review* (1886–1900) was begun as *Virginia Seminary Magazine* and was under the care of the seminary faculty throughout its life.

The Unitarians had a great literary tradition, but did comparatively little to encourage their journals during this period. The *Christian Register* continued the leading weekly of the society, with the versatile Samuel J. Barrows as editor until 1897. The monthly *Unitarian* (1886–1897) was begun in Chicago by J. T. Sunderland, but in its second year was moved to Ann Arbor, where its editor was pastor of a congregation and secretary of the Western Unitarian Conference. It had some good contributors, but was sold to George H. Ellis and friends, of Boston, and there published until its merger with the *Christian Union*. It was followed by *Unitarian Word and Work* (1898–1923), Boston. The *Pacific Unitarian* (1892–1928) was a San Francisco paper.

[75] *New York Tribune*, April 24, 1890, p. 19.
[76] For example, Bishop William Paret's *Maryland Churchman* (1885–current), Baltimore, Westminster; *St. Andrew's Cross* (1886–current), Boston, etc.; *Detroit Churchman* (1895–1934), latterly *Michigan Churchman*; *Church Militant* (1898–current), Boston. Two high-church exponents should be named: the *Catholic Champion* (1888–1901) and *Holy Cross Magazine* (1889–current).

A much more valuable work was the quarterly *New World* (1892–1900), Boston, successor of the *Unitarian Review*, which had just expired. It was edited by Professors Charles Carroll Everett and Crawford Howell Toy, of Harvard, and President Orello Cone, of Buchtel College, and published by the Houghton Mifflin Company. It declared itself "hospitable to progressive, scientific thought in religion, and . . . the science of religion."[77] Comparative religions, international relations, sociology, and literature were among the topics discussed in the articles; and the book reviews were well done. Among contributors were George Santayana, Josiah Royce, Lyman Abbott, William James, Paul Elmer More, Mrs. Humphry Ward, and L. P. Jacks.

The various Lutheran sects carried on many publications. The weekly *Lutheran* and monthly *Lutheran Observer*, both of Philadelphia, continued to be leaders; the latter eventually absorbed the Dayton *Lutheran Evangelist* (1876–1909), one of the larger weeklies. The honored but sparsely distributed *Lutheran Quarterly* continued to be published from the Gettysburg Seminary, under the direction of Dean P. M. Bikle. Published by the Lutheran Synods of Missouri and other states at St. Louis were two notable journals: the *Theological Quarterly* (1897–1920) and *Concordia Magazine* (1896–1901). The former was edited by the faculty of Concordia University; the latter was a handsome, illustrated family monthly. Several other Lutheran periodicals were begun in this period.[78]

JOURNALS OF OTHER PROTESTANT DENOMINATIONS

Oldest of religious papers in America was the *Herald of Gospel Liberty*, almost a centenarian by the end of our period. It was published at Dayton, Ohio, by the Disciples of Christ. More important was the *Christian Oracle* (1884–current), of Chicago, if we consider later developments: in 1900 it became *Christian Century*, and a year or two later declared itself "undenominational."[79] The *Christian Standard*, of Cincinnati, held one of the largest circulations enjoyed by any denominational paper. The *New Christian Quarterly* (1892–1896), of St. Louis, was considered a sequel to the *Christian Quarterly* published twenty

---

[77] *New World*, v. 1, p. 158, March 1892.

[78] Including the *Luther League Review* (1888–current), a monthly at 50¢ a year, published in New York and other cities; *Lutheran Companion* (1892–current), which began as the *Alumnus* of Augustana College, Rock Island, Ill.; *Lutheran World* (1892–1912), a monthly founded as *Lutheran* in York, Pa., by George S. Bowers; *Lutheran* (1896–1919), Lebanon, Pa., absorbed by the Philadelphia *Lutheran*; *Lutheran Church Visitor* (1904–19), Columbia, S.C., also absorbed by the Philadelphia *Lutheran*. The *Union Gospel News* (1888–1906), Cleveland, was an Evangelical weekly.

[79] To be treated in a separate sketch in the next volume of this work.

years earlier. It was edited by J. H. Garrison, who was also manager of the successful weekly, *Christian Evangelist*. Garrison fought the "higher criticism" valiantly, but lost money on his review, which had a short postscript in the *Christian Quarterly* (1897–1898), of Columbia, Missouri.

Most successful of Swedenborgian weeklies during the nineties was the *New Church Messenger*, edited and published during that decade by Charles H. Mann at Orange, New Jersey. A newcomer in the late eighties was S. H. Spencer's *New Christianity* (1888–1906), of Germantown, Pennsylvania. In Boston, the church's leading review, the monthly *New Jerusalem Magazine*, was succeeded by the quarterly *New-Church Review* (1894–1934) under the same editorship — that of Theodore Francis Wright. At Urbana, Illinois, John Whitehead founded *New Philosophy* (1898–current), a quarterly exposition of the works of Swedenborg; it was soon moved to Boston, and later, like the *New Church Life*, to Bryn Athyn, Pennsylvania, where the New Church Academy is located. *New Earth* (1889–1900) was a monthly devoted to Swedenborgianism and the single tax, and edited by Lemuel Wilmarth, the artist, and others.

The *Friend* and the *Friends' Intelligencer*, of Philadelphia, continued to represent the Society of Friends, usually called Quakers. The *Friends' Review* was succeeded in 1894 by the *American Friend*, edited by Rufus Jones; the Chicago *Christian Worker* was merged with the new journal. The *Pacific Friend* (1892–1930) was published at Whittier, California.

There were interesting new ventures by other sects. The *Quarterly Review of the United Brethren in Christ* (1890–1908), was founded by J. W. Etter at Dayton, Ohio; it was called *United Brethren Review* after 1901. The *Universalist Leader* was begun in Chicago in 1898 as a merger of the *Gospel Banner* and the *Universalist*; it was later to be moved to Boston and called the *Christian Leader*. *To-day* (1894–1896) was an all-too-brief Universalist literary monthly edited and published by Frederick A. Bisbee as successor to *Manford's Magazine*. The *American Sentinel* (1886–1904) began at Oakland, California, to represent the Seventh-Day Adventists; it later varied its title and moved to New York. The *Way of Faith* (1890–1931) was a Holiness paper at Columbia, S. C.

### MORMON PERIODICALS

The Latter-day Saints at Independence, Missouri, published the literary monthly *Autumn Leaves* (1888–1932), called *Vision* in its last few years; and *The Evening and the Morning Star* (1900–1916), the church's official periodical; along with the venerable *Saints' Herald*.

The Mutual Improvement Associations of the Mormons issued at Salt Lake City the *Improvement Era* (1897–current) for young men, and the *Young Woman's Journal* (1889–current) — both of which contained much Mormon doctrine as well as attractive literary miscellany.

### CATHOLIC PERIODICALS

The Catholics were served by many journals, numbering more than a hundred at any time in the period. These included many small diocesan weeklies, but not the considerable number of local newspapers which were labeled "Democratic and Catholic."[80] This large output was not satisfactory, however, to the leaders of a growing American church, and there was much discussion of possibilities of the expansion of the Catholic press. In 1894 the *American Ecclesiastical Review* printed an article on "The Weak Points in the Catholic Press," by Louis W. Reilly, in which he pointed out lack of recognition by the church, want of adequate financial support, and mediocrity (and worse) in editorship as the main shortcomings of the Catholic papers.[81] Of course, many editors replied, and eventually an eminent contributor to the controversy ended it. A papal encyclical of 1895 urged greater "concord of minds" among American Catholic editors and more sincere obedience to the bishops.[82] All this may have resulted in some check on the founding of new Catholic papers, but the total of periodicals published in the church's name remained about the same throughout the present period — compared with a decrease in the number of Protestant journals.[83]

The most literary of the Catholic weeklies was the Boston *Pilot*. It did not neglect the religious and political controversies on which it had been founded; but under the successive editorship of two poets — John Boyle O'Reilly until his death in 1890, and then James Jeffrey Roche — it had a strong literary flavor, with contributions from W. B. Yeats, John B. Tabb, Louise Imogen Guiney, and others. When President Roosevelt appointed Roche consul to Genoa in 1904, Katherine Eleanor Conway, who had long been assistant editor, filled out the paper's remaining four years.

The fiery James Alphonsus McMaster, editor of the *Freeman's Journal*, of New York, died in 1886. His assistant, Maurice Francis Egan,

[80] See Appollinaris W. Baumgartner, *Catholic Journalism* (New York, 1931), ch. 3; Paul J. Foik, *Pioneer Catholic Journalism* (New York, 1930), chs. 24, 26; James J. Dunn, "Journalism of the Catholic Church in the United States," *Chautauquan*, v. 20, pp. 712ff, March 1895. The last-named claims that there were 215 Catholic serials currently published in the United States, 143 in English; of these 101 were English-language weeklies.

[81] *American Ecclesiastical Review*, v. 10, pp. 117–25, Feb. 1894.

[82] Foik, *Pioneer Catholic Journalism*, pp. 52–53.

[83] Calculations based on counts in Ayer's *Directory*. Rowell seems to have missed many.

succeeded him for two years, after which the paper came into the hands of Patrick and Brendan Ford, of the *Irish World,* who made Louis A. Lambert editor. Father Lambert had been editor of the *Catholic Times* (1893–1895), just merged with the *Catholic Standard,* of Philadelphia, which now became *Catholic Standard and Times,* George Deering Wolff, editor. The New York *Catholic Review* enjoyed much prestige; after Patrick V. Hickey's death in 1889, it was edited by J. Talbot Smith. The *Review* was merged in the Milwaukee *Catholic Citizen* in 1898. Another journal founded by Hickey was the *Illustrated Catholic American,* which perished in 1896.

The *Pittsburgh Catholic* was one of the highly regarded weeklies of the church in the nineties. One of the handsomest was the Buffalo *Catholic Union and Times,* edited by Patrick Cronin.

The outstanding new Catholic weekly in our period was the *Catholic News* (1886–current), founded by the publisher of the country's leading German-language daily, Herman Ridder, and brought to a record-breaking circulation of a hundred and fifty thousand by the mid-nineties. It carried ten newspaper-size pages, and sold for a dollar a year. Other new weeklies were mostly local news and political papers.[84]

The *Catholic World* still led the church's reviews. Its founder, Father Hecker, died in 1888 and was succeeded by A. F. Hewit, who had long been editor *de facto*; Alexander P. Doyle followed him in 1897. The *American Catholic Review* was edited through most of our period by Archbishop Patrick John Ryan; unlike the *World,* it was not a "popular" review. Still less "popular" was the *American Ecclesiastical Review* (1889–1929), published first in New York and Cincinnati under the editorship of H. J. Heuser, and later under various auspices, eventually dropping the word *American* from its title. It was devoted mainly to pastoral theology. The *Homiletic Monthly* (1900–current) was also a pastoral journal.

Through the nineties *Donahoe's Magazine* continued to be conducted, nominally at least, by its venerable founder, and as a general family magazine. *Ave Maria* continued as a literary monthly at Notre Dame University, and the *Messenger of the Sacred Heart* was still published by the Jesuits at Woodstock, Maryland. The *Rosary* (1891–current) was a literary monthly published by the Dominican Fathers at Somerset, Ohio. *Benziger's Magazine* (1898–1920), New York, began as *Our Boys' and Girls' Own: An Illustrated Catholic Monthly*; but after a year and a half it became a general magazine for Catholic families

---

[84] We may list the following: *Sacred Heart Review* (1885–1918), Boston; *New Century* (1886–1919?), Washington, Milwaukee; *Southern Messenger* (1891–current), San Antonio; *New World* (1892–current), Chicago; *Sentinel of the Blessed Sacrament* (1897–current), New York.

under the new title. Francis J. Finn and Maurice Francis Egan were leading contributors, and there were many departments and much variety. *Benziger's* experienced many variations of editorial policy, format, price, and so on, and eventually deteriorated into a medium for cheap serials. *Men and Women* (1902–1914) was an attractive Catholic home journal conducted by S. A. Baldus at Cincinnati.[85] There were other monthlies and quarterlies, chiefly connected with colleges.[86]

ANTI-CATHOLICISM

What was known as "the Catholic question" was widely discussed in the secular reviews and magazines of the times. In the very first number of the *Forum*, for example, R. Heber Newton answered in the affirmative the question "Is Romanism a Baptized Paganism?" and the next issue carried a reply. The growth of the Catholic church in America alarmed many Protestants, but on the whole the magazines were increasingly tolerant. To the *North American Review*, George Parsons Lathrop in 1894 contributed an exposé of the "A.P.A.," that belligerent anti-Catholic society whose initials stood for American Protective Association. Lathrop told how the A.P.A. circulated reports of storing arms and munitions in Catholic church basements against the day when the Pope would order an uprising to take over the American government, how bogus papal encyclicals were passed along, how the rumor was put abroad that Cardinal Gibbons had set a time in the fall of 1893 to exterminate all non-Catholics, how lectures by "escaped nuns" and "converted priests" spread the hatred. W. J. H. Traynor, president of the association, made reply, rather moderately, in the next number. "The A.P.A.," he said, "continues to grow and thrive amazingly, including in its ranks scholars of the first magnitude."[87]

The leading anti-Catholic magazine was still the *Converted Catholic*, though it had a circulation of less than ten thousand. The monthly *American Protestant* was continued at Melrose, Massachusetts, until 1898, and the *Protestant Standard* (1877–1899) at Philadelphia through the nineties. Two A.P.A. journals were published in St. Louis — the

---

[85] Among contributors were Egan, John Uri Lloyd, and John P. Murphy (later editor). George Randolph Chester was managing editor under Baldus. After a suspension June 1906 to Oct. 1908, it was reorganized under Frank X. Piatt.

[86] Such as *Catholic University Bulletin* (1895–current), which, before 1914, contained many studies by scholars in theology, literature, history, and so forth, but since then has been mainly a news bulletin. See William L. Lucey, "Catholic Magazines, 1880–1890," *Records of the American Catholic Historical Society*, v. 63, pp. 65–109, 1952. The *Working Boy* (1884–1912) was a bulletin of the Boston Working Boys' Home.

[87] *North American Review*, v. 158, pp. 563ff, May 1894; v. 159, pp. 67ff, July 1894. But Traynor had a later and more virulent article in v. 161, pp. 129, Aug. 1895, on "The Menace of Romanism." To this Catholic priests made reply, and the fight continued.

*Protestant American* (1889–1898) and the *True American* (1893–1901). Among the longer-lived "anti-Roman" journals were the Brooklyn *Primitive Catholic* (1884–1901) and the Omaha *American* (1891–1906).

### JEWISH PERIODICALS

In New York the *Jewish Messenger* continued a leader under the enlightened conservatism of Abram S. Isaacs. The *American Hebrew* was still an important journal. The largest circulations among Jewish periodicals were those of the Chicago *Occident* (which ended in 1895) and the Cincinnati *American Israelite*. There were many Jewish newspapers, printed in English, German, Hebrew, and Yiddish, some of which were orthodox and strong in religious attitudes.

New weeklies published for the increasing numbers of Jewish people in the United States were scattered far and wide. The *Jewish Spectator* (1885–1926) was begun in New Orleans and later moved to Memphis. The *Jewish Exponent* (1887–1935) was published first in Philadelphia and then in Baltimore. The *Reform Advocate* (1891–1939) was edited until his death in 1923 by Rabbi Emil Gustav Hirsch, of Chicago. The *Modern View* (1901–1943) was a St. Louis weekly edited by Abe Rosenthal for its first thirty years; it presented a variety of matter for Jewish families, and was much concerned with Zionism and international affairs. A number of fairly successful Jewish weeklies were begun in and about 1895.[88] *The Maccabeean* (1901–1920) was the organ for the American Federation of Zionists.

Chief Jewish monthly was *Menorah* (1886–1907), of New York. Until the last few years of its life it was the organ of the B'nai B'rith. It was a high-class magazine of the review type, strong in history, biography, and literature, and supported by some of the leading Jewish writers of the country. Benjamin F. Peixotto was editor until his death in 1890. The *American Monthly Jewish Review* (1904–1911) was the less distinguished organ of an organization after which it was called, for its first three years, the *Israelite Alliance Review*. *Helpful Thought* (1896–1906), New York, was called *Jewish Home* in its last three years. There were several periodicals devoted to the conversion of Jews to Christianity.[89]

[88] For example, *Jewish Review* (1893–1926), Cleveland, which absorbed the *Hebrew Observer* (1889–99) and became *Jewish Review and Observer*; *Emanu-El* (1895–1946), San Francisco; *Chosen People* (1895–1924), Brooklyn; *Jewish Comment* (1895–1918); *Jewish Criterion* (1895–1939), Pittsburgh; *Jewish Ledger* (1895–1942), New Orleans.

[89] A good example is the *Jewish Era* (1892–1921), which contained much material about the Jews, but was intended more for supporters of the mission which issued it than for the Jews. *Salvation* (1899–1905) was William Cowper Conant's New York paper devoted to "evangelization of the Jews"; it absorbed the *Jewish Christian* (1895–96). The *Jewish Evangelist* (1902–17) was a Brooklyn paper.

Several famous religious journals appealing to all Protestant denominations continued in the nineties from earlier periods — such reviews as the *Independent* and *Outlook*; and such family weeklies as the New York *Witness* and *Christian Work*, the Albany *Zion's Watchman*, and the New York *Christian Herald*. The last-named was edited in the nineties by T. DeWitt Talmage; it carried on a remarkable program of benevolences. Out on the West Coast, P. H. Bodkin published his *California Independent* in Los Angeles through 1896–1920.

A remarkable crusading weekly was Frederick L. Chapman's *Ram's Horn* (1890–1910), of Chicago. It was for prohibition, church union, primitive Christianity, "equal purity, equal suffrage," and "the Sabbath for men." It was distinguished by the colored cartoons on its cover, drawn by Frank Beard, and sometimes as lively and caustic as any Nast ever drew in his attacks on Tammany. It was an attractive religious paper, and was sold on the streets and trains as well as by mail subscription; at one time it claimed a circulation of over fifty thousand.[90] A more modest evangelistic periodical in Chicago was the *Institute Tie* (1900–current), of Moody's Bible Institute, which was later to be called *Moody's Monthly*.

The *Magazine of Christian Literature* (1889–1897), of New York, at first consisted entirely of selected matter, except for some book reviews; later there were a few original articles. For the first ten months of 1893 the English *Thinker* was adopted into the file, title and all; after that it took in the English *Review of the Churches* for a year, calling the merger *Christian Literature and Review of the Churches*. There were several homiletical "pastors' assistants" for help in sermon writing.[91]

In 1893 the *Biblical World* adopted a new series and title.[92] Its editor, William Rainey Harper, had become the first president of the University of Chicago two years before; and he broadened the journal to bring in some social criticism, an advocacy of Sunday School reform,

---

[90] In its last three years the *Ram's Horn* was called *Home Herald*. R. A. Torrey, the evangelist, was a contributor and much lauded in the paper.

[91] Gustav Holzapfel, at Cleona, Pennsylvania, had the *Pulpit* (1889–1909) for sermonizing, and the *Preacher's Helper* (1894–1911) for homiletics; both were monthlies, and for the latter he claimed a circulation of 12,000. This was much larger than the *Preacher's Magazine* (1891–1902), of New York, or the *Preacher's Assistant* (1889–1906), of Reading, Pa. *Twentieth Century Pastor* (1898–1921) was a Philadelphia monthly. *Church Economist* (1897–1906), of New York, was edited by Henry R. Elliott as a trade journal for church officers. The *Expositor and Current Anecdotes* (1899–current), of Cleveland, was a kind of *Gesta Americana* until it was broadened in 1902.

[92] See Mott, *op. cit.*, v. 3, p. 84.

and much about science and religion. The *American Journal of Theology* (1897–1920) was edited by the faculty of the University of Chicago Divinity School and associates in other faculties.

## PHILOSOPHICAL JOURNALS

The *Open Court* (1887–1936) was the successor of the well-known Boston *Index*, organ of the Free Religious Association,[93] and its first editors were the junior editor of that journal, Benjamin F. Underwood, and his wife Sara A. It was brought to Chicago and generously supported by Edward Carl Hegeler, a publisher of that city. After some ten months, the Underwoods were supplanted by Paul Carus, a German scholar who had come to America to find a better welcome for his liberal ideas than the Germany of those times afforded. This proved to be a happy choice, both for Carus and for the magazine. *Open Court* soon changed from fortnightly to weekly publication, with eight pages quarto; then in 1897 it became a monthly with full illustration in the regular magazine size at a dollar a year. In its twentieth anniversary number, the magazine reiterated its devotion to "an earnest and thoroughgoing reformation of religion under the influence of science." The editorial went on to say:

> It discusses the philosophical problems of God and soul, of life and death, and life after death, the problems of the origin of man and the significance of religion, and the nature of morality, occasionally including political and social life, without, however, entering into party questions.[94]

This does not convey the full scope of *Open Court's* offering, which included literary essays, poetry, some fiction, accounts of travel, articles on the American Indians, discussions of East Indian literature and ideas, criticism of Greek drama and philosophy, and much about German philosophy. With all this breadth, it was rarely dull. It was full of ideas; it was an intelligently edited, civilized magazine. After improvements in format in the latter nineties, it increased somewhat in circulation, but it never quite reached five thousand.[95]

---

[93] For the *Index*, see Clarence L. F. Gohdes, *The Periodicals of American Transcendentalism* (Durham, 1931), ch. 11.

[94] *Open Court*, v. 21, p. 1, Jan. 1907.

[95] Prominent among earlier contributors were Moncure D. Conway (whose "Roman Journal" was serialized in 1890), Theodore Stanton, B. F. Underwood, John Burroughs, Woods Hutchinson, E. C. Hegeler, Friedrich Max Muller, and E. P. Powell. Among later contributors were Frederick Starr, Victor S. Yarros, Florian Cajori, and many foreign scholars. After Carus' death in 1919, his family continued to edit the magazine, his daughter, Elizabeth Carus, acting as editor in the 1930's. See "The Work of the *Open Court*" in *Twenty Years of the Open Court: An Index* (Chicago, 1907).

Hegeler also founded the *Monist: A Quarterly Magazine Devoted to the Philosophy of Science* (1890–1936), a less popular journal also edited by Carus, with Mrs. Mary Carus and Hegeler as associate editors.

The *Philosophical Review* (1892–1926) was founded by a group of adherents of the Kantian and Hegelian philosophy of idealism, with Ginn & Company, Boston, as publishers. It was a bimonthly edited by Jacob Gould Schurman, the new president of Cornell University, who was joined after a year and a half by James Edwin Creighton, also of Cornell.[96] The scope of this journal was increasingly broad after its first few years. Leading philosophers at home and abroad were its contributors, including John Dewey, Morris Jastrow, Wilhelm Wundt, and Paul Carus.

William T. Harris' distinguished *Journal of Speculative Philosophy*[97] was continued through 1893. Just before the end of the present period, the *Journal of Philosophy, Psychology, and Scientific Methods* (1904–current) was begun by the Science Press, New York, under the editorship of F. J. E. Woodbridge.

### PSYCHOLOGICAL JOURNALS

The *Psychological Review* (1894–current) was begun in New York as a bimonthly under the editorship of J. McKeen Cattell and J. Mark Baldwin. In 1904 the "Article Section" and the "Literary Section" were divided, the latter being issued as the *Psychological Bulletin* (1904–current), a monthly. The *Bulletin* became an important journal in its own right, prefacing the reviews by important survey essays; the first of these was one on "The Chicago School" contributed by William James.

The *American Journal of Psychology* (1887–current) was founded at Ithaca, New York, by G. Stanley Hall, with much dependence on the experimental laboratories of Cornell and Vassar. When Hall became president of Clark University, he took the *Journal* with him. Its scope has been broad, including the arts, communications, experimental methods, and reviews.[98] Hall also founded at Clark the *American Journal of Religious Psychology and Education* (1904–1915).

[96] Schurman dropped out of the editorship after 1902. Creighton remained to the end, assisted by James Seth and Ernest Albee. The *Review* was taken over by the Macmillan Company, New York, in 1898, and by Longmans, Green & Company, New York, in 1908.

[97] See Sketch 8 in Mott, *op. cit.*, v. 3.

[98] Hall resigned in 1921, to be replaced by the junior editor, Edward B. Titchener (1922–26), who was followed by Karl M. Dallenbach and others. The *Review* published a Golden Jubilee volume in 1937. It was moved to Austin, Texas, when Dallenbach joined the Texas University faculty.

### PSYCHICAL PHENOMENA AND SPIRITISM

Elizabeth Stuart Phelps wrote in the *Forum* in 1886 that "the class of phenomena which for the want of a better term we have taken to calling psychical has come to the front of thought." [99] Editor Flower, who was vice-president of the American Psychical Society, wrote in his *Arena*, "We are on the threshold of a new world," [100] and Albert Shaw pointed out in the *Review of Reviews* in 1891 that there was "an unmistakable growth of interest in the strictly scientific investigation of various kinds of psychical phenomena." [101]

The short-lived quarterly *Psychical Review* (1892–1894) was published by the American Psychical Society. The Reverend T. E. Allen, secretary of the society, was editor and had it printed at Grafton, Massachusetts, where he had a pastorate; the president of the society, Hamlin Garland, was a contributor. It printed chiefly reports of inspections of seances, accounts of experiments, and proceedings of meetings.

It is not easy to tell when the spiritistic journals were sincerely scientific, when they were impelled by an idle interest in spooks or a sentimental hopefulness about the dear departed, or when they were mainly humbug. There were many such periodicals, some of them centering on the activities of individual mediums.[102] The largest circulation (over a hundred and fifty thousand) was reached by the *New York Magazine of Mysteries* (1901–1914), which satisfied in some measure curiosities about dreams, telepathy, hypnotism, and such, as well as devoting a large part of its space to records of psychic phenomena.

### MISSIONARY MAGAZINES

The scores of foreign missionary magazines begun during this period serve to emphasize the world-wide view that America was coming to take as the century ended. These journals often described interestingly the life and society of foreign lands, although sometimes such matter was crowded out by the procedures and propaganda of fund-raising.

---

[99] *Forum*, v. 1, p. 377, June 1886.
[100] *Arena*, v. 7, p. 242, Jan. 1893.
[101] *Review of Reviews*, v. 4, p. 412, Nov. 1891.
[102] *Carrier Dove* (1884–1893), of Oakland, Cal., was issued by the medium Elizabeth Lane Watson. *Sunflower* (1890–1909) was issued by various publishers, but chiefly by W. H. Bach, Lily Dale, N.Y. *Eltka* (1901–06), of Corry, Pa., gave attention not only to psychic phenomena but also to "physical, mental and soul culture." The anti-Blavatsky *Esoteric* (1887–99) was purchased by H. E. Butler, Applegate, Cal., from Charles H. Mackay, Boston, in 1892; it was superseded by the *Occult and Biological Journal* (1900–02), which was followed by *Bible Review* (1902–23). B. F. Austin's *Reason* (1902–30) began as *Sermon* at Rochester, N.Y.; its title was changed in 1905; it was moved to Los Angeles in 1913, and there it became very much a New Thought magazine.

Many of the missionary magazines noticed in earlier volumes of this work continued throughout the present period. Some changed form or title; for example, the *Heathen Woman's Friend* (1869–1940), of the Methodist Episcopal church, became *Woman's Missionary Friend* in 1896. The *Missionary Review of the World* (1878–1939), of Princeton, which was interdenominational despite its Presbyterian leanings, was greatly enlarged in 1888, and adopted illustration in the latter nineties. The *Baptist Missionary Magazine* celebrated its seventy-fifth anniversary in 1892. The *Review of Missions*, a Southern Methodist magazine issued from Nashville, was discontinued in 1903.

Among the more important missionary journals founded in the latter eighties were the *Friends' Missionary Advocate* (1885–current), Chicago; *Woman's Work* (1886–1924), New York, Presbyterian; *Missionary Intelligence* (1887–1918), Cincinnati, Christian; *Pilgrim Missionary* (1888–1909), Boston, Congregational; *World-Wide Missions* (1888–1912), New York and Chicago, Methodist.[103]

The home missionary journals were integrated with the awakening social consciousness in the churches. For example, the Methodist Board of Church Extension published in Philadelphia a bimonthly at fifty cents a year called *Christianity in Earnest* (1889–1906), which was a discussion and a record of social efforts. In New York the monthly organ of similar activity was called first *Aggressive Methodism* (1889–1896) and then *Christian City* (1897–1916). *Our Home Field* (1888–1916) was the home missionary journal of the Southern Baptist Convention. The Methodist Episcopal church had its *Christian Educator* (1889–1931) as the organ of its Freedmen's and Southern Education Society.[104]

[103] For other foreign missionary journals, see page 238, footnote 59.
[104] See also pages 195–96, footnote 17.

# CHAPTER XVII

## GENERAL SCIENCE AND MEDICINE

THE American Association for the Advancement of Science celebrated its semicentennial in 1898. The occasion was widely called America's Jubilee of Science, and brought forth many of those articles characteristic of *fin de siècle* writing — articles that began as factual résumés and ended with rhapsodies of pride and hope. For example, the famous anthropologist W J McGee wrote for the *Atlantic Monthly* an article entitled "Fifty Years of American Science," which ended with the enthusiasm so common in the closing years of the century:

> In truth, America has become a nation of science. There is no industry, from agriculture to architecture, that is not shaped by scientific research and its results; there is not one of our fifteen millions of families that does not enjoy the benefits of scientific advancement; there is no law in our statutes, no motive in our conduct, that has not been made juster by the straightforward and unselfish habit of thought fostered by scientific methods. . . . The trebling of population in a half-century, raising the republic from an experiment in state-making to a leading place among the nations, is the wonder of history; the thrice-trebled wealth and educational facilities gained through application of the new knowledge are a marvel before which most men stand dazzled at home, and wholly blinded abroad; the three times thrice-trebled knowledge itself, lifting the nation high in enlightenment and making way for still more rapid progress, is a modern miracle wrought by scientific work. . . .[1]

All the boasts of achievement that were uttered everywhere in America at the turn of the century placed scientific activity high on the honor roll. The people in general, and certainly the magazines that served them, were very science-conscious in these years.

### SCIENTIFIC JOURNALS

James Dwight Dana and his son Edward S. were editors of the *American Journal of Science* after the death of Benjamin Silliman, Jr., in 1885.[2] The *Scientific American*, famous popular weekly of general

---

[1] *Atlantic Monthly*, v. 82, p. 320, Sept. 1898.

[2] See F. L. Mott, *A History of American Magazines* (Cambridge, 1930) v. 1, pp. 302–05. Another Yale periodical was the *Yale Scientific Monthly* (1894–1918), published by senior students of Yale's Sheffield School, and called during its last five years the *Yale Sheffield Monthly*. Other student-alumni magazines were the *Journal of the Worcester Polytechnic Institute* (1897–current) and the *California Journal of Technology* (1903–14).

science and mechanics, issued a fiftieth-anniversary number on August 7, 1896. J. McKeen Cattell came into control of *Popular Science Monthly* in 1900.[3]

Cattell was already conductor of the great weekly *Science* when he took over the monthly. *Science* had a predecessor that had been founded on July 3, 1880, by Thomas A. Edison and edited by John Michels. It was rather heavy, being composed mainly of papers read before scientific associations. Edison kept it going about a year, and then paid up the editor's salary and made him a present of the paper. A few months later Alexander Graham Bell bought it for five thousand dollars but let it lapse with the number for December 31, 1881. All Bell had wanted was the title and good will, for he had plans for a new weekly on different lines.

The new journal began on February 9, 1883 in Cambridge, the home of its editor, Samuel Hubbard Scudder, distinguished entomologist and assistant librarian of Harvard. The twenty-five thousand dollars of capital used to start the magazine was furnished by Bell and his father-in-law Gardner Greene Hubbard, later the founder of the *National Geographic Magazine*. Heading the publishing company was Daniel Coit Gilman, president of Johns Hopkins. The scope of the journal was broad, even the new sciences of sociology, psychology, and public health being included, and America's leading scientists were contributors. In 1885 N. D. C. Hodges, librarian and physicist, succeeded Scudder as editor, and the journal was moved to New York; but Bell and Hubbard had to continue with donations, eventually putting some eighty thousand dollars into the venture. In 1893 the American Association for the Advancement of Science made it a gift of seven thousand dollars, and Bell made it another gift, but in March of the next year it suspended publication. At this crisis Cattell, head of the department of psychology at Columbia University, came to the journal's aid, with his ability in organization, his youthful drive, and his dominant personality. The new series began January 4, 1895. An editorial committee included most of the leaders in the various fields of science in the nineties. News of associations, domestic and foreign, with reports, papers, addresses, and symposiums originating at these meetings, furnished the chief materials for *Science,* with book reviews, digests of other scientific journals, correspondence, and news notes from universities and research institutions. In 1900 *Science* became the official organ of the A.A.A.S., and each member received the forty-page

[3] For *Scientific American*, see Mott, *op. cit.*, v. 2, Sketch 8; for *Popular Science Monthly*, see *ibid.*, v. 3, Sketch 24.

weekly for only two dollars a year. It was now an established and successful journal.[4]

A short-lived quarterly of high quality called the *New Science Review* published seven numbers beginning in July 1894. Its editor was Joseph Marshall Stoddart, who had been managing editor of *Lippincott's*. Angelo Heilprin conducted a department. James Dewar, famous for one of the popular science sensations of the times, liquid air, used the quarterly for his quarrels; and there were other famous contributors, such as William Crookes, Charles Barnard, and John Andrew.

Many local associations of scientists, usually connected with colleges, began journals, which commonly lasted only a few years, serving as repositories for papers read at meetings. Of these the *Technology Quarterly* (1887–1908), of the Massachusetts Institute of Technology, and the *Ohio Journal of Science* (1900–current), representing the state university and the Ohio Academy of Science, were the most distinguished and longest-lived.

It is not necessary to recapitulate here those leading journals in the different sciences which were founded in preceding periods and are therefore treated in earlier volumes of this work.[5] Only those founded in the years 1885–1905 will be mentioned specifically in the following paragraphs.

The *American Anthropologist* (1888–current) began as the quarterly organ of the Anthropological Society of Washington, D.C.; later it was adopted by the American Anthropological Association and other societies in ethnology and anthropology. Leaders in those fields were contributors, such as W J McGee, A. L. Kroeber, Ales Hrdlicka, Frederick Webb Hodge, and Franz Boas. It tried monthly publication from 1896 to 1898.

The *Astrophysical Journal* (1895–current) was begun at the University of Chicago as a bimonthly devoted to the review of spectroscopy and astronomical physics, with international scope. Chief founders were George E. Hale and James E. Keeler. *Popular Astronomy* (1893–current) is published monthly through the school year by the

[4] In the war years issues were reduced in size; in the twenties the journal prospered again, receiving $3.00 from each A.A.A.S. subscriber, and reaching about 17,000 circulation at Cattell's death in 1944. At that time the journal was made over to the A.A.A.S., which paid the widow, Josephine Owen Cattell, who had shared since the nineties the editorial and business conduct of the publication, a life annuity equal to half its annual net profits averaged over the five years preceding Cattell's death. Executive editors under direction of a board appointed by the association have since been in charge. Circulation rose to over 30,000 by 1950. There was a tendency to use more articles and digests in the fields of medicine and biochemistry in later years, chiefly because of the preponderance of physicians and chemists in the membership of A.A.A.S. See Cattell, "The Journal *Science*," v. 64, n. s., pp. 342–47, Oct. 8, 1926; Edwin G. Conklin and others, "James McKeen Cattell: In Memoriam," v. 99, n. s., pp. 151–65, Feb. 25, 1944.
[5] Chiefly in Mott, *op. cit.*, v. 3, pp. 109–13.

Goodsell Observatory, Carleton College, Northfield, Minnesota. *Word and Works* (1888–1922), published by Irl R. Hicks, St. Louis, was a curious, unreliable mixture of astronomy, meteorolgy, and religion.[6] *Terrestrial Magnetism* (1896–1930) was an important quarterly published by the Johns Hopkins Press.

The *American Geologist* (1888–1905), of Minneapolis, was conducted by a staff of seven editors connected with various educational institutions, chiefly in the Midwest. Newton Horace Winchell became managing editor. The *Journal of Geology* (1893–current) was a University of Chicago publication, at first semiquarterly and then bimonthly. Thomas Chrowder Chamberlin was editor for its first thirty-five years.

The *Physical Review* (1893–current) was founded by Edward L. Nichols and associates, of Cornell University. Begun as a bimonthly, it later became a monthly and then a semimonthly.[7] The *Journal of Physical Chemistry* (1896–current) was also begun at Cornell; it was a monthly without summer issues, long edited mainly by Wilder D. Bancroft.[8] The *Journal of Analytical and Applied Chemistry* (1887–1893) was a monthly conducted by Edward Hart, of Lafayette College, Easton, Pennsylvania; it was merged in the *Journal of the American Chemical Society*, of which Hart then became editor. The *Review of American Chemical Research* (1895–1906) was a quarterly journal of abstracts conducted by a Massachusetts Institute of Technology staff.[9]

The *Aquarium* (1890–1897) was a modest periodical dealing with goldfish, house plants, and so on. The *Biological Bulletin* (1898–current) is published by the Marine Biological Laboratory at Woods Hole, Massachusetts. The *American Museum Journal* began in 1900 as the organ of New York's American Museum of Natural History; in 1919 it adopted its present name, *Natural History*. The *Asa Gray Bulletin* (1893–1900) was merged into the *Plant World* (1897–1919), of which Charles Louis Pollard was founder. Willard N. Clute, who began

---

[6] Hicks abandoned the ministry to conduct this household monthly, for which he claimed a large circulation. "We have been compelled, some months ago, to retire from regular pastoral work in answer to the call of God in this work," he wrote in his magazine (v. 3, Jan. 1889, p. 2); and he added: "We will prove to any of our friends who will call at our office that our congregation is now numbered by the millions instead of hundreds." He printed scientific and literary miscellany, along with long-range weather predictions based chiefly on observation of "sun spots." Hicks engaged in many controversies with newspapers that called him a faker.

[7] In 1903 it became the organ of the American Physical Society, and later of the American Physical Institute.

[8] Latterly published under the auspices of the American Chemical Society, the Chemical Society, the Faraday Society, and others. Now published under the direction of Johns Hopkins faculty as *Journal of Physical and Colloidal Chemistry*.

[9] See list of chemistry journals in E. J. Crane and A. M. Patterson, *Guide to the Literature of Chemistry* (New York, 1927).

business at Binghamton, New York, and later moved to Joliet, Illinois, and other places, was publisher of the *Plant World*, the *Fern Bulletin* (1893–1912), and the *American Botanist* (1901–current). The *Bryologist* (1898–current) has been devoted to North American mosses, lichens, and so on. The *Journal of Mycology* (1885–1908) was published first at Manhattan, Kansas, and then at Columbus, Ohio. The *Rhodora* (1899–current) has been the journal of the New England Botanical Club; and the *Erythea* (1893–current), Berkeley, has specialized in Western American flora.[10]

The *Journal of Experimental Zoology* (1904–current) began at Yale University, to be taken over by the Wistar Institute, Philadelphia, in 1908. There were a number of periodicals in the field of ornithology.[11]

The *American Mathematical Monthly* (1894–current) was founded at Kidder Institute, in the village of Kidder, Missouri, by Benjamin F. Finkel and the next year moved to Drury College, at Springfield in that state. Finkel published the monthly himself for some twenty years, engraving the woodcuts with which it was illustrated with a penknife. In 1916 it was enlarged, made the organ of the Mathematical Association of America, and thereafter moved about with the organization's secretariat.[12]

### MEDICAL PROGRESS

Certain of the improvements in medicine and surgery during our period became, as one writer in the *Forum* declared, "a part of the common knowledge of the people." [13]

The discoveries and reforms of Joseph Lister, who became Lord Lister in 1897, had a profound effect on surgery the world over; and the asepsis in which he was the great leader made possible the safe

[10] For a description of current botanical periodicals, with names of editors, see *Scientific American Supplement*, v. 50, p. 20567, Aug. 4, 1900.

[11] Notably *Birds* (1897–1907), of Chicago, later called *Birds and Nature*; *Bird-Lore* (1899–current), of New York, the name of which was changed to *Audubon Magazine* in 1940; and *Wilson Bulletin* (1889–current), organ of the Wilson Ornithological Club. Note also *By the Wayside* (1897–1914), issued by the Wisconsin and Illinois Audubon Societies; *Condor: A Magazine of Western Ornithology* (1899–current), organ of the Cooper Ornithological Club of California; and the *Warbler* (1903–13), published by the Long Island Natural History Club.

[12] See B. F. Finkel, "The Human Aspect in the Early History of the *American Mathematical Monthly*," in the *Monthly* for June 1931, v. 38, pp. 305–20. The *Bulletin of the New York Mathematical Society* was begun in 1891, becoming three years later the *Bulletin of the American Mathematical Society*. The *Journal of the New-York Microscopical Society* (1885–1903) was a monthly for its first two years, and then a quarterly. *Publications of the American Statistical Association* was the title of a Boston quarterly during 1888–1917; moved to Columbia University, its name was changed in 1922 to *Journal of the American Statistical Association*.

[13] George F. Shrady, "Recent Triumphs in Medicine and Surgery," *Forum*, v. 23, p. 28, March 1897.

practice of certain operations, such as appendectomy, which had been fraught with dangers before. Thus, in the latter nineties, to quote Dr. George F. Shrady, editor of the *Medical Record,* the abdomen "is virtually a thoroughfare, any portion of which may be invaded with impunity," although before the comparatively recent developments in asepsis and anesthesia abdominal operations had been rarely attempted.

A second discovery much publicized in the magazines was that of X-rays. "The scientific world has been stirred and quickened as rarely before by this remarkable discovery," said a writer in the *Arena*.[14] The story was indeed exciting, even in those years before the development of roentgenology had shown the extent of its value in diagnosis.

A third development was the war against tuberculosis. "Consumption is at present the greatest scourge of humanity," declared the *National Popular Review* in 1892;[15] but the *Journal of Tuberculosis* declared several years later that "the indications are plain that a crusade against tuberculosis is being inaugurated"[16] — at the same time that it was beginning its own labors in that direction. The work of the German Robert Koch on the bacilli of diseases, and particularly that of tuberculosis, aroused great interest. In 1890–1891 the papers and magazines were full of the tuberculin treatment, which it was believed spelled the doom of the dread disease. "Undoubtedly," wrote a commentator in the *Chautauquan* for January 1891, "the name most on human lips throughout the civilized world today is that of Dr. Robert Koch, the deviser of the new treatment for consumption."[17] But by May of that year, *Current History* was saying that it was "premature to express an opinion on the merits of the remedy."[18]

Great as was the world-wide disappointment over this "cure," Koch's work in combating other infectious diseases by his discoveries in bacteriology made him one of the great heroes of his age. The threats of epidemics (particularly cholera and yellow fever) were notable in the latter eighties and early nineties. "Cholera" was ever a dreadful word, for the disease was always abroad somewhere in the world; but in 1887, and again in 1892, great alarm was caused when it became known that cholera-infected ships were being detained under quarantine in New York Harbor. In the latter year the *North American Review*

[14] Prof. James T. Bixby in *Arena,* v. 15, p. 871, May 1896.
[15] *National Popular Review: A Journal of Preventive Medicine,* v. 1, p. 8, July 1892. Cf. *North American Review,* v. 168, p. 212, Feb. 1899.
[16] *Journal of Tuberculosis,* v. 1, p. 201, Oct. 1899. This periodical was published at an Asheville, N.C., sanatarium during 1899–1903. Similar was *Outdoor Life* (1904–35), of Saranac Lake, N.Y., which moved to New York in 1910 to become an antitobacco journal.
[17] *Chautauquan,* v. 12, p. 520, Jan. 1891. Cf. Dr. Julian Weiss in *Cosmopolitan Magazine,* v. 11, p. 90, May 1891.
[18] *Current History,* v. 1, p. 112, May 1891.

carried a symposium on the control of the plague.[19] But the always unterrified editor of the New York *Citizen* wrote:

I am not a bit afraid of the cholera. It may kill me if it comes, but I am not going to allow the fear of it to kill me when the reality is not here at all. I do not see that there is much to be afraid of in the "cholera scare." It will, as the old people used to say, be time enough to bid the devil good morning when he knocks at the door.[20]

### MEDICAL JOURNALS

"There is a strange fondness among us for starting medical journals," wrote the editor of *American Medicine* in its first number; and he added that such journals were soon attacked by "periodically recurrent nausea. . . . In some cases this symptom lasts during the rest of life, with complete literary anorexia and anemia."[21] Fishbein, in his history of the American Medical Association, refers to the middle nineties as "the days of competitive journalism in American medicine," in which, he says, "the battle raged continuously."[22]

Estimates on the basis of lists in the directories indicate that in the neighborhood of a thousand journals in medicine and related fields, such as pharmacy and dentistry, were published for shorter or longer periods during the years 1885 to 1905. In the former year there were about a hundred and fifty such periodicals, and in the latter about two hundred and twenty-five. The American Medical Publishers' Association was founded in the early nineties. It was chiefly concerned with the business side of medical journalism, and it issued its own *Bulletin* from 1895 to 1898. There was also an *American Medical Journalist* from 1897 to 1907.

Dr. J. C. Culbertson, a former editor of the *Journal of the American Medical Association*, criticized the advertising practices of the medical journals in general in his 1893 presidential address before the association. He called for the complete elimination of the "reading notice" (in which advertising masqueraded as editorial comment), and he protested against the journals published by manufacturers of medicines as "literary quacks."[23] About the same time the *British Medical Journal* (which Culbertson, incidentally, had called "the king of medical journals") declared that the profession in America suffered

[19] *North American Review*, v. 155, pp. 483ff, Oct. 1892. *Harper's Weekly* carried a story on the outbreak of yellow fever in Jacksonville (v. 32, p. 687, Sept. 15, 1888).
[20] *Citizen*, v. 1, p. 246, April 4, 1885.
[21] *American Medicine*, v. 1, p. 2, April 6, 1901.
[22] Morris Fishbein, *A History of the American Medical Association* (Philadelphia, 1947), pp. 161, 177.
[23] *J.A.M.A.*, v. 20, p. 672, June 17, 1893.

from "the lack of independent medical journals." [24] As a matter of fact, the majority of the medical periodicals depended for existence upon the advertising of patent medicines. [25]

### LEADING MEDICAL JOURNALS

The *American Journal of the Medical Sciences* [26] continued to be rated as "the best of the monthly medical periodicals." It was under the editorship during the nineties of Edward P. Davis. Sharing honors in age and prestige with this monthly was the weekly *Boston Medical and Surgical Journal*. The *Medical News* was moved from Philadelphia to New York in 1897, and in 1905 was absorbed by the *New York Medical Journal*, edited through the nineties by the able Frank P. Foster. Another good New York weekly was the *Medical Record*, well edited by George F. Shrady. The *Journal of the American Medical Association* became the leader among the weeklies soon after 1900. [27] Other medical periodicals begun in earlier years will not be recapitulated here, [28] and only the most important founded in the present period will be named. [29]

There were many regional, state, and city medical journals. [30] Most

[24] *British Medical Journal*, Dec. 2, 1893, quoted in *J.A.M.A.*, v. 21, p. 1013, Dec. 20, 1893.

[25] See P. Maxwell Foshay (editor *Cleveland Journal of Medicine*), "Medical Ethics and Medical Journals," in *J.A.M.A.*, v. 34, pp. 1041–42, April 28, 1900.

[26] Fielding H. Garrison, *An Introduction to the History of Medicine* (4th edition, Philadelphia, 1929), p. 787. For a short history of this journal, see Mott, *op. cit.*, v. 1, Sketch 49.

[27] See Sketch 16 in this volume.

[28] For these, the inquirer is referred to the earlier volumes of this work, which are fully indexed.

[29] Those named in the text are the journals which Garrison, in *An Introduction to the History of Medicine*, designates as the "best," with a few additions. Others that are of comparatively long life and are found in many libraries are named in footnotes.

[30] Other more or less local journals, most of which were associated with medical societies, and full or partial files of which exist in more than 25 libraries, are listed here: *Journal of Medicine and Science* (1894–1905), Portland, Maine; *Vermont Medical Monthly* (1895–1914), Burlington; *Providence Medical Journal* (1900–16); *Brooklyn Medical Journal* (1888–1906); *Bulletin of the American Academy of Medicine* (1891–1919), New York, a bimonthly called in its latter years *Journal of Sociologic Medicine*; *Pittsburgh Medical Review* (1886–97), succeeded by *Pennsylvania Medical Journal* (1897–current), Harrisburg; *Journal of the New Jersey Medical Society* (1904–current); *Washington Medical Annals* (1902–20); *Old Dominion Journal of Medicine and Surgery* (1902–16), Richmond; *Atlanta Journal-Record of Medicine* (1899–1918); *Alabama Medical Journal* (1888–1911), Birmingham; *Journal of the Arkansas Medical Society* (1890–current), Little Rock; *Southwest Journal of Medicine and Surgery* (1893–1922), Oklahoma City; [F. E.] *Daniel's Texas Medical Journal* (1885–1931), Austin, which underwent many title changes; [Joseph M.] *Mathews' Quarterly Journal* (1894–1938), called *Louisville Monthly Journal of Medicine and Surgery* in 1899–1916 and by other titles at other times, and finally moved to New York as *Medical Life*; *Kentucky Medical Journal* (1903–current), Louisville, etc.; *Medical Fortnightly* (1892–1919), St. Louis; *Journal of the Missouri State Medical Association* (1904–current), St. Louis; *Cincinnati Medical Journal* (1885–96); *Cleveland Medical Gazette* (1885–1901); *Cleveland Medical Journal* (1902–18); *Indianapolis Medical Journal* (1898–1934); *Medicine* (1895–1906), Detroit; *Detroit Medical Journal* (1901–20); *Modern Medicine* (1891–1931), suspended 1909–22 and then resumed as *Bulletin* of the

important of the regional monthlies were *Southern Medicine and Surgery* (1892–current), which began as the *Charlotte* (North Carolina) *Medical Journal*; and *Northwest Medicine* (1903–current), which has come to serve the medical associations of Washington, Oregon, Idaho, and Montana. *California Medicine* (1902–current) has its home at San Francisco. The *New York State Journal of Medicine* has served the state association since 1901. The *Journal of the Boston Society of Medical Sciences* (1896–1924) was called *Journal of Medical Research* beginning in 1901. The *Chicago Medical Recorder* (1891–1927) was the organ of the medical society of that city.

*American Medicine* (1901–1936) was a good monthly "founded, owned, and controlled by the medical profession," thirty thousand dollars having been raised from the sale of stock in it to doctors. Begun in Philadelphia, it was moved to New York in 1908. *Progressive Medicine* (1899–1931) was, on the other hand, begun in New York and moved to Philadelphia. *International Clinics* (1891–current), each quarterly number a volume, was another Philadelphia serial.[31]

Philadelphia was also the home of several important specialized medical journals, some founded there and some moved there to come under the care of the Wistar Institute of Anatomy and Biology. Thus the *Journal of Morphology* (1887–current) was begun in Boston, with Ginn & Company as publishers, the *American Journal of Anatomy* (1901–current) was founded in Baltimore as the organ of the Association of American Anatomists, and the *Journal of Comparative Neurology* was founded at Denison University by Clarence L. Herrick — all of them to be taken over by the Wistar Institute, an endowed adjunct of the University of Pennsylvania, in 1908. The *Annals of Surgery* (1885–current) was begun in St. Louis by Lewis S. Pilcher, who moved

---

Battle Creek Sanitarium and Hospital Clinic; *Journal of the Michigan State Medical Society* (1902–1907), Lansing; *Chicago Clinical Review* (1892–1907); *Illinois Medical Journal* (1899–current), Springfield; *Iowa Medical Journal* (1895–1914); *Journal of the Kansas Medical Society* (1901–current), Topeka; *Western Medical Review* (1896–1930), organ of the Nebraska State Medical Society, Lincoln, Omaha; *Wisconsin Medical Journal* (1903–current), Milwaukee, Madison; *St. Paul Medical Journal* (1899–1917); *Colorado Medicine* (1903–current), Denver, title changed to *Rocky Mountain Medical Journal* in 1937; *Southern California Practitioner* (1886–1923), Los Angeles; *Occidental Medical Times* (1887–1904), Sacramento, San Francisco; *Medical Sentinel* (1893–current), Portland, Ore., title changed in 1931 to *Western Journal of Surgery, Obstetrics and Gynecology*.

[31] Other general medical journals which lasted for more than a decade, and full or partial files of which exist in more than 25 libraries, are listed here: *American Practitioner* (1886–1915), New York; *Clinical Medicine and Surgery* (1894–current), Chicago; *International Journal of Medicine and Surgery* (1888–1935), New York; *Medical Council* (1896–1926), Philadelphia, which became *American Physician* in 1921; *Medical Review of Reviews* (1895–1937), New York; *Merck's Archives* (1899–1914), by the New York pharmaceutical house of that name; *Monthly Cyclopedia of Practical Medicine* (1887–1914), Philadelphia, whose title varied; *Sanitary Era* (1886–1904), New York, which changed title to *Modern Medical Science* in 1896; *Therapeutic Notes* (1894–current), by Parke, Davis & Company, Detroit.

it to Philadelphia in 1893; the J. B. Lippincott Company has long been its publisher.

In 1897 the *Annals of Ophthalmology and Otology* (1892–1917), of St. Louis, divided its fields when the *Annals of Otology and Laryngology* was separated from the parent journal; the next year *Rhinology* was added to the title of the new quarterly, of which Hanau W. Loeb was long editor.[32] The *American Journal of Surgery* (1890–current) was founded in Kansas City by Emory Lamphear; it was later moved to St. Louis, and then to New York.

The *Journal of Experimental Medicine* (1896–current) has long been published under distinguished editorship for the Rockefeller Institute for Medical Research. The *American Journal of Physiology* (1898–1949) began at Boston but was later moved to Baltimore; it was the organ of the American Physiological Society. The *Journal of Infectious Diseases* (1904–current), founded by the John McCormick Institute for Infectious Diseases, is published by the University of Chicago Press.[33]

The *Woman's Medical Journal* (1893–current) was begun by E. M. Roys-Gavit in Toledo, Ohio.[34] The *Trained Nurse and Hospital Review* (1888–current), of New York, finally became *Nursing World*. The organ of the American Nurses' Association and of all the state nurses' organizations is the *American Journal of Nursing* (1900–current), which was published in several different cities but finally, like so many others, gravitated to New York.

HOMEOPATHY, OSTEOPATHY, AND ECLECTIC MEDICINE

A number of homeopathic journals begun in earlier periods extended into or throughout the nineties, such as the veteran *North American Journal of Homeopathy*, of Chicago.[35] The more important of those that began during 1885–1905 were the *Homoeopathic Recorder* (1886–current), Philadelphia and other cities; the *Medical Century* (1893–1915), Chicago and other cities; the *Journal of Ophthalmology, Otolo-*

---

[32] Both journals kept their numbering from 1892. The latter is still published.

[33] Other specializing journals were *American Gynecological and Obstetrical Journal* (1891–1901), New York; *Annals of Gynaecology and Pediatry* (1888–1910), Boston; *Archives of Gynaecology, Obstetrics and Paediatrics* (1886–94), New York; *Pediatrics* (1896–1917), New York and London; *American Journal of Urology and Sexology* (1904–20), New York; *Dietetic and Hygienic Gazette* (1886–1914), New York; *Ophthalmic Record* (1891–1917), Nashville, Chicago; *Ophthalmology* (1904–17), Seattle, Chicago, Milwaukee; *Optical Journal and Review of Optometry* (1895–current), New York; *Laryngoscope* (1896–current), St. Louis; *Psychiatric Bulletin of New York State Hospitals* (1896–current); *Journal of Psycho-Asthenics* (1896–1918), Faribault, Minn.

[34] It moved to Cincinnati in 1909, and changed its title to *Medical Women's Journal* in 1920.

[35] See Mott, *op. cit.*, v. 2, p. 85; v. 3, pp. 142–43. Same for eclectic journals.

*gy, and Laryngology* (1889–1929), New York; and the *Homoeopathic Eye, Ear and Throat Journal* (1895–1910), New York.

Eclectic medicine was also represented by some survivors from earlier periods. The current *National Eclectic Medical Association Quarterly* was begun in 1899 in Cincinnati and later moved to Columbus. Also in Cincinnati was published the *Eclectic Medical Gleaner* (1889–1912).

The *Journal of Osteopathy* (1894–current) is issued from Kirksville, Missouri, home of the leading school of that art; and the *Journal of the American Osteopathic Association* (1901–current) is published at Chicago.

PUBLIC AND PRIVATE HEALTH

State and local boards of health were responsible for a number of magazines. The *Public Health Journal* (1886–1903), of New York, began as *Doctor,* and became the organ of the National Board of Health. The *American Journal of Public Hygiene* (1891–1910), of Boston, began as the organ of the Massachusetts Association of Boards of Health, and eventually represented the American Public Health Association. *Sanitary Inspector* (1887–1901) was published at Augusta, Maine.

Health in the home, physical culture, and exercise for both health and sport became almost a cult in the nineties, increasing every year. Near the end of the century, the magazine *Physical Culture* noted the phenomenal growth of interest in such things, so that by that time "the subject is given almost daily attention by all the prominent newspapers, and the magazines are everywhere taking it up." [36] Many of the "home and health" periodicals were cheap papers that battened on patent medicine advertising, and others represented sanatariums; some had a considerable importance. The old *Water-Cure Journal* [37] had its face lifted and its name changed to *Journal of Hygiene and Herald of Health* in 1893; from 1899 to its end in 1910 it was called *Health. Health Culture* (1894–current), of New York, was subtitled "A Journal of Practical Medicine."

The outstanding magazine in its field was Bernarr Macfadden's *Physical Culture,* bold, crusading, sensational, which began in New York in 1899. [38] It was designed for men; with it was soon associated *Beauty and Health* (1900–1908), for women. *Sandow's Magazine,* published in Boston by the professional strong man, Eugene Sandow, was a 1903 flash in the pan. There were some physical education periodicals

---

[36] *Physical Culture,* v. 7, p. 44, April 1902.
[37] See Mott, *op. cit.,* v. 1, pp. 441–42.
[38] Separate sketch of *Physical Culture* will appear in the next volume of this work.

designed for the schools, which were adopting such training into their curricula.[39] The vegetarians had two magazines — the *Vegetarian* (1895–1899), issued by the New York Vegetarian Society; and the *Vegetarian Magazine* (1896–current), organ of many associations.

### JOURNALS OF DENTISTRY

One could count at least twenty dental periodicals in course of publication at any time in the nineties. The only two that reached a circulation of over ten thousand in that time were the two oldest — *Dental Cosmos*, top of the heap, and *Dental Items of Interest*.[40] The next two, which reached about seven thousand, were *Dental Digest* (1895–current), founded in Chicago by J. N. Crouse and later moved to New York and Pittsburgh, and devoted chiefly to abstracting articles from other dental journals; and W. P. Litch's *Dental Brief* (1896–1913), of Philadelphia, full of news and interesting items.

Many of the newer dental journals were sponsored by societies or schools. The *Penn Dental Journal* (1897–current), for example, came from the Department of Dentistry at the University of Pennsylvania, and *Northwestern Dental Journal* (1903–current) from the Dental School at Northwestern University. The *Pacific Dental Gazette* (1926–1934) was the organ of the Los Angeles County Dental Society. A. W. Harlan's *Dental Review* (1886–1918), of Chicago, which had one of the larger circulations, represented many societies by publishing their proceedings. The *Western Dental Journal* (1887–1917), of Kansas City, was edited by J. D. Patterson; and the *American Dental Journal* (1902–1917), of Chicago, by J. B. Dicus.

### PHARMACEUTICAL PERIODICALS

Journals in the general field of drugs were more or less clearly divided between those having to do with the science of pharmacy and those serving the drug trade. The latter was much the larger group. Indeed, the former group was represented chiefly by the veteran and standard *American Journal of Pharmacy*[41] and the Detroit *Bulletin of Pharmacy* (1887–1928), subtitled "A Concise and Comprehensive Monthly Review of Pharmaceutical Literature, Progress and News." The *Pharmaceutical Era* (1887–1931) was also begun in Detroit, and at the same time as the *Bulletin*, but was moved to New York in

---

[39] See Chap. XV.

[40] These and other journals begun before 1885 and continuing in the present period are mentioned in Mott, *op. cit.*, v. 3, p. 143.

[41] See Mott, *op. cit.*, v. 1, Sketch 43.

1894. The *Era* gave much attention to education for pharmacy; Charles West Parsons was its editor for many years.[42]

Preëminent among journals serving the drug trade were the *American Druggist* [43] and the *Druggists' Circular* [44] (1888–current), of Boston, which began as *New England Druggist*; the *Practical Druggist and Pharmaceutical Review of Reviews* (1896–1935), conducted by Benjamin Lillard, of New York, until his death in 1910; [45] and *N.A.R.D. Notes* (1902–current), organ of the National Association of Retail Druggists.[46] There were other valuable and prosperous druggists' journals, mostly regional in scope.[47]

[42] See *Practical Druggist*, v. 50, p. 13, June 1932. Ezra J. Kennedy succeeded Parsons as editor of the *Era* in 1901 and continued to the end.

[43] Before the present period it had been called *New Remedies*. See Mott, *op. cit.*, v. 3, p. 133.

[44] See Mott, *op. cit.*, v. 2, p. 92.

[45] After his death it was sold to Romaine Pierson, and Reginald E. Dyer, formerly assistant editor, became editor-in-chief. See *Practical Druggist*, v. 50, p. 15, June 1932.

[46] In 1918 it became the *N.A.R.D. Journal*, a handsome and well-edited association organ.

[47] The more important were as follows: *Midland Druggist and Pharmaceutical Review* (1899–1927), Columbus, Ohio; *Northwestern Druggist* (1899–current), Minneapolis, St. Paul; *Rocky Mountain Druggist* (1888–current), Denver; *Pacific Drug Review* (1888–current), Portland. The *Philadelphia Drug, Oil and Paint Reporter* was begun in 1885, to become *Drugs, Oils and Paints* in 1892, and *Paint Industry Magazine* in 1939. *Merck's Report* (1892–current) specialized in market reports on pharmaceutical supplies.

# CHAPTER XVIII

# ENGINEERING, CONSTRUCTION, AND TRANSPORTATION

THE activity of American inventive genius, and, even more, the energy displayed in the development of engineering in the fields of power, communication, and transportation, were leading factors in the revolution in American living conditions which took place in the twenty years ending in 1905. The magazines abounded, especially in the latter half of this period, in articles about inventions and new industrial developments. A chief reason that such matters were discussed more often after the mid-nineties than before was that the great popular ten-cent magazines, closer to the news and the people than the older journals, found in these developments matter that was both meaningful and exciting. S. S. McClure and John Brisben Walker were leaders in the exploitation of such materials.

Walker listed in his magazine, the *Cosmopolitan*, in 1901 what he considered the greatest inventions of the nineties: wireless communication, undersea telephony, the submarine, the twenty-mile gun, the small-bore rifle, the X-ray, the baby incubator, the automobile, and acetylene gas.[1] Whatever the shortcomings of this as a list, it is notable for containing two items that were destined to affect American life profoundly for many generations — the wireless and the automobile. The fact that the automobile appears late in the list does not indicate Walker's lack of interest, for he was soon to engage in automotive manufacture himself. The wireless telegraph interested everyone. Marconi himself did an article telling of its invention and development for the *North American Review*.[2] The first wireless message sent across the English Channel was one from Cleveland Moffett, of *McClure's Magazine*, then in Paris, to S. S. McClure, in London.[3]

But more important to the life of the nineties than the recent inventions were the engineering applications and developments of the inventions of a decade or two earlier — the electric cars and incandescent lighting in the cities, the "self-binding reapers" on the farms, the gas-driven engine, the telephone exchanges in the towns, as well as the more specialized improvements in the steel mills and other factories. "The gas motor is as far beyond any other mode of power as the electric light is superior to the tallow candle," declared the *Gas Engine*

[1] *Cosmopolitan Magazine*, v. 31, p. 556, Sept. 1901.
[2] *North American Review*, v. 168, pp. 625ff, May 1899.
[3] *McClure's Magazine*, v. 13, p. 110, June 1899.

in its first number.[4] Edison, writing in the *North American* in 1888, added to a list of uses for the phonograph which he had furnished to that magazine ten years earlier the item of amusement, insisting on this value while he still adhered to the earlier, soberer uses for his invention.[5] The earliest moving pictures, with sound, were little more than curiosities:

> The latest invention due to the wonderful genius of Thomas A. Edison has been called the "kinetograph," the object of which is to reproduce, in addition to the sounds accompanying the movements of objects, a perfect visual image of those objects *as they appear when in motion.*[6]

It should be added that Machinery Hall at the Columbian Exposition at Chicago did much to impress the American people with a sense of the romance as well as the economic importance of mechanical and engineering achievement.

### MECHANICAL AND ENGINEERING MAGAZINES

The *Scientific American* continued to be the leading popular exponent of mechanical development and invention in the country.[7] Two great popular monthlies in this field began very early in the twentieth century — *Popular Mechanics* and *Technical World*.[8] They were copiously illustrated, clearly written, and carefully authenticated. Both were Chicago magazines. The *Popular Mechanics* file constitutes a kind of history of invention and mechanical contrivance in twentieth-century America. The *American Inventor* (1898–1907) was a New York weekly, and there were several others that furnished information about new patents.[9] Correspondence schools published some mechanical magazines designed as aid and inspiration for their students.[10]

*Cassier's Magazine: An Engineering Monthly* was published in London 1891–1902, in London and New York 1903–1906, and in New York 1907–1913. It was richly illustrated, carried the work of authori-

---

[4] *Gas Engine*, v. 1, p. 7, May 1898.

[5] *North American Review*, v. 146, p. 641, June 1888. For the earlier article, see F. L. Mott, *A History of American Magazines* (Cambridge, 1938), v. 3, p. 120; it appeared in the *Review*. v. 126, p. 527, May–June 1878.

[6] *Current History*, v. 1, p. 320, Aug. 1891.

[7] See Mott, *op. cit.*, v. 1, Sketch 8.

[8] *Popular Mechanics* was begun in 1902 and *Technical World* two years later. The former absorbed the latter in 1923 and has been called *Popular Mechanics Magazine* since 1910.

[9] For example, the *Inventive Age* (1889–1914), founded by James T. DuBois, the financier and diplomat, in Washington, D.C.; and the *Patent and Trademark Review* (1902–current), of New York.

[10] Chief of these was *Home Study* (1896–1903), later called *Science and Industry*, published by the Colliery Engineer Company, at Scranton, Pa. *Technical World* (*supra*) was begun by the American School of Correspondence, Armour Institute, but soon passed into other hands.

tative writers, and possessed great variety. It printed much about machine shops and machines, naval engineering, railway locomotives, education for engineering, and (in later years) automobiles and airplanes.

*Engineering Magazine: An Industrial Review* (1891–1933), of New York, later called *Industrial Review*, was notable for the "Engineering Index" that it published, and that was cumulated in a separate volume each year.[11] *Machinery* (1894–current), of New York, was published for a decade or more beginning in 1902 in separate editions for shops, railroads, engineering abroad, and so on. *Modern Machinery* (1897–1910) was a Chicago monthly selling at a dollar a year. The *Gas Engine* (1898–1923), of Cincinnati, sold at the same price. *Power and Transmission* (1885–1929), called the *Dodge Idea* after 1909, was published by the Dodge Manufacturing Company, Mishewaka, Indiana. The *Journal of the Western Society of Engineers* was begun in Chicago in 1896, and the *Southern Engineer* in Atlanta in 1904; both are still published, the latter under the title *Southern Power and Industry.*

There were many student-alumni journals of engineering.[12] Perhaps the most notable, in this period, were the *Cornell Civil Engineer* (1892–1935) and the *Sibley Journal of Engineering* (1887–1935), also a Cornell publication but devoted to mechanical engineering; the two were eventually combined as the *Cornell Engineer.*

#### THE ELECTRICAL FIELD

Some periodicals devoted to electrical research and industries were carried over from the anterior period,[13] but many more new ones were begun in the nineties. *Electrical Industries* published its first number in New York in December 1889, distinguished itself by publishing a weekly World's Fair supplement in Chicago during part of 1893, and was taken over by James H. McGraw in 1896 and renamed *American Electrician.* It was merged in McGraw's *Electrical World* in 1905. The *Electrician and Mechanic* (1890–1915) absorbed many other periodicals and bore various titles,[14] but it was a great popular monthly under

---

[11] *Engineering Magazine* specialized in scientific management, and in 1916 changed its name to *Industrial Management.*

[12] Among them were *Colorado Engineer* (1904–current), Colorado University; *Harvard Engineering Journal* (1902–14); *Iowa Engineer* (1901–current), Iowa State College; *Michigan Technic* (1888–current), Michigan University; *Minnesota Engineer* (1892–1915), Minnesota University; *Nebraska Blue Print* (1902–current), Nebraska University; *Transit* (1890), State University of Iowa; *Wisconsin Engineer* (1896–current), Wisconsin University.

[13] See Mott, *op. cit.*, v. 3, pp. 121–22.

[14] See *Bulletin of Bibliography*, v. 8, p. 151, April 1915.

the name here given throughout the nineties and afterward. *Electricity* (1891–1906) was born in Chicago but was moved before six months were up to New York. It was a weekly and designed to be "popular and practical, as well as technical and scientific." Other important New York electrical journals were *Electric Power* (1889–1896), founded to promote a "new department" in the industry — power transmission; and the *National Electrical Contractor* (1901–current), begun at Utica.[15]

The *General Electric Company Review* (1903–current) was issued from Schenectady; and the Electric Club, an association of Westinghouse men, published the *Electric Journal* at Pittsburgh.

The *Western Electrician* (1887–1908) was a good general weekly from Chicago; and the *Journal of Electricity* (1895–current) was a San Francisco monthly.[16]

SPECIALIZED ENGINEERING JOURNALS

Periodicals devoted to mining had various points of view — including scientific, engineering, and financial. Several important publications in this field continued from earlier periods,[17] but many new ones were begun in the nineties. The Klondike excitement late in that decade caused a great flurry in the magazines.[18]

Most of the new mining journals were published in the West. There were several in Denver to serve Colorado's active mining operations, and others in Montana and the Far West.[19]

Many special phases of engineering had their own periodicals.[20]

---

[15] It underwent various changes of title, and is called *Electrical Construction and Maintenance* in the 1950's.

[16] Purchased by the McGraw-Hill Publishing Company in 1919, and title changed in 1926 to *Electrical West*.

[17] See Mott, *op. cit.*, v. 2, p. 80; v. 3, p. 114.

[18] See pp. 108–09.

[19] Chief Denver mining journal was *Mining Industry* (1886–98), which was succeeded by *Mining Reporter* (1898–1918), called *Mining American* after 1907. An interesting Denver magazine was P. A. Leonard's *Ores and Metals* (1891–1907); though supported chiefly by gold-mine advertising and smelter "write-ups," its earlier issues were picturesque and valuable. It was merged with *Mining Reporter*. *Western Mining World* (1894–1917) was first published at Butte, Montana, but was moved to Chicago in 1903 and there issued as the *Mining and Engineering World*. The *Salt Lake Mining Review* (1899–current) became *Mining and Contracting Review* in 1934. Two San Francisco mining periodicals began in the exciting year of 1897 — the *Pacific Coast Miner* (1897–1906), called *Mining Magazine* in its last two years; and the *Pacific Miner* (1897–1911). Two Chicago weeklies devoted to the industry were *Black Diamond* (1885–current) and *Fuel Magazine* (1902–13).

[20] *Chemical Engineering* was begun in 1902, as *Electro-Chemical Industry*, by J. W. Richards in New York. It was purchased by the McGraw Publishing Company in 1913. It has had a variety of titles. *Chemical Engineer* (1904–25) was a Chicago monthly. *Insurance Engineering* (1901–current), New York, is now *Safety Maintenance and Production. Heating and Ventilation* (1891–1912), New York, was called *Engineering Review* in the latter half of its life. William Fortune founded *Municipal Engineering* in Indianapolis in 1890 as a $1.00 monthly "devoted to the improvement of cities." Its original title, shortened in 1896, was

The *American Architect* (1876–1938), of Boston, was still the country's leading architectural journal throughout most of the present period,[21] under William Robert Ware's editorship. It had serious competition in the nineties, however, from two other journals. The *Architectural Record* (1891–current), of New York, was founded and long conducted by Clinton W. Sweet, as publisher, and Henry W. Desmond, as editor. It was a quarterly, and each issue was a thick quarto book with variety and good illustration. It was notable in the latter nineties for its occasional extra numbers, which compose its *Great Architects Series*. It became a monthly in 1902.[22] It published some belles-letters. The *Architectural Review* (1891–1921), of Boston, was the successor of M.I.T's *Technology Architectural Review* (1887–1890). It was a quarto and carried four to twelve pages of text and six or eight big full-page plates — an impressive publication.[23]

The *Brickbuilder* was another Bostonian, a modest monthly quarto of a dozen well-illustrated pages, begun in 1892 to work for "the advancement of architecture in materials of clay." It was later to become *Architectural Forum*.[24] *Architecture* (1900–1936) was founded in New York by A. Holland Forbes as a beautifully illustrated quarto of thirty-six pages.[25] The *Quarterly Bulletin of the American Institute of Architects* (1900–1912) began modestly as an index of current architectural literature compiled by the secretary, with news of the society, but was later somewhat enlarged.[26] In Chicago a monthly serial devoted wholly to pictures of buildings in Europe was entitled *European Architecture* (1892–1901). The *Western Architect* (1901–1931) was a good Minneapolis monthly.

---

*Paving and Municipal Engineering.* In 1929 it became *Water Works and Sewerage*, and it ended in 1946. *Water and Gas Review* (1890–1919) was a New York monthly founded and edited by D. C. Toal. *Fire and Water Engineering*, begun in 1886, was the leader in its two fields; in 1926 it was divided into the two current journals, *Fire Engineering* and *Water Works Engineering*. *Power Plant Engineering*, begun in Philadelphia in 1896, is now *Power Engineering*, of Chicago. *Domestic Engineering* (1889–current), of Chicago, was devoted to plumbing, heating, lighting, ventilating, and so on. Through the nineties it published weekly and monthly editions; since 1904 it has been a monthly and has given increasing attention to air conditioning. *Heating and Ventilating* (1904–current), a New York monthly, has been a leader in its field. The *Wall-Paper News and Interior Decorator* (1892–1919) was also a New York monthly.

[21] See Mott, *op. cit.*, v. 3, p. 129.

[22] It was published somewhat irregularly in its early years. See *Periodicals*, v. 1, p. 8, Oct.–Dec. 1917.

[23] Bates & Guild were the publishers. Only eight numbers a year were issued during 1891–98, after which it was a monthly. It was suspended May 1910–Dec. 1911.

[24] It was moved to New York in 1924, and in 1932 it was purchased by Time, Inc.

[25] It was purchased by Charles Scribner's Sons in 1918.

[26] It was succeeded by the current *Journal* of the society.

HOUSE BUILDING AND FURNISHING

Much is to be found about house building in the magazines that served women and the home in the nineties,[27] and in a group of periodicals developed in that decade and the next few years that were devoted to house planning, interior decorating, furnishings, and landscape gardening. The most important of this group were *House Beautiful* and *House and Garden.*

The former was founded by Eugene Klapp, of Chicago, in December 1896 as a poorly printed ten-cent monthly; but when Herbert S. Stone obtained control of it after a few months, it showed great improvement in both form and content. *House Beautiful* became a crusader for simple beauty in household furnishings and against the overdecoration of the late Victorian era. By 1899 it was calling itself "The American Authority on Household Art." [28]

*House and Garden* was founded June 1901 by three Philadelphia architects, and it stated in its initial issue that its "point of view is that of the architect." It was a richly illustrated quarto of thirty-two pages. Though it was to undergo various changes when it changed ownership at the end of the present period, it has always been a high-grade magazine.[29]

*American Homes* (1895–1904) was "A Journal Devoted to Planning, Building, and Beautifying the Home," edited in Knoxville, Tennessee; it was a handsome quarterly edited by George F. Barber and selling for a dollar a year.[30] In Minneapolis Walter J. Keith conducted his *Home-Builder* (1899–1931), later called *Keith's Magazine on Home Building.*[31] It was an attractive ten-cent monthly.

No clear line can be drawn between the architects' journals and those designed for the contracting and building industry. The Architects' and Builders' Edition of the *Scientific American,* begun in 1885, belonged, for example, in both classes; from 1895 to its end in 1905 it was called *Scientific American Building Monthly.* The *National Buil-*

---

[27] See Chap. XXI.

[28] *House Beautiful* will be treated more fully in a separate sketch in the next volume of this work.

[29] The three founders were Wilson Eyre, Jr., Frank Miles Day, and Herbert C. Wise. The Philadelphia publisher John C. Winston took control of it in 1905 and made Charles Francis Osborne editor. It was moved to New York in 1909, to be published by McBride, Winston & Company. Condé Nast became a part of that firm two years later and in 1915 took over the publication; in the year before that Richardson Wright had begun his long and distinguished editorship of the magazine. See historical article in v. 50, July 1926, pp. 68–71, 116.

[30] Charles Hite-Smith followed Barber as editor. Its last few numbers were published in New York under the editorship of William Morris Hayes.

[31] The title was *Keith's Beautiful Homes* during 1926–30. In 1930 it was moved to Chicago and Keith's name was dropped.

*der* (1885–1924) was founded by Thomas E. Hill, of Chicago, as a popular journal including matter about gardens and furnishings; but it came into other hands in the nineties and was made a contractors' journal. There were small periodicals in most large cities and several regional publications [32] that gave the news about new building projects, contracts, and so forth; some of them, like the New York *Real Estate Record and Building Guide* (1868–current), continued for many years. Competitors in Chicago were the semimonthly *Contractor* (1898–1918) and the weekly *Construction News* (1895–1916).

## BUILDING MATERIALS

Several lumber journals from an earlier period continued into the late eighties and nineties.[33] There is some distinction between the trade papers and the manufacturers' periodicals in this field, but often the whole industry was served, from forest to building. The *New York Lumber Trade Journal* has been a leader on the trade side since it was founded in 1886. But lumber journals have been scattered widely over the country.[34] There were also some important periodicals devoted to the cement,[35] brick, and stone industries.[36]

## SPEED AND PROGRESS

The doctrine that increases in speed furnished a chief index to progress was widely held in the nineties. The magazines of 1885–1905 abounded in articles about the breaking of speed records, on the race-

---

[32] Most important were the *Pacific Builder and Engineer* (1902–current), of Seattle, and the *Southern Architect and Building News* (1889–1932), of Atlanta.

[33] Mott, *op. cit.*, v. 3, pp. 127, 130.

[34] Chicago has been the home of some of the chief lumber journals of the country, foremost of which, the weekly *American Lumberman*, was founded by W. B. Judson in 1899. The *Lumber Review* (1897–1929) was begun by William A. Radford, of Chicago, as the *Radford Review*; the title was changed when Benjamin F. Cobb came into control in 1902. It was changed again in a merger with *Lumber World* (1905–11), and has been *Chicago Lumberman* since 1926. The *St. Louis Lumberman* (1888–1932) was founded by W. E. Barns; its title became *Lumber* in 1918, with separate editions for manufacturers and dealers. In the timber country of the Northwest were the *West Coast and Puget Sound Lumberman* (1889–current), at Seattle, which now bears the simpler title *Lumberman*; the *Pacific Lumber Trade Journal* (1895–1913), also of Seattle; and the *Columbia River and Oregon Timberman* (1899–current), of Portland, now called *Timberman*.

[35] The pioneer cement journal was the *Cement and Engineering News* (1896–1924), founded by William Seafert in Chicago. Also published in Chicago was the *Cement Era* (1903–17). New York was the home of *Cement* (1900–13) and *Cement Age* (1904–12). *Concrete* (1904–12) was a Detroit monthly.

[36] The leading brick journal was begun in Chicago in 1892 as the *Clay Record*; since 1910, when it absorbed *Brick* (1894–1910), it has been called the *Brick and Clay Record*. Indianapolis was the original home of *Stone* (1888–1942), which later moved to New York; and Louisville saw the birth of *Rock Products*, (1902–current), which later migrated to Chicago. *Granite, Marble and Bronze* (1891–1939), of Boston, was at first called *Producer and Builder*.

tracks, the high seas, the railways, and the highways. One of the sensations of 1886 was the feat of the steamship *Oregon*, whose name, declared one enthusiastic writer, "is now as familiar as a household word,"[37] in crossing the Atlantic "in less than six and a half days." In 1893, Professor J. H. Biles, noting that crossing time had been reduced to six days, prophesied in the *North American Review* that it would be cut to four days in another ten years.[38] His exuberance was characteristic of the times. About the same time H. E. Prout, editor of the *Railroad Gazette*, said in the same review that the New York Central, then operating a twenty-hour run between Chicago and New York, "the fastest train in the world," occasionally reached a speed of eighty-four miles an hour on that run;[39] and he expected this to be exceeded eventually.

And shortly after the turn of the century, Henry Fournier made some sensational records with his automobile racer at the Coney Island track, as *Collier's* reported. In 1903 he did a mile in forty-six seconds. H. L. Bowden, of Boston, exceeded this mark driving a Mercedes at Daytona Beach in 1905, making the mile in thirty-two and four-fifths seconds.[40] Speed in the air was still a matter for romantic speculation in these years.

### THE CARRIAGE TRADE

The enticements of speed reached drivers on the city streets, who indeed always had liked to show off their fast nags.[41] Many of the urban weeklies complained against such speeding, and also against the reckless driving of horsecars. In 1890 *America*, a lively Chicago journal, advocated barring buggies entirely from the busier streets, as well as arrests of cable-car drivers by police when they became reckless.[42]

In the country, driving conditions grew better and better in the nineties as the roads were improved under the influence of the wheelmen. There were a million bicycles in use by 1895, according to one computation;[43] and "country life will become quite a different matter" as the riders of these wheels become organized behind a nation-wide good roads program, thought Editor Walker, of the *Cosmopolitan*.[44] Road improvement was a common magazine topic in the nineties: for

[37] R. H. Thurston in *Forum*, v. 1, p. 331, June 1886.
[38] *North American Review*, v. 156, p. 727, June 1893.
[39] *Ibid.*, v. 157, p. 75, July 1893.
[40] *Collier's*, v. 30, Jan. 17, 1903, p. 11; v. 35, June 17, 1905, p. 13.
[41] See Mott, *op. cit.*, v. 2, pp. 104–05; v. 3, pp. 26, 216.
[42] *America*, v. 4, p. 685, Sept. 18, 1890.
[43] *Cosmopolitan Magazine*, v. 20, p. 418, Feb. 1896.
[44] *Ibid.*, v. 20, p. 28, Nov. 1895.

example, the lead article in the *Century* for April 1892 was a well-illustrated piece on "Our Common Roads" by Isaac B. Potter, in which he outlined methods to combat the "costly and paralyzing condition" of wretched rural highways.[45]

Some of the older carriage and wagon journals continued through the nineties, such as the old *Hub* and *Carriage Monthly*, and a few new ones were begun.[46]

### THE HORSELESS CARRIAGE

In October 1895 a writer in *Progress of the World*, a short-lived New York monthly, observed that since there had been "occasional references in the daily press to the new-fangled device called a 'horseless carriage,' " he had made a study of automatic vehicles by personal tests and was ready to report on them to his readers. He had no hesitation, he continued,

> in affirming that they must soon come into general use. They have many advantages, being capable of three times the speed of an average horse, always under perfect control, never obliged to stop for rest.
> . . . The most unsettled feature of the new vehicle is what name to give it. The daily press, in a half-joking spirit, has dubbed it "the horseless wagon," while some want to call it "motocycle," "motor carriage," "automobile vehicle," etc. . . .
> Steam, electricity, petroleum, gasoline, compressed air, gas, kerosene, hot air, ammonia, gunpowder, ether, and springs have been tried as power. . . .[47]

This appeared in the month before the first automobile journal was published, under the name of the *Horseless Age* (1895–1918), by E. P. Ingersoll in New York. It explained its breaking of new ground as follows:

> The appearance of a journal devoted to a branch of industry yet in an embryonic state may strike some as premature. . . . But those who have taken the pains to search below the surfaces of the great tendencies of the age know what a giant industry is struggling into being there.[48]

Competitive runs attracted attention in these years. In the Chicago tests on Thanksgiving Day of 1895, a Duryea car won, completing the fifty-mile course at an average speed of seven miles per hour, using three and a half gallons of gasoline and nineteen gallons of water.

---

[45] *Century Magazine*, v. 43, pp. 803–20, April 1892.

[46] For the older journals, see Mott, *op. cit.*, v. 2, p. 92; v. 3, p. 216. The *Carriage Dealers' Journal* (1890–1916), of New York, was the organ of a national association. *Hub News* (1891–97), of New York, was a weekly edition of the monthly *Hub*.

[47] Maurice Delahaye (a manufacturer) in *Progress of the World*, v. 1, pp. 22–24, Oct. 1895. As to a suitable name, cf. *Horseless Age*, v. 1, Jan. 1896, p. 1.

[48] *Horseless Age*, v. 1, Nov. 1895, p. 5.

Only two of the dozen entries completed the run.[49] The *Cosmopolitan* conducted a trial run in New York the next year.[50] The essayist William J. Lampton wrote for the *Home Magazine* an interesting story of a round trip that he and a companion made from New York to Washington by automobile in 1900. This was the third such journey undertaken by adventurous spirits, Lampton tells us. It took five days (of course they did not travel by night) to reach Washington, and eight days to return. They had to be towed repeatedly, and other matters took time:

> It takes time to fill up with gas and water, to grease the working parts of the engine, to tighten nuts, to try bolts, to look after the boiler and the pump and the injector and the valves and the lubricator and the chain and the differential and the guages and the air and the tires, and to heat the torch for vaporizing the gas, and to attend to several other matters incidental to the care of automobiles.

Theirs was "a light steam runabout." It attracted much attention along the route. "Although everybody seemed to know an automobile by name, few had personal acquaintance, and it made little difference where we might stop for a few minutes, a crowd always quickly gathered." [51]

By this time motor vehicles (especially electric runabouts) were "a familiar sight at every street corner in New York City," said a writer in the *Yale Scientific Monthly*.[52] It was in the last two years of the century — 1899–1900 — that a machine that had seemed curious and slightly absurd suddenly became popular, and the basis of an important industry. A writer in *Ainslee's Magazine* in the spring of 1901 tells about it:

> A couple of years ago there were barely a hundred automobiles in the United States, while now there are thousands. . . . "The whole country seems to have gone automobile mad," declared an official of the U. S. Patent Office the other day. . . . Scarcely a day passes that the newspapers do not record the incorporation of a new automobile company. Barely a year ago there were but ten manufacturers of automobiles in America, while now there are more than three hundred.[53]

Now many articles appeared in the magazines furnishing data to readers who might contemplate buying automobiles, and advertising of various makes crept, rather timidly at first, into the magazines.[54]

---

[49] *Journal of U. S. Artillery*, v. 5, pp. 246–47, March–April 1896. Data credited to *Engineering*.

[50] See Sketch 10.

[51] *Home Magazine*, v. 16, pp. 423–34, May 1901.

[52] George N. Crouse, "Horseless Carriages," *Yale Scientific Monthly*, v. 6, p. 1, Oct. 1899. In 1903 a count was made on six New York street corners, which showed nearly one-tenth of passing vehicles to be automotive (*World's Work*, v. 6, p. 3502, June 1903).

[53] Edwin Emerson, Jr., "Automobiles Today," *Ainslee's Magazine*, v. 7, p. 206, April 1901.

[54] See Chap. II.

Cleveland Moffett wrote for the *Review of Reviews* an article entitled "Automobiles for the Average Man" in 1900, in which he says that the only practical "self-propelling carriages" are those powered by electricity, gasoline, and steam. "Other kinds, driven by compressed air, alcohol, acetylene gas, etc., may be disregarded as still in the experimental stage," he writes. He begins the long debate over women's driving by the remark: "No doubt there are men (and many women) quite ùnfit for such responsibility" as driving an automobile carriage.[55] At about the same time a writer in the *Woman's Home Companion* declared:

> It is not surprising that the automobile should be popular with women. Few women are experienced drivers, and as a rule they avoid the responsibility of managing a horse. . . . The horseless carriage is more to their liking, inasmuch as they have only to learn how to handle a convenient lever to ride where they will, without any attendant whatever, and with perfect safety.[56]

An article in *Everybody's* in the summer of 1903 entitled "Can I Afford an Automobile?" summed the matter up by pointing out that a horse and carriage cost about four hundred and fifty dollars, and about the same to maintain, while an electric, gasoline, or steam runabout cost six hundred and fifty to buy and only about half of that to maintain for the same amount of travel. Buy an automobile, was the verdict.[57]

But the automobile was not accepted without many reservations and much criticism from many sources. Wrote a paragrapher in *Town Topics*:

> Every hand is against the automobiles, from the hoodlums who throw stones to the magistrates who inflict fines. The squeaking, snorting, stinking machines are debarred from the ferryboats and have no more right on the streets than the locomotive of the Empire State Express has to steam down the avenue. . . . I am not of those who advocate shooting automobilists when they run down pedestrians. Shooting is too good for them. . . . How such vehicles, in which there is no comfort and no style, have become the vogue is impossible to explain.[58]

John Gilmer Speed, writing in the *Saturday Evening Post* in 1899 under the title, "Is a Horseless Age Coming?" said that people had been disappointed in their expectations of quieter and cleaner traffic with horses off the streets:

[55] *Review of Reviews*, v. 21, pp. 704–10, June 1900. Cf. Moffett's earlier article in *McClure's Magazine*, v. 7, pp. 153ff, July 1896, entitled "The Sudden Rise of the Horseless Carriage."

[56] *Woman's Home Companion*, v. 27, Jan. 1900, p. 39.

[57] Arthur N. Jervis in *Everybody's Magazine*, v. 9. pp. 33–37, July 1903.

[58] *Town Topics*, v. 52, Aug. 11, 1904, p. 11. If this was intended to bring advertisers into line, it apparently served its purpose, and Sept. 15, p. 11, we have the note: "*Town Topics* is in favor of automobiles; they have come to stay; they are necessary to the comfort, luxury and business interests of the country."

No doubt we shall experience in the near future many of these things. At present, however, the trolleys and the automobiles, which we call horseless carriages, are not silent by a great deal. They make noises that are to some as objectionable as the beat of horses' feet and the rattle of wheels over the stones.

Speed concludes that "to do without the horse seems too preposterous to consider seriously." [59] *Ainslee's* pointed out a few years later that "A judge of the Supreme Court in New York has held that the owners of steam automobiles should be required to send a runner with a red flag ahead of the vehicle to warn other wayfarers." [60]

But the good roads movement bade fair to receive far more powerful impetus from the automobile drivers than it had from bicycle riders. In Cleveland Moffett's article in the *Review of Reviews* already mentioned, there is a remarkable passage about a transcontinental highway. This commentator foresaw

a transcontinental highway on which automobiles and bicycles may speed from ocean to ocean under best and pleasantest conditions. This is to be a great recreation highway for the public, the expense of building it to be divided among the benefiting States, counties, and cities along the line. Everything will be provided for needs and comforts of rider and driver — automobile inns and clubhouses, repair shops, recharging stations, etc., and nothing will be allowed to interfere with the primary purpose of making this a great people's highway for self-propelling vehicles — the greatest and finest road seen in the world since Roman conquerors spread their marvellous paved ways across empires . . . Many people will prefer to travel from place to place more slowly than at present rather than to rush blindly along iron rails. If the automobile continues the spirit born of the bicycle and makes us see more of our own country, it will have rendered a splendid service to American life and character.[61]

### AUTOMOBILE JOURNALS

Beginning in the same year with the New York *Horseless Age*, mentioned above, was a Chicago monthly titled *Motocycle* (1895–1900), edited by L. B. McGrath. By 1899, when the flood of automotive journals began, the names "automobile" and "motor" had been pretty well settled upon as designations for the new type of vehicle. Five new journals designed to serve the rapidly growing industry were established in the fall of 1899.

*Automobile* (1899–current), founded by M. G. Gillette, of New York, was at the very beginning devoted rather to the interests of purchasers and drivers of the new vehicles than to the trade or industry; but it

[59] *Saturday Evening Post*, v. 171, p. 826, June 24, 1899.
[60] *Ainslee's Magazine*, v. 7, p. 213, April 1901.
[61] *Review of Reviews*, v. 21, p. 710, June 1900. Cf. John Brisben Walker's earlier article, "Some Speculations Regarding Rapid Transit," *Cosmopolitan*, v. 20, pp. 28–30, Nov. 1895.

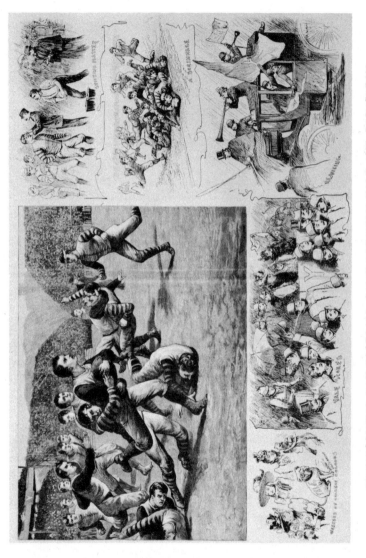

THANKSGIVING DAY FOOTBALL GAME BETWEEN YALE AND PRINCETON

Played on Manhattan Field, New York. From double-page spread in
*Once a Week*, December 15, 1891. See pages 374–376.

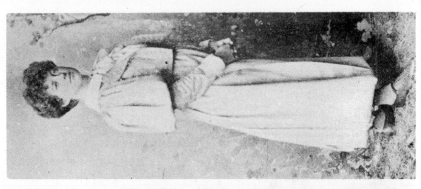

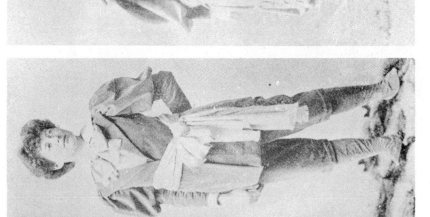

SHOCKING SUGGESTIONS OF A DRESS REFORMER

B. O. Flower, editor of the *Arena*, had the assistance of his wife in designing these costumes. See pages 405–406, and also page 358.

"A PROCESSION OF HORSELESS CARRIAGES"

From the *Cosmopolitan Magazine*, November 1895. See pages 327–330.

OIL-DRIVEN MOTOR OF 1895

From the *Cosmopolitan Magazine*, November 1895.

"PROFESSOR LANGLEY'S AERDROME IN FLIGHT"

From *McClure's Magazine*, June 1897. See page 334.

later broadened its appeal and eventually, under the name *Automotive Industries*, was to become a leader in its field.[62] It absorbed two of the other auto journals that had been established in 1899 — *Motor Vehicle Review*, of Cleveland, merged in 1902; and *Automobile Magazine*, of New York, merged in 1907. In Chicago, *Auto Review* (1899–1908) became *Motor Way* in 1905; and the old *Cycle Age* Company began the publication of the *Motor Age* (1899–current), merging the older publication therein in 1902.

In the next year *Motor World* (1900–1940) and *Automobile Topics* (1900–1949) were begun in New York; and in Philadelphia, *Cycle Trade Journal* (1896–1940) changed its name to take in the automotive trade.[63]

*Motor* (1903–current), New York, was William Randolph Hearst's first magazine. Having seen the new British *Car* while visiting in London, he cabled S. S. Carvalho to start such a magazine in New York. After the first number or two, George d'Utassy was placed in general charge. *Motor* was for many years primarily a consumers' magazine, covering the annual shows, races, endurance runs, tours, and such.[64] It has always been distinguished by rich illustration.

### AMERICAN RAILWAYS

One of the leading topics of the magazines of 1885–1905 was the American railroad — its romance, its mechanics, and its economics. Here was one of the chief political and economic problems of the period, but here was also all the excitement of travel and adventure; and the short stories of Cy Warman and Herbert Hamblen in *McClure's* are quite as important in the magazine offering as those early articles on the subject in *Scribner's* in 1888–1889, or the disquisitions of Henry V. Poor and Edmund J. James in the journals of economics.

"The greatest single industry in the world" was the characterization given to railroading by a contributor to the *Publications of the American Economic Association* in 1891. He went on to say: "It is an industry which in all departments of life — social, political and industrial — is by far the most important of them all, and which, if misdirected, is more disastrous than war." [65] When the *Chautauquan* issued a number wholly devoted to the railways in June 1904, it gave a million and a

---

[62] Founded as a monthly, it became a weekly in 1902. The title change noted above took place in 1917, and the magazine moved to Philadelphia in 1925.

[63] It was *Cycle and Automobile Trade Journal* during 1900–12, and *Automobile Trade Journal* during 1912–40.

[64] In 1924 *Motor* became a trade and industry journal, serving dealers, service operators, and wholesalers.

[65] F. C. Clark in *P.A.E.A.*, v. 6. p. 580, Nov. 1891.

quarter as the number of railroad employees in the United States.[66]

Criticism of the railroads for their discrimination in rates came to a climax in 1886 with the Cullom Committee report, which resulted in the passage of the Interstate Commerce Commission bill the next year.[67] But this did not put an end to "rebates to favored trusts and combinations," according to the *Arena*.[68] That the railroads themselves were combining in great interlocking organizations was pointed out in the *Chautauquan*, which showed that the Harriman-Morgan interests already controlled two-thirds of the railway mileage in the country.[69]

American railways were far from prosperous in the nineties, however. Harry T. Newcomb, a government railway expert, declared in the *North American Review* in 1897 that the I.C.C. had been a failure, that forty thousand miles of railroad (nearly a fifth of the whole) were in receiverships, that solvent lines were unprofitable, and that rates were demoralized.[70] In the Midwest especially, said a writer in the Democratic *Belford's Magazine*, state legislation had so crippled the railroads that they could not remain solvent.[71] The radical *Arena* had an answer: it carried an article in the early nineties claiming that "vast numbers of conservative people" had been converted to a belief in government ownership as a solution to the problem of the American railroad.[72]

### RAILWAY JOURNALS

There was not only a large number, but also a wide variety, of railroad magazines in this period.[73] In any of the twenty years under consideration, the directories listed some thirty-five to forty railroad trade magazines (including the labor union periodicals), as well as ten or fifteen monthly railway guides devoted mainly to timetables and such information. The labor journals [74] were by no means confined to official news of the brotherhoods, but contained a considerable amount of feature material about railroading, sometimes some fiction and verse, and often home departments and such miscellany.

The veteran journals in the general field were the *American Engi-*

[66] George B. Waldron, "Evolution of the American Railroad," *Chautauquan*, v. 39, pp. 316–29, June 1904.
[67] Edmund J. James, "The Railway Question," *P.A.E.A.*, v. 2, pp. 285ff, July 1887.
[68] *Arena*, v. 7, p. 708, May 1893.
[69] Waldron in *Chautauquan*, v. 39, p. 328, June 1904.
[70] *North American Review*, v. 165, p. 591, Nov. 1897.
[71] *Belford's Magazine*, v. 4, p. 227, Jan. 1890.
[72] *Arena*, v. 4, p. 152, July 1891.
[73] See Frank Chapin Bray, "Railroad Trade Journalism," *Chautauquan*, v. 39, pp. 332–37, June 1904.
[74] See Chap. XI.

*neering and Railroad Journal,* edited until 1897 by Mathias N. Forney,[75] and the Philadelphia *Railway World.*[76] But the leading journal of the railways in the present period was the *Locomotive Engineer,* a monthly founded in 1888 by Horace B. Miller and Lycurgus B. Moore, of New York. They brought in as editor a man who had attracted some notice as a contributor to the railroad magazines, a former engineer on the Denver and Rio Grande, named John A. Hill, who was later to become a leading figure in the railroad publishing business. *Locomotive Engineering,* as it was called through the nineties, topped other journals in its field in that decade with twenty to twenty-five thousand circulation.[77]

Railroad journals of shorter lives and smaller circulations tended to serve regional and specialized fields.[78] Also a number of railroads published periodicals intended primarily for their own employees and for promoting the regions in which they operated.[79]

James H. McGraw's *Street Railway Journal*[80] was the leader in that field. It told the story of the electrification of city transit systems in the eighties and nineties. "Time is precious," said a writer in the *New England Magazine* in 1888, pointing out that twenty-one cities had found the old horsecars too slow by that time and had turned to electric power.[81] The *Street Railway Gazette* (1886–1896) changed its name to *Electric Railway Gazette* the year before it was merged in the *Electrical World.* Likewise, the *Street Railway Review* (1891–1908) became *Electric Railway Review* two years before it was absorbed by the *Street Railway Journal.*[82] At the time of this merger the McGraw magazine became *Electric Railway Journal.*

### MARINE ENGINEERING AND SHIPPING

The famous weekly *Nautical Gazette,* of New York, bore the name *Seaboard* from 1888 to 1898 and was edited through the nineties by

[75] See Mott, *op. cit.,* v. 2, Sketch 4.

[76] *Ibid.,* p. 81. Others which continued from the seventies and eighties are mentioned in Mott, *op. cit.,* v. 3, pp. 125–26.

[77] Angus Sinclair was a partner of Hill during 1891–97, both in editing and publishing the magazine; Hill was then sole editor and publisher until his death in 1919. Title was changed to *Railway and Locomotive Engineering* in 1901; the journal ended in Dec. 1928.

[78] For example, *New York Railroad Men* (1887–1933); *Roadmaster and Foreman* (1888–1911), Chicago; *Railroad Car Journal* (1891–1902), New York; *Railway Journal* (1898–1913), Chicago, American Railway Tool Foremen's Association; *Railroad Herald* (1900–33), Atlanta; *Machinery: Railway Edition* (1901–12), New York; *Boiler Maker* (1902–37), begun in New York as *Motive Power,* later moved to Chicago; *Freight* (1904–16), title changed 1914 to *Trade and Transportation.*

[79] For example, *Maine Central* (1893–1905); *Pilgrim* (1895–96), Chicago, Milwaukee & St. Paul; *Book of the Royal Blue* (1897–1911), Baltimore and Ohio; *Great Northern Bulletin* (1900–19); *Earth* (1904–38), Atchison, Topeka and Santa Fe.

[80] See Mott, *op. cit.,* v. 3, p. 126.

[81] Charles L. Holt in *New England Magazine,* v. 6, p. 551, Oct. 1888.

[82] For bibliographical notes on these street railway journals, see *Periodicals,* v. 1, pp. 11–12, Oct.–Dec. 1917.

Alex R. Smith. "American ships for American commerce" was its motto. The *Marine Journal,* a similar publication, was ably edited in this decade by George L. Norton. *Marine Engineering* (1897–current) was founded as a monthly by H. M. Swetland and became an authority in its field.

The *Pacific Marine Review* (1904–1950) was begun in Seattle and later moved to San Francisco. The *Marine Review* (1890–1935), of Cleveland, was devoted to lake shipping and marine news and features; it absorbed the *Marine Record* (1878–1902). The *Waterways Journal* (1887–current), of St. Louis, has long been devoted to commerce of the inland rivers and to flood control.

AIRPLANES AND THE MAGAZINES

In 1891 Samuel P. Langley, superintendent of the Smithsonian Institution, read a paper before the National Academy of Sciences that produced far more comment in the newspapers and magazines than scientific papers usually do. As simplified and condensed for an article in the *Century* for September, it showed that there was already available "mechanical power to sustain in the air (and at great speeds) bodies thousands of times heavier than the air tiself"; all that was necessary now, said Langley, was "the skill to direct this power," and man could fly.[83] Langley himself tried to "direct this power" by means of machines of his construction, and in 1903 made two spectacular failures to fly across the Potomac near Washington. However, Glenn H. Curtiss once told in the *American Machinist* about flying the Langley machine long after the death of the builder, and gave it as his opinion that this pioneer airplane was "inherently right."[84]

But the wits had a barrel of fun with Langley. "Up to the present writing Darius Green's reputation is not in danger," said the *Valley Weekly.*[85] *Electricity* declared, "Few persons have confidence in any form of flying machine," but noted an avid popular interest on the subject.[86]

And so Langley and the English Hiram Maxim (another unsuccessful builder and flyer) contributed a number of articles to leading American magazines about "flying machines." In 1895 Maxim was advising young engineers in the *North American Review* to "turn their thoughts in the direction of the petroleum motor" if they would forward the cause of aerial locomotion.[87]

[83] *Century Magazine,* v. 42, p. 783, Sept. 1891.
[84] *American Machinist,* v. 66, p. 807, May 19, 1927.
[85] *Valley Weekly,* v. 3, Sept. 14, 1904, p. 2.
[86] *Electricity,* v. 1, p. 2, July 22, 1891.
[87] *North American Review,* v. 161, p. 411, Oct. 1895.

Of course, that is what the Wright brothers did. But the Kitty Hawk flights were private, if not secret,[88] and there was little or no magazine comment on the great feat of December 17, 1903, until some five years later.

The pioneer American periodical in the field was *Aeronautics* (1893–1894), which was published by M. N. Forney, of the *American Engineering and Railroad Journal*, and was devoted chiefly to the proceedings of the Conference on Aerial Navigation held during the World's Fair in Chicago. It was a ten-cent monthly of sixteen quarto pages. The *Aeronautical World* (1902–1903), of Glenville, Ohio, was a fifteen-cent monthly of twenty-four large-octavo pages, containing much about Langley and Santos-Dumont. It published articles on ballooning, as did many of the general magazines. The military values of aeronautics were frequently emphasized in army journals[89] and other magazines as well.

### JOURNALS FOR TELEPHONE AND POSTAL WORKERS

A writer in the *New England Magazine* in 1894 called attention to the rapid spread of telephone exchanges in American cities in the eighties and early nineties. "Fifteen years ago," he wrote, "there was not a telephone exchange in the United States. Today there are nearly fourteen hundred exchanges, employing ten thousand subscribers."[90]

The pioneer *Telephone Magazine* (1893–1905) was published in Chicago by Fred De Land under the inspiration of World's Fair exhibits. It was finally merged in *Telephony* (1901–current), another Chicago journal, founded by Harry B. McNeal. Also merged eventually into *Telephony* was the American *Telephone Journal* (1900–1908). *Sound Waves* (1900–1908), of Logansport, Indiana, was subtitled "International Telephone Journal."

Postal workers also had a number of long-lived journals.[91]

---

[88] George Grantham Bain, "The Man Bird and His Flight," *New Broadway Magazine*, v. 21, pp. 170–81, Aug. 1908.

[89] For example, the symposium on observation balloons in *American Cavalry Journal*, v. 37, pp. 103–12, June 1897.

[90] *New England Magazine*, v. 11, p. 461, June 1894.

[91] *Postal Record* (1888–current), National Association of Letter Carriers; *Postmaster Everywhere* (1903–24); *Postmaster's Advocate* (1895–current), National League of Postmasters; *Post Office* (1891–99); *Post Office Clerk* (1901–current), United National Association of Post Office Clerks; *R.F.D. News* (1903–27), National Rural Letter Carriers' Association; *Railway Post Office* (1902–current), Railway Mail Association.

# CHAPTER XIX

## AGRICULTURE, HORTICULTURE, LIVESTOCK

MAGAZINE commentary on "the farm question" has been discussed in early chapters of this volume; it falls naturally into economic, social, and political categories.[1] We may, however, quote in this place a current truism uttered in 1889 by *Belford's Magazine*: "The farmer deteriorates because relatively he is growing poor. The evidence is clear to every beholder." And it added that farm mortgages were often "written in blood; they represent the sweat and tears of a prolonged but utterly hopeless struggle."[2] Six years later the Governor of Kansas, writing in the *North American Review*, said that the farmers' outlook was then "anything but hopeful," and that over ten thousand farmers' families were being dispossessed annually in foreclosure proceedings.[3] At the turn of the century, however, the prospect had been brightened by a more expanded economy and a series of bumper crops.

Impoverished or prosperous, the farmer always had his low-priced periodicals, and plenty of them. In 1885 the Ayer directory listed 139 farm journals of a general character, plus 33 stock and dairy magazines, and several devoted primarily to Grange affairs. In 1905 the same authority showed a 50 per cent increase in general agricultural journals, and 60 per cent in those devoted to livestock and dairying. Perhaps it is unprofitable to attempt any distinction between the general farm journals and those that specialized in the stock and dairy fields, since the former were commonly very inclusive; but there was a constant trend toward emphasis in the periodicals on specific types of farm industry, individual breeds of stock, and particular facets of farm life — all making for specialization. It is safe to say that by 1900 half the agricultural journals were definitely specialized in content.[4]

The figures given above, which do not include horticulture, forestry, poultry, and some other fields, fall far short of those often given for agricultural journalism in this period.[5] Undoubtedly well over a thou-

---

[1] See pp. 176–79.
[2] *Belford's Magazine*, v. 2, p. 645, April 1889.
[3] *North American Review*, v. 160, p. 16, Jan. 1895.
[4] See Jack Vanderhoof, "Eastern and Mid-Western Agricultural Journalism, 1860–1900" (doctoral dissertation, Columbia University, 1951), pp. 15–16.
[5] See Stephen Conrad Stuntz, *List of the Agricultural Periodicals of the United States and Canada Published During the Century July 1810 to July 1910* (U. S. Department of Agriculture, Miscellaneous Publications No. 398, 1941).

sand periodicals, of shorter or longer life, dealing with rural life and industry were published between 1885 and 1905. They depended for their existence on circulation, of course; but many lasted for a long time on a distribution of a few thousand or even a few hundred — enough to attract some advertising business. Their advertising receipts were nearly always far greater than those from circulation. Farm implements, seeds, fine stock, and supplies and gadgets for the farm home were the basis for this advertising. The Frank B. White Company was organized in New York in 1886 as the first advertising agency to specialize in the agricultural field. It issued *Agricultural Advertising* (1894–1918) as its house organ, with its main office in Chicago.

NATIONAL AGRICULTURAL PERIODICALS

Differences in climate, soils, and crops in the various regions of the United States have prevented the development of great national farm journals and fostered, instead, the growth of state and regional periodicals. Apparent exceptions to this rule in the present period were certain holdovers from earlier years.[6] For example, the *Farm Journal*, the unique little Philadelphia monthly, continued with Wilmer Atkinson as senior editor, reaching half a million circulation by the end of our period.

The *American Agriculturist*, of New York, was made a weekly in 1894 and became the central edition of a system of regional journals that included the *New England Homestead*, of Springfield, Massachusetts, and the *Orange Judd Farmer*, of Chicago. The group, which varied in number from time to time, had about two hundred thousand circulation at the end of the present period. *Farm and Home*, semimonthly associate of the *New England Homestead*, had eastern and western editions aggregating over a third of a million at fifty cents a year.[7]

Another fifty-cent semimonthly was *Farm and Fireside*, of Springfield, Ohio, which had maintained a circulation of over half a million throughout the nineties. Phineas Price Mast, a manufacturer of farm implements, had been head of this paper's publishing company when it was started in 1877; he died a millionaire in 1898, and John Stephens Crowell, who had been editor of *Farm and Fireside* from the first, reorganized the firm as the Crowell Publishing Company.[8] This periodical also issued regional editions in the nineties. Its Louisville rival, *Home*

---

[6] See sections on agricultural periodicals in the earlier volumes of this work.

[7] George S. Graves sold control of the entire *Agriculturist* group to Herbert Myrick in 1899 and became president and editor of the Phelps Publishing Company (*New York Tribune*, June 17, 1899, p. 5, col. 2).

[8] See historical sketch in *Farm and Fireside*, v. 25, p. 1, May 1, 1902; also *Publisher's Weekly*, v. 100, p. 555, Aug. 20, 1921.

*and Farm*, circulated somewhat under a hundred thousand in the nineties.

There were a number of nationally distributed mail-order papers designed for farm homes and priced at twenty-five cents a year or less. Several of these were started about the turn of the century, as the Chicago *Farm Life* (1903–1913) and the St. Louis *Farm Progress* (1904–1919).

### COUNTRY LIFE

At the beginning of the new century, when prospects were fair upon the farms, when prices were high and crops large, when roads were being improved and rural free delivery inaugurated, and when President Roosevelt appointed his Country Life Commission to study means for making rural living attractive, three ambitious magazines were begun to exploit this new spirit — *Country Life in America, Suburban Life,* and the *Rural American.*

The editor of the first-named of these wrote in his initial number: "There is a growing interest in country life; this journal would be its representative." Clearly, he meant an interest on the part of city dwellers; *Country Life in America* was not designed for farmers. He continued: "The growth of literature pertaining to plants and animals and the out-of-doors is one of the most emphatic and significant movements of the times."[9] This editor was Dean Liberty Hyde Bailey, of Cornell University, a botanist and chairman of the Country Life Commission. The publishers were Doubleday, Page & Company; and the large-quarto pages, the fine pictures (some in color), and the interesting articles by good contributors made a wonderful beginning for what long continued to be a good magazine.[10]

*Suburban Life* (1903–1917) was a dollar a year in comparison to *Country Life's* four dollars. It was a handsome Boston monthly devoted to homes and gardens.[11] Another Bostonian was the *Rural American* (1900–1904), also a ten-cent monthly; it was "an outgrowth of rural free mail delivery," and was designed to bring commentary on public affairs, as well as some fiction and miscellany, to farm homes. Joe Mitchell Chapple, who also conducted the *National Magazine,* was editor and publisher.

---

[9] *Country Life in America*, v. 1, pp. 24–25, Nov. 1901.

[10] Bailey was editor for only a short time. For list of editors, see *Public Libraries*, v. 14, p. 213, June 1909. There were some changes in title, and the magazine became simply *Country Life* in 1910. It ended in 1942.

[11] The first number (Dec. 7, 1902) was a trial run without title; the name varied somewhat, and in 1914 became *Countryside Magazine.* J. Horace McFarland, president of the American Civic Association, took it over in 1906 and moved it to Harrisburg, Pa., though it kept a Boston office for a time and also had one in New York. At the start, the periodical was really a Boston suburban journal of local appeal; see p. 82.

Some crops had their specialized journals, several of which began in former periods and are mentioned in earlier volumes of this work. *Cotton and Cotton Oil Press* (1900–current) began as *Ginner and Miller* in Memphis and later moved to Dallas. Several tobacco papers were started in this period, chief of which was *Southern Tobacco Journal* (1887–current), of Winston-Salem, North Carolina. The *Louisiana Planter and Sugar Manufacturer* (1888–1929) was published in New Orleans, as was the *Rice Journal* (1898–current) after its early years in the Crowley rice district.

Two journals devoted largely to threshing equipment were *Thresher-men's Review* (1892–1928), of Detroit; and *American Thresherman* (1898–1932), of Madison, Wisconsin.

The reclamation of arid lands was one of the great questions of the new century. Victor H. Smedley, editor of the *Northwest Magazine*, wrote an article for the *World To-Day* shortly after President Roosevelt had signed the new Irrigation Act in 1902, which expressed the matter admirably. That measure, he said,

means more than any other form of progress that could be taken up for that great stretch of country lying west of the Mississippi River. . . . It means a new area of development and enterprise. . . . Irrigation is the great national question of the United States. To at least half of our country it is far more important than the completion of the Panama Canal or the annexation of foreign possessions.[12]

*Irrigation Age*, begun in 1891 in Chicago, was the leading journal in the field, absorbing nine other irrigation and dry-farming periodicals before it moved to Salt Lake City in 1917 and was the next year merged into the *Utah Farmer*. Perhaps the most important of the dry-farming journals was the one that began in Denver as *Arid Region* in 1891 and ended five years later in Omaha as *Arid America*.

Many state and regional farm weeklies begun in the seventies and earlier continued through the nineties.[13] A few may be mentioned here. George M. Whitaker bought the *New England Farmer* in 1885 and also two or three other journals that he consolidated with it, but it was a decaying periodical when it was moved in 1903 to Brattleboro, Vermont, there to perish ten years later. The Tucker family was still in control

---

[12] *World To-Day*, v. 3, p. 1959, Oct. 1902.
[13] For papers named in this paragraph, see earlier volumes of this work, which are fully indexed.

of the old Albany *Cultivator*, which, in line with the improvements in country life, resumed the old name *Country Gentleman* in 1897. Herbert W. Collingwood and Elbert S. Carman edited the *Rural New-Yorker* through the nineties; in 1899 Carman sold his interest to Collingwood and John J. Dillon, business manager. Collingwood's "Hope Farm Notes" made a pleasant, long-continued feature of this great paper.[14] One of the strongest agricultural editors of the period was Miles Evans Williams, of the *Ohio Farmer*, a leading farm paper of the Midwest. The *Michigan Farmer* continued at Detroit, lowering its price to seventy-five cents a year shortly after the turn of the century. Rand, McNally & Company owned that famous champion of farmers' rights, the *Prairie Farmer*, in the nineties; Burridge D. Butler brought it again into a dominant position when he gained control in 1900. It was eventually to absorb the *Farmer's Voice* (1885–1913), spokesman for the Grange, the Alliance, the Wheel, and other groups. James M. Pierce bought the *Iowa Homestead* in 1885; Henry Wallace was its editor until 1894, when he joined relatives on the *Farm and Dairy*, which thereupon became *Wallace's Farmer*.[15] Pierce bought the *Wisconsin Farmer*, of Madison, in 1893.

The important regional and state papers begun in this period were mostly in the West and South. In the Midwest was the monthly *Capper's Farmer* (1893–current), which began in Atchison, Kansas, as the *Missouri Valley Farmer* and was moved to Topeka and built up to a large circulation by Arthur Capper, later United States Senator from Kansas. Three other agricultural periodicals belonged to the Capper group — the famous old *Kansas Farmer*, a semimonthly; the *Missouri Ruralist* (1901–current), a semimonthly published at Kansas City and then at St. Louis before it was moved to Topeka; and *Capper's Weekly*, a rural news and opinion magazine.[16]

*Successful Farming* (1902–current) was founded in Des Moines, Iowa, by Edwin T. Meredith, who was also to serve, though more briefly, as a United States Senator. At first it was a fifty-cent monthly, but it was soon reduced to twenty-five cents a year. A practical and helpful journal, it eventually gained a very large circulation over a wide area.

The *Farmer's Guide* (1889–1917) was started in Huntington, Indiana, by Ben F. Biliter without a subscriber and "on a shoestring." At first it

---

[14] See William Edward Ogilvie, *Pioneer Agricultural Journalists* (Chicago, 1927), pp. 121–28.

[15] *Ibid.*, pp. 102–20.

[16] *Kansas Farmer* grew out of the Topeka *Mail*, later *Mail and Breeze*, which was a combination of the *Topeka Mail* (1882–95) and *Kansas Breeze* (1894–95). Later acquired by a corporation headed by Capper were the *Ohio Farmer*, *Michigan Farmer*, and *Pennsylvania Farmer*. Capper died in 1951. Oscar S. Stauffer bought the original Capper group in 1956.

was half filled with boiler plate, but eventually it became a popular home and farm weekly.

The *Northwestern Agriculturist* (1886–1915) was begun in Jamestown, North Dakota, but soon moved to Minneapolis, where it flourished as a semimonthly at fifty cents a year. In that city also was *Farm Stock and Home* (1884–1929), a semimonthly vigorously edited by Sidney M. Owne, who was the Populist candidate for governor of Minnesota in 1890. A good farm home monthly was the *Farmer's Wife* (1900–1939), founded at Winona, Minnesota, and moved after a few years to St. Paul, where it built up a large circulation at twenty-five cents a year.

In the South were the *Southern Ruralist* (1893–1930), of Atlanta, eventually absorbed by the *Progressive Farmer* (1886–current), of Birmingham; the *National Farmer and Stockgrower* (1899–1926), of Louisville; *Farming* (1902–1926), of Knoxville; and the *Arkansas Farmer* (1899–current), of Little Rock.

Denver had *Field and Farm* (1885–1920) and *Western Farm Life* (1899–current). Spokane had the *Washington, Idaho and Oregon Farmer* (1899–1926) and *Ranch* (1895–current).[17] *Oregon Farmer* (1891–current), of Portland, began as *Rural Northwest*. The *Western Empire* (1898–1924), of Los Angeles, ended life as *California Farmer*.

Many of the state agricultural colleges issued monthlies during the school year, usually student-edited.[18]

### HORTICULTURE AND FLORICULTURE

Though garden magazines were plentiful in the nineties, and the appearance of gardening departments in many more general periodicals attests the popularity of home cultivation of flowers and vegetables, the mortality rate for periodicals in the horticulture field sems to have been unusually high. A number of these, like *Popular Gardening* (1885–1891), of Buffalo, found refuge in the broad bosom of the older *American Garden*,[19] which was itself absorbed, in 1904, by the *Western Fruit-Grower* (1897–1917), of St. Joseph, Missouri. And the *Fruit-Grower* was eventually merged in the *American Fruit Grower* (1883–current), of Chicago, which had begun as *Fruit-Grower's Journal* at Cobden, Illinois.

[17] The former became *Western Farmer* in 1907; and the latter took its present title, *Washington Farmer*, in 1929.

[18] Among them were *Nature Guard* (1899–1914), Rhode Island College of Agriculture; *Penn State Farmer* (1898–current), Pennsylvania State College; *Cornell Countryman* (1903–current), New York State College of Agriculture; *Agricultural Student* (1894–current), Ohio State University; *Illinois Agriculturist* (1897–current), University Agricultural Club; *Iowa Agriculturist* (1902–current), Iowa State College.

[19] See F. L. Mott, *A History of American Magazines* (Cambridge, 1938), v. 3, p. 161. For a table showing consolidations, see *Library Journal*, v. 21, p. 318, July 1896.

Another attractive Chicago magazine in this field was *Gardening* (1892–1925). A sound and well-illustrated magazine at the end of our period was *Horticulture* (1904–current), of Boston, which was the organ of the horticultural societies of Massachusetts, New York, and Pennsylvania. The *California Fruit Grower* (1888–current) was a San Francisco paper.

Though *Park's Floral Magazine* (1871–1925), of Livonia, Pennsylvania, led the flower journals in circulation through most of the nineties, it was generally thought that *Vick's Illustrated Monthly* (1878–1909) was of a higher class. Both originated with seed houses, though by 1900 *Vick's* was claiming to be "unconnected with any seed house or nursery."

Another prominent floral magazine was the *Mayflower* (1885–1906), which claimed three hundred thousand circulation through most of the nineties. It was edited by John Lewis Childs, the seedman of Floral Park, New York, and had some well-known contributors. It specialized in plants and gardening in foreign countries and little-known regions, and printed articles by Henry M. Stanley and George Kennan. It carried a chromolithograph in each number for a long time.

A distinguished floral magazine was *Meehan's Monthly* (1891–1902), of Philadelphia. Thomas Meehan was a nurseryman and a botanist of reputation; he had conducted the *Gardener's Monthly* (1859–1888) and the new periodical bearing his name was an improved version of the older one, dealing with wild flowers, botany, general gardening, and horticulture. It featured chromos by Prang, and engravings on steel and wood. The founder died in 1901 and the magazine was sold soon thereafter, to be continued a few years at Springfield, Ohio, as *Floral Life* (1903–1908).

There were many other flower and fruit journals.[20]

FORESTRY JOURNALS

*Garden and Forest* (1888–1898) was a modest but high-grade Boston weekly consisting of twelve or sixteen pages without illustrations and edited by Charles S. Sargent, director of the Arnold Arboretum.

*American Forests* was begun in January 1895 by John Clayton Gifford, who had just been appointed forester of the New Jersey Geological Survey. Its first title was *New Jersey Forester*, but it was to undergo

[20] *Success with Flowers* (1890–1904), West Grove, Pa., was a small but very practical magazine. It was merged into *Home and Flowers* (1896–1906), Springfield, Ohio, which had begun as *How to Grow Flowers* and was finally absorbed by *Kirk's*. Another practical guide was *Rose Technic* (1891–current), Terre Haute, Ind. More distinctively trade journals were *American Florist* (1885–1931), Chicago, New York; *Florists' Exchange* (1888–current), New York; and *Florists' Review* (1897–current), Chicago. The *Fruit Trade Journal and Produce Record* (1888–1933), New York, was the organ of the National League of Commis-

many changes of name in its first thirty-five years.[21] At first a small monthly of twelve pages at seventy-five cents a year, it gradually increased in size and in 1898 was taken over by the American Forestry Association, moved to Washington, D.C., enlarged and improved, placed under the care of an editorial committee, and priced at two dollars. Its appeal is popular as well as professional, while other journals in the field are more specialized.[22]

HORSE PERIODICALS

Periodicals dealing with the horse are divided rather sharply between those that deal with racing directly and those that are designed for horse breeders and trainers. Most cities had race-track papers,[23] though the older "turf guides" gave way in the mid-nineties to the more statistical "racing forms."[24] Another tendency of the times was the specialization of the older stock-raising journals to serve various classes, and even breeds, of animals. For example, although Judge P. P. Johnston was president of the National Trotting Horse Association, he kept his *Kentucky Stock Farm* a general livestock journal as long as he owned it; but when Samuel G. Boyle bought it in 1888, he made it a trotting horse journal exclusively. *Horse Review* (1889–1932), of Chicago, was also devoted to the light-harness horse. *Horse Show Monthly* (1893–1906), of St. Louis, was, as its name indicates, also a specialist.

The *Horse World* (1889–1920), of Buffalo, was broader in scope, as was the *Northwestern Horseman and Stockman* (1890–1904), of Minneapolis.

DAIRY JOURNALS

Several dairy journals begun in earlier periods continued through the one now under consideration,[25] but the larger circulations belonged to some that began in the nineties, such as the *Practical Dairyman* (1892–1900), of Indianapolis; and the Chicago *Dairy and Creamery* (1898–

---

sion Merchants. *Fruitman and Gardener* (1898–1919) was a modest monthly published at Mt. Vernon, Iowa.

[21] It became *Forester*, 1895; *Forestry and Irrigation*, 1902; *Conservation*, 1909; *American Forestry*, 1910; *American Forests and Forest Life*, 1924; *American Forests*, 1929.

[22] The *Forestry Quarterly* (1902–current), also of Washington, has consisted from the beginning chiefly of technical papers and proceedings of the Society of American Foresters. It adopted the new title *Journal of Forestry* in 1917. The *National Nurseryman* (1893–1939), of Hatboro, Pennsylvania, was the organ of the American Association of Nurserymen. It was eventually merged in the *American Nurseryman* (1904–current), of Rochester, New York, now Chicago. *Modern Cemetery* (1891–current), of Chicago, was mainly devoted to landscape gardening.

[23] For a survey of these papers in 1894, see Oscar Herzberg in *Printer's Ink*, v. 11, p. 867, Nov. 14, 1894.

[24] *Printer's Ink*, v. 13, p. 15, July 24, 1895.

[25] See Mott, *op. cit.*, v. 3, p. 160.

1904). Some creamery and cheese journals are mentioned in this volume in another connection.[26]

When William Dempster Hoard established his weekly newspaper, the *Jefferson County Union*, at Ft. Atkinson, Wisconsin, in 1870, he began a dairy department. Active as a speaker and organizer, Hoard became president of the National Dairy Union and a strong advocate of certain reforms in farming, feeding, shipping, and dairying. He made *Hoard's Dairyman* an independent paper in 1885, and it soon gained a position of leadership in the field. Hoard was governor of Wisconsin during 1889–1891.[27]

There were many local and regional dairy papers, most of which had comparatively short lives and small circulations.[28]

### HOG AND SHEEP JOURNALS

The *American Swineherd* (1884–1929) had a circulation of forty or fifty thousand in the nineties, making it first in its class. Most of the periodicals given over to swine-breeding were specialists, such as the *American Yorkshire Record* (1901–1915), of St. Paul, and the *Duroc Bulletin and Live-Stock Farmer* (1904–1931), of Des Moines.

*Wool Markets and Sheep* (1891–1909), of Chicago, latterly called *Shepherd's Criterion*, was eventually merged in the older *American Sheep-Breeder*.

The *Breeder's Gazette*, perhaps the country's greatest general live-stock weekly in this period, was managed mainly by Alvin H. Sanders, with the assistance of some brilliant writers.[29] The great livestock market papers were dailies, led by the Neff group of Corn Belt Farm Dailies in Chicago, Kansas City, Omaha, and St. Louis.

### BIRDS AND BEES

There was a remarkable spate of poultry magazines in the nineties, most of which had circulations of less than five thousand, and many under a thousand. Advertisers of setting eggs and poultry feeds and appliances kept these smaller journals alive.

[26] See p. 186, footnote.

[27] G. W. Rankin, *The Life of William Dempster Hoard* (Ft. Atkinson, 1925); *Hoard's Dairyman*, v. 81, p. 491, Oct. 10, 1936; *ibid.*, v. 80, pp. 28ff, Jan. 25, 1935 (historical articles); Ogilvie, *Pioneer Agricultural Journalists*, pp. 45–56.

[28] The more important ones were *Chicago Dairy Produce* (1894–1943); [Fred L.] *Kimball's Dairy Farmer* (1903–1929), Waterloo, Iowa, eventually taken over by the Meredith Publishing Company; *Dairy Record* (1900–current), St. Paul; *Northwest Dairyman and Farmer* (1887–1932), Seattle; and *Pacific Dairy Review* (1901–current). The *Holstein-Friesian Register* (1886–1928), of Brattleboro, Vt., was merged with the *Holstein-Friesian World* (1904–current), of Syracuse, New York, etc.

[29] See Mott, *op. cit.*, v. 3, p. 159.

One of the larger circulations was enjoyed by *Farm-Poultry* (1889–1916), edited by A. F. Hunter, of Boston, a small semimonthly at a dollar a year. It claimed twenty to thirty thousand subscribers throughout the nineties. The *American Poultry Advocate* (1892–1927) reached that bracket by 1900, but it was a monthly at twenty-five cents a year; it was really a mail-order journal, and sometimes issued as many as fifty quarto pages a month. The *Reliable Poultry Journal* (1894–1933), conducted by Grant M. Curtis, of Quincy, Illinois, was the leader in the circulation race, however, passing forty thousand at the beginning of the new century; it was a fifty-cent monthly. In Waterloo, Iowa, Fred L. Kimball issued his *Egg Reporter* (1893–current), which was much later to become the *U. S. Egg and Poultry Magazine*, of Chicago. These are only a few of the periodicals in this field.[30]

The pigeon journals were of two kinds — those devoted mainly to homing pigeons, and those aimed at the interests of those who were feeding the birds for the produce market. In the former class were the *Homing Exchange* (1885–current), of Norristown, Pennsylvania;[31] and *Pigeon Flying* (1893–1914), of Philadelphia, the organ of the National Association of Homing Pigeon Fanciers. In the other class were *Pigeon News* (1895–current), of Medford, Massachusetts; and *American Pigeon Keeper* (1898–1940), of Peoria and Chicago.

The two veterans in the aviculture field were still the leaders in the nineties — the *American Bee Journal* and *Gleanings in Bee Culture*.[32] A newcomer was the *Bee-Keepers' Review* (1888–current), which was started by W. Z. Hutchinson in his own home near Flint, Michigan, with only fifty subscribers, lived to become the organ of the National Beekeepers' Association, and later changed title to *Beekeepers' Magazine*, in Lansing. Two others of some importance were the *Nebraska Bee-Keeper* (1890–1910), of York, later moved to St. Joseph, Missouri, and entitled *Modern Farmer and Busy Bee*; and the *Progressive Bee-Keeper*, of Higginsville, Missouri.

[30] Others may be mentioned: *Everybody's Poultry Magazine* (1897–current), Hanover, Pa.; *Michigan Poultry Breeder* (1885–1932), Battle Creek, called *Modern Poultry Breeder* after 1908; *Pacific Fanciers' Monthly* (1885–1938), which began as *California Cackler* at Oakland and underwent many changes of title and place of publication, and was finally combined with *Pacific Poultrycraft* (1895–1939), Los Angeles, to perish the next year; *Pacific Poultryman* (1896–current), Seattle, Palo Alto; *Petaluma* [Calif.] *Poultry Journal* (1895–1929); *Poultry* (1904–16), Kalamazoo, Mich., etc.; *Poultry Culture* (1897–1920), Kansas City; *Poultry Herald* (1888–current), St. Paul; *Poultry Item* (1893–1941), Sellersville, Pa.; *Poultry Success* (1889–1934), Springfield, Ohio; *Poultry Tribune* (1895–current), Freeport, Mt. Morris, Ill.; *Western Poultry Journal* (1888–current), Cedar Rapids, Waverly, Iowa, called *Plymouth Rock Monthly* since 1924.
[31] Called *American Racing Pigeon News* since 1911.
[32] *American Bee Journal*, v. 75, pp. 442–43, Sept. 1935.

# CHAPTER XX

## LAW, BANKING, AND INSURANCE

**M**AGAZINES directed many criticisms at the legal profession at the end of the nineteenth century, but most such strictures were casual rather than studied. The low level of education of lawyers, the common disregard of professional ethics, and the slowness of the courts were objects of animadversion. The editor of the *Century* believed that the law's delays were largely responsible for outbreaks of "lynch law."[1] David Starr Jordan, speaking to the Association of American Law Schools in 1908, told of how even then "a very large number of schools" had faculties of part-time teachers who were judges and practicing attorneys, and "in many law schools thirty years ago a student would read the newspapers and squirt tobacco juice on the floor and pay no particular attention" to the dull lecture that was being read.[2] The law schools professed to require a high-school diploma for admission, but a professor wrote in 1904 that "it is a matter of deep regret that many . . . do not live up to the letter of their professed requirement."[3] In the year of Jordan's address, discussions that had extended over several years resulted in the adoption by the American Bar Association of a Code of Professional Ethics, and the admonition to the law schools that they teach courses based on those canons.

The legal profession was served by an increasing number of journals, many of which were valuable not only for their news of cases and decisions but also for their articles on various phases of the law. There were about thirty legal prediodicals in 1885, and about forty of them twenty years later; but the aggregate circulation in this class increased nearly three and a half times in the twenty years.

In 1885 the largest circulations in this field — in the neighborhood of five thousand — were enjoyed by the *Central Law Journal* and *American Law Review*, of St. Louis; the *Chicago Legal News*; and the *American Law Register*, of Philadelphia.[4] Though all of these except the last kept up their circulations pretty evenly throughout the period, they all fell behind new leaders. These new journals were chiefly case reporters, with some news and commentary. The most important of them had been started in 1879 as the *Syllabi*, a reporter for the northwestern states by

---

[1] *Century Magazine*, v. 37, pp. 632–34, Feb. 1889.
[2] *American Law School Review*, v. 2, 199, Fall 1908.
[3] *Ibid.*, v. 1, p. 176, Spring 1904.
[4] See F. L. Mott, *A History of American Magazines* (Cambridge, 1938), v. 3, p. 144, for notes on these journals.

the West Publishing Company, St. Paul. Other magazines were added to the *Syllabi* (later called *North Western Reporter*), until by 1887 the entire nation was embraced in the "National Reporter System," including seven publications. Later came an eighth for Federal actions and a ninth for Supreme Court decisions. Many other law journals, new and old, were published throughout the country in the nineties.[5]

More general articles, news, and comment, as well as notes of recent decisions, formed the content of another class of legal periodicals. *Case and Comment* (1894–current), a dollar-a-year monthly of Rochester, New York, claimed thirty thousand circulation at the end of our period — greater than that of any other legal periodical. *Law Notes* (1897–1937), long published by Edward Thompson at Northport, New York, had nearly as large a circulation. The *American Lawyer* (1893–1908), of New York, was subtitled "The News-Magazine of the American Bar." *American Legal News* (1899–1925) was a Detroit monthly edited by William C. Sprague, originally called *Collector and Commercial Lawyer*.

The *Green Bag* (1889–1914) was the unique magazine devoted to the lighter side of the law. Its subtitle for its first three years was "A Useless but Entertaining Magazine for Lawyers"; afterward a more inhibited editor deleted the word "Useless." This Boston illustrated monthly printed accounts of *causes célèbres*, anecdotes and facetiae, verse, biographies, and news of law schools. In its later years it lost much of its lightness.[6]

Several of the country's leading law schools began journals in this period, publishing them monthly during the school year. Usually they were edited by students, with more or less faculty direction; students, faculty, alumni, and friends of the school were contributors. The system was a success, and some of these journals gained wide prestige. The *Harvard Law Review* was begun in April 1887 and immediately acquired a notable list of contributors. Sir Frederick Pollock remarked, on the *Review's* semicentennial, that "Hundreds of its pages have been superseded in the most honourable manner by being embodied in books al-

---

[5] Among the older ones, note the *Albany Law Journal* (1870–1908); *New Jersey Law Journal* (1878–current); *Washington Law Reporter* (1874–current); and *Chicago Legal News* (1868–1925). See also Mott, *op. cit.*, v. 2, p. 93; v. 3, pp. 144–45; and Elsie Basset's "List of Anglo-American Legal Periodicals," in Frederick C. Hicks, *Materials and Methods of Legal Research* (Rochester, 2d ed., 1933). Also in Basset, of course, are listed the later journals, the more important of which, in our period, were the *New York State Reporter* (1886–97); the *Montgomery County Law Reporter* (1885–current), covering Philadelphia courts; the *Pennsylvania Justices' Law Reporter* (1902–18); *Virginia Law Register* (1895–1928); *Ohio Legal News* (1894–1902), continued by *Ohio Law Reporter* (1903–34); *Detroit Legal News* (1894–1916); *Kansas City Bar Monthly* (1895–1917); *Nebraska Legal News* (1892–current), and *Oklahoma Law Journal* (1902–16).

[6] Its editors were Horace W. Fuller, 1889–1900; Thomas Tilestone Baldwin, 1901–05; Sidney R. Wrightington, 1906–08; Arthur Spencer, 1909–14. A General Index was published in 1920.

ready classical. Ames's masterly account of the action of assumpsit is the first example that occurs, and not a few of Holmes's essays are there too."[7] Dean Ames's article on trusts in the first number illustrates the *Review's* interest in current economics, politics, and sociology. Its notes, digest, and reviews of books have been outstanding. The *Columbia Jurist* (1885–1887) was supplanted by the *Columbia Law Times* (1887–1893), which was followed in 1901 by the *Columbia Law Review*, a broad and authoritative journal. The *Yale Law Journal* began in 1891 as a quarterly edited and published by students; contributions of faculty members increased as the school came more and more under the care of full-time teachers and scholars.[8] The *Journal* was made a monthly in 1900. In 1897 the old *American Law Register and Review* was taken over by another great law school and titled *University of Pennsylvania Law Review and Law Register*. The *Michigan Law Review* was founded in 1902, with a student editorial board and Professor Floyd R. Mechem as "Manager."[9] These well-established journals at Harvard, Columbia, Yale, Pennsylvania, and Michigan have been designated, with some authority, as "the more important" legal magazines.[10]

The *Intercollegiate Law Journal* (1891–1892) gave way to the *University Law Review* (1893–1897) in New York; but perhaps more important was the *American Law School Review* (1902–1947), published three times a year by the West Publishing Company, St. Paul, as a journal for law teachers and students.

Chief journals specializing in commercial law were the *Banking Law Journal* (1889–current), of New York; and the *Bulletin of the Commercial Law League of America* (1888–current), later called *Commercial Law Journal*, of Chicago. The *Insurance Law Journal* (1871–1938) was chiefly a reporter of decisions in insurance cases. The *Medico-Legal Journal* was a bimonthly of high standing. Many others could be named.[11]

---

[7] *Harvard Law Review*, v. 50, p. 861, April 1937.

[8] *Yale Law Journal*, v. 50, p. 741, April 1941.

[9] Actual control was held by faculty editors until the early 1940's, when students took over the management successfully, with unusually full indexes and digests, as well as outstanding surveys. See E. Blythe Stason, "The *Law Review* — Its First Fifty Years," *Michigan Law Review*, v. 50, pp. 1134–38, June 1952.

[10] E. M. Morgan, "Repositories of the Law," in Hugh E. Willis, *Introduction to Anglo-American Law* (Bloomington, Ind., 1931).

[11] The *Law Bulletin*, published bimonthly (except summer) at the State University of Iowa 1891–1901, and continued as *Iowa Law Bulletin* in 1915 (called *Iowa Law Review* since 1925); *West Virginia Bar* (1894–1917), organ of the state bar association, and since 1917 the *West Virginia Law Quarterly and the Bar*; *Kansas University Lawyer* (1895–1911), after the first two years simply *Kansas Lawyer*; the quarterly *Forum of the Dickinson School of Law* (1897–current), title changing to *Dickinson Law Review* in 1908. *Brief* (1887–1909) was a "legal miscellany" issued by Phi Delta Phi; and the *Law Student's Helper* (1893–1915) was a Detroit monthly.

Perhaps there is no point in separating the banking journals from the more general financial periodicals, but there were some which were directed specifically at bankers as such. Of these, the leaders carried over from an earlier period — the monthly *Bankers' Magazine* and *Rand McNally Bankers' Monthly*, and the weekly *American Banker* and *Banker and Tradesman*.[12] Begun in the present period and continuing in the 1950's were the *Bankers' Encyclopedia*, founded in Chicago in 1895; and *Financial Age*, begun in 1900 chiefly to serve the American Bankers' Association. In addition to these and some ambitious journals of shorter life, there were a number of regional, state, and city banking-and-investment periodicals.[13]

The old *Commercial and Financial Chronicle*, with its full reports, added several monthly and quarterly supplements in the nineties. *Bradstreet's* continued as an authoritative weekly of sixteen quarto pages. The *Merchants' Review* was also a weekly, smaller and cheaper.[14]

A newcomer of 1893 was *Dun's Review*, a small and cheaply printed weekly established by Robert Graham Dun as the organ of his credit agency. The "Story of the Week" in its initial number began with a record of financial disaster. It was not long, however, before the modest weekly improved in appearance, size, and prestige, becoming one of the leaders among the financial journals. The *Financial World* (1902–current), a weekly founded by Otto Guenther in New York, emphasized trends in the markets, stock investment, and so on. A third New York periodical in this field was the *Bulletin of the National Association of Credit Men* (1899–current), which was later to develop along broader lines. In Pittsburgh was *Money* (1902–current); and in Cleveland, *Finance* (1900–1934).[15] All the financial journals gave more or less attention to the stock market and the brokerage business, and some were investment specialists.[16] Most large cities had their own periodicals in

[12] See Mott, *op. cit.*, v. 2, pp. 94–95, and v. 3, p. 147, for the first three. The *Banker and Tradesman* was founded in 1872 in Boston, and later moved to Cambridge.

[13] For example, *Southern Banker* (1904–current), Atlanta; *Northwestern Banker* (1895–current), Des Moines, Iowa; *Pacific Banker* (1902–current), Portland, later *Banker and Business*, Seattle; *Pittsburgh Banker* (1889–1913), various titles; *Michigan Banker* (1904–31), Detroit; *Chicago Banker* (1899–1942); *Banking and Mercantile World* (1897–1918), various titles, but primarily an illustrated local booster journal for Chicago; *California Banker's Magazine* (1890–98), San Francisco.

[14] For these periodicals, see Mott, *op. cit.*, v. 3, p. 147.

[15] The Credit Men's journal was called *Credit Monthly* 1920–31, and after that *Credit and Financial Management*. *Money* became *Money and Commerce* in 1914, and *Finance* changed title to *Finance and Industry* in 1918.

[16] Examples begun in this period were as follows: *United States Investor* (1891–current), Boston; *Bond Buyer* (1892–current), New York; *Bonds and Mortgages* (1895–1922), Chicago; *Knowledge* (1903–17), organ of American Brokers' Association, called *Business and*

this field, some of which represented chambers of commerce, some other organizations, and some the brokerage business in general.[17]

INSURANCE JOURNALS

In a factual and incisive article on the insurance press in 1900, *Printer's Ink* made the following statements:

> There are seventy-five insurance journals, and the number is increasing. In the last two and a half years half a dozen have been started. Every big town has one or more, while New York has twenty. . . . The insurance press is supported by the companies. Very few "lay" advertisements are inserted. Nearly all the papers attempt to cover the entire field of life, fire, and casualty insurance . . . . There are not more than half a dozen which circulate more than twenty-five hundred copies . . . the great bulk have less than five hundred. . . . There are a few journals which are run with a club, and they find it easy to blackmail life companies. . . . Companies are beginning to look upon insurance journalism as a heavy burden on the business. . . . They say there are too many insurance papers.[18]

This tells the story very well, except for omitting the fact that there were some excellent journals in the field.[19]

Perhaps most widely recognized were two or three New York periodicals; most of the others were sectional, despite the occasional use of the words "National" and "American" in titles. Oldest of all was the *Insurance Monitor*, edited at the time of its fiftieth anniversary (1903) by Walter S. Nichols, a recognized expert in the field. The *Spectator*, edited by Clifford Thompson, also enjoyed high standing. *Insurance* was notable for the crusading editorials of Samuel Harrison Davis, who died in 1903. Outstanding among the New York insurance journals begun in the nineties were Patrick J. Hanway's monthly *Vigilant* (1893–1923) and Franklin Webster's *Insurance Press* (1895–1926); the latter was eventually consolidated with one of the veterans, the *Weekly Underwriter*.[20]

---

*Finance* in 1909–17; *Oil Investor's Journal* (1902–current), Tulsa, Okla., called *Oil and Gas Journal* since 1910.

[17] Some of the more interesting or important ones: *Commercial America* (1904–current), organ of Philadelphia Commercial Museum; *Financial Review* (1896–1920), Cleveland; *Michigan Investor* (1903–current), Detroit; *Chicago Commerce* (1904–current), organ of Chicago Association of Commerce; *Clearing House Quarterly* (1895–current), Minneapolis; *Economist* (1888–current), really a Chicago newspaper, eventually becoming daily as *Journal of Commerce*; *Commerce Monthly* (1904–current), St. Louis, changing title in 1913 to *Mid-Continent Banker*; *Financial Bulletin* (1897–1908), Denver; *Commercial Review* (1889–current), Portland, Ore.

[18] *Printer's Ink*, v. 30, Feb. 28, 1900, pp. 3–4.

[19] The best list is in Marion V. Patch, "American Insurance Journals Before 1900" (Columbia University thesis, 1930). For the older journals named in the next paragraph, see Mott, *op. cit.*, v. 2, p. 94, footnote; v. 3, pp. 145–46.

[20] Other long-lived New York insurance journals: *Insurance Advocate* (1890–current),

But not all sections looked to New York insurance papers for leadership, and important periodicals in this field flourished in nearly all regions.[21]

A surprising number of periodicals were published in this period to serve business office workers — stenographers, typists, bookkeepers, filing clerks, accountants, managers, and so on. A large proportion of these were ill-judged ventures of short life, but several lived to become important magazines.

*Business* (1886–1910) was a successful monthly devoted to accounting and office management and edited by A. O. Kittredge. It was called *Office* during its first six years, and *Business World* after 1901. *Book-Keeper* (1888–1915) was a Detroit monthly that swore to a circulation

---

which began as *Echo*, changing title in 1893; *Surveyor* (1892–1917), subtitled "The Insurance Salesman's Weekly," but soon fortnightly; *Interview* (1893–1909), another fortnightly; *Thrift* (1894–1920), Edward Bunnell Phelps's magazine, which changed title to *American Underwriter* in 1902; *Insurance Observer* (1895–1935), founded by W. A. Thomas as a monthly, later a fortnightly; *Assurance* (1896–1912), called *Accident Assurance* until 1903, when William De Matoos Hooper, proprietor, formed a partnership with the poet and insurance agent William E. Underwood, and broadened the journal's scope; *Eastern Underwriter* (1899–current), founded as *Monthly Journal of Insurance Economics* in Boston, but changing to present name in 1904, with the subtitle "A Weekly Newspaper Covering All Branches of Insurance" in New York; *Best's Insurance News* (1899–current), begun as a fire and marine insurance journal, later developing separate editions for life, fire, and casualty, which supplanted the original edition in 1938; *Insurance Engineering* (1901–current), later becoming *Safety Engineering*, then *Safety Maintenance*, etc.; *American Agency Bulletin* (1903–current), organ of the Associated Fire Insurance Agents of the United States. At Rochester, N. Y., the *Fraternal Monitor* (1890–current) was one of few specialized insurance journals.

[21] Henry Worthington Smith's *Insurance Register* (1895–1924) had been started in New York but was soon moved to Philadelphia. *Views* (1889–1921) was a Washington monthly. *Insurance Herald* (1888–1929) was edited by Young E. Allison in Louisville through the nineties; it was later moved to Atlanta, absorbed the Chicago *Argus* (1871–1913) and the Atlanta *Southeastern Underwriter* (1890–1916) and became *Southern Underwriter*. After Allison disposed of the *Herald*, he edited the Louisville *Insurance Field* (1899–1909), a strong paper with two editions. The *Independent*, though born in New York, was a Chicago life insurance monthly nearly all its life. There it was a competitor of the older *Investigator*, the bold Charles A. Hewitt's *Insurance Post* (1892–1941), A. J. Flitcraft's prosperous *Life Insurance Courant* (1895–current), and *Western Underwriter* (1897–current). This last began in Cincinnati by E. J. Wohlgemuth as *Ohio Underwriter*, changed title two years later to *Western Underwriter* and moved to Chicago, where it became *National Underwriter* in 1917. It absorbed *Black and White* (1890–99) and has for some time published separate life and fire-casualty editions. The Detroit *Indicator* (1882–1932) claimed a circulation of 10,000 in 1900 — then the biggest in the field. Other midwesterners were: *Insurance Magazine* (1891–current), Kansas City; *American Insurance Journal* (1894–current), Columbus, Ohio, organ of the American Insurance Union; *Underwriters' Review* (1893–current), Des Moines; *Western Economist* (1895–current), Des Moines, which has been published in Cedar Rapids, Iowa, since 1925 under the title *Fraternal Friend*. In Denver there was the *Insurance Report* (1897–1931). In San Francisco the oldest insurance journal was the *Pacific Underwriter and Banker* (1887–1931); but the most successful one was the *Adjuster* (1891–1928), edited by J. A. Carey, a good writer, and president of the San Francisco Press Club in the nineties. The Denver *Insurance Report* and the *Pacific Underwriter and Banker* were merged in 1931 as *Western Underwriter*, San Francisco. The San Francisco *Insurance Sun* (1892–1905) was a monthly edited by Clara H. Case.

at the turn of the century of fifty thousand.[22] *System* (1900–1929) was a monthly published by A. W. Shaw, of Chicago, chiefly for bookkeepers and filing clerks, though it later broadened its scope to business and trade topics in general. Its inspirational editorials were famous.[23]

Many periodicals devoted to shorthand and typing were published by proprietors of stenographic systems, schools of commercial methods, and typewriter companies. The *New York Sun* was able to count sixteen such journals in course of publication in 1894.[24] Best of them all in the nineties was the *Phonographic World* (1886–1929), edited in that decade by E. N. Miner, a clever journalist.[25] The *National Stenographer* (1890–1900) was a Chicago monthly. Shorthand systems issued the *Munson Phonographic News and Teacher* (1876–1898), the *Gregg Writer* (1899–current), and *Pitman's Journal* (1804–current), all of New York.[26] The *Typewriter Trade Journal* (1904–current), which soon became *Office Appliances*, has been a Chicago periodical.

---

[22] It changed title frequently after 1903; it was *Business Man's Magazine* during 1905–08. E. H. Beach was its conductor.

[23] It changed title in 1927 to *Magazine of Business*. It was purchased by McGraw-Hill in 1929 and moved to New York, to be supplanted later that year by *Business Week*. Its numbering was taken over by the new *System* (1928–35), New York. See *Bulletin of Bibliography*, v. 14, p. 24, May–Aug. 1930.

[24] The *Phonographic World* had many variations in title and ended life (1923–29) as *Journal of Commercial Education*.

[25] Quoted in *Printer's Ink*, v. 11, Dec. 5, 1894, p. 32.

[26] The *Gregg Writer* is now called *Today's Secretary*. For some of the older shorthand journals which continued in this period, see Mott, *op. cit.*, v. 3, pp. 169–70. *Penman Artist and Business Educator* (1895–current), of Columbus, Ohio, has been *Educator* since 1931.

# CHAPTER XXI

## WOMEN'S ACTIVITIES

"THE Era of Women has dawned," declaimed Editor Flower in the *Arena* in 1891, "bearing the unmistakable prophecy of a far higher civilization than humanity has ever known before."[1] Just what this typically Flowerian statement means in realistic terms is hard to say, but the idea seems to be that women were suddenly more prominent in work outside the home, in public life, and in the world of letters than ever before; and that it was hoped that such participation might have a favorable effect on civilization.

The part that magazines played in this emergence of woman was undoubtedly important, though sometimes ambiguous. For a long time there had been what used to be called "a preponderance of female names" on subscription lists,[2] and that disproportion probably increased in the latter eighties. *Woman's Column* quoted Edward Bok as saying in 1890 that "an examination of subscription lists of magazines" showed seven-eighths of the subscribers to be women[3] — an almost incredible figure even when we realize how many of the big-circulation periodicals were among those designed for women and the home. Such a situation might be expected to result in a feminization of magazine content; the periodicals of the nineties, however, were rather definitely virile. The veteran magazinist Oliver Bunce noted this apparent contradiction as early as 1889, and suggested a double hypothesis in the *Critic*: "Has feminine taste undergone a revolution, or have men taken a dominant place among readers?"[4]

The change was in "feminine taste," of course. The new woman found the more scientific, more realistic, more newspaperish new magazine fitted to her needs. Mrs. Belva A. Lockwood, writing in the midst of her second campaign for President of the United States as the candidate of the Equal Rights Party, told in the *Cosmopolitan* of the various educational stimuli that had brought about the new era for women; and one of them was that afforded by the magazines.[5] The emancipated woman wanted to read about the world she now lived and worked in.

---

[1] *Arena*, v. 4, p. 382, Aug. 1891.
[2] See F. L. Mott, *History of American Magazines* (Cambridge, 1938), v. 3, p. 90.
[3] *Woman's Column*, v. 3, Feb. 4, 1890, p. 4.
[4] *Critic*, v. 13, p. 68, Aug. 10, 1889.
[5] *Cosmopolitan*, v. 5, p. 467, Oct. 1888.

WOMAN'S RIGHT TO WORK

It was in the lively pages of the *Cosmopolitan* a decade later that the novelist Olive Schreiner insisted that woman's chief demand was to work and to prepare for work. "This is our Woman's Right," she said.[6] Another popular and brilliant writer on social questions of the times, Robert Grant, agreed in *Scribner's* that, though the vote would come eventually, it could well wait while woman proved that she could "strike out for herself" in many fields of work. "In spite of ridicule, baiting and delay for several generations, she has demonstrated her ability and fitness to do a number of things which we had adjudged her incapable of doing," wrote Grant.[7] And Mary A. Livermore, long a campaigner for the franchise, admitted in the *Bostonian* that, "under cover of the fire for woman's enfranchisement, the door of one opportunity after another has been opened to women, until at the present time they are found in almost every department of the world's work." [8] The right of married women to work was argued in the *North American Review*,[9] and the *Forum* carried a debate on whether women were fairly paid at about half the wages received by men.[10]

An article about women in magazine work in the *Journalist* in 1898 named seven periodicals wholly edited by women, and estimated that four thousand women were engaged in various capacities in New York journalism alone.[11]

The leading periodical for women workers in the business field in the nineties was the *Business Woman's Journal* (1889–1896), founded and conducted until her death in 1893 by Mary F. Seymour, director of a school of secretarial work. In addition to its articles on women in business, it had departments dealing with women's sports, the home, and so on. It gave both sides of "the great social question of woman suffrage." It was "owned, edited and managed by a stock company consisting entirely of women." [12] An amazing number of journals devoted to home training in stenography and office practices sprang up in the nineties.[13] *Far and Near* (1890–1894) was at first conducted by the Association of

[6] *Cosmopolitan*, v. 28, p. 54, Nov. 1899.
[7] *Scribner's Magazine*, v. 18, p. 472, Oct. 1895.
[8] *Bostonian*, v. 1, p. 82, Oct. 1894. Also see *20th Century Monthly*, v. 8, pp. 6–7, Jan. 1897.
[9] *North American Review*, v. 157, p. 451, Oct. 1893.
[10] *Forum*, v. 2, pp. 201–11, Oct. 1886.
[11] *Journalist*, v. 23, p. 9, April 23, 1898.
[12] See *Journalist*, May 21, 1892. The publisher after Miss Seymour's death was Mrs. R. von Horrum Schramm, with Mrs. Helen Kendrick Johnson as editor. The name became *American Woman's Journal — Business Woman's Journal* in 1891, *American Woman's Magazine and Business Journal* in 1895, *American Woman's Magazine* in 1896, and finally *American Magazine*.
[13] See p. 352. The *Business Woman's Magazine* (1903–10) was published in Denver, merging with *Modern World* in 1906. The women employees of the National Cash Register Company, Dayton, Ohio, issued *Woman's Welfare* during 1902–04.

Working Girls' Societies of New York, and later by the National League of Women Workers. Later the League was represented by the *Club Worker* (1899–1921), of which Jean Hamilton was editor from 1902 to 1920.

## VOTES FOR WOMEN

However, as Mrs. Livermore and the others argued, all this emphasis on emancipation from the home carried with it no abandonment of the long fight for the ballot. "Most questions and issues have their seasons," wrote Bishop Doane in the *North American*, "but the issue and question of woman suffrage, like death, seems to have 'all seasons for its own.'"[14] "It would seem that every argument on both sides had been torn to tatters, to very rags, yet the interest flags not," wrote Josephine Henderson in a symposium on the subject in the *Chautauquan*.[15] There was, for example, the standard argument against the vote for women which we find reiterated in *Fetter's Southern Magazine*: "Most of the women do not want it, and all of them are better off without it." But the editor adds: "All that cannot stop the movement."[16] We find the same argument in a remarkable full-page editorial by Editor Bok in his *Ladies' Home Journal*, which began: "From my earliest years I have ever believed in woman. That belief was instilled into me by my mother." It went on to flout the idea that "women of good judgment and refined feelings" wanted to vote, and argued that woman reigned over the land as queen "by her own birthright — womanly, gentle, loving and true."[17] Leading women's voices were heard in most of the important reviews and magazines in behalf of the franchise for their sex; and the journals for the home or the office edited mainly for women were prone to give space to the controversy at the time of a great political campaign — for example, when the *American Woman's Journal* featured J. Ellen Foster and her Woman's Republican Association in the fall of 1892.[18]

Chief woman suffrage periodicals were Mrs. Colby's *Woman's Tribune*, moved to Washington in 1889, and two organs of the American Woman Suffrage Association, published in Boston and conducted by the Blackwells — the veteran *Woman's Journal*, edited with distinction by Lucy Stone and Henry B. Blackwell until the former's death in 1893; and the *Woman's Column* (1888–1904), a cheaper and rather diverting propagandic paper edited by Alice Stone Blackwell. On Lucy Stone's death, the daughter became coeditor with her father of the *Woman's*

---

[14] *North American Review*, v. 163, p. 536, Nov. 1896.
[15] *Chautauquan*, v. 13, p. 76, April 1891.
[16] *Fetter's Southern Magazine*, v. 2, p. 467, June 1893.
[17] *Ladies' Home Journal*, v. 9, Aug. 1892, p. 12.
[18] *American Woman's Journal*, v. 5, pp. 68–69, Nov. 1892.

*Journal*, and thus conducted both periodicals. *Progress* (1902–1910) was a western organ of the association, published at Warren, Ohio; and a leading state organization was the *New York Suffrage Newsletter* (1899–1913).

WOMEN'S CLUBS

"Women's clubs are started nowadays for almost every conceivable object, from the meritorious wearing of a short skirt on rainy days to the study of the *Niebelungenlied*," observed *McCall's Magazine* in 1899;[19] and a few years later the *Arena* pointed out that every village had its woman's club, and in the cities there were swarms of them, "in which the same women are apt to be duplicated and reduplicated."[20]

The General Federation of Women's Clubs was formed with a basis of fifty clubs at a celebration of the twenty-first birthday of Sorosis in 1889. By 1892 the number of clubs in the General Federation had doubled, and ten years later there were 3,358, with a quarter of a million members. It was commonly said in the latter nineties that there were a million clubwomen in the country, federated and independent.[21]

The *Woman's Cycle* (1889–1896) was founded as the organ of the federation, but in October 1890 it was absorbed by Marion Harland's handsome and ambitious monthly called *Home-Maker* (1888–1893). Mrs. Harland was then supplanted in the editorship by Mrs. Jane C. Croly ("Jenny June"), who had been the founder of the pioneer association of women's clubs, called Sorosis. But *Home-Maker* was too general a magazine, and it gave way in 1893 to the *New Cycle*, which lasted three years. It was absorbed by *Lotos* (1887–1896), a handsome, well-edited monthly, shortly before that magazine's end. These had been New York journals. For the next few years the federation was served by the *Club Woman* (1897–1904), of Boston, of which Helen M. Winslow was editor. The *Federation Bulletin* (1903–1920) later became the official organ and was moved about according to the secretary's convenience. Meanwhile, there were several local and regional club periodicals, some allied with the General Federation, some with other organizations, and some independent.[22]

[19] *McCall's Magazine*, v. 26, p. 276, March 1899

[20] *Arena*, v. 27, p. 374, April 1902.

[21] See full account of the women's club federation movement in *Godey's Magazine*, v. 131, pp. 575–87, Dec. 1895; abridged in *Review of Reviews*, v. 12, p. 720, Dec. 1895. Cf. *Arena*, v. 6, p. 362, Aug. 1892; *ibid.*, v. 27, p. 374, April 1902; *Scribner's Magazine*, series "The Unquiet Sex," 1897–98.

[22] *Keystone* (1899–1913), Charleston, S.C., a state federation journal; *Club Notes for Club Women* (1902–12), Cleveland; *Courant* (1899–1913), St. Paul, a regional federation journal; *Club Life* (1902–06), San Francisco, a state federation journal; *Eleanor Kirk's Idea* (1892–1905), New York, an independent woman's paper by Eleanor Kirk Ames; *Practical Ideals* (1900–12), Boston, organ of Women's International League of Right Thinking and

### EDUCATION FOR WOMEN

The adult education movement and Chautauqua and other reading circles are treated in Chapter XV, but note may be made here of the growth of college education for women. A statistical article in the *Saturday Evening Post* at the turn of the century pointed out the indications that the women's colleges were sure to "wane in the future through the increased power and prestige of collegiate coeducation"; already four out of five women in college were enrolled in the coeducational institutions.[23]

It was repeatedly said that girls went to college to prepare themselves for jobs outside the home — especially teaching — and also sometimes to find husbands. But such a popular social philosopher as Robert Grant was inclined to stress the fact that the new education for women came as the result of a change in the mores: "For centuries the women of civilization have worshiped chastity, suffering resignation, and elegance as the ideals of femininity; now we mean them to be intelligent besides, or at least as nearly so as possible." Therefore he advocates that "the choicest girls" shall be "educated to be the intellectual companions of men . . . instead of being limited to the rose garden or the harem."[24] There was much satire, however, on the modern intellectual young lady, who read Ibsen and discussed art and politics with equal facility. "She never plucks daisies and buttercups nowadays and pulls them apart to test her lover's affection for her. You find her instead arranging orchids in a glass and making cynical reflections." Thus, with bitter nostalgia for the lost age of innocence, the editorial essayist of *Scribner's* brooded over the modernism of the nineties.[25] Edward Bok, editor of the *Ladies' Home Journal*, was against "improvements" in the education of girls. "Conditions for training daughters have not changed in the past twenty-five years," he wrote in 1894.[26]

Another kind of education was pointed out in the *Cosmopolitan*: "The summer resort is the great school that is educating the country into accepting the same social standard and customs"; and this writer of 1895 claimed that two million people spent some time at a resort each summer.[27] And the big parties that were the fashion in the New York "sea-

Right Living; *Gulf Messenger* (1888–98), founded in Houston by Laura E. Foute as *Ladies' Messenger*, published in San Antonio 1891–96, edited by Sara Harman after Mrs. Foute's death in 1893.

[23] *Saturday Evening Post*, v. 172, p. 334, Oct. 28, 1899. See, however, a good review of the leading women's colleges in *Bachelor of Arts*, v. 1, pp. 172ff, Nov. 1895.

[24] "Education," in Grant's suggestive series, "The Art of Living," *Scribner's Magazine*, v. 17, p. 496, April 1895.

[25] *Scribner's Magazine*, v. 10, p. 528, Oct. 1891.

[26] *Ladies' Home Journal*, v. 11, Jan. 1894, p. 12.

[27] *Cosmopolitan*, v. 19, p. 316, July 1895.

son" drew the following heartfelt comment from the *Citizen* editor: "What a farce it is! — this gathering of five or six hundred people who go reluctantly and come away gladly, and of whom not more than one-fifth have any enjoyment of the large expenditure of money, time and health required." [28] The scandalous *Town Topics* put it in rhyme:

> Though wicked we may seem to be
> And drink champagne, preferring tea;
> Though we may pass the vulgar jest,
> 'Tis 'cause the fashion says 'tis best:
> It is the mode to be risqué —
> Pour avoir l'air, Ohé! Ohé!
>
> Corseted to the bursting point,
> With unguents nightly we anoint;
> List to the opera they call grand
> We neither like nor understand;
> At erudition then we play —
> Pour avoir l'air, Ohé! Ohé! [29]

### FASHIONS IN DRESS

The dress reformers had much to say about tight corsets, heavy pleating, multiple tight bands, and long skirts. Said Frances E. Willard in the *American Woman's Journal*: "The amount of force exerted at this moment to compress the waists of women by artificial methods would, if aggregated, turn all the mills between Minneapolis and the Merrimac." [30] The *Arena*, which devoted much space to dress reform, claimed that "women have actually died of pleating." [31] The *Arena* devised a reformed dress which it tried to popularize. So did the *Ladies'* (later *Woman's*) *Home Companion*, which believed that "for most of our ill health our clothing is responsible." The recommended costume minimized garters and bands and included divided skirts. "Ah, well," concluded the writer, "I fear my suggestions, like so much other good advice, will go unheeded." [32]

However, the *Business Woman's Journal* believed that the dress reformers were producing results by 1892: "The bathing dress, the tennis suit, the mountain costume, the gym-blouse, and the divided skirt have given a brief experience of untrammeled exercise" and increased discontent with tight waists and heavy, trailing skirts.[33] There was one

[28] *Citizen*, v. 1, p. 151, Feb. 21, 1885.
[29] *Town Topics*, v. 41, Jan. 19, 1899, p. 3.
[30] *American Woman's Journal*, v. 5, p. 16, Oct. 1892.
[31] *Arena*, v. 3, p. 353, Feb. 1891.
[32] *Ladies' Home Companion*, v. 18, Oct. 1, 1891, p. 3.
[33] *Business Woman's Journal*, v. 4, p. 38, Jan. 1892.

periodical devoted mainly to dress reform — the *Jenness Miller Magazine* (1887–1898), published by the manufacturers of combination underwear for women. Mrs. Miller also published a *Quarterly Journal* (1889–1892). Besides their propaganda and advertising, these periodicals printed some fiction and articles on physical education for girls.

But it took courage to depart from the conventional, for the new "fads" in dress were severely criticized. Bok wrote in the *Ladies' Home Journal* that "the vast and overwhelming majority of women . . . prefer to be womanly, and dress tastefully and prettily, as God intended women should dress." [34] *Life* called attention to Ella Wheeler Wilcox's disapproval of bathing costumes and behavior: "Considering the scarcity of raiment on both men and women, it seems to her that they confabulate more than accords with strict decorum." [35] And this was in 1887, when women were always clothed from head to foot when they went on the beach or into the water. The bicycle did more than the beach for sensible dress. Said a writer in *Puck* in 1892:

> The bicycle makers have accomplished more for dress reform in two years than the preachers of that cult have accomplished since clothes began to be the fashion. Today, thanks to the bicycle, there is every prospect that woman will soon be able to dress sensibly, comfortably, and modestly, all at the same time. [36]

Meantime, some censors were much concerned over the fashion of extreme décolleté in evening dress. *Theatre* complained about such costumes, not on the stage, but in the boxes. [37] But when Elizabeth Stuart Phelps Ward wrote severely of "The Décolleté of Modern Society" in the *Forum*, Robert G. Ingersoll is quoted in *Current Literature* as remarking: "What curious opinions dried apples have of fruit on the tree!" [38]

### THE GREAT JOURNALS FOR WOMEN

Some of the women's magazines were among the most important and successful periodicals published in this period. It was a large and highly competitive field, and in it were some of the top circulations among all American magazines.

The famous old "ladies' books," octavo in size, illustrated by "fashion plates" and partly dependent on literary content, were tottering to their graves. *Godey's*, *Peterson's*, and *Arthur's* all succumbed in 1898, and *Demorest's* the next year. The grand old weekly *Home Journal* was edited until 1900 by Morris Phillips. "It is in the very prime of vigorous

---

[34] *Ladies' Home Journal*, v. 9, Aug. 1892, p. 12.
[35] *Life*, v. 10, p. 114, Sept. 1, 1887.
[36] *Puck*, v. 37, p. 391, Aug. 7, 1895.
[37] *Theatre*, v. 1, p. 1, March 20, 1886.
[38] *Forum*, v. 9, p. 670, Aug. 1890; *Current Literature*, v. 5, p. 478, Dec. 1890.

success," said the *Journalist* in 1890, and added, "Scandal finds no haven in these clean columns."[39] It celebrated its semicentennial in 1896; four years later it changed title to *Town and Country*. Then followed a decade of fumbling, after which this journal became well established as the prosperous organ of the country club set.[40] *Harper's Bazaar*, also a weekly in those days, and a purveyor of literature and fashions, was edited through the nineties by Margaret Sangster. It suffered from the Harper financial crisis at the century's end, and became a monthly in 1901. The Butterick Company's *Delineator* was mainly a fashion monthly until Charles Dwyer became editor in 1894, broadening its literary program.[41]

The type of the new magazine for women in the nineties was set by the *Ladies' Home Journal*, which had made the spectacular success in this field. It is treated separately in this volume, as are the *Woman's Home Companian*, *McCall's*, and *Vogue*. The new type was small-folio in size, highly departmentalized, and personal in tone. Some, like *McCall's* and *Vogue*, placed a much greater emphasis on fashions in the nineties.

*Good Housekeeping* was begun in Holyoke, Massachusetts, in 1885 by Clark W. Bryan, and moved to Springfield the next year. It was very scrapbookish, full of household hints, fashions, cookery, puzzles, poetry, and a little fiction. Helen Campbell edited a notable department on "Woman's Work and Wages." It was well printed and interesting, but it did not reach twenty-five thousand circulation until 1900, and it did not become a great national magazine until it moved to New York in 1911.[42]

The *Ladies' World* (1886–1918) was begun by S. H. Moore & Company in New York at fifty cents a year. It absorbed *Fireside at Home* (1879–1886) with the number for January 1887. These were mail-order journals, but they contained some good material; during the nineties Frances E. Fryatt was editor of the *Ladies' World*, and Eben E. Rexford, Sophie Swett, and Mary A. Denison were regular contributors. By 1905 the magazine had improved in appearance and quality, and had reached nearly a half million in circulation.[43]

---

[39] *Journalist*, v. 11, April 12, 1890, p. 2.

[40] See the good historical treatment in *Town and Country's* centennial number of Dec. 1946.

[41] All the magazines named in this paragraph are treated in separate sketches in earlier volumes of this work.

[42] To be treated in a separate sketch in the next volume of this work.

[43] Myrna Drake Moore was editor 1905–06, Charles Dwyer 1907–13, and Frederick L. Collins 1913–18. In its later years it enlisted such contributors as Alice Brown, Zona Gale, Mary Stewart Cutting, Juliet Wilbor Tompkins, Richard Le Gallienne, and Albert Bigelow Paine. It was purchased by McClure Publications in 1912, and reached a million circulation at 10¢ a copy by 1914. Harrison Fisher did covers for it; May Manton ran the fashion department; and Lewis B. Allyn conducted crusades for pure foods — especially a big fight against alum in baking powders.

*Modern Priscilla* (1887–1930) began at Lynn, Massachusetts, with Mrs. F. Beulah Kellogg and Frank S. Guild as editors. It was a sixteen-page quarto devoted to fancywork, dress patterns, china painting, and so on, at fifty cents a year. In 1894 it was moved to Boston, and eventually it was enlarged in scope, in size, in price, and in circulation.

The *Home Magazine* (1888–1908), though supported by mail-order advertising and issued at the low price of fifty cents a year, was a paper of some distinction throughout the nineties. It was edited at Washington, D.C., by Mrs. John A. Logan, who placed much emphasis on national affairs; it carried, however, the multiple departments common in the household magazines. It was very respectable, except for some of the advertising. Arthur T. Vance was editor from 1896 to 1899, and greatly improved the magazine. He was followed by Francis P. Elliott, formerly of *Harper's*. In 1902 the price was lowered to twenty-five cents; and two years later the paper was sold to P. V. Collins, of Minneapolis, publisher of the *Northwestern Agriculturist*, who allowed it to deteriorate. But it spent the last two years of its life under the ownership of the Bobbs-Merrill Company, Indianapolis, who published it on a higher plane than it had ever before known.[44]

The *Chaperone* (1889–1911) was a St. Louis monthly edited by Annie L. Y. Swart, who later married her publisher, Samuel Orff. It changed its name to *American Woman's Review* in 1904. It was a well-printed and fairly well edited magazine, with good variety of home and literary departments. There were occasional contributions from such magazinists as Ella Wheeler Wilcox, Will N. Harben, and Eben E. Rexford.

The *New Idea Woman's Magazine* (1896–1920) was begun at Brattleboro, Vermont,[45] but moved to New York in 1903. Originally a dress-pattern paper, it was broadened and improved when it came to the big city, under the editorship of Mrs. Marie Mattingly Meloney. Thus it made its try in competition with the big national women's magazines, but it failed and in 1920 was merged with the *Designer*.

The *Puritan* (1897–1901) was one of Frank A. Munsey's unsuccessful ventures. It was founded as a forty-page, slick-paper folio at ten cents, "A Journal for Gentlewomen," lavishly illustrated with portraits and art studies, and very miscellaneous. In the fall of 1898 Munsey bought *Godey's* at a bankrupt sale and merged it with the *Puritan*, which he then reduced to regular magazine size. Juliet Wilbor Tompkins became

[44] Bobbs-Merrill combined it with *Madame*, which Arthur S. Ford had begun in Springfield, Ohio, in 1903; and it fell heir to *Madame's* excellent format and its serial voluming, retaining virtually nothing but its own title. In these two years it had covers by Christy, and serials by Zona Gale, Francis Lynde, Grace Macgowan Cooke, and Eben E. Rexford. It was merged with *Uncle Remus' Magazine*, which continued as *Uncle Remus' Home Magazine*.

[45] It was the successor of the *Woman's Magazine* (1877–90), which Frank E. Housh, publisher, and Esther T. Housh, editor, had also produced at Brattleboro.

editor; and Grace Macgowan Cooke, Rheta Childe Dorr, and Matthew White, Jr., were among the contributors. But it was not a success and was merged with the *Junior Munsey*.

Another *Home Magazine* (1893–1902) began at Syracuse, New York, the organ of the Commercial Travelers Home Association of America, which was the agency promoting a home for retired commercial travelers. But it was an entertaining (though largely eclectic) miscellany, and when it was placed under the editorship of Arthur T. Vance and moved to New York in 1898, it became for a few years a first-class magazine.

The *Pictorial Review* (1899–1939) began as a house organ of Albert McDowell's System of Dressmaking and Tailoring. From the first it was rather smart and clever in its notes on books and the drama; but its literary material seems to have been edited chiefly with scissors and pastepot during the present period, and it is included in this group only because it later became one of the great women's magazines.[46]

Some of the most important women's magazines were begun in small cities — like *McCall's* and *Good Housekeeping*. Others were moved to New York, in an effort to make them big national competitors, and failed — such as the *Ladies' World*, *Modern Priscilla*, and the *New Idea Woman's Magazine*. Most cities of any size had women's magazines at some time or another during this period. Any hustling publisher could start such a journal "on a shoestring"; he could get cheap literary help to write and clip miscellany for the household, contract with a printer to issue the new monthly on cheap stock, use the premium system to sell large numbers of subscriptions at twenty-five cents to a dollar a year, and by exaggerated circulation claims attract a flood of cheap advertising. Hundreds of papers made a moderate success in this way: some of them became great mail-order journals; some supplied a fair standard of content and managed to exist over a number of years; some moved ambitiously to larger cities and tried "the big time"; and others failed after a few years. Still others emerged from the crowd of such periodicals through some specialty or by the development of a characteristic personality that found favor.

Of the women's journals that stayed at home, two may be named here. The *Pilgrim* (1899–1907), though born at Marshall, Michigan, spent most of its life at nearby Battle Creek, where it had such good editors as Willis J. Abbot (later editor of the *Christian Science Monitor*), and Karl Edwin Harriman (later editor of the *Red Book*). It emphasized current events, and was a helpful paper for clubwomen and home-makers. The *Household* (1902–current) was begun in Topeka by Arthur Capper as a cheap home monthly; later it became an excellent

---

[46] *Pictorial Review* will be treated in a separate sketch in the next volume of this work.

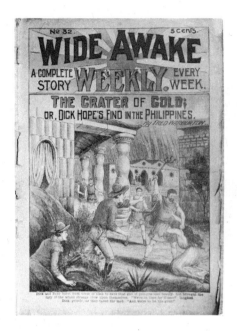

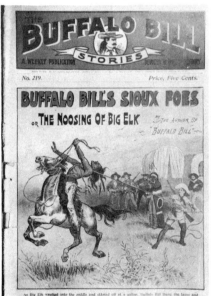
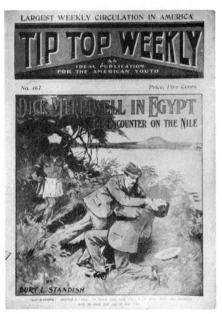

COVER PAGES OF NICKEL THRILLERS

Descendants of the Dime Novel in the Nineties. See pages 118–120.

## EVOLUTION OF THE BICYCLE

Both of these pictures are from *Outing*; the one of the tricycle was printed in 1885 and that of the high-wheeler and the brand-new "safety" in 1893. See page 377.

**BICYCLING IN RIVERSIDE PARK**

From *Munsey's Magazine*, May 1896. See page 378.

**"THREE'S A CROWD"**

From *Life*, November 26, 1896.

BICYCLING COSTUMES FOR WOMEN

From *Cosmopolitan Magazine*, August 1895. See page 378.

periodical as *Household Magazine*. But there were many more,[47] including some that will be noticed later in connection with the great mail-order journals.

## FASHIONS, COOKERY, HOUSES, BABIES

Virtually all women's magazines gave some attention to fashions, and many of them furnished or offered dressmaking patterns. Such famous and successful journals as *Harper's Bazaar*, the *Delineator*, *McCall's* and *Vogue* are treated separately;[48] but a few others that specialized in styles should be mentioned here. The *Designer* (1894–1926), which began as *Standard Delineator*, carried a big folding chromolithographic fashion plate in each number in its early years, and many woodcuts. Later it was a well-printed magazine in handsome large-quarto form, with good color work. It always printed some household helps, besides its fashions. It reached half a million circulation, but was finally merged in the *Delineator*. The *Home Needlework Magazine* (1899–1917), begun in Florence, Massachusetts, was a bimonthly at fifty cents a year and had a steady circulation of somewhat under a hundred thousand. It was moved to Boston in 1912 and an attempt made to exploit its possibilities; it was soon merged in *Modern Priscilla*.[49]

The *American Analyst* (1885–1894) was the pioneer consumer research periodical in the food field. It was the successor of an American edition of the English *Analyst*, a journal of practical chemistry, but it became a pure-food advocate. The outstanding culinary magazine in the nineties was Mrs. S. T. Rorer's *Table Talk* (1886–1920), of Philadelphia, a well-printed dollar-a-year monthly. Mrs. Rorer left *Table Talk* in 1893; and after editing the short-lived *Household News* (1893–1896), she became famous as the cookery expert of the *Ladies' Home Journal*. Meantime, *What To Eat*, which was later to absorb *Table Talk*, was established at Minneapolis in 1896, moved to Chicago in 1900, and to New York in 1913. Designed in the chapbook spirit, it was an attractive magazine.[50] The *New England Kitchen Magazine*

---

[47] *American Home* (1902–08), Waterville, Maine; *Household Companion* (1879–1911), Boston, published during the nineties and afterward by the Budget Company; *Mother's Journal* (1893–1904), New Haven, Conn.; *Southern Woman's Magazine* (1904–18), Atlanta; *American Home Journal* (1902–15), Dallas, reorganized in 1911 as a "booster" magazine; *Southland Queen* (1895–1904), Beeville, Texas; *St. Louis Magazine* (1871–96), which began as *St. Louis Ladies' Magazine* and always emphasized household and fashion articles; *Illustrated Home Journal* (1896–1908), St. Louis.

[48] *Vogue* (Sketch 32) and *McCall's* (Sketch 17) in this volume; *Harper's Bazaar* (Sketch 9) and *Delineator* (Sketch 22) in Mott, *op. cit.*, v. 3.

[49] A few other fashion magazines begun in the nineties should at least be mentioned here: *Browning's Magazine: A Periodical of Fashions and Fancies* (1890–1922), New York; *Fashions* (1891–1916), Philadelphia; and *Modes and Fashions* (1891–1915), New York.

[50] Issued by the Pierce Publishing Company, *What To Eat* was edited during its Chicago sojourn by Rutledge Rutherford. In 1908 it changed title to *National Food Magazine*, and in 1916 it absorbed *Table Talk* and continued its own numbering under the title *Table Talk and*

(1894–1908), of Boston, was established by Estelle M. H. Merrill and Anna Barrows, and later suffered various changes of ownership, title, and policy.[51] *American Cookery* (1896–1946) was long published as the *Boston Cooking School Magazine.*

Leading magazines dealing primarily with the care of children were *Babyhood* (1884–1909), *American Motherhood* (1895–1919), and *Trained Motherhood* (1897–1903). *Babyhood,* of New York, was a good, practical magazine, edited by Dr. Leroy M. Yale and Marion Harland in its early years; it deteriorated toward the end. *American Motherhood* began as *Mothers' Friend,* edited by Dr. Mary Wood-Allen at Ann Arbor, Michigan, and devoted to rather intimate matters, such as how to tell "the facts of life" to young children; in 1896 it was enlarged and made the official organ of the Purity Department of the W.C.T.U. In 1901 it was purchased by Arthur H. Crist, of Coopers-town, New York, who retained Dr. Wood-Allen as editor for some years, but who eventually broadened the scope of the periodical con-siderably under the editorship of Della Thompson Lutes. *Trained Motherhood,* of New York, was a cheap but well-printed and practical journal; it became *Motherhood* in 1901.

*House and Home* (1892–1905) was the successor of the Philadelphia monthly, *Builder, Decorator and Woodworker* (1883–1891); F. Eugene Irvine was editor. Other periodicals dealing with houses and gardens will be dealt with elsewhere in this volume.[52]

### THE MAIL-ORDER JOURNALS

It is not always easy to draw the line between the "mail-order jour-nals" and the more "legitimate" magazines for the home. The best of the women's magazines used advertising that solicited mail orders. The *Ladies' Home Journal,* undisputed leader of the better group, carried many small advertisements of cosmetics, medicines, jewelry, and clothes, to be delivered by mail on receipt of price, as well as calls for agents. The characteristics of the paper that was issued chiefly for the use of such advertisers came to be clear, however: a yearly sub-

---

*National Food Magazine* through July 1920. At the time of the merger, *Table Talk* was being published by Arthur H. Crist, who had bought it in 1909 and moved it to Cooperstown, N. Y., where it was edited by Marion Harris Neil. Marion Harland, drawing near to the end of a long life of writing for the magazines, was associated in the editorship of this one in its last years.

[51] It was *American Kitchen Magazine,* 1895–1903; having absorbed *Motherhood* in 1903, it became *Home Science Magazine,* 1903–05; *Modern Housekeeping,* 1905–06; *Everyday Housekeeping,* 1906–08. Other culinary magazines of some importance were *Table and Home Magazine* (1901–18), New York, and *Cooking Club* (1895–1917), Goshen, Indiana, by Mary and Adella S. Starr.

[52] Those emphasizing the architect's point of view are considered on pp. 324–25, and those emphasizing horticulture on pp. 341–42.

scription rate of twenty-five to fifty cents, poor printing (usually in the folio size), cheap serial fiction, and varied but undistinguished household departments. It would be wrong to shrug these journals off as unimportant. There were hundreds of them within the present period; many attracted great audiences over considerable terms of years, and not a few were well edited within the bounds of a policy appealing to readers of limited education.

Historically, the genre began with the *People's Literary Companion*, published at Augusta, Maine, by E. C. Allen.[53] When Allen died in 1892, he had a round dozen periodicals with an aggregate circulation of over a million, but with three-fourths of his subscribers hopelessly behind in their payments. As a matter of fact, all Allen wanted was a list of mailing addresses good enough to satisfy the Post Office Department; but when Samuel W. Lane, who had been editorial director of the Allen papers for some twenty years, purchased the list in 1894, he killed off all but five — *Golden Moments* (1880), *Sunshine* (1886), *Illustrated Family Herald* (1876), *National Farmer and Home Magazine* (1879), and *People's Literary Companion* (1869).[54] By this time, the big publishers of such papers were selling the circulation of their "lists" to advertisers in single transactions, so that an "ad" would appear in all the papers in a "list" at one price. Hallett's List, of Portland, was consolidated with Allen's List about 1890, and discontinued when Lane took over. It included the *Practical Housekeeper and Ladies' Companion* (1886) and *Our Home and Fireside Magazine* (1873), which were pretty good home papers. Another Portland paper which met the same fate was George Stinson's *People's Illustrated Journal* (1877).

Most important of mail-order journals was *Comfort*, a monthly begun in Augusta in 1888 as a cheap miscellany for the home. Through most of its life it sold at fifty cents a year, though a large part of its circulation was added on the basis of its "four years for a dollar" offer. By 1894 Rowell gave it a rating of 1,300,000 — "largest circulation of any single publication in the world." [55] It continued with about that circulation until 1907.[56] As one turns the leaves of the files (they must

---

[53] See Mott, *op. cit.*, v. 3, pp. 37–39.

[54] Only the beginning dates are given here; they all ended in 1907 with the strict enforcement of the rules of the Post Office Department requiring paid subscription lists.

[55] *Printer's Ink*, v. 10, p. 323, March 21, 1894.

[56] *Comfort* was founded by Morse & Company, and long published by Gannett & Morse, with W. H. Gannett as editor. It met the 1907 postal regulation by lowering its price to 15¢ a year; it always had been stricter than other mail-order papers about making subscribers pay. There came to be more fiction, with contributors like Fannie Hurst and H. H. Knibbs in the twenties and with Anson N. Goddard as editor. W. H. Gannett, Inc., sold *Comfort* to Needlecraft Publishing Corporation, of Augusta, in 1940, and it was merged with *Needlecraft* two years later, just before that journal perished.

be turned carefully, for the wood fibre in the old paper stock breaks easily), one has no trouble in understanding the fascination that *Comfort* had for children or the values that housewives found in it. There were corners for puzzles, quizzes, cycle clubs, comics, palmistry, and so on, in great variety. *Comfort* was among the earliest of publications to offer colored comic strips. For mothers, there were styles, patterns, fancywork, crocheting designs, cookery hints, suggestions for care of children, and helps for flower and vegetable gardens. And there were farming columns for father. There was not so much serial fiction in the nineties, but there were columns of misleading patent medicine and "Agents Wanted" advertising, and the usual cheap watches and diamonds, and such things.

Boston also became a center for the mail-order journals. Among the cheap papers for the home published there were the *Social Visitor* (1872–1907; *Home* (1877–1908), edited for most of its life by Nella I. Daggett; [57] *Woman's Home Journal* (1878–1909), originally issued by the publishers of the *Yankee Blade*; *Household Monthly* (1885–1891), a well-printed quarto; *Cottage Hearth* (1874–1894), which had begun in Providence; *Modern Women* (1902–1907), an unusually attractive paper conducted by George Livingston Richards; and *Columbian* (1893–1907), which experimented at the end with a rate of three years for a quarter. Lynn and Greenfield were other Massachusetts cities that produced notable journals of this class. The *Housewife* (1882–1917) was edited in Greenfield by Kate Upson Clark, and moved in 1891 to New York, where it continued as a very respectable cheap monthly. The *Household Monthly* (1885–1890) was a Lynn magazine by W. N. Swett, and J. F. *Ingalls' Home and Art Magazine* (1887–1894), also of Lynn, was a low-priced, ambitious, cheap magazine of the better class. In Providence, the *Home Guard* (1886–1897) was published by E. J. Smith and edited by his wife.

In New York the leading mail-order paper was the *Ladies' World*, discussed above. F. M. Lupton's *People's Home Journal* (1886–1929) and *Good Literature* (1889–1910) were merged in 1910. Both published much serial fiction by such writers as Mary Jane Holmes, Ann S. Stephens, Mary A. Denison, Charles Garvice, and Metta V. Victor. *Good Literature* was called *Home Guest* until 1895. The *Journal* eventually became a competitor of the greater women's magazines.[58]

---

[57] It began as *People's Fireside Journal*, changed in 1884 to *Home*, and in 1898 to *Home Monthly*. It reprinted much English fiction. In its last years it specialized in poultry care.

[58] When M. B. Gates became president of the publishing company after Lupton's death, there were better contributors, better format, and better paper. The price was raised to 10¢ in 1917 and 15¢ in 1920. Ben Ames Williams, Zoe Beckley, George Madden Martin, and Ellis Parker Butler were among the contributors.

A. D. Porter's *Hearthstone* (1891–1907) was mainly a cheap story paper, originally published in "eight mammoth pages" but later in twenty-four pages of a more modest quarto. It kept over half a million of its list for a goood many years. *Paragon Monthly* (1898–1908) specialized in the strange and curious.[59]

Philadelphia had half a dozen mail-order journals of some importance.[60] Washington had J. T. Latham's *People's Journal* (1885–1901). Chicago became a great center for this type of publication. Perhaps its most famous mail-order journals were George H. Currier's *Woman's World* (1901–1940), which was not very important until, having built up a tremendous circulation at a low rate, it made its bid in the big-time field shortly before World War I; [61] and *Home Life* (1891–1920), which came to Chicago from the hinterlands in 1900, and under Frank O. Balch worked up nearly a million circulation by the use of second-run serials by such popular writers as Robert W. Chambers.[62]

In Minneapolis, the *Housekeeper* (1877–1913) had a long and useful life. In St. Paul, the frankly named *Mail Order Monthly* (1899–1908) was published by J. R. Lovering as a journal of advertisements, fiction, and "condensed information." In Des Moines, the *People's Popular Monthly* (1896–1931) at first emphasized current events, and later household departments. In St. Louis, the *Woman's Magazine* (1898–1910) at one time sold at a cent a copy, ten cents a year.

There were also cheap papers financed by mail-order advertising for the farmers,[63] similar publications in the juvenile field, and so on; but their chief strength was in papers for the home. In 1899 a concern was established called Standard Associated Magazines, which would issue

[59] Others of note: *Welcome Friend* (1879–1902) and *Illustrated Companion* (1882–1907), by Edwin F. Nason; *Metropolitan and Rural Home* (1885–1913), by C. E. Ellis, publisher of the *Paragon* (*supra*); *Modes and Fabrics* (1891–1915), not all fashions; *Modern Stories* (1892–1909), definitely of a lower type; *Cheerful Moments* (1892–1908), notable for its wit and humor columns, which made a brief effort before its end to enter the "big time"; *Home Topics* (1895–1908), which became *Ladies' Home Topics* in 1899; *Indoors and Out* (1902–07), which emphasized sports and health.

[60] *People's Magazine* (1880–94), *Home Queen* (1885–1900), *Household Journal* (1887–1908), *Home Visitor* (1896–1907), *Home Advocate* (1897–1915).

[61] Walter W. Manning headed its publishing company during 1916–32, having purchased control from the Currier-Boyce interests. Editors were Forrest Crissey, 1907–09; Byron Williams, 1909–10; Herbert Kaufman, 1910–13; Charles Dwyer, 1913–16; Hiram Moe Greene, 1916–19; Walter W. Manning, 1919–31; Cora Francis Sanders, 1931–32; Florence Prebeck, 1933–34; Ray Wallace, 1934–40. Thus it was Manning who directed the *World's* chief try for a position among the leaders. In 1910, the periodical claimed "two million a month — the largest circulation in the world" at 25¢ a year, all in advance. Its price went to 10¢ a copy in 1917, 15¢ in 1929, back to 10¢ in 1933; but it sold for 50¢ a year from 1917 on. Its circulation claim had dropped to one million by 1920. Rex Beach, Opie Read, Harriett Prescott Spofford, and Mrs. Wilson Woodrow were among the *World's* contributors.

[62] Other Chicago mail-order journals were *Chicago Household Guest* (1892–1908), sold to Currier-Boyce in 1907 and merged with *Woman's World* the next year; *Homefolks* (1896–1908), which suffered a similar fate; *Ladies' Magazine* (1903–08), a Balch paper.

[63] See pp. 340–41.

for any nominal publisher who wished to make the speculation "a monthly magazine for mail-order advertisers, agents, mixers, and streetmen." Another practice that threatened to destroy what little standing as magazines these cheap publications had left, was the use of premium advertising as a cloak for direct sales. The premium system of soliciting subscribers required a small payment to be added to the negligible subscription price; and then, on some articles, payments were increased out of all proportion to the subscription price. When some papers made it unnecessary to subscribe at all, a catalog-selling business was being conducted under the cent-per-pound mailing rate which the Post Office Department offered magazines and newspapers.

There was much agitation in Congress against this low postal rate, but newspapers and magazines were in a strong position to fight increases — except for the gigantic mail-order papers. The Post Office Department had long had a rule providing that a magazine must have a list of bona fide subscribers in order to make use of the second-class mailing privilege; but in 1907 it strengthened this by requiring that all subscriptions should be paid in advance. This effectively ended the great period of mail-order journals. Those that did not quit outright lowered the price to ten cents a year and made bona fide collections of that amount, and then on the basis of swollen circulations, attempted "the big time." A few of the better ones succeeded for shorter or longer periods, as we have seen.[64]

[64] See above *Ladies' World, Woman's World, Modern Priscilla, People's Home Journal, People's Popular Monthly,* and others.

## CHAPTER XXII

## SPORTS AND RECREATION

OBSERVERS of the mid-nineties agreed that the United States was experiencing a remarkable new enthusiasm for outdoor sports and recreation, which, of course included audience interest, but also extended to wide participation. The *Tammany Times* declared, "Not for years has the country seen such a revival of interest in athletic sports as that which now has possession of every city, and of every interior crossroads." [1] Charles D. Lanier, writing in the *Review of Reviews*, told how this was largely participator interest: "There is an open-air movement almost revolutionary in its degree. . . . People are bicycling, yachting, running, jumping, fishing, hunting, playing baseball, tennis and golf, to an extent which is new in this generation." [2] The magazines all gave increasing attention to sports; *Harper's Weekly, Collier's, Life,* and others established separate departments for notes and news about sports. *Puck* printed a "phrenological" chart of Uncle Sam's cranium, showing it divided into baseball, football, golf, bicycling, and so on. [3]

A writer in the *Chautauquan* pointed out that "the great change which has been going on for the past few years in the field of public interest in sports is mainly due to the shorter hours of work required of the masses and the rapidly increasing number of what are sometimes called our leisure classes." [4] A writer in the *Atlantic* had a different explanation; he thought that the urban craze for games supplied a deficiency left by the disappearance of the physical activities of the frontier. [5] *Scribner's* for 1890 discussed the Amateur Athletic Union, the Turnvereins, and the other athletic clubs, and concluded that over a hundred thousand young men were engaged in organized athletics. [6] Some clubs had their own journals, chief among which was the *Winged Foot* (1892–current), of the New York Athletic Club. As has been already observed, the Y.M.C.A.'s, too, often published bulletin-like periodicals. [7] In 1896 the *American Physical Education Review* remarked

---

[1] *Tammany Times*, v. 1, p. 5, May 14, 1893.

[2] *Review of Reviews*, v. 14, p. 58, July 1896. Cf. statements by Charles P. Sawyer in "Amateur Track and Field Athletics," *Scribner's Magazine*, v. 7, pp. 775–82, July 1890.

[3] *Puck*, v. 21, p. 236, June 1, 1887.

[4] J. H. Mandigo, "Outdoor Sports," *Chautauquan*, v. 12, p. 388, July 1894.

[5] I. N. Hollis, "Intercollegiate Athletics," *Atlantic Monthly*, v. 90, p. 534, Oct. 1902.

[6] Sawyer in *Scribner's*, v. 7, pp. 775–82, July 1890, Cf. Duncan Edwards, "Life at the Athletic Clubs," *Scribner's Magazine*, v. 18, pp. 4–23, July 1895.

[7] See p. 287.

that the Y.M.C.A. "seems destined to fill the position of the Deutsche Turnerschaft in this country. Its growth as an agency of physical training is marvellous." Many athletic clubs, this writer declared, had been ruined by the pursuit of championships, gambling, and so on, but not so the Y.M.C.A.[8] Championships are, nonetheless, inseparable from sports, and the magazines showed great interest in all such, including the "reestablishment of the Olympian Games" at Athens in 1896, which was "received with the greatest enthusiasm the world over," according to the *New England Magazine*.[9]

Physical training came into the schools. "Within a few years," wrote William Dean Howells in *Harper's* in 1893, "the gymnasium has become an important and prominent adjunct to educational institutions." [10] In the colleges, athletic games — especially football, as will be noted a little later — had reached the status of a "problem" in the 1890's.[11]

Women were by no means apart from this great movement. The "athletic girl" began with the bicycle and went on with the tennis racquet, the golf club, the rowing oar, and so on. A rhymester in *Munsey's Magazine* described her:

> With her cycling cap tip-tilted, and her golfing costume kilted,
>     All her lovers she has jilted and forsworn;
> She no more of dancing thinks, and no soda-water drinks,
>     But is found upon the links both night and morn.
> She has tried her hand at boating, and at diving and at floating;
>     Almost everything but voting she controls.
> She's been salmon-fishing, eeling, and of course is skilled at wheeling,
>     And has contemplated sealing at the poles.
>
> Billiards, pool, and otter-hunting, golf, canoeing, paddling, punting,
>     Moose and mountain sheep confronting — and croquet,
> Shuttlecock and battledoring, on the rifle ranges scoring,
>     Sailing yacht or catboat, oaring on the bay;
> Running, jumping, and natation, navigation, ambulation —
>     So she seeks for recreation in a whirl.
> She's a highly energetic, undissuadable, magnetic,
>     Peripatetic, athletic kind of girl! [12]

"Already there is talk of the organization of women's athletic clubs in some of the cities," wrote the editor of the *Woman's Home Companion* in 1897, and added: "A higher physical development is re-

[8] *American Physical Education Review*, v. 1, p. 25, Sept. 1896.
[9] *New England Magazine*, v. 14, p. 261, May 1896.
[10] *Harper's Magazine*, v. 87, p. 961, Nov. 1893.
[11] See, for example, C. A. Young, "College Athletic Sports," *Forum*, v. 2, pp. 142–52, Oct. 1886. The football criticism piled up later.
[12] *Munsey's Magazine*, v. 15, p. 633, Aug. 1896.

quired by the rapid development of the sex in those pastimes and business pursuits formerly monopolized by men."[13] In March 1900 that magazine carried an illustrated article about the Woman's Athletic Club of Chicago, and three years later it initiated a department on "Physical Culture for Women" edited by Mary Perry King. The *Posse Gymnasium Journal* (1892–1920) was the voice of the Posse Gymnasium Club, of Boston, which practiced the Swedish system of physical culture for women, of which Baron Nils Posse was the exponent. Posse contributed to this journal until his death in 1896.

## BOXING

The chief plea for the recognition of pugilism to appear in the magazines of the eighties was one written for the *North American Review* of 1888 by the lawyer-novelist Duffield Osborne. He thought that the laws against the sport did little to prevent fights but much to degrade them. He asked for recognition of the manly art, so "that when we come to die, we shall die leaving men behind us, and not a race of eminently respectable female saints."[14] This eloquent plea was published the year before the last of the great bare-fist fights, in which John L. Sullivan defeated Jake Kilrain in "seventy-five red rounds."

Most magazine comment was, however, adverse to prize fighting. When Sullivan lost his title to James J. Corbett in 1892, the *American Journal of Politics* remarked:

An event that tends to sustain the theory that man has descended from the monkey and, in fact, that he is still descending in some respects, was the recent pugilistic contest in New Orleans. Everything else was eclipsed by this national event.[15]

This fight marked a turning point in the American attitude toward boxing: it began to be popular, if not quite respectable. Kate Field told of the excitement in New York as the reports of the fight were received:

New York's Printing House Square was alive with men, aye, and women and children; every hotel had a special and continuous telegraphic report of an event which cast even cholera in the shade and created more excitement than a Presidential election.[16]

"Gentleman Jim" Corbett was a popular champion. Writing of the interest in the fight in which Corbett lost his title to Robert Fitzsim-

---

[13] *Woman's Home Companion*, v. 24, Jan. 1897, p. 15.
[14] *North American Review*, v. 146, pp. 429–35, April 1888.
[15] *American Journal of Politics*, v. 1, p. 434, Oct. 1892.
[16] *Kate Field's Washington*, v. 6, pp. 162–63, Sept. 14, 1892.

mons in 1897, *Judge* said, "Pugilism is more tolerated today than ever before." But it added: "That may not be a recognition of pugilism as a legitimate amusement, however, so much as an evidence of the decline of public morality." [17] *Judge's* contemporary *Life* was, as usual, more acute in its comment: "There is much to object to about prize-fights; as a rule only one of the contestants is whipped." [18] But again the heavyweight title fight had been a national sensation: "It has completely overshadowed free silver and caused the blessed gold reserve to be forgotten," wrote Brann in his *Iconoclast*.[19]

The next winter the Horton Act passed the New York legislature, and in 1899, when Fitzsimmons lost the championship to James J. Jeffries, the fight was at Coney Island. *Current History* noted that "Chief Devery, of the New York police . . . was present, and took complacent satisfaction in every detail of the exhibition," which consisted of "a bloody contest of eleven rounds." [20]

Chief organ of the ring in these years was the *National Police Gazette*,[21] which gave jeweled belts to champion pugilists, wrestlers, pedestrians, and so on. This weekly, with its pink paper and its pictures of prizefighters and burlesque queens, was to be found in nearly all barbershops and barrooms throughout the length and breadth of the country. The Boston *Illustrated Police News* [22] was similar to its New York contemporary, but had only a sectional circulation. The *Illustrated Day's Doings and Sporting World* (1885–1890), of New York, was issued by Richard K. Fox, publisher of the *National Police Gazette*, in an effort to parlay the winnings of the older journal. Its technique was to take the most sensational news of the day and supersensationalize it. A typical heading:

FRISKY FEMALES;

or,

How an Innocent Young Man Was
Not Done For.

---

A STORY OF AN EXCEEDINGLY FLY
GOTHAMITE AND METROPOL-
ITAN ADVENTURESSES

The slang scattered through the file of this weekly is fascinating; its prizefighting features are inferior; its "sizzling" stories are likely to be tiresome; and its advertising is vile. *Weekly Sports* began in 1889,

---

[17] *Judge*, v. 32, p. 34, Jan. 16, 1897.
[18] *Life*, v. 29, p. 250, April 1, 1897.
[19] *Brann's Iconoclast*, v. 5, p. 160, Oct. 1895.
[20] *Current History*, v. 9, p. 400, 2nd quar., 1899.
[21] See F. L. Mott, *A History of American Magazines* (Cambridge, 1938), v. 2, Sketch 9.
[22] *Ibid.*, p. 187.

later to become *Vanity Fair*.[23] There were many other papers that
gave occasional, and sometimes rather specialized, attention to the
ring.

### RACING AND YACHTING

But a more respectable spectator-sport was horse racing. "It is no
uncommon incident," wrote a leading New York journalist in *America*
in 1889, "for twenty-five thousand people to go to the Coney Island
race-track, to Monmouth Beach, to the Jerome track in Fordham."[24]
Though most of the discussion of racing was left to the newspapers,
there were occasional articles about it in the magazines. A historian of
the trotting horse, writing in *Munsey's Magazine* in 1891, just after
Sunol had clipped half a second off the record of Maud S., declared
with heartfelt enthusiasm that "the evolution of the trotting horse is
one of the most remarkable feats of our civilization."[25]

The old racing journal called *Spirit of the Times* went bankrupt in
1902 and was merged in the Chicago *Horseman* (1881–1915); but
the New York *Clipper*, which covered not only the track but the
theater and the circus, went on throughout the period.[26] *Sports of the
Times* began in 1902 with emphasis on the track, but also much attention to the kennel, the theater, and the early automobiles. In its second
year it absorbed the famous *Turf, Field and Farm*.[27] There were also
a number of journals devoted to horse breeding and showing.[28]

Yachting was a sport of the rich; but it had a popular appeal based
on the international yacht races, in which the *America's* cup was successfully defended in race after race. It was a wave of patriotic pride
that brought an interest in yachting in the late eighties which a writer
in the *Cosmopolitan* compared to New York's madness over Jenny
Lind many years before.[29] Lord Dunraven and George A. Stewart
carried competition from deck to page when they wrote about the
races in the *North American Review* in 1892–1893. *Rudder* was an
illustrated monthly founded in New York in 1890, and still published.
The *American Yachtsman* (1887–1908) was published by a dealer for
eastern yacht clubs. *Motor Boat* (1904–current) covers both pleasure
boating and shipping.

[23] See p. 47, footnote.
[24] Joseph Howard, Jr., in *America*, v. 2, p. 275, May 30, 1889.
[25] *Munsey's Magazine*, v. 6, p. 247, Nov. 1891.
[26] See Mott, *op. cit.*, v. 2, pp. 203–04.
[27] See Mott, *op. cit.*, v. 3, p. 215.
[28] *Racer and Driver* (1890–current), New York, was a fine, well-illustrated journal. *Horse
Show Monthly* (1895–1906), St. Louis, was merged in *Sports of the Times. Trotter and Pacer*
(1894–1926) was a good New York monthly. See also p. 343.
[29] S. G. W. Benjamin in *Cosmopolitan*, v. 5, p. 347, Sept. 1888.

## BASEBALL AND FOOTBALL

But "the one great sport of the day for participants and onlookers alike," said John H. Mandigo in the *Chautauquan*, was baseball.[30] A veteran player writing in the *Nickell Magazine* in 1896 gave some recollections of the game a decade or two earlier: "I remember when the catcher stood behind the batter wholly unprotected. I have seen Snyder playing with one eye closed by a foul tip, a lip swollen to the size seen on a Florida coon, and hands bleeding as well as bruised."[31] From 1884 until 1891 there were post-season playoffs between the National League and American Association pennant winners. These were the first "World Series," and drew great crowds. They were interrupted by the collapse of the American Association in 1891, and were not resumed until two years after the formation of the American League in 1901. Baseball had its organizational troubles in the nineties, with many competing leagues; but support grew steadily. "There is no professional sport which compares with baseball in popularity," declared one observer in the mid-nineties.[32]

Of the many papers founded in this period with the expectation of capitalizing on baseball's popularity, the one that was destined to reach eventual fame and fortune was the *Sporting News* (1886–current), of St. Louis. It was founded by Albert H. Spink in the midst of its city's delirium over the winning of the American Association pennant by Charley Comiskey's Browns. Al's brother Charles C. was business manager of the paper, and took over control of it in 1897. It had much to do with promoting the organization of the American League.[33]

Chief competitor of the *Sporting News* was Francis C. Richter's *Sporting Life* (1883–1926), of Philadelphia. Both were weeklies, but in the earlier nineties *Sporting Life* was somewhat larger, better illustrated, and more expensive.[34] Each had a circulation of about fifty thousand. The *Sporting Times* (1887–1894), of New York, was started by certain National League "interests" that were dissatisfied with their treatment in the other weeklies, but it was never very successful.[35]

Football renounced its rugby infancy in the latter eighties, and

---

[30] *Chautauquan*, v. 15, p. 410, July 1892.
[31] *Nickell Magazine*, v. 5, p. 267, May 1896.
[32] *Ibid.*, p. 269.
[33] See Stanley Frank, "Bible of Baseball," *Saturday Evening Post*, June 20, 1942; reprinted in John E. Drewry, ed., *More Post Biographies* (Athens, Ga., 1947).
[34] It then sold for $4.00 a year, but later came down to $2.00, the price of *Sporting News*. After the failure of the Federal League, which *Sporting Life* promoted, the paper was suspended a few years (1917–22). In its last two years it was titled *Sports Life*.
[35] See Frank in Drewry, *More Post Biographies*, p. 331.

came to be a game of power and speed — a spectacular arena game requiring courage, toughness, and brawn. "Football is typical of all that is heroic in American sport," said an editorial in the Chicago *Graphic* in 1892; [36] and a few years later the *Saturday Evening Post* called football

the game that more than any other brings distinction in athletics. . . . The capacity to take hard knocks which belongs to a successful football player is usually associated with the qualities that would enable a man to lead a charge up San Juan Hill or guide the *Merrimac* into Santiago Harbor.[37]

It was primarily a college game, though high schools and the preparatory academies had their teams by the turn of the century; and those eastern colleges that the *Nickell Magazine* called "the Big Four" — Harvard, Yale, Princeton, and Pennsylvania — dominated public interest.[38] By the end of our period, however, several teams in the Midwest (led by Michigan) had become famous, and the game was well established in nearly all colleges and universities. There were many quarrels between the eastern institutions over rules, and sometimes there were free-for-all fights on the playing field. A Yale student in the *American University Magazine* complained that football in 1894 was "in a muddle. . . . Harvard refuses to play Princeton, Yale refuses to play Pennsylvania," and so on.[39] But Harvard's plaint was the most pitiful. In the first number of the *Harvard Graduates' Magazine*, the editor wrote: "Harvard's almost unbroken series of defeats during the past twelve years in Rowing, Baseball, and Football contests with her old rival Yale have caused her loyal alumni the deepest chagrin." Then to his own question, "What is Harvard's greatest need today?" the editor answered in what to become a characteristic alumni fashion, "Coaches." [40]

On the other hand, "paid coaching" was one of the dangers of football, according to the critics, since it made for commercialism.[41] But the chief evils were physical injuries resulting from the new mass-velocity plays, which had not been properly limited, the unnecessary roughness and rioting, the "celebrating" by spectators, and the use of nonstudents (professionalism), especially by some of the western colleges. The *Pathfinder* gives some details of injuries in the Harvard-Yale game of 1894, in which men were carried off the field with con-

---

[36] *Graphic*, v. 7, p. 408, Dec. 3, 1892.
[37] *Saturday Evening Post*, v. 171, p. 330, Nov. 19, 1898.
[38] *Nickell Magazine*, v. 10, p. 265, Nov. 1898. Cf. *Current History*, which says that the superiority of these teams is being challenged by Carlisle, Brown, Lafayette, and West Point (v. 6, pp. 878–79, 4th quar., 1896).
[39] *American University Magazine*, v. 1, p. 61, Nov. 1894.
[40] *Harvard Graduates' Magazine*, v. 1, p. 31, Oct. 1892.
[41] *Pathfinder*, v. 1, p. 7, Dec. 8, 1894.

cussion of the brain, dislocation of collarbones, smashed noses, gouged eyes, injury to eyeball, sprained knee, sprained ankle. Wrote the editor: "There is a certain nobility that appeals to the masses in these elevens of hard-muscled, stout-hearted men, but it is the nobility of a band of Comanche braves on the warpath — a nobility of barbarism." [42] Moreover, B. O. Flower wrote in his *Arena* in 1893 that after the Thanksgiving Day game, the Yale victors engaged in "bacchanalian revelry the bare recital of which must fill all clean minds with disgust." [43]

OTHER OUTDOOR GAMES

Dr. Willard H. Morse made a novel suggestion in *Outing* in 1887. "If we seek a change in outdoor sports in America," he wrote, "why not welcome Golf? — a noble game. . . . Our prairies and meadow lands give better 'links' than the gorse-covered downs. . . . Is there any reason why we should not have an Americanized Golf?" [44] It was a good suggestion, but five or six years later golf was still almost unknown in this country, and "a solitary golf course in America was a curiosity and a mystery." [45] But in 1895 came a wave of enthusiasm for the game, and the next summer Mrs. Reginald de Koven was writing in the *Cosmopolitan* of "the incredibly rapid spread" of golf among both men and women.[46] In 1900 *World's Work* said: "A competent authority estimates the present number of golfers in the United States at two hundred thousand," many of whom bring to the game an "enthusiasm which leads their families and associates to doubt their sanity." [47]

The *Golfer* (1894–1906) was the organ of the new United States Golf Association. Being superseded in this official capacity by *American Golf* (1900–1902), it turned to other fields of sport, and became *Outdoors* in 1903. Meantime *American Golf* had been supplanted by the *Golfer's Magazine* (1902–1931), edited and published in Chicago by Crofts W. Higgins. It was a handsome illustrated monthly, to which famous golfers contributed. *Golf* (1897–1917), of New York, also claimed to represent the United States Golfing Association; it absorbed *Golfing* (1894–1899). The spread of country clubs, with their golf courses, is shown in the magazines of fashion and the urban weeklies.

---

[42] *Ibid.*

[43] *Arena*, v. 7, p. 372, Feb. 1893.

[44] *Outing*, v. 11, p. 285, Dec. 1887.

[45] *Review of Reviews*, v. 14, p. 61, July 1896. The first course was in Yonkers in 1890, says Henry E. Howland in *Scribner's*, but in 1895 "the tale outruns the telling," v. 17, p. 531, May 1895.

[46] *Cosmopolitan*, v. 21, p. 325, Aug. 1896.

[47] *World's Work*, v. 1, p. 62, Nov. 1900.

"Is lawn tennis dying out in America?" asked the *Saturday Evening Post* in 1899, and replied to its own question, "No! A thousand times no!" What had happened, it explained, was that the initial furor of the faddists had died down, permitting a saner outlook on the sport.[48] Perhaps a franker explanation would have been that tennis was just beginning to emerge from the period in which it was dominated by the amateurs. The United States National Lawn Tennis Association had a *Bulletin* 1894–1897, to be followed by *American Lawn Tennis* (1898–1901) and *Lawn Tennis* (1901–1903).

Organization of the National Cricket League of the United States in 1891 signalized an attempt to revive that game in this country. That fall an American team won an international match with Canada, and a Philadelphia team beat Lord Hawke's famous English team.[49] The *American Cricketer* continued in its valiant effort to rouse American interest in a game that could not compete with baseball as a sport on this side of the Atlantic.

THE POPULARITY OF THE "SAFETY" BICYCLE

"When the social and economic history of the nineteenth century comes to be written," said a commentator in the *Forum*, "the historian cannot ignore the invention and development of the bicycle." [50] Cycles had been popular in America as early as the years immediately following the Civil War, but these were three-wheeled velocipedes. In the latter half of the 1880's there were three kinds of cycles in vogue — the old three-wheeler, used now chiefly by women and children; the high-wheeled bicycle, which seated the rider nearly five feet above the ground and was the wheel of the racing competitions and still used by many amateurs as late as the earlier nineties; and the new "safety" bicycle, so called because its twin-size wheels were low enough so that a tumble did not risk the rider's neck.

It was the "safety," equipped with pneumatic tires instead of the old hard-rubber rims, which brought about the amazing popularity of the bicycle in the nineties. *Outing*, a leading journal of the wheel, reported in 1890 on the "new pneumatic tire" which had "already created a sensation in England." Though some doubted its practicability on American roads, *Outing* prophesied that it would soon make its way on this side of the Atlantic.[51] It did make its way soon indeed. By the mid-nineties America was awheel. More than a quarter of a

[48] *Saturday Evening Post*, v. 172, p. 366, Nov. 4, 1899.
[49] *Current History*, v. 1, pp. 300, 427, Aug., Nov. 1891.
[50] *Forum*, v. 20, p. 578, Jan. 1896.
[51] *Outing*, v. 16, p. 380, Feb. 1890.

million bicycles were sold in 1894, and more in each succeeding year, until it was estimated that ten to twelve million were in use at the end of the decade.[52] Nearly a hundred different makes were shown by eighty manufacturers at the Madison Square Garden Bicycle Show of 1895, priced at a hundred to a hundred and fifty dollars.[53]

Said *Scribner's Magazine*: "On the smoother and more quiet streets of our large cities the crowds of cyclists are so constant and dense during the hours that allow breadwinners to ride, as to form an actual procession in which there is difficulty in moving faster than the pace of one's fellows." [54] Bicycle clubs were organized in cities, towns, villages; and tours were arranged on week-ends and holidays. By the latter nineties the wheel became an immense power for better roads. The membership of the League of American Wheelmen grew to over a hundred thousand, and the organization exerted a strong influence on legislative action.[55]

To women, the bicycle was an emancipating agency. Mrs. Reginald de Koven wrote in the *Cosmopolitan* in 1895; "To men, rich and poor, the bicycle is an unmixed blessing; but to women it is deliverance, revolution, salvation. It is well nigh impossible to overestimate . . . its influence in the matters of dress and social reform." [56] By 1892 the tricycle had been "relegated to the background," and it was "no longer a novelty to see wheel-women in our streets and parks," said the *American Woman's Journal*.[57] Two years later the fashionable world took to cycling in Central Park, New York, and in similar places the country over, stimulated thereto both by the advice of the doctors and by the styles provided by Paris.[58] One admirable observer declared in 1896 that the bicycle had already "done more for dress reform among women than the advice of the medical profession and lecture platform have accomplished in fifty years." [59] Some sincere conservatives and some pseudomoralists objected to women on wheels, however; the *Philistine*, an example of the latter, reported that 30 per cent of the "fallen women" who came to the Women's Rescue League of Boston for help had been "bicycle riders at one time."[60] Nevertheless, the *Wheelwoman* (1895–1902) continued its blithe way under the editorship of Mary Sargent Hopkins, of Boston.

[52] *Scribner's Magazine*, v. 17, p. 696, June 1895; *Chautauquan*, v. 33, p. 207, June 1901.
[53] *Scribner's Magazine, loc. cit.*
[54] *Scribner's Magazine*, v. 20, p. 131, July 1896.
[55] *Chautauquan*, v. 26, p. 101, Oct. 1897.
[56] *Cosmopolitan Magazine*, v. 19, p. 386, Aug. 1895.
[57] *American Woman's Journal*, v. 5, p. 34, Oct. 1892.
[58] *Scribner's Magazine*, v. 17, p. 705, June 1895.
[59] Lt. (later Maj. Gen.) William C. Davis, "The Bicycle and Its Adaptability to Military Purposes," *Journal of United States Artillery*, v. 5, p. 250, March–April 1896.
[60] *Philistine*, v. 1, p. 63, July 1895.

The main functions of the bicycle were social and recreational, but it had a growing use for transportation of workers. "By its use," said one writer, "the business man and workman alike find it possible to reside at greater distances from their places of employment, so that the suburbs are rapidly building up." [61] There was some use of bicycles in the army, and much discussion of it by military authorities.[62]

The magazines of the period were full of comment on the bicycle and its impact on contemporary life. In the mid-nineties, the *Critic, Life, Godey's Magazine,* and other periodicals issued special cycling numbers every year; and such fashion monthlies as *Harper's Bazaar* and *Vogue* put out bicycle-fashion editions every spring. A magazine called *Bicycle Fashions* was published in New York in 1897–1899. There were many accounts of journeys by wheel in the magazines, the most remarkable of which were the long serials in *Outing* by Thomas Stevens and Frank G. Lenz.

The leading wheelman's journal was the *Bicycling World.*[63] Though *Outing* enlarged its scope in the nineties, it always gave much attention to the wheel.[64]

The *American Cyclist* (1890–1898) was published at Hartford, Connecticut, the great bicycle manufacturing center, by Joseph Goodman; it was absorbed by the *Bicycling World*. Four other leaders in the field were the *Wheelman's Gazette* (1886–1908), first published in Springfield, Mass., and then moved to Indianapolis; the *American Athlete* (1887–1895), of Philadelphia; the *Wheel and Cycling Trade Review* (1888–1900), of New York; and *Bearings* (1890–1897), of Chicago, which was merged with *Cycling Life* (1893–1897) and *Referee* (1888–1897) to form *Cycle Age and Trade Review*, merged into *Motor Age* at the end of 1901. There were more than thirty periodicals devoted to bicycle news and miscellany by 1895, and the number grew rapidly. Nearly all cities of much size had their cycling papers by the end of the decade, catering to the interests of riders and battening on the advertising of a highly competitive field. The League of American Wheelmen had its magazine, which was published under various titles[65] — notably *Good Roads* — from 1885 to 1931. It became more

---

[61] Davis in *Journal of United States Artillery,* v. 5, p. 251, March–April 1896.

[62] Davis in *Journal of United States Artillery,* vols. 5–8, 1896–97. Cf. *Cavalry Journal,* v. 8, pp. 235–38, Sept. 1895; *ibid.,* v. 15, pp. 589–604, Jan. 1905; *Army and Navy Journal, passim.*

[63] See Mott, *op. cit.,* v. 3, p. 213.

[64] See Sketch 21 in this volume.

[65] It was *L.A.W. Bulletin* during 1885–88; this was merged with *Bicycling World,* which became the association's organ until 1894. It then resumed separate publication, absorbing *Good Roads* (1892–95) the next year. It was [Sterling] *Elliott's Magazine* 1899–1900, and *L.A.W. Magazine* 1900–01; after this it was called *Good Roads* until its end in 1931. It changed from monthly to weekly issue in 1911. See v. 2, n.s., p. 9, Jan. 6, 1912; and v. 13,

of a popular magazine after about 1898, publishing good articles by prominent writers. *State's Duty* (1889–1900), of St. Louis, though at first devoted to child welfare, later espoused the wheelmen's cause of better roads.

BOWLING; ROLLER SKATING; CROQUET

Bowling was popular in many cities, especially among the German elements of the population. The *Bowlers' Journal* (1893–1934) was the weekly organ of the United Bowling Clubs of New York; it began in German, but was soon shifted to English with a German section.

Roller skating suddenly attained amazing popularity about 1884–1885. Wrote the *Citizen* editor in the latter year:

> That roller-skating is now a popular mania in its zenith no one can doubt. . . . There is a roller-skating rink in every city and town north of Mason and Dixon's line and east of the Mississippi. . . . Almost incredible stories are reported of fortunes realized by opening roller-skating rinks. . . . The mania is not confined to the middle classes, but has apparently affected all grades in the social scale.[66]

Croquet, while still very popular, was commonly regarded less as recreation than as social diversion.[67]

HUNTING AND FISHING

A considerable proportion of the periodicals in the field of sports during the years 1885–1905 were designed chiefly for hunters and fishermen. Many parts of the country still abounded with game, and streams were full of fish. It is true that William T. Hornaday exclaimed with exasperation in the *Cosmopolitan*: "At last the game butchers of the great West have stopped killing buffalo. The buffalo are all dead!"[68] But hunting, though unlike what it had been on the frontier, was still good.

Several of the older hunting and fishing periodicals continued during some years of the present period.[69] One of the most important of the newer magazines in this class was the *Sportsmen's Review* (1890– current), founded in Chicago as *Sporting Review* by Harry C. Palmer. After a couple of years it became *Sportsmen's Review and Bicycle*

n.s., p. 9, Jan. 6, 1917, for historical sketches. *Bassett's Scrap Book* (1900–23), of Newton-ville, Mass., was a notes and queries type of monthly; it moved to Boston in 1904 and claimed to represent the L.A.W.

[66] *Citizen*, v. 1, p. 104, Jan. 31, 1885. Cf. *Outing*, v. 5, p. 300, Jan. 1885; *Brooklyn Magazine*, v. 1, p. 118, March 1885.

[67] *Journal of Social Science*, v. 12, p. 141, 1880.

[68] *Cosmopolitan Magazine*, v. 4, p. 85, Oct. 1887.

[69] See Mott, *op. cit.*, v. 3, p. 210.

*News,* featuring cycling, trapshooting, and hunting. Then in 1898 it was bought by Emil Werk, changed from monthly to weekly publication, shorn of the bicycle part of its title, and moved to Cincinnati. It survived these basic changes to become a leading hunting and fishing journal of the early decades of the twentieth century.

*Recreation* (1894–1912) was a New York ten-cent monthly founded by G. O. Shields. It was attractive and varied in content, and had many departments, including one on photography.[70]

Several hunting and fishing magazines were regional. A few began as regional periodicals and later reached out for national audiences. *Western Field and Stream* was begun in St. Paul in 1896 by John P. Burkhard; two years later it was moved to New York and the *Western* dropped from its title. In the twentieth century it became one of the greatest of all American magazines devoted to hunting and fishing.[71] *New England Sportsman* (1899–1941), of Boston, became *National Sportsman* after two years, and made a moderate success. *Sports Afield* (1887–current) was at its beginning a regional magazine, published first in Denver, then in Chicago, and later in Minneapolis. *Hunter-Trader-Trapper* (1900–current) was published first in Columbus, Ohio, and later in Chicago.[72]

### BOARD AND CARD GAMES

The great whist craze began about 1890 and continued progressively for many years. Frank W. Crane, writing in the *Cosmopolitan Magazine,* declared:

Never before has there been anything like the present enthusiasm for whist in the United States. . . . The whist boom has extended all over the country from

[70] W. E. Annis became publisher and Edward Cave editor in 1905. Two years later it absorbed the *Illustrated Outdoor News,* having been purchased by the owners of that magazine. Shields claimed to have started *Recreation* on $3,000 (v. 5, p. 54, Jan. 1897); the *Illustrated Sporting News* was founded in 1903 by a stock company that had raised $50,000. It was a handsome weekly edited by Julian A. Ripley. It changed its title to *Illustrated Outdoor News* in Oct. 1905.

[71] To be treated in a separate sketch in the next volume of this work.

[72] *Maine Sportsman* (1893–1908), Bangor, was the organ of the Maine Ornithological Society. The *Sportsman* began in New York in 1901, but moved to St. Louis in 1905 and ended life as *St. Louis Sportsman and Amateur Athlete* in 1908. The *Northwestern Sportsman* (1901–27), of Milwaukee, became *Outer's Book* in 1907; ten years later it absorbed *Recreation* and added its title. It ended as *Outdoor Recreation,* Chicago. The *Recreation* here referred to began in New York in 1888 as the *Sportsman;* it changed title to *Illustrated Outdoor World* in 1912 and, absorbing *Recreation,* became *Outdoor World and Recreation,* and finally *Recreation.* *Outdoor Life* was begun in Denver in 1897 by J. A. McGuire, absorbed *Outdoor Recreation* thirty years later, and is now, in the 1950's, a large-circulation New York magazine. Two San Francisco sporting monthlies were *Field Sports* (1890–1900) and *Western Field* (1902–14). *Gameland* (1892–98) was a New York periodical. The *American Rifleman* (1885–current), New York, was called *Rifle* in its first two years, *Hunting and Fishing* 1888–1906, and *Arms and the Man* 1906–23; it is now issued from Washington as the organ of the National Rifle Association of America.

the Atlantic to the Pacific. Although barely of five years' growth, the interest has been continually progressive.[73]

Several periodicals were devoted to the game, most important of which was *Whist* (1891–1903), of Milwaukee, edited by C. M. Paine.

More than a dozen chess journals were published during the present period, devoted to problems of the game and news of tournaments. Perhaps three which came from New York were most important — *International Chess Magazine* (1885–1891), conducted by William Steinitz; [Emanuel] *Lasker's Chess Magazine* (1904–1909); and the *American Chess Bulletin* (1904–current). The *Corsair* (1902–1910) was a Boston chess periodical.

The leading checker-players' journals, from among ten or a dozen, were the *American Checker Review* (1888–1894), of Chicago; and the *Checker World* (1895–1910), of Manchester, New Hampshire.

### DOGS, CATS, FIGHTING COCKS

*Field and Fancy* (1900–1928), founded by G. M. Carnochan in New York, was interested chiefly in dogs, but gave some attention to cats and other pets. Battle Creek, Michigan, was the home of two famous dog journals — the cheap but attractive *Dog Fancier* (1891–1936) and the well-illustrated *Dogdom* (1900–1941) — both monthlies. The *American Kennel Gazette* (1889–current) does little more than list the registrations of the American Kennel Club. Leading magazines for cat lovers were the *Cat Journal* (1901–1912), of Palmyra and Rochester, New York; and the *Cat Review* (1903–1931), of Dayton, Ohio.

Ten or a dozen periodicals were devoted to fighting cocks, as the monthly *Game Bird* (1892–1910?), of Derby, Indiana; and *Dixie Game Fowl* (1894–1907), of Columbus, Tennessee. They were mainly advertising sheets.

[73] Frank W. Crane, "Whist in America," *Cosmopolitan Magazine*, v. 19, p. 196, June 1895.

# CHAPTER XXIII

## HUMOR AND HOBBIES

A WRITER in *Drake's Magazine* made a survey in 1888 covering the production of humor the world around. He found the comic muse in rather feeble health everywhere else; but, said he, "in this great and glorious country the humorist flourishes like the green bay tree. Here he attains his best development, in quantity as in quality."[1] Whatever may be said about the European humor of the period, the *Drake's* writer was surely right about the abundance of it in America. James L. Ford later pointed out in *Collier's* that a phenomenon of the eighties was "the establishment of pages or columns of original humorous matter in a vast number of periodicals."[2] He ascribes this largely to the influence of *Life*, *Puck*, and *Judge*; but with Mark Twain and a host of minor humorists in full production, it seems impossible to narrow the activating influence to these three great periodicals.

It is to be noted that the period now under consideration (1885–1905) is unique in having so many humorous journals of high quality in course of publication. To the three named above should be added *Truth*; and, for the years 1884–1890, *Tid-Bits*.[3] These five were satirical, varied, and extremely well illustrated weeklies. Many of the colleges had their comic monthlies, too, led by the *Harvard Lampoon*. Not infrequently the urban weeklies, which were a feature of this period,[4] turned markedly to social satire. And many of the *bibelots* that flourished at the turn of the century[5] were essentially journals of satire. All these, with a swarm of minor humorous periodicals, made a very considerable showing for magazines in the lighter vein.

### COMIC CHARACTERS

The characters around which jokes centered in this period were somewhat different from those of earlier times. The Irish were still butts of jokes in infinite variety. Jews came on the comedy stage more

---

[1] *Drake's Magazine*, v. 6, p. 249, April 1888.
[2] *Collier's*, v. 30, Jan. 31, 1903.
[3] For *Tid-Bits, Harvard Lampoon*, and other humorous papers that held over from the preceding period, see F. L. Mott, *A History of American Magazines* (Cambridge, 1938), v. 3, pp. 268–70. In the same volume, see separate sketches of *Puck* (30) and *Judge* (36); in the present volume, see Sketch 15 for *Life*, and pp. 83–85 for *Truth*.
[4] See pp. 77–78.
[5] See pp. 386–91.

and more frequently. Negroes furnished fun in picture, story, and joke. There seems to have been little self-conscious sensitiveness to this fun-making on the part of the nationalities and races involved: the Irish flocked to see the Harrigan comedies, and there were many straight Negro minstrel shows. There was, however, some resentment against the *Arkansaw Traveler* and against the "Arizona Kicker" on the part of the people of those states.[6]

Two new characters used often in the jokes of the period were the Yellow-Kid type, which has already been discussed,[7] and the "dude." The *American Quarterly* said in 1883 that "dude" was "a new name for a large class of very young, very senseless, very soulless, very snobbish, and altogether very stupid and would-be smart specimens of manhood who have afflicted society here, especially during the last season."[8] More and more the silly, fashionably dressed "dude" became a comic character — in Palmer Cox's "Brownies,' in *Life* and *Puck*, and in the joke columns. Noah Porter, editor of *Webster's Unabridged Dictionary*, writes that the name "dude" in 1887 "conveys a specific idea" — to which the *Woman's Tribune* replies: "Whoever heard of a dude conveying 'a specific idea'? It would make him tired."[9]

### CURRENT SLANG

Much of the slang of the day came from the argot circulating in the three fields of the theater, sports, and crime. Files of such periodicals as *Today's Doings* and the *Police Gazette*, the *Clipper*, and *Sports of the Times* are therefore especially good repositories of such language. Popular songs were responsible for the circulation of such phrases as "Shoo-fly, don' yo' boddah me!" and "Where did you get that hat?" Chimmie Faddens "nit!" and the somewhat later "twenty-three-skiddoo!" had a great vogue for a decade or more. "Skiddoo," popularized by "Tad" Dorgan, the comic artist,[10] is an example of slang spread by the "funnies." "Well, I should smile" to express enthusiatic assent, and "daisy" as a term of approval were current in the nineties. "Fake" is said to have been taken by the public from the "vocabulary of the playhouse."[11]

[6] Gov. Irwin, of Arizona Territory, protested against the latter, which was a feature of M. Quad's *Detroit Free Press* column; see *Current Literature*, v. 9, p. 478, March 1892. For objections to *Arkansaw Traveler*, see, Mott, *op. cit.*, v. 3, p. 270.

[7] See pp. 196–97.

[8] *American Quarterly*, v. 10, p. 46, March 10, 1883. Cf. Julien Gordon in *Cosmopolitan Magazine*, v. 10, p. 580, March 1891.

[9] *Woman's Tribune*, v. 5, Dec. 17, 1887, p. 1.

[10] See H. L. Mencken, *The American Language* (New York, 1938), pp. 560–61.

[11] Brander Matthews, "The Function of Slang," *Harper's Magazine*, v. 87, pp. 304–12, July 1893.

Slang terms were sometimes printed on "buttons" to be pinned on coats or dresses. The "button" fad had its origin in political campaigns, and it spread widely in the mid-nineties. It was considered smart in some circles to wear "buttons" carrying such legends as "You ain't my girl," "Talk fast," "23," "This is my busy day," and so on.[12]

### HUMOROUS PERIODICALS

*Commodore Rollingpin's Illustrated Humorous Almanac* was published annually for more than twenty years before it was made a monthly in 1895. It was edited by John Henton Carter, a St. Louis novelist and poet, and was a handsome quarto with chromolithographic cover and center spread. The editor wrote most of its stories and poems.[13]

The Philadelphia *Jester* (1889–1891) was at first distinguished by the drawings of Matt Morgan, Albert D. Blashfield, and Charles Howard Johnson; latterly it was distinguished by neither art nor prose. It was cheap — five cents a week. The Boston *Jester* (1891–1892), which followed it, cost ten cents a number, but was no better.

*Chicago Figaro* (1888–1893) was at first largely produced from plates arleady used by *Life*; but under the editorship of J. C. B. Andrews in 1890, the *Life* pictures were dropped and the local Chicago matter was increased. Thus *Figaro* became a society and amusement journal of the urban weekly type, but with emphasis on the prose contributions of J. Percival Pollard (who was part-owner for a time) and the poetry of Francis S. Saltus. Caroline Kirkland wrote about books; Charles Emory Shaw discussed art; G. E. Montgomery furnished a New York letter, and so on.

Frank Tousey published some cheap comic weeklies in New York in the mid-nineties — the *Comic Library* (1894–1898) and *Snaps* (1899–1901). These sold for five cents a number; Thomas Worth was the chief illustrator. A much better nickel weekly was *Clips* (1895–1897), which described itself as "A pictorial eclectic, a review of the best current wit, verse, story, and illustration to be found in the press of the world . . . fads and fancies of everywhere, from Canton to London." It was well printed and clever, and carried an increasing amount of original matter; but it lasted only a little over a year. *Twinkles* was the "serio-comic supplement" of the *New York Tribune*,

---

[12] *Munsey's Magazine*, v. 16, p. 121, Oct. 1896; v. 16, p. 251, Nov. 1896.
[13] For many years its annual editions were devoted to the St. Louis fall festival, the Pageant of the Veiled Prophet. It was an annual 1871–94, monthly 1895–96, and quarterly 1897–98, ending with an annual number for 1899.

sold separately during 1896–1897, later called simply the "Illustrated Supplement."

The *Verdict* (1898–1900) was a satirical-political paper along the lines of *Judge* and *Puck*. Its cover and center spread were in color, and its cartoonists were George B. Luks, Horace Taylor, and others. Alfred Henry Lewis was its editor, and it was often said to represent "the Alfred Henry Lewis faction of the Democratic party"; but as a matter of fact it was financed by Oliver H. P. Belmont largely to fight the Vanderbilt interests, and it carried much about New York transportation problems. It hated Cleveland, and accepted Bryan with reluctance. Its "Chucky," from Mulberry Bend (later "Tammany Tim"), discoursed on politics from Lewis' liberal and reform point of view. There were also short stories by Lewis, including some of his famous "Wolfville Nights." Its editor resented the designation of "comic" as applied to the *Verdict*, and considered it primarily a political journal; for it he wrote some rather fine editorials based on his brand of political idealism. The following lines from an essay in the last number furnish an example:

> Be pure, and your government will be pure; be brave, and it will have courage; be free, and freedom will abide in your high places and descend therefrom to the rabble least among you. Be dogs, and you will have a dog government — a kennel, a collar, a bone to gnaw and a chain to clank.[14]

W. J. Arkell, recently supplanted as publisher of *Judge*, launched several humorous magazines in the first decade of the new century. *Sis Hopkins' Own Book and Magazine of Fun* (1899–1911), a ten-cent bimonthly (later monthly) was the most successful of them. *Just Fun, That's all* (1903–1904) took over Eugene Zimmerman and Grant E. Hamilton from *Judge* and scrapped editorially with that journal. The *Foolish Book* (1903–1904) and *Fun Quarterly* (1903–1904) were two other Arkell ventures in this field.

The *Arkansas Thomas Cat* (1890–1948), by J. Davis Orear, of Hot Springs, Arkansas, yowled for more than the normal term of a cat's nine lives. Its editor was a nonconformist and vulgarian who at one time had many followers. There were also many comics of shorter life.[15]

### "EPHEMERAL BIBELOTS"

What Faxon called "ephemeral bibelots," and others nicknamed "fadazines," "chapbooks," or "little magazines," formed a curious and not unimportant feature of the magazine offering of the nineties. "They

[14] *Verdict*, v. 4, Nov. 12, 1900, p. 3.
[15] *Bee* (1898–99), New York; *Broadway* (1892–94), witty New York society journal con-

owe their origin probably to the success of the *Chap-Book*," said Faxon in introducing his bibliography of them.[16] Most of them followed that archetype by providing a small or odd-shaped page, fine typography and printing, and cleverness and radicalism in criticism. This triple characterization of the chapbooks is too simple, for they were nothing if not original, and no two were alike; they might be eccentric in format, printing, method of distribution, ideas, content. As *Le Petit Journal des Refusées*, which was published in a single number on wallpaper by James Marrion, of San Francisco, existed to tell the world, these ephemerae were printed (sometimes, at least) because their editors and contributors could not get their work published in established magazines. They were, in general, issued in the amateur spirit; and their editors were concerned less with making money from them than with merely keeping them alive as vehicles for their expression and that of their friends. Usually they did not keep them alive long.

The chapbooks seem to have come to a peak in number and queerness in the fall and winter of 1896. Said *Munsey's* in the summer of that year:

> A fad of the past year, and one that seems to be still on the increase, is what may be termed the "freak periodical." Its name is legion, and each new representative of the species is, if possible, more preposterous than the last. . . . They rave furiously, tearing at popular idols and beating in impotent rage at accepted standards. . . . And so these little magazines arise and rave and vanish into the oblivion from which they came. . . . They die almost as fast as they are born.[17]

The *Critic* complained that because "any youth just out of college, or any freshman just in college" could have his own magazine if he had a little money, "print has lost much of its dignity." This was a blow at the *Chap-Book*, whose publishers were collegians, though the *Critic* conceded that the *Chap-Book* was the best of the lot to date.[18]

There was a lull in the *bibelots* in 1898–1899, but a revival of them

---

ducted by Lew Rosen; *Fun* (1891), New York, C. L. Riker's unsuccessful attempt to introduce "the English brand of humor" into the United States; *Hallo* (1903–04), by Carl Hauser, formerly of *Puck*; *Hot Solder* (1901–04), Chicago, containing the "Sandy Pike" papers detailing the adventures of a country boy in Chicago, issued to advertise the hardware supplies of J. L. Perkins & Son; *Jolly Joker* (1899–1900), New Orleans, Edwin D. Elliott's weekly of politics and wit; *Kansas Knocker* (1900–01), Topeka, "A Journal for Cranks"; *Lies* (1889), told by the New York journalist, Alfred Trumble; *Light* (1889–91), begun in Columbus, Ohio, as *Owl*, then moved to Chicago, given the format of *Puck* and *Life*, losing $30,000 before it was abandoned (*Journalist*, July 11, 1891, p. 7); *Nast's Weekly* (1892), thirteen numbers of a political journal made notable by Thomas Nast's strong cartoons attacking Cleveland, etc.; *Pick* (1894), a primitive comic using old cuts; *Portland* (Maine) *Figaro* (1890–91), society and humor; *Sagebrush Philosophy* (1904–10), Douglas, Wyo., by M. C. Barrow; *Sam the Scaramouch* (1885–86), an ambitious Cincinnati weekly; *Texas Sifter* (1896), a brief attempt by Alex Sweet after he withdrew from *Texas Siftings*.

[16] *Bulletin of Bibliography*, v. 3, pp. 72ff, May 1903.
[17] *Munsey's Magazine*, v. 15, p. 374, June 1896.
[18] *Critic*, v. 30, p. 12, Jan. 2, 1897.

in 1900. They were the forerunners of the "little magazines" of a later date. The most important were the *Chap-Book*, the *Philistine*, and the *Bibelot*, each of which is treated separately in this volume.[19]

It may be that the *Lark* should be ranked with these leaders. It was unique in its high spirits and its freshness; and it was as clever as the best of them — one of the most charming magazines ever published. There were twenty-four monthly numbers, beginning with the one for May 1895, and followed by a twenty-fifth called the *Epilark*. Each number consisted of sixteen square twelvemo pages printed on one side of brownish bamboo paper, a bale of which Burgess had found in San Francisco's Chinatown, and which, remarked Carolyn Wells forty years later, "today disintegrates when you look at it. . . . I always turn my head when I pass the shelf that holds my copies." [20] Editors and chief writers of the first three numbers were the San Francisco muralist Bruce Porter and a young civil engineer named Gelett Burgess, who was doing a spot of teaching at the University of California. In the later numbers, Burgess' name appeared alone, though Porter continued to do sketches and fables for the little magazine. The boys began the venture with a hundred dollars, "just for a lark," and did not expect to issue a second number; but it was so well received that William Doxey took over its publication. At its end it had a circulation of five thousand; but, as Burgess said, he "wanted it to die young and in its full freshness."

Covers and other sketches were by the editors and Ernest Peixotto, Florence Lundborg, and Willis Polk. Yoni Noguchi, Carolyn Wells, Porter Garnett, and Juliet Wilbor Tompkins were outside contributors. But the fame of the little magazine was made by the quatrains, villanelles and rondeaux, fables and aphorisms, nonsense rhymes and children's verse by the editors. The very first number contained the "Purple Cow" quatrain, and the last one a sequel:

> Ah, yes, I wrote the Purple Cow!
> I'm sorry now I wrote it;
> But I can tell you anyhow,
> I'll kill you if you quote it!

Quoting Burgess and improvising *Lark*-like verses became a popular fad, if we are to believe the writer of the "Book Chat" in *Munsey's*:

During the last month or so we have heard them [Burgess rhymes] repeated far and near, in literary sancta, in business circles, in the thick of the social maze.

---

[19] In Sketches 8, 22, 4, respectively.

[20] See Carolyn Wells, "What a Lark!" in *Colophon*, part 8, 1931; also Claude Bragdon, "The Purple Cow Period," *Bookman*, v. 69, pp. 475–78, July 1929. C. A. Murdock & Company were the publishers; Burgess supervised typesetting and makeup in the shop. The *Lark* sold for 5¢ a copy its first year; the price was then doubled.

To exchange these ditties, to learn them by heart, to invent others like them, is a fad of the day. Someone has paraphrased one of Mr. Burgess' jingles in a way which seems to throw light on his literary methods:

> I write my verses in the dark
> And do not have to think;
> I make my fingers chase the pen
> And the pen pursue the ink! [21]

A kind of postscript to the *Epilark* was *Enfant Terrible*, edited by Burgess, Oliver Herford, and Miss Wells in a single number for April 1, 1898.

One of the earliest of these amateur magazines, antedating the *Chap-Book* and likewise edited by young Harvard men, was the brief *Mahogany Tree* of 1892, to which Algernon Tassin and Herbert Bates, of Harvard, and Jesse Lynch Williams, of Princeton, contributed. Unlike the "fadazines," it was a handsome quarto. Just before its end, Mildred Aldrich, Boston writer, took it over. The *Fly Leaf* (1895–1896) was Walter Blackburn Harte's hard-hitting "pamphlet periodical of the new." Percival Pollard, Arthur Grissom, and Bliss Carman were contributors. Harte claimed that Hubbard "murdered" it by offering a phony merger with his successful *Philistine*.[22] *Bradley, His Book* (1896–1897), of Springfield, Massachusetts, was the beautifully designed magazine of the artist Will H. Bradley. It had a tall page that lent itself to the poster effects of the editor. No two numbers were alike in formula. There were good contributors, with much literary comment; but the magazine's chief interest was in art. Apparently an imitator was the Chicago *Four O'Clock* (1897–1902), published by A. L. Swift & Company, manufacturers of college annuals. It was printed on a thick wood-pulp paper, with illustrations on calendared paper usually pasted on or tipped in. Writers were chiefly beginners, some of whom were later famous, as J. Oliver Curwood, Zona Gale, and Samuel Merwin. Henry Justin Smith was editor and publisher in the magazine's last months.

Of unusual typographic beauty were the nine numbers of the *Cranbrook Papers* (1900–1901), produced in the Cranbrook community near Detroit and sold at fifty cents a number. It was a quarto on handmade paper, using a Jenson type and illuminated captials, everything done by hand with great effectiveness. Much of the content related to printing arts, but there were some short stories and verse.

The *Blue Sky* (1899–1902) was conducted by Thomas Wood Stevens and Alden Charles Noble in Chicago. Frank W. Gunsaulus and James

---

[21] *Munsey's Magazine*, v. 15, p. 637, Aug. 1896.
[22] See *Lotus*, v. 2, p. 31, Jan. 1897.

Lane Allen were among the contributors. Also a Chicagoan was the *Goose-Quill* (1900–1904), of Cowley Stapleton Brown, whose *Anti-Philistine* (1897) had been published a few years before in London. Subtitled "An Anglo-American Magazine," it was notable for the editor's sharp literary criticism under the heading "Reading and Rot," later continued in the *10 Story Book*, which Frank Harris called, in retrospect, "about the best book criticism written in the United States." [23] *Goose-Quill* had wit, a certain literary quality, and boldness — nothing if not boldness. Among its contributors were Eugene Field, Opie Read, Clarence Darrow, Michael Monahan, and William Marion Reedy.

But there were hundreds of these little periodicals, every one of which seemed important to someone at some time.[24] In Faxon's admittedly incomplete list, compiled in 1903, there were two hundred and twenty-eight entries. Some of these seem interesting today chiefly for their choice of names, such as *Angel's Food* (1901), Los Angeles; *Buzz Saw* (1897), New York; *Clack Book* (1896–1897), Lansing, Michigan; *Fad* (1896–1897), San Antonio, Texas; *Freak* (1902–1903), Sharon, Massachusetts; *Jabs* (1902–1904), Chicago; *Stiletto* (1900–

---

[23] *Pearson's Magazine*, v. 39, p. 152, July 1918.

[24] Some which seem worth mentioning are listed here: *Alkahest* (1896–1903), Atlanta, according to its boast, "The Leading Literary Gossip Book of America"; *Bauble* (1895–97), Washington, whose only good feature was its biting literary criticism; *Burr McIntosh Monthly* (1903–10), New York, narrow-octavo, mostly an exhibit of photographic art, though Ethel Watts Mumford was a leading contributor to early numbers and George Jean Nathan was the dramatic critic later; *Cornhill Booklet* (1900–14), Boston, which followed the *Bibelot's* example in reprinting choice and little-known material, but was suspended 1906–14; *Echo* (1895–97), Chicago, Percival Pollard's magazine, which specialized in its department "Poster Lore"; *Ghourki* (1901–09), Morgantown, W. Va., printed on butcher's paper, emphasizing wit and inspiration; *Good Cheer* (1900–01), Boston, Nixon Waterman's "Magazine for Cheerful Thinkers," to which Sam Walter Foss, Hezekiah Butterworth, and Opie Read contributed; *Honey Jar* (1898–1911), Columbus, Ohio, not always so sweet as it sounds; *Ishmaelite* (1896–99), Indianapolis, edited by H. H. Howland, with such contributors as Maurice Thompson, Meredith Nicholson, Elbert Hubbard, and W. B. Harte; *Kiote* (1898–1901), Lincoln, Neb., to which such Nebraskans as Edwin Ford Piper and Hartley Burr Alexander were contributors; *Knocker* (1901–04), another Nebraskan, edited by a vituperative writer named Will A. Campbell (*Grit* once said it was impatiently awaiting "the news that someone had introduced a bullet into Campbell's gizzard with fatal results"); *Lotus* (1895–97), Kansas City, a collaboration of several Kansas collegians; *Lucky Dog* (1900–10), Springfield, Ohio, and Winchester, Mass., literary and inspirational, revived 1940–44 as an annual; *Muse* (1900–02), Oakland, Cal., "a journal of art and letters"; *Papyrus* (1903–12), Mt. Vernon, N.Y. (single issue at Newburg in 1896), "a magazine of individuality"; *Philharmonic* (1901–03), Chicago, devoted to literature, music, art, and drama (called *Muse* in final numbers); *Philosopher* (1897–1906), Wausau, Wis., edited by William H. Ellis, with the motto, "Thoughtful, but Not Too Thoughtful"; *Seen and Heard by Megargee* (1901–08), Philadelphia, the continuation of a column in the *Philadelphia Times* by Louis N. Megargee; *Time and the Hour* (1896–1900), Boston, edited during at least part of its life by Edwin M. Bacon, with contributions from Margaret Deland, Robert Grant, Frank B. Sanborn, and Ruth McEnery Stuart; *What's the Use?* (very irregularly 1901–04), East Aurora, N.Y., iconoclastic and socialistic; *Whim* (1901–05), Ridgewood, N.J., edited by Ernest Crosby and Benedict Prieth under Tolstoian influence. See Frederick Winthrop Faxon, *Modern Chap-Books and Their Imitators* (Boston, 1903), a reprint of bibliography first entitled "Ephemeral Bibelots," cited in footnote 16, *supra*.

1901), New York; *Tabasco* (1902), Lapeer, Michigan; *Wet Dog* (1896),
Boston; *Yellow Dog* (1901), Chicago. Some of these were criticisms
of the movement — satires on themselves.

COLLECTORS' JOURNALS

The veteran *American Journal of Philately* and a few others begun
in preceding periods [25] held over into the present one; but the lives of
these journals, issued mostly by dealers or as media of exchange
among amateurs, were commonly short. The organ of the American
Philatelic Association was the *American Philatelist*, founded in 1887.
*Mekeel's Weekly Stamp News* (1891–current), which was published in
St. Louis through the present period and after,[26] was one of the most
successful magazines in the field. Charles Haviland Mekeel also published now and again the monthly *Philatelic Journal of America* (1885–
1917). One of the western stamp-collectors' journals was *Filatelic
Facts and Fallacies* (1892–1901), a San Francisco monthly. There
were some two score others in the period.[27]

There were also a few coin-collectors' magazines, chief of which was
the old *American Journal of Numismatics* (1866–1919), of Boston.
The leading journal of the autograph hunters was the interesting
*Collector* (1887–current), published in New York by the well-known
dealer, Walter Romeyn Benjamin. Arthur Chamberlain's *Mineral
Collector* (1894–1909) succeeded William M. Goldthwaite's *Minerals*
(1892–1893) in New York. The *Nautilus* (1886–current) is considerably more than a journal for the collector of shells.

The *Sphinx* (1902–1921) was the organ of the Society of American
Magicians.

[25] See Mott, *op. cit.*, v. 3, p. 113, footnote.
[26] It later moved to New York, Boston, Portland.
[27] Among them: *American Philatelic Magazine* (1892–1902), Omaha; *Metropolitan Philatelist* (1890–1920), New York; *Philatelic Bulletin* (1897–1902), Newmarket, N. H., which
absorbed *Eastern Philatelist* (1887–99); *Philatelic Era* (1889–1904), Portland, Maine;
*Philatelic West* (1896–1930), Superior, Neb.

# SUPPLEMENT

For an explanation of the organization of the supplement, see the preface to this volume. For comment on the method of the bibliographical treatment, which appears as footnote 1 of each sketch, the reader is referred to the first volume of this work, page 69.

The following magazines began in the period 1885–1905 but were much more important later, and are therefore designated for separate sketches in the next volume of this history: *American Boy, Appleton's Booklovers' Magazine, Christian Century, Editor & Publisher, Everybody's Magazine, Field and Stream, Good Housekeeping, Hampton's Broadway Magazine, House Beautiful, Metropolitan Magazine, Pearson's Monthly, Physical Culture, Pictorial Review, Red Book, South Atlantic Quarterly, Success, Yale Review.*

# THE ANDOVER REVIEW [1]

WHEN the *Bibliotheca Sacra*, which had been published at Andover for forty years, was moved to Oberlin, there to enjoy an atmosphere of more assured liberalism than seemed possible amid the theological conflicts which beset the older seminary,[2] a new faculty started a new journal. Not all the Andover Theological Seminary faculty was new: Egbert C. Smyth, its president and the professor of ecclesiastical history, had been at Andover for twenty years, and William Jewett Tucker had been professor of sacred rhetoric five years when the *Andover Review* was founded. But George Harris had just been inducted into the chair of theology; John W. Churchill and Edward Y. Hincks were likewise newcomers; and it was generally recognized that a new era was opening for Andover with the beginning of the fourth quarter of her first century.

The *Andover Review's* first number was a handsome 120-page magazine, octavo in size. It was issued, as were all the following numbers, by Houghton, Mifflin & Company, of Boston, who were also the publishers of the *Atlantic Monthly*. It announced itself as a monthly, to be had at four dollars a year. Since the first number foreshadows in many respects the entire file, it may be examined in some detail.

It opens with an introductory article by Smyth,[3] "The Theological Purpose of the Review," which said:

The editors of this Review will welcome to its pages the contributions of men of various schools of thought who are seeking with them to develop a truly

[1] TITLE: *The Andover Review: A Religious and Theological Monthly.* (The last word waš changed to "Bi-Monthly" on the half titles but not on the title page of the last volume.)
FIRST ISSUE: Jan. 1884. LAST ISSUE: Nov.–Dec. 1893.
PERIODICITY: Monthly, 1884–92; bimonthly, 1893. Vols. 1–18, regular semiannual vols., 1884–92; v. 19, regular bimonthly numbers, 1893.
PUBLISHER: Houghton, Mifflin & Company, Boston.
EDITORS: Egbert Coffin Smyth, William Jewett Tucker, John Wesley Churchill, George Harris, and Edward Young Hincks. Assistant Editors: John P. Gulliver, John Phelps Taylor, George Foot Moore, and Frank E. Woodruff. (William Hering Ryder took the place of Woodruff in 1893.)
INDEXES: Index to vols. 1–10 in v. 10. Indexed in *Poole's Index* and *Review of Reviews Annual Index.*
REFERENCES: Daniel Day Williams, *The Andover Liberals* (New York, 1941); Egbert C. Smyth and others, *The Andover Defence* (Boston, 1887).
[2] For *Bibliotheca Sacra*, see Mott, *A History of American Magazines* (Cambridge, 1939), v. 1, pp. 739–42. This journal ended in 1943, after 90 years of publication. It was published during 1930–33 by the faculty of Pittsburgh-Xenia Theological Seminary, and during 1934–43 by Dallas (Texas) Theological Seminary. Editors: M. G. Kyle, 1922–33; Rollin T. Chafer, 1934–40; Lewis S. Chafer, 1940–43.
[3] *Andover Review*, v. 1, pp. 1–12, Jan. 1884.

Christian theology. . . . We seek to promote large-minded, large-hearted discussions of Christian truth. . . . To our thought, there is a preparation and demand for better statements of Christian doctrine in the religious life of our time.

President Smyth, while welcoming the study of natural science, added:

But the attempted identification of natural law with supernatural, of the forces with which physical science deals and those which rule in the spiritual sphere, is but a new instance of an old peril. Calvinism cannot be established by Darwinism, admitting Darwinism itself to be established.

This position with regard to the theory of evolution was maintained consistently by the *Andover Review* throughout. Herbert Spencer's metaphysical applications of that theory were often attacked, and a student of the file tells us that "more of the polemics in the *Andover Review* are directed against Spencer than any other thinker." [4] But the passage that indicated the thinking which was to make Smyth's journal the center of the bitterest theological quarrel of the times is found in the middle of his introductory essay:

Ideally the phrase "Christian Doctrine" denotes something perfectly true, a correct reflection of the truth revealed in Christ. Experimentally and practically it includes that appropriation and explication of this truth which has been going on in the Church to the present time. It means revealed truth interpreted, applied, logically developed, formally stated, by Christian minds. . . . It cannot reasonably be questioned that every reader of these pages is now holding some belief as a part of his Christian faith, some dogma as a part of his theology, which Christian men of later generations will reject. This experimental law of belief should teach modesty.

Perhaps more shocking because more specific was the article entitled "The Doctrine of Sacred Scripture" by Harris, which was a discussion of George T. Ladd's new book of that name. Dartmouth Congregational theology had once fought that of Yale; now, in certain modernities, they embraced. Harris noted with approval Ladd's argument that the Biblical account of the creation was scientifically incorrect, that Joshua's feat in making the sun stand still was literary rather than factual, that while a whale could doubtless swallow a man, the story of Jonah was important mainly as an allegory.

There is other theological and religious matter in this first number. The Editorial Department, which runs to a dozen or more pages, has a history of the new German revision of the Bible; editorials in later issues were often to take more space and give more of what they took to theology. A department called "Theological and Religious Intelligence" was devoted to an account of the Sixth International Congress

[4] Williams, *The Andover Liberals*, p. 15.

of Orientalists and to news of several missionary conventions. This department was later irregular, dealt often with foreign movements, and came to be used for series on missions. Another department, conducted by Professor John Phelps Taylor, one of the assistant editors, was called "Archaeological Notes," and told of developments in that field which were related to studies of the Scriptures. The department of book reviews was occupied chiefly with theological works. In the first number, a review of Henry Drummond's *Natural Law in the Spiritual World* gave Smyth an opportunity to reiterate his warning against "premature recasting of Christian dogma in scientific molds."[5] The department of "Biblical and Historical Criticism," important though irregular in later volumes, was not begun with Volume I, Number 1; "Sociological Notes," edited by Samuel W. Dike, and "Notes from England," by Joseph King, appeared even less frequently.

The second article in the first number of the *Review* was Washington Gladden's "Christianity and Aestheticism." The author was well known as a clergyman-journalist of advanced social views, and this article was rather an attack on the "luxurious classes" and their pleasures than the philosophical discussion suggested by its title. Gladden's recently published *Things New and Old in Discourses of Christian Truth and Love* is noticed favorably in the review department. The progress made by the *Andover Review* in its own thinking in its ten years of life is well illustrated by the contrast between the review of Gladden's 1883 book and that of his 1893 book, *Tools and the Man*, published in the journal's last number. The latter review is chiefly a warning to "zealous philanthropy" that "economic and in a growing measure social problems are scientific problems."[6]

Another clerical publicist was in the *Review's* first number — Charles H. Parkhurst, with "A Bible Study — The Unjust Steward." Here was Parkhurst's favorite solution of the labor question — love and sympathy of the employer for the employed, of the rich for the poor. It was to become a favorite doctrine of the *Andover Review*.

An article on "The Religious Condition of France" serves to indicate the future course of the journal in stressing studies of religion abroad. Andover was founded for the training of missionaries quite as much as for the education of men for American pulpits, and the *Review* is definitely a missionary magazine. A question of administration in this field was soon to involve both the seminary and the *Review* in bitter controversy.

In this first number appeared two poems by Caroline Hazard, later

[5] *Andover Review*, v. 1, p. 107, Jan. 1884.
[6] *Ibid.*, v. 19, p. 759, Nov.–Dec. 1893.

president of Wellesley College. Poetry is not common in the file of the
*Review*, but John G. Whittier and Paul Hamilton Hayne contributed
verse to it. There was no literary criticism of note in the first number,
but in each of the ensuing issues there was, as a rule, one such essay.
Charles F. Richardson, Hamilton Wright Mabie, George R. Carpenter,
Edward Everett Hale, and others contributed articles of this character.
Biography was not uncommon through the decade; Gamaliel Bradford,
Jr., and Henry Cabot Lodge wrote in this field, and Wendell Phillips
Garrison's series on John Brown in 1890–1891 was notable.

It is easy to compile a considerable list of distinguished writers whose
articles on religion and theology, education, philosophy, economics, sociology, history, and so on, lent importance to the pages of the *Andover
Review*. On that list were such scholars as Daniel Coit Gilman, first
president of Johns Hopkins; Arthur Twining Hadley, not yet president
of Yale; John Dewey, then of the University of Michigan; President G.
Stanley Hall, of Clark; Mark Hopkins, of Williams; Andrew Preston
Peabody, then retired from the Harvard faculty; President E. Benjamin Andrews, of Brown; Asa Gray and N. S. Shaler, famous Harvard
scientists. An important *Review* writer on theological topics was Francis
Howe Johnson. C. C. Starbuck wrote much on missions and other topics.
Other well-known contributors were Lyman Abbot, Julius H. Ward,
George Herbert Palmer, and Vida D. Scudder.

In its second year, the *Review* was said by a discriminating commentator, the *Critic*, to "strike a happy mean between the learned review and the magazine." The same writer went on: "It deals much with
theological topics, but aims to treat them with compactly uttered, sound
commonsense. . . . It comes home closely to the average educated
man."[7] Throughout its life the *Review* was concerned with social problems; to use a term then much in vogue, it was devoted largely to "social
Christianity" and to altruistic reform in general.

But it was after the period referred to in this perspicuous statement
by the *Critic* that the *Andover Review* gained such fame — or notoriety,
at least — as has been accorded to few religious magazines. This came
not from its excellence as a magazine, but from the "Andover trials."

The doctrinal positions taken by the *Review*, especially in a series of
articles first printed in the Editorial Department and later issued in
book form under the title *Progressive Orthodoxy*, gave great offense to
many prominent supporters of Andover Seminary. Complaints were
made in the Board of Trustees against the five editors, and in 1886
these complaints were carried to the Board of Visitors, the body with
power to remove offenders from the faculty for cause. Technically, the

[7] *Critic*, v. 6, p. 192, April 18, 1885.

charges were mainly unfaithfulness to the Andover Creed, which, as a matter of fact, had been an 1808 compromise between Old Calvinism and Hopkinsianism. Now, however, there was to be no new compromise with the old compromise: truth was eternal, i.e., truth in the words of the Andover Creed. The talk in the journal about "experimental laws of belief" was the "most stupendous breach of truth of a century." There was a trial before the Board of Visitors; it was a full-dress affair, with testimony, statements, and arguments. The chief prosecutor was a former Attorney General of the United States, Judge E. Rockwood Hoar. The trial attracted national attention, the newspapers as well as the religious press devoting many columns to it. The orthodox argued that the Andover professors were dishonest because they had accepted the creed with their jobs and now forswore it; on the other hand, liberals hoped that Smyth and his associates might lead the people out of medieval superstitions. Wrote the vivacious Gail Hamilton in the *North American Review*:

> Mr. Samuel Jones [the revivalist Sam Jones] lately electrified to shrieks a Boston congregation with a story of a thoroughly materialistic Devil chasing a lost and departing soul around a woodpile and through a window — which is in line with the Andover Creed.[8]

The immediate result of the trials was the action of the board removing Smyth; the others would doubtless have been disposed of later if the Smyth verdict had been effective. But appeal was immediately taken to the courts on the question of the powers of the board. It was not until 1891 that the Supreme Court of Massachusetts set aside the decision of the board. The next year some attempt was made to revive the charges; but the board finally dismissed the whole case, and what Gail Hamilton had called "that everlasting Andover controversy" was finished at last.

The *Andover Review* was deeply involved in another great controversy. The American Board of Foreign Missions, strongly rejecting the Andover doctrine of future probation, rejected also certain graduates of that seminary who were candidates for appointment to the mission field. The idea of future probation was an invention of theologians who could not face the idea that uncounted millions of heathen had all been condemned to endless torment because they had never heard of the gospel of Christ; it was conceived that these souls would have an opportunity after death to know and confess the love of God. The American Board took the position that such a doctrine made a mockery of the whole missionary movement. Andover won this controversy also. In 1893 the

---

[8] Gail Hamilton, "That Everlasting Andover Controversy," *North American Review*, v. 144, p. 481, May 1887.

board accepted William H. Noyes, Andover graduate, who had not changed his opinion after three former rejections by the ruling body; as a result the home secretary of the board resigned.[9]

Throughout these conflicts, the *Andover Review* kept an admirably calm and equable course. There was no vilification, personalities were absent, all was on a high plane of stoutly maintained position without undue attack. The *Review* cannot be said to have been primarily a controversial journal; and yet it was probably controversy that made it prosperous in the late eighties, and it was the end of controversy that ended the *Review*. Late in 1892 it was determined to make the journal a bimonthly. "The long season of controversy in connection with the Seminary, which necessitated the frequent and possibly disproportionate treatment of controversial subjects, is practically over."[10] Now every other month was often enough, and besides such a plan would make a reduction to three dollars a year in the subscription price possible. So the *Review* continued through 1893, and then succumbed, saying that the editorial work was too great a load for full-time teachers.[11]

The *Andover Review* stands, after all, as a symbol of the transition from the older Calvinism to more modern religious views. It printed much that was not theological, and only a comparatively small part of its file bears directly on the "Andover case"; yet it is chiefly notable as the mouthpiece of the men involved in that once famous controversy.

[9] See Williston Walker, *A History of the Congregational Churches in the United States* (third edition; New York, 1898), p. 421. For the Smyth trial, see *ibid.*, p. 416.
[10] *Andover Review*, v. 18, p. 526, Nov. 1892.
[11] *Ibid.*, v. 19, p. 713, Nov.–Dec. 1893.

2

# THE ARENA[1]

THE *Arena* was founded by B. O. Flower and was conducted by him throughout most of its career of two decades. Though ten or a dozen other persons were associated with the management of this monthly magazine during those years, as coeditors, associate editors, publishers, and business managers, and though for a few years of its life Flower was not even on the staff, his was always the dominating personality. Whatever significance the *Arena* had was based upon editorial policies for which Flower was chiefly responsible.

Benjamin Orange Flower was a member of a notable Illinois family. His grandfather and great-grandfather had come from England to the prairies of the Midwest, to found the town of Albion, Illinois, to sell to Robert Owen the land for his socialistic community at New Harmony, Indiana, and to leave their impress for liberalism and intellectual progress on the Illinois frontier. Benjamin's father was a minister of the Disciples of Christ, and educated his son for similar service. In those days educational requirements for the ministry were often low, and B. O. Flower had only one year of college work, which he spent at the Bible School of Transylvania University. His experience as a clergyman

[1] TITLE: *The Arena.*

FIRST ISSUE: Dec. 1889. LAST ISSUE: Aug. 1909.

PERIODICITY: Monthly. Vols. 1–10, regular semiannual vols. beginning with Dec. and June, Dec. 1889–Nov. 1894; 11, Dec. 1894–Feb. 1895; 12, March–May 1895; 13, June–Aug. 1895; 14, Sept.–Nov. 1895; 15, Dec. 1895–May 1896; 16, June–Nov. 1896; 17, Dec. 1896–June 1897; 18–40 regular semiannual vols. beginning with Jan. and July, July 1897–Dec. 1908; 41, Jan., Feb., March, July, Aug. 1909.

PUBLISHERS: Arena Publishing Company, Boston, 1889–99; Alliance Publishing Company, New York, 1899–1904; Albert Brandt, Trenton, N. J., 1904–09.

EDITORS: Benjamin Orange Flower, 1889–97, 1900–09 (with Charles Brodie Patterson, 1900–04); John Clark Ridpath, 1897–98; Paul Tyner, 1898–99; John Emery McLean, 1899–1900; Neuville O. Fanning, 1900.

INDEXES: *Poole's Index, Cumulative Index, Jones' Legal Index, Review of Reviews Annual Index, Readers' Guide.*

REFERENCES: B. O. Flower, *Progressive Men, Women and Movements of the Past Twenty-Five Years* (Boston, 1914); H. F. Cline, "Benjamin Orange Flower and the *Arena*, 1889–1909," *Journalism Quarterly*, v. 17, pp. 139–50, June 1940; H. F. Cline, "Flower and the *Arena*: Purpose and Content," *ibid.*, pp. 247–57, Sept. 1940; H. F. Cline, "Mechanics of Dissent" (unpublished honors thesis, Hist. Dept., Harvard University, 1939); David H. Dickason, "Benjamin Orange Flower, Patron of the Realists," *American Literature*, v. 14, pp. 148–56, May 1942; David H. Dickason, "The Contribution of B. O. Flower and the Arena to Critical Thought in America" (unpublished dissertation, Ohio State University, 1940); Roy P. Fairfield, "Benjamin Orange Flower, Father of the Muckrakers," *American Literature*, v. 22, pp. 272–82, Nov. 1950; Fred C. Mabee, "Benjamin Orange Flower and the Arena, 1889–96" (unpublished thesis, Columbia University, 1938). (Note: Grateful acknowledgment is made to Howard F. Cline, chief authority on Flower and the *Arena*, for the use of his notes, clippings, and correspondence.)

was likewise short. His call to the ministry was not very clear, but there was no doubt about the clarity or urgency of his call to journalism. At the age of twenty-two he and another young fellow founded a weekly family newspaper and miscellany at Albion called the *American Sentinel* (1880–1882). It was Republican in politics and devoted to the cause of temperance. His ambitions made him impatient with small-town journalism, however, and he soon joined a brother in Philadelphia.

This brother, Dr. Richard G. Flower, after brief experiences in law and the ministry, had taken a course at the "Cincinnati Health College," and now, in 1881, was running a business professing to cure nervous disorders. He had offices in Philadelphia and New York and was planning to open one in Boston.[2] He had a big mail-order business, and offered his younger brother a secretarial job. The business prospered greatly, and Dr. Flower built a magnificent new sanitarium in Boston. He also took care of his brother's special interests by starting, or allowing Benjamin to start, a dollar monthly for the family, which was amply justified by its advertising of Dr. Flower's flourishing enterprises. This periodical was the *American Spectator*, of Boston, which began in 1886 and was merged in the *Arena* when that magazine was founded three years later. Apparently, however, the *Arena* did little or nothing for brother Richard, and the *Spectator* had a brief postscript career in 1890–1891. Thereafter Richard was frequently in trouble for practicing without a proper license, for fraud in connection with selling mining stock, for alleged swindles in connection with an artificial diamond formula, and so on. Twice he escaped when under indictment, forfeiting bail.[3]

All this family background of reformatory zeal, intellectuality, religion, and quackery are important in understanding the career of B. O. Flower's *Arena*, a review of importance in its times, which gave space to articles conforming to all these background elements. According to the apparently unanimous testimony of those who knew him well, B. O. Flower was sincere, altruistic, and zealous for the reform of all abuses; but his mind was neither profound nor ordinarily critical. It must be remembered, however, that it is a dictum of the free-press hypothesis that all views must have a hearing; and the very title of Flower's review predicated the clash of truth and error in open conflict.

The *Arena* first appeared as a monthly octavo of something over a hundred pages in Boston in December 1889. At first there was a good

<hr />

[2] Richard Herndon and Edwin M. Bacon, *Boston of To-Day* (Boston, 1892), pp. 227–28.

[3] "Dr. Flower of Boston Arrested," *Boston Globe*, Feb. 27, 1892, p. 1; "The World Finds Dr. Flower in Philadelphia," *New York World*, Jan. 5, 1907, p. 1; "Stock Swindler Arrested," *Boston Evening Transcript*, Jan. 5, 1907, part 2, p. 8; "Dr. Flower Forfeits Bail," *ibid.*, April 9, 1907.

deal of religion in the magazine's contents, but it soon became apparent that social reform was the chief interest of the editor. When the magazine was about a year and a half old, W. T. Stead, an English critic who watched American magazines carefully and commented on them wisely, wrote that the *Arena* was already established in the first rank. Some of Stead's observations are well worth quoting:

Mr. Flower, its editor, impresses his personality upon its pages, which is more than can be said of the editors of either the *Forum* or *North American*. If we may judge of the editor from the magazine he edits, we should say that Mr. Flower is a young man with strong sympathies for the people, whose humanitarian instincts have not yet crystallized. . . . He has great sympathies with socialism, especially in its protests against the slavery of women, but he recoils against any system which destroys liberty and cripples individualism. He is a man with an open mind, who, if he does not believe in millionaires, nevertheless is quite open to believe in ghosts. He does not bar his magazine to the orthodox, but they never seem to be quite at home in his pages. . . . The *Arena* is never *dull*, although it is sometimes mad, or, to speak more correctly, it sometimes publishes a mad article, which, after all, is rather welcome. . . . It is an open arena for the discussion of subjects tabooed by the *Forum* and the *North American*. There is more audacity about the *Arena* than its older rivals.

The *Arena* for June is even more desperately strenuous than usual. . . . I am tolerably strenuous, but I cannot hold a candle to Mr. Flower of the *Arena*, whose magazine from the first page to the last is strained almost to the breaking point with overcharged earnestness.[4]

This is all very well said, and it applies as well to all the first half and last fourth of the *Arena* file as to the early months. The comparisons with the *Forum* and *North American* are appropriate, because the *Arena* was highly conscious of a rivalry with these reviews, especially with the *Forum*.

Let us look now at some of the doctrines and crusades that filled the pages of the *Arena*. We might as well begin with religion, which was prominent in the file from first to last. In the very first number, three of the eight articles were in this field — Minot J. Savage's "Agencies That Are Working a Revolution in Theology," in which this prominent Unitarian clergyman, who was to continue one of the most faithful contributors on religious, social, and literary topics throughout the *Arena's* first phase, discussed the effect of scientific discovery on ideas of the nature of God, of man, and of the Scriptures; W. H. H. Murray's "The Religious Question," one of the eloquent but overrated Boston Music Hall addresses of that odd genius; Hurson Tuttle's "A Threatened Invasion of Religious Freedom," in which a prominent reformer and spiritualist sounded an alarm against the movement to introduce the

---

[4] *Review of Reviews*, v. 4, pp. 51–52, July 1891.

name of God into the Constitution. Tuttle's article was followed, in the next issue, by one on the same subject from the pen of that spokesman of the agnostics, Robert G. Ingersoll.

This proportion of articles on religion was not maintained in the face of growing variety in the *Arena's* pages; but there was never a number of this review which did not deal at some length, directly or indirectly, in article, book review, symposium, or editorial, with the grand subject of religion. Says Howard F. Cline, the most industrious and discriminating analyst of the *Arena* file:

a high percentage of the contributors came from the clergy. They differed radically among themselves; but no denomination, faith, or creed, however exotic, was excluded. Rabbi Solomon Schindler could be found between Episcopal Canon Freemantle and Catholic Bishop Spalding. . . . Religions of other lands were thoroughly treated, from Judaism to Mohammedanism, and increasing tolerance was spurred by reports from the World Congress of Religions.[5]

The relations of theology and religious movements to science, the so-called higher criticism of the Bible, missionary effort, spiritism, theosophy, ethical culture, Christian Science, and social Christianity were prominently and repeatedly stressed. And the *Arena* joined in the heated discussion of whether the Chicago World's Fair should be open to the public on Sundays.

"Christianity must take off its kid gloves," Flower was soon declaring, and meet the underprivileged "as man to man, or they will rot in the slums of our present civilization."[6] Moreover, Flower practiced what he preached: he took off his kid gloves, and went after Boston slums, which were owned in some cases by pillars of Back Bay society. *Arena* exposés were reprinted in a widely distributed pamphlet entitled *Civilization's Inferno*. Press and pulpit were aroused, there was a legislative investigation, and helpful housing and sanitation laws were enacted. So moving were the articles published during this crusade that more than three thousand dollars came to the *Arena* in cash contributions to relieve the immediate want of Boston slum dwellers.[7]

Poverty, sweatshops, slum clearance, unemployment, and child labor were important topics throughout the life of the *Arena*, but particularly during the hard times of the mid-nineties. Among the writers on these subjects were such scholars and reformers in the field of social investigation as Helen Campbell, N. P. Gilman, Frank Parsons, Walter Blackburn Harte, Edward Everett Hale, and, most important of all, Flower himself. "During the first five years of the *Arena*," Flower wrote later,

---

[5] Cline in *Journalism Quarterly*, v. 17, p. 253, Sept. 1940.
[6] *Arena*, v. 3, p. xxii, April 1891. For other comment on *Robert Elsmere*, see pp. 280–81.
[7] Flower, *Progressive Men*, p. 123.

"we published over fifty carefully prepared contributions dealing with the problem of advancing poverty and its attendant evils."[8]

One of the "attendant evils" was prostitution, which was discussed more frankly than it had ever been before in any magazine designed for the general public. Theodore Schroeder, for example, tried to encourage a scientific rather than a sentimental view of the matter in his "Prostitution as a Social Problem."[9] There was no *Arena* tabu on discussions of sex matters, wherever they cropped up. Birth control was openly advocated. "If children are not wanted," wrote Sydney Barrinton Elliot, M.D., as early as 1894, "then those responsible for them should see to it that their *conception is prevented,* since there are harmless, effectual, and entirely satisfactory means to this end."[10] In 1908–1909 Rabbi Schindler debated "race suicide" with John Haynes Holmes, Rose Pastor Stokes, and Helen Campbell. Some *Arena* articles supported "advanced" ideas — the use of hypnotism in surgery, socialized medicine, and opposition to medical monopoly, and printed much nonsense about prenatal influences.

Filling many pages of the earlier *Arena* was a crusade for raising the "age of consent" to eighteen by state laws; thus intercourse with girls under that age would be rape by legal definition. This was a long campaign, which ran through the first half of the nineties and beyond. The Woman's Christian Temperance Union joined in it, and strong pressures were exerted on state legislatures. The laws sought were enacted in six states in the course of this crusade.

Women were very important in the pages of the *Arena.* They were important as subject matter, as contributors, and even as editors. Almost a fourth of the contents of the first twenty volumes were written by women.[11] For the very first number Mary A. Livermore wrote, on request, an essay entitled "Centuries of Dishonor," in which she reviewed the wrongs that women had suffered throughout the ages. Chief *Arena* topics in this field were divorce, the education of women, women's clubs, female labor in factories, the rights of women in marriage, suffrage, and dress reform. The issue for August 1891 contained articles by eight women. Flower himself contributed a paper to that number entitled "The Era of Women," which W. T. Stead criticized as a "beatific vision," because "all women do not have wings under their stays."[12]

Whatever was under them, the stays themselves were a major concern of Editor Flower, who was an ardent dress-reformer. The *Arena* pub-

---

[8] *Ibid.,* p. 120.
[9] *Arena,* v. 41, pp. 196–201, Feb. 1909.
[10] *Arena,* v. 10, p. 668, Oct. 1894. See also v. 12, p. xvii, May 1895.
[11] Cline, "Mechanics of Dissent," p. 72.
[12] *Review of Reviews,* v. 4, p. 298, Sept. 1891.

lished scores of articles by men and women — doctors, clergymen, artists — vigorously attacking tight lacing and long skirts. Flower declared repeatedly, "Women cannot have brains till they have ankles." He and his wife even designed reform garments, which were pictured in the *Arena*; and patterns for them were widely distributed. The reformers expected to receive much help from the popular enthusiasm for bicycling, for which they planned what they thought were suitable costumes. This dress-reform campaign was another of the *Arena's* ambitious and intensive crusades.

But the biggest crusades, after all, were those which Flower and his staff conducted in the fields of politics and economics. Henry George's single-tax doctrine, Edward Bellamy's "Nationalism," W. T. Stead's socio-economic reform ideas, the city "settlement house" movement, General James B. Weaver's Populism, and the propaganda for the free coinage of silver were all in general circulation when the *Arena* was founded; they were all challenging and controversial concepts, most of them gaining in popularity. Then, soon after the review began, the hard times of the early nineties came on, emphasizing the need for reform and building up strong popular antagonisms against trusts and other combinations of wealth. All these things operated to make the *Arena* what it was in the nineties.

Among the magazine's chief "causes" in the field of political-economic reform were free silver, agrarian reform, the single tax, the antitrust war, the initiative and referendum, primary elections, the reform of municipal governments, and prohibition of the liquor traffic. Not that the *Arena* was consistently dogmatic. It took sides, both editorially and by means of a kind of unplanned allotment of space; but the other side occasionally got a hearing. Thus Henry George's chief contribution was an article in the second number advocating the removal of all restrictions on the sale of intoxicants in order to annihilate the "rum power" in politics. Even more striking was "The Unrighteousness of Government, as Viewed by a Philosophical Anarchist," by one Charles Clark Rodolf, M.D. The Utah, or Mormon, question was one on which sharply divergent opinions were expressed by such men as Joseph F. Smith, of Salt Lake City, and Theodore Curtis, of Boston. Symposiums, which were common in the *Arena*, were designed, of course, to bring together differing viewpoints; but beyond this, there was a studied liberty of the contributor in *Arena* policy that was Flower's honest tribute to freedom of the press. Hamlin Garland tells, for example, of the letter Flower wrote to him in accepting his first contribution, in which he noted that certain paragraphs of social commentary had been marked out; the editor remonstrated, expressing the fear that the suppressions had been made to avoid violating *Arena* policy, and urged: "I do not wish you to feel, in writing for the *Arena*, at any time the slightest restraint." [13]

Garland, who entered the pages of the magazine as a writer of literary and imaginative pieces, remained for a time as a social and political reformer. His special interest was in populism and the single tax. Flower, who seems to have regarded Garland with the enthusiasm of a leader for a talented disciple, financed a journey for his new writer to the Midwest and Southwest to view at first hand the phenomena of the agrarian revolt. Congressman John Davis, of Kansas, if not as talented, was quite as prolific, particularly in discussions of the currency problem. In fact, the *Arena* became a kind of textbook of the populist movement. Flower later quoted a Kansas worker for the Farmers' Alliance as saying of the magazine, "We took it with us everywhere, and clinched our arguments with quotations from it." [14]

Municipal government was a continuing subject. Josiah Quincy, of Boston, and Hazen S. Pingree, of Detroit, reform mayors both, told how they did it in the *Arena*. Such was not the method later used by the muckraking magazines; that was, however, approximated in Rudolph Blankenburg's serial exposé of the Philadelphia machine in 1905, and a little later in J. Warner Mills's "The Economic Struggle in Colorado."

Direct legislation, as a means of combating the power of the "interests" in legislative halls, was one of the magazine's favorite topics. "Ours is not a government of the people, but of the corporations, and for the millionaires" [15] was a kind of assertion common in the magazine in the mid-nineties. W. D. McCrackan, an authority on Swiss Government, discussed in several articles the methods of initiative and referendum used in that country. The *Arena* published *A Primer of Direct Legislation*, which enthusiasts circulated widely.

Many other developing fields of thought received attention in Flower's review. Criminology and penology, with prison reform and strong opposition to capital punishment, were often prominent. There was some discussion of the press, with more than a little condemnation of what *Arena* writers were already calling "gutter journalism" in the early nineties. Various "isms" appeared, as mesmerism, theosophy, and spiritualism. Throughout virtually its whole file, the *Arena* was deeply interested in psychic phenomena; Camille Flammarion, Richard Hodgson, Alfred Henry Wallace, Minot J. Savage, T. Ernest Allen, Flower

[13] Hamlin Garland, *Broadside Meetings* (New York, 1930), p. 176; *A Son of the Middle Border* (New York, 1917) pp. 410–11. Cf. Flower's account in *Arena*, v. 28, pp. 103–04, July 1902.

[14] Flower, *Progressive Men*, p. 100.

[15] *Arena*, v. 18, p. 614, Nov. 1897.

himself, and many others wrote on the subject for the *Arena*. In 1891 Savage, Flower, and Allen organized the American Psychical Society, of which the three became respectively president, vice-president, and secretary-treasurer.[16]

Labor unionism was generally defended, usually without reservations. Notable articles were Associate Editor Harte's "Review of the Chicago Strike of 1894" in the September number for that year, and a January 1903 symposium on the recent coal strike. Government ownership of utilities and industries was occasionally suggested in discussions of strikes, and the *Arena* published a number of articles advocating this basic phase of socialism.

Flower once reviewed sympathetically a book on palmistry (July 1895), and his interest in astrology is shown repeatedly.

But in all this welter of religion, sociology, economics, politics, and what not, were there no belles-lettres? What of fiction, poetry, and criticism? Well, in the first place, Flower thought all literature should be didactic — all novels and all poems should have a Social Purpose. This idea is well set forth in an editorial titled "The Highest Function of the Novel" in the fifth number of the *Arena*, in which Victor Hugo's dictum that "the beautiful must be the slave of the good" is quoted, the practice of "art for art's sake" is excoriated, and the *Arena* itself is dedicated to the reform of current evils by a literature and art which will be "the champions of the world's helpless millions."[17]

We may assume that great literature of this type was not available to the *Arena*. The very long "prose poems" by W. H. H. Murray, based on Indian legends, were neither good literature nor good anthropology, and Flower's admiration for Murray seems unreasonable. On the whole, poetry was uncommon in the *Arena*. Joaquin Miller contributed two or three western pieces; Ella Wheeler Wilcox had several didactic poems well adapted to the magazine; Edgar Fawcett wrote some rather striking pieces in both verse and prose on New York crimes and foibles, and others who are as well forgotten did iambics and spondees occasionally for the *Arena*.

The magazine's chief service to contemporary literature was its encouragement to Hamlin Garland, some of whose best short stories, such as "The Return of a Private" (December 1890) and "Lucretia Burns" (published as "A Prairie Heroine" in July 1891), appeared in the *Arena*. Flower, struck by the propaganda strength of these simple and tragic stories of Midwestern farm life, undertook to recruit Garland for service to the reform movements and at the same time to build

---

[16] *Arena*, v. 5, p. xlv, Feb. 1892; *Boston Globe*, Dec. 22, 1891.
[17] *Arena*, v. 1, pp. 628–30, April 1890.

up his literary reputation. The new author's first contribution to the *Arena* was an essay on Ibsen in the number for June 1890, and his second was an Ibsenian play which the magazine published in full the next month with the title "Under the Wheel"; changed from dramatic into fictional form, this was issued by the Arena Publishing Company in paper binding as *Jason Edwards*. Garland's early short stories were published in the magazine from December 1890 through December 1891 and then issued with the title *Main Travelled Roads*, a dollar in cloth and fifty cents in paper. Garland's western trip was undertaken mainly to get material for a serial, *A Spoil of Office*, which he wrote for the *Arena* and which the magazine company then published in paper covers at fifty cents. Whatever all this meant to "the cause," it meant rather less than first appears to Garland's reputation and pocketbook. To be sure, these first acceptances by a magazine "changed the world" for him, and seventy-five dollars for a story was good pay; [18] but Garland never got any royalties from those books,[19] and he soon realized that the career of the literary propagandist was not going to be satisfying to him. The fact is that Gilder was "refining" him with *Century* blandishments.[20] After his serial had run its course, Garland contributed only half a dozen articles to the *Arena*.

Flower doubtless had some thought of duplicating his success with Garland when he published the southern sketches and stories of Miss Will Allen Dromgoole in the early nineties; but they were not of such stern and meaningful stuff as that which made the early Garland stories distinctive and memorable.

From time to time the *Arena* printed a considerable amount of literary criticism. Hamlin Garland's discussions of regionalism in "The Future of Fiction" (April 1893) and "The Land Question: Relation to Art and Literature" (January 1894) were notable. The relations of literature with science and religion were sometimes discussed, particularly in a late series on the religion of famous writers. Contemporary and emerging literary figures were often assessed, such as Howells, James, and Mrs. Wharton. Archibald Henderson, the young mathematics professor at the University of North Carolina who wrote

---

[18] Garland names this amount in *Roadside Meetings* (p. 176), though he says $100 in *A Son of the Middle Border* (pp. 410–11). In both these accounts he indicates that his first contribution was "A Prairie Heroine," and in the former he gives the date of acceptance as May 1, 1890. "Ibsen as a Dramatist" appeared in the June 1890 issue, and "A Prairie Heroine" not until July 1891, as noted above. It was probably the Ibsen article for which he received his first *Arena* acceptance and the check in question. Garland's first story was not published in the *Arena* but in *Every Other Saturday*, March 28, 1885. See C. E. Schorer, "Hamlin Garland's First Published Story," *American Literature*, v. 25, pp. 89–92, March 1953.

[19] *A Son of the Middle Border*, pp. 442–43.

[20] *Roadside Meetings*, pp. 182–83.

brilliantly of modern literature and drama, became a prominent contributor to the *Arena* in its latter phase. English, French, German, Austrian, and Russian writers received much attention in the magazine. Edmund Gosse, Frederick J. Furnivall, Edmund Clarence Stedman, Moncure D. Conway, Horace Traubel, Wilbur L. Cross, Nathan Haskell Dole, and Edward Everett Hale are also found among the contributors of literary criticism and comment in the *Arena*.[21]

Dramatic literature and the theater were occasionally discussed. James A. Herne, Dion Boucicault, Charles Klein, and A. C. Wheeler were leading commentators in this field. Mme. Modjeska's "Reminiscences of Debuts in Many Lands" appeared in the *Arena* in 1890. The Shakespeare-Bacon controversy occupied an amazing amount of space in 1892–1893.

Book reviews, handled in various ways at various times during the magazine's career, are an important part of the file. They come from many hands and are very uneven. Flower wrote a majority of them; and such literary judgment as he had was sadly warped by his social, economic, and political enthusiasms.

From the foregoing notes on what the *Arena* published, especially in its first phase, 1889–1896, it will be seen that here was a crusading magazine, dedicated to active campaigns for a number of definite reforms. The technique of multiple crusades had been developed by certain newspapers in the eighties — particularly by Joseph Pulitzer's *St. Louis Post-Dispatch* and *New York World* and by the Scripps papers. Its adaptation to the national magazine was new, if not unique.[22] There had been plenty of reform journals in the past — many antislavery and many temperance periodicals, as well as papers devoted to free trade, civil service reform, labor unions, and so on — but the *Arena* was a multiple-crusade magazine of general circulation — and that was something new.

It was in earnest in its crusades, with its supplements, pamphlets, paper-covered books, and clubs and societies. Two of its books were novels of protest by the obscure Elbert Hubbard, whom Flower installed in a position in his publishing company. The publication of a series of articles on poverty, the slums, and child-slavery, under the title "The New Time: A Plea for the Union of Moral Forces," resulted in the formation of Arena Clubs throughout the country. The first was in

---

[21] See Dickason, "The Contribution of B. O. Flower." An abstract of Dr. Dickason's dissertation is found in *Abstracts of Doctoral Dissertations*, No. 32 (Ohio State University Press, 1940).

[22] Perhaps the old *Phrenological Journal* (see F. L. Mott, *A History of American Magazines*, Cambridge, 1939, v. 1, pp. 447–48) comes as near to being a multiple crusader as any earlier periodical, but its "causes" were chiefly in the physiological realm.

FOUR MAGAZINE EDITORS OF THE NINETIES

Upper left: Frank A. Munsey, of *Munsey's* and *Argosy*.
Upper right: Walter Hines Page, of *Forum, Atlantic,* and *World's Work*.
Lower left: Benjamin O. Flower, of *Arena*.
Lower right: Samuel S. McClure, of *McClure's Magazine*.

"TEDDY" ROOSEVELT WAS ALWAYS A GOOD SUBJECT FOR THE CARTOONIST

These are newspaper cartoons dealing with T. R.'s experiences as New York police commissioner, as reproduced in the *Cosmopolitan Magazine* for November 1895. See pages 169–170.

New Orleans, the second in Mead, Kansas. Flower objected, with remarkable disinterest in the promotional value of the clubs for the magazine, that the name "Arena Club" narrowed the scope of the interests of the association and repelled some joiners. He first suggested "League of Love,"[23] but fortunately this found little acceptance, and "Union for Practical Progress" was settled upon. At its height in 1894–1895 the union had about eighty chapters in some twenty-five states and Canada.[24] Flower was national treasurer, and there was an active national speakers' bureau. This organizational movement was similar to that of the Bellamy Clubs and local Nationalist Societies, many of which still flourished on the ideas of *Looking Backward*. The study programs provided by the *Arena* were reminiscent of those which the *Chautauquan* had long furnished and which it and the *Bay View Magazine* were still furnishing, though less extensively.[25]

In 1896 the *Arena* suddenly found itself the only magazine or review of national importance supporting William Jennings Bryan for the presidency, or giving much space to the free-silver propaganda. Since its third volume, Flower's review had paid some attention to this currency problem, and by 1893 it was clearly on the side of the silver men. Bryan himself contributed four articles to the *Arena*, the most important of which was the one on "The Currency Question" that appeared in the midst of the presidential campaign, in September 1896.

Flower, writing about the *Arena* some twenty years later, claimed that the stand taken in support of free silver in the campaign of 1896 "led to a serious cutting off of advertising patronage, and was in other ways unfortunate for the success of the magazine."[26] It may be doubted, however, whether a slight reduction in advertising, which never amounted to much in the *Arena* anyway, was really an effective cause of the crisis that overtook the magazine at the end of 1896. The subscription price had been reduced from five dollars to three in November 1895, in an effort to bring the circulation above the twenty-five thousand figure, where it seemed to be stuck. During the presidential campaign a six-months subscription had been offered for one dollar. It is doubtful that these devices increased the *Arena's* permanent circulation,[27] and they probably impaired further the magazine's financial situation. Flower was ill during at least a part of 1895–1896; and

---

[23] *Arena*, v. 8, p. xxiii, June 1893.
[24] Flower, *Progressive Men*, pp. 128–33.
[25] For the *Chautauquan*, see Mott, *op. cit.*, v. 3, Sketch 34; and for the *Bay View Magazine*, p. 54 of this volume.
[26] Flower, *Progressive Men*, p. 109.
[27] See the Rowell and Ayer directories. The *Arena* claimed 35,000 in the 1897 Ayer (for 1896), but the more conservative Rowell refused to quote circulation for the *Arena* in that year, on the basis of unsatisfactory information.

Helen H. Gardner and Walter Blackburn Harte, associate editors, had to relieve him of most of his work. About this time, Mrs. Flower had to be taken to an institution for the mentally unsound. The prospect was dark indeed when the Arena Publishing Company went into a receivership at the end of 1896, owing between sixty and seventy thousand dollars.[28]

The "angel" of the original venture had been Gideon F. T. Reed, a public-minded Boston merchant connected with Tiffany and Company. He had died in 1892, and his widow had taken his place as president of the publishing company.[29] It was generally thought then that the new magazine had made an auspicious beginning. "Seldom has a periodical met with such success from the start," said the *Journalist*.[30] It had achieved in two years a circulation of twenty thousand, which was almost as much as its New York rival, the *Forum*, and more than any other Boston monthly (including the *Atlantic*) — though only a tenth of the giant circulations of the *Century* and *Harper's*. The *Arena* and *Forum* were five-dollar magazines, while the *Atlantic, Century*, and *Harper's* sold for four dollars.

The *Arena's* loss in its first year had been $37,809. This had been cut in half the next year, and had steadily declined thereafter, until 1894 showed a profit of over $3,000.[31] But the hard times of the mid-nineties had caught up with it; Mrs. Reed appears to have quarreled with Flower; and no rich radical turned up to subsidize a nonconformist review. It was not to perish, however, for a new purchaser with a new editor in tow (or vice versa) appeared in the nick of time.

The purchaser was John D. McIntyre, a New York manufacturer, and the editor was John Clark Ridpath. Ridpath had been an English professor at DePauw University and was well known as a popular historian and compiler of textbooks. He had written free-silver articles for the magazine in 1896. Under his editorship, the *Arena* continued to be radical politically: "The *Arena's* mission is to place before the American people facts that the plutocratic press and magazines withhold, and for their own sordid purposes ignore." [32] Flower returned to write a monthly article for the magazine in 1898. He still insisted that "the titanic struggle of the present" was "between corporate power in the hands of a few on the one side and public interests and the people's

---

[28] *New York Tribune*, Dec. 2, 1896, p. 1, col. 3.
[29] *Arena*, v. 5, April 1892, p. xxxiii; v. 6, p. 772, Nov. 1892. For Reed see also Mabee, "Benjamin Orange Flower and the *Arena*, 1889–96," pp. 21–22; *Boston Globe*, Feb. 26, 1892.
[30] *Journalist*, v. 7, May 10, 1890, p. 9.
[31] These figures were brought out in a suit brought against Flower and C. S. Smart, business manager, tried March 12–16, 1897. See Boston newspapers, especially *Daily Advertiser*, March 13, p. 10. For the later receivership, see *New York Tribune*, Dec. 2, 1896, p. 1, col. 3.
[32] *Arena*, v. 18, p. 720, Nov. 1897.

rights on the other." [33] In the face of the oncoming war with Spain, Ridpath was chauvinistic, and the anti-McKinley *Arena* was a good war magazine. It absorbed the *American Magazine of Civics*; [34] and though it expected to be a kind of official transmitter of information to members of the American Institute of Civics, it received little support from that organization. It also absorbed *New Time*, a short-lived reform monthly with which B. O. Flower had been connected.[35] It enlarged its page, lowered its price again (this time to two dollars and a half), and made a special drive for farmers' subscriptions. In the summer of 1898 it printed articles by Senator William M. Stewart, of Nevada, and by Editor Ridpath, purporting to show a conspiracy on the part of international bankers to enslave the world in gold-standard chains. Cried Ridpath:

> Men of my country! Men of the world! You can accept this situation if you want to accept it. If you have no more love of freedom, no more patriotism, no more sense than to accept it, why, then, accept it, and be slaves forever. If nothing will arouse you, why, then, sleep, sleep! [36]

But nothing aroused them, and they slept, and the *Arena* announced that it would suspend publication with the issue of September 1898. But again a rescuer appeared, this time from Denver. Paul Tyner had been editing in that city a small magazine of the New Thought school called *The Temple*, "A Monthly Magazine Devoted to the Fuller Unfoldment of the Divinity of Humanity" (1897–1898), which was now merged with the *Arena*, taking in also the *Journal of Practical Metaphysics* (1896–1898), of Boston, and later the *Coming Light* (1896–1899), of San Francisco. Tyner and his associate editor, Horatio W. Dresser, declared the magazine's independence from parties and factions, promising that it would seek out the facts and the truth on all sides of all questions. It leaned toward the "expansion" of the McKinley policy. It made a notable attack on Christian Science with an article on Mrs. Eddy in the number for May 1899. Later Flower was to defend Christian Science in the *Arena*; now, finding many points of difference with the magazine, he dropped out as a contributor and joined Mrs. Calvin Kryder Reifsnider as coeditor of a monthly devoted

---

[33] *Arena*, v. 19, p. 218, Feb. 1898. At this time Flower was also a staff contributor to the *Non-Conformist* (1897–98), an Omaha weekly edited by C. Vincent.

[34] See p. 204.

[35] Founded January 1897 with Frederick U. Adams as editor and a Mr. McBride, of Canada, as "angel." Flower joined Adams in June 1897, after being deposed as editor of the *Arena*, but stayed less than a year. Though *New Time* reached 30,000 circulation, it was never out of debt. See *New Time*, v. 3, Aug. 1898, p. 91. It was merged with the *Arena* in Dec. 1898.

[36] *Arena*, v. 19, p. 840, June 1898.

largely to spiritism, called *The Coming Age*.[37] Tyner's ownership of the *Arena* lasted only a year, and it then came into the hands of John Emery McLean and his Alliance Publishing Company.

This concern issued *Mind*, a twenty-cent monthly of liberal ideas, New Thought, and occultism, published in New York.[38] It moved the *Arena* to New York, and attempted to build it up again along the lines on which it had attained its former standing. Symposiums became common once more and the standard *Arena* topics reappeared, but the contributors were not, in general, distinguished. The war in the Philippines was opposed; the currency question was still discussed, but from both sides; the Mormon problem, divorce, and criminology were leading subjects.

Neuville O. Fanning soon relieved McLean of most of the editorial work on the *Arena*. He projected an *Arena Quarterly*, labeled "A Magazine of Civic Progress," and published a single issue in June 1900.[39] But by November 1900, Charles Brodie Patterson, a lecturer on New Thought, had become supervising editor of both *Mind* and the *Arena*, with Flower back as managing editor of the latter and Dresser still on the job as an assistant. Flower now wrote a "Topics of the Times" department, as well as extensive book reviews. In the next two or three years, the *Arena* resumed somewhat the flavor and attitudes that had made it a distinguished production a decade before. It was a rather chastened *Arena*, however, lacking both the wildness and the variety of its youth.

In 1902 the magazine reached what was probably its highest circulation mark, at a little less than thirty thousand.[40] But this was not

---

[37] *The Coming Age: A Magazine of Constructive Thought*, Boston and St. Louis, Jan. 1899–Aug. 1900. Mrs. Reifsnider had contributed the serial "Between Two Worlds," a spiritistic romance, to the *Arena* in 1896. Many former *Arena* contributors wrote for the *Coming Age*. Perhaps a series of "Conversations" with notable men was the magazine's best feature. It called itself "a magazine with a mission," but it lacked the aggressive attack of the *Arena*. It was published monthly at $2.00 a year.

[38] *Mind*, "devoted to science, religion, metaphysics, philosophy, psychology, and occultism," and calling itself "the world's largest and most important review of liberal and advanced thought," was published from 1897 to 1906.

[39] Fanning was editor and McLean associate editor. This single number had articles about municipal problems by such distinguished contributors as Henry Clews, Charles T. Yerkes, Alfred Henry Lewis, and Frances A. Kellor.

[40] It is sometimes said that the *Arena* had a circulation of 100,000. This is an absurdity based on Flower's reference to a time "when the *Arena* was being read by over one hundred thousand of the most thoughtful Americans every month" (*Arena*, v. 29, p. 670, May 1903). It was common in these times to estimate that each copy of a magazine or newspaper was read by at least five persons (see note on that practice, *Printer's Ink*, v. 28, July 5, 1899, p. 36), and that is what Flower was doing here. In Rowell's *American Newspaper Directory* for 1908, it was shown that the only satisfactory circulation reports the *Arena* had ever made were two: that of 1895, showing 24,612, and that of 1902, showing 28,161 (p. 701). Note conspectus of quotations from all the directories in Cline, "Mechanics of Dissent," p. 123.

enough to represent prosperity, or even solvency. It is doubtful, indeed, if the *Arena* showed an actual profit for more than three or four years out of its twenty.

Accordingly, in 1903 the magazine changed hands for the fourth time in seven years. The purchaser, Charles A. Montgomery, kept it for less than six months before disposing of it to Albert Brandt, of Trenton, New Jersey. Brandt was a printer, and a publisher of books in a modest way; he was deeply sympathetic with liberal ideas and was an admirer of Benjamin Orange Flower. He immediately placed Flower in sole editorial charge of the *Arena*, enlarged the page to a double-column format, and added some illustration. It had in its earlier years carried some portraits; now Ryan Walker's cartoons were a feature, and there were other pictures. Thus during its last lustrum the *Arena* was more handsome than it had ever been before, some of its better-known contributors returned, and Flower himself wrote voluminously. Professors Parsons and Henderson, Miss Dromgoole, poets Edwin Markham and Joaquin Miller, Rabbi Schindler, George Wharton James, William Kittle — these were some of the names familiar to readers of the last ten volumes of the *Arena*; but there were many other scholars, statesmen, and publicists who occasionally contributed pieces. Leading topics were the trusts, socialism, the Negro problem, direct legislation, the railways, literature, and the stage.

Belated use of the muckraking techniques came in 1905 and 1906, with the Blankenburg and Mills articles already referred to. Critics have sometimes regarded the *Arena* as a muckraking magazine from its beginning;[41] that is, of course, a matter of definition. The *Arena* was a journal of protest from the start, but its writers did not often use the method of elaborate factual exposé, which had been flourishing in certain magazines for several years before Theodore Roosevelt fitted the epithet "muckraking" to it.[42] Doubtless Clinton Rogers Woodruff's article, "Philadelphia's Election Frauds" (October 1900), Thomas Elmer Will's piece on what he called "The College Trust" (September 1901), and even Charles Frederick Holder's brief "The Dragon in America" (August 1904) might qualify as "muckraking" in the narrower sense indicated, and perhaps other essays in the earlier *Arena* as well; but in the main the magazine was a sharpshooter, not a raker.

Flower wrote editorials, book reviews, dramatic criticism, and philosophic, literary, and economic essays for the last five years of the

---

[41] This is the attitude of C. C. Regier in his valuable *The Era of the Muckrakers* (Chapel Hill, 1932).

[42] See pp. 209, 494–95.

magazine. His "In the Mirror of the Present" was an important department, which, fragmentary as it was, probably came to occupy too
much space.

Publisher Brandt filed a petition in bankruptcy in the fall of 1909.
The *Arena* was discontinued with the August number that year, and
was merged thereafter with *Christian Work*.[43] The last lines by Flower
in the last number commend a book by Orison Swett Marden for the
cheer which it affords "those who are becoming discouraged after long
grappling with the perplexities of present-day life."[44]

The best brief summary of the *Arena's* significance is one written by
Flower himself; "Believing that in the crucible of free discussion is
found the gold of truth, I sought in the *Arena* to cultivate intellectual
hospitality."[45] Sometimes it was not so much intellectual as simple and
uncritical hospitality; but on the whole the *Arena* was a truly liberal
and significant journal. Its circulation was never large, but it reached
many leaders of American thinking and (through schools, editorial
offices, and libraries) many leaders-to-be.

Flower's subsequent life was not especially edifying. Two months
after the *Arena* was discontinued, he was back in Boston founding the
*Twentieth Century Magazine* (1909–1913), a reform monthly that he
edited for two years. Meantime he became president of the National
League of Medical Freedom, which had been organized to fight the
American Medical Association, which it called "the medical trust." In
1916 he became president of the company that published that egregious
anti-Catholic journal, the *Menace*, of Aurora, Missouri. He was still
ranting against the Pope in the tawdry pages of the *Menace* when he
died, on December 24, 1918.

[43] See Mott, *op. cit.*, v. 3, pp. 82–83.
[44] *Arena*, v. 41, p. 600, Aug. 1909.
[45] Flower, *Progressive Men*, p. 19.

# 3

## THE ARGOSY [1]

AUGUSTA, Maine, in 1882 was a town of less than ten thousand people; but it was the seat of a very profitable publishing business. Certain mail-order periodicals that boasted world-beating circulations made their home at Augusta.[2]

> This was the great business of the city, completely overshadowing everything else, and making vastly more money than anything else. Moreover, it had about it an element of romance and picturesqueness that was startlingly and abnormally interesting because of the smallness of the town.[3]

The quoted sentences were written by Frank A. Munsey after he had himself attained a phenomenal success as a publisher; but they harked back to the days when, an impressionable youngster in charge of the telegraph office at Augusta, he found his ambition fired by what he saw going on about him. They show clearly the romantic idea which young Munsey had of the publishing business; indeed, the autobiographical notes from which they are taken depict their central figure as the hero of another "Rags to Riches" novel. It is appropriate that in this same sketch Munsey should pay a "little tribute" to Horatio Alger, a faithful contributor for many years to the Munsey publications.

[1] TITLES: (1) *The Golden Argosy, Freighted With Treasures for Boys and Girls*, 1882–March 6, 1886; (2) *The Golden Argosy*, March 13, 1886–Nov. 24, 1888; (3) *The Argosy*, Dec. 1, 1888–July 17, 1920; (4) *Argosy All-Story Weekly*, July 24, 1920–Sept. 28, 1929; (5) *Argosy*, Oct. 5, 1929–current (*New Argosy*, March–July 1942).

FIRST ISSUE: Dec. 9, 1882. Current.

PERIODICITY: Weekly, 1882–March 1894, Oct. 1917–Oct. 1941; monthly, April 1894–Sept. 1917, May 1942–current; biweekly, Nov. 1941–April 1942. Vols. 1–6, annual vols., Dec. 1882–Nov. 1888; 7–11, semiannual vols., Dec. 1888–May 1891; 12, May 30–Aug. 22, 1891; 13–16, semiannual vols., Aug. 1891–Aug. 1893; 17, Aug. 26, 1893–March 24, 1894; 18–23, semiannual vols., April 1894–March 1897; 24–85, 3 vols. yearly, April 1897–July 1917; 86, Aug.–Sept. 1917; 87–133, 6 issues per vol., Oct. 6, 1917–May 7, 1921; 134–315, 6 issues per vol., May 14, 1921–Oct. 1943; 316–21, 4 issues per vol., Nov. 1943–Aug. 1945; 322, Sept. 1945–July 1946; 323, Sept.–Dec. 1946; 324–current, semiannual vols., Jan. 1947–current.

PUBLISHERS: E. G. Rideout & Company, 1882–83; Frank A. Munsey, 1883–1925; William T. Dewart, 1926–41; Henry Steeger (Popular Publications), 1942–current. All New York.

EDITORS: Frank A. Munsey, 1882–1925; Matthew White, Jr., 1925–28; A. H. Bittner, 1928–30; Don Moore, 1930–31; Albert J. Gibney, 1931–36; Chandler H. Whipple, 1937–39; George W. Post, 1940–42; Henry Steeger, 1942–48, 1955–current; Jerry Mason, 1948–53; Howard J. Lewis, 1953–54; Ken W. Purdy, 1954–55.

REFERENCES: Frank A. Munsey, *The Story of the Founding and Development of the Munsey Publishing House* (New York, 1907); William T. Dewart, "The Story of the *Argosy*," *Argosy*, v. 234, pp. 142–45 (Dec. 10, 1932); George Britt, *Forty Years — Forty Millions* (New York, 1935), chs. 5–6.

[2] See, for the Augusta papers, F. L. Mott, *A History of American Magazines* (Cambridge, 1938), v. 3, pp. 37–39.

[3] Munsey, *Story of the . . . Munsey Publishing House*, p. 10.

The Augusta telegraph boy, his mind full of the dream of millions to be won by the publication of a popular weekly, gave all his leisure to a study of the operation of the Augusta periodicals, and even some of his working hours to daydreaming about his own plans. Gradually those plans became definite: he would start a weekly for boys and girls in New York (not in Augusta) and would make it more attractive than any of its competitors by means of lithographed covers and many woodcuts. He persuaded an Augusta broker to put twenty-five hundred dollars into the venture; a young New York acquaintance, formerly an Augusta boy, was to put in another thousand; and Munsey had five hundred in cash and a vast fund of enthusiasm. He proceeded to spend most of his own five hundred for manuscripts, packed his bag, and arrived in New York in the fall of 1882 with forty dollars in cash and a portfolio of stories for boys and girls. But alas, when he set up shop and called on his Augusta backer for money, none was forthcoming. Then his New York friend backed out, and there was young Frank Munsey with his bundle of manuscripts and a rapidly dwindling cash reserve, friendless in a great city.

"Chapter Two" shows Frank interviewing publishers, expounding his Plan. On second thought he had discarded the lithographed cover, and most of the woodcuts; he would publish a five-cent weekly of inspirational fiction. And he did manage to interest a publisher, E. G. Rideout, already proprietor of *Rideout's Monthly* and two women's periodicals. Frank must have been a persuasive talker; he had, moreover, those object lessons back at Augusta to point to — money-coining object lessons. So the great day came — December 2, 1882 — when the first number of the *Golden Argosy, Freighted with Treasures for Boys and Girls* was issued, bearing the date a week in advance, as was the custom. It was an eight-page small-folio containing the opening of a serial by Horatio Alger, Jr., entitled "Do and Dare, or a Brave Boy's Fight for a Fortune," which began on the front page. Beginning on an inside page was another serial, with the inspiring title "Nick and Nellie, or God Helps Them That Help Themselves," by Edward S. Ellis, famous dime-novel author and former editor of *Golden Days*, of Philadelphia,[4] which was really the model for the Munsey venture. Along with these serials were two or three short stories, a puzzle department, a section devoted to amateur journalism, and other miscellany. A score of numbers had been regularly issued; "Do and Dare" was drawing to an end; plans were already made to follow it with another story from the same teeming fancy, when suddenly Rideout, the publisher, went bankrupt, leaving the *Golden Argosy* high and dry.

[4] See Mott, *op. cit.*, v. 3, p. 178.

"Chapter Three" of Munsey's own "Fight for a Fortune" finds our hero stepping in and buying the paper from the receiver. With what? With the sum the bankrupt publishers owed him on his editorial salary. Then we see him working desperately, writing as well as editing, doing a publisher's and clerk's work, keeping the paper barely alive. He borrowed three hundred dollars from a friend back in Maine; the paper came out regularly, and after a year or two credit was less difficult to obtain. He hired an office editor, Malcolm Douglas, at ten dollars a week, and began to write some of the *Argosy's* serial stories himself; the second was called "Afloat in a Great City," and the young publisher based his first advertising campaign upon it. This campaign cost him ten thousand dollars and involved the free distribution of a hundred thousand copies of the number containing the first installment of his own serial. That was in the spring of 1886. As a result his circulation increased to the point at which he was making a hundred dollars a week profit.

But it also threw him deeply into debt. He had owed $5,000 before his campaign; now he owed $15,000. His answer was another campaign the next fall. He doubled the size of the paper, increased the price from a dollar and seventy-five cents to two dollars a year, and put out during five months 11,500,000 sample copies. He kept fifteen to twenty men on the road in charge of the proper distribution of these papers. He had no clerks in the home office, not even a bookkeeper; he did all the work himself, and even ground out another serial.

Five years of poverty, five years of awful struggle, and now the earth was mine! Rich at last, richer than I had ever dreamed of being — a thousand dollars a week net, and every week adding to it by leaps and bounds — fifty thousand dollars a year, and all mine — next week sixty thousand, then seventy, and a hundred — a million, maybe — GREAT HEAVENS, AND IT WAS ALL REAL!

. . . But the money to work it out, thousands of dollars every day? Where could I get it? How could I get it? And it meant riches, power, position, the world, the great big world!

With all these thoughts, these feelings, and a thousand others, and the work and the energizing of everybody, and the enthusing of everybody, and the tension and intensity of it all, it was one great, dizzy, dazzling, glorious intoxication.[5]

This campaign cost Munsey $95,000 and brought the *Golden Argosy* a circulation of 115,000, which represented a profit of $15,000 a week. But he was still borrowing to the limit, "kiting" checks, and taking desperate financial chances.

Munsey soon discovered that the publisher of a juvenile was never on a secure footing. The best advertisers kept aloof because boys and

---

[5] Munsey, *Story of the . . . Munsey Publishing House*, pp. 27-28.

girls are not buyers; and children do not stay children, and by and by they put away childish things, including their childhood papers — thus making it impossible to build up a stable subscription list. Munsey turned his thoughts to the publication of cheap books and adult periodicals. He put out his own stories in book form, as well as other serials that had appeared in *Golden Argosy*. Then in 1889 he founded *Munsey's Weekly*, which, two and a half years later, became *Munsey's Magazine*.[6]

In the meantime, the juvenile declined. In 1886 the subtitle referring to boys and girls was dropped, though the magazine still seemed to be aimed chiefly at a juvenile audience. Two years later, the name was shortened to simple *Argosy*: "Golden," said Munsey, made it sound like a child's paper, while it really was an adventure magazine. The size was increased to thirty-six pages quarto with a cover, and the price again raised — this time to four dollars. Another two years, and the number of pages and the price were halved, so that it again sold for a nickel on the stands. Still the curve was downward. Other minor changes were made, to no avail.

It was the success of *Munsey's Magazine* that saved the *Argosy*, which had dropped to nine thousand circulation by 1894. This success inspired Munsey to make the *Argosy* an adult monthly in the large octavo size then universal among regular magazines, and at the ten-cent price per copy. The circulation immediately went up to forty thousand. But *Argosy* remained merely a weak imitation of *Munsey's* until, in 1896, it was made an all-fiction magazine. If not the first magazine of this type, it was at least the first successful all-fiction "pulp." For it was now successful; it ran up to eighty thousand, and, after hesitating there for a few years, began a steady ascent to the half-million mark, which it attained in 1907. By that time it was earning a profit of about three hundred thousand dollars a year.[7]

Matthew White, Jr., who had come to Munsey in 1886, had been managing editor of the *Argosy* since 1889, writing serials for it and planning its successive numbers.[8] Besides Alger and Ellis, and Munsey and White, the earlier juvenile paper had printed serials by such writers as Harry Castlemon, Frank H. Converse, Mrs. Henry Wood, Oliver Optic, G. A. Henty, and Richard H. Titherington. A serial by

---

[6] See Sketch 19 in this volume.

[7] Munsey, *Story of the . . . Munsey Publishing House*, p. 52.

[8] R. H. Titherington wrote to the author of these pages on Sept. 12, 1933, as follows: "I went into Mr. Munsey's office in September, 1886. White joined us in December of that year, and all three of us worked on the *Argosy*, without any titles, although of course Mr. Munsey was the publisher and chief editor. In 1889 . . . White took hold of the *Argosy*, and I think his managing editorship should be dated from 1889 to 1928." For White, see *Bookman*, v. 32, p. 663, Feb. 1911.

P. T. Barnum, the showman, called "Dick Broadhead," ran in 1887. After the change to the status of an adult monthly, its contents were highly varied, with copious halftone illustration, and articles and fiction by well-known writers. But it was after the change to an all-fiction monthly that the typical later *Argosy* format and table of contents were developed. No pictures, "pulp" paper, a plethora of adventure stories — this was the *Argosy*. There were few love stories, but exotic adventure, mystery, and action set the tone. It was a men's and boys' magazine. Frederick Van Rensselaer Dey, probably the most prolific fictionist who ever wielded pen, author of both the "Nick Carter" and the "Duchess" series, was a valued contributor, as were William Mac-Leod Raine, Albert Payson Terhune, Louis Joseph Vance, and Ellis Parker Butler. Many writers who were later to make considerable reputations did early work for the *Argosy* — James Branch Cabell, Sidney Porter (not yet "O. Henry"), Charles G. D. Roberts, Susan Glaspell, and Mary Roberts Rinehart. Young Upton Sinclair wrote serials for the magazine at the turn of the century. Rates were not high: one leading contributor has named five hundred dollars as *Argosy's* top payment for a serial.[9]

The circulation of the *Argosy* declined somewhat from 1907, and in 1917 it was made a weekly, keeping the same octavo format. Three years later it was merged with the *All-Story Weekly*, another Munsey periodical, under the name *Argosy All-Story Weekly*. Munsey's habit of buying older periodicals and combining them with his own, and re-combining his own — what he called "cleaning up the field" — caused several magazines to be absorbed by *Argosy All-Story* — chief among them the old *Peterson's*. Before the mergers and afterward, the magazine printed fiction by such writers as Frank Condon, Courtney Ryley Cooper, Captain A. E. Dingle, Arthur Somers Roche, Edison Marshall, Octavus Roy Cohen, Max Brand, and Zane Grey. Matthew White remained as managing editor until 1928, though he spent a year or two abroad in 1913–1914 as Munsey's literary representative in London.

Munsey died in 1925. Appraisal of his estate after it had been put in order by the executors placed its value at about twenty million dollars.[10] There were bequests to Bowdoin College, which he had never attended, and to certain hospitals in which he had never been a patient; but the bulk of the estate was left to the Metropolitan Museum of Art, which he had never frequented.

Under the will, *Argosy All-Story*, like everything else Munsey owned, was to be converted into cash. It was purchased, along with the other

[9] Albert Payson Terhune, *To the Best of My Memory* (New York, 1930), p. 168.
[10] Britt, *Forty Years — Forty Millions*, p. 301.

Munsey magazines and the New York *Sun,* by William T. Dewart, who had been general manager of Munsey's various businesses, and who was executor of his estate.

In 1929 *Argosy* was again separated from *All-Story.* Besides many of the old favorites, the authors whom *Argosy* readers could now follow in their quest for "decent, red-blooded fiction for the millions" were H. Bedford-Jones, T. S. Stribling, Erle Stanley Gardner, C. S. Forester, Robert Carse, Theodore Roscoe, Luke Short, Van Wyck Mason, Achmed Abdullah, W. C. Tuttle, and many others. *Argosy* had long been a habit with many men and boys. Its distribution in the twenties held at about four hundred thousand; but the depression hit it hard, and by the end of the thirties circulation had fallen to a tenth of that. Other Munsey publications had fared no better, and something had to be done. So all of them were sold at the end of 1941 to Popular Publications, a New York "pulp" group.

The organization of cheaper magazines into groups, or "combinations," for facility in selling advertising, in manufacture, and in handling circulation, is a feature of modern mass publication of periodicals. In this case, the Munsey Combination, consisting of *All-Story, Munsey, Argosy, Railroad Magazine,* and *Detective Fiction Weekly,* was sold as a unit to Popular Publications, which included a score of other magazines.

*Argosy* was under the close personal supervision of Henry Steeger, president of Popular Publications, for several years after it was made a part of that group. For a time, under the title of *New Argosy,* Steeger stressed features linked to world news and the war, as well as true adventure stories, without too much neglecting the old stand-by for which the name *Argosy* was a kind of trade-mark — the exciting adventure story of struggle and melodrama. The gradual transformation was from "pulp" to "slick"; an observer in the publication field remarked that Steeger had undertaken the task of easing *Argosy* into a white collar.[11] One of the features of this period was the department conducted by Erle Stanley Gardner, in which that super-anodynist of the detective story field presided over a "Court of Last Resort." In this department cases of men considered unjustly convicted of crimes were considered; some were freed as a result of this publicity.

An outstanding development of the period immediately following World War II was the rapid growth of the men's magazines. The leading exemplar was *Esquire,* though *True* (of the Fawcett Combination) and *Argosy* were not far behind. Under the editorship of Jerry Mason, a former associate editor of *This Week,* the transformed magazine,

[11] *Magazine Industry,* v. 1, Winter 1950, p. 13.

now called *Argosy — The Complete Men's Magazine,* installed strik-ing four-color layouts, began spending more for contributions, in-creased stress on humor, and generally made a more brilliant and arresting magazine. The response, even with the price raised to twenty-five cents, sent the magazine's circulation soaring toward the million mark, which it reached in 1951. A temporary ban by the prim Post-master General Frank Walker probably did it no harm, and by 1953 it was asking $5,250 for one full-color page, on a guaranteed circulation of 1,250,000.

With all its changes, *Argosy* has never quite lost its old seasoning of strange and tough adventure, which has made it favorite reading for men and boys through two generations.

## THE BIBELOT [1]

TOM MOSHER, of Portland, Maine, went voyaging with his sea-captain father instead of going to school. Thus he never had any "prep" school, and, as he said later, was "saved" from college. He was an omnivorous reader, however, developing marked tastes and strong personal preferences in literature.

Seafaring over, Thomas Bird Mosher served as a clerk and later a partner in a firm of Portland printers and stationers that went bankrupt in 1890. Since the stationery business, which Mosher did not like, had treated him so unkindly, he decided to try to make a start in an occupation that would bring him rewards in pleasure whether it fetched in shekels or not. So in October 1891 he published, in a most pleasing format, with excellent typography and presswork, that early tragic masterpiece of George Meredith, *Modern Love*, which had never been reprinted since its first issue thirty years before. This was a choice characteristic of his later work as publisher and anthologist, for Mosher was to show a predilection for verse and essay of a somber cast, for work that had been allowed to languish in obscurity, and for performances of high literary quality. *Modern Love* was only a moderate success, but enough to make it possible for the publisher to continue. The second book was James Thomson's *The City of Dreadful Night*, an offering of even more despairing mood. In the next few years Mosher built up a considerable list, chiefly of small books, appealing to somewhat precious tastes, always beautifully printed.

Encouraged by the growing response to his book publishing, and answering too to the anthologist's urge that was basic in his feeling about literature, he began in January 1895 the publication of a series of monthly brochures in duodecimo, each number containing twenty-four to forty-eight pages in which was reprinted some choice piece of

[1] TITLE: *The Bibelot: A Reprint of Poetry and Prose for Book Lovers, Chosen in Part from Scarce Editions and Sources Not Generally Known.*
FIRST ISSUE: Jan. 1895. LAST ISSUE: Dec. 1914.
PERIODICITY: Monthly. Annual vols., 1–20 ("Testimonial Edition" reprint by W. H. Wise & Co., New York, 1924, included an index volume as v. 21).
EDITOR AND PUBLISHER: Thomas Bird Mosher, Portland, Maine.
INDEXES: Index to vols. 1–12 in v. 12; *General Index* to vols. 1–20, compiled by Milton James Ferguson, separately published by T. B. Mosher, Portland, 1915. In "Testimonial Edition," the Ferguson index is called "Analytical Index."
REFERENCES: Keith Gibson Huntress, "Thomas Bird Mosher: A Biographical and Literary Study" (unpublished doctoral thesis, University of Illinois, 1942); *Abstract* of same (published, Urbana, 1942).

literature. "To bring together the posies of other men bound by the thread of one's own choosing is the simple plan of the editor of the *Bibelot*," said the first number.[2] These "posies" were poems, poem-sequences, one-act plays, single acts from longer dramas, essays, short stories, or prose poems. The first number contained "Lyrics from William Blake"; the second, "Ballades by François Villon," in John Payne's translation; and the third was devoted to "Medieval Latin Students' Songs."

Each number sold for five cents, and a year's subscription cost fifty cents, while a year's issues in permanent library binding could be bought for a dollar and seventy-five cents. It seems amazing that these charming, beautifully printed booklets ever sold for a nickel; but it is a basic fact in the printing art that it is as cheap to print tastefully as vulgarly. Mosher tried to show "by example that choice typography and inexpensivness need not lie far apart";[3] and show it he did, for these little fascicles, on pages measuring about four by six inches, perfectly printed (often from Oldstyle brevier) satisfied the eye by their form at the same time that they pleased the mind and fancy by their contents.

Mosher wished to print work that was "not generally known," and at the same time to maintain a high esthetic level. He offered "the less accessible things 'which perish never.' "[4] Outstanding in the file were such things as the early William Morris material, dug out of a college magazine, the work of the authors of the Celtic revival, such as Yeats, Synge, "AE," Lionel Johnson, Ernest Rhys, and "Fiona Macleod," as well as the writing of the symbolists, the vers librists, and so on. The little magazine afforded great variety. It ranged from Theocritus to Swinburne, from Sir Philip Sidney to Arthur O'Shaughnessy, from Marcus Aurelius to Walter Pater. Yet Mosher's discriminating choices gave the whole a certain unity. At the end of the file, the editor wrote: "The content of the *Bibelot* possesses unity of purpose: it represents what I have personally accepted as specimens of the finer spirit."[5] Christopher Morley was later to recognize in Mosher's work as anthologist that sureness of judgment which knows excellence as a fact at first sight.[6]

The *Bibelot* may have been suggested by the *Chap-Book*; it was one of several artistic periodicals of small page-size that followed closely

[2] *Bibelot*, v. 1, intro., Jan. 1895.
[3] *Ibid.*
[4] *Ibid.*
[5] *General Index*, p. xii.
[6] Christopher Morley, "A Golden String," in "Bowling Green" dept., *Saturday Review of Literature,* v. 1, p. 892, July 11, 1925.

upon the heels of that magazine's success.[7] But the *Bibelot* had a true vocation of its own, and only one of the many "fadazines" of the period equaled its length of life: Hubbard's *Philistine* and Mosher's *Bibelot* enjoyed almost exactly the same span of existence.

The Mosher periodical had something most of its rivals in this field lacked — a legitimate appeal to the self-culture motive of the nineties. It supplemented the *Chautauquan*, the *Bay View Magazine*, the *Arena*, and so on, with their study clubs.[8] Of this reading public Mosher was well aware. "If the *Bibelot* means anything," he wrote, "it means definitely an aid to self-culture in literature." [9]

Its cheapness, too, was important. It began in the "hard times" which also saw the advent of the fully illustrated ten-cent magazine — years when a nickel was real money. In the midst of a later and less traumatic depression, the annual subscription price was raised from fifty to seventy-five cents; by that time there was little newsstand sale.

Of course, the price was possible only because Mosher, in most cases, paid nothing to his authors. The international copyright agreement, which became effective in the same year that Mosher began publishing, provided that if no American edition of a book was produced within sixty days of the publication of the foreign edition, the work was virtually in the public domain. Thus great numbers of little boats were set afloat on the high seas of literature without protection; and it was these little and obscure craft that our bold, bad buccaneer particularly coveted. Best sellers were immediately published in America, and thus protected; the poets (especially the new ones) were with difficulty printed on the other side, and they were ready prey for literary piracies.

It is not strange that some writers protested strongly against the Mosher ethics, or lack of them. Andrew Lang was shrill in his denunciation of the Portland publisher when his *Aucassin and Nicolette* was appropriated. Thereby the little book received a generous gift of publicity, and, as we are told by the best of the Mosher students, the publisher

calmly continued to reprint items by Lang. Almost the same thing happened in 1906, when Hilaire Belloc protested against Mosher's edition of his *Tristan and Iseult*, threatening, not legal action, but what must have been corporal punishment for any other infringements on his rights. Mosher responded by pirating two other items by Belloc.

But on the other hand, continues Dr. Huntress, the poet Le Gallienne wrote Mosher: "Not to be robbed by you would be a great disappoint-

---

[7] See Sketch 8 in this volume.
[8] See pp. 54–56.
[9] *General Index*, p. xi.

ment." [10] Nor was Le Gallienne the only writer who considered it to be a great honor to be pillaged by a pirate who handled his loot so beautifully. It should be explained that later, whether by necessity or choice, Mosher used more and more material which was under copyright, and, of course, had to pay for it.

For each of his two hundred and forty numbers, the editor wrote an introduction or notes; and in this apparatus he showed himself a critic of fine sensitiveness and rare perceptions. In the valedictory number of the *Bibelot* — the *General Index* — Le Gallienne paid tribute to that ability as well as to Mosher's genius as an anthologist. He spoke for many when he said that for him personally, the *Bibelot* was "the most fascinating miscellany of lovely thought and expression ever compiled." [11]

But the editor was sixty-two and thought it time to quit. In Portland, said a friend, he "lived a life withdrawn. . . . His little shop of a few simple rooms up a dusty flight of stairs . . . contained none of the elaborate machinery of modern business." [12] He had accumulated a competency, if not a fortune. Twenty fat little volumes stood on the shelf, and there was a kind of completeness about the full score.

There are those who find the *Bibelot* a little too "precious"; and, of course, there are others who are offended by its literary piracy. But many had and have an affection for it. When a New York publisher, some years after Mosher's death, brought out a reprint of the whole file, a surprising number of reviewers had pleasant things to say about the editor and his unique magazine. But perhaps William Marion Reedy's piece on "The Ending of the *Bibelot*," which appeared in that farewell issue, is most quotable:

For twenty years no month has passed that I have not had one certain joy. It was in the reading of the dainty, blue-covered *Bibelot* that came from Mr. Mosher, of Portland, Maine. . . . a body of literature which, but for the resurrectionist Mosher, we might never have known. Burns in it all the flame of the spirit, in the urn of form . . . and to that union he added another element — beautiful, chastely beautiful, printing. . . .

In the wide range of the *Bibelot's* contents, one finds a fugue consistent. Each selection conforms to an underlying, informing purpose — to touch the soul to finer issues, to acquaint it with the ecstasies of life lived and contemplated. . . .

We readers of the *Bibelot* came to know and love Mosher, his work made such a beautiful exhibition of his own soul.[13]

[10] Huntress, *Abstract*, p. 5.
[11] *General Index*, p. 416. See also Richard Le Gallienne, "In Praise of a Literary Pirate," *Literary Digest International Book Review*, v. 2, p. 778, Oct. 1924.
[12] Anon., "A Tribute from a Friend," *Publishers' Weekly*, v. 104, p. 787, Sept. 15, 1923.
[13] *General Index*, pp. 423–26.

# THE BLACK CAT [1]

THE founder of the *Black Cat* was an advertising man named Herman D. Umbstaetter. After a short newspaper career in Cleveland and New York, Umbstaetter established an advertising office in Baltimore and became internationally famous as an "ad writer." Joseph Pulitzer, penning a note of introduction directed to George Augustus Sala, of the London *Daily Telegraph,* declared: "Mr. Umbstaetter is undoubtedly the greatest advertising genius in this or any other country." [2] Many years later Harry Leon Wilson was writing an article entitled "Advertising" for the *Saturday Evening Post* and in a nostalgic mood recalled the work of an "ad writer" unknown to him by name. Wrote Wilson:

> Would that I had by me the complete works of that anonymous word artist who lauded St. Jacob's Oil in words of acute, slim beauty like unto the legs of Chippendale. That man knew how to say it in short words! I mourn his passing. After earnest effort I can recall no abler writer of prose. He had the virtues of Ruskin and Pater and the vices of neither. [3]

Wilson did not know that the object of his dithyrambic tribute was Herman Daniel Umbstaetter, who was not only a great writer of advertising copy, but the founder and editor of the *Black Cat.*

Umbstaetter made a fortune in advertising and publishing by the time he was forty, but lost it in similar ventures in London, along with his health. Returning to America, he first went west to regain his health, and then located in Boston to make another fortune. This he proposed to do by the publication of a magazine devoted wholly to short stories and selling at five cents a copy.

Two facts bearing on this decision should be noted here. First, the

---

[1] TITLE: *The Black Cat.*
FIRST ISSUE: Oct. 1895. LAST ISSUE: April 1923 (?).
PERIODICITY: Monthly 1895–1920, semimonthly 1922–23. Vols. 1–25, annual vols., 1895–1920; suspended Nov. 1920–Dec. 1921; 26–27, 1922–23.
PUBLISHERS: Shortstory Publishing Co. (H. D. Umbstaetter, owner), Boston, 1895–1912; Shortstory Publishing Co. (Samuel E. Cassino, owner 1913–15; Herman E. Cassino, owner 1915–19), Salem, Mass., 1913–19; Black Cat Publishing Company, New York, 1919–20; Black Cat Magazine, Inc., New York, Feb.–Oct. 1920; William R. Kane, Highland Falls, N. Y., 1922–23.
EDITORS: Herman Daniel Umbstaetter, 1895–1912; Theresa E. Dyer, 1913; T. H. Kelly, 1914; Harold E. Bessom, 1915–20; William R. Kane, 1922–23.
REFERENCE: Harold E. Bessom, "The Story of the *Black Cat,*" in Twenty-Fifth Anniversary Number, *Black Cat,* v. 25, Oct. 1920, pp. 84–92.
[2] Quoted by Bessom, *ibid.*
[3] *Saturday Evening Post,* v. 192, July 26, 1919, p. 115.

cheap-magazine idea was in the air. It had just been demonstrated that big, illustrated magazines could be published successfully for ten cents; [4] Curtis had built up the *Ladies' Home Journal* at an initial price of five cents; and more recently the *Chap-Book* and the *Bibelot* had appealed to more literary tastes with nickel monthlies.[5] In the second place, there was also in the air an enthusiasm for the short story, which had only recently achieved recognition as a distinctive art form in American literature.[6] It was not only an attractive form, but it looked like an easy one for both practiced writers and amateurs.

And Umbstaetter's idea was to get these amateurs to furnish the stories for his magazine through prize offers. He planned to pay out in prizes about as much as it would cost him to buy established names; but at the same time he would be interesting a considerable audience in the contests, and he thought he would actually get more lively and original stories.

Accordingly, during the first year of publication, the *Black Cat* paid over seven thousand dollars to its contributors,[7] and during the next eight years more than four thousand annually, in prizes ranging from a hundred to two thousand dollars, from a typewriter to an expense-paid tour of the world.[8] In the first contest, the top prize of fifteen hundred dollars was won by Henry J. W. Dam, later a well-known dramatist. These contests attracted an amazing number of entrants. The editor himself read most of the manuscripts. By no means all of its stories came to the *Black Cat* through its contests, but clever and ambitious amateurs discovered the magazine chiefly through its competitions.

In its latter years the *Black Cat* was fond of listing the famous authors who had begun their careers by writing for that magazine, most of them as entrants in the contests. Among these authors were, according to such claims, Jack London, Rupert Hughes, Ellis Parker Butler, Susan Glaspell, Octavus Roy Cohen, Alice Hegan Rice, Will N. Harben, Cleveland Moffett, Harry Stillwell Edwards, Sewell Ford, and Holman Day. One of the most successful of these — Jack London — testified repeatedly to the debt he felt he owed to the *Black Cat* for the encouragement afforded by its acceptance of his work. In *Martin Eden* he tells the story of his sale of a short story to the *Black Cat*, calling it *"The White Mouse"*; but the better account is found in an introduction he wrote for a volume of short stories written by Umbstaetter. Here he declared:

[4] See Chap. I.
[5] For various other five-cent magazines, see pp. 47–51.
[6] See Chap. VIII.
[7] *Black Cat*, v. 1, Oct. 1896, advertising page 58.
[8] Bessom in *Black Cat*, v. 25, Oct. 1920.

In the field of the short story the *Black Cat* is unique, and a *Black Cat* story is a story apart from all other short stories. While Mr. Umbstaetter may not have originated such a type of story, he made such a type possible. I know he made me possible. He saved my literary life, if not my literal life.

Then London went on to tell how he was sick, mentally and physically, and in despair because he could not sell anything he wrote, when he got a letter from Umbstaetter offering him forty dollars if he would cut the manuscript submitted in two! This gave the young writer something to live for again. London added:

To many a writer with a national reputation, the *Black Cat* has been the stepping stone. The marvellous, the unthinkable thing Mr. Umbstaetter did was to judge a story on its merits and to pay for it on its merits. Also, and only a hungry writer can appreciate this, he paid immediately on acceptance.[9]

This explains something of the special flavor of the magazine, though it cannot be admitted that the *Black Cat* story was a type. There was too much variety. The editor himself said that what he was looking for was the story that would hold the interest of the reader. He wanted plenty of incident and movement, and preferred tales somewhat off the beaten path.[10] This last preference resulted in stories that were often somewhat bizarre; this, combined with an amateurish lack of adept writing, was perhaps more the *Black Cat* trade-mark than anything else. Some readers got the idea, doubtless from the name of the magazine, that it capitalized on the weird and gruesome; but that was a mistake.

Two of the prize stories most popular with readers were Clifton Carlisle Osborn's "A Few Bars in the Key of G," and Cleveland Moffett's "The Mysterious Card" — both clever, tricky, sentimental stories such as O. Henry taught a wide public to like a few years later. Umbstaetter himself wrote short stories, contributing a good many to early numbers of the *Black Cat*; indeed, he wrote three of the seven tales in the first number.

The magazine caught on rapidly, helped by advertising of its contests. It claimed a circulation of over 150,000 throughout 1896,[11] and 186,000 in 1897–1898; and apparently it kept up a fairly good pace until the financial crisis of 1907. In 1908 it followed the example of other magazines and raised its price to ten cents. It had been from the start a small-octavo of fifty or sixty pages; the sable feline on the cover took many forms.

[9] Herman Daniel Umbstaetter, *The Red-Hot Dollar and Other Stories from The Black Cat* (Boston, 1911), pp. v–ix.
[10] *Black Cat*, v. 25, Oct. 1920, p. 91.
[11] See Rowell directories. Reports for 1897 were considered unsatisfactory by Rowell. But see Ayer reports for 1898–1924.

Umbstaetter's health declined in 1912, and he died the next year. Samuel E. Cassino, of Salem, Massachusetts, publisher of books and of the *Little Folks' Magazine* (1897–1926), purchased the *Black Cat* at the end of 1912. Theresa E. Dyer, who had been Umbstaetter's assistant for many years, went to Salem as editor, but soon resigned in favor of T. H. Kelly. In 1915 Cassino's son Herman took the magazine over, making Harold E. Bessom editor. It was now printed on "pulp" paper.

In 1918 another nickel was added to the price of the *Black Cat*, which had been claiming a circulation of about 50,000 since the Salem migration. Its traditional contests, failing in their drawing power in the midst of World War I, were discontinued. In 1919 the magazine was moved to New York and refinanced. There were some good contributors, and for a time the old *Cat*, which had undoubtedly lost two or three of its nine lives, seemed somewhat sleeker. But in 1920 there was another change in management (though Bessom was still retained as editor) and the price went up to twenty cents. The contests were now resumed, $7,500 being announced in prizes, and later in the year $2,500 more.

But times had changed, and the dizzy twenties did not take to this technique. The magazine was published for a few months under its second New York management, its circulation quoted at fifteen thousand. It was suspended late in 1920, but in January 1922 it was revived as a semimonthly of thirty-six pages by William R. Kane, of Highland Falls, New York. Kane was editor and publisher of the periodical *Editor*, which was issued in the interests of amateur writers. He afforded the *Black Cat* one more life, the last of its quota, and it perished in the spring of 1923.

# 6

## THE BOOKMAN[1]

FOUNDER of the *Bookman* was Frank Howard Dodd, president of Dodd, Mead and Company, New York book publishers. He placed in the editorial chair a brilliant professor of Latin language and literature at Columbia University — Harry Thurston Peck.

The early success of the *Bookman* was due mainly to the literary and editorial genius of Professor Peck. "For some issues he wrote a good part of the contents himself," says a biographer; "and his taste, knowledge, and lightness of touch set the tone of the whole magazine."[2] He had a certain professorial arrogance, especially in regard to relatively inconsequential matters of English usage; but he had also a variety of interests and a literary catholicity unusual in a scholar. Furthermore, he possessed the born publicist's instinct for catching and holding the interest of his readers. "His taste," writes Thomas Beer, "kept the magazine from the pretentious heaviness which marked earlier literary reviews; in fact, there was nothing heavy about Peck. His coat had a flower; some of his waistcoats were illustrious of their kind."[3] He was a great teacher at Columbia, an erudite and industrious editor of encyclopedias and anthologies, a good classical scholar, and he had a remarkable grasp of both the esthetic and practical sides of contemporary publishing.

As his "junior editor," Peck was given a young Scotsman, James MacArthur, who was also literary adviser to the book-publishing firm. It was a good idea to have a mon wha kenned the writers and the talk of

---

[1] TITLE: *The Bookman.* Subtitles: "An Illustrated Literary Journal," 1895–99; "A Review of Books and Life," 1899–1933.

FIRST ISSUE: Feb. 1895. LAST ISSUE: March 1933.

PERIODICITY: Monthly. Vol. 1, Feb.–July 1895; 2, Sept. 1895–Feb. 1896 (Aug.–Sept. combined); 3–73, semiannual vols. beginning in March and Sept., March 1896–Aug. 1931; 74, Sept. 1931–March 1932 (Jan.–Feb. combined); 75, April–Dec. 1932; 76, Jan.–March 1933. Succeeded by *American Review.*

PUBLISHERS: Dodd, Mead & Co., New York, Feb. 1895–Aug. 1918; George H. Doran Co., New York, Sept. 1918–Aug. 1927; Bookman Publishing Co. (Seward Collins, pres.), New York, Sept. 1927–March 1933.

EDITORS: Harry Thurston Peck and James MacArthur, 1895–99; H. T. Peck and Arthur Bartlett Maurice, 1899–1907; A. B. Maurice, 1907–17 (with Frank Moore Colby, 1907–10); G. G. Wyant, 1917–18; Robert Cortes Holliday, 1918–20; Henry Litchfield West, 1920–21; John Chipman Farrar, 1921–27; Burton Rascoe, 1927–28; Seward Collins, 1928–33.

INDEXES: *Poole's Index, Annual Library Index, Readers' Guide, Cumulative Index, Review of Reviews Annual Index, A.L.A. Portrait Index,* and *Dramatic Index.*

REFERENCES: A. B. Maurice, "Old Bookman Days," *Bookman,* v. 66, pp. 20–26, Sept. 1927; "More Old Bookman Days," v. 70, pp. 56–65, Sept. 1929.

[2] George Harvey Genzmer, in the *Dictionary of American Biography.*

[3] Thomas Beer, *The Mauve Decade* (New York, 1926), p. 189.

the Kailyard School on the staff of a publishing house, in those days of Maclaren and Barrie and Crockett; and MacArthur was a genial and industrious editor.

The first number of the *Bookman* was issued for February 1895. It had seventy-two double-column, small-quarto pages, well printed and inviting, and sold for fifteen cents, raised a year later to twenty cents. There were only two or three illustrations; and though this number was somewhat increased in succeeding issues, the *Bookman* did not have a great many pictures during its first four or five years. In this first phase, the magazine was extremely miscellaneous — almost fragmentary. It began with ten or a dozen pages of "News Notes," soon to be called "Chronicle and Comment," which consisted of items from three lines to half a column in length, passing on announcements of publishers and retailing the gossip and chatter of writers and critics. It continued with short articles of two or three pages each about writers and literary and critical matters, followed by correspondence from London and Paris. Then came twenty pages or more of book reviews, the longest running to a page and a half. Finally there was "The Book Mart," with records of rare-book sales, bookstore reports from a score or more of American cities naming the best-selling books at the moment, and a "List of Books Published During the Month." This set a pattern which, though altered here and there, was generally maintained for the next five years. The ruling principles were short pieces, bright reporting, a considerable emphasis on English, Scottish, and Continental authors, frank attention to the business of publishing and selling books, and a basic appeal to what may be called the bibliophilic sentiment.

Author of the London letter in the first number and, with fair regularity, for the next five years was W. Robertson Nicoll, friend of Frank Dodd's,[4] editor of the London *Bookman*, and a leading figure in British book-publishing circles. At the very beginning the American magazine used a few articles from the English *Bookman*, but that did not last long. There were some articles in these early years by English critics — Clement K. Shorter, George Saintsbury, Edmund Gosse, Andrew Lang — and much attention to British books and writers. Stevenson had died just before the *Bookman* was founded, and with its first number the magazine enclosed an illustrated Stevenson supplement reprinted from the London *Bookman*. Professor Peck disapproved the ensuing Stevenson cult, but he could not keep it out of his magazine. It was the Kipling mania which was the more prominent, however; Kipling material continued almost unabated until about 1914. Other favorites were Hardy and Meredith and Conan Doyle.

[4] See memorial sketch of Dodd, *Bookman*, v. 43, p. 197, April 1916.

There was much also about French, Italian, German, and Russian literature. Robert Sherard was the magazine's first Paris correspondent; Alfred Manière was writing from that city in 1897, and Adolph Cohn at the end of the century.

But the chief interest of the *Bookman,* however international its outlook, was current American literature; and this it faithfully discussed throughout its four decades. No literary journal is infallible, and few have maintained a high and consistent average of perceptive, fair, and adequate book reviewing over a long term of years; but the *Bookman,* on the whole, did very well. It is appalling to consider that more than five thousand books were weighed in the balances of *Bookman* reviewers. But there seems to have been a minimum of log-rolling and clique-claques. Such prejudice as is discernible seems to have been intelligent prejudice. Among the reviewers in the first number were Brander Matthews, Albert Shaw, Lionel Johnson, William H. Carpenter, and "Nym Crinkle." This brief list serves to indicate the caliber of the critics who, for several years, signed the more important book reviews. The *Bookman* drew its reviewers from far and wide; though its own staff did many of the notices, it looked to various fields and countries for reviewers of the more important books. An index to its reviewing is its quickness to praise the very first work of Edith Wharton (June 1899) and that of Edwin Arlington Robinson (February 1897).

Of course, Peck and MacArthur wrote many reviews themselves. Indeed, Peck contributed all kinds of material but fiction — reviews, critical articles, gossip, essays, poetry, and history. As Tom Masson, who was one of many who were offended by Peck, made him declare:

> There isn't a thing I cannot do
> With my active pen laborious,
> From poetical stuff
> To fulsome puff,
> Or a talk on words vainglorious.[5]

In July 1896 the editor started his "Bookman Letter Box," in which he quoted from letters received, and commented on them. Later he also had a brief editorial department called "Here and There." In such commentary he was dogmatic in regard to matters of English usage, manners, literary values, and public questions. Peck in the *Bookman* of the nineties was not unlike Richard Grant White in the *Galaxy* of the seventies — perhaps more a wit and less a savant than White. A lady from Philadelphia writes saying that her uncle, who is a great reader, objects to Peck's placing Balzac above Dickens as a novelist. The editor replies:

---

[5] *Life,* v. 38, p. 9, July 4, 1901. Elbert Hubbard lambasted him occasionally; see *Philistine,* v. 10, Jan. 1900, pp. 42–47.

Your uncle is doubtless a good man, and we can only explain his objection to our comparative estimate of Balzac and Dickens in one of two ways. Possibly he has not read Balzac. On the other hand, perhaps he has not read Dickens.[6]

Peck had a strong feeling for history; and old authors, old books, old magazines, old publishers and booksellers occupy many pages in the *Bookman*. Nor was Peck's interest in history limited to the field of literature; the *Twenty Years of the Republic*, which was for some time the most popular book on general American history after 1885, appeared serially in the *Bookman* in 1905–1906. After Peck's retirement, the *Bookman* continued this interest. In 1910 it published Arthur Hoeber's "History of Art in America"; in 1915, Algernon Tassin's "The Magazine in America," and so on.

One feature that began with the very first number was destined to introduce a new angle of interest to the book trade and to readers in general. It was the *Bookman* which first made booksellers and readers best-seller conscious. It adopted from the first the policy of publishing titles of books "in the order of demand" in various cities, a plan which had been used for some years by the London *Bookman*; thus it listed for each of sixteen cities of the United States the six best-selling books of the preceding month, numbered one to six. Eventually thirty cities were covered by the lists, which were based on booksellers' reports. At first there was no national summary; but for the issue of November 1897 MacArthur began such a résumé, which was printed at the end of the city lists under the heading "Best Selling Books." Then in 1899 the *Bookman* began its series of annual lists based on the monthly summaries. It now seems remarkable that the *Bookman* never used the term "best seller" in these lists, though it began a series of articles, "Best Sellers of Yesterday" in 1911 — the year in which the term was introduced by *Publishers' Weekly*. The *Bookman* abandoned its lists of "Best Selling Books" when it was sold by Dodd, Mead and Company in 1918.[7]

A feature perhaps off the true course of a critical journal was the serial story, but the *Bookman* used such fiction throughout much of its life. Its first story was Ian Maclaren's "Kate Carnegie," of 1896, which was followed by a couple of undistinguished historical novels, and then, in 1899, by Paul Leicester Ford's "Janice Meredith," which became a great best seller when Dodd, Mead published it between covers. John Uri Lloyd's popular "Stringtown on the Pike" came along in 1900. But there were many second- and third-raters — long stories by the English Eden Phillpotts, Jeffrey Farnol, and Maurice Hewlett and the American George Barr McCutcheon and Louise Closser Hale, and so on. Then

---

[6] *Bookman*, v. 10, p. 369, Dec. 1899.
[7] See F. L. Mott, *Golden Multitudes* (New York, 1947), pp. 204–06.

from 1910 until the 1918 change in ownership, there was a *Bookman* moratorium on fiction. Hugh Walpole's "Jeremy" was serialized in 1918, and his "Jeremy at Crale" several years later. But serials were uncommon in the twenties, though some outstanding short stories by Theodore Dreiser, Aldous Huxley, Joseph Conrad, Michael Arlen, and Padraic Colum were printed. In 1928 Upton Sinclair's "Boston" made somewhat of a sensation when the *Bookman* serialized it.

Poetry is to be found in the *Bookman* file from one end to the other, but never in large quantity or remarkable quality. Stephen Crane and Richard Hovey were the most notable poets in the early volumes; and there were also represented therein Editor Peck, Clinton Scollard the ubiquitous, Guy Wetmore Carryl, Father Tabb, Myrtle Reed, Arthur Stringer, and Thomas Walsh. Carolyn Wells's parodies made bright spots in many numbers. In the latter volumes of the file, we find John Gould Fletcher, Amy Lowell, Sara Teasdale, and others. In 1917 Edward J. O'Brien edited a "Masque of Poets" department for the magazine; and in 1921–1922 there was another department, "Poems of the Month," for which well-known poets selected the "best" poetry that had appeared in contemporary magazines.

The *Bookman's* special articles were always among its most important offerings. In the early years these were literary and artistic and cultural, and likely to run in series — such as the essays on old booksellers, and those on living critics, American, English, German, French. There was a series on "Foreign Authors in America" in 1901, one on "Great American Newspapers" in 1902, and another in which informed writers discussed various facets of "The American Newspaper" in 1904. The theater was often discussed, and Norman Hapgood wrote a "Drama of the Month" department from 1899 to 1902.

Financially, the *Bookman* was only a fair success during its first five years, reaching, by degrees, a circulation of about fifteen thousand by the end of 1899. Young Frank Crowninshield was its first publisher; he left it to go to the *Metropolitan Magazine* in 1900. Just before that James MacArthur had left Dodd, Mead for the Harper house, and had been followed as junior editor by Arthur Bartlett Maurice.

Maurice was good medicine for the *Bookman*. For seventeen years he served the magazine, bringing indefatigable energy and a great journalistic talent to bear on its lagging fortunes. It improved in illustration and attractiveness as soon as he joined the staff, and its circulation began an upward climb that exceeded forty thousand at the time of the 1907 financial stringency. This was the *Bookman's* highest point of success in both distribution and advertising. Shortly afterward the price per copy was raised to twenty-five cents.

The year 1907 marks Professor Peck's retirement from the *Bookman* editorship. A few years later he was to suffer a strange collapse, which brought in its train divorce, philandering, a sensational breach of promise suit, dismissal from the university, bankruptcy, a physical and mental breakdown followed by an attempt at recovery, and finally, suicide.

After Peck's departure from the *Bookman,* in a flurry of controversy over "fonetic refawm," Maurice took Frank Moore Colby as his junior editor. Colby, probably best remembered as an encyclopedist but also a witty essayist and sound critic, was good help for the next three years. In this period, book reviews were less important in the magazine. Half a dozen or so of the output were reviewed each month in a single article headed "Six Books of the Month" — or four, or nine, or whatever the number of those chosen for careful review. This was supplemented by other articles which were, in effect, but less formally, reviews of interesting books. Frederick Taber Cooper's scholarly and lively articles often commented on half a dozen new books. Cooper had been an assistant of Peck's in the Latin Department at Columbia and had later transferred to New York University. He began his contributions to the *Bookman* shortly before the turn of the century and continued them for nearly twenty years.

Other prominent contributors of these years were Lawyer Frederick Trevor Hill, Playwright George Middleton, and Professors Algernon Tassin and Clayton Hamilton. Maurice was very fond of that kind of regionalism which relates literatures to places. He himself wrote "New York in Fiction" and "The Paris of the Novelists," serials in the *Bookman* and later published as books, and other essays of a similar kind. There was a series in 1913–1914 by several writers called "American Backgrounds for Fiction." Floyd Dell wrote about "Chicago in Fiction," and sooner or later most American localities were surveyed for literary associations. Literary history was still prominent, and at the very end of Maurice's incumbency the *Bookman* printed William Lyon Phelps's "The Advance of the English Novel" and a history of Russian literature by Abraham Yarmolinsky. There was also an editorial penchant for articles about illustrators and caricaturists, obviously because they, as well as reviews of the theater, lent themselves to attractive illustration. But *Bookman* illustration, on the whole, declined in the latter years of Maurice's editorship.

Frank H. Dodd, the founder, died in the spring of 1916. Later in that year Maurice resigned to serve with the Belgian Relief contingent under Herbert Hoover. He was succeeded as editor by G. G. Wyant, who continued during 1917 much the same policies that had governed the magazine under his predecessors. The decline in circulation that set in with the panic year of 1907 continued, until circulation had fallen to twenty thousand in 1912; the magazine quoted that figure for several years afterwards, but there can be no doubt that it went lower.

Circulation was probably not over twelve thousand, and only a few pages of advertising appeared in each number, when the *Bookman* was sold in September 1918 to the George H. Doran Company, a ten-year-old book-publishing firm. Illustration was now abandoned, and a thicker, "eggshell finish" paper was adopted in place of the calendered stock that had been necessary to carry halftone engravings. For the illustrated "Chronicle and Comment," which had long been almost a trade-mark of the magazine, was substituted a "Gossip Shop" department at the back of the book. The magazine had an attractive blue cover, and sold for thirty-five cents. At first it carried a hundred and thirty-two pages, but after a year or two it came back to its standard hundred-page size.

The new editor was Robert Cortes Holliday, an accomplished essayist, who had begun his career as an illustrator, had served as a librarian for a time, and was now on the Doran staff. The salutatory of the new owners seemed to promise less history and more of the forward look, and of course the magazine found itself immediately plunged into the midst of war literature and war problems. Some of the older contributors remained, such as Brander Matthews, H. W. Boynton, Padraic Colum, and Carolyn Wells; but Walter Prichard Eaton and Maurice Francis Egan now became familiar names in *Bookman* pages, as well as Joyce Kilmer, Joseph Hergesheimer, Arnold Bennett, Harold J. Laski, and Alfred Noyes. Amy Lowell and Ludwig Lewisohn had an interesting debate on the new poetry in the number for January 1919. Christopher Morley's "Haunted Bookshop" papers appeared in 1918–1919. There was much about French literature, and a regular letter from London.

Holliday resigned in 1920 to join the Henry Holt organization; and after a brief interim editorship by Henry Litchfield West, man of letters and law who was a member of the Doran staff, John Farrar became editor-in-chief of the *Bookman*.

Farrar was a young poet-journalist not quite twenty-five years of age. At once he gave the magazine a somewhat more personal and attractive air, introduced some portrait sketches and other line drawings by William Gropper and William Saphier, and soon made the *Bookman's* pages a kind of working guide to the current literary movements. Departments were reorganized. "Foreign Notes and Comment" was more comprehensive than the former fragmentary treatment of Continental literature, and "The Sketch Book" contained brief and often excellent essays by important writers. "The Literary Spotlight" consisted of short, sometimes caustic, sketches of contemporary writers, with Gropper impressions; this was a series in 1921–1924, rather than a department, and perhaps set the pattern of what was later to be called the "profile." Louis Bromfield's "The New Yorker," a man-about-town department, ran in 1925; it seems to have followed Stephen Vincent Benét's "To See or Not to See." Also, "Murray Hill," who was ex-editor Holliday, wrote an occasional New York letter, and Kenneth Andrews had a Broadway department for a few years. There was a "Literary Club Service," with study outlines, in 1922–1924.

Finally, the best-seller record, which had been thrown out when Doran bought the magazine, and had been referred to only obliquely since then, was resumed in the form of a "Monthly Score" on the library demand for new books. Doran's objection to best-seller lists as such, sustained by the opinions of many in the publishing industry, was based on the fact that booksellers' reports were likely to be casual, or even to reflect efforts to unload items that had been overpurchased.

Farrar's *Bookman* was lightened by humor, such as Donald Ogden Stewart's "Outline of American History" of 1921, Floyd Dell's "Parody Outline of Literature" of 1923, Robert Benchley's travesties of 1925, and Corey Ford's 1926 burlesques. Essays by Ernest Boyd, Branch Cabell, Irwin Edman, and Christopher Morley, often stressing the satirical note, were characteristic of the magazine in this period.

Reviews, once more abundant, were in general sound and interesting. Frank Swinnerton, under the pen name of "Simon Pure," wrote an excellent London letter. Hugh Walpole, Arnold Bennett, and J. B. Priestley were occasional contributors of both criticism and fiction, and Aldous Huxley's "Diary of an Eastern Journey" was a 1926 feature. Among frequent reviewers were William McFee, Louis Untermeyer, Ruth Hale, Sidney Howard, Struthers Burt, Gamaliel Bradford, Robert E. Sherwood, and William Beebe. There were critical articles by Heywood Broun, Henry Seidel Canby, Stuart P. Sherman, John Erskine, May Lamberton Becker, and some of those just named as reviewers. It was a brilliant galaxy, and represented the best literary criticism in America and England.

Some of the serials of these years were notable, such as Theodore Dreiser's "Out of My Newspaper Days," Mary Austin's remarkable essays on the psychology of the writing process, Holliday's somewhat more conventional series on authorship, parts of DuBose Heyward's *Porgy* and Thomas Burke's *The Sun in Splendour*. Short stories by Katherine Mansfield, Elsie Singmaster, and Stephen Vincent Benét belong to the Farrar era.

Farrar was kind to the poets, and the *Bookman* in his lustrum printed much of the newer American verse and some from abroad. Among these poets were Amy Lowell, Carl Sandburg, Witter Bynner, H. D., Maxwell Bodenheim, John V. A. Weaver, Sara Teasdale, Conrad Aiken, Marguerite Wilkinson, Genevieve Taggard, Margaret Widdemer, Jessie B. Rittenhouse, and Joseph Auslander: it is a long and thoroughly representative list.

The numbers of the *Bookman* under Farrar were interesting throughout in somewhat the same way that Peck's early volumes were. It was smoother, and its sophistication of the twenties was different from that of the nineties. It did not have Peck's crudities; neither did it have the first editor's "bounce."

Eugene Saxton and Grant Overton were associate editors during parts of the Doran regime; Miss Amy Flashner was an assistant editor, and Stanley M. Rinehart and Henry T. Downey were business managers. In 1927 Doran merged his publishing business with Doubleday's, taking Farrar with him, and the *Bookman* was sold. Its circulation had improved somewhat under the Doran ownership, but it had never quite reached twenty thousand. The new owner was Seward Collins.

Collins, a literary man of independent fortune, had been on the staff of *Vanity Fair* for two years after his graduation from Princeton. Illness had then sent him west for an enforced vacation of a few years; now he was back in New York with plans for a periodical combining the features of a newsy and interesting literary review with those of a general magazine on a high level. The page size was enlarged and the number of pages increased to a hundred and twenty. With its new brown cover, the *Bookman* now made an impressive appearance and sold for fifty cents. It carried about ten pages of advertising.

Burton Rascoe was the new editor. Rascoe had been a reporter and literary critic on the Chicago *Tribune* and the New York *Tribune* and an associate editor of *McCall's*, and he had achieved a reputation for hailing new talent as soon as it appeared on the literary horizon. He had many friends among the important new writers — an excellent thing in an editor. His first number of the *Bookman* contained a story by Theodore Dreiser, an essay on George Sterling by Upton Sinclair, fantasies by James Branch Cabell and E. E. Cummings, a poem by Dorothy Parker, and reviews of mystery stories by Gilbert Seldes. These were not all, of course, but they were enough to inform the world that this was a new *Bookman*. There were bookish comments by John Farrar in a special department, plenty of reviews, a Walpole serial, more verse than usual, and the "Monthly Score."

Later Thomas Beer, John Macy, and Shane Leslie became prominent in the *Bookman*. In 1928 the magazine began to print in successive numbers newspaper stories adjudged by competent authorities the best pieces of reporting published in American papers, thus bringing some fine pieces into its own pages. In that year also, the *Bookman* serialized Sinclair's novel about Sacco and Vanzetti entitled *Boston*. It all made a good and stimulating magazine, but Rascoe did not stay at the helm very long. The owner wanted some hand in the editorial direction, Rascoe resented interference, they quarreled over editorial policies, and Collins soon found himself editor as well as owner.

The *Bookman* now became a more sober, dignified, and conservative review than it had ever been before. Not that there were not efforts at humor, like Robert Benchley's comedy and H. W. Hanemann's labored historic fancies; but the ready gossip, the pleasing turns of comment, the quick little controversies — what we have called "bounce" in the old *Bookman* — were now smoothed out into the even tenor of the review article. As though to summon again the Peckian genius, the "Chronicle and Comment" department was brought back in 1930, with illustrations on slick paper; but it was at first devoted to a single long editorial article, and it never did succeed in being very lively in its second incarnation.

Nevertheless, Collins' *Bookman* was an important review. In 1929 it had a notable roster of contributors, which included John Gould Fletcher, Aldous Huxley, Mary Johnston, John Macy, T. S. Eliot, Edmund Blunden, and Robert Herrick. Hamlin Garland's *Roadside Meetings* was serialized. Rebecca West wrote an always interesting and often fascinating monthly European letter. But perhaps most important of all, the *Bookman* became the champion of the new and controversial humanist movement led by Irving Babbitt and Paul Elmer More. Not only those leaders, but Stuart P. Sherman, Norman Foerster, Gorham B. Munson, Robert Shafer, and others added fuel to a fire that burned merrily for a year or so. The purpose of the *Bookman* in general seemed to be to squash the nonsense of the twenties, to get back to the verities, and so on. It was an attitude natural enough in the depression thirties.

The depression may have had something to do with Collins' decision to suspend the *Bookman* and supplant it with the *American Review*,[8] a somewhat more modest and less literary venture. Thus the *Bookman* ended with its number for March 1933.

Except for the *Dial*, which had perished only a few years earlier, the *Bookman* was the longest-lived of American monthlies devoted mainly to books and literary matters. It was a faithful historian of contemporary world literature for nearly forty years, and was unsurpassed in variety, attractiveness, and importance in its field.

[8] Published April 1933–Oct. 1937 in 8 vols. and 4 nos. of v. 9.

## BRANN'S ICONOCLAST[1]

WILLIAM COWPER BRANN was born on an Illinois farm in 1855. His mother died when he was only a baby, and his clergyman father placed him in the family of a neighboring farmer, from whom he ran away when he was thirteen. Thereafter he made his own way — as hotel bellboy, house painter, traveling salesman, printer, reporter, editorial writer. He had no schooling, but he became a tremendous reader in every field of literature. He worked for a time under Joseph B. McCullagh, of the *St. Louis Globe-Democrat*, but he found his true newspaper home in the state of Texas.

This background of experience and education explains much about the extraordinary person that W. C. Brann came to be.

He hated established religion; and he was suspicious of all comfortable, stable, "well-off" society. He had made his own way not only in earning a living but in the world of ideas. He considered himself a tough, honest, radical thinker, and prided himself on his disagreements with those who were rich, or respected, or in high place. His immense appetite for reading, which had developed quite without discipline, gave him an uncritical command of words, phrases, and concepts that was amazing. He acquired, to a remarkable degree, the gift of tongues.

In an autobiographical moment, Brann once wrote:

> In the year of our Lord 1891, I became pregnant with an idea. Being at that time chief editorial writer on the Houston *Post*, I felt dreadfully mortified, as nothing of the kind had ever before occurred in that eminently moral establishment. Feeling that I was forever disqualified for the place by this untoward incident, I resigned and took sanctuary in the village of Austin. As swaddling clothes for the expected infant, I established the *Iconoclast*.[2]

[1] TITLES: (1) *Iconoclast*, 1891–94; (2) *Brann's Iconoclast*, 1895–1926; (3) *Windle's Liberal Magazine*, 1926–29; (4) *The Liberal*, 1929–34.

FIRST ISSUE: July 1891. LAST ISSUE: May 1937.

PERIODICITY: Monthly, 1891–1926, 1927–34; Semimonthly, 1926–27. Annual vols., 1–39, 1891–1929; semiannual vols., 40–48, 1930–34. Suspended Oct. 1891–Jan. 1895, but when it was resumed, omitted vols. were counted in the numbering.

EDITORS AND PUBLISHERS: William Cowper Brann, 1891–98 (Austin, Texas, 1891; Waco, Texas, 1895–98); H. S. Canfield, Chicago, 1898–1900; J. C. Hart, 1900–03, Chicago; C. A. Windle, Chicago, 1903–33; C. Pliny Windle, 1934–37.

REFERENCES: Memorial article on Brann, *Iconoclast*, v. 8, pp. 74–76, May 1898; J. D. Shaw, ed., *Brann the Iconoclast*: *A Collection of the Writings of W. C. Brann in Two Volumes, with Biography*. (Knight Printing Co., Waco, Texas, 1898–1903; later editions, Waco, 1911, N.Y. 1938); Hyder E. Rollins, "William Cowper Brann," *South Atlantic Quarterly*, v. 14, pp. 56–67, Jan. 1915; John Randolph, "The Apostle of the Devil" (doctoral dissertation, Vanderbilt University, 1939).

[2] Quoted by Rollins in *South Atlantic Quarterly*, v. 14, Jan. 1915, pp. 54–55.

# PUBLIC OPINION

Volume 20    27 February, 1896    Number 9

PRICE 5 CENTS
$2.50 PER YEAR

## CONTENTS

Yes, here in this poor, miserable, hampered, despicable Actual, wherein thou even now standest, here or nowhere is thy Ideal. Work it out, therefrom, and, working, believe, live, be free. Fool! the Ideal is in thyself, the impediment, too, is in thyself; thy Condition is but the stuff thou art to shape that same Ideal out of. What matters whether such stuff be of this sort or that, so the Form thou give it be heroic, be poetic? O thou that pinest in the imprisonment of the Actual, and criest bitterly to the Gods for a Kingdom wherein to rule and create, know this of a truth: the thing thou seekest is already with thee, here or nowhere, couldst thou only see.—THOMAS CARLYLE, in "Sartor Resartus."

PUBLISHED WEEKLY BY
THE PUBLIC OPINION COMPANY · NEW YORK

TRADEMARK REGISTERED

COVER OF *PUBLIC OPINION* IN MID-NINETIES

See pages 649–651.

WITH SUPPLEMENT.

NEW YORK, MARCH 11, 1887.

PRICE TEN CENTS.

VOL. XXI—No. 521.

PUCK'S SOUVENIR PERFORMANCE.
531st Appearance. 11th Year.

BIRTHDAY COVER OF A LEADING HUMOROUS WEEKLY

NEW YORK

## THE FORUM PUBLISHING COMPANY, Union Square

AGENTS: { LONDON : E. Arnold, 37 Bedford St., Strand    } 1s. 3d. a Copy
           { PARIS : Librairie Galignani, 224 Rue de Rivoli } 15s. a Year

25 Cts. a Copy    [Vol. XVIII., No. 4.]    $3.00 a Year

SOBER MAGAZINES DID NOT REQUIRE PICTORIAL COVERS

For *Arena*, see pages 401–416; for *Forum*, pages 511–523.

---

IS SPIRITUALISM WORTH INVESTIGATING? A Debate By JULIAN HAWTHORNE, Rev. M. J. SAVAGE, In this Number.

## TABLE OF CONTENTS.

## BOSTON, MASS.:

## THE ARENA PUBLISHING COMPANY,

PIERCE BUILDING, COPLEY SQUARE.

LONDON AGENT:—Brentano's, 430 Strand.

PARIS:—Brentano's, 17 Avenue de l'Opera; The Galignani Library, 224 Rue de Rivoli

Entered at the Post Office at Boston and admitted for transmission though the mails as second-class matter

Copyright, 1891, by The Arena Publishing Co.

Single Numbers, 50c.   Published Monthly.   Per Annum, $5.
Full-Page **Photogravures From Recent Photographs of**
REV. M. J. SAVAGE, JULIAN HAWTHORNE, PROF. A. S. ISAACS,
IN THIS NUMBER.

RUSSIA OF TO-DAY, By Prof. EMIL BLUM, Ph. D., Late of Odessa, Russia, In this Number.

The first issue of the Austin *Iconoclast,* which was to express the Brann "idea," was dated July 1891. It was a monthly of twenty quarto pages and priced at a dollar a year.

The *Iconoclast* made a small sensation even in those days of free-wheeling Texas journalism. It attacked hypocrisy, and especially a hypocritical moral code; it lit into the churches, the banks, and the politicians. Austin, a small city of fifteen thousand and the state capital, was shocked. Peyton Brown, editor of the leading daily paper, the *Statesman,* expressed the feeling neatly:

Its mission is evidently to make a large quantity of sheol, and make a good-sized portion of the human race wish they or it had never seen the light of day. It is a veritable "roasting mill," a "skinning machine" with a full set of knives and a revolution like a drunken buzz-saw. It strikes at pretty much everything it sees and at quite a number of things that it don't see but imagines it does, and it strikes below the belt with both fists, and does not scruple to use its teeth.
. . . That he [Brann] is a writer of marked ability no one can deny. He is perhaps the most vigorous manipulator of the English language in the entire South. . . . Sarcasm and ridicule become in his hands veritable whips of scorpions. But unfortunately he is a misanthrope, a pessimist, and takes the very worst possible view of everything.[3]

Neither subscribers nor advertisers flocked to the *Iconoclast* office; and after three months Brann, deciding that there had been a miscarriage, gave it up. He went back to the *Globe-Democrat* for a while, and then got a position as editorial writer on one of Texas' largest papers, the San Antonio *Express.* Also he began to give lectures about the country — lectures of the oratorical-humorous type that was in demand in the nineties. Brann's favorite topics were "Humbugs" and "Gall."

Meantime a young bank clerk in Austin named Will Porter, feeling a strong urge to follow his bent for humorous writing, determined to start a comic weekly of his own, and paid Brann two hundred and fifty dollars for the *Iconoclast* plant. Porter actually brought out, in March 1894, two issues of a new *Iconoclast* series before he changed the name and got off to a better start with the *Rolling Stone.* How his little weekly failed is another story,[4] as is his later career as O. Henry.

Brann decided to make a second try at monthly journalism, this time at Waco, Texas, and in February 1895 he issued the first number of the first series to be entitled *Brann's Iconoclast.* The new paper was like that of 1891 in size, price, and content. It rapidly built up a circulation of over twenty thousand, which was enough to make it profitable.

*Brann's Iconoclast* consisted of a series of editorial essays, most of

[3] *Austin Statesman,* v. 19, July 29, 1891, p. 4, col. 1.
[4] See Sketch 30 in this volume.

them one or two thousand words in length. The favorite topics were
religion, sexual sins, and politics — a trinity universally interesting.

In religion, Brann was antichurch and anticlergy. He was indeed anti-
Christian, but he was also antiatheist. An address to Ingersoll in the
first number, headed "Brann to Bob — The Apostle Writes the Pagan,"
protests against the atheism found in the famous heretic's writings.
"Oratorically," writes Brann to Bob, "you soar like the condor when its
shadow falls on the highest peaks of the Andes, but logically you grope
among the pestilential shades of an intellectual Dismal Swamp, ever
mistaking shadow for substance." [5] A few months later he wrote:

> The Bible is a great gold-mine, in which inexhaustible store of yellow metal is
> mixed with much worthless rubbish that must be purged away by honest criticism
> before the book becomes really profitable, or even fit for general circulation. I
> would rather place in the hands of an innocent girl a copy of the *Police Gazette*
> or *Sunday Sun* than an unexpurgated Bible. It is a book I value much, yet keep
> under lock and key with *Don Juan* and the *Decameron.*[6]

Brann's "Christ Comes to Texas — and Calls Upon the *Iconoclast*" was
an imitation of W. T. Stead's *If Christ Came to Chicago* and E. E.
Hale's *If Jesus Came to Boston*, but it was sacrilegious where the Stead
and Hale books were reverent.[7] But Brann did defend the Catholics,
though he was not so much pro-Catholic as anti-anti-Catholic; he attacked the A.P.A., and one of his most sensational feuds was with an
anti-Catholic lecturer named Slattery, who spoke in Waco, under the
auspices of Baylor University, in 1895.

Brann's preoccupation with sex was noticeable, if not in every editorial, at least in every number of his paper. The leading article in the
first number was headed "Woman's Wickedness — Chastity Going Out
of Fashion"; it was mostly fuss and fustian, intended to interest because of its suggestions of lust and indecencies:

> The history of humanity — its poetry, its romance, its very religion — is little
> more than a Joseph's coat woven of Love's celestial warp and Passion's infernal
> woof in the loom of Time. For sensuous Cleopatra's smiles Marc Antony thought
> the world well lost; for false Helen's favors proud Ilion's temples blazed, and the
> world is strewn with broken altars and ruined fanes, with empty crowns and
> crumbling thrones, blasted by the self-same curse. . . .
> What is it that is railroading so large a portion of the young women to hell?
> . . . Is it lawless lust or force of circumstances that adds legion after legion to
> the cohorts of shame?[8]

[5] *Iconoclast*, v. 5, p. 15, Feb. 1895.
[6] *Ibid.*, v. 5, p. 33, April 1933.
[7] *Ibid.*, v. 6, pp. 117–19, June 1896.
[8] *Ibid.*, v. 5. pp. 1–2, Feb. 1895.

He does not answer his own question very definitely. Discussing it gives him a chance to excoriate hypocritical reformers, rich corruptionists, suffrage leaders, and so on.

Brann loved to discuss the sins of high society, but he also wrote about "the common courtesan" with gusto and bombast. He seems to have thought that most men, as well as most women, were, secretly or publicly, in a pretty bad way. "I suspect," he wrote, "that if any large proportion of benedicts are faithful, it is not altogether their fault."[9] Wit and epigram sometimes took the place of a kind of ranting eloquence that was often tiresome, if not disgusting, and thus furnished a happy change of pace. He did not approve of the new bloomer dress for women:

> Had Queen Elizabeth worn bloomers, Sir Walter Raleigh might have bridged a mud-puddle for her with his costly cloak, but more likely he would have told her to climb upon his back. Leander might have swam the tempestuous Hellespont to bask in the smiles of a beauty clad in breeches, but I think he would have waited for the boat.[10]

Critical reviews of books were concerned chiefly with the passages in them which emphasized sex, and the editor excoriated in unmeasured terms such best sellers as *Quo Vadis* — "just such a book as I would expect a Texas editor to write while enjoying an attack of delirium tremens"[11] — and *Trilby* — "a dirty tale of bawdry."[12]

In politics, Brann was against the gold standard, against Cleveland, against imperialism. He called Cleveland "a tub of tallow," and he talked plainly about the stories of the former president's sexual irregularities, and repeated tales "often asserted" that he got drunk and beat his wife, who "could scarce apply for divorce from a man who has twice been president."[13]

Most shocking of all Brann's crusades was the one against the Negro. He argued that "if the South is ever to rid herself of the negro rapefiend, she must take a day off and kill every member of the accursed race that declines to leave the country."[14] Hatred against the Negro was never more luridly expressed than in that frightful article; infernal thunders rumble all through it, and the flames of hell light up its phrases. (One cannot write of it, alas, without falling into Brann's high-flown diction.)

When Brann used the same techniques in reporting local scandals, he

[9] *Ibid.*, v. 6, p. 339, Jan. 1897.
[10] *Ibid.*, v. 5, p. 155, Oct. 1895.
[11] *Ibid.*, v. 8, pp. 51–52, April 1898.
[12] *Ibid.*, v. 5, p. 76, June 1895; v. 7, p. 41, March 1897.
[13] *Ibid.*, v. 7, p. 214, Oct. 1897.
[14] *Ibid.*, v. 5, p. 9, Feb. 1895.

found himself in serious personal difficulties. A young Brazilian girl, sponsored by Baptist missionaries, enrolled at Baylor University, a Baptist institution located in Waco, and, after an illegitimate child was born to her, brought suit for rape against a relative of the university's president. The scandal divided the Waco community into two factions, and there were street fights and mob violence. The *Iconoclast* attacked the university and its management. In the summer of 1897, Judge G. B. Gerald wrote a letter to the *Waco Times-Herald* defending Brann and his contentions; when Editor J. W. Harris refused to print it, a fist fight ensued and the judge was thrown out of the office. When Baylor opened its fall term with a larger enrollment than ever, Brann wrote:

> This proves that Texas Baptists are determined to support it at any sacrifice — that they believe it better that their daughters should be exposed to its historic dangers and their sons condemned to grow up in ignorance than that this manufactory of ministers and Magdalenes should be permitted to perish. It is to be hoped that the recent exposé of Baylor's criminal carelessness will have a beneficial effect — that henceforth orphan girls will not be ravished on the premises of its president, and that fewer young lady students will be sent home enceinte.[15]

The faculty of the college, wrote Brann, were illiterate; but then they were paid "on the scale of a second assistant bookkeeper of a fashionable livery stable." He offered to set up a night school for them.

As Brann must have expected, this scurrility stirred up more violence. He accounted for the tardiness of the November issue of the *Iconoclast* by explaining that he had been recovering from some "doses of Saving Grace presented by my Baptist brethren," who, he added,

> desired to send me as a missionary to foreign lands, and their invitation was so urgent, their expressions of regard so fervent, that I am now wearing my head in a sling and trying to write with my left hand. . . .
> The same old God-forsaken gang of moral perverts and intellectual misfits who more than two years ago brought a Canadian courtesan and an unfrocked priest [the Slatterys] to Waco to lecture on APAism, and who threatened at one of those buzzard-feasts to mob me for calling the latter a cowardly liar [from the platform] were responsible for my being dragged with a rope by several hundred hoodlums up and down a Baptist college campus in this city October second, and for the brutal assault upon me five days later by a pack of would-be assassins who waited until my back was turned before they had the nerve to get out their guns.[16]

Two weeks later Judge Gerald and Editor Harris had a gun fight on the street, in which Harris and his brother were killed, Gerald badly wounded, and several bystanders struck by stray bullets. For two or three months after that shocking event, hostilities subsided somewhat,

---

[15] *Ibid.*, v. 7, p. 227, Oct. 1897.
[16] *Ibid.*, v. 7, p. 239, Nov. 1897.

and the *Iconoclast* was more moderate; the Reverend R. C. Burleson, who had been president of Baylor for nearly half a century, resigned. But in the spring of 1898, the dogs of war were loose again. In his April issue Brann reviewed the Antonia Tiexeria case again, once more warned parents against sending their daughters to the college, and declared that the institution was "not a proper guardian for any youth whose father does not desire to see him land in the Baptist Pulpit or the penitentiary."[17]

On April 1, Captain T. E. Davis, who had a daughter enrolled at Baylor, shot Brann from behind, on a crowded Waco street. Fatally wounded, Brann turned on his assailant and riddled him with bullets. Both died the next day, and there was more duelling in the streets. Brann's funeral was the largest Waco had ever seen. The procession to the graveyard, which stretched out for two miles, was led by two bands playing dirges. The story in the *Dallas News* said: "Among those who followed the Apostle to his grave were several persons of note whom he had assailed in the *Iconoclast* when, with a pen of fire, he was uttering his brilliant diatribes."[18]

Baylor University at length outgrew its scandal, outlived its traducers, became again a highly respected institution of higher education. But W. C. Brann, whose assault on smug acceptance of the prevailing order with all its abuses was far broader than the incidental attack on the small church college at hand, cannot quite be forgotten. Despite his egregious type of poolroom criticism of persons and institutions, in which sentimentality is mixed with cynicism and noble language with low slang, Brann did challenge, courageously and even recklessly, notable hypocrisies and "humbugs" of his day. Despite his errors of reasoning and taste, he still stands as a martyr to free speech and the free press.

The May 1898 issue of the *Iconoclast*, brought out by his friends, was a memorial number for the late editor. Judge Gerald wrote the chief obituary, in the course of which he declared:

had he lived ten years longer, in all probability the intellectual world would have held him as the grandest writer the earth has known since the days of old Homer. . . . His name and writings will live until the English language dies.[19]

There were tributes from many others to the dead "Apostle," as he liked to call himself ("Apostle of the Devil," he sometimes said) and eulogies came from far and wide — among them some good verses from William

---

[17] Reprinted in the issue for Nov. 1918.
[18] *Dallas News*, April 3, 1898, p. 1. Quoted by Rollins in *South Atlantic Quarterly*, v. 14, Jan. 1915.
[19] *Iconoclast*, v. 8, p. 75, May 1898.

Marion Reedy. Of all the admirers of Brann who have tried to sum him up in a sentence or two, perhaps Michael Monahan did it best some five years later in the first number of his own little magazine:

> He was the most brilliant and daring guerilla-publicist of our time — fantastical, exaggerative, even grotesque, if you please, but not less a writer of genuine potency who had woven of his literary style a whip of scorpions. Brann indeed had power in excess. The weapons of his invective and scorn have not been matched in our day. As an antidote to this pen that dripped poison, to these gifts of vitriolic scorn and hearted hate, the enemies of Brann could propose only the pistol of the assassin — and so they filled the prophet with lead. It is thus, alas! that Texas disposes of a literary style.[20]

But Brann's style, like his passion, is too unbridled. It is too florid, too artificially Ossianic, to please a disciplined taste. It is at its best in Fourth of July eloquence, as in "Old Glory," an address delivered at San Antonio on July 4, 1893, or in attack on hated enemies with what Monahan called his "scorpion-whip." But most of Brann is (except in small doses) tiresome in its sophomoric overwriting. "Mr. Brann," wrote one eastern critic, "never errs on the side of subtlety." [21]

Brann's works were edited in two volumes, and three editions have been published, first in Waco and later in New York. In 1919 a twelve-volume edition of *The Complete Works of Brann The Iconoclast* was published in New York.

In the later publication of the *Iconoclast* the widow of the dead editor was aided for six months after the tragedy by several friends — W. H. Ward, Brann's long-time friend and lecture manager, and a former newspaperman; Judge Gerald, now a veteran of the Brann war; and Henry S. Canfield, who had been a deputy sheriff as well as a newspaper reporter and editor. In July F. T. Marple, of Fort Worth, bought the plant, with the idea of moving it to his city,[22] but Canfield transferred the publication of the journal to Chicago. It is said Waconians extended their good wishes when the *Iconoclast* left Texas, and muttered under their breath, "God help Chicago!"

In Chicago, Canfield's *Brann's Iconoclast* did fairly well. Much of the martyr-editor's stuff was reprinted, and the new pieces were very Brann-like indeed. The memorial article on Ingersoll in the August 1899 number seemed to be Brann at his best. There was a series on "Men Who Ought to be Dead" — Cleveland, John Sherman, Rockefeller, and others. Circulation was under ten thousand when the paper was sold in 1900 to J. C. Hart. It is usually said that at the end of Brann's career

[20] *Papyrus*, v. 1, July 1903, pp. 12–14.
[21] *Echo*, v. 3, p. 232, Nov. 7, 1896. See also Reedy's more careful estimate in his *Mirror*, v. 8, April 8, 1898, p. 1.
[22] *New York Tribune*, July 23, 1898, p. 6, col. 6.

he had brought his circulation to ninety thousand; but the directories do not support an estimate of over fifty thousand,[23] and in Chicago it never reached the Waco circulation.

In 1903 C. A. Windle took over the journal, with J. G. Hoeger as business manager. Wrote the new editor: "In taking up the work of puncturing frauds, exposing fakes, and smashing false idols, where it fell from the dying grasp of the brilliant Brann, I make but one promise — to be as radical, as right, and as uncompromising as Justice." [24] Windle was a picturesque and violent writer, in the Brann tradition. He attacked "Billy" Sunday, opposed prohibition, was against the entry of the United States into the First World War but later supported it, fought President Wilson, defended Catholicism, attacked socialism and Bolshevism. The *Iconoclast* got up to forty thousand circulation on the war issue. C. Pliny Windle, son of the editor, became business manager after the war, and later associate editor.

In 1926 the name was changed to *Windle's Liberal Magazine*; the periodical became a semimonthly for a short time, and later a monthly again at three dollars a year. It was now full of revolt against the "Volsteaders" and the Prohibition Amendment. The "noble experiment" of Hoover became the "hellish adventure" of Windle. In 1929 there was a reorganization, though Windle stayed on as editor. The name was now simply the *Liberal*. Active support of Alfred E. Smith, on the ground of religious liberty, continued after his defeat for the presidency; articles against prohibition went on after repeal. The *Liberal* had a way of flogging dead issues. C. A. Windle died in 1934 and C. Pliny took over. There was now much against Bolshevism. The circulation was down to ten or fifteen thousand in 1937, when the journal quietly subsided — the only quiet thing it ever did.

[23] The figure of 90,000 came from J. D. Shaw, *Brann the Iconoclast: A Collection*. But see Rowell's *American Newspaper Directory* for 1903, in which the average for 1898 is stated as 49,750.

[24] *Iconoclast*, v. 13, p. 2, March 1903.

## THE CHAP-BOOK[1]

**H**ERBERT S. STONE and Ingalls Kimball were Harvard seniors when they began the *Chap-Book* in May 1894. They had already founded a small publishing house, and they planned the magazine chiefly as an advertising organ for that business. But the liveliness and sharp originality of its contents and the distinction of its format and typography made the little magazine immediately popular among the elite, and it was soon an important undertaking in itself. Its page measured four and a half by seven and a half inches, and the stock was antique laid paper with deckled edges. The type throughout was Caslon. The first number carried an article on Francis Thompson's poetry by Bliss Carman, a story by Maria Louise Pool, a poem by Charles G. D. Roberts, "Notes" by the editors, a self-portrait of Aubrey Beardsley, and the announcement of Stone & Kimball books.

The two young men who were so active (prematurely, thought the Harvard authorities) in this original publishing venture had been stimulated thereto by certain literary and artistic movements of the midnineties. There were some American writers breaking new ground, like Crane, Garland, Boyesen, James, Hovey, Carman, and so on; and there were English, Irish, and French writers who were exciting and too little known in the United States. The new poster art was also exciting, as was the "Revival of Printing" in England, already gaining some disciples in America. The English *Yellow Book* undoubtedly had some influence on the *Chap-Book*. Certain Boston publishers — especially Copeland & Day and Lamson, Wolfe & Company — were already bringing out some books showing the influences of these contemporary currents. Stone and Kimball had unlimited enthusiasm and some money, and publishing cost far less than in later years.

After three months, their college days over, the two young men moved both magazine and publishing business to Chicago, where Melville E.

[1] TITLE: *The Chap-Book.*
FIRST ISSUE: May 15, 1894. LAST ISSUE: July 1, 1898.
PERIODICITY: Semimonthly. Vols. 1–8, semiannual, May 15, 1894–May 1, 1898; 9, May 15-July 15, 1898.
PUBLISHERS: Stone & Kimball (Cambridge, Mass., May–June, 1894; thereafter Chicago), 1894–96; Herbert S. Stone & Co., Chicago, 1896–98.
EDITOR: Herbert Stuart Stone.
REFERENCES: Sidney Kramer, *A History of Stone & Kimball and Herbert S. Stone & Company* (Chicago, 1940); Earnest Elmo Calkins, "The Chap-Book," *Colophon*, v. 3, part 10, 1932; Herbert E. Fleming, "The Literary Interests of Chicago," *American Journal of Sociology*, v. 11, pp. 795-805, May 1906.

Stone, Herbert's father and the founder of the *Chicago Daily News*, was now a prosperous banker and general manager of the Associated Press. There the typography of the magazine was under the direction of the great Frederick W. Goudy, and it went on to win the plaudits of the discerning both for its appearance and for its literary offerings.

It would be pleasant to say that it also won large financial rewards; but the facts are that its circulation averaged less than twenty thousand,[2] and though the price was raised from one to two dollars a year (five to ten cents a number) in 1897, it must always have had deficits to pay. After two years in Chicago, Stone and Kimball parted, Kimball taking the old firm name to New York to continue in book publishing,[3] and Stone remaining in Chicago, keeping the *Chap-Book*, and publishing under the style of Herbert S. Stone & Company.

Many authors of standing and ability were printed in the *Chap-Book*. Among the serials were Bliss Carman's "Contemporaries" and Hamlin Garland's "Land of the Straddle Bug," both in 1895; Henry James's "What Maisie Knew," in 1897, and Andrew Lang's "Letters to Dead Authors," in 1898. The level of the *Chap-Book's* short fiction was high; there was more good poetry printed in this magazine, in proportion to the size of its file, than in any other American periodical of its times; and its criticism of books, though not bludgeoning, had a good cutting edge. A few contributors' names may be listed here, chiefly to show the variety of the four years' performance of this magazine: Thomas Bailey Aldrich, Max Beerbohm, Alice Brown, John Burroughs, Richard Burton, George W. Cable, Stephen Crane, Paul Lawrence Dunbar, Eugene Field, Clyde Fitch, Edmund Gosse, Thomas Hardy, Joel Chandler Harris, William E. Henley, Stéphane Mallarmé, Gilbert Parker, Percival Pollard, Arthur Quiller-Couch, William Sharp, Edmund Clarence Stedman, Robert Louis Stevenson, Maurice Thompson, Paul Verlaine, William Watson, George E. Woodberry, W. B. Yeats, and Israel Zangwill.

Carman was associate editor of the first few numbers, and Harrison Garfield Rhodes held that position after the magazine was removed to Chicago. In January 1897 the page size was enlarged and a smooth-finish paper suited to the use of halftones was adopted, thus bringing the magazine more nearly into conformity with those to which the public was accustomed.

Leading artists for the *Chap-Book* were John Sloan, Robert Wagner, E. B. Bird, Frank Hazenplug, Dawson Watson, Claude Fayette Brag-

---

[2] The directories bear this out; but see Fleming, *ibid.*, p. 801.

[3] He published one periodical also, the *Daily Tatler*, a literary paper of eight two-column pages in thirteen numbers, Nov. 7–21, 1896, containing contributions by Howells, Hovey, Maeterlinck, and others. The *New York Tribune* criticized it for its "slangy slap-dash" (*Tribune*, Nov. 11, 1896, p. 8, col. 1).

don, Fred Richardson, and Will Bradley. The caricatures of Max Beerbohm were a feature. The posters designed to advertise the *Chap-Book*
at the newsstands [4] were the most artistic used for any of the magazines.
They were drawn by Hazenplug, Bragdon, Bradley, and Bird. Bradley
built his reputation largely through these posters.[5]

In 1898 the *Chap-Book* was sold to the *Dial*, Chicago's most durable
literary magazine. The first July number of that year, and the last of
the file, was devoted to a valedictory announcement. *Publisher's Weekly*, announcing the end of the *Chap-Book*, said that it had called out
"nearly a hundred and fifty" imitations. Five years later, F. W. Faxon,
compiling his bibliography of "ephemeral bibelots," listed two hundred
and twenty-eight which, as he thought, "owe their origin to the success
of the *Chap-Book*." [6] Most successful of these was Elbert Hubbard's
*Philistine*,[7] but most were weak imitations that the *Chap-Book* had
long since disowned with scorn.[8]

Herbert Stone continued with a modest publishing business in Chicago. In 1915 he happened to be returning from Europe on the same
boat with Hubbard. The boat was the *Lusitania*, and Stone and Hubbard
were two of the almost twelve hundred persons who were drowned when
their ship was sunk by a submarine.

[4] See pp. 19–20.
[5] See F. Weitenkampf, *American Graphic Art* (New York, 1924), pp. 277–78.
[6] Frederick Winthrop Faxon, *Modern Chap-Books and Their Imitators* (Boston, 1905),
p. 3.
[7] See Sketch 22 in this volume.
[8] *Chap-Book*, v. 2, p. 446, May 1, 1894.

## COLLIER'S[1]

PETER FENELON COLLIER was born in County Carlow, Ireland, in 1849 and came to America when he was seventeen years old. He worked hard, got some schooling in a Catholic academy, and at the age of twenty-four was in the publishing business. His first ventures were books with special appeal to Catholics, but after a few years he was issuing popular reprints of standard authors. His business, which depended on low-priced library sets sold on the installment plan by book agents, and a "library" of popular literature sold by mail in series, was extremely successful in the eighties. In the last thirty years of his life, P. F. Collier is said to have manufactured and sold fifty-two million books.

In April 1888 Collier founded a periodical called *Once a Week*, which was sold in conjunction with the biweekly *Collier's Library of* novels and popular books at bargain rates. Separately, *Once a Week* was priced at seven cents, and it was advertised as a magazine of "fiction, fact, sensation, wit, humor, news." Small-folio in size, its sixteen pages were packed with readable material, fiction predominating. In

---

[1] TITLES: (1) *Collier's Once a Week*, 1888–89; (2) *Once a Week, An Illustrated Weekly Newspaper*, 1889–95; (3) *Collier's Weekly, An Illustrated Journal*, 1895–1904 (cover title May 1901–Dec. 1902, *Collier's Illustrated Weekly*); (4) *Collier's, The National Weekly*, 1905–57. (Title on cover, contents page, and page captions since 1949: *Collier's*.)
FIRST ISSUE: April 28, 1888. LAST ISSUE: Jan. 4, 1957.
PERIODICITY: Weekly, 1888–1953; fortnightly, 1953–current. Vols. 1–61, semiannual vols. ending in Sept. and March, 1888–1918; 62, Sept. 14–Dec. 21, 1918; 63, Jan.–June 1919; 64, July–Dec. 1919 (only 21 nos., issues for Oct. 11, 18, 25, Nov. 1, Dec. 27 being omitted); 65–140 (no. 1), regular semiannual vols., 1920–Jan. 4, 1957.
PUBLISHERS: P.F. Collier, New York, 1888–1900; P.F. Collier and Son, New York, 1900–19; P.F. Collier & Son Company, editorial offices, New York; publication offices, Springfield, Ohio, 1919–34; Crowell Publishing Company, same addresses, 1934–39; Crowell-Collier Publishing Company, same addresses, 1939–current. (For officials of the publishing company, see p. 763.)
EDITORS: Nugent Robinson, 1888–90; Mayo Williamson Hazeltine, 1891; Julius Chambers, 1892–93; T. B. Connery, 1893–96; Daniel Lyons, 1896–98; Robert Joseph Collier, 1898–1902, 1912–13; Norman Hapgood, 1902–12; Mark Sullivan, 1914–17; Finley Peter Dunne, 1917–19; Harford Powel, Jr., 1919–22; Richard John Walsh, 1922–24; Loren Palmer, 1924–25; William Ludlow Chenery, 1925–43; Charles Henry Colebaugh, 1943–44; Henry La Cossitt, 1944–46; Walter Davenport, 1946–49; Louis Ruppel, 1949–52; Roger Dakin, 1952–55; Kenneth McArdle, 1953–57. (Paul Clifford Smith, editor-in-chief, 1954–1957.)
INDEXES: *Readers' Guide* and *Dramatic Index* since 1908.
REFERENCES: William L. Chenery, *So It Seemed* (New York, 1952), chs. 16–24; Mark Sullivan, *The Making of an American* (New York, 1938), chs. 23–31; Norman Hapgood, *The Changing Years* (New York, 1930), chs. 12, 13, 15; Hickman Powell, "Collier's," *Scribner's Magazine*, v. 105, May 1939, pp. 19–23ff; Amos Stote, "Case History: Collier's," *Magazine World*, v. 1, Oct. 1945, pp. 10–15; William L. Chenery, "Behind the Scenes at Collier's," *Quill*, v. 22, May 1934, pp. 8ff.

fact, the first number begins four fiction serials and also presents six short stories. The list of contributors in that initial issue is a notable one: the serials are by Amélie Rives, H. Rider Haggard, Dion Boucicault, and James Franklin Fitts. Marion Harland edits a "Woman's World" column, Edgar Fawcett does "Social Silhouettes" (later he did the editorial notes), "Nym Crinkle" Wheeler has a theater department, and Bill Nye writes a weekly humorous feature. Also Julian Hawthorne, Benson J. Lossing, Ella Wheeler Wilcox, James Whitcomb Riley, Maurice Thompson, and George Parsons Lathrop are contributors. There is a double page of comic pictures, and illustration is copious.

For its first few years *Once a Week* was under the editorial charge of a young journalist named Nugent Robinson, who continued until 1892 to make it chiefly a story paper, but one of good standards, with excellent contributors. When Robinson retired in 1892, *Once a Week* claimed a circulation of a quarter-million,[2] which put it in the top bracket for American weeklies of that time.

Robinson's successors were well-known journalists — Mayo W. Hazeltine, long-time literary editor of the *New York Sun*; Julius Chambers, a former editor of the *New York Herald*, who stayed with the paper for only about a year; and finally the man who had once been Chambers' boss on the *Herald*, Thomas B. Connery, a novelist and a former minister to Mexico. These competent newspapermen made *Once a Week* less a story paper, and much more a weekly news magazine. The *Journalist* noted soon after Chambers took over that the new editor was making *Once a Week* "as nearly like a wide-awake metropolitan newspaper as it is possible for a weekly to be."[3] A special local edition was provided for Chicago, under the editorship of Curtis Dunham, from the staff of the *New York World*. What the paper became in these years was a somewhat breezier and lighter *Harper's Weekly*. It was not unlike the *Frank Leslie's Illustrated Weekly* of the early nineties. In 1895 its name was changed to *Collier's Weekly: An Illustrated Journal*. There was still plenty of fiction and humor, but the emphasis was now on news and public affairs; and as the arts of photography and engraving developed, it became a leading early exponent of the halftone news picture.

Whether because of the change in policy or the hard times of the mid-nineties, circulation declined under Chambers, Connery, and a third newsman-editor, Daniel Lyons. It was not until the publisher's son, Robert J. Collier, fresh from college, was put in charge of the journal in 1898 that it began to pick up once more.

Not that Rob Collier stepped from the sacred precincts of Harvard

[2] *Journalist*, v. 17, Feb. 20, 1892, p. 9.
[3] *Ibid.*, June 18, 1892.

into the magazine office a seasoned editor. He told about his editorial beginnings later:

I had just come from Harvard with the idea that popular journalism needed a little true literary flavor. I showed my judgment of the public taste by ordering a serial story by Henry James. The illustrations were by John La Farge, and I have never yet discovered what either the story or the pictures were about. So with the covers. The first one, I remember, was by Wenzell and represented a Greek goddess mounting a hill, which may have been the Acropolis. Underneath was the caption ΑΩΣΟΜΕΝ (We Shall Give). I had selected it from one of the fragments of Sappho, and was so afraid that someone would understand it that I printed it in the original Greek.[4]

But it did not take young Collier long to get his bearings in "popular journalism." He himself, in the same jocular tone, ascribes his awakening to the coming of the war with Spain and a quick appreciation of the possibilities of covering the news of Cuban events in pictures and words for a weekly journal:

It was at that time, when I had been fitting myself to become the editor of the *Athenaeum* or the *Yellow Book*, that the *Maine* blew up and Jimmy Hare blew in. Sending Hare to Havana that morning involved me in more troubles and wars and libel suits than any one act in my life. It turned me from the quiet paths of a literary career into association with war correspondents, politicians, muckrakers, and advertising men.[5]

James H. Hare was the greatest of the early news photographers, and he worked for *Collier's* for many years. For that periodical he covered wars and disasters, ceremonies, conventions, and so on. A pioneer in photo-journalism, Jimmy Hare played no small part in the success of *Collier's Weekly*. In his early years he was the paper's correspondent as well as its photographer. The "Cuban Number," of May 28, 1898, for example, with a striking Stanlaws cover, filled ten of its twenty-four pages with illustrations, many by Hare; and its chief article had Hare's by-line.

"*Collier's* first took its place as The National Weekly by the thorough way in which it covered our war with Spain," wrote the editors nearly fifteen years later.[6] Chief *Collier* correspondent in the field was able Frederick Palmer, twenty-five years old and covering his second war. Palmer's stories and Hare's pictures attracted national attention. Also in the news realm were the articles on public affairs by Henry

---

[4] Cecil Carnes, *Jimmy Hare, News Photographer* (New York, 1940), p. 257. These remarks were made at a dinner given to Hare. The Henry James story referred to was *The Turn of the Screw.*

[5] *Ibid.*

[6] *Collier's*, v. 50, Nov. 9, 1912, p. 23.

Loomis Nelson, recently retired from the editorship of *Harper's Weekly*. By 1902 Walter Wellman was doing a Washington letter for *Collier's*. The same year Peter Finley Dunne wrote *Collier* editorials for six months; over a considerable period he contributed "Mr. Dooley" essays to the weekly.

In those early years of Rob Collier's editorship there was a great improvement in illustration, stories, and articles. The price was increased to ten cents, and the size was brought up to twenty-four pages.

Illustration brightened immediately, and it continued to improve as Collier money was poured into the magazine. Harrison Fisher, Henry Hutt, and Howard Chandler Christy — a popular 1900 trio of specialists in magazine covers adorned by faces of pretty girls — were recruited; later came Will Bradley, Thure de Thulstrup, the Leyendeckers, James Montgomery Flagg, and others. But the sensational "catch" was Charles Dana Gibson, darling of the nineties, who had long been the special property of *Life*,[7] but who in 1903 entered into a contract to draw a hundred double-page "cartoons" for *Collier's*, for a consideration of a hundred thousand dollars, the pictures to be distributed over four years. This generous contract was advertised in the newspapers, and there were special Gibson numbers for October 16, 1904, and October 21, 1905. Gibson was back with a later series in 1908–1912.

*Collier's* became a leader in the new era of color in magazine illustration in the first decade of the new century. Maxfield Parrish furnished imaginative and colorful paintings, and his 1906–1907 series of Arabian Nights pictures was memorable, as were the many double-page illustrations — westerns by Frederic Remington, marines by Henry Reuterdahl, and so on. Jessie Willcox Smith drew delightful pictures of children. E. W. Kemble and A. B. Frost furnished homely comedy in their pictures for the magazine. Kemble also did political cartoons, as did F. T. Richards, J. T. McCutcheon, Boardman Robinson, Art Young, and others.

Young Collier was lavish also in his outlay for stories and articles. Rudyard Kipling and Robert W. Chambers, desirable writers for any magazine in these years, were among his prizes. Hall Caine's *The Eternal City* was a serial in 1901. Frank Norris, Israel Zangwill, and Stanley Weyman were contributors of fiction. There was poetry, too, by Frank L. Stanton, James Whitcomb Riley, and others. There were many "special numbers," devoted to such things as humor, the stage, and women's interests. There were departments for women, for sports, and

---

[7] *Life* had shared him for a time with *Harper's Magazine*, and later he drew for *Harper's Weekly*.

so on. Walter Camp wrote sports articles for *Collier's,* and continued to name All-American teams in its pages for many years.

Circulation was up to three hundred thousand when, in 1902, Collier invited Norman Hapgood to the editorship of the magazine at a salary of twenty-five thousand dollars a year.[8] In this new arrangement, Hapgood's main responsibility was the editorial page; Collier retained an over-all direction, initiating most of the projects, and keeping a hand on all departments.

Hapgood was thirty-four when he joined the *Collier* staff, and he remained for ten years. A singularly humorless young man, a graduate of the Harvard Law School who had deserted the law for journalism, and particularly for theatrical criticism, Hapgood was a remarkable combination of scholar, journalist, and connoisseur of the arts. Collier had hired him, on the advice of Peter Dunne,[9] largely to give tone to the *Weekly*; he wanted more of such prestige as *Harper's Weekly* enjoyed, with its influence on public affairs.[10] Hapgood found an editorial department of two attractively designed facing pages in the front of the magazine awaiting him, and what he did with them we shall see as soon as we have taken a hurried glance at the more general fare offered by the magazine during the Hapgood decade.

Emphasis on fiction continued for a time, chiefly through the promotion of Rob Collier. In 1903 there were new Sherlock Holmes stories, and more Kipling. In 1904 began a series of prize competitions for short stories, which for the next five years brought many excellent stories in *Collier's* pages and helped win the journal a reputation for interesting short fiction. Margaret Deland and Rowland Thomas were top winners in the five-thousand-dollar contest; Thomas was later a staff writer. The roll of distinguished fictioneers in the first few years of the new century is a long one; it will be suficient to name, in addition to writers whose contributions to *Collier's* have already been noted, O. Henry, Frank Norris, Owen Wister, F. Marion Crawford, Edith Wharton, Booth Tarkington, Jack London, Winston Churchill, Rex Beach, Anthony Hope, and P. G. Wodehouse. But by 1909 the importance of fiction in *Collier's* had declined, and for a few years many numbers contained no fiction at all, though an occasional "fiction number" might carry four or five short stories by Charles Belmont Davis, Edwin Balmer, Gouverneur Morris, and others. Fiction serials were dropped.

There was some poetry in these years, by Bliss Carman, Edith

---

[8] Sullivan, *The Making of an American,* p. 237.
[9] Elmer Ellis, *Mr. Dooley's America* (New York, 1941), p. 187.
[10] Sullivan, *The Making of an American,* p. 207.

Wyatt, Edwin Markham, Frank L. Stanton, and Arthur Stringer. News remained important. A "Paragraphic Record of the World's News" was correlated with a "Photographic History of Current Events." Hapgood himself wrote able monthly and yearly summaries of current history.

*Collier's* had excellent coverage of the Russo-Japanese War by special correspondents, artists, and camera men. Richard Harding Davis was paid a thousand dollars a week for his articles,[11] and they were supplemented by those of Frederic Palmer, H. J. Whigham, and Edwin Emerson, while Frederic Remington, Cyrus C. Adams, and others furnished a fine series of pictures to illustrate the stories. But after all, it was the photographic coverage by Jimmy Hare, Robert L. Dunn, James F. J. Archibald, and others which was most effective of all. Davis once referred to Hare as the man who made the Russo-Japanese War famous.[12] "The ubiquitous Mr. Hare," said *Collier's* several years later, "followed the Japanese army across the Yalu and up to Mukden, and the photographs he took have since become valuable historical records." [13]

*Collier's* issued a great San Francisco earthquake number dated May 5, 1906. It was actually out only two weeks after the disaster, with Jack London's story, and no less than sixteen pages of pictures.

A. Radcliffe Dugmore's African jungle pictures — "Ahead of Mr. Roosevelt" — were a feature in 1909. Caspar Whitney, former *Outing* editor, ran a monthly "Outdoor America" section in 1909 and later — a "magazine within a magazine," with its own contributors. There were occasional "dramatic" numbers. An early department by Editor Hapgood, "Seen From My Study Window," dealt with plays and books. Robert Bridges, and later Rowland Thomas, reviewed books. And, of course, there was always some comedy. The "Hashimura Togo" pieces of Wallace Irwin were amusing, and "Mr. Dooley" was both amusing and meaningful. George Ade, George Fitch, Jerome K. Jerome, and Oliver Herford were among *Collier* humorists.

But it was comment on public affairs that gradually came to give *Collier's* its distinctive quality during the first decade of the new century. Carroll D. Wright's series on labor problems in 1903, one on immigration the next year, the monthly forums and the insurance articles of 1905, the stories on the Panama Canal and Theodore Roosevelt in 1906–1907, C. P. Connolly's series on the Moyer-Haywood case in 1907, the articles on the American saloon in 1908, Samuel Hop-

[11] Charles B. Davis, ed., *Adventures and Letters of Richard Harding Davis* (New York, 1917), p. 300.
[12] Carnes, *Jimmy Hare, News Photographer*, p. 225.
[13] *Collier's*, v. 50, Nov. 9, 1912, p. 23.

kins Adams' "The Art of Advertising" in 1909, Will Irwin's great series on "The American Newspaper" in 1911, and Garet Garrett's financial department in 1912 are only a few highlights among *Collier's* offerings, during the Hapgood regime, in the wide field of social-economic problems.

But even more conspicuous and memorable in this *Collier* era were Hapgood's editorials, tied up as they were with the journal's crusades on certain great issues.

The first of these journalistic battles was not waged on a great national issue, however. *Town Topics*, a New York society journal,[14] had said some nasty things about Alice Roosevelt, more innuendo than anything else:

> From wearing costly lingerie to indulging in fancy dances for the edification of men was only a step. And then came a second step — indulging freely in stimulants. . . . Flying all around Newport without a chaperone was another thing that greatly concerned Mother Grundy. There may have been no reason for the old lady making such a fuss about it, but if the young woman knew some of the tales that are told at the clubs in Newport she would be more careful in the future about what she does and how she does it.[15]

Rob Collier pointed out the paragraph to Hapgood, suggesting an editorial. The editor obliged with a couple of paragraphs in which *Town Topics* was called "the most degraded paper of any prominence in the United States" and "a sewer-like sheet." To this Collier himself added a final paragraph, in which the editor of *Town Topics* was said to have a social standing "somewhat worse than that of an ordinary forger, horse-thief, or second-story man." [16] If this seems unreasonable heat to be generated by a paragraph in a gossip-sheet, it should be remembered that (1) loose gossip was less common in the New York press then than it became a generation later, (2) Rob Collier was a gallant young society man, and (3) Colonel William D'Alton Mann, editor of *Town Topics*, was believed by more than one man of wealth and position to edit his social columns with an eye to loans and cash payments — a custom for which there is an ugly name.

At any rate, when Colonel Mann induced District Attorney William Travers Jerome to put the matter before a grand jury and have Hapgood indicted for criminal libel, the *Collier's* attorneys dug up a great quantity of evidence which, while it probably did not prove blackmail, at least caused the jury to sympathize with the original statement

---

[14] For *Town Topics* see Sketch 37 in this volume.
[15] *Town Topics*, v. 52, Oct. 20, 1904, p. 3.
[16] *Collier's*, v. 34, Nov. 5, 1904, p. 9. See also Sullivan, *The Making of an American*, pp. 211–13.

about horse-thieves and to acquit the prisoner.[17] Mark Sullivan later wrote:

> The *Town Topics* suit did for *Collier's* what Collier most desired and needed. The first-page stories and heavy headlines with which the daily papers reported the trial, the parade of names of the best-known figures in New York yielding to intimidation or occasionally resisting it, as the *New York Sun* said, "with courage, celerity, and artistic thoroughness" — all combined to give *Collier's* esteem, éclat, kudos. It became, and for years remained, the most influential periodical in the country, in many respects the most distinguished America has ever had.[18]

Long before Hapgood's trial and acquittal in this case, *Collier's* was knee-deep in a crusade of much wider interest and of greater significance. In his autobiography, Hapgood tells how the weekly blundered accidentally into the fight against injurious patent medicines.[19] In one of those rather labored humorous editorials that he sometimes attempted, Hapgood had poked some fun at William Jennings Bryan's *Commoner*, which, while hammering monopolies, was giving large advertising space to "liquozone," a remedy that claimed to cure more than forty diseases, from cancer to dandruff. Isn't this a monopoly in cures? asked *Collier's*.[20] The witticism did not seem funny to publisher Bryan, or to the manufacturers of "liquozone," who descended upon the humorist in force. This incident made *Collier's* a party to the crusade against the whole patent medicine business, the abuses of which, as exposed in the *Ladies' Home Journal*, had hitherto provoked little more than a casual interest on the part of the weekly. And in the summer of 1905, just as the *Collier's* editors were getting warmed up on the matter, Samuel Hopkins Adams, who had been connected with *McClure's Magazine*, came knocking at the sanctum door with plans for articles attacking the patent medicine business along a wide front. These articles began in October of that year, under the title "The Great American Fraud," and they were concluded shortly before Congress passed a reformatory Food and Drug Act.

It was out of this campaign that the famous suit against the Postum Cereal Company grew. In 1906, *Collier's* lost the advertising of Charles W. Post, of "grape-nuts" fame, presumably because it had protested in November 1905 against medical claims made for that cereal food. Then, in July 1907, *Collier's* carried an editorial by Adams vigorously

[17] For Hapgood's résumé of the case, see *Collier's*, v. 36, Nov. 11, 1905, p. 25.

[18] Sullivan, *The Making of an American*, p. 219. Sullivan's sweeping conclusions about *Collier's* influence may be questioned. But there is no doubt that it won general commendation for the fight against *Town Topics*. See, e.g., *World's Work*, v. 11, p. 7369, April 1906.

[19] Hapgood, *The Changing Years*, pp. 177–78.

[20] *Collier's*, v. 34, March 25, 1905, p. 8; v. 35, April 22, 1905, pp. 9, 27. This was shortly before Sullivan, who assisted the *Ladies Home Journal* in its exposures, joined *Collier's* staff. For the *Journal's* part in the crusade, see p. 543.

attacking the widely advertised claim that a diet of "grape-nuts" would prevent appendicitis. This was answered by an advertising campaign in which it was asserted in many newspapers that *Collier's* had attacked Post products because Post would not advertise in the magazine. This was a clear accusation of blackmailing, and Collier sued the Postum Cereal Company for libel. Early in January 1911 he was awarded fifty thousand dollars damages, which seemed a full justification of *Collier's* course in the matter.[21] But when, on appeal, the verdict was set aside on a technicality, Collier decided he had been vindicated anyway, and dropped the case.

In another widely publicized libel case, *Collier's* was the defendant and William Randolph Hearst the plaintiff. Hearst sued for half a million dollars because he was accused, in Irwin's series on "The American Newspaper," of selling editorial commendation of theatrical productions along with display advertising — a thousand dollars for a Brisbane editorial and a full-page ad. The case was never brought to trial, and the next year the Federal Post Office Act included a regulation that reading notices must be clearly marked "Advertisement." In 1911, the year after the Irwin articles appeared, *Hearst's Magazine* published the famous Archbold letters; and *Collier's* exposed the "liberties" Hearst had taken with the stolen letters in an article (October 5) entitled "Mr. Hearst's Forgeries." Again there was brave talk of libel suits, but this time none was filed.

The crusades against "standpat" leadership in Congress were largely directed by Mark Sullivan. Sullivan had been associated with the *Ladies' Home Journal* in its drive on patent medicine abuses, and it was an article submitted to *Collier's* in connection with that controversy which first brought him to the favorable attention of the managers of the latter periodical. He joined the *Collier's* staff in 1906 and soon made an influential third in the Collier-Hapgood-Sullivan combination. By 1908 he was writing a "Comment on Congress" page; and there he developed an attack on Joseph G. Cannon, Speaker of the House of Representatives, which was supplemented by articles furnished by William Hard and others. Eventually the House took the power to appoint committees out of the Speaker's hands, which sounded the knell of "Cannonism." Said Congressman Samuel W. McCall, during the debate over curtailing the Speaker's powers: "This movement does not originate in the House of Representatives. You are about to do the

---

[21] See *Collier's*, v. 46, Jan. 14, 1911, p. 25; also a pamphlet entitled, *The $50,000 Verdict: An Account of the Action of Robert J. Collier vs. The Postum Cereal Company, Ltd., for Libel, in Which the Plaintiff Recovered $50,000 Damages. Also Ceratin Truths About the Nature of Grape-Nuts, Postum, and C. W. Post*, published by P. F. Collier & Son in 1911.

behest of a gang of literary highwaymen who are entirely willing to assassinate a character to sell a magazine." [22]

In the following issue of *Collier's*, Sullivan's "Comment on Congress" was headed: "Next, Aldrich!" and the journal swung its guns on the Senate majority leader. But Aldrich soon resigned, and the fight merged into a general advocacy of the cause of the "insurgents," later the Progressives, in Congress and before the people.

Closely identified with the contests in Congress was the attack on Secretary Ballinger, whose management of the Department of the Interior, especially in relation to Alaskan resources, came under fire. This eventually became an assault on the whole Taft conservation policy, which was the basis for the Roosevelt repudiation of his protégé in the White House. When the matter had arrived at the stage of hearings before a Congressional Committee, Collier was informed that the plan was first to whitewash the secretary and then to sue the magazine for a million dollars in a personal damage suit to be brought by Ballinger.[23] This forced Collier to employ an attorney to represent him at the hearings, and for this task he secured Louis D. Brandeis. As the hearings proceeded, Brandeis virtually took charge, by virtue of his mastery of the material, and the result was the resignation of Ballinger from the Cabinet and the emergence of Brandeis as a national figure.

Other causes for which *Collier's* fought were the income tax, the direct election of senators, railroad rate regulation, child labor laws, settlement houses and slum clearance, and woman suffrage. Few periodicals in America have exerted, over any decade, as strong and direct an influence on national affairs as that of *Collier's* during the Hapgood regime. To what extent its campaigns are to be classified as muckraking is a question. Perhaps the attacks on Cannon, Aldrich, and Ballinger may be so denominated. In its own pages *Collier's* was called the "last surviving muckraker" in 1909,[24] but muckraking as a movement had by then pretty well beaten itself out.[25]

In the hectic presidential campaign of 1912, an irreconcilable difference of opinion developed between Collier and Sullivan on the one hand and Hapgood on the other. The causes for which the magazine had been fighting were the "my policies" of T. R., and Collier felt thoroughly committed to the "Bull-Moose" side; but the more scholarly Hapgood strongly favored Wilson. In the feud which developed, and which resulted in the firing of Hapgood at the end of October 1912,

[22] Sullivan, *The Making of an American*, pp. 261–62.
[23] Hapgood, *The Changing Years*, p. 183.
[24] *Collier's*, v. 42, Jan. 2, 1909, p. 18.
[25] See pp. 208–09. For an opinion on the influence of *Collier's*, see Will Irwin, *The Making of a Reporter* (New York, 1942), p. 156.

there was too much public acrimony. When Collier took over the editorship, he said that he believed that *"Collier's* attitude in the campaign just closing has not been true to its own best traditions. It has been captious, unresponsive, even sneering" toward the Progressive party. "Since the owner's opinion did not coincide with the former editor's, he has decided to edit his own paper," added Collier. Roosevelt's letter congratulating Collier on his action, which was given a full-page space in the same issue which announced the change in editors, said:

I am deeply pleased. . . . I owe much to *Collier's.* . . . In this campaign the Progressive party has suffered very grave harm through the perpetration of an untruth as to its position on the regulation of trusts. This untruth has been disseminated through two channels — the editorial pages of *Collier's Weekly*, and the speeches of Woodrow Wilson.[26]

Hapgood rejoined in the newspapers with some angry remarks to the effect that Rob Collier's editorial about Roosevelt which had appeared in a recent number was so commonplace that if the office-boy had submitted it, he would have complimented the boy but thrown the editorial into the wastebasket.[27] Hapgood always claimed thereafter that it was not the quarrel over Roosevelt that caused his resignation, but a difference over "business and editorial relations." He intimated at the time that advertising pressures were involved; there was doubtless also some resentment over the growing influence of Sullivan, and there were other differences.[28]

Hapgood, while he was extremely valuable to *Collier's*, was not a great editor. He was, however, a careful, well-balanced liberal. Upton Sinclair's denunciation of him in *The Brass Check* is not quite convincing, and some details of the Sinclair story of *Collier's* handling of the meat-packers' scandal are not borne out by the file of the paper.[29] Hapgood was a reformer, but he had a dislike for rant and fustian. He was not really a muckraker; and, except for the crusade against patent medicine abuses, *Collier's* methods in those years were never precisely the techniques of the muckraking era. When Sullivan, though recognizing Hapgood's talent and "highly civilized touch," declares, "Hapgood was not a journalist at all; he was an essayist," he perhaps overstates the matter, but he is essentially right. Upon Hapgood's death in 1937, the *Nation* said:

---

[26] *Collier's*, v. 50, Nov. 2, 1912, pp. 8–10.

[27] *New York Times*, quoted in *Outlook*, v. 102, p. 473, Nov. 2, 1912. Also see *Collier's*, v. 50, Nov. 9, 1912, p. 8.

[28] Hapgood, *The Changing Years*, p. 222. But see full account of the episode in Sullivan, *The Making of an American*, ch. 30, and *Collier's*, v. 50, Nov. 9, 1912, pp. 8, 31–32.

[29] Compare the scurrilous remarks of Sinclair about the elder Collier with the tributes in *In Memoriam: Peter Fenelon Collier* (New York, 1910).

At the height of his power as editor of *Collier's Weekly* during the administrations of President Theodore Roosevelt and President Taft, Norman Hapgood exercised great public influence. A man of real ability and the finest character, without selfish ambitions, he soon found himself with a tremendous following.[30]

By 1912, when Hapgood resigned, *Collier's* had a little over a half million circulation. At the same time, *Harper's Weekly*, of which Hapgood was now to become editor, was down to seventy thousand and well started on the toboggan slide to oblivion. *Leslie's Weekly*, with a third of a million, was also behind *Collier's*; but the *Saturday Evening Post*, which had been about even with *Collier's* at the beginning of the Hapgood regime, had roared far ahead of all competitors and was now pressing the two-million mark. Of course, *Collier's* was still a ten-cent magazine, and the *Post* sold for a nickel.

In advertising there was a similar pattern. *Collier's* topped its competitors in advertising linage in 1904 and 1905; and in the latter year, according to a statement in Ayer's *Directory* signed by Advertising Manager Condé Nast, it printed "more advertising than any other weekly or monthly publication has ever carried in any similar period." But by 1912 the *Post* was forced to print seventy or eighty pages a week to accommodate its big advertising business, while *Collier's* had to satisfy itself with half that. There were good men on the business side at *Collier's*: Nast was advertising manager and later business manager to 1907; Ellmore C. Patterson had become vice-president and general manager by 1912. By that time A. C. G. Hammesfahr was ad manager; he later took Patterson's place. *Collier's* was the first great advertising medium for the young automotive industry. Its fascinating Automobile Number of January 17, 1903, was a pioneer venture, and was followed by many other such issues, always in January. The one for January 11, 1913, carried forty pages of automotive advertising and thirty pages of articles related to cars and motoring.

In the matter of editorial personnel, there was, as on all magazines, much shifting and change on *Collier's*. Besides the editorial triumvirate of Collier, Hapgood, and Sullivan, there were Associate Editors Arthur Ruhl and Richard Lloyd Jones, who served throughout most of the decade. John Habberton, the novelist, had been managing editor for less than a year when Rob Collier took charge; he remained for only a year or so longer. Albert Lee, coming from *Harper's Weekly* as an associate editor in 1901, served as managing editor from 1903 to 1911. He was followed by Edgar G. Sisson, 1911–1914. Arthur H. Gleason was an associate editor from 1908 to 1913, and J. M. Oskison and Lee

---

[30] *Nation*, v. 144, p. 523, May 8, 1937. The *Nation* comments especially on the following in the Middle West.

Shippey came to similar positions about the same time. Charles Belmont Davis, brother of *Collier's* famous war correspondent Richard Harding Davis, was fiction editor throughout the period. Walter Russell, Will Bradley, and Stuart Benson served as art editors and James H. Hare as staff photographer. Staff contributors throughout most of the decade were S. H. Adams, Will Irwin, R. H. Davis, and Frederick Palmer. Louis D. Brandeis wrote many editorials for the paper, especially in 1912.

Rob Collier's second editorship lasted only about fourteen months, but they were months full of interest. By the end of 1912 Collier had faithful Frederick Palmer covering the start of the great war in the Balkans, with Stephen Bonsal, another experienced war correspondent, and Jimmy Hare, now fifty-six years old but raring to go. The old short-story contests were renewed; James B. Connolly won the first prize of twenty-five hundred dollars. The first of a long series of "Fu Manchu" stories by Sax Rohmer appeared in 1913. Some more Sherlock Holmes stories were printed, and there were serials by Amélie Rives and others. The magazine battled against railway monopoly in New England, established a Pure Foods department edited by Lewis B. Allyn, published a series of articles on arson, and featured an interesting lot of personality sketches by Peter Clark Macfarlane drawn from various parts of the country, titled "Everyday Americans." Grantland Rice ran a comedy page called "Pickups."

In May 1913 Collier took the momentous step of reducing the price of his magazine to five cents. The art work became somewhat less brilliant, news pictures were featured less, and the paper became more like the *Saturday Evening Post*. Circulation began a slow, steady increase which was to bring it to the million mark by 1917.

In 1914 Collier put the editorship in the hands of Mark Sullivan, who held it for three years, and then passed it on to Peter Dunne, who was editor until the sale to Crowell. Palmer and Bonsal were joined by Staff Writers Ruhl, Irwin and Child in writing about the World War, as well as by Stephen Graham, William Slavens McNutt, William Gunn Shepherd, and James Hopper. Editorials featured the Liberty Bonds campaigns, War Savings Stamps, and other home-front activities. There was a special page headed "Seeing It Through." After his resignation as editor, Sullivan continued to write leading political articles for the *Weekly* for several years, and he was *Collier's* special correspondent at the Peace Conference. The magazine opposed Wilson in the 1916 campaign, though it gave space to articles in his favor by Ida M. Tarbell and Ray Stannard Baker. Sullivan wrote articles on the League of Nations toward the end of 1918, but he was not quite favorable to United States participation. Indicating the growing conservatism of the paper were contributions by Thomas W. Lamont, Judge Gary, and Samuel O. Dunn.

In fiction, the chief event of the Sullivan-Dunne lustrum of 1914–1919 was the publication of H. G. Wells's serial "Mr. Britling Sees It Through" in 1916. *Collier's* was partial to English writers at this time, and Arnold Bennett, May Sinclair, Edgar Wallace, and others were prominent. There were also fiction serials by the Americans Holworthy Hall, Jesse Lynch Williams, Meredith Nicholson, Peter B. Kyne, and Booth Tarkington, as well as short stories by Charles E. Van Loan, James Hopper, and other well-known story-tellers of the period. About this time Samuel Hopkins Adams turned from articles on public affairs to fiction.

There was a good deal about sports by Grantland Rice, Will Irwin, and Walter Camp. Julian Street contributed many articles on the American scene; he had a series called "Abroad at Home" in 1914, and another on "American Adventures" in 1916.

It was in 1909 that Peter F. Collier died. He had been an important figure in the field of mass distribution of books and had built a great fortune. His son Robert J. was not a good businessman; he had been trained in the tradition that money came from Dad, and if it ran low there was always more to be had from the same source. When finally Rob had the responsibility for all the Collier enterprises on his shoulders, without his father's steadying hand, he seemed to go to pieces. The evils of dissipation grew on him; when he lost money, he spent more and more lavishly; and he formed the habit of turning to his banker friends for aid much as he had formerly turned to his father. It was Harry Payne Whitney, an intimate friend, to whom Rob turned oftenest; the money was freely loaned, but the debt piled up. The banking house of Lee, Higginson & Company, which handled the loans, soon came to have an important financial interest in *Collier's Weekly*. Their auditors moved in, and Fred W. Allen, a banking partner, became an advisory manager. It was this situation which caused the resignation of Sullivan as editor.[31]

It was natural that Dunne should take over the editorship when Sullivan left. He was already writing many of the editorials and part of the page of "Comment on Politics." He agreed heartily with the Collier-Sullivan attitudes favoring all-out preparedness efforts but opposing Wilson. From this time onward, Rob Collier's mental and physical condition became steadily worse, along with his financial

[31] Sullivan, *The Making of an American*, ch. 29.

position, and he died two days before the Armistice, on November 9, 1918.

In view of an end marked by failure, and the fact that he left *Collier's Weekly* headed toward destruction, Robert J. Collier is often referred to as an incapable and inept magazine editor and manager.[32] Such is far from the truth. In his best years, Rob Collier was a brilliant, capable, and active editor-in-chief. Without him the *Weekly* surely would never have made the extraordinary record of influence and accomplishment that marked its history in the first two decades of the twentieth century. Hapgood wrote in his autobiography, some years after his quarrel with Collier, "I have often said, and the opinion remains, that for a number of years Collier was the ablest magazine journalist in America."[33] Sullivan, in his life story, summed up his opinion of Collier:

> On the whole, I thought that, on many matters, Collier's instinct was better than Hapgood's judgment — and I knew that in matters having to do with journalistic effectiveness, Collier was always right. Collier was a true journalist, of the highest order. . . . It was Collier who made the *Weekly* the most effective journalism of the time.[34]

Though deeply in debt, *Collier's* did not seem to be by any means a worthless property at the time of its owner's death. It had over a million circulation. Its annual automobile number, which was being planned when Collier died, would run to over a hundred pages, more than a third of it advertising. By Collier's will, he left the *Weekly* to three friends who had, in the few years before his death, worked hardest for its success — Dunne, Whitney, and the attorney Francis P. Garvan. But when it was found that the widow was not so well provided for as had been supposed, the heirs turned the magazine over to her.[35] She then sold it in September 1919 to the Crowell Publishing Company, of Springfield, Ohio, and New York. Dunne was disappointed and a little bitter. He wrote to a friend:

> I am out of it . . . she practically gave the property away. She gets very little money, perhaps none, after the debts are paid, and ten per cent of stock in a new company of very doubtful present value. The head of the buying syndicate (which includes . . . Peabody, Houghteling & Co.) is Tom Lamont. Isn't it weird that the property should go to the very man whose attempt to get hold of it in 1912 was the cause of the appeal to Payne Whitney? Collier was in a bad situation then, and the Astor Trust Co., which Lamont controls, called his loan, expecting

[32] See Powell in *Scribner's*, v. 105, May 1939, and Stote in *Magazine World*, v. 1, Oct. 1945.
[33] Hapgood, *The Changing Years*, p. 168. Also see *Collier's*, v. 50, Nov. 9, 1912, p. 8.
[34] Sullivan, *The Making of an American*, p. 229.
[35] Ellis, *Mr. Dooley's America*, pp. 253–54.

of course that he would be forced to throw the property into the hands of the Crowell Publishing Co. (a Lamont concern).[36]

The sale to Crowells was negotiated by Thomas Hambly Beck, who had formerly been a sales manager for *Collier's* but was now vice-president of the Crowell organization. The consideration was said to have been $1,750,000.[37] Thomas W. Lamont and Samuel Untermeyer helped finance the transaction, but the controlling stockholder of the Crowell Publishing Company, and its guiding genius, was Joseph Palmer Knapp.[38] Knapp was the son of a lithographer and printer. A young man of unusual executive force, he soon took over management of his father's business, built it up, and about 1906 gained control of the Springfield, Ohio, concern which had long issued the profitable *Farm and Fireside* and *Woman's Home Companion*, and which was being gradually transformed from the old firm of P. P. Mast & Company[39] to the Crowell Publishing Company. In 1916, this organization had added the *American Magazine* to its list of periodicals, and now it completed its pattern with the purchase of a great national weekly. Knapp was still the dominant force in the publishing concern, and though primarily a manufacturer, he had a shrewd sense of editorial values.

It proved to be a bad moment, however, to make the purchase. In the first three months after the change in ownership, *Collier's* passed through the darkest period of its life. Editorially vague, wobbly on its business feet, it suddenly faced a serious printers' strike. For four consecutive weeks the magazine did not appear at all, and when it was resumed on November 8, it had been reduced to the ignominy of black-and-white covers. It was not until January 1920 that it was on a reasonably even keel again; the annual automobile number appeared on January 3 with 102 pages.

Harford Powel, Jr., a young journalist with several years of experience on other magazines, was editor through this troublous period. Lowell Mellett, recently a United Press war correspondent, was managing editor; Child, now a veteran on the staff, was editor of the editorial pages; and F. De Sales Casey was art editor. The magazine was no longer "liberal" or reformatory, except in its desire to reform by a return to "normalcy." It fought government ownership of railways. Outstanding business leaders of the country wrote a series favoring college education. There was something like a campaign for volun-

---

[36] *Ibid.*, pp. 254–55.
[37] Powell in *Scribner's*, v. 105, May 1939, p. 20.
[38] Chenery, *So It Seemed*, pp. 162–69.
[39] See p. 337.

tary strike arbitration in this period of multiple, country-wide strikes. In the presidential campaign of 1920 *Collier's* was not a pronounced supporter of either the Harding and Coolidge ticket or that of Cox and Roosevelt. It tried, however, to define its editorial position by a "Platform" with three planks, printed at the head of its editorial pages: "(1) Give us less government, and better; (2) Preserve our nation's agriculture; and (3) Bring peace to industry."

In the early twenties Wythe Williams was a special correspondent abroad. Jay Darling's cartoons were an always interesting feature. Arthur Somers Roche, Earl Derr Biggers, H. C. Witwer, and Ring Lardner were among the writers of fiction. Heywood Broun, William Almon Wolff, and Edward Hungerford were also prominent in the magazine's pages. Jack O'Donnell did a series on "rum running," and there were other reflections of the prohibition era. Sports were a major part of the content. Witwer had a series on prize fighting called "The Leather Pushers" in 1920, Camp reappeared with a regular sports page in 1924, and each number had one or two sports articles or stories.

In 1922 Powel was succeeded in the editorial chair by Richard John Walsh, who had been promotion manager for Curtis. But Walsh stayed only two years before he gave place to Loren Palmer, who had held editorial positions on various magazines and had been *Collier's* managing editor since Mellett's retirement from that position in 1921. Thoreau Cronyn now became managing editor. A "gag" went the rounds of magazine circles to the effect that one day when George Creel called to see the editor and was asked to wait twenty minutes, he said, "Tell him I will wait twenty minutes if he will guarantee that he will still be editor at the end of that time!"

But the search for the right editor came to an end in 1924. In that year William Ludlow Chenery was brought to the attention of Lee W. Maxwell, president of the Crowell Publishing Company, who passed him along to Beck, who passed him along to Knapp; after all had okayed him, he was made associate editor, and in January of the next year editor-in-chief. His name was not immediately posted as occupying that position, however; there had been too many failures, and it was not until a couple of years of hard work had passed and Chenery was an unqualified success that readers were informed that he was the editor. In the course of his editorial term he received from $15,000 to $35,000, plus bonus, as annual salary.[40]

Chenery was a thoughtful, well-educated newspaperman who had been managing editor of the *New York Sun*. He began by bringing together a first-class editorial staff. Some of these men were already

---

[40] Chenery in letters to the author.

with *Collier's*, like Charles Colebaugh, who became the capable managing editor, supplanting John B. Kennedy, who remained as a staff writer. Another man already on the staff was George Creel, who was writing a page of political satire under the pen name of "Uncle Henry" and who continued to do that job for two or three years, even after he was writing articles based on information from his high Washington sources. William G. Shepherd, formerly a war correspondent for *Collier's*, now became correspondent from all parts of the United States. Walter Davenport, who wrote chiefly of politics, was a Chenery recruit; the two had been acquainted in New York newspaper work. William B. Courtney, who had been Tom Beck's secretary, became a roving correspondent and later aviation editor. Kenneth Littauer came to the staff as fiction editor in 1927 and remained many years; his apprenticeship had been spent with the pulps. Aimee Larkin was women's editor, and Kyle Crichton wrote many articles on movies and the theater. William O. Chessman became art director. The English-born Jim Marshall was Far Eastern correspondent. Among leading sports writers were the durable Grantland Rice, H. C. Witwer, Frank Condon, Damon Runyon, and Quentin Reynolds. Reynolds was listed as sports editor in 1936, but a few years later he was one of *Collier's* chief war correspondents. Finally, there were the associate editors John T. Flynn and Owen P. White; the former had been managing editor of the *New York Globe*, but the latter was an El Paso, Texas, clerk when he broke into the *Collier's* organization.

The magazine under its new editorship first attracted attention by its campaign for the repeal of the Prohibition Amendment. Its technique was that to which Congress was eventually driven in dealing with the liquor situation — that of surveying the whole country to see how the Eighteenth Amendment and the Volstead Act were working; and *Collier's* correspondents came to the same factual conclusion that the Wickersham Commission later reached — namely, that law was being flouted on every hand. But whereas the commission opposed repeal as a remedy, *Collier's* favored that solution. It was a campaign somewhat in the nature of the crusades in the old Hapgood and Sullivan days, and *Collier's* seems to have taken a repeal position earlier than other important periodicals. Though many readers were offended, and the editor thought that about twenty-five hundred canceled their subscriptions, the gains were much greater than the losses.[41] The magazine was not bitter or intolerant; and it did print articles on the other side, like those by Clarence True Wilson.

*Collier's* was an interesting magazine during Chenery's early years

[41] Chenery in *Quill*, v. 22, May 1934, p. 10.

as editor. The theory behind the building of each number was that fiction was "the backbone of mass circulations,"[42] and the following pattern soon emerged: installments of two serial stories, four short stories, one short short story, four to six articles, and three or four departments.

One of the early serials was Willa Cather's "The Professor's House" (1925), but *Collier's* came to demand more action and more obvious motivations. Valentine Williams, Kathleen Norris, Zane Grey, Peter B. Kyne, and E. Phillips Oppenheim fitted the formula better. Sinclair Lewis' "Mantrap" was a 1926 serial, and John Erskine's "Adam and Eve" came in 1927, the latter illustrated by Frank Godwin. Morals of *Collier's* readers were pretty carefully protected, and the nudities of Godwin's Eve were exceptional in the magazine's pages. But after all, they were Biblical.

But the perennial serialists for *Collier's* were Sax Rohmer, with his "Fu Manchu," and Arthur Somers Roche, specialist in the modern love story in what used to be called "high life." These writers, with unflagging invention, wrote millions of words for *Collier's* over a long series of years. Though there was an essential sameness in the production of each of them, their "fans" seem never to have been sated. And those fans — especially the "Fu Manchu" addicts — were sometimes found in surprising places. Chenery tells of calling on President Coolidge at the White House and being pleased to have him say that he had recently been reading *Collier's* with great attention; indeed, he had been sending a White House messenger out to a dealer on the avenue to get advance copies each week. The magazine was then running an important series by Shepherd, and Chenery ventured to ask the President's opinion on those articles, only to find that all he was reading in the weekly was the current Sax Rohmer mystery; he just could not wait each week to learn whether the hero would foil "Fu Manchu" and how.[43]

The short-story budget in each number came to include, nearly always, one love story, one adventure yarn, one dramatic theme story, one humorous story (often dealing with sports) and one "short short." Among the leading writers of short fiction in Chenery's early years were Albert Payson Terhune, Hugh MacNair Kahler, Zona Gale, Bernice Brown, Samuel Hopkins Adams, H. C. Witwer, Sophie Kerr, Louis Joseph Vance, Courtney Ryley Cooper, Stephen Vincent Benét, Joseph C. Lincoln, Mary Roberts Rinehart, Chester T. Crowell, and James B. Connolly.

[42] *Ibid.*, p. 9.
[43] Chenery, *So It Seemed*, pp. 225–26.

*Collier's* claimed that it "created the short short story." It did not do that,[44] but it was a leader in creating the popularity of that art form. In September 1925 it asked four writers to furnish stories about twelve hundred words in length which could be completed, with a large illustration, on a single page. Those writers were Octavus Roy Cohen, Zona Gale, Rupert Hughes, and Sophie Kerr. Their first series was so successful that the "short short" became a fixture that was never displaced in the magazine. Some other distinguished practitioners of this form (which more often than not has a surprise ending) during the Chenery editorship were Roark Bradford, Katherine Brush, Richard Connell, Corey Ford, John Marquand, Quentin Reynolds, Damon Runyon, and Richard Sherman.

Nonfiction articles were of many kinds. Sometimes they were in series, as Bruce Barton's *The Book Nobody Knows*, a popular serial of 1925–1926, and William Allen White's articles on Coolidge in 1925. More often series were not formally connected, as the pieces on prohibition enforcement, Shepherd's articles on prisons in 1926, Creel's on romantic figures in American history, and the health essays of Lulu Hunt Peters. Stories about men prominent in business, politics, sports, the theater, and so on, based mainly on interviews, were so common as to be almost as much a *Collier's* trade-mark as Sax Rohmer and the "short shorts." All the staff writers did this sort of thing from time to time. These pieces were nearly always a bit eulogistic, well illustrated, and brightly written. A good example (if inaccurate in view of later developments) was John B. Kennedy's "Up the Scale: From Song Writer to Mayor," May 22, 1926, which told how James J. Walker, of New York, was "giving his city a sane and businesslike administration."

In addition to the fiction and articles, there was a good humor department entitled "If You Know What I Mean," by Don Marquis; a popular science page called "Catching Up with the World," by E. E. Slosson (later Freling Foster); and a radio column, "Picked Out of the Air," by Jack Binns. The double-page spread for editorials was maintained for several years, the second page carrying a contributed essay by a well-known man or woman, until the editorial department was reduced to a single page and moved to the end of the book in 1927. There was also a double spread of pictures from photographs — not news pictures now, but feature groups, such as the interesting one of early plane flights, called "When Wings Were Young," September 24, 1927. There were also some comics in the back of the book, by O. Soglow and others. There was a little two-color illustration, but not much before the latter thirties.

[44] See p. 114.

In 1924, when Chenery joined the editorial staff, advertising revenue had fallen below $1,700,000 and circulation had dropped below 1,000,000; but in 1925 a gradual upturn in both advertising and circulation began. The next year the stockholders took up an issue of 25,000 additional Crowell shares, and by 1927 it was figured that in the eight years during which the Crowell Publishing Company had owned *Collier's* it had spent some $10,000,000 on the weekly without getting it on a paying basis.[45] When some stockholders murmured, Knapp pointed to the upward curve then on the charts and offered to buy whatever stock the doubters wished to offer. So another $5,000,000 went into the weekly; and up went circulation, reaching 2,000,000 in November 1929, and an average net for the entire years of 1941 of over 2,250,000. By this time the depression had struck in full force, but *Collier's* was strong enough to withstand it. There was a slight decrease in circulation in 1932–1933, and advertising declined until some numbers ran to only 40 pages; but by 1937 there was a strong rebound, circulation passed 2,500,000, some numbers exceeded 90 pages in thickness, and gross revenues amounted to $13,000,000, with $2,800,000 net.[46] Advertising rates went up to $6,500 a page in 1938 and to $7,000 in 1941. It was in the latter thirties that *Collier's* was able to repay, to some extent at least, and certainly at a crucial time, the help it had received from its sister monthlies in the Crowell organization — the *American Magazine*, the *Woman's Home Companion*, and the farm periodical now called *Country Home*.

*Collier's* in the thirties followed much the same pattern which it had found successful in the latter twenties. In 1933 it was advertising "a new novel every month," which meant that it was running two eight- or ten-part serials all the time. The same tried-and-true fictioneers were doing the serials, with the addition of such writers as George Agnew Chamberlain, J. P. McEvoy, Hugh MacNair Kahler, Max Brand, Mignon Eberhart, and Louis Joseph Vance. New names among writers of shorter fiction were Roark Bradford, Arnold Bennett, Guy Kilpatric, James Hopper, Albert Richard Wetjen, Frederick Hazlitt Brennan, Ernest Haycox, James Hilton, Margery Sharp, William Saroyan, Elmer Davis, and Dashiell Hammett. Dr. Ruth F. Wadsworth wrote on child care, Milton C. Work on bridge, and Henry F. Pringle on motion pictures.

But the great star among *Collier's* contributors of the thirties was Winston Spencer Churchill, famous British statesman and journalist. He was out of office at the time he began writing for *Collier's* in 1930,

---

[45] Powell in *Scribner's*, v. 105, May 1939, p. 20.
[46] *Ibid.*

and he signed a contract to write six articles a year for the weekly at the very reasonable price of fifteen hundred dollars apiece. Subjects were to be agreed upon annually by author and editor. Churchill wrote his memoirs of the First World War, his opinions on many subjects, his impressions of Roosevelt and the New Deal, his observations on the abdication of Edward VIII. He showed himself amenable to editorial criticism, rewriting his article on King Alfonso of Spain no less than five times. "Always make me do it again if it is not right the first time," he told Chenery. "I am a journalist and a professional." [47] When he reëntered the Cabinet in 1938, Churchill broke off a brilliant and memorable *Collier's* series.

In the mid-thirties, the weekly brought both Churchill and H. G. Wells over to evaluate the New Deal and its works. The verdict of Wells was not as favorable as that of Churchill — nor, on the whole, as friendly as that of *Collier's* editors. The weekly was by no means partisan in these years; it never aligned itself with any presidential candidate during the Chenery suzerainty. But in an editorial early in 1935 reviewing two years of the new administration, it spoke of the bold moves that had been necessary, and that had been possible because of "the potent hold which President Roosevelt has had upon the imagination and affection of a vast majority of Americans." [48] Beck and Chenery were good friends of the President, and often at the White House. In December 1939 Roosevelt signed a contract with *Collier's* to become a member of its staff at a salary of seventy-five thousand a year, writing weekly or biweekly articles, effective if and when he retired from the presidency in 1941. [49] In his speech from the White House, July 19, 1940, accepting a nomination for a third term, Roosevelt said:

> Like most men of my age I had made plans for myself, plans for a private life of my own choice and for my own satisfaction — a life of that kind to begin in January 1941. These plans, like so many other plans, had been made in a world which now seems as distant as another planet. Today all private plans, all private lives, have been, in a sense, repealed by an overruling public danger.

The plans Roosevelt referred to were embodied in the contract (a carefully kept secret) with *Collier's*. The weekly did publish in 1941, however, as a series of articles by the President, the introductions he had written to collections of his public papers.

The appearance of the magazine changed greatly in the latter thirties. There was much more color in the illustrations, the printing of

[47] Chenery, *So It Seemed*, ch. 20.
[48] *Collier's*, v. 95, March 9, 1935, p. 58.
[49] Chenery, *So It Seemed*, pp. 259–62.

them was "bled" off the edges of the pages, there was much of the new angled make-up, and illustrators like Gluyas Williams took the pencil and brush from the old-timers. Covers by Ben Jorj Harris, Robert O. Reid, Alan Foster, and others were in this new mood and style.

In 1942, when some issues exceeded three million in circulation, the price per copy was raised from five to ten cents, though the annual subscription was only three dollars. In this increase *Collier's* followed the example set two months earlier by the *Saturday Evening Post*. The *Post* had reached three million circulation five years before, and was now about half a million ahead of *Collier's*; it had more than twice *Collier's* advertising revenue, and thus its weekly numbers were twice as large. But competition was keen between the two great weeklies. Against the *Post's* newsboy solicitation *Collier's* pitted its salesmen who contracted with purchasers for their total annual magazine budget, to be paid for on the installment plan. *Collier's* sometimes lured *Post* contributors into its own pages, and vice versa. *Collier's* was friendly to F. D. R.; the *Post* was inimical to him and to the New Deal.

In 1943 Chenery retired as editor, and for the next six years he served as publisher. For almost two decades he had guided the editorial policy of *Collier's*. In spite of the fact that there was so much weight in the upper echelons of the Crowell-Collier organization, Chenery had been the editor, calling the turns as he saw them.[50] He had been wise as well as enterprising, with a shrewd understanding of the mass audience and also a respect for the magazine and its traditions.

Charles Henry Colebaugh, who had long served the magazine as managing editor, now took the chief editorial position. Death removed him, however, after eighteen months as editor-in-chief, at the age of fifty-one years, more than half of which had been spent on the staff of *Collier's*. Henry La Cossitt, who had come to the weekly a few months earlier from the *American Magazine* to become managing editor, stepped into the top spot; but he remained only two years before being replaced by the veteran *Collier's* staffer, Walter Davenport.

In the first five years after Chenery's retirement, many changes were made, chief of which were a decrease in the emphasis on fiction and a wartime stressing of feature articles from abroad and at home. Now there was only one serial running at a time; there were usually four short stories, and seven or eight articles.

Pearl S. Buck, Lion Feuchtwanger, Erich Maria Remarque, Vickie Baum, Faith Baldwin, and Edwin Lanham wrote serial fiction for *Collier's* in the war years; but the accent was on mysteries, and "whodunits" by Agatha Christie, Margery Allingham, Nevil Shute, and

[50] *Time*, v. 53, April 25, 1949, p. 51.

John P. Marquand were frequently found in the magazine. Editor Allen Marple made a special effort to promote interest in *Collier's* short stories; among his leading writers were Damon Runyon, C. S. Forester, Jessamyn West, and Wallace Stegner.

An early series on the war was the five-part "What Happened to France" by André Maurois of 1942. The next year appeared the notable "Thirty Seconds Over Tokyo" by Captain Ted W. Lawson, "ghosted" by Bob Considine. *Collier's* staff of war correspondents included Frank Gervasi, Frank D. Morris, William B. Courtney, Quentin Reynolds, John Gunther, Robert Bellaire, Edward P. Morgan, and Weldon James. Most of these were staff members, as were, for a time, Martha Gellhorn and her husband Ernest Hemingway, who wrote from England and France. The magazine continued to be nonpartisan in domestic politics. Harold L. Ickes' "Confessions of a Sourpuss" was an interesting feature of 1943, and articles by Wendell Willkie appeared the next year.

Changes were constantly taking place on the staff. La Cossitt's managing editor was Joe Alex Morris. New names among the associate editors in the early forties were Clarence H. Roy and Gurney Williams. Robert McCormick wrote from Washington, as did William Hillman and Robert De Vore a little later, and by the mid-forties James C. Derieux. Ifor Thomas and U. L. Calvosa were photography editors in the early forties. Herbert Asbury and Jim Bishop joined up in 1944. With Chenery's promotion from editor to publisher, Beck changed over to president and Knapp to chairman of the board; and Albert E. ("Cap") Winger, who had been treasurer, became executive vice-president.

In June 1948 President Beck replaced Morris with Oscar Dystel as managing editor; Dystel had been editor of the successful *Coronet*. A few months later *Collier* typography and make-up were redesigned, but the most noticeable change was the use of color photographs for the cover. Tony Palazzo came from *Coronet* as art director. There was color now on nearly every page, and several pages carried four-color pictures. Color photographs — news and feature — were eye-catchers in every number. To match this chromatic glory were the nonfiction serial, "The Secret Papers of Harry L. Hopkins," and the 1948 partisan arguments by Alben W. Barkley for the Democrats and Earl Warren for the Republicans.

In 1949 the magazine was printing the names of no less than thirty associate editors, and most of its articles were written by them. For example, Bert Bacharach was writing occasional articles dealing with men's fashions, as Henry L. Jackson had done before him; and Frederic

B. Neely was doing articles and a column on aviation subjects. Kenneth Littauer was back as fiction editor, and there were stories by Edward Streeter, Louis Paul, George F. Worts, Frank Yerby. Roche had been gathered to his fathers, but Rohmer still spun his romances.

In 1948 Knapp, having reached what he considered a proper age of retirement — eighty-five — turned over his job as chairman of the board to Beck, who held it for the two years of life that remained to him, and Winger became president of the publishing company. The next year there were more changes in the top brackets. Chenery, who had been giving some valuable help on the editorial page, retired as publisher, giving place to Edward Anthony, who was publisher also of the *American Magazine* and *Woman's Home Companion*. At the same time Davenport retired to what he considered a more comfortable position as "senior correspondent," leaving the editorial chair to robust, aggressive Louis Ruppel, a former captain of marines and high-powered Hearst editor.

*Collier's* had been holding its own in circulation (at a little less than three million yearly average) but it had not been gaining. It had raised its single-copy price to fifteen cents in November 1948. Its advertising linage had been slipping, showing a decrease of 15 per cent in 1948; and the Crowell-Collier profits of nearly five million had been cut in half.[51] The weekly's contents were coming to have a certain deadly sameness. Ruppel's idea, shared with Beck, Winger and Anthony, was to do something about these things. Palazzo was replaced by former Art Director Chessman. Littauer, who had returned as fiction editor in 1948, saw Ruppel coming and left his job to Max Burger. There were many brisk and brusque changes, new assignments and cancellations of old ones.

An interesting and significant about-face was a rapprochement with Walter Winchell, who had been offended by a severely critical "profile" the preceding year (February 28, 1948) and was now offered $12,500 for an article attacking the new Department of Defense, "Blueprint for Disaster" (June 18, 1949). Ruppel adopted a slashing exposé program, the most notable result of which was the series published in 1949 and 1950 under the title, "Terror in Our Cities." These studies of crime in the country's largest municipalities were a kind of prologue to the investigations of the Kefauver Committee.

John Denson, who had been managing editor, was sent to Korea as *Collier's* war correspondent in 1950. Lowell Thomas wrote "War Adventures in Burma" in that year. A. J. Cronin was a leading serialist. But the most sensational achievement of Ruppel's editorship was its

---

[51] Chenery, *So It Seemed*, pp. 162–63.

World War III number (October 27, 1951) in which "Russia's Defeat and Occupation, 1952–1960: A Preview of the War We Do Not Want" was given by such writers as Robert E. Sherwood, Hanson W. Baldwin, Edward R. Murrow, Walter Reuther, Lowell Thomas, Arthur Koestler, Allan Nevins, Stuart Chase, Erwin Canham, Philip Wylie, Hal Boyle, J. B. Priestley, and others. Prophetical "correspondence" from the scene of the great conflict, and stories about how the Soviets were managed after the defeat of their attempt to conquer the world were very impressive. The illustrations by Chesley Bonesteel and others were vivid and, for some readers, terrifying. The magazine sold a half million extra copies, but there was wide criticism of the feature. Chief objection was that it appeared to many, and especially to allies and diplomats abroad, to be "warmongering." [52] Editorial motives were patriotic, however, and the symposium was not only sensational but deeply significant.

Tom Beck's passing in 1951 was like the passing of an era. Now Winger succeeded to the chairmanship of the Crowell board; and Clarence E. Stouch, who had begun as private secretary to H. P. Davison, of J. P. Morgan & Company, and had come from there into the Crowell Publishing Company a long time before, became its president. Ruppel resigned suddenly in May 1952. Publisher Anthony carried on for several weeks; and then Roger Dakin, who had been editor in charge of nonfiction articles for the *Woman's Home Companion*, was chosen as editor of *Collier's*.

In the presidential campaign of 1952, the weekly supported Eisenhower; it was the first time it had taken a partisan position since its support of Charles E. Hughes against Woodrow Wilson in 1916. Peter Kalischer wrote from Korea, and Bill Stapleton's color photographs from the war were outstanding. Articles on space travel were featured in 1953. Regional correspondents had been used by *Collier's* for many years; now bureaus were set up, not only in Washington, but in Los Angeles for the West Coast, in Chicago for the Midwest, and in Atlanta for the South.

Sports were still prominent, especially in football previews (by Francis Wallace) and the selection of All-American college football teams. These selections had been a *Collier's* tradition. From 1891 to 1925 Walter Camp did the picking; then Grantland Rice did it for twenty-two seasons. But *Look* stole Rice in 1948, hence *Collier's* team was chosen by a group of well-known coaches and later by the American Football Coaches' Association.

On the whole, contents were a little more sensational, a little sexier,

[52] *Time*, v. 59, Jan. 14, 1952, p. 56.

a little more violent under Ruppel and Dakin than under former editors. There seeemed to be a desperate effort for circulation. A reader who complained of certain "wild tales" in the magazine was assured on the editorial page that whether the stories had "social significance and moral teaching is a matter of exalted indifference to us." [53] At the end of 1952 the trade press carried reports that Crowell-Collier had appropriated three million dollars to correct a downward trend in the circulation and advertising linage of *Collier's*.[54] In August 1953 the magazine was made a fortnightly.

At the end of that year Paul C. Smith was made president of the Crowell-Collier Publishing Company. He had been editor and manager of the *San Francisco Chronicle*, had come to Crowell-Collier as a "trouble shooter," and now tackled one of the hardest jobs in the magazine world, in managing the destinies of the slumping *Collier's*, *American Magazine*, and *Woman's Home Companion*. In July 1954 he assumed the title of editor-in-chief of all three, and about a year later Kenneth McArdle, who had been with Smith on the *Chronicle*, became editor of *Collier's* under Smith's direction. To a policy directed less at space cadets and more at the intelligent middle-class American home, circulation responded favorably; Smith negotiated large loans from New York and Chicago financiers, and in 1955–1956 the *Collier's* annual deficit, which had amounted to $7,500,000 in 1953, was reduced to $1,500,000.[55] But in the latter half of 1956, advertising fell off badly, and publication was discontinued with the number for January 4, 1957. This was a part of the collapse of the Crowell-Collier magazine group, the *American Magazine* having ended in August 1956 and the *Woman's Home Companion* in January 1957.

*Collier's* two great eras — the first under Rob Collier, Norman Hapgood, and Mark Sullivan, and the second under William L. Chenery and Thomas H. Beck — gave it an important position in American affairs and in the history of our magazines. It perished as the result of more than a decade of management which was consistent only in its ineptitude.

[53] *Collier's*, v. 131, March 14, 1953, p. 74.
[54] Don Iddon's letter in *World Press News*, v. 48, Dec. 26, 1952, p. 4.
[55] *Time*, June 6 and July 22, 1955, and July 9, 1956; *Magazine Industry Newsletter*, July 23 and 30, 1955; Nate White in series on the Crowell-Collier Publishing Company, *Christian Science Monitor*, March 1, 2, and 3, 1956.

## COSMOPOLITAN; HEARST'S INTERNATIONAL

THE *Cosmopolitan Magazine*[1] was founded by Paul J. Schlicht and first published in Rochester, New York, by the firm of Schlicht & Field, printers and manufacturers of office supplies. It was designed as

a first-class family magazine. . . . There will be a department devoted exclusively to the interests of women, with articles on fashions, on household decoration, on cooking, and the care and management of children, etc.; also a department . . . for the younger members of the family.[2]

But it turned out to be a general literary magazine rather than a home monthly. Frank P. Smith was editor, and he and Schlicht both wrote for it. The first number, dated March 1886, contained a story by H. H. Boyesen, then a writer for the best magazines, some verses by R. K. Munkittrick, an article on the Irish question by Smith, one on direct elections by Schlicht, some translations by Schlicht, a children's department by Clara F. Guernsey, some home departments as promised, a piece of music, and three or four full-page pictures from wood engravings. There were sixty-four octavo pages, less than half the number in *Harper's* or the *Century*, though the *Cosmopolitan* subscription price was the same — four dollars.

Contents of the following numbers continued readable and attractive. Some well-known writers were published; they included Mary E. Wilkins, Julian Hawthorne, Arlo Bates, Elizabeth Cady Stanton, Har-

[1] TITLES: (1) *Cosmopolitan Magazine*, 1886–1925; (2) *Hearst's International Combined with Cosmopolitan*, 1925–52; (3) *Cosmopolitan*, 1952–current.
FIRST ISSUE: March 1886. Current.
PERIODICITY: Monthly. Vols. 1–4, semiannual vols., March 1886–Feb. 1888; 5, March–Oct. 1888 (omitting June–July 1888); 6–43, semiannual vols., Nov. 1888–Oct. 1907; 44, Nov. 1907–May 1908 (omitting March 1908); 45–67, semiannual vols., June 1908–Nov. 1919; 68, Dec. 1919–June 1920; 69–current, regular semiannual vols., July 1920–current.
PUBLISHERS: Schlicht & Field, Rochester, N.Y., 1886–87; Schlicht & Field Company, New York, 1887–88; Joseph N. Hallock, New York, 1888; John Brisben Walker, 1889–1905 (New York, 1889–94, Irvington-on-the-Hudson, N.Y., 1895–1905); International Magazine Company, New York, 1905–36; Hearst Magazines, New York, 1936–52; Hearst Corporation, 1952–current.
EDITORS: Frank P. Smith, 1886–88; E. D. Walker, 1888; J. B. Walker (with William Dean Howells, 1890, and Arthur Sherburne Hardy, 1893–95), 1889–1905; Bailey Millard, 1905–07; S. S. Chamberlain, 1907–08; C. P. Narcross, 1908–13; Sewell Haggard, 1914; Edgar Grant Sisson, 1914–17, Douglas Z. Doty, 1917–18; Ray Long, 1918–31; Harry Payne Burton, 1931–42; Frances Whiting, 1942–45; Arthur Gordon, 1946–48; Herbert R. Mayes, 1948–51; John J. O'Connell, 1951–current.
INDEXES: *Poole's Index, Readers' Guide, Engineering Index, Dramatic Index.*
[2] Second page of cover of v. 1, no. 1.

riet Prescott Spofford, Louise Chandler Moulton, Maria Pool, and Sophie Swett. William T. Hornaday's travel sketches and wild-animal adventures were a good feature, and Schlicht continued to do translations from the French and German. The art reproductions were good. The magazine bought and announced a romance by George Sand, but found it a forgery before publication; the *North American Review* had not been so fortunate in dealing with the same forger.[3]

When the *Cosmopolitan* was a little over a year old, its publishers claimed a circulation of twenty-five thousand. They were sufficiently encouraged by that response to move to New York, commission a new and handsome cover design (by Stanford White, who had drawn those in current use by the *Century* and *Scribner's*), enlarge the number of pages to eighty, and cut the annual price in two. They made the single-copy price twenty cents, in comparison with thirty-five currently paid for *Harper's* or *Century*, and twenty-five for the new *Scribner's*. Circulation responded, but not sufficiently, for Schlicht and Field's limited resources; and in March 1888 the firm failed and the magazine came into the hands of Ulysses S. Grant, Jr., who became vice-president of the publishing company.[4] This flier in the New York magazine field by the California lawyer with the famous name was not a success, and after three months the *Cosmopolitan* was currently reported as discontinued.[5] But a purchaser was found in the nick of time; he was Joseph Newton Hallock, publisher of the *Christian at Work*, who, according to one observer, kept a kind of literary graveyard for unsuccessful periodicals.[6]

Hallock did not bury the *Cosmopolitan*, however; he kept E. D. Walker, whom the Grant management had placed in charge, as editor, and made notable improvements. Walker had been on the staff of *Harper's*, and he had just attracted some attention by a new book on an old doctrine, entitled *Reincarnation*. He was given leave to introduce several new features in the *Cosmopolitan*, such as serial fiction, book reviews, a department of "Live Questions," and some experiments in color illustration. Size was increased to a hundred pages. The serial story was "Miss Lou," by the popular E. P. Roe; it was the last of a long line of novels, for Roe died while it was running its course through the *Cosmopolitan*.

[3] These forgeries were by Lew Vanderpoole. The *Review* and the *New York Star* had published some of them. See New York *Journalist*, Sept. 24, 1887.

[4] *Critic*, v. 12, p. 146, March 24, 1888; *Journalist*, v. 10, Nov. 9, 1889, p. 10.

[5] *Book Chat*, v. 3, p. 522, July 1888.

[6] *Journalist*, v. 8, April 30, 1892, p. 2. For the *Christian at Work*, see F. L. Mott, *A History of American Magazines* (Cambridge, 1938), v. 3, pp. 82–83. The *Journalist* named *Our Continent* (*ibid.*, pp. 557–59) and the *Manhattan* (*ibid.*, p. 37) as having been interred in Hallock's graveyard. Later the *Arena* met a similar fate (see p. 416).

By the end of 1888 circulation was only twenty thousand, and the plot in Hallock's burying ground was already chosen, when still another nick-of-time purchaser appeared. This one possessed the two necessities to save the situation — money and ideas.

John Brisben Walker was forty-one years old when he bought the *Cosmopolitan* and became its editor. He had left a West Point course for a brief diplomatic and military career in China. He had later made a fortune of half a million in iron manufacturing before he was thirty, and had lost it in the panic of '73. Still later he had made a much larger fortune in Denver real estate. Meantime he had been a successful newspaperman in Cincinnati, Pittsburgh, and Washington.

Though the *Cosmopolitan* "cannot hope to excel the literary or artistic features of its competitors, it will aim to present a series of articles more in keeping with the immediate popular interests of the day," said an early advertisement.[7] A friendly critic, writing about Walker after he had been editor of the *Cosmopolitan* three years, said: "He has introduced the newspaper ideas of timeliness and dignified sensationalism into periodical literature."[8]

Shortly after Walker bought the magazine, he offered the editorship to James G. Blaine, who had journalistic backgrounds.[9] Blaine came near to accepting, but President-elect Harrison was about to offer him the portfolio of state in his new cabinet. E. D. Walker, who was not related to the new owner, was retained as managing editor. Edward Everett Hale was put in charge of a department of "Social Problems." Murat Halstead, famous Cincinnati editor, who had once employed J. B. Walker, now worked for him, editing a "Review of Current Events" in 1890–1892, and continuing for several years as a valued contributor on political subjects. Elizabeth Bisland conducted a book review department; and soon after she departed on her travels in 1890, Brander Matthews became a staff contributor of articles of literary criticism that were usually in the nature of reviews. Travel articles were prominent for several years; among *Cosmopolitan* writers of such features were Miss Bisland, David Ker, Frank G. Carpenter, Ernest Ingersoll, William Eleroy Curtis, and A. S. Hardy.

In fiction and poetry the magazine was good in the first years of the Walker regime, though not on the level of the *Atlantic*, *Harper's*, and the *Century*. Richard Malcolm Johnston, H. H. Boyesen, Gertrude Atherton, John Esten Cooke, and Octave Thanet were among the writers of fiction; and Richard Henry Stoddard, Joel Benton, Edith M.

[7] *Cosmopolitan*, v. 7, Oct. 1889, advertising section.
[8] *Journalist*, v. 8, April 30, 1892, p. 2.
[9] *Cosmopolitan*, v. 23, p. 475, Sept. 1897.

Thomas, John Vance Cheney, and Archibald Lampman were *Cosmopolitan* poets.

In an effort to raise the literary prestige of the magazine, Walker engaged William Dean Howells as joint editor in 1892. Howells considered the arrangement a liberal one, and expected it to be permanent.[10] He had won a position as a leading novelist with *The Rise of Silas Lapham*, *A Modern Instance*, and other works reflecting contemporary America; and he had argued for realism in fiction in "The Editor's Study" department of *Harper's*. The announcement in the February 1892 *Cosmopolitan* that he would begin on March 1 to edit that magazine "conjointly" with Walker excited wide interest. He probably went on the payroll March 1, as Walker said, but his first number was the one for May 1892. This was a notably Howellsian issue, opening with a poem by James Russell Lowell, and containing an article by Henry James, stories by Hamlin Garland, Sarah Orne Jewett, and Frank R. Stockton, essays by Thomas Wentworth Higginson and Brander Matthews, articles by Theodore Roosevelt and Hiram Maxim, poems by Edmund Clarence Stedman and John Hay, and a parlor farce by Howells. This represented much more belles-lettres than was common in the magazine. The June number was rather more Walker than Howells; and the July number was mostly Walker, though a James serial entitled "Jersey Villas" was begun therein and another Lowell poem appeared. As a matter of fact, Howells resigned his position with the *Cosmopolitan* at the end of June, in order, it was announced, to devote his time to the writing of fiction. Howells wrote to his father at the time, however, that his resignation was due to "hopeless incompatibility" between himself and his "fellow editor."[11] It is clear that Walker was very much the boss of the *Cosmopolitan*; his was always a dominating personality, and he maintained a rather rigid discipline about the office. "Nothing," wrote a later assistant editor, "could be accomplished without Mr. Walker's O.K., and manuscripts were held up, awaiting his decision, to the horror of us all." And later, "He was a czar in his own world." The same reporter tells of a "legend to the effect that once, when William Dean Howells was editor of the *Cosmopolitan*, he found a note upon his desk one morning, requesting that he report for duty at the unconscionable hour of eight o'clock. Yes, even Mr. Howells!"[12]

A few years later, Walker tried another experiment in coeditorship.

---

[10] D. M. Rein, "Howells and the *Cosmopolitan*," *American Literature*, v. 17, pp. 49–55, March 1949.

[11] *Ibid.*, p. 53.

[12] Charles Hanson Towne, *Adventures in Editing* (New York, 1927), pp. 35, 40, 25. See also comments of a Howells successor, Arthur Sherburne Hardy, *Things Remembered* (Boston, 1923), pp. 275–80.

Arthur Sherburne Hardy was a versatile scholar, engineer, teacher, and novelist when he joined Walker as editor of the *Cosmopolitan* in the summer of 1893; later he was to have a career in the diplomatic corps. Hardy remained with the magazine for two years, but left soon after the removal to Irvington. Meantime J. Wilson Hart had followed E. D. Walker as managing editor, and in the latter nineties George R. Miner, George Casamajor, and Samuel G. Blythe succeeded to that position. Charles D. Lanier was an assistant editor in 1893, Charles Hanson Towne a few years later, and at the turn of the century L. S. Vassault and H. H. Boyesen.

By the end of 1892, the *Cosmopolitan* had reached a place among the country's leading illustrated magazines. It had been increased in size to a hundred and forty-four pages, and it was "fully illustrated" with half-tones and delicate woodcuts. Among the artists who furnished the illustrations were some of the best — William M. Chase, Harry Fenn, F. G. Attwood, E. W. Kemble, Charles Dana Gibson, Frederic Remington, Howard Pyle, Kenyon Cox, and Frederick S. Church. Its cover had a broad vertical band in red on the left side as a kind of trade-mark. In contents it compared favorably with *Harper's* and the *Century*; it had less fiction than these older monthlies, but more public affairs. It had greater variety than *Scribner's* — less art but more discussions of current economic, political, and social questions. It was superior in quality to *Munsey's* and the *Chautauquan*.

The "extraordinary success" of the *Cosmopolitan* under Walker's management was a subject for frequent comment by the periodicals of the early nineties.[13] Starting with a circulation of 20,000 at $2.00 a year, with an advertising rate of $60.00 a page, in January 1889, it raised its price to $3.00, increased its advertising rate to $200, tripled its circulation in two years, and carried 92 pages of advertising in its issue for December 1892. It went on to a circulation of 100,000 in 1892, doubled that by 1896, and passed 300,000 in 1898.

This was not done without hustling. In 1891 Walker chartered a special railroad coach, which he filled with canvassers, and shuttled through New York cities and towns. In 1892 he offered the Grant, Sherman, or McClellan memoirs as a premium with a year's subscription. In 1893 he gave away a thousand college scholarships to successful salesmen of *Cosmopolitan* subscriptions. He spent $360,000 on the magazine before it began to show a profit. The turning point came in November 1892; thereafter it was a profitable magazine.[14]

---

[13] *Current History*, v. 1, p. 71, Feb. 1891; *Journalist*, v. 8, April 30, 1892, p. 2.
[14] E. W. Bok in the *Epoch*, v. 10, p. 296, Dec. 11, 1891; *New York Herald*, feature article on Walker, Sept. 3, 1893, much of which is quoted in *Journalist*, v. 9, Sept. 9, 1893, pp. 2–3.

Walker later claimed that he had planned the fifteen-cent magazine and that his preparations were betrayed to competitors. But it was after *McClure's* had shown what could be done at fifteen cents that Walker, in July 1893, cut the *Cosmopolitan* price to twelve and a half, though he put it back to fifteen five months later. In July 1895 *Cosmopolitan* joined *McClure's* and *Munsey's* at ten cents per copy.[15] For a few years the annual rate was a dollar twenty; but in 1898 it was a dollar a year, where it remained until 1911 — three years after the single-copy price had been advanced to fifteen cents.

Thus Walker's *Cosmopolitan* saw its greatest days as one of that brilliant group of ten-cent illustrated monthlies which made the latter nineties a distinctive period in American magazine journalism. It conformed less to the pattern than did most of its rivals, however. Walker was an individualist, and he gave his magazine a distinct character of its own.

Himself a modern Odysseus of many devices, Walker made the *Cosmopolitan* sponsor of a succession of interesting and important projects. For example, in October 1895 the magazine published an article on the sufferings of Cuba, and that same year he sent Hobart C. Chatfield-Taylor, a *Cosmopolitan* contributor and a former Spanish consul in Chicago, to Spain to negotiate the purchase of Cuban independence for a hundred million dollars. Spanish statesmen would not listen to the proposition, and Walker did not have to make the offer good financially; but the magazine got some good articles on Spain by Chatfield-Taylor and some excellent publicity by means of the project. At the time of the Venezuela trouble, the *Cosmopolitan* was all girt for war; for the June 1896 number there were articles about the imminent conflict by General Nelson A. Miles and Editor Walker. His own short military career as a youth doubtless led Walker to a lifelong interest in war, and there were many articles in the *Cosmopolitan* on military and naval developments at home and abroad, especially with reference to the organization and equipment of the armies and navies of foreign nations. Napoleon's "autobiography" appeared serially in 1898. On the eve of the Spanish-American War appeared an anonymous prophecy in four parts entitled "A Brief History of Our War with Spain"; its prediction of an invasion of the North American continent was happily far wide of the mark. When the war became a reality, the *Cosmopolitan* covered it with some brilliance, by means of articles about the fighting by such topnotch correspondents as James Creelman and Edward Marshall, stories from the camps by Irving Bacheller, a feature about munitions factories by Theodore Dreiser, and so on. The British war against the Boers brought out some good articles, especially one by Stephen Crane

---

[15] See p. 5.

in June 1900, and a two-part essay on Boer history and character by Olive Schreiner.

In March 1897 Walker offered a nation suffering from a financial panic his plan for a credit system based on convertible bonds; he argued that such provision would prevent similar disasters in the future. In October 1899, the magazine published its editor's suggestion for a national clearing-house bank.

Walker's ardent interest in foreign countries was responsible not only for that emphasis on travel articles and discussions of social and political conditions abroad which made the magazine's title no misnomer, but also for a series of projects dealing with foreign affairs, beginning with the mission to Spain already chronicled. In 1897 the *Cosmopolitan* sent Julian Hawthorne to India, as a good-will ambassador from the magazine and its readers, to view the results of plague and famine and formulate plans for American aid. The next year Walker organized a commission to promote an international language.[16] In 1902 he came out with a proposal for a World Congress.[17]

One of the most interesting and ambitious of Walker's plans was that for his Cosmopolitan University. In August 1897 he announced a free correspondence school under this name. "No charge of any kind will be made to the student. All expenses for the present will be borne by the *Cosmopolitan*. No conditions, except a pledge of a given number of hours of study." Thousands proved to be ready to give such a pledge and accept this free educational opportunity. In six weeks, four thousand students had enrolled, and they continued to come at the rate of nearly two thousand a week for a while. The rush subsided only when the "University" acknowledged it was swamped. Clearly, the original announcement had been made without careful consideration. Walker had appropriated one hundred and fifty thousand dollars for the project, which seemed at the time enough to pay for it over five years. But with twenty thousand enrollees, it was pitifully inadequate; students were asked to pay five dollars a quarter — and most of them unhesitatingly complied. Recruitment of a faculty also presented difficulties. E. Benjamin Andrews, who had just resigned the presidency of Brown University, accepted that of the new *Cosmopolitan* institution; but after a few weeks, his troubles at Brown having been adjusted, he returned to his former position. Eliphalet Nott Potter, former president of Union College, then directed the Cosmopolitan University staff for about a year. But at the end of two years' experience with his correspondence school, Walker gave up his grandiose plans for free, or cheap, education

---

[16] *Cosmopolitan*, v. 24, p. 569, March 1898.
[17] *Ibid.*, v. 32, p. 461, March 1902.

by mail. He maintained a modest school for some years, and he urged Congress to endow a National Correspondence University.[18] The whole incident attracted a vast amount of attention, not all of which was serious. *Truth*, for example, suggested that anyone who wanted knowledge should call up Professor Andrews by telephone and get it; then his degree would be Doctor of Bell-Letters.[19] Walker had been by no means the first to promote education by correspondence, but he gave the idea a great stimulus.

Throughout his editorship, Walker published many articles on educational topics. In 1897 he tried to reform the "frozen curricula" of the great American universities. He asked leading educators to write on the subject, and received and printed a series of articles by them; however, they dodged what seemed to Walker to be the crucial points.

But the subject that increasingly engaged Walker's attention and challenged his imagination was transportation. A series of articles on "Great American Railways," written by railway men, was a feature in 1892–1894. Walker, however, thought that railways had seen their best days. When he described the transportation exhibit at the Columbian Exposition in Chicago, which was largely devoted to railroad displays, he concluded a plea for government ownership by saying that if he owned a railway he would want to get rid of it, anyway, for "it is an hour of change" in transportation.[20]

"Aerial navigation" came into the pages of the *Cosmopolitan* in February 1892, when the magazine announced prizes for three best essays on the subject; the next month it carried the editor's own observations and reflections on the matter; and two months later it published a paper by the great pioneer experimenter in this field, Samuel P. Langley, then secretary of the Smithsonian Institution. The prejudice against "flying machines," said Professor Langley, "will surely be revived if first reports are those of failure. This, be it said, is a more than possible contingency, for it would be little more than miraculous if the way to success were not taught by failures."[21] It was as though he looked forward to his own disappointments of 1903. Then in June 1892 the first-prize paper from the contest appeared; it was by Hiram S. Maxim, and it concluded with the statement that if fifty to a hundred thousand dollars were available, two years would be long enough to work out a practical "aeroplane." This consistent interest in aeronautics on the part of the *Cosmopolitan* was not matched by that of any other magazine in the early nineties. In

---

[18] *Ibid.*, v. 23, p. 460, Aug. 1897 (initial announcement); v. 24, p. 9, Nov. 1897 (Potter appointment); v. 24, pp. 333–40 (change of plans); v. 26, p. 240, Dec. 1898 (final statement).
[19] *Truth*, v. 16, Sept. 18, 1897, p. 3.
[20] *Cosmopolitan*, v. 15, p. 590, Sept. 1893.
[21] *Ibid.*, v. 13, p. 58, May 1892.

1896 Walker urged the collection of a popular fund of a hundred thousand dollars for experiments in aviation, and offered to start it with a five-dollar subscription.[22] As long as he owned the magazine, Walker continued to print occasional articles in this field, but when he offered his five dollars, his enthusiasm for the new "horseless car" had already crowded flying machines into second place.

Following an article on "Progress Toward the Age of the Horseless Carriage," in the issue for February 1896, Walker offered three thousand dollars in prizes for a contest between such cars, to be run on Decoration Day, May 30, between the *Cosmopolitan* office at City Hall Park, New York, and the new Cosmopolitan Building at Irvington, a distance of about twenty-six miles. The award was to be based not on speed alone, but also on safety, cost, and simplicity and ease of operation of the cars driven. Among the judges were General Nelson A. Miles, President Chauncey M. Depew of the New York Central Railroad, and Colonel John Jacob Astor. There were nine contestants. Winner was the Duryea Motor Company, whose carriage was timed for the sixteen and a half miles from Kingsbridge at an hour and five minutes. The contest was considered a great success, though the passengers had to get out and push their cars through one bad piece of road.[23]

It was two years after this that Walker purchased the Stanley Automobile Company and began the manufacture of Locomobile steam cars at a factory on the Hudson. He was the first president of the American Automobile Manufacturers' Association. He organized the National Highway Commission, with General Miles as chairman, in 1903. His factory took a great deal of his time from his magazine, but he did not allow the *Cosmopolitan* to become in any sense an automobile trade journal; indeed there was much more about automobiles in the advertising pages of the magazine after 1898 than there was in the articles.

Railroads continued to be discussed, as well as sailing ships, subways, balloons, and so on. A Cosmopolitan Yacht Cup, with a prize of five thousand dollars, was offered in September 1903. Nor was transportation the only technological subject featured in the *Cosmopolitan*. In the nineties a department called "Progress of Science" was filled with contributions by various writers, especially C. A. Young, George H. Knight, S. E. Tillman, and A. E. Dollbear. After 1897 this department was dropped, but science notes then appeared often in a new back-of-the-book section. A contest for articles about radium was begun in September 1902.

It was this inquiring disposition about modern technological advance

[22] *Ibid.*, v. 21, p. 277, July 1896.
[23] *Ibid.*, v. 21, pp. 544ff, Sept. 1896.

which led the *Cosmopolitan* to give so much space to world's fairs and expositions. The September and December numbers in 1893 were almost wholly given over to articles about the Columbian Exposition at Chicago. The magazine printed articles about this great fair in many other numbers, too, by such famous writers as Paul Bourget, Walter Besant, Robert Grant, A. S. Hardy, F. Hopkinson Smith, Julian Hawthorne, and Franz Boas. The Trans-Mississippi Exposition at Omaha in 1898 and the World's Fair at Paris in 1900 were well treated, and full numbers were devoted to the Pan-American Exposition at Buffalo in 1901 and the Louisiana Purchase Exposition at St. Louis in 1904.

The *Cosmopolitan* was nonpartisan. Though Halstead had been a stalwart Republican when editing a newspaper, he reviewed his "Current Events" with singularly little political bias. He once quoted Joseph Jefferson's observation to Sir Edwin Arnold: "In my judgment, Sir Edwin, the country would have been just about where it is if the other fellow had been elected every time for the past hundred years."[24] Walker was a liberal; and though a man of wealth himself, he was much concerned about the inequalities of distribution. The trusts, he said, organize production on a fine scientific basis, but their gains must be distributed to "the many instead of the few."[25] In an editorial article on "The 'Homestead' Object Lesson" in 1892, he wrote: "In fifty years the creation of wealth has become prodigious; the distribution of wealth has become frightful in its inequalities." And he warned his fellow-plutocrats of impending disaster unless this condition was corrected.[26]

Nearly a decade later he gave the same warning to Rockefeller and Morgan, in reporting a gigantic new combination.[27] In the *Cosmopolitan* for 1901 Richard T. Ely wrote with misgivings about the sinister power of the steel trust.[28] In 1904 a Kansas reformer told about how he had upset a corrupt political machine in his home state.[29]

But so long as it was owned by Walker, the *Cosmopolitan* was not truly a muckraking periodical. The ambitious series of short stories on "Captains of Industry" by Samuel E. Moffett, Julian Ralph, and other good writers in 1902–1914, and the series which began in the latter year on "Great Industries of the United States" by William R. Stewart and others, as well as the articles on great railways already mentioned, were all sympathetic interpretations.

Other notable serials were Camille Flammarion's scientific fantasy

[24] *Ibid.*, v. 12, p. 373, Jan. 1892.
[25] *Ibid.*, v. 29, pp. 310–11, July 1900.
[26] *Ibid.*, v. 13, p. 572, Sept. 1892.
[27] *Ibid.*, v. 30, pp. 677–89, April 1901.
[28] *Ibid.*, v. 37, p. 665, Oct. 1904.
[29] *Ibid.*, v. 27, p. 447, Aug. 1899.

"Omega: The Last Days of the World" (1893); Armando Palacio Valdes' novel, "The Origin of Thought" (1894); a nautical romance by W. Clark Russell (1895); Albion W. Tourgée's history of a Civil War regiment, "The Story of a Thousand"; and Harold Frederic's last novel, "Gloria Mundi" (1898). A series called "The Great Passions of History" ran through 1894: it included an article by J. A. Froude on Antony and Cleopatra, one by Edmund Gosse on Laura and Petrarch, another by Anatole France on Abélard and Héloïse, and so on. Similar was a series by Richard Le Gallienne in 1904 called "Old Love Stories Retold." In 1899 the *Cosmopolitan* began to print Tolstoi's "Resurrection"; but Walker found some of the early parts of the novel improper for his magazine's chaste pages, and he had trouble getting copy on time besides, and finally he abandoned the serial entirely. The genius of H. G. Wells was especially adapted to *Cosmopolitan* concepts, and several of his novels ran through its pages, including "The War of the Worlds" (1897) and "The First Man in the Moon" (1900–1901). Other authors of fiction serials were Israel Zangwill, James Lane Allen, Beatrice Harraden, and Herbert Quick. In 1904 Editor Walker himself contributed a serial story, "A Modern Swiss Family Robinson," to his magazine; it was a sociological account of the behavior of a group of transatlantic passengers marooned on an uninhabited island.

But the "continued story" was not a *Cosmopolitan* stand-by. The short story became important in its pages in the latter nineties, with three or four in each issue. Kipling, Stevenson, Besant, Hardy, Mark Twain, Jack London, Mrs. Wharton, and Octave Thanet were among the magazine's writers of shorter tales. Walker was one of the first to recognize the talents of London, to whom he offered an assistant editorship in 1901,[30] just after William Bayard Hale had left the staff.

In 1893 a department of "Art and Letters" was introduced. It had such contributors as Francisque Sarcey, writing a Paris letter, Andrew Lang, writing from London, and Thomas A. Janvier, H. H. Boyesen, Israel Zangwill, and Agnes Repplier. This department and the one on scientific progress were superseded in 1899 by "Men, Women, and Events," a highly diversified department to which many prominent writers contributed short pieces. The magazine was not distinguished for its verse in the nineties, though most of the leading magazine poets of the time contributed to it. Nor was it notable for literary criticism, outside of the "Art and Letters" section. Newspapers were much discussed by such journalists as James Creelman, John A. Cockerill, and Arthur Brisbane, and by such critics as Harry Thurston Peck, who proposed a new "national newspaper" (December 1897). The theater was

[30] Charmian London, *The Book of Jack London* (New York, 1921), v. 1, p. 347.

given liberal attention in illustrated articles. An essay that provoked much acrimonious discussion was Mark Twain's "Christian Science and the Book of Mrs. Eddy" (October 1899).

The copious illustration of the *Cosmopolitan* seemed to emphasize pictures of the female form a good deal in the mid-nineties, but by the turn of the century there was a fine variety in the magazine's art. There was some interest in caricaturing, and Arthur Young's series of acrid comments on modern sins, in full-page cartoons entitled "Hiprah Hunt's Journey Through the Inferno," appeared serially in 1900.

The circulation of the magazine under Walker's ownership never greatly exceeded half a million; but this distribution, with a hundred pages or more of advertising in each issue, represented substantial prosperity. Eugene W. Spaulding was advertising manager until 1894, when he left to go with the *Ladies' Home Journal*; he was succeeded by Henry D. Wilson. Walker gave the magazine its own plant at City Hall Square, New York, in 1892,[31] but shortly thereafter he began the construction of the Cosmopolitan Center at Irvington-on-the-Hudson. These buildings, designed by McKim, Mead & White, were intended to house the Walker enterprises, including homes for the magazine staff. The main building, devoted to printing and binding the *Cosmopolitan* and other magazines, was long unfinished. *Twentieth Century Homes*, Walker's magazine for women,[32] was published there, and the Cosmopolitan University was housed at the center. Throughout the nineties the *Cosmopolitan* also had a large edition printed in London; James Creelman was its editor in 1893, but he could never stay in one place for long.

Walker had become so involved in automobile manufacturing and allied activities by 1905 that he could pay little attention to the *Cosmopolitan*, and its business showed a sharp decline. In that year, therefore, he sold the magazine to W. R. Hearst, for some four hundred thousand dollars.[33] Walker had been an individualistic and, on the whole, a successful editor. His social sense, his enthusiasm for technological advance, his interest in foreign peoples, and his journalistic flair were assets to him as an editor. He also had a fairly good sense of literary values, though he confessed that he was "no judge of verse."[34] He was a conscientious, perhaps even prudish, editor, censoring not only Tolstoi's "Resurrection" but also Le Gallienne's translation of Omar.[35] He was strong on promotion. Perhaps he put James Brisben Walker forward in his magazine too much, but most of the ten-cent magazines were follow-

[31] *Cosmopolitan*, v. 14, p. 259, Jan. 1893.
[32] Towne, *Adventures in Editing*, p. 22.
[33] Mrs. Fremont Older, *William Randolph Hearst, American* (New York, 1936), p. 257.
[34] Towne, *Adventures in Editing*, p. 38.
[35] *Ibid.*, pp. 39–40.

ing a pattern of personal editorship; and perhaps it was not a bad pattern after all.

The purchase of the *Cosmopolitan* was Hearst's first incursion into the field of the general magazine; the only periodical he had previously owned was *Motor*. He chose Bailey Millard, novelist and littérateur, who had been a reporter and feature writer on his newspapers, as editor. New typography opened up the pages and made them more readable. In the next dozen years, under a succession of editors — S. S. Chamberlain, famous Hearst journalist; Sewell Haggard, who had been an editor on *McClure's* and the *World To-Day*; and Edgar Sisson, who had been a newspaperman and a *Collier's* editor — the *Cosmopolitan* pursued a somewhat irregular path to a million circulation. It went up to 450,000 shortly after the Hearst purchase, but it was not until 1911, when the number of pages was increased to 144 and the price to fifteen cents, that it really began its march to the million goal, which was reached in 1914. Henry D. Wilson, the magazine's great advertising manager, who had been on its staff all through the Walker regime, made the *Cosmopolitan* the advertising leader of the general illustrated magazines by 1909, with over 100 pages of advertising at $448 a page in each issue.[36] Advertising rates increased with circulation to nearly $1,000 when the million mark was reached. In 1912 it was claimed that the International Magazine Company, publishers of *Cosmopolitan*, *Motor*, and *Motor Boating* had cleared over $300,000 the year before.[37]

Under Hearst the *Cosmopolitan* was more sensational than before. Hearst's idea of a magazine was the Sunday supplement raised to a higher degree of literary performance, but just as readable and attractive. Alan Dale, in private life Alfred J. Cohen, long a dramatic critic for Hearst's New York papers, wrote theater articles for the *Cosmopolitan* for more than a decade; and they were copiously illustrated by photography. Ambrose Bierce had a department for a few years, called first "The Passing Show" and then "Small Contributions," in the style of surgical wit for which he was famous. Arthur Brisbane was a contributor for many years. His most notable early work in the magazine was a 1908 series advocating control of the liquor business — prohibition, or at least strict temperance. A fourth Hearst journalist who became a *Cosmopolitan* stand-by was the socialist Charles Edward Russell, whose life of Charlemagne appeared in 1910; and a fifth was Alfred Henry Lewis, whose "Story of Andrew Jackson" was serialized in 1906–

[36] See advertisements in Ayer's *American Newspaper Annual and Directory* for 1909, p. 1228, and for 1911, p. 1401.

[37] Page advertisement for a million-dollar bond issue for *Cosmopolitan*, *Motor*, and *Motor Boating*, advertising section of *Cosmopolitan*, Dec. 1912.

1907, and who later did some new "Wolfville Stories" for the magazine, as well as many articles.

Less journalistic was a western author inherited from Walker's administration — Jack London. The *Cosmopolitan* printed some of London's best stories, though he once declared he would not "stand for" editorial changes that had been made in "The Cruise of the Snark,"[38] and he was almost as much upset by deletions in "The Valley of the Moon" a few years later.[39] Bruno Lessing's admirable stories of the New York ghetto ran for many years in the magazine, and a series of George Randolph Chester's new "Get-Rich-Quick Wallingford" stories attracted many readers. Arthur B. Reeve's "Craig Kennedy" detective yarns were popular. Ellis Parker Butler, E. Phillips Oppenheim, and Mark Lee Luther were typical fictioneers in the early years of the Hearst ownership. In 1910 the editor wrote: "In the next issue we are printing a story by another author now unknown, who, we think, will prove to be a second O. Henry. His name is Wodehouse — P. G. Wodehouse, a name it is well to remember."[40]

The poet Edwin Markham, who had been associated with Hearst's western papers, became an assistant editor of the *Cosmopolitan*, contributing articles and verse, as well as a monthly editorial, more or less regularly through several years. Those editorials, printed with artistic embellishments, written by Markham, Elbert Hubbard, Dr. Frank Crane, or Herbert Kaufman over some two decades, were a little like the old Sunday School lessons: they gave you a moral glow without being very practical. They were more affecting than effective. But they were a nice feature.

The series of personal confessions entitled "What Life Means to Me," published in 1906–1907, attracted much attention. Among contributors to them were John Burroughs, Upton Sinclair, Jack London, Julia Ward Howe, and Editors Millard and Markham. Another much discussed series was the one on Christian Science (1907–1908), which was initiated by articles written by two Scientists, the playwright Charles Klein and the Earl of Dunmore. A third notable series was a defense of Mexico and its government by Otheman Stevens (1910), clearly designed as a reply to the "Barbarous Mexico" articles in *Everybody's* and motivated by Hearst's Mexican interests.

Coverage of the San Francisco disaster in the number for June 1906

---

[38] C. London, *The Book of Jack London*, v. 2, p. 153. The squabble between London and the *Cosmopolitan* over the publication of the "Cruise" is set forth in detail on pp. 145–54, without mentioning the magazine's name. But see also Irving Stone, *Sailor on Horseback* (Boston, 1938), pp. 231–33. The *Woman's Home Companion* was also involved.

[39] C. London, *The Book of Jack London*, v. 2, p. 274.

[40] *Cosmopolitan*, v. 48, p. 260, Jan. 1910.

was admirable; there were articles by David Starr Jordan, Mayor James D. Phelan, General Frederick Funston, and Editor Millard. Captain R. P. Hobson's "If War Should Come" series of 1908, General Miles's autobiography in 1911, and Waldemar Kaempffert's "The Problem of Air Flight" (October 1907) were reminiscent of Walker's editorship. A symposium in June 1910 on the high cost of living was notable: among the contributors were Professor E. R. A. Seligman, Secretary James Wilson, John Mitchell, John Spargo, James J. Hill, and Senator H. C. Lodge.

Important in the *Cosmopolitan* during the early years of Hearst's ownership were the muckraking articles. Muckraking in the magazines was passing its crest in 1905; but during the latter years of the movement, the *Cosmopolitan* played a conspicuous part. An anonymous series purportedly written by a former New York detective about graft in that city was printed in 1905. The next year the magazine's leading contribution to this kind of literature was published. The research on which this series was based was performed by Gustavus Myers. "The Senators are not elected by the people; they are elected by the 'interests,'" which are "as hostile to the American people as any invading army," wrote David Graham Phillips in the first installment, for March 1906. The first broadside of the series, called "The Treason of the Senate," was fired at Chauncey M. Depew. W. R. Hearst, who kept a close watch on the magazine in these years, stopped the presses to change the latter part of this first article. After having read the proof, he telegraphed George d'Utassy, who was the general manager of the Hearst magazines:

> Violence is not force. Windy vituperation is not convincing. I had intended an exposé. We have merely an attack. The facts, the proof, the documentary evidence are an important thing, but the article is deficient in them.

Evidently what Hearst and d'Utassy supplied were some quotations from the hearings of the committee which investigated the Equitable Life Insurance Company; d'Utassy testified that Phillips thought the new ending a great improvement, or so Hearst's "official" biographer reports.[41]

The series went on to attack Senators Aldrich, Bailey, Elkins, Cullom, Foraker, Allison, Platt, and Knox. It was this series by Phillips which moved President Theodore Roosevelt to denounce untruthful and exaggerated attacks on public men, and to introduce for such writing the term "muckraking." Roosevelt did not, however, mention Phillips

---

[41] Older, *William Randolph Hearst, American*, pp. 257–58.

or the *Cosmopolitan* by name in this statement, having been deterred therefrom by the cautious counsel of Senator Root.[42]

The editor of the *Cosmopolitan* made it clear that this series was intended to be the most sensational piece of muckraking — "the most conspicuous act of exposure of corruption" — ever attempted.[43] Brilliant cover designs emphasized the series like "scareheads" in a newspaper. "Never in its history," wrote the editor, "has the *Cosmopolitan* been so eagerly bought and read" as in March and April 1906. Those numbers were sold out, and the printing order increased to half a million.[44] Phillips wrote ten articles, and then, appalled by the bitterness of some of the replies that defended the Senate,[45] refused to furnish more.[46] Six years later the Seventeenth Amendment, providing for the direct election of senators, was passed by both houses, and the next year it was adopted by the states. Phillips and the *Cosmopolitan* may have made a contribution to that reform.

Besides Phillips, the chief muckrakers for *Cosmopolitan* were Alfred Henry Lewis and Charles Edward Russell. Lewis had an unrestrained attack on Senator Platt in the same issue that carried the second of the Phillips series, that of April 1906. It ended with what Hearst might well have called "windy vituperation":

What is he? Nothing. What has he done? Nothing. Who will remember him a day beyond his death? No one. . . . One day he will die, and his epitaph might truthfully be: "He publicly came to nothing, and privately came to grief."

Lewis did a series in 1908–1909 on "The Owners of America," including articles on Rockefeller, Carnegie, Schwab, the Vanderbilts, and so on. Here he was less passionately devastating, but still biting. Some of the articles in this series were by Arthur Brisbane and Emerson Hough. In 1911 Lewis contributed a series on the Mormon church in Utah, under such titles as "The Viper on the Hearth," and "The Viper's Trail of Gold." The articles had appropriate "art" — snakes everywhere. Russell's chief series was entitled "At the Throat of the Republic" (1907–1908); it exposed election frauds in various cities. Edwin Markham got into the game in 1906 with a series on child labor entitled "The Hoe-Man in the Making." The same year (the "muckrakingest" year of the magazine's history) Poultney Bigelow furnished a series about the dirt and graft of the Panama Canal Zone.

[42] Isaac Marcosson, *David Graham Phillips* (New York, 1932), pp. 238–40. See also Ray Stannard Baker, *American Chronicle* (New York, 1942), p. 203.

[43] *Cosmopolitan*, v. 40, p. 478, Feb. 1906.

[44] *Ibid.*, v. 41, pp. 113, 115, May 1906.

[45] Marcosson, *David Graham Phillips*, p. 241.

[46] He may have been offended also by business-office interference. See C. C. Regier, *The Era of the Muckrakers* (Chapel Hill, 1932), pp. 170–71.

The next year — 1907 — Josiah Flynt (Willard) made his last magazine contributions in *Cosmopolitan* articles, attacking race-track poolrooms. In 1909 Harold Bolce wrote some attacks on university scholars for liberal ideas, the first one entitled "Blasting at the Rock of Ages." But the series that climaxed and ended the muckraking history of the *Cosmopolitan* was one that exposed corruption in many cities and states, called "What Are You Going to Do About It?" published in 1911. Various writers — such as Lewis, Russell, and George Creel — exposed graft in various states — Mississippi, Ohio, Wisconsin, Illinois, Colorado, and so on. The public had tired of the muckraking frenzy, however, and circulation response seemed slow.

For several years the magazine carried many two-color illustrations in each issue, and on rare occasions three-color plates of pictures by Emilie Benson Knipe or Frederic Remington. Humorous drawings by E. W. Kemble, Penrhyn Stanlaws, T. S. Sullivant, and others were featured. A series of full-page pictures of stage favorites was offered in every number.

A change came in 1912, when the magazine dropped its muckraking and turned to a major reliance on fiction, which was to last for a third of a century. To be sure, Lewis and Russell kept, for a time, a brief "Progress and Politics" department at the back of the book, and there was a series of friendly articles about politicians by John Temple Graves in 1914. Series of reminiscences by the widows of two Civil War generals — John A. Logan and George E. Pickett — indicate the trend toward feminine appeal. The full-page stage beauties were retired, after long service, but the durable Alan Dale was still allowed half a dozen illustrated pages about the theater. Ella Wheeler Wilcox was a preferred contributor of verse and essays until her death in 1919.

But fiction was now dominant. The change-over was due, first, to the decay of popular interest in muckraking, and, second, to the great success of Robert W. Chambers' serial story "The Common Law," published in 1911. The current report had it that *Everybody's* had declined this novel as unfit for a magazine going into American homes, but that Hearst had paid eighteen thousand dollars for it, and then added ten thousand more for its illustration by Charles Dana Gibson.[47] At any rate, it was "the most successful serial ever published," boasted the editor of *Cosmopolitan* later, when he had found time to look at statistics showing a 70 per cent gain in circulation while the serial was running. "It was a leading factor," the editor continued, "in making *Cosmopolitan* the best-selling magazine in the world."[48] Thereafter, for many

[47] *Jim Jam Jems*, v. 13, Jan. 1913, p. 22.
[48] *Cosmopolitan*, v. 53, p. 721, Nov. 1912.

years, the "Chambers-Gibson serials," as the editor called them, were standard fare in the magazine. Gouverneur Morris, Elinor Glyn, and Amélie Rives were also leading serialists. Not all *Cosmopolitan* fiction dealt primarily with unfaithful wives and courtesans, however: George Ade's "Fables in Slang," with McCutcheon illustrations, were long an amusing feature; Booth Tarkington's "Penrod" stories were popular; Jack London, Gilbert Parker, and Rex Beach wrote about the wide-open spaces; and Chester and Reeve continued industriously in their respective short story patterns. But the dominant subject in every number from 1912 until 1918 was sex — sex in society, sex in adventure, sex in mystery.

The *Cosmopolitan* in these years carried two serials, five or six short stories, and three nonfiction articles besides its piece on the theater, in each number. Manager d'Utassy, who was the magazine's real editor, stated his "successful formula" thus: "Find out what your readers want and give it to them. And give it to them regularly!" [49] To do this it was necessary to contract for the total output of chief contributors; otherwise the magazine could not keep up the steady stream of work by its dozen or so tried and tested favorites.[50]

In the fall of 1916 the page was enlarged to quarto size, giving a better opportunity for layouts and for runovers into the advertising section. The next year the price was raised to twenty cents a copy, and two years later to twenty-five cents. At this time the magazine was printing more than seventy-five pages of advertising at two thousand dollars a page, and the price increases had not reduced circulation. Circulation was about a million, more or less, from 1915 to 1925. *Cosmopolitan* was far ahead of all its monthly competitors in both circulation and advertising, unless we consider (as we probably should) the women's magazines as competitors.[51] Thus it was a prosperous publication that came into the editorial charge of Ray Long in 1918.

Long had been a newspaperman, an editorial assistant on *Hampton's Magazine*, and editor of the *Red Book* for seven years, before Hearst hired him to edit *Cosmopolitan*. Long asked and received a liberal salary, which Hearst raised repeatedly before the expiration of the contract period. It is said that at one time he was receiving $180,000 a year in salary and bonuses.[52] Long has testified that Hearst was "a good boss," "did not question or interfere with my plans," and for

[49] Older, *William Randolph Hearst, American*, p. 259.
[50] *Cosmopolitan*, v. 61, Sept. 1916, p. 25.
[51] *The Ladies' Home Journal, Pictorial Review, McCall's Magazine,* and *Woman's World* were ahead of *Cosmopolitan*, and the *Woman's Home Companion* was only some 50,000 behind.
[52] John K. Winkler, *W.R. Hearst, An American Phenomenon* (New York, 1928), pp. 248–49. See also *Editor & Publisher*, July 16, 1935, p. 32.

months at a time had no idea of what was about to be published in his magazine.[53] Yet we are told on fairly good authority of one incident in which the "Chief" insisted on acceptance of the work of an Englishwoman who had shown him some favors, and did not back down until his editor had proffered his resignation. Then he wired: "After all you and I should not quarrel about a girl at our age — and hers. Don't publish the serial if you feel so strongly about it." [54]

Long discarded the d'Utassy formula of sticking to a few writers, which was wearing out. He was hired because of his reputation for recognizing fiction and fictioneers who would please the general magazine audience. He was a "sixth-sense editor." He once wrote:

> I happen to be an average American who has the opportunity to read a tremendous number of manuscripts. From these I select the stories I like, publish them within the covers of a magazine, and through the facilities of our circulation department put that magazine where people may see it; and there are enough other average Americans who like to read the same thing that I like to read to buy the magazine in sufficient quantities to make me worth my salary.[55]

This sounds as though Long were not a believer in the efficacy of big names in his magazines, but *Cosmopolitan* tables of contents during his editorship do not bear out such a notion. H. G. Wells, Blasco Ibañez, Sir Philip Gibbs, Somerset Maugham, Michael Arlen, Robert Hichens, and Raphael Sabatini were some of his writers from abroad. Among American contributors were Booth Tarkington, Edna Ferber, Sinclair Lewis, Fannie Hurst, Theodore Dreiser, Louis Bromfield, Kathleen Norris, and Roark Bradford. From *Red Book* Long brought writers like James Oliver Curwood and Peter B. Kyne; he raided the *Saturday Evening Post* for such names as Irvin Cobb, Ring Lardner, and Montague Glass.[56]

Nor was the magazine without nonfiction features. Essays by O. O. McIntyre and Berton Braley, poems by Edgar A. Guest, stage pictures, and comics gave variety in entertainment. But a reader devoted exclusively to the *Cosmopolitan* would not have known there was a World War in 1914–1918.

[53] *20 Best Short Stories in Ray Long's 20 Years as an Editor* (New York, 1932), "Introduction" by Ray Long, pp. xiii–xiv.

[54] Winkler, *W. R. Hearst*, p. 250.

[55] Doris Ulmann, *A Portrait Gallery of American Editors* (New York, 1925), p. 92. See also the "Introduction" to the Ray Long anthology cited above. Long repeated this creed in a letter to Theodore Dreiser dated March 28, 1918: "Lorimer has been successful because he followed his own beliefs regardless of what any other editor might think. If I am to be successful I must adhere to that same recipe." (Dreiser Collection, University of Pennsylvania Library).

[56] John Tebbel, *George Horace Lorimer and the Saturday Evening Post* (Garden City, N. Y., 1948), pp. 46, 82.

Treatment of public affairs was reserved for *Hearst's International.*[57] This magazine, which Hearst had added to his string in 1911, was begun in Chicago in 1901 as *Current Encyclopedia.* It was one of the home study periodicals of the end of the nineteenth century, and was closely related in its origins to two others of that class.[58] Its founder was William E. Ernst, who had been on the staff of the Werner Company, then American publishers of the *Encyclopaedia Britannica*; he made his magazine virtually a monthly supplement of any standard encyclopedia, with its information arranged alphabetically by topics. When this heavy offering was not successful, Ernst began arranging his material in departments, with profuse illustrations, cut the fifty-cents-a-copy price in half, and changed the name to *The World To-Day.* Charles H. Dennis, of the *Chicago Daily News*, edited the department of current events; and education, invention, sports, science, books, and so on, had their own sections.

In 1903 the *World To-Day* absorbed *Christendom*,[59] a weekly that had been published briefly by the University of Chicago, and took over not only its modest subscription list but its whole editorial board, mostly members of the university faculty. For the next seven years Professor Shailer Mathews was editor of the *World To-Day*, and President William Rainey Harper was chairman of its editorial committee. A typical number of the magazine began with a double-page editorial by Mathews on some social problem, followed by news departments of "World Politics," "The Nation," "Art and Letters," and "The Religious World." A dozen rather short illustrated articles followed, by well-known professors and journalists, such as Edmund J. James, Russell Sturgis, Trumbull White, Albert Bushnell Hart, and Paul S. Reinsch. Short signed articles in a department entitled "The Making of To-morrow" came next, and then the back-of-the-book sections "Books

[57] TITLES: *Current Encyclopedia*, 1901–02; *The World To-Day*, 1902–12; *Hearst's Magazine*, 1912–14; *Hearst's*, 1914–21; *Hearst's International*, 1921–25.

FIRST ISSUE: July 1901. LAST ISSUE: Feb. 1925. Merged with *Cosmopolitan*.

PERIODICITY: Monthly. Regular semiannual volumes, 1–47 (no. 2).

PUBLISHERS: Modern Research Society (William E. Ernst, pres.), Chicago, 1901; Current Encyclopedia Company (W. E. Ernst, pres.), Chicago, 1902–13; The World To-Day Company (W. E. Ernst, v.-p. and publisher), Chicago 1903–11; International Magazine Company (William Randolph Hearst, owner), New York, 1911–25.

EDITORS: Edmund Buckley, 1901–03; Shailer Mathews, 1903–11; Sewell Haggard, 1911–18; Ray Long, 1918–25 (with Norman Hapgood, 1922–25).

INDEXES: Vols. 1–4 not indexed; thereafter *Poole's Index, Jones' Legal Index, Readers' Guide, Dramatic Index.*

REFERENCE: Herbert E. Fleming, "The Literary Interests of Chicago, VI," in *American Journal of Sociology*, v. 12, pp. 76–89, July 1906 (reprinted in *Magazines of a Market-Metropolis*, Chicago, 1906).

[58] *Modern Culture* and *Progress*, for which see p. 55. Bishop Samuel Fallows, editor of the latter, became a director of *Current Encyclopedia* when *Progress* was absorbed. The publisher of *Current Encyclopedia* had taken his idea from Werner's *Modern Culture.*

[59] Issued four months in the summer of 1903; edited by Shailer Mathews and others.

and Reading," "Calendar of the Month," and "The Encyclopedic Index." Thus it was still rather heavily informative; but for the sober-minded it was a genuinely excellent, well-balanced magazine. Illustration was copious and various, including stage pictures, reproductions of art masterpieces, and cartoons.

In July 1904 the price of the *World To-Day* was reduced to ten cents, and the circulation went up to eighty-five thousand.[60] In March 1906 the rate was set at fifteen cents — then the accepted price for the cheaper illustrated monthly. By that time the magazine carried some eighty pages of advertising per issue, and was showing a profit. But the Chicago businessmen who were its stockholders were dissatisfied with its small and uncertain returns, and in 1911 they readily accepted Hearst's offer of twenty-five thousand dollars for it.[61]

Hearst immediately moved the magazine to New York. His plan was to make it a more personal organ than the *Cosmopolitan*. He began by writing editorials against monopolies, illustrated by Davenport cartoons, in the first numbers under his ownership. In March 1912 he changed the name to *Hearst's Magazine*. He did not long maintain his own regular contributions; but he gave Sewell Haggard, his editor, directions to recruit well-known men as writers on public affairs. Thus Louis D. Brandeis, George W. Perkins, George W. Wickersham, Albert J. Beveridge, J. Laurence Laughlin, and F. W. Taussig wrote on political and economic matters for *Hearst's*, along with such writers from his own stable as Alfred Henry Lewis and Charles Edward Russell.

Featured for many months were Guglielmo Ferrero's articles on Roman history, designed to be a warning to moderns. Symposiums on current issues brought in many famous names. W. Morgan Shuster's own story of his financial adventures was an interesting serial in 1913. Belasco's autobiography in 1914, Marcosson's story of Frohman the next year, and Thomas R. Marshall's recollections in 1922 were all good features. In 1912 the magazine published the famous Standard Oil letters, which had been stolen from the company's files. These were the letters the signatures to which were forged, according to an exposure that *Collier's* published almost immediately.[62]

Besides the editorials of the "Chief," or rather after them, there were editorials by Frank Crane, Elbert Hubbard, "Mr. Dooley," and Norman Hapgood. The last-named was hired as "editor" of *Hearst's* in 1922; but Ray Long was editor-in-chief by then, and Hapgood was

---

[60] Fleming in *American Journal of Sociology*, v. 12, July 1906, p. 88. Ayer (1907) gives 99,222 sworn circulation for the preceding year.

[61] Older, *William Randolph Hearst, American*, p. 347.

[62] See p. 461. Generous quotations from the *Collier's* exposure are found in Ferdinand Lundberg, *Imperial Hearst* (New York, 1936), pp. 125–31.

really political editor. As editor of *Collier's*, Hapgood had been wont to lambaste Hearst; now the "Chief" was able to purchase the Hapgood prestige as a front for his magazine.

Charles Henry Meltzer wrote for *Hearst's* on music, J. B. Kerfoot on books, Gardner Teall on art. There was a summary of the "Play of the Month," and another on the "Book of the Month." The illustration was brilliant and profuse. Much of it came from photographs, but there were drawings by Gibson, Christy, Flagg, Benda, Stanlaws, and others of the best.

Fiction in *Hearst's Magazine* was outstanding from the beginning. Winston Churchill's "The Inside of the Cup" (1912), illustrated by Gibson, was the first great serial success. Rupert Hughes, Edgar Saltus, Robert W. Chambers, Rex Beach, and Jack London were faithful contributors. But the magazine's greatest box-office success in the fiction field was David Graham Phillips' "The Story of Susan Lenox, Her Fall and Rise," published four years after the author's death. This delay was due in part to fears of prosecution on the part of the editors; and indeed as soon as the first installment of the story appeared, the Society for the Suppression of Vice, John S. Sumner, secretary, swore out warrants against Editor Haggard and the business manager, William H. Johnson, for publishing "obscene matter." After a hearing, the defendants were discharged, but when action was later brought against D. Appleton & Company for publishing the book, they were forced to delete large portions.[63] Most of these passages had been omitted from the serial version, for "Susan Lenox" was a long novel, which, even when edited for the magazine, ran through nineteen monthly issues.

About two years after Hearst had bought the *World To-Day* and turned it into a high-powered monthly bearing his own name, his experts assured him that if he placed its major emphasis on public affairs he could not hope to get a circulation much over two hundred thousand for it. Once convinced that this was true, the "Chief" ordered *Hearst's* changed into an entertainment magazine in which big-name fiction should be dominant — a direct competitor of the *Cosmopolitan*.[64] Many of these big names came from overseas — Chesterton, Shaw, Caine, Doyle, Kipling, Wells, Galsworthy, and Merrick from England; Blasco Ibañez, Maeterlinck, D'Annunzio, and Bojer from the Continent. There were many others: in 1918, for example, there were serials by Rex Beach, E. Phillips Oppenheim, Marie Corelli, and Elinor Glyn.

In 1915 *Hearst's* adopted the small-folio size. If this was an imitation of the immensely successful *Saturday Evening Post*, it was not

[63] Marcosson, *David Graham Phillips*, ch. 8.
[64] Winkler, *W. R. Hearst*, p. 245.

the only factor of that emulation. The typography of headings and makeup in general were modeled on the *Post* for a time. The raid on *Post* authors made by *Hearst's Magazine* was even more noticeable than that by *Cosmopolitan*. The title was changed in 1921 to *Hearst's International*. The single-copy price fluctuated between fifteen, twenty, and twenty-five cents, and in April 1920 went to thirty-five. Page size returned to quarto in 1922. Circulation during all these changes stuck at a little below half a million,[65] and finally Hearst decided to consolidate his two general illustrated magazines under the title *Hearst's International Combined with Cosmopolitan*. But *Cosmopolitan* was the displayed word on the cover.

The merger resulted in an immediate increase of nearly three hundred thousand in *Cosmopolitan's* circulation, at the single-copy price of twenty-five cents. It also resulted in an enlarged magazine (two hundred and fifty pages for April 1925) which boasted on its cover: "More novels, more stories, more features than any magazine in the world." Most of the *International's* English fiction writers were taken over, making a remarkable galaxy of contributors. Ida Verdon was managing editor in 1926–1928, and she was followed by Helen Butzgy.

Increasingly by the end of the twenties, "sex o'clock" seemed to strike on every page, in the stories, the articles, or the illustrations, or all three. John Held, Jr., and Gluyas Williams were new artists in the magazine, and Gibson, Flagg, and Fisher kept at work — the last-named furnishing most of the covers. Each number now carried no less than four serials, a dozen short stories, and half a dozen features. The features, on the whole, did not seem very important. George A. Dorsey discussed social and psychological problems with acumen. Calvin Coolidge contributed a series of short articles in 1929.

In 1931 Ray Long resigned. It was announced that he retired so he could pursue his lifelong ambition to become a book publisher, but it may be surmised that the president and editor-in-chief of the International Magazine Corporation sometimes took a little too much credit to suit the top boss. *Fortune's* article, "The *Cosmopolitan* of Ray Long" appeared shortly before its famous editor left it [66] and it became again the *Cosmopolitan* of William Randolph Hearst.

Was Ray Long a great magazine editor? That he estimated readers' likes well enough to maintain the circulation which "*Cosmo*" had when he became editor is true. In fact he increased the readership a little, though most of the gain came when *Cosmopolitan* absorbed the *Inter-*

[65] Except for 1916–17, when it ran up to nearly 600,000.
[66] *Fortune*, v. 3, March 1931, pp. 51, 55.

*national.* Long's "feeling" for a story seems to have been largely a feeling for the author's name. He certainly made no more literary "discoveries" for *Cosmopolitan* than such as fall to the lot of the average editor, though his career on *Red Book* may have been more brilliant. A few years after he went into the book business, his firm failed while he was on a pleasure trip abroad. He later tried the movies, and eventually took his own life.[67]

When Long left the *Cosmopolitan,* it had a circulation of 1,700,000 and probably a gross advertising income of about $5,000,000 based on a page rate of $4,800.[68] But the years of the great depression were just beginning, during which any magazine did well to hold most of its circulation and half or a third of its advertising. *Cosmopolitan* slipped a little in circulation for a few years, but by 1937 it was gaining again in both distribution and "ad" business. By the end of 1942 some issues had reached a circulation of 2,000,000, and its average annual circulation for the next decade was a little over that figure.

Editor during the depression was Harry Payne Burton, who had been a newspaper feature writer and an editor of *McCall's* before he came to *Cosmopolitan.* During his term — which was only two years shorter than Long's — the magazine published many notable serial stories, such as Joseph Hergesheimer's "The Party Dress" (1930), Faith Baldwin's "The Office Wife" (1930), Rebecca West's "War Nurse" (1931), Fanny Hurst's "Back Streets" (1931), Pearl Buck's "Sons" (1932), S. S. Van Dine's "The Kennel Murder Case (1933), Lloyd C. Douglas' "Green Light" (1935), A. J. Cronin's "The Stars Look Down" (1935), Hervey Allen's "Action at Aquila" (1938), Edna Ferber's "Saratoga Trunk" (1941). Sinclair Lewis' later novels were published in *Cosmopolitan,* and there were many by Arthur Somers Roche, Agatha Christie, Ellery Queen, Clarence Budington Kelland, C. S. Forester, Vina Delmar, and Louis Bromfield. For some years the magazine offered three serials and ten short stories in a single number, but in the latter thirties it followed the policy of publishing in each number a "book-length novel," a novelette, six or seven short stories, and about eight nonfiction articles.

The nonfiction was occasionally notable. Bernard Shaw, Albert Einstein, Ida M. Tarbell, Claude G. Bowers, and Frazier Hunt were contributors. "Your New National Leadership," by President-elect Roosevelt in January 1933 attracted attention. Mrs. Roosevelt was a later contributor. The "Autobiography of America" feature was modeled on

[67] *Editor & Publisher,* v. 68, July 13, 1935, p. 32.
[68] *Fortune,* v. 3, March 1931, pp. 51, 55.

the successful "How America Lives" of the *Ladies' Home Journal*. From the beginning of the Second World War, there was some material reflecting that conflict, by Bob Considine and others.

At the beginning of the forties *Cosmopolitan* was using the sectional type of make-up originated by *McCall's* some years earlier. It called itself "The Four-Book Magazine." The first section, entitled "The Magazine," contained one novelette, six to eight short stories, two serials, six to eight articles, and eight or nine "special features." The other three sections contained a complete short novel, a complete "book-length novel," and a digest of current nonfiction books. It was a big offering of two hundred pages or more. The amount of color increased constantly during Burton's editorship, and the magazine was a leader in skillful layout and illustration. The appeal was to entertainment seekers, to the moderately sophisticated, to women. Burton's own adjectives for his book were "current, vital and entertaining." [69]

During the next decade, under a succession of editors,[70] *Cosmopolitan* continued a similar policy though with declining emphasis on fiction. There was much of Hemingway, whose "Across the River and Into the Trees" was a 1950 serial. Elliot Paul, H. Allen Smith, John Hersey, and John P. Marquand were authors now frequently found in the magazine's pages, as well as such names long familiar to *Cosmopolitan* readers as Gouverneur Morris, Margaret Culkin Banning, and Elisabeth Sanxay Holding. The decrease in reader-demand for fiction noted by most of the general magazines at this time brought *Cosmopolitan* offerings in that field down to five short stories and one "complete mystery novel" by the early fifties.

There was, of course, a corresponding increase in articles, features, service departments, and "picture essays." Departments devoted to popular psychology, fashions, travel hints, and so on, gave variety. Louella O. Parsons long provided "Movie Citations," Lawrence Galton wrote "What's New in Medicine," and Dorothy Kilgallen and Dick Kollmar furnished an interesting New York page reminiscent of O. O. McIntyre. Illustration in these years was impressive — brilliant with color in both drawings and photography, and effective with bold full pages. Art features and cartoon sequences became common.

The owners of the *Cosmopolitan* met the phenomenal cost increases of 1953–1955 by cutting its circulation by about 50 per cent. This included a reduction of as much as 80 per cent for a time in the newsstand distribution. Advertising rates were, of course, reduced accordingly. Savings more than offset losses, and a magazine that had been

[69] *Quill*, Sept. 1935, p. 6.
[70] *Magazine World*, v. 3, Jan. 1947, pp. 4–5, 10.

losing money in 1953 at a circulation of considerably over two million was two years later making money on the basis of a little over a million.[71]

*"Cosmo"* has had a long and various history. Under Walker, it was a part of the magazine revolution of the nineties, strong in ideas, individualistic, functioning in many fields. Under the Hearst ownership it has been a striking and entertaining magazine, various and plentiful in its content.

[71] *Magazine Industry Newsletter*, June 4, 1955, p. 4.

## CURRENT LITERATURE [1]

I N CHRONICLING the founding of *Current Literature*, we can do no better than quote Gertrude Atherton's account as given in her autobiography:

I well remember the evening Mr. Frederick M. Somers called on me and asked my help in making an important decision. Formerly the editor of the San Francisco *Argonaut*,[2] of which he was joint founder with Frank M. Pixley, he had retired from that brilliant journal as soon as it was fairly launched, and gone into Wall Street. There he had made a decent little fortune, and knew enough to stop while he still possessed it.

After his twelfth visit to Europe, he began to tire of being a gentleman of leisure; and when I first met him in New York, shortly after my own arrival there, he was already looking for something that would fill his time and exercise his abilities. He said nothing definite for a time, and then one evening he descended upon me with three original ideas, one of which was *Current Literature*. I forget what the other two were, except that they were equally interesting; but of course I decided for the magazine.

Mr. Somers was a person of immense energy when roused, and he started to put his idea into practice the next day. There was much excitement among his friends, I remember; and I know that I felt immensely important in being allowed to help him. . . . The person who gave him real assistance then and later, however, was William George Jordan, who was full of ideas himself.[3]

Through its first two and a half years, *Current Literature: A Magazine of Record and Review* was by far the most attractive and entertaining eclectic journal ever published in the English language; and in value and significance it was at least the equal of the *Littell's* and *Eclectic* then current. The chief advantages of the newcomer over the old stand-bys in the eclectic field were its greater variety, its shorter and more attractively edited pieces, and its better paper and printing.

[1] TITLES: (1) *Current Literature*, 1888–1912; (2) *Current Opinion*, 1913–25.

FIRST ISSUE: July 1888. LAST ISSUE: April 1925. Merged into the *Literary Digest*.

PERIODICITY: Monthly. Vols. 1–5, semiannual, July 1888–Dec. 1890; 6–14, 3 vols. yearly, 1891–93; 15–26, semiannual, 1894–99; 27–28, quarterly vols., Jan.–June 1900; 29–78 (no. 4), semiannual, July 1900–April 1925.

PUBLISHERS: Current Literature Publishing Company, New York (Frederick M. Somers, pres., 1888–91; Thomas Ewing, pres., 1891–1912; E. J. Wheeler, pres., 1912–22; Adam Dingwall, bus. mgr., 1920–25).

EDITORS: F. M. Somers, 1888–91; William George Jordan, 1891–94; Bliss Carman, 1895–96; George Washington Cable, 1897; Harold Godwin, 1897–1900; William Bayard Hale, 1900–01; Jules E. Goodman, 1902–03; Charles Barzillai Spahr, 1904–05; Edward Jewitt Wheeler, 1905–20; E. J. Wheeler and Frank Crane, 1920–22; Frank Crane, 1922–25.

INDEXES: *Readers' Guide, Cumulative Index, Dramatic Index.*

[2] See F. L. Mott, *A History of American Magazines* (Cambridge, 1938), v. 3, pp. 56–57.

[3] *Current Opinion*, v. 54, Jan. 1913, advertising section, under heading, "Our Change of Name." See also Gertrude Atherton, *Adventures of a Novelist* (New York, 1932), p. 146.

The first number, for July 1888, consisted of ninety-six large quarto pages of text (there was a little advertising front and back), printed on a laid paper and arranged mostly in one- to three-page units. It began with no less than nine pages of paragraphs of literary gossip, and then after two pages of magazine poetry, five more pages of current literary news. There were pages of wit and humor scattered through the book, including "cute" sayings of children, a page from the *Arizona Kicker*, and a piece by Bill Nye. Fifteen pages of verse, commonly with three or four poems on the page, afforded a larger poetical offering than any other magazine then published; most of these pieces were new, but some were from the old poets, and they ranged from dialect verse to the classical forms. There were short short stories and sketches, little features on celebrities, a good deal about ghosts and psychic phenomena, a few translations, four pages of "Fads, Foibles, and Fashions," and some historical and some scientific matter.

The magazine was a good social historian of its times. It was full of sidelights on the American scene. A minimum of the selections in these early volumes was taken from English periodicals, and even these were mostly about America. The literary criticism was indulgent; adverse opinion was quoted, to be sure, but the general attitude of *Current Literature* was genial and complaisant.

After thirty months, Somers tired of the magazine and sold it to a joint-stock company. Its page was reduced to octavo; and though the number of pages was increased to one hundred and sixty, it never again gave the impression of copious richness that characterized the early volumes. Jordan was editor until 1894, when he left in order to preach his doctrines of education from the lecture platform and write books on the subject. He gave place to Bliss Carman, the poet, who soon resigned in favor of George W. Cable, the novelist, who had been editing the *Symposium*,[4] an amateurish kind of magazine at Northampton, Massachusetts. Cable was *Current Literature's* editor for only eight months, and then he gave place to Harold Godwin, grandson of the poet-editor Bryant, and son of Parke Godwin, another editor of the *New York Evening Post*. Circulation, at three dollars a year or twenty-five cents a number, was about forty thousand, which represented reasonable prosperity in those times. Advertising consisted largely of publishers' announcements of books, but it would sometimes run to twenty or thirty pages.

Publishers of newspapers, magazines, and books were generous with their material. It was considered good publicity to allow fairly long quotations; indeed most general magazines broadcast extensive clip-

---

[4] See p. 265; also Lucy L. C. Bikle, *George W. Cable* (New York, 1928), p. 220.

sheets, along with free copies, to newspapers. *Current Literature* regularly printed the advertising announcements of the magazines that coöperated with it, and doubtless these easy relations had much to do with the friendly attitude toward all current productions by Somers and his staff.

*Current Literature* had less individuality and brightness after Somers sold it in 1891. Material was more departmentalized, under such headings as "Art, Music and Drama," "Philanthropical and Social," "Biography," "Society Verse," "Drama," and "Adventure and Sport." Readings from new books became a feature. A few illustrations appeared in 1893, chiefly in the magazine's articles about the Columbian Exposition; and for some two years there were many pictures from current books, the engravings obviously loaned by the publishers, and often bunched in an illustrated section. From the first, the magazine had presented a list of new books; but beginning in 1892 this list was more elaborate, and it was accompanied by a "Magazine Reference List," which continued for many years. In 1894 *Current Literature* went back to its quarto form, which it then retained until 1901, when it turned to a large square-octavo.

In March 1903 *Current Literature* absorbed *Current History*,[5] of Boston, and announced that "the record of the month's great events will hereafter be the main feature of *Current Literature*."[6] As early as 1895 the magazine had begun calling itself "semieclectic," marking a change from straight reprint toward comment on current topics. The lead department was "Editorial Comment" in 1901, and after 1903, "Progress of Events." In fact the magazine was increasingly like *Review of Reviews*, though it included more literary gossip, sketches, verse, and quotations from new books. The reproduction of current newspaper cartoons was a feature after 1903. "Books on Vital Issues" was a good department, reflecting a liberal attitude. In the presidential campaign of 1904, the Democratic sympathies of Editor Spahr were apparent, though both sides of the debate were presented through excerpts from the press.

The editorship passed from Godwin to William Bayard Hale, the clergyman-journalist, in 1900, and a year or so later to the dramatist Jules Eckert Goodman. Charles B. Spahr, a specialist in political science and author of *America's Working People*, was at the helm in 1904 and part of 1905.

The fortunes of *Current Literature* declined steadily from about 1895. Magazines were increasingly reluctant to foster a newsstand

---

[5] See p. 71.
[6] *Current Literature*, v. 34, p. 257, March 1903.

rival by allowing immediate reprint of their best articles. That was one reason for turning to the field already occupied by the monthly *Review of Reviews* and the weekly *Literary Digest* — comment on the current scene and reprint of short cuttings from newspapers and periodicals. Another reason was declining readership, which forced the magazine to experiment with various new policies and techniques. By 1905 the circulation had sunk to less than eight thousand.[7]

At this critical juncture Edward J. Wheeler joined the organization. He had served ten years as editor of the *Literary Digest*, and he brought to *Current Literature* an industry and a competent understanding of the magazine field that it badly needed. He became editor in July 1905. At that time he bought some stock in the publishing company, and the next year he brought about a complete refinancing. Thomas Ewing, Jr., patent attorney by profession and poet by avocation, became president; though he resigned that position to Wheeler in 1913, he retained his holdings in the company until 1916.

Wheeler made his "Review of the World" an opening department of real interest. He did not take sides in the presidential campaigns. He was inclined to heterodoxy in politics, showed a considerable interest in Debs, but was never strongly Rooseveltian. He was sympathetic with Wilson, and strongly supported the League of Nations after the war.

The magazine now became more interesting and vital throughout. A monthly condensation and review of a play, with illustration, became a feature. Much attention was given to a contemporary history of sports. A selection of the "best" short stories for monthly publication was undertaken in 1910; these became the O. Henry Prize stories, which, ten years later, began an annual series in book form.

In 1913 the name was changed to *Current Opinion*. The magazine had, in fact, become a kind of monthly *Literary Digest* — a good miscellany, with current verse and its short story and play to remind one of its origins, but above all an epitome of the current scene, with Wheeler's "Review" and many short pieces from current periodicals and newspapers. Once more it was a quarto.

Alexander Harvey, who had been associated with Wheeler on the *Literary Digest*, came with him to *Current Literature* and remained his right-hand man until his chief's death. George Sylvester Viereck became an associate editor in 1907. With his strong German sympathies, he might have been expected to turn the magazine against England in the years before America's entry into the First World War; but

---

[7] An advertisement in Ayer's *Annual* for 1910 says that circulation had multiplied ten times in less than five years. It was then given as 77,000.

Wheeler seems to have kept it on a fairly even keel. Viereck started his propagandic *Fatherland* in 1914, resigning from the *Current Opinion* staff early the next year. He was succeeded by Frank Chapin Bray, who had been on the *Digest* and later editor of the *Chautauquan*, for a year or two; and later by William Griffith, who had occupied various positions in New York magazinedom, and who remained with *Current Opinion* to its end.

The magazine soon began to feel the effects of the Wheeler management; it reached fifty thousand circulation by 1908, and doubled that in two years more. In 1910 it absorbed *Van Norden's Magazine*, another current-affairs periodical, which had been founded in 1906. But *Current Opinion* began slipping again in 1911, and it went down steadily to less than forty thousand by the end of the war.

In 1920 there were some changes. Frank Crane, the famous preacher-journalist whose little sermons, syndicated in the newspapers, had made his name (with the "Dr." prefixed to it) known the country over, became coeditor with Wheeler, and on the latter's death two years later, editor-in-chief. Funk & Wagnalls, publishers of the *Literary Digest*, and William H. Wise & Company, book publishers, became chief owners. The price was raised to thirty-five cents, and the page size reduced again to octavo. *Democracy, A Magazine of Opinion* (1918–1920) was absorbed.

The content remained much the same. Crane's monthly moral essay occupied an introductory page; then followed eight or ten pages of portraits, and fifteen or twenty pages summarizing national and world events, illustrated by current cartoons. Then there were short pieces digesting or extracting articles, books, or plays in great variety, with a "Camera Review," the monthly short story and play, and some wit and humor at the end.

Money and effort were put into promotion, especially through the technique of college scholarships for magazine salesmen, and circulation had pulled up to nearly one hundred thousand again, when, in 1925, a merger was arranged with the *Literary Digest*. It was a fitting end.

# THE FORUM [1]

ISAAC LEOPOLD RICE was a remarkable man. Born in Germany, he was brought to America at the age of six. He early showed a talent in music, which he studied in Philadelphia, where his parents lived, and later in Paris. He taught music and languages for a short time in London, and later combined music-teaching with law studies in New York. After receiving an LL.B. degree from Columbia University, he taught law and political science in that institution, founding a "School of Political Science" there in 1882. But Rice's greatest career was probably in the practice of railroad law and the organization of corporations. It was in connection with his work with the Brooklyn Elevated Railway that he became interested in electrical invention, particularly in the transportation field; as a result he became not only a successful inventor but the manufacturer of his own machines and devices. In the latter part of his life, Rice was president of more than a score of such manufacturing companies and owner of a substantial part of the Philadelphia and Reading Railway. In this

[1] TITLES: (1) *The Forum*, 1886–June 1930, Dec. 1945–1950; (2) *Forum and Century*, July 1930–June 1940; (3) *Current History and Forum*, July 1940–June 1941; (4) *Current History*, Sept. 1941–Aug. 1945; (5) *Forum and Column Review*, Sept.–Nov. 1945.
FIRST ISSUE: March 1886. LAST ISSUE: Jan. 1950.
PERIODICITY: Monthly, March 1886–June 1902, July 1908–Jan. 1950; quarterly, July 1902–June 1908. Vols. 1–32, semiannual vols., March 1886–Feb. 1902; 33, March–June 1902; 34–39, annual vols., July 1902–April 1908; 40–62, regular semiannual vols., July 1908–Dec. 1919; 63, Jan., Feb., March, combined April–May, 1920; 64, July, combined Sept.–Oct., Nov., Dec., 1920; 65–103, regular semiannual vols., Jan. 1920–June 1940; 104, Sept.–Dec. 1945; 105–112, regular semiannual vols., Jan. 1946–Dec. 1949; 113, no. 1, Jan. 1950. Omissions: June and Aug. 1920, July 1940–Aug. 1945. In 1922 and 1923 paging is continuous through the two volumes of the year. Merged into *Current History* in July 1940; resumed as separate publication with old volume numbering Sept. 1945; again merged with *Current History* in Feb. 1950.
PUBLISHERS: Forum Publishing Company, New York, 1886–1910, 1917–40; Mitchell Kennerley, New York, 1910–16; Events Publishing Company, Philadelphia, 1945–50. (Ownership control: Isaac L. Rice, 1886–1910; George Henry Payne, 1920–23; Henry Goddard Leach, 1923–40; *Current History*, 1940–50.)
EDITORS: Lorettus Sutton Metcalf, 1886–91; Walter Hines Page, 1891–95; Alfred Ernest Keet, 1895–97; Joseph M. Rice, 1897–1907; Frederick Taber Cooper, 1907–09; Benjamin Russell Herts, 1909–10; Mitchell Kennerley, 1910–16; H. Thompson Rich, 1917–18; Edwin Wildman, 1918–20; George Henry Payne, 1920–23; Henry Goddard Leach and Frank C. Davidson, 1923–26; Henry Goddard Leach, 1926–40; Daniel George Redmond, 1945–50.
INDEXES: Index to vols. 1–32 (March 1886–Feb. 1902) compiled by Anna Lorraine Guthrie, 1902. Indexed in *Poole's Index, Readers' Guide, Engineering Index, Review of Reviews Annual Index, Annual Library Index, Cumulative Index, Jones' Legal Index, Dramatic Index.*
REFERENCES: Washington Pezet, "Forty Years of *Forum*," *Forum*, v. 75, Illustrated Section, pp. iv–xii, March 1926; "Our Thirty-Fifth Anniversary," *Forum*, v. 65, pp. 104–15, Jan. 1921; Arthur E. Bostwick, "The *Forum*," in *A Life With Men and Books* (New York, 1929).

busy life, his hobby was chess, in which he became an expert, and the inventor of the "Rice gambit."

Rice also found time to write two or three books, including *What Is Music?* as well as several articles for the *North American Review.* It was in connection with these *Review* articles that he made the acquaintance of the managing editor of the famous magazine, Lorettus Sutton Metcalf. Metcalf had conducted a string of suburban weeklies near Boston before he had joined the staff of the *North American,* then published in that city, as business manager. He had come with the review when it moved to New York, and soon became its office editor. He was an indefatigable worker, fourteen to sixteen hours usually comprising a day's work for him. But he wanted a monthly review of his own, and in Isaac L. Rice he found an "angel." In 1886 Rice organized the Forum Publishing Company, with himself as president; and as secretary he brought in an old friend and fellow student from Columbia Law School days, Nathan Bijur, then a New York lawyer and later a justice of the Supreme Court of New York.[2] The founding capital was said to be a hundred thousand dollars.[3]

The editorial policy of the new monthly review may be described by the statement of four basic principles. The first was that of the specialist writer. Metcalf conceived it to be his initial editorial duty to determine what topics were of greatest timely significance and widest public interest, and then to secure experts on those subjects to discuss them in his magazine. This resulted in a very distinguished list of contributors. The second editorial policy was that of the symposium. The *North American* had, for some years past, given both sides of controversial problems a hearing in its pages, but the *Forum* now carried the magazine debate so far as to make it almost a trade-mark. Throughout most of its hundred and twelve volumes, the *Forum* was distinguished by joint debates on all kinds of political, economic, social, religious, scientific, and educational subjects. The review's third editorial principle called for the printing, along with three or four "finished and important essays" in each number, several other articles designed to capture attention — not sensational by any means, but lighter in nature.[4] And finally, Metcalf's formula called for the meticulous and severe editing of the manuscripts of all contributors, however distinguished they might be.

It would be difficult to find a better exposition of the more serious interests of the American mind in the decade 1886 to 1896 than is

---

[2] *Journalist,* Feb. 7, 1891, p. 4.
[3] *New York Herald,* quoted in *Journalist,* v. 9, Dec. 16, 1893, p. 2.
[4] *Review of Reviews,* v. 3, p. 288, April 1891.

afforded by the first twenty volumes of the *Forum*. It would require a long catalogue even to list the varieties of interests comprised in this library of fact and opinion. Political discussion was prominent and evenly balanced in partisanship. The successive presidential canvasses and the issues involved in the hard times of the early nineties were discussed, with many articles on the tariff, free silver, labor unionism, and strikes. The progress of science and industry, education in its many phases, religious controversy, and movements in literature and the fine arts gave variety to *Forum* content.

Much space was given to reform movements. The new review was more reform-minded than the old *North American*, but less radical than a monthly review that was begun when the *Forum* was three years old, and whose title suggested a more violent attack — the *Arena*. Among the reform movements discussed in the *Forum* were prohibition, feminism, divorce, civil service, prisons, socialism, and the Australian ballot. In later decades came discussions of many other reforms — birth control, the "New Deal," revolts in the fine arts, and so on. Like the *Arena*, *Forum* issued occasional pamphlets, and in 1890–1891 a series of *Forum Extras* appeared, featuring "short studies of living problems."

Series of articles by well-known men were interesting features of the magazine. During its first year it ran a series on "How I Was Educated," by such writers as Edward Everett Hale, Timothy Dwight, Thomas Wentworth Higginson, and W. T. Harris. This was followed by one on "Books That Have Helped Me," to which Andrew Lang, A. P. Peabody, Edward Eggleston, and many others contributed. In the early nineties, another on "Formative Influences" brought W. E. H. Lecky, John Tyndall, and F. W. Farrar, as well as several American thinkers, into *Forum* pages. Then there was a series of personal defenses of creeds, called "Confessions of a Catholic," "Confessions of a Baptist," and so on, by prominent churchmen.

Though the *Forum* stuck to prose and nonfiction for more than twenty years, it gave no little attention to discussions of belles-lettres. Thomas Hardy wrote on "The Profitable Reading of Fiction" in March 1888, and the popular E. P. Roe on "Life in Fiction" the next month. Five years later F. Marion Crawford contributed his notable monograph, "The Novel — What It Is," for serial publication in the *Forum*. Edmund Gosse, Andrew Lang, Frederic Harrison, Edward Everett Hale, Charles Dudley Warner, H. H. Boyesen, and Jules Verne wrote much on literary topics.

George W. Cable contributed to the *Forum* some of those articles on the southern Negro which made him *non grata* to his fellow townsmen; and that old war horse, Albion W. Tourgée, wrote on the same topic.

Grant Allen and Lester F. Ward were among those who discussed social questions. Tyndall, Crookes, Lombroso, and many others were scientific writers for the *Forum* in its first two decades.

It was indeed a notable roll of authors. Metcalf had a predilection for United States senators, bishops, college presidents, and well-known novelists. Henry Cabot Lodge was long a faithful contributor, and such colleagues in the Senate as George F. Hoar, J. B. Foraker, and Shelby M. Cullom were with him in the *Forum*. College Presidents Charles W. Eliot, Andrew D. White, Arthur T. Hadley, and F. A. P. Barnard were frequently in *Forum* pages. Bishop A. Cleveland Coxe was in the first number, and Henry C. Potter and John H. Vincent were occasional contributors. Among the novelists who wrote articles for the *Forum* were Hamlin Garland, "Ouida," Edward Bellamy, Paul Bourget, and Elizabeth Stuart Phelps.

Metcalf had been both editor and business manager of the *Forum* for a year and a half when the modest success of the new review (about twenty thousand circulation) was believed to warrant the hiring of a man to relieve him of the burden of business management. The assistant chosen was Walter Hines Page, an energetic young newspaperman in his early thirties. Page's vigor and acumen helped make the magazine the success that it rapidly became. It seems evident that the younger man, with his eyes on the circulation curve, soon pushed the old editor, who resented business office interference, into the discard.[5] Metcalf resigned in 1891.

He had been a good editor, and had made his magazine respected, if not prosperous. The *Review of Reviews*, commenting on the *Forum* at the time of Metcalf's retirement, said:

> Many men in England have pronounced it the ablest and timeliest periodical of its class in the English language. . . . [Page] may safely follow in the general line of policy which has, in five years, brought the *Forum* to so commanding a position among periodical publications and to so strong a place as regards influence with the serious elements of the community.[6]

Metcalf belonged to the order of editor-tyrants; he was absolute dictator over his pages. An assistant editor wrote of him many years later:

> He had succeeded in assembling a notable group of contributors, including some eminent English writers; but he always gave them to understand that after he had accepted an article, it was his absolute property, to do as he liked with. On this theory he did not hesitate to make drastic changes in phraseology and grammar — always, he asserted, in the interest of clearness, which was his hobby. "What do

---

[5] Bostwick, *A Life With Men and Books*, pp. 125–26.
[6] *Review of Reviews*, v. 3, p. 288, April 1891.

you think this means?" he would ask me, reading a passage. I would tell him. "Well, why doesn't he say it plainly then? I wish you would take that passage and rewrite it so that its meaning will be clear to anyone." So I found myself correcting Edmund Gosse and Andrew Lang as if they were the twelve-year-old writers of school compositions. The victims sometimes protested mildly, but they kept on writing for the *Forum*.[7]

One reason for this insistence on clearness was the use of the *Forum* in schools and colleges. Its debates and symposiums were early found useful in connection with school exercises, and it kept its favored position in college libraries for many years.

But when Page became editor, he was not interested in the meticulous work with manuscripts that had taken so much of the time of his predecessor; and Arthur E. Bostwick, whose employment as assistant editor had been chiefly of that kind, soon found his occupation gone. Page's chief interest was in what has been pointed out above as the first plank of Metcalf's editorial platform — the enlistment of famous and expert writers to comment on significant affairs. Page also kept the second plank — the magazine-debate technique. Consequently, Page's editorship seems integral with Metcalf's, but it was more brilliant; and a greater stress on the distinguishing characteristics of the magazine, as well as a more acute sense of promotion and more insistence on timeliness, made a more attractive magazine.[8] Henry Holt, in his reminiscences, comments upon Page's editorship of the *Forum*: "the best editor that, up to that time, America had had," pontificates Holt, who was himself a *Forum* contributor.[9]

The financial stringency brought articles about the problem of poverty, agrarian discontent, and immigration. The World's Fair in Chicago was discussed, and its stimulus to interest in the fine arts is

---

[7] Bostwick in *A Life With Men and Books*, p. 118.

[8] Burton J. Hendrick, in his *The Life and Letters of Walter H. Page* (Garden City, 1922–25), 3 vols., is unfair to Metcalf. It is ungenerous to misprise the achievement of the first 18 months of the *Forum* in order to magnify that of Page. Hendrick says that the choice of a title "that was almost perfection . . . after two years of experimentation, represented about the limit of their achievement. The *Forum* had hardly made an impression on public thought and had attracted very few readers, though it had lost large sums of money for its progenitors" (v. 1, pp. 48–49). In the 18 months before Page joined the staff, the *Forum* had built up a great list of contributors, published three admirable volumes, and won no little praise. Hendrick says: "Before his [Page's] accession it had had not the slightest importance" (v. 1, p. 49). This is ridiculous. See *Review of Review's* evaluation, *supra*. Page did not invent *Forum's* editorial formula, as Hendrick would have us believe; he took it over, doubtless improving it, from Metcalf, who had it from Thorndike Rice, of the *North American Review*. Nor had the great American editors before Page all been examples of that "solemn, inaccessible high priest . . . secluded in his sanctuary" whom Hendrick cartoons so pleasantly but unjustly for his readers. Willis, Graham, Lowell, Holland, Rice, Godkin, and Howells, to name no more, had been successful editors before Page. Hendrick says further that when Page left the *Forum*, it "soon sank into an obscurity from which it has never emerged" (v. 1, p. 53). The *Forum's* high point in circulation, double that reached under Page's management, was attained 30 years later.

[9] Henry Holt, *Garrulities of an Octogenarian Editor* (Boston, 1923), p. 56.

evident. The free coinage of silver, what Bob Burdette in exasperation called "the eternal tariff," [10] and other political topics of preceding years were discussed for *Forum* readers. A student who analyzed the review's file for its first decade found about four hundred articles on economics and sociology, three hundred on politics, one hundred on education; and religion, science, history, and literature (in that order) calling for less than a hundred articles each.[11] Frederic Harrison's series on contemporary literature and art produced some criticism; it was followed by Harrison's papers on famous English authors of the nineteenth century. Theodore Roosevelt and Woodrow Wilson, Senator George F. Hoar, and Professors William P. Trent, Brander Matthews, and John Bach McMaster may be mentioned as frequent contributors.

But however assiduously Page sought famous names, the young editor did not hesitate to turn thumbs down on the contributions of seasoned statesmen and publicists when they did not fit his publishing plans or measure up to the standards he had in mind. His biographer tells the story of one editorial plan that went wrong:

One day he called in one of his associates. "Do you see that wastebasket?" he asked, pointing to a large receptacle filled to overflowing with manuscripts. "All our Cleveland articles are there!" He had gone to great trouble and expense to obtain a series of six articles from the most prominent publicists and political leaders of the country on the first year of Mr. Cleveland's second administration. It was to be the feature of the number then in preparation. "There isn't one of them," he declared, "who has got the point. I have thrown them all away, and I am going to try to write something myself." And he spent a couple of days turning out an article which aroused great public interest. When Page commissioned an article, he meant simply that he would pay full price for it; whether he would publish it depended entirely upon the quality of the material itself.[12]

The prestige of the magazine in these years was extensive. Page's biographer, who is given to superlatives, asserts that "it is doubtful if any review in English exercised so great an influence." [13] In 1893 the magazine began to show some profits.[14] But Page was disappointed in his hope of gaining financial control of Forum Publishing Company, which Isaac Rice did not care to relinquish in order to retain for the magazine the services of an energetic and successful young editor. Therefore Page left the *Forum* for the *Atlantic Monthly*, which he served first as assistant editor, and later, for a brief term, as editor.

[10] *Forum*, v. 9, p. 722, Aug. 1890.

[11] *Forum*, v. 26, p. 211, Oct. 1898.

[12] Hendrick, *The Life and Letters of Walter H. Page*, v. 1, pp. 51–52. Page's article was evidently the one in the number for April 1894 signed "An Independent." But Page did use in the May issue Governor William E. Russell's and Senator Shelby M. Cullom's articles on the subject, which, as they expressed conflicting judgments, he could set against each other in typical *Forum* debate fashion.

[13] *Ibid.*, p. 49.

[14] *New York Herald*, quoted in *Journalist*, v. 9, Dec. 16, 1893, p. 2.

After Page's departure, his assistant, Alfred Ernest Keet, carried on for a couple of years, with Frank Presbrey as publisher 1894–1896; and then Rice made his brother Joseph editor for a full decade, 1897–1907. Dr. Joseph Mayer Rice had practiced medicine in New York for eight years before he yielded to his interest in education and spent some years studying psychology and pedagogy in German universities. Some years earlier, he had written a *Forum* series on school management, which, according to the *New York Herald*, produced a "revolution" in the organization of American schools.[15] Dr. Rice was not an original or aggressive editor, but he continued the traditions of the *Forum* with respect to specialist writers and symposiums. The magazine fell short of its possibilities during the war with Spain, though imperialism and the Philippine question figured largely in its pages. It had never been strong in the field of international relations; now there was more on foreign affairs, by W. T. Stead, Charles Kendall Adams, Abraham Cahan, Prince Kropotkin, and others. The historical novel, which reached flood tide at the turn of the century, received critical attention from Brander Matthews, G. R. Carpenter, and several others. Circulation "slumped badly" in these years,[16] and by the end of Dr. Rice's editorship it probably got down to ten or fifteen thousand.

In 1902 the *Forum* became a quarterly, written, for the most part, by members of the editorial staff. Henry Litchfield West had charge of the politics; A. Maurice Low, the American correspondent of the London *Morning Post*, edited the foreign-affairs department; Alexander D. Noyes, then financial editor of the New York *Evening Post*, took care of finance and economics; Professor H. H. Supplee had the science department; Professor Ossian H. Lang dealt with educational problems; and Russell Sturgis edited the department in which he was a generally recognized authority — that of the fine arts. Literary matters were looked after successively by Frank Jewett Mather, who, in these years between a professorship of English and Romance languages at Williams and one in art and archeology at Princeton, was enjoying a flyer in New York journalism; and Professor William P. Trent, newly come to Columbia from the University of the South. First drama editor was Henry Tyrrell, a feature writer for the New York Sunday *World*; he was followed by Clayton Hamilton, then an extension lecturer for Columbia. *Forum* in these years published some articles contributed from outside this group, but the magazine was mainly staff-written as long as it was a quarterly. The plan cannot be said to have been a

---

[15] *Ibid.* These articles discussed the schools of certain large cities. They appeared in 1892–93.

[16] Pezet in *Forum*, v. 75, Ill. Sec., March 1926, p. lxxv.

success; circulation continued to decline, and the review became dull and routine-ridden.

In 1907 Frederick Taber Cooper became editor of the *Forum*. He had been a professor of Latin and Sanskrit at New York University, and later a member of that lively group which centered around Lincoln Steffens in the editorship of the New York *Commercial Advertiser*. Cooper immediately began to push the departments more or less to one side and gradually to open the pages of the review to outsiders. In 1908 he changed the magazine back to monthly publication, and introduced fiction and poetry to its pages for the first time. Joseph Conrad's "The Point of Honor" was *Forum's* first serial, and J. L. Snaith's "Araminta" followed it. William Lyon Phelps, William G. Sumner, G. K. Chesterton, and Percy Mackaye may be mentioned as contributors.

Cooper resigned in 1909, and after a brief editorship by young Benjamin Russell Herts,[17] Isaac Rice sold a controlling share of the Forum Publishing Company to Mitchell Kennerley. The new owner was English born, but had set up a publishing business in New York in 1905, when he was only twenty-seven years old. He was his own editor; and he established a new pattern for the *Forum*, making it a general magazine, with an emphasis on literature and art, rather than a review. Many of Kennerley's contributors were English, and nearly all the serial fiction was from Britain. The names of Galsworthy, Wells, Meredith, Phillpotts, and Hewlett became familiar to *Forum* readers. Among American writers, Kennerley retained few of the old stand-bys; but he had friendly recognition for the new poets and short story writers who were coming up. Thus, he published Joseph Hergesheimer's first story, Edna St. Vincent Millay's brilliant first poem "Renascence," and Vachel Lindsay's "Adventures While Preaching the Gospel of Beauty" and other early work, as well as youthful and brilliant pieces by H. L. Mencken, Sherwood Anderson, John G. Neihardt, and Witter Bynner. It was in these years that the *Forum* won a reputation for excellence in the field of the short story, which it held for more than a quarter of a century. From the point of view of belles-lettres, the dozen Kennerley volumes in the *Forum* were a distinguished contribution to the periodical literature of the years immediately preceding the First World War.

Yet the magazine still lost money, and in 1916 it came back to the Rice estate. Isaac L. Rice had died in the preceding year; but his widow, herself a writer, and his daughter strove to keep the magazine he

---

[17] He had been editor of the small magazine *Moods*, but was only 21 at the time of his *Forum* editorship. He was later well known as an interior decorator and writer.

had founded alive during the war-filled years, which were difficult for all periodicals. Paper and presswork declined in quality, but the *Forum* discussed war and politics, international relations, and literature and the arts with a good deal of competence. Such topics as the situation in the Far East and the need for airplanes received much attention. Governors wrote on war work in their respective states. United States senators were again prominent in the pages of the *Forum*, along with many professors from leading universities. The review type of article did not wholly drive out short shories and poetry. David Morton, to be long identified with the magazine, made his first appearance as a contributor of verse in these years, and Charles Henry Meltzer wrote criticism of both music and drama.

The editor for a year or two after Kennerley left was H. Thompson Rich, another of the series of youths in their twenties and early thirties who edited the *Forum* for brief terms; he was later to combine business and imaginative writing successfully. In July 1918, Edwin Wildman purchased control. Here at last was a fairly experienced writer and editor; Wildman had edited *Leslie's Weekly* for a short time and had been a war correspondent for the Hearst papers. But he was not much more successful than his immediate predecessors. He was his own editor, though F. S. McLuitock, his chief associate, was sometimes represented as holding that position.

Wildman sold his holdings to George Henry Payne in 1920. Payne had a long record of editorship of magazines and newspapers, and of activity in New York politics. His short editorship saw a strong emphasis on foreign life, literature, and affairs. Such notable writers from overseas as Viscount J. B. S. Haldane, Lady Astor, Arthur Symons, Prince Bibesco, Rolandi Ricci, Stephane Lauzanne, and Edouard Herriot contributed to the *Forum* in the early twenties. In spite of the fact that Payne had been an ardent admirer and friend of Theodore Roosevelt, he seems to have been an economic conservative as an editor, and Frank A. Vanderlip, Otto H. Kahn, and others wrote for big business without challenge or rebuttal. Bolshevism was attacked, and so was the Einstein theory.

A brilliant and successful era came with the purchase of a controlling interest by Henry Goddard Leach. The new owner and editor had been an English instructor at Harvard, and later secretary of the American-Scandinavian Foundation. He immediately resumed the old Metcalf symposium technique with which the *Forum* had won its first success. Under the magazine's name plate he printed this statement: "A nonpartisan magazine of free discussion. It aims to interpret the new

America that is attaining consciousness in this decade. The *Forum* gives both sides. Whatever is attacked by contributors this month may be praised in later issues."

For example, Leach had a symposium on fundamentalism, in which the debaters were William J. Bryan and Newell Dwight Hillis. There was one on modernizing the Monroe Doctrine, in which General C. H. Sherrill said "aye" and Ernest Gruening said "nay." "Was Lenin a Failure?" was debated by Pitirim Sorokin and Anna Louise Strong. The chairman of the national Republican and Democratic committees, John Taylor Adams and Cordell Hull, debated the tariff in the campaign year of 1924. Later air power, cubism, birth control, the possibility of war with Japan, and many other diverse topics were debated in the magazine. Arthur Train took the affirmative of the question, "Can a Rich Man Be Convicted?" and Upton Sinclair the negative. Bertrand Russell maintained that companionate marriage was moral, and Professor William McDougall denied it. One of the hottest debates of all was on a subject that had been argued in the early issues of the *Forum* — Roman Catholicism in America, with Michael Williams on one side and John Jay Chapman on the other, followed by reverberations later.

Leach revived another Metcalf technique when he brought famous contributors together in less controversial series, such as the one on "What Is Civilization?" Dhan Gopal Mukerji gave India's answer, W. E. B. DuBois spoke for Africa, Paul Shorey proposed the Age of Pericles, Maurice Maeterlinck wrote about ancient Egypt, and so on. A literary series was one in which William Lyon Phelps, Arthur Symons, and others named and commented upon "The Fifteen Finest Novels." There was an "Americana" series — bits of American history and biography — and "New Trends in the Theater" discussed current drama in various countries. Reminiscent of early *Forum* years was the sequence that began with G. K. Chesterton's "Why I Am a Catholic," to be followed by such articles as Rufus M. Jones's "Why I Am a Quaker" and Senator Reed Smoot's "Why I Am a Mormon." An interesting series was one called "Definitions," in which well-known writers attempted to clarify the meaning of such words as Americanism, socialism, humor, and immorality. Contests for best definitions were thrown open to readers. But one of the most distinguished of all *Forum* series was the "Living Philosophies" symposium, later brought together in book form,[18] which began in September 1929 with Bertrand Russell's article and was followed by thoughtful essays by Robert A. Millikan, Theodore Dreiser, Irving Babbitt, John Dewey, Dean W. R. Inge, and many others.

[18] *Living Philosophies* (New York, 1931).

In belles-lettres the *Forum* of the twenties was stronger than ever. Most of the contemporary minor poets were represented from time to time. In 1925 a poetry department was begun, edited by Walter S. Hinchman, critic and poet, who was then teaching English at Milton Academy in Massachusetts. The magazine printed some good short stories in the twenties, by Luigi Pirandello, John Galsworthy, Roark Bradford, Rupert Hughes, Fanny Hurst, Willa Cather, Christopher Morley, and others. Its first fiction serial since the days of Kennerley's editorship was Anne Douglas Sedgwick's "The Little French Girl," which was followed by Hamilton Gibbs's "Sundings," Llewellyn Hughes's "Seven Sisters," and so on. Such biographical serials as Emil Ludwig's "Wilhelm Hohenzollern," André Maurois's "Disraeli," Anatole France's "Rabelais," and Constantine Stanislavski's "My Life in Art" gave variety and quality to the *Forum* of the twenties. Book reviews were by a staff of distinguished critics, American and English.

By the middle of the decade, line-cuts were being used freely to open up the pages (which, in the old *Forum* tradition, had been consistently dull-looking), articles were shorter, and the magazine as a whole became more attractive in appearance. Series of block cuts by various artists were reproduced in nearly every number. In 1929 the page was enlarged to small-quarto size, some color was introduced, and improved typographical treatment made the book far more inviting to the eye than it had ever been before.

Circulation had responded to Leach's diligence and skill. When he took the magazine over, it had a little over two thousand distribution.[19] The increase was very slow for the first few years, but by the end of the twenties it had reached the highest point in its history, ninety-two thousand. But for the financial crash of 1929, it would no doubt have continued the rise on which it was well started.

As they did to all periodicals, the depression thirties offered an uphill drag to the *Forum*. The purchase of the list and good will of the *Century Magazine* in 1930 did not help much. The *Century* had a history even more distinguished than that of the *Forum*, but it had been failing long before the depression struck. Usually the combination of two magazines that are on the toboggan only makes the ride the faster.

But the *Forum and Century* was a good magazine in the thirties. John Maynard Keynes's "Causes of World Depression" and Charles A. Beard's "A Five-Year Plan for America" were outstanding articles for 1931. The National Recovery Administration and the New Deal were focal points of argumentative writing in the magazine, and a department called "Calendar of Controversy" presumed to settle each month

[19] Leon Whipple, "The Revolution in Quality Street," *Survey*, v. 57, p. 469, Jan. 1, 1927.

a dozen major and minor disputes which had arisen the country over. Prominent contributors were André Maurois, G. K. Chesterton, Hendrik Willem Van Loon, James Truslow Adams, Jay Franklin, and Paul Hutchinson. Mary M. Colum conducted a good book review department, while Ralph M. Pearson wrote on art and Harry J. Price conducted a section that was a lure for travel advertising. The *Forum* quiz page followed a current style.

Editor Leach had an abiding interest in young authors, and especially in amateur writers of short stories and verse. He attended the summer "conferences" and "workshops" of amateur writers, and was at one time president of the Poetry Society of America. In the *Forum* he set up contests for beginning writers. In the field of short fiction, especially, these contests resulted in the publication of some very good material, and a number of writers who later gained wide recognition made their first appearances in the pages of *Forum*. But the amateur magazine is never the popular magazine, and the paucity of top names in the *Forum* in 1939–1940 gave notice of impending disaster. Circulation had sunk to thirty-three thousand in 1935; and though it had managed an upward curve thereafter, the going was too heavy.

In July 1940, the *Forum* was sold to *Current History*, a magazine that had originally been published by the New York *Times* but had changed hands twice in the thirties. *Current History and Forum* had few characteristics of the elder journal, but it did keep vestiges of the form of the magazine debate. It was soon sold to *Events*, a monthly review of foreign affairs published at Scotch Plains, New Jersey, which was immediately absorbed into *Current History*. In the fall of 1945, Events Publishing Company bought *Column Review*, a pocket-sized monthly that reprinted "columns" from the newspapers; then, splitting off the *Forum* from its own entity, it made a new combination magazine, the *Forum and Column Review*, published in Philadelphia. For this periodical it resumed the old *Forum* numbering, which had ended with the respectable volume number of CIII. After a few months the title was simplified to *Forum*.

This postscript to the file contains articles on important public matters by little-known writers, selections from newspaper columns by somewhat more celebrated authors, a poetry department by David Morton, one on books by Jasper R. Lewis, and one on the theater by John Gassner, together with a news summary. There was a monthly debate — an informative but routine performance by hack writers. In 1948 the magazine increased its page size to small-quarto, dropped its column reprints, and introduced a few line-cuts. But it kept the same staff writers and much the same policy as in its former series. The editor,

D. G. Redmond, an experienced publisher, was part-owner, but the chief mortgagee was Shelby Cullom Davis, the financier and writer, whose holdings dated from the *Current History* phase.

It seems a pity that the *Forum* could not have died peacefully in 1940. The admirer of a magazine that has once enjoyed something of greatness hates to see it kicked around as the football of foredoomed failures; but that happens to many old magazines. In its best days — in the editorships of Metcalf, Page, Kennerley, and Leach — the *Forum* made an admirable contribution to free and open discussion of great public questions. Its many volumes, most of them fat and full, contain much that is of comparatively permanent value.

# JOURNAL OF THE AMERICAN MEDICAL ASSOCIATION [1]

THE first definite action in the chain of events that led to the formation of the American Medical Association was the adoption by the Medical Society of the State of New York in February 1844 of a resolution offered by Dr. Nathan Smith Davis looking toward educational reforms. Davis was then a young practicing physician of Binghamton, New York; later he became dean of the medical school at Northwestern University. His historic resolution demanded a national convention to consider standards of medical education and licensure. Such a convention assembled at New York University on May 5, 1846, and it issued a call for the organization of a national association of physicians to meet at Philadelphia just a year later. At that time and place the American Medical Association was founded.[2]

The proceedings, including papers read at each annual meeting, appeared in a yearly volume of *Transactions*, published by C. B. Norton, of New York. In these volumes, issued from 1848 to 1882 and now much neglected, appeared many important early papers on anesthesia, medical botany, endemic and epidemic diseases, hygiene and sanitation, and so on.

But it was soon recognized that annual volumes were inadequate to keep up with medical progress. The current medical journals, of which there were many, quarterly, monthly, and weekly,[3] were, on the whole, a decentralizing factor; the association needed its own journal if it was

[1] TITLE: *Journal of the American Medical Association.*
FIRST ISSUE: July 14, 1883. Current.
PERIODICITY: Weekly. Vols. 1–117 (July 1883–Dec. 1941), 2 vols. yearly; 118–current (Jan. 1942–current), 3 vols. yearly.
PUBLISHER: American Medical Association, Chicago.
EDITORS: Nathan Smith Davis, July 1883–Dec. 1888; John Brown Hamilton, Jan. 5–Feb. 9, 1889, July 1893–Dec. 1898; Board of Trustees (with assistance of N. S. Davis), Feb. 16–June 19, 1889; John Hamilcar Hollister (acting), June 26, 1889–Dec. 1890; James Coe Culbertson, Jan. 1891–June 1893; Truman W. Miller (acting), Dec. 20, 1898–Feb. 25, 1899; George Henry Simmons, March 1, 1899–Nov. 15, 1924; Morris Fishbein, Nov. 22, 1924–Nov. 26, 1950; Austin Smith, Dec. 3, 1950–current.
INDEXES: Vols. 1–24, 1883–1906 (Chicago, 1906); vols. 25–49, 1906–19 (Chicago, 1919); indexed in *Index Medicus, Quarterly Cumulative Index Medicus.*
REFERENCE: Morris Fishbein, *A History of the American Medical Association, 1847–1947* (Philadelphia, 1947); part of it published serially in *JAMA*, vols. 132–33, Nov. 16, 1946–March 29, 1947.
[2] N. S. Davis, "A Brief History of the Origin of the American Medical Association," *JAMA*, v. 28, pp. 1115–17, June 12, 1897; Lewis S. McMurtry, "The American Medical Association: Its Origin, Progress, and Purpose" (presidential address), *JAMA*, v. 45, pp. 145–49, July 15, 1905; Fishbein, *History of the A.M.A.*, pp. 21–26.
[3] See pp. 312–16.

to draw the profession together effectively. The first suggestion for more frequent publication of the A.M.A.'s papers was made by Dr. J. B. Flint, of Kentucky, in 1852. But, as a later president of the association observed,

> It required years for this proposition to come into effect; and when finally, largely through the efforts of N. S. Davis, the Society voted to journalize its *Transactions*, many had serious doubts as to the outcome.[4]

In 1882 the association set up a Board of Trustees to take the responsibility for its *Journal*. It was natural that Davis, father of the association, should be the first editor. Thus the *Journal of the American Medical Association* began July 14, 1883 (a week later than had been planned), as a thirty-two page quarto priced at five dollars a year, a subscription being included in the dues of each regular member of the A.M.A. It started with a circulation of about thirty-five hundred [5] and with a fair advertising patronage.

A subtitle pointed out that the new publication included "the Official Record of the Proceedings" of the national association, with "Papers Presented in the Several Sections" in which the annual conventions were organized. But an editorial said, "We shall need many original papers besides those coming through the National Association, and we specially invite favors in this direction." [6] Most papers of the latter class which *JAMA* published were, naturally, studies that had been presented to local medical societies throughout the country. An early department, later absorbed into other sections of the journal, was called "Medical Progress," and consisted of short quotations from other periodicals, at home and abroad, concerning new developments in medicine, surgery, and so on. Other departments contained proceedings of local and regional societies, news letters from various cities at home and abroad, book reviews, and necrology. Editorials occupied a page or two, and commented on a diversity of subjects. There were discussions of medical education, advocacy of pure drug legislation, continuing attacks upon the Keeley Cure for alcoholism, condemnation of the practice of docking horses' tails, defense of "animal experimentation," talk about the doctor and politics, propaganda for a Department of Health with a Secretary in the President's Cabinet, and comments on new trends and developments scientific and professional. The guerilla warfare between doctors and newspapers, based on mutual lack of understanding and tolerance, was

---

[4] Nicholas Senn, presidential address, *JAMA*, v. 28, p. 1057, June 5, 1897; Fishbein, *History of the A.M.A.*, pp. 106, 108–09.

[5] *JAMA*, v. 1, p. 730, Dec. 29, 1883.

[6] *JAMA*, v. 1, p. 29, July 14, 1883.

perennial. Occasionally the *Journal's* own editorial omniscience faltered, as in a piece favoring the view of a parasitic origin of cancer.[7]

Dr. Davis was editor of the *Journal* for a little more than five years, during which the circulation went up to five thousand. Advertising, however, was disappointing. Davis had counted on about five thousand dollars a year from that source,[8] but only about half that much came in the first year.[9] At the outset, the Board of Trustees had laid down the rule:

> Advertisements from all medical educational institutions and hospitals open for clinical instruction, from book publishers, pharmaceutists, instrument-makers, and all other legitimate business interests [may be solicited]. But all advertisements of proprietary, trade-mark, copyrighted, or patent medicines should be excluded.[10]

But adherence to such fine principles was difficult. Davis was succeeded by three editors serving less than three years each, and the *Journal* declined in both circulation and advertising. The financial uncertainties of the early nineties and the panic of 1893 were reflected in its business. In 1892 the editor defended the advertising of proprietary medicines in his *Journal* on the ground that most physicians were prescribing them anyway.[11] Two years later it was pointed out that the loss of patent medicine advertising would cost the *Journal* about eight thousand dollars a year.[12] There was much objection on the part of members of the association to this flouting of the medical code, with its rule against secret formulas and cures; and by 1895 the board was forced to adopt the policy of refusing all patent medicine advertising the order for which was not accompanied by a statement of the formula.[13] This lost the *Journal* four thousand dollars per year in revenue,[14] but was one of the reforms that gained greater acceptance for it and put it on the high road to success by the close of the century.

But the early nineties were dangerous years for the American Medical Association. There was much agitation for the removal of the headquarters to Washington. New York medical organizations were unfriendly and intransigent. There was much opposition to the code of ethics. Many eastern physicians thought the specialists' societies

---

[7] *JAMA*, v. 20, p. 399, April 8, 1893.
[8] *JAMA*, v. 1, p. 23, July 14, 1883.
[9] Thomas R. Gardiner, "The Business Department of the American Medical Association," in Fishbein, *History of the A.M.A.*, p. 981.
[10] *Ibid.*, p. 980.
[11] *JAMA*, v. 18, pp. 685–86, May 28, 1892.
[12] *JAMA*, v. 22, p. 958, June 23, 1894. This is a quotation from the *American Lancet* about *Journal* affairs.
[13] Fishbein, *History of the A.M.A.*, p. 169. The *Journal* had begun demanding formulas as early as 1892.
[14] *Ibid.*, p. 182.

and publications superior to the A.M.A. and its weekly. No doubt the *Journal* of the national association lacked breadth and thoroughness; it was missing some major discoveries and important new treatments in the medical field.[15]

In July 1893 Dr. John Brown Hamilton, former Surgeon General of the Marine Hospital Service and a famous sanitarian, became editor of the *Journal*. He had held that position for a few weeks early in 1889, but had resigned it to give his full attention to his duties with the government. During his five-year term of editorship, the *Journal* improved editorially and prospered financially. The page size had already been increased slightly, and the number of pages grew year by year to seventy-eight and the circulation to well over ten thousand. The editorial scope broadened. To the subtitle were now added the words "Together with the Medical Literature of the Period," and abstracts of papers from other journals became increasingly important.

At the beginning of the Spanish-American War, the *Journal* urged doctors to volunteer for service in camp and field. War correspondence by Lieutenant Colonel Nicholas Senn, then Chief Surgeon of the Sixth Army Corps, made an important contribution in 1898; and there was much other military and naval news and comment.

Hamilton died in the last week of 1898; and shortly thereafter George Henry Simmons, English-born physician and surgeon from Lincoln, Nebraska, became editor of the *Journal*—a position he retained for a quarter of a century. During the first half of this term he was also general secretary of the association. In these two positions he gave the medical profession of the United States intelligent and aggressive leadership. The *Journal* was now illustrated by halftones (from the first there had been some line-cuts: diagrams, charts, and so on), and soon there was occasional illustration in color. News of local and state associations was still important, "Clinical Reports" became a leading department, abstracts of medico-legal decisions were regularly printed, "Current Medical Literature" was the name of an improved digest of papers from other journals, and a new department of queries and answers was begun. The annual preconvention number was still a *Journal* highlight, there were yearly reports on such topics as medical education and hospitals, and a supplement to the number for May 27, 1899, was filled with articles on medical progress to celebrate the association's semicentennial. The weekly numbers now carried over a hundred pages, and advertising was excellent.

The efforts of Dr. Simmons, his assistant, Dr. Edward Everett Hyde, and the business manager, Will C. Braun, brought an immediate in-

[15] *Ibid.*, p. 154.

crease in the *Journal's* circulation, which by 1900 had passed fifteen thousand and stood at double the membership of the association.

Such a situation obviously indicated the necessity of some promotion of A.M.A. membership, and the reorganization of 1900–1901 followed, with its reform of representation of state societies in the association. The integration of county, state and national societies, promoted by a traveling organizer, eventually resulted in the growth of probably the most powerful professional association in the world. The *Journal* was its official mouthpiece, extremely important to all its activities; and it became, with the growth in membership and consequent increase in circulation, advertising, and prestige, the great financial mainstay and money-maker of the association. It was the income from the *Journal* which enabled the A.M.A. to purchase its own home in Chicago in 1902, and later to build larger and finer quarters for its business. It was chiefly the *JAMA*, too, which supported the less remunerative special journals of the association, which began with the *Journal of Internal Medicine* in 1907 and by the 1940's numbered nine.

In its issue for April 21, 1900, the *Journal* printed the first install-ment of a serial article entitled "Relations of Pharmacy to the Medi-cal Profession." In the second part of the series Castoria and Syrup of Figs were mildly but firmly "exposed." This was the first of the attacks on patent medicines and quack practitioners that became so common later. In 1901 a new formula was found for the exclusion of undesir-able drug advertising when the *JAMA* announced that it would no longer insert announcements of medicines that advertised in the newspapers.

In 1905, the year in which *Collier's* joined the *Ladies' Home Journal* in its crusade against quack medicines with the first of those Adams exposés which were later published under the title, *The Great American Fraud*,[16] the American Medical Association created its Council on Pharmacy and Chemistry as a "reference committee" to examine and report upon medicines and drugs.[17] But it was not until about two years later that all *Journal* advertising of proprietary medicines and drugs was subjected to the approval of this council.[18] Thus, although the *JAMA* was apparently the first magazine to attack patent medi-cines specifically and systematically, it did not find an acceptable method of purifying its own columns until after the passage of the Federal Food and Drug Act of 1906.

An additional source of advertising revenue was found in the advent

[16] See p. 460.
[17] Fishbein, *History of the A.M.A.*, pp. 865–86.
[18] *Ibid.*, p. 297.

of the automobile. The *Journal's* first automotive number was issued April 9, 1910; it carried many pictures, together with stories of doctors' experiences with the new means of transportation.

Under Simmons, the *Journal* achieved a greater variety than it had known before. Then and later there were those who complained of frivolity in the magazine's austere columns; but with numbers running to 136 pages and more, there was room, at least among the advertisements, for a department of wit and humor. The first jokes in *JAMA* were those scattered in the "Miscellany" in 1893. Ten years later came "Clippings from Lay Exchanges," which specialized in funny errors found in newspapers. Then came "Knocks and Boosts," and finally, in 1913, the *Journal's* famous "Tonics and Sedatives." This last was filled with doctors' humor; and if a lay reader has occasionally been shocked by these anecdotes, it has served him right for reading a doctors' journal.

In the First World War, Editor Simmons was a major in the Medical Reserve Corps, served in the Personnel Division, and later received a Distinguished Service Medal in recognition of his patriotic work. Meantime, Dr. Morris Fishbein, who had succeeded Dr. Hyde as assistant editor on the latter's death in 1913, carried on with vigor and ability. Doctors were urged to volunteer for the medical corps. Continuous effort was exerted to obtain more influence by medical officers on the policies governing the regulations as to the health and physical welfare of the men in the services. Coöperation with medical draft boards was a constant topic. A list of doctors in service was published in the number of June 1, 1918. There was a series of articles by Colonel E. W. McKnight on "The Medical Officer," and a regular department began April 14, 1917, under the heading "Medical Mobilization."

When Simmons resigned his editorship in 1924, on account of declining health, he left the *Journal of the American Medical Association* with a circulation of eighty thousand and a patronage that brought in about fifteen hundred pages of advertising a year. It should be pointed out that after the reorganization of 1901, a subscription to the *JAMA* was not a part of a doctor's dues to any association. A doctor belonged to a local or county association, which sent delegates to a state association; and state societies sent representatives to the House of Delegates of the American Medical Association, which became the national policy-making body. The individual doctor paid dues to county or state societies, but not to the A.M.A. But, without the crutch afforded so many association journals by the subscription-with-dues plan, *JAMA* long before Simmons' retirement had reached a distribution far beyond that of any other medical journal in the world. In the early nineties *JAMA* had quoted the *British Medical Journal* as the "king" in its class, but that time was long past. As early as 1905, A.M.A. President Lewis S. McMurtry dared to say of the *JAMA*: "In all that a great weekly medical journal should be, it has no superior in the world." [19]

Dr. Morris Fishbein, who succeeded Simmons as editor, had come to the *Journal* directly from medical college. For more than a decade he had served as assistant to Simmons, and he had taken more and more responsibility as his chief's health deteriorated. Fishbein was a facile writer, and a forceful, dominating personality. He was sincerely devoted to the American Medical Association and its *Journal*. He was self-confident and gregarious, making both friends and enemies readily. His friends thought that he was a genius as writer, speaker, and leader; his enemies thought him insufferably conceited and incredibly short-sighted.[20]

Fishbein's twenty-six-year editorship of the *Journal* was exciting throughout. Highlights were the running warfare with quacks and quackery, the bitter debate over the relations of the doctors with the situation which arose under the Prohibition Amendment, the problems of a depression economy, the activities of a Second World War, and the great campaign against "socialized medicine."

Fishbein followed the Simmons technique of exposing bad medicines and charlatans with enthusiasm, showing himself more belligerent than his predecessor. Some of these articles had provoked libel suits — notably, one about Wine of Cardui, which a jury in 1916 had found to be libelous and to have damaged the plaintiff to the extent of one cent. Both sides accepted this as a victory — an expensive one for the A.M.A., which was taxed with the costs. Two years later the *Journal* was defendant in six more libel suits, totaling $600,000.[21] But this was only a beginning. Fishbein wrote in 1947 that shortly after he "assumed the editorship of the *Journal of the American Medical Association* and undertook an active campaign against quacks, frauds, and nostrums of many types, libel suits began to multiply." [22] By 1938 the association was defending libel suits totaling $3,500,000; [23] in 1940 it was defending $4,500,000 worth of such actions.[24] One of the most famous of these suits was that brought by John R. Brinkley, the goat-gland man, of Kansas and later of Mexico. When the suit came to trial in 1939, how-

---

[19] McMurtry in *JAMA*, v. 45, p. 146, July 15, 1905. *JAMA* stopped its complimentary references to *BMJ* when its English cousin attempted some competitive promotion (see *JAMA*, v. 21, p. 1013, Dec. 20, 1893). *JAMA* passed *BMJ* in the circulation race in 1900.

[20] See Howard Whitman, "Doctors in an Uproar," second of two-part article, *Collier's*, v. 123, May 21, 1949, pp. 21ff; *American Mercury*, v. 70, pp. 182–87, Feb. 1950; Milton Mayer, "The Rise and Fall of Dr. Fishbein," *Harper's Magazine*, v. 199, Nov. 1949, pp. 76–85.

[21] Fishbein, *History of the A.M.A.*, p. 304.

[22] *Ibid.*, p. 499.

[23] *Ibid.*, p. 435.

[24] *Ibid.*, p. 454.

ever, it was not based on the *Journal* exposé but on an article in *Hygeia,* a popular health magazine published by the A.M.A. and edited by Fishbein. Brinkley lost his case, as Norman Baker, the Iowa cancer doctor who utilized the radio to obtain customers, had already lost his in 1931. Then there were "Painless" Parker, the California dentist, who filed suit for $100,000 in 1935 and later withdrew it; Hirestra Laboratories, whose suits totaled $7,000,000, and were also dropped; Dinshah P. Ghadiali, whose suits to protect the good name of "Spectro-Chrome Therapy" did not come to trial before the plaintiff's conviction under the Mann Act, and so on.

During the years that the country lived, worked, and played under the Eighteenth Amendment, physicians were embarrassed by the difficulty of obtaining alcohol for therapeutic purposes. A minority of A.M.A. members repeatedly proposed resolutions in the House of Delegates declaring that alcohol was unnecessary, but one of the association's committees in 1923 induced the Commissioner of Internal Revenue to facilitate procurement of whisky bottled in bond for prescription purposes. Thenceforward the *Journal* was active in movements to discipline physicians who abused this privilege. It made a practice of printing the names of doctors whose licenses to prescribe liquor had been revoked.

When Hitler loosed the dogs of war in Europe, the American Medical Association was fully aware of the dangers and implications of the situation. As early as 1939 it offered its files and lists of physicians to the government for mobilization purposes. It coöperated actively with the Red Cross and with draft boards. The *Journal* began a section entitled "Medical Preparedness" in 1941, and later carried a news department entitled "Medicine and the War." Editorially it was much concerned with the recruitment of doctors, and with regulations to prevent a future shortage of medical service by allowing medical students to complete their courses. Later there was much about the postwar problems of medicine. National shortages of paper and labor affected *JAMA*, as they did all publications in 1942–1946; but the association published a special journal, *War Medicine*, 1941–1945, under Fishbein's editorship.

What later came to be called "socialized medicine" and "state medicine" had been discussed in the *Journal* occasionally and without heat for many years before it became a bitterly controversial issue. Dr. J. Berrien Lindsley, writing on "State Medicine" in the number for July 2, 1892, thought there should be more of it; and that was the general idea behind the A.M.A. Section on State Medicine and its continuous advocacy of a Secretary of Health in the President's Cabinet.

But by far the most important of the discussions of national health systems was the one which was presented to the House of Delegates in 1917 by Dr. Alexander Lambert, chairman of a new Committee on Social Insurance, and which occupied thirty-four pages in the *Journal*. This report contained not only a survey of health, old age, and unemployment insurance in European countries, but also advocated such measures for the United States. The report concluded:

> The profession can, through its influence on the community, prevent for a time these laws being passed, and it can, by a refusal to cooperate, still further retard them; but in the end the social forces that demand these laws, and demand an improvement in the social existence of the great mass of the nation, will indignantly force a recalcitrant profession to accept that which is unjust to it and that which is to its detriment.
>
> The profession today, in certain states, is acting the part that our schoolboy history showed of old King Canute sitting on the seashore bidding the rising tide to stop. And King Canute only got wet for his trouble.[25]

The report was adopted by the House of Delegates, including its resolution to "cooperate, when possible, in the molding of these laws." The next year many committee and council members were absent from the annual meeting on war duty, and proceedings were routine in nature; but Dr. Lambert was elected president of the association. At the general meeting in 1919 the committee's report, instead of being adopted, was referred to another committee and recommended for general study. Meantime various state associations were coming out strongly against "compulsory contributory insurance against illness," and in 1920 the House of Delegates by resolution adopted that position.

The association now gave much attention to "The War Against Socialized Medicine." At the 1925 meeting, Dr. J. Basil Hall, president of the British Medical Association, addressed the House of Delegates. He spoke of "state service — a condition of things we abhorred," and appealed for united action of the medical associations of the two nations. The A.M.A. and its *Journal* now bitterly opposed all governmental proposals looking toward the furnishing of further medical service by the state — the Sheppard-Towner Act for maternity care, legislation for complete medical care of veterans, and poor-relief service.

In the last-named field was the Federal Emergency Relief Administration established by Congress in May 1933. The Judicial Council of the A.M.A. was much concerned over this "invasion" of "basic beliefs and principles of the medical profession"; and though it did not call for a sit-down strike, it did cite the example of some societies that had

[25] *JAMA*, v. 68, p. 1755, June 9, 1917.

refused coöperation. The F.E.R.A., a depression measure, was viewed by the *Journal* as a "gradual extension of medical practice into a function of government bureaucracy." [26] But the attitude changed somewhat as the membership became aware of the desperate nature of the depression, both in the impoverishment of the profession and the sufferings of the very poor. The problem of the costs of medical service was recognized by many as central in the whole matter of "state medicine." In 1932 the Committee on Costs of Medical Care, headed by Dr. Ray Lyman Wilbur, made a report favoring voluntary group medical insurance. This report, Dr. Fishbein said in an editorial in the *Journal*, spoke for "the forces representing the great foundations, public health officialdom, social theory — even socialism and communism — inciting to revolution." [27] At the Milwaukee meeting the next year President-elect Dean Lewis, though severe on propagandists for state medicine, thought a reduction of the costs of medical service was important:

> In some ways the Depression has rendered a great service, as it has been demonstrated that . . . the cost of medical service may be greatly reduced and the quality maintained. . . . Simplification of medical practice should be the aim of this organization. Such simplicity will mean a limitation of specialism and the reduction of specialists.[28]

"Socialization Battle Intensifies" reads the caption over Fishbein's annals of the A.M.A. for 1930–1934. And so it did, up to the beginning of World War II, indeed. The fight became thoroughly political, and Republican Candidate Alfred M. Landon was a speaker at the Milwaukee meeting in 1936, declaring his opposition to "state medicine." The *Journal's* unfavorable verdict on the Wilbur Committee's recommendation of group health insurance was shared by the articulate majority of association members, and such movements were included in the hateful term "socialized medicine." Doctors sometimes refused to service such organizations. When Group Health Association, Inc., was set up in 1937 by some twenty-five hundred government employees in Washington, it was boycotted by the Medical Society of the District of Columbia, a unit of the A.M.A., and the next year the Attorney General brought suit against the District Society, the American Medical Association, Dr. Morris Fishbein, and other officials of the organizations named, under the Sherman Anti-Trust Act, for conspiracy in restraint of trade. The Federal grand jury found a true bill, the trial was held in 1941 with much publicity, and the associations were convicted and

[26] *JAMA*, v. 101, p. 2054, Dec. 23, 1933.
[27] *JAMA*, v. 99, p. 1952, Dec. 3, 1932.
[28] *JAMA*, v. 100, p. 2021, June 4, 1933.

fined while the individuals indicted were acquitted. The decision was later upheld by the Supreme Court.

Thereafter the American Medical Association gradually receded from its position against voluntary group insurance, but it intensified its crusade in opposition to "compulsory insurance" against sickness, and "state medicine." Bad public relations, stemming not only from publicity on the Federal prosecution, but also from the aggressiveness — termed "arrogance" by its critics — of what was now frequently called the "Medical Trust" came to be recognized as a crucial problem. "Authors whose mental processes seem to have been influenced by Moscow or Berlin have written volumes of destructive criticism concerning the policies of the American Medical Association," said Dr. Nathan B. Van Etten in the presidential address of 1941.[29] In 1946 a high-priced public relations man was hired; but as soon as he discovered he was not to be allowed to work on a policy-making level, he resigned.

Dr. Fishbein was really the public relations counsel of the American Medical Association. Some called him "The Voice of A.M.A.," and some "Mr. Medicine." During his quarter-century with the association, he wrote more than a score of books, delivered innumerable speeches from platform and broadcasting booth, and furnished syndicated columns to newspapers and magazines, besides writing editorials and overseeing the publication of A.M.A.'s many periodicals. A bald, stocky, talkative man, he always came out of his corner fighting. His last big campaign was the one against the Wagner-Murray-Dingell Bill for a Federal medical-care program. It was the biggest propaganda crusade of his career, but he was not permitted to remain general-in-charge long enough to see the defeat of the measure he fought. With victory pretty well insured, the Board of Trustees summarily dismissed Fishbein.

The belligerent editor and spokesman had made many enemies. "You've got to get people mad at you in this job," he told one interviewer. "I have the best list of enemies in the country." [30] But more and more of these enemies came to be found in the ranks of the doctors. For at least ten years before the editor was fired, some state delegation — more often California than not — would lead a fight against him at the annual meetings. In 1949 the fight was successful. To many observers it seemed clear that Fishbein, who had got himself hated for his tireless and tiresome devotion to A.M.A. causes, had been sacrificed paradoxically to the cause of better public relations.[31]

[29] *JAMA*, v. 116, p. 2695, June 14, 1941.
[30] Whitman in *Collier's*, v. 123, May 21, 1949, p. 21.
[31] *Time*, v. 53, June 20, 1949, p. 50; *American Mercury*, v. 70, p. 182, Feb. 1950.

When Fishbein was supplanted as editor by Dr. Austin Smith, the *Journal of the American Medical Association* was in excellent condition. It had a circulation of one hundred thirty-five thousand, said to amount to more than the lists of all other weekly medical journals in the world put together,[32] and only five thousand less than the total membership of the association. It was issuing some one hundred fifty pages a week, about half advertising. Distributors of medicines, pharmaceuticals, foods, and physical equipment were able to buy space in the *JAMA* only after the appropriate councils had made laboratory tests and given them the "Seal of Acceptance," and thus much advertising was refused; but there was plenty, and at a good price.

With Fishbein the *Journal* lost the occasional hard-punching editorial, the chatty and too personal "Dr. Pepys' Diary," and a dominant and ebullient editorship. Editor Smith was as retiring and self-effacing as his name. Editorials dealt with scientific matters, and for a time they were signed by well-known physicians. Association presidents, who had formerly been overshadowed by the editor, now had a page (or two pages) of their own, in which they discussed A.M.A. affairs, professional life and ethics, and the eternal issue of "socialized medicine." The editor's former function, partly official and partly self-assumed, was now taken over by the large and expensive Department of Public Relations first set up late in 1948 and now operating in the secretary's office with the aid of professional publicity men.[33]

Under Smith, the *Journal* was handsomer than ever. It was crammed with original articles, clinical notes, special reports of councils and committees, news of meetings and organizations, abstracts of medical literature, queries and answers, news from abroad and from Washington, etc., etc. General approval by the profession was indicated by the fact that circulation in the early fifties advanced to over one hundred sixty thousand.

But for a quotation with which to sum up the influence and intention of the *JAMA*, we turn back to Fishbein:

The *Journal* has been the life-blood and the heart of the American Medical Association. Its earnings have paid not only its own expenses, but those of the Association as well. . . . It has been the powerful voice of the medical profession in raising the standards of medical education, investigating the preparation and composition of drugs, . . . and campaigning for the advancement of medical science and medical care. . . .[34]

[32] Whitman in *Collier's*, v. 123, May 21, 1949, p. 58.
[33] *JAMA*, v. 148, pp. 1129–30, March 29, 1952.
[34] Fishbein, *History of the A.M.A.*, p. 249.

## THE LADIES' HOME JOURNAL [1]

IN 1876 Cyrus Hermann Kotzschmar Curtis, then a young man of twenty-six, moved his story paper and miscellany called *The People's Ledger* (1872–1879) from Boston to Philadelphia. It was the year of the centennial, and Philadelphia seemed a kind of national capital; besides, printing costs were lower there.[2] But Curtis saw that the *Ledger* was not going to make him rich; and he sold it in 1878, founding a farm family paper at fifty cents a year under the name *Tribune and Farmer* (1879–1885) the following year. The new weekly featured the horticultural articles of Thomas Meehan and a women's department edited by the publisher's wife.

It was this "Woman and the Home" section of the *Tribune and Farmer*, edited by Mrs. Curtis, that developed into the *Ladies' Home Journal*. The story has it that young Cyrus himself began the department by clipping matter that he thought would interest women; but when he brought the paper home and showed his wife the column, she laughed at it. "Try it yourself if you think you can do better," challenged the man; and as the result of this dare, Mrs. Curtis entered upon a distinguished editorial career. For the department prospered, and after a few years it was resolved to issue it as an eight-page monthly supplement to the *Tribune and Farmer*, sold, when subscribed for separately, at fifty cents a year.

[1] TITLE: *The Ladies' Home Journal*. Subtitle: *and Practical Housekeeper*, 1884–89.

FIRST ISSUE: Dec. 1883. Current.

PERIODICITY: Monthly, except for 18 semimonthly numbers, Sept. 1910–May 1911. The first few issues bore no serial numbers whatever. Vols. 1–26, annual vols. beginning with Dec. number, Dec. 1883–Nov. 1909; 27, Dec. 1909–Dec. 15, 1910; 28–current, regular annual vols., 1911–current.

PUBLISHERS: Cyrus H. K. Curtis, 1883–84; Curtis Publishing Company, 1884–current (presidents: Cyrus H. K. Curtis, 1884–1932; George Horace Lorimer, 1932–34; Walter D. Fuller, 1934–current). All of Philadelphia.

EDITORS: Mrs. Louisa Knapp (Curtis), 1883–89; Edward W. Bok, 1889–1919; H. O. Davis, 1920; Barton W. Currie, 1921–28; Loring A. Schuler, 1928–35; Bruce Gould and Beatrice Blackmar Gould, 1935–current.

INDEXES: *Readers' Guide, Dramatic Index.*

REFERENCES: Edward W. Bok, *The Americanization of Edward Bok* (New York, 1922); Edward W. Bok, *A Man From Maine* (New York, 1923); John Adams Thayer, *Astir* (Boston, 1910), chs. 5–6; "Mrs. Louisa Knapp," *Journalist*, v. 8, Jan. 26, 1889, pp. 1–2; Richard Pratt, "Friend of the Family," *Quill*, v. 24, July 1936, pp. 6ff; Amos Stote, "Case History: The Ladies' Home Journal," *Magazine World*, v. 2, July 1, 1946, pp. 6ff; "How This Magazine Happened" and "A Few Things We Have Done," *Ladies' Home Journal*, v. 25, Nov. 1908, pp. 1–2; Dorothy Johnson Caldwell, "Education, Citizenship and Vocations in the Ladies' Home Journal" (thesis, University of Missouri, 1954).

[2] Bok, *Man From Maine*, p. 85.

Thus the first issue appeared in December 1883, without serial numbering, "conducted by Mrs. Louisa Knapp." Louisa Knapp was Mrs. Curtis's maiden name. The supplement was called *Ladies' Home Journal,* to which was added in the second issue the words *and Practical Housekeeper.* The early numbers, small-folio in size, carried a woodcut illustration on the front page, an installment of a serial, a short story, and departments of recipes, household hints, fancywork, fashions in brief, and gardening. The first serial was a sentimental two-part story by Ella Wheeler, whose *Poems of Passion* had just brought her a kind of fame.

It was an unpretentious, cheaply printed little paper; but it had variety, and it was skillfully edited to appeal to women in middle-class homes. It was a success almost from the start. At the end of a year it had a circulation of twenty-five thousand, and Curtis had parted company with the *Tribune and Farmer* by making over that paper wholly to the man who had been his partner, and taking the *Journal* and the plant's type for himself.[3] The partner had disapproved founding the *Journal* and had no share in it. So in October 1884, the name Curtis Publishing Company appeared for the first time as the owner, and the *Journal* was no longer used as a supplement to the agricultural paper.

With his decks cleared for action, Curtis was ready to show what he could do in the way of circulation building. His first device was the "club" of four subscriptions for a dollar, designed to make each subscriber a solicitor of three other subscriptions. This worked so well that it doubled the circulation in six months; when the stimulus of a four-hundred-dollar advertising campaign in the newspapers was added, the list doubled again in another six months, bringing it to a hundred thousand at the end of 1884. Advertising in considerably larger amounts doubled the circulation once more in the next half-year. But Curtis knew more than to expect that he could go on indefinitely forcing his list to double itself semiannually by any reasonable advertising expenditure. He saw he had to improve his paper and charge more for it, in order to make it profitable. As a beginning in that direction, he managed, after a personal visit to her home in Massachusetts, to get a short story from Marion Harland, then at the height of her reputation as a writer for women, for ninety dollars; and the ninety dollars was hard to scrape together. With Marion Harland's name, Curtis undertook some more advertising, which brought the list slowly up to two hundred seventy thousand by the spring of 1886.[4] The publisher now

---

[3] *Ibid.,* p. 95.
[4] See sworn circulation in Ayer's directory for 1886, figures as of March–July. Bok tells of

doubled the number of pages in the *Journal*, engaged several well-known writers and advertised them, and discontinued his clubbing rate. This last move amounted to doubling his subscription price, for virtually his whole list had been obtained on the twenty-five cent basis and now everything was straight fifty cents.

The new writers were often difficult to obtain. Two decades later, a President of the United States and the leading writers of the world were happy to contribute regularly to the *Ladies' Home Journal*; but in 1886, established authors felt that they demeaned themselves in allowing their work to appear in a cheap household-hints paper. Adamantine was the refusal of Louisa M. Alcott, who could sell all her work to periodicals of a higher class for at least as much as the *Ladies' Home Journal* could pay. But the resourceful Curtis proceeded to employ with her the kind of argument which Bonner of the *New York Ledger* had used to break down similar author-resistance on the part of Edward Everett years before:[5] he offered to pay a hundred dollars to Miss Alcott's pet charity if she would write one column for the *Journal*. She accepted, and Curtis exultantly added her name to the "List of Famous Contributors" which he was advertising. This list now included Elizabeth Stuart Phelps, Harriet Prescott Spofford, Rose Terry Cooke, Mary Jane Holmes, Mrs. A. D. T. Whitney, Marietta Holley ("Samantha Allen"), Will Carleton, and Robert J. Burdette. It was a varied bill of fare, with plenty of sentiment, some always ladylike thrills, and a dash of humor; but the household and fashion departments were still the backbone of the periodical. The editor's salary was widely advertised as ten thousand dollars,[6] but it was known to some that this was "all in the family." Mrs. Emma C. Hewitt and Mrs. James H. Lambert were associate editors.

After the change in price to fifty cents, with the accompanying enlargement of the paper, the circulation continued its upward trend. In a signed statement in the fall of 1887, headed "A Million Subscribers," Curtis declared, "I am determined to push the circulation of the *Ladies' Home Journal* to the highest possible point this year."[7] He offered cash prizes for the largest lists of new subscribers, and he spent $20,000 on a newspaper advertising campaign.[8] The list went up to 400,000,[9]

---

another semiannual doubling, bringing the figure to 400,000 (*Man From Maine*, p. 110); but the contemporary sworn statements in Ayer do not show *Journal* circulation at that point until 1888.

[5] See F. L. Mott, *A History of American Magazines* (Cambridge, 1938), v. 2, p. 361.

[6] See, for example, the *Journalist*, Oct. 22, 1887, p. 10.

[7] *Ladies' Home Journal*, v. 4, Sept. 1887, p. 8.

[8] *Ibid.*, v. 5, Dec. 1887, p. 5.

[9] *N. W. Ayer & Son's American Newspaper Annual* (Philadelphia, 1888), p. 436. Figures obtained in March–July; sworn circulation.

# The LADIES HOME JOURNAL

## And practical Housekeeper...

Copyrighted, 1887, by CYRUS H. K. CURTIS.   ENTERED AT THE PHILADELPHIA POST OFFICE AS SECOND-CLASS MATTER.

VOL. V, NO. 9.   PHILADELPHIA, AUGUST, 1888.   Yearly Subscription 50 Cents, Single Copies 6 Cents.

## A LOVELY GIRL.

BY ELIZABETH STUART PHELPS.

COVER OF *VOGUE*, JULY 10, 1902

See pages 756–762.

and the advertising rate was raised to $2.00 an agate line. The next year Curtis added premiums as an inducement, publishing a 20-page premium list; and by the fall of 1889 the circulation stood at 440,000.[10]

Now came the great crisis in the Curtis campaign. It was decided to raise the price to $1.00 a year on July 1, 1889, with 32 pages and a cover. The publisher knew that this was a bold move, and that in order to accomplish it successfully he would need to invest huge sums in advertising and also to get liberal credit from his paper-makers. In F. Wayland Ayer, of N. W. Ayer & Son, advertising agents, he found a backer who believed in him and in his project. Ayer not only agreed to advance $200,000 advertising credit from his firm, but he endorsed notes to the extent of $100,000 in favor of the paper-makers.[11] With this arrangement, Curtis was enabled to conduct a smashing advertising campaign. When all the fifty-cent subscriptions had run out in 1890, he found himself with a list of 488,000 on a dollar basis — a larger list at double the price of the year before. But the advertising campaign of 1889–1890 had cost $310,000 instead of the $200,000 originally planned, and it required careful financing for the next few years to consolidate successes. Premiums were still offered for clubs of subscribers for several years; an eight-page premium list was issued each December. A modest British edition was begun. In 1891 a stock company was organized, capitalized at half a million dollars. This signalized the sound establishment of a great publishing business. A majority of the stock in the new corporation was owned by Curtis; the old name — the Curtis Publishing Company — was retained. In this year the circulation went to 600,000 and in the next to 700,000; and in that neighborhood it remained throughout the nineties, retarded, perhaps, but not reduced by the hard times of 1893. Advertising, which in the first year of the magazine had cost $200 a page, rose in the nineties until the back page of the cover was sold for $4,000.

In the meantime, Mrs. Curtis had come to feel that her growing daughter needed her more than the growing *Journal*; and on October 20, 1889, she gave up the editorial chair to Edward William Bok. Bok was at exactly the same age when he came to *Ladies' Home Journal* as that at which his employer, Curtis, had entered Philadelphia journalism — twenty-six. Born in the Netherlands, he had been brought to America at the age of seven, had worked for two or three different book publishers, had edited the *Brooklyn Magazine* for a short time,

---

[10] In *A Man From Maine* (p. 112), Bok gives the figure of 700,000 as the circulation just before the increase of the subscription price (July 1889). In *The Americanization of Edward Bok* (p. 166), he gives 440,000 as the circulation when he took over the editorship in Oct. 1889. Ayer gives the sworn circulation for mid-1889 as 410,000.

[11] *Man From Maine*, pp. 113–16.

and then had founded a newspaper syndicate service. Called to the editorial chair of a periodical that was rapidly becoming the most important journal for women in America, Bok was a bachelor, devoted to his mother, but quite without an intimate understanding of women. To the end of his life he had certain curious ideas about the sex in general: he thought that women arrived at conclusions by something he called "instinct" rather than by reasoning,[12] and he believed that they possessed a sensibility which raised them above selfishness.[13] He was inclined to idealize the average woman of his period; and perhaps it was because he made a magazine for what the women wished to be rather than for what they actually were that he achieved a great success.

There was always something a little funny about Bok as a bachelor-editor for the ladies. One of his very first efforts was a department called "Side Talks with Girls," in which he chatted confidentially with girls about their problems, in an effort to take the place of mothers who were not confidential enough. These letters were signed "Ruth Ashmore." After the first installment appeared, pseudo-Ruth received seven hundred letters from girls, in which they took her at her word and waxed more confidential than the editor had expected! After reading the first two of the seven hundred, the blushing Bok rushed out of the office, took the first train for New York, and there called on Mrs. Isabel A. Mallon, who was a contributor to his syndicate service. He opened the last copy of the *Journal* to the "Side Talks" department.

"Have you read this?" he asked.

"I have," answered Mrs. Mallon. "It's very well done. Who is this Ruth Ashmore?"

"You are!" declared Bok.

The editor himself tells the story in his popular autobiography, *The Americanization of Edward Bok*, and adds:

> From that time on, Mrs. Mallon became Ruth Ashmore, the most ridiculed writer in the magazine world, and yet the most helpful editor that ever conducted a department in periodical literature. For sixteen years she conducted the department, until she passed away, her last act being to dictate a letter to a correspondent. In those sixteen years she received 158,000 letters; she kept three stenographers busy, and the number of girls who today bless the name of Ruth Ashmore is legion.[14]

Many people thought that the department was written by Bok, however, as well as the advice to mothers, the recipes, and the fashion hints;

---

[12] *Americanization*, pp. 151, 158, 176–77.
[13] *Ibid.*, pp. 332–39.
[14] *Ibid.*, p. 171. Mrs. Mallon also wrote a dress department in the *Journal* for some years.

and he soon became a favorite butt of the paragraphers. The *Yellow Book* ran a burlesque of the department in its "Snide Chats with Girls" in 1897. Bok himself said that he encouraged this lampooning because he thought it good advertising for the *Journal*; [15] but there can be no doubt that he suffered under it, and eventually did all he could to end it.[16] One of the worst offenders was Bok's friend Eugene Field, who climaxed a series of comments by the sober announcement in his column [17] in the Chicago *Daily News* that Bok was about to marry "Miss Lavinia Pinkham, the favorite granddaughter of Mrs. Lydia Pinkham, the famous philanthropist." [18] The newspapers picked this up with delight and gave it wide circulation. Field provided interviews with the imaginary Miss Pinkham, stories of her trip to Paris to buy a trousseau, and so on. When this extravaganza was worn out, Field started another. Miss Pinkham could have, at best, but a ghostly notoriety of slightly medicinal scent; but Mrs. Frank Leslie, redoubtable widow, heroine of more than one passionate episode, and still publisher of two or three periodicals,[19] was an actual and highly flavored personality. On June 27, 1893, Field printed the following in his column:

There is now a rumor to the effect that Mr. Edward W. Bok, the talented editor of the *Ladies' Home Journal*, is about to link his destiny with that of Mrs. Frank Leslie. Although the lady in question is Mr. Bok's senior by several years, it is easy to understand how one of his impressionable nature would reverence a woman so long and so conspicuously identified with those reforms in which Mr. Bok himself is interested and of which he writes so sweetly and so forcefully in his excellent journal. It is also easy to understand that the tempest-tossed heart of this superior lady should only too willingly commit itself at last to the tender keeping of this valorous young man whose career so far has been a constant and discreet battle in behalf of womankind.

While we have not always endorsed Mr. Bok's views upon the subjects of corset-covers and toilet soaps, although we have not infrequently criticised his recipes for lemon pie, chapped lips, and angel-food, and although the system advocated by him of pulling out basting threads with forceps instead of with the fingers does not meet with our approval — in spite of all this, we cordially approve of that prospective event which promises to bring two sympathetic hearts into permanent union.[20]

But it was at about this time that the actual engagement of Bok to the daughter of Mr. and Mrs. Curtis was announced, and that ended what

[15] *Ibid.*, pp. 172, 190.
[16] *Ibid.*, p. 320.
[17] Bok says (*ibid.*, p. 181) that Field put the item into the news columns, but in this he was mistaken. For further discussion see Charles H. Dennis, *Eugene Field's Creative Years* (New York, 1924), p. 105.
[18] *Ibid.*
[19] See Mott, *op. cit.*, v. 2, pp. 461–63; v. 3, pp. 511–12.
[20] Dennis, *Eugene Field's Creative Years*, p. 106.

might otherwise have been a long series of Field's "rumors." It did
not, however, end the lampoons, quips, and libels — many of them
personal and even abusive — which followed Bok through his editorship. One other may be quoted — Gilbertian lines put into the mouth
of the ladies' editor by Tom Masson:

> I am Bok, of the *Ladies' Home Journal*,
>     And a nice young man am I.
> My methods are purely supernal;
>     My job is as easy as pie.
> The element religious,
> With a finesse quite prodigious,
>     Is the only affectation I pursue;
> But I do it with persistence
> That admits of no resistance,
>     With a cash accumulation held in view.[21]

Bok was wont to say that he had a dual personality — the Bok that
knew what his audience wanted and gave it to them, and the Bok that
was more intellectual, artistic, and aspiring. When he shot over the
heads of his readers, or allowed his reforming zeal to run away with
him, he was inclined to blame the error on the other Bok. But it seems
to be indicated by his autobiography that intellectually, esthetically,
and sentimentally he was near enough to the level of his audience —
which is commonly the case of a great editor. His idealism, in which he
surpassed his readers, pleased them even when they could not follow
him to the height of his aspiration. His natural appeal, as he phrased
it, was "to the intelligent American woman rather than to the intellectual type." [22] Thus the *Journal's* place was fixed as a periodical for the
middle-class home. In its advertising it often stressed its appeal to
men as well as to women.

Bok began to improve the magazine as soon as he took over the
editorship. He already had a considerable literary acquaintance, which
he enlarged assiduously. T. De Witt Talmage, the popular preacher of
the day, wrote an article for each number. Eben E. Rexford, author of
"Silver Threads Among the Gold" and other sentimental ballads, did
a department on flowers, for which, it was reported, he received one
hundred and twenty-five dollars a column.[23] Margaret E. Sangster, Julia
Ward Howe, Grace Greenwood, Ella Wheeler Wilcox, and Robert J.
Burdette were frequent contributors.

The magazine's keynote became *intimacy*. Soon a department of
"Heart to Heart Talks," edited by Mrs. Margaret Bottome, president

[21] *Life*, v. 38, p. 9, July 4, 1901.
[22] *Americanization*, p. 374.
[23] *Current Literature*, v. 3, p. 443, Nov. 1889.

of the King's Daughters, was begun to supplement Ruth Ashmore's "Side Talks with Girls"; and it was almost equally successful. The journalist Foster Coates did a department called "Side Talks with Boys." The feature articles were intimate personality sketches revealing the private lives of the great and near-great. P. T. Barnum wrote on "How I Have Grown Old," A. Bogardus on "Presidents I Have Photographed," an anonymous writer on "The Story of a Literary Woman." There were series on "Unknown Wives of Well Known Men," "Clever Daughters of Clever Men," "Society Women as Housekeepers," "How I Manage to Be Happy," and "The Woman Who Most Influenced Me." The last-named series began with an article by Eugene Field on "My Grandmother"; Dickens' daughter wrote of her father, and Mrs. Henry Ward Beecher of her late husband. Benjamin Harrison described the life of himself and his family in the White House.

Typography and covers gradually improved. The *Journal* was one of the first magazines — possibly the very first — to change its cover design monthly, though its buff covers of the early nineties were dingy in comparison with those of later years. Illustration became more adequate. Patent medicine advertising was excluded in 1893, and thereafter a running fight was carried on with the makers of nostrums. Mark Sullivan joined the *Journal* staff in 1904, as legal adviser in connection with a libel suit brought by a patent medicine manufacturer, and as a contributor of articles in the magazine's crusade. It was Sullivan who discovered that Lydia E. Pinkham was not "in her laboratory at Lynn, Massachusetts," as the advertisements said, but in her grave in Pine Grove Cemetery near that city, and had been there, according to the date on the tombstone, for twenty years — and a picture of the tombstone, with inscription, was presented to *Journal* readers. Sullivan changed over to *Collier's* shortly after that weekly joined in the crusade in 1905. It was the next year that a Federal Food and Drug Act was enacted by Congress.[24] Bok often told of the sacrifice involved in the refusal of patent medicine advertising: when Curtis once closed his pages to the soothing syrups and sarsaparillas, a certified check for a page advertisement, arriving just before a big payroll was due, had no influence on him.[25]

Howells was Bok's first big literary prize. "The Coast of Bohemia" appeared serially in 1892–1893, and was followed by "My Literary Passions." For the latter Curtis paid ten thousand dollars, and then spent fifty thousand advertising it.[26] Frank R. Stockton, John Kendrick

[24] Mark Sullivan, *The Education of an American* (New York, 1938), ch. 21.
[25] *Americanization*, p. 201; *Man From Maine*, p. 128.
[26] *Americanization*, p. 202.

Bangs, James Whitcomb Riley, Mary E. Wilkins, and Julia Magruder were other literary headliners.

It must be said that the *Journal* of the early nineties looks pretty grey to modern eyes. Its small type, neat make-up, comparatively few and small illustrations made it not unattractive, but certainly not striking.

In 1893 Bok became vice-president of the reorganized Curtis Publishing Company. The next year he visited England and France in search of foreign literary talent, obtaining promises of work from Rosa Bonheur, Kate Greenaway, "Ian Maclaren," and Rudyard Kipling. With Kipling he began an acquaintance that continued for many years and was filled with interesting incidents. There was, for example, the editing out of certain drinking episodes in Kipling's first *Ladies' Home Journal* tale.[27] Another incident relates to the publication of Kipling's poem "The Female of the Species" in the *Journal*. It was doubtless the "other Bok" who accepted a poem containing the refrain, "The female of the species is more deadly than the male." And this in the ladylike *Home Journal*! It is no wonder that the temerarious editor was deluged with protests. "They were delightful," wrote Kipling after he had read some of the indignant letters.[28]

It was not long until the *Journal* was publishing most of the best American writers. Among them were Mark Twain, Bret Harte, Marion Crawford, Conan Doyle, Hamlin Garland, Joel Chandler Harris, Sarah Orne Jewett, Kate Douglas Wiggin, and Anthony Hope. A Sunday School department edited by Dwight L. Moody and called "Moody's Bible Class" was instituted. Musical compositions had been a feature of the magazine for some years, but in the middle nineties new interest was awakened by the publication of John Philip Sousa's marches and Reginald de Koven's new pieces. When Bok was in England he got Sir Arthur Sullivan's permission to present the first correct and properly purchased version of "The Lost Chord." [29] Compositions were printed by Tosti, Paderewski, Moscowski, Strauss, Mascagni, and Josef Hofmann. The last-named became editor of a musical department in the magazine in 1907. An outstanding series of articles in the late nineties was one called "Great Personal Events," by Charles A. Dana. "When Jenny Lind Sang in Castle Garden," "When Henry Ward Beecher Sold Slaves in Plymouth Pulpit," and "When Louis Kossuth Rode Up Broadway" were among the titles. These subjects lent themselves well to pictorial illustration. By this time the art work of the *Journal* had become really distinguished. Edwin A. Abbey, W. L. Tay-

[27] *Ibid.*, p. 220.
[28] *Ibid.*, p. 306.
[29] *Ibid.*, p. 228.

lor, Howard Pyle, Charles Dana Gibson, Will H. Low, and W. T. Smedley were among its artists. The *Journal* was one of the first magazines to take up four-color illustration, and it continued to feature such work longer than the others in this period.

It was in 1895 that the *Journal* began the publication of plans for houses costing from one to five thousand dollars. Complete specifications and estimates were prepared for each house, and these were sold at five dollars a set. Contests for the best homes were part of the campaign. The effect of this propagation of good home architecture upon the country at large was undoubtedly very great. Stanford White wrote, shortly before his death: "I firmly believe that Edward Bok has more completely influenced American domestic architecture for the better than any other man in this generation." [30] Bok followed this campaign with another directed to a reform of interior decoration; still another tried to improve the class of pictures hung on the walls of the average home, in connection with which the *Journal* furnished portfolios of prints approved by its editors at a low price. Fundamentally, Bok was a reformer; and having tasted success, he went on to improve the furnishings in Pullman cars, to banish disfiguring signboards, to clean up ugly and dirty spots in cities, and so on.

In the prosperous years following the Spanish War, the circulation of the *Journal*, already larger than that of any other magazine, resumed its upward trend. In 1900 it went to 800,000, two years later to nine hundred thousand; and in 1903 it reached the long-desired goal of 1,000,000 circulation — the first magazine (except for a few cheap mail-order journals) to attain that pinnacle. One means used to stimulate circulation was particularly effective. It was devised by Editor Bok to take the place of premiums, and consisted of scholarships in colleges and musical conservatories awarded to successful subscription solicitors. The scheme made new subscribers feel like philanthropists because they had helped a bright young man in his struggle to get an education; and they had done this without expense to themselves, because the magazine was well worth the $1.00 paid. But once the million mark had been reached, the price was raised to $1.50 — without greatly affecting the size of the circulation. In 1892 *Journal* advertising amounted to $250,000, in 1894 to $300,000, and in 1897 to $500,000.[31] John Adams Thayer was advertising director during 1892–1898, with Thomas Balmer as western manager — a great team.

The *Ladies' Home Journal* in the first decade of the new century

[30] *Ibid.*, p. 243.
[31] *Printer's Ink*, v. 11, p. 320, Aug. 29, 1894; *ibid.*, v. 24, Aug. 3, 1898, p. 34; *ibid.*, v. 25, Dec. 14, 1898, p. 62; *ibid.*, v. 27, May 17, 1899, p. 4; and Frank Presbrey, *The History and Development of Advertising* (New York, 1929), p. 481.

was a beautiful magazine, riding on the top wave of prosperity. Handsome color work in literary and advertising sections was a distinctive characteristic. W. L. Taylor's illustrations of the Psalms, Jessie Willcox Smith's child pictures, the brilliant work of Maxfield Parrish, Peter Newell's amusing drawings — these were but a few of the attractions. Mrs. S. T. Rorer was at her zenith as the nation's instructress in cookery. Jane Addams wrote "My Fifteen Years at Hull House" for the *Journal*, and Helen Keller her "Story of My Life." The religious element, never quite neglected by Editor Bok, was stressed in Lyman Abbott's "My Fifty Years as a Minister," later published in book form as *Reminiscences*, and Henry Van Dyke's "Out of Doors in the Holy Land." Kipling's "Just So Stories" and "Puck of Pook's Hill," Jean Webster's "Daddy Long-Legs," Kate Douglas Wiggin's "The Old Peabody Pew," and F. Hopkinson Smith's "The Man in the Arm Chair" were other successful serials in these years. Nordica, Melba, Schumann-Heink, and others wrote articles on singing.

The *Journal* had become a forum from which anyone was glad to speak. President Theodore Roosevelt remarked to Bok one day that he envied him his power over the public. "My messages are printed in the newspapers and read hurriedly, mostly by men in trolleys or railroad-cars," he explained, "but you are read in the evening by the fireside." Bok forthwith offered the President a department in his magazine, but Roosevelt snapped, "Haven't time for another thing. Wish I had." Then he reflected, "I have only half an hour, when I am awake, that I am really idle; and that is when I am being shaved." Bok immediately seized upon this half-hour, suggesting that Robert L. O'Brien, Washington correspondent of the *Boston Transcript*, should interview the president during two of those shaving half-hours a month, and obtain from him views that he wished to communicate to the women of America.[32] The barber was not consulted, but T. R. accepted; for a year during 1906–1907 there appeared in the *Journal* a page headed "The President," with the subtitle: "A department which will be presented showing the attitude of the President on those national questions which affect the vital interests of the home, by a writer intimately acquainted and in close touch with him." The department naturally attracted much attention, and made each issue of the magazine news. Ten years later, just after Roosevelt's return from his African safari, he agreed with Bok to write a series of twelve articles for the *Journal* under the strictest anonymity. They dealt with men's interests, men's family and community relations, men's work; and they were published as a department headed "Men." Roosevelt wrote them

[32] *Americanization*, pp. 273–75.

out in pencil, Bok copied the manuscript personally, and the authorship was a complete secret until it was revealed some years after Roosevelt's death in Bok's autobiography. Lyman Abbott and Charles W. Eliot were most frequently guessed to be the author of the articles, but Roosevelt, says Bok, was not suspected. As a matter of fact, the series lacked something of the fire and zest of the younger T. R.

Bok continued his reform crusades. Shortly after the turn of the century, he broke out against pseudocultural activities of some of the women's clubs, following this attack by a similar onslaught upon woman suffrage. In these campaigns he was aided and abetted by such respected and aging gentlemen as Grover Cleveland, Charles W. Eliot, and Lyman Abbott. Cleveland's article on "Woman's Mission" in May 1905 was a red flag to the suffragists. Indeed Bok had, as he wrote later, formed the habit of "jumping from one sizzling firepan into another." [33] Thousands of clubwomen signed petitions begging Curtis to discharge his crusading editor, and whole clubs boycotted the *Journal*. Indeed, Curtis sued one club, under the Sherman law, for boycotting. These campaigns of Bok's took courage, but they did not permanently injure the standing of the magazine. Doubtless the contrary was true, for Bok knew that his audience was conservative. He always *felt* with his readers, and he did not (as has been noted) edit the *Journal* for "the intellectual type."

Bok later retired in good order from some of these positions. Jane Addams was allowed, in the number for January 1913, to favor woman's suffrage as a means of social reform. Although the editor had denied in the mid-nineties that modern girls "required a training any different from that which their mothers were given," and had declared that "perambulating encyclopedias in the guise of women are very uncomfortable things," [34] the *Journal* displayed an educationally liberal article on "The College Girl as Homemaker" in July 1910.

Perhaps the most courageous thing Bok did, however, was to enter the lists for sex education. Here was something that offended the conservatives, and again there was an uproar from shocked readers. Thousands of subscribers whose delicacy was outraged by the mention of syphilis stopped their papers, and thereafter the *Journal* was more guarded in its references to sex and sex diseases. Bok published a little series of books on personal hygiene to aid the cause.

A crusade in favor of American styles to supplant those of Paris was a complete failure. It had been planned carefully. Sentiment was

---

[33] *Ibid.*, p. 297.
[34] *Ladies' Home Journal*, v. 11, Jan. 1894, p. 12. See also Caldwell, "Education, Citizenship and Vocations."

worked up against Parisian fashions as indecent and suited only to the demimondaine, and dishonesty in handling labels of Paris *couturiers* was exposed. The American styles were carefully designed and presented. But all to no avail; not even *Ladies' Home Journal* could wean American women from Paris fashions. There was a similar failure in an attempt to stop the trade in aigrettes, which was shown to be founded on cruelty to birds. Laws against the importation of aigrettes were, however, finally obtained. Another victory through legal enactment was the international agreement obtained to save the beauties of Niagara from the power companies.

One reason for the influence of the *Journal* was that its subscribers looked upon it not merely as another magazine, but as a friend and counselor in the home. This service idea, beginning with the correspondence elicited by the "Side Talks with Girls," was extended to all other departments, and was particularly important in house building and furnishing and in health advice.

Step by step, the editor built up this service behind the magazine until he had a staff of thirty-five editors on the monthly payroll; in each issue he proclaimed the willingness of these editors to answer immediately any questions by mail; he encouraged and cajoled his readers to form the habit of looking upon his magazine as a great clearing-house of information. Before long, the letters streamed in by the tens of thousands during a year. The editor still encouraged, and the total ran into the hundreds of thousands, until during the last year, before the service was finally stopped by the Great War of 1917–18, the yearly correspondence totalled nearly a million letters.[35]

Probably the most remarkable of these services was that which was instituted for the care of mothers in 1910. The work was chiefly under the charge of Dr. Emelyn L. Coolidge. Thousands of prospective mothers were advised by mail each year with great care and detail; reports and advice were exchanged until the child reached the age of two years.

No doubt these services were largely responsible for the fact that the *Ladies' Home Journal* was but little affected by the panic of 1907. It was not making as much money, however, as its associate, the *Saturday Evening Post*, obviously because it had only one shot at the advertising market per month, while the *Post* had four. So for nine months — September 1910 through May 1911 — the *Journal* adventured with semimonthly publication at ten cents a copy. These were all special numbers — "Girls' Number," "Marriage Number," "American Fashions Number," "Spring Romance Number," and so on. But the experiment was not successful, and June 1911 brought a monthly number again, with the price raised from ten to fifteen cents.

[35] *Americanization*, p. 174.

It was in 1910 that the Curtis Advertising Code was framed. It was designed to eliminate fraud, extravagant claims, and immoral and suggestive copy. Special restrictions for the *Journal* banned financial advertising, the offering of tobacco in any form, and all advertising of playing-cards. It was further specified and required that "no reference to alcoholic liquors is allowed — not even illustrations of wine glasses or steins."[36]

By 1912 the *Journal* was well started on its climb to its second million, which it reached for one issue in the fall of 1919. In these years, its monthly numbers frequently ran to over two hundred pages, and its gross advertising revenue for one number to over a million dollars.[37] It was, beyond question, the most valuable monthly magazine property in the world. Its editor, who was also vice-president of the publishing company, drew a salary of a hundred thousand dollars a year.[38]

In 1912 the *Journal* began the publication of the finest series of art works in color that had yet appeared in a general magazine. Four reproductions of famous paintings in American galleries were given in each issue; the work of such painters as Rembrandt, Turner, Velasquez, Hals, Corot, Whistler, and the older masters made a great showing in the magazine, and were framed to hang in many homes.

With the coming of the war in 1917, Curtis and Bok placed all the resources of the magazine at the command of the government. Upon the advice of President Wilson, Bok resolved to do little in the way of portraying the progress of the war at the front, but to support the "second line of defense" at home. In the first war number, Franklin D. Roosevelt, Assistant Secretary of the Navy, explained to mothers why they should allow their sons to enlist. William Howard Taft, chairman of the Red Cross Central Committee, undertook the editorship of a Red Cross department. Herbert Hoover made his first public statement as food administrator through the *Journal*; and the magazine published scores of articles from his department of war work, helping to make the new wartime dishes attractive by presentation in full color. Queen Elizabeth of Belgium asked for help for the children of her country, and readers responded by liberal gifts. McAdoo, Baruch, Gerard, Garfield, and other government officials made statements about war work. President Wilson himself wrote an address to the women about the second Liberty Loan especially for the *Journal*. Altogether, the magazine was probably an extremely effective arm of the national

---

[36] Ralph M. Hower, *The History of an Advertising Agency* (Cambridge, 1949), p. 428.

[37] The number for Dec. 1918 contained 231 pages, and the page rate, without color, was $6,500. The total for that issue was undoubtedly over $1,500,000.

[38] Edward A. Bok, *Twice Thirty* (New York, 1925), p. 172.

defense. In 1919 there were some articles from the front; Catherine Van Dyke was the correspondent of the *Journal.* Also there were some full-page battle pictures in color.

One interesting fact brought out during the war was the popularity of the *Ladies' Home Journal* among young men; it ranked third among the magazines in demand by the soldiers.[39]

After the war, Bok resigned his editorship. For thirty years he had directed the magazine editorially, with uniform success. He was now a wealthy man, and he wished more leisure for writing and philanthropy. There can be no question about Bok's position through these decades as one of America's foremost magazine editors. Central in his work was what Francis Hyde Bangs calls his "passion for intimacy." [40] The close integration of *Ladies' Home Journal* with the lives of its readers was an extraordinary accomplishment. A second technique consisted in obtaining contributions from famous persons, in which Bok was persistent and successful. Once obtained, the great names were well advertised, and Bangs calls Bok the greatest advertising genius in America after the death of Barnum. Clearly, this distinction should be shared with Publisher Curtis, who engineered the magazine's first success through such means, and never lost faith in the efficacy of advertising for building magazine circulation.

Bok was succeeded in January 1920 by Harry Orville Davis, who had been director general of the Panama California Exposition and later had been in the film business. He lasted only four months in the top position, however, and the year was filled out by Manager Editor John E. Pickett, who had been a Missouri newspaperman and later editor of *Country Gentleman.*

In January 1921 Barton W. Currie became editor-in-chief. Currie was also a *Country Gentleman* graduate; before that, he had done newspaper work in New York. Immediately he changed the traditional small-folio page size of the magazine to large-quarto, which had been adopted by many other magazines because it was better suited to advertisers' needs — especially for full-page displays. But Currie continued the policies of his predecessor in the departments and in art work. Gardens were stressed more than ever; landscaping patterns were developed as a new service of the *Journal.* Color illustration of foods and fabrics became a feature. The historical serials of Herbert Quick, novels by such writers as Zane Grey, Corra Harris, and Eleanor Hallowell Abbott, and articles by Harry Emerson Fosdick, Walter Damrosch, and William Lyon Phelps are representative of the literary contents. Phelps continued the literary comment that had been contributed in earlier years by Robert Bridges and Hamilton Wright Mabie.

And yet gradually, with the changing times, *Ladies' Home Journal* changed its character. It inevitably became less Bokish; it was edited less for a special class, i.e., noble but somewhat backward American womanhood. In the fifth year of his editorship, Currie expressed the idea governing the change thus:

> Women's magazines are no longer edited for clinging vines. They are no longer edited for helpless, submerged and inarticulate gentlewomen who in order to maintain gentility and purity of thought must stifle their impulses and disregard their complexes. The intellectual development of American women has jumped forward one hundred years in the past ten. The pose of masculine superiority has lost all its old swagger . . . . Hence seventy per cent of your contents must be devised so that it will catch and hold the interest of both sexes. If you attempt to feminize it all, you become a hopeless bore to the vast majority of alert and intelligent American women. But on the score of the care and education of children, clothes, and household efficiency, feminine is still feminine. . . . You cannot edit down from a lofty masculine plane.[41]

This statement calls for two observations. First, there can be little doubt that men comprised a considerable proportion of the reading audience of *Ladies' Home Journal* from the start; and second, the gap between the interests of women and the interests of men, not very great in 1883, was much less in 1920. It is interesting to note that just about the time the *Journal* was discovering it had men readers, its opposite in the Curtis organization, the *Saturday Evening Post*, was finding that a big proportion of its readership was feminine.[42]

In 1923 the price of the *Journal* was cut back to the dime-a-copy on which the magazine had made its original success.[43] Now the reader got far more for his dime than in the nineties, and indeed the advertiser got more for his dollar when he paid nine thousand dollars for a page in the twenties than he had received when he paid only a few hundred in 1890. Circulation boomed, and some issues went over two and a half million.

In 1928, on the eve of panic and depression, Currie turned the editorship of the *Journal* over to Loring A. Schuler, who, like himself, had been first a newspaperman and then editor of the *Country Gentleman*.

[41] Doris Ulmann, *A Portrait Gallery of American Editors* (New York, 1925), p. 48.

[42] *Magazine World*, v. 2, Oct. 1946, p. 8. Article by Amos Stote.

[43] It was, of course, first priced at 5¢, raised to 10¢ in 1889. The first change from the 10¢ price was made when it was raised to 15¢, in Dec. 1904. It was returned to 10¢ for the magazine's experiment in semimonthly publication, from Sept. 1910 to May 1911, after which the 15¢ price was maintained until the increase to 20¢ in May 1920. It was soon back to 15¢ (July 1921) and then to 10¢ (Oct. 1923). This old price was kept through the depression. In Feb. 1942 it was raised to 15¢, in June 1946 to 25¢, and in Jan. 1953 to 35¢.

In the difficult years of Schuler's editorship, the *Journal* maintained its circulation and standing, though advertising fell off in 1931, and rates had to be reduced, as they were for all magazines. Curtis retired as president of the publishing company in 1932, and George Horace Lorimer, of the *Post*, succeeded him; Walter D. Fuller became president in 1934 and Lorimer chairman of the board.

Service activities were featured — house and garden "patterns," standards and specifications for intelligent buying, and leaflets offering help in a great number of home activities. A department called "The Sub-Deb" was provided for girls in their teens, "The Hostess" was designed to help in entertaining, and "Women in Business" gave vocational aid. A regular correspondent in Hollywood dealt with motion pictures. Mary Roberts Rinehart wrote a special editorial department. The whole tone of the magazine was much smarter than it had been a decade or two earlier. A Paris office was maintained, and the *Journal* made much of its styles direct from the studios of the famous couturiers, undeterred by any memory of Bok's once famous crusade against "cocotte costumes." Public questions involving both domestic politics and international relations were frequently discussed; Calvin Coolidge contributed three articles on world peace immediately on his retirement from the presidency in 1929. Galsworthy, Tarkington, and Wells contributed serials; Willa Cather, Edna Ferber, and Bess Streeter Aldrich were favorite short-story writers.

To the editorial management of the *Journal* in 1935 came a husband-and-wife team, Bruce and Beatrice Blackmar Gould. Both were Iowans, both had been in New York journalism, both had done writing in various fields. They were young and in touch with contemporary interests and ideas, but sympathetic with the traditions of the old magazine whose editorial course they were to direct successfully for many years. Bruce had been for a year and a half an associate editor of the *Saturday Evening Post* under Lorimer, who thought highly of his editorial ability.[44]

The first "hit" which the Goulds made was the enlistment of Mrs. Eleanor Roosevelt as a contributor. Her frank reminiscences, entitled "This Is My Story," were published serially in 1937, while her husband was in his second term as President. Through the forties she wrote for the *Journal* a page called "If You Ask Me," in which she answered all kinds of questions — on politics, internationalism, economics, home life, practical psychology — in her own way, which was often wise, always socially progressive, and sometimes amazingly banal. She parted company with the *Journal* in 1949 when the Goulds suggested that

---

[44] John Tebbel, *George Horace Lorimer* (Garden City, N.Y., 1948), p. 213.

her new autobiographical series was "superficial in respect to some matters." [45] The new articles went to *McCall's*.

It was also in 1937 that Dorothy Thompson began to write her page — a department which stimulated much thinking on national and international politics and produced bags full of mail. The *Journal* — and the American woman — had come a long way since Edward Bok had allowed the presidential campaign of 1892 to pass without a line of mention. The Goulds had a series of polls made to discover what women were thinking about — an interesting feature for the magazine, but even more valuable as a chart for the editors. A new campaign against syphilis had nothing Bokish about it, but was bold and aggressive; Dr. Thomas Parran, Jr., Surgeon General of the United States Health Service, and Paul de Kruif, famous writer on medical subjects, collaborated on the new *Journal* series. The magazine's staff writer on health was Dr. Herman N. Bundesen.

But the biggest feature of all was one called "How America Lives," each article of which considered in detail the situation and life of some more or less "typical" American family. One was a family all members of which had jobs, one the family of an alcoholic, another a young preacher's family, still another the family of a "grass widow." In each case, besides the description and elaborate picturing of the family's life, there is an attempt to solve its chief problems, by advice, a suggested budget, and sometimes direct aid. This series began in 1940, with plans for a year if it worked out well; it has become a permanent feature of the magazine. Its revealing and personal nature gives it a remarkable human interest impact.

For several years Struthers Burt wrote a series of inspiring moral essays under the title, "This Can Be America." Gladys Taber began in 1938 her department called "Diary of Domesticity" — an intimate and altogether charming account of a family's life. Mrs. Taber has also written short stories and serials for the *Journal*. Harlan Miller is a later comer, whose page, "There's a Man in the House," began in 1949. It is the kind of "column" which, by simply putting together commonplace matters of home and family, achieves a pleasant minor miracle of wit and wisdom. "The Sub-Deb" is continued from former years; it was written for several years by Elizabeth Woodward, a staff member. The always important subjects for home magazines, food and fashions, have been treated attractively during the Gould regime, with the aid of color illustration and clever writing.

Serial fiction in these years has sometimes been nothing less than distinguished. Franz Werfel's "The Song of Bernadette" (1942), Jesse

[45] *Time*, v. 53, June 13, 1949, pp. 79–80.

Stuart's "Taps for Private Tussie" (1943), Nevil Shute's "Pastoral" (1944), Margery Sharp's "Cluny Brown" (1944), Taylor Caldwell's "This Side of Innocence" (1945), Christine Weston's "The Dark Wood" (1945), George Stewart's "Fire" (1947), Elizabeth Goudge's "Wayward Pilgrim" (1947) and "Gentian Hill" (1949), John P. Marquand's "Point of No Return" (1948) and "Melville Goodwin, USA" (1951), Jan Valtin's "Wintertime" (1949), Rumer Godden's "A Candle for St. Jude" (1948) and "A Breath of Air" (1950), and Daphne du Maurier's "My Cousin Rachel" (1951) and "No Motive" (1952) make an impressive list of fiction serials. For some years the *Journal* published a complete novelette in each number, and later a long book digest or "condensation." Since 1948 the topnotch nonfiction serials have perhaps outnumbered the distinguished serials. No catalogue can be attempted, but a few 1949–1952 successes may be named: John Gunther's "Death Be Not Proud," Margaret Mead's "Male and Female," Pearl Buck's "The Child Who Never Grew," George and Helen Papashvily's "Thanks to Noah."

By the beginning of 1942, the circulation of *Ladies' Home Journal* had passed 4,000,000. Newspaper advertising had again been employed, and a large part of the increase had come from newsstand sales. In February 1942 the price per copy was again raised to $.15, and the advertising rate to a new high of $9,200 for a black-and-white page. But both circulation and advertising volume continued to increase. In June 1946 the price was raised to $.25, but by fall of that year the circulation had passed 4,500,000, the base page rate was $13,510, and single numbers were being issued that carried over $2,000,000's worth of advertising. Advertisers were taking very seriously the *Journal's* slogan: "Never underestimate the power of a woman." In January 1953, when the single-copy price was raised to $.35, circulation increased to over 5,200,000, with a newsstand sale of over 2,000,000.

The attentive student of the history of *Ladies' Home Journal*, which covers over seventy years of publication at this writing, cannot but note the remarkable homogeneity of the entire file. Intimacy, name writers, services, and advertising made up the Curtis-Bok formula in the early years; intimacy, name writers, services, and advertising do the job today under Fuller and the Goulds. Not that there are not differences. Names are actually somewhat less important than they once were. Women are no longer placed on pedestals. Even the character of the intimacy on which the magazine is founded has changed. Of course, the most obvious alterations are those that have been wrought by improved typography and layout, omnipresent color, and skillful art work wedded to clever editing.

The "services" of a magazine like the *Journal* are very real and very important in many lives. In the days of Bok and Ruth Ashmore and Mrs. Bottome and Foster Coates, the influence of the *Journal* on character was deep and lasting, and the effect on homes and home life was extraordinary. The "services" and the intimacy of the appeal have made the magazine's hold on its readers continuous. Its effect today may be a little more on women's thinking and a little less on their fancywork and rules of etiquette, but in kind it is the same authority and control.

Intimacy has always been the trademark of the *Journal*. It is quite as notable in the series "How America Lives" and in the departments of Gladys Taber and Harlan Miller, and on many other pages of the *Journal* under the Gould editorship, as ever it was when Bok was shaping the magazine. It was a feature, for example, of that charming 1950 series on the upbringing of the present Queen of England and her sister, "The Little Princesses." Even the "international intimacy" of the Goulds had its counterpart in the Bok era. In 1915 Algernon Tassin wrote in the *Bookman* with characteristic sarcasm about Bok's early editorship:

He immediately began that series of novel series which effected the introduction of everybody to everybody else and placed the two hemispheres on a family basis. . . . Unknown Wives of Well-Known Men, Unknown Husbands, Famous Daughters of Famous Men, How I wrote This and Did That — . . . . One touch of Mr. E. W. Bok had made the whole world kin. It seemed as if the possibilities of the genre might never be exhausted. . . . The fever for fellowship spent itself in time, of course. . . .[46]

But Professor Tassin was wrong there. That fever has never spent itself, and we may reasonably doubt if it ever will. The globe-circling tour of the Goulds in 1952, the world consciousness of many *Journal* writers, and indeed the extension of the interests of a large proportion of *Journal* readers tend to make this magazine, in the words of Padmaja Naidu, "one dedicated to the larger problems of women all over the world." [47] To place the two hemispheres on a family basis would, in all seriousness, be an object fitting the traditions and worthy of the highest exertions of the *Ladies' Home Journal*.

[46] *Bookman*, v. 42, p. 404 (Dec. 1915); also in Tassin's *The Magazine in America* (New York, 1916), p. 355.
[47] *Ladies' Home Journal*, v. 69, July 1952, p. 4.

15

# LIFE [1]

*LIFE* began on this planet on January 4, 1883. In those azoic ages of the soul before the appearance of *Life*, comic weeklies had been very uncertain phenomena indeed. The good among them had invariably fulfilled the proverb as to early death, while the uncouth and banal and cheap had occasionally dragged out a curious longevity of stifled yawns. *Puck*, "our colored contemporary," blatant with chromolithography, had, however, passed its first lustrum with every expectation of a long life and a jocular one; its imitator *Judge* was a yearling.

> When *Life* began, experienced persons said:
> "Swift move Lachesis' shears toward that slim thread!
> A line so slender can't protracted be:
> Lo *Punchinello's* early tomb! and see
> Yon tumulus whose cut-off hump declares
> How premature an end was *Vanity Fair's*.
> Brightness and brevity as surely mate
> As pork and beans. It isn't chance; it's fate!
> A few brief months of coruscation, then
> *Life* will go out." So said experienced men.[2]

So they said also to young John Ames Mitchell when he first talked his plan over with them in the summer of 1882. Mitchell had been graduated in science at Harvard, had studied architecture in Paris, practiced it in Boston, gone to Paris again to study painting, and settled in New York to do illustrating. One day in May 1882, while he was drawing a picture for *Our Continent* — a new weekly, but already started down toward the graveyard at the bottom of the hill — Mitchell

---

[1] TITLE: *Life*.
FIRST ISSUE: Jan. 4, 1883. LAST ISSUE: Nov. 1936.
PERIODICITY: Weekly 1883–1931; monthly 1932–36. Vols. 1–98, regular semiannual vols., 1883–1931; 99–103, no. 11, regular annual vols., 1932–Nov. 1936.
PUBLISHERS: J. A. Mitchell and Andrew Miller, 1883–1918; Andrew Miller, 1918–19; C. D. Gibson, pres., 1920–28; Clair Maxwell, pres., 1928–36.
EDITORS: John Ames Mitchell, 1883–1918 (literary editors — Edward S. Martin, 1883, Henry Guy Carleton, 1883–84; John Kendrick Bangs, 1884–88; Frank Marshall White, 1888–94; Thomas L. Masson, 1895–1922); Andrew Miller and James S. Metcalfe, 1918–19; Edward S. Martin, 1920–22; Louis Evan Shipman (Oliver Herford and Lucinda Flynn, associate editors), 1922–24; Robert E. Sherwood (Lucinda Flynn, managing editor), 1924–28; Norman Anthony, 1929–30; Bolton Mallory, 1930–32; George T. Eggleston, 1932–36.
REFERENCES: Jubilee Number, *Life*, v. 21, Jan. 1893; Twenty-Fifth Anniversary Number, *Life*, v. 51, Jan. 2, 1908; Fortieth Anniversary Number, *Life*, v. 81, Jan. 4, 1923; Fiftieth Anniversary Number, *Life*, v. 100, p. 23, Jan. 1933; "*Life*, Dead and Alive," *Time*, v. 28, Oct. 19, 1936, pp. 61–63.
[2] Edward S. Martin, "Retrospectively Speaking," *Life*, v. 21, p. 5, Jan. 1893.

indulged in some reflections. How much more fun it is, he thought, to draw pictures of life and character than to paint — what a pity there are few or no good mediums for such work in America — why not start a picture weekly myself? — it's worth trying — I'll do it! Thus ran the thoughts of this brash young man.[3] He had a legacy of ten thousand dollars in the bank [4] and this idea in his head when he called upon Henry Holt, a publisher for whom he had been illustrating books. Holt said that Brander Matthews [5] was also thinking about starting a periodical, and that the two should get together; indeed, he gave a luncheon for them, but Matthews was thinking about one kind of periodical and Mitchell another. By this time Mitchell's resolution was definitely taken to begin in the following January a satirical weekly to be illustrated by line drawings in black and white. Seeking a partner who should attend to the literary side of the magazine while he devoted himself to its art, Mitchell felt out various literary young men; but the perilously high death rate of such periodicals in the past made them all hesitate, until Edward Sanford Martin was sought out at Cambridge and inoculated with Mitchell's enthusiasm. Martin had been an editor of *Harvard Lampoon*, and had lately been trying, without conspicuous success, to bring it out of Harvard Square into the big world. After more seeking, the two discovered, shortly before the date of the first issue, a business manager in Andrew Miller, another Harvard man. Mitchell, the moneyed man of the three, arranged quarter interests for his partners; and the plans went forward.

When it came to getting a printer, further difficulties were encountered; the venture was too shaky to suit hardheaded businessmen. Mitchell later wrote out his interview with one of these men:

He listened politely to a description of the aims and hopes of the future paper; then, after a few intelligent questions, said:

"As I understand, you mean to give the public a periodical about half the size of *Harper's Weekly*, *Puck* or *Judge*, and yet ask the same price for it. Now, to get that price, your smaller publication must be unquestionably better in quality, both artistic and literary. Have you secured the men whose work and reputation will assure you that position?"

"No. The artists are not to be had."

"And the literary men?"

"The same with them."

"That's bad enough. Is your own experience in journalism such as to warrant you in going ahead under such — peculiar circumstances?"

"I have had no experience in journalism."

[3] This incident and others respecting the founding of the paper are related in *Life*, v. 21, p. 16, Jan. 1893, by Mitchell himself.

[4] *Life*, v. 81, p. 16, Jan. 4, 1923.

[5] Mitchell refers to his meeting with "M," but Matthews' own article in *Life*, v. 81, p. 9, Jan. 4, 1923, makes the identification clear.

"None whatever?"

"None whatever."

The man of experience indulged in a smile, but a smile of indulgence and pity.

"Would you mind telling me," he asked, "just to gratify my curiosity — on what you are building your hopes for success?"

"On the fact of there being an unoccupied field for it. If such papers can thrive in Europe, there must be some place for one in America."

"Previous efforts have demonstrated the reverse, and they have done it pretty clearly."

"But this paper will be a very different thing from any of its predecessors — of a higher grade and far more artistic."

"How can that be when the best men hold aloof?"

"That will occur only in the beginning. I think it will prove an opportunity for talent now unrecognized to come to the front."

Again the business man smiled the sorrowing smile.

"All that you have said is pure theory, without a single solid fact on which it would be safe to risk a dollar. Take my advice and drop the whole business while you can. A year from now you will be amazed that you ever thought of it."

When the writer stepped out upon the sidewalk after this interview, he said to himself: "Probably the advice is good, but if I listen to reason I shall weaken." [6]

So he closed his ears to the folly of common sense, and finally secured Gilliss Brothers as printers, bills to be paid weekly in advance. The first number was duly offered to a mildly interested public. But of the second issue, three-fourths were returned from the newsstands unsold; while of the third, practically all came back.

And when the returns of the fourth and fifth came in, the three anxious men who counted them made the blood-curdling discovery that the unsold copies outnumbered the edition printed! Six thousand had been issued, and there were six thousand two hundred returns. It seemed for a moment that miracles were being resorted to that *Life's* defeat might be the quicker. A more careful examination, however, showed the extra copies were from previous editions. [7]

And so it went for weeks, and then months. The public had apparently determined to ignore the gay little magazine, but it went on being gay and its money went on into the pockets of the printers. The hardheaded man with his common-sense advice was by way of being vindicated. But with May came a little upturn. In June the improvement was marked. "At least," said the partners, "this encouragement will stiffen our backs for the seasonal summer slump." But there was no summer slump. By August the circulation figures were still mounting; in September the finances of the paper had at last reached the point where they broke even. The battle was won, and early in its second year *Life* passed the twenty-thousand mark.

[6] *Life*, v. 21, p. 16, Jan. 1893.
[7] *Life*, v. 21, p. 18, Jan. 1893.

Just about the time the paper showed its first faint signs of success, Martin's health forced him to leave New York. He turned in his quarter-interest, and thereafter Mitchell and Miller were partners. They secured Henry Guy Carleton, whose Negro-and-poker sketches were clever, to oversee the literary contents, but Carleton proved to be "the most irresponsible editor ever known." [8] Nevertheless, they kept him on until John Kendrick Bangs came to them in the spring of 1884.

Said the *Critic*, early in February, 1883: "*Life*, the new comic paper, is real, *Life* is earnest, and the grave is not its goal." [9] It was earnest — not yawnfully so, but built around ideas. It was not a mere joke book. The pun was not its *raison d'etre* — though it did have a little pun department, which began with the observation that "the pun is mightier than the sword." The magazine had a certain light cleverness decidely reminiscent of the old *Vanity Fair*, and its satire really bit. It began its thrusts at Society with a capital S and at addlepated clubmen in its very first number. Brander Matthews wrote sharp theatrical reviews for some of the early issues, signing them "Arthur Penn." George T. Lanigan and William L. Alden, both of whom had some reputation as humorists, were contributors to the first number; as were John T. Wheelwright, another *Lampoon* recruit, and George Parsons Lathrop.

But *Life* had been founded as a picture paper, and it was upon illustration that the founder Mitchell lavished his care. His plan was to utilize the new method of reproducing line drawings directly (the zinc etching process) instead of having them engraved on the wood block. At first it seemed that Mitchell himself would have to do most of the drawing, for the best draughtsmen were monopolized by *Puck* and *Judge* and *Century* and the Harper periodicals.[10] But F. G. Attwood, full of ideas and with a good sense of comedy, came to *Life* from the old *Harvard Lampoon* group; and after some months others came in increasing numbers. Mitchell "developed his own school of artists by a system of encouragement that was unique," wrote Tom Masson after the death of his old chief. "He never flattered, but he would invariably select some good quality in those who served him, and define it." Thus he "was constantly bringing out latent talent." [11] His standards were high, and he knew what he wanted. He himself wrote:

It was necessary that drawings representing scenes in high life should be of a style and quality unlike anything then published this side of the Atlantic. . . . For *Life's* uses, such drawings, while being true to nature and clever artistically,

---

[8] *Life*, v. 81, p. 18, Jan. 4, 1923.
[9] *Critic*, v. 2, p. 16, Feb. 3, 1883.
[10] See Mitchell's article, "Contemporary American Caricature," *Scribner's Magazine*, v. 6, p. 734, Dec. 1889.
[11] *Bookman*, v. 48, p. 698, Feb. 1919.

must show a lightness of touch, an ease, brilliancy, and force of expression which are not demanded in other work. Moreover, a sense of humor, a playfulness, and a gentle exaggeration are indispensable to the perfect work.[12]

*Life's* history before John Kendrick Bangs came to the magazine as literary editor in the spring of 1884 may be thought of as a preliminary period of struggle. But when Bangs came, *Life* had begun to flourish abundantly: its circulation grew apace, it was beginning to make profits, a distinctive and distinguished art staff was in the making, and writers of verse and sketches were eager to get into the brilliant new paper. Mitchell had met Bangs at the Gilliss printing establishment, where the *Acta Columbiana* — that college paper with a name smelling of dust and cobwebs but with pages lively with fresh wit [13] — was also printed. *Puck* had raved against the "silly" *Acta* and all college funny papers [14] (thereby delivering a tangential blow at its rival, which had sprung from the bosom of the *Harvard Lampoon*), but *Life* made this college boy its literary editor less than a year after his graduation. Bangs proved to be at once a brilliant writer and a consistently faithful worker — a combination necessary to satirical journalism, but all too rare. He wrote the editorials, as well as many long and short pieces of prose and verse, frequently signed "Carlyle Smith"; and he also conducted the oft-quoted "By the Way" page. He worked closely with Mitchell, who was always editor-in-chief.

Robert Bridges (Princeton, '79), later editor of *Scribner's Magazine*, began doing a book review department for *Life* during its first year, under the signature "Droch." Of him Bangs once wrote:

> He sits in judgment on our works:
> One in a hundred wins caresses,
> The other ninety-nine he dirks,
> And spurns our well beloved MSS.[15]

Alfred J. Cohen followed Matthews in the middle eighties with dramatic criticism, under the pen name of "Alan Dale"; and "Tricotrin" (W. J. Henderson) wrote on sports. Robert Grant, F. J. Stimson ("J. S. of Dale"), and Curtis Guild, Jr. — all schoolmates of Mitchell and Miller at Harvard — were frequent contributors. Frank Dempster Sherman and H. L. Satterlee had been associates of Bangs at Columbia. Henry A. Beers, of Yale, wrote condensed novels and a Yale undergraduate diary. Obviously, *Life* in its early years was a product of the

---

[12] *Life*, v. 21, p. 18, Jan. 1893.
[13] See Francis Hyde Bangs, *John Kendrick Bangs: Humorist of the Nineties* (New York, 1941), ch. 3.
[14] *Puck*, Aug. 1 and 22, 1883.
[15] *Life*, v. 81, p. 23, Jan. 4, 1923.

university wits;[16] it was the first comic of general circulation to recognize and use those bubbling founts of humor.[17] There were contributors from outside the charmed circles, of course — notably James Whitcomb Riley, who was represented in the magazine's third number; and Thomas L. Masson, later to become its literary editor.

The leading artists were, besides Mitchell and Attwood, Harry W. McVickar, who had made his beginnings on the Columbia *Spectator*, and who had an eye for society figures and scenes; W. A. Rogers, *Life's* chief cartoonist, notable for the vigor and originality of his conceptions; E. W. Kemble, whose pictures of darkies were delightful; Palmer Cox, a versatile contributor from the early numbers; W. H. Hyde, sure delineator of high society; Charles Kendrick, who had a gift for likenesses and became an important cartoonist; and C. Gray-Parker, whose horses and equipages were a joy to *Life's* readers for many years.

It was a wedding of delicacy to force that made the *Life* of the eighties and nineties the distinctive magazine that it was. "There is a charm about *Life*," remarked a contemporary, "an aroma all its own, a quality as distinct from any other publication as if it were alone among magazines."[18] It had something of what Meredith called the "comic spirit" — "the silvery laughter of the mind." It had standards and backgrounds and culture that its predecessors and contemporaries knew not of. Not that it did not print a good deal of burlesque and the more vigorous and less reflective types of humor: it never got far enough away from the general public to check its circulation rise, which reached fifty thousand in 1890.

The paper kept abreast of current events, of developments in morals and manners, of politics, of drama, literature, and the arts. It refused partisan allegiance in political contests, though it had its favorite leaders and its principles. It liked Cleveland, though it did not always take him seriously; it supported him in 1884 by dint of opposing Blaine, and four years later it advocated his reëlection "because we need Mrs. Cleveland in the White House four years more to teach conduct and manners to American society."[19] It never lost an opportunity to get in a blow against the protective tariff. It was all for hanging the Chicago anarchists high as Haman. It liked to poke fun at Boston, to hammer

[16] The author is indebted to Francis H. Bangs for some notes on this subject, and for materials about his father's connection with *Life*. See also *Yale University Library Gazette*, v. 7, pp. 53ff, Jan. 1933, as well as Bangs, *John Kendrick Bangs*.

[17] George Frisbie Whicher appears to be mistaken in his assertion in the *Cambridge History of American Literature* (New York, 1921, v. 3, p. 22), that *Puck* and *Judge*, as well as *Life*, "took their cue" from "the best of the college funny papers." He is, of course, correct in pointing out that they owed little to *Punch*.

[18] *Quarterly Illustrator*, v. 1, p. 123, June 1893.

[19] *Life*, v. 12, p. 72, Aug. 9, 1888.

Ben Butler, to stir up a pretty quarrel with Dana and his *Sun*. Ward McAllister and his "four hundred" it satirized mercilessly, along with the "dudes" and all Anglomaniacs. It badgered Christian Science, and asked pity for mistreated horses. It conducted a long fight against the trustees of the Metropolitan Art Museum, first against the acceptance of General di Cesnola's collections of specimens in art and archeology, much of which it thought spurious; and later against the rule closing the museum to the public on Sundays. Rigid sabbatarians always aroused its wrath; and Anthony Comstock, protector of the nation's virtue, suffered from its shafts.

The editor's own favorite crusade was that against vivisection: "He wrote scarcely anything for *Life*," Masson tells us, "except paragraphs showing up the cruelty of vivisection." [20] He would not argue the matter scientifically or statistically, but by barbed paragraphs and by pictures that were sometimes really distressing. Doctors were often angered by all this, and perhaps they were sometimes annoyed by other gibes; but thousands of them kept the attractive little periodical in their waiting rooms, thus dispensing a wit often more therapeutic than medicine.

But *Life's* satire was ordinarily far more gentle: the flirtatious summer girl, the vagaries of the rich, the expensiveness of marriage, the poker club on Thompson Street, calf love, the wistful humors of the poor — these were treated with more kindly pen and pencil. In 1887 *Life* instituted its Fresh Air Fund, taking up a collection among its subscribers that annually sent thousands of children of the slums to the country for a short time in the hot-weather period. And thus the procession of *Life's* interests passed:

> Fair Chloe, both ways drawn, choosing by toss
> 'Twixt Strephon's ardor and old Bullion's dross;
> Lucy and Jack kept single by the curse
> Of large requirements and a slender purse;
> The joys ornate in which the rich compete;
> The simple pastimes of a Thompson Street;
> Shanty-bred Romeo's high-flown speeches poured
> Into the infant ears of his adored;
> Cesnola's fragments joined with too much skill;
> The summer-girl, by ennui driven to kill
> The sluggish hours by stirring with her fan
> The smouldering passion of the casual man;
> The Sabbatarian, aye obtusely prone
> To estimate the Lord's Day as his own;
> The anxious tests the newly married make
> To learn what course two lives when lumped must take;

[20] *Bookman*, v. 48, p. 697, Feb. 1919.

In all his uses in recurring course,
That dearest quadruped to man, the horse;
Dudes, chappies, flunkies, bishops, statesmen, sports;
Brusque millionaires; professors of all sorts;
Managing matrons, doctors, perfect dears;
Prudes, politicians, fortune-hunting peers;
Prigs, flirts, small boys chock-full of devilment;
Wrong-headed folks who err with good intent;
Policemen, parsons, all the recurring train
That cross the boards of time, and come again,
While down in front, in strongest light, confer
The score-score stars of the McAllister.[21]

In 1888 Bangs resigned to join the Harper organization. Frank Marshall White took over his executive work, and Edward S. Martin returned to the magazine to write editorials and other pieces for it continuously thereafter. Martin's little essays on politics, lterature, art, and manners seemed to belong to *Life* by some kind of organic connection. Mitchell once wrote to him:

I can truthfully say of Martin that his civilizing influence has done much toward keeping *Life* from the gallows — the rest of us out of jail. . . . The moderation, justice, quiet humor, sanity, and moral tone of his editorials have proved a benign influence toward counteracting certain pugnacious antics in the other pages of the paper.[22]

It was about this time — in 1887, to be exact — that Charles Dana Gibson, not yet twenty-one, appeared in *Life*. Elated by his first acceptance, a check for four dollars, and Mitchell's praise, he immediately offered a dozen more drawings — "which were not unkindly declined." [23] But he had found his proper market, and his work continued to appear at intervals in *Life*. One can trace its evolution through 1889–1890, and ere long "the Gibson girl came shining like a bride." She was not always represented as a bride, of course — this serene, self-reliant, beautiful American girl — but she always had something of the radiance and sweet confidence of the bride. She had a real character; she was entirely convincing. "When Mr. Gibson undertakes to depict in the pages of *Life* a woman of refinement and gentle breeding," wrote Mitchell in *Scribner's*," he does it in such a manner that we have no suspicion of her using bad grammar when out of the picture." [24]

[21] *Life*, v. 21, p. 5, Jan. 1893.
[22] *Life*, v. 51, p. 14, Jan. 2, 1908.
[23] *Collier's*, v. 30, Nov. 29, 1902, p. 8. See also Fairfax Downey, *Portrait of an Era — as Drawn by Charles Dana Gibson* (New York, 1936), for details about Gibson's connection with *Life*.
[24] *Scribner's Magazine*, v. 6, p. 744, Dec. 1889. For some good comments on the "Gibson girl," see *Monthly Illustrator*, v. 3, pp. 3–8, Jan. 1895; and Anthony Hope's "Mr. C. D. Gibson on Love and Life," *McClure's Magazine*, v. 9, p. 870, Aug. 1897.

Through the pages of *Life* week after week for nearly twenty years (or until Gibson went abroad in 1905) tripped the Gibson girl — with the Gibson man, who was scarcely less a type. The man was square shouldered, firm jawed, handsome, well groomed, self-possessed. If both were a bit priggish, it was because they had been born to the purple, and knew it.

In the middle nineties, the American people took the Gibson girl to their hearts. She and the Gibson man became popular middle-class ideals. The girl of the nineties tried to dress and to stand like the popular idol, and to hold her chin as the picture girl held hers; she sang: "Why do they call me a Gibson girl, a Gibson girl, a Gibson girl?" while all the time she was doing her best to act so "they" would bestow that compliment upon her. The men squared their shoulders (with the help of their tailors), stuck out their chins, shaved off their mustaches. No doubt Gibson's ability to tell a story in a single black-and-white picture had much to do with this immense popularity; and thousands of homes were decorated with framed pictures from *Life* showing the Gibson girl and the Gibson man and the Gibson dowager and the Gibson rich old gentleman implying a whole drama by their attitudes and the expressions on thier faces. This led eventually to series of pictures; and "The Education of Mr. Pipp," printed in *Life* in 1898, was so popular that it was dramatized and staged by Augustus Thomas in New York.

The art work in *Life* developed to a very high point in the nineties. Halftones had come in during the preceding decade, the first double-page engraving of that type appearing in the Christmas number for 1886. Wash drawings became common. The lively fancy of Oliver Herford, M. A. Woolf's love of children and sympathy with the foibles of older children, S. W. Van Schaick's understanding of gentlefolk, and F. P. W. Bellew's ingenious devices were well known to readers of *Life* before 1890; they were continued, along with the work of Wilson de Meza, Alfred Brennan, Charles Howard Johnson, Albert B. Wenzell, and many others. In the later nineties, Henry Mayer, Penrhyn Stanlaws, Albert N. Blashfield, and T. S. Sullivant were prominent. "Great stress," says one editor, "was laid upon the right wording under the pictures"; [25] and the brevity and succinctness of these "cut lines" — excellent wit in themselves — added to the verve and sureness of the pictures.

James S. Metcalfe took over the theatrical reviewing in 1888, and for thirty years he discussed plays in *Life*. He was "a constant treader up-

[25] *Yale Review*, v. 15, p. 120, Oct. 1925.

on tender toes," [26] but a healthful influence on the theater. He was in the thick of the fight against the theatrical trust, banished from their houses, threatened with jail; but he was unterrified, and the monopolists finally dropped a libel suit brought against *Life* in 1907. "Droch" continued his book department until he was succeeded by J. B. Kerfoot in 1900.

*Life* was much interested in the exposition at Chicago in 1893 — particularly in its art and manners. It maintained a constant testimony against David B. Hill, William Jennings Bryan, Anthony Comstock, and the prohibitionists. It showed strong anti-Semitic feelings. The perennial summer girl kept her place in its pages, more and more often in bathing suits as bathing suits became more revealing and attractive. With the coming of the Spanish War, there was some interesting philosophic comment on patriotism, as well as a reflection of the exuberance of the times.

*Life* was one of the magazines whose prosperity was securely based on circulation. That knowledgeable gossip, *Printer's Ink*, said in 1894 that in the preceding year *Life* had made a profit of nearly a hundred thousand dollars, one-third of which came directly from circulation.[27] The magazine weathered the panic of 1907 easily, keeping its long-time circulation of sixty to seventy thousand. Mitchell thought the depression a good time to "splurge," so he put in more pictures than ever.[28] The newly arrived automobile was a great boon to *Life*: it not only brought joy to the advertising manager's heart, but it furnished a new theme for writers and artists. *Life's* famous automobile trip from New York to Paris afforded in 1908 one of the best satirical series the magazine had printed for years. Wallace Irwin's "Hashimura Togo" pieces were a great hit of 1912 and thereafter for several years. Harrison Fisher and James Montgomery Flagg made reputations drawing summer girls; and Orson Lowell, Albert Levering, and William L. Jacobs did amusing work.

Circulation went up and up in the second decade of the new century, reaching 150,000 in 1916. "The most successful ten-cent weekly is *Life*," wrote Colonel George Harvey somewhat enviously just before he sold *Harper's Weekly* in 1913; "it is crisp as a doughnut and as full of spice as a cooky." [29] It was full to bursting, also, with advertising, in which automobiles and liquors figured largely.

*Life* reached the height of its success just before the United States entered the First World War. It had then completed two full decades

[26] *Life*, v. 51, p. 14, Jan. 2, 1908.
[27] *Printer's Ink*, v. 10, p. 176, Feb. 14, 1894.
[28] *Bookman*, v. 48, p. 695, Feb. 1919.
[29] *Harper's Weekly*, v. 57, May 31, 1913, p. 3.

of very general acceptance by the more discriminating classes of American readers. It had become one of the two or three greatest satirical weeklies ever published in this country. Its very name was a token of smartness and wit without vulgarity. Some twenty-five volumes of selections from the magazine's pictures, verse, short stories, and so on, appeared during these twenty years, usually around Christmas time.[30]

Then came the World War. Mitchell, remembering perhaps his student days in Paris, was a vigorous champion of France and the allies from the beginning. *Life* issued a "John Bull Number" on January 27, 1916; it assailed the kaiser in a "Life of Attila the Second," which ran serially with pictures by Otho Cushing; it took up collections for French orphans; in 1916 it was filled with appeals to the United States to arm. But Mitchell did not live to see Germany humbled; he died in July 1918.

It is no reflection on the men who followed him to say that the loss of Mitchell was a crushing blow to *Life*. He had been so fully its guiding spirit that it was difficult for others to carry on without him. In the reorganization of the company, Miller became president and Metcalfe secretary, while Masson continued as managing editor. Then the next year Miller died; and, "as the result of much thought and many efforts,"[31] Charles Dana Gibson was brought in as chief owner and president of the publishing company in 1920, and Martin was installed as editor. F. de Sales Casey became art editor, and Robert C. Benchley theatrical reviewer. Martin remained as editor for only two years, after which Louis Evan Shipman, playwright and magazine writer, was editor for an equal period.

The new owner's career had been a romantic one: he had married the beautiful Irene Langhorne, of Virginia, had acquired a competency from his art, and had gone to Europe to paint and travel. But the financial stringency of 1907 brought Gibson back to America and to *Life*. Then when the magazine was up for sale in 1920, his friends rallied about him and enabled him to outbid the agents of F. N. Doubleday. The price was a round million dollars.

In the ensuing years, besides some of the older contributors, the readers of *Life* had sketches and poems by such writers as F. P. Adams, Corey Ford, Montague Glass, Rollin Kirby, Will Rogers, and Dorothy Parker. Prominent among the newer artists were Louis Raemaekers, Gluyas Williams, Coles Phillips, Will James, C. H. Sykes, and John

[30] See Library of Congress catalog. Most important of these was the series "The Good Things of *Life*," which was published annually by White, Stokes & Allen, of New York, beginning in 1884 for ten years or more.

[31] *Life*, v. 81, p. 18, Jan. 4, 1923.

Held, Jr. Percy L. Crosby's "Skippy" pictures won a following from
their beginning in 1923. There were picture-title contests, question contests, and movie directories. Under Mitchell's editorship, *Life* had never
taken motion pictures very seriously, but now "The Silent Drama"
was an important department, conducted by Robert E. Sherwood. In
1924 Sherwood became editor of the magazine — a position which he
held for four years. Skits by Ring Lardner became a feature. Baird
Leonard's "Mrs. Pep's Diary," a satire on the fashionable woman's
occupations, ran for several years. In an effort to make a wider geographical appeal, *Life* in 1928 began a department called "Neighborhood News," containing personal gossip from various cities written
after the fashion of the old country newspaper. In the same year Walter
Winchell began his "Along the Main Stem," which was also a gossip
page. But *Life's* most spectacular feature for 1928 was its nomination
of Will Rogers for president. The magazine now had decidedly more
variety than in earlier years; but it had lost, perhaps in gaining that
variety, the more or less insulated distinctiveness which had been
characteristic of it. Now much the same group of artists and wits were
working for it as contributed to *Judge.*

From the editorship of *Judge* came Norman Anthony in 1929, to be
editor of *Life.* Baird Leonard took over theaters, and Harry Leonard
movies. With Delevanter to portray the new bootleg society, R. B.
Fuller to work out really funny ideas of one kind and another, and
Ralph Barton to caricature actors and other public figures, *Life* kicked
up its heels. But it was a new *Life*, a *Life* of the era of bootleg and
other legs, a *Life* which, forgetful of the old delicacy, was not averse to
a bit of ribaldry now and then. The radio, crossword puzzles, the
careering stockmarket, the "speaky," and all in all a somewhat maud-
lin society furnished its materials. Editor Anthony was happy to see
his newsstand sales doubled and still going up; but his rejoicing was
cut short by a summons from President Gibson, who told him to forget
the newsstands and remember *Life's* traditions. It seems that advertisers were complaining about the change in the character of *Life's*
readership and therefore of the character of the market offered them.[32]
Editorial effervescence subsided; circulation declined, though it still
managed to keep above a hundred thousand. But the grand crack-up
was coming anyway.

Just before the stock-market collapse, Gibson turned over the presidency of the publishing company to Clair Maxwell, who, with Henry
Richter and Frederick Francis, became the new owner. Came the
crash, and *Life's* advertising, like that of most other magazines, tobog-

[32] Norman Anthony, *How to Grow Old Disgracefully* (New York, 1946), pp. 94–108.

ganed. Anthony gave up his editorial seat in 1930 to Bolton Mallory, and Mallory resigned two years later in favor of George T. Eggleston. In 1932, weekly publication, which had been maintained at five dollars a year for almost half a century, was abandoned; and *Life* became a fifteen-cent monthly.

Meantime, it crusaded against the Fourteenth Amendment. In 1929–1930 it inserted a series of five full-page advertisements in thirty-seven metropolitan newspapers protesting against the iniquities of prohibition. In 1932 it used a similar advertising campaign to influence the Democratic national convention to adopt a strong repeal plank in its platform.

Milt Gross, Don Herold, and Dr. Seuss were stand-bys; "Edwina" did her excellent "Sinbad" dog pictures, "Marge" satirized society, Percy Crosby's "Skippy" was introduced, and E. S. Martin continued his unruffled observations upon the passing scene. Frank Sullivan, Robert Benchley, and Dorothy Parker made a good trio.

Nevertheless, as the writer of *Life's* obituary in *Time* observed, the paper "had passed its prime, was definitely on the downgrade. The *New Yorker*, coming smartly into the field in 1925, was setting the pace for the New Humor. Later appeared such crude periodicals as *Ballyhoo* and *Hooey*, with their backhouse atmosphere. *Esquire* joined *Life's* competitors in 1933." [33] But *Life* was not bankrupt, and was indeed making a small profit when, in October 1936, with its November issue on the presses, it decided to give up the battle and accept an offer from Time, Inc. That corporation sold *Life's* subscription list, features, and goodwill to *Judge*, long its competitor; its name, for which it had been purchased, was reserved for the new picture magazine to be launched in November.

*Life* might well have ended its fine career in 1928. In its last decade it was a strayed reveler, having lost its way in a confused world. E. S. Martin came out of his octogenarian retirement to write the last words for the old paper, and he added his blessings on the new *Life* in these words: "I wish it all good fortune; grace, mercy, and peace; and usefulness to a world which does not know which way to turn nor what will happen to it next." [34]

[33] *Time*, v. 28, Oct. 19, 1936, p. 62.
[34] *Ibid.*, p. 63.

## THE LITERARY DIGEST [1]

ISAAC KAUFFMAN FUNK, founder of the *Literary Digest*, was a Lutheran clergyman, a publisher of books and periodicals, and a leader in the Prohibition party. He resigned from the regular ministry to enter that of religious journalism in 1872. Four years later he began a journal of his own; it was a repository of sermons, first called the *Metropolitan Pulpit* and later the *Homiletic Review*. This was a successful venture, and in 1877 Funk was joined by a former schoolmate in broadening his base of operations. This friend was Adam Willis Wagnalls, who had been practicing law for some years at Atchison, Kansas; and the broadening took the form of publication of standard books in cheap paper covers — a kind of publishing that was flourishing mightily in those years. In the presidential campaign of 1884, Funk & Wagnalls began a Prohibition paper called the *Voice*, later expanded and continued with great success as an organ of the party. In 1888 the firm took over publication of the *Missionary Review of the World*.

All of these enterprises seem to have been successful. Doctor Funk had an acute perception of the demands of middle-class culture in America. He did not, however, hesitate to take over for publication English works then in the public domain, or to defend his course against the rising tide of opinion that favored international copyright. One of the advocates of this reform, noting that the firm had reprinted the *Encyclopaedia Britannica* in a low-priced edition, used language that the publisher and his lawyers considered libelous. Funk thereupon sued

[1] TITLES: (1) *The Literary Digest: A Repository of Contemporaneous Thought and Research as Presented in the Periodical Literature of the World*, 1890–99; (2) *The Literary Digest: A Weekly Compendium of the Contemporaneous Thought of the World*, 1900–01; (3) *The Literary Digest*, 1902–July 10, 1937, Nov. 13, 1937–1938; (4) *The Digest: Review of Reviews, Incorporating The Literary Digest*, July 17–Nov. 6, 1937.

FIRST ISSUE: March 1, 1890. LAST ISSUE: Feb. 19, 1938. Merged with *Time*.

PERIODICITY: Weekly. Vol. 1, March–Oct. 1890; 2–14, Nov. 1890–April 1897, semiannual vols.; 15, May–Dec. 1897; 16–55, 1898–1917, regular semiannual vols.; 56–113, 1918–June 1932, quarterly vols.; 114–23, July 1932–June 1937, semiannual vols.; 124 (nos. 1–2), July 3, July 10, 1937; new series, v. 1 (nos. 1–24), July 17–Dec. 25, 1937; old series, v. 125 (nos. 1–8), Jan. 1–Feb. 19, 1938.

OWNERS AND PUBLISHERS: Funk & Wagnalls, 1890–92; Funk & Wagnalls Company (Robert Joseph Cuddihy, pub. 1905–37), 1892–1937; Review of Reviews Corporation (Albert Shaw, Jr., pub.), 1937; The Literary Digest, Inc. (George F. Havell, pub.), 1937–38. All New York.

EDITORS: Isaac Kauffman Funk, 1890–95; Edward Jewitt Wheeler, 1895–1905; William Seaver Woods, 1905–33; Arthur S. Draper, 1933–35; Morton Savell, 1935; Wilfred John Funk. 1936–37; Albert Shaw, 1937; David Perkins Page, 1937–38.

INDEXES: *Readers' Guide, Dramatic Index, Engineering Index*.

his critic, who was Edwin Lawrence Godkin, of the *New York Evening Post*, for libel; and only the courtroom genius of Joseph H. Choate, the defense attorney, saved Godkin from having to pay damages.[2]

In 1894 the *Standard Dictionary*, said to have cost a million dollars to produce, was published by Funk & Wagnalls under the general editorship of the senior partner.

Thus it was in the midst of arduous lexicographical labors that Funk undertook to edit the *Literary Digest*, a weekly eclectic of twenty-eight quarto pages, the first issue of which appeared under date of March 1, 1890. The periodical was quite in line with Funk's free-borrowing creed. The very idea was borrowed, for the early *Literary Digest* was clearly an imitation of the weekly *Current Opinion*, of Washington, and W. T. Stead's monthly *Review of Reviews*, which had begun publication in London two months before the *Literary Digest* began.

Funk's periodical was very well put together. The editor was a compiler of no mean ability, with wide interests, encyclopedic knowledge, and strong feelings. The orderliness of the *Digest* was almost repellent, and its want of illustration gave the whole a grey appearance; but the fact is that nearly everything in the magazine was worth reading.

The first and most important section, occupying more than half the magazine, was entitled "The Reviews," and consisted of condensations (not excerpts)[3] of articles that had recently appeared in American, English, Canadian, German, French, and Italian periodicals, with occasional pieces from those of other countries. More than a score of journals were thus laid under tribute in each issue; the editor was not a player of favorites, and he boasted that "173 of the leading periodicals of the world" had been drawn upon during the *Digest's* first year. A typical number in the early nineties would contain about ten condensations from American magazines, five each from England and Germany, and three or four from France, Italy, Canada, or perhaps Turkey, Russia, or Norway. The abstracts ranged in length from one to two thousand words. "The Reviews" section was divided into six parts: "Political," "Sociological," "Education, Literature, Art," "Science and Philosophy," "Religious," and "Miscellaneous." The politics always included something of foreign affairs; the sociology contained a good deal of ethics; and the religious selections generally had a rather liberal point of view.

[2] *Journalist*, Feb. 25, 1893; Allan Nevins, *The Evening Post, A Century of Journalism* (New York, 1922), pp. 560–62.

[3] There seems to be a general idea on the part of those who have not examined the file that the early *Literary Digest* was a mere paste-up of clippings — a complete misconception.

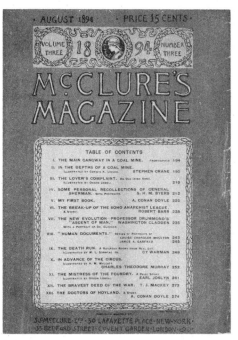

THE CHRISTMAS
MUNSEY 1896

If you have a son
or a sweetheart in
you why—if

Ten Cents A Copy—Yearly Subscription One Dollar
Frank A. Munsey III Fifth Avenue, New York

COVERS OF THE THREE LEADING TEN-CENT MAGAZINES OF THE 1890's

Together with that of *Scribner's*, the lowest-priced "quality magazine." See pages 3–6.

CHARLES A. DANA, JOSEPH PULITZER, AND HENRY WATTERSON

A cartoon from *Puck* (May 18, 1887) showing these editors trying to
dam the flood of Cleveland's popularity. See pages 240–243.

The remainder of the early *Digest* was always occupied by two departments — "Books" and "The Press." The former was allotted two pages and offered three to five reviews, usually of serious books. The latter, which was eventually to develop into the premier department of the magazine, at this time contained only clippings from American newspapers — seven pages of them, with three columns in small type to each page. These, too, were in categories — politics, foreign affairs, religion, "The Liquor Issue," and so on. On the last two pages was an "Index to Periodical Literature," citing some of the leading articles in American and foreign magazines; a list of new books; and a column in which the leading events of the preceding week, to within four days of the publication date, were recited.

In its first two or three years the *Literary Digest* made a very modest success. It circulated only a few thousand copies, at three dollars a year or ten cents a number, and it carried four pages of advertising per issue. In December 1893, stimulated perhaps by the establishment of an American edition of the *Review of Reviews*, it made some improvements. It began to use some illustration — portraits of public figures by halftone, and newspaper cartoons reproduced by line-cuts. Quite as important was a modernizing of the arrangement of departments and an improvement in typographical layout. "Questions of the Day," later called "Topics of the Day," now supplanted "The Reviews" as the first department in the magazine; and the informational introductions to quoted newspaper editorials, which were later to become an effective part of *Digest* articles, now made their first trial appearances. There remained, however, for a few years longer, some mere consecutive printing of digests on given questions. "Topics of the Day" nearly all came from newspapers; but the magazines made their showing under "Literature and Art," "Science and Invention," and "The Religious World." Under "Foreign Topics" the newspapers were back again.

By 1895 the *Digest*, despite the hard times, had won a circulation of twenty-five thousand. For five years Doctor Funk, with the aid of such office assistants as Edwin Munsell Bliss (1890–1891) and J. T. Wright (1890–1895), had edited [4] the magazine in connection with many other duties. Now Edward Jewitt Wheeler, who had been editor of the *Voice* since its beginning, took over also the editorship of the *Literary Digest*. He was to keep that position for ten years, and to give the *Digest* its characteristic pattern.

Wheeler's great contributions were two — one relating to form, and the other to the quality and spirit of the editing. Under "Topics of

---

[4] *Public Libraries*, v. 14, p. 213, June 1909.

the Times" the *Digest* now carried a series of articles on the four or five leading events of the week in the United States, each having an informative news summary arranged as an introduction and leading into the exact quotation of parts of a document, an interview, or a news story, or of any two or all three of these, and followed by reprints of related newspaper editorials in whole or substantial part. For example, the leading story on April 9, 1898, was on the report of the United States Naval Court of Inquiry into the destruction of the battleship *Maine* in Havana harbor. It began with some facts about the investigation, passed rapidly to the data of the report itself, and then quoted half a dozen paragraphs from it; then it gave something about President McKinley's message transmitting the report, with quotations from it, after which it quoted some paragraphs from the Spanish Naval Commission on the same subject. This article, longer than most, then ended with two pages of comments on the report and the President's reaction to it, from the *Philadelphia Press*, the *Boston Journal*, the *New York World*, the *Chicago Journal*, the *Detroit Journal*, and the *New York Tribune*. Thus the quotations from both documents and newspapers were woven into a single comprehensive article, with skillful introductory and transitional paragraphs by the editor. This was Wheeler's contribution to form in the *Digest*; the other element he added was greater editorial skill in selection and presentation of material which would interest as well as inform. Thus the periodical became livelier in content, arrangement, and typography under his editorship.

The departments which were entitled "Letters and Art," and "The Religious World" did not lend themselves so well to the weaving process as did "Topics of the Times," unless, as occasionally happened, the articles under those headings were of a controversial nature and more than one commentator could be quoted. In those departments, however, it was usually a matter of digesting a single article very summarily, and then working in a fairly long quotation or two. "Science and Invention," long edited by Arthur E. Bostwick, used a similar treatment.[5] But in "Foreign Topics" the editor could again use the techniques of "Topics of the Times," with translated paragraphs from papers in various languages. The *Digest* continued its summary record called "Current Events," and its chess page, and added a department of personal notes about famous people, which was to become a fixture, and one on business and finance.

Wit and humor columns were also developed. One made up of the

[5] See Arthur E. Bostwick, *A Life With Men and Books* (New York, 1939), pp. 147–64, for the author's reminiscences of this editorship.

paragraphic wit of the newspaper editorial pages was called "Topics in Brief." In 1900 "More or Less Pungent" was begun, to be followed by the famous "Spice of Life," which was composed of bits from newspapers and magazines the country over, and eventually picked up by the motion picture films. "Slips That Pass in the Type" was the heading of a budget of typographical misfortunes funny to everyone but the proofreader.

Circulation advanced steadily but slowly, reaching sixty-three thousand by 1900. About that time several improvements were made. For one thing, there was more illustration, much of which came from the same sources that were drawn on for the articles quoted and digested. Also, the magazine became somewhat more literary in flavor, with the introduction of a new and excellent department of "Current Poetry" in 1901 and more or less regular book reviews two years later. The interesting query-and-answer department called "The Lexicographer's Easy Chair" began in 1904; it was conducted by Frank H. Vizetelly, then managing editor of Funk & Wagnalls' *Standard Dictionary.* Doctor Funk came out for "simplified spelling" in 1900,[6] and the *Digest* adopted the limited list of twelve spellings of common words endorsed by the National Education Association.

In 1905, much to the surprise of many who had considered him a fixture on the *Literary Digest* staff,[7] Wheeler resigned to accept the editorship of *Current Literature,* later called *Current Opinion.*[8] Though not precisely forced out, Wheeler had doubtless felt that the time and opportunity for a change had come. A new aggressiveness had come into the top management, centering in Robert Joseph Cuddihy. Though he still came regularly to the office, Funk had virtually retired, to devote his few remaining years to the investigation of psychic phenomena. Cuddihy, who had come to the firm at sixteen as an office boy long before the *Literary Digest* was born, and whose drive had made him business manager, was now publisher. His Catholic morality was quite as marked as Funk's Lutheran ethics: the ban against smoking in the editorial offices was maintained, and it is said that divorce and drinking were equally disqualifying habits on the *Digest* staff, and that female secretaries sometimes were required to occupy offices separate from those of male editors.[9] But more important than these peccadilloes was the promotion program that Cuddihy devised for the magazine. In 1906 he bought *Public Opinion* and combined it with the *Digest,* and then he embarked on an advertising campaign which was so ex-

[6] *Literary Digest,* v. 20, p. 515, April 28, 1900.
[7] *Critic,* v. 49, p. 198, Sept. 1906.
[8] See pp. 509–10.
[9] *Newsweek,* v. 9, June 26, 1927, p. 24.

pensive that it terrified his partners,[10] but which brought the magazine up to two hundred thousand by 1909, to double that seven years later,[11] and eventually to a million and a half average annual circulation.

A publishing embarrassment of 1919 should be mentioned, chiefly because it served to bring out an interesting printing technique. A strike of compositors caused the *Digest* to employ a method called "callitypy" to bypass the linotype. This was merely a combination of typewriting and zinc etching.[12] It was less satisfactory than the "cold type" method evolved by strike-bound Chicago newspapers in 1948, but it served well enough for the duration of this strike.

Wheeler's successor as editor was William Seaver Woods, who had come to the *Digest* from newspaper work in 1897; he was to serve as editor-in-chief for more than a quarter-century — through the magazine's period of greatest prosperity.

Probably the *Literary Digest's* coverage of the First World War did more to establish it in a high place among American periodicals than anything else. Its maps were made by professional cartographers; they were usually in two or more colors, and they were very frequent. On July 31, 1915, it published its "History of the First Year of the European War," and this was followed by other more elaborate annual résumés. The magazine collected about ten million dollars during the war for Belgian and Near East relief.

By the end of the war, the *Digest* was claiming nine hundred thousand circulation, and it went on from there to a million and a half by 1927. The twenties were the great period of the magazine. *Time* later declared: "In the 1920's the *Literary Digest* had become one of the greatest publishing successes in history." [13] In the weekly field, it was surpassed in circulation only by the runaway *Saturday Evening Post*. The advertising in the *Digest* was one of the wonders of the decade. It had issued a hundred-page number as early as August 26, 1913; on April 17, 1920, it had one hundred and seventy-four large-quarto pages, and there were a good many other issues of over a hundred and fifty pages throughout the early twenties. In 1922 the yearly subscription price was raised to four dollars, without changing the single-copy rate of ten cents.

The abundance of advertising made it necessary to increase the text, adding new departments and expanding the old ones. Sections devoted

---

[10] *Ibid.*

[11] See Ayer's directory, remembering that figures are, in this period, generally for approximately the year preceding that given on the title page.

[12] *Literary Digest*, v. 63, Nov. 15, 1919, pp. 44–50.

[13] *Time*, v. 31, March 7, 1938, p. 55.

to sports and to "Birds, Beasts, and Trees" ran through the advertising pages; but perhaps the most popular for a few years was "Personal Glimpses," which often occupied over twenty columns with its sketches of men and women of all classes, taken from books, magazines, and newspapers. In these years covers were usually color reproductions of good paintings.

One of the reasons for the *Digest's* great popularity was its reputation for impartiality. If it quoted a Republican paper on a controversial question, it would immediately balance that quotation with one from a leading Democratic organ, and add a third from an Independent paper for good measure. A student of magazines in the twenties declared: "No faction, whether political, religious, or intellectual, may honestly assert prejudice by the *Literary Digest* for or against its cause." [14]

This quality, and its high moral tone and interesting variety, as well as the lucidity of its presentations, combined to make the *Digest* acceptable for use in schools, and in the twenties it had a circulation of over one hundred thousand among students in schools and colleges.[15]

But the activity that was most generally identified with the *Literary Digest* in the popular mind during the twenties and the early thirties was the taking of election polls, or "straw votes," as they were then called. In the years immediately preceding World War I, the *Digest* refined its techniques of collating editorial opinion by occasionally telegraphing editors for an expression of opinion on some crucial question as a short cut over the usual method. This led to questioning others by wire and mail, and that soon developed into small "straw votes." Thus, the issue for April 29, 1916, carried a poll of members of state legislatures the country over on their choices for the party nominees for President; and on October 7 of that year there was a poll of labor union officials on the impending election. The polls of 1916 were then climaxed by a vote of fifty thousand *Digest* readers in Illinois, Indiana, Ohio, New Jersey, and New York, regarded as key states, on the presidential contest. This proved a good barometer, and four years later the same method was successfully used, with California added.

In the meantime, the *Digest* had taken other votes. It found its polls profitable in three ways: the results were highly interesting to its own readers; the newspapers gave them a good "play" as real news, and this was fine promotion for the magazine; and, finally, with every

---

[14] John E. Drewry, *Some Magazines and Magazine Makers* (Boston, 1924), p. 13.

[15] *Literary Digest*, v. 75, Nov. 18, 1922, p. 44. See also "The Literary Digest as a Text-Book," *ibid.*, v. 46, Nov. 11, 1913, p. 81.

ballot sent out there was an attached subscription blank, and the operation paid as a solicitation campaign. And so such issues as the veterans' bonus, the Mellon plan for tax reduction (fifteen million ballots), and the enforcement or repeal of the Prohibition Amendment were made the subjects of such voting. Prohibition polls were taken in 1922, 1930, and 1932, from eight to twenty million ballots being mailed out to automobile owners and telephone subscribers. All resulted in "wet" victories — an ironical turn when we consider the traditions of the *Digest* management.

Though there had been a national poll in 1920 on presidential nominations, in which eleven million ballot cards had been mailed, the first nation-wide *Digest* poll on a presidential election was that of 1924, with sixteen and a half million ballots mailed. In this vote the medial average plurality error per state was 12 per cent; it ranged as high as 45 per cent for Connecticut and as low as 1 per cent for Michigan and South Dakota. This was not really good predicting; but the only other agency making a national poll was the Hearst Newspapers, and their average error was the same, with a state range from 0 to 62 per cent.[16] The *Digest* error favored Coolidge, giving him too large a proportion of the vote in all but seven states.[17] But the interest was encouraging, and eighteen million ballots were distributed in the campaign four years later. Again the medial average plurality error per state was 12 per cent; again it was the Republican candidate (Hoover) who was favored — this time in every state in the union.

But the *Digest* was inclined to poke fun at criticism and the niceties of the statisticians. It took the attitude that predicting the leader in most of the states and, most important, the winner in the electoral college was all that was necessary. In 1924 it had predicted the electoral vote totals exactly three days before the general election (November 1, 1924); and when the prediction of 1928 was almost equally accurate, some papers suggested calling off the elections and substituting *Digest* polls.[18] In 1932, when it actually polled the largest number of votes — over three million — which it ever recorded on any question, the *Digest* was even more fortunate than previously on state predictions, though it went wrong on Pennsylvania. "Not even Franklin D. Roosevelt can feel more triumphant that the editors of the *Literary Digest*," observed the *Kansas City Journal-Post*. And the editors in question,

[16] Claude E. Robinson, *Straw Votes: A Study of Political Prediction* (New York, 1932), p. 67. The table on this page is the source also for the 1928 percentage of error.
[17] *Ibid.*, p. 72.
[18] *Literary Digest*, v. 110, Nov. 17, 1928, p. 9.

quoting the *Journal-Post*, showed how triumphant they felt by promising: "When better polls are built, the *Digest* will build them." [19]

Pride goeth before falling flat on one's face, however. In 1936, the *Literary Digest*, sending out ten million ballots but receiving less than a fourth of them back, showed Landon a victor by four votes out of seven, and represented him as carrying New York, Pennsylvania, California, Ohio, Illinois, etc. In the election he carried only Maine and Vermont. "The *Digest* mispredicted a Landonslide," said *Time*.[20]

The lists of those to whom the *Digest* sent ballots for its polls before 1936 were derived from telephone books, the registers of automobile ownership, and their own subscription rolls. In 1936 the telephone lists, which were hard to keep up to date, were largely discarded.[21] The spectacular debacle of 1936 has generally been ascribed to the failure of the sample to reach the lower economic brackets of the voting population. The *Digest* could explain the fiasco only by the theory that for some occult reason Republicans answered a mail questionnaire more readily than Democrats.[22]

It has often been conjectured that the *Literary Digest's* collapse in 1937 was due to its loss of prestige through the notorious poll of the preceding year. Of course, that was no help, but the old magazine had been on the way out previously. As the president of the publishing company wrote later, the *Digest* was already punch-drunk, and this was the last blow.[23] It was a victim of the depression and of the competition of *Time* and *Newsweek*, fresher and sprightlier weekly news magazines. Its decline was apparent as early as 1932, when it dropped some circulation, despite the facts that it was using insurance-policy premiums and that a presidential campaign was in full blast. It lost advertising heavily in the early thirties.

Woods retired as editor in 1933, and Arthur S. Draper, an assistant editor of the *New York Herald Tribune*, succeeded him. William Morris Houghton, *Herald Tribune* editorial writer, joined the staff in 1934, to do a page called "At the Observation Post." About the same time Robert Winsmore, of the *Philadelphia Inquirer*, joined as financial and industrial editor. The familiar fare of the *Digest* table — diverse editorial comment — was reduced to a minimum. Articles appeared by well-known writers on current topics — Edward Price Bell, Silas Bent, Joseph Cummings Chase, and so on. A poll of California in the fall of

[19] *Literary Digest*, v. 114, Nov. 26, 1932, p. 6.
[20] *Time*, v. 29, June 28, 1937, p. 40.
[21] Memorandum from Wilfred Funk.
[22] *Literary Digest*, v. 122, Nov. 14, 1936, p. 7.
[23] Memorandum from Wilfred Funk.

1934 indicated the impending defeat of Upton Sinclair and his EPIC program. Draper's *Digest* was an attractive magazine, and circulation responded for a time, exceeding a million a week; but it was down again in 1935, and the magazine had a new editor by midyear — Morton Savell. But after a few months Wilfred J. Funk, son of the founder, president of the firm since 1925 with about 43 per cent of its stock, took over as editor-in-chief. He dropped the by-lined articles and made the weekly more *Time*-ly than ever, but circulation continued downward with discouraging consistency.

With the number for July 17, 1937, the *Literary Digest* came into the hands of the Review of Reviews Corporation, of which Albert Shaw, Jr., was president. Funk & Wagnalls actually gave the *Digest* to the *Review of Reviews*, although less than ten years earlier Cuddihy had offered Funk five million dollars for his 40 per cent interest.[24] In its last number under the Funk & Wagnalls Company, the *Digest* announced the sale and called attention to the fact that its own backgrounds and history were almost identical with those of the *Review of Reviews*.[25]

The monthly and the weekly were now combined in a weekly entitled *The Digest: Reviews of Reviews Incorporating the Literary Digest*. And to complicate further the question of which periodical had absorbed the other, a new numbering was adopted beginning with Volume I, Number 1. The elder Albert Shaw, now an octogenarian, took on the new editing job. His former associates, Howard Florance and David Perkins Page, were installed as managing editors, John T. Hackett as news editor, John Bakeless as literary editor, Roger Shaw (the other son of the editor-in-chief) as foreign editor, Sigmund Spaeth as music editor, and so on. Thus fully staffed, the weekly emphasized amusing illustration, a "Pro" and "Con" double page on controversial issues, and features. There was no doubt, however, where the magazine stood on the New Deal; it was a loyal adherent of President Roosevelt.

But in October 1937 the *Digest* was sold again, and it resumed the old title of *Literary Digest* on November 13. At a price again reported as two hundred thousand dollars [26] George F. Havell, former managing editor of the *Forum*, and a group of associates had purchased the merged news magazine. Page, who had been associate editor of the *Review of Reviews* under Shaw, took over the top editorship of the *Digest* from his chief at the time of the sale and determined to make it less partisan and more newsy. But now it was short of money; capital it had hoped

[24] *Ibid.*
[25] *Literary Digest*, v. 124, July 10, 1937, p. 3.
[26] *Time*, v. 30, Oct. 25, 1937, p. 71.

to attract was shy of a magazine whose circulation had dropped to less
than half a million, which carried only a few pages of advertising, and
which was able to issue a mere twenty-four pages in comparison with
the hundred or more in the weekly numbers of other news magazines.
So after the issue of February 19, 1938, publication was suspended —
temporarily, it was hoped. A letter sent as a test to ten thousand subscribers begged for help:

> *Literary Digest* is not just another magazine; it is an American Institution of
> major importance. *It cannot be allowed to die.* . . . We ask you to put a dollar
> in the enclosed return envelope. . . . Your dollar will be credited to your sub-
> scription as an increase in rate.[27]

The appeal brought many dollar remittances and some outright gifts;
then the Audit Bureau of Circulations stepped into the picture, forbidding such an irregular tampering with rates and circulation methods.
It was ironic that the A.B.C., which Funk had fought to the end of his
life, should deliver the *coup de grâce* to the periodical he had founded
and so long nurtured. For now Havell returned the gifts, and petitioned
the court for permission to reorganize under the Bankruptcy Act.
*Time*, candid reporter of good and evil to decrepit ancient and brash
youngster alike, willingly recorded the fatal statistics:

> Against liabilities of $1,492,056 (including a $60,000 demand note to Funk &
> Wagnalls — original *Literary Digest* publishers — $63,000 for paper, $30,000 for
> printing, $612,000 to readers for paid-up subscriptions), the *Digest* listed assets
> of $850,923: cash on hand, $222,293; mailing lists, furniture, machinery, $377,-
> 794; deferred charges, $160,821; goodwill, $90,015.[28]

After three months' suspension, the *Digest* was taken over by *Time*,
which filled out the 250,000 unexpired subscriptions.[29]

Publisher Havell was right in his claim that the *Literary Digest*
was an American institution. For almost half a century it was a depend-
able and impartial recorder of public opinion as expressed in the press,
as well as a repository of digests of, and extracts from, current informational literature.

It was the typical periodical of a generation which placed a high
value on ordered information in many fields, presented seriously for
leisurely study.

[27] *Time*, v. 31, March 28, 1938, p. 44.
[28] *Ibid.*
[29] *Time*, v. 31, May 23, 1938, p. 47.

## McCALL'S MAGAZINE [1]

J AMES McCALL learned the tailor's trade in Scotland, where he
had been an orphan apprentice. When he had become a full journeyman tailor, he came to America. After he had tried country towns
in New York and Ohio, he was able to set himself up in business in
New York through the income from certain improvements he had
made in the sewing machine.[2]

And so by 1869 McCall was a New York tailor, and agent for the
"Royal Chart" in the United States. The "Royal Chart" was a system
for drafting dressmaking patterns, and it opened a successful career to
the young tailor. He soon went back to Jefferson, Ohio, and married a
Miss Abel, and together they built up a pattern business that was
destined to reach large proportions and to persist up to the present
writing, and doubtless many years longer.

Having developed their own patterns, James McCall & Company
felt the need of a fashion sheet to promote them. It was probably in
the fall of 1873 [3] that the first number of *The Queen: Illustrating
McCall's Bazar Glove-Fitting Patterns* was issued. Consisting of four
small-folio pages, printed on pink paper in ten monthly issues each
year, this fashion paper carried some notes dealing with the latest

---

[1] TITLES: (1) *The Queen*, 1873–91; (2) *The Queen of Fashion*, 1891–97; (3) *McCall's
Magazine*, 1897–current. (Title on cover and contents page since 1950: *McCall's*.)
FIRST ISSUE: Sept. (?) 1873 (?). Current.
PERIODICITY: Monthly; annual vols. Early vols. (1–14?) omitted Jan.–Feb. and July–Aug.
each year; 15–21 omitted only July–Aug. each year; 22–24 (Sept. 1894–Aug. 1919) regular
annual vols. beginning with Sept. and ending with Aug.; 47, Sept. 1919–Sept. 1920; 48–cur-
rent (Oct. 1920–current) regular annual vols. ending with Sept.
PUBLISHERS: James McCall & Company, 1873–90; McCall Publishing Company, 1890;
Bladworth & Company, 1890–92; Page & Ringot, 1892–93; J. H. Ringot & Company, 1893;
McCall Company (James H. Ottley, 1893–1913; White, Weld & Company 1913–36), 1893–
1936; McCall Corporation, 1936–current. All New York, but office of publication Dayton,
Ohio, 1924–current.
EDITORS: James McCall and wife (?), 1873–84; "May Manton" (Mrs. George H. Blad-
worth), 1885–91; Frances M. Benson, 1892–96; Miss E. B. Clapp, 1897–1911; William Grif-
fith, 1911–12; Alice Manning, 1912–16; Myra G. Reed, 1916–18; Bessie Beatty, 1918–21;
Harry P. Burton, 1921–27; Otis L. Wiese, 1928–current.
INDEX: *Readers' Guide*.
REFERENCES: *McCall People* (Dayton, Ohio, 1949), sec. 1; *The Pace and the Pattern*
(New York, 1950), promotion brochure.
[2] Clipping from *Jefferson* (Ohio) *Gazette*, undated, furnished by Clifton Krausz, of the
McCall organization.
[3] Until 1920 the entries in the periodical directories uniformly carried the date of founding
as 1873; it was then changed to 1870 for no discoverable reason. Certainly 1873 more nearly
agrees with volume numbering, which ended v. 47 with Sept. 1920. An issue bound in with the
Oct. 1888 number of *Arthur's Home Magazine* is called v. 15, no. 10.

modes on the first page, but was otherwise devoted to woodcut pictures of the garments for which patterns were offered. McCall patterns were said to be superior to those of competitors because they made no allowances for seams, leaving that matter to the individual dressmaker to adjust according to her materials. As the business prospered, the McCalls added certain semiannual publications, issued in spring and fall, so that by the late eighties they were offering for the sum of one dollar ten numbers of the *Queen*, published monthly except for two summer months; two issues of the *Bazar Dressmaker*, each containing a thousand illustrations of fashions from Paris, London, Berlin, Vienna, and New York; two semiannual catalogs; and two "magnificent colored fashion plates."

In 1884 James McCall died and his widow became president of the company. It may be conjectured that Mrs. McCall had been for some time editor of the *Queen*, which now consisted of eight smaller and more manageable pages of fashions and fashion news, issued monthly in an edition (so it claimed) [4] of three hundred thousand copies. At any rate, the editorship was now confided to Mrs. George H. Bladworth, wife of one of the chief members of the McCall organization, who wrote under the name "May Manton." A little more variety, in the way of household helps, fancywork suggestions, and so on, was introduced.

In 1890 George H. Bladworth became president of the concern, which was now called the McCall Publishing Company; and the next year the title of the magazine was enlarged to *The Queen of Fashion*.[5] The periodical now had twelve pages, and could be taken separately for thirty cents a year. These were not prosperous years, however, and in the fall of 1892 the company was bought at sheriff's sale by Page & Ringot, which next year became J. H. Ringot & Company. Mrs. Bladworth yielded the editorial tripod to Frances M. Benson.

Miss Benson continued as editor when the McCall Company was taken over by James Henry Ottley in 1893. It was about time a strong businessman took control, for the circulation of the *Queen of Fashion*, on which the pattern business was largely based, had dropped to twelve thousand.[6] Ottley was good medicine. He raised the annual subscription price to forty cents, increased the size to sixteen pages,

---

[4] Letter to an advertiser, Dec. 31, 1884, in files of company. Subsequent circulation figures are from current directories.

[5] Leslie & Company had published a *Queen of Fashion* during 1883–85, apparently unconnected with McCall's *Queen*.

[6] "James Henry Ottley," in *National Cyclopaedia of American Biography* (New York, 1935), v. 24, p. 65. Rowell's directory for 1893 gives the circulation as "over 75,000 not guaranteed." The *Remington Bros. Newspaper Manual*, 1893, carries an advertisement of Page & Ringot (p. 477) claiming 200,000!

and improved the editorial variety. Circulation responded, going to seventy-five thousand in a year. Pattern prices were cut in half (all of them now sold at ten or fifteen cents), and agencies were established throughout the country, with branch offices in Atlanta, Chicago, San Francisco, and Toronto. The *Queen of Fashion* now became a five-cent monthly (fifty cents a year), offering sixteen to thirty-two small-folio pages of fare somewhat more varied than formerly, with some illustration by woodcuts. The first fiction *McCall's* ever printed was a short story in the number for August 1894, which had won a prize of ten dollars offered by the magazine. The publishers were now insisting that the *Queen* was "not a mere fashion journal, but it contains other news and articles of interest to women." And it did — a "Children's Corner," a fancywork department, a column of literary notes, a budget of jokes, and a few editorials — but fashions were still the chief offering, and the chief function of the periodical was the promotion of McCall's pattern business. The front-page feature was a large fashion picture.

In 1896 the *Queen* was reduced to the quarto size common to the women's magazines of the period. As a forty-page book with "fashion plate" cover, it was greatly improved in appearance. A further change came in the next year, when the title became *McCall's Magazine: The Queen of Fashion*; the subtitle was carried for seven years. With change of title came change of editors, and Miss E. B. Clapp was installed for a term of fifteen years. It was not until 1911 that she gave place to the poet William Griffith, who came from *Hampton's* and *Travel,* had a short tenure with *McCall's,* and went to *Current Opinion* and *Author's Digest.*

But with changes in names, formats, and editors, there was little alteration in editorial policy. *McCall's* remained a cheap magazine for women, with emphasis on styles and patterns, as long as Ottley owned it. It still sold for fifty cents a year, with a free dress pattern as a bonus, and larger premiums offered for clubs. Subscribers could buy McCall patterns illustrated in the magazine at half price. But the printing of *McCall's* showed a marked improvement over that of the old *Queen of Fashion* in typographical design, presswork, paper stock, and illustration. At the end of the nineties the outstanding items of content were two big fashion plates in each number, produced in brilliant chromolithography. Also there were more articles and fiction, all by unknowns, but interesting and informative and sentimental. There was more content (often as much as seventy-two pages by 1900) because there was more advertising, and there was more advertising because there was more circulation.

Circulation reached a hundred thousand in 1899, doubled that in the next two years, and then advanced steadily to a million in 1908. Charles D. Spaulding became advertising manager and vice-president in the latter year, succeeding B. L. Davis; and soon hundred-page issues, carrying sixty or seventy pages of advertising, were common. Even in the first and most difficult years of the Ottley ownership, the magazine had accepted "no unguaranteed patent medicine advertisements," [7] thus beginning a tradition of careful supervision of advertising pages.

In 1913 Ottley decided that his magazine, though reasonably prosperous, had reached the point where it required generous refinancing if it were to go ahead in competition with the standard women's journals of the country. He therefore sold the whole concern — magazine, pattern business, *McCall Book of Fashions,* and so on — to White, Weld & Company, a banking firm. In his ten years of ownership, Ottley had brought the circulation of the magazine from twelve thousand to a million and a quarter, and the number of company employees from thirteen to seven hundred. He had worked intimately with the entire organization, had watched all details of operation, and had become a fellow workman with printers, draftsmen, and editors.

The new president of the McCall Corporation, as it was now called,[8] was Edward Alfred Simmons, who was also president of the Simmons-Boardman Company, publishers of the *Railway Age.* After a year or two he was succeeded by Allen H. Richardson. These were fumbling, experimental years which had now come upon *McCall's.* Its owners wanted to make it a major magazine, but they did not know how. Cash prizes were offered for the best essays with the title "If I Were Editor," and many suggestions of questionable value were collected. Some changes were adopted. For example, name writers were introduced by 1915; Editor Alice Manning bought serials and short stories from Mary Imlay Taylor, Eunice Tietjens, Nathalie Sumner Lincoln, Zona Gale, and other well-known magazinists.

Then in February 1917 *McCall's* took the important step of raising its single-copy price to ten cents, which took it once and for all out of the cheap-household-journal class. The mail subscription price was juggled for a few years between seventy-five cents, a dollar, and a dollar and a half. Toward the end of World War I, *McCall* circulation showed a decline instead of an advance, for the first time in many years; and advertising in 1919 dropped to an average of less than twenty-five pages an issue. Danger signals were out.

---

[7] "James Henry Ottley," in *National Cyclopaedia.*

[8] The name of the over-all organization was changed to McCall Corporation with the reorganization of 1913, but the magazine continued to be published by the McCall Company, a subsidiary, until 1936.

At this juncture, William Bishop Warner was brought into the organization and elected president of the corporation. His background was in the merchandising business, but he was a great organizer and he proved to be a great publisher. One thing he did soon after taking up his new responsibilities was to part company with the dictatorial American News people and organize the S-M News Company for the distribution of the McCall periodicals and those of the Popular Science Publishing Company. But even more important were his courage in pouring the company's money into the editorial department of *McCall's* and his audience sense in respect to the spending of those funds.

Myra G. Reed had followed Miss Manning as editor for two years, 1916–1918; and Bessie Beatty, well-known newspaper writer and foreign correspondent, lasted a little longer than that, 1918–1921. Then Harry Payne Burton, who had been a foreign correspondent and a feature writer for the Newspaper Enterprise Association, became editor for a six-year period, with a mandate to bring famous and popular writers into *McCall's* pages. Thus E. Phillips Oppenheim, one of the earliest *McCall* authors of this type, seemed to lead (with a serial illustrated by Montgomery Flagg) a procession of the successful writers of the day — Robert W. Chambers, Ethel M. Dell, Emerson Hough, Samuel Merwin, Louis Joseph Vance, Arthur Somers Roche, Gilbert Parker, Dorothy Canfield, Kathleen Norris, Booth Tarkington, Mary Roberts Rinehart, Harold Bell Wright, Zane Grey, James Oliver Curwood, Joseph Hergesheimer, Juliet Wilbor Tompkins, and so on and on.

Nor was the magazine all fiction. During World War I there had been many articles and features dealing with the various "war efforts"; and articles by Henry Van Dyke, Albert Bigelow Paine, Mary Heaton Vorse, and others mingled with the fiction. In October 1920 appeared a Fiftieth Anniversary Number; [9] it led off with an article by George Bernard Shaw which was entitled "Woman Since 1860," and which began: "I was born in 1856. Shortly after this I became conscious of women . . ." Lady Astor wrote on "Woman's War For Peace" in January 1928, and Margot Asquith, on "American Women," led the number for July 1922. Gene Stratton-Porter had a special page in the early twenties for her "messages" to *McCall* readers. Also there were always a dozen pages of fashions, a trade-mark of the magazine; new McCall patterns were now printed in its pages. Beginning in March 1921 there were four-color fashion plates, and by the mid-twenties *McCall's* pages were brave with color. Indeed, the whole magazine

---

[9] The editors anticipated. See note 3, *supra*.

was very handsome, with beautiful covers by Neysa McMein and others.

In 1924 the printing of the magazine was transferred to the large plant that the McCall Corporation had just erected at Dayton, Ohio, and that city became the official publication point for all the concern's periodicals.

In the twenties *McCall's Magazine* began the accent on nation-wide coverage and nation-wide appeal that was to become characteristic. In that decade this national audience was often referred to as "McCall Street," for the magazine's statisticians had figured out that its readers might occupy houses every twenty-five feet on both sides of a street from Boston to San Diego, California. What *McCall* editors were visualizing was a middle-class audience living on an American street in ordinary houses anywhere in the country.

Otis Lee Wiese was appointed editor in January 1928. He had been graduated from the University of Wisconsin less than two years before, had become associate editor of *McCall's* in 1927, and was now editor-in-chief at twenty-three — the youngest magazine editor in America, said the newspapers, which made much of the matter. It turned out to be a good appointment, for Wiese had imagination, initiative, and a mind of his own.

Margaret Ostenso, Temple Bailey, Faith Baldwin, Margaret Culkin Banning, and Alice Duer Miller made up a quintet of popular female serialists whose work was familiar to *McCall* readers in the thirties. Heywood Broun, F. Scott Fitzgerald, J. P. Marquand, Octavus Roy Cohen, and Wallace Irwin might be said to make up a balancing male quintet. And there were many other well-known contributors in that depression decade, though the new editor was not really a big-name man. He had inherited that editorial theory from Burton and Warner; and he was later fond of saying that he had been fired at least six times during his first year because of his rebellious notions, but always rehired after a few days "because there was nobody else around the place with ideas." [10]

One of those ideas made a minor revolution in magazine journalism in the women's field. In 1932 Wiese introduced the "three-way make-up" in *McCall's*, which gave readers three magazines in one, each with its own cover-page and distinctive contents. The first section was "Fiction and News," that is, it contained the serial, short stories, and reviews of motion pictures, books, and public affairs; second was "Home Making," primarily a service section; and third was "Style and

[10] *Time*, v. 49, Jan. 6, 1947, p. 68.

Beauty," with matter on health, cosmetics, and hairdressing, and the traditional *McCall* fashion and pattern departments. Whether or not this new idea in magazine making was an advantage to the reader, it did help the advertiser by breaking up the old text-in-front, ads-in-back make-up. It brought the advertising forward; and even when the triple-magazine plan was abandoned in 1950, the advertising remained in the forepart of the book. This innovation of *McCall's* had an influence on all of the women's magazines and some of the others, and magazine advertising was never again relegated to posteriority.

A new departure of December 1937 was the "complete novel," or novelette, in each issue. This had been tried a few years before by *Redbook* (which, along with *Blue Book*, had been purchased by the McCall Corporation in 1929) with immediate stimulus to newsstand sales. It worked also for *McCall's*, which soon became the first woman's magazine with newsstand sales of over a million.

A venture of the late thirties was a series of youth conferences arranged by the editor and his staff, and reported in the magazine by Mrs. Banning and others. Though a separate public service, these conferences were magazine stuff and they were also reflected in magazine prestige and popularity. Readership research was a specialty with *McCall's* from 1934 onward, and its continuing reader-interest surveys by the interview method constitute a record in the publications field.

The year before Wiese became editor, *McCall's* had counted a yearly net paid circulation of 2,225,000; it had printed an average of 52 pages of advertising in each issue; and its advertising revenue had totaled $6,265,304. The curve continued upward, and the March 1930 issue had considerably over 100 pages of advertising in a 192-page number. Circulation continued to advance long after the financial crash, and up to the bank moratorium; even then there was only a slight sag, and it recovered in 1937 and started up again, to reach 3,000,000 in 1940.

Wiese had his way on the big-name question in the forties. Fiction was becoming less important anyway, and staff contributors were much relied upon for features. The magazine's "National Defense" section was initiated in the summer of 1940, to do valuable service after the entry of the United States into World War II. A bureau was established in Washington to supply a regular newsletter from the capital. Service material was adapted to the needs of women in a war period. After the war was over, the magazine turned to community and social problems; one of the most important was the "Yardville" project for city planning "beginning in your own back yard."

In 1949 Mrs. Eleanor Roosevelt became a regular contributor to

*McCall's.* The first series of her memoirs had been published in the *Ladies' Home Journal,* but when the editors of the *Journal* suggested that editorial changes in the second series would be desirable, she changed over to *McCall's,* which not only printed the memoirs (and spent a hundred and twenty thousand dollars advertising them) but took over the monthly page in which Mrs. Roosevelt offered succinct and common-sense answers to correspondents under the title "If You Ask Me."

The price per copy was increased to fifteen cents in 1942 and to twenty-five cents in 1946; but circulation advanced steadily to reach four million in 1951. The next year it added another quarter-million, and enjoyed a whacking twelve and a half million dollars of advertising revenue that year.[11]

William B. Warner died in 1946. He had retired as president of the corporation only a few months before his death. He did not live to see the completion of the eleven-million-dollar addition to the Dayton plant, which was to print so many periodicals, including *Reader's Digest, Newsweek,* and a score of others. He was succeeded in the presidency by Marvin Pierce, who had begun as Warner's assistant twenty-five years earlier and had been vice-president for a decade. Wiese was elected vice-president in 1949, and publisher as well as editor of *McCall's Magazine.* It was in the next year that Wiese brought Daniel D. Mich over from *Look* to be "editorial director," and a little later Henry Ehrlich, *Look's* managing editor, to take a similar position with *McCall's.*

Emphasizing its effort to keep a national coverage, the magazine set up a West Coast editorial office in 1950; for fifteen years it had maintained a field editor with staff to keep in touch with the various cities and regions of these United States. In the fifties, a series of *"McCall's* Personal Stories" gave intimate experiences of various types of persons like you and me in various situations such as you or I might be in, or at least interested in. Inserts, or "extras," appeared in the early fifties, giving special treatments to such matters as home decoration and new food ideas. In short, the book was crammed with household and home matters, foods and child care and dressmaking, styles and fashions, in the true tradition of *McCall's* through its eighty years and more — but at the mid-century far more attractive, more lively and colorful than in its early phases. For several years its research had centered on what is called "reader traffic" through the book; and in the fifties the service matter was made equal with fiction and articles, thus "pacing"

---

[11] *Magazine Week,* v. 1, Feb. 28, 1953, p. 1. The yearly rate was set at $2.50 in 1946, but raised to $3.00 in 1953.

the reader's progress through the magazine's offerings. Colorful? Eighty per cent of its pages commonly had some color besides the black on white. It would be enough to make austere, industrious, bearded old James McCall open his eyes very wide to see this magazine and to know of its prosperity in the 1950's. In 1956, the year of its striking "togetherness" program, *McCall's* reached the circulation figure of 4,750,000.

# 18

## McCLURE'S MAGAZINE [1]

SAMUEL SIDNEY McCLURE, born in Ireland and reared in poverty, and John Sanborn Phillips, midwestern born and bred but educated at Leipzig and Harvard, had been classmates at Knox College and partners in the business of syndicating fiction and other feature material to newspapers for eight years, when, in 1893, they decided to start a magazine. Between them they had $7,300 to put into it, of which $4,500 was Phillips' and $2,800 McClure's.[2] They planned to make the magazine a kind of appendage to their syndicate business, filling it with material already purchased and widely used, and paying its staff from syndicate profits. With such economical plans, and with illustration provided chiefly by the new, cheap halftone engravings, it was resolved to put the price very low.

Already there had been cheap class periodicals in America, one of them greatly successful; and in England two years earlier a cheap general illustrated magazine had made a success.[3]

---

[1] TITLES: (1) *McClure's Magazine*, June 1893-June 1928; (2) *New McClure's Magazine*, July 1928-March 1929.

FIRST ISSUE: June 1893. LAST ISSUE: March 1929. Merged with *New Smart Set*.

PERIODICITY: Monthly. Vols. 1–6 (semiannual), June 1893-May 1896; 7, June-Oct. 1896; 8–49 (semiannual), Nov. 1896-Oct. 1917; 50, Nov., Dec. 1917; 51, 1918; 51A, 1919 (individual numbers continue v. 51, but title page has v. 51A); 52, 1920; 53, Jan.-Sept. 1921; 54, March 1922-Feb. 1923 (susp. Oct. 1921-Feb. 1922); 55, March-Dec. 1923; 56, Jan.-April 1924; 57, May-Aug. 1924; new series 1, May-Oct. 1925 (susp. Sept. 1924-April 1925); new series 2, nos. 1–3, Nov. 1925-Jan. 1926; 57A, July-Dec. 1926 (susp. Feb.–June 1926); 58–61 (semiannual), Jan. 1927-Dec. 1928; 62, nos. 1–3, Jan.-March 1929.

PUBLISHERS: The S. S. McClure Company (John S. Phillips was McClure's chief partner until 1906), 1893–1911; The McClure Publications, 1911–21 (Frederick L. Collins, pres.); The McClure Publishing Company (Moody B. Gates, pres.), 1922-April 1924; McClure Press (S. S. McClure owner), May-Aug. 1924; S. S. McClure Company (S. S. McClure, owner), May 1925-Jan. 1926; International Publications (W. R. Hearst, owner), 1926–28; Magus Publishing Company (James R. Quirk, pres.), 1928–29. All New York.

EDITORS: Samuel Sidney McClure, June 1898-Aug. 1913, March 1922-Jan. 1926; Cameron Mackenzie, Sept. 1913-April 1915; Frederick L. Collins (Charles Hanson Towne, managing editor), May 1915-Feb. 1920; Herbert Kaufman, March 1920–March 1927; Arthur McKeogh, July 1926-March 1927; Arthur Sullivant Hoffman, April 1927-June 1928; James R. Quirk, July 1928-March 1929.

INDEXES: *Index to McClure's Magazine, Vols. I–XVIII, 1893–1902* (New York, 1903). *Poole's Index, Readers' Guide, Engineering Index, Jones' Legal Index, Cumulative Index. Review of Reviews Annual Index, Annual Library Index.*

REFERENCES: S. S. McClure, *My Autobiography* (New York, 1914), chs. 7–8 (also in *McClure's*, vols. 42–43, April-May 1914); Ida M. Tarbell, *All in the Day's Work* (New York, 1939), chs. 8–13; Ray Stannard Baker, *American Chronicle* (New York, 1945), chs. 9–24; Lincoln Steffens, *Autobiography* (New York 1931), part 3, chs. 1–26; Charles Hanson Towne, *Adventures in Editing* (New York, 1926), pp. 165–81.

[2] McClure, *My Autobiography*, p. 208.

[3] For a description of the situation out of which the American general illustrated magazine of low price grew, see pp. 2–5.

Thus, when *McClure's Magazine* issued its first number, for June 1893, it was priced at fifteen cents, or a dollar and a half a year. It contained just under a hundred pages and carried one hundred illustrations, almost half of them halftones. Unfortunately, however, it was in May 1893, about the time the new magazine was placed on the newsstands, that the first shocks of a great financial decline occurred, to be followed rapidly by a general collapse. Twelve thousand of the twenty thousand copies of the first number printed were returned unsold. When the syndicate's bills were uncollectible, and no money was to be had anywhere, the scientist-theologian Henry Drummond volunteered a loan of three thousand dollars out of the unexpectedly large profits of an American lecture tour. Drummond was a contributor to *McClure's* pages as well as to its exchequer; and so was Conan Doyle, who put in five thousand dollars, also out of American lecture receipts.[4] Colonel A. A. Pope, the bicycle manufacturer, a benefactor and former employer of Sam McClure,[5] advanced a thousand dollars, which he planned to take out in advertising. And so, often uncertain whether another number would be forthcoming, McClure and Phillips managed to keep the new magazine afloat for more than a year at thirty to forty thousand circulation.

The first real taste of popular approval came to *McClure's* as a result of the publication of Ida M. Tarbell's "Napoleon" and the pictures from the Hubbard collection that illustrated it. The genesis of this feature was characteristic of the McClure editing methods. From the first number of the magazine, an interesting section had been the few pages devoted to what were called "Human Documents," each of them a series of three to six portraits of some famous man taken at different ages. Today these pictures, technically ill produced, make a rather poor impression, seeming to emphasize badly fitting clothes and untrimmed beards; but the passion of readers of the mid-nineties for portraits of the great and near-great would be hard to overstate, and these pictures at once became one of the most popular features of the new magazine. An Omaha reader wrote to the editor suggesting a series of portraits of Napoleon, whose reputation, on the centennial of his first military successes, was undergoing a kind of renascence called in France the "Napoleon Movement."[6] McClure thought the suggestion from Omaha a good one, and looked up a remarkable collection of prints owned by Gardiner Green Hubbard, of Washington. These were

[4] McClure, *My Autobiography*, pp. 212–17.
[5] See F. L. Mott, *A History of American Magazines* (Cambridge, 1938), v. 3, pp. 213–14, footnote; McClure, *My Autobiography*, ch. 5.
[6] See p. 230 for note on the repercussion in the United States.

so impressive that McClure thought they should be accompanied by an elaborate text, and he engaged the English Robert Sherard to do a study of Napoleon. But when the manuscript came to hand, it embodied all the anti-Bonaparte feeling of John Bull at Waterloo, and Hubbard would not permit his pictures to be used with such a text. Then McClure, who had the year before found Miss Tarbell in Paris writing a life of Madame Roland and been much impressed with her ability and character, insisted that she do a biography of Napoleon forthwith, to begin in November 1894 and to be published serially with the Hubbard pictures. The result doubled the circulation of *McClure's Magazine,* and set it well on its way to its first hundred thousand.[7]

Meantime Miss Tarbell had joined the editorial staff of the magazine, and McClure was urging another project upon her. Let her tell it:

> The Napoleon sketch had not been finished before Mr. McClure was urging me into a new job — not writing this time, but editing — editing according to his recipe. "Out with you — look, see, report." Abraham Lincoln was the subject. . . . Lincoln was one of Mr. McClure's steady enthusiasms. . . . His insight told him that people never had had enough of Lincoln. Moreover, he believed that there was to be had for the seeking a large amount of "unpublished" reminiscences. It was on this conviction that he started me off. He was right about "unpublished" material. Lincoln had been dead only about thirty years, and hundreds of those who had known him in one connection or another were still living.[8]

The "Early Life of Lincoln" began in November 1895, when the magazine's circulation was 175,000: the next year it was 250,000. In 1898–1899, a series on Lincoln's later life was published. These great series were embellished with a large number of Lincoln portraits, many of which had never been published before. It is hard to tell whether the text, which embodied the recollections of scores of people, or the picture series was the more exciting; but together they helped to put *McClure's* in the forefront of American magazines in circulation, advertising patronage, and prestige.

It was, of course, not alone Miss Tarbell's serials, with their portrait illustration, which made the success of the early *McClure's.* The first fiction serial was "The Ebb Tide," by Robert Louis Stevenson and Lloyd Osbourne (1894); it was followed by Anthony Hope's "Phroso" (1896) and "Rupert of Hentzau" (1897–1898), the latter illustrated by Charles Dana Gibson; by Kipling's "Captains Courageous" (1896–

---

[7] McClure, *My Autobiography,* pp. 219–20; Tarbell, *All in the Day's Work,* pp. 147–53.

[8] Tarbell, *All in the Day's Work,* p. 161. In an interesting interview with McClure in the *New York Tribune* (Oct. 10, 1897, suppl., p. 7, col. 1), the connection between the "Human Documents" and the "Lincoln" is emphasized.

1897) and "Stalky & Co." (1898–1899); and by Stevenson's "St. Ives" (1897). The roll of McClure's short-story writers is quite as imposing, including Thomas Hardy, Israel Zangwill, Stanley Weyman, Conan Doyle, Walter Besant, Robert Barr, Gilbert Parker, Stephen Crane, and Joel Chandler Harris. Two series of short stories of the middle nineties require special mention: Kipling's "Jungle Tales" and William Allen White's "The King of Boyville." Most of the authors named were relatively unknown when *McClure's* first published them. One who was quite unknown, even to the editors, was O. Henry, whose "Whistling Dick's Christmas Stocking," written in the Federal penitentiary at Columbus but mailed to the magazine through a New Orleans intermediary, was the author's first short story to be printed in a national magazine.[9] It appeared in the issue of December 1899.

It will be noted that most of these were English writers. McClure had become acquainted with them in the course of his work for his syndicate; and in the magazine's first year or two he followed the original plan and printed much material that was already in circulation through syndication to American newspapers. This hurt both magazine and syndicate, however, and the system was abandoned by 1895.

Besides its Tarbell series and its unusually fresh and lively fiction, the early *McClure's* was notable for four things: its scientific articles, highlighting new discoveries; its emphasis on locomotives and trains, in stories and features; its articles on wild animals and exploration; and its stress on personalities.

In the very first number of the magazine appeared two articles under the covering title, "On the Edge of the Future": one was an interview with Thomas A. Edison about the inventions on which he was currently working, and the other was based on a talk about the future of science with Alexander Graham Bell. In nearly every number thereafter appeared a scientific article. The first contribution of Miss Tarbell, in September 1893, was related to Pasteur's work in his Paris laboratory. Two years later appeared the first article by Henry J. W. Dam, then a student of science in England, who was soon to become one of the editors of *McClure's*. All the magazine's editors wrote science articles now and then, but preëminent among them in that field were Dam and Cleveland Moffett. The latter's pieces on Roentgen rays in 1896 and on Marconi's invention of wireless telegraphy in March 1897 were really distinguished reporting. Dam left *McClure's*

---

[9] Robert H. Davis and Arthur B. Maurice, *The Caliph of Bagdad* (New York, 1931), pp. 190–91. For Bynner's experiences with O. Henry while an editor of *McClure's*, see *ibid.*, pp. 263–68.

in 1898 for his true vocation of playwriting, but Moffett remained to write of the "horseless carriage" and the various experiments in flying, of the developments of wireless, of liquid air and radium and other wonders.

McClure knew that America was fascinated by its own railroads — the technology of steam locomotion, the romance of railroading, the economics of railway financing and organization. Moffett wrote some of the early railroad articles. Cy Warman's stories began in 1894 and continued a long time. Herbert Hamblen's railroading reminiscences made a fine series for 1898.

*McClure's* wild animal articles began with the initial number in a series based on interviews with Karl Hagenback. Staff members and others furnished material about beasts, birds, and reptiles for many years, and Kipling's "Jungle Tales" were at home in *McClure's*. From 1900 on, William Davenport Hulbert contributed many articles in this field. Exploration and adventure in far places furnished material for many contributions. The search for the North Pole was the subject of articles by Greely, Nansen, Cook, Peary, and Wellman.

But perhaps the largest element in Sam McClure's pattern for a magazine was the exploitation of human personalities. The "Real Conversations" with notables were a leading feature of the early numbers; Howells, Edison, and Holmes were among the great men interviewed. The pictorial "Human Documents" already mentioned, the occasional character sketches and biographical studies by W. P. Trent, A. B. Hart, and others, the great Tarbell series with their portraits, such serials as William Wright's "The Brontës," Elizabeth Stuart Phelps's autobiography, Hamlin Garland's "Grant," General Miles's recollections, Charles A. Dana's "Men and Events of the Civil War," and John (Ian Maclaren) Watson's "The Life of the Master" — all with copious illustration — reflect the magazine's interest in great personalities.

In poetry, *McClure's* was very uneven. It published Kipling's "The Merchantman" in its second number, his "Recessional" in October 1897, and "The White Man's Burden" in February 1899. But many numbers in the early years contained no verse, or nothing except some that was reprinted from the older poets.

Among all the organizations preparing magazines, at home or abroad, it is safe to say that the McClure editorial staff was unique. Sam McClure himself, whom Steffens called "the wild editor," was driven by an ever active dynamo of nervous energy. "Blond, smiling, enthusiastic, unreliable, he was the receiver of the ideas of his day. . . . He was rarely in the office. 'I can't sit still' he shouted. 'That's your job, and I don't see how you do it!'" He spent most of his time dashing across the United States, England, Europe. On his return, "he would come straight from the ship to the office, call us together, and tell us what he had seen and heard, said and done. With his valise full of clippings, papers, books, and letters to prove it, he showed us that he had the greatest features any editor had ever had — the most marvelous, really world-stunning ideas and stories."

McClure told Steffens that in judging manuscripts, "I go most by myself, for if I like a thing, then I know that millions will like it. My mind and my taste are so common that I'm the best editor." [10]

Such an erratic character, however, needed a counterbalance, and it was fortunate that McClure had John S. Phillips for partner and adviser. "Mr. McClure was always peering over the Edge of the Future," wrote Miss Tarbell in her autobiography; [11] but Phillips

was the focus of every essential factor in the making of the magazine: circulation, finance, editing. Into the pigeon-holes of his old-fashioned roll-top desk went daily reports of bank balances, subscriptions received, books sold. I doubt if he ever went home at night without having a digest of those reports in his head. . . .

To those of us on the inside it was always a marvel that John Phillips found time to be an editor as well as a focussing center for everything that went on. At the bottom of his constant editorial supervision was, I think, a passion for the profession. He was unmistakably the most intellectual, as well as the best intellectually trained, person in the office. . . .

He was an invaluable aid to the group of staff writers the magazine was building up. He was no easy editor. He never wheedled, never flattered, but rigidly tried to get out of you what he conceived to be your best. . . . I never had an editor who so quickly and unerringly spotted weaknesses, particularly in construction.[12]

They never agreed on titles at the office of *McClure's*, but Phillips may be said to have been general manager and supervising editor. Albert Brady, another Knox College classmate, who had left the publisher's job on an Iowa newspaper, the *Davenport Daily Times*, to join *McClure's*, became advertising manager; his salary was five thousand a year, so that his first year's pay represented about two-thirds of the initial capitalization of seventy-three hundred. Brady died in 1899. Art editor was Auguste F. Jaccaci, whom Miss Tarbell calls "a brilliant artist and art editor, as well as one of the most versatile and iridescent personalities I have ever known." [13] He was

---

[10] Steffens, *Autobiography*, pp. 361–63, 393. See also Tarbell, *All in the Day's Work*, pp. 118–19, 154–55, 199; Baker, *American Chronicle*, pp. 95–98; William Allen White, *Autobiography* (New York, 1946), pp. 386–87.

[11] Tarbell, *All in the Day's Work*, p. 154.

[12] *Ibid.*, pp. 157–58. See also Baker, *American Chronicle*, p. 98; White, *Autobiography*, p. 387.

[13] *Ibid., p.* 158. See also Steffens, *Autobiography*, pp. 358–59.

more than an art editor: he was one of the makers of *McClure's*, and a powerful binding force in the staff. The fiction editor was a remarkable woman, Viola Roseboro, who found the search for good stories a continuing adventure. Like all "readers," she took many manuscripts home in the evening; the morning after she discovered "The Gentleman from Indiana," she marched into the office crying out, with tears in her eyes, "Here is a serial sent by God Almighty for *McClure's Magazine!*" [14]

McClure was always appointing managing editors, and associate and assistant editors; but they nearly always turned out to be contributing editors. Miss Tarbell was one of the first members of the staff, and she was soon put on special jobs of investigation and writing. McClure wrote in one of his occasional "Editorial Notes":

> Awaiting the special writer who can prove his right to it, we have a standing special prize. That is a position on the staff of the magazine, for anyone who can do such work as we are now having done by other members of the editorial staff, such as Miss Tarbell and H. J. W. Dam. [15]

Steffens tells of two nameless young men whom McClure had persuaded to leave their homes somewhere in the West to help edit *McClure's*, who wandered about the office for awhile without finding anything to do, and who were then helped to find satisfactory jobs elsewhere. [16]

Ray Stannard Baker left the *Chicago Record* in 1898 to become one of the most valuable members of McClure's staff. It was the next year that John H. Finley, another Knox College recruit, became "managing editor"; he stayed only a few years, however, leaving to become president of the City College of New York. J. Lincoln Steffens, who had been city editor of the *New York Commercial Advertiser*, took his place, but was soon "on the road," gathering material for a series of articles that was to make him famous. His place was taken in 1903 by a true managing editor, Albert A. Boyden, who had been an office man in the McClure organization since his graduation from Harvard, and who had already won a reputation for both efficiency and kindness. John M. Siddall, a Tarbell discovery, joined *McClure's* in 1904. H. H. McClure, a cousin of the editor, was on the staff from 1901 to 1906, and Samuel Hopkins Adams from 1903 to 1905.

The magazine these men and women produced cannot be described by merely listing the names of some leading authors and the titles of features. It had a fresh and challenging quality; it was alive. The

[14] *Ibid.*, pp. 197–98.
[15] *McClure's*, v. 10, p. 289, Jan. 1898.
[16] Steffens, *Autobiography*, pp. 362–63.

*Review of Reviews* said of its very first number, "It throbs with actuality from beginning to end,"[17] and it continued to vibrate with the times. Its close relationship with the newspaper was recognized at once. Baker, Steffens, Moffett, and others recruited from the daily press brought with them a keen interest in the current scene and "the edge of the future." Immediate topics — the opening of the Klondike, the war with Spain, the lost polar explorer Andrée — came across the tracks from the newspaper to the magazine.

Coverage of the Spanish-American War was chiefly by means of eyewitness accounts obtained from various observers. "*McClure's Magazine* has representatives, contributors, artists, and photographers with every branch of the army and navy," wrote the editor.[18] The number for June 1898 contained no less than eight articles about the war. Perhaps Stephen Bonsal and James Creelman were the magazine's most distinguished war correspondents. In 1898–1899 *McClure's* published Admiral Mahan's "The War on the Sea and Its Lessons." Some of its war numbers showed a gain of over 100,000 copies more than the corresponding months of the preceding year,[19] and by 1900 *McClure's* had reached the remarkable circulation of 370,000 — larger than that of any other general monthly magazine except *Munsey's.*[20]

*McClure's* was one of the trio of great illustrated ten-cent monthlies of the mid-nineties,[21] the others being *Munsey's* and *Cosmopolitan.* *Munsey's* was the first to cut to that price, in October 1893, and it then proceeded to gain a circulation lead on *McClure's* that it did not relinquish until 1912. *McClure's* did not drop to the ten-cent price until July 1895, but a higher type of content brought it a better standing among advertisers of the mid-nineties than *Munsey's* was able to reach. The December 1895 issue of *McClure's* carried 150 pages of advertising; and an editorial boast a few months later claimed that, in the last three months of that year, "we had, month by month, more pages of paid advertising than any other magazine at any time in the history of the world." [22] But at that time they were actually losing money on the magazine because of unexpected increases in circulation; advertising contracts made on a basis of 80,000 had to be carried out

---

[17] *Review of Reviews*, v. 8, p. 91, July 1893.
[18] *McClure's*, v. 11, p. 206, June 1898.
[19] *Ibid.*
[20] *Munsey's* had 650,000. Two women's magazines exceeded *McClure's* — *Ladies' Home Journal* with 880,000 and *Delineator* with 480,000; and the *Farm Journal* had 450,000. Among the weeklies, the only one to top *McClure's* was *Youth's Companion*, with 540,000. These figures do not include circulations of the cheap "home" monthlies supported by mail-order advertising.
[21] See pp. 5–7, and also Sketches of *Cosmopolitan* (10) and *Munsey's* (19).
[22] McClure, *My Autobiography*, p. 222.

when twice that number were being issued, or, for a special issue like that of December 1895, three times that many. Thus at the end of 1895 Phillips and McClure were $287,000 in debt. But in 1896 rates were adjusted to rising circulation, and the publishers began making large profits. In 1898 the magazine was printing an average of 100 pages of advertising every month, and five years later the average was nearly 150, at $375 a page, and an occasional number would carry close to 200 pages of advertising. And this was in a magazine with 112 pages of text, and quite without the assistance of such devices, then unknown, as tailing a story into the advertising section. *Printer's Ink* declared that, in the years 1895–1899, *McClure's* "carried the greatest quantity of advertising of any magazine in the world." [23]

Even before the magazine's balance sheets were safely in the black, Phillips and McClure acquired their own printing plant. One result of this change was much more brilliant reproduction of the portraits that meant so much to *McClure's,* but the whole magazine underwent technical improvement, and at the same time costs were reduced, all under Phillips' watchful eye. A failure of 1895 was *McClure's Quarterly,* which contained the Napoleon story entire; only two numbers of it were issued.[24] In the autumn of 1897, McClure joined with Frank Nelson Doubleday to form the firm of book publishers called Doubleday & McClure Company; two years later Doubleday joined Walter Hines Page in forming another publishing house, and McClure, Phillips & Company founded their own book business.

It was in 1902 that *McClure's* discovered, somewhat to its own surprise, a new pattern of magazine journalism that was to become immediately and spectacularly important. That discovery was recorded in an editorial note in the number for January 1903:

> We did not plan it so; it is a coincidence that this number contains three arraignments of American character such as should make every one of us stop and think. "The Shame of Minneapolis" [by Steffens], the current chapter of the history of Standard Oil by Miss Tarbell, Mr. Ray Stannard Baker's "The Right to Work" — they might all have been called "The American Contempt of Law." Capitalists, workingmen, politicians, citizens — all breaking the law or letting it be broken. Who is there left to uphold it? . . . There is no one left — none but all of us.

The fact is that Sam McClure was no single-minded reformer. He was primarily a magazine-maker. He did a great deal for reform causes by illuminating some dark corners where crime and crookedness and corruption flourished. Perhaps that made him a reformer, in a

[23] *Printer's Ink*, v. 28, Aug. 30, 1899, p. 13.
[24] McClure, *My Autobiography*, p. 222.

practical sense; but he did it because he thought his readers would be interested in such revelations, and excited by them. He thought also that they ought to be interested in them, but there can be no doubt that his chief motivation was practical rather than ethical. This consideration would perhaps be unimportant except for later developments.

What came to be called muckraking began, as far as *McClure's* was concerned,[25] in the mind of Ida M. Tarbell. In the magazine's first phase, Miss Tarbell had been its leading contributor, with her "Napoleon" and "Lincoln." As a wit of the time put it, "Tarbell discovered Napoleon, but McClure discovered Tarbell." [26] In looking about for another subject that would combine an opportunity for original historical research with sure-fire reader interest, Miss Tarbell was strongly drawn to the beginnings of the oil industry, because she had grown up in the midst of the initial development of the Pennsylvania oil fields, and her family had been involved in the early struggles between the independents and the combinations. She discussed the matter at length with the staff, and finally persuaded Phillips that, with the growing interest in the threat of trusts and combinations in America's economic life, there would be a popular response to a serial history of the Standard Oil Company. McClure was in Europe, and thither Miss Tarbell went to talk the project over with him and eventually to gain his approval of it.[27] The research and writing of the series required more than four years and cost *McClure's* close to fifty thousand dollars.[28] But it was money well spent, for the Tarbell "History of the Standard Oil Company," which ran for two years, was one of the greatest serials ever to appear in an American magazine. It was a significant socio-economic document; though subject to later correction in some respects, it represented good historical investigation; it was interesting reading for all, and for some it was nothing less than sensational; and it was an important factor in the upward march of *McClure* circulation.

Miss Tarbell thought of her work as history — which it was — but Lincoln Steffens thought of his articles about municipal corruption as exposés. Steffens, having learned that "editing" *McClure's* meant riding the trains and getting about the country, had gone out to St. Louis to check on the reports about reformer Joseph W. Folk. Then

[25] For earlier inception of the movement, see p. 207.

[26] *Philistine*, v. 1, p. 69, July 1895.

[27] Tarbell, *All in the Day's Work*, chs. 11–12.

[28] *McClure's*, v. 24, p. 112, Nov. 1904. But in his *Autobiography* McClure raises the price to $4,000 apiece for 15 articles (there are 18). Other figures are named by other writers, but they usually approximate those given above.

he had engaged a local newspaperman to write an article on Folk's crusade; but later he contributed some facts of his own, and signed the story as coauthor. It appeared in the issue for October 1902 and is sometimes called "the first muckraking article"; [29] but if muckraking is a magazine's own exposé of abuses, then this celebration of Folk's exploits at St. Louis scarcely qualifies. It led, however, to one of the chief muckraking series in the whole movement — Steffens' "The Shame of the Cities," which began in January 1903 with an arraignment of Minneapolis, and continued that year with analyses of corruption in St. Louis, Pittsburgh, and Philadelphia; and in 1904–1905 with articles about corrupt state machines in Illinois, Wisconsin, Rhode Island, New Jersey, and Ohio.

Meantime Ray Stannard Baker's series on labor union leaders and "rackets" in 1903–1904 and on the railroads in 1905–1906 were going full blast. McClure wrote Baker that the fortuitous Tarbell-Steffens-Baker trio of exposés in the number for January 1903, already mentioned, had made "the greatest success we have ever had." [30] The pattern thus set and found greatly successful was, of course, continued, and it made *McClure's* the leader of the muckraking magazines. These articles were all based on sound and extensive research. None of them, said an editorial note, "has cost *McClure's Magazine* much less than a thousand dollars, and fully half of them have cost as high as twenty-five hundred dollars each." [31]

But it was money well spent. Circulation went up to nearly half a million by the time of the 1907 panic. In a 1908 advertisement *McClure's* boasted that for the preceding ten years it had "carried more advertising each year than any other magazine." [32] Its advertising must have grossed close to a million dollars in 1906.

But Sam McClure, unstable, enthusiastic, plagued by ill health, was a better leader in adversity than in triumphant success. He came home from one of his journeys one day early in 1906 with a fully developed, grandiose plan calling for major changes in the whole organization, on which he had not consulted Phillips or any of the staff. It was a blueprint for a great industrial combination, to include an expanded magazine, distributed from various points; a publishing company, also expanded, to include textbooks and reference works; a McClure Life Insurance Company, to pile up funds for loan to the other enterprises; a McClure Bank, for ready financing; and eventually, with surplus

[29] Steffens, *Autobiography*, p. 373; C. C. Regier, *The Era of the Muckrakers* (Chapel Hill, 1932), p. 59.
[30] Baker, *American Chronicle*, p. 168.
[31] *McClure's*, v. 24, p. 112, Nov. 1904.
[32] *Ayer's American Newspaper Annual and Directory*, 1908, p. 1233.

profits, such benevolent foundations as settlement establishments and ideal housing projects. It was an even bigger expansion than the one Walker had attempted or the one Munsey was currently working out. His great plan "seemed to possess him like a religious vision which it was blasphemy to question." It did no good to point out to him that *McClure's* had long been fighting all such trusts and combinations of wealth; he thought the time for that was past, and the thing to do was to furnish competition to the great combines.[33]

The result was that Phillips and McClure, who had been so closely associated for twenty years, parted company, McClure buying the Phillips interest. With Phillips went Steffens, Baker, Miss Tarbell, Boyden, Siddall, and H. H. McClure. They enlisted William Allen White, who had contributed analyses of political bosses (Platt, Hanna, Croker) to *McClure's*, and Finley Peter Dunne, who, if not a muckraker, was a friend and abettor of the genus; and together they purchased the *American Magazine*.[34]

McClure did not at once abandon the great plan. In 1907 he built a big new plant at Long Island City at a cost of seven hundred thousand dollars.[35] In October the single-copy price of the magazine was raised to fifteen cents, though both *Munsey's* and *Cosmopolitan* kept to ten cents a few years longer. Perhaps this increase affected sales, perhaps it was the loss of the famous trio of contributors, or perhaps it was the financial crisis of 1907; but circulation declined somewhat, and advertising with it. McClure laid aside his grand design and tried to get the magazine back on the up-curve.

Muckraking was not abandoned because of the defection of Tarbell, Steffens, and Baker, the undisputed leaders in that profitable field. McClure recruited George Kibbe Turner, a midwestern newspaperman; C. P. Connolly, a Montana lawyer and businessman; and Burton J. Hendrick, who came from the staff of the *New York Evening Post*. For managing editor, Will Irwin was persuaded to transfer from the *New York Sun*. Turner wrote a typical exposé of the combination between vice, politics, and business in Chicago for the April 1907 number. Later (June 1909) he turned his attention to New York and Tammany. In February 1908, he viewed with alarm the decline of American naval power; in November 1909, prostitution in New York occupied his attention. With John Moody, he did a series on "Masters of Capital in America" in 1910–1911. And so on. Occasionally McClure himself supplemented the Turner articles with sequels, as in "Chicago as Seen by

[33] Tarbell, *All in the Day's Work*, p. 256.
[34] See F. L. Mott, *op. cit.*, v. 3, pp. 512–13.
[35] *McClure's*, v. 29, p. 582, Sept. 1907.

Herself" (May 1907) and "The Tammanyizing of a Civilization" (November 1909).[36] Connolly's chief contribution was a series on Montana politics and the "copper kings" in 1906–1907. Hendrick wrote some articles on the life insurance companies, published in the same years; this was followed by a series on "Great American Fortunes," 1907–1908. Harry Orchard's "Confession and Autobiography," serialized in 1907, was an exposé of labor union methods in the Western Federation of Miners; and Judson C. Welliver's article on "The National Water Power Trust" (May 1909) was in the muckraking pattern.

After about a year of editorial service, Will Irwin decided he could no longer endure Sam McClure's extravagances and resigned. "As a curb on genius I was not a success," he later confessed.[37] Sewell Haggard, a New York newspaperman, succeeded him. On the staff at that time were the faithful Miss Roseboro; Miss Willa Sibert Cather, whose first nationally circulated short stories were published in *McClure's*; Turner and Hendrick, leading article writers; Cameron Mackenzie, who came over from the *Sun* and was later to play an important part in the magazine's fortunes; and Witter Bynner, poetry and features editor.

In detailing the leading content of the magazine dealing with public affairs — the articles that tied in with newspaper journalism — we have neglected *McClure's* belles-letters of this period. Its fiction offering was distinguished, including such serials as Kipling's "Kim" (1900–1901), and Tarkington's "The Two Vanrevels" (1902), and such short story "firsts" as Helen R. Martin's "The Conversion of Elviny" (May 1902, followed by many other New Mennonite stories), Myra Kelly's "A Christmas Present for a Lady" (December 1902, followed by other "Little Citizens" stories), and Willa Cather's "A Sculptor's Funeral" (January 1905). Stewart Edward White became a frequent contributor; his "Arizona Nights" was printed in 1906. Mrs. Humphry Ward's "The Case of Richard Meynell" was serialized in 1910–1911, Owen Johnson's controversial "Stover at Yale" in 1911, and Miss Cather's "Alexander's Masquerade" (in book form *Alexander's Bridge*) in 1912. Remembered with pleasure by all readers of *McClure's* in the first decade of the new century are Jack London, whose "God of His Fathers" appeared in May 1901; Josephine Dodge Daskam, with her stories of children; Edith Wyatt, with her short stories of immigrants; George Madden Martin and her "Emmy Lou" stories; Norman Duncan and his dramatic sea stories; Mary Stewart Cutting and her stories of married life; Herminie Templeton and her Irish fairies; James Hopper and his stories of Filipinos; Henry Wallace Phillips, with his humorous

---

[36] See McClure, *My Autobiography*, pp. 256–59.
[37] Will Irwin, *The Making of a Reporter* (New York, 1942), p. 137.

westerns; as well as short fiction by O. Henry, Alice Brown, Rex Beach, Mrs. Wilson Woodrow, George Randolph Chester, Arthur Train, Harvey J. O'Higgins, George D. Paine, and so on.

Bynner improved the quantity and quality of *McClure's* poetry. He was largely responsible for introducing A. E. Housman's *Shropshire Lad* to America, though it had been published in book form some years earlier.[38] Many of the newer poets were represented; favorites seem to have been William Butler Yeats, Moira O'Neill, and Florence Wilkinson.

Biographical serials continued to be prominent in the magazine, as Clara Morris' lively recollections of the stage (1900–1906), George W. Smalley's English reminiscences (1901–1903), Carl Schurz's tiresome "Memoirs" (1905–1917), Georgine Milmine's critical and detailed "Mary Baker G. Eddy" (1907–1908), the suppressed Kuropatkin "Memoirs" (1908), George F. Parker's series on Grover Cleveland (1908–1909), and the autobiographies of Thomas C. Platt and Goldwin Smith in 1910. George E. Woodberry contributed a series on "Masters of Literature" in 1905–1916.

Watson's "The Life of the Master" had been illustrated by color plates from paintings by Corwin Knapp Linson in 1900, and fine illustration in color was supplied also for John La Farge's "Great Artists" series of 1901–1902. *McClure's* continued its brilliant illustration, though it was now by no means so outstanding in that respect as formerly; competition in that department, as indeed in all departments of magazine-making, had increased tremendously. But its portraits from photographs were still excellent; and such artists as Maxfield Parrish, Albert Sterner, Oliver Herford, A. B. Frost, Dan Beard, Jessie Willcox Smith, Alice Barber Stephens, Howard Chandler Christy, Charles Dana Gibson, Henry Hutt, and W. T. Benda kept high standards of illustration. Several of these artists specialized in the pretty-girl covers that adorned *McClure's* for many years.

The second phase of *McClure's Magazine* ended in 1911. The health of the editor-owner was bad, his financial affairs were involved, and the magazine's business had declined slowly but steadily since 1908. Cameron Mackenzie, brilliant writer and editor, had married McClure's daughter, and for two or three years had been acting as general manager of the magazine, much as Phillips had once done. In 1911 he interested Frederick Lewis Collins in *McClure's,* and the two purchased it under the name of McClure Publications. Collins and Mackenzie were of the same age — twenty-nine. Both young men were able, ambitious,

[38] A. E. Housman, *A Shropshire Lad*, Jubilee Edition, with Notes and a Bibliography by Carl J. Weber (Waterville, Maine, 1946), pp. 120–21.

and already highly regarded in the magazine field. Collins came to *McClure's* from the Crowell Publishing Company, of which he had been secretary, and for which he had been editing the *Woman's Home Companion.* "How fast he could do everything!" exclaimed one of his editors some years later. "Frederick Collins, with his terrific health and youth and energy, was a dynamo who never seemed to tire." [39] The partners had the Crowell idea of conducting two or three magazines in a group, and bought the *Ladies' World* at the time they acquired *McClure's,* obtaining with it Arthur S. Moore as business manager. Sam McClure remained as titular editor for two years, and H. H. McClure came back from the *American* to lend a hand, but Mackenzie had to take over the editorship in 1913. Two years later, anxious to devote more of his time to writing, he yielded the top editorship to Collins, who brought Charles Hanson Towne, poet and experienced magazine man, into the staff as managing editor.

The financing that Collins had been able to arrange made *McClure's* more comfortable in its editorial and publishing operations, but it continued to decline for two or three years. The fact seems to be that the editorship which produced what the *Nation* called *"McClure's* Periclean age" [40] was now outmoded: top popular interests were no longer public affairs and muckraking, but fiction and lighter matters. After McClure left the staff there was an upward turn, more marked after Mackenzie's departure, and under the Collins-Towne editorship. The quarto size now demanded by the advertisers was adopted May 1915; even before that, Advertising Manager Ernest F. Clymer had instituted the policy of combining text and advertising in the back of the book.

For a few years, during the McClure-Mackenzie editorship, there was some grappling with political and social problems. Hendrick had a series on the initiative, referendum, and recall in 1911, and one on political leaders in 1912–1913. Jane Addams contributed some articles on commercialized vice in 1912. But the muckraking days were over. The *Nation,* true to its sworn enmity against the "interests," said that *McClure's* had now come "under the control of the forces of predatory privilege with which it had been battling." [41] The collapse of muckraking, in *McClure's* and other magazines, was due, however, not only to the need for large capital to meet the mass publication problems, but also to shifting popular interest in an era of prosperity and apparent security. At any rate, when Steffens returned to *McClure's* pages, it was with short stories and a "constructive" series called "The Fame of the Cities."

[39] Towne, *Adventures in Editing,* p. 169.
[40] *Nation,* v. 113, p. 219, Aug. 31, 1921.
[41] *Ibid.*

The great crusade of 1912 was one in favor of Mme. Maria Montessori's educational system. The crusade was an effective piece of propaganda, and perhaps the most important contribution among the many that *McClure's* made to educational theory and method. James H. Collins and Edward Mott Woolley wrote on business topics for most of the decade ending in 1921. Cleveland Moffett became a staff contributor once more, writing on science, industry, and other topics. Waldemar Kaempffert was often seen in *McClure's* pages, with his excellent science and automobile articles, and Hugo Munsterberg wrote on psychological matters. Inez Milholland edited a woman's department in 1913, and Marion Hill wrote on child care; but Anna Steese Richardson became the efficient editor for women's interests in 1915–1920. Samuel Hopkins Adams rejoined the staff in 1912 to edit a health department, and H. Addington Bruce wrote in the same field. Lewis B. Allen was director of the McClure–Westfield Standard of Pure Foods, a guaranteed-advertising agency. A book department was edited by Jeanette L. Gilder, one on finance by Albert W. Atwood, and later Paul Tomlinson; Grantland Rice wrote on sports.

Leading features of the decade were "Great Cases of William J. Burns" (1911–1912) by Dana Gatlin, Harvey J. O'Higgins, and Arthur B. Reeve; Marie Belloc Lowndes's "Great French Mysteries" (1912); S. S. McClure's autobiography (1913–1914); sketches of the old home town by Eugene Wood; and the victory-crusade articles of the war years. Just before the war, the magazine published a sensational series by Cleveland Moffett on what would happen if Germany should invade the United States. "McClure's Win-the-War Magazine" of 1918 was filled with patriotic articles, chiefly about doing one's bit on the home front; the magazine, said one observer, "was mobilized from cover to cover." [42]

There were fiction serials and short stories by Arnold Bennett, Jeffrey Farnol, Leonard Merrick, Mary Roberts Rinehart (her "K" was a 1914–1915 serial), G. K. Chesterton (some of his "Father Brown" stories appeared in 1912–1913), Kathleen Norris, Samuel Merwin, Cameron Mackenzie (the former editor), Sax Rohmer, Perceval Gibbon (an old favorite), Julian Street, Sophie Kerr, Ward Muir, Owen Johnson ("The Salamander," 1913–1914), Basil King, and so on. Among the humorists often found in *McClure's* in these months were Wallace Irwin, Orson Lowell, P. G. Wodehouse, and Oliver Herford.

During the war *McClure's* circulation reached a higher point than at any other time in its history — an annual average (sworn) of 563,-000 in 1918. But what would have been a big and profitable circulation

---

[42] *Ibid.*

twenty years earlier was now quite inadequate to compete in the advertisers' market; and when there was a decline of twenty thousand in 1919, Collins thought it time to get out. He sold to Herbert Kaufman, advertising man and writer of an inspirational type of feature editorial, widely syndicated, at the end of that year. The single-copy price, which had fluctuated capriciously — lowered to ten cents in 1916, brought back to fifteen cents in 1917, twenty the next year, and twenty-five in 1919 — was now advanced to twenty-five cents; in January 1921, it was set back to fifteen cents. The magazine looked fine in 1920–1921, with Tarkington, Ibañez, Cabell, Ferber, Merwin, Zane Grey, Mrs. Rinehart, and so on; but it was the flush of death. Circulation was down eighty thousand in 1920, and nearly that much in 1921; and now advertising really fell away. McClure Publications petitioned for a receiver in bankruptcy in the fall of 1921. The *Nation* wrote its epitaph: "The soul of *McClure's* had long since fled. It was a good magazine when it had one." [43]

But at least one man thought that the magazine was not dead beyond resuscitation. That was Moody B. Gates, editor and publisher of the *People's Home Journal* and president of the F. M. Lupton Company, which published the *Journal,* cheap books, and so on. Gates had the idea of bringing S. S. McClure back as editor and chairman of the board, and recreating the old magazine.[44] McClure had been experimenting in the daily newspaper field, somewhat in the style of his ancient rival Munsey, though on a smaller scale; [45] but he came willingly back to the magazine. Kenneth W. Payne, managing editor of the *Journal,* took over similar duties on *McClure's.* Page size was reduced to small-quarto when the magazine appeared again in March 1922. The autobiographies of Henry Ford (ghosted by Samuel Crowther) and Frank W. Woolworth, of five-and-ten fame, were features; but there were few well-known names, and there was little sparkle to articles, stories, or illustration.

In the spring of 1924, the Lupton interests, having lost all the money they cared to, turned the magazine over to McClure, who became editor and publisher, with Sonya Levien as managing editor and the faithful Viola Roseboro as associate editor and contributor.

Perceval Gibbon, Samuel Crowther, and Max Bentley were among the writers, most of whom were unknowns. Page size went back to the old-fashioned royal-octavo, presswork was bad, illustration was inadequate, and advertising came to be almost nonexistent. Circulation was

---

[43] *Ibid.*
[44] *New York Times,* Nov. 30, 1921, p. 19, col. 7.
[45] With some assistance, he bought the *New York Evening Mail* in 1916. It had a bad war record.

no longer quoted, but it must have dropped to about a hundred thousand when the magazine was suspended with the number for August 1924, after a trial of the new form lasting only four months.

But McClure managed to get new financing and revived the magazine a second time, with a new series beginning May 1925. This was a little more promising. It began with a serial life of Judge Gary by Miss Tarbell, and several old writers reappeared. Herbert Hoover contributed two or three articles. Chief problems discussed were prohibition, education in child welfare, and the crime situation. Once more Sam McClure galloped over the country from coast to coast, following various enthusiasms that might lead to feature series or promising fiction. He told Harry Harrison Kroll, whose "The Mountainy Singer" he serialized, that he was going to bring to him such fame as he had created for Tarkington and Cather. But efforts to repeat a success on the basis of a failure are rarely successful; the old magic did not suit the new times, and the aging editor's struggle was pathetic. He had to give up with the January 1926 issue. He lived for twenty-three years longer, occupying his mind with ineffectual studies of modern civilization which he published at his own expense, and died at the age of ninety-two.

But still they would not let the magazine die decently. A third time it was revived, after eight months' lingering on the Stygian shore, by a strong injection of William Randolph Hearst's money. About all there was for Hearst to buy was the name, which still had a real value; to it was now added a subtitle "The Magazine of Romance." Hearst first put Arthur McKeogh in charge, bringing him over from his *Cosmopolitan*. Under McKeogh, the magazine was cheap and vulgar, and its format matched its contents. It was, as the *Independent* observed, "distinguished by an almost incredibly even vulgarity and ineptitude." [46] In January 1927 the magazine was running three serials — Vida Hurst's "The Demi-Bride," Elmer Davis' "Without Marriage," and Warwick Deeping's "The New Eve." Short stories in these months had such titles as "The Girl Who Walked Home," "She Got What She Wanted," "Trial Love," and "The Bad Little Nice Girl." Illustration was mostly by photographs, including that provided for fiction, and printing was by rotogravure. There were some good writers — Sara Haardt, Wallace Irwin, Berton Braley, James Warner Bellah, Nina Wilcox Putnam, and others. Louella O. Parsons wrote pretty regularly about motion pictures. Cosmo Hamilton and P. C. Wren contributed serials. John Held, Jr., did most of the covers. But advertising rarely exceeded twenty pages, and circulation was under a hundred thousand.

In December 1927 McKeogh gave place to Arthur Sullivant Hoffman,

[46] *Independent*, v. 117, p. 5, July 3, 1926.

an experienced magazine man. The magazine improved at once in content and appearance. Carl Sandburg, Frazier Hunt, Konrad Bercovici, A. E. W. Mason, and Ethel Watts Mumford were leading contributors. Just as it was getting to be an attractive and well-balanced magazine, Hearst, tiring of its red balance sheets, sold it to the Magus Magazine Corporation, whose president was James R. Quirk. It then had a circulation of about sixty thousand.

Quirk had been in the magazine business for some twenty years, and was at the moment publisher of *Smart Set* and *Photoplay*. With T. Howard Kelly, a newspaperman, brought in as associate editor of both *McClure's* and *Smart Set*, Quirk set out to exploit whatever possibilities were left in both or either of these famous names. The *New McClure's — A Man's Magazine!* was, according to the *Saturday Review* "the greatest mess of shrieking type and bad illustration" on the newsstands.[47] It was really not quite that bad. O. O. McIntyre's autobiography was serialized. Fiction was contributed by E. Phillips Oppenheim, James Hopper, Edison Marshall, and Rupert Hughes; and special articles were furnished by Herbert Asbury, Jackson Gregory, James H. Collins, and Gene Tunney. There was humorous writing from Donald Ogden Stewart and Irvin S. Cobb. But the *New McClure's,* like most "revived" magazines, was a lost soul with nowhere to go. After the issue for March 1929 it was combined with the *Smart Set,* which lasted a little more than two years longer.

The history of *McClure's* falls into three periods. The first and second were each about nine years in extent, and the third includes the remainder of the magazine's thirty-six years of life. In the first period it set the pattern for the golden age of the ten-cent illustrated magazines, and was marked by freshness, brilliance, and abundance of life in all departments. The second was the great muckraking period, in which *McClure's* exerted a tremendous influence on the thinking of the American people, "hardly less important than that of Roosevelt himself," according to some observers.[48] The third period was one of decline. Under Collins, from 1911 to 1919, it was still an excellent magazine; but after that it was kicked about, knocked out, revived, and knocked out again — a sad spectacle as far as Samuel McClure's part in it was concerned, and a ridiculous one in other aspects.

[47] Quoted in *Bulletin of Bibliography,* v. 13, p. 108, May-Aug. 1928.
[48] Mark Sullivan, *Our Times* (New York 1930), v. 3, p. 85; William Archer, "The Cheap American Magazine," *Fortnightly Review,* v. 93, p. 923, May 1910, and *Living Age,* v. 265, p. 581, June 4, 1910.

## MUNSEY'S MAGAZINE [1]

FRANK A. MUNSEY liked money for the power and prestige that it brought him, but he loved most of all the romance of making it. For this reason, he had the strongest feeling for the *Argosy*, among all his magazines: *Argosy's* early history was his own rags-to-riches story, and it seemed to him altogether the most dramatic romance of modern life.[2] But it was *Munsey's Magazine* that "saved the day for the *Argosy*," as their owner himself asserted; [3] and it was *Munsey's Magazine*, the great general, illustrated monthly, that became the chief money-maker of all its owner's publications — weekly, monthly, and daily. Munsey himself was wont to call it the "flagship" of his fleet.

During his early years in New York, Munsey did not have the audacity to challenge such great magazines as *Harper's* and the *Century* in their field, and so his three ventures of the eighties were weeklies. Thus his new adult periodical, first issued February 2, 1889, was called *Munsey's Weekly* [4] — a thirty-six-page quarto selling for ten cents. Clearly, it was an imitation of the satirical weekly *Life*, which was then at the peak of its success, with a dash of *Harper's Weekly*. In

[1] TITLES: (1) *Munsey's Weekly*, 1889–91; (2) *Munsey's Magazine*, 1891–1918; (3) *Munsey*, 1918–29.
FIRST ISSUE: Feb. 2, 1889. LAST ISSUE: Oct. 1929. Merged with *Argosy All-Story*.
PERIODICITY: Weekly, 1889–91; monthly, 1891–1929. Vols. 1–5 (semiannual vols., Feb.–Aug. and Sept.-Jan.), Feb. 2, 1889-Aug. 18, 1891; 6–49 (semiannual vols., Oct.-March and April-Sept.), Oct. 1891-Sept. 1913; 50–98, no. 1 (3 vols. yearly, Oct.-Jan., Feb.-May, June-Sept.), Oct. 1913–Oct. 1929.
PUBLISHERS: Frank A. Munsey & Company, 1889–95; Frank A. Munsey, 1895–1902; The Frank A. Munsey Company (F. A. Munsey, owner, 1895–1925; William T. Dewart, pres., 1925–29), 1895–1929. All New York.
EDITORS: Frank A. Munsey, 1889–1925; Robert H. Davis, 1925–29. Managing editors: John Kendrick Bangs, 1889; Richard H. Titherington, 1891–1925.
INDEXES: *Poole's Index, Readers' Guide, Cumulative Index, Annual Library Index.*
REFERENCE: George Britt, *Forty Years, Forty Millions* (New York, 1935).
[2] This does not fully agree with a statement by the competent biographer of Munsey (Britt, *Forty Years, Forty Millions*, p. 88). But it seems to be borne out by a comparison of pieces that Munsey himself wrote about the two magazines. Munsey's little monograph, *The Founding of the Munsey Publishing-House* (New York, 1907, also published in *Munsey's*, v. 38, pp. 417–32, Dec. 1907), has for its subtitle, "The Story of the *Argosy*, Our First Publication, and incidentally the Story of *Munsey's Magazine*." See history of the *Argosy* (Sketch 3) for Munsey's early experiences in New York.
[3] Munsey, *The Founding of the Munsey Publishing-House*, p. 37.
[4] *Munsey's Illustrated Weekly* was an earlier periodical — a Blaine campaign paper published from Sept. 6 to Nov. 8, 1884. Blaine, a fellow Maine man, was one of Munsey's heroes; the paper was not endowed by party funds. "Honestly and handsomely Republican," as the *New York Tribune* said (Sept. 3, 1884, p. 4, col. 5), it thus differed editorially from the paper it resembled in format — *Harper's Weekly*. Well illustrated, it published much undistinguished miscellany.

make-up, paper, and illustration, it was like the former; in its commentary on public affairs it was more like the latter. For managing editor, Munsey hired young John Kendrick Bangs, who had been an associate editor of *Life,* and more recently conductor of the "Editor's Drawer," humorous department of *Harper's Monthly.*[5] There was much satirical humor in the new weekly, with excellent illustration by E. L. Durand, A. E. Fenner, and others. There was an extensive Washington department — four pages of gossipy social and political items.

Munsey himself contributed serial stories. He had begun writing the Alger type of story for the *Argosy* as an economy measure, and had continued with stories of New York society and business life whose only virtues were that they were moral and had a good flow of incident. In the *Weekly,* Munsey advertised a new book-publishing business founded on his own *Afloat in a Great City* and *The Boy Broker,* in cloth, and a fifteen-cent series of books for boys by Horatio Alger, Jr., Matthew White, Jr., Frank H. Converse, and others — reprints of stories published serially in the *Argosy.* But when Munsey handed his new society novel, "A Tragedy of Errors," to his new editor to use as a serial for the *Weekly,* Bangs thought the title apropos less to the events narrated than to the literary performance, and rejected it. That was carrying an editor's prerogatives too far, thought the author, and Bangs resigned after four months' service.[6]

Munsey carried on, with the aid of the small group of editorial workers he had gathered for the *Argosy.* The *Weekly* was, on the whole, a good paper of handsome appearance; but it was expensive, it reached less than forty thousand circulation, and it lost money consistently. After more than two and a half years of losses, totaling over a hundred thousand dollars,[7] Munsey made a radical change; in October 1891, he changed his periodical to monthly publication, making its page size that of *Harper's* and other standard magazines, and its price twenty-five cents a copy.

Managing editor of the new monthly was Richard H. Titherington, who was to retain that position for twenty-two years. This young Englishman had been marking time teaching when he had become acquainted with Munsey in the early days of his struggle to get the *Golden Argosy* afloat. The two young men were patrons of the same boardinghouse; they talked over Munsey's problems and goals, and Titherington became so deeply interested that he offered to work for

[5] F. L. Mott, *A History of American Magazines* (Cambridge, 1938), v. 2, pp. 399–400. For *Life,* see Sketch 18 in this volume.

[6] Francis Hyde Bangs, *John Kendrick Bangs* (New York, 1941), pp. 102–03.

[7] Munsey, *The Founding of the Munsey Publishing-House,* p. 32; *Munsey's,* v. 13, p. 103, April 1895.

his friend without pay in his spare time. This led to steady employment. As the Munsey projects multiplied and business expanded, editors were needed. "Though he was always chief editor in much more than name," wrote Titherington after Munsey's death, "he had less and less time for the details of the work." [8]

The new monthly began with ninety-six pages of reading matter, rather sparsely illustrated with halftone engravings. Except for Horatio Alger, Jr., no well-known writers appeared in its pages. There was a serial story with the scene laid in Russia by William Murray Graydon. Munsey himself contributed some articles; theatrical reviews, followed after a few months by a regular department entitled "The Stage," were written by C. Stuart Johnson. The magazine had a strong New York flavor, with articles about Central Park, Fifth Avenue, the Metropolitan Museum, and so on. In 1892 it made a specialty of novelettes, running to about fifty pages each — " a complete novel in each number." In April 1892 it absorbed the *Epoch,* a weekly journal of news and opinion. For a few months in 1892–1893 it experimented with a big section of news commentary from the newspapers, in imitation of the *Literary Digest,* which crowded out most of its fiction; but this was soon abandoned, leaving a series of long-lived departments — "Literary Chat," "The Stage," "Impressions by the Way" (editorial paragraphs), and "Etchings" (humor in anecdote, verse, and picture).

But the magazine did not catch on, and all of Munsey's deep cogitations that had led him into the monthly field [9] seemed wasted. The financial panic, which tightened the loan situation, added to his embarrassments. One recourse was left — to try an experiment in the low-price field. Many periodicals were making a variety of trials based on new and cheaper processes of production,[10] but no general illustrated magazine had ever made a success at ten cents. Munsey decided on such a venture. However, the periodical-distributing agency which had a virtual monopoly of that business — the American News Company — refused to handle a ten-cent magazine for much less than they got out of the higher-priced periodicals; at any rate, the terms they offered were ruinous. Munsey then determined to handle his own distribution, promoting it by direct-mail circulars and newspaper advertising. When these produced results, and the News Company's clients demanded the new ten-cent magazine, Munsey coolly lowered the rate of three and a half cents that he had originally proposed to allow the distributors to

---

[8] *Munsey's,* v. 87, supplementary pages in front of the number for March 1926.
[9] Munsey liked to speak of that reasoning in later years; it was possibly rationalization about a successful venture. See Munsey, *The Founding of the Munsey Publishing-House,* pp. 34–35.
[10] See pp. 3–6.

three cents,[11] and when that was rejected he organized his own Red Star
News Company.[12]

Not only was the first edition of 20,000 copies of the October 1893
*Munsey's*, at the epochal ten-cent price, disposed of, under the impact
of its advertising; but 20,000 in new printing were called for. The next
month 60,000 were sold, and in December 1893, 100,000.[13] The ten-cent
magazine was a success. Average circulation for 1895 was nearly 500,000
a month. For December 1895, 600,000 copies were printed, and the
figure went on up to 700,000 in 1897. Meantime advertising revenue
totaled $25,000 to $35,000 a month,[14] and later much more. In October
1898 Munsey, in an address before the chief New York advertising
club, stated his belief that the system of agency commissions, according to which fees were paid by the medium rather than by the client,
was unjust and dishonest, and declared that after the end of that year
he would pay no more such commissions.[15] In an editorial note in
December, he said that he had taken that stand "to stay, and to stay
forever." However logical his stand, he soon learned that it was not wise
to antagonize the agencies; and he surrendered to the prevailing custom
within the year, before he had lost much.

What kind of magazine was this, which made such a success in the
closing years of the century? It had a hundred and sixty pages of text
and eighty to a hundred pages of advertising. The leading article each
month was a department entitled "Artists and Their Work," copiously
illustrated by good halftone reproductions of paintings and portraits of
artists. In this illustration, and that which accompanied the departments called "The Stage" and "Types of Fair Women," as well as
articles on artists' models and such, there was no little emphasis on the
female form divine in the seminude. The *Independent* complained of
*Munsey's* "half dressed women and undressed statuary." [16] This was
most noticeable in 1893–1895; later, when the magazine had won a
circulation of half a million, anatomical display was toned down
greatly; but the reputation for naughty pictures that it had gained was
hard to shake off. Libraries sometimes reacted unfavorably to such
reader-lure; and as late as 1898 the Wilkes-Barre Public Library cut
*Munsey's* off its list "because of the many illustrations . . . which are
on the nude order." In an editorial note, Munsey advises Wilkes-

[11] Munsey, *The Founding of the Munsey Publishing-House*, pp. 42–47; *Munsey's*, v. 13,
p. 103.

[12] *Munsey's*, v. 18, p. 479, Dec. 1897.

[13] Munsey, *The Founding of the Munsey Publishing-House*, p. 47; *Munsey's*, v. 22, p.
338, Dec. 1899.

[14] *Munsey's*, v. 14, p. 760, March 1896.

[16] *Independent*, v. 47, p. 867, June 27, 1895 (p. 11).

[15] The address is printed in *Munsey's*, v. 20, pp. 476–86, Dec. 1898.

Barreans to bring up their boys in a glass case: "they would be such sweet boys . . . would do well for a sideshow to some back-street menagerie." [17]

The art department, with decreasing sex appeal, continued to take premier position through 1896 and 1897. In those years the magazine's illustration consisted chiefly of the reproduction of works of art, theatrical pictures, and portraits. Articles on European royalty and nobility, on dogs and horses, on American statesmen and industrialists, and on literature and music were standard fare. Departments were much shifted about. "In the Public Eye" was a section devoted to famous personalities, begun in late 1894 and destined to be important over several years. Most of the special articles were apparently written by "hacks" on assignment; and leading names were those of Munsey, Titherington, Morris Bacheller, George Holme, Harold Parker, Anna Leach, James L. Ford, and Arthur Hornblow. A series on "Prominent American Families" was written by various authors, and Theodore Dreiser did a series on American authors at home.

Fiction serials were written by Munsey, whose "Derringforth," a Wall-Street-and-society story with a sad ending, was in the course of writing and publication at the time the price of the magazine was lowered to ten cents; by Matthew White, Jr., editor of the *Argosy*; and by several obscure fictioneers. *Munsey's* first serial by a well-known writer was a great hit — Hall Caine's "The Christian" (1896–1897). Soon after it had begun, F. Marion Crawford's "Corleone" started its course through the magazine, and serials by H. Rider Haggard and Anthony Hope followed. Juliet Wilbor Tompkins, Myrtle Reed, and Grace MacGowan Cooke contributed short stories, though most *Munsey* writers in this field were unknowns. "Etchings" had by this time been turned into a poetry department, to which Frank Dempster Sherman, Bliss Carman, C. G. D. Roberts, Guy Wetmore Carryl, Ella Wheeler Wilcox, Clinton Scollard, and others contributed light verse.

Hall Caine seems to have been the herald of a more brilliant set of writers of both fiction and articles in *Munsey's Magazine*. In 1897 a number of public men were induced to write short pieces for its pages — Theodore Roosevelt on "The Ethnology of the New York Police Force," Chauncey M. Depew on the Supreme Court, Thomas B. Reed on "The Making of the Constitution," and so on. A number of famous writers were asked to furnish essays on "My Favorite Novelist and His Best Book"; and thus William Dean Howells, Paul Bourget, S. R. Crockett, Brander Matthews, Frank R. Stockton, Bret Harte, Conan Doyle, and many others were lured into *Munsey's*.

[17] *Munsey's*, v. 18, p. 798, Feb. 1898.

With the coming of the war with Spain, there was a shift to somewhat more serious content. War articles crowded the art department out of first place in 1898, and soon "In the Public Eye" was occupying that position regularly. There were great quantities of military and naval pictures, some of them by the pioneer movie-news photographer, J. C. Hemment. Titherington's careful history of the war was a serial from October 1898 to August 1899.

But the chief characteristics of *Munsey's Magazine* continued to be found in the pictures — whether of the battlefield or the stage — and the various illustrated departments. Munsey himself wrote in the number for April 1897 that those departments, next to the pictures, "have done more than anything else to individualize the magazine, to popularize it, and to give it its strength with the people." [18] A few months later he enlarged on the topic:

> We would not do away with our dozen departments for any amount of the best work of noted writers. The strength of this magazine lies in the short, unsigned work. It ranks as better journalism, and is closer to the people's wants, than the pretentious articles.[19]

There was much truth in this. The departments of "Literary Chat" and "The Stage," for example, contained from month to month, over a number of years, many items of information that reflected very well the literary and dramatic currents of the times, and occasionally a bit of acute and sensible criticism. Besides the departments that have already been named, the magazine contained at this time "In Vanity Fair," with bits in prose and verse about social happenings and fads; "The World of Music," with short pieces about events and personalities; and "The Publisher's Desk," in which Munsey talked intimately with his readers. But "the section devoted to the drama," declared the publisher, "has a wider following than any other feature of *Munsey's*." [20] "In the Public Eye" continued to be a good illustrated department of current events until 1905, and was later revived as a picture section.

The average circulation that *Munsey's* claimed [21] for 1897 was higher than that of any other monthly magazine except the *Ladies' Home Journal*, and it was about even with that great leader in the women's field. In all Munsey's boasts about the circulation preëminence of his *Magazine*, he never mentioned the *Journal*; in fact, he did not consider it a "magazine" at all. That term he always reserved, even in speaking of his own publications, for the monthly of royal-octave size. Among

---

[18] *Munsey's*, v. 17, p. 159, April 1897.
[19] *Munsey's*, v. 17, p. 478, June 1897.
[20] *Munsey's*, v. 24, p. 308, Nov. 1900.
[21] Munsey did not furnish sworn circulation figures until 1918.

what Munsey called "magazines," his own got a head start on competitors at ten cents by almost two years, as he was fond of pointing out. This lead it maintained for a full decade, yielding it only to *Everybody's* during the "Frenzied Finance" period.

*Munsey's* circulation declined somewhat in the years 1898–1905, but it seemed to make little difference in the advertising. Liquor and patent medicine ads were outlawed in 1905. The rate was low, at $500 a page on a claimed circulation basis of 700,000, but there were 90 to 100 pages of advertising every month. The magazine was economically produced in its own printing establishment, which it called the "largest magazine plant in the world." [22] Its editorial costs were not extravagant; except for some of its authors of fiction serials, it used writers who were satisfied with modest fees. Munsey, who was always ready to prove that the cheapest way was the best way, boasted in 1900 that his magazine was "written by trained journalists" rather than by famous men of letters.[23] Nor was there much outlay for art: illustrations were from photographs by halftones — "truer to life" than artists' work, said Munsey.[24] Book paper prices were low. The fact is that *Munsey's Magazine* was a great money-maker, and so were the *Argosy* and, probably, the two new magazines Munsey started in 1897 — the *Puritan* and the *Quaker*. He may have been making a profit even on his book publishing — cloth-bound novels for twenty-five cents and 150–page paperbacks for two cents. He later claimed that he was clearing over $500,000 a year from his publishing enterprises by 1900,[25] and he did not at that time own any newspapers. In 1899 he started a London edition of *Munsey's Magazine,* distributed in England by Horace Marshall & Son, but printed and bound in New York. The ragged urchin who had started the *Golden Argosy* on $40.00 and faith was now a proud millionaire. As he wrote in January 1899, the ten-cent magazine was "the road to wealth, fame, power." [26]

Munsey had always been interested in millionaires and an admirer of them; from boyhood he had aimed to be one. Eulogistic articles about "kings of finance" and "masters of money" were common in his magazine in the nineties, and after he had joined the fraternity they were even commoner. Arthur Reed Kimball's series entitled "Our American Millionaires" was published in 1907, and Isaac F. Marcosson's similar series appeared in 1912.

---

[22] *Munsey's*, v. 17, p. 160, April 1897.
[23] *Munsey's*, v. 24, p. 159, Oct. 1900.
[24] *Ibid.*
[25] Munsey, *The Founding of the Munsey Publishing-House,* p. 52; *Munsey's*, v. 38, p. 431, Dec. 1907.
[26] *Munsey's*, v. 20, p. 661, Jan. 1899.

This was after the movement known as muckraking was in full swing — had, indeed, passed its peak. No muckraker was Munsey. In 1910 he wrote:

I am keenly interested in the advance of this country — keenly interested in a constructive policy, not a destructive policy. *Munsey's Magazine* has never been committed to the muck-raking theory, and never will be. Muck-raking is one thing, and progress is quite another.[27]

There had been one number, however, which seemed to indicate that *Munsey's* was going to commit itself to what was then known as "trust-busting." In January 1900, Arthur E. McEwen's article, "The Trust as a Step in the March of Civilization," brought strong accusations against the corporations and advocated the trust type of organization to fight them. In the same issue Senator William E. Chandler's "Free Competition versus Trust Combinations" showed how monopolies operated against the interests of consumers. But although this looked like the start of a crusade, it was a beginning without a sequel.

In the early years of the century Munsey contributed an occasional article to his magazine on politics or finance. He became an ardent supporter of Theodore Roosevelt, following him into the "Bull Moose" party. He was able to subordinate his high-tariff and prorailroad views to his admiration of T. R.; and in the campaign of 1912 he contributed to the cause not only a substantial portion of the party funds, but also the enthusiastic support of his newspapers and *Munsey's Magazine*. In the magazine for March appeared an article, "Catching Up with Roosevelt," by Judson C. Welliver, then editor of Munsey's *Washington Times*, which was designed to persuade the businessman that Roosevelt was not dangerous, and which was widely distributed during the summer and fall by the Progressive campaign committee. Other articles by Welliver, and short editorial pieces in departments, gave the *Magazine* a political tinge during the campaign. After the slaughter of the bull moose at the polls, Munsey contributed a series of large-type editorials in 1913 proposing three "amalgamations" among political parties. He thought that politics should pursue the same path of combination and "clean-up" that he found so necessary in the fields of newspapers, magazines, and grocery stores; but his major proposal was the formation of a political "holding company" to take over the assets of the Republican and Progressive parties, and form a new Liberal party. The idea met with some favor, but the old-timers scoffed. After 1914 partisan politics disappeared from the magazine's pages, though Welliver's occa-

[27] *Munsey's*, v. 44, p. 217, Nov. 1910.

sional articles on public problems and personalities continued as a strong feature.

*Munsey's* leading serial writers in the first dozen years of the new century were F. Marion Crawford, Stanley Weyman, Anthony Hope, Max Pemberton, Lloyd Osbourne, Louis Joseph Vance, and James Oliver Curwood. For a few years the "storiettes" seemed to crowd out the short stories; but when Robert Hobart Davis, fiction editor extraordinary, joined the staff in 1904, the magazine began to display a quality in short fiction equal or superior to that shown in the continued stories. Susan Keating Glaspell, Dorothy Canfield, Clarence B. Kelland, Charles E. Van Loan, and Montague Glass were some of the writers, soon to be well known, who made early appearances under the aegis of Bob Davis. William Sidney Porter ("O. Henry") was a special protégé of his. The magazine had already published a few O. Henry stories before Davis became fiction editor of the Munsey publications; but in January 1905 it contracted with him to be allowed the first reading of all his stories, and to pay him ten cents a word for all that Davis accepted. Thus a dozen O. Henry stories were purchased between 1905 and 1910.[28]

*Munsey's* always printed a few pages of verse in each number. For several years the department called "Etchings" carried half a dozen poems; in 1906 the title was changed to the more appropriate "Light Verse." In 1904 there were several contests for the best "topical verse." Such minor poets were represented in the magazine after the turn of the century as Sarah N. Cleghorn, Theodore Roberts, Joel Benton, John Kendrick Bangs, and — yes, Mary Roberts Rinehart.

In an effort to end a circulation slump that had extended over several years, *Munsey's* in 1905–1906 shifted departments, improved paper and presswork, added some color in illustration, and brought in several high-powered writers on public affairs. Thus Herbert N. Casson's series entitled "The Romance of Steel and Iron in America" appeared in 1906, and soon Welliver and Marcosson became regular contributors. Dr. Woods Hutchinson wrote on medical subjects, and John Grant Dater began in 1910 a "Financial Department" of several pages in which investment advice was freely given. T. P. O'Connor wrote a few articles on English affairs, and F. Cunliffe-Owen wrote mostly about European royalty. But the outstanding series in these years was one on "Famous Affinities of History," in which outstanding love affairs of the past were celebrated through the magazine's numbers for nearly four years by Lyndon Orr. This, with its illustrations from paintings and prints, was 100 per cent *Munsey*.

[28] Robert H. Davis and Arthur B. Maurice, *The Caliph of Bagdad* (New York, 1931), chs. 13–14.

Circulation swung upward in 1906, almost equaling the seven hundred thousand peak of 1897; but after that it declined slowly but consistently until in 1912 the business manager claimed only four hundred thousand a month. That year the price per copy was raised to fifteen cents. Munsey was still "Chief," but he gave less and less attention to his "flagship" in the coming years. He had launched no less than a dozen other magazines,[29] though he never had that many afloat at once. He had a successful chain grocery. He had just been knee-deep in politics and daily journalism, and in 1916 he was to enter his second and mammoth series of newspaper ventures. The faithful Titherington, whom O. Henry, in one of his more ebullient moments, once called "Colonel Titherington, than whom the Flatiron holds none more worthy of being Second Cousin to the Moon and Brother-in-Law to the Sidereal System,"[30] was managing editor for a third of a century. With him had been associated many assistant editors — among them, C. Stuart Johnson, Harold Parker, Jerome Case Bull, J. Hayden Clarendon, Frank Crowninshield (1903–1907), Richard Duffy (1906–1909), Issac F. Marcosson (1909–1913), Robert McKay (1909–1915), Bannister Merwin, and Robert H. Davis.

With the coming of the First World War, the successive numbers of *Munsey's* were very martial. Government heads wrote articles — Secretaries Lansing, Gage, Redfield, and Lane, Senator Lodge, Chairman Edward N. Hurley, of the Shipping Board, and so on. Welliver was a stand-by, as well as several writers from Munsey's *New York Sun* — notably Willis J. Abbot and Frank M. O'Brien. Illustrations were now grouped, so that there would be sections of several pages in rotogravure, such as a dozen camera shots of war scenes or a series of portraits of President Wilson and his "chief advisers"; and other sections of combined letterpress and halftones on highly calendared paper, such as the never-failing department "The Stage," now edited by Matthew White, Jr. "Editorials" now claimed ten pages of large-size type; not all of them dealt with the war. "The Odd Measure" was a second editorial department. The single-copy price, which had been dropped back to the traditional ten cents in 1916 in order to stimulate circulation, failed of that purpose and was raised to twenty cents in 1918; at the same time the number of pages was increased to an amazing two hundred and sixty for occasional issues.

[29] Munsey's magazines may be listed as follows: *Golden Argosy*, 1883, name changed to *Argosy* in 1888, current; *Munsey's Illsutrated Weekly*, 1884; *Munsey's Weekly,* 1889–1929, name changed to *Munsey's Magazine* in 1891; *Puritan*, 1897–1901; *Quaker*, 1897–1902, name changed to *Junior Munsey* in 1900; *All-Story Magazine*, 1905–current, many changes; *Railroad Man's Magazine*, 1906–19; *Scrap Book*, 1906–12; *Woman*, 1906–07; *Ocean*, 1907–08, name changed to *Live Wire* 1908; *Cavalier*, 1908–14.
[30] Davis and Maurice, *The Caliph of Bagdad*, p. 221.

The nonfiction in *Munsey's* during the war and immediately after it seems more than usually interesting and varied. Richard Le Gallienne, Brander Matthews, Frederick Austin Ogg, Frederick M. Davenport, and Anne O'Hagan had been reliable contributors for several years; and they all wrote well on social, political, and literary topics. O'Brien's history of the *New York Sun* was a 1917 serial. But the magazine was on the lethal toboggan. Its average circulation in 1920 (sworn) was a hundred and thirty thousand, and it carried only twenty pages or so of advertising. Meanwhile the all-fiction *Argosy* was doing nicely with nearly half a million circulation. Would the *Magazine* do better under a plan in which fiction dominated?

The "complete novel in each number" policy, which had been tried briefly many years before, was adopted in 1913–1917; and P. G. Wodehouse, George Barr McCutcheon, Gilbert Parker, Joseph Conrad, Arnold Bennett, E. Phillips Oppenheim, and Rupert Hughes wrote some of the novelettes. Various combinations were tried — novelettes without serials; serials without novelettes; serials, novelettes, and short stories. In July 1921, *Munsey's Magazine* was made an all-fiction monthly, without illustration, printed on wood-pulp paper — a two-hundred-page packet of varied fiction at twenty-five cents. During most of its remaining years it offered in each number installments of five serials, a novelette, nine short stories, and some poems. Sometimes there were "true stories," and in 1928 some articles on sports and the theater were added; but for its last eight years *Munsey* (as it had long been named on the cover) was devoted to fiction. Leading writers for the "pulps" were represented, and some well known in the "slicks," such as Louis Tracy, T. S. Stribling, Charles Francis Coe, Edwin L. Sabin, Octavus Roy Cohen, Ellis Parker Butler, Jack Bechdolt, Elisabeth Sanxay Holding, Max Brand, Homer Croy, Edgar Rice Burroughs, and Frank R. Adams.

Frank A. Munsey died in 1925, and William T. Dewart succeeded him as publisher. "Bob" Davis, who had been an editor of Munsey's magazines since 1904, was now in chief editorial charge. The magazine's circulation got down to sixty-four thousand in 1924, and thereafter it was not reported separately. After October 1929, *Munsey* was merged with the weekly *Argosy All-Story* to form the *All-Story Combined with Munsey's* while the *Argosy* was resumed as a separate publication. The Munsey name was soon dropped, but *All-Story,* with mutations, continued for a long time.

*Munsey's* was never a first-class magazine. It was chiefly notable for introducing the ten-cent price in the general illustrated magazine field, and thereby attaining, for a few years at the turn of the century, a top

circulation and large profits. It did this largely by liberal illustration
of art subjects, by a great variety of content in which light but rather
unoriginal writing predominated, and by printing more pages than
other magazines. Munsey continually boasted of the number of pages
in his magazine — 160 for a long time, then 192, and then as many as
265. At least once he counted not only pages, but articles and pictures
in the various magazines, and printed a table showing how much more
*Munsey* readers were getting.[31] Sometimes there was quality as well as
quantity in the magazine, but there was a shocking amount of mediocrity; and *Munsey's* compares unfavorably with such ten-cent magazines as *McClure's, Everybody's,* and Walker's *Cosmopolitan.*

[31] *Munsey's,* v. 19, p. 317, May 1898.

# THE NATIONAL GEOGRAPHIC MAGAZINE [1]

T HE National Geographic Society was organized in Washington in January 1888. Its stated aim was "the increase and diffusion of geographic knowledge," and its chief functions, in the beginning, were the holding of public lectures in Washington and the publication of a magazine. These two activities were closely related, since the former was to furnish a body of content for the latter.

First president of the society was Gardiner Greene Hubbard, a lawyer-capitalist who had financed the great invention of his son-in-law, Alexander Graham Bell, and had thereupon become the first president of the Bell Telephone Company. Among the other incorporators of the society were General A. W. Greely, who had gained fame as the leader of a polar expedition several years before and was now chief of the Signal Service Corps; Major J. W. Powell, explorer of the Grand Canyon and at this time director of the United States Geological Survey; George Kennan, famous for his recent travels in Siberia; Henry Gannett, distinguished cartographer with the Census Bureau and the Geological Survey; O. H. Tittmann, leader of many surveying expeditions in the West and a member of the Coast and Geodetic Survey staff.

[1] TITLE: *The National Geographic Magazine.*

FIRST ISSUE: Oct. 1888. Current.

PERIODICITY: Irregular, vols. 1–6, 1888–95: 1, Oct. 1888, April, July, Oct. 1889; 2, April, May, June, Aug. 1890, April 1891; 3, March 28, May 29, 1891, Jan. 28, 1892; 4, March 26, March 21, March 18, March 31, May 15, 1892, Feb. 8, 1893; 5, April 7, March 20, April 29, July 10, 1893, Jan. 31, 1894; 6, Feb. 14, March 17, April 25, May 23, June 22, Nov. 1, Dec. 29, 1894, April 20, 1895. Monthly, annual vols. 7–24, 1896–1913; monthly, semiannual vols., 25–current, 1913–current.

PUBLISHER: National Geographic Society, Washington, D.C. (1901–02, published by McClure, Phillips & Company, New York, for National Geographic Society).

EDITORS: Henry Gannett, secretary, 1888–90; Marcus Baker, secretary, 1891; W J McGee, chairman publication committee, 1892–95; John Hyde, 1896–1900; Henry Gannett, 1901–02; Gilbert Hovey Grosvenor, 1903–1954; John Oliver La Gorce, 1954–current.

INDEXES: Henry Skadsheim, comp., *Topical Index of the National Geographic Magazine, 1888–1912* (Berrien Springs, Mich., 1935); *Cumulative Indexes*, 1899–1946, 1947–1951, 1952–1954, published by the society; *Poole's Index, Jones' Legal Index, Contents–Subject Index, Engineering Index, Readers' Guide.*

REFERENCES: Gilbert Grosvenor, *The National Geographic Society and Its Magazine* (Washington, 1936), reprint of article in *NGM*, v. 69, pp. 123–64, Jan. 1936 (Much of this appears also in Grosvenor's "The National Geographic Society," *Proc. of Am. Antiq. Soc.*, v. 52, pp. 325–49, Oct. 1942, and Introduction to *Cum. Index*, 1899–1940, *supra*); Geoffrey T. Hellman, "Geography Unshackled," *New Yorker*, v. 19, Sept. 25, 1943, pp. 26ff, Oct. 2, pp. 27ff, Oct. 9, pp. 27ff; Ishbel Ross, "Geography, Inc.," *Scribner's Magazine*, v. 103, June 1938, pp. 23ff; Edwin C. Buxbaum, *Collecting National Geographic Magazines* (Milwaukee, 1936).

It will be noted that these men were mostly connected with government bureaus; in the main, they were distinguished scientists. For its first decade the society had little claim to the name "National," except for the fact that it functioned in the national capital; the word in its title represented rather a hope for the future than a reality of 1888.

For its first seven years the *National Geographic Magazine* was published irregularly, as material accumulated. Its first number was dated October 1888, and the second was not issued until the next April. These numbers, or "brochures," as the officers liked to call them, were printed in New Haven from 1888 to 1891, and later by Judd & Detwiler, Washington. They were tall-octavo in size, contained anywhere from sixteen to a hundred pages, and were bound in rather forbidding terra-cotta covers. From the first, there were many maps and charts, usually bound in, folded, at the back of the "brochure." The articles were chiefly technical and scientific papers, though Robert E. Peary's "Across Nicaragua with Transit and Machete" (April 1891) points toward the type of more popular article that was later characteristic of the *Geographic.* Another prophetic note was the studied variety of the society's early work: originally there was a vice-president for the geography of land (Herbert G. Ogden), another for that of the sea (George L. Dyer), a third for that of the air (A. W. Greely), and finally a vice-president for the geography of life (C. Hart Merriam). Later Gannett was added as head of a section devoted to the geography of art. It was apparent that these men, explorers all, were willing to strike out on new and non-academic roads in geographic science.

Each of the first two volumes contained four rather large numbers; the next four were, by plan,[2] more irregular in size and frequency, Volume Six containing eight parts. There was much of Alaskan exploration and the Bering Sea controversy, by Greely and others. The society's expeditions to Mount St. Elias, Alaska, financed by President Hubbard, furnished no little material. Other common subjects were meteorology, geology, oceanography, volcanology, population, and the history of exploration and discovery.

The society's membership reached a thousand in 1894. Dues were five dollars, three of which went to the magazine. But it was evident that if this publication were to be truly "National," and really a "Magazine" instead of a series of reports and monographs, something had to be done about it. Accordingly, it was made a regular monthly at the beginning of 1896, with a halftone frontispiece and gradually increasing illustration. A better looking cover was provided, and newsstand sales were attempted. In a ringing declaration of Americanism, the

[2] See the detailed plans for the publication in *NGM*, v. 2, pp. 287–88, 311–14, April 1891.

editor declared: "It will be the aim of the *National Geographic Magazine* to be American rather than cosmopolitan, and in an especial degree to be National."[3] And then it started off its first monthly number with an article on "Russia in Europe," by President Hubbard, while the lead article the next month was one by William Eleroy Curtis on Venezuela, and so on. In other words, available material gave the magazine a world view in spite of itself. But there were some articles about individual states by their United States senators or representatives, and many about national resources, such as Bernhard E. Fernow's papers on our forests. There was much about the national capital from time to time: the number for December 1897 was almost wholly devoted to Washington. In 1898 the war brought articles on Cuba and Porto Rico, and began an emphasis on the Philippines that continued for several years. Anthropology and ethnology were leading subjects, and such articles as J. B. Hatcher's illustrated paper on "Patagonia" (November 1897) were typical. There were back-of-the-book departments of "Geographic Notes" and "Geographic Literature."

Editors of the earlier numbers of the magazine had been the recording secretaries of the society, Henry Gannett and then Marcus Baker. From 1892 to 1895, a "publication committee" had been in charge; its chairman had been that remarkable, self-educated geologist and ethnologist, W J McGee. When the magazine became a monthly, it was given an editor-in-title (though at first called "honorary editor" because the secretary was still expected to do most of the work) in the person of John Hyde, who had been associate editor of the *Bankers' Monthly*. But Hyde was not a full-time, paid editor, for he was currently chief of the Department of Agriculture's Bureau of Statistics.

The belief grew that the society and its magazine would never make a success until it had an aggressive, full-time man in charge. Newsstand sales had been a failure, and society membership had stalled at nine hundred to a thousand. This was the conviction, especially, of the new president of the society, Alexander Graham Bell.[4] Bell was a genius whose interests, far from being limited to the field of the physics of sound, or even of physics in general, ranged freely over the whole world of ideas. It had seemed natural that, on the death of President Hubbard in December 1897, the succession should fall upon his son-in-law. Bell immediately began to look for a young man to broaden and popularize the magazine, in the hope that thereby he would at the same

---

[3] *NGM*, v. 7, p. 2, Jan. 1896.

[4] The society's presidents have been Gardiner Greene Hubbard, 1888–97; Alexander Graham Bell, 1898–1903; W J McGee, 1904; Grove Karl Gilbert, 1904; Willis Luther Moore, 1905–09; Henry Gannett, 1910–14; Otto Hilgard Tittmann, 1915–19; John Elliott Pillsbury, 1919; Gilbert Hovey Grosvenor, 1920–54; John Oliver La Gorce, 1954–current.

time broaden the scope of the society to national proportions and provide the financial support that such an organization would need in order to function properly. Bell bethought himself of the twin sons of his friend Professor Edwin A. Grosvenor, of Amherst; they had been graduated *magna cum laude* from that college the year before and had subsequently been house guests of the Bells at their summer home in Nova Scotia. Brilliant young men, identical twins, Gilbert and Edwin Grosvenor could substitute for one another in most capacities; but when Bell's offer came to them jointly, there was an end to all comedies of errors based on identity. For an attachment had developed between Gilbert and one of the Bell daughters, and Edwin stuck to his law career while his brother went to Washington on April 1, 1899. Bell personally paid young Grosvenor's salary of a hundred dollars a month for the first five years in the editorship of the magazine; but it was soon "all in the family," for Gilbert Hovey Grosvenor and Elsie Graham Bell were married in 1900.

When Bell suggested the job to the Grosvenor boys in 1899, he said that one of them "might find in this position a stepping-stone to something better." [5] But it was realized long before Doctor Grosvenor celebrated in 1949 his golden jubilee of service to the *Magazine* and society, in the midst of world-wide acclaim,[6] that what he had actually found at that time was a steppingstone to an enlargement of his original job, though the proportions of it were then undreamed of and are even now difficult to believe.

In the summer of 1899 Grosvenor became assistant editor of the *National Geographic Magazine*. He was not given the title of editor until 1903; but, with the advice of President Bell, he was the organizing and driving force behind the magazine. At first he did not even have a clerical assistant, and he did everything himself — even to addressing the monthly copies to be mailed to the nine hundred members. From Bell he accepted the doctrine and technique of member-subscribers with enthusiasm. Since this is the cornerstone of the *National Geographic's* success, it must be explained with some care.

The concept envisions a society national — even world-wide — in scope, whose functions are the diffusion of geographic knowledge through the publication of a magazine, monographs, manuals, bulletins, and so on; [7] the support of expeditions of exploration and discovery, archeological researches, and surveys of many kinds; and aid to the preservation of national resources and to the government and its vari-

---

[5] Grosvenor, *The National Geographic Society and Its Magazine*, p. 136.
[6] *NGM*, v. 96, pp. 252–61, Aug. 1949.
[7] The traditional National Geographic Society afternoon and evening lecture courses are still maintained in Washington, for an additional fee.

ous departments in war and peace. It was thought that such a large project could be financed by the annual dues of members (lowered to two dollars in 1900) if membership could be made sufficiently attractive through the appeal of a popular magazine of geography. Therefore, the newsstands were forgotten; regular "subscriptions," though accepted at fifty cents extra, were not encouraged; and solicitation took the form of invitations to membership in the National Geographic Society. The invitations, which begin, "I have the honor to inform you that you have been recommended for membership," perhaps sound pretentious; they are designed to convey the perfectly genuine idea that membership in the society means participation in, and support of, its wide-flung activities, as well as a subscription to the *Magazine*. The membership idea also helps in renewals, and makes for a far more permanent list than most magazines have. And finally, as a selling device, when applied to a really excellent magazine, it is matchless.

Of course, the plan required skillful popularization of scientific knowledge, and there are those who say that popular science is never good science. It is recalled that Hubbard, beginning his first address as president of the society, said, "I am not a scientific man." [8] This was undue modesty, in view of his later papers in the *Magazine*; but that initial remark emphasizes the view held by the society, even in those early days when the published papers were largely technical, to the effect that the bare facts, the exhaustive data, and the technical phraseology of exact science were not required in the society or its magazine. And it soon became clear that under Grosvenor's editorship, such things not only were not required, they were not permitted. It was, of course, a matter of adjusting content to a different audience; the early numbers had been designed chiefly for technical readers, while those after 1899 were suited to the more general public. Wrote Grosvenor some years later:

> Dr. Bell had a revolutionary idea: Why not popularize the science of geography and take it into the homes of the people? Why not transform the Society's *Magazine* from one of cold geographic fact, expressed in hieroglyphic terms which the layman could not understand, into a vehicle for carrying the living, breathing, human-interest truth about this great world of ours to the people? [9]

This does not mean that either truth or substantial accuracy was ever sacrificed. As Grosvenor sets forth his editorial formula, he names accuracy as "the first principle." The second one is "abundance of beautiful and instructive illustration." A third is the avoidance of controversy,

[8] *NGM*, v. 1, p. 1, Oct. 1888.
[9] *Proc. Am. Antiq. Asso.*, v. 52, p. 327, Oct. 1942. Cf. Grosvenor, *The National Geographic Society and Its Magazine*, pp. 137–38; *Cum. Index*, 1899–1940, p. 19.

while at the same time "the content of each number is planned with a view to being timely." Another factor striven for is permanence, and the lively business in supplying back numbers of the *Geographic* testifies to the popular agreement about the enduring value of its contents. Finally, the magazine is faithful to this article of its creed: "Only what is of a kindly nature is printed about any country or people." [10] Doubtless it has been impossible to keep out all offense to any people whose land and life have been discussed, but the fact is that a one-world sympathy pervades the whole file of the *National Geographic* and that kindliness has rarely given way to asperity. Indeed, there is a certain sentimentality in the magazine's continual emphasis on friendliness, beauty, and loving-kindness in the various aspects of this our world.

For many years most of the contributors to the *National Geographic* were connected with the departments and bureaus of the government, including members of both houses of Congress and justices of the Supreme Court, members of the Cabinet and of the diplomatic corps, and officers of the armed services. Emphasis on exploration and discovery was noticeable. Admiral Peary was a member and contributor long before he was famous. At the time of the Peary-Cook controversy over the discovery of the North Pole, the society offered to decide the case if the explorers would submit their records to its research committee. Dr. Cook's "proofs" never were submitted to it, but it hailed Peary as the discoverer in January 1910.[11] Greely, Peary, Cook, Amundsen, Stefansson, Byrd, Shackleton, MacMillan, Ellsworth, and Wellman were among the explorers of polar regions to write for the *National Geographic*. To the expeditions of some of these men the society made important contributions. Wrote Byrd on one occasion: "Other than the flag of my country, I know of no greater privilege than to carry the emblem of the National Geographic Society." [12] But by 1902 there was a trend to more material of the travelogue type — such as S. P. Langley's "Voyage from San Francisco to Tahiti and Return" (December 1901), Congressman Ebenezer J. Hill's "A Trip Through Siberia" (February 1902), and David G. Fairchild's "Travels in Arabia" (April 1904). Ministers to foreign countries, such as William Eleroy Curtis, John W. Foster, and John Barrett furnished similar reports of their observations.

Soon there was a noticeable enlargement of interests, with articles about jade, reindeer in Alaska, the construction of kites, immigration,

[10] *Proc. Am. Antiq. Asso.*, v. 52, p. 333, Oct. 1942. Cf. Grosvenor, *The National Geographic Society and Its Magazine*, p. 149; *Cum. Index*, 1899–1940, pp. 25–26.

[11] Reports of Peary and Cook, *NGM*, v. 20, pp. 892–916, Oct. 1909; society's handling of the case, v. 20, pp. 921–22; decision, v. 21, pp. 63–82, Jan. 1910.

[12] Grosvenor, *The National Geographic Society and Its Magazine*, p. 124.

distribution of insanity in the United States, eugenics, American industries, "Queer Methods of Travel," "How the World Is Shod," "Children of the World," and so on. Secretary William Howard Taft wrote "Some Recent Instances of National Altruism: The Efforts of the United States to Aid the Peoples of Cuba, Porto Rico, and the Philippines" in the number for July 1907; and after Taft had taken over Roosevelt's quarters in the White House, Sir Harry Johnston, later Commissioner for Uganda, contributed an article, "Where Roosevelt Will Hunt" (March 1909). Still later the magazine published T. R.'s own "Wild Man and Wild Beast in Africa" (January 1911). Besides Taft and Roosevelt, Presidents Coolidge and Hoover were faithful contributors to the *Magazine* and members of the society.

The "geography of the air" became a favorite field for the *Magazine*; writing in 1936, Grosvenor declared that "the *Geographic* has published more about aviation than any other magazine of general circulation." [13] From Alexander Graham Bell's early articles on man-lifting kites (July 1903, January 1907) to the later narratives by Charles A. and Anne Lindbergh, Auguste Piccard, Dr. Hugo Eckener, Captain Albert W. Stevens, General William L. Mitchell, and General H. H. Arnold, the *Geographic* has given full treatment to the development of aeronautics. The July 1924 number was all aviation: it led off with John A. Macready's "Non-Stop Flight Across America." The December 1953 issue was also an aviation number, celebrating the airplane's semicentennial in articles by Hugh L. Dryden and Emory S. Land.

In the first decade of the new century there was also much about the American dependencies — Alaska, Hawaii, the Philippines, and the Canal Zone. Several articles on the Panama Canal by George W. Goethals and Theodore P. Shonts were important and well illustrated.

Illustration improved gradually in brilliance and in amount. By 1908 pictures were occupying more than half the space in an eighty-page magazine. But it was the advent of color in the next decade that really transformed the *Geographic* into a kind of periodical never before known. Its first color pictures appeared in the number for November 1910. They were made from photographs taken by William Wisner Chapin, and illustrated his article entitled "Glimpses of Korea and China"; while by no means up to standards later developed, these were attractive pictures — thirty-nine of them, mostly full pages. Again in 1911 and 1912 the November issue (which was the Christmas number) contained similar Chapin pieces, one about Japan and the other about Russia.

[13] *Ibid.*, p. 129. See also the account of the society's work in the encouragement of aviation, *NGM*, v. 52, pp. 233–42, Aug. 1927.

Then in June 1913 began a long series of occasional articles about birds, the earlier ones by Henry W. Henshaw with colored drawings by Louis Agassiz Fuertes, and the later ones by Alexander Wetmore with color "portraits" by Major Allen Brooks. This first article was called "Fifty Common Birds of Farm and Orchard," and subsequent installments were similarly grouped. The bird articles were special favorites of Editor Grosvenor, and they beautified many numbers. The editor wrote the caption for a reprint from a book by Frank M. Chapman directly from the heart: "Birds May Bring More Happiness Than the Wealth of the Indies" (June 1913). Later there were comprehensive pieces on pigeons, ducks, geese, tropical birds, poultry, etc.

Similar series on wild flowers, illustrated in color, began in 1915, with notes by N. L. Britton and illustrations from the water colors of Mary E. Eaton. These naturalists were from the New York Botanical Garden; later Edith S. and Frederick E. Clements, of the Carnegie Institution, furnished similar pictures and notes.

There were many other extended forays into the natural history field by naturalist-and-artist teams. One of the most popular single numbers ever issued was that of March 1919, containing descriptions and illustrations in color (by Fuertes) of seventy-three of the common breeds of dogs, together with an article by Ernest Harold Baynes with the characteristic NGM title: "Mankind's Best Friend, Companion of His Solitude, Advance Guard in the Hunt, and Ally of the Trenches." This had eleven illustrations; and an editorial article entitled "Sagacity and Courage of Dogs: Instances of the Remarkable Intelligence and Unselfish Devotion of Man's Best Friend Among Dumb Animals" had fourteen more. In later years field dogs, hounds, terriers, and sheep dogs have been celebrated, many of these articles illustrated from paintings by Edward Herbert Miner. Even more exciting, as far as pictures are concerned, than the famous dog number, was the horse number of November 1923, with its spirited Miner illustrations, twenty-four of them in color. The text, entitled "Story of the Horse: The Development of Man's Companion in War Camp, on the Farm, in the Marts of Trade, and in the Field of Sports," was by General William Harding Carter. "The Taurine World" followed in December 1925, with nearly a hundred illustrations of cattle, twenty of them in color from Miner paintings; the text was by Alvin Howard Sanders, of the *Breeder's Gazette*. Then there were the two magnificent numbers on the wild animals of North America by Edward William Nelson, issued November 1916 and May 1918, with Fuertes paintings, said to have cost the magazine forty thousand dollars. The number of July 1929 was brilliant with no less than two hundred and sixty-nine color pictures of insects, some from photographs by Edwin L. Wisherd, and many from paintings by Hashime Murayama. These artists, together with Else Bostelmann, illustrated many of the resplendent articles about fishes that appeared in the twenties. Then there were colorful pieces, of this same handbook kind, about butterflies, vegetables, trees, shrubs, berries, fruits, reptiles, cats, and so on.

Many of the articles and pictures mentioned above have been edited and published by the society in book form. Outstanding is the two-volume Grosvenor-Wetmore *Book of Birds,* with nine hundred and fifty "color portraits" by Major Brooks, first published in 1937.

Franklin L. Fisher was the able "illustrations editor" from 1915 to 1953. Some notable photographers and technicians have worked in this division of the magazine's staff. Melville Bell Grosvenor, son of the editor-in-chief, began as an assistant in illustrations in 1924; he was made assistant editor of the magazine in 1935 and associate editor in 1954. A third-generation Grosvenor, Gilbert Melville, started in illustrations shortly after the mid-century. B. Anthony Stewart, chief of the staff photographers, joined the staff in 1927 and has had more pictures published in the magazine than any other camera man. Maynard Owen Williams, chief of the foreign staff from 1930 until his retirement in 1953, published in the magazine about sixty-five articles illustrated by his own photographs. Walter M. Edwards, who joined the illustrations staff in 1933, became the senior editor in that group on Fisher's death in 1953.

Equally distinguished has been the leadership in the *Geographic's* photographic laboratory, a pioneer in processing film for magazine use. Charles Martin was chief of this laboratory from 1915 to 1942, and he was succeeded by Edwin L. Wisherd.

The magazine claims many firsts in photographic illustration. One of these is the first publication of flashlight photographs of wild animals in their natural habitats; such pictures, by George Shiras, were a feature for twenty-five years, beginning in 1906. The *Geographic* also published the first pictures taken from the stratosphere, and the first natural-color photographs of undersea life. Beginning in 1913, the number of issues in the year that carried color sections increased gradually, until half of them had such illustration in 1924, and all of them by 1928.

In 1913, Grosvenor was in Europe, where he heard rumors of war on every hand. Coming home, he immediately ordered the preparation of a big new map of Europe, which he held until the assassination at Sarajevo and its sequel sent readers to atlases that they commonly found sadly out of date. With the outbreak of the European war, the *Geographic* was at once full of articles about European countries, and its map-makers worked overtime. Its sympathies in the conflict were indicated by the articles about France, like Arthur Stanley Riggs's "The Beauties of France," occupying a hundred pages, with color pictures, and accompanied by the editorial article, "The World's Debt to France" (November 1915). Carl Holliday's "Our Friends, the French" (November 1918), Herbert Hoover's "Bind the Wounds of France" (May 1917), and Ambassador J. J. Jusserand's "Our First Alliance" (June 1917) came later. The number for October 1917 displayed no less than 1,197 flags and standards of the world in colors; this, said the editors, was "the most expensive as well as the most instructive and beautiful number in the world history of periodical literature." [14] It was accompanied by an article by Franklin K. Lane, a frequent contributor to the magazine in these years, on "The Makers of the Flag." And the entire number for December 1918 was given to Edwin A. Grosvenor's remarkable article, "The Races of Europe," with lavish illustration and several maps.

It was in the year of the flag number that the society membership (and magazine circulation) reached half a million; though dues were raised to three dollars in 1920, membership went on to reach a million by 1926.

Meanwhile exploration, discovery, and travel were not neglected. Expeditions to Peru, sponsored jointly by the society and Yale University, resulted in several articles during 1912–1916; in the ensuing five years the expeditions to the Mount Katmai volcanic region in Alaska produced a number of articles about the "Valley of Ten Thousand Smokes," by Robert F. Griggs. Besides the excavations of the Incan sites by Bingham, there were major archeological expeditions to Pueblo Bonito, in northwestern New Mexico, resulting in articles by the leader of the researches, Neil M. Judd; and others in 1938–1941, in which the society joined with the Smithsonian Institution in sending a party to Vera Cruz, led by Matthew W. Stirling, who furnished a number of articles about Mayan monuments and other topics. Sylvanus Griswold Morley and others added to the articles about the Mayan civilization, and the color reproductions of H. M. Herget's paintings were striking. Also undertaken with the Smithsonian's coöperation was the 1948 expedition to Arnhem Land, in Australia, with its magazine articles the next year. In the latter forties and early fifties the archeologists represented in the *Magazine* included Stirling (Panama, March 1949, February 1950), Judd (Indian mounds, January 1949), Don Watson (Mesa Verde, September 1948), Frank M. Setzler (gravel effigies, September 1952), William Duncan Strong (Peru, April 1947), Henry

[14] *NGM*, v. 32, p. 283, Oct. 1917.

Field (Palestine, December 1948), and George C. Cameron (Iran, December 1950).

The great variety and large number of articles on travel and adventure in foreign lands can be indicated here by mention of only a very few articles: General William Mitchell's "Tiger Hunting in India" (November 1924), Felix Shay's "Cairo to Cape Town, Overland: An Adventurous Journey of 135 Days, Made by an American Man and His Wife Through the Length of the African Continent" (February 1925), Hans Hildenbrand's "Through Germany With a Color Camera" (December 1928), Joseph F. Rock's "Carrying the Color Camera Through Unmapped China" (October 1930), Captain A. W. Stevens' "Flying the 'Hump' of the Andes" (May 1931), Amos Burg's "Inside Cape Horn" (December 1937), W. Robert Moore's "In the Land of Moses and Abraham" (December 1938), La Verne Bradley's "Scenes of Postwar Finland" (August 1947), Andrew H. Brown's "Quebec's Forests, Farms, and Frontiers" (October 1949), and Burt Kerr Todd's "Bhutan, the Land of the Thunder Dragon" (December 1952). Especially notable were Mrs. Grosvenor's articles on an "African Safari" (August 1953, December 1954), illustrated by her husband's color photographs.

The color illustration that now brightened nearly every article made it possible to reproduce national costumes much more effectively. The quaintness of dress of foreign peoples had long been emphasized by the *Geographic's* pictures. And undress had been a feature in illustration, too; pictures of dusky, bare-breasted belles and young men with robust black torsos representing native tribes in obscure parts of the world had come to be expected in occasional articles. There were reports also of botanical and biological expeditions sent by the society to China, the Netherlands Indies, Brazil, and Venezuela.

But, despite all its loot from far places, the *Geographic* has never neglected its own land. It has published a remarkable series of articles about the various states, and its descriptions of the national parks and reserves and the resources and flora and fauna of the United States continue frequent and copious. Stirling's "Indians of Our Western Plains," with W. Langdon Kihn's paintings of Indian faces and figures (July 1944); Frederick G. Vosburgh's "Fabulous Yellowstone" (June 1940); Jack Breed's "Utah's Arches of Stone," with the author's kodachromes (August 1947); Mason Sutherland's "Adobe New Mexico," with Justin Locke's kodachromes (December 1949); Howell Walker's "You Can't Miss America by Bus," with photographs by the author (July 1950); Leo A. Borah's "From Sagebrush to Roses on the Columbia" (November 1952), with ektachromes by Ray Atkeson, are examples named at random.

During the Second World War, the *Geographic's* files of photographs, then including some 350,000 pictures, were made available to the government, which found them

a veritable gold mine of factual values to the intelligence sections of our armed services. Some were guideposts to enemy industrial or waterfront targets; other sets, besides reconnaissance photographs, were capable of unmasking camouflage.[15]

Further, the society was able to supply thousands of maps for the army, navy, and air force. The big eight-color maps went out also to members, month after month, as supplements of the magazine. There was much, in these war years, about the homelands of our allies, about the war industries at home, and about certain combat techniques — especially aviation and photography. Notable were William F. Draper's naval paintings (October 1944); and even more outstanding was the series on everyday life in ancient times — Egyptian (October 1941), Greek (March 1944), Roman (November 1946), Mesopotamian (January 1951) — with text by Edith Hamilton and other scholars, and illustration from Herget paintings. General Arnold was a faithful contributor on air power in the war, Owen Lattimore wrote much on Siberia and other subjects, and Lt. Col. Frederick Simpich, Jr., reported on life with the troops.

After the war, the *Geographic* was more colorful than ever. In 1946 it began some "bleeding" of color pages, eliminating margins and giving the effect of the larger page that the magazine has never been willing to adopt; and in a year or two nearly all color pages were given that treatment. The color pictures of Bikini in April 1947 were extraordinary.

The society and its magazine grew constantly and steadily in prosperity and in popular prestige. The Hubbard Memorial Building, which the Hubbard and Bell families had erected at the beginning of the century to house the society's activities, had been outgrown in less than a decade, and much more extensive and elaborate quarters had been provided from magazine profits. Circulation suffered scarcely at all in the great depression. Advertising, which never included liquors or cigarettes and which was limited to 20 per cent of the magazine's pages, showed no decline; and the magazine as a whole seemed to improve. After the Second World War the subscription rate, or (more properly) the annual membership fee, was raised to five dollars, and eventually to six; but circulation went forward steadily to about two million by the fifties. Nonprofit, untaxed, the society turned its earn-

---

[15] *NGM*, v. 83, p. 277, Feb. 1943.

ings into the improvement of its magazine and the prosecution of its projects in exploration and discovery.

About half the magazine was now written by staff members. Among assistant editors were Ralph A. Graves (1916–1932), Jesse Richardson Hildebrand (1919–1951), William Joseph Showalter (1914–1935), Maynard Owen Williams (1919–1953), Frederick Simpich (1927–1950), Frederick G. Vosburgh (1933–1957), Leo Arthur Borah (1928–1956), F. Barrows Colton (1935–1954), Mason Sutherland (since 1942), W. Robert Moore (since 1931), George W. Long (since 1945), Robert Leslie Conly (since 1951), and Franc (since 1953). Elsie Graham Bell Grosvenor has had an unofficial but important connection with the magazine ever since her marriage to Dr. Grosvenor. She has accompanied him on nearly all of his travels for the society and has herself been a notable contributor.

Grosvenor retired from the editorship of the magazine and the presidency of the society in May 1954, and John Oliver La Gorce was chosen to fill both positions. La Gorce had been assistant and later associate editor of the *National Geographic* for forty-nine years, having joined Grosvenor in its management when it had a circulation of only ten thousand. As La Gorce became editor, Melville B. Grosvenor became associate editor and his father chairman of the Board of Trustees of the Society. This arrangement lasted less than three years, however, for La Gorce, aged seventy-six, retired in January 1957 to become vice-chairman of the Board. Melville Bell Grosvenor thereupon became editor of the magazine and president of the society. At the same time, Frederick G. Vosburgh became associate editor, and Thomas W. McKnew vice-president and secretary of the society.

There is really nothing like it in the world. For more than half a century the *National Geographic Magazine* has not published a single monthly number that has not been interesting and informative, with some measure of permanent value. If it has seemed to some critics too much a picture book, even they have had to admit that in this it is in harmony with its times, and that its pictures are educational in a high degree. By the middle of the twentieth century it had attained the largest monthly circulation in the world at its price, and it had an assured position among the top ten monthly circulations at any price. This is a fabulous record of success, especially since the magazine is founded upon an editorial conviction that rates the intelligence of the popular audience fairly high. The *National Geographic Magazine* has long represented an achievement in editorship and management outstanding in the history of periodicals.

# OUTING [1]

OUTING was founded in Albany, New York, by William Bailey Howland, a young publisher who was to become general manager of the *Outlook* and later of the *Independent*. The first number, dated May 1882, was a twenty-four-page quarto, priced at twenty cents, or two dollars a year. The subtitle was "A Journal of Recreation," and there were articles on hunting and fishing, bicycling, college athletics, and yachting, with news from the pleasure resorts and some fiction and verse. The illustrations, by Dan Beard and others, were attractive, and the periodical was nicely printed.

Early numbers brought several well-known writers into *Outing's* pages — George Parsons Lathrop, Kate Upson Clark, Sophie Swett, and John Boyle O'Reilly. But Howland did not have the resources to build the circulation necessary for the production of a first-class magazine.

Five months after *Outing* was founded, another recreation magazine was begun on somewhat the same lines, but giving more emphasis to the popular interest in bicycling. This was the *Wheelman*, of Boston, published by the famous bicycle manufacturer, Colonel Albert A. Pope, and edited by a young employee later to be celebrated in the magazine world, Samuel S. McClure. This "high-class American organ of bicyclical and tricyclical operation and sentiment" [2] had been no more successful than Howland's venture, and Pope decided at the end of 1883 to merge the two and see what might happen. He kept Howland on as partner and editor. McClure resigned, though he later said he had a chance to be joint editor with Howland.[3]

[1] TITLES: (1) *Outing*, May 1882–Dec. 1883, April 1885–March 1906, May 1913–April 1923; (2) *Outing and The Wheelman*, Jan. 1884–March 1885; (3) *The Outing Magazine*, April 1906–April 1913.

FIRST ISSUE: May 1882. LAST ISSUE: April 1923.

PERIODICITY: Monthly. Vol. 1, May 1882–April 1883; 2, May–Dec. 1883; 3, Jan.–March 1884 (the consolidated magazine took over *Wheelman* numbering, and the Oct.–Dec. 1883 numbers of *Wheelman* are usually counted as v. 3, nos. 1–3, of the consolidated magazine); 4–82, no. 1, semiannual vols., April 1884–April 1923.

PUBLISHERS: W. B. Howland, Albany, 1882; Outing Publishing and Printing Company, Ltd. (W. B. Howland), Albany, 1882–83; The Wheelman Company (Albert Augustus Pope), Boston, 1884–85; Outing Publishing Company (Poultney Bigelow, 1886–88; J. H. Worman, 1888–1900; Caspar Whitney, 1900–09; Thomas Harper Blodgett, 1909–15; Albert Britt, 1916–23), New York, 1886–1923.

EDITORS: William Bailey Howland, 1882–85; Poultney Bigelow, 1886–88; Sylvester Baxter, 1888; James Henry Worman, 1888–97; Ben James Worman, 1897–1900; Caspar Whitney, 1900–09; Albert Britt, 1909–23.

INDEXES: *Poole's Index, Readers' Guide, Cumulative Index.*

[2] *Wheelman*, v. 1, p. 2, Oct. 1882.

[3] S. S. McClure, *My Autobiography* (New York, 1914), p. 159.

The new magazine was issued from the *Wheelman's* office by the *Wheelman's* publisher, and it kept the *Wheelman's* volume numbering and very handsome format; the *Wheelman* would, therefore, seem to have absorbed *Outing*. But the merger immediately adopted *Outing's* editor and his broader editorial policy, and it placed *Outing's* name first in the new title, and soon dropped "Wheelman" altogether. So *Outing's* later and greater career seems to have stemmed from the Albany rather than from the Boston periodical.

Such a question is bibliographical. The important development after the magazine got its new start was in content. Besides the sports already named, the magazine now gave attention to tennis, rowing, canoeing, lacrosse, and cricket. It also contained much about travel and exploration, forestry, amateur photography, and true experiences in connection with sports. "Our Monthly Record" included detailed reports of athletic events. Both McClure and Howland had included fiction, verse, humor, and news in their initial ventures; and these now became more important. Maurice Thompson and Julian Hawthorne contributed serial stories; and Arlo Bates, Joseph Pennell, Clinton Scollard, Frank Dempster Sherman, and R. K. Munkittrick were among *Outing's* writers. In 1885 Thomas Stevens began his long serial — it ran for some three years — entitled "Around the World on a Bicycle."

The size of the magazine had to be increased, of course; it grew from eighty pages in 1884 to a hundred and twenty-four the next year, the price being raised to twenty-five cents. It was expensive to produce, and it had reached only eight thousand circulation by 1886. Colonel Pope is said to have lost sixty thousand dollars on it [4] before he sold it in January 1886 to Poultney Bigelow, of New York.

The new owner and editor was a son of the famous journalist and diplomat, John Bigelow, and was himself a world traveler and adventurer. A devotee of amateur sports, he took on the direction of the magazine as a labor of love. "All our staff was working on a practically honorary basis," he wrote later; and added, "For three years I edited *Outing* without drawing any salary." [5]

The scope of sports treated (sometimes cursorily, indeed) was broadened. Chief interests were hunting and fishing, cycling, yachting, and travel; but there was also something about college sports (especially football and baseball), fencing, archery, polo, ballooning, skiing, coaching, camping, and even roller-skating. Walter Camp, "the father of football in American colleges, and for many years head of the Yale team" was early announced as a member of the staff. Captain R. F.

---

[4] *Outing*, v. 18, p. 346, July 1891.
[5] Poultney Bigelow, *Seventy Summers* (New York, 1925), v. 1, p. 300.

Coffin, long recognized as the foremost writer on sailing and other water sports for the New York press, contributed a serial "History of American Yachting" in 1886. Stevens' story of his bicycle tour was still running. Theodore Roosevelt wrote for *Outing* in the same year a series on "Ranch Life and Game Shooting in the West"; for these articles, much to Bigelow's disgust, the author sent the struggling magazine a bill for a hundred dollars apiece.[6] Illustration also improved; some of young Frederic Remington's first westerns appeared in *Outing*.

"There can be no question of the improvement of *Outing* since Poultney Bigelow assumed the management of the magazine," said the *Critic* late in 1886.[7] It was indeed more attractive, and it had more character as a magazine for the amateur sportsman. "Everything appealing to the gentleman sportsman was represented by the best amateur names in America," wrote Bigelow in his autobiography.[8] Professional sports were beneath its pitch. The prize ring, its activities largely illegal, was banned. Henry Chadwick, pioneer baseball reporter, wrote for the magazine; but he devoted himself therein chiefly to the diamonds of Harvard, Yale, and Princeton, leaving the vulgar professional contests to the newspaper. League baseball was under a cloud, anyway, during much of the nineties.[9]

Circulation rose to twenty thousand, but that was not enough to balance the budget; and one day Bigelow called his small staff together and gave them the magazine.[10] This was a fine gesture, but, under the circumstances, no kindness. When Bigelow walked out, Sylvester Baxter, a newspaper foreign correspondent and traveler who had been on the *Outing* staff for a year or two, served as editor until an "angel" could be found.

James Henry Worman, who saved the magazine from bankruptcy in 1888, was an educator and journalist long connected with the Chautauqua movement, and recently a professor at Vanderbilt University. He had made a fortune writing schoolbooks,[11] and supporting a high-class magazine of limited appeal was a good way to redistribute it. He was said to be hard to work for and had one managing editor after another for a few years.[12] He was his own managing editor for a time, and later his son, Ben James Worman, was his chief lieutenant.

The Worman management resumed the monthly record of amateur

[6] *Ibid.*
[7] *Critic*, v. 9, p. 235, Nov. 13, 1886.
[8] Bigelow, *Seventy Summers*, p. 300.
[9] See p. 374 of this volume; also *American Quarterly*, v. 5, Spring 1953, p. 48, which comments on *Outing's* attitude toward professional baseball.
[10] Bigelow, *Seventy Summers*, p. 301.
[11] *Pocket Magazine*, v. 3, p. 153, March 1897.
[12] Richard Neville, Francis Trevelyan, Charles E. Clay, and Alfred Balch.

sports events that Bigelow had discontinued, and this twenty-page section became an important part of the magazine. By 1893 it had seven departments — college athletics, including football, baseball, and track in season; amateur photography, consisting of instructions rather than reports; "Aquatics," divided among yachting, rowing, and canoeing; cycling, filled with news of tours and the activities of organizations; "Rod and Gun," devoted to counsel and news of the suppliers of guns, tackle, and so on; "Kennel and Loft," with news of dog shows and pigeon records; and "Equestrian Sports," including coaching, polo, and hunts. By the end of the nineties, the "Monthly Review" occupied thirty pages, with departments for yachting, canoeing, lawn tennis, track athletics, polo, croquet, rowing, photography, rod and gun, kennel, football, golf, cycling, and cricket. Camp left *Outing* with Bigelow in 1888, but he was back two years later, writing annual football reviews. John Corbin covered college athletics, R. B. Burchard and A. J. Kenealy wrote on yachting, Price Collier on golf, Edwyn W. Sandys on hunting and fishing, and so on. There were short departments for books, the theater, and humor.

There also was a short story (sometimes two) based on travel or sport in every number throughout the nineties, and there were a few fiction serials. But the important serials were nonfiction, and told of long cycle trips in the United States and abroad. The Stevens opus did not end until 1892, and by that time Frank G. Lenz's "World Tour Awheel" had begun — a series that was to last for five years. It was not Lenz who finished it, however, for he was lost in Kurdistan, presumably killed by the natives, in March 1895. But another "special correspondent" eighteen months later picked up where he had left off. The mystery of Lenz's disappearance furnished no little publicity for the magazine. Mr. and Mrs. Trumbull White cycled "Through Darkest America," Grace E. Denison wrote "Through Erin Awheel," Sidney Cross told about his "Five Weeks Awheel in France," F. M. Turner wrote "In the Land of the Breadfruit." Travelers sometimes carried cameras, and by the mid-nineties illustration was chiefly by halftone, and was more copious. Before that, A. W. Van Deusen and Henry S. Watson had been leading artists for *Outing,* with Gean Smith for horses and Herman Simon for dogs.

*Outing* was a fairly prosperous magazine in the later nineties. By 1896 it had reached a circulation of about ninety thousand, with some forty pages of advertising a month. The next year J. H. Worman "retired from the active management" of the magazine,[13] and a little later was appointed by President McKinley consul to Munich. Ben James

[13] *Outing,* v. 35, p. 623, March 1900.

Worman, who became editor and manager, was "a partial invalid."
And so, in February 1900, the Wormans sold *Outing* to a group of
wealthy sportsmen [14] headed by Caspar Whitney, well-known traveler,
explorer, and hunter, and one of the country's leading writers on outdoor recreation.

Whitney was a good editor, and for the next decade the magazine
was at the highest point of excellence in its history. It was intelligent,
lively, varied, and attractive in appearance. Whitney's editorial department, which occupied a dozen or more pages, set the tone for the magazine. It was called "The Sportsman's View-Point," and it was personal,
incisive, informative. When Roosevelt raised the question of "nature
faking," Whitney sided with the President; but he was not indignant
against good story-tellers and thought the whole commotion a "fool
controversy." [15] Assistant Editor Leonidas Hubbard, Jr., wrote much
about different parts of the United States; in 1905 he made an expedition into Laborador and lost his life in a snowstorm. His diary of the
trip was published in April 1905 and his companion's story was a serial
in 1906–1907. Eben E. Rexford ran a farm and garden department.
The old record and review departments were abandoned, though sports
summaries were sometimes printed. Herbert K. Job and Gene Stratton
Porter wrote about birds, Agnes C. Laut and George Wharton James
about Indians, E. P. Powell about country life, Dan Beard about camping, William C. Harris and Henry W. Lanier about fishes and fishing,
Joseph A. Graham about dogs, and F. M. Ware about horses. The
cycling fervor declined; little by little the automobile supplanted the
bicycle as the touring vehicle, and articles about motor carriages began
to appear in *Outing.*

There were some contributors whose fame extended beyond *Outing's*
sports, nature, and travel. Theodore Roosevelt was both writer and
subject in the magazine. Jack London's "White Fang" was a serial in
1906, and Stewart Edward White's "Round-Up Days" the next year.
Owen Wister, Zona Gale, Charles G. D. Roberts, William Beebe, Vance
Thompson, and Gouverneur Morris were frequent contributors. Ralph
Henry Barbour wrote football stories. While the illustration could not
be called profuse, it was good; and there were some color plates.
Among the leading artists were Frederic Remington, N. C. Wyeth,
Arthur Heming, A. B. Frost, and Charles Livingston Bull.

---

[14] Robert Bacon (who became vice-president), Fletcher Harper (who became secretary),
C. C. Cuyler, S. Reading Bertron, all of New York; S. F. Houston and T. D. M. Cardeza,
of Philadelphia; David M. Goodrich, of Boston; Walter Camp, of New Haven; and Charles
Hodgman, of St. Louis. Harper was doubtless drawn in because Whitney had been a member
of the staff of *Harper's Weekly.*

[15] *Outing,* v. 50, pp. 748–52, Sept. 1907.

*Outing's* largest circulation was a little over a hundred thousand in the five years 1905–1910. Whitney and his fellow sportsmen were tired of the game by 1909, when they sold the magazine to Thomas Harper Blodgett and Albert Britt.

These men had been fellow-students at Knox College. Blodgett had become western representative of *Outing* and other magazines after finishing a law course at Michigan, and Britt had been editor first of *Public Opinion* and then of the *Railroad Man's Magazine*. Taking over *Outing*, Blodgett, of course, became publisher and Britt editor. Some of the older contributors remained faithful to the magazine under the new management, but the better-known names tended to disappear. E. P. Powell on farming, Williams Haynes on dogs and other topics, and Harold Whiting Slauson on automobiles were prominent. Stewart Edward White, E. Alexander Powell, and Walter Prichard Eaton were among the more famous authors. There was a short news department giving records, and an equally short editorial department.

Blodgett withdrew in 1917, leaving Britt as editor and publisher. The magazine enlarged its pages to the quarto size, which had become prevalent. There was something of the war, and there was much of outdoor scenes in the United States. Full-page pictures in series, produced by an offset process, made impressive showings. Horace Kephart, sportsman and expert on guns, and Elon Jessup, a roving correspondent, were members of the staff. *Outing* "service," designed to promote advertising more than to serve readers, occupied much space. But circulation declined, both editorial and production quality declined, and (worst of all) advertising declined. An increase of price to thirty-five cents after the war did not help matters, circulation had fallen to thirty thousand, and the last number appeared in April 1923. The name was revived for a brief period when it was taken over in December 1924 by the *Athletic World*.[16]

*Outing* was throughout a gentleman's outdoor magazine; and, during the Bigelow and Whitney editorships, it was a distinguished periodical.

[16] A Columbus, Ohio, periodical, begun Sept. 1921 as *Football World*; continued 1922–24 as *Athletic World*. As *Outing* it lasted to Feb. 1926.

22

# THE PHILISTINE [1]

ELBERT HUBBARD was a soap salesman until he was thirty-seven years old. From boyhood he had been in the soap business with relatives. He had helped found J. D. Larkin & Company at Buffalo and had been chiefly responsible for devising the remarkable sales system of that concern, which later made it so widely known and prosperous. But in 1893, when the Larkin company was on the verge of its greater success, Hubbard, who had for some time been feeling the urgings of a mind and spirit above the soap business, suddenly sold out his half-interest for seventy-five thousand dollars and enrolled at Harvard College. But he did not stay long at Harvard. He was too impatient; he wanted to travel, to write fiction and history and criticism and philosophy, and to read whole libraries. He was a big, handsome man, dominating any group of which he was a part; and he was terribly ambitious to be a part of cultural movements.

On a trip to England, Hubbard visited many literary shrines, for which he had deep sentimental feelings. Most important of these visits, perhaps, was the one to the home of William Morris; he was greatly impressed by the community and the crafts at Kelmscott. Coming back to New York, he tried to sell to magazines and book publishers a series of essays he had written about his English tours — "Little Journeys to the Homes of Good Men and Great." In this he was unsuccessful until he had two of the essays produced by a firm of East Aurora printers; then G. P. Putnam's Sons took them over and began in December 1894 to publish them in monthly numbers.[2]

The *Little Journeys*, which were a compound of eulogy and information in quaint and tricksy style, were a success, and Hubbard was quick to follow them with a little magazine that was also quaint and tricksy. It has been said by Hubbard's biographer that when the *Philistine* was started, "the newsstands and mails were cluttered with small side-pocket magazines";[3] but, as a matter of fact, the vogue for the *bibelot* type of periodical did not really begin until the impressive success of

[1] TITLE: *The Philistine: A Periodical of Protest.*
FIRST ISSUE: June 1895. LAST ISSUE: July 1915.
PERIODICITY: Monthly. Vols. 1–41, no. 2, semiannual vols. beginning in June and Dec.
PUBLISHER: Elbert Hubbard, East Aurora, New York.
EDITORS: Harry Persons Taber, 1895–96; Elbert Hubbard, 1896–1915.
REFERENCES: David Arnold Balch, *Elbert Hubbard* (New York, 1940), esp. ch. 5.
[2] The *Little Journeys* continued to be published until 1909. The Roycrofters took over the publication in 1900.
[3] Balch, *Elbert Hubbard*, p. 160.

the *Philistine* had stimulated imitation.[4] The English *Yellow Book* and the American *Chap-Book* had been going for a year or so, and may have afforded Hubbard some suggestion; but they were both larger in size and more serious in intention than the *Philistine*. The only "side-pocket" periodical then in course of publication was Mosher's *Bibelot* (which, incidentally, was advertised in the first number of the *Philistine*), but it was devoted wholly to the reprinting of choice literature.[5]

When the *Philistine* appeared in June 1895, it measured four and three-quarters by six and a quarter inches, and was bound in cream-colored covers. After the first three numbers it was a trifle smaller, and brown "butcher's wrapping paper" covers were adopted. The type for the text was a Jenson, or something similar, with a rather black and squarish effect; and large ornamental factotums were used for initials. The printing on the cover was in black and red, and the magazine was thereon announced as "Printed Every Little While for the Society of the Philistines and Published by Them Monthly." It was not that the publication was to be more regular than the printing, but the way of telling about it was a Hubbardism. Fra Elbertus was later fond of telling about how he had at the beginning no intention of issuing more than one number of the *Philistine*, which he printed merely to get some things off his mind; how he was amazed to find that people sent in subscriptions for it; how he then decided to keep it going a year, and how the flood of subscribers forced him to continue it thereafter. It made a good story. He explained the facts that the first issue was given a serial number, and that monthly publication and yearly and monthly prices were specified, merely as a trick to get the Post Office Department to allow him second-class mailing privileges.[6] But it is clear that really Hubbard was trying the *Philistine* out as a magazine. In the first number he explained:

> It is the business of the true Philistine to rescue from the environment of custom and ostentation the beauty and goodness cribbed therein. And so the Philistines of these days, whose prime type is the Knight of La Mancha, go tilting at windmills and other fortresses — often on sorry nags and with shaky lances, and yet on heroic errand bent. And to such merry joust and fielding all lovers of chivalry are bidden: to look on — perhaps to laugh, it may be to grieve, at a woeful belittling of lofty enterprise. Come, such of you as have patience with such warriors! It is Sancho Panza who invites you.[7]

After the first five months, Hubbard was able to take the printing of the *Philistine* away from the East Aurora shop he had been patron-

[4] See pp. 386–91.
[5] See Sketch 4 in this volume for the *Bibelot* and Sketch 8 for the *Chap-Book*.
[6] Balch, *Elbert Hubbard*, p. 163.
[7] *Philistine*, v. 1, p. 20, June 1895.

izing and handle it in his own establishment. He had purchased second-hand equipment of his own, Harry Taber had installed it in a barn, and it had become a part of the developing Roycroft community.

The windmills at which Hubbard tilted were mainly the leading literary reputations, the established publishing houses and magazines, and the colleges, doctors, lawyers, and preachers. Chief individuals attacked were William Dean Howells, Hamlin Garland, Brander Matthews, Edward Bok of the *Ladies' Home Journal,* Harry Thurston Peck of the *Bookman,* Richard Watson Gilder of the *Century,* S. S. McClure, Bernard Shaw, Count Tolstoi, and Rudyard Kipling. These are only a few; there were biting attacks, especially in the earlier volumes, on many others. In his slashing criticism, which always mingled eloquent tirade with cutting sarcasm or raucous laughter; in his constant references to literature, history, philosophy, art, and music, which often show superficial knowledge in those fields; in his free-thinking on religious matters, in his exploitation of sex problems, in his inexhaustible grandiloquence, and in his technique of capitalizing his animosities, Hubbard resembles no other writer so much as his contemporary of the mid-nineties, Brann the Iconoclast.[8] This resemblance is more noticeable in the early volumes; after a few years Hubbard swung the tomahawk somewhat less, ran more to epigrams, and gave more space to the glorification of business success.

One of the *Philistine's* attacks would commonly be about a thousand words long, occupying five or six pages. The introduction would be philosophical or topical — at least innocuous — and then, whoosh! and wham! The tomahawk would swing with coruscating verbiage. A few passages at random:

> I know of no publication in America that inculcates in its pages so much hate, venom, vengeance, invective, imprecation, truth-perversion, and downright falsehood as the newspaper entitled *The Menace.* It is rightly named. . . . It is a menace to the civilized world.[9]

> •     •     •     •     •

> A short time ago I saw a hundred colored men clearing Harvard Yard of snow. I asked a certain professor of Political Economy why the students did not do this work. He looked at me in pity and replied, "Here teachers, tutors, professors, students, and parents have entered into a pact to the effect that at college no useful thing shall be done."[10]

> •     •     •     •     •

> Newell Dwight Hillis is a type of the genus Pharisee. He is also the paid and hired president of a social club called the Plymouth Church. This institution used

[8] See 442–49.
[9] *Philistine,* v. 40, p. 80, Feb. 1915.
[10] *Ibid.,* v. 41, pp. 27–28, June 1915.

to stand for free speech, generosity, truth, and liberty. It does not now. It is only a smug collection of grannies, male and female, who patronize the poor and live on the record of a great man gone. . . . Had Hillis been present nineteen hundred years ago when the mob crowned with thorns the Man whom he now calls Master, Hillis would have denied him seventeen times before cock-crow.[11]

. . . . .

The dear American public has gagged at last on the blood-boltered gospel of Ruddy Kipling. After so much raw meat, it is expiating its gluttony by a horrible attack of indigestion. . . . And so it leaves, sick and surfeited, the raw head and bloody bones it has greedily munched for a dozen years, and vomits its rage on the Laureate of Slaughter.[12]

. . . . .

Every lawyer is an officer of the court, yet fully one half of all the lawyers in the land are thorough rogues. And the curious fact is, all lawyers admit it. A lawyer is a moral strabismic, who revels in sharked-up reasons. Lawyers are the jackals of commerce, and get their living by preying on the people.[13]

. . . . .

And my opinion of Harry Thurston Peck, the man who wrote it [a criticism of Robert Ingersoll] is that he is one no woman can love, no man respect, and no child trust.[14]

. . . . .

Only one glimmer of sanity is found in Mark's article [Mark Twain's *Cosmopolitan* piece on Christian Science] and that is where he tells of being found by a Swiss peasant who was looking for a lost ass.[15]

. . . . .

George Bernard Shaw is a diabolic moralist, as hopelessly unintellectual as Savonarola, saved from the gallows or the insane asylum by a paradoxical mind. In him middle-class idealism finds its vengeful messiah.[16]

. . . . .

Tolstoy's demon-like frenzy before the flesh and the devil — and may their kingdoms never be lessened! — would have made even Mephistopheles serious. . . . Had he ever had mankind in his keeping for a single year, Saint Bartholomew night and Kishineff would have been enacted twenty times over, and Salem and Tyburn and Toledo and Cordova would have come back reinvested with their ancient glory — all in the name of "social purity" and the "spiritualization of humanity."[17]

[11] *Ibid.*, v. 13, pp. 22–25, June 1901. This was called forth by Hillis' refusal to speak from the same platform as George D. Herron.
[12] *Ibid.*, v. 13, pp. 129–30, Oct. 1901.
[13] *Ibid.*, v. 13, p. 165, Nov. 1901.
[14] *Ibid.*, v. 10, pp. 45–46, Jan. 1900.
[15] *Ibid.*, v. 10, p. 58, Jan. 1900.
[16] *Ibid.*, v. 40, p. 24, Dec. 1914.
[17] *Ibid.*, v. 40, pp. 27–28, Dec. 1914.

Ham Garland has gone up the coulee to his farm near La Crosse and is writing another novel. He is daily in receipt of letters and telegrams from people in all parts of the country asking him to pull the coulee up after him.[18]

Of course, literature and society need sharp-tongued satirists, and many readers welcome such criticism. It has been said that Hubbard "was scorned by the cultured public as a blatant ignoramus." [19] That is not quite true. A good many intellectuals, while never approving him completely, derived no little pleasure from the half-truths that he blazoned across the *Philistine's* small pages.

It would be possible to place a higher value on Hubbard's writings, essentially vulgar though they were, if one could believe in the man's sincerity. The *Philistine's* subtitle was "A Periodical of Protest"; it might more precisely have been called "A Magazine of Resentments." The Fra's towering egotism could not brook criticism of anything he had done, or even a failure to admire him and his works. It seems clear that the *Philistine* was started in order to afford a medium for his resentments against the magazine editors and book publishers who had turned down his novels and essays, the critics of the day of whom he was jealous, and the colleges (especially Harvard) that had failed to welcome him with open arms.[20] Kipling was a target after he had sued Hubbard for using a poem of his without copyright permission. Shaw was a butt after he had protested against unauthorized changes that Hubbard had made in a Shavian essay reprinted in the *Philistine*.[21] And so one comes to expect an ulterior motive behind every attack.

And then, when Hubbard turns from his assaults upon "the Superior Class" to become a special pleader for wealth, one is inclined to believe, even without the documentation furnished by Norman Hapgood in *Harper's Weekly*,[22] that the reason for his change was the discovery of the profits in his "little journeys" to the homes of millionaires. The socialist of 1903 could write, "The Superior Class is a burden. No nation ever survived it long, none ever can"; [23] and ten years later the same man as spokesman for the great corporations could write:

The most important move in the interests of peace is for the Government to cease making war on our men of enterprise, the men of initiative, the men of originality, and we will have peace and also plenty. Trust-busting attorneys, intent on barratry, working under the protection of an obsolete law, have wrought havoc and worked a dire wrong to the working people. The endeavor to destroy our

[18] *Ibid.*, v. 1, p. 103, Aug. 1895.
[19] Frederick Lewis Allen, in an excellent study of Hubbard, *Scribner's Magazine*, v. 104, Sept. 1938, p. 12.
[20] Balch, *Elbert Hubbard*, pp. 161, 166.
[21] *Ibid.*, p. 182.
[22] *Harper's Weekly*, v. 60, p. 112, Jan. 30, 1915.
[23] *Philistine*, v. 10, p. 134, April 1903.

Captains of Industry — our creators of wealth — has been a blunder, vast and far-reaching in its malevolent effect.[24]

"Hubbard," said Harold Bolce, in the *Cosmopolitan* in 1911, "is a Moses turned real-estate promoter and booming lots in the Promised Land. He is a vaudeville performer with a message — a jester pointing the way to the Infinite!"[25]

It was as early, however, as 1899 that Hubbard had emerged as a "business philosopher." In March of that year he published in the *Philistine* a fifteen-hundred-word essay entitled "A Message to Garcia," telling of the devotion to duty of a youth named Cowan, who had carried a message from President McKinley to the leader of the Cuban insurrectionists, and applying the lessons of loyalty and faithfulness found in that incident to employer-employee relations in business and industry. Immediately there was a tremendous demand for reprints of this piece for distribution by banks, insurance companies, and manufacturing concerns the country over. From this time onward, Hubbard rode two horses — socialism and big business. Perhaps his socialism was never much more than occasional rhetoric in the *Philistine,* plus the pseudo-Morris community at East Aurora, which was profitable financially. And after a few years most of the complaint against the superior class disappeared; by 1914 the Fra was playing golf with John D. Rockefeller.

Thus Hubbard's economic philosophy seems to have been governed by personal advantage. Probably the slaps he took at monogamy time and again were motivated by his own marital situation; they seemed to decrease after his wife divorced him and he married his mistress. A characteristic Hubbardism may be quoted from a 1900 essay on free love — typographical flowers, simplified spelling, and all:

 And now I boldly hazard the profecy that members of the American Academy of Immortals [subscribers to the *Philistine*] who avail themselves of the ninety-nine year limit [life subscribers] will witness planks introduced into all great party platforms endorsing Soul Gravitation and Sykik Communion Not only this, but that church which has not in its creed a tenet advocating Cellular Correspondence will have nothing better to boast of than a beggarly array of empty pews.

 I have spoken.[26]

Though the *Philistine* was Elbert Hubbard from beginning to end, many writers were associated with it as assistant editors and contributors. The printer-poet Harry Persons Taber, an early member of the

[24] *Ibid.*, v. 37, pp. 133–34, Oct. 1913.
[25] *Cosmopolitan*, v. 50, p. 516, March 1911.
[26] *Philistine*, v. 10, p. 74, Feb. 1900.

Roycroft community, was listed as editor and datary of the first eight numbers. Taber's first title was nominal, and his second, borrowed from that of the papal secretary for benefices, was doubtless merely a Hubbardism. Four years later, Hubbard reviewed some of the assistance that he had received on the magazine. "Starting with Harry Taber," he wrote, "to whom I paid four dollars a week and board, my cubbard (also my buffet) has been made desolate." And soon Harry associated himself with another little-magazine venture — the *Echo*, whose editor, Percival Pollard, wrote that "we owe the inception and whatever cleverness was ever in the *Philistine*" to Taber.[27] But Hubbard goes on with his review:

I gave Harry Taber just one kick in the pants and continued serenely on my way. Next Walter Blackhart Burns [Walter Blackburn Harte] came down upon me, and he was the finest o' the lot. He remained in East Aurora two weeks (lacking one day) & didn't do a thing while he was here but tie firecrackers to my coat tail. He then touseled his hair like a boofay artist, curst in falsetto, & rusht into *Footlights* and another sheet like it called *The Critic* telling why East Aurora was no place for a man of genius & declaring I was a big What-D'ye-Call-It[28]. . . .

After Blackhart had gone back to Bloomingdale, there arrived three rogues in buckram suits, by name Hamlin Whidden, Steve Crane, and John Jerome Rooney. None of them could write much better than Philip Becker Goetz, but all had ambitions, & a Thirst.

Strict East Aurora asceticism was not to Stevie's taste. He went down to New York in search of Local Color & evidently found it, for he came back daubed all over — his karacter speckled as a turkey's egg.

Stevie's next move was to pinch eight thousand dollars that Amy Leslie had entrusted him to carry to the bank. It was Amy's whole month's salary as editor of the *Chicago News* Society Page. Steve did not get away with the boodle, however. . . . After that, I positively refused to have anything more to do with Steve: had he secured the eight thousand (or Amy) it might have been different.

Marco Morrow and Bliss Carman then came to take Steve's place. Neither one proved facile or felicitous in handling a pitchfork, and Ignorance (which is Bliss) was so bright that he would not get up mornings until noon, as he said he wished to give the Dawn a chance.

I do not care to speak ill of any one, but truth compels me to say that Richard Hovey, whom I carried thru two hard winters, showed his total unfitness for community life by refusing to churn; & Tudor Jenks wrote no poetry after the cider barrel was empty. So I trun 'em both out. . . . These batty poets, who soar high and dive deep and never pay cash, have pusht the game just a little too far. I am done with the whole regiment of Ruf Writers; & all parties are notified not to hitch their wagon to this Star.[29]

Nevertheless, it was after this outburst that Richard Le Gallienne and Michael Monahan became members of the Roycroft community

[27] *Echo*, v. 3, p. 217, Oct. 24, 1896.
[28] *Critic*, v. 28, pp. 372–73, May 23, 1896.
[29] *Philistine*, v. 8, pp. 33–39, Jan. 1899.

and writers for the *Philistine*; but Hubbard eventually quarreled with them, too, and drove them out.[30] With Stephen Crane he had an off-and-on friendship for several years. He often poked fun at Crane and his work; but he did something to help his literary reputation,[31] regarded him as a protégé, and printed a rather touching piece about him when he died. "I have gibed Stephen Crane and jeered his work, but beneath all the banter there was only respect," wrote Hubbard then. "Within the breast of that pale youth there dwelt a lion's heart."[32] The whimsical and sharp essays of Walter Blackburn Harte were among the best contributions to the early *Philistine*, which in April 1896 took over Harte's own Boston periodical, the *Fly Leaf*. After his brief sojourn at East Aurora, Harte wrote in his *Lotus* that Roycroft was an "intellectual poppycock shop,"[33] and in the *Critic* he claimed that Hubbard had offered him an equal partnership in the magazine and then, when he had taken over the *Fly Leaf*, refused to carry out the bargain. Harte printed an interesting letter in which Hubbard had suggested they could "do a John Ruskin-William Morris work, or better."[34] Other occasional contributors were Joaquin Miller, Carolyn Wells, William Marion Reedy, Eugene Field, Hugh O. Pentecost, and a variety of versifiers unknown to fame.

According to its own claims,[35] the *Philistine* had reached a circulation of sixty thousand by 1900, and in 1903–1906 it went up to its highest point, about a hundred and twenty-five thousand. After the 1907 panic it declined somewhat, but was at a hundred and ten thousand when the periodical was discontinued in 1915. The price was maintained at a dollar, "including Health, Success, and Love vibrations that are sent daily to all subscribers at 4:00 P.M., Eastern Time. (If shy on vibrations, please advise.)" When the Roycrofters took over the publication of the *Little Journeys* in 1900, a combination price of the two series for a dollar was made for a short time, without vibrations.

The subscription "come-on" was a Hubbardism of purest ray serene. On the inside of the cover appeared the statement:

American Academy of Immortals, otherwise the Society of the Philistines. An association of Book Lovers & Folks who Write, Paint and Dream. Organized

---

[30] Balch, *Elbert Hubbard*, pp. 226–28, 261–63, 274–81.
[31] See *ibid.*, pp. 184–94, 217–18; and for the dinner given to Crane, see Claude Bragdon, "The Purple Cow Period," in *Bookman*, v. 69, p. 478, July 1929. But the best treatment of the relations of Hubbard and Crane is David H. Dickason, "Stephen Crane and the *Philistine*," in *American Literature*, v. 15, pp. 279–87, Nov. 1943.
[32] *Philistine*, v. 4, p. 84, Feb. 1897.
[33] *Lotus*, v. 2, p. 62, Feb. 1897.
[34] *Critic*, v. 28, pp. 372–73, May 23, 1896.
[35] It did not quote circulation for Ayer until 1901 (for 1900), and it never swore to its circulation. *Little Journeys* claimed 60,000 during 1908–12. For *Philistine* claims, see also its v. 11, Nov. 1900, p. 17 of advertising section; and v. 14, p. 32, Dec. 1901.

to further Good-Fellowship among men and women who believe in allowing the widest liberty to Individuality in Thought and Expression.

Art. xii. Sec. 2. — The annual dues shall be one dollar. This shall entitle the member to all documents issued by the Society, together with one copy of the incomparable Philistine Magazine, monthly, for one year.

Art. xii. Sec. 7. — A Life Membership in the Society of the Philistines is Ten Dollars. This entitles the member to every number of the Philistine Magazine, with bound volumes already issued, and that shall be issued, for ninety-nine years.

Art. xix. Sec. 4. — The duties of each member shall consist in living up to his highest Ideal (as nearly as possible) and attending the Annual Dinner (if convenient).

In the matter of advertising, Hubbard made a bargain with a national representative early in the magazine's history, contracting its advertising space for a figure much below what its circulation soon came to warrant, and it was only after much litigation and a considerable payment of money by Hubbard that he regained control of his advertising pages.[36] In its prosperous years the *Philistine* carried thirty or forty pages of advertising divided pretty evenly between the Roycrofters' offerings and those of outside firms.

The success of Hubbard's little magazine called forth a horde of imitators about the turn of the century, as well as some parodies and an *Anti-Philistine* in London. The best parody was the *Bilioustine,* of Chicago, of which two numbers were published in May and October 1901. It was written by Bert Leston Taylor ("Fra McGinnis"), originally published in B. L. T.'s "Line-o'-Type" column in the *Chicago Tribune*, then printed on fine paper, bound in burlap, and issued at Evanston (masquerading as East Aurora, Illinois) by William S. Lord. Later Taylor did some more of this satire for Puck.[37]

In its last years, the *Philistine* was filled with thoughts and ideas and stories which Hubbard picked up on his lecture tours and the vaudeville stage. Epigrams, which he must have turned out about one to each ninety seconds of working time, were abundant; and occasionally one of them, dressed up in impressive typography, seems memorable:

When what you have done in the past looks large to you, you have not done much today.

Be at peace with yourself and you will be at peace with the world.

Remember the Week-Day to keep it holy.

I would rather appreciate the things I do not have than to have things I do not appreciate.

These are taken from back cover pages of 1903 issues, merely as a sample. Borrowing and adaptation are easy in the field of epigrammatic

[36] Balch, *Elbert Hubbard*, pp. 194–96.
[37] See, for example, *Puck*, v. 56, Aug. 3, 1904, p. 6.

literature, and how much originality there was in these utterances of Fra Elbertus is hard to say; but many readers found them wise and witty.

The January 1915 issue of the *Philistine* was a "War Number." It had a ravening devil overprinted in red on the front cover, and its motto was "Hell Was Made in Germany." The pages were dressed in mourning for Belgium by means of black borders, and "Bill Kaiser" was excoriated on every page. Hubbard was strongly against American entry into the war: "A 'successful' war is a contradiction in terms. . . . All war, whether 'successful' or not, destroys productive power."[38]

A few months later, when the *Lusitania* was sunk, Elbert Hubbard went down with the ship, becoming one of the early American casualties in the First World War. Some followers of the Fra thought that the German emperor, stung by the *Philistine's* invective, had decreed the sinking of the great passenger ship because Hubbard was aboard.

The little magazine was discontinued after the death of its founder — out of respect, it was said, to his memory. In the number for July 1915, subscribers read: "The *Philistine* had been Hubbard's armor, his shield, his sword for long years. He has left us for a Little Journey, we know not where. He may need his *Philistine*, and so with tears on it we give it to him."[39]

The writer of these words was probably Edward (Felix) Shay, who became editor of *The Fra* after Hubbard's death, and conducted it for about two years, when was discontinued. In his encomiastic biography of Elbert Hubbard, Shay wrote:

> The *Little Journeys* were a search for an education.
> The *Philistine* was a whim, a gesture 🖉
> *The Fra* was a purpose.
> The three together were a highly profitable business.[40]

[38] *Philistine*, v. 41, p. 41, Jan. 1915.
[39] *Philistine*, v. 41, insert in the number for July 1915.
[40] Felix Shay, *Elbert Hubbard of East Aurora* (New York, 1926), p. 485.

## PUBLIC OPINION [1]

FRANK PRESBREY, an ambitious young newspaperman from Youngstown, Ohio, came to Washington in 1886 and started a weekly journal. He had tried to buy the *Critic*, of New York, but finally organized a stock company to publish a weekly news magazine in Washington, with a "simultaneous edition" in New York.[2] This journal was modeled on a London weekly, from which it took its title, its subtitle, its editorial policy, and its style of make-up.

Thus was born the American *Public Opinion: A Comprehensive Summary of the Press Throughout the World on All Important Current Topics*. A quarto of twenty pages, it sold at ten cents a copy or three dollars a year. It was remarkably unattractive in appearance, set in small type, with two very wide columns to the page and extremely modest headings. Its material, most of which consisted of short quotations from the American press, was arranged in departments, chief of which were politics, science (with emphasis on medicine), finance and commerce, capital and labor, railroads, education, and sociology. There were also some "notes" on literature, drama, art, and music, as well as occasional statistical pieces, comments on journalism, a résumé of "Events of the Week" and a rather sober collection of "Wit of the Week."

In its early years, *Public Opinion* was largely concerned with politics and public affairs, and gave comparatively little attention to literature, the theater, or lighter topics. Nor was it much concerned with foreign affairs; such articles on events abroad as it printed were found in the political department. The distinction of the magazine at this time was found in the incredibly large number of separate items. Almost any twenty-page issue in the first dozen volumes contained more than three

[1] TITLE: *Public Opinion: A Comprehensive Summary of the Press Throughout the World on All Important Current Topics.*
FIRST ISSUE: April 15, 1886. LAST ISSUE: June 30, 1906.
PERIODICITY: Weekly. Vols. 1–16, semiannual April–Sept. and Oct.–March, April 1886–March 1894; 17, April–Dec. 1894; 18–40, regular semiannual vols., Jan. 1895–June 1906. Merged with *Literary Digest*.
PUBLISHERS: The Public Opinion Company, Washington, D.C., 1886–94; same, New York, 1895–1906. Chief owners, Frank Presbrey, 1886–94; Wesley Marion Oler, 1895–98; Hazlitt Alva Cuppy, 1898–1905; J. M. Hill Company, 1905–06.
EDITORS: Frank Presbrey, 1886–94; Ernest E. Russell, 1895–98; H. A. Cuppy, 1898–1906.
INDEX: Vols. 1–23 in *Poole's Index.*
[2] *Journalist*, v. 7, May 5, 1888, p. 2.

hundred and fifty items, of which about half were "notes" of from one to three sentences.

*Public Opinion* attained a circulation of nearly ten thousand in its first year, and doubled that by 1890.[3] This was higher than the *Critic's* figure, and about the same as that of the *Literary Digest*. It carried a little advertising, and was a moderate success when Presbrey left it in 1894 to become publisher of the *Forum* and later to found an advertising agency. His stock control in *Public Opinion* was purchased by Wesley Marion Oler, a Baltimore banker-publisher, who reduced the price to five cents a copy, moved the office of publication to New York, installed Ernest E. Russell as editor and H. D. Slater as associate editor, and himself removed to New York to function as president of the company.

The magazine was now a little more pleasing in appearance — an effect due chiefly to better departmental headings and the arrangement of "notes" in logical paragraphs. Each department was now preceded by an "Editorial Summary," strictly nonpartisan, which explained more fully than the routine news résumé what had occurred during the preceding week. "Foreign Affairs" now occupied two or three pages, and there was a department of book reviews. But the chief emphasis was still on domestic politics, and the multiplicity of items remained a feature.

Circulation, however, did not respond to such treatment; it seemed impossible to keep the annual average even as high has twenty thousand. Oler had become president of the Knickerbocker Ice Company, and it was soon apparent that an iceman's career was more pleasant and far more profitable than that of a publisher of a quality weekly.

The new purchaser, in 1898, and the magazine's editor and publisher for nearly all the remainder of its career, was Hazlitt Alva Cuppy, a scholar who had studied at Oxford and Heidelberg, who had later founded and edited the *Altruistic Review,* and who came to *Public Opinion* from the directorship of the University of Chicago Press. Cuppy immediately restored the ten-cent price, though he put the annual rate at two dollars and a half in 1900–1901 and sold short-term trial subscriptions as low as twenty-five cents. As circulation increased (it reached about fifty thousand in 1903), the advertising effort was extended; but the magazine never carried more than five to ten pages of "ads."

Up to this time, *Public Opinion* had not been illustrated. Now polit-

---

[3] See Ayer directories; but also Rowell's *American Newspaper Directory* for 1898, in which it is noted that the "largest circulation ever accorded" *Public Opinion* by that authority up to that date was 21,000 in 1891 (p. 659). See Ayer for figures on later circulation.

ical cartoons taken from the newspapers were added, with a few portraits. Late in 1900 the magazine began to print more and more illustration, using pictures that had appeared with the articles reproduced from other magazines, or in books under review — an editing technique long employed by *Current Literature, Literary News,* and other review periodicals. Linked with this development was a growing emphasis on the "Letters and Art" department.

Cuppy also introduced the "condensed" magazine article. Previously, the magazine had emphasized its claim that articles were never rewritten, the original language always being preserved; now most leading articles were labeled "Condensed for *Public Opinion*." The editorial summaries that started off departments were now less formalized, and were sometimes abandoned altogether. Despite the prominence of book reviews and articles condensed from other magazines, however, politics and public affairs remained the chief preoccupation of *Public Opinion,* and quotations of newspaper comment its chief stock in trade.

In 1905 the J. M. Hill Company, book-dealers and publishers, took over the Public Opinion Company [4] and made a gradual change in editorial policy. The subtitle on the cover became "News of the World Weekly Magazine," and original magazine articles were featured. The economic liberals and reformers were definitely favored, and there were some ventures in muckraking. Denis Donohoe's exposure of exposer Thomas W. Lawson was a series which attracted much attention. Harvey W. Wiley's series on food frauds and William J. Bryan's articles on public affairs were first-class magazine material. Elisha W. Kelly's "Gambling and Horse Racing" (July 22, 1905) was a notable study. Other well-known contributors were H. Addington Bruce, Cy Warman, and Arthur B. Reeve. At the same time, the magazine continued to print a certain amount of the comment on events and affairs which was expected by its readers.

All this was fine but expensive. By February 1906 the journal had been forced to return to its old tradition and was again wholly eclectic. It looked and read more like the *Literary Digest* than ever. But it had less than a third of the circulation of that rival in 1906; and after completing the first half of that year, it did the logical thing and merged with the *Digest*. For twenty years it had been a good periodical, but never a very successful one.

[4] *Critic,* v. 49, p. 198, Sept. 1906.

# REEDY'S MIRROR [1]

ONE of the most remarkable of the periodicals of the urban weekly class through some three decades was *Reedy's Mirror*, of St. Louis. It was remarkable chiefly because of the personality of its editor, William Marion Reedy. Son of an Irish policeman, educated at St. Louis University, a reporter on the St. Louis papers for several years, Reedy came to the *Mirror* a talented and experienced writer with strong convictions and an independent habit of mind. He came also as a seasoned roué, whose life in the bars and brothels of his native city was well known. In the year in which he became editor of the *Mirror*, he married a woman who kept a house of prostitution. His wife spent much of her fortune trying to cure Reedy of his drinking habits; when he finally took the Keeley Cure and returned to St. Louis determined to lead a more "respectable" life, he separated from his wife and she divorced him. Soon afterward, Reedy married a girl from a good St. Louis family; after her death four years later, his drinking increased. "The passion for drink is a divine passion," he once wrote.[2] He took for his third wife another mistress of a house of ill fame, who survived him.

These things, baldly stated, doubtless give a false idea of Reedy's lusty and gusty personality. The epithet "naughty little boy," used to describe him by a later editor,[3] seems inept: in the first place, he was a man of Falstaffian proportions; he himself, with the polysyllabic humor he often affected, spoke of his figure as "the pachydermatous ponderosity of the hippopotamus." And secondly, his vices do not seem to be those of immaturity. His capital faults were closely integrated with his preëminent virtue — his love of people. "Billy Reedy," wrote Mitchell Kennerly in the memorial number of the *Mirror*, "was the greatest human being I have ever known — a man like Shakespeare."

[1] TITLES: (1) *Sunday Mirror*, 1891–93; (2) *The Mirror*, 1893–1913; (3) *Reedy's Mirror*, 1913–20; (4) *St. Louis Mirror*, 1920.

FIRST ISSUE: March 1, 1891. LAST ISSUE: Sept. 23, 1920.

PERIODICITY: Weekly. Vols. 1–23, annual vols., 1891–1914; 24, Feb.–Dec. 1915; 25–38, annual vols., 1916–19; 29, Jan.–Sept. 1920.

PUBLISHERS: A. B. Cardoner and A. LeBerton, 1891–92; James Campbell, 1893–96; W. M. Reedy, 1896–1920; John P. McGowan, 1920.

EDITORS: Michael A. Fanning, 1891–92; William Marion Reedy, 1893–1920; J. J. Dickinson, 1920.

REFERENCES: Fred W. Wolf, "William Marion Reedy: A Critical Biography" (doctoral thesis, Vanderbilt University, 1951); Marjorie Eileen Fox, "William Marion Reedy and the St. Louis Mirror" (master's thesis, University of Illinois, 1947); John T. Flanagan, "Reedy of the *Mirror*," *Missouri Historical Review*, v. 43, pp. 128–44, Jan. 1949.

[2] *Mirror*, v. 8, June 9, 1898, p. 3.

[3] J. J. Dickinson in *Mirror*, v. 36, p. 701, Sept. 9, 1920.

And then he added a wonderful statement which might well stand as Reedy's epitaph: "He had a genius for understanding everybody." [4] That genius, which was more than mere gregariousness, was of the essence of Reedy's greatness.

It had much to do with his achievement as an editor and a literary critic. With a circulation that never rose much above thirty thousand and was in many years about half of that,[5] Reedy had to depend on personal friendships and, latterly, the prestige of appearing in the *Mirror*, for contributions. *"Pay* anything?" he wrote explosively to Theodore Dreiser. "Heavens! Money is in the vocative with a vengeance out here. . . . It is hard work to pay the electric light bill." [6] Yet Reedy built up an enviable list of contributors for the *Mirror*. In his editing and in his articles of literary criticism and his book reviews, he was, in general, friendly to newcomers in the literary field, especially if they showed original talent. He could swing the tomahawk: "It is sad that an author like Benj. Rush Davenport should be where his readers cannot get at him to testify to their appreciation of his efforts — with an ax." [7] But commonly he liked to be kind to new writers.[8]

The St. Louis *Sunday Mirror* began in 1891 as an urban weekly of society, politics, the arts, and sports and amusements. "Mike" Fanning and James M. ("Red") Galvin, with "Jack" Sullivan as advertising manager, were the founders.[9] They were enterprising newspapermen. The new paper's society gossip and sports stories created some stir, but available funds ran out in two years. An "angel" was found in James Campbell, who had made a fortune in various speculative enterprises, and who now, as part owner, lost a substantial chunk of it through *Mirror* deficits.

Reedy became editor some weeks before Campbell's advent in *Mirror* affairs; and when the paper went into bankruptcy in December 1893, Campbell bailed it out and a little later gave it to Reedy. "Tell Billy the damn paper is his; he can keep it," he said to Sullivan, after three weeks of paying $18,000 deficits.[10] It was not, however, until 1913 that

---

[4] *Mirror*, v. 29, p. 607, Aug. 5, 1920.

[5] The sworn circulation in Ayer's directory for 1900 was 30,815, though the *Mirror* claimed a little more by "publisher's detailed statement" later. See also Wolf, "William Marion Reedy," p. 60; and *Mirror*, v. 8, June 9, 1898, p. 1.

[6] Letter dated Sept. 16, 1915, in Dreiser Collection, University of Pennsylvania Library. Dreiser then submitted a one-act play "for free." Reedy rejected this, but later accepted some Dreiser sketches.

[7] *Mirror*, v. 8, Sept. 1, 1898, p. 4.

[8] See a good résumé of Reedy's literary criticism in the *Mirror* in Flanagan, *Missouri Historical Review*, v. 43, pp. 133–37, Jan. 1949.

[9] Harry B. Winkeler in *Mirror*, v. 15, n.s., June 1946, pp. 3–5.

[10] *Ibid.*, and also *Wolf*, "William Marion Reedy," p. 58.

it adopted the title *Reedy's Mirror,* though by that time Reedy's name was better known than that of his paper, and for some three years the subtitle "Reedy's Paper" had been appearing on the cover. Sullivan also had an interest in the *Mirror*; and it was his never flagging effort to get advertising that put the paper on its feet financially. About a third of its pages were given to advertising. Sullivan's persuasiveness with the railways and insurance companies, his enterprise with "mug" numbers,[11] and his redoubled industry when the editor was absent from his post kept the *Mirror* solvent. In 1905 the paper was rescued again from a receivership by a loan of $5,000 from the woman who was to be Reedy's third wife.[12] The single-copy price was increased to ten cents in 1917, apparently without much loss in circulation.

Contributors to the *Mirror* during the twenty years beginning with 1898 make a fine list — which is much more impressive, however, in the second of the two decades. Perhaps the most notable of them all was Edgar Lee Masters, whose "Spoon River Anthology" was begun with seven epitaphs signed "Webster Ford" in the issue for May 29, 1914, and continued through nearly eight months. It was Reedy who gave the poet, who had been an earlier contributor of both verse and prose, a copy of the Greek *Anthology* and suggested the use of local subject matter for something similar in English.[13] At the same time the *Mirror* was publishing a column by Harris Merton Lyon called "From an Old Farmhouse," along with some of that author's brilliant short short stories and essays. In these months and years it was also publishing some of the work of Vachel Lindsay, Edwin Arlington Robinson, Carl Sandburg, and Robert Frost — a great quartet of a great period in modern American poetry.

The poems of Ernest McGaffey began in the latter nineties and continued for many years. Percival Pollard's "The Imitator" was one of the few fiction serials published in the *Mirror*; it appeared serially in 1901. Pollard also wrote a number of articles on American letters, later collected in the volume *Their Day in Court.* George Sylvester Viereck's criticism of Americans in his clever serial "Confessions of a Barbarian" (1901) stirred many readers of the *Mirror* to reply. Several St. Louis writers later to become famous tried their wings in their home weekly — Fannie Hurst, Orrick Johns, Sara Teasdale, and Zoë Akins among them. Other prominent contributors were Edna St. Vincent Millay, John Hall Wheelock, Witter Bynner, Ezra Pound, Louis Untermeyer, Babette Deutsch, Yone Noguchi, James Huneker, Vincent Starrett, Eunice Tietjens, Opie Read, and Bliss Carman. There were always

[11] See p. 77.
[12] Wolf, "William Marion Reedy," p, 162.
[13] *Mirror*, v. 25, Aug. 29, 1915, p. 2.

some reprinting of the older poetry, some borrowing from English periodicals, and some translations of European moderns.

Michael Monahan wrote a New York letter for the *Mirror* in 1899. The paper always carried a few columns of local society items — "Folks in Society," later "The Fashionables," by "Daisy Miller," and beginning in 1905 the spicy "Blue Jay's Chatter." There was, of course, much about the Louisiana Purchase Exposition. As early as 1901, Reedy was warning the managers that "the World's Fair must be beautful or it cannot be a success"; when it was ready, he found it beautiful as a dream.

But whatever else appeared in the *Mirror*, the three or four pages of "Reflections," by "Uncle Fuller," or whatever Reedy preferred at the moment as a pen name, were the heart of the magazine. Reedy wrote on topics in many fields — social, economic, artistic, literary — but he seemed to revel in politics with a devotion not given to other matters. Fred W. Wolf, author of the best study of Reedy, calls him an "Independent Democrat," which means that he did not support all Democratic nominees and officeholders. Indeed, Reedy found it hard to support any political leader at all times and in all his activities: he came nearer doing so with Theodore Roosevelt than with anyone of his own party. He liked Bryan, but found him full of faults; he thought Wilson too cold and formal; he once spoke of Cleveland's "fatuous fatness." He was an expansionist, but he wrote of McKinley's Philippine policy as "Imperialism Gone Mad" (February 22, 1900). He wrote editorials about corrupt politics in his home city in a series that ran in 1899–1901 under the title "What's the Matter With St. Louis?" These articles pointed the way for Lincoln Steffens' exposés in *McClure's* two years later and for subsequent reforms. But Reedy could never approve Joseph Folk, the Missouri reformer, because of a mistrust of his "unscrupulous ambition." He was uncompromising in his support, year in and year out, of the single tax.

Reedy wrote much for his paper besides the editorial department entitled "Reflections." Sometimes he wrote more than a third of the magazine — articles, editorials, chitchat, verse. One of the matters which enlisted his deepest interest and on which he wrote many columns in the years 1915 and 1916 was the literary performance of "Patience Worth," communicated from the spirit world through the planchette of a St. Louis medium, Mrs. Curran. The poems and stories of the seventeenth-century Patience provoked the curiosity of many scholars and spiritists, and have never been satisfactorily explained.

Some of Reedy's most popular editorials were published in a series of "Mirror Pamphlets" from time to time, and in 1902 the editor and his friends were encouraged to start the monthly *Valley Magazine*, which was, however, not a success.[14]

Reedy had suffered with illness for several years, and in January 1920 lost the sight of one eye. He determined to take a vacation, and prevailed on Charles J. Finger, long a friend and contributor, to take over the editorship of the *Mirror* for a short time. He began his vacation by going out to San Francisco to attend the Democratic national convention, and he died in that city on July 28, 1920. The memorial number that Finger edited August 5 contained much eulogy, and showed how highly his friends valued William Marion Reedy.

It is almost inevitable to compare Reedy with four other individualists of his times — Brann, Bierce, Hubbard, and Mencken. He and Brann were friends in their early newspaper days in St. Louis, and later wrote for each other's weeklies; but Reedy seldom carried hyperbole and invective and overwriting so far as Brann, and on the latter's death, wrote a just and sound criticism on his old friend.[15] Bierce was a more skillful literary craftsman than Reedy, who, though he occasionally wrote well and effectively, was too often sloppy and pretentious. Hubbard and Reedy exchanged contributions,[16] but the *Philistine* editor was far less sincere than his friend of the *Mirror*, who was a true liberal. Mencken is suggested for comparison because his love for curious and effective vocabulary was like Reedy's, and also because of their common liking for criticism of the lambasting kind; but Mencken was, after all, sounder in scholarly backgrounds, more restrained in general, and superior in the critical faculty. It was palpable exaggeration for Masters to call the *Mirror* "the most influential weekly in America for nearly twenty years,"[17] but the magazine was an effective encourager of a new movement in American poetry, and it probably had some local political influence.

Finger had hoped to continue the *Mirror*, but it was sold to John P. McCowan, who made Major J. J. Dickinson editor. It lasted, however, for only two months under the new management. Finger tried to continue the tradition of the *Mirror* with his magazine *All's Well*, at Fayetteville, Arkansas. A new series of the *Mirror* was published monthly in St. Louis 1929–1947 by Jack Sullivan and Rose M. Wertheimer. It republished many of Reedy's more famous articles, but it appeared very irregularly, with long gaps toward the end.

---

[14] See p. 101.

[15] *Mirror*, v. 8, April 8, 1898, p. 6.

[16] Hubbard printed a long attack on Reedy in 1901, in which he said: "That Reedy will set up a hierarchy as soon as he loses his capacity to sin there is no doubt" (*Philistine*, v. 13, p. 152, Oct. 1901).

[17] *American Speech*, v. 9, pp. 96–98, April 1934.

## THE REVIEW OF REVIEWS [1]

THE *Review of Reviews* was founded in London in January 1890 by William Thomas Stead, famous journalist, daring social reformer and aggressive crusader for the unity of English-speaking peoples. Stead was a man of great ideas, often at once grandiose and altruistic, and his magazine salutatory was true to character:

There exists at this moment no institution which even aspires to be to the English-speaking world what the Catholic Church in its prime was to the intelligence of Christendom. To call attention to the need for such an institution . . . to enlist the co-operation of all those who will work towards the creation of some such common centre . . . are the ultimate objects for which this *Review* has been established. . . .

Among all the agencies for the shaping of the future of the human race, none seems so potent now, and still more hereafter, than the English-speaking man. Already he begins to dominate the world. The Empire and the Republic comprise within their limits almost all the territory that remains empty for the overflow of the world. Their citizens, with all their faults, are leading the van of civilization. . . .

To establish a periodical circulating throughout the English-speaking world, with its associates or affiliates in every town, and its correspondents in every village, read as men used to read their Bibles, not to waste an idle hour, but to discover the will of God and their duty to man, — whose staff and readers alike are bound together by a common faith, and a readiness to do common service for a common end, — that, indeed, is an object for which it is worth while to make some sacrifice.[2]

Stead's magnificent plan bore fruit in an eighty-four-page, small-quarto monthly, rather poorly printed on inferior paper, and sparsely

[1] TITLES: (1) *The Review of Reviews*, Jan. 1890–June 1897; (2) *The American Monthly Review of Reviews*, July 1897–May 1907; (3) *The American Review of Reviews*, June 1907–1928; (4) *Review of Reviews*, 1929–Aug. 1932; (5) *Review of Reviews and World's Work*, Sept. 1932–July 1937.
FIRST ISSUE: Jan. 1890 (first American issue: April 1891), LAST ISSUE: July 1937. Merged with *Literary Digest*.
PERIODICITY: Monthly. Vol. 1, Jan.–June 1890; 2, July–Dec. 1890; 3, Jan.–July 1891 (March omitted, and American edition begun with April); 4, Aug. 1891–Jan. 1892; 5, Feb.–July 1892; 6, Aug. 1892–Jan. 1893; 7, Feb.–June 1893; 8–95 (regular semiannual vols.) July 1893–June 1937; 96, no. 1, July 1937.
PUBLISHERS: Review of Reviews, London (W. T. Stead), 1890–Feb. 1891; Review of Reviews, New York (Albert Shaw), April 1891–1893; Review of Reviews Company, New York (Albert Shaw), 1894–an. 1923; Review of Reviews Corporation, New York (Albert Shaw, Albert Shaw, Jr.), Feb. 1923–July 1937.
EDITORS: William Thomas Stead, 1890–91; Albert Shaw, 1891–1937.
INDEXES: *Poole's Index, Annual Library Index, Readers' Guide, Cumulative Index, Jones' Legal Index, Engineering Index, A.L.A. Portrait Index.*
[2] *Review of Reviews*, v. 1, pp. 15–20, Jan. 1890. Reprinted in v. 3, pp. 2–4, Jan. 1891.

illustrated. But the journal was crammed with information, ideas, and challenging suggestions. It began with an editorial news-and-comment department entitled "The Progress of the World," which was usually followed by some matter about Stead's reform activities. Then came the "character sketch" of the month, about a great world figure, followed by some thirty pages of "Leading Articles," condensed (often with considerable extracts) from the chief reviews and magazines of the world. Then, in a section of similar length, called "The Reviews Reviewed," appeared a remarkably careful series of summaries and evaluations of the current numbers of English and American periodicals, and somewhat briefer notes on French, German, Russian, Italian, Spanish, Portuguese, Scandinavian, Dutch, and Belgian reviews. Following this section came a condensation of a new book, usually a novel; for this purpose Stead chose in his first year such remarkable works as Tolstoi's *The Kreutzer Sonata* and *The Journal of Marie Bashkirtseff*. For the Tolstoi novel Stead wrote an enthusiastic introduction, which itself must have shocked the more staid readers of his review. Finally, the magazine contained an annotated list of new books and a check list of magazine articles.

Thus it was a large and varied table that the *Review of Reviews* spread. Though a moralist like Stead's friend Tolstoi thought that the diversification destroyed any grand central purpose,[3] and the more snobbish type of British critic thought that the compilation was best adapted to below-stairs intelligence,[4] the *Review's* increasing circulation testified to the approbation of the rank and file. In the summer Stead bought out his partner, Sir George Newnes, for three thousand pounds.[5] When one hundred and forty thousand copies of the November 1890 number were disposed of, Stead became overoptimistic and printed two hundred thousand of the special December issue,[6] thus justifying Newnes's fears by almost capsizing the project when it was a year old. Forty per cent of the Christmas number remained unsold,[7] and plans for expansion had to be abandoned. Some months later, Stead was joined in the enterprise by E. H. Stout, who had a better head for business management.

Stead's original plan envisaged "associates or affiliates" in all English-speaking countries; but the only ones ever set up were those in the United States and Australia.[8] For editor of the American affiliate,

[3] Frederic Whyte, *The Life of W. T. Stead* (London, 1925), v. 1, p. 313.
[4] *Critic*, v. 19, p. 132, Sept. 12, 1891.
[5] Whyte, *The Life of W. T. Stead*, p. 319.
[6] *Critic*, v. 18, p. 17, Jan. 10, 1891.
[7] *Ibid.*, p. 321.
[8] The *Review of Reviews for Australasia*, edited by Dr. Fitchett, was issued July 1892–Aug. 1914 under that name at Melbourne; under the later titles of *Stead's Review* and *To-Day*

Stead chose Albert Shaw,[9] who had studied political science under Jesse Macy at Grinnell College and won a doctorate under Richard T. Ely at Johns Hopkins. Later he had been a newspaper editor in Minneapolis. Now at thirty-four, he moved to New York and undertook the editing and publishing of an American *Review of Reviews*, which began with the issue of April 1891.

Throughout 1890, the Critic Company had produced an American edition of Stead's magazine from sheets sent over from London. In announcing the Shaw venture, the *Critic* said, "Mr. Shaw will be responsible only to his chief in London." [10] That Mr. Shaw, however, was answerable from the first only to himself seems certain. He received virtually no financial aid from Stead, who wrote him June 3 that he was "at present about as hard up for money as any human being can be." [11] There was a close relationship between the two magazines for many years, however; and until his death Stead's own articles, and for several years some by his leading contributors, continued to be printed in Shaw's *Review of Reviews*. When Stead was lost in the *Titanic* disaster, Shaw wrote: "Although wholly independent of each other in editorship and control, and quite different in method and appearance, there has been a close and unbroken coöperation between Mr. Stead's English *Review* and its American namesake." [12]

Moreover, Shaw kept the departmentalization and content types of the original *Review*, with only slight changes; also he took over the title and the volume and page numbering of the London progenitor. The only awkwardness in the transition was the missing of March in dating. But the American magazine was far superior to its English parent in nearly every respect. It sold for twenty cents, in comparison with the English *Review's* sixpence. It was better printed on superior paper stock, and its illustrations "came up" much better — all of which Stead was happy to acknowledge with even a little envy.[13] Pictures soon became much more plentiful. Political cartoons reproduced from the newspapers and humorous journals of the world, which had been sparingly introduced by Stead in the fall of 1890, became, in the Amer-

it continued through Aug. 1934. There was a *Revue des Revues* in Paris 1890–1900 edited by Jean First; it was continued as *Revue Mondiale* to March 26, 1936. It owed much to Stead; see *American Review of Reviews*, v. 46, p. 105, July 1912.

[9] For Shaw, see *National Cyclopaedia of American Biography*, v. 9, p. 469; *American Historical Review* (obituary), v. 53, pp. 220–21, Oct. 1947; *Outlook*, v. 53, p. 139, Jan. 25, 1896; *Everybody's Magazine*, v. 26, pp. 53–56, Jan. 1912; *Bookman*, v. 12, pp. 358–59, Dec. 1900; *The American Review of Reviews: A Brief Sketch* (New York, 1923), 19 pp.

[10] *Critic*, v. 18, p. 62, Jan. 1891.

[11] Whyte, *The Life of W. T. Stead*, p. 321.

[12] *Review of Reviews*, v. 45, p. 692, June 1912.

[13] Whyte, *The Life of W. T. Stead*, p. 323.

ican magazine, an attractive four-page section, eventually to be enlarged to eight pages.

What the American magazine lacked, of course, was the ebullient personality of W. T. Stead; but in its place there was the "high standard of fairness and unemotional rationality"[14] that distinguished "The Progress of the World" during the period of almost half a century when Dr. Albert Shaw wrote its many pages every month. The editor of the *Outlook* said of Shaw in 1896:

> He is entirely free from short-sighted partisanship . . . and he appreciates to the full the power of intelligent, judicial statement. His opinions, therefore, carry great weight, and it is not too much to say that he has not his superior in the field of American journalism.[15]

Shaw once wrote that an editor "ought to know almost everything that it is possible to learn about some one form of human activity, and then something at least about almost every other form."[16]

"The Progress of the World," which eventually came to occupy some thirty pages of the magazine each month (a third of it illustration) was devoted mainly to government and economics, at home and abroad. Shaw inherited from Stead an emphasis on foreign affairs, which were also discussed chiefly from political and economical angles. There was occasionally something about education or religion or even sports; but such things were commonly left to other pages, and Dr. Shaw's sixty to eighty editorial paragraphs (each with a title in a little indented square at the left of the top three lines) stuck pretty much to the editor's own interests. They were mainly informative in type, but full of mild — and, on the whole, wise — comment. Shaw was against free silver, and he favored prohibition. He was a fairly consistent Republican; he was apparently for McKinley in 1896 and 1900, for Theodore Roosevelt in 1904, and Taft in the 1912 campaign — and so with later Republican candidates, including Hoover and Landon. But his advocacy of a presidential candidate was nearly always temperate, and the arguments of the opposition were, as a rule, not unfairly presented. Shaw's strong disapproval of F. D. Roosevelt was responsible for a less balanced presentation of the political picture in the thirties than in earlier years.

The "Leading Articles of the Month" continued to be informative and interesting, and "Current History in Caricature" entertaining. "The New Books" department gained in importance in the early nineties; it came to consist of sixteen pages of book lists arranged in categories,

[14] *American Historical Review*, v. 53, pp. 220–21, Oct. 1947.
[15] *Outlook*, v. 53, p. 139, Jan. 25, 1896.
[16] Doris Ullman, *A Portrait Gallery of American Editors* (New York, 1925), p. 134.

with annotations which sometimes amounted to short reviews. A subject index to the periodicals of the preceding month was a helpful feature for librarians and readers. Like all American magazines, the *Review of Reviews* gave much attention to the Columbian Exposition in 1893. The problems attendant on the hard times of the early nineties, plans for the relief of the unemployed, agrarian unrest, the free coinage of silver proposal, and social reforms in the cities were prominent. The monthly "character sketch" was always an interesting feature. For a few years beginning in 1895 there was special correspondence from London and Paris.

In 1897 the magazine adopted the title *The American Review of Reviews*. It had been drifting further and further away from its English progenitor, and it now marked its parting by a separate title.[17] Up to this time it had never been able to attain a circulation much larger than ninety thousand; now it went ahead quickly to a hundred thousand, and by 1906 to double that figure. This was excellent for a review — "the largest circulation in the world for any magazine not publishing fiction," boasted the publisher.[18] Advertising followed in great quantity. In the last three months of 1906, the *Review of Reviews* carried an average of one hundred and eighty-six pages of advertising per number, which its "ad" manager claimed was the "largest amount of paid advertising in any magazine in the world." [19] It had raised its single-copy price to twenty-five cents in 1892.

The war with Spain reacted favorably on the popularity of a magazine that stressed foreign affairs. Besides careful editorial coverage of the war by Shaw, the day-to-day "Events" record, and the cartoon history of the war, the *Review of Reviews* presented a number of good original articles about the campaigns on the various fronts and the chief military and naval figures. Winston Churchill wrote an admirable character sketch of Commodore Dewey and also an article about the defeat of Admiral Cervera's fleet. James Creelman wrote about the Santiago campaign and John A. Church about Porto Rico. There was also much about the Philippines.

Gradually the *Review of Reviews* had come to use more of these original articles. In addition to the monthly "character sketch," it carried half a dozen special articles by 1900, and ten years later it had twice that many. About a third of these features dealt with affairs in foreign countries. Though the political-economic bent of the magazine was

---

[17] The English *Review of Reviews* had a later career not dissimilar to that of the American magazine. It was united with the *World Review of Reviews*, later *World Review*, and perished in 1936.
[18] Advertisement in Ayer's *American Newspaper Annual and Directory* for 1910, p. 1257.
[19] *Ibid.*, 1907, p. 1255.

apparent in the subject matter of these original contributions, there was, after all, a good variety in them; and art and literature, education, religion, social reform, women's rights, and so on, all had their places in the *Review's* richly furnished pages. For these contributions, Shaw drew chiefly on university professors and well-known journalists; a short but representative list might include Arthur T. Hadley, John R. Commons, Woodrow Wilson, Edmund J. James, J. Laurence Laughlin, Richard T. Ely, Jesse Macy, David Starr Jordon, Albert Bushnell Hart, E. Benjamin Andrews, John Bassett Moore, Julian Ralph, Judson C. Welliver, Cleveland Moffett, Adachi Kinnosuke, Murat Halstead, Jacob A. Riis, and Theodore Roosevelt. Jack London, then an unknown, contributed an article on "The Economics of the Klondike" to the number for January 1900.

The *Review of Reviews* did not join in the journalistic movement known as muckraking. Its readers were informed of the abuses of concentrated wealth and the miseries of poverty; they learned of the corrupt alliances between politics and business, especially in municipal government; and they were kept aware of the agrarian revolt. All these great matters were by way of being specialties of Shaw and his review. But Shaw preferred constructive suggestions and planning to exposés and all-out attacks. Perhaps the nearest the magazine came to muckraking was in a series published in the latter half of 1912 entitled "The People and the Trusts." These articles were written by Holland Thompson, Albert W. Atwood, and others; and they advocated an interstate trade commission whose chief business should be giving publicity to the operations of trusts and industrial concerns.

The international interests of the *Review of Reviews* were always notable, and that feature of the journal was emphasized during and after the war with Spain. "An International Magazine" was the subtitle it bore, and the whirling globes on its cover were symbolic.

The index to periodicals was dropped in 1904, the *Readers' Guide* having made it unnecessary. The next year the section called "The Periodicals Reviewed" was abandoned; after all, the magazine got enough out of current periodicals in its "Leading Articles of the Month" department, and it needed the room for its own original contributions.

These were the years in which a very fat *Review of Reviews* was made up of 128 text pages and 160 to 190 pages of advertising. They were profitable years indeed; but there was a shrinkage in circulation in 1909–1914, which should have been a warning that times and tastes were changing faster than Albert Shaw and his review. World War I, with its intensified interest in world affairs, brought a reprieve. In 1917–1918 the circulation went over 240,000, which was the highest point of its history. Frank H. Simonds was the *Review's* staff expert on the war; and his articles and those of other reporters, together with the many pictures, made a great war history.

In the twenties, Shaw deplored the deadlock between President Wilson and the Senate. He was for the League, but he maintained his Republicanism in the presidential campaigns of 1920 and 1924. He was a supporter of the Prohibition Amendment and its enforcement laws. Simonds was still a contributing editor, with a roving assignment that took him chiefly to European capitals. William Hard and Charles H. Sherrill contributed with some regularity; and there were occasional articles by well-known scholars and men of affairs.

But circulation slipped after the war. A reorganization in 1923 seemed to help, and the slump of that year was followed by a gain in 1924. Albert Shaw, Jr., brought new vitality when he came in as secretary and treasurer of the Review of Reviews Corporation, but circulation soon resumed its slow and steady decline. With the beginning of 1929 the magazine was redesigned in a new and handsome full-quarto form, and its hundred and sixty-four pages made a good showing. The single-copy price had been raised to thirty-five cents in 1923.

The period of free-and-easy borrowing from other magazines was now long past. A busy staff had to write and compile the monthly story of activity in many departments. The result was a little like *Time* and a little like *World's Work,* but still a good deal like the old *Review of Reviews.* In 1932 the two monthlies just named were merged under the name *Review of Reviews and World's Work,* but the combination did little to stop the steady circulation decline or the even more marked advertising losses.

The *Review* was no New Dealer. It chronicled patiently the phenomena of the great depression. It was amazed at the "Blue Eagle," which "burst upon the country like one of the astronomical apparitions that overwhelmed superstitious multitudes in former times." [20] It gave more and more attention to business and finance, apparently veering toward the field of the businessman's journal. Staff writers were Shaw, whose "Progress of the World" was shorter than it had once been; Raymond Clapper, writing on politics; Joseph Stagg Lawrence and Howard Florance, dealing with finance and industry; Roger Shaw, young son of the editor, now foreign correspondent; and Jo H. Chamberlin, specialist on labor and social questions. But the magazine grew slimmer, and by 1934 was down to sixty-two pages for one issue after another.

In 1937, its circulation less than it had been since the nineties, the

---

[20] *Review of Reviews,* v. 90, Nov. 1934, pp. 20–21.

monthly *Review of Reviews* was merged into the weekly *Literary Digest,* which had for many years followed much the same editorial pattern as the *Review* and which was now in similar straits. But two failures never yet added up to a success. As a later commentator put it, "the *Review of Reviews* and the tottering *Literary Digest* staggered into each other's arms and over the brink." [21] The combined periodical lasted only eight months.

The *Review of Reviews* rarely talked about itself; but when it changed to the quarto size, it observed, modestly and truly:

> Its aim has always been to bring to its readers a monthly statement of events at home and abroad, with a reasonable interpretation of those transactions that constitute history in the making. We have sought to support an intelligent and high-principled conduct of the governmental and social affairs of the United States, regardless of party. Furthermore, it has always been an object of this magazine to promote international good-will.[22]

But its polysyllabic fairness and sweet reasonableness seemed out of date in the thirties. When one looks upon its whole file, however, one is impressed with the extraordinarily valuable record and commentary that it furnishes of "history in the making."

[21] *American Historical Review,* v. 53, p. 221, Oct. 1947.
[22] *Review of Reviews,* v. 79, Jan. 1929, p. 29.

## THE ROLLING STONE [1]

IN 1894 William Sidney Porter, whose short stories written under the pen name of "O. Henry" were later to furnish pleasure to millions of readers, was a young bank clerk in Austin, Texas. He had been a clerk in the First National Bank of Austin for three years, was happily married, and had one child. He had a strong penchant for writing, especially for dashing off short pieces of a humorous sort, and he earned a small supplement to his regular income by selling such squibs to the New York *Truth*, the *Detroit Free Press*, and other periodicals with notable humor departments.

Then in March 1894 he had the opportunity to purchase for only two hundred and fifty dollars the printing office in which W. C. Brann had produced his *Iconoclast* a few years earlier.[2] Porter borrowed the money, two friends signing the note with him;[3] he bought the little plant and immediately began making plans for the publication of a new weekly. Like Brann's paper, it was to deal somewhat with politics, with an emphasis on satirical comment; but it was to be funnier than Brann ever could be. For the first two issues Porter kept the Brann title, *Iconoclast*; then Brann, who had moved to Waco, wrote to him, apparently protesting that the name did not go with the plant. Porter was not fond of the name anyway: "I didn't think much of it and let him have it," he said later.[4]

Accordingly, Number Three of the new paper appeared as the *Roll-*

[1] TITLES: (1) *Iconoclast*, April 14–21, 1894; (2) *The Rolling Stone*, April 28, 1894–April 27, 1895.
FIRST ISSUE: April 14, 1894. LAST ISSUE: April 27, 1895.
PERIODICITY: Weekly. Vol. 1, 36 numbers, April 14–Dec. 21, 1894; vol. 2, 12 numbers, Dec. 28, 1894–April 27, 1895. Omitted: Nov. 10, 17; Jan. 5, 12, 19; March 16, 23; April 23. (Since March 16 is given a number [v. 2, no. 8], when we are told in the issue for March 30 that it was missed, we may suspect that other numbered issues were missed. In the only file known to exist — the one at the University of Texas — 12 numbers do not appear, in addition to seven skipped weeks for which there are no numbers allowed. Thus we can say only that from 37 to 48 numbers were published.)
PUBLISHER: William Sidney Porter, Austin, Texas (with Hec A. McEachin, March 30–April 27, 1895). Branch office at San Antonio, Jan. 26–April 27, 1895.
EDITOR: William Sidney Porter (with Henry Rider-Taylor, Jan. 26–March 9, 1895).
REFERENCES: Paul Aubrey Tracy, "A Closer Look at O. Henry's Rolling Stone" (master's thesis, University of Texas, 1849); O. Henry, *Rolling Stones* (Garden City, 1920), with Introduction by Henry Peyton Steger.
[2] See Sketch 7 in this volume.
[3] Edmund Travis, "O. Henry's Austin Years," *Bunker's Monthly*, v. 1, p. 506, April 1928.
[4] This is from the article on O. Henry by George MacAdam in the Sunday *New York Times*, April 4, 1909, later reprinted and enlarged in the pamphlet *O. Henry Papers* (Garden City, n.d.). Though the article is a mélange of misinformation designed to conceal Porter's prison years, there seems to be no reason whatever for doubting this statement. No copy of either of the first two numbers (published as *Iconoclast*) seems to be extant.

*ing Stone,* with a kind of subtitle, carried for a few months, "Out for the Moss." It was an eight-page small-folio, with five columns to the page, printed on inferior news stock. The only illustrations were from single-column stereotype plates furnished by one or more of the "boiler-plate" houses, the pictures borrowed from the standard humor magazines. In this first phase of the paper, there was perhaps more comment on news events and less belles-lettres and illustration than in later numbers. Much of this comment was sharply satirical, and some of it shows plainly the strong sympathy of the editor with the downtrodden that was later to be a characteristic of O. Henry's short stories. An example is the following comment on the arrest of "General" Coxey, who had led the march of the unemployed on Washington:

> General Coxey and a few other leaders of the "commonweal army" have been found guilty in a Washington police court of having had the temerity to put sacrilegious foot upon the sacred grass of the Capitol grounds, and are to be punished for the heinous crime unless the higher courts intervene. . . .
> General Coxey has made a great blunder. He and his fellows should have gone to Washington clad in broadcloth and fine garments, and backed by a big bankroll, as the iron, steel, sugar, and other lobbyist delegations do. He should have taken apartments at the Arlington, and given receptions and dinners. That's the way to get legislation at the hands of the American congress.
> This thing of leading a few half-clothed and worse fed workingmen to the Capitol grounds to indulge in the vulgar and old-fashioned peaceable assemblage for redress of grievances, with not a dollar of boodle in sight for the oppressed and overworked members of congress, was of course an outrage, and so the perpetrators were promptly squelched by the strong hand of the "law."
> Mr. Coxey now knows more than he did. He knows that the law must not be infringed — by the poor.[5]

There were many other comments in this vein. Yet the *Rolling Stone* was far from following the current leaders of socialistic politics. It considered the Populists as figures of fun, and one of its more elaborate travesties was a parody of Poe's detective stories, in which the famous sleuth Tictocq ferreted out a pair of socks belonging to "Sockless Jerry Simpson," the Populist leader.[6] A parody ridiculing the Populists ran as follows:

> On a tree by Salt River a Populist sat
> Singing silver, free silver, free silver;
> And I said to him, Do you know where you are at,
> Singing silver, free silver, free silver?[7]

There was a considerable amount of verse by the editor in the *Rolling Stone* throughout its short life. Much of it was humorous in intent, and

[5] *Rolling Stone,* v. 1, May 12, 1894, p. 4.
[6] Reprinted in O. Henry, *Rolling Stones,* pp. 146–56.
[7] *Rolling Stone,* v. 2, Sept. 8, 1894, p. 2.

Porter showed himself a parodist of ability. Also, of course, he wrote limericks, one of which may be quoted as an example:

A seedy old farmer in Md.
Moved West and took up some Prd.
Where he prospered so well
That he went back to tell
How at last he had lighted in Fd.[8]

Nearly everything in the paper was written by the editor. Most of the politics had to do with state affairs; Governor James Stephen Hogg was a favorite target. There was also much comment on Austin matters. Indicative of the habits that were later to influence O. Henry is a remarkable essay entitled "Vagrant Remarks," which begins: "Like the Calif Haroun al Raschid, but without his power of relieving distress or punishing wickedness, I often stroll about Austin studying nature and reading many pages in the great book of Man." Most of what follows deals with poverty and squalor in his home city of fifteen thousand.[9] Altogether, the reader is amazed at the amount and variety of writing — some of it sparkling — that Will Porter was able to perform outside of his hours of service in the bank. Of course, much of the wit seems strained, and there is nothing so flat as an unsuccessful "gag"; but the marvel is that there was so much that was genuinely amusing and good.

There was a good showing of advertising for the first month or two. In fact for two issues advertising reached a proportion of nearly a third of the total column-inches of the paper — a mark which probably would have meant long life, if not prosperity, had it been maintained. But *Rolling Stone* advertising, having no sound basis of circulation, was inconsistent and by July 1894 had dropped to less than one-sixth.[10] It was then that Porter decided on a new format, and the paper entered on its second phase.

The main features of the new *Rolling Stone* were a change to twelve pages of quarto size, a better quality of paper stock, and a profusion of illustration, most of it original. The increase in pictures meant still more work for Will Porter, who each week drew five or ten of them on chalk for Dixie Daniels, a member of his business staff, to engrave by the cheap but not always satisfactory method known as "chalk-cuts." [11] Some of these line drawings were political cartoons, some illustrated local happenings, but most were pictures to accompany jokes.

[8] *Ibid.*, v. 1, May 26, 1894, p. 4.
[9] *Ibid.*, v. 2, Aug. 18, 1894, p. 1. For further comment on Porter's "bumming" in Austin, see account of Dixie Daniels, *Dallas Morning News*, Feb. 25, 1912, part 3, p. 2, quoted in Arthur W. Page, "Little Pictures of O. Henry," *Bookman*, v. 37, p. 507, July 1913.
[10] Tracy, "A Closer Look," p. 252.
[11] Page, in *Bookman*, v. 37, p. 506, July 1913.

The abandonment of the newspaper-size page for that more often used for humor journals indicated a certain change in general content. There were somewhat more sketches and short stories; indeed, a few of the pieces that appeared in the fall of 1894 and the spring of 1895 now seem to presage the later O. Henry, with their sharp drama, humorous touches, and occasional surprise endings. The poetry seems more ambitious, too. Some of the verse in the journal was signed "Ten Eyck White," Porter's first pseudonym. A large number of the poems, including the longer ones, were either parodies or imitations, such as "Fra Giacamo," a curious dramatic monologue in the number for January 26, 1895, apparently inspired by Browning.

Editorial commentary on political and social questions continued to be a feature, especially on page four. Lotteries, then legal in Texas, were strongly attacked. Lynching was defended as the only effective weapon for the defense of southern womanhood. The governorship campaign of 1894 received much attention; personalities were not spared. The German immigrants who had flocked into Texas in the eighties were frequent butts of Porter's satire, and some of his ridicule of *Saengerfeste* is said to have affected the *Rolling Stone's* circulation adversely.[12] Other objects of Porter's barbed satire were the modern girl, the "dude," and the college graduate.

The issue for October 13 carried the beginning of a comic feature that was to continue as long as the paper lasted. This was the weekly page from "The Plunkville Patriot," a travesty on the most primitive kind of crossroads newspaper. It was not a new comic device; it had been employed by the *Knickerbocker Magazine* (with far less typographical fireworks) as early as 1853,[13] and by other periodicals later. But Porter's burlesque was a work of grotesque art (see the reproduction in this volume). It was a typographer's nightmare, with more wrong fonts, "typos," and general compositor's cussedness than any printer has ever condensed into such a limited space before or since. Besides all this, the content itself was often genuinely funny — accounts of social affairs; the political adventures of the editor, Colonel Aristotle Jordan, and his subsequent crusades to clean up pigpens, and so on; and some marvellous obituary verse — imitative, of course — from which we may quote a few lines of one widow's lament:

> I will miss you, Jabez, miss you
> When the stars begin to shine,
> In fact It will be hard to get along without you
> But I will have to be resign.

---

[12] See discussion of this matter in Tracy, "A Closer Look," pp. 136–50.
[13] See F. L. Mott, *A History of American Magazines* (Cambridge, 1931), v. 1, p. 610.

You will wait for me in heaven
Just with in the pearly gates
He died just a quarter past seven
But Providence rules our fates.

But true hearts death cannot sever
There never was a kinder man,
I never expect to do better ever;
But I'll try and do the best I can.[14]

Porter's work at the bank had been growing increasingly unsatisfactory, not only because it interfered with his work on the paper but
also because of that irregular conduct of the bank's business which later
led to his arrest and imprisonment for defalcations.[15] In December 1894,
he resigned his clerkship. Now he devoted all his time to the *Rolling
Stone,* and immediately enlarged its page to the former folio size, keeping the same quality of paper at first and occasionally publishing as
many as twelve pages, but usually only eight. There was the same prodi-
gality of illustration, and the belles-lettres count was high. In the latter
part of January, Porter made arrangements with Henry Rider-Taylor,
a San Antonio journalist, to open a branch office in that city and to edit
a San Antonio page; and this arrangement continued during the few
remaining months of the *Rolling Stone's* existence. But if circulation
and advertising help was expected from the larger city (as was doubtless the hope), the venture was a disappointment, and advertising declined instead of advancing.

On March 2 the paper changed back to quarto size. But bad luck
pursued the editor. In the March 30 number appeared the apology:

The person who sweeps the office, translates the letters from foreign countries,
deciphers communications from graduates of business colleges, and does most of
the writing for this paper, has been confined for the past two weeks on the under-
side of a large red quilt with a joint case of la grippe and measles.

We have missed two issues of The Rolling Stone, and we are now slightly convalescent, for which we desire to apologize, and express our regrets.[16]

The paper's affairs also seemed "slightly convalescent," since the same
issue carried the announcement:

With this issue Mr. Hec A. McEachin assumes the position of associate in the
business and management of this paper. Mr. McEachin is an experienced journalist and will contribute all his time and energy to the success of the paper.[17]

[14] *Rolling Stone,* v. 1, Oct. 13, 1894, p. 3.
[15] See standard biographies of O. Henry, such as C. Alphonso Smith, *O. Henry Biography*
(New York, 1916) and Robert H. Davis and Arthur B. Maurice, *The Caliph of Bagdad*
(New York, 1931); and also Luther W. Courtney, "O. Henry's Case Reconsidered," *American Literature,* v. 14, pp. 361–71, 1943.
[16] *Rolling Stone,* v. 2, March 30, 1895, p. 1.
[17] *Ibid.,* p. 5.

But on April 27 the *Rolling Stone* came to a standstill, quite without moss.

It probably never had as many as fifteen hundred subscribers,[18] and it was never a financial success; but it was an amusing paper, with occasional flashes of the great talent O. Henry was later to display. It was an amateur performance in the writing and the illustration; but the work of true amateurs should not be undervalued. As Paul Aubrey Tracy, leading student of this periodical, concludes, editing the *Rolling Stone* was the most significant phase of "the development of Will Porter into O. Henry." [19]

[18] Tracy, "A Closer Look," pp. 49–50, 262.
[19] *Ibid.*, p. 269.

# THE SATURDAY EVENING POST [1]

ROBERT S. COFFIN was a romantic soul. He learned the printer's trade in his boyhood, then went to sea for a while, and later wandered about New England, New York, and eastern Pennsylvania practising the printer's art; and throughout his short life (he died when he was thirty) he was continually inditing verses. He called himself "The Boston Bard," though he had been born in Maine, had served his apprenticeship at the types in Newburyport, and

[1] TITLES: (1) *The Saturday Evening Post*, 1821–30, 1839–42, 1845–current; (2) *Atkinson's Saturday Evening Post*, 1830–32, 1833–39; (3) *Atkinson's Saturday Evening Post and Bulletin*, 1833; (4) *Atkinson's Evening Post and Philadelphia Saturday News*, 1893; (5) *The United States Saturday Post and Chronicle*, 1842–43; (6) *The United States Saturday Post*, 1843–45.

FIRST ISSUE: August 4, 1821. Current.

PERIODICITY: Weekly. Vol. 1, Aug. 4, 1821–Dec. 28, 1822; 2–10, 1823–31, regular annual vols; 11, Jan. 7, 1832–July 14, 1832; 12, July 21, 1832–Dec. 30, 1832; 13, Jan. 5–Dec. 27, 1833; 14, Jan. 3, 1834–Jan. 2, 1835; 15, Jan. 9–Dec. 31, 1836; 16, Jan. 7–Sept. 2, 1837; 17, Sept. 9, 1937–Dec. 29, 1938; 18, Jan. 5–Nov. 30, 1839; 19, Dec. 7, 1839–Oct. 31, 1840; 20, Nov. 7, 1840–April 24, 1841; 21, May 1–Oct. 30, 1841; 22, Nov. 6, 1841–Nov. 5, 1842; 23, Nov. 12, 1842–Sept. 23, 1843; 24, Sept. 30, 1843–April 27, 1844; 25, May 4–Oct. 26, 1844; 26, Nov. 2, 1844–Aug. 9, 1845; 27, Aug. 16, 1845–June 24, 1848; 28, July 1, 1848–Aug. 4, 1849; 29, Aug. 11, 1849–July 6, 1850; 30, July 13, 1850–June 28, 1851; 31, July 26, 1851–July 3, 1852; 32, July 10, 1852–July 23, 1853; 33, July 30, 1853–July 29, 1854; 34, Aug. 5, 1854–June 30, 1855; 35–50, vol. numbering abandoned (single-issue numbers 1823–2609), July 7, 1855–July 29, 1872; 51–76, Aug. 5, 1871–June 26, 1897, regular annual vols. of 52 numbers each; 77, July 3, 1897–June 25, 1898, changed Jan. 29, 1898, to v. 170; 171–current, July 2, 1898–current, regular annual vols. July–June.

PUBLISHERS: Atkinson & Alexander, 1821–28; Samuel Coate Atkinson, 1828–39; Du Solle & Graham (John S. Du Solle and George Rex Graham), 1839–40; G. R. Graham & Company (Graham and Charles Jacobs Peterson), 1840–43; Samuel D. Patterson & Company (Patterson and Graham), 1843–48; Deacon & Peterson (Edmund Deacon and Henry Peterson), 1848–65; H. Peterson & Company (Peterson and Bella Z. Spencer), 1865–73; Saturday Evening Post Publishing Company (owners: R. J. C. Walker, 1874–75, with C. McF. Reed and Joseph P. Reed, May–Aug. 1875; Charles I. Wickersham and Joseph P. Reed, 1875–76; Bennet & Fitch, 1876–77; Andrew E. Smythe, 1877–97), 1874–97; Curtis Publishing Company, 1897–current (presidents: Cyrus Hermann Kotzschmar Curtis, 1897–1932; George Horace Lorimer, 1932–34; Walter Deane Fuller, 1934–current). All of Philadelphia.

EDITORS: T. Cottrell Clarke, 1821–26; Morton McMichael, 1826–28; Benjamin Mathias, 1828–39; George Rex Graham, 1839–46 (with John S. Du Solle, 1839–40; with Charles J. Peterson, 1840–43); Henry Peterson, 1846–73 (with Edmund Deacon, 1848–65; with Bella Z. Spencer, 1865–?); R. J. C. Walker, 1874–75; Joseph P. Reed, 1875–76; Orlando Bennet, 1876–77; Andrew E. Smythe, 1877–97; William George Jordan, 1897–99; George Horace Lorimer, 1899–1936; Wesley Winans Stout, 1937–42; Ben Hibbs, 1942–current.

INDEX: *Readers' Guide.*

REFERENCES: Edward W. Bok, *A Man From Maine* (New York, 1923); John Tebbel, *George Horace Lorimer and the Saturday Evening Post* (Garden City, 1948); [Frederick S. Bigelow], *A Short History of the Saturday Evening Post* (Philadelphia, 1936); Roger Butterfield and *Post* editors, *The Saturday Evening Post Treasury* (New York, 1954), especially headnotes to selections; Eugene H. Munday, "The Saturday Evening Post," *Proof Sheet*, v. 3, pp. 69–72, March 1870, reprinted in the *Saturday Evening Post*, Oct. 7, 1871; James Playsted Wood, *Magazines in the United States* (New York, 1949), ch. 13. (Except for Munday, these are all valuable only for the Curtis-Lorimer regime.)

spent much of his life in Pennsylvania. His poem "On Presenting a Lady with a Cake of Soap" achieved a modest success, but we may surmise that his talents were not always appreciated from the lines entitled "Ode to Genius, Suggested by the Present Unhappy Condition of the Boston Bard, an Eminent Poet of This Country." Coffin's greatest literary success was made when he was employed on the *Village Record* of West Chester, Pennsylvania. The proprietor of that paper had a daughter who was blind, but who had become a skilled typesetter. Coffin's poetical sentiments were stirred by this situation, and he wrote some stanzas called "A Blind Girl," which the young lady put into type herself when they were recited to her.

Coffin was encouraged by the acclaim that met this effort, and shortly thereafter he came to nearby Philadelphia and announced that he was going to edit and publish there a weekly miscellany to be called the *Bee*. He got the paper out in the spring of 1821, but the subscribers did not flock in as he had expected. Indeed the *Bee* buzzed but briefly; its editor had no resources for the promotion of his venture, and he was lucky to find a fellow-printer who was willing to pay him something for the two hundred subscribers who had signed his subscription list. Let us hope Coffin got enough out of it to pay for his passage back to Boston.[2]

The printer who obtained the *Bee* list and undertook to furnish a paper to the disappointed subscribers was Charles Alexander. He was of the same age as Coffin, twenty-four. He had been apprenticed to Zachariah Poulson, of the *American Daily Advertiser*, at sixteen; now, having been a full journeyman for a few years, during which he had saved a few dollars, he was anxious to get into a business of his own.[3] Weekly literary miscellanies were springing up all over the country; they were easy to start, and many of them were successful.[4] There were then no Sunday editions of daily papers, and Saturday papers for Sunday reading had become popular.

Alexander formed a partnership with another printer, Samuel Coate Atkinson, who was associated with the printing business being conducted in the old plant of the then defunct *Pennsylvania Gazette*, the paper which Benjamin Franklin had once owned.[5] Atkinson & Alexander now made arrangements to take over this plant for the publication of their new miscellany.

And so, on August 4, 1821, Volume I, Number 1 of the *Saturday Eve-*

---

[2] Coffin, his poem "A Blind Girl," and the *Bee* are mentioned by Munday in *Proof Sheet*, v. 3, March 1870, as is the sale of the *Bee's* list to Alexander.

[3] *American Annual Cyclopaedia*, v. 6 (1866), 578; Munday in *Proof Sheet*, v. 3, March 1870.

[4] See F. L. Mott, *A History of American Magazines* (Cambridge, 1930), v. 1, p. 354.

[5] See pp. 682–83.

*ning Post* was published in a two-story brick building "back of No. 53, Market Street." The first floor was all pressroom, with two Patrick Lyon presses; the upper story was divided into two composing rooms, and the editorial department was in the attic.[6] The paper was a modest four-page small-folio, with five columns to the page, and without illustration. It adopted newspaper form and called itself a newspaper chiefly, no doubt, because the postal rate on newspapers was lower than that on other periodicals. It did indeed carry a considerable amount of news on the second and third pages, but at least half of its columns were filled with literary miscellany for Sunday reading. For the first five years most of the contents of the *Post* consisted of matter compiled by Editor Thomas Cottrell Clarke by means of scissors and pastepot, short articles from Clarke's own pen, and stories and poems either contributed by amateur writers or borrowed from other periodicals. Most of the news was in the form of single-paragraph "items." All "political controversy" was, by editorial promise from the first, taboo. Fiction was generally limited to an occasional tale; but a serial story entitled "Guilt Triumphant Over Innocence; or, The Story of Emma Somerton" — a seduction novel in the pattern of the best sellers *Charlotte Temple* and *The Coquette* — began its course in the *Post* June 22, 1822. It was signed "D."; everything in the paper was anonymous and much of it was apparently the product of amateur effort. The *Post* in these early years paid nothing to its contributors, and chatted informally in its editorial columns with those who had submitted tales and verse, praising one and condemning another. In the fall of 1822 a "Dramatic Summary" was begun, to continue for many years; plays at the New-Theatre and the City-Theatre in Philadelphia, and occasionally performances in other American cities, were reviewed. "The Moralist" was the heading of a department of periodical essays by various hands over several years, and "The Ladies' Friend" was a column of household hints.

At the end of five months of publication, the *Post* claimed to be a success: "We have the gratification of finding the attempt at the publication of a family newspaper successful in its very incipiency." However, the publishers added the plea that was so common in both the newspapers and the magazines of the time:

We respectfully take leave to remind our friends, that without the stipendiary equivalent for our labour, we may ultimately encounter the fate, which has attended many of our predecessors, whose attempts, in consequence of their not having any "backing" from their patrons, have resulted in abortion.[7]

[6] *Proof Sheet*, v. 3, pp. 69–72, March 1870.
[7] *Saturday Evening Post*, v. 1, Jan. 5, 1822, p. 3.

Later such notices were to become less rhetorical and more mandatory.[8] At the end of its first year, the *Post* was exultant because "The list of our subscribers, at present, is rising ONE THOUSAND."[9] This, at two dollars apiece, even if there were no "delinquents" among them, seems a modest beginning. But it was at least enough to keep the paper alive, and two years later the paper was claiming "between three and four thousand" circulation and boasting of "unprecedented patronage."[10]

Indeed, by the time the *Post* was four and a half years old, Atkinson & Alexander testified to their prosperity by founding a monthly magazine as companion to their weekly. This was the *Casket*, which was edited by Atkinson, and which continued for more than twenty years, through various shifts in ownership and editorship, to have a close connection with the *Post*. Even for eight years after it had come into a richer life as *Graham's Magazine,* the monthly continued in an interlocking management with the *Post*, and was published from the same plant.

The association was helpful to the *Post*. More commodious quarters were found at 112 Chestnut Street, and moves were made again in 1833 and 1840, each time with improvement of plant and housing. The content of the paper improved, and its page size was increased to six columns. Possibly a change of editors helped in that regard; Clarke left to found his own weekly, the *Album,* and his place was taken by a young law student, Morton McMichael, nineteen years of age. McMichael was admitted to the bar midway of his three-year term as the *Post's* editor, but he never practised law much; he lived to become a distinguished journalist, a notable orator, and mayor of Philadelphia. After he left the *Post* in 1828, he was associated with three other Saturday papers in succession, and for the last twenty-five years of his life he was editor and publisher of the *Philadelphia North American,* a famous daily newspaper.

A typical number of the *Saturday Evening Post* in 1827 gave a column and a half of the front page to poetry, and the remainder of the six columns to tales and essays. On the second page there would be two columns of miscellaneous feature material, with the remainder of the space given to domestic and foreign news items. The third was the editorial page; it had one or two columns of nonpolitical editorials, and the rest of the page was filled with news and advertisements, including death and marriage notices. On the back page readers found more feature stories and more advertisements. These paid notices were all set

---

[8] Note, for example, *ibid.,* v. 6, Jan. 20, 1827, p. 3.
[9] *Ibid.,* v. 1, July 27, 1822, p. 3.
[10] *Ibid.,* v. 4, Dec. 4, 1824, p. 3.

single-column width, and in them patent medicine and lottery advertising predominated.

A few woodcuts now appeared, especially in "The School of Flora" department; these increased, and by the end of 1829 the front page was often "adorned" with a double-column illustration, though the engraving was usually pretty bad. There was still some "selected" material, but much of it was original. The *Post* management was strong on prize contests for the best essay, American tale, biography, metrical composition. Prizes were modest indeed, mostly consisting of bound volumes of the *Casket*; and then both the weekly and the monthly printed the winning pieces, apparently without further compensation to the writers. By 1831, however, the *Casket* was paying a dollar per printed page, and Graham eventually competed with Godey for the title of the best paymaster among magazine editors. The *Post* used much *Casket* material; and when the monthly's name was changed to *Graham's Magazine* in 1840, it continued to make free with the contents of its associate. Or, in some cases, and especially with serials, the *Post* might present material first, and the monthly reprint.

In 1828 Alexander sold out to his partner Atkinson in order to found a newspaper, the *Daily Chronicle*. "Charles Alexander is no common man," wrote Louis A. Godey some years later, and went on to enumerate eight magazines that he had had a hand in starting, beginning with the *Saturday Evening Post* and *Casket-Graham's*, and ending the list with *Godey's Lady's Book* itself, of which Alexander was one of the original "joint proprietors." [11] But he was evidently one of those entrepreneurs who are better at starting things than at seeing them through; at any rate, after eight years of the *Post* and two of the *Casket,* he left both to Atkinson and adventured in new fields.

Thus began the second phase of the *Post's* history, in which Atkinson had complete control, with Benjamin Mathias as his editor. Mathias was another of those young journalists who got their start on the *Post*; he eventually left it to edit a rival weekly, the *Saturday Chronicle,* which was finally merged with the *Post* in 1842. Atkinson put his own name into the titles of both his periodicals, so the weekly appeared for several years as *Atkinson's Saturday Evening Post.*

The contents were not yet very distinguished. Mark Bancroft's "The Vendue" was a serial story of 1829, and there was apparent an effort to make the *Post* distinctively American in its literary features. Music was presented on page one in the thirties: nearly every issue had either a double-column woodcut or some music on that page. Lambert A. Wilmer did a stint as an editorial assistant on the *Post* in the thirties;

[11] *Godey's Lady's Book,* v. 23, p. 192, Oct. 1841.

he was a great complainer, and his contention that he was underpaid need not be taken too seriously. But it seems evident enough that he was right in his statement that the periodical was "conducted by Mr. Atkinson on the most economical plan"; and though we may have some doubts about the corollary, "and his profits must have been extremely great," [12] we find that Atkinson was getting on well enough, at least, to buy one of his rivals, the *Saturday Bulletin* (1827–1832), at the end of 1832. The circulation of the *Post* had been increasing steadily; its publisher was claiming fifteen thousand in 1832, and he expected the *Bulletin* to bring him five thousand more. And twenty thousand, he declared, would be the greatest circulation of any weekly "on the continent of America." [13] The *Post* at that time was no doubt among the leaders of American weekly miscellanies in circulation. The subscription list of the *New York Mirror* may have been greater; its literary standard was certainly higher. But the *Post,* increasing its page size, its illustration, and its literary variety, became at last a nationally important periodical — "the most popular weekly paper in the United States," declared Wilmer.

The third period of the history of the *Saturday Evening Post,* from 1839 to 1848, was dominated by the bold and romantic personality of George Rex Graham. Graham had come to Philadelphia from a country town as an orphan boy of nineteen, with eight dollars in his pocket. He got a job with a cabinet-maker, but every night, after a long day's work, he would spend six hours in reading and study. Thus, in 1839, by the time he was twenty-six, he was admitted to the practice of law; and in January of that same year he seized an opportunity to realize his chief ambition by entering magazine journalism. Atkinson hired him as editor of the *Post.*

It is likely that the hard times of the late 1830's affected Atkinson's business adversely; at any rate, he sold both his periodicals in November 1839. Not much is heard of him later. He was associated with the *Journal of Health* (1829–1833) and later with the *Temperance Advocate* (1841–1845). But eventually he lost all his money, and ended his career as a humble typesetter. A fellow-printer wrote many years later of knowing Atkinson in this late phase — a portly, benevolent-looking old gentleman, "more cheerful in adversity than many are in success." [14]

The new purchaser of the *Post* was John S. Du Solle, a Philadelphia newspaperman, who took Editor Graham as a partner. The two did not get along well, however, and after four or five months Du Solle sold

[12] Lambert A. Wilmer, *Our Press Gang* (Philadelphia, 1859), pp. 19, 41. In his statement about the *Post's* popularity, Wilmer was referring definitely to the period of the 1830's.
[13] *Saturday Evening Post,* v. 12, Dec. 22, 1932, p. 3.
[14] *Proof Sheet,* v. 3, p. 69, footnote.

out. Meantime, Atkinson had sold the monthly *Casket* to Graham, and Graham had employed Charles Jacobs Peterson as coeditor of that magazine. Graham and Peterson were birds of a feather, sanguine, energetic, full of ideas; and so when Du Solle wanted to get out, it was Peterson who bought his interest in the *Post*.

Charles J. Peterson was with Graham only three years, but during that time he was an able lieutenant on both periodicals. He helped transform the monthly from the rather shabby *Casket* into the brilliant *Graham's Magazine*, one of the four best American monthlies of the second quarter of the nineteenth century.[15] He helped to raise the *Saturday Evening Post* out of the ruck of undistinguished week-end papers and prepare it for its most brilliant pre-Curtis period. Peterson was a brother of the three men who composed the important Philadelphia book-publishing firm of T. B. Peterson & Brothers. Like so many *Post* editors, he had been admitted to the bar but had soon deserted the courtroom for an editorial sanctum. He is chiefly remembered for the magazine that he founded, on a suggestion from Graham, as a rival to *Godey's*, and which made a great success under the name of *Peterson's Magazine*.[16]

Before he sold the *Post*, Atkinson had taken over the list of the defunct *Saturday News* (1836–1839), one of Louis A. Godey's failures.[17] Late in 1839 Graham enlarged the page size of his weekly to what was called in those days a "blanket sheet." He also used better paper, and the printing was improved. But best of all, the literary level of contributions improved; this was largely under the influence of *Graham's Magazine*, which passed on to the weekly the work of Nathaniel Parker Willis, James Kirke Paulding, H. T. Tuckerman, John Neal, Edgar Allan Poe, and many others. Rufus W. Griswold was literary editor of both the *Post* and *Graham's* in 1842–1843.[18] Sometimes the weekly was permitted priority with an important contribution. This was the case with Poe's "The Black Cat," published in the *Post* in 1843. News was still a feature of the paper.

In 1842 Graham bought up two more of Philadelphia's Saturday papers — Mathias' *Saturday Chronicle* (1836–1842) and the *United States and Dollar Newspaper* (1837–1842), issued by the owners of the *Philadelphia Public Ledger* and the *Baltimore Sun*. These were successful papers, and the consolidation of three strong weeklies put the resultant *United States Saturday Post and Chronicle* in a favorable com-

[15] For a history of *Graham's*, see Mott, *op. cit.*, v. 1, Sketch 45.
[16] For a history of *Peterson's*, see Mott, *op. cit.*, v. 2, Sketch 6.
[17] In its issue of Jan. 5, 1839, the *Post* said the *News* had suspended publication. The next week it said the *News* had been merged in its own publication.
[18] See Mott, *op. cit.*, v. 1, pp. 550–51.

petitive position, with forty or fifty thousand circulation. And then, when Charles J. Peterson left the *Post* to conduct his own magazine, the paper was fortunate in his successor.

In 1846 the *Post* was twenty-five years old. Mere survival in a highly contested field was something; the *Post* was now Philadelphia's oldest week-end paper, as well as much the largest in point of circulation. Several factors had worked against its development into a great periodical. One of them was the competition: at any time in the forties and fifties, the Post could count more than a dozen Philadelphia rivals in the field of the weekly miscellany. Also the connection with a monthly magazine, though it had its advantages, tended to restrain any original and aggressive spirit on the part of *Post* editorship. But worst of all, throughout its quarter-century of publication, the *Post* had suffered from a lack of continuous and devoted editorship. It had had five owners and six editors in those years, nearly all of whom had been distracted by other editorial ventures. But just three months after its twenty-fifth birthday, the *Post* was joined by a young man who was to direct its fortunes for the next twenty-seven years, and make it a journal of real distinction.

This man was Henry Peterson, a cousin of Charles J. At the age of twenty-one, Henry had formed a partnership with Edmund Deacon for the publication of cheap reprints and manuals. That business had prospered; but in the course of time it became possible to leave it largely to the efficient Deacon, and Peterson took a position as editor of the new *Saturday Gazette* (1844–1853). When Graham offered him the editorship of the *Saturday Evening Post* (it had now resumed the old title) Peterson was quick to accept. This was in 1846, and two years later the firm of Deacon & Peterson bought the *Post*, thus separating it at last from *Graham's Magazine*. Though both partners were nominally editors and publishers, Deacon had charge, in the main, of the business and Peterson of the literary and editorial side.

The *Post* now entered upon the golden period of its early history. It had only four pages — but what pages! They measured two feet wide by a yard long. The paper called itself "A Family Newspaper, Neutral in Politics, Devoted to Morality, Pure Literature, Foreign and Domestic News, Agriculture, the Commercial Interests, Science, Art, and Amusement." In other words, it strove for all the variety required of a Saturday miscellany. Its premier contributor in the fifties was the great Mrs. E. D. E. N. Southworth, who turned out one long serial after another, and who, at the mid-century, shared with Charles Dickens the palm as the most popular writer for the American middle-class audience. An advertisement setting forth the prospectus for 1854 will show what the publishers considered to be their most important offerings:

THE SATURDAY EVENING POST

Offers the Following Brilliant Array of Genius:

MRS. SOUTHWORTH; EMERSON BENNETT;
MRS. DENISON; GRACE GREENWOOD;
AND FANNY FERN

Mrs. Southworth, whose fascinating works are now being rapidly republished in England, also will maintain her old and pleasant relation with the POST. The next story from her gifted pen will be

MIRIAM, THE AVENGER; OR, THE FATAL VOW
By Emma D. E. N. Southworth

$2.00          Deacon & Peterson[19]

Though Mrs. Southworth's very first novel appeared in the *National Era,* of Baltimore, her second was a *Post* serial; and one of her most popular stories, "The Curse of Clifton," was printed in the *Post* in 1852. The *New York Ledger,* a weekly that was just beginning to pay extravagant rates to authors, took Mrs. Southworth away from the *Post* in the latter fifties. It also robbed them of Mrs. Sara Willis Eldredge (later Parton), whose "Sketches by Fanny Fern" had formed a regular department for some years. Other popular writers found regularly in *Post* pages in the years before the Civil War were Mrs. E. F. Ellett, Augustine J. H. Duganne, Mary Irving, and T. S. Arthur. Illustration, by engravings on wood, was increased somewhat; each issue usually contained a woodcut in the center of page one, a cut or two of some invention or building or place, and (on the last page) a comic picture.

At the end of 1855, the *Post* was proudly advertising a circulation of "between 80,000 and 90,000"[20] — its greatest pre-Curtis distribution. At this time it made a marked change in format, becoming an eight-page small-folio. The price was still two dollars a year. English serials now became common. Dickens' "Tale of Two Cities" was published in 1858; and Charles Reade, Mrs. Mulock, "Ouida," and G. P. R. James became contributors — some of them perhaps involuntarily, though Deacon & Peterson followed the example of other reputable publishers of the fifties and, in the absence of an international copyright agreement, often paid English writers for "advance sheets."

During the Civil War, the *Post* carried regularly some news of military operations, accompanied by woodcut illustrations of battle scenes, often taken from *Frank Leslie's Illustrated Newspaper.* By 1863 the big picture, four columns wide, on the front page, had become a feature

[19] Advertisement on the cover of the *Ladies' Wreath* for Dec. 1853.
[20] *Saturday Evening Post,* v. 6, p. 391, Dec. 13, 1855.

of the *Post*. But the paper was more and more a fiction periodical. Mrs. Henry Wood's first novel was serialized in 1860, and the next year her "East Lynne" made its melodramatic and tearful way through *Post* columns. Virginia F. Townsend, Marion Harland, and the younger Pierce Egan also wrote serials for the paper. For many years some good poets had appeared from time to time in the pages of the *Post*: Poe, Emerson, Lowell, and Bryant may be mentioned, along with Gerald Massey, T. B. Aldrich, and Alice Cary. Farmers' notes continued to appear, with some household hints, humor, and riddles. Editorials, once a regular feature, were resumed when the eight-page format afforded more space.

In 1865 the *Post* was forced by the fiscal inflation to raise its subscription price to two dollars and a half. Page borders, in imitation of the *New York Ledger*, dressed up the paper, but the literary standard tended to decline. In June of that year Mrs. Bella Z. Spencer purchased Deacon's interest and became nominal editor of the *Post*. She was the young wife of an army officer, and had written a novel called *Ora; or, The Lost Wife*, which had been widely praised. For her own paper she now wrote "Lucile Rembrandt"; she appears to have been an imitator of Mrs. Wood, who continued to write for the *Post*. Emerson Bennett, Captain Mayne Reid, Mrs. Mary A. Denison, Louise Chandler Moulton, and "Sophie May" were faithful contributors for the next few years. Editorials were again omitted; the amount of news declined in 1865 to a column or so of deaths, marriages, and markets; and even these were finally dropped in 1871.

At the end of 1873 Henry Peterson closed his long editorship of the *Post*, and sold the paper to a publishing company headed by Robert J. C. Walker, a Philadelphia merchant and politician. In the next four years six men in rapid succession were editors and publishers of the declining periodical, ending with Orlando Bennet. Captain Bennet, a famous naval "wrecker," had saved many a hulk from the bottom of the sea, but it looked as though this one was a total loss when he and his partner Fitch sold it at a sheriff's sale in 1877.

The purchaser, and the owner and editor for the next twenty years, was Andrew E. Smythe. The serials were now by unknowns; and though the page was larger and the price was back to two dollars, the *Post* was merely another cheap story paper. The circulation fell below thirty thousand. At the end of 1879 Bennet made the *Post* a sixteen-page large-quarto. Though the price was two dollars, most of its circulation came from "clubs" of ten at a dollar each.

Smythe claimed to have a subscription list of thirty-five thousand in the late eighties. There were commonly three fiction serials running at a time, all by writers now deservedly forgotten. There were columns of miscellaneous items, facetiae, household hints, and so on. There was some verse, and a moral essay appeared each week on the editorial page. "Nothing impure or debasing will be permitted to defile its pages," said a declaration at the head of its editorial department; certainly nothing of notable quality distinguished its pages. Its advertising consisted chiefly of patent medicine testimonials, free offers, and announcements that agents were wanted to sell various articles from door to door. The *Post* was proud of its age; its subtitle read, "The Oldest Literary and Family Paper in the United States. Founded A.D. 1821." Its age was about all it had left to be proud of.

The story goes [21] that Smythe, on the verge of bankruptcy, went to Chicago in 1897 to raise money on some gas company holdings or prospects, but died in August of that year without having been able to provide for the continuance of the publication. His only heir was a sister who was unwilling to risk any money on a failing magazine. Six weeks went by after Smythe's death, and his friends and the old office force got out six issues, sometimes tardily, while the executor took out his papers and began a search for a purchaser for the *Post*. There were a supply of worn type, an old press, and other printers' tools; and there were the name (uncopyrighted) and the prestige (tarnished) and traditions (including a current story of some connection with Benjamin Franklin) of the *Saturday Evening Post*. There was a subscription list of about two thousand names. For more than twenty years the paper had made a mere pittance for its owner; it was generally believed that the weekly of literary miscellany had had its day and was now outmoded; and nobody could be found to take a chance on a proven failure. A seventh number was issued on October 2, and the printers and office force declared that this was the last unless someone appeared who could meet payrolls every week.

In desperation, the executor called on Cyrus H. K. Curtis, who had made the most astounding success in recent publishing history with his monthly *Ladies' Home Journal*, and begged him to buy this ancient and honorable periodical and save it from shipwreck. The conversation must have gone somewhat like this: "And how much do you want for this bankrupt old paper?" "Mr. Curtis, you can just about name your own price!" "Well," and Mr. Curtis smiled through his beard, "I'll give you a thousand dollars." "Sold!" Actually, at this time in the fall the *Ladies' Home Journal* was taking in a good many thousand dollars

---

[21] See Bok, *A Man From Maine*, p. 152. A notice of Smythe's death appears in the *Post* for Aug. 14, 1897. His name as publisher had been removed from the masthead in the issue of Aug. 7.

a day for subscriptions alone, and two thousand a day on the year-long average. In other words the price paid for the *Post* by Curtis, though it may have meant something to the Smythe estate, was peanuts to Curtis. He forthwith wrote a check to bind the bargain and sent a draywagon to the *Post* office to haul away the printing materials he had purchased. With those materials the October 9, 1897, issue of the *Post* was printed in the *Journal* building; it was copyrighted by the Curtis Publishing Company, but contained no other notice of a change in management.

It is clear that Curtis did not know what to do with the *Post* after he had bought it.[22] He put William George Jordan, of the *Journal* staff, at work editing it; it took three months for Jordan to shake off the old *Post* and put on the new; and even then the new proved to be only a kind of weekly *Ladies' Home Journal*. On January 22, 1898, the paper came out in a new dress of type, and from that date it was vastly improved. It was *Journal*-ish to be sure, but the *Journal* standard was far higher than that of the old *Post*.

A new dress and improved editorial content were not all the benefits the *Post* received in January 1898; it also officially acquired a tradition. For half a century it had printed in its date line or in bold black letters under its name plate the information that it had been founded in 1821. (See illustration in this volume.) This was done for more than three months after it had come under the Curtis management; then abruptly a change was made. Under the name plate on January 22 were the words, "Founded A. D. 1821"; on January 29 this line read, "Founded A. D. 1728." Thus the paper picked up ninety-three years in a week. The volume number was conformably changed from 77 to 170, and in smaller blackface type under the name plate appeared this historical note:

In 1729 this paper was purchased by Benjamin Franklin, and published by him as "The Pennsylvania Gazette" until 1765, when it passed into other hands. On August 4, 1821, the present title was adopted, and the office of publication was the one occupied by Benjamin Franklin, in the rear of 53 Market Street, Philadelphia.

A year later this note was dropped and the whole matter was simplified in the line: "Founded A° D¹ 1728 by Benj. Franklin."

Now, it must be understood that neither Curtis nor any of his lieutenants invented this remarkable fable of the identity of the *Saturday Evening Post* with the *Pennsylvania Gazette*. They derived it from

---

[22] Bok, in his romantic biography of Curtis, indicates that the publisher had definite plans for the *Post* long before he bought it, but the files are the best evidence in this matter. See Bok, *A Man From Maine*, pp. 149–50.

The COLLEGE MAN'S NUMBER

# THE SATURDAY EVENING POST

### An Illustrated Weekly Magazine
### Founded Aᵒ Dᴵ 1728 by Benj. Franklin

Volume 172, No. 18       PHILADELPHIA, OCTOBER 28, 1899       5 Cents the Copy; $2.50 the Year

The Curtis Publishing Company, Philadelphia

THE CENTRAL NEWS COMPANY, PHILADELPHIA, GENERAL AGENTS

THE FIRST SATURDAY EVENING POST COVER

See page 682.

THE SATURDAY EVENING POST
FOUNDED, A.D. 1821
THE GREAT PIONEER FAMILY PAPER OF AMERICA

Vol. 77 PUBLISHED WEEKLY, AT 425 ARCH STREET Philadelphia, Saturday, January 22, 1898 FIVE CENTS A COPY $2.00 A YEAR IN ADVANCE No. 30

Entered at the Philadelphia Post-Office as Second-Class Matter



## The Turning of the Tide

*THE STORY OF AN AMBITIOUS WOMAN*

*By Florence Stacpoole*

CHAPTER I

BEATIE, dearest, don't! Don't cry so, dear—it unnerves me, and I want you to help me, love!"

These words had a magical effect, for Beatrice's sobs stopped, and about a minute afterward she could speak calmly.

"Poor Eric! Poor, dear Eric! With your examination before you, and starting at six in the morning, too! What a selfish, selfish creature I am!"

Eric took the soft little hand that lay on his arm and kissed it.

"My darling, you are not selfish—don't say that! No wonder you feel as you do, for the affair has been very sudden."

These two young people were walking on the short, soft grass of a little lawn which was in front of an old-fashioned, pretty country house. The air of the May evening was sweet with the breath of the hawthorn hedges surrounding the lawn and separating it from the garden and fields that lay around the dwelling, and an unseen nightingale's song was the only sound that broke the stillness when Eric's voice ceased. But before he had time to resume he and his companion were startled by hearing a woman's shrill tones coming from the porch of the pretty villa.

"Beatrice! Beatrice! Where on earth are you? Come in this instant!"

◆

Eric drew the girl's arm within his, and, turning toward the house, they met a plain little person, in a brown serge gown, coming forward to meet them.

"You ought to be ashamed of yourself, walking about at this hour of the evening with a young man!" she exclaimed.

Eric burst into a hearty, good-humored laugh.

"I think it is pleasanter for her than walking about without a young man!" he cried. "But, my dear Miss Steet, there's not the slightest reason for you to be shocked. We are engaged! We became engaged an hour ago, and the reason why we have stayed strolling about here so late, instead of coming in and sitting in the drawing-room, is that I've been trying to convince Beatrice that we must be married in three weeks. I want to speak to Mr. Burton about it."

The person in the brown serge dress gave a convulsive gasp, and her swarthy, sallow face turned very pale, but it was not noticeable in the dusk. She did not speak for a few moments; then, recovering herself, she said, not so shrilly, but much more viciously than before:

"Well, you can't see grandpapa to-night—he has gone to bed; you'll have to wait till to-morrow!"

"To-morrow!" exclaimed the young man blankly. "To-morrow! But I'm going away in the morning by the six o'clock train!"

"That's not my fault—you should have come in sooner! But the postman's not going away, I suppose?" and the next moment, with an indignant sniff, the young lady addressed as Miss Steet had vanished into the house.

"Yes, I must write, love," said Eric, taking his sweetheart's hand in his again. "I must explain everything to your grandfather—that the practice would have been snapped up if I had not secured it at once, even before I was qualified, and that you are willing to stand by me in the first bit of the stiff pull up the hill until the fees come rolling in. There will be nothing to fear, dear, because you'll be by my side—won't you, dear?" he rattled on enthusiastically.

As Beatrice did not speak he continued:

"You've decided, dearest, haven't you, that it's better for us to be married in three weeks' time than to have to wait months and months before there's a chance of our seeing each other again—you down here with 'dear Cousin Harriet'"—and he laughed as he mimicked Miss Steet's shrill treble—"and I up there, facing my strange patients, and living in my new house all alone? Only think, Beatie, it is May now! Well, before we should see each other again—that is, if I settle in Birmingham alone on the first of June—there would be June, July, August, September, October, Nov——"

"Oh, stop—stop, Eric! I could not bear it!" ejaculated the girl, quite overcome by the prospect. "I could not live all through the long summer and autumn——"

"And winter, too, without seeing me!" interrupted Eric triumphantly. "And how could I live without seeing you, my darling? No, no—we could not do it. You'll be my wife this day three weeks! It's settled, remember, with your grandfather's consent or without it! But I'll write and ask for it, as it would be only proper to obtain it!"

"Ah," sighed Beatrice, "I don't suppose there'll be so much trouble to get it now as there would have been this time last year!"

"Before 'dearest Harriet' came?" inquired Eric.

"Yes," assented Beatrice. "I was all in all to grandpapa, Eric, till this time last year; and now Harriet is everything to him—everything! He won't mind in the least my leaving him!"

"Well, you're going to be all in all to me now! It's much more convenient as it is, for it would have been awful for me if he had wanted to keep you with him. There's one thing—he won't find any one troubling him to take Miss Harriet off his hands. But I am afraid he'll think me a very bad match for you, love. I'm not a very great catch, I know!" murmured the young man.

Just then Beatrice interrupted him by putting her hand on his lips.

"Don't," she implored—"don't let us talk about money! I am tired of hearing about it, for Harriet talks of hardly anything else all day long. Don't let us spoil this evening, especially, by doing so!"

◆

The city was hot, stifling and dusty as Eric Kenlis trudged every day from his lodgings in a quiet street to the College of Surgeons, where he was undergoing an examination previous to becoming qualified to act as a medical practitioner.

Eric was not uneasy on the score of not passing, for he felt pretty confident that he would do so. He was well up in his work, so it was not any doubt on that point that made his heart sink occasionally, as he diverted his attention now and again from abstruse physiological questions to his own private affairs.

Nor was it any qualm as to his biological or anatomical knowledge that made him uneasy, which he certainly was pretty frequently; his disquietude came from the same plain, prosaic and unpoetical cause which has worried millions of lovers since banking-accounts first came into existence. Indeed, Eric's balance at his banker's was not of quite the amount which would really warrant a young medical man in plunging recklessly into matrimony with a girl who did not possess sixpence of her own.

His financial position was this—he had signed a check for the purchase of a practice in Birmingham, and when his examination fees were paid the exact amount remaining to his credit at Messrs. Goldsworthy's bank would be a few hundred dollars only.

"Don't let us talk about money!" Beatrice had said on that sweet evening when the two had wandered together by the hawthorn hedges; nevertheless, he could not help thinking about it.

"What's the matter, old man?"

The speaker was another student, also up for his examination. They had known each other in hospital days, and Gregory Hardcastle and Eric Kenlis had been great chums.

"Oh, my thoughts weren't exactly unpleasant!" returned Eric, with a little laugh.

"A girl? I thought as much!" remarked the astute Gregory. "But there's something else, I can tell by the look of your face!"

"Yes, there is," admitted Eric. "You are right, as usual, Gregory. Well, to begin with, I'm engaged!"

"I'm not surprised to hear it. You're not the fellow to be in love long without clinching the matter. You always were too impulsive, old boy."

"I think you might give me your congratulations first and the lecture after," remarked Eric.

"That's true," responded his friend. "I'm afraid I was rather rude. Well, I congratulate you heartily, old man, and the young lady, too, as far as that goes!"

"That's a very pretty compliment, Gregory; it quite takes away the sting of the lecture you were beginning. Thank you very much!"

"Well, go on with the sequel," urged Hardcastle. "The engagement was only the first part of the story."

"And the best part, too!" ejaculated Eric. "Well, I've bought a practice, too!"

"Great Scott!" exclaimed Gregory. "You take my breath away! A practice! Before you have got your diploma! This is impetuosity with a vengeance! I must have something to settle my nerves after that," he remarked, lighting a cigar. "If you'll take one, my boy"—handing Eric the case—"it will soothe the system, and enable you the better to tell the story. And where is the practice?" continued Hardcastle.

"In Birmingham," replied Eric.

◆

Gregory made a grimace as he asked, after a moment's silence:

"How much did you give for it?"

"Oh, I think I've got a bargain—twenty-five hundred dollars."

"You've seen the books, of course?"

"No—no," said Eric hesitatingly. "I have not."

"You haven't! But why didn't you make the fellow show them when you inspected the place? You should have looked to the takings before anything else."

"But I haven't inspected the place! In fact, I've never been in Birmingham!"

"Good gracious!" cried young Hardcastle. "Are you a born idiot, Eric? You're not serious, surely?"

He looked so astonished that Eric's uneasiness, which before had been vague, began to assume a more definite form; but he replied firmly:

"If I had waited till I had seen the place and inspected the books, I should probably have lost the chance of it, and most likely have lost my examination, too!"

"How so?" asked Gregory, who had actually let his cigar go out; his anxiety for his friend had made him forget even the delights of good tobacco.

"Well, the way it happened was this," proceeded Eric, drawing intricate geometrical designs with the ferrule of his walking-stick on the gravel at his feet. "About a fortnight ago I saw the advertisement regarding the practice, and wrote about it. The holder is in bad health, and sent word back that it brought in over twenty-five hundred dollars a year, and was worth eight thousand dollars, but that he'd take twenty-five hundred dollars from an immediate purchaser if he could get one."

"So you agreed?" queried Hardcastle.

"Yes," replied Kenlis.

"And paid cash down?"

"I sent off the check the next day. Well, my dear fellow," Eric continued deprecatingly, as Gregory's face looked anything but encouraging, "if I had not made up my mind at once, the other fellow would have got the practice. If I had gone to Birmingham to inspect the books, my reading would have been thrown out of gear. If I had kept the money, I might have been tempted into spending some of it, and, once I had done that, all hope, for this year at least, would have been over."

"All hope of what?" asked Gregory, though he knew pretty well what the answer would be.

"Well—of getting married this year," answered Eric, a little shamefacedly.

"Ah, that's it! Well, humph! I suppose I must congratulate you! You've got through a lot of work in a short time at all events—that's more than every one can say!"

Gregory did not like to question his friend too closely as to his private affairs, but he would have liked to ask if the girl had money, who she was, and so forth.

"When is it to be?" he inquired presently.

"'It'? What do you mean?" Kenlis demanded, reddening a little.

"Your wedding, of course!"

"Oh, in about three weeks."

Gregory Hardcastle threw up his hands in amazement.

"I always said you were the most reckless, impetuous fellow I ever met. Come on! I don't know whether love takes your appetite away, but I need something to eat at once." And he strode off.

◆

More than two hundred years ago the well-known lines were written:

"Heaven has no rage like love to hatred turned,
Nor hell a fury like a woman scorned,"

and the words are as true of the women of the nineteenth as they were of those of the seventeenth century.

Miss Harriet Steet had not been scorned; indeed, the man upon whom she had set her love was not even aware of that fact. But the affection she undoubtedly bore Eric turned to virulent hatred when she found that he, whom she had endeavored to attract by various smiles and graces, had not only been utterly oblivious of them, but had actually engaged himself to a minx of seventeen! That the "minx" was her own cousin made no difference, unless in the way of making her hatred more bitter.

Beatrice Somerville had always been a source of irritation to Miss Steet. Beatrice's pretty face vexed that young lady vastly; so did Miss Somerville's blue and white muslin gowns, as serge would, Harriet argued, have been more useful and would never want washing. Even the plain, coarse straw hats Beatrice wore—and they were as plain and coarse as they well could be—were an eyesore and an abomination to Miss Steet, for under them her cousin's fair face looked so innocent.

For twelve months Harriet Steet had been keeping house for her grandfather. Before that time she had seen little and thought less of him, and Mr. Burton's domestic arrangements had been managed partly by an old servant, Marjory, and partly by Beatrice, who had lived with him since her babyhood, when she had been left in his charge by her dying mother, herself a young widow.

In all these years Miss Steet's family had thought little of old Mr. Burton. He was a commonplace man, being only a retired contractor, and their status, in the eyes of their neighbors, was not raised by the relationship. He was living in a dull, out-of-the-world place, on a small annuity, which died with him. This probably was the most uninteresting fact about him, for, living as he did, he would have nothing in the shape of money to leave behind him. So neither old Mr. Burton nor Beatrice Somerville was taken any notice of by the nearest relatives that they had in the world.

◆

A sudden change, however, came over the aspect of affairs.

"John Burton's two sons have just been killed in a railway accident in Santiago!" exclaimed Mr. Thomas Steet, Harriet's father—a struggling solicitor in a small county town—one morning.

He had been reading the newspaper to himself while at breakfast—indeed, he literally devoured it with his toast, coffee and eggs—quite undisturbed by the cackle which Harriet and her sisters and mother kept up all the time.

"Dear me! How awful!" ejaculated Mrs. Steet.

"How shocking!" "Poor fellows!" and "When did it happen?"

Such were the observations that fell from the lips of Harriet's sisters, but she herself

FRONT PAGE OF *POST* ABOUT FOUR MONTHS AFTER IT WAS BOUGHT BY CURTIS

The founding date is displayed in the nameplate, as it had been for many years. This is the issue for January 22, 1898.

Volume 170, No. 31

FIVE CENTS A COPY
$2.00 a Year in Advance

# THE SATURDAY EVENING POST

## Founded A.D. 1728

In 1729 this paper was purchased by Benjamin Franklin, and published by him as "The Pennsylvania Gazette" until 1765, when it passed into other hands. On August 4, 1821, the present title was adopted, and the office of publication was the one occupied by Benjamin Franklin, in the rear of 53 Market Street, Philadelphia.

Philadelphia, Saturday, January 29, 1898

Copyright, 1898, by The Curtis Publishing Company — PUBLISHED WEEKLY AT 425 ARCH STREET — Entered at the Philadelphia Post-Office as Second-Class Matter

## *Doctor Langdon's Dilemma*

*BETWEEN FRIENDSHIP AND LOVE*

*By Kate Erskine*

THE Doctor was very busy that evening, more so than usual; there had been an epidemic of measles in the town among the children, and to use Parson Brown's expression, "Providence has seen fit to grievously afflict us." The Parson was a thoroughly good man, none better, but he had acquired the habit of laying everything to Providence, and if one should have ventured to speak to him of natural laws, or to have reminded him that the disease in question was brought into town by Mrs. Stimpson's little niece, and possibly not sent directly from above, he would have questioned that person's religious principles, or at least thought him not strictly orthodox. But finally the last visit was made, the last little patient relieved, with cheery assurances of a speedy recovery, and the Doctor sprang into his buggy, turned the horse's head toward home, and gave him the rein.

•

It was a beautiful evening; the moon shining clear and full, causing the trees to cast their shadows weird and fantastic across the road, and the mountain plainly visible in the distance. The Doctor, leaning in a corner of the carriage with the reins loosely held in his hand, sat buried in thought. He had much to think of—every good physician has, and his whole heart and soul were in his work.

But this evening they were bent in another direction: old associations were flooding his memory, causing his pulse to beat now slow, now fast, and once a great wave of color passed over his face; he put up his hand as if to conceal it, although there was no one to see. The stars still twinkled cheerily, and the moon now put forth an increase of brightness, which seemed to wrap him alone in its tender light. And so he was carried along until the sudden stopping of the horse and Allan Wycoff's voice roused him from his reverie.

It was a warm welcome that passed between the two men: only a few words, but the strong grasp of the hand and look of confidence told volumes. It spoke of the long friendship of the past, and faith in the present, notwithstanding the years that had intervened since they last met.

Such strong natures as these two had always change as they approach middle life; it is not until they have mingled freely with the world, used it, been used by it; tasted the sorrows as well as the joys of life that they feel at liberty to say, "I think this," or, "I have made up my mind to that," and even then with the air of the taught—never of the teacher. For is not life a continual study, an inspiration? This being the belief and doctrine of both, it was with a considerable degree of curiosity and interest that they looked for the developments sure to take place during the summer months they were to pass together.

"You remember, Allan, that I have often written you of the Sherwins who live here, and of a few of our people who meet at the Sherwins' once a week to have what we term 'a literary evening.' Well, this is the regular night, and I want you to go and get acquainted with those who will form your immediate circle while here."

•

Dr. Langdon spoke these words with some hesitation, and when his friend had accepted, and they were driving toward their destination, there was the same undercurrent of doubt in his thoughts.

Had it been a wise move after all on his part, this urging his friend to pass the summer with him? Was there sufficient to interest and divert the mind of a man accustomed to such different surroundings, and would the pleasure of having this companion of his youth with him counterbalance his anxiety of mind?

Let us take a look at them while they are busily talking, and first as to their appearance. The moon is just touching Allan Wycoff's face. Five feet nine in height, broad-shouldered and lithe, the kind of man who appears to equal advantage in a tennis or dress suit. Medium complexion, inclining toward the dark; gray, restless eyes, and brown wavy hair and mustache. A strong light shows that the hair is slightly streaked with gray; but that is not always a sign of age, and Allan Wycoff carries his thirty-six years with the youthfulness of air that marked him ten or more years before.

•

Doctor Langdon is a decided contrast to his friend. Two inches taller when standing perfectly straight—but that he seldom does, having a slight stoop, but without being round-shouldered—he is also broad, and somewhat stouter. Very fair hair and close-cut beard, not of the auburn shade, but the silvery, which has the darker skin, and now that he is tanned, makes it appear still darker. His eyes are a deep blue; quiet eyes, with a kindly light in them. This summer he will be thirty-eight.

These men had always known one another, first as little fellows at school where they fought for and against each other—in short, conducted themselves as most small boys do, without exactly knowing why they liked or felt drawn toward one another—but as they grew up and entered college this uncertain feeling strengthened into the strongest of friendships, marked with a thorough respect for the views and sentiments of the other, to be accepted or repulsed as his light showed, but never to be scoffed at.

After leaving college Allan Wycoff studied law, and passed his examination for the Bar in such a manner as to cause the old lawyers to shake their heads and warrant him great success in his profession; and this prophecy he had thus far fulfilled, for at the present time he is a lawyer of growing reputation in New York with an already large practice. This summer, however, feeling the need of a long rest, he had come into the country.

•

Doctor Langdon commenced his practice in Brooklyn, but before the second winter was passed the severe winds warned him that he could not stand the climate and must go elsewhere. How he came to be still in that "heathenish place in the mountains," as his friends called it, after ten years had passed and his health was fully established, was a problem they could not solve; indeed, they had given it up long ago, but a few knew part of his reason for remaining, and suspected the rest. This was, that before the two years had passed which he had pledged himself to remain, he felt convinced that here lay his life-work. In this little mountainous town, surrounded by so many others like it, needing and longing for the services of a good physician—yes, here he would spend the rest of his days, driving over the hills and through the valleys, bringing life to this one and comfort to that one to whom it had been denied.

This decision had not been an easy one. If Doctor Langdon had been enough of a recluse to feel that, outside of his practice, his only wish was to spend his time in study, such a place would have made but little difference to him, but with a social nature craving congenial company when it often could not be had, there must, in consequence, be a great void felt.

The horse stopped before a farmhouse by the side of the road. The clear night showed Wycoff that it was quite large, white, with green blinds, and the light shining from the windows gave it a cheerful, home-like look.

It was a pleasant sight that met their eyes as they entered the room where the others were gathered. Mrs. Sherwin, in furnishing the farmhouse for the summer home, had endeavored to do so in the simplest manner possible and yet give it an attractive, home-like appearance. This she had succeeded in doing with straw mattings, bright rugs, wicker furniture, and other little contrivances for comfort. On the evening in question, the weather being quite cool, a bright wood fire burned in the large open fireplace.

"It is so pleasant sitting around the fire," said Mrs. Sherwin as she conducted the two gentlemen into the room, "that I told the others we would not light the lamps until your arrival."

"And what have we done that we should be deprived of that pleasure? Let us enjoy it for a few minutes," said the Doctor, smiling on his assembled friends.

"Very well, we will postpone lighting them for a while if Mr. Wycoff will allow me to treat his introduction to these people in the same way, for if I should attempt it now there would have to be a repetition or a most confused medley of names and people would exist in his mind. In the meantime Di will find a seat for him beside her."

"Di," she said, turning to her daughter who now approached, "I want to introduce you to Mr. Wycoff; it will devolve on you first to make him feel he is still among the civilized. And you, Doctor," she continued with a laugh, "I shall allow to do as you please."

•

If it could be said that there was one chair any more comfortable than the others in the room, it was the one Di placed for Mr. Wycoff by the side of the chimney, a little back, so that his face was shaded, but several of the others he could see quite clearly. Wycoff wondered whether this was intentional on her part; if it were not a little feminine manœuvring brought about that he might satisfy any curiosity he might have as to their looks before he knew their names. But, however that might be, he felt well satisfied with his position, and leaning back in his chair became lost in a dreamy reverie of his surroundings—an unusual condition for him to be in, but the long journey in the cars, followed by the evening drive with the breeze blowing full in his face, had produced a soothing effect—and he was well content now to remain quiet and only think, while his glance wandered around the pleasant room, resting occasionally on the faces near him.

And so he had really entered Jack's life at last—dear old Jack! And into one of its brightest spots, too, for he knew how he always anticipated the family's coming in the spring; well, he would do all he could while he was with him to make the summer unusually pleasant. Why, it almost seemed as if they were boys again; by putting up his hand he could shut those strangers off from view and only see him on the other side of the fireplace, just as they used to sit at college. Mrs. Sherwin seemed pleasant. "A little loquacious," perhaps, but it was too soon to judge. "And Di?" He did not remember that there was a young lady in the family, but there was a little girl—could it be?—why, of course, he was always forgetting that he was not the only one growing old. This was the little girl he used to hear about, now grown into a charming young lady without doubt. He wondered——

•

"Mr. Wycoff, did you find your journey to our little village a long and tiresome one?"

Wycoff roused himself, and answered the question put to him by the young lady of his thoughts with the unpleasantly conscious feeling that she had been reading them and that he had been rude in not noticing her before.

"I wonder," she continued, "how you are going to like up here—not only the place, but us—that is, I mean," with a little laugh, "everybody in this room, for we are a regular 'We, Us & Co.'"

"And the Co., I hope," Wycoff returned, "will now include my name."

"Oh, yes, but you do not want to do anything rash; remember you will be held liable. Now, with a full understanding of the risk you run, do you still wish to join us?"

Wycoff signified that even after this warning he had made up his mind to join them.

Only a little passing fun on both sides, enjoyed by each, and then forgotten by one, perhaps: yes, but by the other to be remembered long afterward when its full significance was understood.

The lamps were brought in and placed at either end of the room, the shades to the windows drawn, and fresh logs thrown on the fire. The ladies took out their fancy-work, drew up around the tables, and commenced a little conversation in a low voice among themselves on the usual domestic topics. They did not mind the interruption, however, when Mrs. Sherwin brought Mr. Wycoff up to be introduced; in fact, what woman does object, be she young or old, married or single, to meeting a fine-looking man, fresh from the best the world affords, and with its flavor still pervading his air and conversation.

"Mrs. Allyn, of Boston, Mr. Wycoff; Miss Howard, of the same city; Mme. Vandeville; Mr. Platt," and so on, in the usual perfunctory manner of society introductions.

•

Mr. Wycoff seated himself beside Mrs. Allyn, thinking as he did so that she was very attractive, and so she certainly was. No one denied it, not even the lady herself. So it was taken quite as a matter of course that Allan Wycoff should seat himself beside her. Miss Howard surveyed them across the table; good old Mme. Vandeville gave a satisfied purr—a queer little noise she always made when well content—and smoothed down the folds of her one black silk. She had known Edith Allyn for twenty years and had loved her with a strong love. It was a pretty sight always to see them together, for Edith returned with equal ardor the warm affection of her old teacher.

"My friends," called out the hostess at this point, "the hour of grace has extended itself this evening thirty minutes—Mr. Wycoff, we hold you responsible for that. It is now nine o'clock, and I move that we proceed to business," and she handed a copy of Browning's Poems to the Doctor. "The Doctor does not enjoy Browning very much," she explained to Mr. Wycoff, "so we think it very good of him to read his poems to us, but before long we shall read something he does like and so try to repay him."

It was a refreshing sight, when she had concluded, to see Mr. Platt come forward, take a chair, and place it directly in front of the reader, determined to do his duty, at least, as a listener.

But this trait was only one of the many that were peculiar in the character of Mr. Platt. He wore, for instance, the same clothes summer and winter; not meaning, literally, that he never replaced them by new ones, but they were always of the same texture—heavy broadcloth—and his boots of the thickest. He had evidently given this subject of dress a great deal of consideration, for ever since he was a young man (and he was now sixty-five) he had never changed it.

Mr. Platt was the brother of Mrs. Stimpson, at whose house Doctor Langdon lived and where the others boarded in summer. He had gone to the city when quite a boy, and by dint of close application to business had amassed a snug little fortune. Every summer, on the first day of July, he came up to Jenkins' Centre, and remained until the twenty-fifth of September; he had made up his mind that was the correct and fashionable time to be away, and so never deviated from it. Everybody liked him for his sterling qualities, overlooking his little weaknesses, so he was always invited to Mrs. Sherwin's with the others, especially as his great desire to be literary had caused him to think he really was inclined that way, besides possessing the critical faculty in a high degree.

It took a reader of strong nerves not to quail as he sat before him with folded arms and a sternly judicial look in his eye. The Doctor confessed that the cold chills ran all over him if he happened to catch his eye, but he usually avoided it.

•

The evening passed very pleasantly, all entering with interest into the discussion of the different conceptions of the poem, and none with more than Di Sherwin. Wycoff thought her very charming, and Browning seemed rather more interesting than he had ever found him before; he would make it a point to read more of his poetry.

On the ride home the Doctor said that he wished he cared more for poetry, and his face wore a puzzled, uncertain expression.

[TO BE CONTINUED]

FRONT PAGE OF THE *POST* ONE WEEK LATER: IT HAS PICKED UP 93 YEARS

The founding date has been changed to introduce Franklin as a kind of patron saint of the *Post*. See pages 682–685.

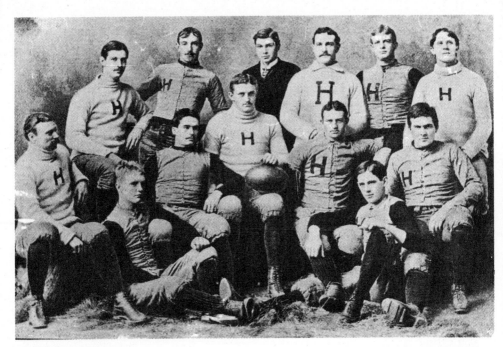

YALE AND HARVARD FOOTBALL TEAMS OF 1889

From *St. Nicholas Magazine*, December 1889. See pages 374–376.

others, as will be explained. Moreover, there is a real, though tenuous, connection between the two papers.

The *Pennsylvania Gazette* was founded in 1728 by Samuel Keimer, purchased the next year by Benjamin Franklin and Hugh Meredith, and published from 1732 to 1748 by Franklin alone. In 1748 Franklin formed a partnership with David Hall, who became sole owner when Franklin withdrew entirely from the printing business in 1766. David Hall, his partners, and his sons and grandsons and their partners conducted the *Gazette* until it was discontinued in 1815.[23] Thereafter a third David Hall, grandson of Franklin's partner, continued to conduct a printing business in the plant "back of 53 Market Street," and for that purpose took in Samuel C. Atkinson as partner. David Hall died in 1821,[24] and a few months later Atkinson formed a partnership with Charles Alexander to found the *Saturday Evening Post*. To that partnership Alexander brought the list of subscribers he had secured from the poet Coffin, and Atkinson brought his interest in the old *Gazette* printing plant. Atkinson had not been associated in the management of the *Gazette*; whether he was ever a printer on that paper is pure conjecture.

Thus the only connection of the *Post* with the *Pennsylvania Gazette* or its illustrious early editor was the fact that it was first published from the shop in which the *Gazette* had perished six years before, and one of its founders had been a partner of the grandson of Franklin's partner, in a printing business.

The *Post* was published for considerably more than half a century before it occurred to any of its managers that it might make capital out of the Franklin name. In 1870–1872, Eugene H. Munday, editor of a trade paper published by a firm of type founders, wrote for that paper, called the *Proof Sheet*, a series of articles about Philadelphia newspapers and periodicals, including one that set forth very well the history of the *Saturday Evening Post*.[25] This article was reprinted in the *Post* the next year, with due credit, as a part of the *Post's* observance of its fiftieth anniversary; then it was reprinted again, with no credit whatever but with very little abridgment, in Scharf and Westcott's big three-volume *History of Philadelphia*, published in 1884. All this was harm-

[23] See Clarence S. Brigham, *History and Bibliography of American Newspapers* (Worcester, 1947), v. 2, p. 934. The final issue, for Oct. 11, 1915, is to be found in the files of the Historical Society of Pennsylvania and the Rutgers College Library. In it is a statement that the paper would probably be resumed in May, but there is no record whatever of any such resumption or of any continuation of the *Pennsylvania Gazette* after Oct. 11, 1815.

[24] See obituary notice, *American Daily Advertiser*, May 29, 1821.

[25] Citations of this important article are given in footnote 1, *supra*, under "References." The *Proof Sheet* was a bimonthly (Philadelphia, 1867–82), half of its 16 pages devoted to advertising the Collins & McLeester type foundry.

less thus far; but Scharf and Westcott, or one of their compilers, seem to have assumed that when Munday named Hall & Atkinson as "successors to" the former publishers of the *Pennsylvania Gazette,* and said they "carried on the printing business" at the old stand, he meant that they continued to print the *Gazette;* and so, in writing the section about the *Gazette* for their omnibus history, they said that the old Franklin paper was continued by Hall & Atkinson "after 1815 or 1816" (which was entirely false), and that following David Hall's death in 1821 it "survived to Mr. Atkinson," who formed a partnership with Charles Alexander and started a new weekly "on the venerable foundation of the *Pennsylvania Gazette* . . . to which they gave the name of the *Saturday Evening Post.*"[26] Munday, whose article presumably gave rise to this story, had not connected Atkinson with the publication of the *Gazette* at all: he had said that David Hall "inherited the remains of the old *Pennsylvania Gazette* office," and that Hall & Atkinson "carried on the printing business in the office once occupied by Benjamin Franklin."

But once set forth in a respectable historical work, the story of the continuity of the *Gazette* and the *Post* was bound to gain currency. Paul Leicester Ford wrote a little article called "History of a Newspaper" for the *Magazine of American History*[27] based on the Scharf and Westcott version of the *Pennsylvania Gazette's* story. Eventually Andrew Smythe, publisher of the *Post,* picked it up, and advertised his paper as follows: "Originally established by Benjamin Franklin in 1728, and appearing in its present character in 1821, it has had an uninterrupted career of 162 years."[28]

Thus the Franklin legend was ready-made to the hand of Curtis when he bought the *Saturday Evening Post* in 1897. A great advertiser and promoter, he made the most of it. The story was told and retold with added flourishes, most notably by William Perrine in the *Post* for May 28, 1898. Never an issue since 1898 has appeared without the name of Franklin as founder, and 1728 has thus become the best-known date in the history of American periodicals. The *Post* type, first cut for the name plate and headings of the magazine, was supposed to be modeled upon, or at least to remind the reader of, the typography of Franklin and his newspaper; it became so popular with other papers and magazines that the *Post* in a few years was claiming that it had "brought about a typographical revolution."[29]

[26] J. Thomas Scharf and Thompson Westcott, *History of Philadelphia, 1609–1884* (Philadelphia, 1884), v. 3, p. 1987.

[27] *Magazine of American History,* v. 15, p. 452, May 1886.

[28] Advertisement of the *Post* in N. W. Ayer & Son's *American Newspaper Annual,* 1891, p. 1330.

[29] *Saturday Evening Post,* v. 173, Jan. 26, 1901, p. 14.

But Franklin gave the rejuvenated *Post* something more than a promotional symbol and a slogan; he gave it a goal and a standard. In an editorial boasting of its increase in circulation to three hundred thousand in January 1901, it added this declaration of faith: "When the *Post* gets closer to the standard of Benjamin Franklin, it will have a million circulation." [30] And as we trace the development of the periodical under Lorimer, it will be evident that, consciously or unconsciously, large portions of the plain common sense, homely democracy, shrewd pragmatism, and faith in the recognized virtues which we think of as characteristic of Franklin have been consistently worked into the editorial pattern of the *Saturday Evening Post*. One of the severest critics of the *Post,* Benjamin Stolberg, once pursued an analogy between Franklin and Lorimer interestingly and at length.[31] In following such a parallelism, one soon senses the approach to absurdity, however: Lorimer was certainly not the representative of a new Age of Enlightenment to twentieth-century America.

But the *Post* was under Curtis ownership seventeen months before Lorimer became its editor. In that term it published such things as Theodore Roosevelt's "Hunting on the Little Missouri," a piece by General A. W. Greeley on arctic exploration, and Morgan Robertson's realistic sea stories; but there was much more material which fitted the *Ladies' Home Journal* formula — "At Home With" articles on Queen Victoria, Rosa Bonheur, Marie Corelli, Prince Bismarck, Jules Verne; "Courtships of our Presidents," "Favorite Works of Famous Authors," and "Men and Women of the Time"; essays by Cardinal Gibbons and Theodore L. Cuyler, a good deal of travel, and many short stories. The most distinguished serial was Harold Frederic's "The Market-Place." Other contributors of fiction were Will N. Harben, Ian Maclaren, Francis S. Saltus, Grant Allen, Sarah Grand, Stanley J. Weyman, Arthur Morrison, Emerson Hough, Octave Thanet, Will Allen White, Robert J. Burdette, and "Josiah Allen's Wife" — a real galaxy of popular writers of the late nineties. There was also some eclectic material from books, magazines, and even newspapers. In short, a great quantity of good material was going into the *Post* from week to week; but it had no plan or pattern. It was on its way, but it did not know where.

The illustration improved. There was some trial of pictures from posed photographs, but these were soon supplanted by halftones of wash drawings by good artists, such as Alice Barber Stephens and Harrison Fisher. By the summer of 1898 no page was without excellent illustration.

[30] *Ibid.*
[31] Benjamin Stolberg, "Merchant in Letters," in *Outlook,* v. 155, pp. 83–84, May 21, 1930.

The subscription rate was raised in February 1898 from two dollars to two and a half, the single-copy price remaining what it had been since the beginning — five cents. *Collier's* and *Leslie's* each sold for ten cents; but Curtis, who had made a great contribution to the cause of cheap periodicals by the maintenance of his ten-cent price for a high-grade woman's monthly, was now to show what could be done with a quality nickel weekly. But the immediate response was disappointing. The faithful two thousand or so who comprised the *Post* subscription list when Curtis bought the paper had liked the long melodramatic serials that had been its staple fare, and many of them dropped away as the changes were made, until in June 1898 only twelve hundred were left. But in that month a strong circulation drive on the basis of an 1899 prospectus was begun, and by the end of the year the list had reached two hundred and fifty thousand [32] — a figure far beyond anything the *Post* had ever before known.

Curtis was dissatisfied, however, with the unsure, groping editorial policy of his weekly. He had an editor of genius for his monthly, and he felt that he must have comparable editorial strength at the head of the *Post* if it was to be a success. He had been much impressed with the work of Arthur Sherburne Hardy during the two years when that versatile genius edited the *Cosmopolitan,* and now decided to get him for the *Post.* But Hardy had recently accepted an appointment as minister to Persia and was at Teheran. Curtis got in touch with him, however, and made an appointment to meet him in Paris in the spring of 1899. Then Hardy's portfolio was suddenly changed to Greece, and he was unable to keep his date with Curtis; but by that time Curtis had found another editor right at home.

The man he found was George Horace Lorimer, a young Boston newspaperman, son of a famous Baptist preacher of that city. Thirty-one years old, Lorimer had had a year at Yale and another at Colby; and he had worked for three or four years in Armour's packing plant in Chicago, becoming assistant manager of the canning department. But he wanted to write and to be associated with writers; and when he learned that Curtis was looking for help for his newly acquired *Saturday Evening Post,* he applied, had an interview, and was hired as a "literary editor." Before Curtis left for Europe to see Hardy, he let Jordan go and put Lorimer, who had then been on the *Post* staff for two or three months, in temporary charge. Lorimer made the most of this trial period, and Curtis liked the young man's work so well that soon after he returned from his trip abroad he installed Lorimer as editor-in-chief.

Two factors made Cyrus H. K. Curtis America's most successful

[32] *Saturday Evening Post,* v. 171, p. 376, Dec. 10, 1898.

magazine publisher. First, he showed remarkable ability in choosing his editors; and once chosen and their trial periods passed, those editors were given virtually complete carte blanche. If Bok asked him a question about some editorial problem, Curtis would say, "I don't know. Why should I?" It was the perfect answer for a publisher. "I was one of his editors for thirty years," said Bok, "and not once in all that time was I made to feel that his authority was greater than mine. Not a single time did he try to influence my editorial judgment."[33] Once in the early years of Lorimer's service on the *Post*, Curtis remarked in regard to a story in the current issue, "My wife doesn't think it's a very good piece to be in the *Post*." Lorimer replied, "I'm not editing the *Post* for your wife." Curtis turned away without saying more; shortly thereafter he raised Lorimer's salary to two hundred and fifty dollars a week.[34]

Bok quotes Curtis as saying, "Get the right editor and you'll have the right magazine. Then it's only a selling proposition."[35] This points to the second factor in Curtis' success: he was a bold and brilliant advertiser and promoter. Once given a popular editorial formula for the *Ladies' Home Journal,* he poured money into newspaper advertising and into a country-wide local selling organization until he had given that magazine the premier circulation in the country, with an astounding advertising patronage. Most observers doubted whether he could repeat that success with a nickel weekly; but repeat it he did, in almost precisely the same pattern. Biographer Bok dramatizes the story. He tells how money was poured into the *Post* in the years at the turn of the century,[36] despite the fears of all Curtis' assistant managers, until he had lost eight hundred thousand dollars on the paper; how he then remarked to his distraught treasurer that he had two hundred thousand to go before his losses reached a million and proceeded to plan an advertising campaign in that amount; how indications then appeared that a turn was coming, and he tossed in another quarter-million dollars; how success then came "with such a rush that the presses could scarcely keep up with the demand."[37]

The story is substantially true, but it oversimplifies the record of the *Post's* growth. We shall try in the next few paragraphs to correlate a description of the paper's editorial policies with the story of its growth in circulation and advertising.

What Lorimer brought to the *Post*, even before he was officially

---

[33] Bok, *A Man From Maine*, p. 165.
[34] Tebbel, *Lorimer and the Post*, p. 25.
[35] Bok, *A Man From Maine*, p. 169.
[36] According to *Printer's Ink*, v. 30, Jan. 10, 1900, p. 36, Curtis had spent $1.50 for each of the 200,000 subscribers and buyers he had found for the *Post* by the end of 1899.
[37] Bok, *A Man From Maine*, pp. 159–62.

named as editor, was a resolution to part company with the other Curtis publication: he was resolved that the *Post* should not be a weekly *Ladies' Home Journal*. Logical as that decision now seems, it was then nothing less than astounding. The *Journal* formula had been immensely successful; it was tried and reliable. The *Saturday Evening Post* had always been a home-and-family paper; its subtitle up to the time Lorimer took over was "The Great Pioneer Family Paper of America." But Lorimer made it definitely a man's magazine. Of course, it was expected that some women would read it; and perhaps they read it, even during its first decade under Lorimer, as much as men did; but the chief themes of the new periodical were chosen for their appeal to ambitious young men of the great middle-class American public.

The editorial plan on the basis of which the *Saturday Evening Post*, in the opening years of the twentieth century, achieved one of the outstanding successes in the history of American magazines was not a strict formula; but its elements are easily recognizable. First and foremost, there was an emphasis on three types of subject matter — business, public affairs, and romance. These overlapped and mingled. Thus business articles tended to emphasize the romance of large fortunes and the rise of a young man from the bottom of the ladder to the topmost rung of millionaireship; discussions of public affairs tended to stress current ideas for control of trusts and government handling of large sums of money; and even the romantic fiction was often based on financial deals and the pursuit of wealth. All three of these themes were so handled as to emphasize personalities to a remarkable degree. And there was more variety than the foregoing analysis suggests; such factors as sports, humor, science, photography, the theater, literature, and foreign affairs had notable parts in the program, perhaps more or less in an order of importance as listed. But the three elements named — business, public affairs, romance — dominated the subject matter and ideology of the magazine.

Of the three, business is properly named first. Business success was the most interesting subject in the world to the young man of the turn of the century, except perhaps for a bout with romance in the spring of the year; it fitted the mood of what Senator Beveridge called in an article in the *Post* "this money-age." [38] The *Post* became the prophet of business success in its articles, its stories, and its advertisements; also it practiced what it preached and became itself a great example and exemplar of success.

For the first year of Lorimer's editorship, the public affairs theme was rather more prominent than that of business. Grover Cleveland,

[38] *Saturday Evening Post*, v. 178, Nov. 18, 1905, p. 5.

Thomas B. Reed, and Albert J. Beveridge were contributors of series of articles; and there was a Washington column written by that old *Sun* man and long-time congressman, Amos J. Cummings. But there were also such articles as "Our New Prosperity," by Frank A. Vanderlip; "Getting and Keeping a Business Position," by Robert C. Ogden; and, in the annual "College Man's Number" for 1899, "Why Young Men Fail," by Roswell Miller and others. There was a roll of good contributors of fiction, including Hamlin Garland, Charles G. D. Roberts, Morgan Robertson, Robert Herrick, Bret Harte, and Arthur Stringer. Robert W. Chambers was a stand-by. There were few serial stories, but several excellent series of articles presenting recollections of men distinguished in various fields, as Julian Ralph's "The Making of a Journalist," J. B. Pond's reminiscences of a lyceum manager entitled "Eccentricities of Genius," and Alexander K. McClure's political reminiscences.

In 1900 there was a series on railway management by top railway executives; Frank G. Carpenter wrote a sequence on business conditions in the Orient; there was another called "American Kings and Their Kingdoms," which dealt with Astor, Rockefeller, and others, and finally one on "How I Made My First Thousand Dollars" by various successful men. The business theme was emerging; but there was much variety, with departments of current events, public personalities, book reviews, and poetry "of the sort that workaday men and women can understand." Serials were by Hall Caine, Gilbert Parker, and Cyrus Townsend Brady; short stories by Rudyard Kipling, Stephen Crane, Joel Chandler Harris, Jerome K. Kerome, Charles Egbert Craddock, and so on. There were an occasional supplement for amateur photographers, some articles on sports, and a series on famous actors of the past by stage stars of the present.

Illustration improved, with the work of Henry Hutt, the Leyendeckers, Harrison Fisher, George Gibbs, and others. The first colored cover came on September 30, 1899, and thereafter there was about one a month until they became the rule in 1903.

But the *Post's* circulation seemed to stick at the two hundred and fifty thousand that it had reached shortly after the editorial changes of 1898. Even lowering the annual subscription rate to a dollar in the fall of 1900 did not help much. Advertising also lagged. Eight pages in a thirty-two page issue represented the high point for the ad men until the pre-Christmas number of 1900, when they made it fourteen pages out of thirty-six. The *Post* and *Journal* had just moved into a new eight-story building and installed ten new presses.

It was in 1901 that the theme of business success really became dominant in the *Post's* editorial policy. James J. Hill wrote on "Young Men and Speculation," Sir Thomas Lipton on "The Lipton System of Business," President William R. Harper on "The Business Side of a University," Mayor Charles A. Schieren on "Why Young Men Should Begin at the Bottom." "Why Millionaires Can't Stop Making Money" was a little symposium by financial leaders telling why they did not retire. In 1902 this emphasis was even stronger. Senator Beveridge did a series on "Winning the Markets of the Orient," in which he predicted the Russo-Japanese War and its outcome; Paul Latzke wrote on "The Unknown Captains of Industry" and "The High-Rolling Steel Rollers — Plutocrats of Labor"; a Wall Street broker told "How J. Pierpont Morgan Does Business"; David Graham Phillips entered the pages of the *Post* with a "Pen Picture of George W. Perkins"; William T. Stead had a series on "Money Kings of the World," and Forrest Crissey wrote on "Sons of American Millionaires." And these are only high spots.

Quite as striking was the development on the fiction side. Henry Kitchell Webster and Samuel Merwin contributed their "Calumet K: A Romance of the Great Wheat Corner" to the *Post* in 1901. It made a hit with readers, and was followed by Webster's "The Copper King" the next year. In the fall of that year appeared Frank Norris' "The Pit," second in the author's trilogy dealing with wheat, later a great success as a book and a play. Even more important to the *Post* was Lorimer's own contribution to 1901–1902 issues, "Letters of a Self-Made Merchant to His Son," a series of witty, down-to-earth, Franklinian essays about business and life. Both this series and *The Pit* were in the *Bookman's* list of the ten best-selling books of 1903.

There was some poetry, too, in the *Post* in these early Lorimer years. Edwin Markham's work was occasionally featured. John J. Ingalls' "Opportunity" appeared in the number for January 13, 1900. Paul Laurence Dunbar, Frank L. Stanton, Bliss Carman, Richard Hovey, Madison Cawein, Clinton Scollard, and Guy Wetmore Carryl were *Post* poets.

In the fall of 1901 *Post* circulation at last began a modest upward curve, reaching three hundred thousand; next year, with "The Pit" and the "Merchant's Letters," and with generous newspaper advertising, it continued to advance until it reached half a million early in 1903. Its own advertising soon reached twenty pages in occasional issues.

The year 1903 was a good one for the *Post* on both the editorial and the business sides. Jack London's "The Call of the Wild" (for which the author was paid seven hundred dollars), David Graham Phillips, "The Golden Fleece" (first of six *Post* serial stories by Phillips), and Lorimer's own "Old Gorgon Graham" (a sequel to the "Letters") were among the serials. Zona Gale, Harold McGrath, Alfred Henry Lewis, and Frank H. Spearman were other fiction writers. Paul Latzke and Robert Barr wrote series on modern advertising. Edwin Lefèvre began a long connection with the *Post* with his articles on "Wall Street and Prosperity." Arthur E. McFarlane told of the origin of great fortunes in a series, "Where the Money Came From." By the end of 1903 *Post* covers announced that circulation had passed six hundred thousand.

The *Post* had now found its stride editorially, the Curtis advertising campaign was going full blast, circulation was rising steadily, and there was confidence that the sales-resistance dam against big advertising in a cheap weekly would soon break. The boy-merchants who worked for the *Post* Friday afternoons and Saturdays now numbered six thousand and were scattered all over the country. Curtis always furnished a beginner his first week's supply of ten copies free, and paid good commissions and cash prizes. Letters of prize-winners were published; some were making fifteen dollars a week. Many a hustling boy found his first interest in business or journalism (or both) through selling the *Post* after school. Older boys worked for college scholarships by canvassing for annual subscriptions; more than a thousand such scholarships were awarded for 1903–1904. Also, the individual subscriber was given an incentive to get another reader by a special price of a dollar and a half in "clubs" of two. Thus by March 19, 1904, the *Post* was able to announce on its cover a circulation of seven hundred thousand. Next year the annual subscription price was juggled again, "club" rates were withdrawn, and the paper sold at a dollar and a half, or four years for five dollars.

The panic of 1907 slowed the *Post's* advance somewhat, but it had no effect on the rich editorial table that the editor spread. In the years 1904–1908 there were such serials as "The Eagle's Shadow," by James Branch Cabell; "Hurricane Island," by H. B. Marriott Watson; "Lady Baltimore," by Owen Wister; "Gaspar Ruiz," by Joseph Conrad; "The Cry of the Children," by Mrs. John Van Vorst; and others by Hamlin Garland, Robert W. Chambers, and so on. George Randolph Chester began his short stories of yeggmen and swindlers, and followed them with "Get Rich Quick Wallingford." Arthur Train began his "Tricks of the Trade" series in 1905; "Mr. Tutt" came a little later, in no less than eighty-three stories. Ephraim Tutt, says one commentator, became the best-known lawyer in America. When Train wrote an article for the *Post* of February 26, 1944, making it plain that Tutt was fiction and not fact, some readers would not believe it, and one wrote indignantly, "The fact is Mr. Tutt invented Train." [39]

[39] Butterfield, *Saturday Evening Post Treasury*, p. 250.

Will Payne wrote a series of articles from Washington in the first decade of the new century; and there was a department of gossip from the capital entitled "The Senator's Secretary," written but not signed by Samuel G. Blythe, who was destined to write for the *Post* for many years. William Allen White began his stories of life in Emporia, which were later published in the volume *In Our Town* in 1905. Booth Tarkington, Ernest Poole, O. Henry, George Fitch, Rex Beach, Emerson Hough, Lloyd Osbourne, and Edwin L. Sabin also contributed short stories. There was some humor in every issue; a "Sense and Nonsense" page began in 1906. Carolyn Wells contributed "The Rubáiyát of Wall Street" in 1908. Senator Beveridge was still preaching in 1907. In that year Isaac F. Marcosson, long to be a leading contributor, began his department "Your Savings." Illustration by A. B. Wenzell, F. R. Cruger, N. C. Wyeth, May Wilson Preston, Anton Otto Fischer, Charles Livingston Bull, and others was attractive. Harry Arthur Thompson, who joined the *Post* editorial staff in 1903, took over the art direction of the magazine 1906–1912.

On April 11, 1908, the *Post* cover announced a new high point in circulation at 905,400; and on December 19 of that year it blazoned forth the news: "More than a Million a Week Circulation." The long march to a million had been made in ten and a half years. Advertising answered the call of circulation, though slowly and reluctantly, and in 1909 the rate was raised to three thousand dollars a page.[40] The pre-Christmas number of 1909 carried thirty-three pages of "ads" in a sixty-four-page book; and a few months later, on April 2, 1910, in an issue of seventy-two pages and cover, there were forty-two pages of advertising.

In the years 1909–1913, the editorial policy of the *Post* had crystallized, had come to be regarded by many as more or less a fromula, and was strongly supported by a group of able contributors.

The pattern had been changed somewhat from that which had been set by Lorimer ten years earlier. Then it had seemed necessary, in order to divorce *Post* policy from that of the *Ladies' Home Journal*, to make a dead-set at the young man and his interests. Even in fiction, virile writers such as Rudyard Kipling, Morgan Robertson, Gilbert Parker, Cy Warman, Cutcliffe Hyne, Stephen Crane, Rex Beach, and Jack London, had been prominent. Now there was more recognition of women readers. "Who says that the *Saturday Evening Post* is a magazine for men only?" asked an editorial in a summer number in 1908, and then boasted, "we number women readers not by tens but by hundreds of

[40] *Printer's Ink*, v. 66, p. 38, Jan. 6, 1909.

thousands." [41] Another variation in the pattern was a growing stress on humor. Lorimer had had this in mind from the first; now he was better able to realize his plan, with contributors like Irvin Cobb, Montague Glass, George Randolph Chester, George Fitch, Wallace Irwin, Ring Lardner, and many others (like Lorimer himself) who mixed into their contributions a large amount of humor, though not enough to make that element predominant. A third change was that which was apparent in the length of articles. At first, in a magazine of twenty-four pages, everything was almost necessarily short; now, with numbers fattening to eighty pages in some issues, need was increasingly felt for stories and articles that could "tail" through the advertising section in the back of the book. The result, at this time, was beneficial. "Nobody can really tell a story in less than three thousand words," Lorimer once remarked to Ben Ames Williams. "Maupassant did," said Williams. "Maupassant's dead," retorted Lorimer.[42]

The writers whom the editor had recruited as regular contributors were not bound to the *Post* by contract; Lorimer always insisted that each and every piece should be submitted on a free-lance basis. But favorite contributors knew that their work would be welcome. Thus a group of unofficial staff contributors grew up, under the stimulus of good pay (about five hundred dollars as a top short-story price) and mutual understanding of what was wanted. Mary Roberts Rinehart brought her "Tish" stories to the *Post* in 1909; and though she always insisted on her own rights as a free lancer, she wrote thereafter chiefly for the *Post* and *Journal*. In 1910 Corra Harris made the first of her many contributions to the *Post* — "A Circuit Rider's Wife." It was in 1909 that Montague Glass began his long series of funny stories about Potash & Perlmutter, partners in the New York cloak-and-suit trade. The first of George Fitch's stories of "Old Siwash" had appeared in 1906. A third humorist, Irvin S. Cobb, made his first contribution in 1912. George Randolph Chester and Arthur Train were already members of the group. Samuel G. Blythe, Isaac F. Marcosson, Will Payne, Edwin Lefèvre, and George Pattullo wrote regularly on politics, business, and world affairs, Marcosson and Pattullo spending most of their time abroad. Emerson Hough was a constant contributor on the American outdoors and conservation.

Meanwhile there were the continued stories of Robert W. Chambers (for the ladies?), as well as the more stinging serials of David Graham Phillips. The latter's "The Grain of Dust" was running in the *Post* in 1911, when the author was murdered on the street by a paranoiac

---

[41] *Saturday Evening Post*, v. 180, June 20, 1908, p. 1.
[42] Tebbel, *Lorimer and the Post*, p. 73.

who thought his sister had been maligned in one of Phillips' novels. G. K. Chesterton, Leonard Merrick, William J. Locke, and E. Phillips Oppenheim were four English authors who wrote much for the *Post* in these years. Tarkington serials appeared in 1912–1913. Other new names that were to grow familiar in the magazine's columns in these years were those of Charles E. Van Loan, Eugene Manlove Rhodes, Richard Matthews Hallett, Peter B. Kyne, and Melville Davisson Post.

In the years 1910–1913 there was an annual advance in circulation of about a quarter-million, and on December 20, 1913, the *Post* was able to print on its cover: "Circulation More Than Two Millions a Week." This was the greatest magazine circulation in the world [43] — considerably more than that of the *Ladies' Home Journal,* which offered its audience to advertisers only once a month. Advertising grew apace, the annual revenue from that source passing five million dollars in 1910 and doubling that by 1914. The first hundred-page number was issued for April 3, 1915; it contained sixty-nine pages of advertising. It is clear that the *Post* owed much of its growing success to the burgeoning automotive industry. The first auto advertisement in the *Post* was a modest inch-and-a-half announcement by W. E. Roach in the issue for March 31, 1900, headed "Automobiles That Give Satisfaction," and illustrated by a cut of an open runabout with right-hand, horizontal-bar steering, at a thousand dollars. The first full-page automobile advertisement in the *Post* was for a new Winton model in the issue for January 24, 1903. By 1915, about one-fourth of the advertising space in the *Post* was occupied by announcements of automobiles and their accessories. In the April 3 number, Chalmers and Overland each took two pages, and there were page ads for Ford, Maxwell, Hupmobile, Cole, Detroit Electric, and Milburn Light Electric. Next to automotive advertising ranked that for clothes, food, cameras, insurance, patent razors, and books; this was about the order of advertised articles in the *Post* during the first two decades under Curtis. No advertising was accepted for liquors, cigarettes, or patent medicines.

It may be instructive to examine the content of this epochal hundred-page Easter issue for April 3, 1915. There was an Easter cover in two colors by Leyendecker, showing a cherub in top hat with a bouquet of

---

[43] *Woman's World*, Chicago, and *Fashion Book*, New York, also claimed somewhat over 2,000,000, but they were mail-order monthlies at 35¢ a year. Frank Presbrey, in *The History and Development of Advertising* (New York, 1929), p. 483, gives a table of five-year records of the *Post*:

| Year | Avg. Circ. | Advtg. Revenue | Year | Avg. Circ. | Advtg. Revenue |
|---|---|---|---|---|---|
| 1897 | 2,231 | $ 6,933 | 1917 | 1,883,070 | $16,076,562 |
| 1902 | 314,671 | 360,175 | 1922 | 2,187,024 | 28,278,755 |
| 1907 | 726,681 | 1,266,931 | 1927 | 2,816,391 | 53,144,987 |
| 1912 | 1,920,550 | 7,114,581 | | | |

flowers. Clarence F. Underwood, Harvey Dunn, and Henry Raleigh were the chief illustrators. Many photographs were used.

The lead article was titled "A Talk with the King of the Belgians," and represented one of the best of Mrs. Rinehart's performances as *Post* correspondent in Europe during the First World War. Other articles were Will Payne's "Competition in Oil," Isabel Brush's "Russia's Stake in the War," Emerson Hough's "The Yosemite," Enos A. Mill's brief "The Black Bear" in the back of the book, and George Pattullo's "Consider the Calf" (on the beef and cattle business). Two serials were running — E. Phillips Oppenheim's "The Double Traitor" and Eugene Manlove Rhodes's "Hit the Line Hard!" — the latter a humorous story of gamblers and swindlers. Short stories were "Blue Motors," a business romance with liberal dashes of humor, by Edgar Franklin; a love story by David Gray; "The Professional Game," a golfing story, the very first Joseph Hergesheimer contribution to the *Post*, which was later to run "Java Head" and other distinguished work by this author; and an outdoor love story, with dialect, by William R. Lighton. There was no verse. The editorial page contained some short and unremarkable editorials; and there was one department — "What Next?" — about new inventions. It was a big, rich, various, and entertaining book. A few years later a French commentator was to define the *Post* type of periodical as "a monthly magazine appearing every week." [44] Certainly no monthly offered a bigger book. A little later the *Post* printed up its March 22, 1919, number in octavo form with binding, under the title *One Issue*, to show what a sizable book it made; without the advertising there were three hundred eighty-two pages.

The years just before the entry of the United States into the European war were marked by the first "You Know Me, Al," stories by Ring Lardner (bought by Lorimer against his staff's protests),[45] Harry Leon Wilson's "Ruggles of Red Gap" and "Ma Pettingill," P. G. Wodehouse's "Jeeves," Peter B. Kyne's "Cappy Ricks." Enough to send America into the war in high spirits, especially when added to the production of Cobb ("Speaking of Operations" appeared in 1915), Glass (Abe and Mawruss were still active), and others. Octavus Roy Cohen came along in 1917 with Florian Slappey and his crowd. Sinclair Lewis, Clarence Budington Kelland, Earl Derr Biggers, Stewart Edward White, and Basil King were other new contributors. Arthur Stringer's "The Prairie Wife" was a distinguished serial of 1915, and John Taintor Foote's fine horse stories came in the same year.

---

[44] "En somme on pourrait définir ces revues-là des Monthly Magazines qui paraissent toutes les semaines" (Albert Schinz, *Revue Politique et Littéraire*, v. 58, p. 551, Sept. 18, 1920).

[45] Butterfield, *Saturday Evening Post Treasury*, p. 135.

During the war, Cobb, Marcosson, and Mrs. Rinehart and Mrs. Harris were *Post* correspondents. Blythe was in England. Arnold Bennett presented the British side in the early fall of 1914, Bernhard Dernburg the German case, and Georges Clemenceau "The Cause of France." After the United States entered the conflict, Pattullo was the magazine's accredited correspondent with the A.E.F., Will Payne and Will Irwin had roving commissions, and Kenneth L. Roberts had the Siberian assignment. Henceforth Roberts became one of the inner circle of *Post* contributors, along with Garet Garrett, political and economic writer. William Allen White reported on the Peace Conference for the *Post* in 1919.

In 1917–1918 there was a recession in the *Post's* circulation, but it was back to 2,000,000 in 1919. Average net paid circulation throughout the twenties was about 2,440,000. There was a drop of nearly 500,000 in 1927, but this was more than regained the next year; and at the time of the financial collapse at the end of the decade, the *Post* was reaching for an average annual sale of 3,000,000 copies a week. This figure was not to be obtained until 1937, however. The book got fatter and fatter with advertising throughout the decade following World War I. The first 200–page issue came out on November 22, 1919; it had 111 pages of advertising at $5,000 for a black-and-white page and $7,000 for one in two colors. Now automotive advertising (including accessories) often amounted to a third or more of the total. All this was immensely profitable. It was reported that in 1924 Curtis was one of four men in the United States whose incomes exceeded $5,000,000 a year.[46] In December 1925 the Curtis Publishing Company declared one of the largest stock dividends on record, when preferred stock was increased by 700,000 shares at $100 each and the new shares distributed among the holders of common stock. The earnings of the company were then estimated at over $16,000,000 a year. The next year advertising rates were raised to $8,000 a black-and-white page, and in 1927 the *Post's* advertising revenue amounted to over $50,000,000.

The most important fiction serials of the early twenties were Emerson Hough's "The Covered Wagon" and Harry Leon Wilson's "Merton of the Movies." Wilson's "Oh, Doctor!" and "Professor, How Could You!" came a little later, as did Katharine Brush's "Young Man of Manhattan." J. P. Marquand and C. E. Scoggins made their first bows to a *Post* audience in these years. "Short Turns and Encores," a humor page later called "Post Scripts," made its debut in 1922; it was better than the old "Sense and Nonsense" department. Will Rogers made a great hit in 1926 with his travel articles, under the title "Letters of a

46 *Nation*, v. 136, p. 683, June 2, 1933.

Self-Made Diplomat to His President." Thomas Beer contributed his
Mrs. Egg stories. Serial reminiscences were especially strong in this
decade, including H. H. Kohlsaat's "From McKinley to Harding,"
James J. Corbett's "The Roar of the Crowd," Alonzo A. Stagg's "Touch-
down!," Corra Harris' "My Book and Heart," Herbert Quick's "One
Man's Life," and the memoirs of Mme. Emma Calvé, Augustus
Thomas, John Philip Sousa, Harry Lauder, Weber and Fields, and
Irving Berlin. The last two were written by Alexander Woollcott.

It was in the twenties that the detective mystery came into first-rate
importance in the *Post*, though the time was to come when that genre
would flower still more prolifically. Earlier detective series were Jacques
Futrelle's "Thinking Machine" stories of 1906, G. K. Chesterton's
Father Brown tales of 1910–1911, and in the following years the Judge
Priest stories by Irvin Cobb and those centering about Randolph Mason
by Melville Davisson Post. But some kind of climax was reached with
Frances Noyes Hart's "The Bellamy Trial," of 1927, "suggested by the
Hall-Mills case," [47] and a classic in this kind. A little later came Earl
Derr Biggers' Charlie Chan serials, to the delight of murder-mystery
fans. Biggers, Rex Stout, J. P. Marquand, and Mary Roberts Rinehart
wrote detective serials for the *Post* in the thirties. Stout's "The Rubber
Band" and Marquand's "Thank You, Mr. Moto" were running at the
same time in 1936. It is appropriate that Somerset Maugham's famous
defense of murder mysteries should have appeared in the *Post*. That
notable essay ended with a prediction that was by no means pure
whimsy:

It may well be that posterity, turning a cold shoulder to the more pretentious
efforts of our day, will acclaim the crime story as the most characteristic and
remarkable feature of English literature in the twentieth century.[48]

Among short-story writers of this period may be mentioned James
Warner Bellah, whose "Fear" was an outstanding tale of a war aviator;
Ann Cameron, whose stories of Mrs. O'Malley were well suited to the
*Post's* favorite formula of humor in a distinctively American frame-
work; Donn Byrne's romantic stories of the Irish, and I. A. R. Wylie's
distinguished stories of Germans. It was commonly said that the *Post*
encouraged its writers to make their short stories too long; certainly
Lorimer's three thousand words seemed often to stretch to six, eight, or
even ten thousand. An English critic overstated the matter in a review
article:

All the articles and stories have to be long in order that their tails may provide
the reading matter against which the advertiser pays to put his announcement in

[47] [Bigelow], *Short History of the Post*, p. 29.
[48] *Saturday Evening Post*, v. 213, Dec. 28, 1940, p. 49.

the hinder part of the compendium. The consequence is that length, in an American short story or article, positively assumes the aspect of a virtue.[49]

Payment to writers, which had been liberal from the time Curtis had purchased the *Post*, perhaps reached its peak at the end of the 1920's. Top writers then received as much as $6,000 for a short story and $60,000 for a serial.[50] Coolidge's first article after he left the presidency was contributed to the *Post*, which paid $10,000 for it. The same price was paid for Hoover's first postpresidential article, but when Lorimer learned that a competitor (probably *Liberty*) had made a higher offer but had been refused by Hoover in favor of the weekly that had long been faithful to him, the *Post* insisted on paying an additional $5,000 for it.[51] This amounted to $3.00 a word, and it may be supposed that the second article was paid for at the same rate.

During the four years following the summer of 1926, the two-hundred-page *Post* issue became common. The number for December 7, 1929, carried two hundred seventy-six pages. (At midcentury this still held the record as the biggest of all *Posts*.) As usual, about 60 per cent was advertising,[52] but more striking was the fact that about half the advertising in this issue used color. Some of these pages were two-color jobs, but many were in "full color." Such chromatic brilliance came to the advertising pages and the covers before it penetrated the body of the book.

*Post* covers for two decades had been attractive productions in black and orange, sometimes with a third color added. The earliest covers were mostly of a rather formal poster type, but pretty girls lent their charm from about 1907 to 1912. In these years such artists as J. C. Leyendecker, Paul Bransom, Harrison Fisher, George Brehm, Oliver Kemp, and S. M. Arthurs contributed cover pictures for the magazine. But from about 1912 onward, the *Post* began to use Americana themes for its covers — bits of homely American life from country, village, and city. The master of this genre was Norman Rockwell, whose work began to appear in 1916. "Full color" brought new effectiveness to the Rockwell and Leyendecker covers that adorned so many of the fat numbers of the late twenties.

For 1929 the Curtis Publishing Company, which then issued the *Post*, the *Journal*, the *Country Gentleman* and *Jack and Jill*, reported net earnings of $21,534,265, "an all-time high for any publishing enter-

[49] Ward Muir in *Nation and Athenaeum*, v. 32, p. 155, Oct. 28, 1922.
[50] Tebbel, *Lorimer and the Post*, pp. 59, 71.
[51] *Ibid.*, p. 197.
[52] That was the usual proportion of *Post* advertising according to statistics presented in the *Journal of Applied Psychology*, v. 10, p. 64, March 1926.

prise."[53] The *Post* again was said to have sold $50,000,000 worth of advertising in that year.[54] Came the shocking financial crash of late fall, with its many fiscal casualties; but it looked for a time as though the *Post* might weather the storm without hurt. Many of the April and May numbers in 1930 ran over 200 pages; circulation for 1930 showed even a slight gain over that for 1929. When receipts for the first six months of 1930 showed a 5 per cent decline from the corresponding period in 1929, the publishers promptly initiated a million-dollar newspaper advertising campaign, which worked wonders. And yet, with bank failures the country over, *Post* advertising by the summer of 1931 had fallen to such an extent that some numbers had less than a hundred pages altogether. The decline continued, and by the end of 1932 some issues had only 60 pages, with twelve to fifteen pages of advertising. In 1933 advertising revenue had declined to less than $18,000,000.[55] It was in 1931 that the outdated taboo against cigarette advertising was removed, but that did not help much. Liquor announcements were still banned, depression or no depression.[56]

Circulation held up remarkably well. There was a slight decline in 1933–1935, but an upturn began in 1935, which brought the list in 1937 to the long-coveted goal of three million copies. This was done by the tried-and-true Curtis method — newspaper advertising supported by newsboy solicitation — to which was now added telephone solicitation. A million and a quarter dollars was put into the *Post's* own advertising campaign in 1937, and that did much to break whatever threat the great depression held for the *Saturday Evening Post*.[57]

The man who brought *Post* advertising through the depths of the depression was Fred A. Healy, who had begun as a solicitor in Chicago, had managed the Chicago office of the *Country Gentleman* for Curtis, and had then suggested to him the opening of a Detroit office in order to get a bigger share of automotive business. Healy managed the new office so successfully that he was made advertising director of the Curtis Publishing Company in 1928, succeeding William Boyd. Healy had been on the top of the wave for a while, then deep in the trough, and now was slowly winning back to figures that represented prosperity for Curtis stockholders. The year 1936 brought great encouragement: the *Post* boasted at the end of that year that its advertising revenue had amounted to $26,384,013, topping that of 1935 by approximately

[53] *Time*, v. 34, Dec. 4, 1939, p. 78.
[54] *Time*, v. 16, Nov. 24, 1930, p. 32.
[55] *Time*, v. 30, Nov. 1, 1937, p. 51.
[56] As late as 1943, a stockholder's proposal to open the *Post* to liquor advertising was defeated by a large majority (*New York Times*, April 22, 1943, p. 35, col. 6).
[57] *Time*, v. 31, Jan. 10, 1938, p. 22.

$4,250,000. That was an advance of 17.2 per cent. "This increase exceeds the gain of any two other magazines," declared a trade advertisement,[58] which continued: "It gives the *Post* a total advertising revenue that exceeds the combined total of all other weekly magazines." The next year was a tough one, with a minor panic in the fall; however, the *Post* not only held its advertising gains, but made a slight advance of 1.6 per cent.[59] After that increases were steady.

During these depression years there was no decline in the level of contents. Of course an issue of sixty pages contained far less textual matter than one of two hundred seventy-five pages; the fattest and slimmest numbers in the four years 1929–1932 offered a hundred and eight as compared with forty-five pages of text. But tables of contents showed about the same types of material in about the same proportions. Perhaps there was a little more nonfiction, but the *Post* kept up its reputation as an always diverting magazine.

There was, for example, a continuation of the series of leaders in the sports world: Jack Dempsey's "In This Corner" and James J. Jeffries' "Inside These Ropes," assisted respectively by Francis Coe and Eddie Orcutt; Bozeman Bulger's "Along Came Ruth," and the autobiographies of Helen Wills and Sir Thomas Lipton. A series of football coaches made their way through the pages of the *Post*, assisted by "ghost writers" — Harry Kipke, Bob Zuppke, Fritz Crisler, Jock Sutherland, Harry Stuhldreher, Pop Warner, and so on. Series reflecting popular interest in European affairs were Leon Trotsky's story of the Russian revolution and the autobiography of Queen Marie of Roumania. Dorothy Thompson wrote a series of articles reporting on the situation in Germany, and Katherine Dayton contributed her amusing satires on domestic politics called "Mrs. Democrat and Mrs. Republican."

The fact that the three series last named, all dealing largely with politics, were written by women directs our attention to the fact that the *Post* was no longer chiefly a man's magazine. The editors (two of them were women) recognized that they had about as many women readers as men. "There is no natural sex division in magazine reading," wrote one of the editors boldly.[60]

Four of the leading fiction serials in the *Post* during the depression years were by women — Katharine Brush's "Red-Haired Woman," Rose Wilder Lane's "Let the Hurricane Roar," Mrs. Rinehart's "Miss Pinkerton," Agatha Christie's "Murder in the Calais Coach." Other

[58] *Advertising and Selling*, v. 28, Jan. 14, 1937, pp. 14–15.
[59] *Time*, v. 31, Jan. 10, 1938, p. 22.
[60] [Bigelow], *Short History of the Post*, p. 25.

were Phil Stong's "Farmer in the Dell," and another headliner in that growing rout of detective stories — Rex Stout's "The Frightened Men." Norman Reilly Raine began his amusing Tugboat Annie stories, and other writers of shorter fiction not already familiar in *Post* pages were Walter D. Edmonds, William Faulkner, Oliver LaFarge, Ben Hecht, and Paul Gallico. Stephen Vincent Benét's "The Devil and Daniel Webster," a short-story masterpiece, was in the number for October 24, 1936. Nordhoff and Hall's nonfiction series "Men Against the Sea" was followed by "Pitcairn's Island."

In the summer of 1932, as he was about to start on a cruise on his yacht *Lyndonia*, Cyrus H. K. Curtis suffered a heart attack. In the following October he was relieved at his request of the duties of president of the Curtis Publishing Company and became chairman of the Board of Directors. He died on June 7, 1933, ending a career as the most successful publisher in the history of American magazines. Though he gave away close to ten million dollars in benefactions in the latter years of his life, he left an estate valued at many times that figure.

Curtis had to go in the midst of the *Post's* hardest struggle against the forces of the depression; Lorimer, who became president of the company when Curtis resigned, lived to see the magazine well on the way to a new prosperity. Lorimer carried the presidency of the company and the editorship of the *Post* for a little over two years; then he turned the presidency over to Walter D. Fuller and became chairman of the board. But at the end of 1936, at the age of sixty-nine, he retired both as chairman and as editor. The next year he died after a short illness with pneumonia.

Evaluation of George Horace Lorimer's life work as editor of the *Saturday Evening Post* is not so simple and easy as it may appear at first thought. That he was extraordinarily successful as the editor of a popular magazine is shown by the *Post's* circulation figures. How great his influence was upon American thought and American culture, and in what directions that influence was exerted, are questions much more difficult to answer.

When Lorimer died, the *New York Times*, acknowledging that the *Post* "probably had more influence on the cultural life of America" than any other periodical, summed up the editor by calling him "a sort of Henry Ford of American literature." [61] This was in line with a common criticism of Lorimer and the *Post*, though much of that criticism had been more bitter — and even abusive. Lorimer's adherents, and the *Post's*, have been accustomed to say that such comment was mostly founded on envy. Bernard De Voto once wrote that there

[61] *New York Times*, Oct. 23, 1937, p. 1, col. 4.

were only two classes of writers who did not contribute to the *Post* —
those who were financially independent, and those who could not "make
the grade." [62] This rather oversimplified things, but there was much
truth in it. Certainly the banishment of *Post* stories from the O'Brien
collection of "bests," the highbrow snobbery that always lifts the nose
at writing which large numbers of people buy, and much of the railing
against Lorimer and *Post* literary standards through the years, have
been based largely on a sour-grapes sophistry.

But not all criticism can be shrugged off so easily. Perhaps the fault
oftenest alleged against Lorimer's *Post* was that it was largely devoted
to a "crass materialism." [63] Moreover, we have been told, this was
commonly mixed with romance that was often more "crass" than the
materialism. Thus business success, romance, sports, humor, and public affairs were said to constitute the *Post* pattern; and short stories,
serials, and articles were alleged to be created and repeated according
to a few variants of a successful formula, thus killing originality, new
ideas, and the art impulse in general. The *New York Times* obituary
said that Lorimer

> built up a long list of writers who knew how to pour their words into a form
> which the *Saturday Evening Post* found profitable. . . . Week after week there
> sprang from his editorial assembly line technically perfect stories and articles,
> wedged between costly advertising, illustrated by the best artists in the coun-
> try. . . .[64]

One of the most extreme critics of the *Post* was Upton Sinclair, who
wrote that its "stuff is as standardized as soda crackers; originality is
taboo, new ideas are treason, social sympathy is a crime, and the one
virtue of man is to produce larger and larger quantities of material
things." [65] And then Sinclair printed George Sterling's ballad "The
Black Hound Bays," which he justly called "a wild and terrible poem,"
but from which a few lines may be quoted here, without agreement, but
as representative of one phase of contemporary thinking:

> The Lords of the Nation go hunting with their dogs;
> Some have the hearts of tigers, and some the hearts of hogs.
> On the path of the quarry the yapping mongrels pour,
> And the keenest of the pack is the great dog Lorrimor.
> "Woo-hoo-hoo-hoo! O Lords, spare not the spur!
> Give me the white doe Freedom, that I flesh my fangs in her!
> I ha' hate for all wild hearts!" bays the dog Lorrimor. . . .

---

[62] "Writing for Money," *Saturday Review of Literature*, Oct. 29, 1937.

[63] One of the best articles on this line is Leon Whipples' "Saturday Evening Post," in
*Survey*, v. 59, p. 699ff, March 1, 1928.

[64] *New York Times*, Oct. 23, 1937, p. 1, col. 4.

[65] Upton Sinclair, *Money Writes!* (New York, 1927), p. 68.

Oh, lavish is his tongue for the feet of all his Lords!
And hoarse is his throat if a foot go near their hoards.
Sharp are his teeth and savage is his heart,
When he lifts up his voice to drown the song of Art.

.    .    .    .    .

If the young folk build an altar to their vision of the New,
Be sure the great dog Lorrimor shall lift a leg thereto.

Now, envy and passion aside, is it true that Lorimer's *Post* was wholly materialistic? Or standardized by formulas? Or unfriendly to new ideas? Or inimical to literature and the artistic impulse?

The *Post* made its first spectacular success by a wholehearted devotion to material prosperity, and by directing young men to that goal. But the loaf of materialism was, as a matter of fact, leavened by something more than patterned romance. The frequency with which articles by Albert J. Beveridge, William Allen White, and (somewhat later) Corra Harris reappear in Lorimer's *Post* show an interest in the more altruistic phases of American life.

The allegation of a moldlike formula for fiction and also one for nonfiction is likewise overdrawn. For a decade or more at the beginning of Lorimer's editorship, there was an easily discernible pattern in many numbers; it became less apparent in the twenties and thirties, and it is clear that there was never an obligatory formula. Many smart critics have tried in vain to suit the editors with stories and articles done according to the principles they imagined were sure-fire *Post* material. Of course, there were and are certain things the *Post* likes, but they have never comprised anything quite so precise as to be called a formula.

Lorimer's *Post* was, on the whole, conservative; it became increasingly so after it had become greatly successful. But it was never really inhospitable to new ideas; and even when it disagreed with new points of view, it often gave space to a spokesman for them. Diversified examples are Clarence Darrow's article on the open shop in 1904, Joseph Medill Patterson's "The Socialist Machine" in 1906, W. J. Bryan's articles on the Wilson administration in 1916, Leon Trotsky's series on the Russian revolution, and Gertrude Stein's essays on money in 1936.

The Stein series was an exception, however; Lorimer bought it as humor rather than as examples of a new literary departure. He had no interest in literature as such, and he was even wary of the term itself. He once wrote Mrs. Harris regarding her "The Circuit Rider's Wife," "I am a little uneasy because every now and then someone says that it is literature. . . . Literature is never discovered until it has been a hundred years dead and there is nothing but the bones of it left." [66] The important thing about this concept is that it reveals Lorimer's overpowering interest in what commanded the interest, thinking, and emotions of people week by week. He once wrote a curiously defensive article about his editorial practice in which he stated the faith that every good editor of a popular magazine must have:

> I have learned during the twenty-five years that I have been editing to have confidence in the good sense, good judgment, and good taste of our popular audience. It is true that many of them like an occasional story dealing with American business. But why not? If literature has any relation to life, the American writer cannot pass it by.[67]

Lorimer, clearly, did not edit the *Post* with what he considered to be "literary" intentions; but he did manage to get a considerable amount of writing into the pages of the magazine that represented very well the better American and English literature, in fiction at least, of the first third of the twentieth century. Repetition of the roll of contributors is scarcely necessary here; but it is easy to name such distinguished American writers for the *Post* in these years as Frank Norris, Jack London, Stephen Crane, Theodore Dreiser, F. Scott Fitzgerald, O. Henry, David Graham Phillips, Sinclair Lewis, Joseph Hergesheimer, Edith Wharton, Ellen Glasgow, Stephen Vincent Benét, William Faulkner, James Branch Cabell, Hamlin Garland, Joel Chandler Harris, Booth Tarkington, Willa Cather, and William Allen White; and such English contributors as Rudyard Kipling, Hall Caine, Joseph Conrad, G. K. Chesterton, H. G. Wells, Arnold Bennett, John Galsworthy, and Gilbert Parker. It is absurd to suggest that these writers merely wrote words to a pattern set by Lorimer — the "assembly line" concept of the *Times*. Of course, the *Post* did not publish masterpieces by all these writers. It did, however, publish masterpieces by some of them and work of good literary standards by most of them.

It has been said, in further criticism, that Lorimer was a big-name hunter, willing to take third-rate material when a famous author signed it. This also appears to be quite unjust. There is every reason to believe Lorimer sincere when he said to Marcosson:

> One of the greatest fallacies in making magazines is the "big name" fallacy. When you get a good story under a big name you have the ideal combination. But when you have the big name and a bad story, you simply disappoint the high

---

[66] Tebbel, *Lorimer and the Post*, p. 134; for the Stein articles, p. 160.

[67] Doris Ullmann, *A Portrait Gallery of American Editors* (New York, 1925), p. 99. Also see Lorimer's article, "Beveridge: A Study of the Self-Made Man," *Appleton's Magazine*, v. 6, pp. 709–17, Dec. 1905.

expectations of your readers. I should always prefer a good story by an unknown man to a moderately good story by Kipling.[68]

Some credit is due Lorimer for being a consistently generous and prompt paymaster. He raised authorship, said Frank Parker Stockbridge, with some exaggeration, "from a starveling trade to a lucrative profession." [69]

Much of the criticism levied against Lorimer was based on his political positions. He made the *Post* a political periodical from the first, taking a strong position on many of the partisan issues before the country. He would often present the other side, especially in a national campaign; but that was rather in the nature of a sop to the opposition, and there was never any doubt not only about the position of Lorimer's editorial page, but about the side taken in most of the political and economic articles.

The *Post* maintained a consistent position on some issues throughout Lorimer's editorship; on others there were notable changes. On conservation, *Post* advocacy was clear and persistent. Emerson Hough wrote to Lorimer in 1921: "I believe the *Saturday Evening Post* is about the only branch of the government which is going to be of much use in saving the wild animals and the outdoor sport of America." [70] The magazine's long-term campaign extended to reclamation, parks, and water power. Another persistent fight was against unlimited immigration. Lorimer contended that America should be kept for Americans, that "Amerikanskis" with un-American ideas and ideals were dangerous, and that the only beneficiaries of unrestricted immigration were the great industries that wanted cheap labor. This doctrine was closely related to the isolationism that characterized Lorimer's ideas in the field of foreign relations. The *Post* was a hundred per cent loyal in the First World War; but it never forgave Woodrow Wilson, whom it had supported in his 1916 campaign on the platform "He Kept Us Out of War," for what it considered his about-face on entanglement in European quarrels, and it never supported another Democratic candidate for the presidency.

But on the grand issue that has dominated our domestic politics since the 1890's — the question of government controls in the economic field — the Lorimer course made a wide swing from left to right. As the young man's magazine at the turn of the century, the *Post* was for opportunity and against "aggrandized wealth." When Theodore Roosevelt became President in September 1901, the *Post* wished him well

[68] Isaac Marcosson, *Adventures in Interviewing* (New York, 1920), p. 63.
[69] *New York Times*, Nov. 3, 1937, p. 30, col. 1.
[70] Tebbel, *Lorimer and the Post*, p. 140.

editorially, and made a place in its annual College Man's Number two weeks later for Owen Wister's "Theodore Roosevelt, Harvard '80." In the 1904 campaign, the aging Cleveland, who had already written two or three partisan pieces for the *Post*, was permitted to speak for the foredoomed Alton B. Parker, while young Senator Albert J. Beveridge presented T. R.'s case. Beveridge was to become a constant contributor for many years of articles for the Progressive cause and of a kind of practical moral essay of which he showed himself a masterly writer. In the years 1902–1905, David Graham Phillips wrote some fifty articles for the *Post*, many of them very critical of what he called "Swollen Fortunes." In this early Roosevelt period, William Allen White was a frequent writer of both articles and signed editorials. A remarkable editorial titled "Why the Nation Will Endure" in the issue for March 4, 1905, published on the date of Theodore Roosevelt's inauguration, was a kind of new Gettysburg Address. It ended with these sentences:

And as the years of this century pass, this nation, peacefully, soberly, and with humility, will decimate aggrandized wealth and will put the benefits of the civilization which all have builded within the reach of every hard-working, industrious man or woman, reserving the higher prizes — the higher rewards — for those who have honestly earned them in great social service, and giving them to no one else. And so this nation shall not crumble, and this people shall not be blown away upon the four winds of Heaven.

Of course the *Post* was roundly attacked for this kind of "socialism." Some advertisers did not like it, but what could they do? *Post* circulation was growing during these years, marching steadily toward its first million, and advertising had to follow along. At length, goaded by criticism, the *Post* gave its entire editorial page one week to a reply to the critics of its liberal politics. It argued that the popular periodicals that were so generally espousing the Progressive cause were merely following the overwhelming sentiment of the people: not the editors but the people were leading the movement.

The people are beguiling them [the editors] from the strait and narrow path that leads to the standpat Heaven, from which pauper angels are rigidly excluded, and where a select group of seraphim discourse sweet music on their harps — 45% ad valorem — at Paderewski prices.[71]

Of course, big business had its spokesmen in the *Post* during these years; Philip D. Armour, Lorimer's old friend, had a series of articles in the early weeks of 1906 defending the beef trust on all counts. And after the defeat and decimation of the Progressive party in 1912, the *Post* was not so sure about the direction in which the people's mandate

---

[71] *Saturday Evening Post*, v. 183, Dec. 10, 1910, p. 18.

pointed. It stood with Wilson on what it thought was an isolationist platform in 1916, it supported Harding as an exponent of nationalism and domestic "normalcy" four years later, and it liked Coolidge for his ideas about the repayment of the war debts — a subject on which the *Post* was long insistent. Garet Garrett had now joined Samuel G. Blythe as a leading writer of political articles for the magazine.

Lorimer was a close friend of Herbert Hoover, one of the first to propose him for the presidency, and an active leader in the campaign to nominate and elect him. President Hoover later offered Lorimer the ambassadorship to Great Britain, a position suited neither to his liking nor to his abilities. Much as Lorimer was displeased with Hoover's moratorium on the war debts, he favored his friend for reëlection in 1932. That fall Calvin Coolidge presented "The Case for the Republicans" in the *Post*; but Alfred E. Smith, who had promised to write the piece for the Democrats and his one-time supporter Franklin Roosevelt, begged off at the last and sent an article about veterans' bonuses instead, and Governor Albert C. Ritchie gave the Democrats their inning just before the election. Lorimer was against Franklin D. Roosevelt and the New Deal from the very beginning of the first F. D. R. term, up to and including the last editorial he ever wrote for the *Post*. This was not a mere presidential campaign fight; it was a week-to-week feud. His main quarrel with the Roosevelt administration was that he believed it was "Stumbling Into Socialism," to use the title of a lead article by David Lawrence (July 20, 1935).

That a periodical with three million circulation could maintain steadily such a strong partisan stand, with bitter attacks on a man who was repeatedly returned to the highest office in our government by large majorities (the biggest majority of a popular vote in our history in 1936) without suffering in circulation or prestige seems one of the miracles of modern mass communication. Certainly a large segment of *Post* readers disagreed with its political opinions and policy. One is forced to the conclusion that the modern American reader is not too much disturbed by party attitudes that differ from his own, and that, in the case of the *Post*, they like the nonpolitical contents so well that they continue to read the magazine despite some resentment against its politics. It is probable that the least-read department in Lorimer's *Post* was its editorial page, and it was easy to pass over the political articles, too.

Thus, while we may be skeptical about the political influence of George Horace Lorimer, evidence of his greatness as editor of a popular literary miscellany seems overwhelming. He was a great editor because he had faith in the "good sense, good judgment, and good taste of our popular audience." Indeed, like all great editors, he was himself a representative of the audience he served; and Irvin Cobb was probably right when he said that "Lorimer more nearly approximates the popular conception — and the proper one — of the typical American than any other man I have known." [72]

The man who succeeded Lorimer as president of the Curtis Publishing Company in 1934 was Walter D. Fuller, who had been with the company for a quarter of a century and knew the business well from salesman's job to executive's responsibility. The man who succeeded Lorimer as editor of the *Post* was Wesley Winans Stout, who had come to the magazine from newspaper work and had served under Lorimer for fourteen years.

When Stout first came to the *Post*, its editorial staff included a trio who had been with the magazine since the early years of the century — Churchill Williams, who was relied on for outside contacts, and retired in 1925; Frederic S. Bigelow, an old newspaper friend of Lorimer's, who was office editor, and retired in 1929; and Adelaide W. Neall, long a kind of unofficial managing editor, who stayed on as Stout's "right-hand man," and withdrew in 1942. Other associate editors may be named. Helen D. Walker had retired shortly before Stout came to the *Post*. Arthur McKeogh, versatile in art, journalism, the law, and military life, was lost in 1923 in the raid that Hearst made on the *Post* staff and contributors when he was recruiting editors for his own magazines. Thomas B. Costain had joined the staff in 1921, the year before Stout's advent. He was an aggressive editor, going out after new talent, and was long the heir apparent to the Lorimer throne; but he was lured away in 1934 by Hollywood and best-seller authorship. Thomas L. Masson came to the *Post* from thirty years as one of the editors of that incomparable satirical weekly, *Life*, and for seven years gave special attention to *Post* humorous features. W. Thornton ("Pete") Martin joined the staff in 1929 and was art editor from 1936 to the end of Stout's editorship; later he was to do nearly every job on the paper, and to become one of its more brilliant contributors.[73] Graeme Lorimer, son of the chief, was an associate editor from 1932 to 1938; he came to the *Post* from the *Ladies Home Journal*, and resigned to rejoin the *Journal*. Bruce Gould, a *Post* associate editor in 1934–1935, also withdrew to join its sister magazine, of which he and his wife Beatrice Blackmar Gould became editors-in-chief.[74] Erdmann N. Brandt, partner in the famous firm of literary agents known as Brandt & Brandt,

[72] *Bookman*, v. 48, p. 390, Dec. 1918.
[73] Butterfield, *Saturday Evening Post Treasury*, p. 444.
[74] See Sketch 14.

began a long term as associate editor in 1934. Marione V. Reinhard came in 1935 and Richard Thruelsen and Martin Sommers in 1936. Thus when Stout succeeded to the editorship of the *Post*, he had as associates Graeme Lorimer, Brandt, Thruelsen, Sommers, and Misses Neall and Reinhard, with Martin as art editor.

Stout's *Post* was very much like Lorimer's. During Stout's five years, leading writers of fiction serials were Kenneth Roberts, Walter D. Edmonds, J. P. Marquand ("The Late George Apley"), Nordhoff and Hall, Ben Ames Williams, C. E. Scoggins, Rose Wilder Lane, James Warner Bellah, James Boyd, Bess Streeter Aldrich, and so on. Agatha Christie and Leslie Ford were leaders in the detective story field. William Hazlitt Upson wrote stories of Alexander Botts and his tractors. There were short stories by Stephen Vincent Benét, Margery Sharp, Fannie Hurst, Sophie Kerr, and Philip Wylie. There was lots of Kelland. There were fifty "Glencannon" stories by Guy Gilpatric between 1930 and the author's death in 1950. Humor was furnished also by Corey Ford, Paul Gallico, J. P. McEvoy, and P. G. Wodehouse. "The Story of Will Rogers" by his wife was a 1940 serial. Jack Alexander and Demaree Bess became constant contributors, and soon associate editors. Alva Johnston continued his "profiles," Edgar Snow wrote on foreign topics, Frank J. Taylor contributed features from the West, and Albert W. Atwood continued to do politics and economics. Garet Garrett became "editorial writer in chief" and did many articles as well. Ex-President Hoover and Senator Arthur H. Vandenberg were contributors. Former N.R.A. Administrator Hugh S. Johnson and former Assistant Secretary of State Raymond Moley, after they had resigned, became *Post* writers. But on the whole there were not many exciting new contributors to the *Post* during Stout's lustrum.

Politically, Stout followed his illustrious chief. An article in one of his first numbers drew a rebuke from President Roosevelt. Stanley High's "Whose Party Is It?" which attempted to "read the Democrats out of the Democratic party," was introduced by an editorial note, which said that High had "the Washington reputation of being one of the President's close advisers." The White House statement was a repudiation of High as a spokesman.[75] The *Post* was the leading mouthpiece of the isolationists as the guns began to thunder in Europe. "Let us jealously mind our own defense in the great manner of a great people resolved to be let alone," it urged in the troublous months of 1940.[76] The magazine was attacked in the Canadian Parliament by

[75] See *New York Times*, Feb. 5, 1937, p. 1, col. 3; *Saturday Evening Post*, v. 209, Feb. 6, 1937, p. 11.
[76] *Saturday Evening Post*, v. 213, Sept. 7, 1940, p. 26. See DeWitt S. Snell's pamphlet *The Isolationism of the Saturday Evening Post* (Schenectady, N. Y., 1941).

Senators who accused it of criticizing the war effort in that country and
who thought it should be excluded from the Dominion.[77]

The greatest improvement in the magazine in these years was in
page layout and color. When Stout first took over, he introduced a
slightly larger and more readable type and began to experiment with
double-page designs, cuts bled off the edge of the page, and variation
in angles and placement of pictures. Lorimer had always stuck to the
old rule of rectangular layouts on all pages, marching with order and
regularity; and the *Post* had fallen behind other magazines in the
attractiveness of its pages. There had been color in both typography
and illustration before Stout's term, as in some of Anton Otto Fischer's
marines; but it was not until 1938 that Lewis W. Trayser, director of
manufacturing at the Curtis plant, and his staff succeeded in printing
four colors, on top of each other, on fast presses with instantaneous
drying and accurate register. This miraculous performance enabled the
*Post* to offer at least one full-color page in each number from mid–1938
onward. The next year there were more angled and bled cuts and two
full-color pages in each number, as well as many two-color pages. In
1940 these improvements were even more marked, and so it went.

But *Post* affairs were not going well in the spring of 1942. The bitterly
isolationist *Post* had found it necessary to change its tune when the
Lend-Lease agreement was signed:

> Everything we said on the losing side we still believe . . . . Yet . . . whether
> we were right or wrong no longer matters. . . . We shall have to make up our
> minds to go on at any cost, to reconquer Europe and destroy Hitler there, even
> with American man power. . . .[78]

Then had come the attack on Pearl Harbor and the declarations of
war. Some staff dissensions developed, advertising declined, while a
few stockholders complained that their investment was being ruined
by the *Post's* isolationism. There was even a proposal that a stockholders' censorship committee be set up. But restraining actions in
the courts and uprisings in stockholders' meetings came to naught: a
large majority stood by the management.[79] As far as circulation was
concerned, the *Post* was doing well. In every year of the Stout editorship, average annual net circulation had increased from 50,000 to
100,000; it passed the 3,000,000 mark in Stout's first year, and it was
over 3,400,000 in 1942. And in March 1942 the *Post* doubled its 121-
year-old price per copy of five cents. The ten-cent *Post* was a sensation,

[77] *New York Times*, July 19, 1940, p. 8, col. 2.

[78] *Saturday Evening Post*, v. 213, May 24, 1941, p. 28.

[79] See *New York Times*, April 7, 1942, p. 9, col. 6; April 16, 1942, p. 17, col. 2; April
22, 1943, p. 25, col. 6.

but it was in line with rising prices in a war economy. Yes, circulation was doing well enough, but advertising in the first eleven issues of 1942 had declined 20 per cent.[80] Furthermore, the Curtis Publishing Company actually lost money in the first three months of 1942,[81] and that was enough to make many jobs insecure. It was thought by some that the furor produced by the third of a series of articles about the American Jews [82] had something to do with the explosion which blew Stout out of the *Post's* editorial chair; but this was a misconception, since, though he bought and scheduled the article, he resigned before it actually appeared.

At any rate, Stout withdrew at the end of March 1942 because of "a firm but friendly disagreement with the Curtis Publishing Company on policy." [83] With him went editorial writer Garrett and the senior among the associate editors, Miss Neall. Stout had been attacking the Willkie one-world doctrines: "Shouldn't we be better employed in giving the same thought and fervor to American democracy at home?" [84] Two months later his successor wrote: "Whether we like it or not, international politics will dominate the rest of our lives, out-ranking in public concern most, if not all, our domestic issues." [85] And in the next issue, the *Post* was apologizing for Milton Mayer's piece on the Jews: "We deeply regret this misunderstanding." [86]

The new editor, Ben Hibbs, came to the *Post* from the editorship of the *Country Gentleman*. Like his predecessor, he was a native Kansan with newspaper backgrounds. Curtis President Fuller had been born in Iowa; Advertising and Circulation Manager Healy was a native of Illinois; and the new managing editor, Robert Fuoss, had come from Michigan. The Midwest had apparently taken Independence Square. Meanwhile, Wesley Stout got out his automobile and set off for the Far West, declaring he was going to be a tramp for a while. The Chrysler Corporation did not long permit him to be a tramp.

Many a magazine has been wrecked by clinging just a little too long to the traditions of a past success. A few months, a year or two, on the toboggan can mark the beginning of the end; and the quick, defi-

[80] *Time*, v. 39, March 23, 1942, p. 40.
[81] *New York Times*, April 22, 1943, p. 35, col. 6.
[82] The three articles appeared in March 1942. They were by Jerome Frank, Waldo Frank, and Milton Mayer. It was Mayer's "The Case Against the Jew," March 28, that drew widespread criticism. See Harry Serwer's pamphlet *The Case Against Milton Mayer and the Saturday Evening Post* (n.p., n.d.). Bigelow, in his *Short History of the Saturday Evening Post*, p. 19, claims that Montague Glass's Potash and Perlmutter stories, accepted by Lorimer over the protest of his whole staff, were a "success . . . with Jews and Gentiles alike."
[83] *New York Times*, March 13, 1942, p. 21, col. 2.
[84] *Saturday Evening Post*, v. 214, March 7, 1942, p. 26.
[85] *Ibid.*, v. 214, May 9, 1942, p. 20.
[86] *Ibid.*, v. 214, May 16, 1942, p. 18.

nite, but not too disturbing change is vitally important. By June of his first year, Hibbs had made a daring break with the past — with the glory that was Lorimer. There were changes in typography, layout, illustration, titling of stories and articles, and content itself. The symbol of the whole change-over was the discarding of the old Post Style type for headings and even on the cover in favor of the bright and beautiful Bodoni. Page layout and the handling of illustration were more imaginative, departments were reorganized, comics and verse bloomed in the rearward pages. Stories and articles were shortened, so that in Hibbs's first year the number of articles increased by 52 per cent and short stories by 13 per cent.[87] Hibbs relied much on weekly reader-interest surveys; he did not follow them slavishly (a process which might impair the character of a magazine) but used them constantly for their monitorial and suggestive value.

Hibbs's initial staff included Fuoss as managing editor (a new position) and James Yates as art editor, while the associate editors were Brandt, Thruelson, Martin, Bess, Alexander, Frederic Nelson, Martin Sommers, Stuart Rose, and Alan R. Jackson. Some important changes took place in 1944, Kenneth Stuart becoming art editor, Sommers foreign editor, and Davis Washington editor; while Day Edgar became assistant to the editor, Marione Reinhard Derrickson rejoined the staff, and Edgar Snow, long a valued contributor, became an associate editor.[88] In June of that year, Glenn Gundell became the magazine's advertising and promotion manager. In 1955 a new position was again made for Fuoss — executive editor — Robert Lee Sherrod becoming managing editor.

During the war, the *Post* printed many articles about the fighting, about industrial production in support of the war effort, about the ideological background of the conflict, and about the state of the nation in war times. Altogether, considerably more than half of the magazine's contents may be said to have been devoted to the war during the three years beginning in June 1942. The *Post* had Edgar Snow, Ernest O. Hauser, Robert Carse, John Lardner, Charles A. Rawlings, John Bishop, William Worden, and Demaree Bess abroad as correspondents at various periods of the war.

Through Hibbs's first decade it was the rule that each number should include installments of two fiction serials, four or five short stories,

---

[87] *Magazine World*, v. 2, October 1946, p. 8.

[88] Warner Oliver was an associate editor during 1943–45. Newcomers to the board of associate editors in the latter 1940's were Wesley Price (1945), John Bailey (1945), Robert M. Yoder (1945), Peggy Dowst Redman (1945), Ernest O. Hauser (1946), H. Ralph Knight (1946), Steven M. Spencer (1947), Hugh Morrow (1948), Harry T. Paxton (1948), Ashley Halsey, Jr. (1949). Thruelsen, who had resigned in 1942, returned to the staff during 1947–52. Beverly Smith succeeded Forrest Davis as Washington editor in 1946.

and eight or ten articles. On the whole, there was less emphasis on fiction than in the older *Post*. Detection mysteries and westerns predominated among the fiction serials; leading authors of continued stories were C. S. Forester, Erle Stanley Gardner, Leslie Ford, Agatha Christie, Ngaio Marsh, Martha Albrand, and Clarence Budington Kelland. Prominent among short-story writers in the forties were such favorites as Dorothy Thomas, Paul Gallico, Kay Boyle, Dana Burnet, Storm Jameson, I. A. R. Wylie, Mackinlay Kantor, Wilbur Schramm, William L. Worden, Upson with Mr. Botts, and Raine with Tugboat Annie. "Complete novels" or novelettes of twenty-five thousand words were published occasionally in the mid-forties: Kantor's "Happy Land" was an outstanding example.

Associate editors furnished many of the nonfiction articles, though the names of a number of nonstaff writers became — or continued — familiar in *Post* pages — Stanley Frank, Henry F. Pringle, Frank J. Taylor, Alva Johnston, Boyden Sparkes, Joseph and Stewart Alsop. Articles on sports were more frequent than ever; science and industry were well represented. There were somewhat fewer serial memoirs, though "Eisenhower's Diary," Admiral Halsey's recollections, and "We Barrymores" (by Lionel) were notable. For the first-named, the *Post* paid what is perhaps a record price for a magazine famous for its liberality to authors — $175,000 for the ten installments.[89] The longest series of the forties and fifties was the one about American cities by a variety of writers. These articles were almost invariably exciting to readers in the cities treated, and they were interesting and informative to the general reader. One of the most striking series was that of Associate Editor Snow, interpreting Russia to America — articles appearing irregularly from 1942 through 1945. And perhaps the most sensational series was the 1952 presentation of Whittaker Chambers' story of the Hiss case under the title "I Was the Witness," for the ten installments of which Hibbs paid $75,000.[90]

Verse became somewhat more important in the *Post* in these years, though it was still little more than a variety-maker in the back of the book. Lorimer, after the first few years, had, at rare intervals, given prominent space to a poem, such as Alfred Noyes's "A Victory Dance" in 1926 or Arthur Guiterman's "Pershing at the Front" the next year. But most of the verse used in the *Post* when he was editor was of a humorous sort, by S. E. Kiser, Wallace Irwin, Frank L. Stanton, and others. Ogden Nash was a favorite in the magazine in the thirties. In

---

[89] Information derived from staff talks before the annual convention of the American Association of Teachers of Journalism, Philadelphia, Dec. 29, 1947.

[90] *Time*, v. 59, Feb. 11, 1942, p. 73.

the forties and fifties most of the *Post's* verse was merely amusing, but among the half dozen or more little poems in each issue there was occasionally one of real charm and value — perhaps by Charles Hanson Towne, Dorothy Hughes, Arthur Stringer, or Joseph Auslander. The last-named contributed a series of odes in 1943 addressed to the "Unconquerables" of Greece, Chekoslovakia, Netherlands, Poland, and Norway.

Hibbs and his staff also introduced little back-of-the-book series such as "The Role I liked Best," by actors; "The Perfect Squelch," by volunteer contributors; "You Be the Judge," on points of law; and quizzes, especially in spelling. A picture story in color became an occasional *Post* feature in the fifties.

But most scintillating in brightening up the dreary behind-spaces of the magazine were the so-called "cartoons" — the little pictures that made satiric comments on some phases of contemporary life — pricked a bubble, guffawed at a popular absurdity, or merely pointed out a frailty of which all readers knew very well they too were guilty. Carl Anderson had begun his "Henry" pictures as early as 1933; "Marge" had come along the next year, but had not introduced *Post* readers to "Little Lulu" until 1935. Sixta's dog "Rivets" delighted many, and Ted Key's "Hazel" became the perennial favorite of favorites. At first "Henry" was the sole comic in the book, and he was centered on the last page; through the thirties there were rarely more than two such pictures in a number. Toward the end of the Stout regime there were more, and Hibbs increased their number by a third in the first year of his editorship and accented many of them with a bit of color.

The sudden departure of Editor Stout had pleased some of the friends of the current administration at Washington; but anyone who hoped that the *Post's* anti-Roosevelt guns had been spiked was surprised unpleasantly and soon. Editorials against F. D. R. were standard procedure on the editorial page in 1944, and there was an article each week in favor of the Republican cause for two or three months before Roosevelt was reëlected to a fourth term in November of that year. In the 1948 campaign National Chairman J. Howard McGrath wrote for Truman and Senator Robert A. Taft for Dewey, but there was a strong editorial barrage against Truman. The next year the editorial page was shifted to the front of the book (where it was preceded only by the new and popular "Letters" department) and there, with the aid of a weekly cartoon, it went after Truman and the Democratic administration regularly and with increasing intolerance. In the 1952 campaign, the *Post* published articles friendly to Stevenson as well as to Eisenhower; editorially it was strongly Republican in both 1952 and 1956.

There was, of course, no circulation advance during the war years; but 1946 saw the upward curve started again. In November of the following year the price was raised to fifteen cents;[91] but this had only a brief adverse effect, and in 1949 the magazine reached an average annual net circulation of over four million. It reached five million in February 1954. More than half of this was still sold by mail subscriptions.

Not until 1946 did the *Post* regain something like the corpulence of the late twenties. In 1947 advertising rates were raised to about $10,000 for a black-and-white page, and the issue for May 17 of that year carried the largest advertising business, counted in dollar value, in the history of the magazine — $1,625,000. This issue contained 200 pages, of which 126 were given to advertising. But the *Post* did not let that record stand. It took page ads in the papers on October 17, 1951, to announce that in its issue for October 20 it was carrying "the biggest dollar volume of advertising in its entire history." This was in a 224-page number with 139 pages devoted to advertising, and the value referred to was $2,098,729.[92] In 1952 a black-and-white page sold for $13,710, and the fourth cover page for $26,325.

On the other hand, paper and labor costs continued to advance alarmingly. By 1947 the *Post* was paying twenty million dollars a year for paper, and increases continued. It was estimated at that time that each copy of the magazine delivered in the home cost almost thirty cents; thus advertising paid half of the cost to the reader. Advertising accounted for three-fourths of the publisher's revenue.[93] But by 1951 the Curtis Publishing Company, issuing the *Post*, the *Ladies' Home Journal*, the *Country Gentleman*, *Holiday*, and *Jack and Jill*, was able, for the first time in many years, to figure earnings on its common stock. Its gross income for 1950 had been about a hundred and fifty million dollars and its net just short of six and a quarter million.[94]

A "new dress" in October 1955 gave the *Post* wider margins and more pictures — "an easier-to-read, more beautiful magazine," said Editor Hibbs.

The history of the *Saturday Evening Post* falls into certain fairly

[91] The annual rate had been raised from $3.00 to $4.00 in 1944; now it was increased to $6.00. The two-year rate had then been raised from $5.00 to $6.00; now it was jumped to $10.00.
[92] *Printer's Ink*, v. 237, Oct. 19, 1951, p. 14.
[93] Staff talks: see note 89 *supra*.
[94] *New York Times*, March 23, 1951, p. 29, col. 4.

well defined over-all periods. During its first quarter-century it was a weekly paper of news and miscellany whose chief distinction was that it had managed to survive longer than its fellows in the highly competitive Saturday paper field. Its second twenty-five years were a kind of golden age of its career as a Saturday miscellany, when it proudly displayed the work of contributors who are still famous in American literature, as well as popular features by lesser writers. Its third quarter-century was spent obscurely, as one of the decreasing number of representatives of an out-dated type of week-end paper, now crowded by the great Sunday editions of the newspapers. This was followed by the Curtis-Lorimer era, which lasted for forty-five years, including the Stout editorship. In this period the *Post* became an American institution, and it was so recognized by both its admirers and its critics. Definitely a young man's guide to success at the beginning of this stage, it gradually broadened its appeal. The modern, or recent, period began in 1942, when Ben Hibbs took the helm. The *Post* is now a magazine for the man and his family. At this writing we have some perspective from which to view the Hibbs regime, and it seems to be continuing, with intelligent modern adaptation, in the great tradition of the *Post*.

"The great American nickelodeon" it was once called. The term is long out-dated, and we have no Will Rogers to make us another one for today. But it must be generally agreed that the *Saturday Evening Post* is as American as the public school, the big department store, the television network program, the hot dog and the ice cream cone. For many years it has set a long and wide table with a great diversity of offerings. The *Post* has amused and informed and taught our people for a longer time than any other American general magazine.

## SCRIBNER'S MAGAZINE [1]

WHEN Scribner & Company sold their magazine to the newly formed Century Company in 1881, and *Scribner's Monthly* became the *Century Illustrated Monthly Magazine*, it was part of the bargain that the Scribner name should not reappear in the magazine field for at least five years.[2] But as soon as the stipulated lustrum had passed, Charles Scribner's Sons, book publishers, began planning a new *Scribner's Magazine*. As editor they chose Edward L. Burlingame, a member of their own staff. It was an excellent choice. Son of the famous diplomat Anson Burlingame, educated in American and European universities, experienced in both newspaper work and book publishing, the new editor was enterprising and aggressive but insistent upon literary and artistic standards.

When the first number of *Scribner's Magazine* was issued, in January 1887, there were already three general magazines published in the United States in the "quality" bracket. The *Atlantic Monthly* carried no illustration, published 144 pages a month, claimed a circulation of 12,500, and was a faithful heir to a fine literary tradition. The *Century* was copiously and beautifully illustrated, published 160 pages monthly, had a circulation of over 222,000, and had good literary standards as well as an interest in some current problems. *Harper's New Monthly Magazine* was the oldest of the three, despite its title; it gave its readers 168 large pages a month of richly illustrated articles and stories, had a circulation of 185,000, and appealed to a very wide American audi-

[1] TITLE: *Scribner's Magazine.*
FIRST ISSUE: Jan. 1887. LAST ISSUE: *May* 1939.
PERIODICITY: Monthly. Vols. 1–104, regular semiannual, Jan. 1887–Dec. 1938; 105, Jan.–May 1939. Merged with the *Commentator* in Nov. 1939.
PUBLISHERS: Charles Scribner's Sons, New York, 1887–1937; Harlan Logan Associates, New York, 1937–39.
EDITORS: Edward Livermore Burlingame, 1887–1914; Robert Bridges, 1914–30; Alfred S. Dashiell, 1930–36; Harlan de Baun Logan, 1936–39.
INDEXES: *Index to Vols. I–X, Jan. 1887–Dec. 1891* (New York, 1891). Indexed in Poole, *Readers' Guide, Cumulative Index, Annual Library Index, A. L. A. Portrait Index, Review of Reviews Annual Index, Contents-Subject Index, Engineering Index.*
REFERENCES: *A Brief Retrospect of Scribner's Magazine* (New York, 1905); Frederick Lewis Allen, "Fifty Years of *Scribner's Magazine*," *Scribner's*, v. 101, Jan. 1937, pp. 19–24; Marion Ives, "*Scribner's* — Surveyor of the American Scene," *Quill*, v. 23, Dec. 1935, pp. 8ff.
[2] See F. L. Mott, *A History of American Magazines* (Cambridge, 1938), v. 3, p. 468. George F. Rowell, in his *Forty Years An Advertising Agent* (New York, 1906), p. 415, says that Roswell Smith "never quite forgave the Scribner firm for starting *Scribner's Magazine*. He thought they had no right to do so."

ence on a cultural level slightly lower than that of its competitors. Each of the three sold for thirty-five cents a copy, or four dollars a year.

This was the group of which *Scribner's Magazine* was designed to make a fourth. The talk of the trade was to the effect that its backers had set aside half a million dollars to place it in that position, and that it spent the last dollar of that fund before its losses were changed to profits.[3]

Burlingame said repeatedly that his formula was popular topics with literary treatment — "intrinsic interest" and "pure literary work." [4] By this he did not mean, however, that topical matters (that is, matters of immediate interest and the frequently berated ephemera of the newspapers) were to occupy much space. On the contrary, the early *Scribner's* gave less attention to public affairs and social causes than the *Century*; it was only after it became well established in the literary and art fields that it gave any very considerable space to treat, with dignity, what Burlingame called "the great working life and practical achievements of the country." As to "pure literary work," it was not always as successful as the *Atlantic*; but it generally kept to a good standard and sometimes reached a very high one.

But the Scribner ace in this competitive game was the magazine's price of twenty-five cents a copy instead of thirty-five, and three dollars a year instead of four. True, it was a little smaller than its rivals; but it was well illustrated, and every one of its 128 pages bespoke modest but insistent "quality." The hypothesis on which the Scribner house bet its half million was that readers of the upper middle class, at which the magazine was aimed, would be happy to save a dollar a year even at the sacrifice of thirty to a hundred pages per issue, if the content was attractive and on a good cultural level.

A hundred thousand copies of the widely publicized first number were distributed; and though it was more than two years before the average circulation reached that figure, *Scribner's Magazine* appeared to be a success from the very first. Let us take a look at this Volume One, Number One. The cover was designed by Stanford White, who had made the one used by the *Century*; many years later, *Time* was to take occasion in its obituary article on *Scribner's* to speak of the "the ugly yellow cover designed by Stanford White." [5] The color of the cover stock was a light buff, and White's neoclassic design was far from displeasing to magazine readers for over half a century. The

---

[3] J. B. Walker in *Cosmopolitan*, v. 14, p. 261, Jan. 1893; E. W. Bok, in the *Epoch*, v. 10, p. 296, Dec. 11, 1891. "Money flowed like water before the first issue came out," wrote Bok.

[4] *Current Literature*, v. 2, p. 93, Feb. 1889; *Scribner's* v. 73, p. 121, Jan. 1923.

[5] *Time*, v. 33, May 15, 1939, p. 60.

number opens with an installment of E. B. Washburne's recollections of what he had seen in the Paris of the Commune when he was minister to France, with illustrations by Howard Pyle and Thure de Thulstrup. This is followed by the initial installments of two serial stories — Harold Frederic's fine novel of rural New York, "Seth's Brother's Wife," and H. C. Bunner's historical romance, "The Story of a New York House." The former is not illustrated, but Bunner's work has some pleasing woodcuts after F. Hopkinson Smith, A. B. Frost, and G. W. Edwards. Three elegiac sonnets by Arlo Bates follow; there are two other poems in the issue — one by Austin Dobson and the other by Maybury Fleming. Then comes one of the two articles in the first number that may be said to deal with public affairs — Captain F. V. Freene's "Our Defenceless Coasts," illustrated by maps and diagrams. The other article is "Socialism," by President Francis A. Walker, of the Massachusetts Institute of Technology; it reads very much like appeals for "free enterprise" seventy-five years later. A second serial of the autobiographical type is introduced in the first installment of excerpts from the Paris diaries of another minister to France, this time not from the Commune period but from an earlier disturbance known as the French Revolution. There are two short stories — Thomas A. Janvier's tragic and colorful "In Mexico," and a shorter, sentimental piece with musical theme by Margaret Crosby. The article on the fine arts is by William Hayes Ward, and is illustrated by photographs of pieces from the author's collection reproduced by halftone.

An illustrated article on some phase of the fine arts in each number came to be characteristic of *Scribner's*. John C. Ropes, historian, supplied articles on likenesses of Caesar and Napoleon to the first volume; later he contributed several studies in his favorite field of Napoleonic investigation. E. H. and E. W. Blashfield provided art-and-travel articles, with illustrations, for many numbers in the early nineties; W. C. Brownell had a series on French art and artists in 1892, and P. G. Hamerton one on "Types of Contemporary Painting" in 1894. Robert Blum's "Artists in Japan" was an attractive feature of 1892.

"The strength of *Scribner's* lies in the illustrations," pontificated W. T. Stead in his English *Review of Reviews* in 1890.[6] Possibly, but it was several years before the new magazine could be said to be abreast of the *Century* in this regard. Josiah B. Millet was the first art editor. He was succeeded in April 1888 by O. H. Perry. In the early volumes woodcuts predominated, by such engravers as W. B. Closson, G. T. Andrew, George Kruell, Frederick Juengling, and Elbridge Kingsley. But in the early nineties, photography through a screen upon

[6] *Review of Reviews* (London), v. 1, p. 67, Jan. 1890.

metal, developed as halftone engraving, came to be used more and more; and the engravers and printers of *Scribner's* did amazingly fine work in this kind. Besides the artists already mentioned, the following were prominent in the first ten or twelve years: J. W. Alexander, W. L. Taylor, R. F. Zogbaum, C. D. Gibson, Kenyon Cox, Will H. Low, W. T. Smedley, A. B. Frost, Peter Newell, W. D. Stevens, and Maxfield Parrish. A few chromolithographs were used, by Blum and others, in 1892–1893. The number for May 1893 was designed for exhibition at the World's Fair; it represented most of the leading illustrators and was called by one good critic an "exponent of the highest stage we have reached in the art of illustrating."[7] There were several articles about the fair in 1892–1893. A series on American illustrators in 1892 and one on wood engravers in 1895 gave special opportunities for attractive illustration, and Ernest C. Peixotto began in 1898 a long series of travel articles illustrated by the author — a kind of offering with which *Scribner's* long delighted its readers. In 1896 the magazine began its department called "The Field of Art," for many years signed by a variety of critics — Russell Sturgis, Frank Weitenkampf, Will H. Low, and others.

Chief literary triumphs of the early *Scribner's* were "Unpublished Letters of Thackeray," begun in the fourth number, and illustrated by the author's own sketches and by a fine Kruell engraving of the Laurence portrait; and some essays and a serial story by Robert Louis Stevenson. The serial was "The Master of Ballantrae" (1887–1888), and a few years later the magazine published "The Wrecker," by Stevenson and his stepson Lloyd Osbourne. Indeed, *Scribner's* was long the R. L. S. magazine. In 1899 it printed letters of Stevenson, edited by Sidney Colvin, with sequels in 1911 and 1923; then came Osbourne's recollections of his stepfather in 1923–1924, and other R. L. S. material.

George Meredith's "The Amazing Marriage" was a serial of 1895. There were three or four by Frederic, some comparatively undistinguished ones by Mrs. Humphry Ward and William Dean Howells, and George W. Cable's "John March, Southerner" in 1894. In 1896 the magazine made a great hit with J. M. Barrie's "Sentimental Tommy," and later followed it with "Tommy and Grizel" in 1901. In 1897 it printed an early "Jerry" serial by Sarah Barnwell Elliott and Richard Harding Davis' popular "Soldiers of Fortune." Thomas Nelson Page's historical "Red Rock" came the next year. A. T. Quiller-Couch's Cornish tales began in 1899.

There were some really notable short stories — Octave Thanet's

---

[7] *Review of Reviews* (New York), v. 7, p. 609, June 1893.

"Stories of a Western Town" (1892), Bunner's "As One Having Authority" (August 1892), Page's "The Burial of the Guns" (April 1894), Ernest Thompson Seton's "Lobo" (November 1894), Stephen Crane's masterpiece "The Open Boat" (June 1897), and Rudyard Kipling's ".007" (August 1897). Most of the well-known fictioneers of the time contributed to *Scribner's*. Besides those already named, we must list F. J. Stimson, Edith Wharton, Joel Chandler Harris, Henry James, Robert Grant, Bret Harte, Sarah Orne Jewett, Frank R. Stockton, F. Hopkinson Smith, Robert Herrick, William Allen White, and Julian Ralph. It would almost seem as though *Scribner's* discovered the short story of newspaper life, what with such famous stories as Richard Harding Davis' "Gallegher" (August 1890), Jesse Lynch Williams' "The Stolen Story" (August 1897), and many others in between.

The magazine was strong in biography and autobiography. Henry M. Stanley, Lester Wallack, Mrs. John Drew, Hugh McCulloch, and George F. Hoar wrote their recollections for readers of the nineties. William C. Church's "John Ericsson" (1890) and A. T. Mahan's "John Paul Jones" (1898) showed *Scribner's* interest in the navy as well as in biography. Two serial histories should be mentioned: E. Benjamin Andrews' "History of the Last Quarter Century" (1890) and Henry Cabot Lodge's "The Story of the Revolution" (1898).

A number of articles about steamships, mechanics and invention, and industry appeared in early volumes. In 1891 there was a series on ocean travel and commerce. But the series in this field that attracted the greatest attention was one on railroads in 1888–1889, by various writers. This was not a muckraking venture, but a good collection of analytical and expository articles. One of the best of them was Charles Francis Adams' "The Prevention of Railroad Strikes," which advocated recognition of employee organizations. This series was said to have increased *Scribner's* circulation by twenty-five thousand.[8] Later came some articles on electricity in industry, and in 1897 a symposium on "The Conduct of Great Business," such as hotels, factories, department stores, and banks.

But *Scribner's* appeared to be interested in the poor as well as in the rich. A success in 1889 was Jacob A. Riis's "How the Other Half Lives," followed three years later by "The Poor in Great Cities," by Riis and others. "Men's Occupations" was also an 1892 series; and in 1898 appeared Walter A. Wyckoff's articles on "The Workers," the third of which was a notable discussion of "The Army of the Unemployed."

President Walker continued to write his conservative articles on economic and social topics through the nineties. There were pieces on

[8] *Current Literature*, v. 1, p. 369, Oct. 1888.

forestry, irrigation, and so on, by N. S. Shaler and other scientists. William James contributed several articles on psychological subjects. In the latter nineties much attention was paid to colleges and universities, and there was a series on "Undergraduate Life in America" in 1897.

Theodore Roosevelt wrote on "Six Years of Civil Service Reform" in August 1895; this was the beginning of a long series of contributions by T. R., including his chronicle of the "Rough Riders" (1899) and those of his later hunting expeditions to Brazil and Africa. The story of Roosevelt's famous regiment in Cuba was only one of the many features that *Scribner's* published about the war with Spain. In 1898 the magazine averaged three articles about the war in each issue — by Richard Harding Davis, John R. Spears, Captain Mahan, and many others.

*Scribner's* continued the older magazine tradition of emphasis on accounts of travel in far-away places. Its interest in foreign countries during the nineties was pictorial and curious rather than political and sociological. Brownell's articles on French life and character (1887–1888) were later included in his volume *French Traits*. A member of Charles Scribner's Sons editorial staff for nearly forty years, Brownell commonly wrote his literary and art criticism for the magazine, and collected it later in volumes that the firm published. William F. Apthorpe's series of 1892 on the theaters of Paris was attractive, and suited the magazine's special predilection for France. In the same year there were articles on "The Great Streets of the World." Sir Edwin Arnold wrote on picturesque Japan in 1890.

The literary type of essay, in the field of criticism of life or letters or both, was common in *Scribner's*; August Birrell, Bliss Perry, Brander Matthews, E. S. Martin, Robert Grant, and W. C. Brownell were frequent contributors of such essays. The department called "The Point of View," written by Editor Bridges and others — sometimes even by writers quite outside the Scribner House — was begun in 1890 and continued for more than thirty years to provide *Scribner's* readers with urbane, intelligent, conservative comment, to the extent of three or four pages a month.

*Scribner's* poetry was occasionally distinguished. Charles Henry Lüders' "The Dead Nymph" (December 1888) and Rudyard Kipling's "McAndrew's Hymn" (December 1888) represent both the wide range and the high quality of the verse in the early volumes. Julia C. R. Dorr, Edith M. Thomas, Charles Edwin Markham, Andrew Lang, Archibald Lampman, Susan Coolidge, Richard Hovey, Oliver Herford, and Mrs. James T. Fields were frequent contributors of verse.

By the mid-nineties, *Scribner's* was well established both as a quality magazine and as a money-maker. Frank N. Doubleday, later a famous book publisher, was business manager; and the first advertising manager was J. Rowland Mix.[9] The magazine's October 1891 number circulated 124,850 copies, and the average for that year was 110,000.[10] Its slogan "When in doubt, buy *Scribner's*," was widely advertised. It carried about 100 pages of advertising monthly, at $200 a page. In 1891 it adopted the plan (far ahead of its time) of inserting a few comic drawings in the advertising section, thus making a hit with the space-buyers. English and Australian editions were set up when the magazine was only a year or two old.

But the "quality group" suffered in the mid-nineties from two causes — the hard times and the advent of the ten-cent general illustrated magazines. Like *Harper's* and the *Century*, *Scribner's* declined somewhat in circulation at this time; but *Scribner's* recovered better than the others and passed its thirty-five cent rivals at the end of the century with an annual average circulation of 165,000, in comparison with the 150,000 that they each claimed.

The first ten or fifteen years of the new century comprised the period of *Scribner's* highest circulation, which went to two hundred thousand and over in 1909–1911, and its best advertising patronage, which ran to well over a hundred pages a month at three hundred dollars a page. On *Scribner's* twenty-fifth anniversary, in 1912, the *Outlook* printed a congratulatory editorial in which it stated a common opinion of the magazine:

> Ably edited, representing the best standards interpreted by the most original writers, thoroughly artistic in illustration, *Scribner's Magazine* must be counted not only among the publications which belong to periodical literature, but also as an important contribution to permanent literature.[11]

Leading authors of serial stories in this period were F. Hopkinson Smith, Maurice Hewlett, John Fox, Jr., Edith Wharton, and John Galsworthy. Fox's "Little Shepherd of Kingdom Come" (1903) and "The Trail of the Lonesome Pine" (1908) were major successes. It was Editor Burlingame who suggested a fine title for a fine novel [12] when he accepted Mrs. Wharton's "The House of Mirth" (1905); later the magazine published other serials of hers, including the novelette "Ethan Frome" in August–October 1911. Of Galsworthy's novels *Scribner's*

[9] Earnest Elmo Calkins, "Magazine into Marketplace," *Scribner's*, v. 101, Jan. 1937, p. 112.
[10] Advertisement in Ayer's *Directory* for 1891, p. 1369, gives the Oct. 1891 circulation and the advertising rate.
[11] *Outlook*, v. 100, p. 65, Jan. 13, 1912.
[12] Allen in *Scribner's*, v. 101, Jan. 1937, p. 24.

also printed several, from "Dark Flower" (1913) to "The White Monkey" (1924).

Some of these novelists also contributed frequent short stories to *Scribner's*, as did Katharine Fullerton Gerould ("Vain Oblations," March 1911), Mary R. S. Andrews ("The Perfect Tribute," July 1906), Robert Herrick ("The Master of the Inn," December 1907), Mary Synon, Arthur W. Colton, James B. Connolly, Cyrus T. Brady, James G. Huneker, Kate Douglas Wiggin, Alice Brown, and other prominent writers.

Best of the *Scribner* poets of these years was Edwin Arlington Robinson, who sent some of his finest short poems to the magazine. Others were Henry Van Dyke, David Morton, Arthur Davison Ficke, Sarah N. Cleghorn, Edith Wharton, and Katharine Lee Bates. *Scribner's* was never averse to making a striking display of a chosen poem, as when it presented Maxwell Struthers Burt's "Pierrot at War" in April 1916 with two full-color plates by Elenore Plaisted Abbott.

These were the years of the prosperity of muckraking. *Scribner's* did not share in the movement or in the affluence which it sometimes brought. It printed some articles in the field of industry and labor, like Wyckoff's "London Wage Earners" (1902) and a second railroad series (1906), which did not duplicate the success of the earlier one; but in the main its interests were belletristic [13] and its mood urbane, in a magazine era generally characterized by attacks and exposés in many fields.

A count of pages in 1906, at the climax of the muckraking movement, shows that almost exactly half of *Scribner's* contents were then devoted to fiction and poetry; about a fourth to art, travel, and the wild-animal studies of Thompson Seton; and about an eighth to biography and literary criticism — leaving only about an eighth for economics and sociology, foreign affairs, railways (nearly all foreign), army and navy, and mechanics and industry.[14] Even when *Scribner's* dealt with social and industrial problems — as it did again and again, and effectively — its attitude was likely to be reasonable, polite, and slightly professional.

Theodore Roosevelt, who gave impetus and a reproachful name to muckraking, was *Scribner's* outstanding contributor during the first two decades of the twentieth century. His "African Game Trails," for which the magazine paid $50,000, was published serially in 1910 and

[13] C. C. Regier, *The Era of the Muckrakers* (Chapel Hill, 1932), p. 11.

[14] Fiction occupied 697 pages out of 1536, and poetry 53. Such classifications are never trustworthy, but this count gives a pretty reliable general idea of contents for the year in which Roosevelt gave vent to his famous outburst against muckraking.

resulted in newsstand sellouts of every issue in which it appeared.[15]
Thus it was responsible for the largest annual average in the magazine's
history — 215,000.[16] There was not the same response to "A Hunter
Naturalist in the Brazilian Forest" when it was serialized in 1914;
there was a great difference between the adventures of a romantic figure
just out of the White House, and the less exciting experiences of a
half-forgotten man in a continent far removed from a Europe then
bursting into flame.

Frederick Funston's Philippine recollections were a good feature in
1911; and George W. Goethals' "The Building of the Panama Canal,"
the first installment of which was illustrated by full-color reproductions
of a series of paintings by W. B. Van Ingen, was the major nonwar
magazine feature of 1915. Other autobiographical serials were the recollections of Mrs. Burton Harrison (1911), Henry Cabot Lodge (1912–
1913), Richard Harding Davis (1914), and Edward H. Sothern (1914).
Dealing with the more distant past were Roosevelt's "Oliver Cromwell"
(1901), Mahan's "The War of 1812" (1904), and the artist-author
W. J. Aylward's beautifully illustrated article on the clipper ships
(April 1917).

An attractive series, with fine illustrations, was the one about American wild animals by Ernest Thompson Seton, published in 1907. William T. Hornaday was also a contributor in this field.

In the second decade of the century there was much about the automobile. From 1906 on, an early issue of each year commonly featured
motoring articles and advertising. A travel series entitled "The Motor
and the Highways," by writers who had driven the roads in various
countries, was a 1914 feature. Thus was *Scribner's* traditional interest
in travel adapted to the motor age. Its illustration of such articles also
showed new developments, as the scenery of western America and
Canada came to be depicted by the camera rather than by painters.
The photographic studies of Indians by E. S. Curtis had been a striking feature of the magazine in 1906; in 1915 Dwight L. Elmendorf's
pictures of American scenery were notable. But the travel article illustrated by the author's sketches or paintings was still characteristic of
*Scribner's*; Edward Penfield did many of them, and Peixotto more.
Kenyon Cox's "The Golden Age of Painting" (1917) was illustrated
through photography of masterpieces, as was the "Field of Art"
department.

But the outstanding feature of illustration, and perhaps the most
striking thing about the whole magazine in this period, was its full-

---

[15] *New York Herald Tribune*, Sept. 3, 1941, p. 16, col. 2.
[16] See Ayer's *Directory*, 1910, advertisement on p. 1291.

color pictures. There had been early ventures, already noted, in chromolithography, and from 1897 onward there were some colored borders
and decorations. In the Christmas number for 1899 there were some
effective two-color pictures, and a year later John La Farge's article
on Puvis de Chavannes, with its full-color plates, was a sensation in
the magazine world. In the next few years the color illustrations of
Quiller-Couch's Cornwall stories by Howard Pyle and Maxfield Parrish, Frederic Remington's "Western Types" (October 1902), A. B.
Frost's "The Farmer's Seasons" (August 1906), N. C. Wyeth's bold
and sparkling illustrations of Connolly's sea stories, Jessie Willcox
Smith's children, and Howard Chandler Christy's mannered drawings
of the life of fashion — all in full color — made *Scribner's* resplendent.

Burlingame retired from the editorship in 1914. He was sixty-six and
had been at the magazine's helm for over a quarter of a century. A
decline in circulation had set in. Reducing the advertising rate to two
hundred and fifty dollars [17] a page had not increased linage: the magazine now ran about eighty pages of advertising a month. In the reorganization, Robert Bridges, who had been associate editor since the
magazine had been founded, and a newspaperman before that, took the
top editorial post.[18] He was only ten years younger than Burlingame,
and he continued the traditional policies of *Scribner's* without much
change.

The outbreak of the European War, as it was then called in the hope
that the United States might not be drawn into it, brought to America
a competition in British and German propaganda. English thinking
was reflected in *Scribner's Magazine* by John Galsworthy's effective
"Thoughts on This War" in the issue for November 1914; its sequel
came more than a year later in "Second Thoughts" (January 1916).
Edith Wharton's observations of France at war were printed in 1915,
and were followed by Herbert Ward's "War-Time Sketches in France"
(June 1916). On the other side, there were such pieces as Price Collier's
"Germany and the Germans" (1913) and Oswald Garrison Villard's
"Germany Embattled" (December 1914), but the weight was on the
side of the Allies. From the field, *Scribner's* had Richard Harding
Davis's vivid articles, H. G. Dwight's reports from the Near East,
James F. J. Archibald's articles from the German side, and a varied lot
of reports from such observers as E. Alexander Powell, Charles Lincoln
Freeston, and Alexander Dana Noyes. From their Washington offices,
Franklin D. Roosevelt wrote an appeal for the navy with the title "On

---

[17] See Ayer's *Directory*, 1914, advertisement between pp. 1392 and 1393.
[18] The best biography of Bridges is a two-column obituary notice in the *New York
Herald Tribune*, Sept. 3, 1941, p. 16.

Your Own Heads" (April 1917), and Henry L. Stimson sent a contribution on military training for the same number.

In 1918–1919 each number of *Scribner's* contained four to six war pieces: many phases of the conflict were treated by many writers. Outstanding were the articles of Raymond Recouly ("Captain X") on the French fighting, Winston Spencer Churchill's "A Traveller in War-Time" (1918), and the battle front paintings of F. C. Yohn. There were groups of war poems — a technique followed later in presenting contemporary poetry.

When the war was over, *Scribner's* followed its traditional path with respect to contents. There were new writers in the twenties, but there were also contributions by many whose names had become familiar in the magazine's pages before the war — Mrs. Wharton and Mrs. Gerould, Brownell, Galsworthy, Van Dyke, and so on. The most striking change was a decline in illustration. Full-color plates had gradually disappeared during the war, and even the number of fine-screen halftones had been greatly reduced. By the end of 1924 most of the magazine was printed on a paper suitable only for the reproduction of line drawings; and there were only two sections on better paper — one for three or four illustrated articles, and the other for the "Field of Art" department. The latter was edited after 1923 by Royal Cortissoz. *Scribner's* still liked articles illustrated by their authors, and it found several new writer-artists who contributed to its pages in these years and in the following decade. John W. Thomason, a captain of the marines, began in 1923 a series of contributions, illustrated by his own sketches, which were to continue almost as long as the magazine did. They dealt with the war at first; later there was a life of General J. E. B. Stuart (1930) and some fiction. Will James, the cowboy artist, was another who wrote pieces to go with his pictures; he also began in *Scribner's* in 1923, and his contributions — including "Smoky" in 1926 — covered nearly a decade. In the late twenties there were many groups of illustrations, such as Doris Ulmann's "Kentucky Mountains" (June 1928).

"Theodore Roosevelt and His Time" was the title given T. R.'s letters, edited by Joseph Bucklin Bishop and published in 1919–1920. Corrinne Roosevelt Robinson contributed her recollections of her brother in 1921. Chauncey M. Depew's reminiscences made a serial in 1921–1922. And one of the best in *Scribner's* long line of autobiographies was Michael Pupin's "From Immigrant to Inventor" (1922–1923). Edward P. Mitchell's "Recollections of an Editor" appeared in 1924, and there were some of General Lee's letters, edited by Douglas Freeman, in 1925–1926.

Henry Van Dyke's "Guide-Posts and Camp-Fires" made an essay

series in 1919–1921, and John Burroughs also wrote several nature essays for *Scribner's*. Gordon Hall Gerould and Brander Matthews were old favorites among the essayists. William Lyon Phelps began his "As I Like It" department in 1922; it was to continue for fourteen years, lauded by some and berated by others. Brownell's serial dissertation on "Style" was a 1924 offering. Walter Prichard Eaton and Arthur Hobson Quinn wrote on the drama. There were still plenty of travel articles — Mrs. Wharton's "In Morocco" (1919), Recouly's occasional articles about French life and affairs, E. Alexander Powell's postwar travels, and Lothrop Stoddard's observations in the Far East and in Europe from 1921 to 1924. Kermit Roosevelt wrote of elephant hunting in 1924, and there were many other articles about far places.

By 1925 a swing toward greater emphasis on public affairs had become noticeable. The January number for that year led off with a political article by Senator William E. Borah, and contained Edmund A. Whitman's "Who Owns the Railroads?" and an article by Robert A. Millikan on electrons, with Edwin Dial Torgeson's "Letters of a Bourgeois Father to His Bolshevik Son." Every number thereafter had two or three good articles on public affairs. Whiting Williams had been writing on labor and industry in Europe for some time, and J. Laurence Laughlin discussed economic problems. Millikan, George Ellery Hale, and Edward M. East contributed articles on recent scientific developments. In June 1926 appeared William Allen White's striking essay, "The End of an Epoch: The Passing of the Apostles of Liberalism in the United States." Frank R. Kent became the chief political writer the next year. Silas Bent did some profiles, and later some critical analyses of developments in newspaper journalism. Will Rose's series on the small town (1926) was pleasantly nostalgic, and Thomas Boyd's "Mad Anthony Wayne" was a good biographical serial.

Mrs. Wharton and Galsworthy remained *Scribner's* leading writers of long fiction in the first half of the twenties — the former with "A Son at the Front" (1922–1923), and the latter with "To Let" (1921), "The White Monkey" (1924), and "The Silver Spoon" (1925–1926). But in 1927 a new element entered *Scribner's* serial fiction that made a palpable hit and eventually exerted a great effect on most general magazines. This was the detective mystery, and the 1927 serial was S. S. Van Dine's "The Canary Murder Case," followed the next year by "The Greene Murder Case." "Perhaps not in our generation has any other novel of this genre been so extensively read and so highly praised," wrote *Scribner's* editor of the former story.[19] Morley Callaghan's "In His Own Country" was a notable serial of 1929, but it was eclipsed

[19] *Scribner's*, v. 83, p. 1, Jan. 1928.

by the great success of that year, Ernest Hemingway's "A Farewell to Arms."

Likewise in the short-story field, the old-timers continued their long acceptable work in the early twenties, joined after a few years by newcomers. Maxwell Burt ("The Blood-Red One," 1918) was a contributor of fiction, poetry, and essays to *Scribner's* over many years. Ralph D. Paine, Armistead C. Gordon, Louis Dodge, Katharine Holland Brown, and Edward C. Venable were long faithful fictioneers for the magazine. But a little later came some newer talents: Conrad Aiken ("Spider, Spider," February 1928), Stark Young, Meridel Le Sueur, André Maurois, and finally Thomas Wolfe, whose first published story, "An Angel on the Porch," appeared in August 1929.

The downward curve in both circulation and advertising that began about 1912 continued steadily. Circulation declined to 100,000 by 1911 and 70,000 by 1924. Raising the single-copy price to thirty-five cents in 1919 apparently had no effect on circulation, one way or the other: the road led downward anyway. In the late twenties, stimulated by Van Dine and Hemingway, there was an upturn, but it was of short duration. By 1930 *Scribner's* was back at an average annual circulation of about 70,000, while *Harper's* had 120,000 and the *Atlantic* 130,000. In that year young Alfred Sheppard Dashiell, twenty-nine, who had been an assistant editor since his graduation from Princeton, was entrusted with the editorship of *Scribner's*.

Under Dashiell, the magazine came out with a whole new set of authors. Most of the new school of fiction writers were attracted to *Scribner's* pages. Hemingway and Wolfe were joined by Sherwood Anderson, D. H. Lawrence, Erskine Caldwell ("Kneel to the Rising Sun," February 1935), Josephine Herbst, Ruth Suckow, Grane Flandrau, Evelyn Scott, Tess Slesinger ("Jobs in the Sky," March 1935), Marjorie Kinnan Rawlings, Sophie Kerr, Langston Hughes, Sara Haardt, William Saroyan, Vardis Fisher, James Boyd, William Faulkner, and August Derleth. A variety, indeed, but mostly a strong peppering of new movements and youthful vigor. F. Scott Fitgerald, who had contributed a very early short story to *Scribner's*, now appeared with the serial "Tender Is the Night" (1934).

In nonfiction, Dashiell was concerned with finding "a new way of life for America." In one of his early numbers, he wrote:

We shall continue to make free discussion an important feature of our editorial programme. We believe that an examination of other points of view than the orthodox can only be helpful, and we have faith in the vitality and sturdy quality of the United States.[20]

[20] *Scribner's*, v. 91, p. 1, Jan. 1932.

It was his youth, as well as his undoubted editorial ability, that had commended Dashiell to the publishers of *Scribner's,* and he made a magazine much of which was aimed at young intellectuals. He looked more to the leftward for his authors than had been common in the Scribner shop. Clarence Darrow, John Dewey, J. J. Spengler, Lewis Mumford, George Seldes, Max Eastman, Waldo Frank, Thomas Beer, Lothrop Stoddard, Stuart Chase, and Edmund Wilson were common names in the early thirties. "Straws in the Wind: Significant Notes in World Affairs Today" was a new department of shorter articles, not all of it comment on foreign affairs; its companion was "Life in the United States." Kent continued to write politics, Howard Mumford Jones and V. F. Calverton wrote on literary topics, Norman Foerster and John R. Tunis on education, W. M. Kiplinger and Edward A. Filene on business, Paul Hutchinson on religion and the lack of it, and Thomas Craven and Gilbert Seldes on art. There was much for and against the "New Deal," by Henry A. Wallace, Charles A. Beard, A. A. Berle, Jr., Upton Close, and others. Malcolm Cowley wrote a defense of bohemianism in "The Village" (January 1933) and Robert Briffault and William C. White discussed "The Plight of the Intellectuals" (August 1932). Henry Hazlitt proposed government without legislature in July 1932; in the following January Ernest Sutherland Bates wrote on "The Passing of the Democratic Fallacy"; and in April, Ella Winter, recently home from Russia, asked, "After the Family — What?" Thus all voices were heard; and the new and old deals, fascism, communism, all brands of socialism, humanism, bohemianism, and even "economic royalism" had their innings.

Among the serials were Galsworthy's last one, "Flowering Wilderness" (1932), Stephen Bonsal's "Heyday in a Vanished World" (1934), Nicholas Murray Butler's recollections (1935–1936), some biographical studies by Henry F. Pringle, and James Truslow Adams' "The Crisis and the Constitution" (1935–1936). Some new poets appeared — Robinson Jeffers, Jesse Stuart, and Robert P. Tristram Coffin.

The effect of this new editorial policy on the circulation of *Scribner's* was deplorable. The old core of faithful subscribers dropped away, and new recruits did not replace the deserters fast enough. In 1936, when the circulation had dropped nearly to 40,000, Dashiell left *Scribner's* for the *Reader's Digest,* where he was later to make a great success as managing editor. The Scribner firm, now discouraged, but willing to give the magazine one more trial, offered the editorship to Harlan Logan, at that time an associate professor of English at New York University. Logan had been a star basketball player at Indiana University and later a Rhodes scholar. At N.Y.U. he had become interested in the study of periodicals, and soon he had won some recognition as a magazine analyst and adviser to editorial staffs; thus he had attracted the attention of the Scribner house.[21]

Logan enlarged the page size again: it had been made a small-quarto in 1930, and now it was full nine by twelve inches. The single-copy price was put back to the original twenty-five cents. Thomas M. Cleland designed the new cover, which presented a timely picture in full color each month. The dull-finish paper of the past decade was supplanted by calendered stock; and again *Scribner's* was a handsome, fully illustrated magazine.

Logan kept the department "Life in the United States," offering prizes for contributions to it; he also kept "Straws in the Wind," which he made over into the semblance of the *New Yorker's* "Talk of the Town"; and he added "Scribner's Presents," a brief section containing stories or pictures or both by new authors, and a fairly extensive "Scribner Quiz," adapted to the current furor of interest in question-and-answer games. The illustration was excellent and often striking, much of it based on photography. Again there were some fine full-color plates — especially the lithographs of modern art illustrating the 1937 series on "American Painting."

Late in 1937 the editor took over financial management under the name of Harlan Logan Associates, and Don Wharton became his chief associate editor. John Chamberlain reviewed books, George Jean Nathan the theater, and Gilbert Seldes motion pictures. Thomas Craven did some good articles on the midwestern painters Benton, Wood, and Curry. For a while Edwin C. Hill had a department of commentary, giving place to "don herold." Most of the magazine was staff-written, and there were progressively fewer well-known names in the tables of contents.

Under the Logan treatment, *Scribner's* circulation quickly advanced to 100,000. Losses, which had been running to $25,000 a month, were cut to $700; but, according to a current report, the Logan Associates "never turned a profit." [22] Soon after the May 1939 number was on the press, the publication company ran out of working capital and announced the suspension of the magazine.

A few months later *Esquire* bought the *Scribner* list of 80,000 subscribers for $11,000.[23] In August the name was sold to the *Commentator*, which became in November *Scribner's Commentator*. Under this name a size and cover not unlike those of *Scribner's* were adopted. The

---

[21] *News Week*, v. 7, June 27, 1936, p. 29.
[22] *Time*, v. 33, May 15, 1939, p. 60.
[23] *Time*, v. 34, Sept. 4, 1939, p. 34.

serial numbering was that of the *Commentator*, however, and *Scribner's Commentator* was in no sense a continuation of *Scribner's Magazine*. This is important because of an unfortunate sequel.

*Commentator* had been founded by Charles Shipman Payson in 1937, and edited successively by Lowell Thomas and Francis Rufus Bellamy. But in 1941, with *Scribner's* name added, it came under other management; and in October 1942 Joseph Hilton Smyth, its publisher, pleaded guilty to an indictment under the Foreign Agents Registration Act for accepting money from Japanese officials to publish propaganda for that government.[24] When a respectable magazine dies it should emulate Stevenson's hunter and lay itself down with a will, and not pass its name on for some other periodical to disgrace.

Throughout its long life, however, *Scribner's* was a credit to the name it bore — a magazine notable for its service to American literature and art, and for its urbane criticism of our national life and culture.

[24] *New York Times*, Oct. 7, 1942, p. 30; Nov. 2, 1942, p. 10.

29

## SEWANEE REVIEW [1]

WILLIAM PETERFIELD TRENT came to the University of the South, at Sewanee, Tennessee, in 1888. That institution published the *University of the South Magazine* from April through December 1890; many universities tried such magazines in this period, and most of them, like this one, were soon abandoned. But Trent was not deterred by such a record of failures. He was working on his life of William Gilmore Simms at the time, and was inspired by his study of the Simms reviews to try his hand at such a journal. In this ambition he was encouraged by a young professor of Greek, B. Lawton Wiggins, an alumnus of the university and soon to be its head. Telfair Hodgson, who had recently resigned as vice-chancellor of the university, offered — rather unexpectedly, it appears — to assume the financial responsibility for a year, provided his name appeared with the somewhat misleading label of "managing editor." And so the quarterly was launched, in November 1892.

"I got out the first number by hook or crook, writing two articles and several reviews," [2] said Trent later. One of those articles was "The Novels of Thomas Hardy" and the other was a review of Thomas Nelson Page's apologia, *The Old South*. Trent could multiply contributions in this way because anonymity was the rule in that first num-

[1] TITLE: *The Sewanee Review*. Subtitles: "A Quarterly Journal," 1892–97; "A Quarterly Journal of Literary Studies," 1898–99; "Quarterly," 1899–1942. Subtitle on cover on half title, "A Quarterly of Life and Letters," 1928–44.
FIRST ISSUE: Nov. 1892. Current.
PERIODICITY: Quarterly. Vols. 1–4, annual vols. beginning with Nov., Nov. 1892–Aug. 1896; 5–current, annual vols. beginning with Jan.
PUBLISHERS: Financially responsible in earlier years were Telfair Hodgins, 1892–93; B. Lawton Wiggins, 1893–1902; various faculty members and alumni of the University of the South, 1902–17, including small university subsidy as editor's salary, 1900–13; Sewanee Review, Inc., 1913–26; University of the South, 1927–current. The Imprint of Longmans, Green & Co., New York, was carried during 1899–1917, but publication from the beginning has been at Sewanee, Tenn.
EDITORS: William Peterfield Trent, 1892–1900 (with Benjamin Willis Wells, 1897–99); John Bell Henneman, 1900–08 (with Burr James Ramage, 1900–03); faculty of the University of the South, 1909; John McLaren McBryde, Jr., 1910–19; George Herbert Clarke, 1920–25; William Skinkle Knickerbocker, 1926–42; Tudor Seymour Long, 1942–44; Allen Tate, 1944–46; John James Ellis Palmer, 1946–52; Monroe K. Spears, 1952–current.
INDEXES: *Poole's Index, International Index*. General index of vols. 1–10 in v. 10.
REFERENCES: John Bell Henneman, "Ten Years of the *Sewanee Review*: A Retrospect," *Sewanee Review*, v. 10, pp. 477–92, Oct. 1902; Alice Lucile Turner, *A Study of the Content of The Sewanee Review, with Historical Introduction* (Nashville, Tenn., 1931); Franklin Trenaby Walker, "William Peterfield Trent: A Critical Biography" (dissertation, George Peabody College for Teachers, 1943).
[2] Henneman in *Sewanee Review*, v. 10, p. 480, Oct. 1902.

ber; later, however, most articles were signed. Trent wrote five of the thirty articles in the first volume of the *Review*, and twenty-one during his eight years' editorship. These had a remarkable range of subject matter, from the Greek elegy to the political issue of imperialism. Trent's brother-in-law and colleague, Benjamin W. Wells, wrote two articles for the first number, and six for the first volume; from 1897 through 1899 (after which he left Sewanee to become associate editor of the *Churchman*), Wells served as Trent's associate in the editorship of the *Review*.

"This *Review* has been established under the auspices of the Faculty of the University of the South, at Sewanee, Tennessee," said the prospectus printed on the inside of the cover of the first number. And then followed:

> It will be devoted to such topics as General Theology, Philosophy, History, and Literature as require fuller treatment than they usually receive in the popular magazines, and less technical treatment than they receive in specialist publications. In other words, the *Review* will conform more nearly to the type of the English reviews than is usual with American periodicals.

But literature should have been placed first in the list, for the *Review* has always been preëminently a journal of literary criticism. A computation covering its first 37 years shows about 60 per cent of its articles dealing directly with literature, with English letters far in the lead, and America slightly behind Europe. History comes next, then contemporary questions, biography, education, philosophy and theology, and fine arts, in that order.[3]

There were a hundred and twenty-eight octavo pages, one-fourth of them given to book reviews and notes, the whole bound in a brown cover and priced at seventy-five cents a number, or three dollars a year. With the second volume, Wiggins took over the business management, and he continued with that responsibility, including finding the funds for the annual deficit, for some ten years. The circulation during the nineties was not over five hundred copies per issue.

The *Review* found some important friends, however, and without doubt exerted a good influence on taste and scholarship. Trent wrote to a later editor that "the most hearty northern support" came from Theodore Roosevelt and Brander Matthews.

> They never ceased to praise and encourage. Roosevelt wrote an article, and on more than one occasion praised the *Review* in public. Matthews did likewise, and was constantly suggesting articles and writers.[4]

[3] Turner, *The Content of The Sewanee Review*, p. 273.
[4] Henneman in *Sewanee Review*, v. 10, p. 483, Oct. 1902.

Roosevelt's article was a letter to a committee in charge of the Lee centennial, published in April 1907 as "Robert E. Lee and the Nation." Other writers active in the pages of the early *Review* included William Norman Guthrie, Burr James Ramage, Thomas F. Gailor, Francis A. Shoup, William P. Du Bose, and John Fearnley, all of the faculty of the University of the South. The faculty contributors made the *Review* in its early volumes, and its excellence at that time is a tribute to the liberal attitudes as well as to the learning of the university at Sewanee.[5]

Trent was not only a distinguished scholar, a great teacher, and a discriminating critic; but he was always a kindly gentleman as well. Highly characteristic is his review of Edwin Arlington Robinson's privately printed *The Torrent and the Night Before*, in which he said of Robinson:

> We fancy that he is young, for we detect the influences of other poets in his work; and if he is, we have decided hope of him — nay, we have not only hope of him, which is what almost any kindly critic may say of any fledgling poet, but we have a positive desire to see his next volume. . . . We think that he handles the sonnet very well indeed. . . . We do not wish our readers to suspect us as posing as a "poet-finder." Our purpose is a more modest one — namely, to encourage Mr. Robinson with the thought that he has at least one interested reader.[6]

Trent's own slender volume of *Verses* appeared some two years after this; it was not noticed in the *Review*.

The allegiance of the *Review* to certain English forms, and its continuing interest in English literature and English culture, were perhaps due in some measure to the university's affiliation with the Church of England. The magazine also had an acknowledged allegiance to the South, and gave much attention to the history and literature of that region. Yet, chiefly through its broad sympathies, it avoided being sectional.

When Trent was called to Columbia University in 1900, his place as editor of the *Sewanee Review* was taken by John Bell Henneman, who had held the chair of English language and literature at the University of Tennessee, and who was invited to a similar post at Sewanee when Trent left. Henneman, like his predecessor, was a scholar and a gentleman.[7] He wrote with ease and authority on many subjects, and had been a contributor to the *Review* before assuming its editorship; his favorite topics were Shakespeare, education, and the literature of the South. For the first three or four years of his editorship, he had Ramage

---

[5] See William S. Knickerbocker, "Trent at Sewanee," *Sewanee Review*, v. 48, pp. 149–50, April 1940.
[6] *Sewanee Review*, v. 5, p. 246, April 1897.
[7] *Ibid.*, v. 17, pp. 107ff, Jan. 1909.

as an associate and a ready writer on historical, political, and economic subjects.

Henneman died in November 1908, and for a year thereafter the journal was edited by faculty committees; then for a full decade the editor was John McLaren McBryde, Jr. (son of the famous botanist of the same name), who, like his predecessors, was the ranking professor of English at Sewanee. McBryde was much interested in folklore; and there were contributions in that field by such authors as William Hand Browne, Henry Marvin Belden, and John A. Lomax. The *Review* was by this time printing more and more contributions by writers outside of Sewanee. It could command such articles not by payment in money, for it never paid its contributors, but because of the prestige that it had attained.

During McBryde's editorship the journal celebrated its twenty-fifth anniversary. During all this time (and, indeed, for nearly twenty years longer) its circulation was not often more than four hundred copies. A large share of these copies, however, went into libraries, where they found many readers.

The financial difficulties of such a journal are set forth in a revealing letter by McBryde:

When I took charge, the University did not claim ownership and was unwilling to assume any financial responsibility, as the University itself was then having to meet an annual deficit of a good many thousand dollars. Even the annual stipend of three hundred dollars which the University had paid as an editorial salary for several years was stopped when Bishop Albion W. Knight became chancellor in 1913. It happened, however, for several years, that one good friend after another came forward to pay the deficit on the *Review*. There was no managing editor, no treasurer, no regular business manager. . . . As a consequence, subscriptions lapsed and the deficit increased. There was no editorial board, no secretary to carry on correspondence. The full burden of editing, reading proof, making up each issue, carrying on the correspondence was borne by the sole editor, who was like the famous crew of the Nancy Brig. When the good friends of the magazine left the mountain [the campus] and there was no one to assume the deficit, the University authorities refused to assume it, and certain alumni agreed to meet it, so that it struggled on for one more year, expecting each to be the last. When the alumni failed to meet their obligations, five members of the Faculty, including myself, agreed to underwrite it, and carried it for two years, meeting the deficit out of our own pockets. Finally, "The Sewanee Review Incorporated" was formed. . . . Through the efforts of this corporation, advertisements were secured and the *Review* was at last able to meet its obligations at the end of each year.

When I was connected with the *Review*, it was printed at the University Press on the mountain, under the able direction of Mr. A. C. Sneed, a man of unusual artistic taste. . . . The printed page of the *Review* compared favorably with that of any other magazine in the land. The four issues were printed at the amazing price of eight hundred dollars, four hundred copies of each issue.[8]

[8] Turner, *The Content of The Sewanee Review*, pp. 17–18.

Such is the remarkable inside story of Professor McBryde, the man who saved the magazine during the difficult years of World War I. Under his editorship, contributions came increasingly from writers unconnected with the University of the South. For example, in the twenty-fifth volume (1917), of the thirty-one authors represented, only five were from Sewanee. In this year appeared articles by Killis Campbell, Norman Foerster, Joseph Wood Krutch, Grant Showerman, and Thomas J. Wertenbaker. Most of the *Review's* contributors were members of university faculties, and more than half of them from northern and western institutions. Among the leading nonacademic writers for the *Review* were Gamaliel Bradford, Arthur Colton, and Alexander Harvey.

When McBryde left Sewanee for Tulane University, he was succeeded as editor of the *Review* throughout the early twenties by George Herbert Clarke, who had just come to Sewanee from the University of Tennessee to head the English department. Clarke was a poet as well as a scholar in the English field, and he not only emphasized contemporary and Victorian poetry in the articles and reviews, but introduced original poems into the *Review's* own pages for the first time. Only four appeared during his first year: they were by Eden Phillpotts, Morley Roberts, Clinton Scollard, and Clarke himself. Later Clarke published verse by John Jay Chapman, Theodosia Garrison, Gamaliel Bradford, John Crowe Ransom, and many others. Not only was original poetry an innovation in the *Review*, but so were English contributors, such as Phillpotts and Roberts, and later Rowland Thirlmere and others. Clarke also emphasized contemporary movements in literature to a greater extent than had before been known to readers of the *Review*.[9] Ludwig Lewisohn, Clayton Hamilton, and Carl Holliday, contributors for some years past, wrote on European and American literature.

The University of the South was continually losing its leading English professors to other institutions. At the end of 1925, Clarke (who was Canadian-born) removed to Queen's University, Kingston, Canada. His successor as editor of the *Review* (and head of the Sewanee English department) was William Skinkle Knickerbocker, who had been a member of the Syracuse University faculty after studying under Trent at Columbia. For the first year of his editorship he was assisted by Associate Professor Tudor Seymour Long.

Knickerbocker was himself a writer of some grace and charm, as well as a good critic. An editorial department, "Asides and Soliloquies," dealt with a considerable range of topics, but after a few years

---

[9] W. S. Knickerbocker, "Asides and Soliloquies," *Sewanee Review*, v. 38, p. 3, Jan. 1930.

appeared with increasing irregularity. Knickerbocker wrote much for the *Review*, however. His interest at first appeared to be in Victorian and American literature, with some emphasis on contemporary writers. He followed his predecessor's trend in the observation of contemporary literary movements, and when the neohumanist controversy developed in the latter twenties, he made the *Sewanee Review* available to debaters on all sides of the issue — Paul Elmer More, Norman Foerster, Gorham B. Munson, Allen Tate, C. Hartley Grattan, W. E. Collin, and many others. Knickerbocker himself participated: he approved much of Babbitt, "written in a day before humanism became frozen into a false finality, before it became a cult"; [10] but he published his "Farewell to New-Humanism" in July 1930. The farewell was not final, however, and there was comment diminuendo on the subject through the thirties.

Among the poets represented in these years were Merrill Moore, Allen Tate, Norman MacLeod, and David Morton. T. S. Eliot contributed an article on Matthew Arnold to the number for October 1935. Among writers on contemporary literary movements were Robert Spiller, Charles I. Glicksburg, Allen W. Porterfield, I. Robert Lind, and Louis Untermeyer. In other fields, Henry S. Pritchett, Merle Curti, Roscoe Pound, Benjamin T. Spencer, and A. M. Schlesinger, Jr., were contributors. Leading topics, as humanism receded into the background, were the perennial one of the South and its culture, poetry old and new, literary criticism in systematic treatments and in book reviews, and colleges and universities, with the problems of higher education.

When Knickerbocker retired in 1942, Professor Long carried on as "acting editor" for about two years. There was a considerable emphasis on war literature in the magazine under Long, and more of philosophy and religion than for some time. Poetry continued a major topic, and there was much of European literature and of the older authors. Cleanth Brooks made his debut in the *Review*, with Willard Thorp, Richard M. Weaver, Reinhold Niebuhr, Theodore Spencer, and so on.

For over half a century the *Sewanee Review* had kept a remarkably consistent course as a fairly conservative literary quarterly with a circulation of less than 500 at $3.00 a year ($2.00 back in the years of the First World War). But now, at the end of the Second World War, a change was determined upon, and Allen Tate, well-known young poet and critic, was brought in as editor. In his salutatory, Tate spoke of the difficulties of accepting either a nationalistic or a Southern point of view — or both — in editing the *Review*, and added:

[10] *Ibid.*, p. 351, July 1930.

A more serious difficulty lies in the mediation between good writing which has not yet got on the New York market (some of it does get there) and an audience which is not only small but scattered, and, without high-pressure advertising, hard to reach. Apart from libraries, the audience for magazines like the *Sewanee Review* is largely made up of writers, and it will not increase until there is enough money for enough advertising to tell more people that such magazines are available (and not unreadable) to persons over twenty-one who wish to keep up their education. For although the University of the South is handsomely supporting this *Review*, no university can afford to advertise its publications.[11]

Probably no university can *not* afford to advertise its publications if it wishes to remain in the publishing business; but the point is that the *Sewanee Review* had never been advertised enough, nor was it properly promoted until 1945, when more extensive efforts brought circulation to 2,250, and a few years later to 2,750 — the highest figure it has ever reached.

Tate's *Review* was well worth advertising. Criticism by Jacques Maritain, Wyndham Lewis, W. H. Auden, T. S. Eliot, Wallace Stevens, Marianne Moore, E. E. Cummings, John Crowe Ransom, Cleanth Brooks; short stories by Katharine Ann Porter, Eudora Welty, Caroline Gordon; poems by Cummings, Ransom, John Gould Fletcher, Mark Van Doren, Genevieve Taggard — these represent only a sampling.

In November 1946 Tate yielded his tripod to J. E. Palmer, who had been an Oxford scholar and later managing editor of the *Southern Review*, and who was now an assistant professor on the Sewanee faculty. Palmer made the journal even more an exponent of the "new" criticism of the "new" poetry, and a spokesman for ideas underlying contemporary literary movements at home and abroad. It fulfilled the statement that the editor made in taking office — namely, that it would "remain primarily a literary journal," but concerned with education, philosophy, religion, and "perhaps even politics." "We expect," he added, "to have a part in promoting an international community of letters." [12] Many of the contributors under Tate's editorship were retained, to be supplemented by such writers as Eliseo Vivas, William Carlos Williams, F. R. and Q. D. Leavis, Robert Penn Warren, Robert B. Heilman, F. Cudworth Flint, and Philip Wheelwright.

In his introductory editorial, Palmer showed how well he understood the new *Sewanee Review* by the following perspicacious remark:

The chief criticism which a journal of this nature encounters can be reduced to the comprehensive charge of *austerity*: it dislikes more frequently than it likes; it rarely waxes enthusiastic; the writers it chooses to exhibit are difficult in style,

[11] *Sewanee Review*, v. 52, pp. 608–09, Oct. 1944.
[12] *Ibid.*, v. 54, pp. 732–33, Nov. 1946.

not content with easy patterns of language, given to much wrestling with terminology.[13]

Gone were the generous encouragements of a Trent, a Henneman, a Knickerbocker. No commendation was set down without immediate conditioning and restriction; adverse criticism was freer and easier. It was not so much that standards were high, as that praise was considered an evidence of lowbrowed, if largehearted, enthusiasm. Tate's statement that the *Review* was for writers and libraries may be extended to the observation that here were poets writing for poets; story writers providing entertainment for their kind; and poets, story writers, and critics writing for critics. If the circle was small, it was at least select, and it was free from the horrors of mass communication.

In 1952 Palmer resigned the editorship of the *Review* in order to accept a naval post in England. He was succeeded by Monroe K. Spears, who announced that he would continue the Tate-Palmer editorial tradition for the sake of the readers who had been loyal to the *Review* during the preceding decade, but that he would try to attract the academic group by more critical writing about the older literature. At the same time, he hoped to afford some aid in "revitalizing the religious imagination," as befitted a journal supported by the University of the South.[14] The *Review* continues to be distinguished by the contributions of Tate, Ransom, Warren, Eliot, Spender, Vivas, and other well-known writers.

[13] *Ibid.*
[14] *Sewanee Review*, v. 60, pp. 746–48, Autumn 1952.

## THE SURVEY AND RELATED MAGAZINES [1]

IN 1897 Edward Thomas Devine, thirty years old, was general secretary of the Charity Organization Society of the City of New York and professor of social economy in Columbia University. He was at the beginning of a notable career in the field of social service. In December of that year, with promised support from Robert Weeks de Forest, a wealthy corporation lawyer who was president of the Charity Organization Society, Devine started a modest "official organ" for the society called *Charities: A Monthly Review of Local and General Philanthropy*. It was a square-octavo of sixteen pages, and because a famous advertising agent, George P. Rowell, was a member of the society's board and active in the publication's support, a third of its pages were filled with advertising. The second number was reduced a little to a royal-octavo size, but the magazine seemed a going concern at a dollar a year. Its circulation at the end of a year was said to be 4,750, and it was then made a weekly at two dollars. But Rowell, having lost $6,000 on it, withdrew in 1898.[2]

If it had been no more than the organ of the New York society, *Charities* would never have been very well known; but it did not keep within local bounds. It reported meetings and conferences of social service workers the country over, published abstracts of addresses made at such gatherings, and furnished varied news and clipped comment in many fields of social reform. Its articles and items were short in these early years; but when it was a little over three years old, with its issue for March 2, 1901, it absorbed the monthly *Charities Review* and underwent a radical change in policy.

The *Charities Review* [3] had also been published by the Charity

[1] TITLES: (1) *Charities*, 1897–Oct. 1905; (2) *Charities and The Commons*, Nov. 1905–March 1909; (3) *The Survey*, April 1909–1937 (cover title 1933–37, *Midmonthly Survey, Journal of Social Work*); (4) *Survey Midmonthly*, 1938–48; (5) *The Survey*, 1949–52.

FIRST ISSUE: Dec. 1897. LAST ISSUE: May 1952.

PERIODICITY: Monthly, 1897–Nov. 1898; weekly, Dec. 1898–May 1922; semimonthly, June 1922–1932; monthly, 1933–52. Vol. 1, Dec. 1897–Nov. 1898; 2–4, semiannual vols., Dec. 1898–May 1900; 5, June–Dec. 1900; 6–11, regular semiannual vols., 1901–03; 12, Jan.–Sept. 1904; 13–67, semiannual vols., Oct. 1904–March 1932; 68, April–Dec., 1932; 69–87, regular annual vols., 1933–51; 88, nos. 1–5, Jan.–May 1952.

PUBLISHERS: Charity Organization Society of the City of New York, 1897–1912; Survey Associates, New York 1912–52.

EDITORS: Edward Thomas Devine, 1897–1912; Paul Underwood Kellogg, 1912–52.

INDEXES: *Poole's Index, Readers' Guide*.

[2] George P. Rowell, *Forty Years an Advertising Agent* (New York, 1906), p. 296.

[3] TITLE: *The Charities Review: A Journal of Practical Sociology*. (Continued on next page.)

Organization Society, and it had been edited gratuitously by John H. Finley from 1891 through 1896, de Forest paying the deficits.[4] In 1897 it had absorbed *Lend a Hand*,[5] Edward Everett Hale's Boston monthly devoted to philanthropy and reform. *Lend a Hand* "had never been a mere adventure, seeking gain":[6] it had been started as an organ for Hale's Lend-a-Hand clubs and the Ten-Times-Ten clubs founded by Etta Russell in connection with Sunday School work; then it had come to intersperse reports on Boston charities and philanthropical societies with some poetry and fiction and Hale's leading articles; and finally it had become an organ for the New England Conference of Charities, Correction, and Philanthropy. Its reformatory zeal and its interest in Negroes, Indians, and immigrant groups had made its merger with the New York monthly in the same field, the *Charities Review*, a logical development.

But when this happened, the *Charities Review*, which had maintained a similar relation to New York organizations, abandoned its character as an organ of local groups and aimed to publish "an international record of social experiments," becoming the successor, in some respects, of the *International Record of Charities and Corrections* (1886–1888). Thus in 1897 the *Review* had a new policy, a new block of readers and contributors from Boston, a new typographical dress, and a new editor — the clergyman, sociologist, and statistician, Frederick H. Wines. Slums and playgrounds, the church and charities, unemployment, inebriation, industrial insurance, strikes and labor, organization, penology, child study — such were some of the topics treated in the magazine, chiefly by practical workers in the field. Devine, Wines, Hale, Francis G. Peabody, and Homer Folks were among the contributors. There were book reviews, editorials, and a department of news. But when it became evident, after a year or two, that the new profession of social

---

FIRST ISSUE: Nov. 1891. LAST ISSUE: Feb. 1901. Merged in *Charities*.

PERIODICITY: Monthly, but during 1892–96 it omitted numbers of July, Aug., Sept., and Oct. Also omitted Nov. 1896–Feb. 1897. Vols. 1–5, annual vols., Nov.–June, 1891–96; 6, March–Aug. 1897; 7, Sept. 1897–Feb. 1898; 8–10, annual vols., March 1898–Feb. 1901.

PUBLISHER: Charities Organization Society of the City of New York.

EDITORS: John Huston Finley, 1891–96 (with Paul Leicester Ford, 1893–94); Frederick Howard Wines, 1897–98; Herbert S. Brown, 1898–1901.

INDEXES: *Poole's Index, Readers' Guide*. Index of vols. 1–8 in v. 8.

[4] See obituary article about de Forest by Finley, in *Survey*, v. 66, p. 439, Aug. 1, 1931.

[5] TITLE: *Lend a Hand*. Subtitles: "A Journal of Organized Philanthropy," 1886–89; "A Record of Progress," 1890–97.

FIRST ISSUE: Jan. 1886. LAST ISSUE: Feb. 1897. Merged in *Charities Review*.

PERIODICITY: Monthly. Vols. 1–5, annual vols., 1886–90; 6–17, semiannual vols., 1891–96; 18, nos. 1–2, Jan.–Feb. 1897.

PUBLISHER: J. Stillman Smith, Boston.

EDITOR: Edward Everett Hale.

INDEX: *Poole's Index*.

[6] *Lend a Hand*, v. 1, p. 703, Dec. 1906.

work was not going to rally to the support of the *Review*, it declined, and after the issue for February 1901 it was merged, as has been said, with the weekly *Charities*.

As a matter of fact, *Charities* had been born to take the place of *Charities Review* as an organ for the New York society when the latter monthly made its plans to occupy a larger sphere. Now that it had absorbed the monthly, it initiated a system that it was to follow for many years, of making its first issue of the month more a magazine, while the three or four other issues kept the character with which it had begun — that of a bulletin of news and information designed for social workers and their organizations. Thus, the first, or magazine, number was enclosed in a cover, had forty-four pages, plus advertising, carried some illustration from the start and much more somewhat later, and published full-length articles, as well as departments that pointed out sociological materials in other magazines and in books. The bulletin numbers, which ran to sixteen pages, also sometimes carried regular articles, and eventually became departmentalized for workers in various fields of social service. Devine was assisted at first by W. Frank Persons, and later by Paul U. and Arthur P. Kellogg.

Among the leading topics were housing reform, child labor, the battles against tuberculosis and other diseases, temperance, unemployment, penology, playgrounds and recreation, settlement work, and labor organizations. Immigration and immigrant groups received much attention; the Slavic peoples were studied in a series by Emily Greene Balch in 1905–1906, and later the Italians, Bulgarians, Servo-Croats, and others, were discussed. Devine's editorials, under the heading "Social Forces," were a feature, and a broad program of service and reform was emphasized continually. There were occasional special numbers, like the one on the Negro on October 7, 1905, to which Booker T. Washington and W. E. B. Du Bois contributed.

On November 4, 1905, *Charities* absorbed *The Commons*,[7] Graham Taylor's Chicago magazine, which was the leading exponent of the settlement movement. Begun by John Palmer Gavit as a bulletin of the Chicago Commons, a settlement house on North Union Street, its scope had been broadened when Taylor had taken it over in 1900 to include "industrial justice, efficient philanthropy, educational freedom, and the people's control of public utilities." With the Chicago magazine

---

[7] TITLES: (1) *Chicago Commons*, April 1896–March 1897; (2) *Commons*, April 1897–Oct. 1905.

FIRST ISSUE: April 1896. LAST ISSUE: Oct. 1905. Merged in *Charities*, which became *Charities and The Commons*.

PERIODICITY: Monthly. Semiannual vols., 1–10, April 1896–Oct. 1905.

PUBLISHERS AND EDITORS: John Palmer Gavit, April 1896–March 1900; Graham Taylor, April 1900–Oct. 1905.

and its list came its editor, to become a staff writer for *Charities and The Commons*. Then in March 1906 *Jewish Charity* [8] was also absorbed, and its founder, Lee K. Frankel, became an associate editor of the surviving magazine. Frankel did not remain on the staff for long, but Taylor was a valuable associate (later contributing) editor for many years. His special interest was the social service of the churches, but he wrote on other subjects as well.

When the former of these mergers was made, a new Publication Committee was set up, headed, of course, by de Forest, and including such leaders in the field of social work as Jane Addams, Joseph Lee, Simon N. Patten, Daniel C. Gilman, Jacob A. Riis, and Robert Treat Paine. These notable persons became contributors as well as consultants in the publication of the magazine, the first three of them for many years. No less than fourteen departmental editors were named in 1905, including several well-known writers who remained faithful contributors, such as Ben B. Lindsey, Lilian Brandt, Mary E. Richmond, Florence Kelley, Samuel J. Barrows, and Homer Folks. Paul U. Kellogg now became managing editor and his brother Arthur P. business manager, while Graham Romeyn Taylor, son of the former editor of *The Commons*, and later an important writer and social worker in his own right, was assistant business manager, located in Chicago.

*Charities* now began to attract attention by some of its special numbers, like those of 1906 on the care of the blind (February 3), visiting nursing (March 7), and municipal parks (July 7). Rita Teresa Wallach contributed a series on "The Settlement Movement" in that year, and there was also much about the San Francisco disaster and the relief agencies there. An important number of 1907 was the one on child labor (October 5). In the next few years an already distinguished list of contributors received such accessions as Henry S. Pritchett, John R. Commons, and Charles Mulford Robinson. But the greatest project of these years, and one that changed the whole course of the magazine (even its name) was a social survey of the city of Pittsburgh. Special funds were contributed by the Russell Sage Foundation for this task, which was directed by Paul Kellogg and which enlisted the work of such men as Commons, Robert A. Woods, Samuel Hopkins Adams, and so on. The results of the study, always called "the survey" in the magazine, furnished a very well illustrated series in 1909, and later filled six volumes issued by the Charities Publication Committee.

So successful was this venture that the Publication Committee determined to turn its attention more and more to social surveys, and in

[8] Founded as *Charity Work* Jan. 1902; title changed to *Jewish Charity* Jan. 1904. Final issue, Feb. 1906.

April 1909 changed the magazine's name to *The Survey*. The page size was enlarged to quarto, and the subscription price was increased from two to three dollars. Circulation, which in the early years had amounted to only a thousand or two, was now over twelve thousand. Living up to its name, the *Survey* published many valuable and comprehensive social studies, often dealing with great metropolitan centers, like G. R. Taylor's series on "Satellite Cities" in 1912; but the only city on which it did a study at all comparable to the one on Pittsburgh was Birmingham, Alabama (January 6, 1912). It did help to set up other surveys, however, and to organize the Russell Sage Foundation's Department of Surveys. The magazine's staff — a dynamic group — now became active in many fields. They set on foot a national investigation of jail conditions, as a result of *Survey's* reports of the 1910 meeting of the International Prison Congress, of which a departmental editor, Samuel J. Barrows, was president. The magazine printed much on the Lawrence mill strike, and even more on the McNamara dynamiting case; and the creation of the Federal Commission on Industrial Relations was the direct outgrowth of a *Survey* symposium on "The Larger Bearings of the McNamara Case" (December 30, 1911).[9] The magazine's editors — Kellogg, Owen P. Lovejoy, Miss Addams, Mrs. Kelley — were active in formulating the "industrial standards" that played a prominent part in the presidential campaign of 1912. Under the leadership of Associate Editor Taylor, the *Survey* was closely identified with the "Men and Religion" movement, and its campaign teams, which swept the country in 1911–1912. In the years 1910–1912, Charles M. Cabot contributed a fund that enabled the *Survey* to study the labor and welfare conditions in the United States Steel plants and communities. This was really an extension of the Pittsburgh study, and was under the charge of John A. Fitch, an associate editor who had been a member of the staff that had conducted the earlier survey.

All these activities, in which *Survey* articles and editorials usually spearheaded movements largely conducted by various reform organizations of which the magazine's associate editors were leaders, convinced many thinking people of the value and significance of this lively periodical. And yet *Survey* circulation was less than twenty thousand, and there was a continual struggle with deficits. In the summer months especially, operating capital was depleted, and the weekly bulletin numbers were then "reduced to practically a news basis."[10] But such was the regard in which many socialminded readers held the magazine that, when the Survey Associates, Inc., was set up as a financing organi-

---

[9] See *An Announcement of Survey Associates, Inc.* (New York, 1912), p. 5.
[10] *Charities and The Commons*, v. 16, p. 391, June 30, 1906.

zation in 1912, nearly seven hundred persons paid in ten dollars each
— three dollars for their annual subscriptions and the remainder as a
donation — and twenty-five made gifts of a hundred to a thousand
dollars each. The next year there were nearly a thousand "associates,"
and just before the financial crash of 1929 there were two thousand.[11]

Kellogg became editor-in-chief in 1912, and Devine, Taylor, and Miss
Addams were associate editors and constant contributors. The subtitle
"A Journal of Constructive Philanthropy" gave place to "A Journal of
Social Exploration."

The weekly numbers were a little more departmentalized than formerly: "The Common Welfare" was news and comment; "Editorial
Grist" contained short pieces by members of the staff; and there were
departments of "Civics," "Industry," "Church and Community," "Education," and "Jottings." All departments were not represented in each
issue, but they were scattered through the three or four "weekly"
numbers.

The magazine number (now the first issue of each month) came to
be a very handsome production; this was especially true after a larger
page size was adopted in October 1913, and both typography and illustration were improved. The magazine was also broadening its contents
base; and there was more about politics, socialism, social insurance,
industrial reform, labor strikes, child welfare, health, and phases of
sex and prostitution. Though careful to avoid partisan alliances, *Survey*
felt "a new social consciousness" in the Progressive party in 1912.[12]
There were occasional set debates in the magazine on social and economic problems. Well-known names were common in the tables of
contents of the magazine number; among the new ones in this period
were Edwin R. A. Seligman, Sidney Webb, John Dewey, Vida D.
Scudder, and Rufus M. Jones.

When the Great War broke out in Europe, the *Survey* took strong
pacifist grounds. Miss Addams inspected conditions overseas in the
summer of 1915 and wrote some antiwar articles as a result of what
she saw, and Mary Chamberlain was a London correspondent in the
peace campaign in that year. But when the United States entered the
war, *Survey* was fully loyal. Editor Kellogg served with the Red Cross
in France and Italy during 1917–1918. From abroad he wrote about
his observations, and he contributed a remarkable section on "Free
Belgium" to the number for March 30, 1918. After the war, *Survey*
was urgent in its pleas for aiding European countries to reëstablish

[11] *Survey*, v. 29, verso of illustrated insert opposite p. 267, Dec. 7, 1912; v. 31, p. 31, Oct. 4, 1913; v. 66, p. 113, April 15, 1931.
[12] *Survey*, v. 29, p. 10, Oct. 5, 1912.

their several economies. "Shall We Turn Our Backs on Europe?" asked Henry P. Davidson (April 24, 1920). The League of Nations was stoutly supported; and after it was established, Bruno Lasker, an associate editor, contributed reports of its proceedings.

Postwar inflation almost drove the *Survey* out of business. "The rise in publication costs is little short of staggering," wrote Kellogg.[13] The paper was poorer in quality, and illustration declined. In October 1921 it was decided to make the magazine a semimonthly instead of a weekly, the bulletin issues to be consolidated in a "Midmonthly Number," with the service departments for social workers; while the magazine issue was to be called the "Graphic Number" because of its emphasis on illustration. The subscription price had been raised to four dollars in 1918 and five dollars two years later; now the fifteen thousand subscribers could have the Graphic and the Midmonthly for five dollars, or either one separately for three. From the first, the Graphic sold 50 per cent better than the Midmonthly.[14] The semimonthly was a good idea as it worked out; it could not have been successful, however, but for the faithfulness and increased generosity of the Survey Associates, who were furnishing over a hundred thousand dollars by 1929, nearly half the magazine's total revenue.[15] In the twenties, coöperating members paid ten dollars, sustaining members twenty-five, contributing members one hundred — and for those who paid up to three thousand dollars annually the managers seem to have been able to find no appropriate adjective.

Until his death in 1931 de Forest remained president of Survey Associates, Inc.; he was succeeded by Lucius R. Eastman. For a few years after the war the associate editors had been listed as Devine, Lasker, William L. Chenery, and Winthrop D. Lane; with Taylor, Fitch, Miss Addams, and Mrs. Kelley as contributing editors. Few if any of the *Survey's* associate, contributing, or departmental editors were ever full-time workers, and many changes took place in the list in the ensuing thirty years.[16]

The *Survey* was more attractive in the 1920's than in any other decade of its history. Paintings and drawings by such artists as Joseph Stella, Howard N. Cook, Boris Grigorieff, George B. Luks, and S. J.

[13] *Survey*, v. 44, p. 459, July 3, 1920.
[14] *Survey*, v. 49, p. 51, Oct. 1922.
[15] *Survey*, v. 63, p. 244, Dec. 1, 1929.
[16] Following is a list of departmental editors in the twenties: Paul L. Benjamin, Joseph K. Hart, Arthur Gleason, Neva R. Deardorf, Robert W. and Martha B. Bruère, Geddes Smith, Mary Rose, Leon Whipple, Haven Emerson, Sara Merrill, Beulah Amidon, Grace Hathaway, John D. Kenderdine, Halle Schaffner, John Palmer Gavit, Loula D. Lasker, Florence L. Kellogg, Gertrude Springer. A number of these continued on the staff through the thirties and forties — some to the end of the magazine.

Woolf, with the photographic studies of Lewis W. Hine and woodcuts of J. J. Lankes, Rockwell Kent, and others added much to its appeal as a quality magazine. Most of these were not drawn especially for the *Survey*, but were reproduced from murals and exhibitions. Leon Whipple, professor of English at New York University and a journalist of some experience, edited a good "Letters and Life" department, written partly by himself and partly by others. Verse had appeared occasionally in the *Survey* for many years — some by Sara Teasdale, Sarah N. Cleghorn, and other good minor poets. Now there was somewhat more for a few years, by Clement Wood, Robert P. Tristram Coffin, William E. Brooks, and others. But social service was still the great theme.

A few highlights in Graphic numbers may be mentioned. The number on coal mines and miners (April 1921) attracted much attention. Robert S. Lund's exposé of conditions in the Elk River Basin oil fields led to a reply by John D. Rockefeller (November 1922). There was a number about the Russian experiment (March 1923). A fine Negro number (March 1925) contained contributions dealing with Negro culture by leaders of that race. Mahatma Gandhi wrote an article entitled "Untouchable" for the issue of December 1925. The "Family Life in America" number (December 1927) was excellent, yet no more notable than many other illustrated special numbers. As early as 1928 the *Survey* pointed with alarm at the growing unemployment; it issued a special number containing studies of the subject April 1929 — six months before the crash. Frances Perkins contributed an article on unemployment insurance in November 1931. A feature of 1932 was the series of articles that Walter Duranty wrote giving a sympathetic picture of Russian social and economic life. Other *Survey* writers in the twenties included George E. Vincent, Oswald Garrison Villard, John Palmer Gavit, W. F. Ogburn, Stuart Chase, Bertrand Russell, William Bolitho, Mary Austin, Zona Gale, and Dorothy Canfield Fisher.

In the depression thirties, another change in the *Survey* was determined upon. The Graphic Number was made a separate monthly magazine under the name *Survey Graphic*,[17] in the hope of building a more popular support for it. The Midmonthly Number, which retained

[17] TITLE: *Survey Graphic.*
FIRST ISSUE: Jan. 1933. LAST ISSUE: 1948.
PERIODICITY: Monthly. Annual vols., numbered 22–37. There actually were no vols. 1–21 of *Survey Graphic*, and the Graphic Number of *Survey* was paged and volumed (semiannually) as a part of *Survey*, and is always so bound. Vols. 1–21 may be accounted for in two ways: (a) The Graphic Number of *Survey* began Oct. 1921, and thus Jan. 1933 should be v. 24, no. 4; (b) Semimonthly publication began Oct. 1922, and if this beginning date was used, Jan. 1933 should have been v. 22, no. 4.
PUBLISHERS: Survey Associates, Inc., New York.
EDITOR: Paul Underwood Kellogg.
INDEXES: *Readers' Guide, Index to Labor Articles, Index Medicus.*

the title and numbering of the *Survey*, had never been suitable for a popular appeal; it was a professional journal, and it continued in that character. In fact, it had reverted to its first status — that of a monthly periodical for social workers.

The new *Survey Graphic* began with a special number wholly devoted to summaries of the reports of President Hoover's Committee on Social Trends. Felix Frankfurter, Robert F. Wagner, Samuel S. Fels, William Hard, A. A. Berle, Jr., and Henry Pratt Fairchild were contributors to the first volume; but most of it was written by the magazine's editorial staff. Whipple continued his book department for several years. Victor Weybright was managing editor, followed by George Britt, 1947–1950.

The highlights of the whole *Survey Graphic* file are the series of special numbers under the general title "Calling America." These began in February 1939 with one on democracy in Europe and America — an extraordinary symposium by important writers and observers. Raymond Gram Swing was the special editor, collaborating with the regular staff. One or two of these numbers now appeared each year, well illustrated, and each with a special editor and a selected group of well-qualified contributors. They dealt with many topics, from Russian relations to food.[18] The fourteen numbers of the series (1939–1948) sold an aggregate of over half a million copies.[19] At its highest point the average annual circulation of the *Graphic* was nearly thirty-five thousand.

Meanwhile the *Midmonthly Survey* had pursued an even course, with thirty-six pages to the number, some illustration, and its regular news-and-comment departments, supplemented by occasional special articles by authorities outside the magazine's regular staff. News from Washington, so important to social workers in this period, was supplied first by Glen Leet and then by Rilla Schroeder. Besides the topics that have been named already as staple content in *Survey*, there was now much discussion of the Work Projects Administration, medical costs, old age security, social insurance, city planning, and the many phases of unemployment and relief. Throughout World War II there was a regu-

---

[18] Following are the subjects (not necessarily the titles), special editors, and dates: democracy in Europe and America, Raymond Gram Swing, Feb. 1939; schools, Beulah Amidon, Oct. 1929; homes, Albert Mayer, Feb. 1940; North and South America, Victor Weybright, March 1941; arsenal for democracy, William H. Davis, Nov. 1941; health in wartime, Victor Weybright, March 1942; Negroes, Alain Locke, Nov. 1942; conversion from war to industry, Stuart Chase, May 1943; American-Russian relations, Albert Rhys Williams, Feb. 1944; the British and ourselves, Victor Weybright, Ferdinand Kuhn, and Lewis S. Gannett, March 1945; the right to know, Henry Christman (under a Brandeis bequest), Dec. 1946; segregation, Thomas Sancton, Jan. 1947; education, Beulah Amidon, Nov. 1947; food, Paul Kellogg, Helen Hall, and George Britt, March 1948.

[19] *Survey*, v. 85, p. 5, Jan. 1949.

lar "War and Welfare" department. The *Midmonthly* had about half the circulation of the *Graphic*.

Postwar inflation, with its high printing and publishing costs, forced an increase in subscription prices of both journals; both went to four dollars in 1947. Then at the beginning of 1949, in a further effort to find a formula that would make both ends meet, the two monthlies were merged. The new *Survey*, dropping the word "Graphic" and contenting itself with meager illustration, consisted of forty pages a month, and sold at fifty cents, or five dollars a year. Joseph P. Chamberlain, of Columbia University, was now president of the publishing board. Frequent contributors were Henry S. Commager, H. A. Overstreet, Beulah Amidon, and Gertrude Springer.

But this was the last phase of a long and heroic struggle to keep a valuable periodical alive. Its last number was the one for May 1952, at which time Paul Kellogg had been connected with the magazine for almost exactly half a century. He had been editor for forty years, during which *Survey* had reflected his ideals, his hopes, his reformatory drive, his personality. As the *Nation* said, "It was the devastating combination of rocketing costs and Mr. Kellogg's serious illness that finally defeated the valiant efforts of the *Survey's* friends to raise the necessary funds" to keep it alive. And the *Nation* added mournfully: "It filled a place no other journal occupies, and filled it with integrity and distinction."[20]

[20] *Nation*, v. 174, p. 539, June 7, 1952.

## TOWN TOPICS [1]

Wsociety in Cincinnati in 1874. He called it *Andrews' Bazar.*
It was a quarto of only sixteen pages, with woodcuts, and
sold for a dollar a year. Encouraged by a circulation of some thirty
thousand, reached in four years, Andrews decided to take his journal
to New York, there to enter the lively competition in dressmaking
patterns and fashion periodicals. He had devised "Andrews' Pinned
Paper Fashions," and had big ideas for varied types of publication.

In New York, Andrews sold his patterns, continued his journal for
a time as *Andrews' Fashion Bazar,* and published an *Encyclopedia of
Fashion,* a *Code of Manners,* and other books; but perhaps his most
ambitious undertaking was the founding, in 1879, of a women's magazine which he called *Andrews' American Queen: A National Society
Journal.* It was issued twice a month at three dollars a year and consisted of sixteen small-folio pages, carrying society notes from some
fifty cities in the East, South, and Midwest. In each issue there were
whole pages giving lists of guests and descriptions of costumes at hundreds of parties all over the country. It now seems incredibly dull.

However, foreign correspondence, which was a little livelier, became
more important after a year or two. Weekly publication at four dollars
a year or ten cents a copy was adopted in 1880 and remained the rule
for thirty years. Fiction borrowed from English, French, and German
magazines and a humor department on the last page entitled "The
Queen's Jester" brightened the magazine. Gradually the great expanses
of society notes from Pittsburgh and Keokuk and so on diminished,
and the *Queen* became more a New York journal, with reviews of
music and the theater. The Gray-Parker drawings of coaching and
society events, which occupied page one, were an excellent feature in

[1] TITLES: (1) *Andrews' American Queen,* 1879–83; (2) *American Queen,* 1883–84;
(3) *American Queen and Town Topics,* 1885; (4) *Town Topics,* 1885–1937.
FIRST ISSUE: Jan. 1, 1879. LAST ISSUE: Nov. 1937.
PERIODICITY: Semimonthly, 1879; weekly, 1880–1931; biweekly, 1931; suspended Oct.
1931–Jan. 1936; monthly, Feb. 1936–Nov. 1937. Regular semiannual vols. 1–104, 1879–
1931; v. 105 irregular, with 56 numbers.
PUBLISHERS: W. R. Andrews, 1879–82; W. P. Shannon, 1882–83; Ernest F. Birmingham, 1883–84; E. D. Mann, 1885–90 (with Paul M. Potter, 1885–87; W. D. Mann, 1885–
90); William D'Alton Mann, 1891–1920; Town Topics Publishing Company, 1920–31;
Washington Publishing Corporation, 1936–37. All New York.
EDITORS: W. R. Andrews, 1879–83; Ernest F. Birmingham, 1883–84; Paul M. Potter,
1884–86; Alfred Trumble, 1886–88; George Wotherspoon, 1888–94; Charles Bohm, 1895–
1920(?); A. R. Keller, 1920(?)–31; J. C. Schemm, 1936–37.

1881. There were literary notes and reviews, home departments, and light editorial comment.

But both ends were not meeting. Gray-Parker disappeared and so, at the beginning of 1883, did Andrews. Ernest F. Birmingham became owner and editor in that year; and under his management the title was *American Queen: A Journal of Home and Society*, but the news was no longer national, being limited to that of New York, Boston, and the fashionable eastern resorts. Portraits of social leaders now occupied the first page. But the Birmingham management lasted only a year. Telling about what happened at this juncture, a later editor said, "The amateur journalists who started *Town Topics* . . . lost all the money their confiding backers could be induced to put up. Then a real journalist stepped in." [2]

This was E. D. Mann, who bought the paper at the beginning of 1885, changed its name to *Town Topics*, made it a quarto, and brought in contributors who gave more zest, wit, and cleverness to its pages. There were, for example, Count Chapolsky's series on New York society in 1886; the "Foghorn Stories" by Alfred Trumble and Paul Potter, said to have been written at a resort of wits known as Foghorn Tavern, Ninth Avenue and Twenty-Third Street; and the art reviews of James B. Townsend, of the *New York World*. The social gossip department now came to be called "Saunterings"; it was written by Ed Fox ("Modoc") and contained an increasing amount of scandal — little excited barks and some sharp bites. Other contributors were Alfred Thompson, whom one of the owners described as "an admirable painter of the nude in letters"; [3] the caustic and racy Fred Schwab; and Arthur Joseph, who began the periodical's long record as "financial tattler."

In the fall of 1885, E. D. Mann sold a third-interest in *Town Topics* to his older brother William, and another third to Paul Meredith Potter. Potter, later to become a famous playwright, was then a young dramatic critic, lately come to New York from England. He was responsible for much of the cleverness of *Town Topics* for a year or so, while he was editor; but he had many irons in the fire, and the editorship was soon put into the hands of Alfred Trumble, a bright young journalist not much troubled by scruples. He had edited *To-Day* (1885–1886), a weekly review of society, the stage, art, and literature, which was said to have been first issued under the tentative title of *Lies*.[4] At any rate, it was accused of being a "libel sheet." [5]

[2] *Journalist*, Oct. 16, 1886, p. 2.
[3] *Journalist*, Sept. 24, 1887, p. 9.
[4] Joseph E. McCann was a cofounder who soon retired. Weston Coyney was publisher.
[5] *Journalist* reported (May 22, 1886) that *Theatre* had made that accusation in print.

With the Mann brothers as managers and Trumble as editor, *Town Topics* printed more and more scandalous gossip. The *New York Star* attacked the paper, accusing it of blackmail. The situation soon became distasteful to Potter, who pulled out. The *World* said that the immediate breach was caused by a letter Potter received from E. D. Mann proposing to "shake down" some leading New York politicians.[6] As a result of Potter's withdrawal, the publishing company was thrown into a temporary receivership. But despite such troubles — perhaps because of them — *Town Topics* gained in circulation, passing fifty thousand in 1890, and increased its number of pages.

It was in those hectic years of the latter eighties that the journal established its reputation for good writing, on the one hand, and outrageous scandal on the other. Under its editorial "flag," it called itself

The newsiest, brightest, wittiest, wisest, cleverest, most original, and most entertaining paper ever published. A complete and perfect journal for cultivated men and women, being a topical and outspoken critic and chronicle of the events, doings, interests, and tastes of the fashionable world. It is always up to date, and carries with it the atmosphere of the metropolis.

An informed writer in the *Journalist* was quite as flattering in some respects, but more realistic in others. He called the *Town Topics* of this period

The best written paper in the English language . . . written by gentle folk for gentle folk, on topics of interest to gentle folk, and as such it has won a phenomenal success. . . . It became famous, even notorious. No scandal was too salacious for it to handle, no joke too risqué for its print. It gathered about it some of the most brilliant writers in the metropolis. It made the reputation of Francis S. Saltus. . . .[7]

In 1891, Colonel William D'Alton Mann bought a controlling interest in the journal. The new proprietor had gained his title in the Civil War, had made a fortune in cottonseed oil in Mobile after the war, and had practiced politics and journalism there. He claimed election to Congress from the Mobile district, but he was not seated. He invented the Mann Boudoir Car, and always claimed he was cheated of a fortune from it by Wall Street; eventually he sold his patents to the Pullman Company. Later he was to found the magazine *Smart Set*.

Throughout the third of a century in which Colonel Mann controlled its destinies, *Town Topics* followed a pattern that varied but little. "Saunterings," the department of social items, gossip, and scandal, was for many readers the most important part of the journal and came

---

[6] Quoted in the *Journalist*, Sept. 17, 1887, p. 6.
[7] "The Tale of Town Topics," in *Journalist*, v. 22, p. 36, Nov. 20, 1897.

to occupy nearly half of its pages. But there was also some excellent and lively reviewing of New York theaters, art exhibits, and opera and concert music. James Huneker contributed a remarkable annual review of music for a number of years, as well as other pieces. Percival Pollard was the magazine's brilliant literary critic. Pollard also sometimes contributed fiction. The short stories in *Town Topics* had a flavor all their own: they were always sophisticated, usually light, often technically very well done. Well-known writers like Amélie Rives, Edward S. Van Zile, and Justus Miles Forman were found in the magazine, but many of its authors were evidently beginners. There were many translations, especially in later years, and these were all by well-known masters. So popular was this fiction that Mann began in 1891 to issue *Tales from Town Topics* as a quarterly publication.[8]

He also issued for several years after the turn of the century an annual entitled *Fads and Fancies of Representative Americans at the Beginning of the Twentieth Century*. This book was lavishly illustrated, sumptuously bound in crushed levant elaborately tooled in gold, and sold for fifteen hundred dollars or more a copy — more if the victim was well able to pay. In the famous Collier trial, it was asserted that the publication of this volume was a blackmailing enterprise.

The trial referred to was on an action for criminal libel brought against *Collier's* in 1905 on the complaint of Colonel Mann. *Town Topics* had printed a nasty paragraph about the behavior of Alice Roosevelt at Newport. Young Rob Collier sprang to Miss Roosevelt's defense, and observed that Colonel Mann's reputation in New York was somewhat lower than that of a horse thief. The incident is detailed, with quotations, in the history of *Collier's* in this volume,[9] and it is enough to say here that, while the defendant was acquitted, District Attorney Travers Jerome was able to declare at the trial that "there is not a scintilla of evidence Colonel Mann blackmailed anyone." [10] However, the stigma of blackmail will always stick to *Town Topics*, and its famous annual will continue to be referred to as "that highjacking book."

----

[8] *Tales from Town Topics* contained a novelette in each number, with short stories, sketches, verse, and humorous bits. From Sept. 1891 through June 1902, each square-octavo number was called a volume (1–44), but when it was enlarged to small-quarto, the preceding file was regarded as having two numbers to a volume, and it continued: 23–27, Sept. 1902–Dec. 1904, two numbers to vol.; 28, March 1905; 29–35, June 1905–Sept. 1907, four numbers to vol.; 36, Oct. 1907; 37, Nov. 1907–Feb. 1908, four numbers; 38, March 1908. It became a monthly under the title *Tales* June 1905. With the issue for Oct. 1906 the title became *Transatlantic Tales*, and the contents were almost wholly translated stories. It ended with March 1908.

[9] See pp. 459–60. Incidentally, *Town Topics* announced, apparently in earnest, the engagement of Alice Roosevelt and Senator Albert J. Beveridge (March 30, 1905).

[10] *Collier's*, v. 55, March 1, 1906, p. 3.

On the other hand, a thoughtful critic of American literature has written:

Until the end of the [First] World War, *Town Topics* continued a school of critics and short story writers, and its columns should one day be sedulously analyzed for the brilliant light that would thus be thrown upon our cultural history during certain years.[11]

Colonel Mann died in 1920. His famous weekly declined for a decade, was suspended for five years, and was then revived as a monthly by the publishers of the *American Sketch and Washington Mirror*, though it was still left in New York. It ended with the issue for November 1937.

[11] Ludwig Lewisohn, *Expression in America* (New York, 1932), pp. 315–16.

# VOGUE [1]

VOGUE began in 1892 as a society weekly designed to serve wealthy New Yorkers. The names of most of the two hundred and fifty stockholders of its publishing company were in the *Social Register*, and included Mrs. Stuyvesant Fish, Cornelius Vanderbilt, D. Percy Morgan, and so on.[2] The founders were Arthur B. Turnure, a young clubman from a wealthy family, who had already had some experience in the periodical field, and who became publisher of the new magazine; and Harry McVickar, whose great-grandfather was the merchant prince Stephen Whitney, and who had studied art in Europe and now became art director of *Vogue*. The weekly had at first only sixteen quarto pages, but was well printed and handsome typographically. The cover was adorned by one of those urbane but not very vigorous drawings such as *Life* had made currently popular, with a witticism in dialogue beneath it. The price of ten cents indicates the design to tempt persons of slender means to buy the periodical in order to find out what Society was doing.

The weekly set out to be "a dignified, authentic journal of society, fashion, and the ceremonial side of life." [3] There was a story by Thomas A. Janvier in the first number, but fiction found no permanent place in the periodical. It was well illustrated; there were some drawings of costumes, though, as one observer remarked, the new magazine's portrayals of what smart people wore were not "fashion plates" in the accepted sense of the day.[4] In fact, it was clear from the first issue that this was not merely another journal devoted to ladies' fashions, but

[1] TITLE: *Vogue.*
FIRST ISSUE: Dec. 17, 1892. Current.
PERIODICITY: Weekly, 1892–1910; semimonthly, 1910–current. (Issues for May, June, July, 1945; June, July 1946 were monthly; since then Jan., June, July, and Dec. have been monthly.) Vol. 1, Dec. 17, 1892–June 24, 1893; 2–current, regular semiannual vols., July 1893–current.
PUBLISHERS: Arthur B. Turnure, 1892–1907; Condé Nast, 1909–42; Iva Sergei Voidato-Patcèvitsch, 1942–current. All New York, though the publication office has been Greenwich, Conn., since the twenties.
EDITORS: Mrs. Josephine Redding, 1892–1907; Marie Harrison, 1907–14; Edna Woolman Chase (Newton), 1914–48; Jessica Daves, 1948–current.
INDEXES: *Readers' Guide* (since 1953), *Dramatic Index.*
REFERENCES: Edna Woolman Chase, "Fifty Years of Vogue," *Vogue*, v. 102, Nov. 15, 1943, pp. 33ff; Walter G. Robinson, "With the Makers of *Vogue*," *Vogue*, v. 61, Jan. 1, 1923, pp. 74ff; Edna Woolman Chase, *Always in Vogue* (Garden City, 1954).
[2] Robinson in *Vogue*, v. 61, Jan. 1, 1923, p. 75; Chase in *Vogue*, v. 102, Nov. 15, 1943, p. 35; *Vogue*, v. 1, p. 16, Dec. 17, 1892.
[3] *Vogue*, v. 1, p. 16, Dec. 17, 1892.
[4] *Book Chat*, v. 8, p. 11, Jan. 1893.

a modest and respectable periodical filled with news and notes about fashionable New York. Though modest, it was clearly of a high class of excellence; that it was respectable set it off from such sensational journals of New York's *haute monde* as *Town Topics*.[5] There were reports from the theaters and from concerts and art exhibitions, and some notes on new books, a London letter, and so on.

But perhaps the most characteristic item in the early *Vogue* was the column "As Seen by Him," written by Walter C. Robinson. For the magazine's thirtieth anniversary number, Robinson told of how he came to write these "notes," as he called them:

> A number of the members of the Calumet Club, where I then lived, contributed to the new magazine. It was James B. Townsend who suggested that I write the notes for men. I had been in Europe, was on the staff of the *Times*, and was a member of the same clubs as Turnure, McVickar and Townsend. A new genera- tion of men of leisure was springing up. The city had emerged from its Age of Innocence, and was becoming quite metropolitan. I had several friends who talked of nothing but proper clothes, amateur sports, entertaining, manners, and so forth, and their point of view amused me. I thought *Vogue* might have a series of papers on the fads and fancies of the men of the day. . . . I suppose it was because I wrote in a new vein, and with an assumption of authority, that the articles took well.[6]

It was this authoritative manner, and also the occasional satire, which was sometimes so light and subtle that some readers doubtless failed to perceive it, that gives much of the flavor to the older *Vogue*. Many years later Mrs. Chase, distinguished editor of the magazine, wrote something about those first numbers, and observed: "*Vogue* took such little cracks at the public as this, 'Now that the masses take baths every week, how can one ever distinguish the gentleman?'"[7] (But, Mrs. Chase, isn't that rather a "crack" at the gentleman, whose Saturday-night ablutions alone distinguish him from *hoi polloi*?) At any rate, *Vogue* was, in those days, not above needling the fashionable clubmen, whose point of view, as Robinson says, amused the editors. Not that the magazine was not serious in its role of reporter and even arbiter of the fashionable world of New York: it spoke with authority on the modes, it mentioned Delmonico's with respect, and it gave the details about the soirees and coming-out parties of the social leaders. This record was found in the magazine's Social Supplement, along with ac- counts of dinners, dances, and deaths; betrothals, brides, and births, and something of the travels of those who were socially important.

After about two years, many of the original stockholders were very

---

[5] See pp. 753–54.
[6] Robinson in *Vogue*, v. 61, Jan. 1, 1923, pp. 75–76.
[7] Chase in *Vogue*, v. 102, Nov. 15, 1943, p. 33.

willing to sell at a sacrifice, and a new and tighter "Vogue Company" supplanted the original "Fashion Company" as the publishing concern, Turnure retaining the management. Circulation did not exceed ten thousand until after the turn of the century; through most of the nineties it was considerably below that.

Editor of *Vogue* in these years was Mrs. Josephine Redding, who is described as "a violent little woman, square and dark, who, in an era when everyone wore corsets, didn't." But, it appears, she did always wear a hat, "in or out of the office; and once when she was ill in bed, she received one of her staff in her nightgown and a hat." [8] Mrs. Redding and her publisher initiated the system of part-time editorial assistants, which was to be carried on by later management for many years. Thus many an "elegant amateur" was able to patronize the best restaurants and the fashionable dressmakers or tailors, and "to live a round of country week-ends at the big Long Island houses, and still get a salary on Fridays." [9]

*Vogue* scored a coup when it presented, in the number for November 14, 1895, drawings of the three-thousand-dollar trousseau of Consuelo Vanderbilt, whose impending marriage to the Duke of Marlborough was a great event. *Vogue* artists were permitted to sketch the lingerie, all in cambric, lace, and embroidery. That was a remarkable achievement for Mrs. Redding and her staff; for any other periodical it would have been inconceivable. *Vogue* was a champion of the growing country club movement, and a leading reporter of the early golf matches. It was strongly antisuffragist, but it carried the torch for the Society for the Prevention of Cruelty to Animals. There was something of the old-fashioned bridge and whist, but the new bridge madness did not come in until well after the turn of the century, when *Vogue* gave it full sway. In short, the magazine uttered the *dernier cri* in every department of social life. A tuxedo, said Meadows, the valet created for Robinson's column, must always be referred to as a dinner coat; there was never any relaxation of *Vogue's* tutelage in such matters. It had its duty to perform.

But it had become apparent ever since the reorganization of 1894 that *Vogue* was now primarily a fashion journal. At that time, or soon after, such departments made their appearance as "Smart Fashions for Limited Incomes," "Vogue Designs for the Seamstress" "The Paris Letter," "The New York Letter," and so on. But *Vogue* policy called for a higher grade of modern fashion illustration than was found in other women's magazines, as well as for selection of superlative fashion

---

[8] *Ibid.*, p. 35.
[9] *Ibid.*, p. 110.

designs. In its tenth anniversary number, the magazine declared that "all fashions proceed from the top downwards, and really our only guide in fashion lies in those of the highest standard, from which ideas are derived by suggestion, adaptation, and modification." [10]

When Turnure died in 1907, *Vogue* circulation had grown to about twenty-five thousand; [11] its advertising business had never been properly developed, and its income from that department amounted only to about fifteen hundred dollars a week. [12] In 1909 the magazine was purchased by Condé Nast, who had made a reputation in the publishing world as advertising director (and later business manager) of *Collier's*. About a year after he bought it, Nast made *Vogue* a semimonthly of sixty-four pages, selling it at fifteen cents — raised some months later to twenty-five cents.

The magazine became more than ever before a portrayer and interpreter of styles, though it was still aimed at readers of the higher income brackets. "It is the purpose of the magazine to hold the mirror up to the mode," wrote the editor, "but to hold it at such an angle that only people of distinction are reflected therein." This was not pure snobbery, for the editor again explained: "It is really the smart women who create the mode," and therefore "what they wear smartly and do smartly is what the discriminating eye of *Vogue* should constantly record." [13] Almost since the beginning, the magazine had printed in each issue a full-page portrait of a society leader, in suitable costume, naturally.

Nast inherited an editor who had succeeded Mrs. Redding after Turnure's death; she was Marie L. Harrison, a sister-in-law of the deceased publisher, one of the first of the women golf champions, and an editor of enthusiasms curbed by good sense. It was under her direction that patterns were first included in the magazine; thus she initiated what was to become an immense and very profitable business in *Vogue* dressmakers' patterns.

Two or three years after Nast made *Vogue* a twenty-five-cent semimonthly of styles, it established itself on that steadily rising curve of circulation and advertising in which it has maintained itself ever since. Its strategic and dramatic exploit of 1914, when it organized the first New York fashion show, marked the beginning of its greater prestige and of the era of its major business prosperity. With French importations cut off by the war, and therefore with a forced interregnum in the dictatorship of Paris over the world of fashion, *Vogue* originated "The Fashion Fête," which brought together society, led by Mrs. Stuyvesant

---

[10] *Vogue*, v. 20, p. 828, Dec. 4, 1902.
[11] See Ayer's directories.
[12] Robinson in *Vogue*, v. 61, Jan. 1, 1923, p. 170.
[13] Doris Ulmann, *A Portrait Gallery of American Editors* (New York, 1925), p. 20.

Fish and Mrs. Vincent Astor, and the trade, led by Bonwit Teller and B. Altman.

To the position of editor-in-chief of *Vogue* came, in 1914, Mrs. Edna Woolman Chase, who had been a member of the staff for a decade or more. A hard worker, intelligent, with wide interests and understanding, and an able executive, Mrs. Chase was the ideal editor for the period of expansion on which the magazine was entering.

In 1916 Nast established a British *Vogue* in London, with William Wood as editor. This was in the middle of World War I; shortly after the end of the war, in 1920, a Paris *Vogue* was founded, under the editorship of Phillipse Ortiz. These overseas *Vogues* have continued ever since, though the French publication was, of course, interrupted during the German occupation in the Second World War. There was also a Spanish edition for South America, and a fifth one for Germany, in the twenties; but they were short-lived. In 1925 the semimonthly *Vogue Pattern Book* was begun; it was a great success from the start, soon forging ahead (though temporarily) of *Vogue* itself in circulation. A great thirty-acre printing and publishing plant was built at Greenwich, Connecticut.

In 1918 the price per copy of the American edition of *Vogue* was raised to thirty-five cents. It was well worth the money throughout the twenties, when two hundred pages were issued in each number. To be sure, nearly four-fifths of it was advertising, but what advertisements! It seemed that the ad-copy artists were in competition with the artists whom Heyworth Campbell, the magazine's art director, and Mrs. Chase employed to illustrate the editorial articles. Campbell was a genius at page layout; Helen Dryden's covers were striking; and George Plank, Claire Avery, and Miss Dryden made attractive drawings, some of which were produced in color. Then Mrs. Chase employed a group of French artists who had come to New York to work on Nast's abandoned *Gazette du Bon Genre*; and they not only gave real distinction to their portrayals of such unpromising subjects as the modes of that strange decade, but exerted a notable influence on American advertising art.

Early in the twenties, *Vogue* was publishing two million dollars' worth of advertising a year;[14] and its patronage remained steady throughout the decade. Of course it suffered from the impact of the financial crash of 1929 and the depression which followed; but by the mid-thirties it was back on the climb, and before the end of the decade it had reached two hundred thousand circulation and its issues were again fat with advertising. It helped, of course, to receive the list of *Vanity Fair*, which was merged with *Vogue* in 1936. Nast had owned *Vanity Fair* for several years and had despaired of making it pay, excellent magazine though it was; now he brought Editor Frank Crown-

[14] Robinson in *Vogue*, v. 61, Jan. 1, 1923, p. 170.

inshield to the staff of *Vogue* as a special writer. Indeed, for two or three years, the general editorial base of *Vogue* was broadened, and a number of the well-known writers who had brought distinction to *Vanity Fair* were found in *Vogue*, such as Thomas Wolfe and William Saroyan; but this flier into literature did not last, and by 1940 the magazine was again following its tried and fabulously successful pattern of quality presentation of top styles, by editors "who understand journalistically the place and value of chichi," as Mrs. Chase once said, "but are never taken in by it."[15]

Nast died in 1942. No more after-theater parties in the Nast penthouse, with notables from stage, finance, letters, politics, in attendance; no more of that promotion and publication and advertising "knowhow" that had been synonymous with the name of Condé Nast. But long before his death, he had put the finger on an assistant to be his successor; this was Iva Sergei Voidato-Patcèvitsch. The new editor was son of a White Russian civil governor, a former manager of the Paris *Vogue*, and had been for some years Nast's executive assistant in New York. Under his guidance *Vogue* demonstrated in the early years of World War II that patriotism was smart and smartness was patriotic.[16]

In the forties, though the magazine continued to be mainly staff-written in the demonstrated formula of success, other writers were occasional contributors. Bertrand Russell, Philip Wylie, Ilka Chase (daughter of *Vogue's* editor), and Robert Littell wrote articles on a great variety of subjects. The number and scope of these features by well-known writers increased, so that in the number for July 1945, for example, Owen Lattimore wrote on "China Is Changing," Jean-Paul Sartre on "New Writing in France," and Senator Fulbright on "The Price of Peace." During the war Mary Jean Kemper was *Vogue's* roving correspondent in both Asia and Europe. After the war the magazine did not abandon internationalism, which was more or less a tradition with it anyway. In 1949, for example, there was Jean Cocteau's "The Best of Talk" (February 15), Richard Hughes's "The Phoenix City of Warsaw" (March 15), and a striking anthropological essay by Margaret Mead (February 1).

There is one type of article that has been staple throughout the whole history of *Vogue*; in it two or three or more notables are discussed and pictured together—not precisely as a group, but as more or less related personalities. Thus three leaders of fashion, half a dozen debutantes, four patrons of the Metropolitan, or three young polo players may be brought together in three or five pages of pictures and text. For example, two women war photographers, Margaret Bourke-White and Therese

---

[15] Chase in *Vogue*, v. 102, Nov. 15, 1943, p. 110.
[16] *Time*, v. 40, Sept. 28, 1942, pp. 50–53.

Bonney, with six pictures, were shown on four pages of the number for July 1, 1943; Harold Nicolson wrote a piece about England's leading political figures for July 1945; in the issue for July 15, 1953, there was a feature about three society beauties, another about four debutantes, and still another about two interesting and prominent families in France. Such features give an opportunity to picture and discuss costume, social events, art, politics, and so on.

If the advertising sections were striking in the twenties, what shall we say of the forties, when color came into its own and made *Vogue* gorgeous throughout? In editorial illustration, there was much attention given to modern art reproductions — Van Gogh, Covarrubias, Grant Wood, and so on. There was a fine section on the Museum of Modern Art, with illustrations in full color, in the July 1945 number. In the advertising, color was used with extraordinary effectiveness. By 1950, about one-fourth of *Vogue's* pages used color, and within the ensuing years the proportion increased.

In 1948 Jessica Daves, who had long been the managing editor of *Vogue*, was named as editor of the American edition, while Mrs. Chase became editor-in-chief of all editions. Later the terminology made Miss Daves editor-in-chief of the American *Vogue* and Mrs. Chase chairman of the editorial board. Again the magazine was mainly staff-written, and well-known names were found infrequently in the tables of contents. A distinguished series of 1953 consisted of engagingly written essays on the "arts of living" by various authors, such as John Mason Brown, Charles Poore, and Malcolm Muggeridge.

The single-copy price had been raised again in 1947, but at fifty cents circulation was greater than ever before in the magazine's history, passing four hundred thousand for the issue of January 1953.

*Vogue's* extraordinary advertising record is due largely, we are told, to the fact that it has built up a large and faithful following among buyers for large stores the country over. Some great retail stores buy as many as a hundred copies of the magazine regularly for their buyers in various departments.[17] It is partly, then, to reach this audience that advertisers were willing to pay two thousand dollars per black-and-white page in *Vogue* in 1940, and thirty-four hundred dollars in 1953.

For more than sixty years *Vogue* has been a faithful recorder of fashions and fashionable life on a high plane of excellence in production and intelligence in writing. "The world's No. 1 fashion magazine," *Time* called it, in reviewing Mrs. Chase's autobiography in 1954.[18]

---

[17] Henry F. Pringle, "High Hat," *Scribner's Magazine*, v. 104, pp. 20–21, July 1938.
[18] *Time*, v. 64, Nov. 1, 1954, p. 50.

## WOMAN'S HOME COMPANION [1]

THE success of the early mail-order monthlies in Augusta,
Maine,[2] stimulated adventurous young publishers in many other
cities to try their luck at the same game. Among those who
started home magazines of this type "on a shoestring" in the mid-
seventies were two brothers in Cleveland, Ohio, S. L. and Frederick
Thorpe. Their monthly, entitled *The Home*, was begun early in 1874,
probably in January of that year.[3] It was an eight-page paper, folio in
size, with a subscription price of fifty cents a year. It was printed on
cheap paper, carried some household departments and some fiction by
unknowns, and was supported by several columns of small advertisements of "agents wanted," cheap jewelry, cosmetics, patent medicines,
and so on. Most of these items were to be ordered directly by mail.

The paper did fairly well, apparently, and advertising increased somewhat, despite the hard times. Frederick Thorpe died in 1877, and the
next year the surviving brother acquired another Cleveland monthly,

[1] TITLES: (1) *The Home*, 1874–78; (2) *Home Companion*, 1878–86 (in the latter
half of 1883 it was called *Our Young People*); (3) *Ladies' Home Companion*, 1886–96;
(4) *Woman's Home Companion*, 1897–1957.
FIRST ISSUE: Jan.(?) 1874. LAST ISSUE: Jan. 1957.
PERIODICITY: Monthly, 1874–80; semimonthly 1880–96; monthly, 1896–1957. Regular
annual volumes.
PUBLISHERS: Thorpe & Bro., Cleveland, Ohio, 1874–77; S. L. Thorpe, Cleveland, 1877–
81; Harvey & Finn, Cleveland, 1881–83; Mast, Crowell & Kirkpatrick, Springfield, Ohio
(and Philadelphia in 1891–95), 1883–98; Crowell & Kirkpatrick Co., Springfield, 1898–
1901; Crowell Publishing Co., Springfield (editorial office in New York), 1901–39; Crowell-
Collier Publishing Co., New York and Springfield, 1939–current. (Presidents: S. L. Thorpe,
1874–81; E. B. Harvey, 1881–83; P. P. Mast, 1883–98; John S. Crowell, 1898–1906; George
H. Hazen, 1906–18; George D. Buckley, 1918–23; Lee W. Maxwell, 1923–34; Thomas H.
Beck, 1934–47; Albert E. Winger, 1947–53; Paul Clifford Smith, 1953–57.)
EDITORS: S. L. Thorpe, 1874–77; E. B. Harvey, 1881–83; T. J. Kirkpatrick, 1883–96;
Joseph Franklin Henderson, 1896–1900; Arthur Turner Vance, 1900–06; Frederick L.
Collins, 1906–11; Gertrude B. Lane, 1912–41; Willa Roberts (Plank), 1941–43; William
A. H. Birnie, 1943–52; Woodrow Wirsig, 1953–56; Theodore Strauss, 1956–57.
INDEXES: *Readers' Guide, Dramatic Index.*
[2] See F. L. Mott, *A History of American Magazines* (Cambridge, 1938), v. 3, pp. 37–39.
[3] For many years the *Woman's Home Companion* gave the year 1873 as its founding
date. However, George P. Rowell & Co.'s *American Newspaper Directory* for 1878 gives the
founding date of the *Home Companion* as 1874. This was the periodical's first listing in any
directory. Rowell continued to give this founding date for the *Home Companion* until after
it was moved to Springfield. So did N. W. Ayer & Son's *American Newspaper Annual* after
it began publication in 1880. Moreover, the earliest extant volume — the one for 1891 — is
numbered 18, which would mean that vol. 1 would be that for 1874 if regular annual numbering had been maintained. It is highly probable that the new Springfield publishers, in
figuring the founding date when the periodical changed hands in 1883, noted that the current
volume was numbered 10, and simply subtracted 10 from the year 1883 — a common type
of error in computing birth dates of periodicals.

which M. A. Beebe had been publishing, called *Little Ones at Home*; after consolidating the two under the new title *Home Companion: A Monthly for Young People*, and lowering the price to thirty-five cents a year, Thorpe claimed a circulation of eighty-eight thousand.[4] By 1880 the paper was issuing two editions, one a monthly and the other a semimonthly, thus increasing the advertising receipts; but soon it dropped the monthly and continued the semimonthly at sixty cents. But evidently S. L. Thorpe had not intended, from the first, to make a career of publishing. He had been studying medicine; and when he hung out his shingle as a doctor in 1881, he sold his paper to E. B. Harvey and Frank S. Finn. Under its new management, the *Home Companion*, though still designed for the juvenile audience, was, as Rowell's *Directory* said, little more than "an advertising sheet."[5]

In 1882 Harvey & Finn started another juvenile of a somewhat higher class, entitled *Young Folks' Circle*, published monthly without advertising; and the next year they sold the *Home Companion* to Mast, Crowell & Kirkpatrick, of Springfield, Ohio.

Phineas Price Mast had begun his career as the manufacturer of a patent cider-mill, and he had gone on to become one of the most successful producers of agricultural machinery in the country. In 1877 he began the publication of a farm paper, *Farm and Fireside*, challenging the successful *Home and Farm*, published at nearby Louisville, Kentucky.[6] T. J. Kirkpatrick, a nephew of Mrs. Mast, was active in the management of the new paper, and induced John S. Crowell, an editor of the Louisville rival, to come to Springfield, where the publishing firm of Mast, Crowell & Kirkpatrick was formed in 1879.[7] When the firm bought the *Home Companion*, its farm paper had a hundred and fifty thousand circulation and it was occupying a new four-story printing plant.

Two months after the Mast firm bought the "subscription list, goodwill, etc." of the Cleveland paper, it purchased the *Youth's Home Library*, a similar paper selling for fifty cents a year, which had been published in Boston since 1877. The two were then merged in an illustrated semimonthly called *Our Young People*, which Kirkpatrick had started the year before, and for which the publishers now claimed a circulation of thirty thousand.[8] *Our Young People* as a name for the consolidation of the three papers was obviously wrong. The merger was

---

[4] Most of the data about the early history of the *Home Companion* is derived from directories of the city of Cleveland, 1876–82.

[5] See Rowell's entries for the *Home Companion*, 1880–82.

[6] Mott, *op. cit.*, v. 3, p. 156.

[7] *Farm and Fireside*, v. 25, p. 1, May 1, 1902; *Publishers' Weekly*, v. 100, p. 555, Aug. 20, 1921.

[8] Ayer's *American Newspaper Annual*, 1883, p. 689.

advertised as "a journal suited to the entire family and read by all," and it soon switched to the proper title, *Home Companion*.

Harvey & Finn's *Young Folks' Circle* was purchased by the Springfield firm in 1884 and was continued for a year and a half as a lowpriced monthly designed for an urban juvenile audience, while the *Home Companion* was the company's general family magazine. Then at the beginning of 1886, *Young Folks' Circle* was absorbed by the *Home Companion*, and in November of that year the name was changed to *Ladies' Home Companion*. The size was also changed, and the paper now carried thirty-two small-quarto pages; it was published semimonthly at fifty cents a year. It still printed a lot of mail-order advertising — as, indeed, nearly all women's magazines of the time did — but its contents had been improved by the addition of some of the *Circle's* rather competent writers, such as Maria Louise Pool, James Otis, and Eben E. Rexford. Mrs. Eliza R. Parker had begun a "Practical Housekeeping" department that was to be an important feature of the magazine for a number of years, and other departments lent variety, while a limited number of woodcuts made the text pages more attractive. For several years the *Companion* occasionally reprinted articles from other magazines.

In 1888 the format was again changed, this time to sixteen small-folio pages, and the quality of the paper improved. More space was given to fashions and to foods, and there were more illustrations. Advertising patronage advanced in amount and in quality. Serial fiction became important; a story by John Habberton was printed in 1889–1890.

Like most of its contemporaries, the *Companion* issued an illustrated premium list as a supplement to one of the fall numbers, and made frequent premium offers in other issues. It was willing, for example, to give her own subscription free to any reader who found one new subscriber. In 1889 circulation reached eighty thousand, and the next year a hundred thousand,[9] making the *Companion* one of the leaders in its field.

Throughout the early nineties, departments were strong. Articles were usually very practical — on household budgeting, the servant problem, home furnishing, house building, and so on. Fashions and fancywork continued to be important, and there were contributions on health, child care, and etiquette. Travel articles were not infrequent, many of them written by Jessie Ackermann. Serial fiction and short stories were by Harriett Prescott Spofford, Edgar Fawcett, Will Allen Dromgoole, J. L. Harbour, Abbie Farwell Brown, Sophie Swett, and others. There was verse by James Whitcomb Riley, Eugene Field ("Little Boy Blue," April 1, 1893), Susan Coolidge, Ella Wheeler Wilcox, Helen Hunt

[9] *Printers' Ink*, v. 28, Nov. 16, 1898, p. 43.

Jackson, and Frank Dempster Sherman. The first cover appeared on the Christmas issue for 1891, but covers did not become the rule until three or four years later. The first halftone pictures made directly from photographs appeared in 1894.

In October 1893 the price of the *Companion* was raised to a dollar a year. That was the price of the *Ladies' Home Journal*, of whose competition the *Companion* was fully conscious. The *Journal* advertised frequently in the *Companion*; it had twice as many pages, but the *Companion* was issued twenty-four times a year instead of twelve. The *Journal* had a more luminous galaxy of writers and four times as much circulation, but the differences in both those matters were being reduced a little by the mid-nineties. In March 1896, the *Companion* changed to monthly publication, with thirty-two pages per number; five months later, it resumed its old price of fifty cents a year, and at the same time increased the quality of its contents. As a result it went to over three hundred thousand circulation by the end of 1898 — about half that of the *Ladies' Home Journal*. It then raised its price to the *Journal* level again — a dollar a year and ten cents a number. The price per copy was not very important, since only 8 per cent of its sales were on the newsstands.[10] In January 1897 the name was changed to *Woman's Home Companion*, partly, without doubt, in order to mark a difference from the *Ladies' Home Journal*, and partly because of a real objection to the word "lady" for "woman." Said the editor:

The indiscriminate use and abuse of the term "lady" has robbed it of so much of its meaning that it has been in a measure tabooed by those who deserve the title in its best sense. The noblest ambition of our end-of-the-century femininity is to be a "woman." . . . "Woman" is an honest Anglo-Saxon word, and has no synonym. The use of "lady" as a synonym for "woman" is vulgar.[11]

The editor who may be presumed to have written the above was Joseph F. Henderson, who came to the *Companion* in 1896. Before that, the general editor had been the junior member of the publishing firm, T. J. Kirkpatrick. Henderson was a former newspaperman, who had written dime novels in his youth.[12]

The *Woman's Home Companion* was now a handsome small-folio not unlike the *Youth's Companion*, of Boston, in appearance. The well-known writers mentioned as contributors in the early nineties nearly all continued to be found in the magazine's pages to the end of the decade. In addition, Lilian Bell wrote often and cleverly on feminism ("The

[10] *Printers' Ink*, v. 25, Dec. 21, 1898, pp. 18–19.
[11] *Companion*, v. 24, Jan. 1897, p. 15.
[12] Albert Johannsen, *The Home of Beadle and Adams* (Norman, Okla., 1950), v. 2, pp. 139–40.

New Woman," February 1897) ; Mary Jane Holmes, Will N. Harben, and Mrs. Burton Harrison furnished fiction serials; Octave Thanet, Opie Read, Stanley Waterloo, Marietta Holley, Julia Magruder, and others wrote short stories; and there was a full set of departments, including "Literary Chat," "Our Boys and Girls," and Mrs. Ella M. Kretschmar's housekeeping hints. College education for girls, women in art, women in the civil service, sight-seeing abroad, women's clubs, and athletic exercises for girls were leading topics. Except for an article on the Red Cross (September 1898) there was almost nothing about the war with Spain. Illustration was much improved; the halftones were well printed, and among the artists who illustrated the fiction were Albert D. Blashfield, Jessie Willcox Smith, and W. P. Snyder. There were striking covers by Leyendecker and others. The attractiveness of the advertising also became noticeable; the Ivory Soap "ads" in chromolithography were charming.[13]

Arthur T. Vance became editor of the *Companion* in 1900; he had been editor of the *Home Magazine*, and later associate editor of the *New England Magazine*. He emphasized a broadening of the *Companion's* field: it was now, he said, designed not for women alone, but for all members of the family. "Every month," said Vance, "we print some story or article particularly aimed at the man of the house."[14] A series on "Great Movements Which Are Making the World" marked an increasing interest in public affairs. A crusade against "child slavery" was a feature of the magazine in 1906–1907; there were well illustrated articles about child-workers in the cotton mills, canning factories, tailoring, sweat shops, and so on, by John Spargo, Samuel McCune Lindsay, Owen R. Lovejoy, and others. Even President Theodore Roosevelt made a statement on child labor for the *Companion* in January 1907. This crusade represents Vance's nearest approach to the muckraking common in the magazines of the time. In the same issue that contained the T. R. contribution appeared an article on "The Human Side of John D. Rockefeller."

Editor Vance was especially interested in the short story. New names in the tables of contents were those of Francis Lynde, Frank H. Spearman, Hamlin Garland, Sarah Orne Jewett, Bret Harte, Robert Grant, Eden Phillpotts, Morgan Robertson, and Rafael Sabatini. Jack London's "The Apostate" appeared in September 1906, and a few months later some of the results of his famous *Snark* cruise began to appear under the title "Round the World for the Woman's Home Companion." Myrtle Reed's "Romances of Famous Americans" was a 1903 serial,

---

[13] Examples in the issues for Sept. 1896, April 1897.
[14] *Critic*, v. 44, April 1904, p. 319.

and the next year appeared "Visits to the Homes of Great Americans."
Forrest Crissey wrote on Hull House in 1898 and Edward A. Steiner
continued European studies begun earlier. There was much on art and
music, as well as books, and the regular departments on fashions and
household matters were maintained. Verse was not neglected; grouping
three or four lyrics on a page was a favorite editorial device. "Carmen
Sylvia" was featured, and the older stand-bys were joined by such poets
as Charles Hanson Towne and Clinton Scollard.

Mast died in 1898, leaving an estate of a million and a half dollars.[15]
Kirkpatrick sold out his interests in the publishing house in 1901, leaving Crowell as president and general manager. In 1901 the main editorial
offices were moved to New York. By that time each issue contained
some twelve pages of advertising; this increased slowly for a year or
two, and then more rapidly, until at the end of the Vance editorship in
1907 the *Companion* occasionally carried well over seventy-five pages of
advertising. This made a fat and prosperous magazine.

In 1906 Joseph P. Knapp paid $750,000 for a majority interest in the
Crowell Publishing Company.[16] Vance resigned to go to the *Pictorial
Review*; and for the five years 1906–1911 the editor was Frederick L.
Collins, who made few changes in his predecessor's editorial policy. The
venerable Edward Everett Hale wrote an editorial page, and Mrs. Margaret E. Sangster contributed "Talks with Mothers." Gelett Burgess
and R. K. Munkittrick contributed some humor, as John Kendrick
Bangs had in earlier years ("The Idiot at Home," 1899). Kate Douglas
Wiggin, Alice Brown, and Elizabeth Stuart Phelps made a notable trio
of new contributors. There were many "Special Numbers," for spring
fashions, Valentine's Day, Easter, outdoor life, love stories, and so on.
Advertising boomed; though the rate was raised from $1,750 to $2,100
per page in 1908, the number for September 1909 had 100 pages of paid
matter. This was on the basis of 564,000 average circulation, sworn
statement.[17]

Gertrude Battles Lane, who was to serve as editor-in-chief of the
*Companion* for thirty years, was named to that position in 1911. She had
entered the Crowell organization in 1903 at eighteen dollars a week, a
twenty-year-old girl who had already had a taste of magazine editorship
on the *Boston Beacon*, a weekly society paper. Before her death she was
receiving a salary of fifty thousand dollars a year,[18] and was recognized
as one of the greatest woman editors of her generation. Miss Lane once
stated her editorial creed as follows:

---

[15] *Publisher's Weekly*, v. 100, p. 555, Aug. 20, 1921.
[16] Amos Stote, "Crowell-Collier, et al.," in *Magazine World*, v. 1, Aug. 1945, p. 9.
[17] See Ayer's *Directory*, 1908, including advertisement, p. 1326.
[18] *Time*, v. 28, July 27, 1936, pp. 43–44; v. 38, Oct. 6, 1941, pp. 65–66.

In editing the *Woman's Home Companion*, I keep constantly in mind a picture of the housewife of today as I see her. She is not the woman who wants to do *more* housework, but the woman who wants to do *less* housework so that she will have more time for other things.

She is intelligent and clear-headed; I must tell her the truth. She is busy; I must not waste her time. She is forever seeking new ideas; I must keep her in touch with the best. Her horizon is ever extending, her interest broadening: the pages of the *Woman's Home Companion* must reflect the sanest and most constructive thought on the vital issues of the day.[19]

Miss Lane's editorship covered the First World War, the roaring twenties, and the great depression. During the war, Margaret Deland wrote some fine articles from France for the *Companion*. Miss Lane herself spent much time in Washington on special duty with the Food Administration. "Ideas for War Work at Home" was a continuing department. The magazine managed a Treasure and Trinket Fund, for which women sold or melted down jewelry in order to offer special aid to the Air Force.

Mrs. Anna Steese Richardson was an able staff member who conducted the magazine's Good Citizenship Bureau for a number of years. In the thirties Mrs. Eleanor Roosevelt had a page, and Walter Lippmann was an occasional contributor. Presidents Taft, Wilson, Coolidge, and Hoover wrote for the *Companion* at one time or another. Mrs. Sangster continued her "Talks," Anne Bryan McCall conducted a "Tower Room" department of advice and essays, Jeanette L. Gilder had a book page, Dr. Roger H. Dennett had a department entitled "The Healthy Baby," Caroline French Benton made suggestions for club programs, and Sam Lloyd had a puzzle page for the youngsters. Later Grace Tabor wrote on gardens and Alice Bradley on cookery.

For a good many years the Lane formula was two serials, four or five short stories, six special articles, and a full complement of service departments for each number. The serial fiction was an important feature of the magazine; and it was said that such popular writers as Kathleen Norris, Edna Ferber, Dorothy Canfield Fisher, and Sophie Kerr were sometimes paid as much as eighty-five thousand dollars for a serial story.[20] In the twenties and thirties there was fiction of distinction in the *Companion* by Willa Cather, Sherwood Anderson, Booth Tarkington, Ellen Glasgow, Sinclair Lewis, Margaret Deland, Mary E. Wilkins Freeman, Pearl S. Buck, John Galsworthy, Arnold Bennett, and many others. Illustration was rich, with growing use of color by the beginning of the forties.

---

[19] Undated promotion piece. See also editorial in Sixtieth Aniversary Number, v. 60, Nov. 1933, p. 4.

[20] *Time*, v. 28, July 27, 1936, pp. 43–44.

A spectacular editorial feature of 1935 was some hitherto unpublished correspondence of Robert and Elizabeth Browning. For the serial rights to these letters, which ran through three numbers, the *Companion* was said to have paid twenty-five thousand dollars.[21] Another notable series was one which appeared in 1948 entitled "Too Many Churches," which advocated unions of religious bodies.

In the second decade of the new century a great race developed between the four leading women's magazines, for circulation and advertising. *McCall's*, at $.50, had reached the 1,000,000 mark as early as 1908, and it did not change to $1.00 a year until 1916. *Pictorial Review*, which had been $1.00 a year from the first, touched its first million in 1915. Thus, in 1916, when *Woman's Home Companion* attained the 1,000,000 mark, *Ladies' Home Journal* had 1,500,000, both selling for $1.50 a year; and *McCall's* ($1.00) and *Pictorial Review* ($1.50) each had about 1,250,000.[22] The *Companion* gained on its competitors in the twenties, however. It was still a little behind when, having been reduced to $1.00 a year, it reached 2,000,000 in 1927; but in the thirties it led the entire field by a slight margin. Its average circulation (sworn) in 1938 was 3,000,000.

World War I inflation made trouble for the magazines. The *Companion* raised its single-copy price to twenty cents in August 1918, but in March 1922 it was back at fifteen cents; and in July 1926 it met the *Ladies' Home Journal* and *McCall's* newsstand price of ten cents. Page size had been reduced to the large-quarto used by most of the other women's magazines in 1921. Advertising zoomed. The May 1927 number ran to 172 pages and cover, and that of April 1930 set a record, with 204 pages and cover; the basic black-and-white advertising rate for 1930 was $9,400. The depression thirties brought these giant issues down, however, despite the remarkable record the *Companion* made in holding its circulation — and even gaining substantially in the latter thirties. Depression reductions pushed the advertising rate down to $8,550 in 1932, and the next year to $7,700.[23] In 1934 it went up again to $8,250,[24] and thereafter the curve was always upward. In 1939, with the *Companion* still slim, but showing unmistakable signs of recovery, the management was reorganized as the Crowell-Collier Publishing Company.

On Miss Lane's death in 1941, Willa Roberts was editor for a few years; she was a writer, and had been on the staff of the *Companion* for more than twenty years. Edward Anthony was publisher. These were

[21] *Ibid.*
[22] Circulations in this paragraph are derived from Ayer's *Annual*, which at this time, gave the average of any six months in the year preceding the date of the current *Annual*. *Good Housekeeping* got into the million circulation class in the mid-twenties.
[23] *Editor & Publisher*, v. 65, April 15, 1933, p. 11.
[24] *Ibid.*, v. 66, Feb. 10, 1934, p. 10.

difficult years, with the country entering another World War. There were interesting letters from the fighting fronts, for which the magazine gave prizes in war bonds. Doris Fleeson was a war correspondent in the European theater of operations in the early forties, to be succeeded by Helen Huntington Smith and later Patricia Lockridge. There was much about war gardens, the canning of vegetables and fruit, and many other activities in support of the general war effort. The magazine grew more brilliant with color, in the illustrations of articles and fiction, in the fashions, and in the advertising pages. The single-copy price went up once more to fifteen cents in March 1942.

William A. H. Birnie became editor of the *Companion* in 1943. A former newspaperman, he had been assistant editor of the *American Magazine* and then managing editor of the *Companion*. As article editor, Birnie chose another newspaperman, Roger Dakin; and the two made a good team for remaking the magazine into a more aggressive campaigner for causes — "a fighting lady," as it was sometimes called. There was one article, entitled "Get the Children Out of the Jails," which resulted in the passage of a law in New York designed to prevent children being confined in jails with adults. There were many articles on sex and marriage, as "What Do You Know About Divorce?" and "Too Many Miscarriages"; and an answer department called "Marriage Clinic" became a fixture for some years. Mrs. Glenn Frank's "Fraternities and Sororities Must Go" created no little excitement in April 1945. Opinion polls became a regular feature.

Such fiction writers as Mary Roberts Rinehart, Kay Boyle, Clarence Budington Kelland, Nelia Gardner White, Faith Baldwin, and Taylor Caldwell contributed to the *Companion* in the forties; but the nonfiction movement had set in, and more emphasis was now given to features, service articles, and so on, than to serials and short stories. Birnie adopted the make-up style, then novel in the magazine world, by which advertising moved forward in the book. Double-page layouts in color became common.

In 1946 the price was increased to twenty-five cents, and in 1953 to thirty-five. In 1950 circulation reached four million. In October 1951, and again in March 1953, the *Companion* reached new heights in advertising revenue. In the latter year the rate for a black-and-white page was $12,880. But thereafter advertising declined alarmingly, and the magazine faced hard times. In July 1954, Paul C. Smith, who had become president of Crowell-Collier several months before, was installed as editor-in-chief of the *Companion, Collier's,* and *American Magazine*. Woodrow Wirsig, who had followed Birnie as *Companion* editor in 1953, was himself supplanted three years later by Theodore Strauss.

At mid-century, service to the modern home was the keynote of the *Companion.* Only three short stories were published each month. Big-name authorship was no longer relied upon for circulation, though a famous personality was occasionally a contributor. Margaret Thompson Biddle wrote regularly from Paris. Inviting layout and plenty of color made an attractive magazine.

But mounting costs and Crowell-Collier organizational difficulties brought the *Companion's* troubles to a climax in the years 1954–1956. In July of the latter year, it was calculated that the annual loss would reach three million dollars,[25] and in December it was announced that the number for January 1957 would be the *Companion's* last.

The passing of this periodical was mourned by many readers, for it had long been a lively, interesting, and helpful member of the group of leading magazines for women and the home.

[25] *Magazine Industry News Letter,* July 7, 1956.

## THE WORLD'S WORK[1]

A CHIEF object that Walter Hines Page had in mind when he joined Frank N. Doubleday in 1900 in establishing the new publishing house of Doubleday, Page & Company was the founding of a quality magazine over which he should have full control.[2] He had left the editorship of the *Forum* because he had been disappointed in plans for a share in its ownership, and he had made a similar break with the *Atlantic Monthly* because of the uncertainty of the position of a "hired editor."[3] But when *World's Work* was begun in November 1900, Page was not only editor but part-owner and the undisputed manager in design and execution. He came to the task supported by capital, prestige, and unusual self-confidence.

Page's introductory editorial was a clarion manifesto of optimistic America entering upon the twentieth century. The "richest of all countries," he wrote, with the best workmen in the world and the best organization of industry, was changing the very nature of man.[4] "It is with the newly organized world, its problems and even its romance, that this magazine will eagerly concern itself, trying to convey the cheerful spirit of men who do things."[5] This was indeed the spirit of the magazine throughout most of its history. Page set upon it the seal of his own expansive, bold, clear-speaking personality.

Some friends of Page's *Atlantic* years were disappointed at the lack of definitely literary values in the new magazine. William Roscoe Thayer, trying hard to praise the first numbers, wrote: "It is bound to have a large clientele, whom it will help, but what opening does it

---

[1] TITLE: *The World's Work, A History of Our Time.*
FIRST ISSUE: Nov. 1900. LAST ISSUE: July 1932. Merged with *Review of Reviews.*
PERIODICITY: Monthly. Vols. 1–56 (semiannual vols., May–Oct., Nov. April), May 1900–Oct. 1928; 57, Nov., Dec. 1928; 58–60 (annual vols. divided into Part I, Jan.–June, and Part II, July–Dec.), 1929–31; 61, Jan.–July 1932, complete in 7 numbers. Vols. 1–22 are paged continuously, pp. 1–15010.
PUBLISHERS: Doubleday, Page & Co., 1900–26; Doubleday, Doran & Co., 1927–32. New York.
EDITORS: Walter Hines Page, 1900–13; Arthur Wilson Page, 1913–26; Carl C. Dickey, 1927–28; Barton Currie, 1928–29; Russell Doubleday, 1929–31; Alan C. Collins, 1931–32.
INDEXES: *Poole's Index, Readers' Guide, Annual Library Index, Engineering Index, Review of Reviews Annual Index.*
[2] Burton J. Hendrick, *The Life and Letters of Walter H. Page* (New York, 1922), vol. 1, p. 66.
[3] *Ibid.*, pp. 67–68.
[4] See p. 168.
[5] *World's Work*, v. 1, p. 3, Nov. 1900.

afford for the *best* work — which is, after all, deliberate, sober, mellow, imaginative?"[6] There was no reconciliation here: Page wanted his articles to be thoughtful, to be sure; but he wanted them on top of the event, with quick, bright reports. In spite of his success with the *Atlantic*, Page was not a literary soul; at the end of the first year of *World's Work*, he declared that his magazine had

> a more original aim than to thresh over old straw and call the chaff "Literature." . . . It is a confusion of ideals that has caused so little heed to be paid to the literature of achievement. Most men among us who write well are yet writing about subjects of no earthly concern to anybody but their own craft; and most men who feel the thrill of our expanding life cannot write well. Our life, therefore, is one thing — a thing of extraordinary accomplishment, full of the healthful joy of growth. And most of our contemporary literature is another thing — a thing that lags far behind our work. . . . Into the midmost field of cheerful and significant work this magazine has tried to carry its readers, and to interpret the far-reaching meaning of it — to present the literature of action.[7]

In this point of view, Page agreed with another successful editor of his times, George Horace Lorimer, of the *Saturday Evening Post*.[8]

And so, when the magazine appeared, it lived up to its name by its emphasis on work in many fields and on world-wide interests. Each number began with a department of news and comment entitled "The March of Events," which occupied some twenty pages and was written in Page's virile style. The short articles in the body of the book dealt much with industry and industrialists, and there was a department of short sketches called "Men Who Work: Among the World's Workers." More than a third of the first number had an international angle — if we include the articles on the position of the United States in world affairs, and those dealing with the possessions so recently taken from Spain. Most of the magazine was staff-written (much indeed was by Page himself),[9] and unsigned, though Professor Mark H. Liddell contributed a number of pieces from the first, and Joel Chandler Harris furnished a series in which "Billy Sanders" expressed his views about current events and public affairs. This latter feature, which lasted for about a year, was suggested by Henry Wysham Lanier,[10] son of the poet, secretary of Doubleday, Page & Company, and active himself as a contributor to the magazine and as an associate in its editorial man-

[6] Charles Downer Hazen, ed., *The Letters of William Roscoe Thayer* (Boston, 1926), p. 99.
[7] *World's Work*, v. 2, p. 1257, Oct. 1901.
[8] See p. 704. Cf. also the views of Flower, of the *Arena*, on literature for its own sake, p. 408.
[9] *World's Work*, v. 21, p. 13907, Jan. 1911.
[10] Julia C. Harris, *Life and Letters of Joel Chandler Harris* (Boston, 1918), p. 431.

agement. Indeed business and editorial conduct were always closely integrated on the staff of *World's Work*.[11] Frank Doubleday, president, Herbert S. Houston, secretary, and S. A. Everitt, treasurer, participated in editorial conferences; and Page was a vice-president as well as the editor.

The early numbers of the magazine were very handsome, each with a hundred and sixteen small-quarto pages, well illustrated and well printed, with sewn rather than flat-stapled binding, and priced at twenty-five cents a copy. There were illustrations on about half the pages; some were political cartoons from the newspapers, but most were halftone engravings from photographs. Two articles in the first number — A. Radclyffe Dugmore's "A Revolution in Nature Pictures" and A. J. Stone's "A Day's Work of an Arctic Hunter" — were especially well illustrated. The latter was the first of many "day's work" articles in which the jobs of a stockbroker, public-school administrator, a traveling man, and so on, were detailed. Thus this first number set the pattern which, filled out and proportioned, determined *World's Work* editorial content, illustration, and form for its first fifteen years.

There was a considerable resemblance between the new magazine and the *Review of Reviews*. Albert Shaw's "The Progress of the World" was more comprehensive than Page's "The March of Events," and the older magazine was more eclectic and miscellaneous than the new one. On the whole, the *Review of Reviews* had a few more pages and more stuff crowded into them; but *World's Work*, with a little larger type and greater vigor, was more original and attractive.

*World's Work* began just before the great outburst of muckraking, but at a time when many magazines and newspapers were examining reform proposals in various fields. Page was interested in reform movements, too, and his magazine was by no means uncritical; but in the main *World's Work* was an apologist for the trusts and for current trends in big business. Page in 1900 thought that things were going pretty well in this best of industrial worlds. In the magazine's second number Henry Harrison Lewis, writing in answer to the question "Are Young Men's Chances Less?" decided that consolidations of industry had not crowded out beginners. In the following number, however, the editor recorded his belief that the "doctrine of room at the top" was true only if a young man had good training, diligence, and balanced judgment.[12] In the number for March 1901, Henry Grafton Chapman expressed his pleasure at "The Progress of Honesty" in big business. In the same issue appeared H. I. Cleveland's "Philip Armour, Merchant,"

[11] *World's Work*, v. 21, p. 13909, Jan. 1911.
[12] *World's Work*, v. 3, p. 1413, Jan. 1902.

while the next month the magazine published sympathetic personality sketches about no less than three leaders of industry and finance — Morgan, Schwab, and Carnegie.

What Page liked best to do was to present the details of some successful reform as a model; the "uplift" number of July 1904 presents an outstanding example of this policy. Therein appeared more than a dozen articles telling of improvement in many fields; J. Horace McFarland wrote on "The Uplift in American Cities," Thomas F. Woodlock on "The Uplift in Business," Page himself on "The Cultivated Man in an Industrial Era," Charles Henry Caffin on "How American Taste is Improving," Lyman Abbott on "The Advance of Women," and Dallas Lore Sharp on "Our Uplift Through Outdoor Life." Charles W. Eliot was an occasional contributor to *World's Work*; his essays suited Page's mood of optimism in the face of American industrialization. Eliot concluded an article on "Great Riches" by declaring: "All signs indicate that America will meet this test" of great fortunes in the hands of comparatively few. He saw the rise of a "numerous class of superior persons — rich, well off, comfortable, or just self-supporting."[13] George W. Perkins contributed a series on business ethics in 1911, and William G. McAdoo discussed the management of his Hudson and Manhattan Railroad in the number for March 1912 under the title "The Soul of a Corporation." Clement Melville Keys, formerly on the staff of the *Wall Street Journal* and now financial editor of *World's Work*, wrote on "The New Democracy of Business" in February 1913 in the conviction that businessmen had become "builders instead of exploiters." There is little room for doubt that Walter Hines Page, and also his son and successor Arthur Wilson Page, were sincere in their belief in an altruistic, or at least a philanthropic, wealthy class as a paramount factor in our socio-economic progress, and in their desire that *World's Work* should perform a public service by encouraging such attitudes.[14]

Though their method was constructive, and though their sympathies seemed really to be with successful men rather than with the "have-nots," their magazine did engage from time to time in campaigns of exposure. Tammany, wrote the editor in 1901, was "the most loathsome fact in American life."[15] A staff member, Adele Marie Shaw, wrote in February 1904 of "The Public Schools of a Boss-Ridden City," and did not hesitate to speak of the corrupt practices in Philadelphia municipal government. Eighteen months later Isaac F. Marcosson, another staff

[13] *World's Work*, v. 11, p. 7460, April 1906.
[14] See Isaac F. Marcosson, *Adventures in Interviewing* (New York, 1923), pp. 42–44; *World's Work*, v. 25, pp. 265–68; Doris Ulmann, *A Portrait Gallery of American Editors* (New York, 1925), p. 116.
[15] *World's Work*, v. 3, p. 1361, Nov. 1901.

writer, was able to write an article about current reforms in that city, entitled "The Awakening of Philadelphia." Henry Oyen's 1911 series on "The Awakening of the Cities" was followed by a regular department headed "The March of the Cities."

An abuse against which *World's Work* waged a long war was the "padding" of pension rolls and the growth of the pension burden on the taxpayers. Robert Lincoln O'Brien fired the first gun in May 1904 with his article entitled "Our Enormous Pension Roll." When William Bayard Hale was the magazine's staff representative in Washington, from 1909 to 1913, he delivered many volleys against pension legislation; he was reinforced by Charles Francis Adams, whose "Pensions — Worse and More of Them" appeared in January 1912. Page claimed in 1913 that there had been "a decided stiffening of courage and opinion" on this reform as a result of his magazine's articles. In 1915 Associate Editor Burton J. Hendrick continued the crusade with a series on "Pork-Barrel Pensions."

A series signed "Q. P." exposed life insurance abuses in 1905–1906; and the issue of April 1906, following the report of the Armstrong Insurance Investigation Committee of the New York legislature, was a kind of readers' guide to life insurance problems. In 1907–1908 Keys had a series on "The Money Kings," suggested by the financial troubles of that year and explaining for the average reader the values and dangers of trust companies, savings banks, and speculative stocks; he declared that some banks had made immense profits from speculation during the recent panic. Keys's 1910 series, "How the Railroad Works with the Trust," was equally bold, clear, and convincing.

Thus it is evident that the statement sometimes made[16] to the effect that *World's Work* performed a sharp about-face in its attitude toward muckraking in 1906, being prevailingly liberal before that time and conservative afterward, is a fallacy. Page was a strong believer in the greatness and the essential honesty of American industry and industrialists, but from time to time he attacked abuses of the system. When the Archbold-Foraker letters were published, *World's Work* was printing Rockefeller's reminiscences, which constituted a defense of Standard Oil, as a serial; but Page did not hesitate to condemn the corruption on the part of the company's top officials indicated in the correspondence that Hearst had printed, and to add "A Word to the Standard Oil Company" that did much to ruin the public-relations effect of the Rockefeller serial.[17] There were those who said that "John D." had paid *World's*

---

[16] William Kittle, "The Making of Public Opinion," *Arena*, v. 41, p. 448, July 1909; same author in *Twentieth Century Magazine*, v. 2, p. 127, May 1910.

[17] *World's Work*, v. 17, pp. 10851–54, Nov. 1908.

*Work* to publish his recollections, but Page stated categorically that, on the contrary, Doubleday, Page & Company paid Rockefeller their regular rate for articles contributed to the magazine.[18] A similar balancing of viewpoints occurred in 1910, when, shortly after it had printed James J. Hill's recollections, the magazine published an article by Keys showing how the railroads gave special privileges to the trusts (November 1910).

Doubleday, Page & Company made one of its early successes by publishing Upton Sinclair's *The Jungle*, an exposure in fictional form of abuses surrounding the meat industry in Chicago. *World's Work* followed this up with three articles on meat inspection in Chicago, authoritative and well illustrated, in the number for April 1906. In spite of an editorial preface which denied that all this was part of the "literature of exposure," and the lead editorial in "March of Events," which condemned Lawsonism and "the yellow magazines," these articles were very effective exposés, and as truly muckraking as anything in *McClure's*. Page's editorial was probably written under the influence of the Gridiron Club "preview" of Roosevelt's famous speech in which he gave the term "muckraking" to the "literature of exposure"; but the articles on meat inspection were doubtless already in process before that pronouncement or any earlier form of it.

Page printed a number of articles on socialism in those years, including Sinclair's "The Socialist Party" (April 1906). More comprehensive and less propagandic was Professor Samuel P. Orth's "The World-Wide Sweep of Socialism," a serial of 1912.

Integrated with the deep and constant interest of *World's Work* in industrial management and leadership was its advocacy of the improvement of the lot of the laborers. In early numbers appeared articles on "The Betterment of Working Life" (December 1900) and "Self-Help for Employees" (February 1901) by R. E. Phillips, but organized social work occupied little space in comparison with such problems as labor unionism and immigration. Michael Glen Cunniff, who had come to *World's Work* from an English instructorship at Harvard to become the magazine's first "literary editor" at twenty-six years of age, apparently took his cue from an article on "How Labor Organized," by Ray Stannard Baker (August 1902), and was soon writing articles on labor unionism derived from his own first-hand investigations. He became managing editor of the magazine in 1903 and continued his studies of labor; four years later he resigned to follow a short but brilliant career in Arizona mining and politics. Page was less tolerant than the objective Cunniff in dealing with unionism and strikes, and the magazine eventually gave

[18] *World's Work*, v. 21, p. 13907, Jan. 1911.

much space to its opposition to the closed shop and other union principles. Doctor Eliot, who felt so optimistic about the contributions of the rich to American civilization, was more than dubious about labor unions, which he condemned for their adherence to the principle of "the uniform wage," for their "intentional limitation of output," and for "the extraordinary surrender of individual liberty to which all union men consent."[19] Professor Orth had a series on "The Labor War" in 1913.

Commentary on immigration at first took the form of pride in the American "melting pot" — witness Hutchins Hapgood's article on "The Rise of the Russian Jew" in April 1901 — but eventually the magazine took a strong position in favor of severe restriction of immigration, coming back to the subject again and again.

Agriculture was an important subject in *World's Work*. Page was especially interested in new scientific methods of farming; an example among scores of articles explaining such developments is Herbert Quick's article on the Campbell system of dry farming in the number for August 1906. The farmer's lot as a human being was also discussed with intelligent interest; and when farm land values rose sharply in the first decade of the new century, Page thought that "what orators and poets have said about the farmer for a thousand years seems at last to be coming true."[20] A notable feature of 1909 was Edward Berwick's autobiography of a farmer. "Going Back to the Soil" was the title of an article in the third number of the magazine, and it expressed a recurring theme. Secretary of Agriculture James Wilson was an occasional contributor.

Also in the third number appeared an article on "Park Making as a National Art," and the national parks continued to furnish illustrated features for many years. When Arthur Page joined the staff in 1905, the first subject that engaged his attention as contributor was the conservation of natural resources, and for several years he was the magazine's leading writer on that issue. Gifford Pinchot did a series on conservation in 1909. Scenic regions the country over were exploited in the magazine, and the growing American habit of summer vacationing was encouraged. "The American masses have discovered Summer," wrote Page, in introducing a section on "The People at Play" in the August 1902 number, which included articles and pictures about vacation sites from coast to coast. This national and interregional point of view was a characteristic of *World's Work* from the beginning. "At least one editor of the magazine shall visit every section of the country at least once a year, and, of

[19] *World's Work*, v. 28, pp. 575–85, Oct. 1914.
[20] *World's Work*, v. 12, p. 8042, Oct. 1906.

course, at times other countries also," wrote the editor.[21] The number for June 1901 contained an article entitled "The Wonderful Northwest," and that for October of the same year had one called "The Blooming of a Sahara" about the Southwest.

It was natural that such a loyal Southerner as Page should see to it that the South was well represented in his magazine. Fully conscious of the backwardness of the South educationally and industrially, he gave many pages to various plans for the advancement of that great region. "Wherever Walter H. Page hung his hat, that place became automatically the unofficial capital of the New South," wrote Isaac F. Marcosson, who had been for a few years a member of the *World's Work* staff.[22] Page saw the salvation of the Negro in his learning the trades and habits of thrift and self-support, in the Tuskegee pattern. Washington's *Up From Slavery* was one of Doubleday-Page's early successes in book publishing, and its sequel was printed serially in *World's Work* in 1910. W. E. Burghardt Du Bois and Robert R. Moton were talented Negro writers whose work dealing with racial problems appeared occasionally. Edwin Mims's 1911 series, "The South Realizing Itself" was a comprehensive, optimistic set of essays.

But the scope of Page's magazine was, as its title indicated, worldwide. There were occasional foreign contributors, such as Winston Spencer Churchill, who wrote about Lord Roberts in the magazine's third number, and Lord Curzon and Baron Kaneko, who contributed brief statements. But there were many articles by American journalists about British and European personalities, about international trade and politics, and about social and economic movements in various countries. Stanley Brooks wrote a series of articles in 1901 about "The Political Status of Europe." The Boer War, and later the Russo-Japanese War, occupied much space. The number for April 1904 was almost wholly devoted to the war in the Orient. Latin-American countries also received copious attention, for Page was an ardent Pan-American, who saw in the southern continent marvellous opportunities for expansion in trade, wealth, and power.

In spite of his contempt for much of what was called literature, Page did not wholly neglect contemporary books. A small department of book notices was added, as a kind of afterthought, in the second number, including a list of best sellers; in its reviews of new books, the magazine showed no favoritism for those issued by its own publishers. This department ended in 1905, however, and was not resumed until many years later. There were a few short articles in the early years on literary subjects — one on "The True Reward of the Novelist" by Frank Norris,

[21] *World's Work*, v. 25, p. 265, Jan. 1913.
[22] Marcosson, *Adventures in Interviewing*, p. 43.

who was a Doubleday-Page employee when his essay was published in November 1901; one on Tolstoi by Henry Dwight Sedgwick in April 1902; and in February 1903 one by Owen Wister on Norris' *The Pit,* which had just been published by the Doubleday house. Page occasionally noticed literary events in his editorial department. Rather out of line with the other contents of *World's Work* were three or four minor poems by Rudyard Kipling, the leading author of the Doubleday, Page & Company list, which were presented over a term of years, each with special typographical display.

On the whole, more attention was given to art than to literature in *World's Work*. Such sculptors as Barnard, MacMonnies, Saint-Gaudens, and Solon Borglum, and such painters as Whistler, Sargent, Alexander, and Eastman Johnson were discussed in the years from 1902 to 1905, with copious illustrations from their work. Caffin wrote more of these articles than anyone else; and in May 1905 he contributed a piece entitled "A Money Test of Art Appreciation," in which he pointed out the growing importance of New York as an art market. During the next eight or ten years there were many similar studies of individual artists, exhibitions, and architectural achievements, by Caffin, Frank Jewett Mather, Arthur Hoeber, and others. Elihu Vedder's reminiscences appeared in 1910.

Such articles lent themselves well to illustration, as did so many of the magazine's outdoor features. Some articles in 1903–1905 were accompanied by art sections: Norman Duncan's "The Codfishers of Newfoundland" (July 1903) was illustrated by sixteen full-page reproductions of photographs by Richard Byron; and Charles M. Harvey's "The Louisiana Purchase" (May 1903) was accompanied by pictures of the Northwest. The articles on big-game hunting, which were rather frequent in the magazine, were always interestingly illustrated. In 1907 *World's Work* began using at the front of the book a feature that distinguished it for many years, the "portrait gallery"—a series of a dozen or more full-page pictures, nearly all portraits, which accompanied the editorial department, "March of Events."

Education was an important theme in Page's magazine from the first. One of the best series of its early years was Miss Shaw's about the public schools of large American cities, which has been mentioned in connection with the magazine's reformatory activities. Page was himself a member of the General Education Board, whose work he described in an article entitled "A Comprehensive View of Colleges" (July 1906). The development of the free public library received much attention. The subject of health was also prominent, and for several years Dr. Luther H. Gulick and others edited a department headed "The Way to Health."

Another topic, approached in various ways, was that of mechanical progress. The great fairs were given special numbers of the magazine — the Pan-American Exposition at Buffalo (August 1901), the Louisiana Purchase Exposition at St. Louis (August 1904), the Lewis and Clark Exposition at Portland (August 1905), the Jamestown Tercentenary Exposition (June 1907), the Alaska-Yukon-Pacific Exposition at Seattle (August 1909), and the Panama-Pacific Exposition at San Francisco (July 1915). The telephone, steamships, building the Panama Canal, street railways, and agricultural and industrial machinery were common topics. The railroads were a continuing subject, in respect to both their development and their financial problems. James J. Hill wrote some recollections of railway building in 1910, and in 1916–1917 the magazine published the story of his life by Joseph Gilpin Pyles. On the whole, *World's Work* was sympathetic with the railroads and their management. It was also greatly interested in the progress of the automobile, and in December 1906 it published its first comprehensive article on "aerial navigation." In the next decade appeared an occasional comment, picture, or feature about the development of the airplane, but it was not until the First World War stimulated popular interest in aeronautics that aviation received its due in *World's Work*. In 1914 the magazine began a department headed "Man and His Machines," which ran for several years.

But comment on politics and government furnished, of course, a large proportion of the contents of *World's Work*. The magazine supported Republican candidates for President in 1900, 1904, and 1908 — and this despite its editor's Democratic family and tradition. But a magazine which was engaged in glorifying American achievement at century's end, and which could print such an expansionist series as Frederic Emory's "The Greater America," found support of McKinley for reelection in 1900 inevitable. Then Page's long friendship with Theodore Roosevelt predisposed him in favor of McKinley's successor. Page found T. R. conservative by nature, by training, and by choice; and at the end of his first year in the White House, Page thought him more popular and trusted "than any other President in recent times." [23] It was natural that Page should also support Roosevelt's choice for his successor, and in 1907 the magazine published serially Eugene P. Lyle's "Taft: A Career of Big Tasks." On the whole, Page was disappointed in the Taft administration, though the general arbitration treaties called forth a notable World Peace Number in December 1911. It was no easy choice that he made in 1912, especially in view of differences of opinion among his associates on the magazine; but Page had entertained a high regard for Wilson for many years and had maintained a fairly close relation-

[23] *World's Work*, v. 4, pp. 2471–72, Sept. 1902.

ship with him. In 1911 *World's Work* published a serial biography of Wilson by Staff Writer Hale; and during the campaign the magazine, if not an ardent backer of the Democratic candidate, was at least a friendly commentator and well-wisher. It was as though, after the perennial candidacies of Bryan, Page was relieved to find a Democratic leader he could support with satisfaction. Shortly after Wilson's inauguration, Page was appointed ambassador to Great Britain.

Thus ended the first period of the history of *World's Work*. It had been a moderate success from the beginning, attaining a circulation of 100,000, with 50 to 100 pages of advertising per issue by 1907. The page size had been reduced slightly in 1910. When W. H. Page went to London, Arthur Page succeeded his father as editor. Circulation and advertising were down a little at the time of the outbreak of the European War in 1914; but with the first news of hostilities, Editor Page stopped the presses which were then rolling out the September issue, remade it in the form of a separately paged *War Manual*, and hit the newsstands with a 136-page compendium crammed with data about European armaments, personalities, military strategy, war machines, and food supply, with pictures and maps. Nearly 300,000 copies of this number were sold, and during the war the average circulation of *World's Work* was about 140,000 — the largest of any five-year period in its history.

In these years the magazine was filled with war material — military and naval analyses, atrocities, laws of war, the conflict in the air, letters from Americans overseas, Arthur Sweetser's "Diary from the Front," military movements (with maps), correspondence from England, France, Germany, Russia, Turkey, China, Canada, and so on. John R. Rathom's series "German Plots Exposed" caused a sensation in 1917; but editorial difficulties with the author caused the substitution of a series of spy stories by the magazine's own French Strother. Arno Dosch-Fleurot, Frank Simonds, J. B. W. Gardiner, John M. Oskison, Alfred Ollivant, Carl Crow, and Charles W. Furlong were leading writers from abroad. Chief staff writers at home were Lanier, Hendrick, Strother, Walter F. Wyman (finance), James Middleton (politics), and Walter A. Dyer (education). George Marvin, who had covered the 1914 war with Mexico, contributed a series on "The Mississippi River" in 1915.

"The March of Events" occupied much less space after the departure of Walter Hines Page, but there was the same picture gallery. President Wilson's "The New Freedom" was featured as a 1913 serial. The first color portrait was that of James J. Hill, which accompanied the December 1916 installment of Pyles's life of the empire builder, and thereafter there were color pictures of war leaders and scenes, as well as two-color maps. The campaign of *World's Work* for a national budget was a feature of the years 1915–1916; Hendrick wrote a series of articles entitled "Shall We Have Responsible Government?" on the subject of budgeting. Ambassador Morgenthau's recollections furnished a 1918 serial. George MacAdam's "Life of Pershing" was published in 1918–1919, and Admiral William S. Sims's "The Victory at Sea" in 1919. Charles Phelps Cushing contributed photographs and articles, many of them on health topics. Automobiles and the motor industry received more and more attention. In 1917 the small-quarto page size was resumed. Four pages were in full color. The price was raised to thirty-five cents in 1918, which was probably the magazine's most prosperous year.

Lothrop Stoddard, who had been writing much on foreign affairs, began a department called "The World As It Is" in 1919. Samuel Crowther was a staff writer on politics, and Frank Parker Stockbridge was a roving American correspondent. As the war ended, Strother was listed as managing editor and Hendrick as associate editor. In 1919 there were two series on Mexican affairs, one favoring intervention and the other opposing. Full-color illustration was dropped in 1919, poorer paper was used, and circulation began a slight but steady decline over a five-year period.

*World's Work* favored the Prohibition Amendment. In the years just before the United States entered the First World War, it published several articles and editorials urging the reform. In October 1920, with the amendment passed, it was acknowledged that "Prohibition will not come in a day, but it is certainly well started," and the editors had faith that, with the traffic in liquor disorganized, the cause would rapidly "gain new recruits."[24] But MacAdam's "Our Year of Prohibition" (March 1921) was less optimistic. By 1925 when Rollin Lynde Hartt, former clergyman and now a roving reporter for *World's Work*, wrote up his findings on a three-thousand-mile trip of observation under the title "Prohibition As It Is," it had become evident that resistance to the amendment was general, and that enforcement was a failure in many states. The next year, an editorial declared that neither enforcement nor repeal was possible, and that nullification was the right answer.[25] In 1930, the magazine suggested a national referendum,[26] but it perished before the amendment was repealed.

*World's Work* was increasingly nonpartisan in the twenties. It had stuck with Wilson in his second presidential campaign, though it had disapproved his "unreasoning pacifism" during most of his first term.[27]

[24] *World's Work*, v. 40, p. 534, Oct. 1920.
[25] *World's Work*, v. 53, pp. 5–6, Nov. 1926.
[26] *World's Work*, v. 59, March 1930, p. 40.
[27] *World's Work*, v. 32, p. 600, Oct. 1915.

It approved the President's participation in the treaty-making at Versailles, and its number for February 1919 was devoted to the League of Nations. It strongly favored the League editorially that year,[28] but it gave a mild support to Harding in 1920. In the following campaigns, it was nonpartisan. Mark Sullivan was the magazine's Washington correspondent during most of the twenties, and Frank R. Kent and Samuel Crowther also wrote much on national politics.

In the early years of that decade, a department called "The Council Table" occupied a prominent place in the magazine; it carried short contributions from such men as Charles W. Eliot, Herbert Hoover, Booth Tarkington, Henry Morgenthau, and others, who were listed as members of the "Council." An effort was made for variety; and E. E. Slosson contributed his series on "Science Remaking the World," Floyd W. Parsons wrote on health and industry, and the letters of Walter Hines Page and of Franklin K. Lane were published. Carl E. Akeley's series on big-game hunting appeared in 1922, and in that year began also the articles about Martin Johnson's African exploits, which were to continue for a long time. Edwin Mims told "Why the South Is Anti-Evolution" in September 1925; this attitude, recently publicized in the Scopes trial, was blamed on the uneducated masses. MacAdam did some articles on education in 1920; and William McAndrew contributed a series entitled "Planning the Upkeep," on training for citizenship in the schools, in 1923–1924. John K. Barnes, a staff writer, was the author of an extensive survey of the international oil situation in 1920.

The war had brought an even greater emphasis on international matters to a magazine that had from its beginning taken a deep interest in the affairs of foreign countries. England, where the editor emeritus represented his country during the war, was well interpreted to American readers in the pages of *World's Work*. Martyred Belgium and France were also well represented. France was glorified in the number for October 1917, which included four full-color pages; interest in France continued after the end of the war, and André Tardieu was a 1921 contributor. There was much on Russia — its part in the war, its revolution, its people, and the problem of Bolshevism. Arno Dosch-Fleurot, J. B. W. Gardiner, Samuel N. Harper, and A. J. Sack were writers on Russia for *World's Work* in 1917–1918. The socialist John Spargo was author of an article for the November 1919 issue entitled "Bolshevism: A Caricature of Marx's Theories," and two years later a strongly anti-Bolshevik series on Russia was contributed by Hugo W. Koehler. In that same year Count Sergius Witte's memoirs were published serially. There was also

---

[28] *World's Work*, v. 37, pp. 605–10, April 1919.

a good deal about the Orient, including the Japanese articles of William H. Gardiner in 1922.

The magazine continued to be greatly interested in Pan-Americanism and in the opportunities for trade between North and South America. The issue for December 1914 was devoted to that matter; and in the next year Doubleday, Page & Company began the publication of a Latin-American edition of *World's Work*, called *Revista del Mundo*, which began as a quarterly and was published for a little over six years.

Labor also continued a prominent topic. Hendrick and Crowther were leading writers in this field. They took what they liked to think of as the reasonable employers' point of view, urging arbitration, stressing abuses of labor management, and pointing out that the public was the chief sufferer from strikes. "England Has Industrial Peace—Why Not We?" asked Hendrick in March 1918. Charles C. Dickey's two-part article in the spring of 1924, entitled "Must Murder Be the Price of Coal?" drew a reply from the editor of the *United Mine Workers' Journal*, which was duly printed and answered.

In the fall of 1923, *World's Work* was again down to its before-the-war circulation of about a hundred thousand; at that time it made several changes, so that it seemed to become almost a new magazine. What it did, chiefly, was to resume the use of color illustration and to add some new departments in the advertising section. The number for October 1923 had a full-color cover and carried nine pages of color illustration to accompany James B. Connolly's "Mariners of Gloucester." In 1924 there was an outburst of features on art subjects, all beautifully illustrated. The portrait painter Walter Tittle provided some of these articles, and other well-illustrated pieces had to to with birds, flowers, and scenery. Special departments in the advertising section were not new to *World's Work*, which had long given advice on insurance, investment problems, and automobiles in that position; it now placed there an editorial department called "The World's Workshop," and a "Red Letter Book Guide." The latter was under the editorship of Thomas L. Masson, veteran critic and humorist, who had been contributing occasional short pieces on literary subjects to the magazine for the preceding year or two. Gino Speranza's articles on "The Immigration Peril," Dickey's "The Truth About the Newspapers," and Hartt's "The Negro Comes North" and "The War in the Churches" were series that distinguished this episode in the history of *World's Work*.

For it was only a brief episode. In November 1924 color was again abandoned; and indeed for the next two years there was no illustration at all except for one sixteen-page section of halftones in each issue, frontispiece portraits by gravure, and a few line and crayon portraits and diagrams. Departments were shuffled again. Cameron Rogers edited the book reviews for a while, and then they disappeared as a department, to be used as occasional separate articles. The "Workshop" and the investment service were moved out of the advertising section. An interesting new department called "Personalities" appeared. There were more Page letters in 1924, and a series of Joseph Conrad letters in 1926–1927. David F. Houston's "Eight Years With Wilson" was a 1926 serial. Albert Edward Wiggam, Frederick Palmer, Henry F. Pringle, and Gregory Mason were prominent contributors. But on the whole, the magazine in 1925–1926 was an inferior performance.

At the end of 1926, Arthur W. Page resigned from the editorship of *World's Work* to become a vice-president of the American Telephone and Telegraph Company, his place in the publishing house being taken by George H. Doran. It was announced that the magazine would be edited "under the personal supervision of F. N. Doubleday," but the active editor was Carl C. Dickey, who had been managing editor during 1926. The magazine now became once more a fully illustrated, attractive "history of our time."

The great feature of 1927 was Colonel Thomas E. Lawrence's narrative of his war adventures in Arabia. The "Next War" number, of April 1927, passed in review the danger spots of the world, but seemed to center on Asia as the scene of the next great conflict. In 1928 Lord Beaverbrook's "Political Battles of the World War," Warden Lewis E. Lawes' story of Sing-Sing, and the continuation of a series on great American cities were notable.

In August 1928, Barton Currie came from the editorship of the *Ladies' Home Journal* to supplant Dickey as editor of *World's Work*; but he stayed for less than a year, yielding in the summer of 1929 to Russell Doubleday, brother of Frank N., and an officer of the publishing company. Alan C. Collins and Lawrence M. Conant were associate editors. The page size was now enlarged to quarto; each number had 140 to 200 pages, including over 60 pages of advertising. Circulation rose to 150,000 in 1929, and advertising revenue amounted to over $500,000.[29] A new group of men were writing about the same topics to which the magazine had been devoted from the first — business and industry, science and machinery, politics, foreign affairs, and so on. There was now more of aviation and of travel, and perhaps more of books, than in the file as a whole. Lowell Thomas, Theodore Joslin, Freeman Tilden, and T. R. Ybarra were leading writers, as well as such older favorites as Crowther and William L. Ripley.

But the financial crash and the ensuing hard times spelled disaster

[29] *Time,* v. 20, July 25, 1932, p. 24.

for a magazine that had been unstable for several years. Circulation and advertising declined. Doubleday turned his editorship over to Collins in 1931, but the next year the magazine was sold to the *Review of Reviews*, which had been its competitor throughout the whole of its existence.

Always a "quality magazine," *World's Work* made, for a third of a century, a notable contribution to the intelligent discussion of public affairs in America.

INDEX

# INDEX

A. E. See Russell, George William.
*A. I. U. Magazine,* 351 *n.*
Abbey, Edwin Austin, 151, 544.
Abbot, Willis John, 362, 617.
Abbott, Edward, 124.
Abbott, Eleanor Hallowell, 550.
Abbott, Elenore Plaisted, 724.
Abbott, John Stevens Cabot, 293.
Abbott, Lyman, 59, 295, 398, 546, 547, 776.
Abdullah, Achmed, 114 *n,* 422.
*Academy,* 268.
*Accident Assurance,* 351 *n.*
*Acetylene Journal,* 184 *n.*
Ackermann, Jessie, 765.
*Acme Haversack of Patriotism and Song,* 254 *n.*
*Acta Columbiana,* 560.
Adam, G. Mercer, 54 *n.*
Adams, Brooks, 225.
Adams, Charles Francis, 721, 777.
Adams, Charles Kendall, 517.
Adams, Cyrus Cornelius, 458.
Adams, Frank Ramsay, 618.
Adams, Franklin Pierce, 566.
Adams, Frederick Upham, 204.
Adams, Henry, 136.
Adams, Herbert Baxter, 181, 263, 264.
Adams, James Truslow, 522, 730.
Adams, John Coleman, 194.
Adams, John Taylor, 520.
*Adams' Magazine,* 139.
Adams, Samuel Hopkins, 458–59, 460, 465, 466, 471, 595, 604, 744.
Adams, William Taylor, 274, 420.
Addams, Jane, 192, 195, 546, 547, 603, 744, 745, 746, 747.
Ade, George, 196, 458, 497.
*Adjuster,* 351 *n.*
Adler, Felix, 200, 278, 279.
*Advance* (Chicago), 292–93.
*Advance* (New Orleans), 93.
*Advance* (San Francisco), 175.
*Advance Advocate,* 221 *n.*
Advertising, general review of, 20–34. See separate Sketches in Supplement for advertising in individual magazines.
  Abuses of, 31–32, 245–46.
  Medical advertising, 312–13.
*Advertising Age,* 247 *n.*
*Aeronautical World,* 335.
*Aesculapian,* 143 *n.*

*African Repository,* 238.
*Aggressive Methodism,* 305.
Agnosticism, 277–78.
*Agora,* 97.
*Agricultural Advertising,* 337.
*Agricultural Student,* 341 *n.*
Agriculture. Comment on, 336; periodicals of, 336–41. See Populism.
Ahern, Mary Eileen, 143.
Aiken, Charles Sedgwick, 105.
Aiken, Conrad, 440, 729.
*Ainslee's Magazine,* 49.
*Ainslee's Smart Love Stories,* 49 *n.*
Akeley, Carl Ethan, 785.
Akins, Zoë, 654.
*Alabama Medical Journal,* 313 *n.*
*Alabama School Journal,* 270 *n.*
*Alarm,* 172–73.
Alaska-Yukon-Pacific Exposition, 782.
*Alaskan Magazine,* 109.
*Albany Law Journal,* 347 *n.*
Albee, Ernest, 303 *n.*
Albrand, Martha, 713.
Albrecht, Heinrich, 58 *n.*
*Album,* 674.
Alcott, Louisa May, 538.
Alden, Henry Mills, 35, 36–37, 43, 114, 190.
Alden, William Livingston, 559.
Aldrich, Bess Streeter, 552, 709.
Aldrich, Mildred, 389.
Aldrich, Nelson Wilmarth, 462, 494.
Aldrich, Thomas Bailey, 35, 451, 680.
Alexander, Charles, 671 *n,* 672–75, 683–84.
Alexander, Hartley Burr, 390 *n.*
Alexander, Jack, 709, 712.
Alexander, John White, 151, 720.
Alger, Horatio, Jr., 274, 417–18, 609, 610.
*Alkahest,* 92 *n,* 390 *n.*
Allen, E. C., 246, 274, 365.
Allen, Fred W., 466.
Allen, Grant, 51, 514, 685.
Allen, Hervey, 503.
Allen, James Lane, 93, 113–14, 389–90, 490.
Allen, Samantha. See Holley, Marietta.
Allen, T. Ernest, 304, 407–08.
Allingham, Margery, 475.
Allison, Young E., 351 *n.*
Alliston, William O., 188.
*All-Story Weekly,* 421, 618.
Allyn, Dwight, 115.

Pulitzer, Joseph, 410, 428.
*Pulp and Paper Magazine*, 184 *n*.
*Pulpit*, 301 *n*.
*Pulpit Herald and Altruistic Review*, 284.
Pupin, Michael, 727.
Purdy, Ken W., 417 *n*.
*Puritan*, 361, 614.
*Purity Journal*, 200.
Putnam, Nina Wilcox, 606.
*Putnam's Historical Magazine*, 140.
*Putnam's Monthly*, 46.
Pyle, Howard, 151, 484, 545, 719, 726.
Pyles, Joseph Gilpin, 782.

Quad, M. See Lewis, Charles Bertrand.
*Quaker*, 117, 273, 614.
Quaker Periodicals, 296.
"Quality Magazines," 7–9.
*Quarterly Bulletin of the American Institute of Architects*, 323.
*Quarterly Illustrator*, 154.
*Quarterly Journal* (Jenness Miller), 359.
*Quarterly Journal of Economics*, 182.
*Quarterly of the Texas State Historical Association*, 139.
*Quarterly Register of Current History*, 71.
*Quarterly Review*, 228.
*Quarterly Review of the United Brethren*, 296.
Queen, Ellery (Frederic Dannay and Manfred Bennington Lee), 503.
Queen, Frank, 260.
*Queen*, 580–81.
*Queen of Fashion*, 582.
*Queries*, 55.
Quick, Herbert, 46 *n*, 490, 550, 697, 779.
Quiller-Couch, Arthur Thomas, 114 *n*, 451, 720, 726.
Quincy, Josiah, 161, 407.
Quinn, Arthur Hobson, 728.
Quinn, Thomas C., 50.
Quirk, James R., 589 *n*, 607.
*Quiver*, 229 *n*.
*Quo Vadis*, 141, 260.

*R. F. D. News*, 335 *n*.
*Racer and Driver*, 373 *n*.
Racing, 373.
*Radford Review*, 325 *n*.
*Radiant Centre*, 285 *n*.
Raemaekers, Louis, 566.
*Railroad Car Journal*, 333 *n*.
*Railroad Herald*, 333 *n*.
*Railroad Magazine*, 422.
*Railroad Man's Magazine*, 422, 617 *n*.

Railroads, 326, 331–32 (main entry), 487, 782; periodicals devoted to, 332–33.
*Railway and Locomotive Engineering*, 333 *n*.
*Railway Carmen's Journal*, 221 *n*.
*Railway Clerk*, 221 *n*.
*Railway Journal*, 333 *n*.
*Railway Post Office*, 335 *n*.
*Railway Telegrapher*, 221 *n*.
*Railway Times*, 175.
*Railway World*, 333.
Raine, Norman Reilly, 701, 713.
Raine, William McLeod, 79 *n*, 421.
Raleigh, Henry, 695.
Ralph, Julian, 66, 226, 233, 489, 662, 689, 721.
Ramage, Burr James, 733 *n*, 735.
Ramée, Marie Louise de la, 51, 514, 679.
*Ram's Horn*, 301.
*Ranch*, 341.
*Rand McNally Bankers' Monthly*, 349.
Randall-Diehl, Anna, 125.
Rankin, Jeremiah Eames, 52 *n*.
Ransom, John Crowe, 737, 739, 740.
Rascoe, Burton, 432 *n*, 440–41.
Rathom, John R., 783.
*Raven*, 117 *n*.
Rawlings, Charles A., 712.
Rawlings, Marjorie Kinnan, 729.
Read, Opie, 48 *n*, 93, 100, 114 *n*, 115 *n*, 367 *n*, 390, 654, 767.
Reade, Charles, 679.
*Reader*, 46.
*Reader's Digest*, 587.
*Real Democracy*, 283.
*Real Estate Record and Building Guide*, 325.
Realf, Richard, 65.
*Reason*, 304 *n*.
Reavis, Holland S., 184 *n*.
Reavis, L. U., 261 *n*.
*Records of the American Catholic Historical Society of Philadelphia*, 138.
*Records of the Past*, 140.
Recouly, Raymond, 727, 728.
*Recreation*, 381.
*Red Book*, 116, 393.
*Red Man*, 215.
Redding, Mrs. Josephine, 756 *n*, 758–59.
Redfield, William Cox, 617.
Redman, Peggy Dowst, 712 *n*.
Redmond, Daniel George, 511 *n*, 523.
Reed, C. McF., 671 *n*.
Reed, Gideon F. T., 412.
Reed, Joseph P., 48 *n*, 671 *n*.